PEOPLES
OF THE
BUDDHIST WORLD

By this gift, whatever reward I seek,

It is the best of rewards to profit all;

But this abundant merit I desire

Here or later no angelic pomp

Or splendours of a monarch, no, not even

To be a pupil of a conqueror.

But I would build a bridge straight across

The river of Samsara, and all folk

Would speed across it until they reach

The Blessed City. I myself would cross,

And drag the drowning over.

Yes, myself once tamed, would tame the rebels;

Comforted, would comfort the weak;

Alive, would raise those dying;

Cool, would cool the burning,

Free, to set free the bound.

Alaungsithu, King of Burma (1112–1167)

PEOPLES OF THE BUDDHIST WORLD
A Christian Prayer Diary

PAUL HATTAWAY

PIQUANT
editions

Copyright © 2004 by Paul Hattaway

This edition copyright © 2004 by Piquant Editions Ltd
4 Thornton Road, Carlisle, CA3 9HZ
www.piquanteditions.com
info@piquant.net

ISBN 1-903689-90-2

Co-published in the USA by Authentic Media
129 Mobilization Drive, Waynesboro GA 30830
authenticusa@stl.org

and William Carey Library
PO Box 40129, Pasadena, CA 91114
www.wclbooks.com
ISBN 0-87808-361-8

British Library Cataloguing-in-Publication Data:

Hattaway, Paul, 1968–

Peoples of the Buddhist world : a Christian prayer diary
1.Buddhism – Social aspects 2.Buddhism – Customs and practices 3.Missions to Buddhists
4.Christianity and other religions – Buddhism 5.Buddhism – Relations – Christianity
I.Title
294.3'37
ISBN 1903689902

Cover image: 'Praying Buddhist nun', photograph copyright © by Create International.
Used with permission.

Cover design by Projectluz

Book design by 2aT (www.2at.com)

Maps copyright ©2004 by Valerie Lim. Used with permission

Printed in Singapore

For my son Taine,
whose name means 'mighty warrior'.

He was born about the time I accepted the challenge to write
this book and celebrated his third birthday as the manuscript
was being fine-tuned for publication. Many times he came and sat
on my lap while I was typing away.

May you grow up true to your name, a warrior for God with a heart of
compassion for the nations.

Contributors

Nyima Chothar is a converted former Tibetan Buddhist monk.

Dr Ralph Covell has been a missionary in China and Taiwan for 20 years. After returning to the US he taught missions at Denver Seminary from 1966 to 2002 and was Academic Dean from 1979 to 1990. He returns often to China and Taiwan. In Taiwan he continues to consult on the translation of the Old Testament into the Taruku language. He has written five books on China and from 1982 to 1988 was editor of *Missiology*, the journal of the American Society of Missiology.

Dorje is a recognized expert on Tibetan Buddhism who lives and travels extensively among the Tibetan Buddhist peoples of Asia.

Dr David J Hesselgrave is Professor Emeritus of Mission at Trinity Evangelical Divinity School in Deerfield, Illinois. He and his wife Gertrude served as missionaries in Japan for 12 years with the Evangelical Free Church. David has authored several mission books and was the first director of the Association of Evangelical Missions.

Vijay Karunaratne is a Christian scholar living in Sri Lanka. He has been actively involved in ministry to Buddhists for many years.

Hugh P Kemp is Dean of Studies at the Manawatu Centre of the Bible College of New Zealand. He grew up in India, and during the 1990s he worked in Mongolia as a Christian educator and church planter. He is the author of *Steppe by Step* (London: Monarch / OMF / Interserve, 2000), an overview of Christianity among the Mongol peoples from the 12th century to the present day.

Bryan Lurry, as a young graduate from Irving in Texas, spent several months sharing the gospel with monks in a Shan Theravada Buddhist monastery.

Dr Ubolwan Mejudhon is a Thai Christian married to a former Buddhist. Her doctoral dissertation examines the heart of what it means to be a Christian and Thai in a Thai way.

Tilak Rupasinghe is a Christian scholar living in Sri Lanka. He has been involved in ministry to Buddhists for many years.

Steve Spaulding was raised on the mission field, and has spent his life on three continents. He has served with Dawn Ministries and the DAWN movement since the early 1990s. In 1999 he encouraged a group of church leaders in Asia to consider the needs of the Buddhist world. SEANET (South East Asia Network) has become a key gathering for the formulation of strategies to reach Buddhist peoples.

Dr Alex G Smith is Minister-at-Large for OMF International in the USA. He and his wife joined OMF in 1964 and spent 20 years in Thailand. Subsequently Alex served as Northwest Director in the USA for 18 years. He is the author of two Thai books on church growth and evangelism, as well as several English titles including *Siamese Gold: A History of Church Growth in Thailand*, *Strategy to Multiply Rural Churches*, *The Gospel Facing Buddhist Cultures* and *Buddhism through Christian Eyes*.

Gyalsang Tamang is a Nepali man who was converted from Buddhism in his youth.

Contents

ARTICLES

PHOTO INSERTS

Foreword

It's with tremendous enthusiasm that I introduce you to this volume, a combined labour of love and credible research. It grows out of several streams and concerns that converged in the latter 1990s and early months of this millennium.

This book is about *passion*

To be honest, those of us in the English-speaking world have often proven stereotypically unimpassioned by the things that cause God's heart to break. We need to continually reignite the fire of our passion for the peoples of the earth who 'sit in darkness', whose minds a sinister enemy has blinded from entrance to the good life of God. This passion will drive us to prayer, which will further enliven this heart- and heaven-rending passion. If this book does not touch a chord of passion within the intercessor's deepest being, we have in some way failed here. Come, Holy Spirit, and anoint this resource with your presence.

This book is about *prayer* and *power*

There is, in fact, one great cosmic struggle going on between the powers. We are helpless as human agents caught in this 'time between the times' without prayer, our only access to the power and presence of God, our King. More than anything, this book, while a comprehensive information resource on the peoples of the Buddhist world, is first and foremost a resource for prayer. We now know beyond any measure of doubt that there has been, especially in the past 15 years, an observable cause-and-effect relationship between fervent, sustained, united intercession of the body of Christ for specific peoples and those same peoples' increased responsiveness and Christ-ward movement. Conversely, we have found ourselves time and again engaged in labour- and resource-intensive activities for decades, with little or no appreciable Kingdom fruit because of a lack of prayer. If this is the case, why are we not generating volumes of material on these peoples and getting it into the hands of intercessors around the world? We know (from, for example, the multiple 'Pray Through the Window' projects of the 1990s) that there are tens of millions of Christians who pray regularly for world mission concerns. We also (perhaps reluctantly) acknowledge that intercession is decidedly not the purview of a handful of specialists in our churches or institutions. Every believer is to use the dynamic and indispensable spiritual power of prayer to advance the Kingdom.

Are we in fact praying for the arrival of the Kingdom? If so, it behoves us to look most intently at those corners of the globe where the Kingdom most poignantly lacks expression, where peoples remain fundamentally ignorant of the path to true enlightenment, where the opportunity to encounter that Kingdom is least evident. If our prayer is 'Thy Kingdom come!' then surely we must attach the focus of that coming Kingdom to real places, real localities, real peoples to whom this just and goodly rule is yet a distant longing, a shrouded, illusory dream.

This book is about *profiling*

This book will bring a fresh understanding of the unfinished task of bringing the gospel to Buddhists around the world from a people-group perspective.

Peoples of the Buddhist World will prove invaluable for world Christians everywhere and will doubtless provide more than motivational material for those needing strategic and up-to-date data on the hundreds of peoples in this mega sphere.

This book is about *people(s)*

Every page features a particular human face of the Yet-Buddhist World. The photos are prominent and intentionally personal, to move us to prayer for *people*. After all, Jesus sends us to disciple the *ethne* (Greek for 'people') of the whole world — not even so much individuals per se, but *panta ta ethnae* — all the peoples. What would a 'discipled people' really look like? This is a valid question that we do not often ask but should ask, especially at this juncture of history when local language and cultural loyalties have been revived in a post-colonial era of clashing civilizations and supposedly pluralistic societies. Jesus calls us to disciple peoples, not just people. To disciple peoples we must know how to make individual followers of Jesus, but this will always be a corporate and 'peoples-focused' activity if it's to be true to the Great Commission. And it is the Great Commission which guides, personalizes and gives an earthed, incarnational dimension to the commission. Lift up your eyes and look on the peoples of the earth, for they are ripe for harvest. Let that be the love-powered stimulus that communicates to you from the eyes, smiles or haunting gaze of the people pictured herein.

This book is about *participation*

Lastly, this book is specifically network-driven. A group of people calling themselves SEANET (South, East and Southeast Asia Network) has, since 1999, made a commitment to global-level intercession on behalf of the entire Buddhist populace, everywhere, as one of its three primary ministry focuses in relation to the Buddhist world. This particular work forms a part of our wider individual and corporate efforts. We are a diverse group representing a wide spectrum of theological, denominational and ministry streams and emphases. But our goal is the same. The material here in *Peoples of the Buddhist World* is based on contributions from various people and agencies who share a burden for the salvation of all of these peoples. There has been a beautiful surge in global prayer on behalf of the Muslim, and later Hindu, mega blocs, as people have petitioned the Lord of the harvest for new breakthroughs in these least-reached sectors of humanity. Part of our motivation is to help facilitate the same prayer movement for the Buddhist sphere.

So we call you, reader, to become a full participant in this groundswell of intercession for the dear peoples pictured and described here, many of them from the remotest families on the earth, that they will experience the fullness of the answer to our prayer, 'Thy Kingdom come, Thy will be done—among the Drukpa, Newar, Mongol, Buriat and Tibetans as in heaven!' And we will fully expect, in the intervening months and years, a thousand stories of wonder at the ways of God to open, enlighten and transform the peoples of the Buddhist world, as his undeniable answer

Steve Spaulding

Peoples of the Buddhist World will take you on an exciting journey through the Buddhist world. You will encounter groups and cultures as diverse as the Buriat and Tuva of the frozen Siberian plains, the Chuanlan of China (among whom only the women believe in Buddhism while the men do not), the oppressed and hardy Tibetans living on the 'roof of the world', numerous Buddhist groups living among the valleys and mountain slopes of the Himalayas in Nepal and India, the unique people of Bhutan—the mysterious 'land of the thunder dragon', the smiling and gentle Buddhists of Southeast Asia—all the way south to the Sinhalese people of beautiful Sri Lanka, guardians of the Theravada tradition.

When I was first asked to consider writing this book I hesitated, believing I was unqualified to undertake such a task. I felt this lack of confidence in spite of the fact that I had spent my entire adult life living in Buddhist nations. I first served as a missionary in Hong Kong and China as a teenager, frequently interacting with people influenced by Mahayana Buddhism. Even though I am from New Zealand and my wife Joy is an American, we met in Hong Kong. Indeed, when I first met her she was living in an apartment just a stone's throw away from the Ten Thousand Buddhas Temple in the New Territories.

Years later, after we were married, we relocated to Chiang Mai, northern Thailand, which is a major centre for Theravada Buddhism. Our two sons were born in Chiang Mai, delivered by doctors and nurses who were Buddhists. Every day we spoke with Buddhist people: our landlord, printer, gardener, plumber, babysitter, electrician. Our little home outside Chiang Mai was located in a village near a huge 100-foot high idol of Buddha that overlooked the area. The 20-minute daily drive from my house to my office took me past several Buddhist temples and numerous prayer shrines. Buddhist philosophies dominated the lives of tens of thousands of people all around us. Over the years our travels frequently took us into Buddhist nations throughout Asia, such as Laos, Myanmar, Tibet, Thailand, Nepal, Sri Lanka, Japan, South Korea and north India.

Yet I still felt completely inadequate to write this book. As I pondered the reasons why, I began to realize that so little heart-warming Christian material had ever been produced about the Buddhist world. Certainly there were numerous academic papers and doctoral dissertations about various aspects of Buddhism, but very little prayer material that touches people's souls. I found it ironic that the Buddhist world was so full of vibrancy, smiling people and splashes of colour, yet the overwhelming majority of information that the Christian world had produced on them was grey, technical and not particularly motivational.

I wanted to produce something that people from all walks of life would want to read. My target audience is not so much professors of Buddhist philosophy, but housewives in Wisconsin, school kids in Singapore and prospective missionaries in Manila. For me, the benchmark of the book's success is not so much whether it is accepted by scholars and academics, but whether it touches the hearts of common Christians. To achieve this it was obvious that lots of colour pictures needed to be included—not pictures of grim-faced camera-shy people, but pictures that portray the normal everyday life of Buddhist people. I am a firm believer in the saying, 'A picture paints a thousand words'. Flicking through these pages you will see smiling men and women, a monk mowing the lawn, children sleeping, Mongolians riding horses and wrestling, even someone taking a shower! And my favourite image of all—a group of beaming Buddhist monks sitting in a circle on the floor while scoffing down boxes of pizza from Pizza Hut, washed down with cans of Coca Cola!

To me, this is the real Buddhist world. Buddhists are normal people with the same desires as you and me. They enjoy sunny days, they want the best for their children's futures and they struggle with the daily grind of life.

Somehow the Buddhist world, particularly monks and nuns, have come to be viewed as unreachable and untouchable by many Christians. With their shaved heads, orange or saffron coloured robes and mysterious rituals, the millions of Buddhist monks in Asia are almost totally left alone by Christians. Yet didn't Christ command his followers to go into 'all the world' and preach the good news 'to every creature'?

Many of the articles inserted throughout the book give a rare, down-to-earth insight into the lives of the Buddhist clergy, especially Bryan Lurry's 'Behind the White-Washed Walls'. Lurry simply and honestly shares his testimony of how he befriended a group of Buddhist monks in Southeast Asia and ended up holding Bible studies with them inside their temple. Ubolwan Mejudhon's 'Love Letters from Afar' gives a tremendously touching account of her conversion to Christianity from a Thai Buddhist background, and a fascinating record of the long struggle she and her fiancé experienced as she gently tried to share Jesus Christ with him.

The Buddhists constitute a major block of humanity—hundreds of millions strong—that Christians seem to know little about beyond a few basic facts. In the past decades, large-scale initiatives have been launched to mobilize prayer and take the gospel to Muslims, Hindus, Communists, Jews . . . but the hundreds of millions of Buddhists seemed to rarely rate a mention. Part of the reason for the blasé attitude that much of the body of Christ has towards the Buddhist world may be because of the general perception that Buddhists are peaceable, relaxed and friendly. They do not threaten national security, and they are not likely to hijack airplanes, launch wars or invade nations. Consequently Buddhists tend to be overlooked by Christians and viewed as a less important priority, even though Christian missionary history among the Buddhist world has generally been one of failure and lack of progress.

This realization stirred me to accept the challenge to write this book. It is time for the approximately 700 million Buddhists to gain a rightful place in the prayers, activities, knowledge and allocation of resources of the Christian world. Most Buddhist people will probably not be saved by grandiose evangelistic plans or mass media saturation. They will be reached when humble individuals, whose lives have been touched by the love and grace of God and transformed by the truth of his word, befriend and lovingly express this truth to those who have yet to believe. This is how the kingdom of God has always advanced throughout history, and this is how his kingdom is coming throughout the Buddhist world today.

Bob Pierce, the founder of World Vision, often prayed, 'Let my heart be broken with the things that break the heart of God.' Does it break God's heart today that hundreds of millions of Buddhists are marching to hell with little or no gospel witness? Does it break the Saviour's heart that millions worship lifeless idols instead of the true, glorious Heavenly Father? Does it pain the heart of the Father that so few Buddhists have ever heard the Name of his beloved Son?

May we pray the same prayer and, equally importantly, may we possess the same determination and motivation to do something about it as Bob Pierce did.

Paul Hattaway

Acknowledgements

Any project of this size requires the partnership and assistance of numerous people and organizations. I was overwhelmed with the level of help and support that came from God's people in many places.

First and foremost I thank my beautiful wife Joy. She is truly the unseen contributor to all my books. Without her support, encouragement and selfless work behind the scenes, I would not be able to write anything at all.

My heartfelt appreciation goes to Steve Spaulding, Tom and Liz, and others who encouraged this project and showed me its importance.

The office staff at Asia Harvest in Thailand all contributed to the book's production in different ways, whether by long journeys through parts of the Buddhist world, or through menial tasks such as photocopying and scanning pictures. Thank you especially to Harley Hochstetler, Dwayne and Tamara Graybill and Angela Li.

To George, Christine and the fellowship in the basement who pray for us every day—thank you for throwing us a lifeline!

Valerie Lim of Global Mapping International kindly gave much of her time and energy to produce all 238 maps that appear in this book. These are a vital addition to the project that will be appreciated by all readers. Thank you, Valerie!

Numerous gifted photographers freely loaned many superb photographs. They are masterpieces, vividly portraying the heart of God for the Buddhist peoples. Each image used in *Peoples of the Buddhist World* lists the name of the photographer, but in particular I would like to thank Dwayne Graybill, Julian Hawken, David Treat, Nancy Sturrock, Khun Xay of Xayographix and Midge Conner.

Christian organizations and publications who provided pictures for this book include the International Mission Board (Southern Baptists), Create International, Myanmar Faces and Places, China Advocate, Asian Report, Gospel Recordings (Nepal), The Voice of the Martyrs, Christian Far East Ministries, Revival Christian Church (Hong Kong) and the Cooperative Baptist Fellowship. On a few occasions CDs containing images and information were sent to me by missionaries who didn't care to be acknowledged, just as long as their contribution helped the kingdom of God. I thank you all, and the God who knows you all by name will surely reward you!

A number of writers kindly penned articles for this book, or allowed me to adapt articles they had published elsewhere. These gems give backbone to this book, providing sharp insight into specific areas of the Buddhist world. I am greatly indebted to Dr Alex Smith, Hugh Kemp, Dorje, Dr Ralph Covell, Dr David Hesselgrave, Dr Ubolwan Mejudhon, Tilak Rupasinghe, Vijay Karunaratne and Bryan Lurry.

Finally and not least, I would like to express my deep appreciation to Pieter and Elria Kwant and the staff of Piquant for your values, patience, hard work and commitment to the Lord Jesus, and for the way you express these attributes through your publishing ministry.

I hope you will be encouraged and challenged by reading this book and moved to prayer and involvement to reach all Buddhist peoples with the gospel, until *'the kingdom of the world has become the kingdom of our Lord and of his Christ, and he will reign for ever and ever'* (Rev 11:15, NIV).

Overview of Buddhist Peoples

Classification by Population (Projected for the year 2010)

Note: For qualification for inclusion in this book an ethnic group needed to have 50% or more of its population as professing Buddhists, or have a total number of Buddhist adherants greater than 500,000.

People Group	Buddhism	Population (2010)	Professing Buddhists	B %	Primary Country	Language Family	Professing Christians	C %
Han Chinese, Mandarin	Mahayana	947,648,700	236,912,200	25%	China	Sino-Tibetan	75,000,000	7.9%
Japanese	Mahayana	130,779,800	91,545,900	70%	Japan	Japanese	2,000,000	1.6%
Vietnamese	Mahayana	83,340,700	54,171,500	65%	Vietnam	Austro-Asiatic	6,500,000	7.8%
Burmese	Theravada	35,309,500	34,956,400	99%	Myanmar	Sino-Tibetan	40,000	0.1%
Thai, Central	Theravada	30,060,200	29,459,000	98%	Thailand	Tai-Kadai	100,000	0.4%
Han Chinese, Wu	Mahayana	92,600,000	27,780,000	30%	China	Sino-Tibetan	6,000,000	6.5%
Han Chinese, Cantonese	Mahayana	68,156,500	27,262,600	40%	China	Sino-Tibetan	2,500,000	3.7%
Isan	Theravada	23,888,700	22,694,300	95%	Thailand	Tai-Kadai	50,000	0.2%
Korean	Mahayana	84,414,100	21,103,500	25%	South Korea	Korean	17,000,000	20.2%
Han Chinese, Min Nan	Mahayana	60,939,500	18,281,900	30%	China	Sino-Tibetan	3,000,000	5.0%
Sinhalese	Theravada	17,098,500	15,388,650	90%	Sri Lanka	Indo-European	620,000	3.7%
Khmer	Theravada	14,283,400	13,712,000	96%	Cambodia	Austro-Asiatic	100,000	0.7%
Han Chinese, Xiang	Mahayana	40,752,000	12,225,600	30%	China	Sino-Tibetan	400,000	1.0%
Han Chinese, Jin	Mahayana	60,368,000	12,073,600	20%	China	Sino-Tibetan	2,000,000	3.4%
Han Chinese, Gan	Mahayana	41,306,000	10,326,500	25%	China	Sino-Tibetan	1,500,000	3.7%
Thai, Northern	Theravada	7,116,800	6,761,000	95%	Thailand	Tai-Kadai	40,000	0.6%
Mongol	Tibetan	10,564,000	5,810,200	55%	China	Altaic	31,000	0.3%
Thai, Southern	Theravada	5,973,200	4,181,200	70%	Thailand	Tai-Kadai	27,000	0.5%
Hakka	Mahayana	40,745,200	3,667,100	9%	China	Sino-Tibetan	900,000	2.2%
Lao	Theravada	3,823,000	3,555,400	93%	Laos	Tai-Kadai	50,000	1.4%
Shan	Theravada	3,663,000	3,479,850	95%	Myanmar	Tai-Kadai	30,000	0.9%
Han Chinese, Min Dong	Mahayana	10,379,100	3,113,700	30%	China	Sino-Tibetan	600,000	5.8%
Rakhine	Theravada	2,397,200	1,797,900	75%	Myanmar	Sino-Tibetan	19,100	0.8%
Manchu	Mahayana	16,340,100	1,617,700	10%	China	Altaic	22,000	0.2%
Khampa, Eastern	Tibetan	1,535,200	1,458,400	95%	China	Sino-Tibetan	400	0.1%
Tibetan, Central	Tibetan	1,282,000	1,256,300	98%	China	Sino-Tibetan	200	0.1%
Bai	Mahayana	2,470,600	1,235,300	50%	China	Sino-Tibetan	50,000	2.0%
Han Chinese, Hainanese	Mahayana	5,931,200	1,186,200	20%	China	Sino-Tibetan	300,000	5.1%
Mon	Theravada	1,274,800	1,083,600	85%	Myanmar	Austro-Asiatic	10,000	0.8%
Lu	Theravada	1,208,600	1,063,600	88%	China	Tai-Kadai	2,500	0.2%
Han Chinese, Min Bei	Mahayana	2,909,200	872,800	30%	China	Sino-Tibetan	150,000	5.2%
Han Chinese, Huizhou	Mahayana	4,121,400	824,300	20%	China	Sino-Tibetan	250,000	6.1%
Tibetan, Gtsang	Tibetan	814,900	806,750	99%	China	Sino-Tibetan	50	0.1%
Tamang, Eastern	Tibetan	1,086,600	760,600	70%	Nepal	Sino-Tibetan	70,000	6.5%
Han Chinese, Puxian	Mahayana	2,976,100	744,000	25%	China	Sino-Tibetan	120,000	4.1%
Amdo, Hbrogpa	Tibetan	719,200	712,000	99%	China	Sino-Tibetan	100	0.1%
Han Chinese, Pinghua	Mahayana	2,642,000	660,500	25%	China	Sino-Tibetan	10,000	0.4%
Taungyo	Theravada	629,400	616,800	98%	Myanmar	Sino-Tibetan	3,000	0.5%
Pa-O	Theravada	763,000	610,400	80%	Myanmar	Sino-Tibetan	12,000	1.6%
Chuanqing	Mahayana	981,600	539,900	55%	China	Sino-Tibetan	25,000	2.6%
Newar	Mahayana	1,736,200	520,300	30%	Nepal	Sino-Tibetan	20,000	1.2%
Tai Mao	Theravada	566,500	481,500	85%	China	Tai-Kadai	600	0.1%
Kalmyk-Oirat	Tibetan	538,700	457,900	85%	Mongolia	Altaic	1,800	0.4%
Chakma	Theravada	471,900	448,300	95%	Bangladesh	Indo-European	12,000	2.6%

People Group	Buddhism	Population (2010)	Professing Buddhists	B %	Primary Country	Language Family	Professing Christians	C %
Phuan	Theravada	357,600	339,700	95%	Thailand	Tai-Kadai	800	0.2%
Palaung, Pale	Theravada	337,100	333,700	99%	Myanmar	Austro-Asiatic	300	0.1%
Tamang, Western	Tibetan	481,500	313,000	65%	Nepal	Sino-Tibetan	30,000	6.3%
Buriat, Russia	Tibetan	510,600	280,800	55%	Russia	Altaic	1,000	0.2%
Drukpa	Tibetan	380,100	266,000	70%	Bhutan	Sino-Tibetan	800	0.2%
Tsangla	Tibetan	315,100	252,100	80%	Bhutan	Sino-Tibetan	100	0.1%
Khampa, Western	Tibetan	254,200	251,600	99%	China	Sino-Tibetan	10	0.1%
Tu	Tibetan	250,200	245,200	98%	China	Altaic	10	0.1%
Tuva	Tibetan	258,800	232,900	90%	Russia	Altaic	2,000	0.8%
Phutai	Theravada	460,900	230,450	50%	Laos	Tai-Kadai	900	0.2%
Chuanlan	Mahayana	367,000	220,200	60%	China	Sino-Tibetan	20,000	5.5%
Kui	Theravada	292,700	219,500	75%	Thailand	Austro-Asiatic	9,500	3.3%
Palaung, Shwe	Theravada	209,900	201,500	96%	Myanmar	Austro-Asiatic	500	0.2%
Torgut	Tibetan	188,300	188,300	100%	China	Altaic	0	
Intha	Theravada	192,000	188,200	98%	Myanmar	Sino-Tibetan	200	0.1%
Gurung, Eastern	Tibetan	311,000	186,600	60%	Nepal	Sino-Tibetan	200	0.1%
Jiarong, Situ	Tibetan	199,550	179,600	90%	China	Sino-Tibetan	2	0.1%
Amdo, Rongmahbrogpa	Tibetan	180,800	179,000	99%	China	Sino-Tibetan	20	0.1%
Chaungtha	Theravada	165,600	160,600	97%	Myanmar	Sino-Tibetan	200	0.1%
Golog	Tibetan	164,600	158,000	96%	China	Sino-Tibetan	10	0.1%
Palaung, Rumai	Theravada	159,000	155,800	98%	Myanmar	Austro-Asiatic	600	0.4%
Amdo, Rongba	Tibetan	156,500	155,000	99%	China	Sino-Tibetan	10	0.1%
Kayah, Western	Theravada	302,600	151,300	50%	Myanmar	Sino-Tibetan	4,000	1.4%
Khampa, Northern	Tibetan	145,900	145,900	100%	China	Sino-Tibetan	0	
Nyaw	Theravada	136,000	129,200	95%	Thailand	Tai-Kadai	100	0.1%
Khun	Theravada	131,700	125,100	95%	Myanmar	Tai-Kadai	2,000	1.6%
Tibetan, Jone	Tibetan	123,400	117,200	95%	China	Sino-Tibetan	200	0.2%
Tavoyan	Theravada	112,900	110,650	98%	Myanmar	Sino-Tibetan	100	0.1%
Danau	Theravada	115,200	109,400	95%	Myanmar	Austro-Asiatic	500	0.4%
Khampa, Southern	Tibetan	119,200	107,300	90%	China	Sino-Tibetan	7,500	6.3%
Gurung, Western	Tibetan	213,300	106,700	50%	Nepal	Sino-Tibetan	200	0.1%
Ladakhi	Tibetan	128,000	102,400	80%	India	Sino-Tibetan	220	0.2%
Amdo, Rtahu	Tibetan	97,100	97,100	100%	China	Sino-Tibetan	0	
Khamti	Theravada	97,900	96,900	99%	Myanmar	Tai-Kadai	30	0.1%
Bulang	Theravada	120,050	96,000	80%	China	Austro-Asiatic	100	0.1%
Sherpa	Tibetan	95,400	93,500	98%	India	Sino-Tibetan	40	0.1%
Buriat, China	Tibetan	127,600	89,300	60%	China	Altaic	100	0.1%
Tibetan, Shangri-La	Tibetan	92,100	87,500	95%	China	Sino-Tibetan	2,000	2.2%
Tai Nua	Theravada	172,800	86,400	50%	China	Tai-Kadai	20	0.1%
So	Theravada	165,800	82,900	50%	Laos	Austro-Asiatic	3,000	1.9%
Tamang, Southwestern	Tibetan	163,900	81,950	50%	Nepal	Sino-Tibetan	7,000	4.3%
Ergong	Tibetan	74,500	73,800	99%	China	Sino-Tibetan	1	0.1%
Tibetan, Nghari	Tibetan	61,500	61,500	100%	China	Sino-Tibetan	0	
Kheng	Tibetan	64,400	61,200	95%	Bhutan	Sino-Tibetan	50	0.1%
Han Tai	Theravada	70,700	56,550	80%	China	Tai-Kadai	200	0.3%
Lepcha	Tibetan	83,800	54,500	65%	India	Sino-Tibetan	18,000	21.5%
Lao Krang	Theravada	55,100	54,500	99%	Thailand	Tai-Kadai	100	0.2%
Tamang, Northwestern	Tibetan	82,600	53,700	65%	Nepal	Sino-Tibetan	2,000	2.5%
Mosuo	Tibetan	53,700	51,000	95%	China	Sino-Tibetan	100	0.2%
Lao Wieng	Theravada	54,600	49,150	90%	Thailand	Tai-Kadai	300	0.6%

People Group	Buddhism	Population (2010)	Professing Buddhists	B %	Primary Country	Language Family	Professing Christians	C %
Huayao Tai	Theravada	89,200	49,050	55%	China	Tai-Kadai	200	0.2%
Kucong	Theravada	88,500	48,700	55%	China	Sino-Tibetan	1,500	1.7%
Lawa, Western	Theravada	68,700	48,100	70%	China	Austro-Asiatic	10,000	14.6%
Pumi, Northern	Tibetan	48,100	48,100	100%	China	Sino-Tibetan	0	
Sogwo Arig	Tibetan	47,700	46,250	97%	China	Sino-Tibetan	0	
Bumthang	Tibetan	48,300	45,900	95%	Bhutan	Sino-Tibetan	50	0.1%
Song	Theravada	49,600	44,650	90%	Thailand	Tai-Kadai	400	0.9%
Mru	Theravada	75,100	41,300	55%	Myanmar	Sino-Tibetan	5,000	6.7%
Buriat, Mongolia	Tibetan	81,900	41,000	50%	Mongolia	Altaic	50	0.1%
Kinnaura	Tibetan	73,500	36,750	50%	India	Sino-Tibetan	100	0.2%
Mongour	Tibetan	49,800	34,850	70%	China	Altaic	0	
Loba	Tibetan	33,700	33,350	99%	Nepal	Sino-Tibetan	10	0.1%
Mongol, Sichuan	Tibetan	35,000	33,250	95%	China	Sino-Tibetan	5	0.1%
Sikkimese	Tibetan	33,300	32,600	98%	India	Sino-Tibetan	200	0.7%
Matpa	Tibetan	32,200	32,200	100%	Bhutan	Sino-Tibetan	0	
Lao Ngaew	Theravada	33,100	32,100	97%	Thailand	Tai-Kadai	60	0.2%
Zangskari	Tibetan	32,750	29,480	90%	India	Sino-Tibetan	0	
Padaung	Theravada	56,200	28,100	50%	Myanmar	Sino-Tibetan	8,000	14.3%
Dainet	Theravada	28,100	28,100	100%	Myanmar	Sino-Tibetan	0	
Tinan	Tibetan	34,400	27,500	80%	India	Sino-Tibetan	20	0.1%
Qiang, Yadu	Tibetan	38,200	26,750	70%	China	Sino-Tibetan	0	
Tak Bai Thai	Theravada	26,600	26,330	99%	Thailand	Tai-Kadai	20	0.1%
Lao Lom	Theravada	27,300	26,200	96%	Thailand	Tai-Kadai	0	
Thet	Theravada	25,800	25,800	100%	Myanmar	Sino-Tibetan	0	
Minyak	Tibetan	25,750	25,750	100%	China	Sino-Tibetan	0	
Zhaba	Tibetan	25,750	25,750	100%	China	Sino-Tibetan	0	
Tibetan, Shanyan	Tibetan	24,600	24,600	100%	China	Sino-Tibetan	0	
Dzala	Tibetan	24,100	24,100	100%	Bhutan	Sino-Tibetan	0	
Yakha	Tibetan	43,200	23,760	55%	Nepal	Sino-Tibetan	900	2.1%
Tebbu	Tibetan	24,600	23,370	95%	China	Sino-Tibetan	0	
Angku	Theravada	24,000	22,800	95%	Myanmar	Austro-Asiatic	0	
Dariganga	Tibetan	40,800	22,400	55%	Mongolia	Altaic	50	0.1%
Puman	Theravada	21,300	21,300	100%	China	Austro-Asiatic	0	
Qiang, Luhua	Tibetan	23,300	20,970	90%	China	Sino-Tibetan	0	
Tai Wang	Theravada	20,600	20,200	98%	Laos	Tai-Kadai	40	0.2%
Saek	Theravada	36,400	20,000	55%	Laos	Tai-Kadai	50	0.2%
Qiang, Mawo	Tibetan	19,950	18,950	95%	China	Sino-Tibetan	0	
Walung	Tibetan	19,700	18,700	95%	Nepal	Sino-Tibetan	10	0.1%
Helambu Sherpa	Tibetan	18,200	18,000	99%	Nepal	Sino-Tibetan	40	0.3%
Kaleung	Theravada	18,400	17,480	95%	Thailand	Tai-Kadai	0	
Ersu	Tibetan	34,350	17,180	50%	China	Sino-Tibetan	0	
Thami	Tibetan	29,600	16,280	55%	Nepal	Sino-Tibetan	300	1.1%
Kurtop	Tibetan	16,100	16,100	100%	Bhutan	Sino-Tibetan	0	
Nyenpa	Tibetan	16,100	16,100	100%	Bhutan	Sino-Tibetan	0	
Jiarong, Chabao	Tibetan	17,450	15,700	90%	China	Sino-Tibetan	0	
Kyerung	Tibetan	13,700	13,700	100%	Nepal	Sino-Tibetan	0	
Yong	Theravada	13,100	13,100	100%	Thailand	Tai-Kadai	0	
Guiqiong	Tibetan	12,020	12,020	100%	China	Sino-Tibetan	0	
Ghale, Southern	Tibetan	23,700	11,850	50%	Nepal	Sino-Tibetan	300	1.3%
Groma	Tibetan	18,390	18,390	100%	China	Sino-Tibetan	0	

OVERVIEW OF BUDDHIST PEOPLES

People Group	Buddhism	Population (2010)	Professing Buddhists	B %	Primary Country	Language Family	Professing Christians	C %
Xiangcheng	Tibetan	13,750	13,050	95%	China	Sino-Tibetan	5	0.1%
Samtao	Theravada	14,400	12,960	90%	Myanmar	Austro-Asiatic	120	0.9%
Lap	Tibetan	12,800	12,800	100%	Bhutan	Sino-Tibetan	0	
Dolpo	Tibetan	12,950	11,650	90%	Nepal	Sino-Tibetan	20	0.2%
Qiang, Cimulin	Tibetan	16,300	11,400	70%	China	Sino-Tibetan	0	
Khorat Thai	Theravada	11,000	10,900	99%	Thailand	Tai-Kadai	50	0.5%
Queyu	Tibetan	10,420	10,420	100%	China	Sino-Tibetan	0	
Thakali	Tibetan	20,600	10,300	50%	Nepal	Sino-Tibetan	70	0.4%
Khuen	Theravada	12,850	10,300	80%	Laos	Austro-Asiatic	200	1.6%
Monpa, Kalaktang	Tibetan	9,850	9,850	100%	India	Sino-Tibetan	0	
Jirel	Tibetan	12,950	9,060	70%	Nepal	Sino-Tibetan	200	1.6%
Monpa, Tawang	Tibetan	8,550	8,460	99%	India	Sino-Tibetan	10	0.1%
Chong	Theravada	8,420	8,250	98%	Cambodia	Austro-Asiatic	50	0.6%
Lhomi	Tibetan	10,290	8,230	80%	Nepal	Sino-Tibetan	300	3.0%
Brokpa	Tibetan	8,050	8,050	100%	Bhutan	Sino-Tibetan	0	
Yoy	Theravada	9,250	7,400	80%	Thailand	Tai-Kadai	0	
Lawa, Eastern	Theravada	8,600	7,300	85%	Thailand	Austro-Asiatic	100	1.2%
Yugur, Saragh	Tibetan	11,880	7,130	60%	China	Altaic	50	0.5%
Bonan, Tongren	Tibetan	7,100	7,100	100%	China	Altaic	0	
Monpa, Medog	Tibetan	8,200	7,000	85%	China	Sino-Tibetan	0	
Tai He	Theravada	11,350	6,800	60%	Laos	Tai-Kadai	0	
Monpa, Dirang	Tibetan	6,500	6,450	99%	India	Sino-Tibetan	5	0.1%
Tsum	Tibetan	6,400	6,400	100%	Nepal	Sino-Tibetan	0	
Tai Bueng	Theravada	6,200	6,200	100%	Thailand	Tai-Kadai	0	
Jiarong, Sidabao	Tibetan	6,850	6,160	90%	China	Sino-Tibetan	0	
Champa	Tibetan	5,830	5,830	100%	India	Sino-Tibetan	0	
Jiarong, Guanyingqiao	Tibetan	6,300	5,670	90%	China	Sino-Tibetan	0	
Manangba	Tibetan	5,940	5,940	100%	Nepal	Sino-Tibetan	0	
Qixingmin	Mahayana	5,890	5,890	100%	China	Sino-Tibetan	0	
Aiton	Theravada	5,450	5,450	100%	India	Tai-Kadai	0	
Tai Phake	Theravada	5,400	5,400	100%	India	Tai-Kadai	0	
Hdzanggur	Tibetan	5,380	5,380	100%	China	Sino-Tibetan	0	
Gahri	Tibetan	7,050	4,940	70%	India	Sino-Tibetan	15	0.2%
Tamang, Eastern Gorkha	Tibetan	5,900	4,720	80%	Nepal	Sino-Tibetan	300	5.1%
Nubri	Tibetan	4,700	4,700	100%	Nepal	Sino-Tibetan	0	
Mugali	Tibetan	4,610	4,610	100%	Nepal	Sino-Tibetan	0	
Jiarong, Shangzhai	Tibetan	5,040	4,530	90%	China	Sino-Tibetan	0	
Singhpo	Theravada	4,600	4,510	98%	India	Sino-Tibetan	70	1.6%
Dokhpa	Tibetan	4,600	4,140	90%	India	Indo-European	0	
Tai Khang	Theravada	7,090	3,900	55%	Laos	Tai-Kadai	0	
Yugur, Enger	Tibetan	5,800	3,770	65%	China	Altaic	50	0.9%
Ghale, Northern	Tibetan	3,750	3,560	95%	Nepal	Sino-Tibetan	0	
Sherdukpen	Tibetan	3,540	3,470	98%	India	Sino-Tibetan	20	0.6%
Shixing	Tibetan	3,430	3,430	100%	China	Sino-Tibetan	0	
Nyahkur	Theravada	3,430	3,250	95%	Thailand	Austro-Asiatic	0	
Gongduk	Tibetan	3,200	3,200	100%	Bhutan	Sino-Tibetan	0	
Dura	Tibetan	6,350	3,170	50%	Nepal	Indo-European	30	0.5%
Stod Bhoti	Tibetan	3,100	3,100	100%	India	Sino-Tibetan	0	
Wutun	Tibetan	3,070	3,070	100%	China	Unclassified	0	

People Group	Buddhism	Population (2010)	Professing Buddhists	B %	Primary Country	Language Family	Professing Christians	C %
Kagate	Tibetan	3,100	3,040	98%	Nepal	Sino-Tibetan	20	0.7%
Dowaniya	Theravada	3,500	2,970	85%	India	Sino-Tibetan	0	
Tai Gapong	Theravada	3,690	2,770	75%	Thailand	Tai-Kadai	0	
Chak	Theravada	2,730	2,700	99%	Myanmar	Unclassified	10	0.4%
Baragaunle	Tibetan	2,700	2,700	100%	Nepal	Sino-Tibetan	0	
Kaike	Tibetan	2,650	2,650	100%	Nepal	Sino-Tibetan	0	
Tai Pao	Theravada	4,680	2,570	55%	Laos	Tai-Kadai	0	
Nupbi	Tibetan	2,550	2,550	100%	Bhutan	Sino-Tibetan	0	
Yonzhi	Tibetan	4,030	2,420	60%	China	Sino-Tibetan	0	
Monpa, Lishpa	Tibetan	2,400	2,400	100%	India	Sino-Tibetan	0	
Man	Theravada	4,200	2,100	50%	India	Indo-European	250	6.0%
Lao Ga	Theravada	2,000	2,000	100%	Thailand	Tai-Kadai	0	
Ghale, Kutang	Tibetan	1,900	1,900	100%	Nepal	Sino-Tibetan	0	
Chali	Tibetan	1,600	1,600	100%	Bhutan	Sino-Tibetan	0	
Dakpa	Tibetan	1,600	1,600	100%	Bhutan	Sino-Tibetan	0	
Lemo	Theravada	2,670	1,600	60%	China	Sino-Tibetan	0	
Tai Loi	Theravada	2,250	1,240	55%	Myanmar	Austro-Asiatic	0	
Manmet	Theravada	1,700	1,190	70%	China	Austro-Asiatic	0	
Turung	Theravada	1,160	1,160	100%	India	Tai-Kadai	0	
Gara	Tibetan	1,150	1,150	100%	India	Indo-European	0	
Khamiyang	Theravada	1,150	1,140	99%	India	Tai-Kadai	0	
Hu	Theravada	1,890	1,130	60%	China	Austro-Asiatic	0	
Mpi	Theravada	1,710	1,110	65%	Thailand	Sino-Tibetan	0	
Na	Tibetan	1,230	1,230	100%	India	Sino-Tibetan	0	
Monpa, Chugpa	Tibetan	950	950	100%	India	Sino-Tibetan	0	
Thavung	Theravada	1,250	940	75%	Thailand	Austro-Asiatic	0	
Khowa	Tibetan	950	920	97%	India	Sino-Tibetan	0	
Monpa, But	Tibetan	870	850	97%	India	Sino-Tibetan	0	
Mon, Ladakh	Tibetan	840	840	100%	India	Indo-European	0	
Ole	Tibetan	800	800	100%	Bhutan	Sino-Tibetan	0	
Barua	Theravada	930	740	80%	India	Indo-European	0	
Za	Tibetan	610	610	100%	China	Sino-Tibetan	0	
Malimasa	Tibetan	600	600	100%	China	Sino-Tibetan	0	
Huay	Theravada	570	480	85%	Thailand	Austro-Asiatic	0	
Brokpa, Brokkat	Tibetan	480	480	100%	Bhutan	Sino-Tibetan	0	
Zakhring	Tibetan	380	380	100%	India	Sino-Tibetan	0	
Tangsa, Tikhak	Tibetan	620	370	60%	India	Sino-Tibetan	50	8.1%
Chimtan	Tibetan	370	370	100%	Nepal	Sino-Tibetan	0	
Beda	Tibetan	460	320	70%	India	Sino-Tibetan	15	3.3%
Tai Laan	Theravada	570	310	55%	Laos	Tai-Kadai	0	
Tai Doi	Theravada	450	310	70%	Laos	Austro-Asiatic	0	
Chhairottan	Tibetan	240	240	100%	Nepal	Sino-Tibetan	0	
Gong	Theravada	230	230	100%	Thailand	Sino-Tibetan	0	
Lao Ti	Theravada	220	220	100%	Thailand	Tai-Kadai	0	
Tangsa, Yongkuk	Tibetan	90	85	93%	India	Sino-Tibetan	2	2.2%
Totals		1,878,278,990	687,439,675	36.6%			119,711,090	6.4%

Methodology and Terminology

Before you begin reading through this book it will be helpful to take a few minutes to read this section so that you can have a fuller understanding of the methodology and terminology employed in *Peoples of the Buddhist World*.

The profiles

In addition to the articles by various writers that are distributed throughout the book, *Peoples of the Buddhist World* contains one-page profiles of 238 distinct ethnolinguistic Buddhist people groups. They are arranged in alphabetical order, from the Aiton of north-east India to the Zhaba of western China. Each profile has been assigned a date. This is to help readers who wish to pray daily (or read the book in bite-size chunks) to complete the whole book over a period of one year. Because the number of days in a year exceeds the number of groups profiled in the book, I have allocated three days of prayer for groups that number in excess of one million Buddhists, and two days of prayer for groups with between 50,000 and one million Buddhists. All groups with less than 50,000 professing Buddhists have been assigned one day a year. Dividing the book this way, the entire year of 365 days covers the 238 groups.

Alongside a map for each group, a statistical box gives quick and easy access to the essential data for each group's population estimates for the years 2000, 2010 and 2020; countries where they live; the type of Buddhism they adhere to (Mahayana, Theravada or Tibetan), and the present number of Christians among them.

An overview table provides more vital data, including a list of all alternative names by which the group is known; their linguistic affiliation; the number and names of dialects (if any); estimates of the percentage of professing Buddhists and practising Buddhists; and a further percentage for the number of professing Christians. Next, four listings related to the availability of Christian resources for each group are given: details of any Christian Scripture that has been translated for them; whether the *Jesus* film is available in their language; a list of any cassette tapes produced by Gospel Recordings in this language; and whether any Christian radio broadcasts are available in the language. More detailed explanations of each of these categories appear below.

Finally, each profile contains a status of evangelization graph, displaying three estimates: the percentage of people in each group who have never heard the gospel; the percentage of those who have heard but have not become Christians; and the percentage of those who are believers in Christ.

Group names

In Asia, where all Buddhist people groups have their genesis, a particular people group may be known by several different names. When selecting the name for each group, the group's autonym (self-name) has been used as far as possible. The exception to this rule is when a group has become so well known by another name that it would be counter-productive to present the group by their autonym. For example, more than 1.5 million Newar people are the original inhabitants of the Kathmandu Valley in Nepal. According to how they spell their name in the Nepali language, Newar should actually be spelled Newah, and a Newah Association now exists that is actively promoting this name change. For the past 300 years, however, practically all books, magazine, journals and other literary sources have labelled this group *Newar*, so for now it was considered more prudent to continue with this commonly used spelling. Other groups may use a certain name among themselves, but sometimes these names are little known outside the inner circle of the group itself.

If a group is profiled because its members speak a distinct language, the language name is listed after the ethnic name—for example, *Palaung, Pale* or *Han Chinese, Cantonese*. The same applies to a group that is classified by geographical considerations such as a location—for example, *Tibetan, Nghari*; or direction—for example, *Thai, Southern*. The 'Index of Alternative Names' in the back of the book lists approximately 1,700 alternative names and spellings for the 238 groups profiled in *Peoples of the Buddhist World*.

Criteria for inclusion

In 1982, a group of mission leaders created the following definition of a 'people group':

'A significantly large ethnic or sociological grouping of individuals who perceive themselves to have a common affinity for one another because of their shared language, religion, ethnicity, residence, occupation, class or caste, situation, etc. or combinations of these. For evangelistic purposes, it is the largest group within which the gospel can spread as a church-planting movement without encountering barriers of understanding or acceptance.'[1] Missiologist Lawrence Radcliffe has poignantly stated, 'Ethnic identity is not so much in the blood as it is in the head (or in the heart) of the subject, or the observer.'[2]

Using these criteria, 238 distinct Buddhist people groups are profiled in *Peoples of the Buddhist World*. This book is believed to be the first ever attempt to profile *all* of the Buddhist peoples of the world. Information has been gathered from literature in numerous countries. In addition, the author and his wife have lived in predominantly Buddhist countries since they were both teenagers, conducting on-site field research and interacting with Buddhist culture in numerous Asian nations.

A group needed to meet one of two main criteria to qualify for inclusion in this book. First, groups that have 50 per cent or more of its population as professing Buddhists have been included, regardless of size. It was necessary to draw the line at 50 per cent as otherwise *Peoples of the Buddhist World* would have had to profile a few thousand more ethnic groups in Asia and around the world. If inclusion was based just on a group having Buddhist members, I would have had to produce separate profiles for Dutch Buddhists, Norwegian Buddhists, French Canadian Buddhists, Buddhists on each of the Pacific Islands and so on. The list would be endless.

Second, all groups with more than 500,000 professing Buddhists have been included regardless of what percentage of their population the Buddhists represent. The figure allowed me to include many large groups that are viewed as Buddhist, but which today have less than 50 per cent of their people professing faith in Buddhism. Some examples include the approximately 230 million Mandarin-speaking Han Chinese people who profess Buddhism as their religion (this figure equates to just 25 per cent of the group's overall population) and the more than 20 million Korean Buddhists.

Population trends

Some readers may be surprised to find only 238 people groups profiled in a book covering the entire Buddhist world. For a number of years there has been a misconception that more than 1,000 Buddhist groups exist in the world. As this book shows, however, many of the Buddhist peoples of Asia have huge populations, such as the various Han Chinese language groups, the 130 million Japanese, 80 million Vietnamese, 80 million Koreans, 35 million Burmese and so on.

These mega-peoples probably owe their cohesiveness and size to Buddhism. As the Buddhist religion swept across Asia, countless once-segregated tribal groups found a common faith and a unified creed by which to live. Buddhism became a huge linguistic, cultural and ethnic melting pot. This process of assimilation and fusion is still taking place today in numerous countries throughout Asia.

In Sri Lanka, which is widely recognized as a Buddhist country, it may surprise some readers to learn that there is just one Buddhist people group—the 17 million Sinhalese. A small number of animistic tribes have managed to hang on against the influence of Buddhism, while the Hindu Tamils inhabit the northern areas of the island. In Laos, also considered a Buddhist country, only about 30 of the approximately 130 ethnic groups could be described as Buddhist—the majority of groups are animist with minimal Buddhist influence.

In summary, then, although the number of distinct Buddhist people groups may not be particularly high, many of them are densely populated, with almost 700 million professing Buddhists living in people groups that by the year 2010 are expected to have a total population of 1.87 billion people.

A statistical summary of the 238 groups profiled in *Peoples of the Buddhist World* reveals some surprising trends. Mahayana Buddhism has by far the largest number of professing Buddhists (approximately 527 million), yet they are distributed among just 23 distinct people groups (an average of almost 23 million Buddhists per group). The huge mega groups such as the Chinese, Koreans, Vietnamese and Japanese are all Mahayana Buddhists. Conversely, Tibetan Buddhists number less than 17 million adherents, yet these are distributed in 129 different people groups (an average of just 130,000 Buddhists per group).

Many groups that have embraced Tibetan Buddhism have tended to retain their distinctiveness, and consequently they usually have smaller populations. Many distinct Buddhist peoples in Nepal, Bhutan, northern India and the Tibetan Plateau often have populations of a thousand or even less.

Type of Buddhism		Population (2010)	Professing Buddhists	B %	Professing Christians	C %
Mahayana Buddhists	23 groups	1,701,910,890	526,891,190	31.0%	118,367,000	6.9%
Theravada Buddhists	86 groups	153,085,440	143,900,240	94.0%	1,165,770	0.8%
Tibetan Buddhists	129 groups	23,277,280	16,642,865	71.5%	178,320	0.8%
Totals	**238 groups**	**1,878,278,990**	**687,439,675**	**36.6%**	**119,711,090**	**6.4%**

Supporting evidence

Dozens of pages of notes are included in the back of this volume—the author sought to provide as much documentation and corroborating evidence for the existence of, and material about, these groups as possible. An extensive bibliography, listing the titles of more than 1,000 books and articles, will help both students and missionaries to find more information about particular groups. *Peoples of the Buddhist World* presents a considerable amount of brand-new material on the ethnography and anthropology of the Buddhist peoples. Approximately 40 of the groups profiled have never before appeared on any Christian people group lists.

More than 100 Buddhist groups have communities in China. Writing this book just a few years after I compiled *Operation China*, it was difficult in some cases to create completely new profiles of Buddhist groups that were profiled in *Operation China*—especially with the almost complete lack of information available on many of the smaller groups. I have tried to give as much new information as possible in the China profiles, and the photographs are all new, but any careful reader of the two books will soon spot similarities between some of the profiles of Buddhist groups in *Operation China* and those in *Peoples of the Buddhist World*. This book updates and corrects some of the information that appeared in *Operation China*, and it also introduces several completely new Chinese Buddhist groups that had not yet been discovered when *Operation China* was published.

Population estimates

The profiles in this volume use the most recent, documented population figures for each group. Each profile features a coloured box with three population estimates: for the years 2000, 2010 and 2020. The base source for these estimates is listed in the overview section of each profile. It is important to note that the figures for each group refer to their worldwide population. Many groups have members living in more than one country (see Appendix 3: Distribution of Buddhist Peoples by Country). As a result of the hand over of Hong Kong to China in 1997—and that of Macau in 1999—the populations of Buddhist groups living in Hong Kong and Macau have been incorporated into figures for China.

Language

Each profile also provides the linguistic affiliation of each group. In most cases, this information comes from Barbara Grimes' *Ethnologue: Languages of the World*. Linguists have researched the relationship between different languages and dialects, providing valuable analysis which indicates linguistic intelligibility and reveals something of the historical relationship between different groups. The Buddhist people groups of the world speak languages stemming from five main families. Of the groups profiled in *Peoples of the Buddhist World,* 148 speak languages belonging to the Sino-Tibetan family, followed by Tai-Kadai (40 groups), Austro-Asiatic (24), Altaic (14) and Indo-European (8). Japanese and Korean are not listed under any of the above families as they are considered 'language isolates' by many linguists. Two other languages have yet to be classified. The Language Family Index, Appendix 2 at the back of the book, has been compiled to help readers see the linguistic relationship between various groups.

When considering groups for inclusion in this book on linguistic grounds, I was primarily concerned with mutual intelligibility. From the Christian perspective, this is vital in determining how far the gospel can spread from one people to another before it encounters linguistic barriers, which impede the spread of Christianity. In simple terms, if two people cannot understand each other's speech, this book considers that they speak different languages.

A number of Buddhist groups have been profiled separately because of linguistic differences. For example, many researchers place all the Khampa Tibetans together, but this book has separated them into four linguistic groupings: Northern Khampa, Western Khampa, Eastern Khampa and Southern Khampa. Although there is some mutual intelligibility between speakers from each of these four groups, their communication is often hampered by great difficulty. Christian ministries like Gospel Recordings have found it necessary to produce media in numerous languages in order to effectively communicate to people from different areas who may use the same ethnic name.

Similarly, the Han Chinese are the largest ethnic group in the world and Mandarin is spoken as a first language by more people than any other language. The Han are proud of their long history and ancient customs, and they display a very strong sense of ethnic unity. Suggestions that the Han Chinese from different regions of China may speak distinct languages are often met with mocking and disdain by the Chinese themselves, who insist that they are one people who speak one language.

Despite this bravado, the fact remains that Cantonese-speaking Han people from Guangdong Province in the south of the country have no success at all communicating with Wu-speaking Han people from Shanghai (unless they revert to speaking Mandarin, the national language). Neither of these Han groups can understand the speech of the Xiang-speaking Chinese of Hunan Province, and so on. This book has therefore profiled the various linguistic components of the Han Chinese separately.

The three main branches of Buddhism

Mahayana Buddhism: Mahayana means 'greater vehicle'. It is practised in Japan, Korea, Vietnam, China and wherever communities from these nations have dispersed around the globe. This sect believes that the fate of an individual is linked to the fate of others. Mahayana Buddhism 'is replete with innumerable heavens, hells and descriptions of *nirvana*. Prayers are addressed to the Buddha and combined with elaborate ritual'.[3] Mahayana further divides into numerous smaller sects. In Japan alone there are dozens of various Buddhist sects and sub-groups—Christianity in the West has fragmented in a similar way into numerous denominations.

Theravada Buddhism: Theravada, or 'doctrine of the elders', is the sect of Buddhism practised in Thailand, Myanmar, Laos, Cambodia and Sri Lanka, as well as among several minority groups in China's Yunnan Province. It is also known as Hinayana Buddhism, or 'lesser vehicle'. Most Theravada Buddhists reject the term Hinayana, however, claiming that it has derogatory connotations. Theravada Buddhism 'holds that the path to *nirvana* is an individual pursuit. It centres on monks and nuns who make the search for *nirvana* a full-time profession.'[4]

Tibetan Buddhism: Although technically Tibetan Buddhism falls under Mahayana Buddhism, it should be considered a distinct branch of the Buddhist world. It has become highly distinctive, with numerous practices, beliefs and systems not seen among other Buddhists. Tibetan Buddhism is also called Vajrayana Buddhism. One source states, 'Vajrayana Buddhism emphasizes life in the fast lane, with the object of reaching Nirvana within one lifetime instead of enduring countless rebirths. In mountaineering terms, it can be compared to the perilous direct ascent of a sheer face, as opposed to a safer indirect route.'[5] The Dalai Lama is the supreme ruler of Tibetan Buddhists, whereas there is no one such figurehead among the Theravada or Mahayana schools. Tibetan Buddhism divides into numerous sects, of which the Gelukpa ('Virtuous'), Sakya ('Grey earth'), Nyingmapa ('Ancient') and Kagyupa ('Oral transmission') are the main schools. The Nyingmapa, Kagyupa and Sakya schools are sometimes referred to as the Yellow Hat schools, according to the colour of the hats worn by the lamas, while the Sakya worshippers are also known as the Red Hat sect. However, Tibetans generally do not view the differences between the two groups of coloured hats as being as great as many Western scholars do. In fact, the red hats have a yellow lining, and the yellow hats have a red lining!

When Buddhism arrived in Tibet around AD 600, it was incorporated into the ancient religion of Bon, which had already been entrenched in the hearts of Tibetans for centuries. Bon was characterized by the worship of demons, ghosts and fearsome and wrathful deities who demanded regular animal and even human sacrifices. Tibetan Buddhism—also called Tantric Buddhism and Lamaism—today retains many of the features of Bon.

Status of Evangelization graphs

Each profile provides estimates of the status of evangelization. It has been my approach to portray the level of awareness of Christ among each group rather than attempt to determine the spiritual merits of their form of Christianity. In *Peoples of the Buddhist World,* Christians are simply defined as those who make a profession of faith in Christ, regardless of their particular set of doctrines or methods. Overall, it should be

METHODOLOGY AND TERMINOLOGY

acknowledged that only God knows the true number of people who have appropriated Christ's salvation. The aim is to present estimates that show the degree of penetration the gospel has made among Buddhist peoples. As the reader will discover, many groups have few people who have heard of Christ.

Each profile includes an easy-to-use graph, which shows estimates of the status of evangelization among each group. This graph is intended to provide the reader with a quick visual impression of the awareness of the gospel in each group. In one or two countries, including India, the official census forms ask people to declare their religion, making estimates for the numbers of Christians a simpler task. This is not the case in the majority of Asian countries.

Estimates take into consideration factors such as the history of mission work among a people group; the proximity of other Christian communities; reports and interviews with people who know the group or geographical region where the group is located; data I gathered during travels throughout Asia over many years; the linguistic variety present in each group; the level of interaction with other communities; and geographical isolation—many mountainous regions are unable to receive short-wave Christian radio broadcasts, for example.

Each graph lists the following three percentages:

A = the percentage of people who have never heard the gospel or the name of Christ. These are people who are completely unaware of Christianity.

B = the percentage of people who have been evangelized but have not yet become Christians. This does not necessarily reflect the percentage of people who have received a thorough presentation of the gospel but rather the percentage of people estimated to be aware of the existence of Christ. Many people in Asia have become aware of Christianity through gospel radio broadcasts and the showing of the *Jesus* film, for example. This form of ministry may have exposed a significant number of people to the Christian message for the first time, but it does not necessarily mean that the individual or community understood the message well enough to make an intelligent decision to accept or reject Christ.

C = the percentage of people who adhere to any form of Christianity. This indicates the total percentage of people who profess to be Christians, regardless of their denomination or adherence to any particular creed or doctrine. This figure does not necessarily portray the true number of people in a living relationship with Christ. *Note:* Decimal points have been rounded up to the next percentage point. Only those groups without any known churches or believers have 0% here. This helps readers identify quickly which groups are completely untouched by the gospel and without any Christian witness.

Maps

Each profile contains a map, lovingly and skilfully produced by Valerie Lim of Global Mapping International. The geographical extent of each group is shown, while a small inset map of Asia shows the reader which countries the group inhabits.

Overview data

Each profile also provides an overview listing twelve fields of information:

Other Names: Listing all alternative names by which the group is known. An additional index of approximately 1,700 alternative names appears as Appendix 1 at the back of this volume.

Population Source: The figure used as population base for the group is listed, followed by the date and source from which it was quoted. The figures for all members of the group living in each country are provided.

Language: The genetic affiliation of each language first lists its family and then all corresponding branches. See the Language Family Index (Appendix 2) for a more complete picture of how each language relates to others.

Dialects: Where available, all dialects spoken by a group are listed.

Professing Buddhists: This percentage is an estimate of how many members of each group profess Buddhism as their primary religion.

Practising Buddhists: This percentage is an estimate of how many people from each group participate in Buddhist rituals and actively express their faith. Some of the indicators for such expressions of faith include visiting Buddhist temples or monasteries, sending family members to join the monastic order, striving to obey Buddhist precepts and laws and involvement in Buddhist ceremonies and other religious activities. Among some groups, the percentage of practising Buddhists is considerably lower than the percentage of professing Buddhists. This usually reflects a situation in which, although a community still respects

Buddhism, its daily use is in decline. Birth ceremonies, weddings and funerals may involve hiring a Buddhist official, but the religion no longer plays a dominant role in the daily lives of members of the community. A similar dynamic is seen in other world religions. In the American 'Bible belt', for example, 90 per cent of a community may profess Christianity as their faith, but just 10 per cent to 15 per cent may actively attend a Christian fellowship or seek to obey the teachings of the Bible.

Christians: The percentage listed is the figure for all professing Christians among a particular group. This reflects the broadest definitions possible and includes Protestants, Catholics and other groups broadly defined as Christians.

Scripture: All available translations of the Bible, New Testament or books of the Bible (portions) are listed, including the first year of their publication. Where orthographies used in the past are now obsolete, or out of print, these are noted.

Jesus film: This category indicates whether the *Jesus* film (a powerful visual portrayal of the Gospel of Luke distributed by Campus Crusade for Christ) has been translated into the language spoken by the group. Currently the film is available in about 30 languages spoken by Buddhist people groups, but plans are underway for many more translations in the future.

Gospel Recordings: The Christian ministry Gospel Recordings has produced recordings in thousands of languages around the world. Most of them are short, 10- to 15-minute gospel messages including testimonies, songs and outlines of the life of Christ in each native tongue. This tool is especially valuable among tribal groups where there is a high rate of illiteracy.

Christian Broadcasting: This category gives details of any gospel radio broadcasts that are available in a group's language. There are numerous organizations broadcasting the gospel by radio today, but the Far East Broadcasting Company (FEBC) is widely recognized as having the greatest zeal to reach smaller tribal groups throughout Asia, many of which are Buddhists.

ROPAL code: ROPAL stands for the Registry of Peoples and Languages. It is used by Christian researchers to identify and classify the world's people groups, languages and dialects.

Notes

1. Ralph D Winter, 'Unreached Peoples: Recent Developments in the Concept', *Mission Frontiers* (August–September 1989) 12.
2. Lawrence B Radcliffe, 'A Field Worker Speaks out about the Rush to Reach All Peoples', *Mission Frontiers* 20.1–2 (January–February 1998), cited from the electronic edition.
3. Robert Storey ed., *China: A Travel Survival Kit* (Hawthorn, Australia: Lonely Planet Publications, 1994) 75.
4. Ibid.
5. Michael Buckley and Robert Strauss eds., *Tibet: A Travel Survival Kit* (Hawthorn, Australia: Lonely Planet Publications, 1986) 39.

Abbreviations

The following abbreviations have been used in the text and notes:

ABWE—Association of Baptists for World Evangelism
AMO—Asian Minorities Outreach
BWPC—Bethany World Prayer Center
CASS—Chinese Academy of Social Sciences
CCCOWE—Chinese Coordination Centre of World Evangelism
CHT—Chittagong Hill Tracts
CIM—China Inland Mission
CMA—Christian & Missionary Alliance
COI—Cooperative Outreach of India
CPLMR—Chinese Prayer Letter and Ministry Report
DAWN—Discipling a Whole Nation
EDCL—Encyclopedic Dictionary of Chinese Linguistics
FEBC—Far East Broadcasting Corporation
GEM—Global Evangelization Movement
IDP—Internally Displaced Peoples
IMA—India Missions Association
IMB—International Mission Board
km—kilometres
KNNP—Karenni National Progressive Party
LAC—Language Atlas of China
LBTA—Linguistics of the Tibeto-Burman Area
MARC—Missions Advanced Research Center
mi.—miles
n.d.—no date
NEFA—North East Frontier Agency
OMF—Overseas Missionary Fellowship
ROPAL—Registry of Peoples and Languages
SIL—Summer Institute of Linguistics
SPCK—Society for the Propagation of Christian Knowledge
sq. km—square kilometres
sq. mi.—square miles
STEDT—Sino-Tibetan Etymological Dictionary and Thesaurus
UBS—United Bible Societies
UN—United Nations

The Aiton ethnic group inhabits villages in the Jorhat and Karbi-Aleng districts of Assam State in north-east India. The Indian government does not recognize the Aiton at all, so reliable information about them is scarce. The linguist Anthony Diller in 1990 estimated that there were 'several thousand speakers and semi-speakers' of Aiton.[1]

The ancestors of the Aiton originated in northern Myanmar, where they lived for centuries along with other Tai-speaking groups. 'In the latter part of the eighteenth century, the Aiton entered Assam as political refugees from the Shan State in Burma... . They speak the Aiton language among themselves and Assamese, Hindi and English with others.'[2] The Aiton language is part of the Northwest branch of the Southwestern Tai family. It is one of nine different languages that share this affiliation, including Ahom, Khamti, Tai Phake and Khamiyang, all of which are spoken by other ethnic groups in this part of India. Aiton is believed to be similar to the Shan language spoken in Myanmar, China and Thailand, but after more than two centuries of separation from their homeland, the Aiton language, culture and identity have gradually been assimilated.

Elders among the Aiton are responsible for handing the oral traditions, folk tales and songs about their origin and migration down to the next generation. Their songs tell of oppression in their original homeland, which led to their long and difficult journey across the mountains into India.[3]

Until the past decade all Aiton were farmers, fishermen and hunters, but in recent years an increasing number of people have become businessmen, teachers and labourers in the nearby townships in both the government and private sectors.

Despite their small population, there are 14 different clans among the Aiton. These days the people use their respective clan names as their surnames. The strict marriage customs of the Aiton mean that a young man must marry his maternal uncle's daughter. A bride price is required, whereby the family of the groom must pay an agreed-upon amount of cash and goods to the family of the bride. In part this is an expression of gratitude to the bride's family for their years of expense in raising her. Buddhist monks are called upon to officiate at the wedding ceremony, which is held at the bride's house. After giving birth an Aiton woman must not interact with other members of the community for a full month, as she is considered 'polluted'. After the month has passed a ritual is performed and the new mother is free to return to society.

All Aiton are followers of Theravada Buddhism, which they brought with them when they migrated into India more than 200 years ago. They also 'worship Medham Medhphi, their deity, every morning and evening. The *vyas-chow chanq*, the diviner, is called for treatment of the indisposed.'[4] There are no known Christians among the Aiton. They have never appeared on lists of unreached people groups in India, but God has not forgotten them and desires that they may know him as Lord and Saviour.

Population:
4,600 (2000)
5,450 (2010)
6,300 (2020)
Countries: India
Buddhism: Theravada
Christians: none known

Overview of the Aiton

Other Names: Aitonia

Population Sources: 'several thousand speakers' in India (1990, A Diller)

Language: Tai-Kadai, Kam-Tai, Be-Tai, Tai-Sek, Tai, Southwestern, East Central, Northwest

Dialects: 0

Professing Buddhists: 100%

Practising Buddhists: 65%

Christians: 0%

Scripture: none

***Jesus* film:** none

Gospel Recordings: none

Christian Broadcasting: none

ROPAL code: AIO

Status of Evangelization

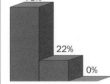

78%
22%
0%

A   B   C

A = Have never heard the gospel
B = Have heard the gospel but have not become Christians
C = Are adherents to some form of Christianity

Population:
583,700 (2000)
719,200 (2010)
886,000 (2020)
Countries: China
Buddhism: Tibetan
Christians: 100

Overview of the Hbrogpa Amdo

Other Names: Brogpa, Made, Anduo, Ngambo

Population Sources: 538,500 in China (1987, *Language Atlas of China*)

Language: Sino-Tibetan, Tibeto-Burman, Bodic, Bodish, Tibetan, Northern Tibetan

Dialects: 15

Professing Buddhists: 99%

Practising Buddhists: 95%

Christians: 0.1%

Scripture: Tibetan Bible 1948; New Testament 1885; Portions 1862

***Jesus* film:** available

Gospel Recordings: Amdo; Zang, Anduo

Christian Broadcasting: none

ROPAL code: ADX01

Status of Evangelization

91%

8%

1%

A   B   C

A = Have never heard the gospel
B = Have heard the gospel but have not become Christians
C = Are adherents to some form of Christianity

Hbrogpa Amdo is one of four main languages spoken by the Amdo Tibetans in western China. *Hbrogpa*, which means 'nomad' or 'herder' in Tibetan, is the largest of the Amdo languages. Linguistically, Amdo is very different from other languages within the Tibetan group. Within Amdo there are four mutually unintelligible languages, of which Hbrogpa is the most widely spoken.[1] Various linguistic sources mention 15 dialects within Hbrogpa.[2] Most Amdo are semi-nomadic herders of sheep, yaks and goats.

Approximately 600,000 Amdo speak the Hbrogpa language. They live in a vast, sparsely populated area of eastern Qinghai Province, as far north as the Qinghai-Gansu border. Significant numbers also live in southwest Gansu Province and in adjacent parts of northern Sichuan. The Hbrogpa region ranges from Qinghai Lake in the north — which at 4,000 square kilometres (1,560 sq. mi.) is the largest lake in China — to the town of Songpan in Sichuan in the south.[3] The Amdo region was incorporated into the Chinese empire in the early 1700s. Horrendous clashes with the Chinese have resulted in massive loss of Amdo Tibetan life. The Dalai Lama listed 49,049 deaths from battles within the Amdo regions before 1983, in addition to 121,982 deaths from starvation.[4]

The overwhelming religious majority of the Hbrogpa Amdo people practise Tibetan Buddhism. Recent years have also witnessed a revival of the ancient pre-Buddhist Bon religion, which is a combination of black magic, demon worship and shamanism.[5]

Several Christian organizations worked in the Amdo area prior to 1949. Cecil Pohill of the China Inland Mission established a mission station in Xining in 1888. Later he 'opened up Songpan as a center for Tibetan work'.[6] In 1922 it was reported, 'The confidence of the people has to a great extent been achieved, and not a few have an intelligent knowledge of the way of salvation.'[7]

According to a 1986 report, 'A few Christian households in Gansu Province gathered to worship during a Chinese New Year's celebration. Their neighbors, seeking to wipe out Christianity, told them to disperse. The Christians were unwilling to stop their meeting and were severely beaten by the crowd. The next morning the persecutors found their sheep, cows and horses were dying. Their family members also began to die one by one. Realizing that the wrath of God had fallen upon them, they pleaded with those who believed in Jesus to pray. The Lord heard the believers' prayers, and the sick and dying were healed. As a result, over a hundred Amdo Tibetans turned to the Lord!'[8]

Today there are at least five small churches among the Amdo Tibetans.[9] Approximately 200 Tibetan believers attend a church in Lintan County in southern Gansu, but they are Jone Tibetans, not Amdo.[10]

Photo credit: Nancy Sturrock

MONGOLIA

Qinghai

Gansu

CHINA

Sichuan

Amdo Rongba

Population:
127,000 (2000)
156,500 (2010)
192,700 (2020)
Countries: China
Buddhism: Tibetan
Christians: 10

Overview of the Rongba Amdo

Other Names: Rongba, Rongpa

Population Sources: 97,600 in China (1987, *Language Atlas of China*)

Language: Sino-Tibetan, Tibeto-Burman, Bodic, Bodish, Tibetan, Northern Tibetan

Dialects: 2

Professing Buddhists: 99%

Practising Buddhists: 95%

Christians: 0.1%

Scripture: Tibetan Bible 1948; New Testament 1885; Portions 1862

Jesus **film:** none

Gospel Recordings: none

Christian Broadcasting: none

ROPAL code: ADX02

Status of Evangelization

90%

9%

1%

A   B   C

A = Have never heard the gospel
B = Have heard the gospel but have not become Christians
C = Are adherents to some form of Christianity

A 1987 report listed 97,600 speakers of the Rongba Amdo language living in eastern Qinghai Province of western China.[1] In many locations in the province, Han Chinese and Muslims inhabit the towns, while the Rongba Amdo live in the countryside. Most are farmers (indeed, the name *Rongba* means 'farmer' in Tibetan[2]), while some dwell in semi-nomadic communities, relocating their tents whenever their livestock need new pasture. They mostly herd yaks, sheep and goats. For centuries, the Amdo roamed the borderlands of the Tibetan-Chinese world. Their menacing reputation struck fear into all who dared to venture, unwelcome, into their realm.

The Rongba Amdo primarily live in Hualong, which is an autonomous county of the Hui Muslims, and in Xunhua County, partly administered by members of the Salar Muslim minority. The northernmost point of Rongba inhabitation is the small township of Ledu. Although many Rongba are nomadic, they still confine their movements within long-established geographical parameters. One family may be allowed to graze its herds up to a certain river, or a mountain pass, and is careful not to take advantage of a neighbour's land, for fear of retribution.

When the Communists took over all of Tibet in the 1950s, thousands of Tibetans were butchered. The official Chinese version of these events is markedly different: 'This rebellion accelerated the destruction of Tibet's reactionary forces and brought Tibet onto the bright, democratic and socialist road sooner than expected.'[3]

The Rongba Amdo language has two dialects and uses more Chinese loanwords than any other Tibetan language in China. Rongba is only partially intelligible with the three other Amdo languages. All Tibetans, however, use the same written script.

The Tibetan New Year, which falls in February according to the Tibetan lunar calendar, is an occasion for great celebration among the Rongba Amdo. In the past, celebrations commenced the moment the peach tree blossomed. It is a time for relatives to get together and celebrate the past year's events.

The Rongba Amdo adhere to Tibetan Bud-

Nancy Sturrock

dhism, also known as Tantric Buddhism. Marku Tsering has written, 'Tantra's most striking feature is its technique of occult visualization. The tantric master gives each student a deity which the student has to visualize. These deities, most of which appear in wrathful or monstrous forms, are supposed to be able to help the student achieve liberation. As the student visualizes, he tries to become what he sees, and in fact some Tibetan Buddhists claim to be able to actually materialize demons in front of them.'[4]

There are about ten known Christians among the Rongba Amdo today. During the missionary era (which in China lasted until the arrival of Communism in 1949), the Christian and Missionary Alliance had a few workers in the area, but little outreach was made to the Rongba Amdo. In recent years the Chinese house churches have sent evangelists to this group, with little success.

Amdo, Rongmahbrogpa

A 1987 linguistic survey of China listed 112,800 speakers of the Rongmahbrogpa Amdo language.[1] The main centre is the picturesque town of Xiahe in south-west Gansu Province. The language is also spoken in Tongren County in neighbouring eastern Qinghai Province.

Although ethnically and culturally the Rongmahbrogpa Amdo belong to the Tibetan nationality, they speak a language that is distinct from other Tibetan languages.[2] The name Rongmahbrogpa is a combination of the Tibetan words *rongba* ('villager', or 'farmer') and *brogpa* ('nomad', or 'herder').

The Labrang Monastery in Xiahe was built by E'ang-zongzhe in 1709. Presently it houses about 1,700 monks, drawn from Qinghai, Sichuan, Gansu and Inner Mongolia. These days the monastery is 'the largest learning institution of the Gelug (Yellow Hat) sect of Tibetan Buddhism. It is comprised of Wensi (literally, "listening and meditating") College, Lower and Upper Colleges for continued studies, Shilun College, Xijingang College and a Tibetan medicine school.'[3]

In recent years Labrang has developed into a major tourist attraction, especially for budget travellers, thousands of whom come to soak in the town's unique atmosphere and beautiful scenery. Thousands of Tibetan pilgrims journey to Xiahe each year. They spin prayer wheels as they encircle the Labrang monastery. The Tibetan prayer wheel, or *manichorkor*, can be turned by hot air, hand, wind or water. As it spins, the scroll contained in the cylinder is believed to release prayers to the heavens.

The Amdo and Hui Muslims have had numerous violent clashes in the past.

In 1919 the Hui sacked the Labrang Monastery, burned to death hundreds of monks, and dumped their corpses on the temple grounds. In 1929, Joseph Rock witnessed the carnage of one battle in Xiahe: '154 Tibetan heads were strung about the walls of the Moslem garrison like a garland of flowers. Heads of young girls and children decorated posts in front of barracks. The Moslem riders galloped about the town, each with 10 or 15 human heads tied to his saddle.'[4]

Almost all Amdo are Tibetan Buddhists, but the ancient Bon religion has experienced a resurgence of growth in recent years. Bon religious rites are led by shamans, whose job in the past, as it is now, was to 'present the sacrifices, appease the spirits with magic, heal the sick and even control the weather. The shaman specialized in a kind of ecstatic trance that let him travel to the spirit world and serve as a medium for the ghosts of the dead. In addition to the shamans there were also magicians and healers who had the power to control gods, demons, and locality spirits.'[5]

The Christian and Missionary Alliance opened a mission base in the town of Xiahe in the early 1920s. They made little progress against the Buddhist stronghold. One missionary wrote that one of the main difficulties was 'The food question. The food of the Tibetans is such that for a foreigner it is very hard to partake of, and still harder to digest . . . yet the itinerating missionary in this district has to eat it, for if he does not, he greatly offends his host and gets no opportunity to preach the Gospel.'[6]

Julian Hawken

Population:
146,800 (2000)
180,800 (2010)
222,700 (2020)
Countries: China
Buddhism: Tibetan
Christians: 20

Overview of the Rongmahbrogpa Amdo

Other Names: Made, Labrang Amdo, Rongmahbrogpa
Population Sources: 112,800 (1987, *Language Atlas of China*)
Language: Sino-Tibetan, Tibeto-Burman, Bodic, Bodish, Tibetan, Northern Tibetan
Dialects: 2
Professing Buddhists: 99%
Practising Buddhists: 95%
Christians: 0.1%
Scripture: Tibetan Bible 1948; New Testament 1885; Portions 1862
Jesus **film:** available
Gospel Recordings: none
Christian Broadcasting: none
ROPAL code: ADX03

Status of Evangelization

92%
7%
0%

A   B   C
A = Have never heard the gospel
B = Have heard the gospel but have not become Christians
C = Are adherents to some form of Christianity

Approximately 70,000 Tibetans in western China's Sichuan Province speak the Rtahu Amdo language. They live primarily on grasslands along the banks of the turbulent Xianshui River in Dawu and Luhuo counties. These two counties form part of the huge Garze Tibetan Autonomous Prefecture in north-west Sichuan, which is home primarily to the fierce Khampa Tibetans.

Rtahu is the southernmost of the four Amdo groups. Linguists have identified Rtahu as a variety of Amdo, but the Rtahu claim to belong culturally to the Khampa Tibetans. The Rtahu language seems to be transitional between Amdo and Khampa Tibetan; these two are reported to have about 70 per cent lexical similarity.[1] There are two dialects of Rtahu: Braghgo and Tahu.[2]

Tibetan history closely reflects the religious journey of the people as they have sought for spiritual enlightenment. Padmasambhava, a Tibetan sage, gave the following prophecy in the 8th century: 'When the iron bird flies and horses run on wheels, the Tibetan people will be scattered like ants across the world and the Dharma will come to the land of the Red Man.[3] In October 1950 the Chinese army invaded Tibet from Sichuan. Another garrison moved southward from Xinjiang into western Tibet. Tenzin Gyatso, the 14th Dalai Lama — who himself is an Amdo Tibetan — fled into India. From his base in Dharamsala, northern India, the Dalai Lama has continued to lobby for the liberation of his people.

Nancy Sturrock

Between 1913 and 1950 Tibet tried to assert its authority as a separate nation, with its own flag, passports and currency. Tibetan passports were only accepted as legal documents by Great Britain, India and the United States. A Tibetan stamp was printed in India in 1910, bearing the image of the Dalai Lama. 'These were rejected by the Tibetans. . . . The Dalai Lama could not be placed on a stamp as it might get trodden underfoot, which would bring dishonor to him. Besides, who was going to strike his head with a great metal franking hammer?'[4]

All Rtahu Amdo Tibetans are fervent Tibetan Buddhists. No more than a handful have ever heard of the existence of Jesus Christ. Geographic, social, linguistic and cultural barriers make communicating the gospel to the Rtahu Amdo extremely difficult. Chinese house church evangelists in recent years have tried to live among the Rtahu Amdo, but their presence in the area has raised suspicion among the authorities and the Tibetans alike.

The criteria used in the 1920s for missionaries among Tibetan peoples still applies to would-be labourers—whether foreigners or Chinese—today: 'In sending out missionaries for work among the Tibetans, candidates with a strong constitution should be chosen, as missionary work in Tibet is more strenuous than in most places. Missionaries that are afraid to expose themselves to hardship and even danger should not be sent to Tibet.'[5]

Overview of the Rtahu Amdo

Other Names: Tahu

Population Sources: 60,600 (1987, *Language Atlas of China*)

Language: Sino-Tibetan, Tibeto-Burman, Bodic, Bodish, Tibetan, Northern Tibetan

Dialects: 2 (Braghgo, Tahu)

Professing Buddhists: 100%

Practising Buddhists: 95%

Christians: 0%

Scripture: Tibetan Bible 1948; New Testament 1885; Portions 1862

***Jesus* film:** none

Gospel Recordings: none

Christian Broadcasting: none

ROPAL code: ADX04

Population:
78,800 (2000)
97,100 (2010)
119,600 (2020)
Countries: China
Buddhism: Tibetan
Christians: none known

Status of Evangelization

95%

5%

0%

A   B   C

A = Have never heard the gospel
B = Have heard the gospel but have not become Christians
C = Are adherents to some form of Christianity

Angku

CHINA
Yunnan

MYANMAR
Shan

LAOS

Angku
THAILAND

Population:
20,300 (2000)
24,000 (2010)
28,500 (2020)
Countries: Myanmar, China, Laos, possibly Thailand
Buddhism: Theravada
Christians: none known

Overview of the Angku

Other Names: Kiorr, Con, K'ala

Population Sources:

10,000 in Myanmar (2000, P Hattaway)
6,113 in China (1995, Global Evangelization Movement)
2,359 Kiorr in Laos (1985, F Proschan)
possibly also in Thailand

Language: Austro-Asiatic, Mon-Khmer, Northern Mon-Khmer, Palaungic-Khmuic, Palaungic, Western Palaungic, Angkuic

Dialects: 4 (Angku, Kiorr, Amok, Pou Ma)

Professing Buddhists: 95%

Practising Buddhists: 65%

Christians: 0%

Scripture: none

***Jesus* film:** none

Gospel Recordings: none

Christian Broadcasting: none

ROPAL code: ANG

Status of Evangelization

84%

16%

0%

A   B   C

A = Have never heard the gospel
B = Have heard the gospel but have not become Christians
C = Are adherents to some form of Christianity

More than 20,000 Angku people live near the common borders of the three nations of Myanmar, China and Laos. The majority live in Shan State of northern Myanmar, while in China they inhabit six villages in southern Yunnan Province.[1] Linguist Frank Proschan listed a 1985 population of 2,359 Angku in Laos, where they are also known as the Kiorr.[2] Unspecified smaller numbers of Angku people may also live in Thailand.

Julian Hawken

The Angku in China are located on the western banks of the Lancang (Mekong) River in Xishuangbanna Prefecture of Yunnan Province. In China the government has officially counted the Angku as members of the Bulang nationality, but the Angku language is not mutually intelligible with Bulang and in fact is more 'closely related to De'ang [Palaung] . . . which is spoken in Yunnan and Myanmar'.[3] There are four Angku dialects, some of which may also qualify as distinct languages.[4]

The Angku, in addition to the Wa, Bulang and De'ang minorities, were originally part of a large Austro-Asiatic group that occupied much of Yunnan before the Dai and Yi people arrived. 'They were driven out of their habitats by the invaders, dispersed and split into the isolated groups they are

today.'[5] Ethno-historian James Olson, who calls the Angku in China by the name K'ala, further explains, 'More than two thousand years ago, Han expansion reached K'ala [Angku] country. By the Tang dynasty of the seventh and eighth centuries, [Angku people] had begun to distinguish themselves ethnically from surrounding peoples, acquiring a sense of group identity based on language and religion. During the centuries of the Tang dynasty, they found themselves under the political domination of the Nanzhao Kingdom. The Dai Kingdom controlled them during the Song dynasty from the tenth to thirteenth centuries.'[6]

Angku women are fond of chewing betel nut, which blackens their teeth and gums. Stained teeth are considered a mark of beauty among Angku women. Since the betel juice only stains temporarily, some women use black dye to artificially stain their teeth.

The Angku, like their Bulang counterparts, are staunch followers of Theravada Buddhism. Angku life revolves around the local temple. Traditionally all Angku boys become novice monks and live in the temple until they are 12 years old. The Angku obey the three tenets of Buddhism: practising self-discipline, teaching and discussing doctrine. Buddhist temples are found in most Angku villages.

Few Angku have ever been exposed to the gospel. Their villages are away from the mainstream of travellers; therefore, it takes a specific effort to make contact with the Angku. So far, the few Christian workers who have laboured in the region have preferred to target the larger minority groups, leaving the Angku without any witness or church. The nearest Christian community to the Angku are the approximately 1,500 Tai Lu and Han Chinese Christians living in Jinghong. There are no Scriptures or ministry tools available in the Angku language.

More than two million members of the Bai ethnic group live in south-west China. They primarily inhabit the Dali Bai Autonomous Prefecture in central Yunnan Province. Dali has been continuously inhabited for 3,000 years. More than 120,000 Bai are located in Guizhou Province.[1] Smaller numbers of Bai also live in Sichuan and Hunan provinces.[2]

David Treat

The Bai helped established the powerful, far-reaching Nanzhao Kingdom, which was centred south of Dali. The kingdom grew so strong that they were able to defeat the Tang Dynasty armies in the mid-700s. The kingdom flourished for 400 years until it collapsed in the 10th century and was replaced by the Kingdom of Dali. Dali, in turn, lasted until AD 1252, when it was overrun and destroyed by the all-conquering Mongol armies. Yunnan—the home province to the majority of Bai—was devastated by a plague, which began in Dali and lasted from 1812 to 1903. The population of Yunnan was reduced from eight million to three million. During the many centuries the Bai have inhabited Dali, they have gradually assimilated to Chinese culture. Dali has always been famous for its prolific supply of marble, which gave the people their name (*Bai* means 'white' in Chinese). Some of the

marble used in the great Taj Mahal of India was obtained in Dali and transported over the Himalayas.

Although the Bai have been given status as a minority nationality in China, they are one of the best assimilated to Chinese language and culture of China's 55 official minorities. In the past, various experts questioned whether the Bai were any different from the Chinese at all. 'During the 1940s . . . the Bai people denied their non-Chinese origin and would show offense if regarded as a minority.'[3] Others commented, 'The Bai like to be called Chinese';[4] 'The Bai nationality as an ethnic label was unknown to the Bai themselves until late 1958';[5] and, 'The Bai are not quite a minority, but not quite Chinese either.'[6]

The Bai speak a language from the Tibeto-Burman family.[7] In the 8th century they possessed their own script, which expressed Bai words by means of Chinese characters. This script is now extinct. Sixty per cent of Bai vocabulary today is Chinese.[8] There are four Bai dialects, all of which 'could be separate languages'.[9]

Many Bai people are followers of Mahayana Buddhism, unlike other Buddhist groups in Yunnan such as the Lu, Tai Mao, Palaung and Bulang who are Theravada Buddhists. The Bai mix their Buddhism with Daoism and ancestor worship, yet many still reply 'Buddhism' when asked what their religion is.

George Clarke of the China Inland Mission was the first Protestant missionary to the Bai in 1881. Recent estimates of Bai Christians include figures of 20,000;[10] 30,000;[11] and 50,000.[12] Most of the Bai believers live in rural areas in the mountains and in Fugong County to the west.[13] Most Bai, however, have yet to receive an intelligible gospel witness. The words of John Kuhn 60 years ago remain true today, 'No wide-spread work of evangelization will ever be done among them until the message is taken to them in the Bai tongue.'[14]

Population:
1,915,200 (2000)
2,470,600 (2010)
3,043,800 (2020)
Countries: China
Buddhism: Mahayana
Christians: 50,000

Overview of the Bai
Other Names: Pai, Minchia, Minkia, Dali, Labbu, Nama, Leme, Baini, Baizi, Baihuo

Population Sources:
1,594,827 in China (1990 census)

Language: Sino-Tibetan, Tibeto-Burman, Bai

Dialects: 4 (Dali, Jianchuan, Lanbi, Bijiang)

Professing Buddhists: 50%

Practising Buddhists: 20%

Christians: 2.6%

Scripture: none

***Jesus* film:** none

Gospel Recordings: Bai: Dali

Christian Broadcasting: none

ROPAL code: PIQ

Status of Evangelization

62%

35%

3%

A   B   C

A = Have never heard the gospel
B = Have heard the gospel but have not become Christians
C = Are adherents to some form of Christianity

Baragaunle

A linguistic source in 1990 estimated a population of '1,600 to 2,200 or more'[1] Baragaunle people living in north-central Nepal. One researcher records that they inhabit 18 villages 'above the Thak Khola River and to the south of Lo Manthang in Mustang District'.[2] More specifically, there are 650 Baragaunle people in Kagbeni village, 530 to 1,140 in Jharkot, and 400 in Purang village—all places located 'in the Kali Gandaki Valley and on the hillsides north of Jomson up to Kagbeni, and east to Muktinath; on the plains and along the river'[3] and within the Mustang District of the Dhawalagiri Zone in Nepal. The name *Baragaun* means 'twelve villages', and for a long time the people from this tribe occupied that many communities. They have now grown to occupy 18 villages, but they ares still called Baragaunle.

Oddly, despite the remote location of their area, the Baragaunle people see many foreigners because they are based along the famous Annapurna trek.[4] Since it opened to foreigners in 1977, it has become the most popular trek in Nepal. Mt Annapurna is one of the highest mountains on earth at 8,090 metres (26,535 ft.). One guidebook notes, 'If you have time, it's worth making the side trip to the mediaeval-looking village of Kagbeni at 2,810 metres [9,217 ft.]. This very Tibetan influenced settlement is as close as you can get to Lo Manthang, the capital of the legendary kingdom of Mustang further to the north, without paying a $700 permit fee. . . . The trail climbs through a desert landscape then past meadows and streams to the interesting village of Jharkot at 3,500

metres [11,480 feet].'[5]

The classification of the Baragaunle is problematic, even though they have been acknowledged by the government as one of the 61 tribes in Nepal (under the name *Bahra Gaunle*). Except for their language and history, the Baragaunle 'resemble Lobas in facial features, language and clothes. They also build their homes in the style of the Lobas of Lo Manthang.'[6]

Until the 1980s, the Baragaunle provided a large number of bondservants to their rich Thakali neighbours. 'It was said that Purang alone, a village of 100 houses, had 35 men and women working as bond servants to a single rich Thakali household in Tukche. . . . Almost every household in the villages of Baragaun had to supply an adult member of the family to its Thakali money lending masters.'[7]

All Baragaunle people profess Tibetan Buddhism as their religion, although there are also many influences from the Bon religion, which pre-dates Buddhism. The Baragaunle area contains the famous Buddhist temple of Muktinath, which is popularly known as Chhume Gyatsa throughout the Tibetan-speaking world.

Very little gospel witness had ever gone out in this remote part of Nepal until recent years, when the more relaxed political situation has allowed various Christian ministries to operate freely. Although approximately a third of the Baragaunle people have now heard the gospel through literature and evangelists, most are unable to grasp the message. So far, no known Baragaunle people have believed in Jesus Christ.

CHINA
Xizang (Tibet)
Dhawalagiri
NEPAL
INDIA
Baragaunle

Population:
2,200 (2000)
2,700 (2010)
3,350 (2020)
Countries: Nepal
Buddhism: Tibetan
Christians: none known

Overview of the Baragaunle

Other Names: Baragaun, Baragaon, Bhoti Gurung, Bahra Gaunle, Panchgaunle, Panchgaun, Baragaunle: Mustang

Population Sources:

'1,600 to 2,200 or more' in Nepal (2000, B Grimes [1990 figure])

Language: Sino-Tibetan, Tibeto-Burman, Himalayish, Tibeto-Kanauri, Tibetic, Tibetan, Central

Dialects: 2 (Jharkot, Kagbeni)

Professing Buddhists: 100%

Practising Buddhists: 70%

Christians: 0%

Scripture: none

Jesus film: none

Gospel Recordings: none

Christian Broadcasting: none

ROPAL code: BON

Dwayne Graybill

Status of Evangelization

69%
31%
0%

A   B   C

A = Have never heard the gospel
B = Have heard the gospel but have not become Christians
C = Are adherents to some form of Christianity

Approximately 800 people belonging to the Barua ethnic group live in the north-east India state of Tripura. They live intermingled in villages with people from other ethnicities, in the Sadar Subdivision of the West Tripura District (also known as Agartala) and the Udaipur Subdivision of the South Tripura District. K S Singh notes, 'Though their total population is not known, it is said that the number of Barua families in Tripura would not exceed 150'.[1]

The name Barua is derived from two words, *bara* meaning 'renowned', and *ua* meaning 'ruler'[2]. In ancient times, the most highly ranked military ruler of Chattagram under the king of Arakan was a man called Barua.[3]

The Barua are unique among all the peoples of India in that they are Buddhists who speak the Bengali language, which is spoken by more than 200 million people in India and Bangladesh. Although almost all Bengalis are Hindus or Muslims, for historical reasons that are not clear the Barua have survived as a Buddhist enclave in the midst of the two giants of Islam and Hinduism.

Dwayne Graybill

After Barua women marry they wear vermilion and conch-shell bangles as marriage symbols and as a sign of their unavailability to men. 'Residence after marriage is patrilocal. Although either spouse can seek divorce, its incidence is rare. . . . Nowadays, the practice of paying bride-price in cash is being replaced by that of dowry.'[4]

Traditionally the Barua earned their livelihood through farming, fishing and hunting. As waves of migrants have entered Tripura the number of wild animals has diminished, making hunting a fruitless exercise unless the participants are willing to trek deep into the forests. The Barua raise goats and chickens today as their main sources of protein.

In the past 20 years, as education levels among them have improved, a number of Barua men and women have obtained jobs as office workers, teachers and administrators in the towns of Tripura.

Perhaps the most fascinating mystery concerning the Barua people is their belief in Theravada Buddhism. The nearest Buddhist communities to them are probably the Chakma and other Theravada Buddhist peoples in the Chittagong Hill tracts of Bangladesh. Just how the Barua came to believe in Buddhism, and equally how they have managed to preserve their faith under pressure from all sides, is difficult to ascertain because they have no written history. 'The Barua are Buddhist. The families linked with a Buddhist temple are brought under their traditional association, which is headed by a *marubbi*. They worship . . . at the family level and participate in traditional festivals.'[5]

As the Barua have slowly lost their culture and language (which has now been completely lost), their Buddhist beliefs have gradually become mixed with Hinduism. The Barua are now allowed to marry people from non-Buddhist communities such as the Brahman, Kayastha and Magh, which means that Buddhism may become extinct in the next generation of Barua. There are no known Christians among this interesting and unique unreached people group.

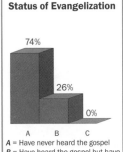

Overview of the Barua

Other Names: Baraua

Population Sources:
150 families in India (1996, K S Singh)

Language: Indo-European, Indo-Iranian, Indo-Aryan, Eastern Zone, Bengali-Assamese

Dialects: 0

Professing Buddhists: 80%

Practising Buddhists: 35%

Christians: 0%

Scripture: none

***Jesus* film:** none

Gospel Recordings: none

Christian Broadcasting: none

ROPAL code: none

Population:
800 (2000)
930 (2010)
1,080 (2020)

Countries: India

Buddhism: probably Theravada

Christians: none known

Status of Evangelization

74%

26%

0%

A   B   C

A = Have never heard the gospel
B = Have heard the gospel but have not become Christians
C = Are adherents to some form of Christianity

Beda

Jammu & Kashmir

Himachal Pradesh

PAKISTAN

INDIA

Beda

Population:
400 (2000)
460 (2010)
540 (2020)
Countries: India
Buddhism: Tibetan
Christians: 15

Overview of the Beda

Other Names: Bodh, Bhot, Bhotia, Jyali, Jyayi, Bedar, Beta

Population Sources:

400 in India (2000, P Hattaway)

Language: Sino-Tibetan, Tibeto-Burman, Himalayish, Tibeto-Kanauri, Western Himalayish, Kanauri

Dialects: 0

Professing Buddhists: 70%

Practising Buddhists: 40%

Christians: 4%

Scripture: none

***Jesus* film:** none

Gospel Recordings: none

Christian Broadcasting: none

ROPAL code: none

Status of Evangelization

50%
46%

4%

A   B   C

A = Have never heard the gospel
B = Have heard the gospel but have not become Christians
C = Are adherents to some form of Christianity

According to Indian researcher S R R Prasad, the Beda tribe number approximately 300 people in Ladakh.[1] Their population has decreased over the decades. The 1931 census in India listed 414 Beda people, of which 70 stated they were Buddhists, and the rest Muslims. This religious adherence is the reason for the diminishing numbers of Beda people. Most of those who believe in Islam change their identity and start calling themselves Balti. An additional small number of Beda, perhaps 100, inhabit a few small villages of the Kullu and Shimla districts of the state of Himachal Pradesh.[2] The Beda in Himachal Pradesh are Hindus.

In 1989 the Beda were granted status in India as a Scheduled Tribe. The Beda in Ladakh have been living there for approximately 200 years, having migrated from the Lahaul and Spitti area of Himachal Pradesh.

In Jammu and Kashmir the Beda are thinly scattered in villages around Leh, the capital of Ladakh and former home of the Ladakhi monarchy. Because of their role as musicians and beggars, the Beda spread themselves out over a number of villages in order to obtain maximum exposure and economic benefit. Usually no more than a few Beda families live in the same village, alongside Ladakhi and people from other ethnic groups.

The Beda have been described as a 'wandering musician community of Ladakh. Their chief occupation is begging. They play on the *surna* (clarinet), *daman* (drum) or *duff* (tambourine) in public places or near a house. Usually the male members play . . . while the females dance on the beats of the tambourine. On the completion of their musical renderings they beg. Due to their occupation of begging, they rank lowest in the Ladakhi society.'[3]

In the past the Beda wandered over a vast territory, playing their music all the way to the Tibetan border.[4] 'They used to pack their belongings over mules and asses staying on the outskirts of Bot [Tibetan] villages for a few days before moving on to the next village. They traversed throughout the Ladakh, Nubra and Zangskar valleys visiting far-flung villages in the course of their annual cycle of migration. . . . On the completion of their renderings they would beg collection food grains from Bot households . . . so that they could sell the surplus food grains in the market place in Leh and purchase necessary items like clothes and utensils.'[5]

Despite their small population, there are Beda who follow each of the four major world religions. Nominally, the majority of Beda families believe in Tibetan Buddhism. Some are Muslims, and the Beda living in Himachal Pradesh are Hindus, while a few families are Moravian Christians. The Moravians first sent missionaries to Ladakh in 1852, and through bringing humanitarian aid they soon won the respect of the community. By 1922 there were 158 Ladakhi Christians, a few of which were Beda people.[6]

Asian Report

Population:
5,500 (2000)
7,100 (2010)
8,740 (2020)
Countries: China
Buddhism: Tibetan
Christians: none known

Overview of the Tongren Bonan

Other Names: Tongren, Buddhist Bonan, Bao'an, Qinghai Bonan

Population Sources:

4,000 in China (1987, *Language Atlas of China*)

Language: Altaic, Mongolian, Eastern Mongolian, Mongour

Dialects: 5 (Tongren, Nianduhu, Dunmari, Gajiuri, Bao'an Xiazhuang)

Professing Buddhists: 100%

Practising Buddhists: 90%

Christians: 0%

Scripture: none

***Jesus* film:** none

Gospel Recordings: none

Christian Broadcasting: none

ROPAL code: PEHO2

Status of Evangelization

94%

6%   0%

A   B   C

A = Have never heard the gospel
B = Have heard the gospel but have not become Christians
C = Are adherents to some form of Christianity

Tongren County, in the eastern part of China's remote Qinghai Province, is home to more than 5,000 people of the Bonan minority group. Tongren is a crossroads for many different peoples, including the Salar, Tu, Hui, Amdo Tibetans and Wutun.

The Tongren Bonan are part of the larger Bonan minority in China, but the Buddhist Bonan living in Tongren consider themselves a separate people from the Muslim Bonan in Gansu. Their languages are now also different. Using the definition of a people group as 'a significantly large ethnic or sociological grouping of individuals who perceive themselves to have a common affinity for one another',[1] the Tongren Bonan definitely qualifies as a distinct people group.

The Bonan language spoken in Tongren County of Qinghai is distinct from the main body of Bonan spoken across the border in Gansu Province. The Gansu Bonan language has been influenced by Chinese, while Tongren Bonan has been heavily influenced by Tibetan and Tu. Various linguists note that sound structure and grammar also differ between the two areas.[2]

The Tongren Bonan are the descendants of Mongolian troops who were stationed in the region during the Mongolian empire of the 13th and 14th centuries. After the collapse of Mongol rule in 1368 most soldiers retreated to Mongolia, but a few remained behind. After centuries of intermingling with the Tibetans, the Tongren Bonan have culturally become almost indistinguishable from their neighbours. 'Those Bonans who retained their Buddhist faith became strongly acculturated to their neighbors . . . as a result, only a small number of persons remain in Tongren who from an ethno-linguistic point of view can still be considered Bonan.'[3]

The Tongren Bonan are Tibetan Buddhists

and mix spirit worship and shamanism into their observances.[4] In the early 1800s, some of the Bonan converted to Islam, 'an event that put them at odds with their Tibetan and Tu neighbours, all of whom were Buddhists. The friction between Buddhists and Muslims occasionally erupted into violence. In the late 1950s and early 1960s the confrontation became so violent that the Islamic Bonan decided to move . . . they gradually migrated down the Huang [Yellow] River into Gansu Province,

International Mission Board

where they live today.'[5]

The first foreign missionaries among the Tongren Bonan were workers affiliated with the Christian and Missionary Alliance. They commenced work in Bao'an Township around 1910. Despite being in the Bonan neighbourhood, the missionaries' primary target was the Tibetans, not the Bonan. By 1922 the mission was closed due to a lack of workers.[6] The mission did open again, but after years of slow and unfruitful labour the work gravitated towards the more receptive Han Chinese.[7] Today, there are no known Christians among the Tongren Bonan. Because of the geographic, cultural and linguistic barriers, they could be classified as one of the most difficult Buddhist groups in the world to reach with the gospel.

Brokpa

A 1991 linguistic study listed 5,000 speakers of the Brokpa language living in eastern Bhutan.[1] George van Driem writes, 'Brokpa is spoken in and around Mera, where there are approximately four hundred Brokpa households with an estimated two thousand inhabitants, and in and around Sakteng where there are approximately six hundred Brokpa households with an estimated three thousand inhabitants.'[2] These two locations are within the Trashigang District in eastern Bhutan, close to the border with the Indian state of Arunachal Pradesh.

People use the word *brokpa* (also *brogpa* or *hbrogpa*) in different ways throughout the Tibetan-speaking world. It can simply mean 'nomad' or 'herder'. In this case, however, people in Bhutan use the word as the name of their ethnic group. Getting to the Brokpa area requires some bone-jarring travel by jeep. Because of the rough roads, it can take over four hours to drive the 92 kilometres (57 mi.) from the town of Mongar. The Brokpa are a nomadic people who live at an average altitude of 3,000 metres (9,840 ft.) above sea level.

For several reasons, it is extremely difficult to identify and classify people groups in Bhutan. Foreigners are welcomed in Bhutan only if they join an organized tour group, which can cost US$200 per day. Visitors are only allowed to enter more remote areas of the country, such as Trashigang District where the Brokpa live, with special permits from the government. In the late 1990s, one intrepid team of Christian researchers did get permission to go to this part of

Bhutan. They reported, 'We headed to the Sakteng Valley with the permission and help of the Governor of East Bhutan. We were told it was politically incorrect to be talking about tribes or people groups in a country whose motto was "One country, one people"! The huts of the Brokpa were empty when we at last arrived as they are nomadic people following their yaks into the high mountains until snow forces them down to their winter "residences". This was disappointing, but we trekked to one hut and had a prayer meeting in it—a shanty of woven bamboo, very rough thatched roof, a slat floor and nothing at all inside. We met a number of Brokpa on our way down the trail again. They were bringing their horses up to go into the mountains and collect the yaks. Their clothes were very distinctive, especially their five-spout yak-hair hats.'[3]

The Brokpa refer to their language as 'Brokpake'. In Dzongkha (the national language of the Drukpa people in Bhutan), the Brokpake language 'is called *Bjokha* and its speakers are known as *Bjop*. . . . The [Brokpa] language is also known by the loconym Mera-Sakteng-kha "the language of Mera and Sakteng".'[4]

Tibetan Buddhism mixed with ancient spirit worship is the religion of the Brokpa people. Although the members of this group say they are Buddhists, shamans are more prevalent than Buddhist lamas. There has never been a church or even a known Christian believer among this unique and precious group.

Population:
  6,250 (2000)
  8,050 (2010)
  10,300 (2020)
Countries: Bhutan
Buddhism: Tibetan
Christians: none known

Overview of the Brokpa

Other Names: Brokpake, Mira Sagtengpa, Dakpa, Dap, Mera Sagtengpa, Sagtengpa, Meragsagstengkha

Population Sources:
5,000 in Bhutan (2001, G van Driem [1991 figure])

Language: Sino-Tibetan, Tibeto-Burman, Himalayish, Tibeto-Kanauri, Tibetic, Tibetan, Southern

Dialects: 0

Professing Buddhists: 100%

Practising Buddhists: 50%

Christians: 0%

Scripture: none

***Jesus* film:** none

Gospel Recordings: none

Christian Broadcasting: none

ROPAL code: SGT

Status of Evangelization

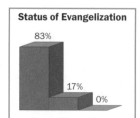

A = Have never heard the gospel
B = Have heard the gospel but have not become Christians
C = Are adherents to some form of Christianity

Approximately four hundred people belonging to the Brokpa ethnic group in Bhutan speak a distinct language called Brokkat. There are more than 6,000 other Brokpa people in Bhutan who speak a language called Brokpake. Although they are culturally and ethnically related to the Brokkat-speaking Brokpa, the two languages are so different that speakers from each group cannot communicate if they only use their own vernaculars.

The Brokkat Brogpa inhabit 'an estimated seventy-odd households in Dur, roughly

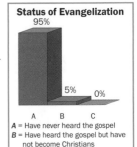

International Mission Board

two thirds of which are Brokpa households and one third of which are Bumthang households'.[1] Dur is within Bhutan's Bumthang District, in the north-central part of Bhutan. Bumthang is known as the cultural heartland of Bhutan. The district consists of four valleys 'dotted with palaces, ancient temples and monasteries. . . . [It] is believed to be the first part of Bhutan to be inhabited, with evidence of prehistoric settlements in the Ura valley of Bumthang and the southern region of Khyeng. These and many other valleys were separated principalities ruled by independent kings.'[2]

The respected Dutch linguist George van Driem was the first scholar to identify and study the Brokkat Brokpa language. He notes, 'Brokkat is what the Brokpas of Dur call their language. . . . The nomadic Brokpa yakherds in northern Bumthang have all been linguistically assimilated to the Bumthang speaking majority. Curiously, only the Brokpas who have taken up a sedentary lifestyle and live in the conglomeration known as Dur have retained their language.'[3]

Brokkat Brokpa is part of the Southern Tibetan branch of the Tibeto-Burman language family. There are seven languages in Bhutan that fall within the Southern Tibetan classification, one of which is the main Brokpa language. Van Driem, however, insists that Brokkat 'is distinct from the Brokpa language of Mera and Sakteng, and the language does not seem to have been very heavily infiltrated by loanwords from Bumthang. Many of the words in the language do not show the apophony typical for Central Tibetan dialects. . . . The Brokpas of Dur refer to [the national language] Dzongkha as *Ngalongkha*, although the Bumthang term *Mengkat* is also used. Interestingly, the Brokpas of Dur refer to their Bumthang speaking neighbours as *Monpa* and to the Bumthang language as *Monkat* "Monpa language".'[4]

All Brokkat Brokpa families profess Buddhism as their religion. For countless centuries Buddhism has been their way of life, and the religion is intricately woven into their cultural fabric.

Christianity has made little impact in the valleys of north-central Bhutan. Few members of this group have ever heard the name of Jesus Christ. Missionary endeavour in Bhutan only really began in 1960, when Bhutan ended its policy of isolation. Indian Christians entered the country as development workers, and Bhutanese students travelled abroad to study. Some returned home as Christians, and the gospel has slowly started to take root.

Population:
370 (2000)
480 (2010)
620 (2020)
Countries: Bhutan
Buddhism: Tibetan
Christians: none known

Overview of the Brokkat Brokpa

Other Names: Brokskad, Brogpa, Brokpa of Dur

Population Sources:
300 in Bhutan (2001, G van Driem [1991 figure])

Language: Sino-Tibetan, Tibeto-Burman, Himalayish, Tibeto-Kanauri, Tibetic, Tibetan, Southern

Dialects: 0

Professing Buddhists: 100%

Practising Buddhists: 65%

Christians: 0%

Scripture: none

Jesus film: none

Gospel Recordings: none

Christian Broadcasting: none

ROPAL code: BRO

Status of Evangelization

95%

5%

0%

A   B   C

A = Have never heard the gospel
B = Have heard the gospel but have not become Christians
C = Are adherents to some form of Christianity

Bulang

Approximately 100,000 Bulang people live in three different countries. The majority (over 80,000) live in Yunnan Province, China—especially in Menghai, Zhenkang, Shuangjiang, Lincang, Lancang and Mojiang counties. In China their villages are often located in extremely remote mountains, some three or four days' walk from the nearest road. Bulang history in China dates back as early as AD 220.[1]

Eastern Shan State in Myanmar is home to about 14,000 Bulang, especially in the Mong Yang area and near the city of Kengtung. Of the three countries inhabited by the Bulang, Thailand has the smallest number, with 1,200 people. Of these, 1,000 live outside Mae Sai City near the Golden Triangle where Thailand, Laos and Myanmar meet.[2] Approximately 200 Bulang work as gardeners in Bangkok. The Bulang in Thailand fled China in the 1960s because of persecution from the Communist authorities. About 200 families first moved into Myanmar, before entering Thailand in 1974.

The Bulang language is of great interest to scholars because of its uniqueness and variety.[3] It is a part of the Mon-Khmer linguistic family, related to Wa and Palaung. Despite the relatively small population, the Bulang in China use two different

alphabetic scripts: the *Totham* script is used in the Xishuangbanna Prefecture, while the *Tolek* script is used in Dehong Prefecture. Among the small number of Bulang in Thailand there is remarkable linguistic variety, with one report listing between six and ten dialects spoken in just one Bulang refugee village.[4]

Dwayne Graybill

For centuries the Bulang have been ardent followers of Theravada Buddhism. They were first converted by their Lu and Tai Mao neighbours. Today, 'Temples and idols are scattered throughout their communities. Many Bulang men enter the Buddhist monkhood, which brings great honour to their families. Few Bulang have

ever heard of Christ, and few care to seek for anything beyond what they already believe. They strive to observe the Buddhist *tripitaka* (three baskets) teaching: self-discipline, preaching and discussing doctrine. The Bulang believe that right thinking, sacrifices and self-denial will enable the soul to reach *nirvana*, a state of eternal bliss.'[5]

Most Bulang also observe animistic rituals. Since the arrival of Buddhism they have cloaked their spirit worship with a veneer of Buddhist teachings, but they still fear and appease a large number of spirits. When a Bulang person dies, the family members of the deceased 'kill a chicken to call back the soul of the deceased, bath the body, dress it in new clothes and finally wrap it in white sheets. The [animistic] Bulang usually bury the dead in a wooden coffin on their village burial ground. The Buddhist Bulang, however, burn their deceased community members at the temple compound.'[6]

There are perhaps 100 Bulang Christians today: 50 in China and a few dozen in Myanmar and Thailand. Protestant missionaries reached out to the Bulang in China prior to the Communist takeover in 1949, and 30 families were converted.[7] Most of them gave up their faith during the horrific persecution of the Cultural Revolution.

Overview of the Bulang

Other Names: Blang, Pulang, Pula, Plang, Kawa, Kontoi, Sen Chun, Hkawa, K'wa, Khon Doi, Plaang, Braang, Bprang, Brang, Prong, Hkun Loi, Loi, Tai Loi, Lo, Lua

Population Sources:

79,850 in China (2000, P Hattaway)[8]

14,000 in Myanmar (2000, B Grimes [1994 figure])

1,200 in Thailand (1998, SIL)

Language: Austro-Asiatic, Mon-Khmer, Northern Mon-Khmer,

Palaungic-Khmuic, Palaungic, Western Palaungic, Waic, Bulang

Dialects: 2 (Phang, Kem Degne)

Professing Buddhists: 80%

Practising Buddhists: 35%

Christians: 0.1%

Scripture: work in progress in Thailand

Jesus film: none

Gospel Recordings: Blang: Blang-Shan

Christian Broadcasting: none

ROPAL code: BLR

Population:
95,050 (2000)
120,050 (2010)
146,100 (2020)
Countries: China, Myanmar, Thailand
Buddhism: Theravada
Christians: 100

Status of Evangelization

74%

25%

1%

A   B   C

A = Have never heard the gospel
B = Have heard the gospel but have not become Christians
C = Are adherents to some form of Christianity

CHINA
Xizang (Tibet)

Bumthang

BHUTAN

Bumthang   Trongsa   INDIA

Population:
37,600 (2000)
48,300 (2010)
62,000 (2020)
Countries: Bhutan
Buddhism: Tibetan
Christians: 50

Overview of the Bumthang

Other Names: Bumthangkha, Bumtanp, Bumthapkha, Bumtang, Kebumtamp, Bhumtam, Bumtangkha

Population Sources:

30,000 in Bhutan (2001, G van Driem [1991 figure])

Language: Sino-Tibetan, Tibeto-Burman, Himalayish, Tibeto-Kanauri, Tibetic, Tibetan, Eastern

Dialects: 4 (Ura, Tang, Chogor, Chunmat)

Professing Buddhists: 95%

Practising Buddhists: 60%

Christians: 0.2%

Scripture: none

***Jesus* film:** none

Gospel Recordings: none

Christian Broadcasting: none

ROPAL code: KJZ

Status of Evangelization

80%

19%

1%

A   B   C

A = Have never heard the gospel
B = Have heard the gospel but have not become Christians
C = Are adherents to some form of Christianity

Approximately 40,000 people living in east-central Bhutan belong to the Bumthang ethnic group. They take their name from their main habitation, Bumthang District, and they call themselves Bumthangpa ('People of Bumthang'). The Bumthang language 'is spoken on either side of the lofty Thrumshingla . . . extending as far east as Senggor and as far west as Trongsa. Bumthang is most closely related to Kheng and Kurtop. The two peaks that loom prominently to the south of Senggor mark the boundary between the Kheng and Bumthang speaking areas.'[1] The Bumthang also spill over into the eastern part of Trongsa District.

Bumthang is believed to have been the first inhabited place in Bhutan. Its ancient capital of Jakar (also spelt J'aga) lies at the foot of the Choskhor Valley and is a major trading centre. Its population of about 2,000 swells on market days, as people from various ethnic groups converge on the town. It was also the location for many fierce battles in history, especially in the 1600s when Tibetan armies invaded Bhutan in an attempt to bring it under the rule of Lhasa. A small pagoda near the bridge outside Bumthang marks the spot where a Tibetan general's head was buried after the locals defeated his army during one of these 17th-century raids.

The Bumthang language is part of the Eastern Tibetan branch of the Tibeto-Burman family. There are eight languages in this branch, all of which are spoken only in Bhutan. One linguist says, 'Although it could be argued that the two languages Kheng and Kurtop are dialects of Bumthang on grounds of mutual intelligibility, there are

essential differences between the phonologies of Kheng and Kurtop on one hand and that of Bumthang on the other. Moreover, the speakers of these three languages identify strongly with their respective homelands in Bumthang, Kurto and Kheng.'[2] Bumthang is believed to be similar to the Monpa language spoken in Cuona County of Tibet. It reportedly has 92 per cent lexical similarity with Kheng, but just 47 per cent to 52 per cent with Dzongkha (Bhutan's national language).[3]

Bumthang has been an important Buddhist centre for centuries. According to legend, 'when the lamas assembled in about 1549 to select a site for a monastery, a big white bird rose suddenly in the air and settled on a spur of a hill. This was interpreted as an important omen, and the hill was chosen as the site for a monastery and for Jakar Dzong, which roughly translates as "castle of the white bird". The site chosen for Jakar Dzong is a picturesque location overlooking the Choskhor valley. The current structure was built in 1667 and is said to be the largest *dzong* in Bhutan, with a circumference of more than 1500 meters.'[4] An earthquake in 1897 severely damaged the monastery, but it still operates as an important Buddhist centre, especially in the winter months when many monks take up residence.

There are a small number of scattered Bumthang Christians. They have faced much discrimination from their communities, but they have remained faithful to the Lord Jesus.

Dwayne Graybill

Buriat, China

Create International

Population:
- 98,900 (2000)
- 127,600 (2010)
- 164,500 (2020)

Countries: China
Buddhism: Tibetan
Christians: 100

Russia. They reportedly 'speak a highly distinctive dialect of Mongolian'.[4] The two main dialects of Buriat in China are known as New Bargu (47,000 speakers) and Old Bargu (14,000). Some sources suggest these two dialects are so different that they may represent distinct languages, but more research needs to be done.

The *yokhor* folk dance plays an important role in the lives of the Buriat. Young girls imitate the actions and movements of birds and animals. Most Buriat live in mud and wood houses, although some are still nomads.[5]

Historically, most Buriat believed in shamanism, allowing mediums to control all interactions between the gods and their communities. To be a shaman, a person had to be seen to possess *utkha*, a mystical spiritual energy. In the 1500s, Buddhist missionaries from Tibet travelled into Mongolia and introduced Tibetan Buddhism. It soon grew in influence, and a mixture of Buddhist teachings and shamanist practices emerged. In the past century many Buriat in Russia and Mongolia became atheists under the Communist system, but a significant number of Buriat in China have continued to believe in Buddhism. A new religion called *Burkanism* has also appeared among them in recent years.[6]

A few of the Buriat in China have recently become Christians, resulting from Chinese house church efforts originating in a revival in Heilongjiang Province. Just one city, Daqing, has more than 200,000 Chinese believers. They took responsibility for evangelizing westward into Inner Mongolia, boldly preaching the gospel and seeing thousands of people converted in many locations, including Hulun Buir. The new Buriat believers are hampered by a lack of Scriptures and other resources in their language.

The 1982 China language census listed 65,000 speakers of the Buriat language in China. In later censuses the Chinese authorities did not count the Buriat separately but included them under the Mongolian nationality. Large numbers of Buriat people also live in Russia and Mongolia but, because of historical and political influences, the Buriat in each country now speak different languages and should be considered three different groups from an ethnolinguistic standpoint. The Buriat in China are relatively recent arrivals, having migrated from Siberia to Inner Mongolia in 1917.[1]

The Buriat in China inhabit grasslands in the Hulunbuir region of the Inner Mongolia Autonomous Region. This remote area is located where the three nations of China, Russia and Mongolia meet. The Buriat originally consisted of several Mongolian people groups and clans who were recognized as five distinct tribes.[2] The Buriat—who claim to be descended from either a grey bull or a white swan[3]—still share many common traits and customs with the Mongols.

The Buriat language spoken in China is different from the Buriat in Mongolia and

Overview of the China Buriat

Other Names: Buryat, Northern Mongolian, Buriat-Mongolian, Northeastern Mongolian, Bargu, Bargu Buriat

Population Sources:
65,000 in China (1982 census)

Language: Altaic, Mongolian, Eastern, Oirat-Khalkha, Khalkha-Buriat, Buriat

Dialects: 4 (New Bargu [47,000], Old Bargu [14,000], Khori, Aga)

Professing Buddhists: 70%
Practising Buddhists: 30%
Christians: 0.1%
Scripture: Portions 1827; work in progress
***Jesus* film:** none
Gospel Recordings: none
Christian Broadcasting: none
ROPAL code: BXU

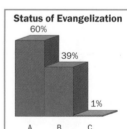

Status of Evangelization

- 60%
- A — 39%
- C — 1%

A = Have never heard the gospel
B = Have heard the gospel but have not become Christians
C = Are adherents to some form of Christianity

The Cross or the Lotus? The Church in Mongolia Today

Hugh P Kemp

At the height of their power in the 13th century, the Mongols held sway over the world's largest ever territory—a vast tract of land stretching from the Danube River in Europe to Korea. Since the time of its eventual demise in 1368, Mongolia has struggled to keep its national identity, bearing the weight of Ming overlords, Manchurian exploitation, feudal poverty and Tibetan-Buddhist theocracy. Mongolia emerged from seven decades of Soviet-styled Communism in 1990, when democratic elections created a new environment that facilitated social and political change. With these changes, the Christian church in Mongolia has sprouted from nothing to a body of somewhere between 12,000 and 35,000 national believers in the country of Mongolia today, with hundreds more Mongol believers inside China.

The veneration of Chinggis Khan

With the collapse of Communism in 1990,

public billboards of Lenin began to be replaced by memorials to Chinggis (sometimes spelled Genghis) Khan (1162–1227). Young people wore lapel badges with the great khan's picture. School textbooks were rewritten, and references to the 'marauding barbarian' were changed to the 'noble statesman'.

It cannot be overstated how much the modern Mongol sees himself in the light of Chinggis Khan. Chinggis is esteemed as a great political figure: the founder of the Mongol nation and the father of its people—the conqueror who established the greatest land empire the world has ever known. Chinggis's military prowess is the object of great pride. After democratic changes, there was much rhetoric about following in the footsteps of Chinggis: 'We were great once, and so we can be great again.'

The glorification of Chinggis Khan during the early 1990s became a quasi-cult. Sons, vodka, furs and travel agencies are named after him. His militant spirit inspires Mongol youth to assert their Mongolian identity in the face of new forces jostling

For countless centuries the free-spirited Mongols have ridden their horses across the wide spaces of the Central Asian steppes.

Asian Report

Mongolian Buddhist monks walking together.

for priority on the nation's agenda. During the last decade of the 20th century Chinggis Khan has been reinvented, reinterpreted and re-venerated.

The influence of shamanism and Tibetan Buddhism

Shamanism and Tibetan Buddhism also play an important role in the shaping of the Mongol world-view. The Mongol *yasa*, a legal framework built on case law from the days of Chinggis, enshrines religious tolerance within the national psyche. The khans did not embrace any one religion out of conviction. Official religious tolerance simply made it easier to govern the conquered. Such tolerance was conditional, however, on absolute obedience to the khan.

The legacy of the *yasa* has influenced Mongolian religious policy and world-view to the present day. The post-Communist constitution of 1992, as interpreted in the Law on the Relationship of Church and State (November 1993) endorses three official state religions: shamanism, Tibetan Buddhism and Islam, and ensures freedom of religious expression for Mongolia's citizens. The apparent tolerance implied by this law is perhaps better described as 'indifference'. As in the *yasa* of Chinggis,

one's religion is seen to be inconsequential to the welfare of the state, so long as the state's citizens are obedient to the law. The law endorses three religions practised by the majority of Mongols. The law's intent was descriptive rather than prescriptive.

Whereas shamanism is the core religion for most Mongols, it is overlaid by Tibetan Buddhism. Outwardly, Tibetan Buddhism might seem to be the dominant partner in this relationship. Tourists walking the streets of Ulaanbaatar today notice the Gandan temple complex dominating the western sector of the city. In the provinces they can visit reopened monasteries and watch novices being trained. This is all encouraged by the periodic visits of the Dalai Lama. On the surface, it seems that Tibetan Buddhism is the main filter through which Mongols interpret their world.

Inwardly, however, most Mongols still view Tibetan Buddhism as a foreign religion. Some are adamant that Buddhism was an import, a convenient way that Kublai Khan (r. 1260–94) used to bring Tibet under his domain without having to conquer it. Many go to a Tibetan Buddhist temple for rites of passage, but shamanistic practices dominate the normal daily rhythms of life. The local Buddhist lama is consulted to find the most auspicious day for a wedding, but the first ladle-full of tea is flicked with the fourth finger to the four points of the compass as an offering to *tenger*, the ancient sky-god whom Chinggis worshipped.

A veneer of Communism

To add to this religious mixture, Soviet Communism has also influenced the Mongol world-view. Communism heavily suppressed all religion with purges in the 1930s, and the 700-odd Tibetan Buddhist monasteries in Mongolia were either demolished or turned into museums. Monks were killed or secularized while most Mongol nomads were organized into work units for the state.

Communism as a world-view led to a pragmatic atheism amongst the Mongols. It bred a class of civil servant in today's post-Communist Mongolia that is neither shamanist nor Tibetan Buddhist. They are disillusioned that the high ideals of the Communist state to which they had given their lives collapsed overnight in 1990. Communism also bred a generation of young people who knew nothing of either ancient shamanism or Tibetan Buddhism. The result was a religious void in society. Certainly the older Mongols still interpret their world through the 'blue spectacles' of the ancient sky-god-based shamanism, while a remnant of priests do so through the 'yellow spectacles' of the Gelugpa sect of Tibetan Buddhism. The dominant world-view, however, became atheism. Communist party officials, bureaucrats and youth viewed the world through the 'red spectacles' of Communism.

Changing economic fortunes since 1990 have brought new challenges to the Mongols: new television programmes,

A young Mongolian boy, identified as a 'living Buddha' blesses an elderly woman.

Training for life as a 'living Buddha'.

An elderly Mongolian monk studies the Buddhist scriptures.

These carefully-preserved sacred Buddhist books have been used by monks for centuries.

easier access to the Internet, freedom to travel and the ever-present lure of materialism. Market reform and profit-driven consumerism have become the key points of reference for a new breed of entrepreneurial Mongol. With the collapse of the state welfare system, the resulting problems of domestic violence, unemployment and underemployment, medical and nutritional mismanagement and a poor work ethic have all contributed to a social agenda that is overwhelming. Inflation, privatization and market reforms have left thousands poorer, indebted, abused and marginalized.

Birth of the modern Mongolian Church

After democratic elections overturned the Communist Mongolian People's Revolutionary Party (MPRP), there were two heady years of political reform. The constitution was rewritten, there was talk of Mongolia becoming an Asian economic tiger,

Asian Report

Most of the Christians in Mongolia today are young people who have broken away from traditional Mongol culture.

the Soviets began leaving and Mongolia opened to the outside world. Progress was checked by the re-election of a restructured MPRP in 1992 but, nevertheless, democratic and open market reforms had come to stay.

These changes were not as sudden as they seemed. During the mid- to late-1980s reform had been in the air. Some Christians had visited the Mongolian People's Republic on tourist visas, praying for the day when it would open. Internal restlessness grew, and news of the changes in Soviet Europe trickled back. A youthful groundswell, inspired by a rock band, picked up momentum, and it is only by the grace of God and the constraint and wisdom of the nation's leaders that Ulaanbaatar did not have a Tiananmen Square-like incident in 1990.[1]

In these first three years, two tools were immediately available for evangelization: the United Bible Societies' (UBS) New Testament (*Shin Geree*) and a film about the life of Jesus produced by Campus Crusade for Christ, simply called *Jesus*.

Both were used extensively throughout Mongolia. Groups of Mongolian Christians showed the *Jesus* film outdoors and in local cinemas, preached, sold copies of *Shin Geree* and gave appeals for conversion. Such endeavours often birthed house groups or churches. The effect of the dual use of the *Jesus* film and the New Testament *Shin Geree* cannot be underestimated: they both received exceedingly wide distribution and have been instrumental in hundreds of Mongolians coming to personally know Christ.

Shin Geree and the *Jesus* film spoke directly to a new generation of Mongolian youth caught in the spiritual void in the wake of Communism. The Tibetan Buddhism of their parents and the shamanism of their grandparents were unattractive, powerless and irrelevant. Consequently, the first three to five years of Mongolian church growth saw many conversions among 14- to 25-year-olds, and especially girls. Nevertheless, by the mid-1990s this disparity had started to even out, with more young men and older people, who were often reached by specialist home groups, in the churches.

From a missions strategy perspective, Mongolia was a clean slate in 1990—full of opportunities. The country had no recent history of missions, no Western colonial history, no established church, no recognizable Christians and no Bible. It was a grand opportunity to get evangelistic strategies right.

It was also a tempting venue to experiment. It is significant that the two key evangelistic tools in the early days, the UBS New Testament and the *Jesus* film, were non-sectarian and interdenominational. Both expatriate and Mongolian Christians were keen to evangelize Mongolia as quickly and effectively as possible. It was no surprise that the period from 1990 to 1993 was characterized by a heady flurry of activity.

State tolerance or persecution?

In December 1993, when local papers published the text of a new 'Law on the Relationship of Church and State', the foreign Christian community reacted immediately, claiming that it discriminated against Christianity on the grounds that the law named Tibetan Buddhism, shamanism and Islam (the latter a concession to the Kazak minority) as Mongolia's official state religions. The law declared Tibetan Buddhism to be the predominant religion that would receive state patronage. The implication was that a genuine Mongol was naturally a Tibetan Buddhist.

The formulation of the law was inevitable. Naming Tibetan Buddhism as the state religion was merely describing what already was, and conceding that there would also be two other official religions alluded perhaps to the indifference embedded in the ancient legal code of the *yasa*. The fact that Christian numbers had been growing so quickly between 1991 and 1993 was certainly a factor in the formulation of the law, and the timing of its publication implied that the government had noticed.

Article 4.2 of the law puts great value on the unity of the Mongol people, their historical and cultural traditions and civilization. The challenge, then, was to present Christ to the Mongolian people in Mongolian ways; the church had to take on a Mongolian face as quickly as possible. Eventually, Christians settled down to wait and see the outcome. Singapore and Hong Kong had similar laws regulating church-state relationships, and Christian churches there seemed to do fine.

Lessons learned in the first decade: 1990–1999

Among all the Tibetan Buddhist people groups in Central Asia, the response of the Mongols to the gospel has been a pleasant reprieve in a hard-fought spiritual battle. In some ways, the people of Mongolia are different from other Tibetan Buddhist peoples. Their background includes, for example, underlying shamanism, recent Communism, the legacy of Chinggis Khan and recent political independence. In other ways, they are very similar to other Tibetan Buddhist peoples.

How can we account for the seemingly sudden success of the gospel? Are there lessons from Mongolia that we can apply to reaching Tibetan Buddhists in other parts of Central Asia?

As we think about these questions, we must first recognize the sovereignty of God in the birth of the church in Mongolia. In many ways it was God's time for Mongolia, and Christians could only stand back, watch God at work and rejoice. There were at least four factors vital to the church's rapid growth:

Most elderly Mongols have little interest in Christianity. This couple have just been given a gospel tract at a festival in Mongolia.

Create International

1. *The New Testament:* In God's timing, there was a colloquial Khalka-Mongol version of the New Testament available as soon as Mongolia opened in 1990. Moreover,

International Mission Board

A happy Mongol nomad mother ready to move to the next location.

almost everyone in Mongolia was literate and could read it. Here was something new to Mongolia, well presented and well distributed. Curiosity drew many to read it. The New Testament had a context; it was usually coupled with the *Jesus* film and good preaching. Any terminology questions were explained or discussed in the context of a worshipping Christian community.

2. *Witness through cooperation:* With a clean missiological slate before them, it was tempting for foreign Christians to act independently in Mongolia. Some did so, but most realized the benefits of working together. There was an encouraging amount of grass-roots cooperation, vision sharing and praying together. Formal and informal partnerships gave rise to various aid and development projects, an international church and an international school, the Bible Training Center (BTC), and the Mongolian Center for Theological Education by Extension (MCTEE). Joint planning also resulted in an annual ministry consultation, city-wide evangelistic campaigns, a unified 'March for Jesus' through the streets of Ulaanbaatar, music-writing workshops, combined worship services, joint Easter and Christmas celebrations and united legal efforts in response to the 1993 Law on the

Relationship of Church and State.

There was cooperation with the government, too. Christian agencies provided English teachers, veterinarians, teacher trainers, agriculturalists, doctors, aid workers, financial consultants and environmental specialists either under direct contract to government departments or in partnership with inter-agency government projects. Christians promoted the spiritual welfare of the nation, but they also witnessed to the love of Christ by providing vital services for the physical welfare of Mongolia. In this way Christians gained credibility with the government.

3. *Church planting:* Church planting has been the dominant mission strategy. With a population of only two and a half million, some saw the possibility of winning the

Asian Report

The Mongols learn to ride horses as soon as they can fit on a saddle, even if the saddle is the same size as they are!

whole nation for Christ. The Mongols themselves kept up the momentum for evangelism. And who better to do it? Some churches systematically prayed, evangelized and established house groups in stairwells, then buildings, housing estates, suburbs and so to whole towns.

Each summer, teams of Mongol Christians travelled to the provinces to preach, distribute literature and show the *Jesus* film. After establishing a house group, they'd stay on to teach the new believers for a number of weeks. This emerging church was encouraged to attend a winter and / or summer camp of the mother church in or near Ulaanbaatar for a week. Leaders were identified and given further training. One Mongolian church, for example, planted 19 daughter churches before its own sixth anniversary. In November 1998, the first daughter church planted a 'granddaughter' church. Immediately after a church was established, it was challenged to reproduce itself and take the gospel into the nations of the world. Mongolian evangelistic teams went to Buriatia (in Russia) and Hohot (in Chinese Inner Mongolia) by 1996. Within Mongolia itself, Mongols began to evangelize the Kazaks, the Chinese and the residual Russian population.

4. *Leadership training:* By the turn of the century, leadership training became a high priority for mission in Mongolia. Individual churches experimented with training their own people as Sunday school teachers and home group leaders. The inter-church and inter-agency Bible Training Center was set up to provide high quality, in-country leadership training. The Mongolian Center for Theological Education by Extension was started in 1995, providing distance-learning courses to pastors who couldn't come into Ulaanbaatar for training. A number of Mongol leaders have won scholarships to seminaries and Bible colleges in America, Singapore, Australia and Europe.

Others have been called to produce resources for the church. A number of translation and

A Mongol man wearing a silver box around his chest. Such boxes contain a miniature shrine and idol, which is believed to ward off evil spirits.

research projects have been started to equip pastors with books in Mongolian so that there would be no need for them to learn other Asian or even European languages in order to use Bible references or to read Christian literature.

The Mongolian church in the new millennium

At the beginning of the new millennium, Mongolian Christians faced three long-term challenges. The first of these is to understand the Mongol Christian church's place in history. Christianity actually pre-dates Tibetan Buddhism. It can be argued historically that Christianity—especially Asian (as opposed to Western) Christianity—has a legitimate place in Mongolia today as the Eastern Syrian church was well ensconced in Central Asia before the rise of the Mongols. Significant Christians were influential during the reign of the Great Khans in the thirteenth and fourteenth centuries. Christian Mongols also need to think clearly about their own culture and experiment with ways of expressing Christian truth and worship in Mongolian ways. The challenge of 'Mongolizing' Christianity into culturally appropriate forms will be ongoing.

A second challenge is the imperative to play a strategic role in nation building. In the late 1990s, Mongolia began 'opening the books' on 70 years of Communism. Atrocities, missing persons, purges and mismanagement began to be addressed. There is now a great opportunity for Mongolian Christians to preach, demonstrate and lead the nation in acts of reconciliation that would bring honour to Christ and his church. With the legal precedent for toleration set down by Chinggis Khan in the legal code of the *yasa*, the Mongolian church has every right to be in the forefront of political and social change.

The third challenge is that of Tibetan Buddhism. The immense social changes of the 1990s have led to a renaissance of Tibetan Buddhism in Mongolia as in other parts of the Tibetan Buddhist world, due to the renewed freedom to express again the religion of pre-Communist Mongolia. Idols have been rebuilt, novices have been recruited and lamas have begun writing in the newspapers and are once again dictating the rhythms of family and national life.

By the end of the 20th century the Mongolian church was aware of, and seeking to address, the great spiritual struggle ahead of it. Opposition from disgruntled Communists is decreasing, while slander from reinstated lamas is increasing.

It is a church born at a time when the nation is at a critical turning point. In God's timing, and in his grace, Mongolia's modern Christian church will continue to bear a solid witness to Christ in the nation and to live out the power and truth of the gospel.

Notes

This article, commissioned for *Peoples of the Buddhist World*, is based on chapter 46 of *Steppe by Step* and parts have also appeared in chapter 10 of Marku Tsering's book *Sharing Christ in the Tibetan Buddhist World* (Upper Darby, PA: Tibet Press, 2nd edn, 1993).

1. In June 1989, thousands of Chinese youth gathered in Beijing's Tiananmen Square to demonstrate in favour of political reform. The Chinese army suppressed and killed thousands of the demonstrators on 4 June 1989; this was the so-called Tiananmen Square Incident. A similar demonstration by Mongolians occurred in 1990 in Ulaanbaatar's Sukhbaatar Square. The demonstrations were allowed to continue and were not suppressed by the army.

Create International

An elderly Mongol lady with prayer beads. Many Tibetan Buddhists chant a sacred invocation 108 times, counting each time by moving one of the 108 beads on the chain.

Population:
70,300 (2000)
81,900 (2010)
95,500 (2020)
Countries: Mongolia
Buddhism: Tibetan
Christians: 50

Overview of the Mongolia Buriat

Other Names: Buryat, Buriat-Mongolian, Northern Mongolian, Mongolian Buriat, Bur'aad

Population Sources:

64,900 in Mongolia (2000, B Grimes [1995 figure])

Language: Altaic, Mongolian, Eastern, Oirat-Khalkha, Khalkha-Buriat, Buriat

Dialects: 2 (Khori, Aga)

Professing Buddhists: 50%

Practising Buddhists: 20%

Christians: 0.1%

Scripture: Portions 1827; work in progress

***Jesus* film:** none

Gospel Recordings: none

Christian Broadcasting: none

ROPAL code: BXM

Status of Evangelization

65%

34%

1%

A   B   C

A = Have never heard the gospel
B = Have heard the gospel but have not become Christians
C = Are adherents to some form of Christianity

Approximately 75,000 Buriat people live in the north-eastern part of Mongolia, near the border with Russia. The Buriat in Mongolia migrated there from their homeland around Lake Baikal in Siberia many centuries ago. Over time, their language and culture have diverged from those of the Buriat in Russia. Today the Buriat of Mongolia, Russia and China should each be treated as separate ethnolinguistic groups. There are two main dialects of Buriat in Mongolia: Khori and Aga. Standard Mongolian has heavily influenced these dialects, and hundreds of loanwords have become part of the Buriat vocabulary in Mongolia.

In the past, most Buriat in Mongolia were nomads, tracking their herds across a wide region of grassland in the north-east of the country. Traditionally, they were 'shepherds who raised horses, cattle, sheep, goats and a few camels. Today, many still raise horses and sheep. Others have jobs in wood-related industries or coal mines; some trap animals; and many work on farms.'[1]

The Buriat along the Russia-Mongolia border were considered strategically important after the 1917 Bolshevik Revolution in Russia. 'By maintaining their influence in Buryatia, the Soviets could keep a tight reign on the Mongolian People's Republic, which most political scientists considered to be little more than a sixteenth Soviet republic. The Soviets feared an independent Mongolia because of the impact it could have on Russian access to the rich natural resources of Siberia.'[2]

Living in one of the coldest places on earth, the Buriat of Mongolia rely on a protein-heavy diet to get them through the winter. They consume 'much fat and meat (mainly mutton) during the winter, and dairy products such as yogurt, cheese and sour cream during the summer. Their favorite drink is *airag*, which is fermented mare's milk.'[3]

Before Communism came to Mongolia, the Buriat were zealous followers of Tibetan Buddhism, which they mixed with their traditional shamanistic practices. During the decades of Marxist rule many became atheists. Temples were demolished and the Buddhist clergy largely disbanded. Since the early 1990s, 'the advent of religious liberty in the former Soviet Union and Mongolia during this period stimulated . . . Buddhists to revive their traditional culture and religion. Monasteries were rebuilt, young men trained as monks, and contacts established with Tibetan Buddhists

Create International

abroad.'[4] The revival of Tibetan Buddhism in Mongolia has been energized by visits from the Dalai Lama.

Because of linguistic differences, the Buriat in Mongolia have been overlooked, and the lack of resources has hindered the small number of Christians among them from growing. The *Jesus* film in Buriat was produced for the Buriat in Russia. Those in Mongolia struggle to understand the dialect used. There are no Scriptures and no gospel recordings produced specifically for the Mongolia Buriat.

25

Buriat, Russia

RUSSIA
Irkutsk · Buryatia
MONGOLIA
CHINA
Buriat Russia

Population:
464,200 (2000)
510,600 (2010)
561,700 (2020)
Countries: Russia
Buddhism: Tibetan
Christians: 1,000

Overview of the Russia Buriat

Other Names: Buryat, Northern Mongolian, Buriat-Mongolian

Population Sources:
422,000 in Russia (1990, *National Geographic*)

Language: Altaic, Mongolian, Eastern, Oirat-Khalkha, Khalkha-Buriat, Buriat

Dialects: 9 (Ekhirit, Unga, Ninzne-Udinsk, Barguzin, Tunka, Oka, Alar, Bohaan, Bulagat)

Professing Buddhists: 55%

Practising Buddhists: 30%

Christians: 0.2%

Scripture: Portions 1827; work in progress

***Jesus* film:** available

Gospel Recordings: Buriat: Eastern

Christian Broadcasting: available

ROPAL code: MNB

Status of Evangelization
57%
42%
1%
A   B   C
A = Have never heard the gospel
B = Have heard the gospel but have not become Christians
C = Are adherents to some form of Christianity

Between 450,000 and 500,000 Buriat people live around the mighty Lake Baikal in the Republic of Buryatia in Siberia, Russia. The main towns in the Buriat area are Ulan Ude and Irkutsk, which lies west of the lake.[1] Lake Baikal is easily the world's largest lake, containing more than 20 per cent of the world's fresh water. During the harsh winter months, when temperatures plummet to minus forty degrees, Russian railway officials save considerable time and distance for the Trans-Siberian Express by relaying the train tracks across parts of the

Nancy Sturrock

frozen lake.[2] Lake Baikal is 636 kilometres (395 mi.) long and 1,600 metres (5,300 ft.) deep. The grasslands around the lake contain numerous 'wolves, jackals, bears, red deer and eagles'.[3]

According to the 1990 census, 381,000 out of the 422,000 ethnic Buriat people (90%) could speak the Buriat language. It has nine dialects, which have come about because of the vast geographical spread of the Buriat. Most young Buriat people are bilingual in Russian. The Buriat language in Russia is considerably different from Buriat in China and Mongolia. They use a different script, styled on the Russian orthography, and there are significant vocabulary differences because of the influence of other languages.[4]

The religious climate of the Buriats is complicated. Tibetan Buddhism entered the area in the 1700s, when 150 monks of the Gelugpa (Yellow Hat) sect of Buddhism travelled throughout what today is Siberia.

Buddhist teaching was placed as a veneer over the existing shamanism. Later, the Russian Orthodox Church converted many Western Buriats to their form of Christianity. There were numerous clashes between the Orthodox priests and the Buddhist lamas. 'Many converted for ulterior motives, such as tax relief. There was a Buriat proverb: "Put a cross on your neck for a piece of land".'[5]

The first Protestant missionaries to the Buriat in Russia were the Stallybrass, Swan and Rahmn families, who worked in Siberia from 1818 to 1840.[6] They reported that the Buriat converts 'rejoiced to know that God did not make any distinctions between rich and poor. They had a new identity as people liberated from the bondage of their past life.'[7] By 1827, the Old Testament and the four Gospels were translated into Buriat.[8] Early missionary William Swan lamented his team's lack of power to combat the authority of the shamans: 'No Christian missionaries, at least none deserving the name, now pretend to the possession of miraculous gifts.'[9]

Since 1990, a partnership of 26 different mission agencies has been working for the salvation of the Buriat people.[10] In 2002 there were an estimated 1,000 Buriat evangelicals. Most are young people with a modern outlook on life. Few of the elderly Buriat have believed in Christ. Numerous resources are available to evangelize the Buriat. They have the *Jesus* film, Christian radio broadcasts, audio recordings and children's Bible stories, and the Scriptures are presently being retranslated. There are high hopes for a bright future among this precious group.

The Burmese are one of the great ethnic groups of Asia. With a population of more than 32 million people, their homeland is the nation of Myanmar (formerly Burma), where they make up about 60 per cent of the population.[1] Hundreds of thousands of Burmese also live in neighbouring countries such as Bangladesh,[2] Thailand, Malaysia and Laos, while tens of thousands more now make their homes in Western nations, especially the United States and the United Kingdom.

The Burmese call themselves Bama, or Bhama. As a national identity they sometimes also refer to themselves as the Myen, from which the new name of Myanmar is derived. The Burmese language is part of the Tibeto-Burman linguistic family, not closely related to other regional giants like Thai, Chinese, Malay or Khmer.

The Burmese are believed to have originated in China and to have made their way into today's Myanmar in the 9th century AD. They quickly established themselves as the major power in the fertile Irrawaddy River Valley, building their greatest capital at Bagan (Pagan) in 1044. The city contained more than 13,000 Buddhist temples before it was sacked by the Mongol hordes in 1287.

The Burmese have zealously followed Theravada Buddhism since the 11th century, when the King of Burma invited the Buddhist monk Arahan from Ceylon (Sri Lanka) to instruct him and his subjects on the teachings

Create International

of Buddha. The Pali script (derived from Sanskrit) was introduced to Myanmar at this time. During the one thousand years since, Buddhism has become intertwined with their ethnic identity to such an extent that it is commonly said, 'To be Burmese is to be Buddhist'.[3] Today, thousands of gold-coloured temple roofs can be seen scattered throughout the country.[4]

Baptist missionary Adoniram Judson, one of the first Protestant foreign missionaries in history, first arrived in Burma in 1813. Facing extraordinary hardships, imprisonment and loneliness, Judson and his family almost single-handedly established the gospel in this seat of Buddhism and translated the Bible into Burmese.[5] Judson was often overwhelmed with the task of bringing the proud Burmese people to Christ, but with eyes of faith he could see the day when the name of Jesus would conquer the teachings of Arahan that flooded the land. Judson boldly said, 'Perhaps we stand on the dividing line of the empires of darkness and light. On shade of Arahan, weep over your falling temples, retire from the scenes of your past greatness. . . . A voice mightier than mine, a still, small voice will before long sweep away every vestige of your dominion. The churches of Jesus will soon supplant these idolatrous monuments and the chantings of the devotees of Buddha will die away before the Christian hymn of praise.'[6] When Judson died, he left behind a church of almost 8,000 members.[7]

The Burmese are one of the largest unreached people groups in the world. They live alongside many Christian people groups, yet most Burmese refuse to consider the claims of the gospel from a tribal person, whom they consider inferior to themselves.

MYANMAR

Burmese

Population:
31,401,000 (2000)
35,309,500 (2010)
39,705,700 (2020)

Countries: Myanmar, Bangladesh, Thailand, China, Malaysia, USA, United Kingdom, India, Cambodia, Sri Lanka, Germany, Laos and many other nations

Buddhism: Theravada

Christians: 40,000

Overview of the Burmese

Other Names: Bama, Bhama, Myen, Myan, Bamachaka, Burman, Man, Bamas, Myanmas

Population Sources:
30,944,900 in Myanmar (2000, GEM)
300,000 in Bangladesh (2001, P Johnstone and J Mandryk)
61,900 in Thailand (2000, GEM)
23,000 in China (2003, Joshua Project II)
20,000 in Malaysia (2003, Joshua Project II)
20,000 in USA (2000, P Hattaway)
12,000 in United Kingdom (2003, Joshua Project II)[8]

Language: Sino-Tibetan, Tibeto-Burman, Lolo-Burmese, Burmish, Southern

Dialects: 4 (Merguese, Yaw, Burmese, Palaw)

Professing Buddhists: 99%

Practising Buddhists: 80%

Christians: 0.1%

Scripture: Bible 1835; New Testament 1832; Portions 1815

Jesus film: available

Gospel Recordings: Burmese

Christian Broadcasting: available

ROPAL code: BMS

Status of Evangelization

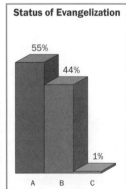

A = Have never heard the gospel
B = Have heard the gospel but have not become Christians
C = Are adherents to some form of Christianity

Chak

Population:
2,370 (2000)
2,730 (2010)
3,120 (2020)
Countries: Myanmar,
Bangladesh
Buddhism: Theravada
Christians: 10

Overview of the Chak

Other Names:

Population Sources: 1,200
in Myanmar (2002, Myanmar
Faces and Places)

909 in Bangladesh (1981
census)

Language: Unclassified

Dialects: 0

Professing Buddhists: 99%

Practising Buddhists: 65%

Christians: 0.4%

Scripture: none

***Jesus* film:** none

Gospel Recordings: Chak

Christian Broadcasting: none

ROPAL code: CKH

Status of Evangelization

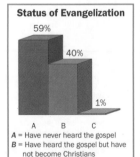

59%
40%
1%

A   B   C

A = Have never heard the gospel
B = Have heard the gospel but have
not become Christians
C = Are adherents to some form of
Christianity

The 2,400 Chak people of western Myanmar and neighbouring areas of south-east Bangladesh comprise one of the least known Buddhist ethnic groups in the world. More than 1,200 Chak live in the Blue Mountains of Rakhine State in Myanmar. They are isolated from outside influence, inhabiting small villages in a tropical forest. The Chak are not officially recognized by the Myanmar government, who acknowledge the existence of just seven tribes in Rakhine State.

A similar number of Chak live across the border in the Chittagong Hill Tracts of Bangladesh. The most recent census in Bangladesh—conducted in 1981—listed 909 Chak people there. In both nations the Chak rely on simple agriculture and hunting to survive. They rarely venture outside their communities. Because of the political instability in this part of the world, the Chak have sometimes found it wiser to stay detached. In June 2001, two Chak people in Bangladesh died when they stood on a landmine while collecting bamboo. Landmines have caused 61 deaths and 125 injuries in this part of Bangladesh since 1993.[1]

There has been very little research done

on the Chak people. The *Ethnologue* lists the Chak people, but it does not identify what linguistic family the Chak language belongs to. It is most likely part of the Tibeto-Burman family, related to other small languages in the area such as Dainet and Thet. The Chak are not the same as the large Chakma Buddhist group of Bangladesh, who speak a language from the Indo-European family.

Several small Buddhist ethnic groups live near the temple ruins of Mrauk-U in Rakhine State, Myanmar. Mrauk-U was once the centre for one of Myanmar's most powerful kingdoms.[2] Founded by the Rakhine king Minzawmun in 1433, Mrauk-U grew in influence throughout central Myanmar and the Indian subcontinent, becoming a centre of wealth and commerce. The kings of the dynasty even hired Japanese samurai as bodyguards to quell the threat of assassination.[3]

The splendour of the Mrauk-U dynasty started to fade in the 1780s, but during its 352 years Buddhism made an impact on all people groups in this area—as a cultural way of life as much as a religious one. Small tribes such as the Chak, Dainet and Thet have remained strong Buddhists to this day.

A Portuguese Catholic monk and envoy visited Mrauk-U in 1630s. They described the royal palaces as having 'massive wooden columns of such extraordinary length and straightness that one wonders there are trees so tall and so straight. . . . In the same palace there is a hall gilt from top to bottom which they call the "Golden House" because it has a vine of the purest gold which occupies the whole roof of the hall, with a hundred and odd gourds of the same pure gold. There are also in that very rich house seven idols of gold, each of the size and proportions of an average man. These idols are adorned on the forehead, breast, arms and waist with many fine precious stones, rubies, emeralds and sapphires and also with some brilliant old rock diamonds of more than ordinary size.'[4]

Create International

More than 430,000 Chakma people inhabit Bangladesh and adjoining areas of north-east India. Approximately 300,000 live in the Chittagong Hills area of south-east Bangladesh, including Chittagong City. They are the largest Buddhist group in that Muslim-dominated country. The Chakma are not the same as the smaller Chak tribe, who inhabit areas further south.

In India the Chakma are a scheduled (official) tribe.[1] They number over 100,000 people spread over five states, including south-western Mizoram along the Karnafuli River (39,900 in 1981), northern Tripura (34,797 in 1981)[2] and Assam (22,789 in 1971, living in the Karbi Anglong, North Cachar and Cachar districts).[3] Small numbers of Chakma live in West Bengal (141 people)[4] and Meghalaya (103 people).

Julian Hawken

The Chakma have inhabited the Chittagong Hill Tracts since long before the region became part of the Mughal empire in 1666.[5] Buddhism flourished in Bangladesh from the 5th to 12th centuries. Since the 13th century, Buddhism has been confined to the Chittagong area. The Chakma 'continued to acknowledge the suzerainty of the Arakanese king until 1784'.[6] They have long found themselves at odds with the predominantly Muslim Bengalis. The construction of the Kaptai Dam in the 1960s caused 18,000 Chakma people to lose their homes, and this is believed to be the origin of the present problems. Since the mid-1970s the Chakma have been involved in a secretive guerilla war against Bangladeshi soldiers. The fighting stems from the influx of large numbers of Bengali settlers, who have moved into the Chittagong area and taken over Chakma land by force. The government does little to stop the illegal settlers, and the Chakma have fought back out of frustration as they see their lives being rapidly decimated. In 1987, Amnesty International reported 'arbitrary arrests, torture and unlawful killings'[7] of tribe members by security forces. Thousands of Chakma have been killed, hundreds of women and girls raped, and Buddhist temples smashed and looted.[8] Tens of thousands of Chakma refugees have fled across the border into India.

According to K S Singh, 'The Chakma are Buddhists and worship Lord Buddha. At the family level they worship deities like Lakshmi and Ganga. . . . The monk, who may be from another Buddhist community, acts as a religious teacher and performs various rites.'[9]

The 1981 census in India recorded 97.62 per cent of the Chakma in Tripura as followers of Buddhism, 2.32 per cent as Hindus and the rest as Christians and Muslims. The 1961 census had returned a higher figure of 99.44 per cent as Buddhists. In Mizoram, 98.83 per cent of Chakma are Buddhists.

According to the India Missions Association, 7,275 Chakma in India are Christians.[10] In Bangladesh, the Christian presence among the Chakma is scarcer, although there are small pockets of believers in scattered villages. Overall, the troubled Chakma people remain a unreached and unevangelized people group. Experiencing turmoil and an uncertain future, they need the inner peace and hope that only faith in Christ can bring.

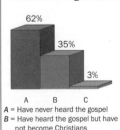

Population:
404,600 (2000)
471,900 (2010)
552,300 (2020)
Countries: Bangladesh, India
Buddhism: Theravada
Christians: 12,000

Overview of the Chakma

Other Names: Takam, Chakama, Thet, Chawngma, Tsak

Population Sources:

260,577 in Bangladesh (1991, United Bible Societies)

103,747 in India (2001, India Missions Association)

Language: Indo-European, Indo-Iranian, Indo-Aryan, Eastern Zone, Bengali-Assamese

Dialects: 6

Professing Buddhists: 95%

Practising Buddhists: 80%

Christians: 2.9%

Scripture: New Testament 1926

***Jesus* film:** available

Gospel Recordings: Chakma: Bangladesh, Chakma: Assam

Christian Broadcasting: none

ROPAL code: CCP

Status of Evangelization

62%
35%
3%

A   B   C

A = Have never heard the gospel
B = Have heard the gospel but have not become Christians
C = Are adherents to some form of Christianity

More than one thousand people belonging to the Chali ethnic group live in eastern Bhutan, the landlocked, mysterious Buddhist Himalayan kingdom. They inhabit a few villages in the Mongar (also spelled Monggar and Mongaa) District.

The linguist George van Driem has provided an extremely detailed description of where the Chali language is spoken. 'The Chali language is limited to a small area north of Mongar on the east bank of the Kurichu. At the southern end, the Chali speaking area proper begins north of Mongar at the Gangg'o La, which is just five kilometers [three miles] south of the village of Chali itself. The Chali speaking villages are Chali and neighboring Wangmakhar. The language is also spoken in the tiny hamlets surrounding these two villages. In the west, the Chali speaking area is bound by the Kurichu and in the north by the Threwenchu, a lateral tributary of the Kurichu. The easternmost Chali speaking hamlet is G'ortshom up on the ridge above Chali village. Outside of the Chali area proper, in the immediate vicinity of Tormazhong village in the Chocangacakha speaking area north of the Threwenchu, approximately one third of the households are also reported to be Chali speaking.'[1]

Mongar is a small, nondescript town with a population of about 1,500 people. It sits on the top of a ridge and is protected from the wind by a row of large eucalyptus trees. Mongar proudly boasts one bank, a hospital and a post office. It also has a small Buddhist monastery, housing fifty or sixty monks, some of whom are young boys not yet in their teens. Although the town itself is of minor interest to visitors, the area has strikingly beautiful scenery, as does most of Bhutan.

The Chali language is different from all other Eastern Tibetan varieties spoken in Bhutan. One source notes, 'The Chali area is bound to the north and west by the Chocangacakha speaking area, and to the south and east by the Tsangla speaking area. . . . Chali has a massive component of loan vocabulary resulting from its location at the crossroads of Tsangla and Chocangacakha speaking areas as well as from historical circumstances.'[2]

Tibetan Buddhism has been the dominant religion in Bhutan since its reported introduction in AD 746, when 'Sendha Gyab, the king of Bumthang, had a conflict with another Indian king in the south of Bhutan. As a result of this dispute, Sendha Gyab became possessed by a demon, and it required a powerful tantric master to exorcise it. The greatest master was the teacher Padmasambhava, better known as Guru Rimpoche (precious master). . . . After an extended process involving trickery and magic dances, the guru captured the demon and converted it to Buddhism. For good measure, he also converted the king and his rival, restoring the country to peace. . . . The first visit of Guru Rimpoche to Bumthang is recognized as the true introduction of Buddhism to Bhutan.'[3]

There are no known Christians among the Chali people. Few have ever heard the gospel in a meaningful manner.

Population:
1,250 (2000)
1,600 (2010)
2,050 (2020)
Countries: Bhutan
Buddhism: Tibetan
Christians: none known

Overview of the Chali

Other Names: Chalikha, Tshali, Chalipkha, Tshalingpa

Population Sources:

1,000 in Bhutan (2001, G van Driem [1991 figure])

Language: Sino-Tibetan, Tibeto-Burman, Himalayish, Tibeto-Kanauri, Tibetic, Tibetan, Eastern

Dialects: 0

Professing Buddhists: 100%

Practising Buddhists: 45%

Christians: 0%

Scripture: none

Jesus film: none

Gospel Recordings: none

Christian Broadcasting: none

ROPAL code: TGF

Photo credit: Dwayne Graybill

Status of Evangelization

87%

13%

0%

A   B   C

A = Have never heard the gospel
B = Have heard the gospel but have not become Christians
C = Are adherents to some form of Christianity

Primarily located along the southern border area between Tibet and the Indian state of Jammu and Kashmir, more than 5,000 Champa people live east and south-east of the city of Leh. One of the alternative names for the Champa is Changtang. The Nghari Tibetans in China are also called Changtang Tibetans, after the massive plain of the same name. More research needs to be done to determine if the Champa people of India are the same (having common origins and speaking the same language) as the Nghari Tibetans of China. The area inhabited by the Champa in Jammu and Kashmir is extremely cold. Living at an average altitude of 4,000 to 5,000 metres (13,000 to 16,000 ft.) above sea level, the Champa's homeland is ravaged by snowstorms during the long winter months.

In 1989 the Champa were granted official status in India as a Scheduled Tribe. Before then they were considered a sub-group of the Ladakhi, but their customs, language and ethnicity are different from those of the Ladakhi. They are also distinct from the Zangskari people, with whom the Champa barter to obtain grain.[1] The Champa come down to trade at the Changthang Nyoma market, where they have also sent some of their children to be educated in Tibetan schools. The diet of the Champa people consists of 'barley (*tsampa*) and the meat of yak and wild horses. Dried cheese and meat boiled with barley flour and seasoned with chilies are also eaten.'[2]

The Champa language is closely related to Ladakhi, and

Julian Hawken

most Champa have no problem understanding Ladakhi when they travel outside their remote valleys for trade. Most Champa people are pastoralists. They raise sheep and goats, and they are particularly noted for the cashmere wool they produce. The Champa can be identified by their conical yak-skin tents called *reboo*. The Champa who live nomadic lives are known as *Phalpa*, while those who have settled down in fixed locations are called *Fangpa*. The ruling aristocracy is known as the *Nono*.

All Champa families profess Tibetan Buddhism as their religion. It 'occupies a central place in their culture. Each tent invariably accommodates the family deity, *Donaq*, and a picture of their spiritual head, the Dalai Lama. The family deity is worshipped on the fifteenth day of the seventh Buddhist month. . . . The Bon heritage is quite conspicuous in the Champa religion despite the efforts of the Buddhists to erase it.'[3] Another source states, 'Buddhism rests quite lightly on them, as they have more faith in their traditional beliefs and practices. In this form of primitive religion, a carry over from the early bon religion, the *lha* (spirits) and *lhu* (serpents) are considered very important. . . . The world of *lhas* and *lhus* is believed to be complex and fearful. For every unwelcome event, be it harsh weather, or death, one of the *lhas* or *lhus* is responsible. The supreme *lha* is known as Changmen, who is believed to control about 360 *lhas* in the Changthang area.'[4]

The Champa could surely be ranked among the most unreached people groups in the world. Because of their remarkably isolated existence, very few have ever been exposed to the gospel, which has failed to penetrate this remote part of the world.

Overview of the Champa

Other Names: Changpa, Champa Ladakhi, Changthang, Changtang, Changtang Ladakhi, Changs-skat, Byangskat, Byanskat, Rong, Rupshu, Stotpa, Upper Ladakhi, Fangpa, Phalpa

Population Sources:
5,000 in India (2000, P Hattaway)

Language: Sino-Tibetan, Tibeto-Burman, Himalayish, Tibeto-Kanauri, Tibetic, Tibetan, Western, Ladakhi

Dialects: 0

Professing Buddhists: 100%

Practising Buddhists: 75%

Christians: 0%

Scripture: none

Jesus **film:** none

Gospel Recordings: none

Christian Broadcasting: none

ROPAL code: CNA

Population:
5,000 (2000)
5,830 (2010)
6,800 (2020)

Countries: India, possibly China

Buddhism: Tibetan

Christians: none known

CHINA
Xinjiang
INDIA
Jammu & Kashmir
Xizang (Tibet)
Champa

Status of Evangelization

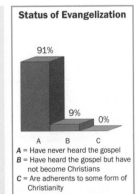

91%

9%

0%

A   B   C

A = Have never heard the gospel
B = Have heard the gospel but have not become Christians
C = Are adherents to some form of Christianity

Chaungtha

MYANMAR
Mandalay
Chaungtha

Population:
147,300 (2000)
165,600 (2010)
186,100 (2020)
Countries: Myanmar
Buddhism: Theravada
Christians: 200

Overview of the Chaungtha

Other Names:

Population Sources:

121,700 in Myanmar (2001, B Grimes [1983 figure])

Language: Sino-Tibetan, Tibeto-Burman, Lolo-Burmese, Burmish, Southern

Dialects: 0

Professing Buddhists: 97%

Practising Buddhists: 75%

Christians: 0.1%

Scripture: none

Jesus **film:** none

Gospel Recordings: none

Christian Broadcasting: none

ROPAL code: CCQ

Status of Evangelization

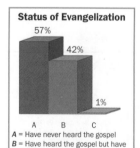

57%
42%
1%
A   B   C

A = Have never heard the gospel
B = Have heard the gospel but have not become Christians
C = Are adherents to some form of Christianity

Approximately 150,000 Chaungtha people inhabit central parts of Myanmar in Southeast Asia. The *Ethnologue* gives a 1983 estimate of 121,700 Chaungtha,[1] while Myanmar Faces and Places extrapolated that figure to give a 2002 population of 153,961 Chaungtha people.[2]

The most recent census held in Myanmar was in 1931, while the country was under British colonial rule. At the time the Chaungtha returned a total of 49,057 people, evenly divided between 24,549 males and 24,508 females.[3]

The name *Chaungtha* means 'people of the valley' or 'people of the stream'. There is a coastal resort town in Myanmar that is also called Chaungtha, but the names are purely coincidental. The Chaungtha are historically and ethnolinguistically related to the Burmese. Because of this, in recent decades their identity has been eroded as an increasing number of Chaungtha choose to identify themselves as Burmese, hoping to benefit from being aligned with the majority ruling people in Myanmar. Because of this transition, it is difficult these days to identify and research the Chaungtha. Today, people in the southern part of the Mandalay Division still identify themselves as Chaungtha.

The principal occupation of the Chaungtha is rice cultivation. 'Some plant rice on mountain terraces, which is the ideal; while others practice "shifting cultivation," moving from one plot to another. Some of the other important crops grown include maize, cotton, tobacco and opium poppies. The amount of tobacco supplied cannot meet the demands made by the many smokers in the region.'[4]

Create International

The central areas of Myanmar are among the most staunchly Buddhist in the nation. Whereas, generally speaking, the mountainous perimeter of Myanmar is occupied by tribal groups who practice animism or Christianity, the heart of the nation where the Chaungtha live is overwhelmingly Buddhist.

One profile of the Chaungtha states, 'Buddhism was introduced into Myanmar in the fifth century; and today, most of the Chaungtha are Buddhist. However, they have also maintained their traditional ethnic belief in evil spirits, or *nats*. They believe that these spirits can do almost anything in nature, such as preventing floods and other natural disasters. Unfortunately, the Chaungtha have no Bible or even portion of the Bible in their language, and no missions agencies are working among them. A greater effort must be made to reach them with the Good News.'[5]

The reason why the Bible has not yet been translated into Chaungtha is probably because they use the Burmese script—so researchers decided that a separate translation is not warranted. Mission agencies may also have decided that the Chaungtha spoken language is close enough to Burmese not to warrant separate audio and video productions for them. In the future, it is possible that the Chaungtha may cease to exist as a distinct ethnicity, as they are already well on the path to being assimilated by the Burmese.

There are believed to be just a few hundred Chaungtha Christians in Myanmar.

CHINA
Xizang (Tibet)
Dhawalagiri
NEPAL
INDIA
Chhairottan

Population:
200 (2000)
240 (2010)
300 (2020)
Countries: Nepal
Buddhism: Tibetan
Christians: none known

Overview of the Chhairottan

Other Names: Chhairo, Chhairo Tibetans

Population Sources:

200 in Nepal (2000, P Hattaway)

Language: Sino-Tibetan, Tibeto-Burman, Himalayish, Tibeto-Kanauri, Tibetic, Tamangic

Dialects: 0

Professing Buddhists: 100%

Practising Buddhists: 90%

Christians: 0%

Scripture: none

***Jesus* film:** none

Gospel Recordings: none

Christian Broadcasting: none

ROPAL code: none

Status of Evangelization

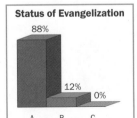

88%

12%

0%

A   B   C

A = Have never heard the gospel
B = Have heard the gospel but have not become Christians
C = Are adherents to some form of Christianity

The 200 Chhairottan people make up one of the smallest ethnic groups in Nepal. They live around the Chhairo village in the Mustang (Lo Manthang) District of Dhawalagiri Zone in north-central Nepal.[1] According to a book published by the Nepal government, the Chhairottan people 'resemble Marphalis and Thakalis in facial features, language and dress codes. Chhairottans are Buddhists though they also practice shamanism . . . The original Chhairottans have migrated from their stronghold at Chhairo village, which is now occupied by a few Thakali households and some ten Tibetan refugee families.'[2]

The existence of the kingdom of Mustang was first mentioned in 7th-century Ladakhi records. Mustang remained apart from the rest of Nepal for centuries, and numerous wars were waged to try and gain control of the low-lying and easily travelled Himalayan corridor.[3] During the 17th and 18th centuries Mustang was continually at war, especially with the kingdom of Jumla to the south-west. 'Jumla managed to take over Mustang only to be repelled when the kingdoms of Ladakh and Parbat came to Mustang's defense. In 1719 Jumla even kidnapped for ransom the future queen (from Ladakh) on her way to marry the king of Mustang.'[4]

Nancy Sturrock

The northern part of the Dwawalagiri Zone, which the Chhairottan people share, juts out into Tibet. When the Chinese occupied Tibet in the 1950s, the king of Mustang 'requested allegiance and protection from the partially democratized government of Nepal and became an official part of Nepal in doing so. . . . The now safe Mustang valley became home to over six thousand Khampa resistance fighters, who waged

a guerilla war against the Chinese and were moderately successful in destroying communications and roads in the Tibetan regions around Mustang. Political pressure from China forced Nepal to take action and Mustang was closed in an effort to alienate the resistance army. This . . . resulted in extreme hardships on the people and lands of Mustang to support this vast army.'[5]

The fighting finally stopped in the early 1970s after a taped plea to lay down arms was received from the Dalai Lama.[6] The king of Nepal was under fierce pressure from Mao Zedong to bring calm to the border area,[7] so the Nepal military waged a brutal campaign against the Khampa, driving most of them back into Tibet where the merciless Communists butchered them.

Fearing the local culture will be overrun by hordes of backpackers and camera-clicking tourists, the government has instituted a tax of US$700 on all foreigners entering Mustang. This has kept the number of visitors down. One guidebook states, 'Mustang has lured trekkers for many years, but was closed for a time both because of a guerilla war that was waged along the border with Tibet, and because of the ecological sensitivity of the region. The area is part of the Tibetan Plateau, and is high, dry and beautiful. . . . It is only possible to enter with an organized group, and permits are a steep $700 for 10 days.'[8]

All Chhairottan people are thought to believe in Tibetan Buddhism.

Chimtan

The Chimtan ethnic group is one of the smallest in Nepal, with a population of approximately 300 people. Despite their tiny size, the Chimtan have been acknowledged as one of the 61 official people groups of Nepal (although many researchers believe the true number of ethnolinguistic groups in Nepal to be 130 or more). Just why the Chimtan have been officially recognized, while many other larger and more obvious groups have not, remains a mystery.

Chimtan people 'are the inhabitants of one of the Panch (five) Gaun or villages between Kagbeni and Tukche in the District of Mustang. Their village is known as Chimada or Chimang. They call themselves Thakalis, and have affinity of language and culture with the Thakalis. Though Buddhists, they also practice shamanism. There are two branches of Chimtans—Bhamphobe and Dhyalkipal Phobe.'[1] The Chimtan language is part of the Tamangic branch of the Tibeto-Burman family.

Mustang District is in the Dhawalagiri Zone of north-central Nepal. They share the area with the Loba (who for centuries had their own kingdom), as well as with Tibetan refugees, Thakali and members of other small ethnicities such as the Chhairottan and Baragaunle.

One of the most interesting customs shared by many of the groups in Mustang is 'the asking of forgiveness after having captured or eloped with a man's daughter. In both cases the girl is kept in the house of one of the boy's relatives either within or outside the village. On the second day some relative or boy is sent (with consent of the captured girl) with a bottle of beer to the house of the girl's parents to apologize. The messenger does not go directly to the house, but stops at a distance of about 100 yards and shouts at the top of his voice, begging forgiveness for the offence and asking the parents to accept the new relationship. Then he walks 50 yards closer and repeats the same plea a second time. Finally he enters the house, anticipating a quarrel or even a fight. The whole day is spent in brawling, abusing each other, or even fighting with knives. In certain cases it takes as long as seven days to calm the offended parents of the girl. Once this is done the payment can be presented and the wedding ceremony proceeds immediately.'[2]

Almost all people living in Mustang follow the Tibetan Buddhist religion, although strong elements of shamanism and Bon (the pre-Buddhist religion of Tibet) are intertwined with their beliefs. This is true of the Chimtan's ceremonies. Some of the obvious differences between Bon and Tibetan Buddhism are that temples and other sacred places are encircled in a counter-clockwise direction by worshippers, 'in direct opposition to Buddhist tradition. That is, the Bon believer must walk to the right of his shrine, whereas the Buddhist approaches from the left. Likewise, the Bon prayer wheels are spun clockwise, the Buddhist counter-clockwise.'[3]

The gospel has not made any impact among the Chimtan people yet. Most are still waiting to hear about Jesus for the first time.

Photo credit: Dwayne Graybill

Population:
300 (2000)
370 (2010)
460 (2020)
Countries: Nepal
Buddhism: Tibetan
Christians: none known

Overview of the Chimtan

Other Names: Chimada, Chimang, Chimtan Tibetans

Population Sources:
300 in Nepal (2000, P Hattaway)

Language: Sino-Tibetan, Tibeto-Burman, Himalayish, Tibeto-Kanauri, Tibetic, Tamangic

Dialects: 0

Professing Buddhists: 100%

Practising Buddhists: 55%

Christians: 0%

Scripture: none

Jesus film: none

Gospel Recordings: none

Christian Broadcasting: none

ROPAL code: none

Status of Evangelization

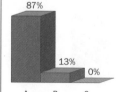

A = Have never heard the gospel
B = Have heard the gospel but have not become Christians
C = Are adherents to some form of Christianity

87%
13%
0%

A   B   C

Population:
7,100 (2000)
8,420 (2010)
10,100 (2020)
Countries: Cambodia, Thailand
Buddhism: Theravada
Christians: 50

Overview of the Chong

Other Names: Shong, Xong, Chawng

Population Sources: 5,000 in Cambodia (2000, B Grimes)

2,000 In Thailand (2000, J Schliesinger [1995 figure])

Language: Austro-Asiatic, Mon-Khmer, Eastern Mon-Khmer, Pearic, Western, Chong

Dialects: 0

Professing Buddhists: 98%

Practising Buddhists: 85%

Christians: 0.6%

Scripture: none

Jesus film: none

Gospel Recordings: none

Christian Broadcasting: none

ROPAL code: COG

Status of Evangelization

71%

28%

1%

A   B   C

A = Have never heard the gospel
B = Have heard the gospel but have not become Christians
C = Are adherents to some form of Christianity

The 7,000 Chong people, who inhabit areas along both sides of the Cambodia-Thailand border, make up one of the lesser-known Buddhist people groups in Southeast Asia.

Approximately 5,000 Chong live in Pursat Province in north-western Cambodia, while an additional 2,000 inhabit four main villages within Thailand's Chanthaburi Province,[1] especially in Makham District. Smaller numbers of Chong also live in Thailand's Trat Province.

Although today they are small in number, the ancestors of the Chong were once wide-spread throughout the region. The Chong today proudly remember the time when they had their own kingdom in Kuankraburi between the 4th and 13th centuries AD. In 1767, 'the Ayutthaya king Taksin fought the Burmese army and ordered the people in Chanthaburi to join the army. Most of the Chong, not willing to join the army, moved to Kichagud . . . to escape the Siamese authorities. Other Chong moved eastward into Trat province where they scattered near the Cambodian border.'[2]

In the past decade the Chong have started to inter-marry with Thai people, though not in great num-bers. The Thais look down on the Chong and consider them socially and culturally beneath them.

The Chong language, which is part of the Mon-Khmer linguistic family, is endangered in Thailand but stronger in Cambodia. In Thailand the Chong have unsuccessfully petitioned the Thai authorities to allow their language to be taught in schools. Now it is mostly elderly people who can still speak the Chong language in Thailand. The

Somray language in Cambodia is closely related to Chong.

The Chong still retain many customs unique to their tribe, including a marriage ceremony called *gatak*. Joachin Schliesinger states, 'Sets of buffalo and ox horns are bound to the heads of two elderly men during the marriage celebration. This custom symbolizes and honors the working capability and strength of buffaloes and oxen. . . . During the meal a young cock and hen are placed face to face. If they continue to look at each other during the wedding meal, the couple will stay together for a long time. If either turns away from the other, it is a bad omen for the outcome of the marriage. To avoid such a fate, some couples use stuffed chickens.'[3]

The Chong have been zealous Buddhists for hundreds of years, although vestiges of spirit appeasement are still found among them. Every Chong house has a Buddhist altar fixed on an inside wall. Many families also build a shrine, which is placed on a platform in the garden. Almost every Chong

Xayographix

family in Cambodia and Laos frequently visits their local Buddhist temple, and they gladly offer food and cash to the monks. Families consider it a great honour to send one of their sons to the temple to be trained as a monk.

Until recently there were no known Christians among the Chong, but since the late 1990s a small number have believed in Christ due to the witness of Christians in northern Cambodia.

Chuanlan

Population:
324,800 (2000)
367,000 (2010)
401,100 (2020)
Countries: China
Buddhism: Mahayana
Christians: 20,000

Overview of the Chuanlan

Other Names: Chuanchun, Ch'uan-chun-tsi, Lao Han, Old Han, Tunbao

Population Sources:
324,800 in China (2000, P Hattaway)

Language: Sino-Tibetan, Chinese

Dialects: 0

Professing Buddhists: 60%

Practising Buddhists: 35%

Christians: 6.2%

Scripture: Chinese Bible

Jesus film: none

Gospel Recordings: Mandarin: Guiyanghua

Christian Broadcasting: none

ROPAL code: none

Status of Evangelization

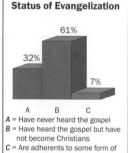

61%

32%

7%

A   B   C

A = Have never heard the gospel
B = Have heard the gospel but have not become Christians
C = Are adherents to some form of Christianity

Approximately 330,000 Chuanlan people are concentrated within Anshun Prefecture in southern China's Guizhou Province. They inhabit Anshun, Pingba and Zhenning counties. The Chuanlan ('Blue-Dressed People') are also known as Lao Han ('Old Han') and Tunbao by people in Guizhou. In the 1950s the Chuanlan applied to the Chinese government for recognition as a separate minority group. Their application was rejected, and they were included as part of the Han Chinese nationality. This upset the Chuanlan, who reapplied in the late 1970s only to be rejected again.

The Chuanlan are a Chinese group who have remained ethnically, linguistically and socially distinct from other Chinese people. It is commonly believed that their descendants were Chinese soldiers from Jiangxi, Jiangsu and Anhui provinces in east China who were sent to Guizhou to quell rebellions many 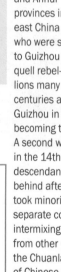 centuries ago. The first soldiers settled in Guizhou in the 8th and 9th centuries, thus becoming the first Chinese in the province. A second wave of 5,000 soldiers arrived in the 14th century. The Chuanlan are the descendants of soldiers who remained behind after military campaigns.[1] Many took minority women as wives and formed separate communities. Because of this intermixing, and centuries of separation from other Chinese people, the language of the Chuanlan developed into a unique form of Chinese. It is not mutually intelligible with Mandarin Chinese.

One visitor to the Chuanlan people commented, 'You find stone-built villages with stone houses and tall watchtowers along a 150 km (92 mile) stretch of karst landscapes. . . . They wear long blue robes with wide sleeves and speak a distinctive language unlike any other, and in all their rites of passage and daily lives they follow their old customs. These people seem old-fashioned, but it is thanks to their ancestors that Guizhou Province was formed and the history of this part of China was changed forever.'[2]

Mahayana Buddhism is the main religion of the Chuanlan people, although somewhat uniquely it is strongly observed by women but not by many men. 'The gender roles are clear cut—men farm and women keep house, men perform opera and women practice Buddhism and everyone is content with their roles. Various festivals and Buddhist activities form an important part of the women's lives. They play the lead in religious activities while the men are either onlookers or at most help keep order. The reason for this goes back to the times when the men tended the farms and kept the frontier areas peaceful. Whenever there were battles, their lives could be endangered. Memories of war have made the women firm believers in Buddhism and they seek Buddha's blessings for peace and safety. . . . The people live freely and have firm beliefs.'[3] The Chuanlan's historic reliance on stone watchtowers gave them their alternate name, *Tunbao*, which means 'stone castles' people.

There are many Chuanlan Christians scattered throughout the region. About half are Catholics and half worship in Protestant government-sanctioned or illegal house churches.

Julian Hawken

Children of the Buddhist World (1)

Birth rates in Buddhist countries are among the highest in the world. Hundreds of millions of children are growing up without any knowledge of the One who created them and loves them. Will you pray for the children of the Buddhist world?

1. A Vietnamese boy in a refugee detention centre receives a Christmas gift from Christians, Hong Kong. [Paul Hattaway]
2. Young Burmese lady, Yangon, Myanmar. [Create International]
3. Monpa girl from a village near Dirang in Arunachal Pradesh, India. [Dwayne Graybill]
4. Monpa baby from Lesba in Arunachal Pradesh, India. [Dwayne Graybill]

5.   Dressed to the hilt. A young Khampa boy at the Yushu horse fair in Qinghai Province, China. [Nancy Sturrock]
6.   Lao boy from central Laos. [Christian Far East Ministry]
7.   A Han Chinese girl. [International Mission Board]
8.   A boy monk from Tawang Monastery in Arunachal Pradesh, India. [Dwayne Graybill]
9.   Shy young Chinese lady. [Julian Hawken]

10. Brother and sister from the Southern Khampa group in Deqen, Yunnan Province, China. [David Treat]
11. Two happy Eastern Khampa girls with their beloved pets. [Nancy Sturrock]
12. Khampa lad from Litang in Sichuan Province, China. [Nancy Sturrock]
13. Novice monks at a temple in Arunachal Pradesh, India. [Dwayne Graybill]

14. Cute as a button Chinese girl from Qingdao in Shandong Province. [International Mission Board]
15. An Amdo girl from a village near Qinghai Lake, China. [Nancy Sturrock]
16. Young novice monks accept food from a Thai woman in Mae Hong Son, Thailand. [International Mission Board]
17. Time for a nap, China. [International Mission Board]

A 1982 study listed 'between 400,000 to 500,000' Chuanqing ('black-dressed people') in Guizhou Province of south China.[1] Most are concentrated in Zhijin and Nayong counties, with others in Dafang, Shuicheng, Guanling, Qingzhen, Puding and Luzhi counties.

The Chuanqing view themselves as a distinct people group. Although they speak a Chinese language and historically belong to the Han ethnicity, the government has placed them in a list of Undetermined Minorities in China.[2] In the 1950s their application for full status as a minority group was rejected. The decision was that the Chuanqing were 'originally members of the Han nationality', and that their characteristics were 'manifestations of the special features of Han in certain regions in an earlier period, not the characteristics of a separate nationality'.[3]

Although some people think the Chuanqing and Chuanlan are the same, and some even call them by the same name, *Tunbao* (which means 'stone castles' people), these two groups view themselves as distinct with separate histories, customs and locations. There were numerous armed clashes between the Chuanqing and Chuanlan in the past. The Chuanqing were formerly known by a variety of names including *Pu Ren* ('garrison people').[4] The Yi call them *Sher-tu* or *Sher-feizu*, meaning 'white-skinned Han' or 'snake-eating Han'. Other locals call them *Da Jiao Ban* ('big foot') and *Da Xiuzi* ('big sleeves').[5]

The Chuanqing (like the Chuanlan) are descended from Chinese soldiers who were sent into Guizhou in the 8th and 9th centuries to quell Miao rebellions. The Chuanqing came from Jiangxi Province and provided forced labour for the army. The Chuanqing 'clung to their own dialect for generations.

The women dressed differently, arranging their hair in three sections. They celebrated separate festivals and followed different marriage customs.'[6]

The long history of religious observance among the Chuanqing is evidenced by the presence of several ancient temples in the Anshun area, including the Wen Miao Confucian Temple built in 1368, the Buddhist White Pagoda dating from the Ming Dynasty, and Tian Tai Shan Buddhist Temple built in 1616. Today approximately half of the Chuanqing people claim to be Buddhists, although the number of practising Buddhists is much lower. One of the most important Chuanqing festivals is called 'Crossing the River'. Its Buddhist origins tell a tale of when a woman was banished by the king of hell to the lowest depths of hell. Her children decided to rescue her. 'One spring day they walked together along the way their mother had taken, broke through 24 barriers, and finally found the King of Hell. When they saw their miserable mother in a river of blood, they denounced the King of Hell for his cruelty . . . retrieved their mother and spirited her across the river back to the human world.'[7]

There are a number of churches in the Anshun area—mostly Catholic—where Chuanqing believers worship. Catholic missionaries were active in the area in the past, resulting in more than 150,000 Catholics spread throughout Guizhou today.[8]

Population:
761,000 (2000)
981,600 (2010)
1,072,900 (2020)
Countries: China
Buddhism: Mahayana
Christians: 25,000

Overview of the Chuanqing

Other Names: Chuangqing, Lao Han, Pu, Pu Ren, Tun, Tunbao, Fang Teo Ren, Old Han, Shertu, Sher-feizu, Da Jiao Ban, Da Xiuzi

Population Sources:
400,000 to 500,000 in China (1982, *Minzu Shibie Wenxian Ziliao Huibian*)

Language: Sino-Tibetan, Chinese

Dialects: 0

Professing Buddhists: 55%

Practising Buddhists: 20%

Christians: 3.3%

Scripture: Chinese Bible

***Jesus* film:** none

Gospel Recordings: Mandarin: Guiyanghua

Christian Broadcasting: none

ROPAL code: none

Status of Evangelization

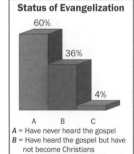

A = Have never heard the gospel
B = Have heard the gospel but have not become Christians
C = Are adherents to some form of Christianity

Dainet

The 25,000 Dainet people of south-west Myanmar are among the least known Buddhist people groups in the world. They live in the mountains of northern Rakhine State and adjacent southern areas of Chin State. Although these areas are close to the Myanmar border with Bangladesh, no Dainet are recorded to be living inside Bangladesh.

The Dainet, along with the Kadu and Ganan tribes, are thought to be the earliest Tibeto-Burman-speaking groups to settle in Myanmar (formerly Burma). The 1931 British-conducted census in Burma combined these three related groups under the heading 'Sak', which had a population of 36,400 at the time.[1] The groups were described as Buddhists, with 'a great reputation for honesty, diligence and reli-ability'.[2] The Dainet are one of the seven ethnic groups of Rakhine State officially recognized by the Myanmar authorities.

Researcher and author Richard Diran visited and photographed the Dainet in his magnificent book, *The Vanishing Tribes of Burma*. He interviewed the leader of a Dainet village on the Lemro (Lemyo) River in Rakhine State. The man was photographed in his traditional Dainet dress, consisting of a white wrap-around robe with red markings and a white headdress.[3]

Unlike other Tibeto-Burman speaking tribes in Myanmar, who migrated southward from China, the Dainet are believed to have come eastward from today's Bangladesh or India 'to escape fighting in Bengal to the west during the fifteenth to seventeenth centuries'.[4]

Create International

Despite the obvious evidence of the existence of the Dainet people in Myanmar, for some reason Christian researchers have never recognized them at all. They have never been listed in the *Ethnologue*, or on any lists of unreached people groups.

For centuries the Dainet have strictly adhered to the teachings of Theravada Buddhism. Indeed, the town of Mrauk-U, south of the Dainet homeland, was one of the most powerful ancient Buddhist kingdoms of Myanmar.[5] It was founded by the Rakhine king Min-zawmun in AD 1433. 'In the next century, the city became a free port that traded with the Middle East, Asia, Holland, Portugal and Spain; elephants were one of the main commodities supplied from the Rakhine region. A Dutchman who visited Mrauk-U in the 16th century described it as one of the richest cities in Asia, and compared it with Amsterdam and London in size and prosperity.'[6] At one time the kingdom created a naval fleet of 10,000 war boats that dominated the Bay of Bengal and the Gulf of Martaban.

It was during the height of this Buddhist kingdom's power that the Dainet migrated into the region, coming under Buddhist influence, which continues to this day. Much later, Baptist missionaries brought the gospel into western Myanmar. They encountered enormous success among animistic groups such as the various branches of Chin, but those tribes like the Dainet who had already embraced Buddhism were difficult to reach.

Today there are no known Christians among the Dainet in Myanmar.

Population:
25,000 (2000)
28,100 (2010)
31,600 (2020)
Countries: Myanmar
Buddhism: Theravada
Christians: none known

Overview of the Dainet

Other Names: Daignet, Daingnet, Dinenet

Population Sources: 25,000 in Myanmar (2002, Myanmar Faces and Places)

Language: Sino-Tibetan, Tibeto-Burman, Jingpho-Konyak-Bodo, Jingpho-Luish, Luish

Dialects: 0

Professing Buddhists: 100%

Practising Buddhists: 75%

Christians: 0%

Scripture: none

Jesus **film:** none

Gospel Recordings: none

Christian Broadcasting: none

ROPAL code: none

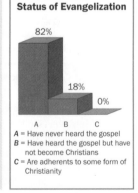

Status of Evangelization

82%

18%

0%

A   B   C

A = Have never heard the gospel
B = Have heard the gospel but have not become Christians
C = Are adherents to some form of Christianity

Population:
1,250 (2000)
1,600 (2010)
2,050 (2020)
Countries: Bhutan, India
Buddhism: Tibetan
Christians: none known

Overview of the Dakpa

Other Names: Dakpakha, Dagpa, Dap, Takpa

Population Sources:

1,000 in Bhutan (2001, G van Driem [1991 figure])

also in India

Language: Sino-Tibetan, Tibeto-Burman, Himalayish, Tibeto-Kanauri, Tibetic, Tibetan, Eastern

Dialects: 0

Professing Buddhists: 100%

Practising Buddhists: 80%

Christians: 0%

Scripture: none

***Jesus* film:** none

Gospel Recordings: none

Christian Broadcasting: none

ROPAL code: DKA

Status of Evangelization

95%

5%   0%

A   B   C

A = Have never heard the gospel
B = Have heard the gospel but have not become Christians
C = Are adherents to some form of Christianity

According to one 1991 source, 1,000 Dakpa people live in the far eastern part of Bhutan as well as adjoining areas of Tawang in Arunachal Pradesh, India. In Bhutan, the Dakpa inhabit the villages of Phongme, Caleng, Yob'inang, D'angpholeng and Lengkhar near the small outpost of Radi, in the Trashigang District.

Radi, which sits at 1,630 metres (5,350 ft.) above sea level, hardly qualifies as a town. 'There are no shops or eating places in Radi; it is just a quiet cluster of houses and a primary school at a bend in the road.'[1] Around Radi, the custom of weaving raw silk into a fabric called *menzimatra* or *lungserma* has been practised for centuries. From Radi it is just nine kilometres (five and a half mi.) from the Dakpa village of Phongme. One guidebook says, 'Beyond Radi the road worsens and climbs through forests interspersed with barren hillsides. This stretch of road is frequently closed by landslides and is usually impassable during the rainy season because it becomes a sea of deep mud. There is a tiny shop and a small *goemba* [monastery] at Phongme. The *goemba* is less than 150 years old and there is no monk body; the caretakers are elderly women. The central statue is of Chenrezig with 1000 arms and 11 heads.'[2]

Few people have ever heard of the Dakpa because most publications list them as part of the Brokpa.[3] One scholar, however, has listed the differences between the two groups, 'The Dakpas . . . like the Brokpas, are itinerant yakherds, but Dakpa is a

Dwayne Graybill

language of the Bumthang group. Although Dakpas and Brokpas share the same characteristic hat known as a *zhamu* and outer garments, there are some differences between the native costumes of the Brokpas and Dakpas. For example, the Dakpas wear *dorma* "trousers", not the *pishu* "leather leg guards" and the *kanggo* "thick white woolen apron covering the loins" worn above the *pishu*, which Brokpas often wear instead of trousers.'[4]

Linguistically, the Dakpa language belongs to the Eastern Tibetan branch of Tibeto-Burman, very different from Brokpa which is a Southern Tibetan language. Despite their small size and remote location, the Dakpa language was first studied by B H Hodgson in 1853.[5]

Although the Dakpa adhere to Tibetan Buddhism, they 'bear allegiance to the reformed Gelup or "Yellow Hat" order of Buddhism which had become victorious in Tibet and not to the "Red Hat" order which is the official state school of Mahayana Buddhism in Bhutan'.[6] In this way the Dakpa are similar to the Sherdukpen tribe and some of the Monpa groups of Aruncahal Pradesh, across the border in India. This came about because while the Bhutanese managed to resist Tibetan attacks throughout the 1700s, thus holding onto their 'Red Hat' traditions, Tawang in India became a vassal state of Lhasa. The part of Bhutan now occupied by the Dakpa people was formerly part of the Tawang District.

There has never been a known Christian among this remote and unique tribe.

Danau

Population:
102,500 (2000)
115,200 (2010)
129,500 (2020)
Countries: Myanmar
Buddhism: Theravada
Christians: 500

Overview of the Danau

Other Names: Danu, Danaw

Population Sources: 100,000 in Myanmar (1998, R Diran)

Language: Austro-Asiatic, Mon-Khmer, Northern Mon-Khmer, Palaungic, Eastern Palaungic, Danau

Dialects: 0

Professing Buddhists: 95%

Practising Buddhists: 60%

Christians: 0.5%

Scripture: none

Jesus film: none

Gospel Recordings: none

Christian Broadcasting: none

ROPAL code: DNU

Status of Evangelization

65%

34%

1%

A   B   C

A = Have never heard the gospel
B = Have heard the gospel but have not become Christians
C = Are adherents to some form of Christianity

According to author and researcher Richard Diran, '100,000 or more' Danau people live in central areas of Shan State and the northern part of Kayah State in Myanmar.[1] One of the main centres for the Danau seems to be the town of Pindaya, located about 50 kilometres (32 mi.) north of Kalaw and Taunggyi. The *Ethnologue*, on the other hand, gives a figure of just 10,000 Danau in Myanmar,[2] which has in turn been used by Christian organizations.[3]

This lower figure is incorrect. The Danau cover a large geographical area. Furthermore, the most recent census taken in Myanmar / Burma—the 1931 census conducted by the British—listed 77,941 Danau people.[4] The name Danau is derived from *donake*, meaning 'brave archers'. One account says: 'In the 16th century the Danau were King Alaungpaya's archers and on returning from wars in Thailand settled in the Pindaya area.'[5]

Pindaya is home to the famous Pindaya limestone caves, overlooking the picturesque Boutaloke Lake. 'Inside the cavern there are more than 8,000 Buddha images—made from alabaster, teak, marble, brick, lacquer and cement—which have been put there over the centuries and arranged in such a way as to form a labyrinth throughout the various cave chambers.'[6]

The Danau speak their own language, which is part of the Mon-Khmer branch of the Austro-Asiatic family. It is related to the Palaung Pale and Riang languages spoken in the same area.

An estimated 95 per cent of Danau people adhere to Theravada Buddhism, mixed with spirit worship and occult practices. Mission Outreach, a New Zealand-based Christian organization, has mentioned the Danau people in one of their newsletters. They asked, 'Who are the Danau?. . . . They are fishermen and cotton growers. They embrace Buddhism and practice witchcraft and black magic. Geographical restrictions coupled with Myanmar's military rule make access to this group quite difficult.'[7]

Myanmar: Faces and Places

Only about 500 Danau people are believers in Jesus Christ, although some encouraging growth has taken place in recent years. Mission Outreach explained how a 23-year-old Lahu pastor named Ahbarel 'longed to reach the 50 or more Danau families in a neighbouring village. He felt that pastoring a Lahu church and reaching the Danau at the same time was much too difficult.'[8] After attending a training course in March 1998, Ahbarel excitedly reported, 'The Lord brought us to the Nong Cho area where some Danau live. Now, we have established a Danau church there with 10 members.'[9] In one of his visits to another area in the Shan State, Ahbarel led a Danau man to the Lord. His name was Soe Aung. 'I enjoyed doing many worldly things,' Soe Aung confessed. 'I habitually drank alcohol and chewed betel nut. When I heard about Jesus, I realized how dirty and sinful I was. I was so happy when I learned that there was someone who can forgive my sins and make me clean. His name is Jesus. That day I received Jesus as my Savior. Today I have the assurance that God will not leave me even when I face difficulties. Before God and man, I declare that I have given my life to Jesus.'[10]

Approximately 35,000 Dariganga people live in and around the town of the same name in south-east Mongolia. They inhabit areas on a volcanic plateau in the southern part of Mongolia's Sukhbaatar Province (also spelled Suhbaatar and Sukhbator).

The Dariganga language is closely related to standard Hahl Mongolian and has been listed in some sources as a dialect of Mongolian.[1] Despite this linguistic relationship, it seems that the people of Dariganga possess a different sense of identity and ethnicity. While acknowledging their link with the larger Mongol group, they also value their unique culture and history.

In the late 1600s, the region now known as Sukhbaatar Province was called Dariganga Khoshun. It was named after the majestic mountain Dari Uul and the tranquil Ganga Lake. A local legend says that 'long ago a man returned to his native Dariganga after years of study in India. He took water from the Ganga River, placed it in the sand, and Ganga Lake was formed.'[2]

The Dariganga region is both barren and beautiful. 'The resplendent slopes of eastern Mongolia and the Moltsog, Ongon and Suj sand dunes stretch across the province's southern reaches. One can see hundreds if not a thousand gazelles frolicking together in the warmer months. Foxes, wolves, marmots and Palla's cats, to name but a few, are also numerous in this province.'[3] There are more than 220 extinct volcanoes in the area, the most famous of

which is Altan Ovoo.

The Dariganga traditionally married when they were very young. 'The girls were usually 13 or 14, and the boys were only a few years older. Today, couples usually marry while they are in their early-to-mid-twenties, then immediately begin having children.'[4]

Shamanism was the traditional religion of the Dariganga in the ancient past, until Buddhism was introduced from Tibet. During the harsh years of Communism, many Dariganga people gave up all religious faith and became atheists. The Yeguzer Khatagtyn Monastery is the focal point of Buddhism in the Dariganga region. The monastery's last lama, Galsandash, was severely persecuted by the Communists in the 1930s. He was taken away and 're-educated'. From the 1930s until the collapse of Communism, the monastery was left unattended. In the early 1990s the new government allowed restoration work on the monastery to begin, and today it again attracts Buddhist pilgrims and worshippers from throughout south-east Mongolia. Tibetan Buddhism is flourishing again among the Dariganga people.

Although there has been encouraging Christian growth in Mongolia since the early 1990s, the gospel has failed to make the same kind of impact in this remote corner of south-east Mongolia as it has in the nation's capital. There are just a few known Dariganga Christians today. Most people have never heard the gospel in a way that enables them to make an intelligent decision to accept or reject Christ.

Create International

Population:
35,000 (2000)
40,800 (2010)
47,500 (2020)
Countries: Mongolia
Buddhism: Tibetan
Christians: 50

Overview of the Dariganga

Other Names: Dariganga Mongols

Population Sources:
32,300 in Mongolia (2000, B Grimes [1995 figure])

Language: Altaic, Mongolian, Eastern, Oirat-Khalkha, Khalkha-Buriat, Mongolian Proper

Dialects: 0

Professing Buddhists: 55%

Practising Buddhists: 30%

Christians: 0.1%

Scripture: Portions 1952; New Testament 1979

Jesus **film:** available (Mongol)

Gospel Recordings: Mongolian

Christian Broadcasting: available (Mongolian)

ROPAL code: KHK02

Status of Evangelization

68%
31%
1%

A   B   C

A = Have never heard the gospel
B = Have heard the gospel but have not become Christians
C = Are adherents to some form of Christianity

Dokhpa

Approximately 4,000 Dokhpa people live in northern India, along the Indus River in Ladakh and Kargil districts of the state of Jammu and Kashmir. Their villages are named Garkun, Darchik, Chulichan, Gurgurdo, Batalik and Da. They formerly lived in Hanu village as well, but now no Dokhpa people appear to live there. There may be a small number of Dokhpa living in Pakistan-controlled Kashmir.[1]

Interestingly, K S Singh, in his authoritative book on India's tribes, says, 'Their population for the 1981 census is not available as the community was notified as a scheduled tribe only in 1989.'[2] The official classification of the Dokhpa in India appears to include three sub-ethnicities: the Brokpa, Dard and Shin. The Dokhpa should not be mistaken for other similarly named groups in the Himalayan Region, including the Drokpa people of Nepal and the Brokpa of Bhutan. Brokpa is a name also given to this group by the Ladakhi people.

The Dokhpa's language is called Brokskat. It is part of the Shina branch of the Indo-European linguistic family—the only one of the seven Shina languages that is spoken in India. Five of the Shina languages are spoken in Pakistan and one in Afghanistan. This linguistic link confirms the suspicions of K S Singh, that the Dokhpa 'are the descendants of the Dards and have migrated from Gilgit. The history of their migration is preserved in their folk literature.'[3]

Although they live in the same area as the Ladakhi, the Dokhpa are distinguished by their linguistic differences and also by appearance. The Dokhpa 'wear headgear and a gown, the former being decorated with flowers, beads,

needles, ribbons and buttons. Both men and women are particularly fond of flowers. Women style their hair in plaits while men shave the front portion of the head and have a long pigtail. The men and women cover their body with goat skin, lined inside with fur.'[4] The main staple food of the Dokhpa is roasted barley flour, called *sattu*. Certain foods, such as beef, cow's milk, birds and eggs, are strictly taboo because of religious and superstitious beliefs.

While all of the closest ethnolinguistic relatives of the Dokhpa people are Muslims living in Pakistan and Afghanistan, most Dokhpa in India follow the Tibetan Buddhist religion. 'The deities worshipped by them are La, Dogla and Sapdak, to whom animal sacrifices are offered. They also believe in demons. . . . Marriage ceremonies are conducted by the Buddhist priest, the lama, at the bride's place. When a death occurs, the lama is called upon to assist the chief mourner to conduct the funeral rites. The dead are cremated in a lying posture and a member of the clan lights the funeral pyre. The remains of the bones and ashes are buried.'[5] Smaller numbers of Dokhpa people follow their traditional animistic religion, while a few have converted to Islam.

Few Dokhpa people have ever been exposed to the gospel. Although there are more than 200 Christians among the neighbouring Ladakhi, few are engaged in sharing their faith.

Overview of the Dokhpa

Other Names: Drokpa, Brokhpa, Brokskat, Brokpa, Brokpa of Dah-hanu, Dokskat, Kyango, Broqpa, Minaro, Brukpa, Drukpa

Population Sources:

3,000 in India (1981 census)

possibly also in Pakistan

Language: Indo-European, Indo-Iranian, Indo-Aryan, Northwestern Zone, Dardic, Shina

Dialects: 0

Professing Buddhists: 90%

Practising Buddhists: 65%

Christians: 0%

Scripture: none

Jesus **film:** none

Gospel Recordings: none

Christian Broadcasting: none

ROPAL code: BKK

Population:
3,940 (2000)
4,600 (2010)
5,360 (2020)

Countries: India, possibly in Pakistan

Buddhism: Tibetan

Christians: none known

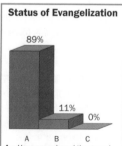

Status of Evangelization

89%

11%

0%

A   B   C

A = Have never heard the gospel
B = Have heard the gospel but have not become Christians
C = Are adherents to some form of Christianity

CHINA
Xizang (Tibet)

NEPAL
Karnali

INDIA

Dolpo

Population:
10,450 (2000)
12,950 (2010)
16,000 (2020)
Countries: Nepal, possibly China
Buddhism: Tibetan
Christians: 20

Overview of the Dolpo

Other Names: Phoke Dolpa, Dolpa, Dolpa Tibetan, Kaikhe, Kaike, Dhopa, Dolpali, Dolpali Bhote

Population Sources:
5,000 to 10,000 in Nepal (2000, B Grimes [1998 figure])
also possibly in China
Language: Sino-Tibetan, Tibeto-Burman, Himalayish, Tibeto-Kanauri, Tibetic, Tibetan, Central
Dialects: 0
Professing Buddhists: 90%
Practising Buddhists: 60%
Christians: 0.2%
Scripture: none
Jesus **film:** none
Gospel Recordings: Dolpo, Dolpa: Phoke
Christian Broadcasting: none
ROPAL code: DRE

Status of Evangelization

71%

28%

1%

A   B   C

A = Have never heard the gospel
B = Have heard the gospel but have not become Christians
C = Are adherents to some form of Christianity

Approximately 10,000 Dolpo people live in the Karnali Zone in north-west Nepal, all the way up to the border between Nepal and China. This has led some to speculate that the Dolpo may also be found inside Tibet.[1] The Dolpo inhabit the villages of 'Goomatara, Kola, Tachel, Kani, Bajebara, Laun, Chilpara, Bantari and Byas . . . beyond the mountains west of the upper Kali Gandaki River valley. . . . [The Dolpo] live in about 24 villages scattered over 500 sq. miles in Namgang, Panzgang, Tarap and Chharbung subdistricts.'[2] Dolpo people also live within the Dhawalagiri Zone, west of the Loba people. The name Dolpo comes from Dolpa—the historical name for their area.[3]

Most Dolpo people these days have settled down in permanent villages, but some continue to lead a nomadic existence, travelling around with their herds ten months every year. The Dolpo villages are situated between 3,660 and 4,720 metres (12,000 to 15,500 ft.) above sea level. 'The terrain is rather bare, with almost treeless grassland valleys, which take on a colourful luster in July and August with a carpet of bright alpine flowers. The rough stone houses of Dolpo are all clustered into a narrow space, making the villages look like forts. Some of them are probably among the highest human settlements in the world.'[4] The Dolpo say it takes seven days to walk from one end of their region to the other.

There seems little doubt that the ancestors of the Dolpo originated in Tibet, before coming south in search of better pastures. They have been in Nepal now for many centuries, although they still retain many of their traditional customs and oral legends of their long migration.[5] The Dolpo are regarded as the original inhabitants of their region.

Severe winter temperatures have made the Dolpo a hardy people. Their houses are built with no windows at all, as every inch of insulation helps them survive the brutal weather. Ceilings are built low to the ground to retain warmth. Cattle and other animals are housed in the ground floor during the winter months.

Tibetan Buddhism and Bon exist harmoniously side by side among the Dolpo. Buddhist and Bon lamas often combine their duties. 'Not only do these lamas handle the religious works and celebrations of the community, but they also act as faith-healers in times of sickness. Without the direction of the lama, these people neither perform any big ceremonies, nor go on journeys and in fact do not decide on anything at all.'[6]

Nancy Sturrock

In the mid-1990s a missionary organization noted, 'This group is totally untouched with the gospel. They still have no written language or Christian literature. There are no known Dolpo believers. In order for a church to be established within this people group, there must be a movement starting with the village leaders and working down from there. Because of their culture, it will do little good for a few individuals or young people to accept Christ.'[7] Since that time a few Dolpo people are known to have started following Christ, but this group remains in great need of the gospel.

Dowaniya

CHINA
INDIA
Assam
MYANMAR
Dowaniya

Population:
3,000 (2000)
3,500 (2010)
4,050 (2020)
Countries: India
Buddhism: Theravada
Christians: none known

Overview of the Dowaniya

Other Names:

Population Sources:

3,000 in India (2000, P Hattaway)

Language: Sino-Tibetan, Tibeto-Burman, Jingpho-Konyak-Bodo, Jingpho-Luish, Jingpho

Dialects: 0

Professing Buddhists: 85%

Practising Buddhists: 45%

Christians: 0%

Scripture: none

Jesus film: none

Gospel Recordings: none

Christian Broadcasting: none

ROPAL code: none

Status of Evangelization

77%

23%

0%

A   B   C

A = Have never heard the gospel
B = Have heard the gospel but have not become Christians
C = Are adherents to some form of Christianity

Approximately 3,000 members of the Dowaniya community live in the north-east Indian state of Assam. They inhabit a number of different locations on the Assam plain, but many live in the district of Sibsagar, a short distance from the Brahmaputra River.

In India the government has not recognized the Dowaniya as a Scheduled Tribe, so their unofficial designation has caused them to be largely forgotten by the outside world. Knowledge of the Dowaniya's existence comes from the work of eminent Indian anthropologist K S Singh,

Dwayne Graybill

who included them in his massive project identifying nearly 5,000 distinct ethnic communities in India.[1]

The Dowaniya have a history closely linked to that of the Singhpo, a tribe of similar size who live in the neighbouring state of Arunachal Pradesh. The Singhpo are cousins of the large Jingpo tribe of northern Myanmar and southern China, who number more than half a million people. The forefathers of the Singhpo migrated from northern Myanmar (then Burma) to north-east India in 1793 to flee persecution and terror caused by the Ahom king Gaurinath Singha. The Singhpos disposed the Khamtis from their land and settled in their present location.

The ancestors of the Dowaniya people were also among those early Singhpo settlers. Singh comments, 'It is said that the mingling of the Singhpo with the members belonging to several other communities, such as the Moran, Matak, Mishing, Kachari, Chutiya and Ahom, brought the Dowaniya into existence. In 1825 and 1826, Captain Neufville released several thousand Singhpo serfs. The descendants of these serfs constitute the Dowaniya community. . . . In the Singpho dialect *dua* means leader or head, and *ni* denotes its plural form, hence, the word *dowani* means headmen or leaders.'[2]

The Dowaniya language is part of the Jingpo branch of the Tibeto-Burman family. Despite coming from the same roots as the Jingpo, more than 200 years of separation has now made Dowaniya very different from its original form. The Singhpo language in India today reportedly only has 50 per cent lexical similarity with Jingpo of Myanmar.[3] The Dowaniya also speak Hindi and Assamese and use the Assamese script for writing.

The Dowaniya people retain their traditional customs to this day. They have managed to keep the all-pervading Hindu culture at arm's length, especially those Dowaniya living further away from the towns. One source notes that 'they are experts in woodcraft, basketry and weaving'.[4]

When the Singhpo first entered India they brought their belief in Theravada Buddhism with them. Most Dowaniya have continued as Buddhists, although their faith is now mixed with Hinduistic and animistic influences. They have their own Buddhist monks, who preside over birth rituals, weddings and funerals, and are also entrusted with the preservation of the ancient Buddhist texts.

There are no known Christians among the Dowaniya people. Throughout their long and troubled history they have been waiting to hear the good news that Jesus loves them and has made a way for them to know the true God.

The Name above All

The Testimony of Gyalsang Tamang— Nepal

This is the testimony of a young Buddhist man living in the mountains of northern Nepal who found Christ in a most remarkable way. Living in a remote tribal area, Gyalsang Tamang had never heard the name of Jesus and had no access to the gospel until God supernaturally intervened in a most astonishing way—using Gyalsang's interaction with spirit 'shadow men' to teach him and his family about Christ and the way to eternal life. For many Western Christians, spiritual reality is sometimes hard to grasp, but for people living in the deeply oppressive regions of Asia where no spiritual light from God has ever shone, the reality of the spiritual world is ever-present. Gyalsang's testimony has been investigated by several respected missionaries and local pastors who travelled to Gyalsang's village. They interviewed family members and others in the community who were witnesses to these events. In fact, the whole village testified to the three years during which Gyalsang received visions from the spirit world. The team of investigators completely verified Gyalsang's account. The strongest evidences of God's involvement are the changed lives of Gyalsang and his family. They love Jesus Christ as Lord and Saviour, and today they follow him with all their heart.

I'd like to share with you the account of how God lovingly reached down to me, my family and our Tamang and Sherpa people in perhaps the only way we would have listened.

My story really begins with my ancestors and my father, Lharkyal. Ten generations ago, the Tibetan border was moved after a war and our citizenship changed to Nepalese. At that time our ancestor, Kham Sung Wang Di, brought a gold-covered Buddha idol for the temple in the forest near Big Syabru.

My father, like his forebears, was guardian of the key to this temple and faithfully carried out his duties as the temple's main keeper. Life was often austere, and in times of famine they subsisted by eating wild grass and nettle soup. By the age of 19, my father realized he would never become a lama himself.

Father is from the Tamang tribe, so when he displeased his family by marrying Dolma, a Helambu Sherpa, his family gave him a home where only one other house had been built. It was on the least desirable land, a hillside near the temple where ghosts and demons were said to live. A village idol, where chickens were sacrificed, stood on the other side of the house. It wasn't surprising that father usually held out his big, curved Gurkha knife in fear as he entered the house. Like others in the area, he drank a lot of millet and wheat whiskey.

At that time father's major religious duty was to lead the worship songs at *Gyawa* festivals—rituals held for 49 days after someone dies. For income our family also kept *jomos* (females from a cross of cows and yaks). When father was 20 and my mother was 24 my oldest brother, Angdawa, was born. He was followed three years later by Mingmar, then a sister who died, and finally, after seven years, I was born. Originally I was named Khaji, but my parents renamed me Gyalsang when, after a serious fall, I stopped breathing for a time. My new name, meaning 'Fainting', was fitting, for I passed out very easily as a boy.

I attended school along with about 20 other village boys, but I learned little. At home we spoke the Sherpa and occasionally Tamang languages, but at school all the classes were conducted in Nepalese.

A Buddhist monastery in Nepal.

What's more, I was careless about attendance—we all were—making it to class only about one in every eight days.

One partly cloudy day in May of 1983 we were out with the herd, mother in front and the stragglers and I bringing up the rear. Around noon I lay down in the grass to doze for a few minutes. After a while

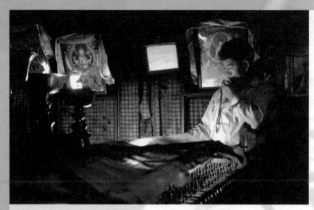

I felt like I had woken up. Although I could neither see nor hear, I felt the presence of two shadowy figures that surged back and forth in front of my face, as fast as lightning. They wore crowns and capes stretching from their shoulders to their feet.

Mother said she heard me shouting in the field and she came running to see what the problem was. By the time she reached me I had passed out. She splashed cold water on my face to revive me, like she had so many times when I fainted as a child. This time, however, it didn't help me recover and she became deeply concerned. She called others who were grazing their herds nearby, and they carried me home, still unconscious. By the time we reached our home it was getting dark and too late to fetch the witch doctor, so mother and father slept on each side of me on the floor.

During the night I had a vision. The shadow-men spoke to me in Sherpa, 'Don't worry. We want to use you. We want to show you the Buddhist Way. Your parents are very afraid for you, so tomorrow they will call for the witch doctor. Tell them they must not call for him. Tomorrow you will feel better, but from

A tour guide explains the history of an ancient Buddha image at the Baodingshan Monastery in Chongqing, China.

David Treat

now on you must sleep alone. Tell your parents to prepare a separate sleeping place for you and instruct them to never wake you during your sleep.' Having said that, the shadow-men left and I awoke to find it was morning. What I had seen was much more real than merely a dream. This visitation was to change my life for ever.

I was hungry. While I ate some breakfast, my parents bombarded me with questions: 'What happened?' 'Are you well?' 'What did you see?' I told them all that had happened and everything the shadow-men had told me. Consequently, they didn't call for the witch doctor and they constructed a two-foot-high wall to separate my sleeping area from theirs.

The following night the shadow-men returned, wanting to take me somewhere. They held me, one on each side, as we flew for some time. Finally we arrived at a dark, unnatural place where no other living creatures seemed to exist. It was a place of complete darkness. It was so dark that I couldn't see my escorts, even though I could feel their bodies beside me.

The shadow-men then took me to another place. This was a place of perfect light— a location far more beautiful than I had ever seen before. The shadow-escorts retreated and there in front of me I dimly saw an image of Buddha. A voice spoke, 'From today I want to use you. I'll teach you my way.'

The shadow-men emerged from behind me and took me back to the world. They said, 'From today you are not to mix with outsiders. Stay alone with your parents. Whenever your father and mother enter the room they must first cover themselves with incense.' After that, I slept with a butter lamp near my head for every night for three years. Every night the shadow-men took me to the place of perfect light I had seen on my first night's travel. There I learned Buddhist doctrine. Each morning I recited to my father what I had learned during the previous night. He was astonished and said it corresponded perfectly with what he had learned in the Buddhist monastery years before. My parents knew very well that I had never learned to read, so they realized I could only have learned these things by supernatural means. We purchased religious clothes, drums and bells. Father was amazed that I could play the instruments, even though I had never been taught to do so.

One night the shadow-men told me to get a special pot that we had in our home. On the night of the full moon I was to clean it and set it, empty, on a shelf near my head. They said the following morning it would be brimming with water. My family and I were to wash our faces and drink as much of the water as we were able. On the morning after the full moon, sure enough, the pot was full of water. There was always enough for us to wash and drink liberally. After three months a green tree branch sprouted from the pot's spout, even though there was no soil inside for it to take root.

After some time of receiving Buddhist doctrine and experiencing such wonders, the shadow-men again took me to the Buddha image. On this occasion I could see a shiny plate, looking a bit like a computer screen, appearing at the Buddha image's knee-level. Letters were etched on it, and a voice explained the meaning. I couldn't read or write Nepalese, but nevertheless every day I clearly and neatly wrote down the messages I had received from Buddha's 'screen'. I wrote in a language which, to this day, no one has been able to identify. I could always read what I had written and from these words could tell my parents amazing things, such as their present inner thoughts and their past sins. I also gave them instructions concerning how they could atone for their sins: They had to daily bow down 108

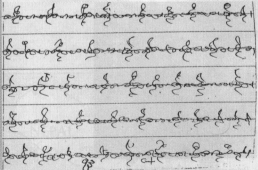

A sample of Gyalsang's writing.

times, first on their knees, then prostrate themselves with their foreheads to the ground. Mother did this so diligently that she developed a callous on her forehead. They also had to buy strings with 108 beads and go through each one saying the traditional Buddhist chant.

A shop selling idols in Kathmandu, Nepal.

We travelled to Kathmandu and purchased two Buddhist idols. We were told to replace the pot we had been using with these two idols. Every Saturday we performed a special ceremony worshipping the idols.

As the weeks and months passed, these extraordinary experiences continued and news spread quite far that Buddha was visiting my family with a special blessing. We carried out more and more rituals.

Then the true God began to intervene in our whole experience!

One day the shadow-men gave me a list of the names of 35 gods. Each night my family and I were instructed to prostrate ourselves three times for each of the gods, speaking the god's name as we bowed. The Dalai Lama was number 35, the lowest rank among the gods. Then one day my notebook said, 'After the Dalai Lama bow down to Yesu.' I didn't know that Yesu is Sherpa for Jesus. In fact, I had never heard of Yesu (Jesus) before.

Every Saturday we opened my notebook for teaching and, week by week, month by month, the name of Jesus rose higher in rank. With the name of Yesu came teaching about this unknown God. We learned of Adam and Eve and the first sin, we learned about Yesu the Son of God, his crucifixion and resurrection, and much more. We were also told that God would come to judge the world.

All of this was completely new to us. For generations our ancestors had been Buddhist, worshipping Buddha and a variety of spirits that helped us grow a successful crop, avoid sickness and so on. None of us had ever met a follower of Yesu and we had never learned his teaching before, until his name started to climb up the list of gods I had been given by the shadow-men.

It was now 1985. As we always did in the autumn, we moved our home down closer to Big Syabru in time for the cold winter months. Father was glad to be able to take a gift to his old friend, the owner of the Yeti Hotel. While there, father noticed a Tibetan booklet lying on the table. He was immediately interested, not only because he could read Tibetan, but more so because he saw the name 'Yesu' on the cover. Father asked the hotel owner about the booklet. It had been left by some tourists and he didn't want it. Father brought it home, and I looked in my special notebook for guidance regarding the booklet. My notebook told me, 'Keep it—it is good. Read it.' We did. In our ignorance we bowed down to the booklet at the same time we bowed down to the idols.

Two months later, my brother Mingmar wanted to quit his job at the cheese factory in order to reopen our house as a lodge. He asked me to look in my notebook for guidance in this matter. I bowed down three times and began to read, 'If Mingmar wants to open a lodge that is fine, but tell him not to sell alcohol. When the lodge is opened, followers of Jesus will meet you.' Mingmar happily opened the lodge, and six months later the disciples of Jesus came.

Many lodges had opened along the well-travelled Lantang Trek. The lodge and hotel owners had a system of lining up for chances to meet trekkers on the trail in order to invite them to stay in their accommodation. On that particular day Mingmar was late in the line so he opted to stay at home. But while at home he spotted three foreigners walking on the less-travelled trail from Sing Gompa to Big Syabru. He ran out to meet the young men, inviting them to stay at his lodge.

The previous night the three men had stayed at a tiny lodge run by two young women who had eagerly requested, 'When you go through Big Syabru, please stop at our cousin Mingmar's lodge.' Jon, his brother Dan, and Jay intended to go farther than just to Big Syabru, but they hadn't wanted to hurt the women's feelings so they promised nothing. However, the following day they made slow progress as snow and rain had made the mud paths slippery. The three Christian men were wet, cold and tired, so at my brother's invitation they decided to stop for the day. They didn't yet realize that Mingmar's lodge was the very one my cousins had recommended the previous evening. They also didn't know how God had gone before them to prepare the way for the Sherpas to hear the good news of Christ.

Actually, Jon and Dan had been praying specifically for the Helambu Sherpa people for two years. It had also been about two years since the name 'Yesu' first entered my visions. Jon and Dan had been sent to Nepal by a Christian mission called Gospel Recordings. Their aim was to learn the Nepalese language and then make gospel message tapes for evangelism in the lesser known languages and dialects of the land. Knowing that there were not yet any Christians among the Helambu Sherpas, they had contacted a translator working with that people group with the hopes of making a recording. Her Sherpa friends refused to cooperate in making a recording.

Buddhist prayer wheels outside a temple in Kathmandu, Nepal.

Paul Hattaway

Arriving at the lodge, the three men changed into dry clothes and ordered instant noodles and hot lemon drinks. Before the meal they bowed for a prayer of thanks in Jesus' name. Mingmar noticed.

Later Dan and Jay went out to explore the village and Jon stayed at the lodge. He struck up a conversation with Mingmar.

'What religion do you observe?' asked Jon.

'Buddhism,' Mingmar replied, giving his full attention. 'Is that all right?'

'What's really all right is what saves your soul,' Jon told him. Then Jon continued, telling him about God, creation, sin and finally about Jesus—his life, death and resurrection which had opened the way for us to come to God.

'The things you've told me and the things my brother has told me are identical!' Mingmar exclaimed.

'Where is your brother?' asked Jon. 'Can we meet him?' Mingmar prepared to take the three foreigners on the three-hour walk up the mountains to meet me. Jon, Dan and Jay were thrilled and curious to meet me.

Two weeks later, Jon returned with Barnabas, a Nepalese Gospel Recordings leader. By that time the name of Jesus had moved up to second in rank on the list of gods we were bowing down to. I was also told that when the followers of Jesus came they should be allowed to enter our house without the customary waving of incense over their bodies. Father, mother, Mingmar and I took our turns bowing down before Jon and Barnabas, but they stopped us, saying, 'Don't bow to us. We are just people like you.'

I still couldn't speak Nepalese, so Mingmar and my father translated as our visitors talked with us. Barnabas began by telling how Jesus was born, lived, was crucified and, three days later, rose again. They also played a gospel tape in the Tamang language for us. Most of the evening I sat quietly, intent to hear

Prayer flags with Buddhist inscriptions reflect the setting sun.

International Mission Board

every word, but finally I was so excited that I jumped up and got my notebooks. Flipping through the pages, I found and read some sections corresponding to what we had heard. (During a later visit from Jon and a Nepalese co-worker, I read from one of my notebooks the complete accounts of how sin entered the world in the Garden of Eden, and of Jesus' life, death and resurrection. Jon, amazed, said I had confused Pilate's name with Caesar's in the part about Jesus' trial, but everything else was just as recorded in the Bible.)

That night the shadow-men came as usual and escorted me to the Buddha image. A voice said, 'Today my kingdom is finished in you and you no longer need to serve me. One has come after me who is greater than I. You must do what the men say and follow Jesus.' The shadow-men took me back. It was my final vision. Morning came, and I felt like a great heaviness was gone from my life.

The next day was warm and pleasant, with plenty of time to talk further with our guests. Jon told us that God doesn't want us to bow down to the idols—nor even to things written about Jesus—as we had been doing. Barnabas explained more about why Jesus had to die in our place, how he had fulfilled all the requirements of righteousness, ritual and law. He also clarified that believing in Jesus means entrusting ourselves to him. Though no one suggested I do it, I yanked the charms and beads from my neck and I told Jesus I would follow only him.

Mother had been out milking the *jomos*, so Jon

and Barnabas gave her the good news of the gospel too. She also wanted to follow in faith, and by herself she prayed a beautiful prayer from her heart: 'From now on Jesus, you are my Lord. I don't know much, but you are my Lord.'

Leaving the Buddhist way, the way of our ancestors, was a struggle at first—especially for father. After Jon and Barnabas had left I saw him light some coals and incense in a pot, bow down three times, then sob uncontrollably. I hated to hear him cry and went to him, telling him the words I had heard in the Buddha vision two nights earlier. He grew calm and peaceful again, and he stopped doing the ritual.

By now the weather was getting too warm for the *jomos,* so we had to move to the higher shelter. Before doing that we burned our religious things, including most of the notebooks. I saved only the smallest notebook, which contained the messages about Jesus.

From that time on, what I had written in the notebook became to me as a completely foreign language most of the time, although I was still occasionally able to read parts of it. I understood that my ability to read it from time to time would only last until I could read a Bible myself and my faith was stronger. The last time I was able to read it was during the monsoon of 1993, the day my mother went to be with the Lord Jesus after a long battle with cancer.

My mother is perhaps the very first Helambu Sherpa to stand before the throne of God in praise.

God has been good to us! My father composes Sherpa and Tamang hymns and leads the worship when the believers from our area gather together. Mingmar and his wife Karmu

Sunset over a Buddhist pagoda in Kathmandu, Nepal.

Julian Hawken

have been able to attend Bible school in Pokhara. God helped me to learn Nepalese and made it possible for me to record gospel message cassettes in Sherpa and later the translation of the New Testament into that, my heart language.

Maybe this testimony is difficult for you to accept. I can show my notebook as proof, and if you ask, I'm happy to give you the names and addresses of those I've mentioned in this account. Many who have stayed at my brother's Goshen Lodge, or at Peace Lodge, which my wife Nimbuti and I run, have heard our story. What's more, my whole village can testify to the three years during which I received visions while living there.

Many people ask who I thought the 'shadow-men' were—angels or demons. I don't know. All I know is that God used this whole strange process to tell us about Jesus and help us to gain everlasting life in him. He was patient with us, realizing that we came from a background of complete darkness and ignorance of his word. He gradually revealed the truth to us, shedding just a little more light day by day, until we found him.

I strongly believe that God can do anything at all if it's his will. God has poured his grace out on us, but we have also encountered much opposition since becoming Christians. The Buddhist lamas consider me a bad example for Buddhists.

If you are a believer in Jesus, I ask you to please pray for us, the Christians at Syabru. Pray also for our people who don't yet follow Jesus. Just as it was impossible for me to become a believer in Jesus and yet I have, please pray that others in Syabru will also follow him.

One day you may hear that, according to God's will, everyone in our village has begun to follow Jesus, the Name above all.

Notes

This article has been adapted with permission from a 1995 booklet by the same title which may be ordered from Samdan Publishers, PO Box 2119, Kathmandu, Nepal.

More than 300,000 Drukpa people are dispersed across the three Asian nations of Bhutan (160,000 people in 1991), India (105,066 in 2001) and Nepal. They are found throughout Bhutan, but are especially concentrated in the western districts of Ha, Paro, Thimphu, Gasa, Punakha, Chhukha, Dagana and Wangdue Phodrang. The Drukpa do not refer to their country as Bhutan, but rather as *Druk-yul*—'land of the thunder dragon'.[1]

In India, some of the Drukpa have not been given status as a Scheduled Tribe, while others appear under the generic term Bhotia, which includes various groups of Tibetan origin. One source states, 'They inhabit hilly terrains of high altitude marked by extreme cold, high rainfall, medium snowfall and dense forests.'[2] The Drukpa live in the Indian states of Arunachal Pradesh, Assam, Meghalaya, Sikkim and West Bengal. The first Drukpa moved to India during the latter half of the 7th century, when they conducted raids into today's north-east India. Some Drukpa have migrated into Nepal where they primarily operate as traders out of Kathmandu.

The language of the Drukpa is called Dzongkha, which comes from two words, *kha* ('language') and *Dzong* ('fortress'). Therefore Dzongkha is 'the language spoken in the fortress'. These stone fortresses 'dominate the

mountainous landscape of Bhutan from east to west and have traditionally been both centers of military and political power as well as centers of learning.'[3]

Bhutan was closed off to the rest of the world for centuries, as the dragon held this group under his tight grip of Buddhism. The Drukpa believe that they have been Buddhists since the Tibetan sage Padmasambhava flew across the Himalayas on the back of a tiger and introduced Buddhism to Bhutan in AD 746. Only in recent years has the gospel started to gain a foothold. Today, between 500 and 600

Christian Drukpa people live in Bhutan, where they 'face many hardships such as ostracism from their family and friends, educational and job advancement difficulties and isolated job placement. Young men are required to make an oath of allegiance to Buddha at the age of 15.'[4] In India, where at least five ministries are working among them, there are an estimated 210 Drukpa Christians.[5]

One Drukpa recalls how he came to faith in Christ: 'In 1992 I was riding my motorbike on a very clear sunny day. Suddenly, my vision went blank followed by a gripping sense of darkness. I crashed my motorbike and could not move half of my body. I was a devout Buddhist and faithfully served our god. I sent my wife to ask the lama concerning my condition. The lama told my wife that some people had sent an evil spirit to kill me and that I would die within a week. My sister-in-law was already a Christian. When she heard of my condition, she brought along her Christian friends to my house. They started praying and applied oil on the paralyzed part of my body. Immediately I was able to move. I was completely healed. They preached Christ to me and I readily gave my life to Jesus.'[6] He later went on to help translate the New Testament into the Dzongkha language, and he has personally led more than 100 Drukpa people to faith in Christ.

Overview of the Drukpa

Other Names: Dzongkha, Ngarung, Sharchop, Kebumtarp, Drukke, Drukha, Dukpa, Bhutanese, Jonkha, Bhotia of Bhutan, Bhotia of Dukpa, Zongkhar, Rdzongkha, Druku, Yul-Mi, Drukpha, Ngalong, Ngalop

Population Sources:

160,000 in Bhutan (2001, G van Driem [1991 figure])

105,066 in India (2001, India Missions Association)

also in Nepal

Language: Sino-Tibetan, Tibeto-Burman, Himalayish, Tibeto-Kanauri, Tibetic, Tibetan,

Southern

Dialects: 3 (Wang-the, Ha, Northern Thimphu)

Professing Buddhists: 70%

Practising Buddhists: 60%

Christians: 0.3%

Scripture: New Testament 2000; Portions 1970

Jesus film: available

Gospel Recordings: Dzongkha, Ngalong

Christian Broadcasting: available

ROPAL code: DZO (Dzongkha); LYA (Layakha); and LUK (Lunanakha)

Population:
305,700 (2000)
380,100 (2010)
487,600 (2020)

Countries: Bhutan, India, Nepal

Buddhism: Tibetan

Christians: 800

CHINA
Xizang (Tibet)

Sikkim

BHUTAN

NEPAL

Arunachal Pradesh

Assam

W Bengal

Meghalaya

INDIA

Drukpa

Status of Evangelization

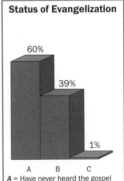

60%

39%

1%

A   B   C

A = Have never heard the gospel
B = Have heard the gospel but have not become Christians
C = Are adherents to some form of Christianity

Dura

Approximately 5,000 Dura people inhabit the Lamjun District in the Gandakhi Zone of central Nepal.[1] According to the respected contemporary linguist George van Driem, 'Their homeland comprises all the territory between the Paudi and Midim rivers and encompasses the ridge which runs from Dura Dada proper via Turlunkot. . . . The Dura homeland affords splendid views of Lamjun Himal, Annapurna II and IV, the eastern flank of Machapucchre and Manaslu.'[2] These peaks represent some of the highest mountains in the world, with Annapurna II rising to 7,937 metres (26,033 ft.).

The Dura were originally a group with their own Tibeto-Burman language. According to one source, 'Round-faced, flat-nosed and short in stature, Duras have their own unique traditions and culture though their religious and cultural formalities are quite akin to Gurungs. Their sons are fitted with bows and arrows on the very day of their naming ceremonies, a fact that reflects on their martial heritage.'[3]

The Dura are believed to have originated in Dullu Dailekh to the west. They migrated to their present location at various stages between the 8th and 12th centuries AD. At the time they had a far larger population than they do today. Over the course of the centuries the Dura area has been inundated with Hindus from the south. Gradually they lost the use of their mother tongue and now the Dura can only speak Nepali although, as van Driem notes, 'There are Dura who still remember bits and pieces of the language.'[4] Concerted efforts have been made to try to record as much

of the Dura language as possible, including a list of more than 200 words, but these seem destined for historical use only.

Despite the loss of their language, the Dura remain a proud and unique people. Another part of their identity that is presently undergoing a process of assimilation is their religious belief. For centuries, Buddhism played the dominant role in Dura spiritual life. They lived at the southern end of the Tibetan Buddhist world, but after centuries of pressure from Hindu migrants, many of the Dura's Buddhist practices have now been subsumed into a complicated Hindu-Buddhist mix. The Dura worship many Hindu deities alongside images of Buddha.

The Dura still have lamas who serve the community's Buddhist needs, and most of their birth and funeral rituals are Buddhist in nature. When someone dies, a lama is summoned to 'perform the last rites and they do not do anything without their presence or permission'.[5] It is noteworthy that the Dura go back to their Buddhist roots at times of death. On other important occasions, however, Hindu rituals are performed, especially matrimonial rituals that have been adopted from the Nepalis.

For more than a thousand years the Dura have been waiting to hear the gospel. In recent years a very small number have believed in Christ, but most of this fascinating group have yet to hear the good news.

CHINA
Xizang (Tibet)

NEPAL
Gandaki

INDIA

Dura

Population:
5,150 (2000)
6,350 (2010)
7,850 (2020)
Countries: Nepal
Buddhism: Tibetan
Christians: 30

Overview of the Dura

Other Names: Durra

Population Sources:
4,500 in Nepal (1994, R Gautam)

Language: Indo-European, Indo-Iranian, Indo-Aryan, Northern Zone, Eastern Pahari

(Dura was traditionally a Tibeto-Burman language which is now extinct.)

Dialects: 0

Professing Buddhists: 50%

Practising Buddhists: 15%

Christians: 0.5%

Scripture: none

Jesus film: none

Gospel Recordings: none

Christian Broadcasting: none

ROPAL code: none

Photo credit: Dwayne Graybill

Status of Evangelization

64%

35%

1%

A   B   C

A = Have never heard the gospel
B = Have heard the gospel but have not become Christians
C = Are adherents to some form of Christianity

According to one researcher in 1991, there were 15,000 Dzala people living in the north-east part of the Buddhist kingdom of Bhutan.[1] They inhabit the highlands along the upper course of the Kholongchu River in the Yangtse District. In 1995, Yangtse was granted administrative status as a fully-fledged district of Bhutan. It was previously a sub-district of Trashigang, and it is often referred to as Trashi-Yangtse. The part of Bhutan inhabited by the Dzala is extremely poor. Many visitors say it is like stepping back to medieval times. Life is simple and slow-paced. One tourist publication unflatteringly describes the main town of Trashi Yangtse: 'It takes 10 minutes to visit the entire town. . . . Just north of the *chorten* is a bazaar area with a few shops. A tall, elaborately decorated Bhutanese-style *chorten* sits beside a small stream, spanned by a concrete bridge, and doubles as the town's vegetable market. A few eating and drinking shops and a spartan guesthouse mark the end of the town.'[2]

about 8 kilometres [5 mi.] upstream from its confluence with the Kurichu. According to local lore, the village is named after *khoma* 'desirable one' coveted by [the Buddhist sage] Padmasambhava during his legendary peregrinations through Bhutan.'[3]

The Dzala language has yet to be placed in a specific linguistic group by researchers. It seems to share many characteristics with other Tibeto-Burman languages in the area, but it also displays significant differences. The Tsangla people, who are found in large numbers in eastern Nepal, 'make a perennial joke about the Dzala and their language because of the near homophony of the name Dzala and the Tsangla word *zala* "monkey".'[4]

Tibetan Buddhism has been the spiritual stronghold over the Dzala people for more than 1,300 years. Buddhism entered Bhutan from Tibet, and visits from lamas and monks from Tibet, India and Nepal maintained and strengthened Buddhism here over the centuries. The Dzala people

Population:
18,800 (2000)
24,100 (2010)
31,000 (2020)
Countries: Bhutan
Buddhism: Tibetan
Christians: none known

Overview of the Dzala

Other Names: Dzalakha, Dzalamat, Yangtsebikha

Population Sources:

15,000 in Bhutan (2001, G van Driem [1991 figure])

Language: Sino-Tibetan, Tibeto-Burman, Himalayish, Tibeto-Kanauri, Unclassified

Dialects: 1 (Khomakha)

Professing Buddhists: 100%

Practising Buddhists: 70%

Christians: 0%

Scripture: none

Jesus film: none

Gospel Recordings: none

Christian Broadcasting: none

ROPAL code: DZL

Dwayne Graybill

Yangtse—which shares the name of China's longest river by coincidence—borders the north-east Indian state of Arunachal Pradesh. The Dzala language is also spoken as far west as the Kurichu River in Lhuntse District. The speakers of Dzala in Lhuntse, however, refer to themselves as the Khoma, and to their language as Khomakha. Khomakha has been listed as a dialect of Dzala. 'The villages on the southern slopes overlooking the Khomachu River are also Khomakha speaking. The most prominent Khomakha speaking village is the village of Khoma itself, located on the Khomachu

see their identity and culture as completely intertwined with Buddhism.

At the town of Duksum, it is said that anyone who can climb the rock face to the top of the hill overlooking the Buddhist temple will be forgiven all of the sins they have committed up until that point. Few Dzala people have ever heard of the true forgiver of sins, who gave his life that they may be free. There has never been a church fellowship in this remote corner of Bhutan, and at present there are no known Christians among the Dzala people.

Status of Evangelization
90%
10%
0%
A   B   C
A = Have never heard the gospel
B = Have heard the gospel but have not become Christians
C = Are adherents to some form of Christianity

Recent research has revealed the existence of approximately 60,500 Ergong people living in remote parts of western Sichuan Province in western China.[1] In 1983, Chinese scholar Sun Hongkai listed 35,000 Ergong people in China.[2] The county with the largest number of Ergong people is Daofu (28,000), followed by Danba (17,000), Luhuo (6,500) and Xinlong within the Ganzi (Garze) Prefecture; while in neighbouring Aba Prefecture the Ergong are dispersed in Jinchuan (also known as Guanyingqiao) (5,000) and Zamtang (Shangzhai) (4,000) counties.[3] All of these areas were formerly part of Kham Province in Tibet.

Officially the Ergong have been included as part of the Tibetan nationality in China, even though they speak their own distinct language. The Ergong are also widely known as Hor, or Horpa. The Ergong language, called Daofuh Hua by the Chinese, is related to Jiarong in western Sichuan.[4] It is a member of the Qiangic branch of Tibeto-Burman. Linguists have studied Ergong for a surprisingly long time. B H Hodgson first described them in 1853.[5] The Ergong speak their mother tongue within their own communities but use Chinese or Tibetan when speaking with outsiders.

The cultural centre of the Ergong people is the town of Daofu, a two-day bus journey from Chengdu City, the capital of Sichuan Province. The Ergong live in distinctive white, flat-roofed houses, supported with red timber. Inside their homes are elaborate paintings depicting Buddhist scenes. These paintings are usually done by a family member and sometimes take many months to complete.

Practically all Ergong adhere to Tibetan Buddhism. A large temple is located in Daofu, 'providing a place for about 200 monks to worship and study each day. Most monks are Ergong, with a few being Zhaba. In the mornings you can watch the monks, young and old, chant and read scriptures in the big temple rooms. You can also walk to the second floor of the temple which houses some enormous god statues, masks and yak-butter sculptures.'[6]

China Advocate

In 1903, two French Catholic priests settled in Daofu. They built a church, which included ten classrooms and an orphanage. The local government and people welcomed the missionaries because of the social benefits they brought to the area. 'Seventy percent of the Chinese in town were Christians, [but] only a handful of Tibetans were Christian believers. Some Tibetans accepted some of the Christian beliefs, but still held onto Tibetan Buddhism. In 1949, the [new Communist] government told the Frenchmen to leave the country. There were no new believers after this time. The church was destroyed and changed into a children's dormitory for a school. Later it was rebuilt into a Tibetan Buddhist temple, which it remains to today. . . . Some of the people in town believe there may be a few old Chinese Christians in town, but there is only one known Ergong Christian.'[7]

Population:
60,500 (2000)
74,500 (2010)
91,800 (2020)
Countries: China
Buddhism: Tibetan
Christians: 1

Overview of the Ergong

Other Names: Daofuhua, Bopa, Hor, Horpa, Horu, Hor-ke, Taofu, Pawang, Gesitsa, Bawang Rong-Ke, Hórsók, Western Jiarong

Population Sources:
60,500 in China (2000, *Qiangic Speaking Tibetans*)

Language: Sino-Tibetan, Tibeto-Burman, Tangut-Qiang, Gyarong

Dialects: 3 (Danba, Daofu, Northern Ergong)

Professing Buddhists: 99%
Practising Buddhists: 65%
Christians: 0.1%
Scripture: none
Jesus film: none
Gospel Recordings: none
Christian Broadcasting: none
ROPAL code: ERO

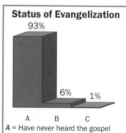

Status of Evangelization

A = Have never heard the gospel
B = Have heard the gospel but have not become Christians
C = Are adherents to some form of Christianity

Qinghai

Sichuan

Ersu

Population:
27,850 (2000)
34,350 (2010)
42,300 (2020)
Countries: China
Buddhism: Tibetan
Christians: none known

Overview of the Ersu

Other Names: Duoxu, Ersu
Yi, Tosu, Buerzi, Ersubuerzi,
Lusu, Lisu

Population Sources:

20,000 in China (1983, Sun
Hongkai)

Language: Sino-Tibetan,
Tibeto-Burman, Tangut-Qiang,
Qiangic

Dialects: 3 (Eastern Ersu
[13,000], Central Ersu [Duoxu]
[3,000], Western Ersu [Lisu]
[4,000])

Professing Buddhists: 50%

Practising Buddhists: 15%

Christians: 0%

Scripture: none

Jesus **film:** none

Gospel Recordings: none

Christian Broadcasting: none

ROPAL code: ERS

Status of Evangelization

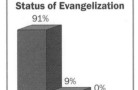

91%

9%

0%

A   B   C

A = Have never heard the gospel
B = Have heard the gospel but have
   not become Christians
C = Are adherents to some form of
   Christianity

A 1983 study listed 20,000 speakers of
Ersu living along the lower reaches of the
Dadu River, in seven different counties
of southern Sichuan Province in western
China.[1] The Dadu River originates at Mount
Golog on the Sichuan-Qinghai border and
runs a total of 1,155 kilometres (713 mi.)
before emptying into the Min River. Despite
their relatively small population, the Ersu
inhabit a widespread area. The main
centre of Ersu habitation could be said to
be Ganluo County, which is an eight-hour
train ride from the provincial capital city of
Chengdu.

The Ersu are
officially consid-
ered part of the
Tibetan nationality
in China, but in the
1980s they asked
the government
to create a new
minority, called
the Xifan, and
to include them
under it. 'As of
yet the central
government has
not agreed with
them.'[2] The linguist
Sun Hongkai says,
'Ersu speakers at
different localities
have different
autonyms: those
living at Ganluo,
Yuexi and Hanyuan
call themselves
Ersu, Buerzi or
Ersubuerzi; those
living at Shimian
use Lusu, and those living at Muli, Jiulong
and western Mianning Lisu. These different
autonyms are dialectal variants of the same
word, originally meaning "white people".'[3]

The Ersu language contains three tones
and three dialects, all of which reportedly
contain 'great differences'.[4] The Ersu
are noted for their use of an ancient
pictographic script. This has baffled and
amazed scholars who have speculated on
how the Ersu came to possess their unique
orthography. One scholar suggests, 'Ersu
is perhaps an indirect descendant of the
extinct Xixia language, spoken in a once-

China Advocate

powerful empire in the Tibetan-Chinese-
Uighur border regions, finally destroyed by
the Mongols in the 13th century. A large
literature in Xixia survives, in a logographic
writing system invented in the 11th century,
with thousands of intricate characters
inspired by, but graphically independent of
Chinese, the decipherment of which is now
well-advanced by Japanese and Russian
scholars.'[5]

The origins of the Ersu are uncertain, but
many Ersu themselves believe their ancestors came from Lhasa about 200 years ago.
Since that time
they have lived
in communities
alongside the
Chinese, Yi
and Tibetans,
and they have
assimilated
parts of all
three cultures
into their own
identity.

The Ersu are
nominally
Tibetan Bud-
dhists, though
in reality few
take religion
seriously. 'They
do not have
any temples,
but worship in
their homes. . . .
The 3,000 Ersu
in Mianning
only have
two monks,
both living in
Mianning City. They come to the villages to
help with burials. Their last Bon temple (in
Huyi) was destroyed [during the Cultural
Revolution] in the 1960s.'[6]

There has never been a known church
or Christian among the Ersu. The Border
Mission of the Church of Christ in China and
the American Baptists worked among the
related Jiarong people until 1949, reporting
34 converts in 1934.[7] No outreach,
however, was ever reportedly undertaken to
the Ersu.

Gahri

Population:
5,880 (2000)
7,050 (2010)
8,350 (2020)
Countries: India, China
Buddhism: Tibetan
Christians: 15

Overview of the Gahri

Other Names: Bunan, Lahuli of Bunan, Ghara, Lahul, Lahouli, Lahuli, Boonan, Punan, Poonan, Erankad, Keylong Boli, Lahaula

Population Sources:

4,000 in India (2000, B Grimes [1997 figure])

1,467 in China (1995, Global Evangelization Movement)

Language: Sino-Tibetan, Tibeto-Burman, Himalayish, Tibeto-Kanauri, Western Himalayish, Kanauri

Dialects: 0

Professing Buddhists: 70%

Practising Buddhists: 60%

Christians: 0.2%

Scripture: Portions 1911

Jesus film: none

Gospel Recordings: Lahouli: Bunan

Christian Broadcasting: none

ROPAL code: BFU

Status of Evangelization

89%

10%

1%

A   B   C

A = Have never heard the gospel
B = Have heard the gospel but have not become Christians
C = Are adherents to some form of Christianity

Approximately 6,000 Gahri people live on both sides of the remote India-China border in the western Himalayan mountains. The *Ethnologue* lists a 1997 estimate of 4,000 Gahri living in the Gahr Valley in the north Indian state of Himachal Pradesh.[1]

A further 1,500 Gahri people live across the border in an extremely isolated area of western Tibet. Western Tibet is separated from Xinjiang to the north by the imposing Kunlun Mountains, and in the south Himalayan peaks rise over 7,000 metres (23,000 ft.) above sea level. China and India had several military border clashes here during the 1950s and 1960s. China has since claimed thousands of square miles of territory from India, including the area inhabited by the Gahri. The Gahri's isolated homeland is so remote that few outsiders have ever travelled there. The Indian government, who also claim the territory inhabited by the Gahri, did not find out that the Chinese had built a road there until two years after it was completed.[2]

The Gahri people are known by a variety of ethnic names, including Bunan[3] and Lahul. In India they form part of the Lahaula Scheduled Tribe. The word Lahaula is 'derived from two local words, *hya-hul*, meaning deities or spirits (divine or supernatural, generally of the malevolent type) and *hul*, meaning land or abode'.[4]

The Gahri language is a part of the Kanauri arm of the so-called *Himalayish* branch of Tibeto-Burman. It is one of a number of different languages located in the linguistically diverse western Himalayan region. This diversity can be seen in linguistic

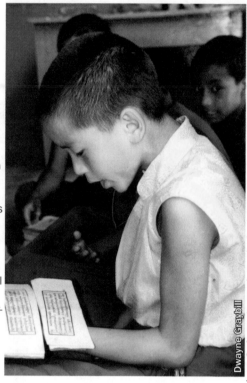

Dwayne Graybill

surveys that find the Gahri language has 39 per cent lexical similarity with Sunam, 26 per cent to 39 per cent with varieties of Chamba Lahuli, 37 per cent with Tinan Lahuli, 26 per cent to 34 per cent with varieties of Central Tibetan and 23 per cent with Kanauri.[5]

Gahri culture has been heavily influenced by the people's devotion to Tibetan Buddhism. Many Gahri make annual pilgrimages to Lake Manasarovar and Mount Kailas—two holy Buddhist sites in western Tibet. Among the Gahri on the Indian side of the border there is some Hindu influence, although the majority are adherents of Tibetan Buddhism. Both the Buddhist and Hindu Gahri retain elements of the spirit-worship that dates back thousands of years. K S Singh states, 'The ancient faith of the area was based on the Loong Pai Chos creed, a form of belief centering around the propitiation of spirits and demons. Many elements of that creed have been incorporated into the Buddhist and Hindu faiths of the area, though the followers of that faith have long ceased to exist as a separate entity.'[6]

The Gahri had portions of the Bible translated into their language by missionaries in 1911, but these have been out of print since 1923. Today there are a handful of Gahri believers, but they are rarely able to fellowship with each other because of geographical separation. Most Gahri in both India and China remain completely unaware of the claims of the gospel of Jesus Christ.

Approximately 1,000 people belonging to the Gara ethnic group live in the Leh and Kargil districts of the north Indian state of Jammu and Kashmir. An unknown (probably very small) number also live in the Lahul and Spitti districts of Himachal Pradesh.[1] The exact population here is uncertain as they were only recognized as a Scheduled Tribe in India in 1989—too late to be counted separately in the last census taken in India in 1981. Ethnologist Sachchindan-andra Prasad estimated a 1998 population of 1,000 Gara people.[2]

Few sources have ever mentioned the Gara as a distinct ethnic-ity—making it even more surprising that the Indian authorities have granted them official status. Those few sources that do mention the Gara usually list them as a sub-group of the Ladakhi. While it is true that much of their culture mirrors Ladakhi culture, there are significant social differences between the two peoples. The main difference is a linguistic one. The Gara speak an Indo-European language, totally distinct from the Tibeto-Burman Ladakhi.

Population:
1,000 (2000)
1,150 (2010)
1,360 (2020)
Countries: India
Buddhism: Tibetan
Christians: none known

The Gara serve the Ladakhi as blacksmiths. Traditionally there was a clear distinction between the Ladakhi and smaller servant groups in the area. K S Singh notes, 'The Ladakhis traditionally did not participate in the marriage and death rituals of the Gara, Mon and Beda. Secular attitudes have brought neighbouring communities closer to each other socially.'[3] Today, even though the Gara live in ethnically mixed communities, the Ladakhi consider the Gara the lowest social class. The Gara are still not allowed to hold any position in the village or monastery administration. They supply the Ladakhi with iron implements. In return, they usually receive a fixed amount

of grain as payment.

Ceremonies are organized throughout the year in which Gara youth are afforded the opportunity to search for a spouse. Young women wear their best traditional clothing to these ceremonies, as a display of their needlework goes a long way to attracting a prospective suitor. Marriages are arranged 'through negotiation, elopement, exchange, courtship, etc. . . . Bride price is paid both in cash and kind. The reasons for seeking divorce are adultery, barrenness, maladjustment, impotency, cruelty and inability to meet the wife's expenses, and remarriage is permissible.'[4]

Most Gara families follow Tibetan Bud-dhism, while a few are Hindus, especially among the Gara in Himachal Pradesh. One source notes, 'They observe all the Buddhist festivals and celebrate *Losae* and *Budh-Purnima*.'[5]

Influences from Bon, the pre-Buddhism religion, can still be seen in the rituals and ceremonies of the Gara. Bon is basically a belief in spirit worship and demonism. Powerful demonic spirits are called upon for assistance and protection. Gruesome masks are worn, and occasionally the lamas go into a demonic trance during which they predict the future and give guidance to the community.

Although more than 200 Ladakhi people believe in Christ today, and the gospel has been established in the area for 150 years, there are no known Christians among the Gara. The social divisions between the different groups create barriers for the gospel.

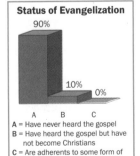

Julian Hawken

Overview of the Gara
Other Names: Garba, Garra
Population Sources:
1,000 in India (1998, S R R Prasad)
Language: Indo-European, Indo-Iranian, Indo-Aryan, Northwestern Zone, Dardic, Shina
Dialects: 0
Professing Buddhists: 100%
Practising Buddhists: 85%
Christians: 0%
Scripture: Portions 1904 (Ladakhi)
Jesus **film:** available (Ladakhi)
Gospel Recordings: Ladakhi
Christian Broadcasting: none
ROPAL code: none

Status of Evangelization

A = Have never heard the gospel
B = Have heard the gospel but have not become Christians
C = Are adherents to some form of Christianity

In 1992, there were reportedly 1,300 speakers of the Kutang Ghale language living in the northern Gorkha District of the Gandaki Zone in central Nepal. They inhabit the Buri Gandaki Valley, from Nyak northward to and including the village of Prok. The Kutang Ghale inhabit villages up to 4,100 metres (13,450 ft.) above sea level.

The authorities in Nepal do not acknowledge any of the three distinct Ghale language groups; they have, rather, included them as part of the large Gurung ethnicity, which numbered more than 449,000 people at the time of the 1991 census. Although there are definite historical and cultural links between the Ghale and the main body of Gurung people, their languages are markedly different.

Linguistic research into the Kutang Ghale language, which is part of the Tamangic branch of Tibeto-Burman, has found that Kutang Ghale shares only between 39 per cent and 49 per cent lexical similarity with Southern Ghale, between 45 per cent and 61 per cent with Northern Ghale, and only 18 per cent with the variety of Gurung spoken in the Banspur area.[1] By way of comparison, English and German share a 60 per cent lexical similarity. When people from one Ghale group try to communicate with other Ghale people they cannot, and they must revert to Nepali to be understood. There is surprising diversity even among the three reported dialects of Kutang Ghale (Bihi, Chak and Rana). These three dialects reportedly share only a 62 per cent to 76 per cent lexical similarity with each other.[2] The Kutang Ghale call their language the 'thieves' language' because they think they have stolen vocabulary from many other neighbouring languages. The Ghale languages were studied by the Christian missionary Larry Seaward between 1971 and 1973. He compiled a 276-page Ghale dictionary, which has not yet been published.

The history of the three Ghale language groups is uncertain, although one source states, 'According to their legend, the Gurung were a wandering tribe that traversed west across Tibet prior to their entry into Mustang. Their Tibetan sojourn pre-dates the introduction of Buddhism there (7th century) as the Gurung religious traditions are basically animist. . . . From Mustang, Gurungs moved to Manang where they came under the domination of Klye (Ghale) chiefs, later migrants from Tibet. . . . In the early 16th century, the Ghale ruler of Lamjung was defeated and replaced by a Thakuri prince from Kaski.'[3]

The term 'Ghale' therefore refers to a ruling class of Gurung people, who appear to have come from Tibet at a different time than the Gurung and brought with them a different language and different customs. There are also historical records of Ghale rulers among the neighbouring Tamang tribe.

All Kutang Ghale people believe in Tibetan Buddhism. They have their own lamas, and their ceremonies and rituals are all Buddhist. There are no known Christians among this ancient and intriguing ethnic group.

Ghale Kutang

Population:
1,550 (2000)
1,900 (2010)
2,350 (2020)
Countries: Nepal
Buddhism: Tibetan
Christians: none known

Overview of the Kutang Ghale

Other Names: Bhotte, Bhotte Ghale, Ghale, Bote Ghale, Bote, Lila, Bhingi, Galle, Galle Gurung, Ghale Gurung

Population Sources:

1,300 in Nepal (2000, B Grimes [1992 figure])

Language: Sino-Tibetan, Tibeto-Burman, Himalayish, Tibeto-Kanauri, Tibetic, Tamangic

Dialects: 3 (Bihi, Chak, Rana)

Professing Buddhists: 100%

Practising Buddhists: 80%

Christians: 0%

Scripture: none

Jesus film: none

Gospel Recordings: Ghale

Christian Broadcasting: none

ROPAL code: GHT

Photo credit: Dwayne Graybill

Status of Evangelization

81%

19%

0%

A　　B　　C

A = Have never heard the gospel
B = Have heard the gospel but have not become Christians
C = Are adherents to some form of Christianity

Ghale, Northern

Ghale Northern

Population:
3,030 (2000)
3,750 (2010)
4,650 (2020)
Countries: Nepal
Buddhism: Tibetan
Christians: none known

Overview of the Northern Ghale

Other Names: Bhotte, Bhotte Ghale, Ghale, Bote Ghale, Bote, Lila, Bhingi, Galle, Galle Gurung, Ghale Gurung

Population Sources:
2,500 in Nepal (1991, H Smith)

Language: Sino-Tibetan, Tibeto-Burman, Himalayish, Tibeto-Kanauri, Tibetic, Tamangic

Dialects: 5 (Khorla, Uiya, Jagat, Philim, Nyak)

Professing Buddhists: 95%

Practising Buddhists: 60%

Christians: 0%

Scripture: none

***Jesus* film:** none

Gospel Recordings: Ghale, Ghale Gurung

Christian Broadcasting: none

ROPAL code: GHH

Status of Evangelization

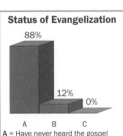

A = Have never heard the gospel
B = Have heard the gospel but have not become Christians
C = Are adherents to some form of Christianity

Approximately 3,000 Northern Ghale people live in the Gorkha District of the Gandaki Zone in central Nepal. They inhabit villages throughout the Buri Gandaki Valley.

The Northern Ghale are one of three distinct Ghale language groups in Nepal. George van Driem notes, 'The Ghale are ethnically classed with the Gurung, who live to the west of them, and are also even called "Ghale Gurung". Traditionally, the Ghale constitute one of the four patrician divisions of the Gurung. Linguistically, however, the Ghale and Gurung are entirely distinct.'[1] This group do not refer to themselves as 'Ghale' but use the ethnic name *Lila*.[2]

Dwayne Graybill

The Ghale are considered the aristocrats among the larger Gurung group. They observe many ritual taboos that are similar to Brahman and other ruling caste rituals. For example, they do not eat the meat of chickens or water buffaloes, as other Gurung do.

The Northern Ghale vernacular is the most distinct of the Ghale languages. This is proven by linguistic research, which shows Northern Ghale shares just 65 per cent to 81 per cent lexical similarity with Southern Ghale, 45 per cent to 61 per cent with Kutang Ghale and 29 per cent to 37 per cent with Western Tamang.[3] The Northern and Southern Ghale speakers are able to hold simple conversations with each other, but they must use Nepali or Tibetan to communicate with the Kutang Ghale or the Gurung. Not many Northern Ghale people

have more than a moderate understanding of Nepali, however, making communication an arduous task.[4]

The Northern Ghale are the most isolated Ghale group in Nepal. Accordingly, their customs have been preserved better than the other groups. One writer notes, 'The young women and girls are notably flirtatious with young men and even strangers; they will make jokes and coy advances to the traveller passing through a village or by the fields where they are working, and they can be heard laughing and joking loudly among friends of both sexes while fetching firewood on the forested hillsides. They are generally a very attractive people, with round faces, bright eyes and broad smiles.'[5]

The Ghale prefer to marry their second cousins, but they are not permitted to marry their first cousins for genetic reasons. When a boy chooses a girl, his parents send one of their friends or male relatives to the girl's parents' house with a present of one rupee and a bottle of liquor. 'The visitors are entertained with food and drink if the girl's parents accept the proposition, but are curtly dismissed if they do not. When the girl's parents have agreed, the boy can make arrangements to fetch the bride at his convenience.'[6]

Tibetan Buddhism is the religious stronghold of the Northern Ghale people. Hinduism has made little impact on them compared to the influence it has had on the Southern Ghale further down the valley.

Although in recent years some Christian organizations have tried to take the gospel to the Northern Ghale, they have yet to successfully penetrate into the society. There are no known Christians among this group.

In 1975, the Japanese linguist Yoshio Nishi estimated a population of 12,000 Southern Ghale people in Nepal. They live in the Gorkha District of the Gandaki Zone, especially in the hills south of Macha Khola. The main centres of the Southern Ghale are considered to be the towns of Barpak and Mandre. The Southern Ghale live at a lower altitude than the other Ghale groups, and consequently they have been exposed to more outside cultural and religious influences. Southern Ghale villages are situated between just 600 and 1,800 metres (1,970 to 5,900 ft.) above sea level. Presuming the Southern Ghale population has grown at the national average rate, in 2000 their population was estimated to have surpassed 19,000, and by 2010 they would number 23,700 people.

Culturally the Ghale are considered part of the Gurung ethnicity, but their languages are very different. The Southern Ghale language has three dialects, which are quite different and only share between 75 per cent and 78 per cent lexical similarity with each other.[1]

The Ghale are different from the Gurung in that they 'consider themselves superior in the Gurung tribal structure. . . . The Ghale, or Kle are traditionally a clan of chieftains by birth. The term *kle* emerges from *Khle* (an old Gurung word) which means something equivalent to master or king.'[2] The Ghale will intermarry with the Gurung on occasion, 'but only those of patrician status. Ethnic Gurungs who take up residence in the Ghale area east of the Darondi become Ghale speakers, while Ghale settling west of the Darondi become Gurung speakers.'[3]

Southern Ghale culture has come under strong pressure

Julian Hawken

from Hindu groups over the last century. As a result, many Ghale ceremonies are now linked to Hindu rituals. One such custom is called '*pud-pude*, the celebratory reception of the first-born male child in the family. Another is *ghatu*, a dance drama performed by virgin girls in spring. The performance is done under trance and the story relates to Pasaram, a one-time king of Gorkha.'[4]

The traditional dress of Ghale men consists of a short shirt tied across the front, 'and a short skirt of several yards of white cotton material wrapped around the waist and held by a wide belt. . . . Women have not cast off their traditional costume, despite their own contact with the outside. . . . They almost always wear a cotton or velveteen blouse tied at the front and a sari skirt of printed material, usually of a dark reddish colour. Their ornaments include gold and coral necklaces, which represent the wealth of their husbands, and gold ear and nose rings given to them at the time of marriage. Their ears and noses are pierced when they are small girls. Like almost all women of Nepal, they delight in coloured bangles.'[5]

The Southern Ghale religion is a fusion of three elements. 'They mix Hinduism, Buddhism and animism, worshipping and trying to placate a host of evil spirits.'[6] There are a small number of Christians among them. The Southern Ghale New Testament was printed in 1992, and theirs remains the only Ghale language with Scripture.

Overview of the Southern Ghale

Other Names: Bhotte, Bhotte Ghale, Ghale, Bote Ghale, Bote, Lila, Bhingi, Galle, Galle Gurung, Ghale Gurung

Population Sources:

12,000 in Nepal (1975, Y Nishi)

Language: Sino-Tibetan, Tibeto-Burman, Himalayish, Tibeto-Kanauri, Tibetic, Tamangic

Dialects: 3 (Barpak, Kyaura, Laprak)

Professing Buddhists: 50%

Practising Buddhists: 20%

Christians: 1.6%

Scripture: New Testament 1992

Jesus film: none

Gospel Recordings: Ghale, Ghale: Southern

Christian Broadcasting: none

ROPAL code: GHE

Population:
19,100 (2000)
23,700 (2010)
29,300 (2020)
Countries: Nepal
Buddhism: Tibetan
Christians: 300

Status of Evangelization

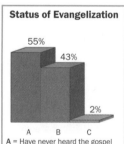

55%
43%
2%

A = Have never heard the gospel
B = Have heard the gospel but have not become Christians
C = Are adherents to some form of Christianity

Population:
127,600 (2000)
164,600 (2010)
202,800 (2020)
Countries: China
Buddhism: Tibetan
Christians: 10

Overview of the Golog

Other Names: Ngolok, Mgolog, Golok, Lhardi, Ngura, Amchok, Rimong, Kangsar, Kanggan, Tsokhar, Ngawa, Gatse, Butsang, Shahrang, Jazza, Ggolo

Population Sources:

80,000 to 90,000 in China (1982, G Rowell)

Language: Sino-Tibetan, Tibeto-Burman, Himalayish, Tibeto-Kanauri, Tibetic, Tibetan, Northern

Dialects: many

Professing Buddhists: 96%

Practising Buddhists: 55%

Christians: 0.1%

Scripture: none

Jesus film: none

Gospel Recordings: none

Christian Broadcasting: none

ROPAL code: GOC

Status of Evangelization

A = Have never heard the gospel
B = Have heard the gospel but have not become Christians
C = Are adherents to some form of Christianity

The February 1982 *National Geographic* listed a figure of between 80,000 and 90,000 Gologs, living in six counties of the remote Golog Tibetan Prefecture in Qinghai Province, China.[1] A total of 100,343 people lived in the Golog Prefecture in 1953, but by 1964 the population had diminished to only 56,071.[2] Thousands of Golog migrated from the area. Thousands more were either killed in battle or starved to death by the Chinese army. The Golog region's extreme isolation was described by a visitor in the late 1920s: 'A miserable land it is, of poverty and incredible filth; a land cut off from the modern world, a region which, for uncounted centuries, has had its own forms of government, of religion and social customs; yet a region which knows no railway, no motor car, no radio, or aught of all that science and invention have given the world since Marco Polo's day.'[3]

According to one source, *Golog* means 'those with heads on backwards'.[4] This name comes from their reputation as an extremely stubborn and rebellious people. Many wild animals inhabit the Golog region, including 'blue sheep, gazelles, bears, wolves, and deer'.[5]

The Golog language is 'largely unintelligible to most Tibetans'.[6] It is a variety of Amdo, with differences that make communication between the Golog and Amdo difficult. There are numerous dialects spoken by dozens of different Golog tribes and clans.[7]

The Golog are the descendants of Tibetan warriors sent to guard the northern borders. 'In the seventh century AD, the Tibetan king dispatched his fiercest warriors, ancestors of the present-day Gologs and neighbouring Khampas, to guard the country's mountainous northern frontier against Chinese invasion. When the Tibetan kingdom eventually collapsed, the Gologs stayed in their mountain retreat, defiant of outside authority.'[8]

Almost all Gologs are Tibetan Buddhists. Many Golog women have 108 braids of hair, considered an auspicious number by Tibetan Buddhists. Few Golog have ever heard of Jesus Christ or his offer of salvation. They have been separated from all outside influence, including Christianity, for centuries. In 1921 some missionaries passed through the Golog area and distributed gospel literature. They later received the following letter from Kurung Tsering, the head lama at a monastery in Kokonor: 'I, your humble servant, have seen several copies of the Scriptures and having read them carefully, they certainly made me believe in Christ. I understand a little of the outstanding principles and the doctrinal teaching of the One Son,

Julian Hawken

but as to the Holy Spirit's nature and essence, and as to the origin of this religion, I am not at all clear, and it is therefore important that the doctrinal principles of this religion should be fully explained, so as to enlighten the unintelligent and people of small mental ability. The teaching of the science of medicine and astrology is also very important. It is therefore evident if we want this blessing openly manifested, we must believe in the religion of the only Son of God. Being in earnest I therefore pray you from my heart not to consider this letter lightly. With a hundred salutations!'[9]

Gong

The Gong are one of the smallest distinct Buddhist people groups in the world. In 1995 they numbered just 200 individuals living in two villages in western Thailand. Thirty Gong families live in Ban Kok Chiang in the Dan Chang District of Suphan Buri Province. Their village is located just a mile or so from the site of the 1991 Lauda Air disaster, in which all 223 people on board died. An additional ten Gong families inhabit Ban Khog Kwai in the Ban Rai District of Uthai Thani Province. In both villages the Gong live in community with Thai people. Intermarriage with the Thai is widespread, so that today there are only a few Gong people who are considered pure-bred.

achieved many soldiers were left behind in southern Yunnan, where they intermarried with local women and gradually formed into the Jino tribe.[1] Could it be that some of those early settlers moved into Myanmar and—many centuries later—ended up as the Gong people in western Thailand?

The Gong language is still spoken by all adults in this people group, although Gong children reportedly now speak Thai as their main language at home. Despite their small numbers, researchers have discovered linguistic differences between those living in the two Gong villages and have separated them as two dialects. The two villages have minimal contact with each other.

Xayographix

The origins of this small tribe are a mystery. It appears that they were once much more numerous, inhabiting many villages in Kanchanaburi Province and westward towards today's border between Thailand and Myanmar. The Gong say they moved to Thailand from Myanmar about 100 years ago, but it appears there are no people identified as Gong living in Myanmar today.

Clues as to the origins of the Gong may be found in their language, which is a unique variety within the Southern Lolo branch of the Tibeto-Burman linguistic family. The most closely related language to Gong appears to be Jino, spoken by about 23,000 people in far-away Yunnan Province in south-west China. The Jino claim their ancestors were soldiers who fought in Kong Ming's army during its southern conquests around AD 200. After the peace was

Throughout their history the Gong were animists, worshipping and being enslaved by a large number of spirit-beings. About 70 years ago the Thais converted the Gong to Buddhism, and they willingly accepted. Although all Gong people now profess Buddhism as their religion, they have retained many of their traditional animistic beliefs. 'They believe in supernatural powers that inhabit the sky, forest, trees, water and other natural surroundings.' Once a year, the entire village 'brings chickens and pig heads to make sacrifices to the village spirit. The chickens are killed near the spirit house, and placed together with the pig heads inside the spirit house. After the shaman has completed the rituals, the villagers take the chickens and pig heads back to their homes, where they are eaten.'[2]

There are no known Gong Christians. Few have ever heard the gospel. Most mission organizations consider them a low priority because of their small population.

Population:
210 (2000)
230 (2010)
250 (2020)
Countries: Thailand
Buddhism: Theravada
Christians: none known

Overview of the Gong

Other Names: Ugong, Lawa, Ugawng, U Gong, Giong, Kwang, U Kwang

Population Sources: 200 in Thailand (2000, J Schliesinger [1995 figure])

Language: Sino-Tibetan, Tibeto-Burman, Lolo-Burmese, Loloish, Southern

Dialects: 2 (Kok Chiang, Suphanaburi)

Professing Buddhists: 100%

Practising Buddhists: 65%

Christians: 0%

Scripture: none

Jesus film: none

Gospel Recordings: none

Christian Broadcasting: none

ROPAL code: UGO

Status of Evangelization

85%

15%

0%

A   B   C

A = Have never heard the gospel
B = Have heard the gospel but have not become Christians
C = Are adherents to some form of Christianity

Approximately 1,000 Gongduk people live in a few extremely isolated villages in Bhutan's Mongar District. Nothing was known about this small ethnic group until the Dutch linguist George van Driem discovered them in 1991. Van Driem wrote, 'The Gongduk language is spoken by a dwindling population in a remote enclave along the Kurichu [River] in east-central Bhutan. . . . In May of 1991, I discovered this previously unknown language in a remote portion of Mongar District, where I was conducting a linguistic survey of the country in the serve of the Royal Government of Bhutan. . . . Gongduk can be reached on foot from Jepzh'ing, from which it is two or three days' journey to the south. It is also about a two days' journey up from the Manas River in the plains. This accounts for the fact that the Gongduk have remained largely unknown outside of the Gongduk area itself and its immediate environs.'[1]

As van Driem studied Gongduk, he excitedly realized that he had found a unique language that appears to be the sole representative of a branch of the Tibeto-Burman family.[2] Another source has said that Gongduk 'retains the complex verbal agreement system of Proto Tibeto-Burman. It is said to belong to one of the ancient populations of Bhutan.'[3] Part of the reason the Gongduk remained undiscovered for so long is because the people pass themselves off as Kheng when they meet outsiders. Just why they do this is uncertain, as they have their own unique culture and language that is not mutually intelligible with Kheng. Van Driem further notes, 'There are currently just over a thousand speakers of the Gongduk language. According to one legend Gongduk was once long ago a small independent kingdom. The Gongduk themselves repeat that they are of aboriginal Dung lineage, or Dungjüt, and that their ancestors were semi-nomadic hunters.'[4] In these respects they are similar to the Lhokpu people of Bhutan.[5]

One has to wonder how many other small tribes and language groups exist in the hundreds of isolated valleys of the Himalayan Range. The Gongduk may have been one of the earliest people groups in Bhutan, but for uncertain historical reasons they were driven to their present location centuries ago. Bhutan was completely closed off to outside influence for centuries until 1960, when the king allowed more freedom.[6] Little has changed in rural areas of the nation for centuries. When the Earl of Ronaldshay entered Bhutan in 1921 he reported, 'With our passage through the bridge, behold a curious transformation. For just as Alice, when she walked through the looking-glass, found herself in a new and whimsical world, so we found ourselves, as though caught up in some magic time machine fitted fantastically with a reverse, flung back across the centuries into the feudalism of a mediaeval age.'[7]

The religious belief of the Gongduk is Tibetan Buddhism mixed with animistic spirit worship. Throughout two thousand years of Christianity, the good news that Jesus Christ died for the sins of the world has never once entered the remote enclave inhabited by the Gongduk.

Population:
2,500 (2000)
3,200 (2010)
4,100 (2020)
Countries: Bhutan
Buddhism: Tibetan
Christians: none known

Overview of the Gongduk

Other Names: Gongdukpa, Gongdubikha, Gongdupkha

Population Sources:

2,000 in Bhutan (2001, G van Driem [1991 figure])

Language: Sino-Tibetan, Tibeto-Burman, Himalayish, Tibeto-Kanauri, Tibetic, Tibetan

Dialects: 0

Professing Buddhists: 100%

Practising Buddhists: 70%

Christians: 0%

Scripture: none

***Jesus* film:** none

Gospel Recordings: none

Christian Broadcasting: none

ROPAL code: GOE

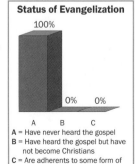

Status of Evangelization

A = Have never heard the gospel
B = Have heard the gospel but have not become Christians
C = Are adherents to some form of Christianity

Groma

CHINA
Xizang (Tibet)

NEPAL
Sikkim
BHUTAN

INDIA

Groma

Population:
14,920 (2000)
18,390 (2010)
22,650 (2020)
Countries: China, India
Buddhism: Tibetan
Christians: none known

Overview of the Groma

Other Names: Trowoma, Chomo Tibetan, Chomo, Gromo, Tomo, Zhuomu Tibetan, Chuo-mu Tibetan, Chumbi Tibetan

Population Sources:

12,840 in China (2000, B Grimes [1993 figure])

also in India

Language: Sino-Tibetan, Tibeto-Burman, Himalayish, Tibeto-Kanauri, Tibetic, Tibetan, Southern

Dialects: 4 (Upper Groma, Lower Groma, Spiti, Tomo)

Professing Buddhists: 100%

Practising Buddhists: 90%

Christians: 0%

Scripture: none

***Jesus* film:** none

Gospel Recordings: none

Christian Broadcasting: none

ROPAL code: GRO

Status of Evangelization

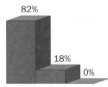

82%

18%

0%

A   B   C

A = Have never heard the gospel
B = Have heard the gospel but have not become Christians
C = Are adherents to some form of Christianity

The *Ethnologue* cites a 1993 source stating that there are 12,840 speakers of Groma living in southern Tibet,[1] in the Chambi Valley between Bhutan and the former independent nation of Sikkim—now a state of India. The valley is located within the Chomo (Yadong) County in Tibet's Xigaze Prefecture. A French Catholic missionary to Tibet, Monsieur L'Abbé Desgondins, graphically described the region: 'Take a piece of paper in your hand. Crumple it up and then open your hand and let it fall out! Nothing is flat—all you have is high points and low depressions—the steep, inaccessible, rugged mountains and the deep valleys.'[2] An unspecified number of Groma reportedly live on the Indian side of the border.[3] In India it seems they have simply been classified as Tibetans, as they do not appear in official government lists.

Much of what is known about the Groma comes from a linguistic study done in 1905.[4] The Groma have been counted as part of the Tibetan nationality in China and may be culturally and ethnically indistinguishable from other Tibetans in the region. They are different because of their language, which is a member of the Southern Tibetan branch. It has two dialects, Upper and Lower Groma, with two others, Spiti and Tomo, listed as 'possible dialects or related languages'.[5]

The cornerstone of emerging Tibetan civilization was the Yarlung Valley area,

China Advocate

about 80 kilometres (49 mi.) south-east of Lhasa. There, according to tradition, the union of a monkey and a she-devil created the Tibetan race. Around AD 600, the warrior-king Namri Gampo began the work of unifying the clans of Tibet. It was his son, Songtsen Gampo, who consolidated the empire and established Tibet as a military power to be reckoned with. Sikkim was nominally independent—although always under Indian influence—until it was annexed in 1975 and integrated into India. Tibetans began entering Sikkim in the 10th century. The Nepalese did not come until the 19th century, but now they make up 75 per cent of Sikkim's population.[6]

The Groma lead typical Tibetan lives. They herd yaks, sheep and goats. Groma women do most of the work. The men often spend their days drinking and gambling with their friends. Tibetan Tantric Buddhism dominates the Groma. Devoted pilgrims undertake pilgrimages to holy sites (such as Mt. Kailas). The Groma also observe many animistic rituals related to spirit propitiation.

There are no known Christians today among the Groma. The little mission work that *has* targeted the area invariably resulted in severe persecution. 'Converts did not easily forget the Christian who was sewn into a fresh yak skin by merciless shaman priests and placed in the broiling sun until the contraction of the skin squeezed the life out of his frame.'[7] In 1997 neighbouring Sikkim counted 250 churches, but almost all the believers were ethnic Nepalis. The north district where the Groma live is completely unreached.[8]

A 1983 study listed 7,000 Guiqiong people in China.[1] They inhabit the tablelands along both banks of the Dadu River, north of Luding County in the Garze Tibetan Autonomous Prefecture in western Sichuan Province. There are also a few Guiqiong located further to the east in north-western Tianquan County. The great Dadu River, which surges each summer as the ice fields in the mountains begin to thaw, is the source of life for the Guiqiong. The river cuts a path through the rocky terrain of western Sichuan. As a result, plateaus have formed on both sides of the river.

China Advocate

The Guiqiong have been officially included as part of the Tibetan nationality in China. As early as 1930, however, Chinese researchers recognized that 'The language and customs of the Guiqiong are distinct from those of either the Chinese or Khampa Tibetans. The people here are actually a unique ethnic group.'[2]

The Guiqiong language has four tones and is part of the Qiangic branch of Tibeto-Burman. Linguist Sun Hongkai says, 'speakers of Guiqiong live in small communities interspersed among larger Chinese communities. They use Chinese outside of their own villages. The Guiqiong language they speak is under heavy influence from Chinese, containing many Chinese loanwords.'[3]

The historical border region between the Chinese and Tibetans has witnessed the fusion and assimilation of numerous tribes. The area inhabited by the Guiqiong was formerly part of the province of Xikang. In the 1930s Xikang was a lawless place that few outsiders dared to enter. 'Aborigines [tribal peoples] seize and kill members of other nationalities. . . . In parts of Xikang, abandoned hovels and wasteland due to pillage are common sights. Violent attacks on communities by "aborigines", as well as government punitive actions against them, cost many tens of thousands of lives.'[4]

One of the main reasons for the extreme violence throughout Xikang in the 1930s and 1940s was the drug trade. Large quantities of opium were manufactured throughout the region until the Communist takeover in the early 1950s. The new government forced the people of western Sichuan to destroy their opium crops. Today most Guiqiong grow maize and barley, while those living near the river grow vegetables.

The Guiqiong, who are nominally Tibetan Buddhists, have no understanding of the gospel or the name of Jesus Christ. They have been cut off from the message of eternal life for centuries. James O Fraser described the tenacity needed to reach groups such as the Guiqiong: 'Evangelistic work on the mission field is like a man going about in a dark, damp valley with a lighted match in his hand, seeking to ignite anything ignitable . . . here a shrub, there a tree, here a few sticks, there a heap of leaves take fire and give light and warmth, long after the kindling match and its bearer have passed on. And this is what God wants to see . . . little patches of fire burning all over the world.'[5]

Overview of the Guiqiong

Other Names: Guichong

Population Sources:
7,000 in China (1983, Sun Hongkai)

Language: Sino-Tibetan, Tibeto-Burman, Tangut-Qiang, Qiangic

Dialects: 0

Professing Buddhists: 100%

Practising Buddhists: 60%

Christians: 0%

Scripture: none

Jesus film: none

Gospel Recordings: none

Christian Broadcasting: none

ROPAL code: GQI

Population:
9,760 (2000)
12,020 (2010)
14,800 (2020)
Countries: China
Buddhism: Tibetan
Christians: none known

Status of Evangelization

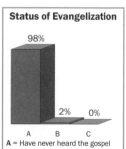

98%

2%   0%

A   B   C

A = Have never heard the gospel
B = Have heard the gospel but have not become Christians
C = Are adherents to some form of Christianity

More than a quarter of a million Eastern Gurung people live in the Gandaki Zone of central Nepal. They primarily inhabit the Lamjun, Tanahu and western Gorkha districts and possibly also Manang District. The homeland of the Eastern Gurung consists of rolling hills and mountain slopes, averaging between 1,500 to 3,000 metres (4,920 to 9,840 ft.) above sea level. After the Gorkha conquest, Gurung people spread far from their homeland into southern Bhutan and north-east India.[1] A small number may also live in Bangladesh.[2]

The name *Gurung* is believed to come from *gu* ('nine') *rong* ('chiefs'), who formed a confederacy in Gandaki many centuries ago. However, 'The term Gurungs use for themselves is *Tamu*. It is a tonal variation of one used by their neighbours, the Tamang, and may be simply rendered as 'highlander' (*ta* = up, *mu* = people).'[3]

The Eastern Gurung were not counted separately in the 1991 Nepal census, but were part of an overall figure of 449,189 people in the Gurung ethnic group, which includes the Western Gurung, three Ghale language groups and possibly others.[4] Out of the 449,189 Gurung in 1991, there were 227,918 (slightly more than half) who could still speak a Gurung language. Gurung people of all ages are bilingual in Nepali. The Eastern and Western Gurung languages have diverged. Today, speakers of the two varieties are able to make simple conversation, but 'do not have adequate intelligibility to handle complex and abstract discourse'.[5]

There are conflicting reports regarding the origins of the Gurung. Some say their ancestors came from Tibet, which would explain why their language is part of the Tibeto-Burman family, while others say their ancestors came from India. Today, most Eastern Gurung are farmers, growing their crops on hillsides.[6] One source notes, 'Most of them are very poor. The meager amount of food that they are able to produce is barely enough to sustain them. Their main food sources are millet, maize and some rice. They also raise soybeans, grains and strong beans.'[7]

The religious belief systems of the Eastern Gurung are complicated. Originally they were shamanists, before being converted to Tibetan Buddhism. Since the encroachment of the Hindu world into their area in the 18th century, the Gurung have gradually become Hinduized. Their religious beliefs are therefore a mixture of Buddhism, Hinduism and shamanism. Generally speaking, those Gurung living in the lowlands and towns are more Hindu, while those in mountain communities are more Buddhist.

The gospel has encountered strong opposition from the Gurung people. The small numbers of Gurung Christians today have faced beatings and other persecution. 'The vast majority of Gurungs have little or no concept of who God is and have never even heard the name of Jesus. In many Gurung villages they outwardly persecute and harass Christians. Often, however, Gurungs show an interest when the gospel is shared and many are open to listen and ask questions.'[8]

Nancy Sturrock

Overview of the Eastern Gurung

CHINA
Xizang (Tibet)
Gandaki
NEPAL
BHUTAN
INDIA
Gurung Eastern

Population:
251,200 (2000)
311,000 (2010)
385,100 (2020)
Countries: Nepal, India, Bhutan, possibly Bangladesh
Buddhism: Tibetan
Christians: 200

Other Names: Gurung, Gurun, Tamu, Daduwa

Population Sources:
207,000 in Nepal (1991, P Hattaway)
105,000 speakers in Nepal (1991 census)
also in India, Bhutan and possibly Bangladesh
Language: Sino-Tibetan, Tibeto-Burman, Himalayish, Tibeto-Kanauri, Tibetic, Tamangic

Dialects: 3 (Lamjung Gurung, Gorkha Gurung, Tamu Kyi)

Professing Buddhists: 60%

Practising Buddhists: 15%

Christians: 0.1%

Scripture: none

Jesus **film:** available (Gurung)

Gospel Recordings: Gurung: Eastern, Gurung: Gorkha, Gurung: Lamjung

Christian Broadcasting: none

ROPAL code: GGN

Status of Evangelization

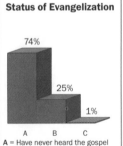

74%

25%

1%

A   B   C

A = Have never heard the gospel
B = Have heard the gospel but have not become Christians
C = Are adherents to some form of Christianity

Population:
172,300 (2000)
213,300 (2010)
264,000 (2020)
Countries: Nepal, India, Bhutan, possibly Myanmar
Buddhism: Tibetan
Christians: 200

Overview of the Western Gurung

Other Names: Gurung, Tamu Kyi, Tamu, Gurkhal

Population Sources:

141,900 in Nepal (1991 census)

72,000 speakers in Nepal (1991 census)

also in India, Bhutan, possibly Myanmar

Language: Sino-Tibetan, Tibeto-Burman, Himalayish, Tibeto-Kanauri, Tibetic, Tamangic

Dialects: 2 (Southern Gurung, Northwestern Gurung)

Professing Buddhists: 50%

Practising Buddhists: 15%

Christians: 0.1%

Scripture: New Testament 1982

***Jesus* film:** available (Gurung)

Gospel Recordings: Gurung: Kaski, Gurung: Syangia

Christian Broadcasting: none

ROPAL code: GVR

Status of Evangelization

80%

19%

1%

A   B   C

A = Have never heard the gospel
B = Have heard the gospel but have not become Christians
C = Are adherents to some form of Christianity

Approximately 180,000 Western Gurung people live in the Kaski, Syangia and Parbat districts of the Gandaki Zone in central Nepal. According to the 1991 census, 72,000 people can still speak the Western Gurung language, just over 50 per cent of the population. The rest speak Nepali as their first language.

Over the past two hundred years the Gurung have migrated into surrounding nations. There is a community of Gurung living in the Samtsi District of south-west Bhutan, where they are commonly labelled as Nepalis. In India, Gurung communities can be found in the hilly terrain of the South, West and East districts of the state of Sikkim, throughout the Darjeeling District of West Bengal, and around the city of Dehra Dun and throughout the Pithoragarh District in Uttar Pradesh.[1] In India, the Gurung have not been recognized as a Scheduled Tribe. Consequently population figures are not available for them, but they probably total a few thousand.

Gurung history is clouded with uncertainty because of their lack of a written script in the past. Legends were handed down orally from one generation to the next. We do know that, during the 15th century, a Gurung king named Ghale Raja was overthrown by a Nepali king. In the 16th century the Khasa armies took over large tracts of land in Nepal and the Gurung came under their control. The Gurung were highly regarded as fighters and many of them were enlisted in the Khasa's armies. Later, after the British took control of India, many Gurung men were enlisted as Gurkha soldiers in the British army. Thousands have served in places from Hong Kong to Bosnia and the Falkland Islands.

Religion plays an important role in the everyday lives of most Gurung people. Their belief system is a mixture of Buddhism,

Hinduism and shamanism. As one researcher wrote, 'Buddhism is followed by the Gurungs today although in ancient times they practiced the animistic and shamanistic form of religion similar to the pre-Buddhist Bon religion of the Himalayan regions. The northern areas of the kingdom

Nancy Sturrock

are populated with people of mongoloid stock who are mostly followers of Tibetan Buddhism, and so these Gurungs can also be included within this category, though currently Hindu Gurungs have also emerged due to their contact with the Hindu lowlanders.'[2]

The ceremonies and rituals that the Gurung perform also have mixed origins. One interesting custom, called *tuno bandhane*, takes place three days after the birth of a baby. 'This entails wrapping the newborn baby (after it has been washed in either cow's milk or cow's urine) in a long piece of cloth.'[3]

Less than one out of every thousand Western Gurung people are Christians today. One source found there to be just 23 known Western Gurung believers in 1997,[4] but this number has increased in recent years. The Western Gurung New Testament was first published in 1982, but it has fallen out of print since because of the small number of Western Gurung Christians and because there is no demand for it.

Approximately 36 million Hakka people are scattered throughout the world. More than 31 million inhabit over 200 cities and counties spread throughout seven provinces of China: Guangdong, Jiangxi, Guangxi, Fujian, Hong Kong, Hunan and Sichuan. An additional two million Hakka live in Taiwan, 1.4 million in Malaysia, 800,000 in Indonesia and 170,000 in Singapore.[1]

There is much speculation concerning the historical roots of the Hakka. Some claim they were the first Chinese people to arrive in China. Others claim the Hakka are the descendants of the Xiongnu tribe. This much is agreed upon: at various stages between the 4th and 13th centuries AD, large numbers of people were forced to flee their homes in the war-torn Yellow River valley to seek refuge in southern China. These war refugees came to be known as *Kejia*—a Hakka word meaning 'strangers', or 'guests'.[2] When the savage Mongol hordes swept across China in the 13th century, many Hakka fled to the south to escape the carnage.[3] Although proud of their cultural differences, the Hakka have never claimed to be non-Chinese. Many famous Chinese have been Hakka, including Deng Xiaoping, Lee Kwan Yew and Hong Xiuquan (the leader of the Taiping Rebellion).

The Hakka are proud of their language and say they would 'rather surrender the ancestral land, but never the ancestral speech'.[4] As part of the careful preservation of their language, when a non-Hakka woman marries into a Hakka family she is required to learn the Hakka language. In the past, many Hakka mothers in China killed their female babies. 'Sooner than sell their daughters into slavery or concubinage, Hakka mothers prefer to kill them soon after birth.'[5] The Hakka never practised foot binding like most other Chinese.

Buddhism is followed by relatively few Hakka, about 8 per cent (which amounts to nearly three million people). Buddhism is stronger among the Hakka in Taiwan and Southeast Asia than it is in China. Most Hakka 'are involved with shamanism (belief in gods, demons, ancestral spirits) and sorcery. . . . A few Hakka are Buddhists, but their faith is mixed with shamanistic rituals and traditions.'[6]

Rev T H Hamburg and Rudolf Lechler were the first missionaries sent out by the Basel Mission. They arrived in China in 1846 to commence work among the Hakka. They experienced great success, and by 1922 the Hakka Christians numbered 30,000.[7] In the 1800s a Hakka leader, Chung Wang, pleaded for missionaries to have patience with his people. 'You have had the gospel for upwards of 1,800 years; we only, as it were, eight days. Your knowledge of it ought to be correct and extensive, ours must necessarily be limited and imperfect. You must therefore bear with us for the present, and we will gradually improve. . . . We are determined to uproot idolatry, and plant Christianity in its place.'[8]

Today, most of the estimated 150,000 Hakka Christians in China are located in southern Guangdong.[9] Outside China, the percentage of Hakka Christians is much higher, as many as 30 per cent in some Southeast Asian nations.

Overview of the Hakka

Other Names: Hakka Chinese, Han Chinese: Hakka, Hokka, Kejia, Kechia, Ke, Xinmin, Majia, Khek, Kek, Kehia

Population Sources:

25,725,000 in China (2000, B Grimes [1984 figure])

2,240,000 in Taiwan (2001, P Johnstone and J Mandryk [2000 figure])

985,635 in Malaysia (1980 census)

640,000 in Indonesia (1982, CCCOWE)

170,000 in Singapore (2001, P Johnstone and J Mandryk [2000 figure])

58,000 in Thailand (2000, B Grimes [1984 figure])[10]

Language: Chinese, Hakka

Dialects: 12 (Jiaying, Xinghua, Xinhui, Shaonan, Yuezhong, Huizhou, Yuebei, Tingzhou, Ninglong, Yugui, Tonggu, Hailu)

Professing Buddhists: 9%

Practising Buddhists: 5%

Christians: 2.5%

Scripture: Bible 1916; New Testament 1883; Portions 1860

Jesus film: available

Gospel Recordings: Hakka, Hakka: Mei Shan, Hakka: Moali

Christian Broadcasting: available

ROPAL code: HAK

Population:
36,059,500 (2000)
40,745,200 (2010)
44,745,400 (2020)

Countries: China, Taiwan, Malaysia, Indonesia, Singapore, Thailand, French Polynesia, Panama, Suriname, French Guiana, Brunei, Mauritius, New Zealand, South Africa, United Kingdom, USA, Canada, Jamaica, Sri Lanka, Philippines, Australia, Kenya, Netherlands, France, Germany, Brazil, Trinidad and Tobago

Buddhism: Mahayana

Christians: 900,000

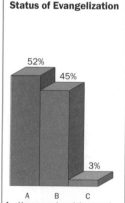

Status of Evangelization

52%
45%
3%

A   B   C

A = Have never heard the gospel
B = Have heard the gospel but have not become Christians
C = Are adherents to some form of Christianity

Buddhism and the Gospel in China

Ralph Covell

The Buddhist faith probably entered China a century or two before the Christian era, but it did not root itself deeply or spread widely until about AD 150. Its greatest growth came after the fall of the later Han dynasty (AD 25–200) and reached its ascendancy and glory during the Tang dynasty (AD 618–907). Ultimately, Buddhism became very popular both among the masses and the official gentry classes and was accepted as an indigenous Chinese faith.[1] The Buddhism which entered China was predominantly Mahayana, although the first books translated into Chinese by monks from India followed the original Pali tradition (Theravada) espoused by Gautama Buddha.

Theravada (also known as *Hinayana*, or 'small vehicle') Buddhism is found today in China largely along the border between Yunnan Province and Myanmar (Burma) and Thailand, particularly among the Dai minority group. Mahayana ('greater vehicle') Buddhism is found among the remainder of China proper and has expressed itself in several different schools.

The Jing Tu (Pure Land), or the Lotus School, became the most popular of the Chinese Buddhist sects and was the one to which the Christian faith related the best.

The Buddhism found in Tibet and Mongolia, although broadly Mahayana, is referred to as Tibetan or Tantric Buddhism. The Chinese prefer to refer to it as Lamaism, a term disliked by the Tibetans themselves. It has proved very resistant to the Christian faith.

The cross and the lotus: Nestorian Christianity enters China

Arriving in China in AD 635 from their home base in present-day Iran, Nestorian missionaries were probably the first representatives of the Christian faith in the middle kingdom. Welcomed and favoured by a tolerant Chinese emperor and his successors, the Nestorian faith prospered. At the time of its demise in China proper, under a severe persecution in AD 845, it had hundreds of monasteries, two thousand religious workers, monks and teachers, and tens of thousands of adherents. The Nestorian Stone, a kind of time-capsule tablet describing the Nestorian work for later generations and now preserved in the provincial museum in Xian, speaks about Christian salvation in terms that would have appealed to both a Buddhist and a Confucian audience.

For example, the tablet states that when Jesus had 'taken an oar in the vessel of mercy and ascended to the palaces of the light above', referring probably to the ascension, 'those who have souls were then completely saved'. Here the figure of speech describes the Buddhist concept of humankind hopelessly lost in a sea of suffering and sin and headed for shipwreck. The compassionate Saviour, filled with mercy, provides a vessel for salvation.

This initial contact of Christianity with Buddhism has raised two important questions. Did Nestorian Christianity contribute to some of the important 'Christianlike' emphases of Mahayana Buddhism and, if so, to what extent? Or was Nestorian Christianity a syncretistic mix with Buddhism which compromised its purity and vitality? This may have been the case by the time of the 9th century, but we know too little of the precise historical situation to give a definitive answer.

Praying to Buddha at a temple in Shanghai.

As Samuel Moffett observes, 'The line between distortion and adaptation or contextualization is difficult to define.'[2]

Matteo Ricci and Buddhism

Roman Catholic missionaries who came to China in the 13th century do not appear to have had much significant contact with Buddhism. Most of their efforts seem to have been directed towards the Mongol court and its leaders. This undoubtedly led them to relate in some way to Tibetan Buddhism, but there is no specific record of this. Referred to by the Mongol name *Ye li ko wen*, the Christianity of this period established no ongoing church among either the Han Chinese or the Mongols and the other tribal groups in the north that they dominated. Nestorian Christianity gained great success among the Uygur, Ongut and Keirat tribes, but the original faith of these groups was probably a folk religion and not Buddhism.

When Matteo Ricci and his companion Michele Ruggieri first arrived in Zhaoqing, a few miles north of Guangzhou (Canton) in 1582, they assumed that Buddhist monks and their faith were highly respected by the local populace. Adopting the lifestyle of these religious figures, they wore long, tattered grey gowns, shaved their faces clean and had their hair closely cropped. They lived wherever they could find space in a variety of temples and adopted a lifestyle of poverty. This was a true immersion, but in the wrong pool! As they eventually found out, Buddhism and its leaders were not respected, but despised. So Ricci and Ruggieri did a total about-face and identified themselves with the Confucian scholars. They did not, however, totally neglect Buddhist leaders.

Ricci noted external ways in which Buddhism resembled Catholicism: the masses, pious images, chants, almsgiving, celibacy, paradise and hell. To the missionaries, these were but 'traps set by the devil' to delude people.[3] Some converts from Buddhism

People light incense sticks.

International Mission Board

to Catholicism reflected that their former faith was really a degenerate form of Christianity.

Jesuit missionaries in Tibet

Catholic missionaries had entered China in the 13th and 14th centuries under the Mongol leaders and once again in the 16th century. However, they made no effort to enter Tibet until the 1620s, near the end of the Ming dynasty (1368–1644). The first Jesuit missionaries came to Tsaparang, in the far south-western corner of Tibet, and were permitted to build a chapel. They entered into serious discussions with Buddhist lamas on such weighty topics as the nature of God and reincarnation. This promising beginning fell victim very soon to a local civil war.

Catholic work continued spasmodically on and around the edges of Tibet for the next century. By 1724, missionaries counted 27 baptized adult converts and double that number of interested inquirers. Over 2,500 children, most near death, were baptized to gain eternal salvation. Lack of cultural sensitivity resulted in some unwise actions by a number of converts, such as refusing to revere the Dalai Lama by bowing and not performing some expected activities. In the vicious persecution that followed, the mission closed down and the fathers hastily retreated to Nepal.[4]

Roman Catholic efforts from the mid-19th century until 1949 waxed and waned, with alternate periods of revitalization and persecution. The single status of the missionaries enabled them to penetrate further into frontier areas that were more difficult for the family-oriented Protestants to reach. In their several stations of work, some from bases in India and others from bases in China, the missionaries started schools for young people, held catechism classes for adults and engaged in many ministries of compassion that attracted people to the Christian faith. Initial evangelistic outreach was usually done through catechists, enabling the foreign priests to remain in the background.

The most effective Catholic work in the 1930s and 1940s was done around Yerkalo, along the Yunnan borders of Tibet. Depending on local circumstances at a particular time, this village was either in Chinese Tibet or independent Tibet. Father Maurice Tournay, a St Bernard missionary to Tibet, communicated Christian truth in innovative ways. He wrote plays for his students that resembled the medieval mystery plays, with their drama of the confrontation between angels and devils.[5]

In all their years in Tibet, Catholic missionaries lived a simple life among Tibetan nomads and learned the life and culture of the people well. Their work on both sides of the China-Tibet border has had a more lasting impact than any of the many ministries of Protestant missionaries in the same areas.

The colony approach among the Mongols

When the Mongol dynasty was overthrown in 1368, there were about 30,000 Roman Catholic Christians, many of whom were Mongols. With the advent of the Ming Dynasty in 1368 Christianity in China virtually disappeared, and this seems to have been the fate of the Mongol Christians as well.

When Lazarist missionaries penetrated what is now Inner Mongolia late in the 18th century, it was with high hopes of establishing Mongol churches. But this hope for 'Missions in Mongolia' quickly became 'Missions amongst the Chinese in Mongolia'.[6]

The only significant response among the Mongol peoples came out of the suffering wreaked upon their villages when Muslims from Shaanxi and Gansu provinces burned their temples and monasteries and killed a large number of people. Missionaries were able to form a group of converts in this area which established the foundation for what came to be known as the Mongol Christian community at Poro Balgeson. This became the only enduring work among the Mongols for either Catholics or Protestants.

Each family admitted to the community had to attest in writing to its willingness to convert to Catholicism, to promote the study of the catechism, to observe the regulations of the village and of the church, and to obey the commandments of God. All of the community was expected to observe adoration, praise, the service of God, obedience to the divine commandments and to ecclesiastical discipline; to receive the sacraments; to recite prayers; and to practise works of charity.

A tour guide explains the history of an ancient Buddha carved out of a rock face at the Baodingshan Monastery in Chongqing, China.

International Mission Board

Modern-day Buddhism in China: burning incense, sunglasses, tattoo and handbag.

Catholic scholars have often been critical of such economic motivation (such as giving cheap farm land to lease in return for 'conversions'), but most have concluded that it has been a starting point for a faith that has persevered under severe trials.

Barriers of Buddhism among the Han Chinese

Early Protestant missionaries among the Han Chinese followed the lead of the 17th-century Jesuits in despising Buddhism as a religion. To their supporters at home, they spoke of pagan idols, silly ceremonies, immoral monks, decrepit temples and systems of thought that were dead. Their hope, epitomized by one missionary speaker at the General Conference in 1877 in Shanghai, was that they might 'destroy this fortress of Buddhism'.

Early Protestant literature on Buddhism (usually just called 'idolatry') was heavily judgemental. As scholars translated some of the Buddhist classics and made them more available to the general public in the latter half of the 19th century, a few missionaries developed more open attitudes to Buddhism in China.

Karl Reichelt was a visionary pioneer in charting a new course of approaching Chinese Buddhists. Affiliated initially with the Norwegian Missionary Society, Reichelt focused his effort almost entirely on teaching seekers, or 'friends of the Dao', from among Buddhist leaders and laypeople. To this end, he established a programme that welcomed wandering monks and pilgrims to visit for religious conversation, trained those who made a commitment to Christ and held retreats and conferences for seekers. In 1927, under the name of the Christian Mission to Buddhists, he built a new site near Shatin in the New Territories, Hong Kong, and called it Tao Fong Shan. The centre continues today, but with a very different emphasis from what Reichelt had. (Although it started out as a centre for reaching Buddhists with the gospel, these days it is a liberal Christian-Buddhist place where both sides agree they are one.)

During the pre-Hong Kong ministries and the period in Hong Kong from 1930 to 1950, over two hundred people were baptized and nearly 1,500 came to the centre to study the Christian faith seriously. Reichelt's influence spread far beyond statistics. Those who were converted had extensive correspondence with their former associates; they wrote testimonial letters in the Chinese press and had significant ministries in many places. Reichelt himself travelled widely to temples and monasteries to find serious religious seekers. He made significant friendships with important national Buddhist leaders.

Reichelt probed deeply into Buddhism, seeking to relate God's revelation to many Buddhist concepts. This was no 'proof text' approach and was not argumentative in style. He truly tried to understand Buddhist thinking and relate to sincere seekers wherever he could find them. outgoing and warm personality, he made friends with people in such a way as to draw them to Christ.[7]

Concluding reflections

Can we generalize from the many experiences of God's servants as they have sought for more than a thousand years to carry his message to the Buddhists in China? Let us look at the more obvious of these lessons in outline form.

1. *The message and messenger must be incarnate* in the receptor culture. This includes personal lifestyle, an attitude of empathy and sensitivity to people whose faith is as devout and sincere as their own, and an outgoing, friendly spirit that accepts people (although not all their belief systems) as they are.

2. In order to be incarnate, *witnesses must adopt the role of learner.* This does not mean necessarily that they earn advanced degrees in Western universities, although this is not precluded. Too many young, earnest missionaries are going to the field with only a smattering of what they need in terms of theology, philosophy, history, culture and sociology. A compulsive urgency

A Buddhist monk seeks alms.

International Mission Board

to meet some supposed deadline by which time the task must be completed can only put them into the loop of failure that has characterized most ministries to Buddhists in the past. Where are those who will follow in the train of the missionary scholar-evangelists from China's past Catholic and Protestant mission history?

3. Witnesses need to recognize that *God reached the land of their potential service long before they did!* They will seek out those in whose hearts Jesus the Eternal Logos has been showing his light. They do not begin from scratch. They follow up what God has been doing. This means that they need to identify with these 'seekers' to let them know that they, too, are spiritual and have the authority of Christ to lead them further in their pilgrimage. Western missionaries working among Buddhists, who have a mystical faith, must be men and women of faith—which goes far deeper than gadgets, technique, technology, money and supporting friends from the West who want a part in the action.

4. In limited-access areas of the Buddhist world among resistant people groups, *a unified witness, even among lone individuals from various mission groups, will have much more impact than that made by a number of isolated witnesses.* Such a unified approach will also make it possible to utilize the spiritual gifts of many people and thus provide a far wider range of services for the developing community. As the message and messenger are incarnate within the receptor culture, a *'people movement' to Christ becomes a real possibility.* Sometimes these people movements develop spontaneously—at other times the missionary may need to use specific methods that are unfamiliar and not part of his or her background or expectations.

5. The witness for Christ among Buddhists will include philosophical discussions as well as 'power encounters' with the demonic world. Where confrontation occurs it is not with people, but with ideas and attitudes.

6. If possible, the missionary needs to develop a team that includes non-Western converts from Buddhism. This will enable the white, Western missionary to stay in the background. The best witness, even that aimed at a people movement, will be personal 'people contact' and not merely 'points of contact'. The witness will need to be more visual and less verbal. Although political

A young man finds a quiet place to pray in a Buddhist cave.

stability is not under human control, mission organizations need to plan for a full range of Christian ministries to maintain contact with the people over the long term and not be satisfied with just a fleeting short-term outreach.

7. The witness must not despise Buddhism or the Buddha; it must not stereotype Buddhism, its leaders or its teachings; neither must it confuse assertions of the supremacy of Christ with one's own sense of superiority, assuming an absolute grasp of the truth or that one has all the answers. In the apt phrase of Daniel Niles, all witnesses to Christ are merely beggars telling other beggars where to find bread.

8. Finally, on a more positive note, the message is Christ—not Christianity, or a religion as such. This focus will deliver the witnesses from argumentation and from a religious debate or 'beauty contest' to determining whether Buddhism or Christianity is superior.

Notes

This article, which was originally published in the *International Journal of Frontier Missions* 10.3 (July 1993), was updated and revised for this publication.

1. For a detailed examination of this process, see Ralph Covell, *Confucius, the Buddha, and Christ* (Maryknoll: Orbis Books, 1986) 133–50.

2. Samuel Moffett, *A History of Christianity in Asia,* Volume I, *Beginnings to 1500* (San Francisco: HarperSanFrancisco, 1992) 311.

3. Jacques Gernet, *China and the Christian Impact: A Conflict of Cultures* (Cambridge: Cambridge University Press, 1982) 74–75.

4. The information on these initial Roman Catholic efforts in Tibet come from several sources: C Wesseks, SJ, *Early Jesuit Travelers in Central Asia 1603–1721* (The Hague: Martinus Nijhoff, 1924); M L'Abbe Huc, *Christianity in China, Tartary, and Thibet,* II (London: Longman, Brown, Green, Longmans, and Roberts, 1857) 249–71; and Fillipo de Fillipi, *An Account of Tibet: The Travels of Ippolito Desideri of Pistola, S.J. 1712–1727* (London: George Routledge and Sons, 1931).

5. For Catholic work in Tibet since 1850 several sources are useful: Adrian Launay, *Histoire Tibet; Les Missions Catholiques* (Paris: Propagation de la Foi et de Saint-Pierre Apôtre); Adrien Launay, *Memorial de la Société Missions-Estrangéres* (Paris: Annales de la Propagation de la Foi); various issues of Catholic Missions published by the Society for the Propagation of the Faith in New York, beginning in 1907; and Gaston Gratuze, *Un Pionnier de la Mission Tibetaine le Pére Auguste Desgodins 1826–1913* (Paris: Apostolat des Editions, 1968).

6. J Leyssen, *The Cross over China's Wall* (Peking: The Lazarist Press, 1941) 39.

7. To investigate Reichelt further see the following works: Eric J Sharpe, *Karl Ludvig Reichelt: Missionary, Scholar and Pilgrim* (Hong Kong: Tao Fong Shan Ecumenical Center, 1984); Hakan Eilert, *Boundless Studies in Karl Ludvig Reichelt's Missionary Thinking with Special Regard to Buddhist-Christian Encounter* (Uppsala, Sweden: Forlaget Aros, 1974); and Covell, *Confucius, the Buddha, and Christ,* 122–32.

Approximately 65 million Cantonese-speaking Chinese live scattered throughout dozens of nations in the world. The vast majority (about 62 million) live in southern China, including almost seven million in Hong Kong. The majority of Cantonese live in the south China province of Guangdong, radiating out from the capital city of Guangzhou (also known as Canton). Other significant communities are located in the southern part of Guangxi and on Hainan Island.

Although the Cantonese today proudly consider themselves part of the Han Chinese ethnic group, one ethno-historian has concluded, 'The ethnic origins of the ancient Yue [Cantonese] people . . . may have been Tai, but with a sizable Miao-Yao minority in the hills. . . . The ancient Yue language was definitely not Sinitic. It is estimated that the population of Guangdong was less than 30 percent Sinitic in 1080.'[1]

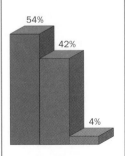

International Mission Board

The large southern city of Guangzhou—which has been continually inhabited for 2,200 years—has always been the centre of Cantonese civilization. In the 33rd year of the reign of Emperor Qin Shihuang (214 BC), the Nanhai Prefecture was established in today's Guangzhou. Large numbers of Han people flooded into the area.[2] Guangzhou became home to numerous foreign merchants in the 9th century until the Tang emperors lost control of it in AD 878. An Arab traveller reported that 'a hundred and twenty thousand Muslims, Jews, Christians and Zoroastrians were slaughtered [in Guangzhou]'.[3]

The dozens of Chinese language groups in China today are considered by linguists to be mutually unintelligible languages. They are not, as official Chinese sources claim, merely dialects of the same language. Cantonese contains up to nine tones—compared to the national language, Mandarin, which has only four. Although they speak different languages and dialects, all Chinese people in China use the same written script.

The Chinese have a saying that to be happy in this life one must be born in Suzhou, live in Guangzhou and die at Suzhou, 'for in the first are the handsomest people, in the second the richest luxuries, and in the third the best coffins'.[4]

Throughout the Communist era the Cantonese have continued to be the most openly religious of all Chinese. Most homes in Guangdong Province have spirit altars. The Cantonese also zealously observe Daoist and Buddhist festivals. Approximately 40 per cent of Cantonese people today profess to be Buddhists—the highest percentage of any Chinese language group.

In September 1807, Robert Morrison landed in Guangzhou. A new era of Protestant missions began in China. Seven years later he baptized his first convert, 'At a stream of water issuing from the foot of a lofty hill, far away from human observation. . . . May he be the first-fruits of a great harvest.'[5] Today there are at least two million Cantonese Christians in China, and another 500,000 living in nations around the world.

Status of Evangelization

- 54%
- 42%
- 4%

A = Have never heard the gospel
B = Have heard the gospel but have not become Christians
C = Are adherents to some form of Christianity

Overview of the Cantonese

Other Names: Yue, Yue Chinese, Yuet, Yuet Yue, Gwong Dung Waa, Cantonese, Yueh, Yueyu, Baihua, Punti, Guangdong Hua, Guangdong

Population Sources:

52,000,000 in China (2000, B Grimes [1984 figure])

748,010 in Malaysia

500,000 in Vietnam

400,000 in Canada

314,000 in Singapore

180,000 in Indonesia

180,000 in USA[6]

Language: Sino-Tibetan, Chinese

Dialects: 7 (Yuehai, Yongxun, Gaoyang, Siyi, Goulu, Wuhua, Qinlian)

Professing Buddhists: 40%

Practising Buddhists: 20%

Christians: 4.0%

Scripture: Bible 1894; New Testament 1877; Portions 1862

Jesus film: available

Gospel Recordings: Cantonese, Toi Shaan

Christian Broadcasting: available

ROPAL code: YUH

CHINA

Guangxi · Guangdong · Hong Kong · VIETNAM · Hainan

Han Chinese Cantonese

Population:
62,123,700 (2000)
68,156,500 (2010)
74,801,500 (2020)

Countries: China, Malaysia, Vietnam, Canada, Singapore, Indonesia, USA, Thailand, New Zealand, Philippines, Costa Rica, Brunei, Nauru, Laos, Panama, Australia, Netherlands, United Kingdom, Honduras, Mauritius, South Africa and many other nations

Buddhism: Mahayana

Christians: 2,500,000

Han Chinese, Gan

Han Chinese Gan

Population:
36,554,000 (2000)
41,306,000 (2010)
45,147,500 (2020)
Countries: China, and many other nations around the world
Buddhism: Mahayana
Christians: 1,500,000

Overview of the Gan Chinese

Other Names: Gan, Kan
Population Sources:
31,270,000 in China (1987, *Language Atlas of China*)
also in many other nations around the world
Language: Sino-Tibetan, Chinese
Dialects: 9 (Changjing, Yiliu, Jicha, Fuguang, Yangyi, Datong, Leizi, Dongsui, Huaiyue)
Professing Buddhists: 25%
Practising Buddhists: 10%
Christians: 4.1%
Scripture: Chinese Bible
***Jesus* film:** available
Gospel Recordings: none
Christian Broadcasting: none
ROPAL code: KNN

Status of Evangelization

63%

32%

5%

A   B   C

A = Have never heard the gospel
B = Have heard the gospel but have not become Christians
C = Are adherents to some form of Christianity

More than 38 million speakers of the Gan Chinese language live in central China's Jiangxi Province and the south-eastern corner of Hubei Province, including Dachi, Xianning, Jiayu and Chongyang counties. The Gan account for approximately 3 per cent of all Chinese in China. The greatest concentrations live along the Fuhe River, the lower reaches of the Gan River and around Poyang Lake. Jiangxi has been described as 'an amphitheater of mountains and valleys, one-fifth larger than England and Wales, draining into a central lake'.[1] Small numbers of Gan speakers also live in eastern and south-western Hunan, southern Anhui and the north-western part of Fujian Province. Tens of thousands of Gan-speaking Chinese have migrated out of China to many nations around the world, but no statistics exist of their dispersion.

Gan Chinese is a distinct language that differs from Mandarin and other Chinese languages. There are nine dialects of Gan Chinese. Almost all Gan are adequately bilingual in Mandarin, the national language that is used throughout China for education and in the media. One scholar states, 'The Gan people have considerably less sense of self-identity than many of the other subethnic groups within China. . . . The name comes from the literary term for the province, a word that is also the name of the [Jiangxi] province's primary river. . . . Only the people of the northernmost and southernmost parts of Jiangxi Province speak any form of Chinese other than

International Mission Board

Gan.'[2]

Jiangxi, where most Gan live, was incorporated into the Chinese empire at an early date but remained sparsely populated until the 8th century. The abundance of silver found in the province is one of the reasons for the influx of immigrants. Extensive mining caused the formation of a wealthy ruling class. Today, Jiangxi is one of the most densely populated provinces in China.

Although the majority of Gan are nonreligious, there has been a revival of Buddhism and Daoism since the relaxing of restrictions on religion in the 1980s. Zhuangzi (369–286 BC) was an early leader of Daoism. His writings introduced the idea of the unity of opposites, *ying* and *yang*, widely used in Mahayana Buddhism to this day. This led to the notion of accepting life without struggle. Approximately 25 per cent of Gan Chinese profess to be Buddhists, although only about one out of ten people (primarily the elderly) participate in Buddhist rituals and ceremonies.

In 1900 the diabolical Boxer Rebellion broke out across China. Thirty thousand Chinese Catholics and 2,000 Protestants were massacred,[3] as anti-foreign and anti-Christian feelings ran rampant. The number of Christians in China more than doubled in the six years following the massacres. In 1901, one missionary in Jiangxi reported 20,000 converts.[4] There are an estimated 1.5 million Christians among the Gan Chinese today, consisting of about 700,000 house church Protestants, 400,000 government-sanctioned church members and 400,000 Catholics. The *Jesus* film has recently been translated into the Gan language.

More than five million Hainanese Chinese are concentrated in the north-eastern parts of China's Hainan ('South Sea') Island. They are located along the coast, from the north-east all the way to the west of the island. Smaller numbers of Hainanese live outside China in Singapore (90,000), Malaysia (7,200) and Thailand (6,700). Unspecified numbers live in Vietnam and Laos.

The Hainanese language (which is also called *Qiongwen*) is widely spoken throughout 14 counties and cities of Hainan. Most Hainanese are bilingual in Mandarin, while many can also speak Cantonese. Hainanese is related to the Min Nan Chinese language of Fujian Province in south-east China. Over the centuries, however, Hainanese 'has evolved in unusual directions and is not at all readily understood by other Min Nan peoples. The early Min Nan peoples who migrated to Hainan could not maintain their family and trade ties with the Min Nan core area [in Fujian Province].'[1]

Considered as part of the Han nationality, the Hainanese are descended from Chinese who migrated from Fujian at various times over the last 15 centuries. Tribal peoples were the main occupants in Hainan for much of its history. The arrival of large numbers of Chinese resulted in conflict as the Chinese forced the tribes off their land and into the desolate mountains. By the time of the Tang Dynasty (AD 618–907), Hainan had a reputation as a place of banishment. Exiled Chinese politician Li Deyi even described it as 'the gate to hell'.[2] By contrast, Hainan is promoted today as a tropical paradise.

Most Hainanese families earn their livelihood from fishing or agriculture. Severe and sudden storms lash the Hainan coastline every summer, causing massive damage to homes and boats. New industry and factories have sprung up on Hainan in the last decade. Significant numbers of Hainanese are employed in the expanding tourist industry, which has catered to a growing number of Chinese and foreign tourists since the early 1980s.

Severe persecution of all religious activity during the Cultural Revolution caused the demise of Buddhism, which was popular on Hainan. Most of the current generation of Hainanese youth are nonreligious, although Buddhism still enjoys significant patronage from many elderly Hainanese.

The first mention of Christianity on Hainan was in 1630 when Jesuit priests came from Macau and constructed a chapel in Fucheng Township.[3] The first Protestant missionary on the island was Carl Jeremiassen, a Danish sea captain who was employed by the Qing government 'to hunt down pirates and smugglers'. Jeremiassen, however, 'changed his mind and his profession upon reaching Hainan in 1881 . . . distributing Bibles with one hand and dispensing medicines with the other.'[4] In 1992 there were at least 37,000 Protestants[5] and 3,000 Catholics[6] on Hainan Island, most of them Hainanese Chinese. In the years since then, tremendous revival has affected many parts of the island as several house church networks from mainland China have focused on Hainan. One trustworthy source counted 360,000 house church believers on Hainan Island in 2000, most of them Hainanese-speaking Chinese.

International Mission Board

Population:
5,247,500 (2000)
5,931,200 (2010)
6,489,000 (2020)
Countries: China, Singapore, Thailand, Malaysia, Vietnam, Laos
Buddhism: Mahayana
Christians: 300,000

Overview of the Hainanese

Other Names: Chinese Qiongwen, Qiongwen, Hainan Chinese, Hainanese

Population Sources:

4,400,000 in China (1987, *Language Atlas of China*)

74,000 in Singapore (2000, B Grimes [1985 figure])

5,880 in Thailand (2000, B Grimes [1984 figure]

5,083 in Malaysia (1980 census) Also in Vietnam and Laos

Language: Sino-Tibetan, Chinese

Dialects: 5 (Fucheng, Wenchang, Wanning, Yaxian, Changgan)

Professing Buddhists: 20%

Practising Buddhists: 10%

Christians: 5.7%

Scripture: none

***Jesus* film:** none

Gospel Recordings: Hainanese, Chinese: Min Nan Hainan

Christian Broadcasting: available

ROPAL code: CFR04

Status of Evangelization

42% A
52% B
6% C

A = Have never heard the gospel
B = Have heard the gospel but have not become Christians
C = Are adherents to some form of Christianity

A 1987 study listed 3.12 million speakers of the Huizhou Chinese language living in eastern China.[1] The majority are located in the southern part of Anhui Province—in an area previously known as Huizhou Prefecture—on the banks of the Xi'nan River. Since 1912, the city of Huizhou has been known as Shexian. In addition, 800,000 Huizhou live in the northern part of Jiangxi Province, especially in Wuyuan, Yuanling and Dexing counties. Small numbers also live in Chun'an County of Zhejiang Province. The Huizhou region was badly hit by the Taiping Rebellion (1851–64) and lost as much as half of its population.[2]

One linguist believes that the Huizhou Chinese should be treated 'as a separate sublanguage and its speakers as a distinct entity within the mosaic of Sinitic peoples'.[3] Huizhou is unintelligible with other Chinese languages. It is spoken in a widespread geographical area of 25,000 square kilometres (9,750 sq. mi.). Its five dialects reportedly 'differ greatly from each other'.[4] The Huizhou use standard Chinese characters like other Han people, but their spoken language is so different from Beijing Mandarin that 'many common spoken words have no written character with which they can be associated'.[5]

The Huizhou have a reputation as expert merchants and businessmen. A Chinese saying says: 'No marketplace is so small there are no Huizhou people.' By the 16th century, Huizhou merchants 'began to assume a major role in the entire national economy [and] soon came to control much of the nation's rice, lumber, and tea trade'.[6] Some early Christian missionaries called them the Jews of China, 'evidently impressed by their role in money-lending

and pawn-brokerage and their strong ties to family and clan—even when widely scattered in the pursuit of business opportunity'.[7]

This incredibly strong sense of identity has allowed the Huizhou Chinese to exist as a distinct group to this day. Leo Moser explains, 'The Huizhou man was not a loner; when alone in a distant city, he worked and thought as a clan member. The extended family and related [Huizhou]-based organizations had financed him. They would rescue him if he was bankrupt or ill. If successful, he was welcomed home a hero. ... This process filled Huizhou with magnificent houses, ancestral temples, and artistic gardens.'[8]

Mahayana Buddhism was formerly strong in Huizhou, but over the last fifty years of Communist rule its influence has waned among the population. During the Cultural Revolution (1966–76), hundreds of Buddhist temples and monasteries were destroyed and thousands of monks sent to prison or forced to leave their religious order. Today, most professing Huizhou Buddhists are elderly people. In the past decade many Buddhists have become Christians. Several former monks are now leaders of the house church in southern Anhui.

Since 1949, Christianity has boomed in the region where the Huizhou live. There are an estimated 250,000 Huizhou believers. The three provinces where Huizhou is spoken contain some of the highest concentrations of Christians in China.

Han Chinese Huizhou

Population:
3,647,300 (2000)
4,121,400 (2010)
4,504,700 (2020)
Countries: China
Buddhism: Mahayana
Christians: 250,000

Overview of the Huizhou Chinese

Other Names: Chinese: Hui, Wannan, Huichou, Hweichow, Huizhou

Population Sources:
3,120,000 in China (1987, *Language Atlas of China*)

Language: Sino-Tibetan, Chinese

Dialects: 5 (Jixi [850,000], Xiuyi [750,000], Qide [700,000], Yanzhou [700,000], Jingzhou [200,000])

Professing Buddhists: 20%

Practising Buddhists: 10%

Christians: 7%

Scripture: Chinese Bible

Jesus **film:** none

Gospel Recordings: Chinese: Huizhou

Christian Broadcasting: none

ROPAL code: CZH

The Voice of the Martyrs

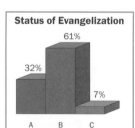

Status of Evangelization

61%

32%

7%

A   B   C

A = Have never heard the gospel
B = Have heard the gospel but have not become Christians
C = Are adherents to some form of Christianity

Han Chinese Jin

Population:
53,423,000 (2000)
60,368,000 (2010)
65,982,000 (2020)
Countries: China
Buddhism: Mahayana
Christians: 2,000,000

Overview of the Jin Chinese

Other Names: Jin, Jinyu
Population Sources:
45,700,000 in China (1987, *Language Atlas of China*)
Language: Sino-Tibetan, Chinese
Dialects: 10 (Bingzhou, Fenzhou, Xingxi, Shandong, Wutai, Dabao, Zhanghu, Cizhang, Huoji, Zhiyan)
Professing Buddhists: 20%
Practising Buddhists: 10%
Christians: 3.7%
Scripture: Chinese Bible
***Jesus* film:** none
Gospel Recordings: none
Christian Broadcasting: none
ROPAL code: CJY

Status of Evangelization

61%

35%

4%

A   B   C
A = Have never heard the gospel
B = Have heard the gospel but have not become Christians
C = Are adherents to some form of Christianity

More than 55 million speakers of the Jin Chinese language, called *Jinyu*, inhabit parts of five provinces in northern China: Shanxi (22.3 million speakers in the year 2000), Hebei (10.6 million), areas north of the Yellow River in Henan (9.4 million), Inner Mongolia (8.2 million), and the northern part of Shaanxi (3.2 million). Jin is spoken in a total of 175 cities and counties throughout northern China.[1]

The province of Shanxi, with its capital at Taiyuan, was the location for one of the most gruesome incidents in Christian history, when thousands of Chinese Christians and almost 200 foreign missionaries were massacred during the Boxer Rebellion in the summer of 1900. Approximately two-thirds of the total population of Shanxi Province are Jin-speaking Chinese.

These days, most visitors find Shanxi people to be friendly and good-natured. One scholar says, 'The people of Shanxi are generally expected to be conservative, simple and thrifty. The man from Shanxi . . . is often the butt of Chinese jokes, taking a role somewhat like that of the Scotsman in the humor of English-speaking peoples. Although the people of Shanxi do have a reputation for being hard-working and good at business, they are also expected to be honest and straightforward in their dealings.'[2]

The Jin language was formerly considered part of the *Xibei Guanhua* dialect of Mandarin, but many scholars now consider Jin a distinct language. Some have even found the Jin language to be similar to Hakka Chinese, now spoken throughout south China. With all education and media in China using standard Mandarin, the Jin language—which contains ten dialects—is confined more and more to home and social use.

The majority of Jin Chinese are atheists. About 20 per cent of people living in the Jin area view themselves as Buddhists, but less than half of that number actually practise their religion. The Jin warrant inclusion in this book, however, because even at 20 per cent the total number of professing Buddhists among the Jin is 12 million people.

Today, there are an estimated two million Jin Chinese Christians. Hebei—where more than 10 million Jin speakers live—is the strongest Catholic region in China with more than 800,000 Catholic church members.[3] Shanxi, Shaanxi, northern Henan and Inner Mongolia have also been experiencing church growth in recent years, as zealous house church evangelists travel all across the breadth of China in search of lost souls to lead to the Master. God has honoured the sacrifice of his servants in 1900, and in numerous locations where Christians were murdered the church today is strong and vibrant. Despite these encouraging events, the majority of Jin Chinese have still to hear the gospel for the first time. The region is densely populated, and the sheer number of people requires a large-scale systematic evangelistic plan in order to make a significant impact among this large group.

International Mission Board

Han Chinese, Mandarin

The Han Chinese are the largest ethnic group on earth, and Mandarin is the world's most widely spoken language. More than 850 million Chinese worldwide speak Mandarin—known as *Putonghua*, meaning 'the common speech'—as their mother tongue. Mandarin-speaking Chinese are found all over China but are mostly concentrated in the northern and eastern provinces. Beijing is the unofficial 'home' of Mandarin, and the Beijing dialect is the standard used in media and education. More than 60 million Mandarin speakers are also found scattered throughout the world, probably in every country on the face of the globe.[1] The name 'China' stems from the Qin (Chin) Dynasty of 221–207 BC. The Chinese call their country *Zhongguo*, 'The Middle Kingdom'.

International Mission Board

There is remarkable linguistic uniformity among Mandarin speakers. Chinese from diverse places such as Urumqi in the north-west, Harbin in the north-east, and Kunming in the south-west—thousands of miles apart—are able to understand each other without too much difficulty.

The Chinese have been most influenced by Mahayana Buddhism, Daoism and Confucianism throughout their history, but since the advent of Communism in 1949 most Mandarin-speaking Chinese inside China could be accurately described as nonreligious. Ralph Covell says, 'The Buddhist faith probably entered China a century or two before the Christian era, but it did not root itself deeply or spread widely until about AD 150. Its greatest growth came after the fall of the later Han dynasty (AD 25–200) and reached its ascendancy and glory during the Tang Dynasty (AD 618–907). Ultimately, Buddhism became very popular both among the masses and the official gentry classes and was accepted as an indigenous Chinese faith.'[2]

Christianity first made an impact on China in AD 635, when Nestorian Bishop Alopen arrived in China. The emperor declared, 'Bishop Alopen of the Kingdom of Ta'chin, bringing with him the *sutras* and images, has come from afar and presented them at our Capital. Having carefully examined the scope of his teaching, we find it to be mysteriously spiritual, and of silent operation. Having observed its principal and most essential points, we reached the conclusion that they cover all that is most important in life. . . . This Teaching is helpful to all creatures and beneficial to all men. So let it have free course throughout the Empire.'[3] By 638 the first church was built in Chang'an, and 21 Persian monks had commenced work in China.[4]

By the time missionaries were expelled from China in the 1950s, it is generally agreed that there were no more than 750,000 Chinese Protestants across the nation. Since that time, China has experienced one of the greatest revivals in church history, with some eastern provinces experiencing continual growth for more than 30 years. Despite these great developments, hundreds of millions of Han Chinese today have yet to hear the name of Christ. Estimates of the numbers of Christians in China today range widely. With the widest definition of Christianity, including all Protestants and Catholics, a worldwide Christian population of 75 million Mandarin-speaking Chinese is probable.

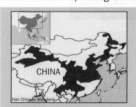

CHINA

Han Chinese Mandarin

Population:
838,512,200 (2000)
947,648,700 (2010)
1,038,672,800 (2020)
Countries: China, Taiwan, Indonesia, Thailand, Malaysia, Singapore, USA, Myanmar, Philippines, Vietnam, Canada, Australia, Cambodia, Japan, United Kingdom[5]
Buddhism: Mahayana
Christians: 75,000,000

Overview of the Mandarin Chinese

Other Names: Mandarin, Pei, Northern Chinese, Guoyu, Putonghua, Potinhua, Beijinghua, Qotong, Hoton, Guanhua

Population Sources:
701,116,436 in China (1990 census)
21,796,000 in Taiwan
8,520,000 in Indonesia
6,447,000 in Thailand
5,650,000 in Malaysia
2,746,000 in Singapore
1,900,000 in the USA
1,596,000 in Myanmar
1,595,000 in the Philippines
1,120,000 in Vietnam[6]

Language: Sino-Tibetan, Chinese

Dialects: 62 (in 8 main dialect clusters)[7]

Professing Buddhists: 25%

Practising Buddhists: 10%

Christians: 8.9%

Scripture: Bible 1874; New Testament 1857; Portions 1864

***Jesus* film:** available

Gospel Recordings: Mandarin, Yunnanese, Chinese: Sichuan, Chinese: Zhangye, Chinese: Ningxia, Chinese: Thongxin, Chinese: Xining

Christian Broadcasting: available

ROPAL code: CHN

Status of Evangelization

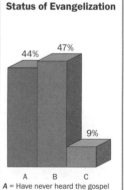

- A = Have never heard the gospel — 44%
- B = Have heard the gospel but have not become Christians — 47%
- C = Are adherents to some form of Christianity — 9%

A 1987 study listed a population of 2,191,000 Min Bei speakers in China.[1] Other publications have listed the much higher figure of 10.29 million Min Bei,[2] but this figure includes the Min Dong group who have been profiled separately in this book. The Min Bei live in eight cities and counties in the north-western part of Fujian Province. Smaller numbers of Min Bei Chinese live scattered throughout Southeast Asia in Singapore, Malaysia, Brunei and Indonesia, where they are commonly known as *Hokchiu*.

Min Bei is one of five distinct languages spoken by the Min Chinese in Fujian. Other scholars divide the Min into 'nine inherently unintelligible varieties'.[3] The Min Bei live both north and south of the Min River. Although most people live in the plains and valleys, there are also some extremely isolated and rugged mountains in this part of China. In 1929, Arthur Sowerby went as far as to say, 'In spite of its comparatively dense population, Fukien [Fujian] is wild, inexpressibly wild, and over the greater part of the province the people live very close to the jungle.'[4] Regarding the variety of ethnic groups in Fujian, Sowerby declared, 'A traveler up the Min will soon realize that there are many types of people in this area, types as distinct as, let us say, the different races in Europe.'[5]

The Min Bei region was first incorporated into the Chinese empire during the Three Kingdoms Period (AD 220–264). However, the Min Bei region 'long remained a frontier zone occupied primarily by barbarian tribes,

peoples presumably similar to the She minority nationality still found in small numbers in the mountains of Fujian. . . . About 300 AD, the political situation in northern China had become very unstable. . . . As a consequence, many Han Chinese families decided to evacuate northern China and take refuge along the open frontier farther south, where the barbarians were more easily controlled. Many established themselves on the lower reaches of the Min River during this period.'[6]

The Min Bei Chinese have practised Mahayana Buddhism for more than one thousand years. Approximately 30 per cent of the population profess faith in Buddhism, although Daoism, ancestor worship, animism and Christianity also have a share on the religious scene.

When Marco Polo arrived in today's Fujian Province, he encountered many Christian communities along the coastal areas. The believers in Fuzhou asked Marco Polo's uncles for advice as to what they should do to gain freedom to worship. They told the Christians to contact the Nestorian Metropolitan in Beijing, 'Explain to him your state, that he may come to know you and you may be able freely to keep your religion and rule.'[7]

Portions of the Bible were first translated into Min Bei in 1852, followed soon after by the New Testament in 1856. The entire Bible was to prove difficult to finish, and it was not until almost half a century more has passed—in 1905—that the whole Bible was available in Min Bei.[8] The *Jesus* film is also available.

International Mission Board

Population:
2,574,300 (2000)
2,909,200 (2010)
3,194,700 (2020)
Countries: China, Singapore, Malaysia, Brunei, Indonesia
Buddhism: Mahayana
Christians: 150,000

Overview of the Min Bei

Other Names: Northern Min, Min Pei, Hokchia, Hockchew, Hokchiu

Population Sources:
2,191,000 in China (1987, *Language Atlas of China*)
11,000 in Singapore (2000, B Grimes [1984 figure])
Also in Malaysia, Brunei, Indonesia

Language: Sino-Tibetan, Chinese

Dialects: 0

Professing Buddhists: 30%

Practising Buddhists: 15%

Christians: 5.8%

Scripture: Bible 1905, New Testament 1856; Portions 1852

***Jesus* film:** available

Gospel Recordings: Chinese: Min Bei Hockchia

Christian Broadcasting: none

ROPAL code: MNP

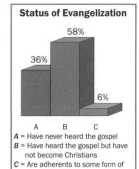

Status of Evangelization

58%

36%

6%

A   B   C

A = Have never heard the gospel
B = Have heard the gospel but have not become Christians
C = Are adherents to some form of Christianity

Han Chinese, Min Dong

More than nine million Chinese people living in eastern China's Fujian Province speak the Min Dong—or Eastern Min—language.[1] People who inhabit 19 cities and counties of Fujian, ranging from the town of Fu'an in the north-east to the large city of Fuzhou on the coast, speak this language. Min Dong speakers are also scattered throughout Southeast Asia. More than 200,000 have made their home in Malaysia, 30,000 in Singapore and at least 20,000 in Indonesia.

Min Dong is part of the Min group of languages that are distinct from Mandarin and other Chinese varieties. The different Min vernaculars 'seem to incorporate remnants of Sinitic offshoots that predate the Sui-Tang era [AD 589]. They may represent variations as old as the Han Dynasty itself—language forms set in place . . . during the Jin Dynasty [AD 265–420].'[2]

Fujian Province seems to have developed separately from the rest of China in many ways. One historian notes, 'Min is another name for Fujian Province. The territory has functioned in Chinese history almost as if it were an island. . . . The Min valley was late to come under Sinitic political control. Access by sea has been the key to its trade and other contacts with the outside world.'[3]

In the past, other Chinese people gave Fujian the nickname 'The province of a hundred dialects'. The complexity of the province has long frustrated the efforts of missionaries trying to learn its languages. J E Walker wrote this colourful commentary after an 1878 trip inland from Fuzhou: 'What a Babel of brogues, and dialects there is among those wild mountains! A

International Mission Board

native can hardly pass the limits of his own village but his speech will betray him. The tones are the most unstable element. . . . They seem utterly lawless. They shoot up to the sky, then plunge into the bowels of the earth, then stiffen straight out, they double up and twist about; they sing, cry, whine, groan, scold, plead; here, are musically plaintive; there, are gruff and overbearing.'[4]

Generally speaking, the Min Dong have proven more receptive to Christianity than Chinese in other parts of China. As early as the 13th century, Marco Polo came across a large body of believers in 'Fugiu' [now Fuzhou City]. 'They had books . . . found to be the words of the Psalter. . . . And thus they had in a certain temple of theirs three figures painted, who had been three apostles of the seventy who had gone preaching throughout the world, and they said that those had taught their ancestors in that religion long ago, and that that faith had already been preserved among them for seven hundred years, but for a long time they had been without teaching and so were ignorant of the chief things.'[5]

Missionaries have worked among the Min Dong for more than 160 years. They translated Scripture portions into Min Dong in 1852, followed by the New Testament in 1856 and the entire Bible in 1884. Today there are at least 500,000 Min Dong believers in China, including more than 100,000 in Fuqing County alone.[6] An additional 100,000 Min Dong-speaking Christians live in Southeast Asia.

Population:
9,164,300 (2000)
10,379,100 (2010)
11,389,600 (2020)

Countries: China, Malaysia, Singapore, Indonesia, Brunei, Thailand

Buddhism: Mahayana

Christians: 600,000

Overview of the Min Dong

Other Names: Eastern Min, Min Dong

Population Sources:
7,526,000 in China (1987, *Language Atlas of China*)
206,013 in Malaysia (2000, B Grimes [1979 figure])
31,391 in Singapore (2000, B Grimes [1985 figure])
20,000 in Indonesia (1982, CCCOWE)
6,000 in Brunei (2000, B Grimes [1979 figure])
Also in Thailand

Language: Sino-Tibetan, Chinese

Dialects: 3 (Houguan, Funing, Manhua)

Professing Buddhists: 30%

Practising Buddhists: 15%

Christians: 6.5%

Scripture: Bible 1884; New Testament 1856; Portions 1852

Jesus film: none

Gospel Recordings: Chinese: Min Bei Fuzhou

Christian Broadcasting: none

ROPAL code: CDO

Status of Evangelization

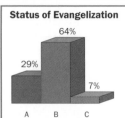

A = Have never heard the gospel
B = Have heard the gospel but have not become Christians
C = Are adherents to some form of Christianity

The Min Nan Chinese language—also called *Hokkien*—is spoken by more than 55 million people around the world. Approximately 33 million of these live along China's eastern and southern coasts. Most Min Nan speakers live in Fujian Province, where they inhabit 53 cities and counties. Others are located in Guangdong, Hong Kong, Zhejiang and Jiangxi.

The Min Nan people are renowned as a great seafaring people, and millions of them have migrated outside the People's Republic of China. Today more than 15 million live in Taiwan, 2.7 million in Malaysia, 1.6 million in Singapore, 1.2 million in Thailand, 880,000 in Indonesia, 820,000 in the Philippines and 15,000 in Brunei.

Julian Hawken

The Min Nan are the largest Chinese group in Taiwan, in Singapore and in the Philippines. Unknown numbers of Min Nan Chinese also live in Western nations around the world.

The Min Nan, or Southern Min, is the largest of the Min Chinese group. During the 10th century, the northern part of the Kingdom of Min in Fujian split off to form the Kingdom of Yin. The line between the Min Nan and Min Bei languages today very closely follows the border between those two kingdoms. Linguists have traditionally separated the Amoy and Shantou (previously *Swatow*) dialects as distinct languages. Hainanese is also related to Min Nan. Amoy and Taiwanese are easily intelligible with each other, while Shantou and Amoy 'have very difficult intelligibilty'.[1]

Christianity among the Min Nan Chinese has a long and distinguished history. A large Christian community existed in Zaitun (now Quanzhou City) in the early 1300s. A Franciscan cathedral was constructed from gifts received from an Armenian woman living in the city.[2] Bishop Andrew of Zaitun wrote in 1326, 'We are able to preach freely and unmolested. . . . Of idolaters a very large number are baptized, but having been baptized they do not walk straight in the path of Christianity.'[3]

The Chinese have historically treated Christianity with suspicion. In 1724, Emperor Yungcheng told Jesuit missionaries, 'You wish to make the Chinese Christians, and this is what your law demands, I know it very well. But what in that case would become of us? The subjects of your kings! The Christians whom you make recognize no authority but you; in times of trouble they listen to no other voice. I know well enough that there is nothing to fear at present; but when your ships shall be coming by thousands and tens of thousands, then, indeed, we may have some disturbances.'[4]

There are approximately three million Min Nan believers worldwide today. Around 1.2 million of these are in China, with significant Christian communities among the Min Nan in all other countries where they reside. Missionaries first translated Scripture portions into Min Nan in 1875, followed by the New Testament in 1896. The full Bible was completed in 1933. Fifty thousand hymnals were printed and distributed for the Min Nan inside China in 1986, using the characteristic Amoy script.[5]

Population:
54,416,800 (2000)
60,939,500 (2010)
66,977,200 (2020)

Countries: China, Taiwan, Malaysia, Singapore, Thailand, Indonesia, Philippines, Brunei, USA, United Kingdom

Buddhism: Mahayana

Christians: 3,000,000

Overview of the Min Nan

Other Names: Min Nan, Southern Min, Amoy, Hokkien, Hoklo, Teochew

Population Sources:

25,725,000 in China (2000, B Grimes [1984 figure])
15,000,000 in Taiwan (1997, A Chang)
1,946,698 in Malaysia (1980 census)
1,482,000 in Singapore (2000, B Grimes [1993 figure])
1,081,920 in Thailand (2000, B Grimes [1984 figure])
700,000 in Indonesia (1982, CCCOWE)
493,500 to 592,200 in the Philippines (1982, CCCOWE)
10,000 in Brunei (2000, B Grimes [1979 figure])

Also in USA, United Kingdom

Language: Sino-Tibetan, Chinese

Dialects: 8 (Fujian, Chaoshan, Hainanese, Zhejiang, Pingyang, Yuhuan, Tongtou, Taishun)

Professing Buddhists: 30%

Practising Buddhists: 15%

Christians: 5.5%

Scripture: Bible 1933; New Testament 1896; Portions 1875

Jesus **film:** available

Gospel Recordings: Amoy, Chinese: Min Nan Teochew, Hokkien

Christian Broadcasting: available in Amoy and Shantou dialects

ROPAL code: CFR

Status of Evangelization

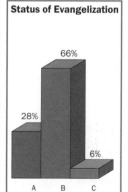

66%

28%

6%

A   B   C

A = Have never heard the gospel
B = Have heard the gospel but have not become Christians
C = Are adherents to some form of Christianity

Han Chinese, Pinghua

CHINA

Guangxi

VIETNAM

Han Chinese, Pinghua

Population:
2,338,000 (2000)
2,642,000 (2010)
2,887,700 (2020)
Countries: China
Buddhism: Mahayana
Christians: 10,000

Overview of the Pinghua Chinese

Other Names: Pinghua, Ping, Pinghwa, Penghua, Penhwa, Pengwa

Population Sources:
2,000,000 in China (1987, *Language Atlas of China*)

Language: Sino-Tibetan, Chinese

Dialects: 2 (Guibei, Guinan)

Professing Buddhists: 25%

Practising Buddhists: 10%

Christians: 0.4%

Scripture: none

Jesus **film:** none

Gospel Recordings: none

Christian Broadcasting: none

ROPAL code: none

Status of Evangelization

77%

22%

1%

A   B   C

A = Have never heard the gospel
B = Have heard the gospel but have not become Christians
C = Are adherents to some form of Christianity

More than 2.5 million speakers of Pinghua Chinese inhabit the Guangxi Zhuang Autonomous Region in southern China. They live primarily along the major traffic routes between Lingchuan (north of Guilin) and Nanning in the south, especially in towns along the railway line. 'A northern subgroup (Guibei) can be found extending from Guilin, through Yangshuo and Pingle, to Fuchuan, Zhongshan and Hexian.'[1] This part of China is spec-tacularly beautiful, with landscapes of karst rocks rising hundreds of metres into the air.

Although the Pinghua Chinese are counted as part of the Han nationality, their language is clearly distinct from all other varieties of Chinese. Pinghua is divided into two dialects: *Guibei* (Northern) and *Guinan* (Southern). These two dialects reportedly 'show significant disparities, though there are a few common features'.[2] The Northern dialect has five tones, while the Southern dialect has eight. One early visitor noted, 'The dialect that results from this mixture of races is called Pengwa [Pinghua]. A large proportion of the people . . . evidently do not speak Cantonese or Mandarin, or at any rate do not speak it freely.'[3]

The Chinese *Book of History* mentions that, at the dawn of Chinese history in the days of Yao and Shuen, around 2200 BC, a terrible inundation was recorded that had once desolated the land. 'In their vast extent the waters embrace the mountains and over-top the hills, threatening heaven with their floods.'[4] Chinese books today

Julian Hawken

have reduced these accounts to a bad flood of the Yellow River.

Buddhism is mixed together with animism, ancestor worship and Daoism to form a complex religious concoction among the Pinghua people. The region is wracked with superstition. It could be said that, when it comes to religion, the Pinghua use whatever works at any given time. If this means consulting a Buddhist monk to divine winning lottery ticket numbers, then they won't hesitate to do so. Although about a quarter of Pinghua Chinese profess Buddhism as their religion, few actually practise it. Most young people refuse to follow the ways of their parents and grandparents. At best they are reluctantly dragged along to observe religious rituals on holidays, but few among the younger generations enter into religion with any zeal.

Guangxi, which means 'vast west', has traditionally been one of the parts of China most neglected by missionaries. In the 1920s workers lamented that there were 'areas inhabited by [minority] tribes where no Christian worker would be familiar with the languages spoken and where the country has not as yet been explored'.[5] Before all foreign missionaries were expelled from China in the early 1950s, the Christian and Missionary Alliance had concentrated their efforts on Guangxi. They had a strategy to plant churches in every part of the province, but they were only able to partially achieve that goal before the Communists came to power.

Today, no more than one per cent of Guangxi's 45 million inhabitants claim to be Christians. The Pinghua Chinese have a small Christian remnant of only about 0.4 per cent of their population.

Approximately 2.8 million Puxian Chinese densely populate a relatively small area in eastern Fujian Province, China. The Puxian take their name from the nicknames of the two counties that they primarily inhabit: *Pu*tian and neighbouring *Xian*you. Xianyou is also under the jurisdiction of Putian City. The Puxian language is spoken in an oval valley about 55 kilometres (34 mi.) wide and 100 kilometres (62 mi.) long.

Scholar Leo Moser, who calls this group by the name *Xinghua*, says that they 'form a special community speaking a rather distinct dialect. In Southeast Asia, the Xinghua people are called the Hinghua and are distinguished sharply from [other Chinese language groups] . . . The city that is now Putian . . . was founded in 567 AD, during the Regimes of North and South, by Emperor Fei of the southern dynasty called Chen. The city of Xianyou, also a county seat, was evidently established in 699 AD, during the Tang Dynasty.'[1] Puxian people are often stereotyped by other Chinese as heroic and athletic people. Many of China's best track and field stars come from Putian.[2]

A Chinese proverb states that for 'every three *li* [about one mile], the dialect is different'. One linguist said, 'People separated by a blade of grass cannot understand each other.'[3] The linguistic diversity among the Chinese of Fujian Province probably exists because the original languages spoken there were non-Chinese minority languages. When the Han Chinese flooded into the province, they formed mixed communities with the original inhabitants. The complex language situation in Fujian today is probably a result of this complicated ethnolinguistic mixing. Most Chinese do not accept the differences between various Chinese languages as being great. For reasons of national pride and unity they downplay differences and claim that languages like Puxian are merely dialects or sub-dialects of Mandarin Chinese.

Marco Polo's description, from his visit to the province over 700 years ago, presents a picture of the peoples who inhabited Fujian. Polo wrote, 'The people in this part of the country are addicted to eating human flesh, esteeming it more delicate than any other. . . . When they advance to combat they throw loose their hair about their ears, and they paint their faces a bright blue colour. . . . They are a most savage race of men, inasmuch that when they slay their enemies in battle, they are anxious to drink their blood, and afterwards they devour their flesh.'[4]

Buddhism is generally on the decline among the Puxian Chinese, and mostly it is only the elderly who still hold to a Buddhist faith. About a quarter of Puxian still profess Buddhism, however, although the number of those who ever attend a temple or participate in Buddhist ceremonies is small.

Today approximately 120,000 (4.6%) of the Puxian Chinese are Christians—including more than 30,000 in Putian City alone,[5] and 90,000 in the whole of Putian County. One source states, 'Of the Christians, about 20,000 adhere to the traditions of the True Jesus Church, while about 2,000 count themselves as members of the Little Flock. The old church building in Putian County gets used well. There are three Sunday services, each of which fills the 1,400-seat church. . . . More than 100 Christian meeting points in Putian have not yet been registered.'[6]

Julian Hawken

Population:

2,633,700 (2000)
2,976,100 (2010)
3,252,900 (2020)

Countries: China, Singapore, Malaysia

Buddhism: Mahayana

Christians: 120,000

Overview of the Puxian Chinese

Other Names: Xinghua, Putian, Hinghua, Pu-Xian, Henghua, Hsinghua

Population Sources:

2,253,000 in China (1987, *Language Atlas of China*)
6,000 in Singapore (2000, B Grimes [1985 figure])
Also in Malaysia

Language: Sino-Tibetan, Chinese

Dialects: 2 (Putian, Xianyou)

Professing Buddhists: 25%

Practising Buddhists: 10%

Christians: 4.6%

Scripture: Bible 1912; New Testament 1900; Portions 1892

Jesus **film:** none

Gospel Recordings: Hing Hwa

Christian Broadcasting: none

ROPAL code: CPX

Status of Evangelization

- 39% — A
- 56% — B
- 5% — C

A = Have never heard the gospel
B = Have heard the gospel but have not become Christians
C = Are adherents to some form of Christianity

The 1987 *Language Atlas of China* listed 70.1 million speakers of the Wu Chinese language.[1] Wu is spoken over a widespread area (137,500 sq. km or 53,600 sq. mi.) in six provinces of eastern China. The majority are located in Zhejiang Province (43 million), southern Jiangsu Province (19.3 million) and the city of Shanghai (13.9 million). Smaller numbers are also located in Jiangxi, northern Fujian and southern Anhui provinces.

The Wu Chinese language is more commonly referred to as the Shanghai dialect, but in fact Wu is spoken in a far greater area than just Shanghai. Wu consists of 14 dialects, all of which are very different from Mandarin Chinese. Most Wu, however, are bilingual in Mandarin because it has been used in all media and education for the past 50 years.

Paul Hattaway

The history of the Wu-speaking people dates back to at least the 7th century BC. Leo Moser says, 'When the kingdom of Wu (also called Gou-wu) first appeared in Chinese annals . . . it was obviously a very foreign state to the Proto-Chinese. The language spoken by the people of Wu at that time was not what we would call a sub-language of Chinese. . . . It could have been a Sino-Tibetan language. . . . A widespread assumption is that it may have been related to the Tai languages.'[2] Over the centuries the Wu were influenced by other Chinese-speaking people groups from every direction, until today the Wu language is related to—though separate from—Mandarin Chinese.

The golden era of Wu culture came during the Southern Song Dynasty (1127–76), 'when the region formed the geographical core of what was surely the most highly cultured state in the world. The Wu-speaking peoples have thus left a major legacy for all human civilization. The Southern Song, with its capital at present-day Hangzhou, played a particularly important role in transmitting Buddhism and other cultural and artistic values to Japan.'[3]

Most Wu Chinese do not practise any religion, although in recent years there has been widespread interest in the magical practice of Qi Gong. Buddhism is the religion of millions of Wu people, especially those living in rural areas, although its influence is waning as the majority of young people are now atheists. Still, the Wu region is home to several famous Buddhist monasteries and centres.

There were Nestorian churches in the region between Nanjing and Shanghai as early as AD 1279. At one time the Nestorians had seven monasteries in and around the city of Zhenjiang,[4] now in Jiangsu Province. In the 1800s, almost all missionaries to China commenced their work in Shanghai, which was the first port of entry for foreigners. As a result, the region has one of the highest concentrations of Christians in all of China today. There are at least six million believers among the Wu, both government-sanctioned church members and illegal house church gatherings. A significant number of Catholics also live in this part of China. Shanghai is one of the strongest Catholic centres in China.

Population:
81,947,000 (2000)
92,600,000 (2010)
101,211,800 (2020)

Countries: China, USA, Canada, United Kingdom, Australia, France, Germany, Italy, New Zealand

Buddhism: Mahayana

Christians: 6,000,000

Overview of the Wu Chinese

Other Names: Wu, Shanghai Chinese, Shanghainese

Population Sources:
70,100,000 in China (1987, *Language Atlas of China*)
also in the USA, Canada, United Kingdom, Australia, France, Germany, Italy, New Zealand

Language: Sino-Tibetan, Chinese

Dialects: 14 (Piling, Suhujia, Tiaoxi, Hangzhou, Linshao, Yongjiang, Taizhou, Oujiang, Wuzhou, Chuzhou, Longqu, Tongjing, Taiguo, Shiling)

Professing Buddhists: 30%

Practising Buddhists: 8%

Christians: 7.3%

Scripture: Bible 1908; New Testament 1868; Portions 1847

Jesus film: available

Gospel Recordings: Chinese: Wu, Chinese: Shanghai

Christian Broadcasting: none

ROPAL code: WUU

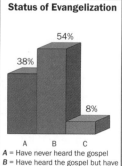

Status of Evangelization

A = 38%
B = 54%
C = 8%

A = Have never heard the gospel
B = Have heard the gospel but have not become Christians
C = Are adherents to some form of Christianity

Population:
36,064,000 (2000)
40,752,000 (2010)
44,541,900 (2020)

Countries: China, USA, Canada, Australia, United Kingdom

Buddhism: Mahayana

Christians: 400,000

Overview of the Xiang Chinese

Other Names: Hunanese, Hunan Chinese, Hsiang

Population Sources:

30,850,000 in China (1987, *Language Atlas of China*)

also in USA, Canada, Australia, United Kingdom

Language: Sino-Tibetan, Chinese

Dialects: 9 (Changsha, Changde, Xiangtan, Yiyang, Yueyang, Linxiang, Shaoyang, Yungshun, Shaungfeng)

Professing Buddhists: 30%

Practising Buddhists: 5%

Christians: 1.1%

Scripture: none

***Jesus* film:** available

Gospel Recordings: Chinese: Hunan Xiangtanghua

Christian Broadcasting: none

ROPAL code: HSN

Status of Evangelization

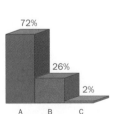

72%

26%

2%

A   B   C

A = Have never heard the gospel
B = Have heard the gospel but have not become Christians
C = Are adherents to some form of Christianity

Approximately 37 million speakers of Xiang Chinese—or Hunanese—live in China.[1] The majority are located in Hunan Province. Others inhabit 20 counties of eastern Sichuan and parts of northern Guangxi and northern Guangdong provinces. There are undoubtedly tens of thousands of Xiang Chinese living in countries around the world, but no record exists showing their dispersion or how many live in each nation.

The Xiang are traditionally acknowledged as the most stubborn and proud of all Chinese peoples. One 1900 report stated, 'The people themselves . . . are the most clannish and conservative to be found in the whole empire, and have succeeded in keeping their province practically free from invasion by foreigners and even foreign ideas.'[2] In 1911 the Xiang were described as 'the best haters and best fighters in China. Long after the rest of the empire was open to missionary activity, Hunan kept its gates firmly closed against the foreigner.'[3]

Xiang is a distinct Chinese language undergoing transition. It is exposed to Mandarin from several directions. Different Xiang dialects 'exist all along the Gan River drainage system in Jiangxi, although most of them are mutually intelligible, at least on a fundamental level. Ethnolinguists divide Xiang into two so-called dialect groups [Old Xiang and New Xiang] although the two are not readily understandable to one another.'[4]

Comparing Xiang with other Chinese languages, one scholar states, 'None of these so-called dialects is mutually intelligible with any other. The people who speak them may very well be united by their Han descent and their shared eclectic mix

of Buddhist, Daoist, and Confucian religious beliefs, but they cannot understand one another's spoken languages, which should render them members of different ethnic groups.'[5]

Recently there has been an upsurge in religious interest in Hunan, as people seek to fill the spiritual void in their hearts. 'A monastery in Hunan . . . has witnessed tens of thousands of pilgrims arriving to worship the three "gods" of Communist China—Chairman Mao, Zhou Enlai and Zhu De. This pilgrimage has set alarm bells ringing in the local government over the revival of superstition.'[6] About a third of Xiang Chinese profess to be Buddhists

International Mission Board

(especially elderly people), although the number of people who practise Buddhism is perhaps no more than one-twentieth of the population.

In 1861, the Welsh missionary Griffith John met a Hunan military mandarin, who 'boasted of the glory and martial courage of the Hunan men, and said there was no danger of their ever believing in Jesus or of His religion taking root there.'[7] The pride of the Xiang has made them the most unreached of all Han Chinese peoples. Today, only about one per cent—or 400,000—Xiang are Christians. Mandarin-speaking house-church Christians in China have struggled to penetrate the Xiang with the gospel because of linguistic and cultural barriers. Because of internal strife, the Hunan church has been described as a 'disaster area'.[8]

Han Tai

Approximately 60,000 Han Tai people inhabit the mountains of Mengyuan County in the Xishuangbanna Prefecture of China's Yunnan Province. 'The area contains 539 species of wild animals and birds, including elephants, wild oxen, tigers, leopards, bears, wild boar, gibbons and monkeys.'[1]

Although the Han Tai have never previously appeared in Christian research lists, they are a people group with their own customs, self-identity and language. While neighbouring Lu (Shui Tai) women wear long, colourful sarongs, and put their hair up in buns, 'Han Tai women wear black, hand-woven sarongs with a bright blue fitted blouse and black turban'.[2]

Over many generations, the Tai race slowly began to separate and form distinctive traditions and languages. They 'eventually evolved into two groups: the lowland farmers or *Shui Tai* and the mountain nomads, or *Han Tai*'.[3] The Han Tai speak their own distinct language. Most (except those living in more isolated villages) are also able to speak the regional Lu language, which serves as the lingua franca throughout the region. The Han Tai speak Lu to outsiders but continue to speak their own language in their villages.

In contrast to the dominant Lu, whose homes are built on stilts, the Han Tai build their homes flat on the ground, often in a long row of houses in which several families live. The Han Tai celebrate the annual *Songkran* festival. People splash water over each other, believing that it cleanses the sins of the past year. A Tai legend tells about a powerful fire-breathing demon who was defeated by Yidanhan, a beautiful Tai maiden. 'One night she made a special feast for the demon and got him drunk. . . . He told her that if someone was able to pull a hair from his head and wrap it around his neck, his head would fall off and he would die. Yidanhan did this, but the demon's head rolled away and set everything on fire. The Tai splashed water on the demon's head to quench the fire, and to wash the blood from Yidanhan's clothes.'[4]

The majority of Han Tai believe in Theravada Buddhism, mixed with spirit worship. During the Cultural Revolution, the Han Tai suffered much persecution. Cadres even dug up the skeleton of a revered Buddhist abbot and used his bones as fertilizer, in a bizarre bid to provoke the people and destroy their faith.[5] Pa Ya Shanmudi, the legendary Tai folk hero, laid down several commandments to ensure the survival of his people. One of these instructs each village to build a shrine, called a *zaixin*, as the symbolic heart of the community. 'It serves as a ritual center. . . . To destroy it or obstruct access to it would be the height of sacrilege.'[6]

An evangelist won a small number of Han Tai Christians who live in the Mengyuan area to Christ in recent years. In the 1960s, the fanatical Red Guards killed many of the Tai church leaders in Xishuangbanna.

Population:
55,500 (2000)
70,700 (2010)
87,100 (2020)
Countries: China
Buddhism: Theravada
Christians: 200

Julian Hawken

Overview of the Han Tai

Other Names: Han Dai, Dai: Han, Dry Land Dai, Mountain Dai

Population Sources:
50,000 (2000, P Hattaway [1996 figure])

Language: Tai-Kadai, Kam-Tai, Be-Tai, Tai-Sek, Tai, Southwestern, East Central, Northwest

Dialects: 0

Professing Buddhists: 80%

Practising Buddhists: 30%

Christians: 0.3%

Scripture: none

Jesus **film:** none

Gospel Recordings: Han Dai

Christian Broadcasting: none

ROPAL code: none

Status of Evangelization

76%
23%
1%

A   B   C

A = Have never heard the gospel
B = Have heard the gospel but have not become Christians
C = Are adherents to some form of Christianity

Children of the Buddhist World (2)

Birth rates in Buddhist countries are among the highest in the world. Hundreds of millions of children are growing up without any knowledge of the One who created them and loves them. Will you pray for the children of the Buddhist world?

1. Two Amdo friends at Choptcha, near Qinghai Lake in China. [Nancy Sturrock]
2. A fashionable young Chinese lady. [Julian Hawken]
3. Wrapped up for winter in China. [International Mission Board]
4. Mongolian girl skipping, Inner Mongolia in China. [International Mission Board]

5. Not happy. Amdo boy at Choptcha, near Qinghai Lake, China. [Nancy Sturrock]
6. Tuva boys from Kyzll in Tuva, Russia. [Nancy Sturrock]
7. Newar girl from Bakhtapur, Nepal. [International Mission Board]
8. Beautiful Khmer girl from Phnom Penh, Cambodia. [International Mission Board]

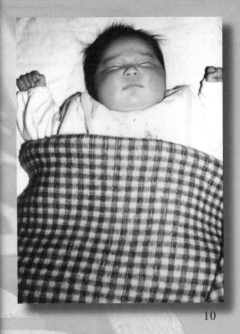

10

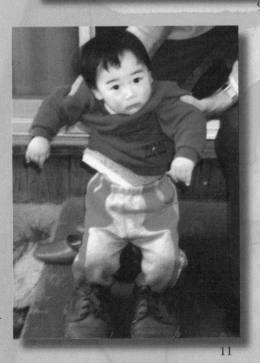

11

12

9. All dressed up: a Khampa girl at the Yushu horse fair in Qinghai Province, China. [Nancy Sturrock]
10. Warm and snug: a Japanese baby in Wakkanai, Hokkaido in Japan. [Paul Hattaway]
11. Following in his father's footsteps, Sapporro in Japan. [Paul Hattaway]
12. A 12-year-old Mon novice monk from Myanmar. [Create International]

13–14. Two little Chinese girls from Kunming in Yunnan Province, China. [both International Mission Board]

15. Lonely and confused: a Vietnamese boy who had lived his entire life in a refugee detention centre in Hong Kong. [Paul Hattaway]

16. All attitude: a Hakka boy from Taiwan. [International Mission Board]

17. A boy from the Sichuan Mongol group, Sichuan Province in China. [China Advocate]

Approximately 5,000 people comprise the Hdzanggur ethnic group in China. This little-known people inhabit a remote part of south-east Qinghai Province, primarily in the Ger Zhung Valley around the Radja (also spelt Ragya) Monastery, north-east of Dawu on the banks of the Yellow River. This area lies within Machen County in the Golog Tibetan Autonomous Prefecture. Hdzanggur territory starts at the banks of the Yellow River and extends for several days' journey by foot to the west. The Yellow River, which originates in the Kunlun mountains further to the west, is the sixth longest river in the world. By the time it empties into the Yellow Sea it has travelled 4,667 kilometres (2,900 mi.).

The Hdzanggur are one of the many sub-groups of Golog Tibetans. They have a reputation for being robbers and murderers. They are heavily armed and practically independent from Chinese rule. One of the first outsiders to visit the Hdzanggur was Joseph Rock in 1929. He wrote, 'I crossed over . . . to see what these almost unknown and wild people were like. Though very suspicious of us, they showed the greatest curiosity about our appearance and clothing. . . . They formed a circle about me, feeling my clothes. My pockets in particular amused them. . . . They followed me about, shaking their heads in bewilder-ment.'[1]

For centuries the Hdzanggur have been cut off from contact with the rest of the world. To this day, they are without telephones, electricity and a postal system. There are few roads in their region, and they practice crude forms of medicine, little changed for centuries: 'I did manage to photograph one wild fellow. . . . His abdomen was covered with straight scars, made when he had held burning rags against his body to cure his stomach ache. These scars were so evenly placed that they looked like tattoo marks. Others had scars on wrists and hands, marks of fiery ordeals to cure rheumatism.'[2] For longer than anyone can remember, the Hdzanggur have employed a unique method for crossing the Yellow River. It has not changed at all since Rock reported in 1929: 'Here a ferry of inflated goatskins supporting a raft of poles was in operation. These skins soon went flat. After each trip the Tibetans had to blow up each skin — excellent exercise for the lungs. As many as 12 people would ride on one of these flimsy rafts.'[3]

The Hdzanggur are fervent Tibetan Buddhists. They also worship a selection of fierce mountain deities, which they have incorporated into their Buddhist world-view. The Radja Monastery is the most influential in the area. Several Westerners are presently studying Tibetan Buddhism at this remote place. The Chinese authorities have strongly persecuted the Buddhist leaders of Radja over the years. Some have been imprisoned and tortured.[4] The local Communist officials have launched a 'love your country, love your religion' campaign in Radja Monastery. In 2003 it was reported, 'Every year, some thirty Chinese officials come to the monastery and stay for a month. During it the monks are made to study anti-Dalai Lama literature and write anti-Dalai Lama write-ups.'[5]

The gospel of Jesus Christ has never penetrated this geographically, politically and spiritually isolated part of the world. There has never been a known Hdzanggur believer.

Julian Hawken

Population:
4,370 (2000)
5,380 (2010)
5,880 (2020)
Countries: China
Buddhism: Tibetan
Christians: none known

Overview of the Hdzanggur
Other Names:
Population Sources:
4,370 in China (2000, P Hattaway)
Language: Sino-Tibetan, Tibeto-Burman, Bodic, Bodish, Tibetan, Northern Tibetan
Dialects: 0
Professing Buddhists: 100%
Practicing Buddhists: 70%
Christians: 0%
Scripture: none
Jesus film: none
Gospel Recordings: none
Christian Broadcasting: none
ROPAL code: none

Status of Evangelization
98%
2%
0%
A   B   C
A = Have never heard the gospel
B = Have heard the gospel but have not become Christians
C = Are adherents to some form of Christianity

Helambu Sherpa

Population:
14,700 (2000)
18,200 (2010)
22,500 (2020)
Countries: Nepal
Buddhism: Tibetan
Christians: 40

Overview of the Helambu Sherpa

Other Names: Helambu, Yohlmu Tam, Sharpa, Sharpa Bhotia, Xiaerba, Serwa, Xiarba

Population Sources:

14,700 in Nepal (1997, Bethany World Prayer Center [2000 figure])

5,000 to 10,000 in Nepal (2000, B Grimes [1998 figure])

Language: Sino-Tibetan, Tibeto-Burman, Himalayish, Tibeto-Kanauri, Tibetic, Tibetan, Central

Dialects: 2 (Eastern Helambu Sherpa, Western Helambu Sherpa)

Professing Buddhists: 99%

Practising Buddhists: 75%

Christians: 0.3%

Scripture: none

Jesus film: none

Gospel Recordings: Sherpa: Helambu

Christian Broadcasting: none

ROPAL code: SCP

Status of Evangelization

46% 53%

1%

A   B   C
A = Have never heard the gospel
B = Have heard the gospel but have
    not become Christians
C = Are adherents to some form of
    Christianity

Approximately 15,000 Helambu Sherpa people live in the Nuwakot and Sindhupalchok districts of the Bagmati Zone in central Nepal. A sizeable community of Helambu Sherpa also lives in the nation's capital, Kathmandu. Most Helambu Sherpa are farmers. Their main crops are potatoes and corn. They often take their produce to the market towns and use it to buy goods or barter for rice.

Despite their names, the Helambu Sherpa are not the same as the main Sherpa group in Nepal, Bhutan, China and India. The term *Sherpa* simply means 'easterners'. Helambu Sherpa is a Central Tibetan language, while Sherpa is a completely unrelated Southern Tibetan language. The two groups refuse to intermarry and have little to do with each other. The Helambu Sherpa 'are believed to have migrated from Tibet to Nepal around the 15th century. The Helambu Sherpa are often confused with the Solokumbu Sherpa because both groups are referred to only as "Sherpa". However, each group is totally distinct from the other, with different cultures and languages.'[1]

The Nepali government has combined the two Sherpa groups together in their official census figure, along with some other ethnic groups such as Khampa and some Tamang. This artificial combination produced an inflated figure of 110,358 Sherpa in the 1991 Nepal census.

Practically all Helambu Sherpa people, except for a few recent converts to Christianity, practise Tibetan Buddhism. One source states, 'The Helambu Sherpa

Nancy Sturrock

migrated from Tibet to Nepal in the 15th century in order to flee religious persecution. At that time, a Mongol king attempted to force them to convert to his sect of Buddhism. The people fled to the Khumbu region, and later moved further into the Helambu region.'[2] In the rural villages, the Helambu Sherpa 'observe all the Tibetan festivals and follow the religion of Tibetan Buddhism, but also put much faith in shamans (witch doctors). One of their festivals, called *Gyawa*, occurs 49 days after a person dies. They gather together and everyone eats as much as they can because they believe that all food eaten at the festival will go directly to the dead person for him or her to eat.'[3]

The gospel has made little impact on the Helambu Sherpa villages, but many of those living in the towns and in Kathmandu have heard the good news and a small number have decided to follow Christ. The new believers have encountered opposition from their fellow tribesmen, who view their belief in Christianity as a betrayal of their ancestors and culture. Gospel recordings are available in the Helambu Sherpa language. One mission agency in the late 1990s wrote, 'Many Helambu Sherpas are aware of Christianity and even know what the cross symbolizes. About half of them have heard the name of Jesus or received Christian literature and about 10% have even visited a church. They are highly protective however, of their religious and cultural identity and are likely to persecute new believers, or those interested in the gospel.'[4]

CHINA

Yunnan

MYANMAR

Population:
1,460 (2000)
1,890 (2010)
2,300 (2020)
Countries: China
Buddhism: Theravada
Christians: none known

Overview of the Hu

Other Names:

Population Sources:
1,000 in China (1984, J-O Svantesson)

Language: Austro-Asiatic, Mon-Khmer, Northern Mon-Khmer, Palaungic-Khmuic, Palaungic, Western Palaungic, Angkuic

Dialects: 0

Professing Buddhists: 60%

Practising Buddhists: 25%

Christians: 0%

Scripture: none

Jesus **film:** none

Gospel Recordings: none

Christian Broadcasting: none

ROPAL code: HUO

Status of Evangelization

89%

11%

0%

A   B   C

A = Have never heard the gospel
B = Have heard the gospel but have not become Christians
C = Are adherents to some form of Christianity

In 1984, linguist Jan-Olof Svantesson estimated that there were 1,000 speakers of the Hu language in south-west China.[1] They inhabit five villages in the Xiaomengyang District of Jinghong County in Xishuangbanna Prefecture of Yunnan Province.[2]

The Hu live near the Manmet people and are also surrounded by Lu and Bulang communities. The area inhabited by the Hu—the extreme south-west of China—is semi-tropical. It is warm and humid most of the year, while the rainy season inundates the crops between May and September every year.

The Hu are a distinct ethnolinguistic people group. Although their language is related to those of the Manmet and Angku who live in the same area, it does have significant differences. The Hu applied to be recognized as a separate minority in the 1950s, but the Chinese government rejected their application. The authorities then offered the Hu a chance to be included as part of one of the several minority groups in the area, which they, in turn, refused to accept. Consequently, in the 1982 Chinese census, the Hu were listed under the *Undetermined Minorities* category.

The tonal Hu language is part of the Angkuic branch of the Mon-Khmer language family. It appears that the Hu language is closely related to that of the Angku, who live in the same part of China. The Hu do not possess their own written script, but some

Myanmar Faces and Places

of the Hu village leaders can read Chinese.

Although little is known about the origins of the Hu, they were probably part of a larger collection of Mon-Khmer peoples in the region who later splintered to become groups like today's Wa, Palaung and Bulang. Lu and Chinese landowners oppressed the Hu until the Communist takeover of China in 1949. The land redistribution programmes of the 1950s ended their oppression. Because they have no official status, few people except those in their immediate neighbourhood know of the Hu's existence.

These days the Hu live in small, secluded communities. Their houses, 'constructed from bamboo, are elevated above the ground, and the area underneath is used for livestock. They are mountain farmers who use agricultural techniques consistent with different ecological settings. Some farmers still use thirteenth-century techniques of slash-and-burn, fertilizing land with ashes and using a stick to plant seeds. . . . Wheat, dry rice, maize, millet, and tubers are the most common crops.'[3]

Although on the surface the Hu claim to be Theravada Buddhists, their daily lives are much more influenced by animistic beliefs. They fear demons and believe all sickness and bad luck comes upon them as a result of upsetting the delicate balance between the natural and spiritual worlds.

The Hu are a people group untouched by the message of the gospel. Few have ever heard the name of Jesus Christ.

Huay

More than 500 members of the Huay tribe live in northern Thailand's Nan Province. They inhabit four main villages (Ban Nam Lieng, Ban Pang Hok, Ban Peen and Ban Huey Kohn) in Thung Chang District, not far from the Thailand-Laos border. About 40 years ago, the Huay moved away from the border area to their present settlements. They share their four villages with Thai and Lu people. Although they get along well with these groups, the Huay retain their own identity. One way they differ is that their women carry loads on their heads, in contrast to most other tribal people in Southeast Asia who carry their loads in baskets on their backs.

The Huay living in Ban Nam Lieng, Ban Pang Hok and Ban Huey Kohn villages all share the family name of Taukam, while the Huay of Ban Peen have the name Hoom Doog.

Xayographix

Little is known about the Huay people. They have never appeared on lists used by Christian organizations of people groups or languages, and so they have never been specifically targeted with the gospel. The ethnographer Joachim Schliesinger, in his 2000 book *Ethnic Groups of Thailand,* was the first to document the Huay as a distinct people group.[1]

Huay, the name this group calls itself, means 'forest stream'. The Thais call them *Kha Hor,* a term that the Huay consider derogatory. 'It is said that they were taken during the troubled times in the middle of the nineteenth century as slaves or war prisoners from Laos to Thailand. . . . Because of their ability to walk fast through jungles and mountainous areas, the Siamese authorities of that time used them as messengers. They walked so quickly that the Thai gave them the name *Kha Hor,* which means "flying slave".'[2]

The Huay used to speak a language from the Mon-Khmer family, related to the Khmu languages. Over the last few generations the Huay language has been spoken less and less, so that today most members of this small group speak Thai, with influences from Lao dialects, in their homes. Today more than 600,000 Khmu people live scattered throughout China and Southeast Asia, but most are either animists or Christians, whereas the Huay are Buddhists.

The Huay outwardly adhere to Buddhism, but they are also strongly influenced by their centuries-old animistic rituals. They have a spirit house located near the Buddhist shrine 'where they offer sacrifices of rice, flowers and, alternatively, chickens or a pig once a year during the Thai New Year (*Songkran*) festival. They do not have altars for ancestor worship nor do they practice any agricultural rituals. In former times, spirit gates were built on the approach to their villages, leading up from the valleys.'[3]

There are no known Christians among this tribal group. Foreign and Thai Christians are working in Nan Province, but they are not known to have taken the gospel to the four villages inhabited by the Huay people. The Huay remain a needy unreached people group.

Population:
520 (2000)
570 (2010)
620 (2020)
Countries: Thailand
Buddhism: Theravada
Christians: none known

Overview of the Huay

Other Names: Kha Hor, Kha Haw, Kha Hao, Kha Hawk

Population Sources: 500 in Thailand (2000, J Schliesinger [1995 figure])

Language: Austro-Asiatic, Mon-Khmer, Khmuic, Unclassified

Dialects: 0

Professing Buddhists: 85%

Practising Buddhists: 30%

Christians: 0%

Scripture: none

Jesus **film:** none

Gospel Recordings: none

Christian Broadcasting: none

ROPAL code: none

Status of Evangelization

86%

14%

0%

A   B   C

A = Have never heard the gospel
B = Have heard the gospel but have not become Christians
C = Are adherents to some form of Christianity

Fifty-five thousand Huayao Tai were reported in a 1990 official Chinese government survey. They live in stockaded villages in the foothills of the mountains in Xinping and Mengyang counties in the southern part of Yunnan Province. The Huayao Tai live in simple, flat-roofed adobe homes that are built on the ground, as opposed to the wooden homes of the neighbouring Lu that are built on stilts. Small numbers of Huayao Tai also live along the banks of the Honghe River in Yuanjiang County.[1]

The Huayao Tai are historically part of the great and ancient Tai race. One writer claimed that the Tai predate even the Chinese. 'Gathered from Chinese and Burmese annals, as well as from their own, this history shows them to be older than the Hebrews or the Chinese themselves, to say nothing of such moderns as the Slavs, the Teutons or the Gauls.'[2] Although the Huayao (Flowery Belted) Tai are a part of the officially constructed Dai nationality in China, they desire to be recognized as a separate minority group. Their language shares some similarities to Lu, but the two are reported to be mutually unintelligible.[3] It is possible that the Huayao Tai were a Tai group who originally lived in eastern Yunnan and migrated to their present location in the Xishuangbanna Prefecture. All

Huayao Tai are also able to speak Lu, which serves as the lingua franca of the region.

Many people mistakenly believe that the term *Huayao Tai* merely represents a social distinction within the Lu, but the Huayao Tai language and self-identity are strongly separate from those of all other groups.

Huayao Tai women are instantly recognizable because of their huge circular hats. They also carry small bamboo baskets containing needle and thread, cosmetics or food. The distinctive dress of the Huayao Tai differs from one area to another, 'by variations in their dress and the ornaments which they wear'.[4] One of the greatest festivals of the Huayao Tai calendar is the annual Flower Street festival.[5]

The Huayao Tai practise a mixture of Theravada Buddhism and animism. Buddhism is more prevalent in locations where the Huayao Tai have been influenced by their Lu neighbours, although few Huayao Tai villages have Buddhist temples. Shamans are also consulted on special occasions. They pray and chant to the tree god, asking for protection from floods and pestilence, and to be bestowed with good luck and prosperity for the coming year.[6]

A small number of Huayao Tai Christians live in Mengyang County. In recent years evangelists have been active among them, establishing several house churches. Few Huayao Tai outside of Mengyang have heard of Christ. The Huayao Tai believers use the Lu and Chinese Scriptures. Gospel recordings have recently been produced in the Huayao Tai language.

Paul Hattaway

Overview of the Huayao Tai

Other Names: Hwayao Dai, Flowery Belt Dai, Flowery Waist Dai, Color Belt Dai

Population Sources:
55,000 in China (1990, official Chinese government figure)

Language: Tai-Kadai, Kam-Tai, Be-Tai, Tai-Sek, Tai, Southwestern, East Central, Northwest

Dialects: 0

Professing Buddhists: 55%

Practising Buddhists: 25%

Christians: 0.2%

Scripture: none

Jesus **film:** none

Gospel Recordings: Hua Yao Dai, Hua Yao Gasa

Christian Broadcasting: none

ROPAL code: none

Population:
70,000 (2000)
89,200 (2010)
109,900 (2020)
Countries: China
Buddhism: Theravada
Christians: 200

Status of Evangelization

A = 71%
B = 28%
C = 1%

A = Have never heard the gospel
B = Have heard the gospel but have not become Christians
C = Are adherents to some form of Christianity

Intha

CHINA
Yunnan

MYANMAR
Shan State

THAILAND

Intha

Population:
170,800 (2000)
192,000 (2010)
215,800 (2020)

Countries: Myanmar
Buddhism: Theravada
Christians: 200

Overview of the Intha

Other Names: Inntha

Population Sources: 141,100
in Myanmar (2000, B Grimes
[1983 figure])

Language: Sino-Tibetan,
Tibeto-Burman, Lolo-Burmese,
Burmish, Southern

Dialects: 0

Professing Buddhists: 98%

Practising Buddhists: 90%

Christians: 0.1%

Scripture: none

Jesus film: none

Gospel Recordings: none

Christian Broadcasting: none

ROPAL code: INT

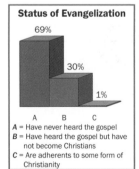

Status of Evangelization

69%

30%

1%

A   B   C

A = Have never heard the gospel
B = Have heard the gospel but have
    not become Christians
C = Are adherents to some form of
    Christianity

Approximately 170,000 Intha people live in south-west Shan State of Myanmar. The 1931 census in Burma (the most recent census held in this troubled land!) recorded 56,901 Intha people.[1] The Intha are one of the most famous ethnic groups of Southeast Asia. Their name means 'children of the lake', and most Intha can be found living in villages surrounding Lake Inle, near Taunggyi. The entire lake and surrounding area is within the Nyaungshwe township. There are 130,000 people from the Intha, Shan, Pa-O, Taungyo, Danau, Kayah and Burmese ethnic groups living in the township. Approximately 70,000 of them live directly around Lake Inle itself. The beautiful Inle Lake is 22 kilometres (13 mi.) long, and 11 kilometres (7 mi.) wide. It has 'very calm waters dotted with patches of floating vegetation and busy fishing canoes. High hills rim the lake on both sides; the lakeshore and lake islands bear 17 villages on stilts, mostly inhabited by the Intha people.'[2]

Linguistically the Intha language is closely related to Burmese. The *Ethnologue* states that it is 'one of the better known varieties of nonstandard Burmese with profound pronunciation and vocabulary differences from Burmese'.[3]

Scholars have long debated the origins of the Intha people, but most seem to agree on two or three main theories. One source says, 'Speaking a distinctive and unusual Burmese dialect, there is mystery over their origins in this area. Like the Pa-Os and Taungyos, it is thought that they arrived from Lower Burma many centuries ago. By one account, they are descendants of southern Burmans who migrated north during the reign of King Narapatisithu (1174–1210), although some scholars

Myanmar Faces and Places

believe they stem from slaves taken captive during on-and-off wars with the Mons and Tavoyans.'[4]

Another source states that the Intha originally came from Dawei in southern Myanmar, 'According to one story, two brothers from Dawei came to Nyaungshwe in 1359 to serve a [local ruler]. The latter was so pleased with the hard-working demeanour of the brothers that he asked them to invite 36 more families from Dawei; purportedly, all the Intha around Inle Lake are descended from these migrant families.'[5]

The Intha are famous for their highly unusual 'leg-rowing' technique. 'Fishermen wrap a paddle around one hand and leg and use this to propel the boat, while balancing precariously on the other. This position leaves them with one hand free, allowing them to drop a large conical net over passing fish in the shallow waters of the lake.'[6]

The Intha people are entrenched in their Buddhist beliefs. For centuries they have clung to their culture and religion, seeing little need for change. Around Lake Inle are at least 100 Buddhist temples and pagodas. Buddhism pervades every part of Intha life and culture, giving them their identity, security and traditions. Consequently, Christianity has failed to make any significant impact among the Intha people. Although there are a few scattered believers here and there, overall only one out of every 1,000 Intha people has put faith in Jesus Christ.

The Isan are the eighth largest Buddhist people group in the world, with a population exceeding 22 million. The overwhelming majority live throughout the provinces of north-east Thailand—a region known as Isan. A further 8,000 spill across the Mekong River into adjacent parts of Laos, while Isan migrant workers can also be found in Singapore, Malaysia and numerous Western nations.

It is difficult to classify and count the Isan, as their language is basically identical to Lao, and their culture and customs are also very similar. The subtle differences that distinguish the Lao from the Isan people are mostly social and historical.[1] The Isan are known as the Lao Isan or Tai Isan, while the most common designation used by the people themselves is *Khon Isan*, simply meaning 'Isan people'. Isan is a Sanskrit word. They 'are named after Phra Isuan, also called Phra Siwa or Shiva, the Hindu god of Destruction'.[2]

In Thailand the Isan are found in at least 17 different provinces, concentrated in the north-east. At least one million Isan live in Bangkok City, where they add their own colour, exotic food and culture to the mix of humanity in the sprawling metropolis. The 7,000 Isan on the Lao side of the border have made their homes in Vientiane City and neighbouring parts of Borikhamxai Province, and in areas of Champasak Province in southern Laos. Thousands of Isan have migrated overseas either as migrant workers or as refugees.

Despite pressure from the Thai government to make Central Thai the standard national language, 88 per cent of Isan people in Thailand continue to speak Isan at home, 1 per cent speak Central Thai exclusively, and 11 per cent use both.[3]

Almost all Isan claim to be Theravada Buddhists but, as one source states, the average Isan person is 'likely to be staunch Buddhist but he is unlikely to have any real understanding of Buddhist doctrine or to be concerned with the long and difficult task of subduing desire and craving. He sees his religion in a much simpler, pragmatic light. He will keep the Five Precepts—don't kill, steal, lie, drink alcohol, or commit adultery (almost certainly unsuccessfully)—and will believe that he should be tolerant, kindly, and generous to others. These attitudes will enable him to acquire a good balance of merit, leading he expects, to a better life.'[4]

Although there are now several hundred small churches among the Isan, Jesus Christ remains a little-known figure among this group. Culturally sensitive Christian radio ministry has proven effective in recent years, but follow-up is difficult because of the meagre human resources available and the vast, widespread area that the Isan inhabit. Just two out of every one thousand Isan people profess faith in Christ, although in recent years some small encouraging signs of growth have appeared, giving hope that this large, precious people group will soon have larger numbers of Christians among them.

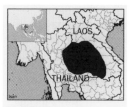

Overview of the Isan

Other Names: Tai Isan, Thai Isan, Lao Isan, Isaan, Northeastern Thai

Population Sources: 20,876,200 in Thailand (1995 census)[5]

7,000 in Laos (1995, Asian Minorities Outreach)

also in Singapore, Malaysia, USA, Canada, United Kingdom, Australia, and many other nations of the world

Language: Tai-Kadai, Kam-Tai, Be-Tai, Tai-Sek, Tai, Southwestern, East Central, Lao-Phutai

Population:
21,854,800 (2000)
23,888,700 (2010)
26,112,000 (2020)

Countries: Thailand, Laos, Singapore, Malaysia, USA, Canada, United Kingdom, Australia, and many other nations

Buddhism: Theravada

Christians: 50,000

Dialects: 3 (North Isan, Central Isan, Southern Isan)

Professing Buddhists: 95%

Practising Buddhists: 80%

Christians: 0.2%

Scripture: Bible 1932; new translation in progress

Jesus **film:** available (Lao)

Gospel Recordings: Lao, Northern Lao

Christian Broadcasting: available

ROPAL code: TTS

Status of Evangelization

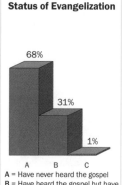

A = Have never heard the gospel
B = Have heard the gospel but have not become Christians
C = Are adherents to some form of Christianity

JAPAN

Japanese

Population:
127,820,200 (2000)
130,779,800 (2010)
133,863,100 (2020)

Countries: Japan, Brazil, USA, Peru, United Kingdom, Mexico, Argentina, Australia, Singapore, Bolivia, Paraguay, Taiwan, Micronesia, Guam, Dominican Republic, Panama, American Samoa, Belize, Canada, Germany, Mongolia, New Zealand, Northern Mariana Islands, Palau, Philippines, China and dozens of other countries around the world

Buddhism: Mahayana

Christians: 2,000,000

Overview of the Japanese

Other Names: Nihonjin

Population Sources:

124,940,200 in Japan (2001, P Johnstone and J Mandryk [2000 figure])
1,400,000 in Brazil
1,200,000 in the USA
120,000 in Peru
55,000 in the United Kingdom
43,000 in Mexico
32,000 in Argentina
30,000 in Australia[1]

Language: Japanese

Dialects: 2 (Western Japanese, Eastern Japanese)

Professing Buddhists: 70%

Practising Buddhists: 20%

Christians: 1.5%

Scripture: Bible 1883; New Testament 1879; Portions 1837

Jesus film: available

Gospel Recordings: Japanese

Christian Broadcasting: available

ROPAL code: JPN

Status of Evangelization

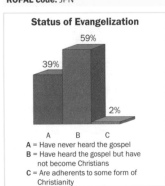

A = Have never heard the gospel
B = Have heard the gospel but have not become Christians
C = Are adherents to some form of Christianity

There are approximately 130 million Japanese people living in dozens of countries around the world. About 125 million of them live in Japan, while other significant Japanese communities are found in Brazil (1.4 million) and the United States (1.2 million). The Japanese are the second largest Buddhist people group in the world, ranking only behind the Mandarin-speaking Chinese.

The long and rich history of the Japanese dates back at least to 1500 BC, when the progenitors of the Japanese are believed to have arrived from mainland north-east Asia. It was not until AD 300 that the Yamato emperors unified the Japanese nation for the first time. Mahayana Buddhism first entered Japan in the mid-6th century, via China and Korea. Prince Shotoku (573–620) instituted Buddhism as the state religion. To this day, the Japanese admire traditional animistic Shintoism. Most Japanese people claim to be both Buddhists and Shintoists. They observe festivals and rituals for both religions, not seeing any contradiction between the two ancient ways.[2]

As a result of the *hakkio-ichiu* (the whole world under one roof) policy, the Japanese military believed they could become the dominant force in the world in the 1940s. Thinking they were invincible because they were led by the emperor—whom they believed was a deity—Japan invaded numerous countries around the Pacific Rim, inflicting untold misery on millions of people. In the decades after the

Paul Hattaway

Second World War, Japan rose from the dust to become the second strongest economic powerhouse in the world. Immediately after the war, there was a tremendous opportunity to evangelize Japan. General Douglas MacArthur, seeing how demoralized the Japanese were, said, 'If I had ten thousand Christian missionaries and one million Bibles, I could change this nation.' Few missionaries came, and the challenge of one million Bibles was never taken up.

Although some scholars suggest that Christianity may have first arrived in Japan in the first century AD, the visit of Francis Xavier to Kagoshima in 1549 is the first recorded instance of someone bringing the gospel here. 'Catholics expanded rapidly, and there were 300,000 baptized by 1593, many in the Nagasaki region. Severe persecution followed. On the morning of 5 February 1597, 26 Catholics (six foreigners and 20 Japanese) were publicly crucified on crosses in Nagasaki.[3] In 1613 the emperor officially banned Christianity. Foreign missionaries were not able to return until 1859, when the present era of missions began.'[4] Protestant missionaries also entered Japan for the first time in that year.

In recent years the Japanese have generally shown more receptivity to Christianity than they had in the past. One poll of Japanese university students found that 53.5 per cent of males and 73.1 per cent of women professed interest in Christianity.[5] There are an estimated two million Japanese Christians of all descriptions today, although one source notes, 'Often there is personal belief in Christ accompanied by disinterest in or rejection of organized Christianity on the grounds that the churches have adulterated the Christian faith by institutionalizing it.'[6]

Reaching Japanese Buddhists

David J Hesselgrave

There it was: 'Training Center for Buddhist Missionaries to North America', just one-half block off Kita-Ooji, the thoroughfare I travelled many times each week en route to our Kyoto Christian Center. The sign was particularly disconcerting and troubling for me, and for more than the obvious reason. It was troubling because what was happening in that Buddhist training centre was in sharp contrast to the training I (and the vast majority of my missionary colleagues) had received prior to being sent to post-war Japan. Here I was, in a bastion of Buddhism surrounded by elaborate temples and with famed Mt Hiei visible from my study window, and my knowledge of Japanese Buddhism was almost entirely restricted to what I had learned *after* my arrival in Japan!

In an attempt to make up for my inadequate knowledge of Buddhism, I began to devote some time every morning to reading a Japanese Buddhist newspaper and other Buddhist literature. That exercise later contributed to a doctoral dissertation on Nichiren Shooshu Sooka Gakkai Buddhism. But all of that is incidental and somewhat beside the point. The fact is that Buddhist missionaries to North America were getting the kind of training that Christian missionaries to Japan so desperately needed. In our case, however, this training had been almost completely overlooked.

As I write now, that first generation of post-war missionaries has been largely replaced by a new generation. They face new opportunities and new challenges. But some things remain the same, and one of them is the challenge of Japanese Buddhism— perhaps more firmly entrenched than ever and certainly more widely disseminated.

Despite more than three centuries of missionary endeavour (indeed, some claim there is evidence that the gospel first arrived in Japan before the end of the first century AD), Japan remains one of the most stubborn Buddhist strongholds in the world as far as the advance of Christianity. *Operation World* (6th edn, 2001) indicates that out of a total population of 126.7 million in the year 2000, Christian adherents in Japan numbered 1,976,742. This figure can be misleading, however. It includes those belonging to all denominations and many fringe groups and cannot reflect adequately the multiple religious loyalties of many who are included—a factor demonstrated by the fact that the editors estimate that Japan may be as much as 85 per cent Buddhist and 90 per cent Shinto.

Three fundamental questions emerge at this juncture. First, how have training programmes fared in the roughly half century that has passed since the vanguard of that earlier generation landed in Japan? Second, what are some of the most important ingredients of a more adequate programme for missionaries going to Japan? And third, what are the prospects for the future? Let's look at these in order.

A Buddhist monk meditates at the Chion-in Temple in Kyoto, Japan.

Paul Hattaway

How has missionary training for service in Japan progressed?

How has training progressed during the past generation? This question merits much more consideration than we can give it here. There can be no doubt that considerable progress has been made in both pre-field and on-field education opportunities for missionaries worldwide. Witness the higher levels of general and theological education undertaken by the average missionary; the increased volume of mission-related books and journals; the added courses in the missions curricula of various

Christ-less gravestones at Nanzen-ji Temple in Kyoto.

schools; the inauguration of masters and doctoral programmes; and the availability of seminars and specialized study programmes. Great progress has indeed been made.

However, it appears that comparatively little progress has been made in one very important aspect of missionary training. With the possible exceptions of training for missionaries to Jews and, more recently, Muslims, we still have very little by way of intensive and specialized training designed to help missionary recruits reach large populations of adherents to the other great religious traditions of the world. As a consequence, the missionary recruit heading for Japan today probably has achieved a somewhat higher level of education and may have had a general course or two in world religions. However, when it comes to preparation specifically designed for effectively reaching Japanese Buddhists, it is unlikely that the average missionary recruit is much better prepared than those missionaries who went to Japan in the 1950s and 1960s.

Effective training for ministry to Japanese Buddhists

What kind of specialized training is necessary for an effective ministry to Japanese Buddhists? Although

education is only one ingredient of solid missionary preparation, to more effectively preach, teach and witness among Japanese Buddhists the missionary must know Buddhism as well as the educated Japanese know it, and they must know it better than less educated Buddhist adherents. Credibility is at stake here. As one Japanese person said to me: 'If the missionary knows little or nothing about my religion, how does he propose to convince me that it should be abandoned in favour of Christianity?'

But it is not only credibility that is as stake here. More than rudimentary knowledge will be required to understand the Buddhist mentality; to compare and contrast Christian truth with Buddhist teachings; and to explain (and, at times, expose) the vagaries of Buddhist myth and history and thought and practice. Specialized training is required for those tasks—training that entails a careful study of both Japanese Buddhism and Japanese Buddhists. Study should highlight the following:

1. *The origin and development of Buddhism,* including its moorings in the Indian world-view, the life and teaching of Gautama Buddha, the origins and distinctives of major schools, the geographical spread of Buddhism and contemporary developments. This may seem ambitious, but nothing is gained and much is lost if one neglects this larger picture. For example, almost without exception, the Western missionary will experience difficulty in coming to grips with Indian monism on the one hand and the type of dualism espoused in Sankya on the other. But unless the missionary is prepared to understand how both play out in Japanese Buddhism, she or he is to that degree ill-prepared to reach Buddhists.

2. *The entry of Buddhism into Japan and something of its tumultuous history in that land.* Japanese people tend to think of Christianity as a foreign religion that is basically unsuited to them and their culture. The missionary needs to know, and

A Buddhist monk chants prayers of blessing for a young Japanese couple.

Japanese should be encouraged to reflect on, the peculiar circumstances surrounding the importation of a foreign (to Japanese) Buddhism from the unlikely (from a Japanese perspective) country of Korea. Japanese need to be reminded of the role that military prowess and power played in the entrenchment of Buddhism in their country. They need to be reminded of the ways in which Japanese Buddhism was informed by Chinese Buddhism and why it was that great teachers such as Saichoo and Kuukai went to China to sit at the feet of the Chinese masters.

What does that history tell us, and them, about 'foreignness'? How is it that times and circumstances have determined what can be deemed 'foreign', and therefore unsuitable, when it comes to the religious preferences of Japanese people?

3. *The developments and teachings of the various schools of Japanese Buddhism.* Schism and strife have plagued Japanese Buddhism almost from the beginning. At times divisions reflect differences that developed

in China and elsewhere, as becomes clear, for example, in a comparison of Joodo and Joodo Shinshu. At times they reflect Japanese nationalism and iconoclasm, as in the teachings of Shinran and Nichiren. Relationships between the schools have at times been amicable, but just as often they have been singularly competitive and highly charged.

Career missionaries especially should be prepared to deal with Buddhist doctrinal and attitudinal distinctives that, old or new, pervade Japanese culture. They should be able to communicate effectively not just with Japanese or just with Japanese Buddhists, but with Tendai Buddhists, Joodo Buddhists, Zen Buddhists and so on. The importance of differences between these groups must be measured by Japanese first and then by missionaries. As measured by Japanese those differences are at certain times rather inconsequential, but in other cases they are critical.

We must remember that Japanese people are not being confronted by a unified

Christianity. This presents missionaries with a problem that is partially resolved by reference to a divided Buddhism in Japan. It can be shown that Christians are not alone in denying certain Buddhist beliefs. Buddhist teachers themselves often cancel one another out.

4. *Basic Buddhist teachings as taught by Gautama Buddha himself.* His teachings are too numerous and even tentative to elaborate here, but missionaries need to understand

and *Obon* (festival for the dead), and who is not familiar with Buddhist rites such as those connected with death and ancestor veneration, is at a great disadvantage. Without this kind of knowledge it is unlikely that he or she will be able to take advantage of certain significant opportunities for Christian evangelism and instruction on the one hand, or to deal with the problems these observances occasion for Christian living and church life on the other.

A very practical illustration might be in order here. One needs to know, for example, how the *danka* system works in Japanese culture. Because Buddhism plays such a singular role in all matters having to do with death and dying, Japanese who do not support a local temple are bereft of special rites, the disposition of their body, and care for their departing spirit when death occurs. The impact of these factors upon Japanese who contemplate conversion to Christ are indeed enormous. A lack of understanding and empathy at this point, as well as a lack of practical answers

Japanese schoolboys write their names and prayers on papers, which are then tied onto a rotating frame. Buddhist monks spin the frame daily, believing this activates the prayers. Sanjusangen-do Temple, Kyoto.

Paul Hattaway

his (presumed) understandings of such things as karma, enlightenment, mercy and buddhahood. How each missionary uses this knowledge must be left to the individual. Nevertheless, to teach, preach and witness in Japan without reference to fundamental Buddhist doctrines is to miss out on one of the most effective methods of gospel communication—namely, comparison and contrast. Remember, we do not really know what something is until we also know what it is not!

5. *Buddhist rituals, practices and behavioural patterns.* The missionary who is oblivious to the meaning and significance of Buddhist celebrations such as Buddha's birthday

to the problem, discredit the work of many missionaries.

6. *Appreciation for the contribution of Buddhism to Japanese culture.* While the religion of the Buddha is idolatrous and inimical to faith in Christ, there is much that can be learned from Buddhist propagation and much that can be appreciated in Buddhist contributions to Japanese art and culture. For example, the propagation strategies and methodologies of some Buddhist cults reveal much that is important about Japanese thinking and motivational patterns important to the ways in which Christians go about evangelism and church development. And much of Japanese art, architecture, decor and etiquette that is

prized and admirable stems from Zen and other schools of Japanese Buddhism. To admit this and to show appreciation by word and deed is not a sign of weakness. It is a sign of strength in the missionary. The Japanese have more respect for missionaries who respect their culture.

Study of Japanese Buddhists

Turning now to a brief study of Buddhism as a religion to the Japanese people, it would be well to consider characteristics such as the following:

1. *Japanese Buddhists as syncretists or 'multi-religionists'.* As noted above, the majority of Japanese are quite firmly convinced that 'though there are many paths on Mt Fuji they all lead to the same summit'. This brings to mind the response of an elderly Japanese man to one of my early evangelistic sermons. With great emotion he said, 'I am so impressed by what you had to say tonight. My family and I have been Buddhists and Shintoists for as long as I can remember. But tonight I have made an important decision. From now on we will be Christians too!' In one sense it is easy to respond to that kind of misunderstanding of what is involved in becoming a Christian. However, careful study will reveal the many implications of that kind of 'decision' and tend to correct our ways of dealing with decision-making in the Japanese context.

2. *Japanese Buddhists as secularists and materialists.* One of my university professors attempted to dissuade me from going to Japan by saying, 'My experience in Japan teaches me that the Japanese are interested in a changed economic picture here and now; not in pie in the sky by and by.'

    He was right, of course. But he was also wrong. Like large numbers of Americans, many Japanese are interested in a religion that promises

prosperity and the good life. But Japanese Buddhists have a basic interest and a primary stake in matters of the spirit and in future existence. It is precisely in these matters that Christian missionaries will experience some of their greatest challenges and some of their greatest opportunities if they are properly attuned to the Japanese mind and spirit.

Conclusion

During my years in Kyoto I became well acquainted with one of Japan's foremost and most wealthy scientists. I led Bible studies in his laboratory and in his home. He listened. He asked questions. He read the Bible. Years passed. One Christmas Eve when visiting us in our home in America he came very close to making a decision for Christ, but he did not do it then and, to my knowledge, he never did.

Subsequently, while on one of my summer trips overseas, I went to his laboratory in southern Honshu. A hostess greeted me, served tea, and summoned the scientist's wife. After a few minutes her chauffeur delivered her to the laboratory entrance. She entered the office area and greeted me warmly with the usual pleasantries. Suddenly she became very sombre and said, 'I regret that in my sorrow and busyness I neglected to write to you. Last Christmas Eve my husband suffered a heart attack and died. Please come with me.'

Her limousine conveyed us up the mountain to the home we had visited a number of times in years gone by. She led me down a narrow corridor to a

Japanese line up to drink holy water believed to have healing qualities. Kiyomizudera Temple at Otawa-no-taki waterfall, Kyoto.

Paul Hattaway

newly constructed and spacious room. It was empty except for a large, ornate Buddhist altar. On the altar there was a large picture of her deceased husband and my scientist friend along with his *ihai* (ancestral tablet), other Buddhist paraphernalia and a copy of the New Testament. She turned to me apologetically and said, 'Please do not misunderstand. I included the Bible that my husband used when attending your studies because he said that was the only religious book he really trusted. As for the other things, please try to understand. I didn't know what to do. But please remember that we are Japanese.'

Will the new generation of Japanese grow up knowing the gospel? Sapporo, Hokkaido.

All sorts of questions flooded into my mind at the time and come flooding back every time I picture that large room with its simple furnishings. Among those questions, two can appropriately be asked here:

First, would that story have been different had I had been more adequately trained to reach Japanese Buddhists? And, second, will future missionaries to Japan have the benefit of better training? If there is a need for special preparation for ministries to Jews and Muslims who share so much of our own religious tradition, how much greater the need for enhanced training when focusing on people with whom we share little more than a commitment to transcendence?

In recent years some encouraging developments have taken place in this regard. The establishment of the Sonrise Center for Buddhist Studies in California; the increase in historical and comparative religious studies that include courses on Buddhism;

the publication of materials designed to focus prayer on Buddhist populations including Japanese—all of this is encouraging. However, still more attention should be given to the Buddhist world generally, and to Japan in particular. World events have conspired to cause missions to focus on other parts of the world. Those areas and peoples are, of course, important. But, as was the case a half-century ago—and perhaps is even more the case now in view of their spiritual dislocation and religious disaffection— the Japanese deserve a fuller measure of missionary interest and involvement. The rancorous division between Nichiren Shooshu and Sooka Gakkai; the meteoric rise of the apocalyptic Nichiren Kenshookai; the deadly chemical gas attack staged by Aum Shinkiryo—events such as these seem to signal both new challenges and new opportunities for Christian ministry in Japan. There may never be a better time for a new effort to understand, and a renewed effort to reach, Japanese Buddhists with the gospel of Christ.

Notes

This article, which was originally published in the *International Journal of Frontier Missions* 10.3 (July 1993), has been revised and updated here.

A family drinks holy water at Kiyomizudera Temple in Kyoto. Will Japan ever find the satisfying living water that Jesus offers?

Approximately 15,000 speakers of the Chabao Jiarong language live in north-west Sichuan Province in western China. They are primarily concentrated in the Longerjia, Dazang and Shaerzong townships in Chabao District. Chabao lies within Barkam County in Aba Prefecture. Barkam is called Ma'er-kang by local Jiarong and Tibetans. One source states, 'Barkam has a mixed population of Chinese, Jiarong, and Khampa Tibetans. The town was constructed in the 1950s on the site of a regionally important monastery after the Chinese built a road to open up this mountainous region.'[1] They live on grassland plateaus between several rivers that run through the region. The Chabao Jiarong dominate the total population of Chabao District.[2]

Wars and diseases have kept the Jiarong population relatively low over the centuries. In the 1930s it was reported: 'Aborigines [minorities] seize and kill members of other nationalities. . . . Abandoned hovels and wasteland due to pillage by them are common sights. Violent attacks on communities . . . as well as government punitive actions against them, cost many tens of thousands of lives.'[3]

The Chabao Jiarong have been counted as part of the Tibetan nationality by the Chinese government, even though the Chabao Jiarong language—which is not mutually intelligible with the other Jiarong varieties—is part of the Qiangic branch of Tibeto-Burman. The Chabao Jiarong have been influenced by the Tibetans more than the four other Jiarong language groups have been. Consequently, most Chabao Jiarong can also speak the local dialect of Khampa. Jiarong adults are reported to have a 27

per cent literacy rate.[4] Most scholars in the West (and some in China) believe that Jiarong is an independent language, while others think it is merely a dialect of Tibetan. 'Political and sociological arguments brought into this discussion tend to cloud objectivity.'[5]

The Chabao Jiarong have survived the extreme Barkam winters for centuries. Very few fruits or vegetables grow in the area. Their main crop is barley. The Jiarong diet mainly consists of fat, meat and soured yogurt. 'The winters are harsh with heavy snows and subzero temperatures in northern regions. . . . Jiarong women wear hand woven belts, head-dresses, and aprons that are uniquely Jiarong. The men wear traditional Tibetan tunic dress. Most of the area does not have running water, electricity, and telephones.'[6]

Approximately 10 per cent of the Jiarong follow the Bon religion.[7] Bon, a mixture of black magic and demon worship, was the religion of all Tibetans before Buddhism arrived from India during the 7th century AD. Buddhism was incorporated into existing Bon rituals.

There are no known Christians among the Chabao Jiarong, and just two individuals among all the five Jiarong language groups are known to believe in Christ! They are an unreached people who have lived and perished in their remote part of China for centuries without any gospel light to show them the way to God.

Julian Hawken

Population:
14,170 (2000)
17,450 (2010)
21,500 (2020)
Countries: China
Buddhism: Tibetan
Christians: none known

Overview of the Chabao Jiarong

Other Names: Gyarong, Gyarung, Rgyarong, Chiarong, Jarong, Chabao, Northeastern Jiarong, Northern Jiarong

Population Sources:
12,197 in China (1993, Lin Xiangron)

Language: Sino-Tibetan, Tibeto-Burman, Tangut-Qiang, Gyarong

Dialects: 0

Professing Buddhists: 90%

Practising Buddhists: 60%

Christians: 0%

Scripture: none

Jesus film: none

Gospel Recordings: none

Christian Broadcasting: none

ROPAL code: JYA

Status of Evangelization

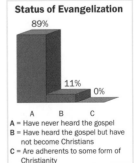

89%   11%   0%

A   B   C

A = Have never heard the gospel
B = Have heard the gospel but have not become Christians
C = Are adherents to some form of Christianity

Jiarong, Guanyingqiao

More than 5,000 speakers of the Guanyingqiao Jiarong language live in the remote north-western part of Sichuan Province in China. According to linguist Jonathon Evans, 'The language is spoken along the tributaries of the Jinchuan River in the south-western tip of Ma'erkang (Barkam) County, north-western Jinchuan County, and south-eastern Zamtang County. It has been named Guanyingqiao after the district in Jinchuan County which is the focal point of the Guanyingqiao-speaking area.'[1] They share this area with Tibetans. Very few outsiders ever visit the Guanyingqiao area.

Although the Guanyingqiao Jiarong have officially been classified as members of the Tibetan nationality, they do not speak a language that is closely related to Tibetan and are known to have a different history, origin and customs. Whereas certain Chinese government experts were in favour of giving the Jiarong status as a distinct minority group, some Tibetan leaders are believed to have campaigned for their inclusion in the Tibetan nationality, fearing that the exclusion of the Jiarong would weaken the Tibetan cause.

Guanyingqiao Jiarong is a member of the Qiangic branch of the Tibeto-Burman language family. It is most closely related to Ergong and Shangzhai Jiarong. Despite their small population, studies indicate the existence of eight dialects within Guanyingqiao Jiarong. 'Representative local varieties of Guanyingqiao, some very

different, include Xiaoyili and Siyaowu in Zamtang County, Muerzong in Barkam County, Guanyingqiao, Ergali, Taiyanghe, Ere and Yelong in Jinchuan County.'[2]

Thousands of years ago, the various branches of the Jiarong in Sichuan were more closely related to the groups in today's Qiang nationality. The Jiarong, however, migrated into Tibetan areas and have been culturally assimilated to Tibetan ways.

Most Jiarong people embrace Tibetan Buddhism today. Polytheism (Bon) and shamanism are also practised among them. The deities most feared by the Jiarong are the mountain gods, which they believe dwell inside large mountains and are responsible for most bad things that happen. 'The most important holy mountain for the Jiarong is Murduo Mountain in Danba County. The Jiarong, Ergong and other Tibetans worship this mountain, trying to appease the spirits and gain protection. The most important monastery is in Guanyingqiao, Jinchuan. The Jiarong take pilgrimages to holy sites and are often seen spinning prayer wheels. Some families send their son to the monastery, both to get an education and as an offering.'[3]

The geographic remoteness of the Guanyingqiao Jiarong has separated them from gospel witness throughout their history. There are few roads in this sparsely populated part of China. Very few Han Chinese have settled in this part of Sichuan, except for government officials and some adventurous merchants. Few Guanyingqiao Jiarong have ever heard the name of Jesus Christ.

Population:
5,110   (2000)
6,300   (2010)
7,750   (2020)
Countries: China
Buddhism: Tibetan
Christians: none known

Overview of the Guanyingqiao Jiarong

Other Names: Gyarong, Gyarung, Rgyarong, Chiarong, Jarong, Chiajung, Guanyingqiao

Population Sources:
5,110 (2000, P Hattaway)

Language: Sino-Tibetan, Tibeto-Burman, Tangut-Qiang, Gyarong

Dialects: 8 (Xiaoyili, Siyaowu, Muerzong, Guanyingqiao, Ergali, Taiyanghe, Ere, Yelong)

Professing Buddhists: 90%

Practising Buddhists: 70%

Christians: 0%

Scripture: none

Jesus film: none

Gospel Recordings: none

Christian Broadcasting: none

ROPAL code: JIQ

Midge Conner

Status of Evangelization

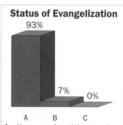

A = Have never heard the gospel
B = Have heard the gospel but have not become Christians
C = Are adherents to some form of Christianity

More than 4,000 speakers of the Shangzhai Jiarong language live in an isolated and sparsely populated part of north-west Sichuan Province in western China. The area inhabited by the Shangzhai Jiarong was previously part of the Tibetan empire but was annexed by the Chinese and integrated into Sichuan Province. The Shangzhai Jiarong are located 'near the confluence of the Doqu River and its tributary, the Zhongke River, in Shili, Zongke and Puxi townships of Shangzhai District, in southern Zamtang County'.[1]

Shangzhai is one of five distinct languages of the Jiarong ethnic group in China (six, if Ergong is included). The Chinese authorities have officially placed the Jiarong under the Tibetan nationality, even though their languages are far removed from Tibetan.[2] There has been some talk in Chinese circles of further investigation being conducted to see if the Jiarong should be classified as a separate minority, but officials in Beijing believe that the task of classifying minorities has been completed and they will not consider any more applications.

Shangzhai Jiarong, and the other Jiarong languages, are members of the Qiangic branch of Tibeto-Burman. Jonathon Evans notes, 'This language remains almost totally unrepresented in the available literature except for isolated words and sample paradigms in one source. Shangzhai seems closer to Ergong than to any other Jiarong languages. The internal diversity of Shangzhai is uncertain but its major local varieties, Dayili, Zongke and Puxi, appear to be quite distinct.'[3] The Dayili dialect was included in a survey of Qiangic languages in 1993.[4]

The Shangzhai Jiarong group is just one of many people groups in the area inhabiting what has been labelled an 'ethnic corridor'. 'This corridor, a borderland of Sino-Tibetan and Yi-Tibetan contact, has been an arena of political tug-of-war. This is also the area where the so-called Qiang, Di, and Rong ethnic groups lived and thrived and where many local governments of varying power and duration have appeared . . . this area should be fertile ground for exploration by historians as well as linguists.'[5]

Tibetan Buddhism and spirit appeasement dominate the daily lives of the Shangzhai Jiarong. They live in three-storey rock houses. 'The bottom floor is for animals, the middle floor for the living area, and the top floor is for grain storage and the god room. The god room is where they burn incense and offer food sacrifices to idols, for protection.'[6]

The region inhabited by the Shangzhai Jiarong has been closed to any Christian presence throughout its history. Lawless bandits, remote mountain ranges rising to 7,000 metres (23,000 ft.) above sea level, few roads and the powerful influence of Tibetan Buddhism have prevented the news of Jesus Christ from ever reaching the ears of the unreached Shangzhai Jiarong.

Population:
4,090 (2000)
5,040 (2010)
6,200 (2020)
Countries: China
Buddhism: Tibetan
Christians: none known

Overview of the Shangzhai Jiarong

Other Names: Gyarong, Gyarung, Rgyarong, Chiarong, Jarong, Chiajung, Shangzhai

Population Sources:
4,090 in China (2000, P Hattaway)

Language: Sino-Tibetan, Tibeto-Burman, Tangut-Qiang, Gyarong

Dialects: 3 (Dayili, Zongke, Puxi)

Professing Buddhists: 90%

Practising Buddhists: 70%

Christians: 0%

Scripture: none

Jesus **film:** none

Gospel Recordings: none

Christian Broadcasting: none

ROPAL code: JIH

Photo credit: China Advocate

Status of Evangelization

93%

7%

0%

A   B   C

A = Have never heard the gospel
B = Have heard the gospel but have not become Christians
C = Are adherents to some form of Christianity

Jiarong, Sidabao

Population:
5,580 (2000)
6,850 (2010)
8,400 (2020)
Countries: China
Buddhism: Tibetan
Christians: none known

Overview of the Sidabao Jiarong

Other Names: Western Jiarong, Western Jyarung, Gyarong, Gyarung, Rgyarong, Chiarong, Jarong, Sidabao

Population Sources:
5,580 (2000, P Hattaway)

Language: Sino-Tibetan, Tibeto-Burman, Tangut-Qiang, Gyarong

Dialects: 2 (Caodeng, Ribu)

Professing Buddhists: 90%

Practising Buddhists: 70%

Christians: 0%

Scripture: none

Jesus film: none

Gospel Recordings: none

Christian Broadcasting: none

ROPAL code: JIW

Status of Evangelization

91%

9%

0%

A   B   C

A = Have never heard the gospel
B = Have heard the gospel but have not become Christians
C = Are adherents to some form of Christianity

Approximately 5,500 Sidabao Jiarong live in an extremely remote and relatively wide-spread area of north-west Sichuan Province in China. 'Most of its speakers live in the three townships of Caodeng, Kangshan and Ribu in the Sidabao District of Ma'erkang (Barkam) County, hence the language name Sidabao. Small outlying communities, however, exist both to the north in certain villages of Kehe and Rongan townships at the southwestern corner of Aba County, and, to the west, along the middle Doqu River between Wuyi and Shili townships in Zamtang County, spilling over even to a small area near the confluence of the Sertar and Doqu rivers in Sertar County. Exact population statistics of Sidabao are not available, but should run to several thousand.'[1]

Although they have been officially included as part of the Tibetan nationality, Chinese scholars have considered the Jiarong distinct for several decades. In 1957, the Chinese Academy of Science listed a population of 70,000 Jiarong. One linguist notes, 'The Jiarong . . . are within the cultural orbit of Tibetan Buddhism but speak distinct languages.'[2]

Sidabao Jiarong is part of the Qiangic branch of Tibeto-Burman. There are two main dialects of Sidabao: Ribu and Caodeng. Ribu further divides into 'several quite different local varieties, such as Shili in Zamtang County, Rongan in Aba County, Ribu proper and Dawei in Barkam County'.[3] The Jiarong are looked down upon by both the Chinese and the Tibetans. 'Those Jiarong in the towns hold no more than low-level clerical jobs, as they are generally poorly educated.'[4]

One Chinese source claims that the Jiarong 'are a branch of Tibetans who moved in remote antiquity from Qungbu in Tibet to live in the Songpan Plateau of northern Sichuan'.[5] Buddhism arrived in Tibet during the reign of King Songsten Gampo (c. AD 605–650). It officially replaced the Bon religion and gradually worked its way to the extremities of the Tibetan world, including the area inhabited by the Jiarong today.

There has been a revival of the ancient Bon religion in recent years among the Jiarong. For the past 13 centuries, Buddhism has been something of a veneer on ancient Bon rituals. The spiritism and black magic still prevalent in Tibetan Buddhism stem from Bon.

The few attempts to evangelize the Jiarong in the past met with some success. In 1934, missionaries listed 34 Jiarong believers.[6] Another book from the 1930s lists a number of Jiarong Christians, but presently there is no indication that there are any believers among them. 'Social ostracism of possible converts, and persecution to the extent of the placing of severe curses by the lamas, or poisoning through family members, are other hindrances to spreading the Gospel.'[7]

There are no Scriptures, gospel recordings or other ministry tools presently available to help evangelize the Jiarong.

China Advocate

Xizang (Tibet)

Sichuan

Jiarong Situ

Population:
161,550 (2000)
199,550 (2010)
245,800 (2020)
Countries: China
Buddhism: Tibetan
Christians: 2

Overview of the Situ Jiarong

Other Names: Eastern Jiarong, Eastern Jyarung, Gyarong, Gyarung, Rgyarong, Chiarong, Jarong, Chiajung, Situ

Population Sources:

139,000 in China (1993, Lin Xiangron)

Language: Sino-Tibetan, Tibeto-Burman, Tangut-Qiang, Gyarong

Dialects: 4 (Lixian, Jinchuan, Xiaojin, Barkam)

Professing Buddhists: 90%

Practising Buddhists: 65%

Christians: 0.01%

Scripture: none

Jesus film: none

Gospel Recordings: none

Christian Broadcasting: none

ROPAL code: JIR

Status of Evangelization

88%

11%

1%

A   B   C

A = Have never heard the gospel
B = Have heard the gospel but have not become Christians
C = Are adherents to some form of Christianity

A 1993 study listed a total of 139,000 Situ Jiarong people in Sichuan Province in western China.[1] The Situ Jiarong group is the dominant Jiarong group in China. The Situ, also known as the Eastern Jiarong, inhabit parts of Li, Wenchuan and Xiaojin counties in central Sichuan, as well as sections of Barkam (Ma'erkang) and Jinchuan counties. Many Situ Jiarong live in a V-shaped valley between the Zagunao River—which originates in the Zhegu Mountains—and the upper section of the Min River.

The name Situ 'refers to the traditional territory of the four chieftaincies of Zhuokeji, Suomo, Songgang and Dangba in the heartland of Jiarong country. The term is adopted since it is now a widely used local label for this language.'[2] The several Jiarong groups in China have been officially counted under the Tibetan nationality. The Jiarong, however, speak their own distinct languages and believe that they are ethnically and historically different from the Tibetans. They have been listed as one of the people groups in China that 'need further investigation'.[3]

The classification of the Jiarong language has baffled Chinese scholars. One scholar reported, 'The languages of the Jiarong who live in Aba and Garze areas of Sichuan are a puzzle. Their language is different from Tibetan in terms of grammar, and akin to the Qiang and Pumi languages. They are considered the "language bridge" between Tibetan and Burmese.'[4] Differences in the five Jiarong languages are great.

China Advocate

Situ Jiarong has only 55 per cent lexical similarity with Sidabao Jiarong and 75 per cent with Chabao Jiarong.[5]

Until 1949, the Jiarong were divided into 18 small kingdoms. They kept the Chinese military at bay for ten years during the 18th century. Today the majority of Situ Jiarong are farmers, herding livestock and growing crops along the river basins in central Sichuan. A number of urban Jiarong are merchants and shop owners.

Most Jiarong are Tibetan Buddhists, but many have also adopted the polytheistic practices of the Qiang. Few have any awareness of Christianity. One source states, 'Compared to other Tibetan groups, the Jiarong are less antagonistic towards the Chinese. Living between the Tibetan and Chinese areas puts them in a great place to be reached by the Chinese.'[6]

The Jiarong were first evangelized in the early 1900s by the American Baptists—who had a mission base at Ya'an—and by the Border Mission of the Church of Christ in China in the 1910s. One writer summarized their efforts: 'In the early half of this century some missionaries stationed in areas relatively close to the Jiarong took some trips into Jiarong territory. This led to the translation of some tracts. It was not until the 1930s that an effort to specifically learn and analyze the Jiarong language got underway. A draft translation of the book of Jonah was in progress when the invasion of the Red Army in 1936 made work impossible. All materials were lost in the war.'[7]

Today, just two Jiarong individuals are known to follow Jesus Christ. May they be the first fruits of a great harvest!

Jirel

CHINA
Xizang (Tibet)

NEPAL

Janakur

Sagarmatha

Jirel

Population:
10,450 (2000)
12,950 (2010)
16,000 (2020)
Countries: Nepal
Buddhism: Tibetan
Christians: 200

Overview of the Jirel

Other Names: Ziral, Jiri, Jirial, Jiripa

Population Sources:

8,000 to 10,000 in Nepal (2000, B Grimes [1998 figure])

Language: Sino-Tibetan, Tibeto-Burman, Himalayish, Tibeto-Kanauri, Tibetic, Tibetan, Southern

Dialects: 0

Professing Buddhists: 70%

Practising Buddhists: 20%

Christians: 1.9%

Scripture: New Testament 1992; Portions 1977

Jesus film: none

Gospel Recordings: Jirel

Christian Broadcasting: none

ROPAL code: JUL

Status of Evangelization

54%

44%

2%

A   B   C

A = Have never heard the gospel
B = Have heard the gospel but have not become Christians
C = Are adherents to some form of Christianity

A 1998 researcher found that there were between 8,000 and 10,000 members of the Jirel tribe living in eastern Nepal.[1] The 1991 Nepal census, however, for some reason officially counted some Jirel villages under other tribes and returned a figure of just 4,889 Jirel people. They inhabit the Jiri and Sikri valleys in the Dolakha District of Janakpur Zone. The largest of their 22 villages are Jiri and Jugu. Dolakha is located about 50 kilometres (32 mi.) east of the nation's capital, Kathmandu.[2] Jirel villages are situated at altitudes between 1,700 and 2,000 metres (5,600 to 6,560 ft.) above sea level. A few Jirel are also found within the Okhaldhunga District of Sagarmatha Zone.

The history of the Jirel is interesting. Scholars record them as one of the ten clans of the Sunwar tribe, who today number more than 40,000 people south of the Jirel region. Unlike most of the other Sunwar groups, the Jirel did not convert to Hinduism but have clung to their belief in Buddhism as well as to their ancient shamanistic rituals. 'The Jirel may therefore, like the Surel, another Sunwar clan, be the products of miscegenation of Sunwar and Sherpa.'[3] The Sunwar generally consider the Jirel to be inferior, and refuse to intermarry with them, 'neither do they eat food cooked by Jirels. In areas where Sunwars do not live in proximity to the Jirel villages, these Jirels call themselves Sunwars, and they also try to remain unconnected and aloof from the Sherpa community, pretending to be superiors.'[4]

The Jirel language is part of the Kanauri branch of Tibeto-Burman.[5] It shares 67 per cent lexical similarity with Sherpa, 65 per cent with Helambu Sherpa and 54 per cent with Central Tibetan.[6] The Jirel have their own script, but only 25 per cent to 30 per cent of Jirel adults are literate, and 60 per cent of younger people.

Some sources state that the Jirel are a Hindu-Buddhist mix, but others firmly state that Tibetan Buddhism is their primary religion. Two Nepali scholars say, 'Jirels are Buddhists. They have their own lamas, gompas and religo-tribal rites and rituals. Lamas and also *jhankris* act as priests in their rites, rituals and festivals.'[7] The animistic roots of the Jirel can also be witnessed in their ceremonies. When a person dies, 'a copper coin is placed in the corpse's right hand, a little mud from the *pindi* (verandah of the house) is placed in the left hand and a smoldering coal from the hearth is placed on the corpse's mouth'.[8] These items are believed to help the ancestors recognize the deceased as one of their own, and to guide the dead person's spirit to the next world.

A small yet strong Christian community exists among the Jirel people. Missionaries have lovingly worked among them for many years. They translated the first Scripture portions into the Jirel language in 1977, and the entire New Testament was printed in 1992. The Old Testament is now being translated. The non-Christians persecuted the Jirel believers at first, but in more recent years there has been a growing acceptance of the Christian faith.

Gospel Recordings Nepal

The small Kagate tribe is divided between the South Asian nations of Nepal and India. In 1974, the linguists Monika Hoehlig and Maria Hari visited the Kagate and estimated their population at about one thousand.[1] In the years since, the number of Kagate people in Nepal is estimated to have grown to approximately 1,500. They reportedly live 'in the mountains between the Likhu and Khimti rivers in the northeastern part of Ramechap district, wedged in between Solokumbu and Dolakha districts'.[2] Another source says that the Nepal Kagate inhabit 'Janakpur Zone, Ramechhap District, on one of the ridges of Likhu Khola'.[3] The Kagate in Nepal live at an altitude of approximately 3,000 metres (9,840 ft.) above sea level. A similar number of Kagate live in India, having migrated there from Nepal. They are found in the North and East districts of Sikkim—the former independent nation that was annexed and incorporated into India in 1975. A few Kagate are also located in the Alubari area of Darjeeling District in West Bengal.

Although this group is widely known by the name Kagate, their self-name is *Syuuba*. Other groups have given them the name Kagate because of their traditional occupation of making paper from a plant called the *kagaj* that grows in the hilly areas of Nepal.[4]

The Kagate language is part of the Tibeto-Burman family. It is closely related to Helambu Sherpa, although it differs 'by using less the honorific system in verbs. People can talk about most common topics in Nepali. . . . Kagate is used at home and to other Kagate.'[5]

Women are hard workers and have a prominent role in Kagate society. They are 'required to collect fuel and fodder, when necessary, and render physical labor in the agricultural process, but are not engaged in plowing or cutting big trees, etc. Women also have a role in animal husbandry, and bring potable water from the spring. Women also have roles in ritual and religious spheres. Some of them take active part in politics too. With a major role in family management, they control the family expenditure.'[6]

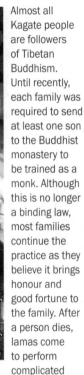

Dwayne Graybill

Almost all Kagate people are followers of Tibetan Buddhism. Until recently, each family was required to send at least one son to the Buddhist monastery to be trained as a monk. Although this is no longer a binding law, most families continue the practice as they believe it brings honour and good fortune to the family. After a person dies, lamas come to perform complicated cleansing rituals for 49 days. 'They burn 108 *chimis* (lamps) at a time, every day, during this period. . . . The lama reads out their religious scriptures. They prepare the *cho* (different fruits offered to the Buddha) and the *torma* (a preparation made of rice, wheat and fruits) for votive offering; and after the rituals distribute these among all the relatives, neighbors and friends. The lama gets some money and a *khada* (scarf) and some food. Generally, a group of six to eight lamas perform all these rituals.'[7]

Most Kagate people have never heard the gospel, although a very small Christian community is believed to exist among them in Nepal. Portions of the Bible were translated into Kagate in 1977.

Population:
2,570 (2000)
3,100 (2010)
3,630 (2020)
Countries: Nepal, India
Buddhism: Tibetan
Christians: 20

Overview of the Kagate

Other Names: Kagati, Yolmo, Shuba, Shyuba, Syuba, Syuuba, Kagate Bhote, Kagatey

Population Sources:
1,000 in Nepal (1976, M Hoehlig and A Hari)
1,000 in India (2000, P Hattaway)

Language: Sino-Tibetan, Tibeto-Burman, Himalayish, Tibeto-Kanauri, Tibetic, Tibetan, Central

Dialects: 0

Professing Buddhists: 98%

Practising Buddhists: 90%

Christians: 0.8%

Scripture: Portions 1977

Jesus **film:** none

Gospel Recordings: Kagate

Christian Broadcasting: none

ROPAL code: SYW

Status of Evangelization

69%

30%

1%

A   B   C

A = Have never heard the gospel
B = Have heard the gospel but have not become Christians
C = Are adherents to some form of Christianity

Kaike

One of the most interesting and little-known parts of Asia is the Dolpa District in the Karnali Zone of north-west Nepal. Massive Himalayan peaks look down on a landscape containing many unresearched ethnic groups and languages. One such language is called Kaike. According to linguist David Bradley, in 1997 Kaike was spoken by 2,000 people in Nepal.[1] The primary location for this group is the village of Tichurong. Three nearby villages are known in Nepali by the names Sartara, Tupara and Densa.

The main source of information about this small language group comes from George van Driem, who profiles Kaike in his comprehensive *Languages of the Himalayas*. He notes, 'A Tamangic language spoken by approximately two thousand people in several villages of Dolpa District . . . is known by the name Kaike.'[2] There has been no grammatical study done of Kaike, although the American anthropologist James Fisher compiled a list of 600 Kaike words in 1971.[3]

Several small Buddhist groups that require further study to determine whether they qualify as distinct ethnolinguistic identities live east of the Kaike area. These include Nyishangba, Narpa and Gyasumdo. One source states, 'The speakers of these three Tamangic dialects practice the Bon religion as well as Mahayana Buddhism and have for centuries formed part of the Tibetan

cultural sphere.'[4] The small tribes in this remote part of the world's largest mountain range rarely travel out of their own area. As a result, other people in Nepal have developed ethnic stereotypes, calling them *Manang*

after a little-visited valley populated by Tibetan Buddhists. In Kathmandu, 'this term is used indiscriminately to designate any large-bodied male of Tibetan appearance with a tendency to bouts of rage and acts of violent crime. The term is also applied to any seedy or unscrupulous youth of Tibetan appearance, even if the lad in question may not have the foggiest notion about where the Manang valley is located.'[5]

It is not surprising, therefore, that the Kaike people have developed a certain insecurity. Even their unique language has been the object of scorn and ridicule. James Fisher has said that other ethnic groups have mocked the Kaike language so that the people now 'view Kaike in low regard because it is felt to be unsophisticated and unexpressive. [The Kaike people have] very low cultural self-esteem.'[6]

The light of the gospel has yet to shine in most of the villages and homes in this impoverished and remote part of the world. The presence of Maoist rebels in western Nepal has complicated evangelistic efforts and made many of the inhabitants of the area fearful of visitors.

There are no known Christians among the Kaike people. No Scripture or gospel messages have yet been translated into their language. For countless generations they have worshipped Buddha, completely oblivious to the existence of Jesus Christ.

Overview of the Kaike

Other Names: Tarali Kham, Tarali Magar, Tichurong, Ticherong, Ka-ne, Khanigaon

Population Sources:

2,000 in Nepal (1997, D Bradley)

Language: Sino-Tibetan, Tibeto-Burman, Himalayish, Tibeto-Kanauri, Kanauri

Dialects: 0

Professing Buddhists: 100%

Practising Buddhists: 85%

Christians: 0%

Scripture: none

Jesus film: none

Gospel Recordings: none

Christian Broadcasting: none

ROPAL code: KZQ (Kaike) and TCN (Tichurong)

Population:
2,140 (2000)
2,650 (2010)
3,280 (2020)
Countries: Nepal
Buddhism: Tibetan
Christians: none known

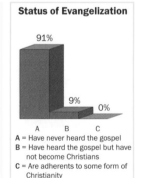

Status of Evangelization

91%

9%

0%

A = Have never heard the gospel
B = Have heard the gospel but have not become Christians
C = Are adherents to some form of Christianity

Kaleung

Population:
15,700 (2000)
18,400 (2010)
21,600 (2020)
Countries: Thailand, Laos
Buddhism: Theravada
Christians: none known

Overview of the Kaleung

Other Names: Kaleun, Tai Kelung, Tai Kaleun, Lao Kaleun, Kalerng, Khalong, Laoeng, Kaleum

Population Sources: 8,000 in Thailand (2000, J Schliesinger [1995 figure])

6,500 in Laos (1995, Asian Minorities Outreach)

Language: Tai-Kadai, Tai, Southwestern, East-Central, Lao-Phutai

Dialects: 0

Professing Buddhists: 95%

Practising Buddhists: 60%

Christians: 0%

Scripture: none

Jesus film: none

Gospel Recordings: none

Christian Broadcasting: none

ROPAL code: TTS02

Status of Evangelization

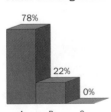

78%
22%
0%

A B C

A = Have never heard the gospel
B = Have heard the gospel but have not become Christians
C = Are adherents to some form of Christianity

More than 16,000 Kaleung people live on each side of the Thailand-Laos border in Southeast Asia. Although the 8,500 Kaleung in Thailand presently outnumber their counterparts in Laos, within ten to fifteen years the Laos Kaleung are likely to outnumber the Thailand Kaleung due to the extremely high birth rate in Laos, where families of ten or more children are not uncommon today.

In Thailand, the Kaleung inhabit the provinces of Mukdahan (Don Tan and Chanuman districts), Nakhon Phanom (Muang District) and parts of Sakhon Nakhon Province. The majority of Kaleung in Laos are located in the Khamkeut District of Borikhamxai Province. A small number also live in the distant Nakay District of Khammouan Province.

Some scholars regard the Kaleung as among the first inhabitants of Southeast Asia. 'Some Kaleung people state that their original homeland is central Laos near the border of Vietnam and that their forefathers migrated into Thailand in the early nineteenth century. They adjusted to Isan culture and gradually gave up their own language.'[1]

Although today the Kaleung language is classified as part of the Tai linguistic family, this is due to the fact that few people can speak the original Kaleung mother tongue, which was part of the Mon-Khmer linguistic affiliation (most people today speak a Tai language instead).[2] Joachim Schliesinger notes, 'For a long time, their language was classified as a Katuic branch among the Mon-Khmer language group . . . closely related to Bru, So and Saek. Therefore it could be assumed that they might have

a common origin with these peoples, especially the Bru. . . . Some elderly members of the Kaleung group in Thailand can still speak their original mother tongue. This language is of Mon-Khmer origin and definitely not a Tai dialect. The change of linguistic classification may have resulted out of the fact that most of the Kaleung people already residing for a long period of time in Thailand have totally forgotten their original tongue.'[3] Despite this fact, the Kaleung do retain a distinct ethnic identity, customs and history.

Kaleung villages are rectangular in shape. In the past their houses were raised on poles, but today most of their homes are similar in appearance to those of their Thai and Isan neighbours. One custom that has remained strong among the Kaleung in

Paul Hattaway

Thailand is the prevalence of matrilineal extended families. Three or four generations of family members live under the same roof. The mother controls the family finances and makes all of the important decisions. When a wedding takes place, the groom's family must pay a bride price to the bride's family. An average price today is around 30,000 Thai *baht* (US$700). After the ceremony, the groom moves into the home of his bride's parents.

The Kaleung are Theravada Buddhists. They also retain many animistic rituals. In Laos they still slaughter pigs and buffaloes as sacrifices to the spirits. There are no known Christians among the spiritually needy Kaleung people.

Approximately half a million Kalmyk-Oirat people live in several different countries in Central Asia. The majority (210,000) live in Mongolia, followed by Russia (174,000), and China (91,300). Smaller numbers of Kalmyk-Oirat live in Ukraine (700) and Uzbekistan (500), while scattered communities can be found in the United States (800), Germany, Kyrgyzstan and Taiwan.

In Russia the Kalmyk-Oirat are concentrated in Kalmykia, on the steppes between the Don and Volga rivers, north of the Caucasus Range and east of the Caspian Sea. The Kalmyk-Oirat in China are concentrated in Qinghai Province, as well as parts of Gansu and Xinjiang. In China many researchers combine the Oirat and Torgut groups, but they are profiled separately in this book. Although the Torgut and Kalmyk-Oirat are closely related and speak the same language, they view themselves as distinct tribes. The Kalmyk-Oirat are one of the main branches of Mongolian people. One expert described the Kalmyk-Oirat as 'physically smaller, more garrulous, friendlier and more inquisitive than [other Mongols]'.[1]

The Kalmyk-Oirat have had a terrible history.[2] From 1755–57, the Chinese Qing armies crushed the Oirat, forcing the survivors to flee to the northern Caucasus Mountains in Russia. Oppression there forced most of them to return to China in 1771. Only a few survived the long journey to Xinjiang. 'The rest died from famine or fell victim to the hostile raids of neighboring tribes.'[3] Those who stayed behind on the Russian side of the border are called Kalmyk, which means 'to remain or stay behind'.[4]

The Kalmyk-Oirat 'burial in the fields' is unique. The corpse is placed on a wooden cart, which is pulled furiously by a horse until the body falls from the back of the cart. Wherever it falls, it is left to be devoured by beasts and birds of prey.[5] The Kalmyk-Oirat have been unflatteringly described as 'a squalid race, reputed never to change their clothes or wash. When one coat wears out, a new one is put over it and not until it rots off do they discard a garment.'[6]

The majority of Kalmyk-Oirat are followers of Tibetan Buddhism. Shamans still perform many rituals and ceremonies. Some Kalmyk-Oirat practise a crude form of black magic under the guise of Buddhism. Every New Year the Kalmyk-Oirat devote their prayers to Okeen Tenger, their female spirit protector. She is believed to have saved the world from evil by bearing, and later killing, the offspring of the Lord of Evil, Erlik Khan.

The Kalmyk-Oirat are one of the least evangelized Buddhist groups in the world. In Russia there are a reported 1,700 Christians among them, but almost all of these are Orthodox believers who were converted under the influence of Russians. That number includes only about 50 evangelical believers. Today there are no known believers among the Kalmyk-Oirat in China. The New Testament was first translated into Kalmyk-Oirat in 1827, but it went out of print in 1894. Work is presently underway to produce an updated version.[7]

Overview of the Kalmyk-Oirat

Population:
477,300 (2000)
538,700 (2010)
607,000 (2020)

Countries: Mongolia, Russia, China, USA, Ukraine, Uzbekistan, Germany, Taiwan, Kyrgyzstan

Buddhism: Tibetan

Christians: 1,800

Other Names: Kalmuk, Kalmuck, Qalmaq, Kalmytskii, Jazyk, Khalmag, Oirat, Volga Oirat, European Oirat, Western Mongolian, Xinjiang Mongol, Weilate, Durbet

Population Sources:
210,000 in Mongolia (2001, P Johnstone and J Mandryk [2000 figure])
174,000 in Russia (1993, United Bible Societies)
91,300 in China (2000, P Hattaway)
800 in USA (2001, Joshua Project II)
700 in Ukraine (2001, Joshua Project II)
500 in Uzbekistan (2001, Joshua Project II)

Also in Germany, Taiwan, Kyrgyzstan

Language: Altaic, Mongolian, Eastern, Oirat-Khalkha, Oirat-Kalmyk-Darkhat

Dialects: 8 (Buzawa, Oirat, Dörböt, Sart Qlamaq, Jakhachin, Bayit, Mingat, Khoshut)

Professing Buddhists: 85%

Practising Buddhists: 40%

Christians: 0.4%

Scripture: New Testament 1827 (out of print); work in progress

Jesus film: available[8]

Gospel Recordings: Kalmyk

Christian Broadcasting: none

ROPAL code: KGZ

Status of Evangelization

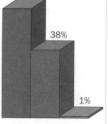

A = Have never heard the gospel
B = Have heard the gospel but have not become Christians
C = Are adherents to some form of Christianity

61% — A
38% — B
1% — C

With a population in excess of a quarter million, the Western Kayah are the largest ethnic group in Kayah State in eastern Myanmar. One source states, 'Myanmar's Kayah State sits on its eastern border with Thailand, directly opposite Mae Hong Son Province. The entire state is consumed by a range of mountains that stretch the length of the eastern section of the country, varying in elevation from 3,000 to 8,000 feet within the Kayah State itself. Two major rivers, the Nampawn and the mighty Salween, run on a north-south route through the area, and have served as geographical landmarks throughout the fierce fighting which has raged here for over 20 years. The majority of the population lives in the military occupied towns and villages of the western third of the state and along the rebel borderlands near Thailand as IDPs (Internally Displaced Peoples). The entire state is off-limits to foreigners.'[1] The main centre for the Kayah people is the town of Loikaw in north-western Kayah State.

An additional 20,000 Western Kayah refugees are presently stuck in refugee camps across the border in Thailand. Large numbers started fleeing Myanmar in the early 1990s, escaping the war between the Burmese military and the KNPP (Karenni National Progressive Party), an anti-government faction operating in the Kayah State. Numerous horrific human rights abuses such as genocide and mass rape have been committed against the Kayah people by Burmese soldiers. Many Kayah are always on the move, travelling just ahead of the war parties from one location to another.

The Kayah are an 'often confused or misunderstood group of people. They are regularly confused with the term *Karenni*, a blanket term used to cover all groups living within the Kayah State of eastern Myanmar. Karenni can include the Padaung, Sgaw Karen, Kayah, and a couple of other small groups. . . . The true Kayah live primarily in the northern half of the State, and speak their own language, though most also speak Sgaw Karen.'[2] The Kayah are also called by the nickname *Red Karen* because of their brightly-coloured red head-cloths and shawls.[3]

The Western Kayah speak a different language from the Eastern Kayah, a group of about 70,000 who live in eastern Kayah State and in Thailand. Speakers of Eastern Kayah 'have difficulty understanding Western Kayah of Myanmar'.[4] The Eastern Kayah have not been included in this book since only a minority believe in Buddhism.

The Western Kayah are 'primarily Buddhist in name, though there are very strong animistic characteristics woven throughout their belief system. They observe Buddhist rituals and make periodic visits to pagodas and monasteries, but almost all villages participate in spirit worship, paying homage to the *nats*, or other spirits.'[5]

Because Kayah State is completely off-limits to foreigners, it is difficult to gauge the number of Christians among the Western Kayah today, though the number is small and not likely to exceed one or two per cent of the population. Perhaps a thousand of the Western Kayah refugees in Thailand have turned to Christ, the result of practical love and evangelism by Karen Christian refugees and foreign missionaries.

Myanmar Faces and Places

Population:
269,867 (2000)
302,600 (2010)
339,600 (2020)
Countries: Myanmar, refugees in Thailand
Buddhism: Theravada
Christians: 4,000

Overview of the Western Kayah

Other Names: Kayah Li, Karenni, Karrenyi, Red Karen, Yang Deang, Karieng Daeng

Population Sources: 249,867 in Myanmar (2003, Myanmar Faces and Places)[6]
20,000 refugees in Thailand (2003, Myanmar Faces and Places)

Language: Sino-Tibetan, Tibeto-Burman, Karen, Sgaw-Bghai, Kayah

Dialects: 0

Professing Buddhists: 50%

Practising Buddhists: 20%

Christians: 1.5%

Scripture: none

Jesus film: available

Gospel Recordings: Kayah

Christian Broadcasting: none

ROPAL code: KYU

Status of Evangelization

48% 50%

2%

A   B   C

A = Have never heard the gospel
B = Have heard the gospel but have not become Christians
C = Are adherents to some form of Christianity

Khamiyang

Approximately one thousand Khamiyang people live in the north-east Indian state of Arunachal Pradesh, inhabiting communities near the Khamtis in the Lohit and Tirap districts. 'They dwell in the plains drained by the Tengapani and Noa-Dihing rivers and within the vicinity of dense tropical moist and deciduous forests.'[1] A small number of Khamiyang live in the Rowai Mukh village within Assam State. The total population of the Khamiyang was listed at 812 at the time of the 1981 census. Out of this number, just three individuals lived in an urban area and 809 were from rural areas.[2]

Few sources have ever mentioned the Khamiyang, although one described them as 'a small Buddhist peasant community with a close affinity with the Khamtis of Arunachal Pradesh and the Aiton and Tai Phake of Assam. They are also called Khamjang and use Shyam as their surname.'[3]

The name *Khamiyang* means 'a place where gold is available'. This name probably comes from their homeland. They are believed to have originally lived in the Patkai mountains, but they left because of oppression from the Singpho and moved to Assam between 1807 and 1814. 'Some of them recall that they subsequently migrated from the Jorhat and Dibrugarh districts of Assam during the great Assam earthquake in the year 1950 and settled down in the plains of the Lohit and Tirap districts of Arunachal Pradesh, where they are now distributed.'[4]

The Khamiyang originally spoke a Tai language, similar to Khamti. Over the centuries, however, the Khamiyang have gradually lost the use of their mother tongue and most have adopted Assamese, which is spoken by more than 15 million people in north-east India.[5] They also use the Assamese script for reading and writing. Their original Tai script is now used only for Buddhist rituals. Despite losing their linguistic identity, the Khamiyang retain their cultural and ethnic distinctiveness, which qualifies them as a mission-significant people group.

Since they live in a place with abundant natural resources, the diet of the Khamiyang includes 'a large variety of wild and domestically grown vegetables, roots and tubers such as pumpkins, brinjals, ginger and onions; mustard leaves; chilies; flower of plantains; mushrooms; shoots of bamboo and cane and many types of leaves. . . . They eat a variety of fish . . . fowls, pigs, goats, wild bears, deer and tigers, but abstain from taking beef.'[6]

Theravada Buddhism is the religious choice of an overwhelming number of Khamiyang people. Each village has its own temple or monastery. The 1981 Indian census records 805 of the 812 Khamiyang as followers of Buddhism. Four individuals listed their religion as Hinduism, and three as followers of 'other religions'. The Khamiyang have been Buddhists since long before their migration from the Shan State area of northern Myanmar many centuries ago. Buddhism forms a major part of their identity and few seem open to change. Consequently, there are no known Christians among the Khamiyang people of India today.

Population:
990 (2000)
1,150 (2010)
1,340 (2020)
Countries: India
Buddhism: Theravada
Christians: none known

Overview of the Khamiyang

Other Names: Khamjang, Shyam, Khamyang

Population Sources:
812 in India (1981 census)

Language: Tai-Kadai, Kam-Tai, Be-Tai, Tai-Sek, Tai, Southwestern, East Central, Northwest

Dialects: 0

Professing Buddhists: 99%

Practising Buddhists: 80%

Christians: 0%

Scripture: none

***Jesus* film:** none

Gospel Recordings: none

Christian Broadcasting: none

ROPAL code: KSU

Status of Evangelization

83% 17% 0%

A = Have never heard the gospel
B = Have heard the gospel but have not become Christians
C = Are adherents to some form of Christianity

Festivals on the 'Roof of the World'

The Tibetan Plateau (known as the 'Roof of the World') is home to some of the hardiest people in the world. Several major festivals each year give the people respite from their struggles. They come from far and wide to eat, drink and have fun with their relatives and friends. These pictures, taken of Amdo and Khampa festivals in western China, display the vibrant colour of these remote people. All the pictures in this 4-page section was taken by Nancy Sturrock, mostly at the Yushu Horse Fair in Qinghai Province, China.

125

CHINA
Qinghai

Xizang
(Tibet)
Sichuan

BHUTAN
NEPAL
INDIA
Khampa Eastern

Population:
1,246,200 (2000)
1,535,200 (2010)
1,891,300 (2020)
Countries: China, Bhutan, India, Nepal
Buddhism: Tibetan
Christians: 400

Overview of the Eastern Khampa

Other Names: Kham, Khams, Khams-Yal, Khams-Bhotia, Kam, Khamba, Kang, Konka, Konkaling

Population Sources:

956,700 in China (1987, *Language Atlas of China*)

1,000 in Bhutan (1995, *Languages of Bhutan*)

Also in India and Nepal

Language: Sino-Tibetan, Tibeto-Burman, Himalayish, Tibeto-Kanauri, Tibetic, Tibetan, Northern

Dialects: 8 (Dege, Karmdzes, Chamdo, Braggyab, Nyingkhri, Batang, Nyagchu, and an unnamed dialect)

Professing Buddhists: 95%

Practising Buddhists: 80%

Christians: 0.1%

Scripture: Tibetan Bible 1948; New Testament 1885; Portions 1862

Jesus film: available

Gospel Recordings: Kham, Khamba

Christian Broadcasting: none

ROPAL code: KHG

Status of Evangelization

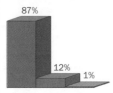

87%

12%

1%

A B C

A = Have never heard the gospel
B = Have heard the gospel but have not become Christians
C = Are adherents to some form of Christianity

Approximately 1.3 million Tibetans speak the Eastern Khampa language. They inhabit a vast area but are primarily concentrated in China's western Sichuan Province as far east as Kangding; in a large portion of eastern Tibet; and in parts of southern Qinghai Province.

There are at least several thousand Eastern Khampa refugees living in Bhutan, Nepal and India today, but their exact numbers are difficult to gauge because in those countries they are usually just identified as Tibetans and no linguistic distinction is made.[1] The Eastern Khampa language is by far the most widely spoken of the Khampa varieties. It is reported to have eight dialects[2] and 80 per cent lexical similarity with Central Tibetan.[3]

In China, the Eastern Khampa town of Litang lies 4,700 metres (15,400 ft.) above sea level. Chamdo is another important town—at an altitude of 3,200 metres (10,500 ft.). The Chamdo Monastery was built in 1473 and now houses 2,500 monks. Other main towns include Bayi and Batang—the latter being 2,700 metres (8,856 ft.) above sea level.[4]

The Khampa have a fearsome reputation for being the most hostile and violent of Tibetans. 'Tall and well-built men, fearless and open of countenance, they resemble Apache Indians, with plaited hair hanging from each side of well-modeled heads.'[5]

The Khampa, like all Tibetan groups, are devout followers of Buddhism. They have a long history of conflict with the Chinese, who annexed most of Kham Province to Sichuan in 1720. Until recently, 'No Chinese dares to enter the territory for fear of being murdered.'[6] Military clashes between the Khampa and the Chinese occurred in 1918,

1928 and 1932. In 1950 the Chinese captured the town of Chamdo without firing a shot. The Khampa fled in terror when the Chinese set off a huge fireworks display on the outskirts of the town. In late 1955 the Chinese authorities ordered the monks of Litang Monastery to produce an inventory for tax assessment. The monks refused to oblige. In February 1956 the Chinese laid

China Advocate

siege to the monastery, which was defended by several thousand monks and farmers. Chinese aircraft bombed Litang and the surrounding areas. In 1959 the Khampa living in Lhasa organized a revolt against Chinese rule. 'The fighting lasted three days with the Tibetans caught up in a religious fervor, not caring whether they lived or died.'[7]

Catholic work among the Khampa commenced in the mid-1800s. The Catholic mission at Batang was demolished in 1873 and again in 1905—after two priests had been killed and converts who would not deny their faith were shot.[8] By 1924 the mission numbered two bishops, 15 French missionaries and 4,800 baptized converts of whom 'about two-fifths were Tibetans'.[9] Today there are 200 Khampa Catholics near Kangding and some near Batang and Yajiang.[10] Protestant work among the Khampa commenced in 1897. Although the missionaries ran hospitals, schools and orphanages, they saw little fruit. By 1922 the Protestant station at Batang had won ten converts.[11]

Khampa, Northern

CHINA
Qinghai
Xizang (Tibet)
Sichuan
Khampa Northern

Population:
118,400 (2000)
145,900 (2010)
179,700 (2020)
Countries: China
Buddhism: Tibetan
Christians: none known

Overview of the Northern Khampa

Other Names: Kham, Khamba
Population Sources:
91,000 in China (1987, *Language Atlas of China*)
Language: Sino-Tibetan, Tibeto-Burman, Himalayish, Tibeto-Kanauri, Tibetic, Tibetan, Northern
Dialects: 4 (Bristod, Khrihdu, Kuergu, Nagnchen)
Professing Buddhists: 100%
Practising Buddhists: 65%
Christians: 0%
Scripture: Tibetan Bible 1948; New Testament 1885; Portions 1862
***Jesus* film:** none
Gospel Recordings: none
Christian Broadcasting: none
ROPAL code: KHG04

Status of Evangelization

97%

3%   0%

A   B   C

A = Have never heard the gospel
B = Have heard the gospel but have not become Christians
C = Are adherents to some form of Christianity

A 1987 linguistic study listed 91,000 speakers of the Northern Khampa Tibetan language in China.[1] They occupy the large, sparsely-populated Yushu Tibetan Autonomous Prefecture in southern Qinghai Province. Northern Khampa is spoken as far north as the 5,214-metre (17,100 ft.) Mount Yagradagze. In addition, a small number of Northern Khampa live over the border in north-east Tibet. The nomadic Northern Khampa live on a high plateau where they herd sheep, goats and yaks.[2]

Northern Khampa is one of four Khampa groups, 'each speaking its own language and living in different areas. Due to the migration of peoples and the many political developments, Tibet has become very ethnically complex.'[3] Anthropologist Michael Peissel described the Khampa in 1964: 'The Khampas stood a good six feet in height . . . wore great heavy boots and flowing khaki robes that flapped like whips as they walked, advancing with their feet slightly apart as if to trample the grass to extinction. . . . Unlike Tibetans of Lhasa, their features were not Mongoloid, but straight, with large fierce eyes set beside beak-like noses, and long hair braided and wound around their heads, giving them a primitive allure.'[4] Khampa men are easily identifiable by the red and black tassels braided into their hair. They say that they wear these to protect their scalps during knife fights. Khampa superstition says that a man without an earring will be reincarnated as a donkey. Turquoise, red coral, bone and silver ornaments decorate

Nancy Sturrock

the hair of the nomad Khampa women.

Heinrich Harrier, famous for his book *Seven Years in Tibet*, walked through Khampa areas in the 1940s. Harrier described the lawlessness and terror that the common people lived under: 'They live in groups in three or four tents which serve as headquarters for their campaigns. . . . Heavily armed with rifles and swords they force their way into a nomad's tent and insist on hospitable entertainment on the most lavish scale available. The nomad in terror brings out everything he has. The Khampas fill their bellies and their pockets and, taking a few cattle with them for good measure, disappear into the wide-open spaces. They repeat the performance at another tent every day till the whole region has been skinned. . . . Stories were told of the cruelty with which they sometimes put their victims to death. They go so far as to slaughter pilgrims and wandering monks and nuns.'[5]

Although they profess to be Buddhists, the Khampa nomads' religion is little more than a crude imitation of the ideals of the pure form of Buddhism. There are few temples or monasteries in this part of the Tibetan world, yet the Northern Khampa still consider themselves believers in Buddha and would not consider any other way. Two thousand years after the birth of Christ, the Northern Khampa remain almost completely untouched by the gospel. Geographic, linguistic, cultural and religious barriers separate them. There has never been any kind of church or lasting Christian witness in this extremely isolated and practically impenetrable Yushu Prefecture.

Khampa, Southern

Much confusion surrounds the classification and population of the Southern Khampa, whom some researchers refer to as *Atuence* people. Atuence is the old name for the Tibetan town of Deqen in northern Yunnan Province. *Operation China* profiled this group as *Tibetan, Deqen,* but I refer to them as the Southern Khampa here in order to remain consistent with the naming of other Tibetan language groups in this book. Some sources list more

than 500,000 Atuence speakers, but our research indicates that there are only around 95,000,[1] in addition to nine villages of Southern Khampa in the northernmost tip of Myanmar.[2] Formerly part of Tibet, the town of Deqen was annexed by the Chinese in 1703 and has since been a part of Yunnan Province.[3] Tibetans had migrated south into the region many centuries earlier. The extreme north of Yunnan is an isolated, mountainous region with abundant rain and snowfall. Hot springs located throughout the region help the people alleviate their winter struggles.[4]

The language and many of the customs of the Southern Khampa are distinct from those of other Tibetan peoples.[5] One Chinese scholar was 'surprised to find that the life and customs of the people of the Deqen Prefecture differ from those of the Qinghai-Tibet Plateau. Besides traditional Tibetan customs, they have developed quite a few of their own.'[6]

Although most Southern Khampa are

Buddhists, this group also has the largest number of professing Christians among any Tibetan group in the world. Three villages with a combined population of 600 people, located on the Tibetan side of the border, are Catholic.[7] Another 700 Tibetans meet in a large Catholic church in Yanjing.[8] The area was first evangelized by workers with the Paris Foreign Missionary Society, who constructed the church building in 1864.[9] The mission lovingly reached out to people all over the Tibetan world. In 1905, Tibetan lamas killed all of the French missionaries and the head of Father Dubernard was hung on the monastery gate.[10] The Chinese authorities responded by demolishing several Tibetan temples in the region. Around the same time, emissaries of the Dalai Lama were dispatched to a Christian village near Yanjing to order the people to renounce Christianity. They shot several Christian families in a field that is known as the 'Field of Blood' to this day. Instead of intimidating the believers, this cruel act solidified their faith and helped them to renounce Buddhism. The village has remained Christian ever since.

By 1922 there were reported to be 1,610 Tibetan Catholic converts in the area.[11] The Pentecostal Missionary Union commenced work in Deqen in 1912 but gained few converts. In recent years Lisu evangelists have been sent to the Deqen Tibetans and have discipled some Tibetans in the ways of Christ. According to a Tibetan Catholic priest, Lu Rendi, there are 6,500 Tibetan Catholics in south-east Tibet and at least a further 3,000 in neighbouring areas of Yunnan Province.[12]

Population:
96,800 (2000)
119,200 (2010)
146,900 (2020)
Countries: China, Myanmar
Buddhism: Tibetan
Christians: 7,500

Overview of the Southern Khampa

Other Names: Deqen Tibetan, Tibetan: Deqen, Atuentse, Atuence, Anshuenkun, Nyarong, Mekong Tibetan, Nganshuenkuan, Deqin Tibetan, Te'ch'in Tibetan, Kangba, Khamba

Population Sources:
95,750 in China (2000, P Hattaway)
1,000 in Myanmar in 9 villages (2000, P Hattaway)

Language: Sino-Tibetan, Tibeto-Burman, Himalayish, Tibeto-Kanauri, Tibetic, Tibetan, Northern

Dialects: 4 (Derong, Deqen, Gyalthang, Phyagphreng)
Professing Buddhists: 90%
Practising Buddhists: 75%
Christians: 7.7%
Scripture: Tibetan Bible 1948; New Testament 1885; Portions 1862
Jesus film: none
Gospel Recordings: Zang: Deging
Christian Broadcasting: none
ROPAL code: KHG02

Status of Evangelization

62%
30%
8%

A = Have never heard the gospel
B = Have heard the gospel but have not become Christians
C = Are adherents to some form of Christianity

Khampa, Western

Population:
206,400 (2000)
254,200 (2010)
313,100 (2020)
Countries: China, India, probably Nepal
Buddhism: Tibetan
Christians: 10

Overview of the Western Khampa

Other Names: Kham, Khamba

Population Sources:

157,700 in China (1987, *Language Atlas of China*)

1,221 in India (1981 census)

Probably also in Nepal

Language: Sino-Tibetan, Tibeto-Burman, Himalayish, Tibeto-Kanauri, Tibetic, Tibetan, Northern

Dialects: 2 (Ger-rtse, Nagchu)

Professing Buddhists: 99%

Practising Buddhists: 75%

Christians: 0.01%

Scripture: Tibetan Bible 1948; New Testament 1885; Portions 1862

Jesus film: none

Gospel Recordings: none

Christian Broadcasting: none

ROPAL code: KHG03

Status of Evangelization

92%

7%

1%

A   B   C

A = Have never heard the gospel
B = Have heard the gospel but have not become Christians
C = Are adherents to some form of Christianity

Approximately 220,000 Tibetans living in the massive Nghari Prefecture in central and northern Tibet speak the Western Khampa language. They have 'a very sparse population in a band to the north-east and extending to the north of almost the entire central Tibetan area'.[1] The region is mostly a high, desolate plateau. 'At 17,000 feet [5,180 metres], the rarefied atmosphere has only half as many oxygen particles as at sea level. As early as AD 100 a Chinese official described the Tibetan Plateau as "Headache Mountains".'[2]

Western Khampa is unintelligible with the Central Tibetan languages or Amdo Tibetan. Despite living in a huge area approximately the size of England, only two dialects are reported within the Western Khampa language.

A small number of Western Khampa live across parts of northern India, predominantly in the states of Himachal Pradesh and Uttar Pradesh.[3] In the 1981 census of India they numbered 1,221 people. The Northern Khampa in India are the descendents of traders from Tibet who settled in India about one hundred years ago. There are probably hundreds more Northern Khampa refugees living in Nepal and India today, but identifying them as such is an impossible task due to their classification simply as Tibetans. There is strong social pressure from within the exiled Tibetan community not to divide the Tibetan peoples by ethnolinguistic classification, as they fear this will weaken their political cause.

The Khampa live in some of the harshest

Julian Hawken

conditions in the world, and they tie their traditional long-sleeved coats with a belt, which conceals a large knife or sword. Many wear lucky charms, magical strings or amulet boxes around their necks. Khampa men, who often get around on horseback, are never without a weapon. Polyandry (the practice of brothers sharing the same wife) still occurs in some places. Life expectancy for Khampa living on the bitter plateau averages only about 45 years.

The Khampa rely on demons, ghosts and the spirits of disembodied deities to guide their decisions. Many monks are able to call up fearsome demons, which sometimes visualize in front of them. The most devout monks are reported to be able to transport themselves spiritually from one place to another, and they have been reputed to appear in different locations, great distances apart, on the same day. The Khampa also worship Yama, the god of death. They believe that he is the king of the underworld and that he controls all the events of their lives.

In the past, missionaries who were frustrated at not being allowed into Tibet loaded up dozens of yaks with Tibetan tracts and sent them randomly into the vast Tibetan frontiers.[4] In the 1920s one writer lamented, 'This region is not only without a resident missionary, but even the scouts of Christianity have barely touched it except at one or two points. . . . All these are realms to conquer in West China. Large areas are unknown absolutely, and still larger ones remain relatively unknown.'[5]

Khamti

More than 80,000 Khamti people live in the area where the three countries of Myanmar, India and China meet. The name *Khamti* means 'a land full of gold' (*kham* means 'gold' and *ti* means 'place'). Most Khamti—approximately 70,000—live in Kachin State of north-western Myanmar, having first settled along the Chinwin River in the 12th century AD.[1] They formed 'three small Khamti Long Thai States and developed a highly advanced civilization. Those who escaped enslavement by the Burmese settled in their present location in the fertile triangle of northern Myanmar, between the Mali and Nmai rivers.'[2] An additional 8,000 or more Khamti people live across the border in north-east India's states of Arunachal Pradesh and Assam, where they are recognized as a 'scheduled' (official) tribe. In Arunachal Pradesh they inhabit the plains of Lohit, Changlang, Lower Subansiri and Tirup districts, as well as the Dibang Valley.[3] Additional numbers of Khamti inhabit Assam State, especially the Lakhimpur, Dhemaji, Dibrugarh and Cachar districts of Assam State.[4]

Historians say that the Khamti migrated to India from the Irrawaddy valley, Myanmar, in 1751.[5] They settled along the Tangapani river.[6] They later moved and now inhabit the 'lower regions drained by the Tangapani and Noa-Dihing rivers. . . . Their territory is surrounded by dense forests of the tropical moist deciduous type.'[7]

The Khamti are one of only a few Tai-speaking people groups found within India's borders. Their language is related to Shan, but after centuries of geographical

separation Khamti has developed its own characteristics. They have their own script, called *Lik-Tai*, which resembles the script used by the Mon in southern Myanmar.

Due to the almost complete lack of ethnographic material available in Myanmar, most of what is known about the Khamti comes from India. One researcher there found that 'though the Khamti are Buddhists, they eat a variety of fish. They consume the meat of fowls, pigs, goats, bears, deer and tigers. Beef is a taboo.'[8] Khamti society is hierarchical, with the village chief at the top, followed by the Buddhist monks, the common people and the former slaves at the bottom.

When a Khamti couple gets married, 'a mediator accompanies the groom's relatives (barring his parents) to the bride's house in a procession. The groom's party offers a basket of dried fish and rice beer to the bride's parents. When the entertainment is over the mediator negotiates with the bride's father, whereupon he hands over his daughter to the groom's party. On its way back with the bride, the groom's party is stopped by the boys and girls of the village demanding a price for the bride.'[9]

Theravada Buddhism is the religion of almost every Khamti person. Each village has its own monastery, where proud parents send their sons to study the teachings of Buddha.[10] In India, out of the 6,181 Khamti people surveyed in the 1981 census, 6,143 stated that they were Buddhist, 28 Hindu, two Muslim and two Christian, while six people did not state their religion.[11] Few Khamti have any awareness of the Son of God who died that they may have eternal life.[12]

Create International (vertical caption on photo)

Population:
86,800 (2000)
97,900 (2010)
110,500 (2020)
Countries: Myanmar, India, possibly China
Buddhism: Theravada
Christians: 30

Overview of the Khamti

Other Names: Khamti Shan, Khampti, Hkamti, Khampti Shan, Khandi Shan, Kam Ti, Tai Kam Ti, Tai Khamti, Kham Tai, Khantis, Tai Kham Ti, Bor-Khampti, Moonglair Khampti, Kmajang, Phakial

Population Sources: 70,000 in Myanmar (2003, Myanmar Faces and Places)
6,181 in India (1981 census)
possibly also in China[13]

Language: Tai-Kadai, Kam-Tai, Be-Tai, Tai-Sek, Tai, Southwestern, East Central, Northwest

Dialects: 3 (Assam Khamti, North Burma Khamti, Sinkaling Khamti)

Professing Buddhists: 99%

Practising Buddhists: 95%

Christians: 0.1%

Scripture: none

Jesus **film:** none

Gospel Recordings: Khamti

Christian Broadcasting: none

ROPAL code: KHT

Status of Evangelization

88%

11%

1%

A   B   C

A = Have never heard the gospel
B = Have heard the gospel but have not become Christians
C = Are adherents to some form of Christianity

131

Kheng

A 1991 source listed a population of 40,000 Kheng people living in south-central Bhutan.[1] It is the most widely spoken of the Eastern Tibetan languages in Bhutan. The Kheng inhabit a widespread area in the south-central part of the kingdom, concentrated in Zhamgang District and western Mongar District. Zhamgang was once a collection of tiny principalities that were absorbed into Bhutan in the 17th century. One source gives specific details regarding the distribution of the Kheng: 'Near Zhamgang, the northernmost Kheng speaking village is Wangdugang on the Mangdechu [River]. Around Zhamgang the Mangdechu forms the boundary between

Population:
50,200 (2000)
64,400 (2010)
82,600 (2020)
Countries: Bhutan
Buddhism: Tibetan
Christians: 50

Bumthang, and just 47 per cent with Dzongkha (the national language of Bhutan).[3] George van Driem says, 'Although it could be argued that the two languages Kheng and Kurtop are dialects of Bumthang on grounds of mutual intelligibility, there are essential differences between the phonologies of Kheng and Kurtop on one hand and that of Bumthang on the other. Moreover, the speakers of these three languages identify strongly with their respective homelands in Bumthang, Kurto and Kheng. . . . The district capital of Kheng is Zhamgang proper. It has three dialects, all of which have significant differences. Within the vast Kheng area there is considerable dialect diversity, both lexically and in the way certain tenses are formed. The differences between the individual Kheng

Dwayne Graybill

the Kheng and Nyenkha speaking areas. South of the village of Takma, however, Kheng is spoken on both sides of the Mangdechu. In the east, the Kurichu River forms the boundary between the Kheng and Tsangla speaking areas. As one crosses the high mountain ridge traveling south from Zhamgang on the main road, one enters Nepali speaking territory.'[2]

The southernmost areas inhabited by the Kheng are off-limits to foreign travellers, because of the threat posed by separatist groups across the border in the Indian State of Assam. Several guerilla groups there have been waging a war against Indian rule, and senseless acts of violence are commonplace.

The Kheng language is part of the Eastern Tibetan branch of Tibeto-Burman. It is closely related to, yet distinct from, Bumthang and Kurtop. Kheng reportedly has 92 per cent lexical similarity with

dialects are in some cases as great as the difference between any one of these and a given dialect of Bumthang.'[4]

Tibetan Buddhism is the professed religion of the Kheng, although the pre-Buddhist religion of Bon also yields great influence. 'The Bon religion is widespread throughout Kheng, where it is practiced in syncretic coexistence with Buddhism, and there is a panoply of different local traditions.'[5] One expert on Tibetan Buddhism noted, 'When tantric Buddhism entered Tibet . . . it began a centuries-long battle with Tibet's native shamanism. In the end, tantric Buddhism prevailed only by absorbing much shamanist practice, and the shamanists survived by adopting a thin veneer of Buddhism.'[6]

In the early 1990s, the first Kheng people believed in Christ. Today there is a small group of believers, struggling to establish the Christian faith among this unreached people group.

Overview of the Kheng

Other Names: Khengkha, Khenkha, Khen, Keng, Ken

Population Sources:

40,000 in Bhutan (2001, G van Driem [1991 figure])

Language: Sino-Tibetan, Tibeto-Burman, Himalayish, Tibeto-Kanauri, Tibetic, Tibetan, Eastern

Dialects: 3 (Pchikor, Nangkor, Tamacho)

Professing Buddhists: 95%

Practising Buddhists: 65%

Christians: 0.1%

Scripture: none

Jesus **film:** none

Gospel Recordings: none

Christian Broadcasting: none

ROPAL code: XKF

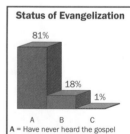

Status of Evangelization

81%

18%

1%

A   B   C

A = Have never heard the gospel
B = Have heard the gospel but have not become Christians
C = Are adherents to some form of Christianity

Approximately 12 million Khmer people live throughout the world today. They are the predominant ethnic group in the nation of Cambodia, where they number 9.3 million (83% of the population). More than 1.2 million Khmer reside in north-eastern Thailand.[1] An additional one million Khmer live in the Mekong River Delta areas of neighbouring southern Vietnam,[2] while a small number (4,000) Khmer live in the southern tip of Laos.[3] In the late 1970s and early 1980s a flood of Khmer refugees travelled to Western nations to avoid the diabolical killing fields of Pol Pot and the Khmer Rouge, when as many as two million people were butchered.[4] Today more than 210,000 Khmer make their homes in the United States, 80,000 in France, 25,000 in Australia and thousands more in Canada, the United Kingdom and many other nations.

Paul Hattaway

The Khmer civilization once ruled much of Southeast Asia. Between the 9th and 13th centuries their kingdom encompassed present-day Laos, Thailand, Cambodia and southern Vietnam. In the 1200s, the Thais and Vietnamese defeated the Khmer and pushed them into Cambodia, where most of them remain to this day. The most significant evidence of the Khmer's great past that survives is the world-famous Angkor Wat complex in Cambodia.

Theravada Buddhism was introduced to the area in the 13th century. The Khmer believe that they will be reincarnated, depending on how they lived their lives. A good person with many merits may come back in a higher social position, but one who was evil may come back as an animal. When they bury their dead, the Khmer place the body in a coffin. Three years after the death, if the Buddhist monks have given their approval through divination, the formal funeral ceremony is held. The body is dug up and cremated, and the ashes placed inside the local pagoda. The children and grandchildren of the deceased are required to then retire to the local monastery or temple to meditate on the good qualities of the deceased person.

The Khmer's Buddhist beliefs are mixed with elements from Hinduism—especially veneration of Siva, the king of Hindu gods. Many elements of animism and spirit worship also remain from the pre-Buddhist era. They worship the *neak*, which is a heavenly dragon the Khmer claim as their progenitor. Carvings of this dragon can be found on the roofs of their homes and temples, and on things such as coffins and the handles of tools.

Because of their strong religious beliefs, throughout history relatively few Khmer have turned to God. In recent years, however, there have been encouraging signs as tens of thousands of Khmer in all areas of Cambodia have decided to follow Christ. The gospel is presently enjoying unprecedented success. Many Khmer refugees found Christ in camps inside Thailand in the 1980s and 1990s. When they finally returned to their homeland, these Christians went as evangelists with a heart of fire for God and a passion for the souls of their countrymen.[5] Today approximately 100,000 Khmer people worldwide are Christians, although this still amounts to less than one per cent of the overall population.

Population:
11,871,600 (2000)
14,283,400 (2010)
17,212,900 (2020)

Countries: Cambodia, Thailand, Vietnam, USA, France, Australia, Laos, Canada, United Kingdom and many other nations

Buddhism: Theravada

Christians: 100,000

Overview of the Khmer

Other Names: Central Khmer, Kmer, Khmer Krom, Cur, Cambodians, Ku, Mien, Kho Me, Cu Tho, Kampuchean

Population Sources:
9,302,700 in Cambodia (2001, P Johnstone and J Mandryk)[6]
1,200,000 in Thailand (2001, P Johnstone and J Mandryk)[7]
895,299 in Vietnam (1989 census)[8]
210,000 in USA (2001, P Johnstone and J Mandryk)
80,000 in France (2001, P Johnstone and J Mandryk)
25,000 in Australia (2001, P Johnstone and J Mandryk)
3,902 in Laos (1995 census)
also in Canada, United Kingdom, and many other nations

Language: Austro-Asiatic, Mon-Khmer, Eastern Mon-Khmer, Khmer

Dialects: 3 (Central Khmer, Southern Khmer, Northern Khmer)[9]

Professing Buddhists: 96%

Practising Buddhists: 70%

Christians: 0.8%

Scripture: Bible 1954; New Testament 1929; Portions 1899

***Jesus* film:** available

Gospel Recordings: Khmer

Christian Broadcasting: available

ROPAL code: KMR (Central Khmer) and KXM (Northern Khmer)

Status of Evangelization

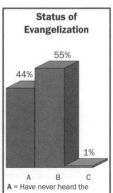

A = Have never heard the gospel
B = Have heard the gospel but have not become Christians
C = Are adherents to some form of Christianity

Khorat Thai

Population:
10,100 (2000)
11,000 (2010)
12,100 (2020)
Countries: Thailand
Buddhism: Theravada
Christians: 50

Overview of the Khorat Thai

Other Names: Thai Khorat, Khorat

Population Sources: 10,000 in Thailand (2001, J Schliesinger [1999 figure])

Language: Tai-Kadai, Tai, Southwestern, East-Central, Lao-Phutai

Dialects: 0

Professing Buddhists: 99%

Practising Buddhists: 75%

Christians: 0.5%

Scripture: none

Jesus **film:** none

Gospel Recordings: none

Christian Broadcasting: none

ROPAL code: none

Status of Evangelization

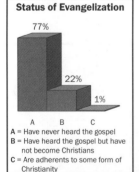

77%

22%

1%

A   B   C

A = Have never heard the gospel
B = Have heard the gospel but have not become Christians
C = Are adherents to some form of Christianity

More than 10,000 Khorat Thai people live in Nakhon Ratchasima Province in central Thailand. They mainly inhabit two large villages, Ban Nung Thap Prang and Ban Nong Samrong, both in the Chok Chai District about 20 kilometres (12 miles) south of the provincial capital. Approximately 4,000 Khorat Thai people live in each village. A few thousand Khorat Thai live in smaller villages in and around Nakhon Ratchasima City.

A lot of confusion exists surrounding the identity and history of the Khorat Thai. Joachim Schliesinger, in his 2001 book *Tai Groups of Thailand: Profile of the Existing Groups,* explains: 'Sei-denfaden[1] described the Khorat Thai as a group of people who are not of pure Thai stock but the descendants of Siamese (Thai) soldiers and Khmer women . . . in the first half of the fourteenth century. Credner,[2] on the other hand, classified the Khorat Thai with the central Siamese. Linguists from the Mahidol University recently classified their language as a central Thai dialect, and the Khorat Thai as an individual Tai-speaking group.'[3]

The Khorat Thai people themselves believe that they are descended from Thai soldiers sent from Bangkok to Nakhon Ratchasima in 1827 to fight against Lao troops. The Khorat Thai attacked and pushed the Lao back across the Mekong River.

This group does not appear on most ethnographic lists of groups in Thailand because their language is only considered slightly different from standard Central Thai.[4] They

do, however, consider themselves a unique ethnic group. Despite being surrounded by Isan (Northeast Thai speakers), the Khorat Thai speak Central Thai. This sets them apart from their neighbours and creates a strong sense of group cohesion.

Elderly Khorat Thai women dress differently from other Thai women. They wear the traditional Khmer-styled *chong kaben*, 'a

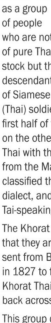

Christian Far East Ministry

long piece of cloth wrapped around the waist and down to the knees, from where it is pulled back between the legs and tucked in at the waist under a silver belt. . . . Old Khorat Thai women report that their mothers decorated themselves with silver anklets and gold armbands and necklaces.'[5] In the past, Khorat Thai men were skilled hunters of deer, wild pigs and other animals, but these have become all but extinct in the area due to over-hunting. They have been forced to feed their families through agricultural means, and now they only hunt for small animals like birds, snakes and rats.

Almost all Khorat Thai families are Theravada Buddhists. In addition to worshipping Buddha, they 'believe in an array of spirits, including those which reside in villages, houses, forests, trees, water and other objects in the natural surroundings. The most important spirit is the spirit of the village, called *jau ban*. Once a year in April, the villagers gather at the spirit house . . . to bring offerings of pigs' heads, chickens, whisky and flowers to appease the protector of the village.'[6]

Very few Khorat Thai have believed in Christ, and there has been little gospel witness among this proud and needy people group.

Population:
820 (2000)
950 (2010)
1,110 (2020)
Countries: India
Buddhism: Tibetan
Christians: none known

Overview of the Khowa

Other Names: Bunun, Khoa

Population Sources:

625 in India (1981 census)

Language: Sino-Tibetan, Tibeto-Burman, Himalayish, Tibeto-Kanauri, Tibetic, Tibetan, Unclassified

Dialects: 0

Professing Buddhists: 97%

Practising Buddhists: 80%

Christians: 0%

Scripture: none

Jesus film: none

Gospel Recordings: Khowar

Christian Broadcasting: none

ROPAL code: none

Status of Evangelization

80%

20%

0%

A   B   C

A = Have never heard the gospel
B = Have heard the gospel but have not become Christians
C = Are adherents to some form of Christianity

Approximately 800 people speak the Khowa language, which is commonly called Bugun,[1] in north-east India. About half of all Khowa people 'reside in the two villages of Wanghoo and Singchung near the district headquarters at Bomdila in West Kameng District'.[2] These communities are on the hillsides along both sides of the Rupa River (also known as Enga). 'The upper reaches of their land are lined by oak forests. The climate of the area is cold. In the upper reaches of the area, snowfall occurs in the months of January and February. The area experiences heavy rainfall in the months of May to August.'[3]

The 1981 Indian census listed 625 Khowa people, down from a figure of 703 Khowa returned in the 1971 census.[4] The Khowa 'are surrounded by the Sherdukpen on the west, with whom they share part of the Tanga valley, by the Monpas on the north, the Mijis or Dhamais on the east, and the Hrusos or Akas on the south'.[5]

The Khowa language—which is an unclassified part of the Tibeto-Burman family—was first studied in the winter of 1913–14, when the British authorities compiled a 100-word list. Little research has been conducted since, except for brief reports by Ivan Simon (1976)[6] and Rinchin Dondrup (1990).[7] J N Chowdhury (1983) briefly mentions that the Khowa have 'a distinctive language which they zealously preserve'.[8]

The Khowa say they originated in the north, in today's Tibet, before they moved southward in search of a new place to live. Locals believe that they arrived in the area before the Sherdukpen. For many years the Khowa were oppressed by the Aka tribe, who used to plunder them on the pretext of

collecting taxes. The Khowa responded by relocating away from them. The Khowa are a colourful people. 'Their dresses during day-to-day occasions are very colourful which they also use during dances and festive occasions. That means they do not have any special dress for their dances and festivals, since they are colourful round the year.'[9]

When the 1981 census was conducted, 606 of the 625 Khowa people stated that Buddhism was their religion. Two individuals said they were Hindus, eight were followers of 'other religions' (i.e., animists), and the remaining nine people did not state their religion. Other sources say that the Khowa believe in a mixture of traditional animism and Tibetan Buddhism. One researcher has found that the Khowa 'believe in one Supreme being who created the universe and life therein. They respect the Supreme God but

Dwayne Graybill

do not worship [him].'[10] Fear of demonic forces plays a major role in everyday Khowa life. For example, children are named immediately after birth, because 'the Khowas believe if there is a delay, some evil spirit will name the baby, and as a result the baby will suffer. . . . When the child grows up to 16 to 17 years, the parents hold a worship called *chhoacshao*. This ritual is performed to please the spirit responsible for the welfare and betterment of the children.'[11] There has never been a known Christian among this small tribe. Gospel audio recordings are available in the Khowa language, but are rarely utilized.

Khuen

More than 10,000 people belonging to the Khuen ethnic group live in the two Asian countries of Laos and China. The majority (approximately 9,000) make their home in Luang Namtha and Oudomxai provinces in north-west Laos.[1] More than 1,200 Khuen people live in nearby areas of south-west China. They inhabit a few small villages within Jinghong County in south-western Yunnan Province.[2] A small number of Khuen families also live on the west coast of the United States in Richmond, California and in Seattle, Washington. They were accepted into America as refugees following the 1975 Communist takeover of Laos.

The Khuen have appeared in published sources under several different spellings. Some publications have listed *Kuan* and *Khuen* as two separate groups, but they are the same people. It is important to note that the Khuen, who speak a Mon-Khmer language related to Khmu, are not the same as two other ethnic groups in Laos with similar names: Tai Kouanne and Khmu Keun. The Khuen are also different from the *Khun*, a Tai group found in eastern Myanmar.

Many aspects of Khuen culture are similar to the Khmu, including their family names—which are taken from the names of sacred animals or plants. For the duration of their lives, the Khuen are not allowed to touch the particular animal or plant that bears their name.

The Khuen in Laos were converted to Theravada Buddhism under influence of the Lu people about 400 years ago. When Christian missionary William Clifton Dodd visited the Khuen more than a century ago, he reported, 'A branch of the Kamu called Kwen [Khuen] have temples and priests teaching the Yun script, and they also have village and household spirits. The other non-Buddhist Kahs have the village and household spirits and then some.'[3] In another Khuen village, Dodd wrote that 'the head man . . . told me that he was the head of nine villages. He and his people are Kwen, who are indigenous to this region. There are five villages that have temples. They are the Buddhists of this region. He says that some time ago there were about seventy houses in this village called Puka. But disease and death have reduced the number to about fifty. . . . I had so many calls for medicine that I hardly had time to eat.'[4] Buddhism enjoys less influence among the 1,200 Khuen people in China. Some have been converted to Buddhism, but most continue to worship a hierarchy of demons and ghosts. Every year, the Khuen hold a festival to worship the spirits of the village and their ancestors.

Today there are between 100 and 200 Christians among the Khuen in Laos. They first received the gospel as early as 1902. Dodd reported, 'I had rapt attention from all. In the evening I had a still larger and more attentive audience. Many stayed after service to talk. They say they understand and would like to listen to such preaching every day. May the time soon come when they can have it. We left feeling that we have many kind friends among the [Khuen] and no enemies . . . they said that if they had someone to teach them they would like to learn Christianity.'[5]

CHINA
Yunnan
MYANMAR
Luang Namtha
LAOS
Oudomxai
Khuen

Population:
10,250 (2000)
12,850 (2010)
16,200 (2020)
Countries: Laos, China, USA
Buddhism: Theravada
Christians: 200

Paul Hattaway

Overview of the Khuen

Other Names: Kuan, Kween, Khween, Khouen, Kuanhua

Population Sources:
8,000 in Laos (1995, L Chazee)
1,000 in China (1991, *Encyclopedic Dictionary of Chinese Linguistics*)
also in USA

Language: Austro-Asiatic, Mon-Khmer, Northern Mon-Khmer, Khmuic, Mal-Khmu, Khmu

Dialects: 0

Professing Buddhists: 80%

Practising Buddhists: 55%

Christians: 1.9%

Scripture: work in progress

***Jesus* film:** none

Gospel Recordings: none

Christian Broadcasting: none

ROPAL code: KHF (Khuen) and QAK (Kuanhua)

Status of Evangelization

68%
30%
2%

A   B   C
A = Have never heard the gospel
B = Have heard the gospel but have not become Christians
C = Are adherents to some form of Christianity

Approximately 120,000 Khun people live in north-east Myanmar (formerly Burma) and areas of northern Thailand. There is some confusion regarding the Khun people. Some sources state that there are 100,000 living in Thailand, but this is not accurate.[1] There are few Khun communities in Thailand, with perhaps a population of only 5,000. The authoritative *Ethnologue*, which lists every known language in the world, doubts there are any Khun in Thailand at all.[2] Joachim Schliesinger says that the Khun in Thailand inhabit four districts (Muang, San Pa Tong, Sam Lang and Hang Dong) in Chiang Mai Province.[3]

Part of the reason for this confusion is that the Tai-speaking groups in the Kengtung valley area in Myanmar's Shan State—where the Khun live—seem to be ethnically, culturally and linguistically interrelated. It is said that the Khun River, which flows through their homeland, lent its name to the Khun people. They are distinguished from the other Tai groups in Shan State by 'slight differences in dialect,[4] physiognomy and the dresses of their womenfolk. The Khun are taller and fairer, and their noses are not so flat.'[5] The Khun should not be confused with the Khouen, Khuen or Tai Khouen people of Laos and Thailand, who speak a Mon-Khmer language.

The Khun people themselves are said to have a 'deep and strongly rooted culture of self-determination. Their homeland . . . has been their center of civilization for many centuries.'[6] Kengtung City has been the main centre of habitation for the Khun since a son of the Lanna King Mengrai founded the Kingdom of Kengtung in the 12th century. The ancestors of the Khun in Thailand were war captives brought from Myanmar in the early 1800s.

Although the large majority of Khun people are Theravada Buddhists, their religious worldview includes strong elements of spirit worship and ancestor worship. 'The most important spirit is the spirit of the land, which has to be propitiated daily with food and beverage, at the spirit house found in almost every Khun compound. The Khun honour ancestral spirits. On the full moon in June, Khun villagers worship their ancestors with offerings of boiled pork meat, chicken, fruit, rice and flowers at a special altar inside their houses.'[7]

In the past few decades a significant Christian church has emerged in Myanmar's Shan State. Thousands of people from ethnic groups such as the Shan, Akha and Lahu have put their trust in Christ. As a result, some Khun have heard the gospel, and about 2,000 are Christians today. In 1997, the Christian mission Asia Harvest supplied New Testaments to the Khun Christians in Myanmar. The Bibles were in the Lu script of 1933, but the Khun were able to read it easily and were deeply appreciative. One Khun pastor said, 'Before now the Buddhist monks mocked us, saying, "If your God is so great, how come his book is not in our language?" Now that we have God's Word in our script, the monks have requested hundreds of copies and are studying the words of Jesus intently.'[8]

Population:
117,400 (2000)
131,700 (2010)
147,900 (2020)
Countries: Myanmar, Thailand
Buddhism: Theravada
Christians: 2,000

Overview of the Khun

Other Names: Tai Khun, Hkun, Khun Shan, Gon Shan, Khuen, Khoen, Tai Khoen, Tai-Khuen

Population Sources: 100,000 in Myanmar (1990, A Diller)
5,000 in Thailand (2003, P Hattaway)

Language: Tai-Kadai, Kam-Tai, Be-Tai, Tai-Sek, Tai, Southwestern, East Central, Northwest

Dialects: 0

Professing Buddhists: 95%

Practising Buddhists: 60%

Christians: 1.7%

Scripture: Portions 1938

Jesus **film:** none

Gospel Recordings: Khun; Khun Shan; Tai Khun

Christian Broadcasting: none

ROPAL code: KKH

Create International

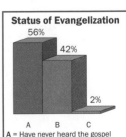

Status of Evangelization

56%
42%
2%

A B C

A = Have never heard the gospel
B = Have heard the gospel but have not become Christians
C = Are adherents to some form of Christianity

Kinnaura

More than 60,000 Kinnaura people inhabit extremely high-altitude locations in the north Indian state of Himachal Pradesh.[1] The Kinnaura are the largest ethnic group in the district that gives them their name—Kinnaur District. The Kinnaura inhabit villages between 5,000 and 6,770 metres (16,400 to 22,200 ft.) above sea level, in an area described as having 'mountainous topography, cold climate, dense forests, low rainfall and heavy snowfall'.[2] The Kinnaura people comprise approximately 70 per cent of the total population in the Kinnaur District. They also inhabit part of the Lahaul-Spiti District, 'from Chauhra to Sangla and north along the Satluj River to Morang and several villages of the upper Ropa River Valley'.[3] Small pockets of Kinnaura also reportedly live in the north Indian states of Uttar Pradesh, Punjab and Jammu and Kashmir.

The classification of the Kinnaura is complicated. Although the Indian government has granted them status as a Scheduled Tribe, there appear to be at least several different language and people groups within this group called Kinnaura.[4] The *Ethnologue*, which attempts to list every language in the world, has several listings. In addition to the main Kinnauri language, they

list Bhoti Kinnauri (6,000 speakers), Harijan Kinnauri (6,331) and Chitkuli Kinnauri (1,060).[5]

From a religious standpoint, the Kinnaura are an extremely interesting group. Their territory forms the

David Treat

border between the Buddhist and Hindu worlds, and accordingly the Kinnaura's religious belief is a fusion of the two. They acknowledge their strong links to Hinduism by claiming that they originated in the shadow of Lord Brahma. Another legend says that 'they have sprung from the toe of Brahma along with the Yakshas'.[6]

Hinduism has gained in popularity in the Kinnaur District in the past few generations, as thousands of Hindus have migrated into north Himachal Pradesh. Previously, Tibetan Buddhism held sway in these remote Himalayan regions. One source notes, 'Kinnaur is a place of curious coexistence of Hinduism and Mahayanist Buddhism. People embracing Buddhism belong to the Nyingmapa, Dukpa, Kargyutpa, and Gelukpa sects. On entering a Buddhist village, one finds a tomb and *chorten* in various [parts] of the village and also in individual houses, which are meant to ward off evil spirits.'[7] Many Kinnaura people do not see a conflict in their mixture of faith. If asked whether or not they believe in Hinduism they reply 'Yes', and if asked if they follow Buddhism they also reply 'Yes!' Many celebrate both Buddhist and Hindu festivals. The Kinnaura also believe and practise animistic rituals in a bid to ward off evil spirits.

The confusion regarding the Hindu-Buddhist mix among the Kinnaura can be seen in figures from the 1981 census, when 31.29 per cent of Kinnaura stated they were Buddhists, compared to 68.71 per cent who said they were Hindus.[8] This accounts for all Kinnaura people, meaning that not a single person believed in Christ at the time. A recent survey indicated there are now 140 Christians in Kinnaura District,[9] about 100 of which are from the Kinnaura ethnic group.

Overview of the Kinnaura

Other Names: Kinnauri, Kinnara, Kinnaurese, Kinara, Kanawara, Kanaura, Kinnaura Yanuskad, Kanorug Skadd, Lower Kinnauri, Kinori, Kinner, Kanauri, Kanawari, Kanawi, Kunawari, Kunawar, Tibas Skad, Kanorin Skad, Kanaury Anuskad, Koonawure, Melhesti, Milchanang, Milchan, Milchang

Kanauri, Western Himalayish, Kanauri

Dialects: 0

Professing Buddhists: 50%

Practising Buddhists: 30%

Christians: 0.2%

Scripture: Portions 1909

Jesus film: none

Gospel Recordings: none

Christian Broadcasting: none

ROPAL code: KFK

Population Sources:

47,913 in India (1981 census)

Language: Sino-Tibetan, Tibeto-Burman, Himalayish, Tibeto-

Population:
63,000 (2000)
73,500 (2010)
85,700 (2020)
Countries: India
Buddhism: Tibetan
Christians: 100

Status of Evangelization

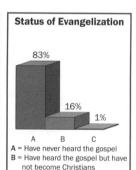

83%

16%

1%

A   B   C

A = Have never heard the gospel
B = Have heard the gospel but have not become Christians
C = Are adherents to some form of Christianity

Festivals of Korea and Japan

Festivals are an important part of Buddhist society. They are times when relatives and friends interact, and when fun and enjoyment are had by all. Many of the festivals that take place among Buddhist groups are religious in nature and reinforce the core values and beliefs of each group's history. In this section we take a pictorial tour of some important festivals in Korea and Japan.

1-5. The Feast of the Lanterns (Buddha's birthday), Beomeosa Temple in Pusan, South Korea. [all by Paul Hattaway]

6. Buddha looks down on his worshippers as monks dance joyously in a Seoul temple, South Korea. [Xayographix]
7. Busy monks cook for hundreds of pilgrims at the Feast of the Lanterns, Beomeosa Temple, Pusan, South Korea. [Paul Hattaway]
8. Hundreds of paper lanterns, Beomeosa Temple. [Paul Hattaway]
9. A kind monk with the author's son, Dalen, at the Beomeosa Temple. [Paul Hattaway]
10. A thousand Buddha idols at a Seoul temple in South Korea. [Xayographix]
11. An elderly Korean woman stops to pray on Buddha's birthday, Pusan. [Joy Hattaway]

12

13

14

15

16

17

12–17. Scenes from a Buddhist ceremony at a temple in Seoul, South Korea. [all by Xayographix]

18-25. The Aoi Matsuri Festival in Kyoto, Japan dates back to the 6th century. This Shinto festival commemorates the successful prayers of the people to stop calamitous weather. Every year more than 600 Japanese dress up in traditional clothing and join a procession behind ox carts and horses carrying imperial messengers. [18-21 by Paul Hattaway; 22-25 by Joy Hattaway]

Approximately 80 million Korean people live in dozens of countries throughout the world. The largest populations of Koreans are found in South Korea (46.7 million in 2000), North Korea (23.8 million), China (2.1 million) and the United States (2.1 million).

According to Korean folklore, the birth of the Korean nation took place in 2333 BC. Constant wars with the Chinese contributed to a strong ethnic identity among the inhabitants of the Korean Peninsula. The first united Korean kingdom was formed in the first century AD in the northern part of the peninsula. The next four centuries 'witnessed a remarkable flowering of the arts, architecture, literature and statecraft. Chinese influences were absorbed, reinterpreted and alloyed with traditional Korean beliefs. Probably the single most formative influence was Buddhism, which in time, became the state religion.'[1]

Paul Hattaway

The Korean language 'does not have tones like Chinese, but certain words have different meanings depending on whether they are pronounced high and short, or low and long'.[2]

The Korean war, which began in 1950, resulted in the break-up of the peninsula into Communist North Korea and democratic South Korea. More than two million people died during the fighting. North Korea has turned into an impoverished, myopic and bizarre place ruled by the tyrannical Kim Il Sung and his son Kim Jong Il. A powerful personality cult emerged, with the two leaders being worshipped as gods.

Mahayana Buddhism entered Korea from China in the 6th century AD. Today there are 18 different sects in Korea. Although atheism and Christianity have made massive inroads into Korean life in the past century, today there remain 11 million Buddhists in South Korea (24% of the population).[3] It is difficult to estimate numbers in North Korea, but there are believed to be more than one million professing Buddhists there,[4] as well as millions more Korean Buddhists around the world.

It is not recorded if Nestorian missionaries penetrated as far as Korean territory during their time in China between the 7th and 14th centuries, but in 1927 archaeologists excavated a tomb near the present North Korea-China border. 'They found the remains of seven bodies and at the head of each a clay cross . . . they were able to date the grave at between 998 and 1006 by Chinese coins of the Song Dynasty left with the bodies.'[5] When the first Catholic missionary entered Korea in 1794, he was greeted by 4,000 Korean believers who had been evangelized by Koreans returning from China.[6] The first Protestants arrived in the 1880s. In the early 1900s a powerful revival saw tens of thousands come to Christ. Prior to the Second World War, Pyongyang, today's capital of North Korea, was known as the 'Jerusalem of the East' because of the large number of churches there. Thousands of North Korean believers have been butchered and tortured in the most demonic ways to the present day, but a secret house church of possibly 300,000 Christians exists in North Korea today, while approximately one-third of the population of South Korea professes faith in Jesus Christ.[7] South Korea has become one of the great missionary sending nations in the world.

Population:
76,208,200 (2000)
84,414,100 (2010)
93,594,400 (2020)
Countries: South Korea, North Korea, China, USA, Japan, Uzbekistan, Russia, Kazakhstan, Brazil, Argentina, Kyrgyzstan, Paraguay, Guam, Singapore, Australia, New Zealand, United Kingdom, Canada and dozens of other countries around the world
Buddhism: Mahayana
Christians: 17,000,000

Overview of the Koreans

Other Names: Chaoxian, Hanghohua, Hanguk Mal

Population Sources:

46,750,300 in South Korea (2001, P Johnstone and J Mandryk [2000 figure])
23,870,900 in North Korea (2001, P Johnstone and J Mandryk [2000 figure])
2,130,000 in China (2000, P Hattaway)
2,100,000 in United States (2001, P Johnstone and J Mandryk [2000 figure])
675,000 in Japan
320,000 in Uzbekistan
110,000 in Russia
109,000 in Kazakhstan[8]

Language: Korean (language isolate)

Dialects: 8 (South Korea [5]: Seoul, Ch'ungch'ongdo, Kyongsangdo, Chollando, Cheju Island; North Korea [3]: Hamgyongdo, P'yong'ando, Hwanghaedo)

Professing Buddhists: 25%
Practising Buddhists: 15%
Christians: 22.3%
Scripture: Bible 1911; New Testament 1887; Portions 1882
Jesus film: available
Gospel Recordings: Korean; Korean: Northern China
Christian Broadcasting: available
ROPAL code: KKN

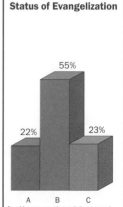

Status of Evangelization

55%

22%   23%

A   B   C

A = Have never heard the gospel
B = Have heard the gospel but have not become Christians
C = Are adherents to some form of Christianity

More than 80,000 Kucong people live scattered around the world. Despite their relatively small population, the Kucong are located in six different countries. The majority (approximately 40,000) live in remote areas of Mojiang, Xinping and Mengla counties of Yunnan Province in south-west China.[1] An additional number of Kucong live in Thailand. There has been a small number of Kucong villages in Thailand for almost a century, but in recent years many Kucong from Laos have found their way to refugee camps along the Thai-Laos border. More than 10,000 Kucong live in Myanmar, near Kengtung City in Shan State, while an additional 5,000 are in north-west Vietnam, located on the banks of the Son Da (Black) River, just west of the town of Muong Te in Lai Chau Province.[2] Approximately 3,000 Kucong live in at least 16 villages of north-west Laos (Luang Namtha[3] and Bokeo provinces). Finally, more than six hundred Kucong have migrated to the United States where they predominantly live in the Visalia, California area.

The Kucong are commonly called Yellow Lahu, yet their language and history are significantly different from those of the other Lahu tribes in Asia. Between the 14th and 19th centuries the Lahu in China took strong leadership in their wars of resistance against their Han and Tai oppressors. 'Not until an irretrievable defeat in 1799 did they begin to collapse. This defeat caused the Lahu to flee into the mountains; from that point on they fragmented as a people. The Black Lahu claim to

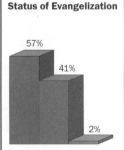

Julian Hawken

be pure Lahu and express contempt for the Kucong for having surrendered to the Qing army. Since that time the Kucong have been hated and oppressed by all other Lahu.'[4]

In China the Kucong lived in dire poverty and isolation for centuries. Due to disease and attacks by wild animals, a third of their population died in just a three-year period between 1947 and 1949.[5] It is primarily because of their struggles that the Kucong have spread out over five countries in Asia as they searched for a better life.

The Kucong are primarily Theravada Buddhists, in contrast to the other Lahu who are either animists or Christians. They also maintain a strong animistic belief system alongside their Buddhist faith.

In the past, Christianity was not able to spread from the Lahu to the Kucong because of the many prejudices between the two groups. Consequently, today there are fewer believers among the Kucong than there are among the Lahu.[6] In Myanmar the Kucong first received the gospel from missionary William Young in 1903. 'By May 1905, Young had baptized 1,623 converts, from both the [Kucong] and Lahu.'[7] H A Baker—the great Pentecostal missionary—left a spiritual legacy at a Kucong village called *Stony Stockade* along a remote mountain ridge in Mojiang County, China. 'The whole village of 29 households were converted after hearing Baker's fiery preaching, and they have earnestly adhered to the faith until this day. Right up to the present, the old inhabitants still enjoy very much recounting to visitors, vividly and nostalgically, anecdotes of "Ben Mooshi" (Pastor Baker).'[8]

Overview of the Kucong

Other Names: Lahu Shi, Yellow Lahu, Kutsung, Shi, Kui, Kwi, Lahu Xi, Kui Sung, Mousseur Luang, Kuy Soung, Lahu Aga, Lahu Adaw-aga, Lahu Shi Bakeo, Kur, Musseh Kwi, Khutsho, Ne Thu, La Hu Si

Population Sources:
40,400 in China (2000, P Hattaway)[9]
20,000 in Thailand (2000, B Grimes [1998 figure])
10,000 in Myanmar (2000, B Grimes [1998 figure])
5,000 in Vietnam (2000, B Grimes [1998 figure])
2,880 in Laos (1999, Asian Minorities Outreach [1995 figure])[10]
600 in USA (1991, J Matisoff)[11]

Language: Sino-Tibetan, Tibeto-Burman, Lolo-Burmese, Loloish, Southern, Akha, Lahu

Dialects: 0

Professing Buddhists: 55%

Practising Buddhists: 25%

Christians: 1.8%

Scripture: work in progress

***Jesus* film:** none

Gospel Recordings: Yellow Lahu

Christian Broadcasting: none

ROPAL code: KDS

Population:
79,900 (2000)
88,500 (2010)
98,300 (2020)
Countries: China, Thailand, Myanmar, Laos, USA, possibly Vietnam
Buddhism: Theravada
Christians: 1,500

CHINA
Yunnan
MYANMAR
Shan
VIETNAM
LAOS
THAILAND
Kucong

Status of Evangelization

57%
41%
2%

A   B   C
A = Have never heard the gospel
B = Have heard the gospel but have not become Christians
C = Are adherents to some form of Christianity

Population:
257,900 (2000)
292,700 (2010)
333,900 (2020)
Countries: Thailand, Laos, Cambodia
Buddhism: Theravada
Christians: 9,500

Overview of the Kui

Other Names: Sui, Suay, Suai, Suoi, Souei, Suei, Soai, Kuoy, Kuy, Cuoi, Kui Souei, Khamen-Boran, Aouei, Dui, Xuay, Xouay

Population Sources:
180,000 in Thailand (2000, J Schliesinger [1995 figure])[1]
45,498 in Laos (1995 census)[2]
15,495 in Cambodia (2000, B Grimes [1989 figure])

Language: Austro-Asiatic, Mon-Khmer, Eastern Mon-Khmer, Katuic, West Katuic, Kuay-Yoe

Dialects: 7 (Damrey, Anlour, O, Kraol, Antra, Chang, Na Nhyang)

Professing Buddhists: 75%

Practising Buddhists: 30%

Christians: 3.5%

Scripture: New Testament 1978, Portions 1965

Jesus **film:** available

Gospel Recordings: Thailand: Kuy, Kuoy, Kui, Kui Antra; Cambodia: Suai, Sui, Suoi; Laos: Souei Bung Sai, Souei Kapeu, Souei Kham Noi, Souei Saneum, Souei Thateng, Sui North, Sui South, Sui Tunla

Christian Broadcasting: available

ROPAL code: KDT

Status of Evangelization

61%

35%

4%

A   B   C

A = Have never heard the gospel
B = Have heard the gospel but have not become Christians
C = Are adherents to some form of Christianity

More than 260,000 Kui people are scattered over three countries in Southeast Asia. The majority (approximately 190,000) live in east-central Thailand in the three provinces of Ubon Ratchathani, Sisaket and Surin.[3] Over 50,000 Kui inhabit more than 70 villages in neighbouring parts of southern Laos,[4] while another 20,000 make their homes in north-east Cambodia.[5] Kui, or Kuy, is the self-name of this group in all three countries where they live. The Thais and Laos call them Sui, or Suay.

Although the origins of the Kui are uncertain, most historians consider them the first inhabitants of parts of Thailand and Cambodia. Later, the Khmer and Thais entered the region and took control. One source states, 'The Negroid features apparent in some Kui may indicate a relationship to the Negroid aborigines of the Malay peninsula. Other Kui are fair skinned, a result from intermixing with Indonesians or Melanesians, driven out or absorbed by subsequent Mon-Khmer invaders.'[6]

In Laos today the Kui are recognized as the best elephant handlers in the nation. Their counterparts in Thailand, however, have been forced to give up this profession due to the deforestation of their habitat. The last wild elephant captured in Surin Province was in 1961.

The Kui (especially those in Laos) have a strongly matriarchal and matrilineal society. 'The wife takes care of her family's finances. All possessions and the family name are handed down through the female side of the family. After marriage, newly-weds must live with the bride's family.'[7]

Although the majority of Kui people profess Buddhism as their religion, for most it seems little more than a thin veneer covering a deeper belief in animism. The Kui in Thailand have been described as practising 'a kind of folk Buddhism, modified with beliefs in spirits, sorcerers, ghosts, evil spells and the like. Therefore, although they are all officially considered Buddhists, the Kui have retained many of their traditional animistic beliefs and superstitious practices and rituals. They feel that many powerful spirits, living in the forest and hills, must be suitably propitiated in order to avoid misfortune.'[8]

Between three and four per cent of Kui people today are estimated to believe in Christ. In Laos there are 'several Catholic villages'[9] among the Kui, while in Thailand, where missionary work can be conducted more freely, there are thousands of Kui Christians of various denominations. The New Testament was translated into Kui in 1978, using the Thai script because the Kui did not have an orthography of their own. Scripture portions were first translated in 1965. Today the Kui have Christian radio broadcasts, the *Jesus* film and more than a dozen gospel recordings in various Kui dialects. Despite the efforts that the body of Christ has expended to reach them, most Kui remain indifferent to the gospel. The Kui Church is generally institutionalized and unable to display a strong vibrant witness to their communities.

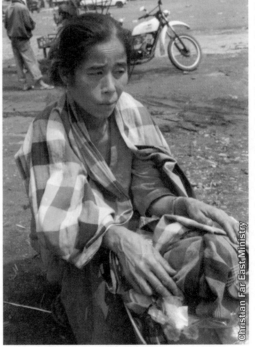

Christian Far East Ministry

Kurtop

CHINA
Xizang (Tibet)

Bumthang   Lhuntse

INDIA

BHUTAN

Kurtop

Population:
12,500 (2000)
16,100 (2010)
20,600 (2020)
Countries: Bhutan
Buddhism: Tibetan
Christians: none known

Overview of the Kurtop

Other Names: Kurtopa, Kurtokha, Gurtü, Kurtopakha, Kurthopka, Kurteopka, Kurthopkha, Kurtobikha, Kurtobi Zhake

Population Sources:
10,000 in Bhutan (2001, G van Driem [1991 figure])

Language: Sino-Tibetan, Tibeto-Burman, Himalayish, Tibeto-Kanauri, Tibetic, Tibetan, Eastern

Dialects: 1 (Tangmachu)

Professing Buddhists: 100%

Practising Buddhists: 75%

Christians: 0%

Scripture: none

Jesus film: none

Gospel Recordings: none

Christian Broadcasting: none

ROPAL code: XKZ

Status of Evangelization

80%

20%

0%

A   B   C

A = Have never heard the gospel
B = Have heard the gospel but have not become Christians
C = Are adherents to some form of Christianity

More than 10,000 Kurtop people inhabit areas of northern Bhutan, as far north as the border with China. Lhuntse District is home to the Kurtop. One scholar has given a detailed description of the extent of the Kurtop territory: 'Kurtop is a language of Lhuntse District spoken to the west of the mighty Kurichu [River] all the way to the Tibetan border in the north. The language is known to its speakers by the names *Kurtötkha* and *Kurtöbi Zhakê*. . . .

Dwayne Graybill

At the southern end, the Kurtop speaking area begins at the village of Tangmachu, south of which Chocangacakha [Matpa] is spoken. The dialect of Tangmachu, located about 5 kilometres [three miles] south of Lhuntse, as the crow flies, differs somewhat from that of the rest of the language as it is spoken elsewhere in Kurto. . . . The Kurichu River separates the Kurto and the Dzala language areas in the east. In the west the Bumthang area begins as one crosses the mountains via the Rodungla.'[1]

Lhuntse District is extremely isolated. As recently as 1998 one book noted, 'It is very rural and there are fewer than five vehicles, including the ambulance, and not a single petrol station in the whole district. Formerly known as Kurtoe, the region is the ancestral home of Bhutan's royal family. Though geographically in the east, it was culturally identified with central Bhutan, and the high route over Rodang La was a major trade route until the road to Mongar was completed.'[2]

Regarding the actual township of Lhuntse, it has been reported, 'There is little to see and do here, but the *dzong* (fort-monastery) is one of the most picturesque in Bhutan. There are a few food shops and food stalls along the road as it enters the town.'[3] Lhuntse is famous in Bhutan for its weaving, embroidery and basket-making. There is no large-scale industry here, but many families earn their livelihood by weaving in their homes.

A two-day walk from Lhuntse up the Kurichu River is the Kurtop village of Dungkhar. Bhutan's royal family, the Wangchuks, trace their ancestry from here. Jigme Namgyal, the father of the first king, was born here in 1825. This fact, understandably, is a cause of great pride among the people in this remote outpost.

Although many Westerners seem to believe the myth that the Buddhist peoples of the world live in perfect peace and harmony with one another, this part of Bhutan has witnessed much death and mayhem during repeated Tibetan invasions. The fifth Dalai Lama 'became jealous of the growing influence of the rival Drukpas on his southern border and mounted further invasions into Bhutan in 1648 and 1649. . . . They were repelled, and the Bhutanese captured large amounts of armor, weapons and other spoils.'[4]

Tibetan Buddhism dominates the lives of all people in this part of Bhutan. It is considered a great honour for a family to send its sons to the monastery for a time. The name of Jesus Christ has rarely been heard in the remote Lhuntse valleys, and there are no known Christians among the Kurtop people.

The little-known Kyerung people live on both sides of the Tibet-Nepal border, not far from Mt Everest. The Global Evangelization Movement estimated a 1995 figure of 6,113 speakers of Kyerung in southern Tibet,[1] along the China-Nepal border. An additional 4,300 Kyerung live in Nepal, especially in the villages of Rasua Gari, Birdim, Thangjet, Syabru and Syabrubensi. These villages

for military assistance when an invading Gurkha army from Nepal was besieging them. After this, Chinese influence in Tibet increased greatly. The states of Sikkim, Bhutan and Nepal splintered and became separate political units.

The Kyerung, like all Tibetan ethnic groups, zealously follow Tibetan Buddhism. They gleefully celebrate all the traditional Tibetan festivals and consider the Dalai Lama their supreme spiritual leader. The remote Kyerung in Tibet often ask visitors if they have any pictures of the Dalai Lama that they can give them.

There are no known Christian

Population:
11,100 (2000)
13,700 (2010)
16,900 (2020)
Countries: China, Nepal
Buddhism: Tibetan
Christians: none known

Nancy Sturrock

are located in the Rasuwa District of the Bagmati Zone in Nepal's Langtang Region. There are also 'large concentrations [of Kyerung] in Kathmandu',[2] the capital city of Nepal.

The Kyerung are considered Tibetans in both China and Nepal; however, they speak their own language, which is unintelligible with other Tibetan languages. The Kyerung make up a significant portion of the 60,000 or more 'Tibetans' in Nepal.

The Kyerung language is part of the Bodic branch of the Tibeto-Burman linguistic family. It is reported to share 68 per cent lexical similarity with Dolpo, Lhomi and Loba; 65 per cent lexical similarity with Central Tibetan; 63 per cent with Helambu Sherpa and 60 per cent with Jirel[3]—all languages spoken in this part of the Himalayan Range.

The 7th and 8th centuries saw rapid growth in the Tibetan empire. Tibet's rule extended into Kashmir, China, Turkestan, Sikkim, Bhutan, Nepal and northern Burma. In 1788 the Tibetans turned to the Chinese

believers among the Kyerung in either Tibet or Nepal. In recent years Christian ministries such as Every Home for Christ have launched large-scale projects to systematically evangelize Nepal. As a result some Kyerung have heard the gospel, but few have understood the heart of the message. This group requires long-term workers who are willing to live among the Kyerung and patiently and lovingly present the gospel to them in deed and in word. Faithful workers like William E Simpson, an American missionary to eastern Tibet who was martyred in 1932, are needed. Simpson summarized his life when he wrote, 'Are not all the trials, the loneliness, the heartache, the weariness and pain, the cold and fatigue of the long road, the darkness and discouragements, and all the bereavements, temptations and testings, deemed not worthy to be compared with the joy of witnessing to this "glad tidings of great joy"?'

Overview of the Kyerung

Other Names: Kyirong, Gyirong

Population Sources:

6,113 in China (1995, Global Evangelization Movement)

4,300 in Nepal (2002, Joshua Project II)

Language: Sino-Tibetan, Tibeto-Burman, Himalayish, Tibeto-Kanauri, Tibetic, Tibetan, Central

Dialects: 0

Professing Buddhists: 100%

Practising Buddhists: 80%

Christians: 0%

Scripture: none

***Jesus* film:** none

Gospel Recordings: none

Christian Broadcasting: none

ROPAL code: KGY

Status of Evangelization

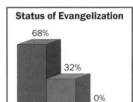

68%

32%

0%

A   B   C

A = Have never heard the gospel
B = Have heard the gospel but have not become Christians
C = Are adherents to some form of Christianity

Ladakhi

According to the Indian Missions Association, more than 100,000 Ladakhi people live in the northern part of the Indian state of Jammu and Kashmir. They inhabit more than 250 villages over a widespread area, radiating out from their historic capital city of Leh. In addition, a few thousand Ladakhi people reportedly live across the border in western Tibet.[1] Before the 1950s, all Ladakhi lived in India. The Chinese invaded northern Ladakh in the 1950s and 1960s, annexing 38,000 square kilometres (14,820 sq. mi.) of the Aksai Chin region in remote Himalayan territory.[2] The Aksai Chin area is so remote that the Indian government did not discover that the Chinese had constructed a road there until two years after it was completed. Consequently, a number of Ladakhi suddenly found themselves living in China, but the border is so porous that it makes little difference to the Ladakhi themselves, who come and go between one country and the other with ease.[3]

The Ladakhi are a Tibetan group but they differ significantly, both linguistically and historically, from their counterparts in Tibet. The Ladakhi language—which shares only 30 per cent to 40 per cent lexical similarity with Central Tibetan[4]—serves as the lingua franca among many people on the southern slopes of the Himalayas.

Life for the Ladakhi is hard. Hidden away in the highest mountains in the world, the region sees little rainfall—no more than three inches per year. Farmers rely on melted snow to water their crops. Not surprisingly for people who long for warm weather, the Ladakhi believe that hell is a miserably cold place.

Leh, the capital of Ladakh, was the home of an independent Ladakhi monarchy for a thousand years.[5] Today a Ladakhi royal family still exists, but their influence has been merely symbolic since the independence of India in 1947.[6] The Ladakhi royal family trace their lineage back to the legendary King Nya Tri Tsanpo, who ruled in the 3rd century BC.

The Ladakhi share the beliefs of their Tibetan neighbours. Tibetan Buddhism, mixed with belief in ferocious demons from the pre-Buddhist Bon religion, has been the stronghold in Ladakh for more than a thousand years. Traces of influence from the dark, distant past are found in the demonic masks and re-enactments of human sacrifices that make up their festivals.

Julian Hawken

The first Christian witness to the Ladakhi probably came from Nestorian traders in the 8th century. Georgian crosses have been found inscribed on boulders in Ladakh.[7] In 1642 a Portuguese Catholic priest, Antonio de Andrade, established a base near present-day Zanda. The king of Ladakh tore the mission down soon afterwards. The Moravians commenced work in Ladakh in 1856, and by 1922 there were 158 converts.[8] They reported, 'There is no very active opposition to Christian work. . . . The people are very willing to accept anything we can give them in the way of medicine, education, or even Scriptures and religious tracts.'[9] The Moravians are still working among the Ladakhi, and in recent years several mission groups from other parts of India have joined them.[10]

Population:
109,700 (2000)
128,000 (2010)
149,500 (2020)
Countries: India, China
Buddhism: Tibetan
Christians: 220

Overview of the Ladakhi

Other Names: Lodokhi, Ladakh, Ladaphi, Ladhakhi, Lodak, Ladwags, Ladak

Population Sources:

102,000 in India (1997, India Missions Association)

2,445 in China (1995, Global Evangelization Movement)

Language: Sino-Tibetan, Tibeto-Burman, Himalayish, Tibeto-Kanauri, Tibetic, Tibetan, Western, Ladakhi

Dialects: 2 (Leh [Central Ladakhi], Shamma [Lower Ladakhi])

Professing Buddhists: 80%

Practising Buddhists: 70%

Christians: 0.2%

Scripture: Portions 1904

Jesus **film:** available

Gospel Recordings: Ladakhi

Christian Broadcasting: none

ROPAL code: LBJ

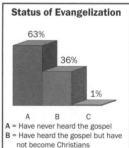

Status of Evangelization

63%

36%

1%

A B C

A = Have never heard the gospel
B = Have heard the gospel but have not become Christians
C = Are adherents to some form of Christianity

Population:
3,077,100 (2000)
3,823,000 (2010)
4,767,500 (2020)

Countries: Laos, USA, Cambodia, France, Myanmar, Thailand, Canada, Vietnam, Argentina, Australia, United Kingdom and many other nations

Buddhism: Theravada

Christians: 50,000

Overview of the Lao

Other Names: Laotian, Laotian Tai, Phou Lao, Eastern Thai, Lum Lao, Lao Wiang, Lao Kao, Rong Kong, Tai Lao, Lao-Tai, Lao-Lum, Lao-Noi

Population Sources:

2,403,891 in Laos (1995 census)[1]
171,577 in USA (1990 census)
55,000 in Cambodia (2003, Joshua Pr II)
49,600 in France (2003, Joshua Project II)
21,000 in Myanmar (2003, Joshua Pr II)
20,000 in Thailand (2001, J Schliesinger [2000 figure])[2]
12,000 in Canada (2003, Joshua Project II)[3]

Language: Tai-Kadai, Kam-Tai, Be-Tai, Tai-Sek, Tai, Southwestern, East Central, Lao-Phutai

Dialects: 6 (Luang Prabang, Vientiane, Savannakhet, Pakse, Lao-Kao, Lao-Khrang)

Professing Buddhists: 93%

Practising Buddhists: 80%

Christians: 1.6%

Scripture: Bible 1936; New Testament 1926; Portions 1906

***Jesus* film:** available

Gospel Recordings: Lao; Lao Phakisan; Lum Lao; Northern Lao

Christian Broadcasting: available

ROPAL code: NOL

Status of Evangelization

71%
27%
2%

A   B   C

A = Have never heard the gospel
B = Have heard the gospel but have not become Christians
C = Are adherents to some form of Christianity

Approximately three and a half million Lao people lend their name to Laos, one of Asia's most unreached countries. The 1995 Laos census recorded 2.4 million Lao people in their homeland. An additional 200,000 have now made their home in the United States, with many arriving in the late-1970s as refugees after the Vietnam War. Significant populations of Lao people can also be found in Cambodia (especially the northern provinces), France, Myanmar, Thailand and in numerous other Western nations.

The ancestors of the Lao people are believed to have migrated southward from China approximately one thousand years ago. As they made their way into today's Laos, they found the land already inhabited by the Khmu. They drove the Khmu into the mountains and took the best land for themselves.[4]

Today the Lao are renowned for being a gentle, friendly and peace-loving people. Their communities revolve around close-knit family ties. It could be said the Lao love their families so much that they choose to have large ones! It is not uncommon to find families with ten or more children in Laos, which has one of the highest birth rates of any country in the world.

Although the overwhelming majority of Lao people consider themselves Theravada Buddhists, their faith is 'interwoven with beliefs in various deities and local spirits. The latter, called *phi*, are ever-present in Lao religious beliefs; they reside in villages, houses, gardens, trees, water, crops and ancestors. They have to be placated by offerings of food placed in small shrines and occasionally with sacrifices, such as chickens and pigs.'[5]

Catholic missionaries first entered Laos in the 17th century, but the Protestant presence never took hold until the late 1800s. Daniel McGilvary and his team travelled north into Laos from their base in the northern Thailand town of Chiang Mai, gaining 3,000 Lao converts over the years.[6]

In recent years, the church in Laos has grown more than it did throughout all of the previous century. The Communist authorities have responded

Paul Hattaway

with sporadic persecution and oppression of the church. Pastors are imprisoned and restrictions are placed on the house churches. Today there are an estimated 40,000 Christians among the Lao in Laos (15,000 Catholics and 25,000 Protestants), in addition to at least another 10,000 Christians among the diaspora Lao scattered around the world.

Despite these impressive gains, the total percentage of Christians is still less than two out of every hundred Lao people. Most Lao have yet to hear the gospel for the first time. The biggest obstacles to the evangelization of Laos are the anti-Christian government and the relaxed, care-about-nothing attitude of many Lao. A missionary once asked a Lao boy what his idea of heaven was. He replied, 'It is like this. A large shade tree that casts a cool shadow under which I can lie and have someone fan me, and bring me water and wait on me generally.' Then he added after a moment's thought, 'And you know, I must have nothing whatever to do.'[7]

Lao Ga

Population:
1,820 (2000)
2,000 (2010)
2,170 (2020)
Countries: Thailand
Buddhism: Theravada
Christians: none known

Overview of the Lao Ga

Other Names: Lao Gao, Lao Go

Population Sources: 1,800 in Thailand (2001, J Schliesinger [1999 figure])

Language: Tai-Kadai, Kam-Tai, Be-Tai, Tai-Sek, Tai, Southwestern, East Central, Lao-Phutai

Dialects: 0

Professing Buddhists: 100%

Practising Buddhists: 60%

Christians: 0%

Scripture: none

***Jesus* film:** none

Gospel Recordings: none

Christian Broadcasting: none

ROPAL code: none

Status of Evangelization

79%

21%

0%

A   B   C

A = Have never heard the gospel
B = Have heard the gospel but have not become Christians
C = Are adherents to some form of Christianity

In 1999, the researcher Joachim Schliesinger estimated a population of 1,800 Lao Ga people living in western Thailand. They inhabit one main village, Ban Tabluang, in the Ban Rai District of Uthai Thani Province.[1]

The Lao Ga speak a language closely related to the Isan language of north-east Thailand. Consequently, most ethnolinguistic studies of Thailand do not mention them at all.[2] One report claims that the Lao Ga 'speak a dialect quite similar to the Lao Krang, but distinguish themselves from the Lao Krang primarily by their loud and croaking voice. This is why other Lao groups call them *Ga* or *Gao*, meaning crow. The designation Ga or Gao is offending for these people. The Lao Ga consider themselves a distinct Lao-speaking group.'[3]

Members of this small group are the descendants of prisoners of war. In the 1800s the Siamese army captured many people during their conquest of Vientiane (the present-day capital of Laos). They forced their captives to march vast distances across Thailand, where they were forced to settle down in remote areas. Over time the people formed a distinct community with their own customs, dialect and common identity as Lao Ga people.

The closely-related Lao Krang people were also captured as prisoners of war at the same time, but their homeland was near Luang Prabang in Laos rather than Vientiane. Therefore, despite their similar history and origins, the two groups consider themselves separate and have no contact with each other, even though both live in Uthai Thani Province. In fact, it could be

Christian Far East Ministry

said the Lao Ga have more in common with the Lao Wieng, who also originated in Vientiane but today speak a different dialect.

Despite their small numbers, the Lao Ga try to intermarry within their own tribe. For many youngsters, however, this is impossible due to the lack of choices, so in recent years the Lao Ga have started to intermarry with the Thai, Lao Wieng, Lao Isan and Chinese. The groom's family is required to pay a price to the family of the bride before the wedding can take place. 'An 84-year-old Lao Ga grandmother still remembers that her parents received a bride price of 12 *baht* when she married. Today, the price has risen to 20,000 to 40,000 *baht* [approximately US$500 to $1,000].[4]

The main occupation of Lao Ga women is spinning, weaving and dyeing. They are skilled producers of blankets, tablecloths and pillows, which they make on traditional spinning wheels and weaving looms. The income they earn from these and other economic enterprises makes the Lao Ga comparatively well off. The men are able to use tractors to cultivate their fields instead of water buffaloes and oxen. The main crops of the Lao Ga are rice, maize, tobacco and sugarcane. The men also use bamboo traps to catch grasshoppers, field rats and red ant eggs, all of which are considered highly-prized delicacies.

One hundred per cent of Lao Ga people are Buddhists. Christianity has yet to make any impact on this people group.

LAOS

THAILAND

Lao Krang

Population:
50,450 (2000)
55,100 (2010)
60,300 (2020)
Countries: Thailand
Buddhism: Theravada
Christians: 100

Overview of the Lao Krang

Other Names: Lao Klang, Lao Khrang, Lao Kang, Krang, Lao Glang, Tai Klang, Tai Krang, Tai Khrang, Tai Kang, Lao Grang

Population Sources: 50,000 in Thailand (2001, J Schliesinger [1999 figure])

Language: Tai-Kadai, Kam-Tai, Be-Tai, Tai-Sek, Tai, Southwestern, East Central, Lao-Phutai

Dialects: 0

Professing Buddhists: 99%

Practising Buddhists: 85%

Christians: 0.2%

Scripture: none

Jesus **film:** none

Gospel Recordings: none

Christian Broadcasting: none

ROPAL code: none

Status of Evangelization

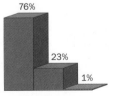

76%

23%

1%

A   B   C

A = Have never heard the gospel
B = Have heard the gospel but have
    not become Christians
C = Are adherents to some form of
    Christianity

More than 50,000 Lao Krang people inhabit a large area of central and western Thailand. Their communities spill into at least eight provinces, including Phichit, Suphan Buri, Uthai Thani,[1] Chai Nat,[2] Phitsanulok, Kamphaeng Phet, Nakhon Pathom[3] and Nakhon Sawan.[4]

The Lao Krang language is closely related to the Lao language of Laos and Isan of north-east Thailand.[5] This linguistic link results from the history of the Lao Krang. They originally lived in the eastern part of Luang Prabang Province in Laos and parts of the neighbouring Houaphan Province. When the Siamese army invaded Laos in the 1770s they captured the forefathers of the Lao Krang and took them as prisoners of war far across Thailand to their present locations. The Thai authorities first used the Lao Krang as labourers, to increase food production to feed the Siamese military. For several generations the Lao Krang were forced to work for their captors, until they were granted freedom by the great King Chulalongkorn in the early 1900s.

The Lao Krang of Thailand are not the same people group as the 5,000 Lao Khang of Laos.[6] The Lao Krang derive their name from their skills in extracting a type of organic paste from the *krang* beetle, which they use to make a bright red dye for their textiles. These days, however, only the Lao Krang in western Thailand continue this custom, as the *krang* beetle is not found in central Thailand. There they use commercial chemical dyes. The traditional dress of Lao Krang women is striking, with vivid orange, red and yellow colours decorating their clothing.

The regions inhabited by the Lao Krang are well-watered and ideal for agricultural production. Their main crops are rice, maize and peanuts, which they produce in commercial quantities. They also raise chickens, ducks, pigs and buffaloes. Many Lao Krang youth have turned away from making their living through farming and have found jobs in the cities and large towns in the region, and also in Bangkok.

Until fifteen or twenty years ago, the Lao Krang married only within their own tribe. A bride price was set depending on the social class of the bride and groom. Wealthy families had to pay a traditional bride price of 3,999 *baht* (about US$90), 1,999 *baht* ($45) for middle-class families and 999 *baht* ($23) for poorer families.[7] These days many Lao Krang youth are intermarrying with the Thai, Isan and other ethnic groups.

The Lao Krang are strong and zealous Theravada Buddhists. 'Until some decades ago, every young Lao Krang man had to enter the monkhood to become a novice before they could marry. In Lao Krang society, Buddhist teachings are the roots for social harmony and an emotionally and physically stable environment. Besides their belief in Buddhism, the Lao Krang honor a multitude of spirits and worship their ancestors. They believe in good and bad spirits who inhabit the house, village, forest, water, trees, etc. The most important of these spirits is the guardian of the village, called *hoo jau nei*.'[8]

The Lao Krang are a needy unreached people group with few Christians and minimal exposure to the gospel.

Christian Far East Ministry

Lao Lom

The Lao Lom people of Thailand had never been studied until Joachim Schliesinger identified and profiled them in 2001.[1]

There are approximately 25,000 Lao Lom living in three distinct areas of northern Thailand: Dan Sai District of Loei Province; Lom Kao District of Phetchabun Province; and Tha Bo District of Nong Khai Province. The Lao Lom in Nong Khai live a stone's throw from the Mekong River, while the other two groups live further inland.

To identify the Lao Lom as a distinct ethnic group, Schliesinger first had to unravel the confusion surrounding their name. He found that they are known by different names in different locations, depending on the name of their village. Those living in Loei Province are often called Tai Loei or Tai Lei, while those in Nong Khai are known as Tai Dan. He discovered that despite this collection of names, the people of all three Lao Lom communities share a common historical link and a common ethnolinguistic heritage.

The Lao Lom were originally Lu people, who over the course of time have formed their own identity and deserve to be considered a distinct people group today. 'Elderly Lao Lom people can still recount reports by their grandparents, who sought refuge across the Mekong River from the Siamese army after the complete destruction of Vientiane during the time of King Anuvong's war for Lao independence against Bangkok. During the following reprisals by the Siamese army in 1828, tens of thousands of people from Vientiane and the Phuan state were taken to Siam.'[2]

In these modern times the Lao Lom women do not wear their traditional dress, but the elderly can still remember the black vest with coloured threads at the hems, thick vertical white stripes and a black turban adorning their heads. The Lao Lom liked to further decorate themselves with silver jewelry around their arms, ankles and waist.

The north-east region of Thailand is the home of some of the most exotic food in the world. The Lao Lom 'hunt in the fields for snakes, rats, grasshoppers, snails and other insects, and catch fish in the rivers with hooks and nets'.[3] They also raise animals such as water buffaloes, ducks, chickens and pigs for consumption.

Traditionally a bride price was required before a Lao Lom woman's family would release their daughter for the wedding. A value was placed on each girl according to her beauty, health and family's social standing. These days a Lao Lom groom may pay as much as 80,000 *baht* (about US$2,000) for an attractive wife. After the wedding it is customary for the newlywed couple to move in with the bride's family.

Like most Buddhist groups in this part of Asia, the Lao Lom also believe in a complicated array of spirits. Ceremonies are held several times each year at which the community must make offerings and prayers to the guardian spirits of the village, in a bid to ensure wealth and prosperity. Failure to fulfill these obligations is believed to bring disaster from the offended demon.

There are no known Christians among the Lao Lom people.

Paul Hattaway

Population:
25,000 (2000)
27,300 (2010)
29,800 (2020)
Countries: Thailand
Buddhism: Theravada
Christians: none known

Overview of the Lao Lom

Other Names: Tai Dan, Tai Loei, Tai Lom, Tai Lei

Population Sources: 25,000 in Thailand (2001, J Schliesinger [2000 figure])

Language: Tai-Kadai, Kam-Tai, Be-Tai, Tai-Sek, Tai, Southwestern, East Central, Northwest

Dialects: 0

Professing Buddhists: 96%

Practising Buddhists: 70%

Christians: 0%

Scripture: none

Jesus film: none

Gospel Recordings: none

Christian Broadcasting: none

ROPAL code: none

Status of Evangelization

79%
20%
1%

A   B   C
A = Have never heard the gospel
B = Have heard the gospel but have not become Christians
C = Are adherents to some form of Christianity

Joachim Schliesinger reported a total of between 20,000 and 30,000 Lao Ngaew people living in central and north-east Thailand. Their main areas of habitation are Lop Buri Province (especially Ban Mi and Khok Samrong districts), the Tha Tako District of Nakhon Sawan Province and scattered parts of Singburi, Saraburi, Chaiyaphum, Phetchabun, Nong Khai and Loei provinces.[1]

Because of their wide geographic dispersion, gaining an accurate population figure for the Lao Ngaew is difficult. Their ancestors lived in the eastern part of Xiangkhoang Province and western Houaphan Province in Laos. In the 1860s they were forced to migrate southward into the Mekong River basin due to pressure from the Chinese who came down into their part of Laos. Later they decided to migrate across the Mekong into Thailand, where they proceeded to form communities in extremely diverse locations. Today the majority live in central Thailand, but several Lao Ngaew villages can be found on the banks of the Mekong River in Nong Khai and Loei provinces.

Although the Lao Ngaew language is considered closely related to Lao and Isan, 'linguistic research found that the main factors influencing the pronunciation of tone in the Lao Ngaew dialect were connected with speech, position of syllables, degree of emphasis and stress'.[2] Several interesting linguistic studies have been made into the Lao Ngaew language.[3]

The Lao Ngaew people have never appeared on lists of ethnolinguistic groups because their language is not considered distinct from other Tai varieties. However, the Lao Ngaew view themselves as a distinct people with a common history and ethnicity. In the majority of their locations they prefer to live with members of their own ethnic group. In other places they share their communities with members of other groups that migrated from Laos, such as the Phuan and Lao Wieng. In those places where Thai people live nearby, the Lao Ngaew seem to be looked down upon by the Thais, who 'consider the Lao Ngaew as a people without their own ethnic culture, who do not preserve their own tradition and customs but too easily adopt the customs of other ethnic Tai groups'.[4]

When a Lao Ngaew couple gets married, the groom's family is required to pay money to the bride's family. These days the bride price may be up to 100,000 *baht* (about US$2,300). A few decades ago the bride price was just 60 *baht* (less than $2)! The Lao Ngaew are able to intermarry with people from other ethnic groups, although not all other groups are keen to marry the Lao Ngaew. This is especially true with the Phuan people, who consider the Lao Ngaew socially and culturally inferior to themselves.

Although almost all Lao Ngaew are professing Buddhists, their beliefs are mixed with numerous animistic rituals and spirit worship. Some of their most revered spirits are those of the village, house, forests, water, trees and sky. 'They honor the most important spirit, called *don hor* once a year with pigs and rice whisky at the village spirit house, often located behind the temple.'[5]

Population:
30,200 (2000)
33,100 (2010)
36,100 (2020)
Countries: Thailand
Buddhism: Theravada
Christians: 60

Overview of the Lao Ngaew

Other Names: Lao Ngiaw, Ngaew, Ngiaw

Population Sources: 20,000 to 30,000 in Thailand (2001, J Schliesinger [1999 figure])

Language: Tai-Kadai, Kam-Tai, Be-Tai, Tai-Sek, Tai, Southwestern, East Central, Lao-Phutai

Dialects: 0

Professing Buddhists: 97%

Practising Buddhists: 70%

Christians: 0.2%

Scripture: none

***Jesus* film:** none

Gospel Recordings: none

Christian Broadcasting: none

ROPAL code: none

Photo credit: Christian Far East Ministry

Status of Evangelization

77%
22%
1%

A   B   C

A = Have never heard the gospel
B = Have heard the gospel but have not become Christians
C = Are adherents to some form of Christianity

THAILAND

MYANMAR

Ratchaburi

Lao Ti

Population:
200 (2000)
220 (2010)
240 (2020)
Countries: Thailand
Buddhism: Theravada
Christians: none known

Overview of the Lao Ti

Other Names: Lao Di

Population Sources: 200 in Thailand (2001, J Schliesinger [1998 figure])

Language: Tai-Kadai, Kam-Tai, Be-Tai, Tai-Sek, Tai, Southwestern, East Central, Lao-Phutai

Dialects: 0

Professing Buddhists: 100%

Practising Buddhists: 85%

Christians: 0%

Scripture: none

Jesus **film:** none

Gospel Recordings: none

Christian Broadcasting: none

ROPAL code: none

Status of Evangelization

83%

17%

0%

A   B   C

A = Have never heard the gospel
B = Have heard the gospel but have not become Christians
C = Are adherents to some form of Christianity

The second smallest of the Buddhist people groups profiled in this book are the two hundred Lao Ti people of Ratchaburi Province in western Thailand. They inhabit just two villages—Ban Goh and Nong Ban Gaim in the Chom Bung District not far from Thailand's border with Myanmar. They share their communities with families from other ethnicities, especially the Central Thai, Northern Thai and Isan. Despite their small numbers, the Lao Ti were first studied by the anthropologist Erik Seidenfaden in 1939.[1]

Although they now live far from Laos, the Lao Ti say their ancestors came from Vientiane in Laos, where they were ox cart drivers 'who transported goods and materials across the countryside. Because of this itinerant occupation, their group name was derived from the Lao term *ti* meaning *pai nai* in Thai or 'where are you going?' in English.'[2] Elderly Lao Ti still recall the oral history of their people. They say their forefathers were slaves of the Lao rulers in the mid-1800s when Vietnamese and Siamese armies laid claim to Laos. During the reign of the great Thai King Chulalongkorn, the Lao Ti were captured by the Siamese army and taken as prisoners of war to their present location in Ratchaburi Province in Thailand.

Although almost all young Lao Ti people today have lost the use of their mother tongue, elderly Lao Ti can still speak their distinct dialect, which is different from that of all neighbouring people including the Lao Song, who live in a nearby village. Because

Paul Hattaway

the Lao Ti vernacular is not being taught to the younger generations, it is likely that the language will become extinct when the present elderly generation dies out.

Animals play an important role in the economy of the two Lao Ti villages. 'They raise buffaloes, oxen, horses, chickens, ducks and pigs, the former as draft animals and the latter for consumption. Occasionally, Lao Ti men hunt deer, wild pigs, rats and snakes to supplement their daily diet. They catch fresh water fish with hooks and traps in streams and ponds.'[3]

Many ethnic groups in Southeast Asia observe the practice of the groom paying a bride price before a wedding can take place, but the traditional bride price paid by the Lao Ti was unique and reflected their history. A young Lao Ti man had to give an ox cart, one pair of draft oxen and 60 *baht* to his parents-in-law. Elderly Lao Ti people can still remember doing this when they were younger, but the custom has gradually died out. In fact, these days the Lao Ti have sold almost all of their traditional carts (which were wooden and made with huge wheels) to be garden decorations in restaurants and private residences.

The Lao Ti say that every single member of their small tribe is a Buddhist. Parents consider it a great honour to dedicate their son to serve in the temple as a monk or novice. Unlike many Buddhist groups in Thailand, the Lao Ti say 'they do not believe in any of the supernatural spirits inhabiting the surroundings. Because of their disbelief, they neither have shamans or religious practitioners to please these spirits nor do they make any sacrifices.'[4]

Population:
50,000 (2000)
54,600 (2010)
59,700 (2020)
Countries: Thailand
Buddhism: Theravada
Christians: 300

Overview of the Lao Wieng

Other Names: Tai Wieng, Lao Wiengchan, Thai Wiengchan, Vieng, Wiang

Population Sources: 50,000 in Thailand (2001, J Schliesinger [2000 figure])

Language: Tai-Kadai, Kam-Tai, Be-Tai, Tai-Sek, Tai, Southwestern, East Central, Lao-Phutai

Dialects: 0

Professing Buddhists: 90%

Practising Buddhists: 70%

Christians: 0.6%

Scripture: available (Lao and Thai scripts)

***Jesus* film:** available (Lao and Thai)

Gospel Recordings: available (Lao and Thai)

Christian Broadcasting: available

ROPAL code: none

Status of Evangelization

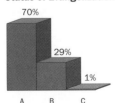

A = Have never heard the gospel
B = Have heard the gospel but have not become Christians
C = Are adherents to some form of Christianity

At least 50,000 people in central and north-east Thailand are known as the Lao Wieng. They inhabit villages in the provinces of Prachinburi, Udon Thani,[1] Nakhon Sawan,[2] Nakhon Pathom, Chai Nat, Lopburi, Saraburi, Phetchaburi and Roi Et. In the past 20 years a significant number of Lao Wieng have moved to Bangkok in search of employment.

The Lao Wieng do not usually appear on lists of ethnic groups in Thailand, but there is little doubt that they are a group with a cohesive self-identity, a common history and a proud culture.

The Thais name this group 'Wieng' because they are the descendants of prisoners of war who originally came from Wieng (Vientiane) in Laos. Joachim Schliesinger, in his excellent book *Tai Groups in Thailand*, recounts the tumultuous time that led to this group being present in Thailand today: 'Because of rivalry for the throne, the once united and power-ful Lao kingdom of Lan Xang split in 1713 into three weak kingdoms. . . . The result was that the rulers of all three states soon had to acknowledge Siamese suzerainty. King Anuvong of Vientiane took offense at the Siamese taking thousands of Lao slaves for doing corvée labor in central Siam. In 1827, he recruited a large army to attack the Siamese garrison in Nakhon Ratchasima and seized vast areas in the Isan region. The Siamese army immediately counterattacked and overran the Lao defense. . . . Within a few days the Siamese sacked Vientiane and following an order from their King Nangklao (Rama III) totally destroyed Vientiane, completely

Paul Hattaway

depopulating it and deporting thousands of its inhabitants—the Lao Wieng—to central Thailand as war captives.'[3]

After generations as slaves, the Lao Wieng and other communities were granted their freedom by King Chulalongkorn. Today they are full citizens of Thailand.

Despite their long separation from their homeland, the Lao Wieng still retain different cultural and linguistic traits from the Thais surrounding them. Until recently Lao Wieng women wore a traditional dress, which consisted of a knee-length *phaa sin*, woven from rough cotton and interwoven with several multi-coloured stripes of cloth. These days the Lao Wieng wear the same clothing as their Thai neighbours (except for certain festivals). The Lao Wieng men who live in farming areas are hard-working agriculturists, while those living in more remote rural locations are skilled hunters and fishermen. They use bamboo traps to catch field rats, the meat of which is consid-ered a delicacy.

From long before their forced departure from Laos, the Lao Wieng have been Buddhists. 'The spirits, however . . . must be propitiated by offerings of food at small spirit houses located in the compound or under the eaves of houses. Every Lao Wieng village has a communal spirit house outside the village, where the villagers meet once a year to bring sacrifices of chicken, pig heads, and rice whiskey to the guardian of the village, to ask for protection and good luck for the community.'[4] There are just a few Christians among this needy unreached people group.

Population:
10,000 (2000)
12,800 (2010)
16,500 (2020)
Countries: Bhutan
Buddhism: Tibetan
Christians: none known

Overview of the Lap

Other Names: Lakha, Tshangkha, Lakhapa

Population Sources:

8,000 in Bhutan (2001, G van Driem [1991 figure])

Language: Sino-Tibetan, Tibeto-Burman, Himalayish, Tibeto-Kanauri, Tibetic, Tibetan, Southern

Dialects: 0

Professing Buddhists: 100%

Practising Buddhists: 75%

Christians: 0%

Scripture: none

***Jesus* film:** none

Gospel Recordings: none

Christian Broadcasting: none

ROPAL code: LKH

Status of Evangelization

80%

20%

0%

A   B   C

A = Have never heard the gospel
B = Have heard the gospel but have not become Christians
C = Are adherents to some form of Christianity

More than 10,000 people belonging to the Lap ethnic group inhabit central areas of the Himalayan Buddhist kingdom of Bhutan. Their language is called Lakha. Little is known about this group, except that they inhabit the eastern part of Wangdue Phodrang District (called Wangdi Phodra on some maps), spilling over into the northern areas of Trongsa District. This group is called Lap ('inhabitants of the mountain passes'), or Lakhapa ('people who speak the Lakha language').

One scholar has noted, 'The Brokpas of Saphu Geo speak a dialect which they call Lakha, literally the "language of the mountain passes" . . . Saphu Geo is situated in . . . the north of the Black Mountains, south of the lofty white peaks of Gangkar Kunzang which separate Bhutan from Tibet. Lakha speaking villages of Saphu include B'uso, Langbji, Brabrak, Dzeri, Darilo, Wangdigom, Rabu, Kumbu, Bati, Nakha, Sekta and Thanya. There are an estimated 1,250 Lakha speaking households in [Saphu] Geo with some 8,000 speakers.'[1] The imposing Gangkar Kunzang (also known as Gangkar Puensum) is a perennially snowcapped peak standing 7,541 metres (24,734 ft.) above sea level.

Tibetan Buddhism is the state religion of Bhutan, and all Lap families follow it. On a local level, spirit appeasement still holds great influence in the people's daily lives. Many 'believe that, when they appear for judgment in the period between death and rebirth, a chicken will put white pebbles onto a scale to represent their good deeds, while a pig shovels on black pebbles to signify evil one has done. Thus almost any

Dwayne Graybill

Bhutanese will happily eat pork. . . . In this perilous time after death, pious Buddhists believe, one's spirit can influence its emergence into a higher life or bring on the disaster of rebirth on a lower plane.'[2]

There are no known Christians among the Lap people of Bhutan. The gospel has struggled to make an impact on this remarkable nation. Few Christian missiologists are aware that the 'father of modern missions', William Carey, visited Bhutan in March 1797, less than four years after his arrival and commencement of missionary work in India. 'In March of 1797, Carey and a friend visited Bhutan, probably with a view towards beginning mission work there. Though favorably received by local officials, Carey's hopes to begin a mission in Bhutan were not realized, and he was forced to remain in his already established work in Bengal.'[3] For the next 163 years, the doors to Christian witness in Bhutan remained firmly closed. In 1960, after Bhutan ended its isolationist policy, several mission groups entered the country. The Leprosy Mission and the Norwegian Santal Mission were invited to set up hospitals in the 1960s and 1970s. Both groups were asked to leave the country after a period of fruitful labour. A 2002 report on Bhutan said, 'In recent years, the growth of Christianity has been seen as a threat to social harmony, and many related debates have taken place in the National Assembly. The possibility of Christian agencies being able to work in Bhutan seems as remote as ever.'[4]

More than 8,000 Eastern Lawa people inhabit villages in northern Thailand, on the border between Chiang Mai and Chiang Rai provinces. The Eastern Lawa are most concentrated in the village of Wiang Papao. Smaller numbers inhabit parts of Mae Hong Son, Lamphun, Lampang, Uthai Thani, Suphan Buri and Kanchanaburi provinces.

The Eastern Lawa language is not intelligible with Western Lawa. Speakers of each language in Thailand can understand some words, but generally they revert to the lingua franca of Northern Thai in order to communicate. A script was invented for the Eastern Lawa, but few have learned how to read it and today less than 1 per cent of the people are literate in their own language.[1] Between one quarter and one half of Eastern Lawa are able to read Thai.

Despite their present small numbers, written records show that the long history of the Lawa dates back at least as far as the Tai kingdom of Kengtung (in today's north-east Myanmar) at the end of the 13th century. Documents from the time record how King Mengrai 'sent troops to expel the Lawa, a tribal group that was formerly very influential in the area. Many Lawa people were exiled to live on mountains outside the city, while others became servants of the royal families at the court of Chiang Mai.'[2]

Like many tribal peoples in Southeast Asia, the Eastern Lawa profess to be Buddhists, but a deeper examination reveals their dependence on animistic practices and spirit appeasement.[3] One source says,

'The Lawa worship a vast array of spirits. They are believed to be in contact with a much greater variety of spirits than many other tribal groups of northern Thailand. . . . Those Lawa living in remote villages still honor all good spirits, who watch over their families, the sky, the jungle, the mountains and the entrance to their village. They sacrifice pigs, chickens, rice wine and, when available, even buffaloes in order to propitiate the spirits. . . . Since most of the Lawa have already been converted to Buddhism, only a few Lawa villages still hold such extensive and costly sacrificial rituals.'[4] The Eastern Lawa also worship their ancestors. Most villages have their own shamans and exorcists to meditate between the people and the spirit realm. Many Lawa wear lucky charms around their necks or waists in a bid to ward off evil spirits.[5]

Both foreign and tribal missionaries have visited the Eastern Lawa with the gospel, but they generally receive a lukewarm reception. The Eastern Lawa community is largely closed to outside influence, and the village leaders have tight control over the people. Change is frowned upon, especially religious change, which many Eastern Lawa fear will bring disgrace on their ancestors and invite retribution on their communities from a host of evil spirits. Despite these pressures, a small number of Eastern Lawa families have embraced the gospel. Some have been forced to leave their village and live elsewhere.

Population:
7,850 (2000)
8,600 (2010)
9,400 (2020)
Countries: Thailand
Buddhism: Theravada
Christians: 100

Overview of the Eastern Lawa

Other Names: Lawa, Northern Lawa, Wiang Papao Lua, L'wa, Lowa, Lavu'a, Lava, Milakkha

Population Source: 7,000 in Thailand (1987, D Schlatter)

Language: Austro-Asiatic, Mon-Khmer, Northern Mon-Khmer, Palaungic-Khmuic, Palaungic, Western Palaungic, Waic, Lawa

Dialects: 2 (Phalo, Phang)

Professing Buddhists: 85%

Practising Buddhists: 45%

Christians: 1.2%

Scripture: none

Jesus **film:** none

Gospel Recordings: Lawa; Lawa: Ban Dong; Lawa: Ban Sam; Lawa: Chang Maw; Lawa: Eastern; Lawa: Eastern Papae

Christian Broadcasting: none

ROPAL code: LWL

Status of Evangelization

62%
37%
1%

A   B   C

A = Have never heard the gospel
B = Have heard the gospel but have not become Christians
C = Are adherents to some form of Christianity

Photo credit: Paul Hattaway

Lawa, Western

More than 65,000 Western Lawa people live in two main regions of Asia. The majority (approximately 55,000) inhabit China's Yongle and Zhenkang counties in Yunnan Province, while numerous Western Lawa villages are also found in northern Thailand's Chiang Mai and Maehongson provinces. The Western Lawa generally inhabit thickly forested mountainous areas. There may also be a small number of Western Lawa in Myanmar. An additional 30,000 Bulang people in China speak Western Lawa as their mother tongue.

The Western Lawa language is unintelligible from the Eastern Lawa language spoken in northern Thailand. The majority of Western Lawa in China are now bilingual in Mandarin, while those in Thailand can speak Northern Thai. Western Lawa is related to other Mon-Khmer languages in southern China and northern Myanmar.

The Western Lawa in China are officially considered part of the Wa minority group, although they never participated in the head-hunting for which other Wa people are infamous. The Western Lawa adopted Theravada Buddhism under the influence of the Tais many centuries ago. Consequently, they became a more peaceful people than their wild head-hunting cousins.

Western Lawa women like to wear lots of jewelry and intricate embroidery and adornment on their blouses and dresses. Large earrings are common, especially in China. In the past the Lawa had no written form of their language, so they communicated by sending objects to other villages. 'Sugarcane, banana or salt meant friendship, but pepper meant anger, feathers urgency, and gunpowder and bullets the intention of clan warfare.'[1]

A curious religious mix exists among the Western Lawa. Although the majority of this group professes Theravada Buddhism, their beliefs are mixed with animistic practices and spirit appeasement. Hundreds of Christian churches are also found among their villages in south-west China. Christianity has made less of an impact among the Western Lawa in Thailand, although there are small pockets of known believers among them.

The forefathers of the 10,000 Western Lawa Christians first received the gospel from the American Baptist missionary William Young in the 1920s. Their conversion was not obtained by forceful preaching as much as by Young's sacrificial love. Once, in 1924, Young came across a sick woman left to die in a ditch outside a Lawa village. Guessing she was a victim of smallpox, 'Young immediately erected a shed and ... washed her sores continuously for three days. To draw out the puss, Young did not hesitate to use his own mouth. His devotion and compassion opened the hearts of countless [Lawa] to receive his message.'[2] Many Western Lawa churches today are liberal and syncretistic. Many people attend church out of tradition rather than in pursuit of a living relationship with Christ.

Population:
62,850 (2000)
68,700 (2010)
75,100 (2020)
Countries: China, Thailand, possibly Myanmar
Buddhism: Theravada
Christians: 10,000

Overview of the Western Lawa

Other Names: Lawa, Mountain Lawa, Lava, Luwa, L'wa, Lavua, Tame Wa

Population Sources: 55,000 in China (2000, P Hattaway) 7,000 in Thailand (1987, D Schlatter) Possibly also in Myanmar

Language: Austro-Asiatic, Mon-Khmer, Northern Mon-Khmer, Palaungic, Western Palaungic, Waic, Lawa

Dialects: 1 (La-Oor)

Professing Buddhists: 70%

Practising Buddhists: 30%

Christians: 15.9%

Scripture: New Testament 1972; Portions 1961

Jesus **film:** none

Gospel Recordings: Lawa: Western, Chang Maw; Lawa: Western, La-oor; Lawa: Western, Kawng Lawi; Lawa: La-oop

Christian Broadcasting: none

ROPAL code: LCP

Status of Evangelization

A 29%
B 55%
C 16%

A = Have never heard the gospel
B = Have heard the gospel but have not become Christians
C = Are adherents to some form of Christianity

Photo credit: Paul Hattaway

Population:
2,140 (2000)
2,670 (2010)
3,290 (2020)
Countries: China
Buddhism: Theravada
Christians: none known

Overview of the Lemo

Other Names: Laimo, Lu-k'ou

Population Sources:

2,000 in China (1997, D Graybill)

Language: Sino-Tibetan, Chinese

Dialects: 0

Professing Buddhists: 60%

Practising Buddhists: 35%

Christians: 0%

Scripture: none

Jesus **film:** none

Gospel Recordings: none

Christian Broadcasting: none

ROPAL code: none

Status of Evangelization

58%

42%

0%

A   B   C

A = Have never heard the gospel
B = Have heard the gospel but have not become Christians
C = Are adherents to some form of Christianity

More than 2,000 people who use the ethnic name Lemo live in the small town of Lemo, 78 kilometres (48 mi.) from Liuku Township in western Yunnan Province, China. The Lemo live along the Nujiang River, near the mountainous China-Myanmar border and close to communities of Lisu and Nu people.

The Lemo appear to be an ethnic group who developed as the result of intermarriage between the Tai Mao and Lisu. Francis Ward, writing in 1913, described them as racially mixed people who spoke Chinese.[1] Today, the Lemo still view themselves as different from surrounding communities, and they still wear their own spectacular ethnic dress. The Chinese authorities have not given minority status to the Lemo but have included them as part of the Lisu nationality.

Being a mix of Lisu and Tai Mao (who speak two completely unrelated languages from two different linguistic families), the Lemo decided to speak Chinese among themselves. Today some Lemo men speak Lisu, but it has been relearned to enable them to trade with the Lisu, who are the largest ethnic group in north-west Yunnan. There are few or no traces of the Tai Mao language remaining among the Lemo.

The Lemo say they were once great hunters who fed their families by killing wild game in the mountains. Hunting parties often travelled away for weeks at a time into northern Myanmar. These days most Lemo

Dwayne Graybill

are agriculturists, although the men still possess bows and arrows and swords. Since the government's inclusion of the Lemo under the Lisu minority—a classification the Lemo strongly disagree with—their identity as a distinct people group has gradually eroded. Neighbouring people, who are forced to believe that China has only 55 minority nationalities, now call them *Lisu*. This has resulted in some comical situations. When several researchers visited the Lemo in 1997, they asked at the home of a Bai man, who said he had never heard of the Lemo. They then knocked on the door of another home about 20 feet away. The family who lived there excitedly said that they were Lemo, and all the people in that particular village were Lemo except the Bai home they first visited![2]

In the 1950s, the Lemo were the focus of a government crop project. With irrigation and the use of 72 tons of manure per hectare, grain output dramatically increased from 100 kilograms (220 lb.) to 1.25 tons (2,750 lb.) per capita.[3]

Most Lemo people, especially the elderly, are Theravada Buddhists. They are superstitious people who believe in ghost-like deities and the existence of good and evil spirits. If someone dies from an accident it is considered a bad omen. Nine grains of rice (seven for women) are placed in the mouth of the deceased to appease the spirit of death.

Although the Lemo live in a strong Christian area with thousands of Lisu, Nu and Han Chinese believers, there are no known Christians among the Lemo. The Lemo's strong belief in Buddhism and their isolated cultural mindset have prevented them from accepting the gospel from their neighbours.

Lepcha

Population:
71,500 (2000)
83,800 (2010)
98,300 (2020)
Countries: India, Bhutan, Nepal
Buddhism: Tibetan
Christians: 18,000

Overview of the Lepcha

Other Names: Rongkup, Rong, Rongke, Rongpa, Nunpa, Mutanchi Rongkup, Lap-cha

Population Sources:

66,649 in India (2001, India Missions Association)

2,000 in Bhutan (2001, G van Driem [1991 figure])

1,272 in Nepal (1961 census)

Language: Sino-Tibetan, Tibeto-Burman, Himalayish, Tibeto-Kanauri, Lepcha

Dialects: 3 (Ilammu, Tamsangmu, Rengjongmu)

Professing Buddhists: 65%

Practising Buddhists: 50%

Christians: 25.1%

Scripture: New Testament 1989

Jesus **film:** available

Gospel Recordings: Lepcha

Christian Broadcasting: none

ROPAL code: LEP

Status of Evangelization

54%
20%
26%

A   B   C

A = Have never heard the gospel
B = Have heard the gospel but have not become Christians
C = Are adherents to some form of Christianity

Approximately 70,000 Lepcha people are found across the three South Asian nations of India, Bhutan and Nepal. The majority live in the Dzongu District of the north Indian state of Sikkim (24,952 in the 1981 census) and the Darjeeling District of West Bengal (23,409 in 1981). There is one village with 106 Lepcha people in Tripura State in north-east India. Smaller numbers live in the valleys of south-west Bhutan[1] (2,000 people in 1991), while approximately 2,000 more inhabit the Ilam District of Mechi Zone in eastern Nepal.[2]

The Lepcha language has been the subject of much discussion since Colonel George Mainwaring first surveyed it in 1876.[3]

Mainwaring wrote the following wonderful comment: 'Of the language I cannot speak too highly. The simple and primitive state in which the Lepchas lived is admirably shown by it. It has no primary words (beyond the words for gold and silver) to express money, merchants or merchandise, fairs or markets. Their gentle and peaceful character is evinced by their numerous terms of tenderness and compassion, and by the fact that not one word of abuse exists in their language. . . . It admits of a flow and power of speech which is wonderful, and which renders it capable of giving expression to the highest degree of eloquence. The language also attests the astonishing knowledge possessed by the Lepchas. . . . It is impossible that a people, with a language so comprehensive; with a manner, though primitive, so superior, as to entitle them to rank high among civilized nations, could be engendered amidst the wilds and fastnesses of the Himalayas.'[4]

The Lepcha, who call themselves *Rong* and their language *Rong ring*, have lived in Sikkim since long before the arrival of Buddhism in the area. They are considered the original inhabitants of Sikkim. The botanist Dr Joseph Hooker, who visited in 1854, wrote, 'The Lepchas possess a tradition of the flood, during which a couple escaped to the top of a mountain (Tendong) near Dorjeeling [Darjeeling]. The earliest traditions which they have of their history date no further back than some three hundred years, when they describe themselves as having been long-haired, half-clad savages. At about that time they were visited by Tibetans, who introduced Boodh [Buddhist] worship . . .'[5]

The Lepcha have been zealous Buddhists since the early 1700s.[6] A unique Lepcha script was invented at that time to help the expansion of Buddhist teaching. The script is still used today. The 1981 Indian census returned 89.3 per cent of the Lepcha living in Sikkim as Buddhists, 8.05 per cent as Christians and 2.65 per cent as Hindus. Among the Lepcha of West Bengal, however, only 57.12 per cent were Buddhists and 35.7 per cent Christians. The West Bengal town of Darjeeling has been a hub of missionary activity for almost 200 years, and today it is one of the most evangelized areas in India. The Lepcha New Testament was translated in 1989 and is widely used among the more than 18,000 Lepcha Christians.[7] The *Jesus* film has also been produced in Lepcha. Despite the exciting Christian growth, the majority of Lepcha people in all three countries they inhabit remain believers in Tibetan Buddhism.

The 14th Dalai Lama: A 'Simple Monk' or a god?

Hugh P Kemp

Millions of people around the globe consider the Dalai Lama to be one of the world's great figures and most popular religious leaders. Small in stature, yet always wearing a warm smile atop his traditional Tibetan robe, he is much loved and respected. Presidents, kings, farmers and nomads alike are eager to meet him, hoping to glean a droplet of spiritual wisdom.

He has received the Nobel Peace Prize, is regarded as a god-king by some and a freedom fighter by others, is the darling of Hollywood, and every book that he authors, or that is written about him, seems destined to be an immediate best-seller.

Many people love the charismatic image of the Dalai Lama, but few know the background behind the man that Tibetan Buddhists from Seattle to Siberia consider their leader.

In 1943, the seven-year-old Tenzin Gyatso was enthroned as the 14th Dalai Lama in the thousand-room Potala Palace in Lhasa, Tibet. Five years earlier in 1938, aged two, he had been identified by a traditional procedure to be the reincarnation of all the previous thirteen Dalai Lamas. At his enthronement ceremony he assumed the mantle as the supreme spiritual leader of the people of Tibet, a country the size of Western Europe and with a population of six million people. When he turned fifteen he became the head of state as well, governing a fragile nation sandwiched between two giant Asian neighbours.

In 1959, His Holiness the 14th Dalai Lama was launched onto the world stage because he had to flee his country after a decade of delicate relationships between India's Nehru to the south and China's Mao to the north. Mao's Communist China proved too strong. Reluctantly, the disguised Dalai Lama was bundled across the border into India to become a refugee, settling in the town of Dharamsala in north India. It is from Dharamsala that he leads his 'government in exile'. In the decades since, more than 100,000 Tibetans have followed the Dalai Lama out of Tibet and have settled in refugee centres throughout India and Nepal.

In the foreword to his autobiography the Dalai Lama writes:

The always smiling 14th Dalai Lama.

Dalai Lama means different things to different people. To some it means that I am a living Buddha, the earthly manifestation of the Bodhisattva of Compassion. To others it means that I am a 'god-king'. During the late 1950s it meant that I was Vice-President of the Standing Committee of the National People's Congress of the People's Republic of China. Then when I escaped into exile, I was called a counter-revolutionary and a parasite. But none of these are my ideas. To me 'Dalai Lama' is a title that signifies the office I hold. I myself am just a human being, and incidentally a Tibetan, who chooses to be a Buddhist monk. [I am] a simple monk.[1]

The word *lama* means literally 'none higher'[2] or 'one who is superior'[3] and signifies a monk 'who can be trusted as a teacher or spiritual friend and guide, and who can show the pure path to enlightenment'.[4] The Sanskrit equivalent is the more familiar word, *guru*, meaning 'teacher'. The term *Dalai* is of Mongolian origin, meaning 'ocean', hence by implication *Dalai*

Lama is he who is an 'Ocean of Wisdom'.

The Dalai Lama is the head of one of four sects within Tibetan Buddhism, namely the Gelugpa, sometimes referred to as the Yellow Hat sect. When he lived in Tibet he was considered to be the reincarnation of Chenrezig (the Tibetan name for the Boddhisatva of Compassion). He explains, 'I am believed to be . . . the reincarnation of the previous thirteen Dalai Lamas, and the seventy-fourth [reincarnation of] a manifestation of Chenrezig . . . I am spiritually connected both to the thirteen previous Dalai Lamas, to Chenrezig and to the Buddha himself.'[5] He dislikes the term 'living Buddha': 'This [term] is wrong. Tibetan Buddhism recognizes no such thing. It only accepts that certain beings, of whom the Dalai Lama is one, can choose the manner of their rebirth.'[6]

If the Dalai Lama himself acknowledges that he means different things to different people, a clear contrast of understanding between East and West has certainly emerged.

In the 'homelands' of Tibet, Nepal, north India, Ladhakh, Bhutan, Mongolia, Inner Mongolia, Buriatia and Tuva he is revered as the reincarnation of the Bodhisattva Chenrezig.

Tibetan Buddhists believe a Bodhisattva is a being close to *nirvana* who in an act of altruism denies himself this privilege in order to assist sentient beings through to *nirvana*. Whereas the historical Buddha did not accept worship or insist on faith as religious principles, the emerging cult of the Bodhisattva historically allowed the expression of this yearning. In due course, the worship of deities arose, perhaps to compensate for the atheistic philosophy of the historical Buddha, and the Lord of Compassion—or Chenrezig—became the patron deity of Tibet.

The metaphysics in Tibetan Buddhism is complex. It understands the historical Buddha as an earthly incarnation of an eternal cosmic Buddha.

The strong implication is that a Bodhisattva is in fact divine and to be worshipped, as this will gain merit for the worshipper. The worship of the Dalai Lama is plainly evident throughout Asia: the honouring of his picture, the desire for his touch, the high regard of his blessing, the pilgrimages to hear him teach and be in his presence. The Dalai Lama's people invest spiritual hope in him.

In assigning the category of Bodhisattva to the Dalai Lama, his devotees perceive him to be exercising a role in the cosmos of directing his spiritual energy towards enlightenment on behalf of all beings. He is motivated by the 'Buddha mind', which is the wish to practise compassion and altruism with the aim of relieving the sufferings

China's Millions

Missionary Frank D Learner gives a Tibetan gospel tract to the three-year-old Dalai Lama in 1939. He had been identified as the next Dalai Lama in 1938, and ascended the throne in Lhasa in 1943, at the age of seven.

of others, thus bringing them to *nirvana,* a state of freedom from all suffering, delusions and karma.[7]

In the West, however, the Dalai Lama certainly appears to be something extraordinarily different. He is a 'political and religious leader of worldwide renown . . . a gentle, decent, unassuming man of considerable shrewdness and enviable tranquility of mind'.[8]

I first met the Dalai Lama in Dharamsala, North India when I was 16 years old. I was on a school field trip and, at the time, I had no idea who he was, except for some vague notion that the Tibetan people had been pushed out of Tibet by the Chinese and that the Dalai Lama was their leader.

I have heard public addresses given by the Dalai Lama on two more occasions since those naïve days— once in 1996 and then again in June 2002. His audience on both occasions was eclectic, but skewed towards the professional strata of society.

On both occasions he presented a message of secular ethics, although he is quite willing to weave Buddhist teaching through his presentations.

When I heard him speak in New Zealand he claimed to have come 'to promote human values', and he taught that to show care and responsibility within the community is the foundation of a happy life. He claimed that 'mental unhappiness' cannot be overcome by wealth but only through 'peace of mind', that we should make every effort to work on 'mental balance', and that people should 'show more interest in the inner life'. Recently he has been talking about education, rather than meditation, as the tool for social change. Is this a concession to the West?

The Dalai Lama is also known as a public advocate for world peace, having been awarded the Nobel Peace Prize in 1989. He believes there is a growing desire for peace in the world. Ironically, and despite this shift, people still like watching violent movies. 'Me too,' he admits. 'I like the shiny polished guns.'

His ultimate solution for world peace, including peace with China, is through the process of dialogue. 'All conflict must be resolved with dialogue, but it is unrealistic to expect to have no problems at all . . . if we all reached *nirvana,* then it will be good.' Both parties in a conflict 'have the right to live, and to live happily. Our humanity means we are interrelated, therefore we must dialogue. Destruction of your neighbor is destruction of yourself. If you can compromise, then dialogue is easily achieved.' We must make every effort to decrease hatred, and we do this by 'inner disarmament, which must go side by side with external disarmament . . . complete

A young 'living Buddha' from the Kham area in Tibet. He is believed to be an incarnation of a former great Buddhist sage.

elimination [of nuclear weapons] should be the goal.'

I was disappointed with the Dalai Lama's reflections on religion, although I admired his bravery (and was irked by his inaccuracy) in commenting on Christianity when he said, 'Religious traditions have the important role to serve and help humanity . . . all religious traditions carry the same message: love, compassion, forgiveness, tolerance, self-discipline, contentment . . . like Christianity and

Another 'living Buddha' in Sichuan Province, China.

Buddhism do.' He believes that all religions have a common message and experience, which may have been his motivation for publishing his commentary on the Sermon on the Mount.[9]

Sincerity is the key commonality: once a person has decided on which religion they will follow, then 'we should not label ourselves Christian or Buddhist

if in daily life there is no practice of it.' Only if we are sincere in our own religion will we then 'gain deeper spiritual experiences which will lead us to see the value of other traditions'. Sincerity, apparently, leads to happiness: 'all people have the same desire, namely happiness . . . If you have a happy life then at the end, you will have satisfaction.'

How could we summarize the main message of the Dalai Lama? Sincerely believe in what you will, as long as you end up happy. Perhaps this is too simplistic, but if I am to believe in what he says I end up with this conclusion.

Two major factors are missing from this message: truth, and moral outrage.

Perhaps the average Westerner isn't particularly looking for truth, and the Western form of Tibetan Buddhism is certainly sympathetic to this non-quest. But is sincerity enough? Surely it matters *what* you believe? Your *sincere* belief that you are Superman is highly unlikely to help you catch a bullet between your teeth.

And moral outrage? This is totally absent. The Dalai Lama instead teaches, 'We should now use our inner potential through training of our mind. We can gain new understanding which will lead to a more open mind . . . mental attitude is the key factor in our inner life. Analyze yourself, then eventually you will gain some benefit.'

Should we then train our minds to have compassion for the Chinese who are raping Tibet, and for Hitler who exterminated six million Jews? Certainly we need to find forgiveness, if possible, but people can only do that because they know that ultimately there is a righteous God who is morally offended and outraged at injustice!

If the Dalai Lama merely 'promotes human values' when in the West, then he has certainly achieved nothing more than this. His calm, stooped, ever-smiling countenance does not lend itself to moral outrage. Where is the passion and conviction of the Christian evangelist who has a life and death message to deliver?

On forgiving the Chinese the Dalai Lama says, 'Forgiveness is the ability to refrain from harboring enmity and losing compassion . . . We must not hate and have anger. We must make a distinction between the government and the [Chinese] people. The Chinese people themselves suffer like us. We must have concern and compassion towards the government officials, and intentionally not allow ill-feeling. They are human brothers and sisters.'

This I find a noble answer, though shallow, lacking any sense of justice, recompense or metaphysical concepts. I still prefer the answer in the 'scandal of the cross', that God in Christ actually achieved a real, forensic, once for all death to animosity, and that the resurrected Christ empowers people now to live in an ongoing forgiven and forgiving state, should they wish to appropriate this forgiveness offered.

On Jesus, the Dalai Lama has stated, 'All religious teachers have beauty and unity. Jesus was a manifestation of Buddha . . . Jesus was a Great Master . . . Whether we can say there is one truth, one religion, or several religions . . . this concept is difficult . . . Religion is like medicine. One particular illness needs one particular medicine to be effective.' A headache is cured with aspirin, but for cancer, you need a different type of medicine. 'So for one problem in society, you need a particular truth, a particular medicine. For another problem, you need another truth, another medicine. In society, there are a variety of problems, therefore we need a variety of medicines.' In 1996 I heard him say that religions were to each other as fingers are to the hand.

The West continues to be enamoured by the Dalai Lama. In 1996, the then Mayor of Christchurch, Mrs Vicky Buck, thanked him for his 'incredibly powerful message'. In June 2002, Sir Paul Reeves, the Anglican archbishop and former Governor General of New Zealand, introduced the Dalai Lama at his Wellington event as one who might help us to consider 'what this experience called life is, and why are we taking part in it . . . what the values and moral framework needed in society are and what is the essence of the creature engaged with the Creator and the cosmos'.

Hollywood continues to flirt with Tibet Buddhism in general and the Dalai Lama in particular. Richard Gere has said, 'His Holiness is the center of the Tibetan universe. He is the *axis mundi* . . . He is the sun itself.'[10] George Lucas, the creator of *Star Wars,* says, 'We're all Buddhists up here [in Marin County].'[11]

Recent Hollywood films have tried to capture the Dalai Lama's life and vision: *Kundun, Seven Years in Tibet* and others promote the simplicity and idealism of Tibetan life or are based on Buddhistic monism (*Star Wars*).

When we consider all the Dalai Lama has become to people around the world it is clear that we have more than a 'simple monk'.

He is a god-king, a secular leader of an exiled nation, a religious leader of a deeply religious people, a reincarnation of the Tibetan god Chenrezig and a world leader expounding the virtues of peace and the brotherhood of man. He is worshipped by his own people, and he is trumpeted by the West.

He has a huge task to do; he must walk the world stage as a politician and statesman, ever defending his own Tibetan people and ever hopeful that he'll get his country back from the Chinese. But the many and varied strands that make him who he is are inextricable.

In the context of a meeting in the West, I witnessed a question that was asked of His Holiness: 'When you reach final enlightenment, what will become of the Dalai Lama and his institution?' His reply revealed a world-view encompassing reincarnation: 'I am only a beginner. I don't know . . . it will take several eons to do. There is no hurry.'

Let us then be alert! Where are the committed Christians of today? Those who live only for the glory of the Lord Jesus Christ and who carry fire from God's altar in their lives and on their lips? Where are those skilled handlers of God's word who can stand up for the truth that Jesus Christ is the apex of all human history, and the only incarnation of God Almighty? Where are those who will proclaim that God himself, in Jesus Christ, took upon himself the sins of the world to release those who believe into eternal life?

As millions of people from both East and West enthusiastically embrace the teachings of the 14th

Dalai Lama, let us commit ourselves to pray: to pray for the Dalai Lama himself, that he would meet the risen Lord Jesus and be confronted with ultimate truth, and for those who have embraced his erroneous 'gospel'. Let us witness to the truth of the cross and the promise of eternal life for all those who place their trust in God's only Son, Jesus Christ.

To the present generation of Westerners, who reject moral absolutes and despise any claim to spiritual exclusivity, it is no wonder the Dalai Lama is so popular.

I've heard the Dalai Lama say, with a casual wave of his hand, 'If you think my message is nonsense, then forget it.'

Thanks, I think I might, and I'll stick with Jesus, the true incarnation of God.

Notes

1. Tenzin Gyatso, *Freedom in Exile: The Autobiography of the Dalai Lama of Tibet* (London: Abacus, 1990).

2. Gabriel Lafitte and Alison Ribush, *Happiness in a Material World: The Dalai Lama in Australia and New Zealand* (Melbourne: Lothian, 2002) 227.

3. Harold A Netland, 'Vajrayana (Tibetan Buddhism)', in *Evangelical Dictionary of World Missions* (ed. A Scott Moreau; Grand Rapids, MI: Baker, 2000) 995.

4. Lafitte and Ribush, *Happiness in a Material World*, 227.

5. Tenzin Gyatso, *Freedom in Exile*, 11–12.

6. Tenzin Gyatso, *Freedom in Exile*, 2.

7. Lafitte and Ribush, *Happiness in a Material World*, 228.

8. Quoted from *New Statesman and Society* in the Dalai Lama's *Freedom in Exile,* jacket.

9. Tenzin Gyatso, *The Good Heart* (Boston: Wisdom Publications, 1996).

10. Ani Pachen and Adelaide Donnelley, *Sorrow Mountain: The Remarkable Story of a Tibetan Warrior Nun* (London: Transworld, 2000).

11. *Time Magazine,* South Pacific Edition (29 April 2002) 50.

China Advocate

A 'living Buddha' visits the Buddhist monastery in Muli County, Sichuan Province. Cash is given to him in return for a spiritual blessing.

Approximately 9,000 Lhomi people live in the three countries of Nepal, India and China (Tibet). The majority are found in Nepal, where they inhabit six villages 'on the steep slopes of the upper Arun above Hedanna in Sankhuva Sabha district as far as the Tibetan border, e.g. in the villages of Cyamtan and Kimathanka'.[1] The Samkhuva Sabha (also spelled Sankhwasawa) District is within the Koshi Zone in eastern Nepal. In recent years some Lhomi men have moved down to Kathmandu, where they work as labourers and builders. In India, 1,000 Lhomi people 'live in the famous tea-growing and tourist region of Darjeeling'.[2]

In 1976 there were reportedly more than 4,000 Lhomi people living in Nepal.[3] No updated figure has been published since that time, as the Lhomi do not officially exist as a distinct entity in the view of all three governments in the countries where they live. In Nepal the Lhomi are officially considered part of the Sherpa ethnic group. In China, the more than 1,500 Lhomi have been included as part of the Tibetan nationality, while in India they have been combined with other Buddhists to form the Bhotia tribe.

The self-name of this group is *Shingsaba*. One linguist notes, 'The Shingsaba or Lhomi are a Himalayan Bodish group with a distinct language. Not much is known about the language, but judging by what little I have heard of Shingsaba, the language seems rather unlike a Tibetan dialect. In Tibetan the people go by the name Lhomi

Gospel Recordings Nepal

'southerner', and in Nepali they are known by names such as *Kath Bhote* 'wood Tibetan' and *Lama Bhote*'.[4] The Lhomi language, which is part of the Central Bodic branch of Tibeto-Burman, is not closely related to any other languages in this part of the Himalayas. Their nearest linguistic relatives are Baragaunle and Dolpo (with which they share 69% lexical similarity). They also share 68 per cent with Loba; 66 per cent with Walung; 65 per cent with Lhasa Tibetan and Kyerung; 64 per cent with Kutang Bhotia; 60 per cent with Helambu Sherpa; 58 per cent with Sherpa and 57 per cent with Jirel.[5]

Although most Lhomi claim to follow Tibetan Buddhism, their practices have been described as 'unrefined Buddhism . . . Their shamans (animistic priests) are as active as the Buddhist lamas. Although animal sacrifice is abhorrent to orthodox Buddhists, the Lhomis make several ritual animal sacrifices during the year.'[6] Before the millet is planted in September, the Lhomi kill three sheep to placate the patron deity of their village.

In recent years, approximately 300 Lhomi in Nepal have become Christians. They are now sending evangelists to other tribes in the area. Faithful believers laboured for years to translate the Scriptures for the Lhomi. In 1976 Bible portions were first printed, and the entire New Testament became available in 1995—a rare occurrence in this part of the world for such a numerically small group. Due to the large Christian presence in Darjeeling, north-east India, 'many Lhomi there have some awareness of the gospel, and a few have believed in Christ. . . . Despite the existence of Lhomi Christians in Nepal and India, it has proven difficult for the gospel to spread to their counterparts in Tibet, due to the political situation there and the tightly controlled borders.'[7]

CHINA
Xizang (Tibet)

NEPAL Koshi

W Bengal

Lhomi INDIA

Population:
8,670 (2000)
10,290 (2010)
12,490 (2020)
Countries: Nepal, China, India
Buddhism: Tibetan
Christians: 300

Overview of the Lhomi

Other Names: Lhoket, Shing Saapa, Kathe Bhote, Kar Bhote, Singsawa, Shingsaba

Population Sources:
4,000 in Nepal (1976, O Vesalainen and M Vesalainen)
1,000 in China (1992, B Grimes [1985 figure])
1,000 in India (1992, B Grimes [1985 figure])
Language: Sino-Tibetan, Tibeto-Burman, Himalayish, Tibeto-Kanauri, Tibetic, Tibetan, Central

Dialects: 0
Professing Buddhists: 80%
Practising Buddhists: 40%
Christians: 3.5%
Scripture: New Testament 1995; Portions 1976
Jesus film: none
Gospel Recordings: Lhomi
Christian Broadcasting: none
ROPAL code: LHM

Status of Evangelization

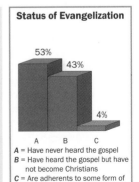

53%
43%
4%

A   B   C

A = Have never heard the gospel
B = Have heard the gospel but have not become Christians
C = Are adherents to some form of Christianity

Loba

In 1998, 26,000 Loba people lived in the Dhawalagiri Zone of north-central Nepal. They inhabit the Mustang (Lo Manthang) and Dolpa districts in the northern part of the region, close to the Nepal-China border. Also known as the Mustang Tibetans and Lopa, the Loba inhabit the Kali Gandaki valley. Their villages sit at an altitude of between 3,400 and 4,000 metres (11,100 to 13,120 ft.) above sea level.[1] The Loba of Nepal are not the same as the Lhoba minority group of southern Tibet.

Until it was incorporated into the Nepali kingdom at the end of the 18th century, the Mustang area was under the control of the Nghari District of Tibet, which was part of the Guge Kingdom. Even today this part of Nepal on the map struts out into Tibet, breaking what is otherwise a fairly straight border between the two nations. This historical fact prompted the Chinese to try to re-establish the Kali Gandaki valley under their control, and several military clashes occurred along the border in the 1960s and 1970s.

The Loba have been the subject of much fantasy in the West. Because of their geographical remoteness, Mustang was viewed as a kind of Shangri-La. Until 1952 this small group had their own Buddhist kingdom and monarchy, which was established around 1380. In 1992 the upper Mustang valley was opened to foreign tourists, although permits are only granted to those who join organized treks at inflated prices.[2]

The Loba language is part of the Central Tibetan branch of the Tibeto-Burman family, although it shares only 65 per cent lexical similarity with Lhasa Tibetan. Other languages spoken nearby include Baragaunle and Dolpo (78% lexical similarity), Helambu Sherpa (63%) and Jirel (62%).[3]

Some Loba practise polyandry, 'where a single woman is the common wife of a group of males . . . A single woman is selected and married to five or six brothers as a common wife, or the eldest brother's wife is also utilized as a wife by his other younger brothers.'[4] This practice probably came about because of the high percentage of Loba men who join the Buddhist monastery for extended periods of time. By having multiple husbands, the women believed they had more chance of surviving and not being abandoned.

Almost all Loba people are zealous believers in Tibetan Buddhism. There are numerous temples and monasteries throughout their territory. A few minor cracks have appeared in the Buddhist stronghold in recent years, however, and today there are a few Loba Christians. A 1998 missions publication noted, 'A few years ago a series of huge floods devastated several Loba villages. Many people died and others lost all their possessions and means of livelihood. The government responded by relocating hundreds of Loba people outside the vast mountains that had separated them from contact with the world for centuries. Because of this God-given opportunity, some Loba have been exposed to the gospel of Jesus Christ for the first time.'[5]

Population:
Population:
27,200 (2000)
33,700 (2010)
41,700 (2020)
Countries: Nepal
Buddhism: Tibetan
Christians: 10

Overview of the Loba

Other Names: Lopa, Loyu, Mustang, Lo Montang, Lo Manthang, Mustang Tibetans, Lhopas, Lowa, Mustang Bhote

Population Sources:

26,000 in Nepal (2000, B Grimes [1998 figure])

Language: Sino-Tibetan, Tibeto-Burman, Himalayish, Tibeto-Kanauri, Tibetic, Tibetan, Central

Dialects: 2 (Lo, Seke)

Professing Buddhists: 99%

Practising Buddhists: 85%

Christians: 0.1%

Scripture: none

Jesus film: none

Gospel Recordings: Mustang

Christian Broadcasting: none

ROPAL code: LOY

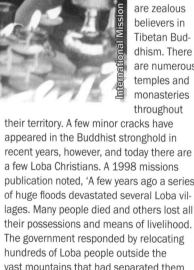

International Mission Board

Status of Evangelization

75%

24%

1%

A   B   C

A = Have never heard the gospel
B = Have heard the gospel but have not become Christians
C = Are adherents to some form of Christianity

More than one million Lu people live throughout the world. The majority (more than 600,000) are concentrated in the south-west part of China, especially in and around the famous Xishuangbanna Prefecture,[1] considered the homeland of the Lu. Xishuangbanna is the Chinese transliteration of the Tai name *Sipsongpanna*, meaning 'twelve thousand rice fields'. This well-watered area is in the Mekong River delta close to the borders of several countries. As a result, significant numbers of Lu people are found across the border in neighbouring countries Myanmar,[2] Laos,[3] Thailand[4] and Vietnam.[5] In each place they are known by different names according to the national language. In Thailand, for example, they are often called Tai Lu, and in Laos they are widely known as the Lao Lu. Several thousand Lu make their homes in the United States, and thousands more inhabit other Western nations. Specific numbers in each country are difficult to ascertain, as in the West they usually identify themselves as Thai or Lao people to avoid having to explain their ethnicity.

The Lu diaspora has occurred because of warfare waged against them by hostile peoples. There is evidence that they were once the dominant people group in the region, having settled there as early as the first century AD. By the 9th century the Lu had a well-developed agricultural system. 'They used oxen and elephants to till the land and constructed extensive irrigation systems.'[6]

The Lu are widely regarded as a peaceful and graceful people. Multitudes of tourists flock to witness their colourful festivals,[7] of which *Songkran* is the most famous. People splash water over each other, believing it cleanses the sins of the past year.

Although the large majority of Lu people call themselves Buddhists, there are certain areas in China and in Vietnam where their Buddhist faith is little more than a veneer thrown over ancient animistic rituals designed to protect them from the threat of evil spirits. At certain times the Lu pay homage to the spirits of those who have contributed greatly to the well-being of their descendants One researcher reported, 'Sacrifices are offered to the spirits [and] the village is shut in on itself; all roads and tracks giving access to the community are blocked with barricades of trees and branches . . . the whole village is encircled with ropes made of straw or a line of white cotton thread, to represent symbolically an encircling wall preventing entry or exit. No outsiders of any description, not even monks or members of the elite ruling class, are permitted to attend these rites.'[8]

The Presbyterian missionary Daniel McGilvary and his co-workers first brought the gospel to the Lu living in the Mekong Delta in 1893. They rode elephants from their base in Chiang Mai, Thailand, distributing Christian literature as they went. The first Lu church was formed in China in the early 1920s. Strong persecution against those who believed in Christ forced the Christians to form their own village, Bannalee, which remains Christian to this day and contains the largest concentration of Lu believers anywhere. The overwhelming majority of Lu people, however, remain oblivious to the gospel.

Myanmar Faces and Places

Overview of the Lu

Population:
1,077,700 (2000)
1,208,600 (2010)
1,358,900 (2020)
Countries: China, Myanmar, Laos, Thailand, USA, Vietnam and other Western nations
Buddhism: Theravada
Christians: 2,500

Other Names: Lü, Tai Lu, Lue, Leu, Dai Lu, Dai Le, Lao Lu, Nhuon, Duon, Pai-I, Shui-Pai-I, Ly, Tai L, Kon, Pai-yi, Sipsongpanna Dai, Xishuangbanna Dai, Shui Dai

Population Sources:
550,000 in China (1986, T'ien Ju-K'ang)
200,000 in Myanmar (1981, SIL)
119,100 in Laos (1995 census)
70,000 in Thailand (1995, Department of Public Welfare)
4,000 in USA (2000, P Hattaway [1998 figure])
3,684 in Vietnam (1989 census)
also in other Western nations

Language: Tai-Kadai, Kam-Tai, Be-Tai, Tai-Sek, Tai, Southwestern, East Central, Northwest
Dialects: 0
Professing Buddhists: 88%
Practising Buddhists: 65%
Christians: 0.2%
Scripture: New Testament 1933 (reprinted 1996); Portions 1921
Jesus film: available
Gospel Recordings: Lu; Thai Lu
Christian Broadcasting: none
ROPAL code: KHB

Status of Evangelization

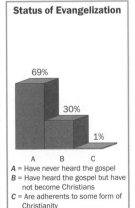

A = Have never heard the gospel
B = Have heard the gospel but have not become Christians
C = Are adherents to some form of Christianity

Malimasa

Population:
515 (2000)
600 (2010)
740 (2020)
Countries: China
Buddhism: Tibetan
Christians: none known

Overview of the Malimasa

Other Names:

Population Sources:[1]

500 in China (1998, Asian Minorities Outreach)

100 families in China (1998, J Matisoff)[1]

Language: Sino-Tibetan, Tibeto-Burman, Lolo-Burmese, Naxi

Dialects: 0

Professing Buddhists: 100%

Practising Buddhists: 85%

Christians: 0%

Scripture: none

Jesus film: none

Gospel Recordings: none

Christian Broadcasting: none

ROPAL code: none

Status of Evangelization

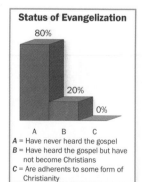

- 80% — A
- 20% — B
- 0% — C

A = Have never heard the gospel
B = Have heard the gospel but have not become Christians
C = Are adherents to some form of Christianity

Approximately 100 Malimasa families inhabit an area near the town of Weixi, in the north-west of Yunnan Province, China.[2] Weixi, five hours by road from the city of Shangri-La (formerly Zhongdian), is at the point where the Tibetan and Chinese worlds intersect. The intrepid explorer and botanist, Joseph Rock, unflatteringly described Weixi in the 1920s as 'a forlorn place of about 400 houses. . . . The town boasts a wall of mud with a few dilapidated gates.'[3] The Malimasa people live in extremely remote communities. Severe snowfall often cuts their villages off from the outside world for weeks during the winter.

Sickness and disease have long plagued people in this part of China. When Rock visited Weixi 70 years ago, he reported, 'Nowhere have I seen goiter so prevalent as here. The people carried regular pouches in their throats, like certain monkeys when they fill up with peanuts.'[4]

The other people in the Weixi region say they have considered the Malimasa as a separate people group for at least a hundred years. The Chinese authorities, however, have included the Malimasa under the official Naxi nationality.

The Malimasa language is part of the Eastern Naxi linguistic branch and is related to Mosuo. The people themselves say their vocabulary is comprised of 30 per cent Tibetan words and 30 per cent Bai words.[5] Despite their small number, the Malimasa have their own 'syllabary script'.[6]

Julian Hawken

The history of the Malimasa is shrouded in uncertainty, but their language suggests that they were once part of the Mosuo people who are today concentrated a considerable distance north-east of Weixi, on the Yunnan-Sichuan border. The Malimasa are still a purely matriarchal and matrilineal society—the women are in complete control of all finances, possessions and decision-making. The Malimasa wear their own traditional dress, which is distinct from that of all other groups in the area. Women wear large turbans wrapped around their heads.

The Malimasa are 100 per cent Tibetan Buddhist. There are a number of Tibetan, Lisu and Naxi Christians in the Weixi area, but they have had little impact on the staunch belief system of the Malimasa.

Catholic missionaries from the Grand St Bernard Order began work at Latsa Pass near Weixi in 1931.[7] Several Protestant families also lived in Weixi prior to 1949. The great missionary statesman Hudson Taylor, writing of China's needs in general, stated, 'The harvest here is indeed great, and the laborers are few and imperfectly fitted for such a work. And yet grace can make a few feeble instruments the means of accomplishing great things—things greater even than we can conceive.'[8] Taylor's passionate desire was that national believers would be given the leadership of their own churches and have control over their own affairs. He wrote, 'I look upon foreign missionaries as the scaffolding around a rising building. The sooner it can be dispensed with, the better; or rather, the sooner it can be transferred to other places, to serve the same temporary use, the better.'[9]

Population:
3,610 (2000)
4,200 (2010)
4,900 (2020)
Countries: India
Buddhism: Theravada
Christians: 250

Overview of the Man
Other Names:

Population Sources:

3,267 in India (1991 census)

Language: Indo-European, Indo-Iranian, Indo-Aryan, Eastern Zone, Bengali-Assamese. (Traditionally, Man was a Tai language.)

Dialects: 0

Professing Buddhists: 50%

Practising Buddhists: 30%

Christians: 6.9%

Scripture: none

***Jesus* film:** none

Gospel Recordings: none

Christian Broadcasting: none

ROPAL code: none

Status of Evangelization

51%

42%

7%

A   B   C

A = Have never heard the gospel
B = Have heard the gospel but have not become Christians
C = Are adherents to some form of Christianity

Approximately 3,500 people belonging to the Man ethnic group live in north-east India.[1] According to the 1991 census, 2,582 Man people lived in Assam State, dispersed in the Karbi Arleng District[2] and North Cachar District.[3] A small number may live in Tinsuria. An additional 585 Man people live in the state of Meghalaya, primarily in the West Garo Hills.[4]

The name *Man* literally means 'a Burmese immigrant'. K S Singh says, 'Legend has it that they came to this part along with an invading army, and were afterwards recruited . . . as sepoys to fight the Garos in the second decade of the nineteenth century. Those who settled down in the Garo hills after relinquishing their duty as sepoys took women from other communities as their wives and formed a separate community. They married Koch, Hajong, Assamese and Bengali women, but they never encouraged marriage with the Muslims.'[5]

Over time, as a consequence of their mixing with other communities, the Man emerged as a distinct people group, and all links to their origins in Myanmar have long been forgotten. Their Tai language has also been lost. They have 'completely forgotten their original language and have adopted Assamese as their mother tongue and use the Assamese script. They sometimes use Bengali and Hindi to communicate with others. The Man have been Assamised to a large extent . . . into the greater Assamese culture.'[6]

Although the majority of Man people say they are Buddhists, Hinduism has influenced their religious belief system and is gradually taking over. 'The life cycle rituals they perform demonstrate much similarity with those of the neighboring caste Hindus of Assam and Meghalaya. The marriage, however, is solemnized by a Buddhist monk or *pathak* reciting hymns from the Pali scripture.'[7]

Despite growing Hindu influence, approximately half of the Man continue to profess Theravada Buddhism. In most of their families the goddesses Lakshmi and Saraswati are venerated. The 1981 census returned 92.04 per cent of the Man in Meghalaya as followers of Buddhism, 3.45 per cent Hindus, 2.55 per cent Christians, 1.05 per cent 'other religions' (i.e., animism), 0.6 per cent Muslims and 0.31 per cent did not state their religion. The 1991 census revealed the inroads Hinduism has made, with the majority of Man in Assam at that time professing Hinduism.

There are approximately 250 Man Christians today in India, a remnant that does not have the resources or motivation to reach the rest of their ethnic group. The 1991 census returned 133 Man Christians living in the Karbi Arleng District and 97 Christians in the North Cachar District, both in Assam State.

Because they do not appear on most missionary lists of ethnolinguistic peoples from India, few Christians have ever heard of the Man and fewer still have tried to reach them with the gospel. About 50 per cent of Man have never heard the gospel in a clear way such that they could intelligently either accept or reject the claims of Christ.

Myanmar, Faces and Places

Manangba

Approximately 5,000 Manangba people live on the slopes of the Nepal Himalayas, at high altitudes of between 3,200 and 3,700 metres (10,500 to 12,100 ft.) above sea level. The botanist Perdita Phole, who has studied the plants and flowers of this remote region, listed a 1988 population of 3,736 Manangba people.[1] They inhabit seven villages along the Marsyangdi River in the Nyeshang area of Manang District. Manang is situated in the north-west of the Gandaki Zone, which has Pokhara as its main city.

Pokhara is many days' trek from Manang for poorer locals, or a short airplane journey for wealthier locals and the foreign trekkers who come to the area to acclimatize to the high altitude before continuing on the world-famous Annapurna Circuit. Manang is a large village of approximately 500 households. The second largest Manangba community is Braga, with 200 houses, while the others are small, averaging 15 to 20 houses in each.

The Manangba people enjoy the enviable privilege of having special trading rights, which they gained way back in 1784. 'Today they exploit these rights with shopping trips to Singapore and Hong Kong where they buy electronic goods and other modern equipment to resell in Nepal. Not surprisingly, they are shrewd traders and hard bargainers.'[2] These special trading privileges have made the Manangba some of the wealthiest people in Nepal. Visitors to this remote Himalayan outpost are often surprised and disappointed to find this tribe wearing Western clothing, with stylish haircuts, polished nails and most of the latest Western music and appliances. Even back in the early 1970s one researcher noted, 'It is remarkable that they are familiar with the modern conveniences of jet air travel, railroads, elevators and automobiles, considering their illiteracy and their primitive way of life and home environment. They trade in semi-precious stones, silk and gold, and return from abroad with transistor radios, wrist watches, cosmetics, silk and general merchandise.'[3] Those rural Manangba who stay closer to home cultivate wheat, potato, barley, maize and radish. They also herd sheep and goats.

The Manangba claim to be close relatives of the Gurung people, although the Gurung deny this relationship. The Manangba language is similar to Gurung, being part of the Tamangic branch of Tibeto-Burman. Culturally the Manangba are closer to the Tibetans, whom they trade with but refuse to marry.

All Manangba people profess Tibetan Buddhism, although traditionally their rituals had a strong Bon spirit-worship influence. Ironically, for a small tribe living on the 'roof of the world', materialism has choked the lives of the Manangba people. One observer states, 'They are nominally Buddhist, but give little thought or care to religion and have allowed their few temples and old monasteries to fall into general disrepair.'[4]

This small, well-travelled tribe has shown little interest in Christianity. Some have been exposed to the gospel on their international travels, but their greed and spiritual blindness have prevented the Manangba from seeing the true spiritual riches available in Christ.

Photo credit: Dwayne Graybill

CHINA
Xizang (Tibet)

NEPAL
Gandaki

INDIA

Manangba

Population:
4,800 (2000)
5,940 (2010)
7,350 (2020)
Countries: Nepal
Buddhism: Tibetan
Christians: none known

Overview of the Manangba

Other Names: Manangay, Manang, Manangi, Nyeshang, Nyishang, Northern Gurung, Manangbolt, Manangbhot, Manangpa, Nesyangba, Neshyangba, Neshyangpa

Population Sources:
3,736 in Nepal (1990, P Pohle [1988 figure])

Language: Sino-Tibetan, Tibeto-Burman, Himalayish, Tibeto-Kanauri, Tibetic, Tamangic

Dialects: 1 (Prakaa)

Professing Buddhists: 100%

Practising Buddhists: 30%

Christians: 0%

Scripture: none

***Jesus* film:** none

Gospel Recordings: Manang

Christian Broadcasting: none

ROPAL code: NMM

Status of Evangelization

62%
38%
0%

A   B   C

A = Have never heard the gospel
B = Have heard the gospel but have not become Christians
C = Are adherents to some form of Christianity

The majority of the more than 13 million Manchu are concentrated in China's north-eastern provinces of Liaoning,[1] Jilin and Heilongjiang—all of which were formerly part of Manchuria. For centuries the Manchu separated themselves from the Chinese and even erected a wooden stockade to keep them out.[2] In 1859 the Chinese were finally allowed to migrate into Manchuria. They entered in such massive numbers that today the Manchu are a minority in their homeland. Small numbers of Manchu may also live in Siberia and North Korea.[3]

Manchu are found in every province of China, and in no less than 2,092 of China's 2,369 counties and municipalities.[4]

Although they are considered China's second largest minority group, most Manchu today are indistinguish-able from the Han Chinese. As one historian notes, 'The Manchus' political and military successes . . . were purchased at the expense of losing their ethnic identity. Long before the Qing Dynasty collapsed in 1911, most Manchus had ceased to be Manchus ethnically, linguistically, and culturally.'[5] The Manchu language is nearly extinct. Various studies have listed 'less than 20',[6] '70',[7] and '1,000'[8] speakers of Manchu remaining among the entire ethnic group.[9] Manchu speakers are located in a few villages in Heilongjiang—Sanjiazi Village in Fuyu County and Dawujia Village in Aihui County. Most of the Manchu speakers use Mandarin as their first language and speak Manchu 'with a pronounced Chinese accent'.[10] Manchu was the only Tungus language to possess a script, but this too is now obsolete.[11]

Although the name Manchu was first used in the early 1600s, their descendants date back 3,000 years to the Suzhen tribe.[12] In 1644, the Manchu broke through the Great Wall and established the Qing Dynasty that ruled China for 267 years.

Before most Manchu were assimilated, they were known as shamanists who also worshiped their ancestors. Some aspects of these practices remain, but today most Manchu are considered nonreligious. One source lists 9.9 per cent of the Manchu as Mahayana Buddhists.[13] North-east China has had less Buddhist influence throughout history than most other parts of China, yet the Manchu warrant inclusion in this book because 1.6 million of them profess to believing in Buddhism—though few go to temples or observe any regular Buddhist ceremonies.

The Catholics began work in Manchuria in 1620. By 1922 they numbered 56,000 converts,[14] most of whom were Han Chinese. Protestant work among the Manchu began in 1869. A revival swept through Manchuria in the early 1900s. A blind evangelist, Chang Sen, won hundreds of converts to Christ. 'Missionaries followed after him, baptizing converts and organizing churches.'[15] In the first half of the 20th century many Manchu Christians suffered severe persecution and torture, especially between 1931 and 1945 when north-east China was annexed by Japan and renamed *Manchukuo*. Today there are at least 22,000 scattered Manchu believers. Many have come to Christ during the great Heilongjiang revival of the 1990s.[16]

Population:
12,666,700 (2000)
16,340,100 (2010)
20,131,100 (2020)
Countries: China, possibly Russia, North Korea
Buddhism: Mahayana
Christians: 22,000

Overview of the Manchu

Other Names: Man, Manchou, Manju

Population Sources:
9,821,180 in China (1990 census)[17]
possibly also in Russia, North Korea

Language: Altaic, Tungus, Southern, Southwest

Dialects: 0

Professing Buddhists: 9.9%

Practising Buddhists: 3%

Christians: 0.2%

Scripture: New Testament 1835; Portions 1822 (obsolete script)

Jesus **film:** none

Gospel Recordings: none

Christian Broadcasting: none

ROPAL code: MJF

Photo credit: Paul Hattaway

Status of Evangelization

69%

30%

1%

A   B   C

A = Have never heard the gospel
B = Have heard the gospel but have not become Christians
C = Are adherents to some form of Christianity

Manmet

CHINA
Yunnan

VIETNAM

MYANMAR

LAOS

Manmet

Population:
1,310 (2000)
1,700 (2010)
2,090 (2020)
Countries: China
Buddhism: Theravada
Christians: none known

Overview of the Manmet

Other Names: Manmi, Manmit, Man Met

Population Sources:

900 in China (1984, J-O Svantesson)[1]

Language: Austro-Asiatic, Mon-Khmer, Northern Mon-Khmer, Palaungic-Khmuic, Palaungic, Western Palaungic, Angkuic

Dialects: 0

Professing Buddhists: 70%

Practising Buddhists: 30%

Christians: 0%

Scripture: none

Jesus film: none

Gospel Recordings: none

Christian Broadcasting: none

ROPAL code: MML

Status of Evangelization

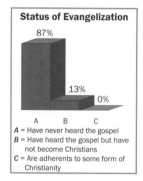

87%

13%

0%

A   B   C

A = Have never heard the gospel
B = Have heard the gospel but have not become Christians
C = Are adherents to some form of Christianity

More than 1,300 members of the Manmet people group live in five villages in the mountains north-east of Jinghong ('City of Dawn')—the capital of Xishuangbanna Prefecture in Yunnan Province, China. Although the Manmet are close to China's borders with the nations of Laos and Myanmar, no communities of Manmet are known to exist outside China.

The Manmet were counted separately in the 1982 Chinese census and then combined into a large group of *Undetermined Minorities*. In the 1950s the Manmet applied to the central government in a bid to be recognized as a distinct minority group, but their application was rejected. Today the Manmet are looked down upon by both the neighbouring Han Chinese and the Lu people.

The Manmet speak a distinct tonal language within the Angkuic branch of the Mon-Khmer linguistic family. Some Manmet men who have spent time as monks in Buddhist temples are able to read the Lu script.

In the 12th century AD, a number of different tribes united with the Tai to establish the *Jinglong Golden Hall Kingdom*. The Nanzhao Kingdom, centred at Dali in central Yunnan, was overthrown by the advancing Mongol hordes of Kublai Khan in AD 1253. Thousands of minority people fled from the savage Mongols. Those who

survived fragmented and evolved into the dozens of ethnic communities that sprang up in southern Yunnan. It was also at this time that the great Mon-Khmer race began to split into smaller, more distinct political units. The Manmet is one group today that may owe its existence to this tumultuous period of history.

The Manmet are experts at tilling their sharply angled fields, which seem to cling to the sides of the mountains. They use every available patch of land near their villages for food production. They grow rice, corn, sugarcane, bananas and various kinds of vegetables. They also raise chickens, water buffaloes and pigs. Most Manmet women stay at home, but some earn an income by selling produce at the Jinghong market. In recent years, many Manmet youth have moved to the cities in search of education and work.

Most Manmet adhere to a mixture of animism and Theravada Buddhism, which is the prevalent religion in the area. Around Jinghong there are numerous temples, which are the focal points for each community's social life as well as places for practising religious rituals.

Presbyterian missionaries in Jinghong established Christian churches, hospitals and schools during the 1930s and 1940s. 'The people readily received the Gospel, but for many, it was very difficult to renounce sin; for them their faith was nominal. . . . During the Cultural Revolution [1966–1976] . . . many leaders of the church were killed.'[2] Although missionaries were active in the Jinghong area, the shy Manmet escaped their attention. Few Manmet people today have any awareness of the gospel or know the name of Jesus Christ.

International Mission Board

More than 25,000 Matpa people are concentrated in the lower areas of Mongar District in eastern Bhutan. Their two largest villages are Tsamang and Tsakaling. A number of Matpa villages are also located within the Lhuntse District further to the north, especially in and around the village of Kurmet.

Matpa is the ethnic name of this group. They have also been listed by their language name, Chocangacakha, which is closely related to Dzongkha, Bhutan's national language spoken by the Drukpa people.

All Matpa people are followers of Tibetan Buddhism.

Despite being a tiny country with one of the smallest populations of any country in the world, 'Bhutan has an enormous number of religious buildings. According to one count, 525 lhakhangs [temples] are owned by the state and another 144 are in the care of reincarnate lamas. In addition, there are another 800 village temples and an estimated 500 privately-owned temples. Each was designed for a different purpose to suit the wishes of the founders, architects or sponsors.'[1] Given that realistic estimates put Bhutan's population at around 600,000, that means there is an average of one Buddhist temple for every 300 people in Bhutan.

The question of Bhutan's population is one of the strangest demographic inconsistencies in the world. Figures given by respected publications range from 600,000 to more than two million. One book, printed in 1998, explains the history behind this odd situation: 'In 1971, when Bhutan applied for UN membership, the population was estimated at just less than one million. No census data existed and government officials estimated the population as best they could, choosing to err on the high side in order to help gain world recognition. Over the years, this nearly-a-million-figure was adjusted upward in accordance with estimates of Bhutan's population growth figures, finally reaching the 1.2 million figure. In some publications, this total was even listed at 1.5 million! The 600,000 estimate is based on the census of 1988 and is now the accepted figure.'[2]

Being an official Buddhist kingdom, Bhutan has been largely locked away from the influence of the gospel for centuries until recent decades, when migrants from Nepal and India have brought Christianity into the country for the first time on any significant scale. The Buddhist groups, however, have remained largely untouched by the gospel. They see Christianity as a foreign religion with little relevance to their lives. Others see Christianity as a threat to traditional Bhutanese values and culture.[3]

The importance of Tibetan Buddhism and the unity that it fosters are best seen among the Matpa people during festivals and ceremonies. The whole community attends, dressed in their festive best. Participants wear gruesome masks depicting powerful demons, and stories are told of how the Buddhist sage Padmasambhava defeated demonic forces with the truth of Buddhism. There are no known Christians among the Matpa people in Bhutan today, and no Scripture translations, *Jesus* film or gospel recordings are available in their language.

Photo credit: Dwayne Graybill

Population:
25,100 (2000)
32,200 (2010)
41,300 (2020)
Countries: Bhutan
Buddhism: Tibetan
Christians: none known

Overview of the Matpa

Other Names: Chocangacakha, Tsamangpakha, Tsakalingpaikha, Maphekha, Rtsamangpa'ikha, Kursmadkha

Population Sources:

20,000 in Bhutan (2001, G van Driem [1991 figure])

Language: Sino-Tibetan, Tibeto-Burman, Himalayish, Tibeto-Kanauri, Tibetic, Tibetan, Southern

Dialects: 0

Professing Buddhists: 100%

Practising Buddhists: 85%

Christians: 0%

Scripture: none

Jesus film: none

Gospel Recordings: none

Christian Broadcasting: none

ROPAL code: CHK

Status of Evangelization
75%
25%
0%

A   B   C
A = Have never heard the gospel
B = Have heard the gospel but have not become Christians
C = Are adherents to some form of Christianity

Minyak

A 1983 study listed 15,000 Minyak living in extremely remote regions of western Sichuan Province in China.[1] They inhabit parts of Kangding, Ya'an, Jiulong and Shimian counties in the Garze Tibetan Prefecture. The Minyak live in the shadow of the mighty 7,556-metre (24,783 ft.) Gongga Mountain (*Minya Konka* in Tibetan). The region was first described in 1930 by explorer Joseph Rock: 'A scenic wonder of the world, this region is 45 days from the nearest railhead. For centuries it may remain a closed land, save to such privileged few as care to crawl like ants through its canyons of tropical heat and up its glaciers and passes in blinding snowstorms, carrying their food with them.'[2]

China Advocate

The Minyak have been described as a 'peaceful, sedentary Tibetan tribe, a most inoffensive, obliging, happy-go-lucky people'.[3] Most of the members of this group call themselves Minyak or Muya, except for those living in Kangding and the Tanggu area of Jiulong County, who call themselves Buoba.

The Minyak language is part of the Qiangic linguistic branch.[4] It has two dialects, Eastern and Western Minyak, which reportedly have significant differences.[5] The Minyak were once part of the now extinct Chiala Tibetan Kingdom in western Sichuan. Ancient *tianlu*, or stone defense towers, still stand in dilapidated condition at strategic locations along the mountain ridges. The Minyak may be descended from survivors of the destruction of Minyak (in present-day Ningxia) by Genghis Khan in 1227. One source states, 'Their culture is essentially Tibetan, with a few local differences. When a [Minyak] boy wants to get married, he takes a wine bottle with a ceremonial scarf tied around it to the house of the girl's parents. He pours them a cup of wine and they drink the cup if they approve of the marriage. . . . When it comes time for the wedding, the boy takes friends to ride horses to the girl's home. The boy must pass three tests at the wedding, and everyone dances all night.'[6]

All Minyak adhere to Tibetan Buddhism. They observe Tibetan festivals and make pilgrimages to Buddhist holy sites. When the Minyak die, 'they are buried with prayer flags to help them make it past the demons, which they will encounter soon after death'.[7]

Although there are presently no known Christians among the Minyak, the China Inland Mission did have a station in Tatsienlu (now Kangding), on the edge of Minyak territory. The mission closed when the missionaries were forced to leave China in the early 1950s. When the explorer Joseph Rock first entered the Minyak region he was besieged for medicine—a sure sign that missionaries had been there before him. 'Whenever we came to a village, the peasants would gather about us and with folded hands would beseech me to dispense medicine to sick relatives.'[8] The Minyak today have no awareness of Jesus Christ. They are ignorant of Christianity, living and dying 'without the slightest knowledge of the outside world'.[9]

Population:
20,900 (2000)
25,750 (2010)
31,700 (2020)
Countries: China
Buddhism: Tibetan
Christians: none known

Overview of the Minyak

Other Names: Muya, Minya, Munya, Miyao, Muyak, Minya Tibetans, Buoba

Population Sources:
15,000 in China (1983, Sun Hongkai)

Language: Sino-Tibetan, Tibeto-Burman, Tangut-Qiang, Qiangic

Dialects: 2 (Eastern Minyak, Western Minyak)

Professing Buddhists: 100%

Practising Buddhists: 65%

Christians: 0%

Scripture: none

Jesus film: none

Gospel Recordings: none

Christian Broadcasting: none

ROPAL code: MVM

Status of Evangelization

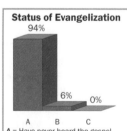

94%

6%

0%

A   B   C

A = Have never heard the gospel
B = Have heard the gospel but have not become Christians
C = Are adherents to some form of Christianity

Population:
1,138,300 (2000)
1,274,800 (2010)
1,428,000 (2020)
Countries: Myanmar,
Thailand
Buddhism: Theravada
Christians: 10,000

Overview of the Mon

Other Names: Talaing,
Mun, Teguan, Taleng, Aleng,
Takanoon, Mou, Rmen, Rman,
Peguan

Population Sources:
1,053,000 in Myanmar (2003,
Joshua Project II)[1]

120,000 In Thailand (2000, J
Schliesinger [1995 figure])

Language: Austro-Asiatic,
Mon-Khmer, Monic

Dialects: 3 (Mataban-
Moulmein [Central Mon]; Pegu
[Northern Mon]; Ye [Southern
Mon])

Professing Buddhists: 85%

Practising Buddhists: 60%

Christians: 0.8%

Scripture: Bible 1928; New
Testament 1847; Portions
1843

Jesus film: available

Gospel Recordings: Mon; Mon:
Thailand; Mon: Takanoon

Christian Broadcasting:
available

ROPAL code: MNW

Status of Evangelization

66%

31%

1%

A   B   C

A = Have never heard the gospel
B = Have heard the gospel but have
not become Christians
C = Are adherents to some form of
Christianity

More than 1.2 million Mon people live along the Myanmar-Thailand border in Southeast Asia. The majority (more than a million) live in the delta regions east of Yangon (Rangoon) in the country of Myanmar. A further 120,000 Mon dwell on the Thai side of the border, especially in Kanchanaburi, Phetchaburi, Ratchaburi, Pha Nakon Sri Ayutthaya, Lopburi and Nakhon Ratch-asima. These provinces are located north and south of Bangkok. The Mon in Thailand are also widely known as the Talaing.[2] In the 1931 census of Burma (Myanmar) the Mon numbered 336,728 people.[3] This Mon group is not related to the small Indo-European Mon tribe of Ladakh, India.

The Mon established the first truly great civilization in the region, with the power of the Dvaravati Kingdom peaking between the 5th and 8th centuries. The Mon are acknowledged as the original Buddhists in Southeast Asia, having accepted Buddhism from present-day Sri Lanka in the 5th century. The Mon gave the region its first alphabet, based on the Indic-based Pali script.[4] In AD 769 the Mon founded a great city in northern Thailand on the site of today's Lamphun. By the mid-13th century, 'the Mon city-state of Haripunjaya had grown into the cultural and religious center of northern Thailand. The Mon . . . maintained contact with Ceylon [now Sri Lanka], and Theravada Buddhist schools taught Buddhism to other ethnic groups—the Lawa and the newly arrived Tai.'[5]

Later Mon history records constant warfare with the Burmese. They were finally

Myanmar Faces and Places

subdued in 1757, and their kingdom was demolished.[6] Many soldiers and civilians fled from the Burmese at the time. Most of those who crossed the border are the ancestors of today's Mon in Thailand. The rest of the Mon in Myanmar were steadily driven south by the Burmese until today most of them inhabit areas in the southern part of Mon State.

Linguistically, the Mon language comes from the Mon-Khmer branch, although less than 50,000 of the 120,000 Thailand Mon are still able to speak their mother tongue. Every year fewer Mon can read their script, making the 1928 Mon Bible increasingly obsolete.

The Mon were the first Buddhists in Southeast Asia, and today the vast majority of people retain their belief in Buddhism.[7] 'Each Mon village has a monastery. Most male children become monks for a time around 10 years of age, and again at 20. At 21, they may choose a lifetime commitment as monks. Females may become nuns. The monastery and its servants are respected, and the local monastery also serves as the village school.'[8] Animistic practices also have a place in everyday Mon life. The Mon 'give offerings to many spirits and observe several kinds of taboos. . . . Buddhist monks are often consulted for advice about the supernatural and they also act as astrologers.'[9]

Although the New Testament was translated into Mon as early as 1847, the gospel has made slow progress among them in both Myanmar and Thailand. Today there are an estimated 10,000 Mon Christians, but this total represents less than one per cent of the population. They remain an extremely needy unreached group.

Mon, Ladakh

The tiny Mon ethnic group of Jammu and Kashmir in northern India is one of the smallest Buddhist groups in the world, yet it has had a large and influential role in history.

The Indian government only recognized the Mon as a Scheduled Tribe in 1989, so no figure was given for them at the time of the 1981 census. The researcher R R S Prasad, however, has estimated a 1998 population of 700 Mon people.[1] They live in Ladakh and Kargil districts of Jammu and Kashmir, in villages along the banks of the Indus River. The area inhabited by the Ladakh Mon is extreme, with temperatures plummeting to minus 20 degrees in the winter and severe snowstorms blocking roads and tracks for weeks at a time.

The Mon are renowned as flute players and musicians. They move about in tandem with the similar Beda tribe. The Ladakhi seem to treat the Mon as a kind of low musician caste. While they utilize their services and appreciate their musical talents, most Ladakhi would not consider to 'eat the food or drink the water touched by them'.[2] The Ladakh Mon 'play the flute and provide music to all those who engage their service on festive and religious occasions, and for this they get an annual payment of grain from all peasant families after the harvest. . . . During dance performances on the occasion of marriage, they play the flute and drums and are paid with money and gifts. During the sowing of crops, they sing *goru* songs and are paid for this too. After the harvest, the Mon visit the houses of the Ladakhi to provide *larango* music and are offered grain and salt. . . . They also perform music on the occasion of childbirth.'[3]

The Mon of Ladakh are not related at all to the identically named Mon of Southeast Asia. While members of this latter group speak a language from the Austro-Asiatic linguistic family, the Ladakh Mon language is part of the Indo-European family.

Despite their tiny size, the Ladakh Mon are an ancient people who played a major role in the history of this part of the Himalayas,[4] 'as is evident from the rock carvings and ruins still known as Mon-castles. They are representatives of Aryan people who inter-mingled with the people of Mongoloid origin.'[5] Wahid Saddiq explains that the term 'Mon' is found in many locations throughout the Himalayas 'and is generally applied to valley dwellers by the Tibetan speaking peoples. The Ladakhi Mon, who were earlier agriculturists, appear to have been important members of society. Today, however, they have been relegated to a low status in Ladakh social system, and are members of the *rignun* or low class.'[6]

All Ladakh Mon believe in Tibetan Buddhism. They call in lamas to officiate at special occasions such as births, deaths and marriages. The major Buddhist festivals celebrated by the Ladakh Mon are the Losar and Purnima.

There are no known Christians among the 700 Ladakh Mon. Despite their distinctive culture, history and language, they have never appeared on Christian lists of unreached people groups in India, so few believers are even aware of their existence.

Population:
720 (2000)
840 (2010)
980 (2020)
Countries: India
Buddhism: Tibetan
Christians: none known

Overview of the Ladakh Mon

Other Names: Mon

Population Sources:
700 in India (1998, R R S Prasad)

Language: Indo-European, Indo-Iranian, Indo-Aryan, Northwestern Zone, Dardic, Shina

Dialects: 0

Professing Buddhists: 100%
Practising Buddhists: 70%
Christians: 0%
Scripture: none
***Jesus* film:** none
Gospel Recordings: none
Christian Broadcasting: none
ROPAL code: none

Status of Evangelization

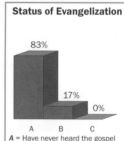

A = Have never heard the gospel
B = Have heard the gospel but have not become Christians
C = Are adherents to some form of Christianity

Approximately nine million Mongol people live in the vast grasslands and deserts of Central Asia. Almost six million Mongols are scattered across a wide area of northern China.[1] Approximately three times as many Mongols live in China as in the nation of Mongolia. An additional 200,000 live in Russia, and smaller numbers live in Kyrgyzstan, Taiwan and the USA. The main Mongol language in China is similar to Khalkha (Halh) Mongol in Mongolia, 'but there are phonological and important loan differences'.[2] The name *Khalkha* means 'shield'.[3]

During the 13th and 14th centuries, the Mongols brutally established the largest empire the world had ever seen, stretching from Southeast Asia to Europe. They instituted the Yuan Dynasty and ruled China from 1271 to 1368. The terrified Europeans called the Mongols *Tatars*, meaning 'people from hell' (*Tartarus*).

At the mercy of their vast and windswept landscape, the ancient Mongols based their religion on the forces of nature. The moon, stars and sun were all revered, as were rivers. The majority of Mongols follow Tibetan Buddhism, which was first introduced from Tibet in the 16th century. It has 'welded them together, has leavened their civilization with religious ideals, and has made them kind and hospitable. . . . But, on the other hand, it has robbed their manhood of its energy and natural ambition. . . . Until the power of

©Create International

Lamaism, with its overgrown, dissolute, and corrupting priesthood, is broken, there can be no hope of arresting the sure decay of the Mongols or of preventing their ultimate extinction.'[4] In the past many Mongols were Christians, converted by Nestorian missionaries between the 7th and 14th centuries. Even a chapel outside the Great Khan's royal tent 'resounded with the sound of public chants and the beating of tablets loudly announcing the appointed hours of Christian worship'.[5] Hulagu Khan's wife was described as 'the believing and true Christian queen'.[6] The Keirats, a Mongol tribe, numbered 200,000 believers in 1007,[7] while there were about 30,000 Mongol Catholics recorded in China by 1368.[8]

At times during the 13th and 14th centuries it seemed that the Mongols were on the verge of adopting Christianity as their religion. Kublai Khan issued this challenge to Marco Polo: 'Go to your Pope and ask him to send me a hundred men learned in your religion, who in the face of these sorcerers . . . will show their mastery by making the sorcerers powerless to perform these marvels in their presence. . . . Then I will be baptized, and all my magnates and barons will do likewise, and their subjects in turn. . . . Then there will be more Christians here than there are in your part of the world.'[9]

In 1992 there were about 2,000 Mongol believers reported in China.[10] Today there are believed to be between 30,000 and 50,000 believers.[11] In Mongolia the early years after the collapse of Communism in 1990 witnessed some exciting developments, with thousands of Mongols professing Christian faith, but in the years since the growth has plateaued as the foreign-dominated church struggles to find a place in Mongol culture. Today there are about 18,000 Christians in Mongolia, most of whom are young adults.[12]

Overview of the Mongols

Other Names: Mongolian, Khalka, Khalkha, Hahl, Hahl Mongol, Halh, Menggu, Meng Zu

Population Sources:
5,811,400 (2000, P Hattaway)
2,395,800 in Mongolia (2001, P Johnstone and J Mandryk [2000 figure])
200,000 in Russia (2001, P Johnstone and J Mandryk [2000 figure])
Also in Taiwan, Kyrgyzstan, USA

Population:
8,456,200 (2000)
10,564,000 (2010)
12,816,200 (2020)
Countries: China, Mongolia, Russia, Taiwan, Kyrgyzstan, USA
Buddhism: Tibetan
Christians: 31,000

Language: Altaic, Mongolian, Eastern, Oirat-Khalkha, Khalkha-Buriat, Mongolian Proper

Dialects: 9 (Chahar, Ordos, Tumet, Shilingol, Ulanchab, Jo-Uda, Jostu, Jirim, Ejine)

Professing Buddhists: 55%
Practising Buddhists: 35%
Christians: 0.4%
Scripture: New Testament 1952; Portions 1979
***Jesus* film:** available
Gospel Recordings: Mongolian, Inner Mongolian Chahar, Sheeringgul: Hohot
Christian Broadcasting: available
ROPAL code: MVF (Mongolian, Peripheral) and KHK (Mongolian, Halh)

Status of Evangelization

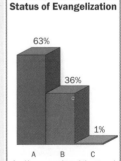

63%

36%

1%

A B C
A = Have never heard the gospel
B = Have heard the gospel but have not become Christians
C = Are adherents to some form of Christianity

Mongol, Sichuan

Population:
27,100 (2000)
35,000 (2010)
43,100 (2020)
Countries: China
Buddhism: Tibetan
Christians: 5

Overview of the Sichuan Mongols

Other Names: Lugu Lake Mongols, Sichuan Mongolians, Hihin, Hii-khin

Population Sources:

21,033 in China (1990 census)

Language: Sino-Tibetan, Tibeto-Burman, Unclassified

Dialects: 0

Professing Buddhists: 95%

Practising Buddhists: 75%

Christians: 0.1%

Scripture: none

Jesus **film:** none

Gospel Recordings: none

Christian Broadcasting: none

ROPAL code: none

Status of Evangelization

89%

10%

1%

A   B   C

A = Have never heard the gospel
B = Have heard the gospel but have not become Christians
C = Are adherents to some form of Christianity

Approximately 30,000 Mongols live in the southern part of Sichuan Province in south-west China. Although a few Mongol villages are within the borders of Yunnan Province—located on the shores of Lugu Lake among the Mosuo people—most are in Sichuan, spread out along two or three valleys in Yanyuan and Muli counties, north-east of Lugu Lake.

The Sichuan Mongols are officially counted as part of the Mongolian nationality in China. They are a distinct ethno-linguistic group, however, from all other Mongolian peoples.[1] They call themselves Mongols and have their own unique clothing, history and language. All other peoples in the region recognize them as Mengzu (Mongols).

Little research has been done on the language of the Sichuan Mongols. In the seven centuries since their arrival in the area, neighbouring languages have heavily influenced their speech. One visitor described their language as 'Neither Mongolian, Mandarin, Yi, Mosuo nor Tibetan. I suspect it is a language taken from all or some of these languages.'[2] The Sichuan Mongol prince could only 'pick out a few words' of a Mongolian cassette played for him.[3]

Joseph Rock was the first recorded foreigner to visit the Sichuan Mongols in 1924. He described the town of Youngning as 'the seat of three chiefs whose ancestors were Mongols, elevated to power by Kublai Khan in the 13th century'.[4] Rock adds, 'When the great Mongol Emperor marched through the territory about Youngning, AD

1253, he left one of his relatives to rule the Hlihin tribesmen.'[5]

Before Communist rule, the Mongol king acted as a warlord over the whole region. 'When the Communists took over, they deposed him, not killing him so as not to make him a martyr in the people's eyes.'[6] The Mongol palace was destroyed and the prince was sent to a re-education camp for several years. The prince, La Ping Chu, is still alive today and respected by his people, although he is not allowed to rule. Many older Mongols still bow their heads in respect when they pass him on the street.

China Advocate

Most Sichuan Mongols are farmers or fishermen, leading quiet lives in their remote villages. They observe Buddhist festivals, 'hoping someday their kingdom will be restored to them'.[7]

Tibetan Buddhism is the spiritual stronghold of the Sichuan Mongols. There is a temple in active use just behind the prince's house. Most temples and altars were destroyed during the Cultural Revolution.

Very few Sichuan Mongols have ever heard the name of Jesus Christ. One person who has heard the gospel is the prince himself, witnessed to by foreign visitors a few years ago. A prayer for healing was offered for the prince, who could not stand up straight because of a stomach ulcer. He was completely healed.[8]

The Sichuan Mongols are surrounded by unreached people groups on every side. There are no Christian communities nearby who could readily reach them.

Festivals of Mongolia

The *Nadam* festival is the greatest occasion on the Mongolian calendar. *Nadam* means 'amusement'. Mongols, young and old, amuse themselves with wrestling, archery, horse racing competitions and the consumption of copious amounts of alcohol.

1

2

3

5

4

6

1&3. [Create International]
2. [Julian Hawken]
4. [Asian Report]
5-6. [International Mission Board]

7

8

9

10

11

12

7, 11 & 12. [Create International]
8, 9 & 10. [International Mission Board]

Festivals in the 'Land of Dawn'

Arunachal Pradesh ('Land of Dawn') is a remote Himalayan state in northeast India inhabited by numerous Buddhist people groups. The Spring Festival in Tawang features masked actors re-enacting the great Tibetan sage Padmasambhava, who is believed to have flown across the Himalayas on the back of a tiger and introduced Buddhism to the region in 746 AD. He first had to defeat powerful demons, which he did by converting them to the truths of Buddhism.

13

14

15

16

17

18

13–18. all by Dwayne Graybill

19

20

21

22

23

24

25

26

19-26. all by Dwayne Graybill

MONGOLIA
CHINA
Qinghai
Mongour

Population:
39,800 (2000)
49,800 (2010)
61,300 (2020)
Countries: China
Buddhism: Tibetan
Christians: none known

Overview of the Mongour

Other Names: Mongor, Monguor, Mongou, Minhe Tu

Population Sources:

30,000 in China (1987, *Language Atlas of China*)

Language: Altaic, Mongolian, Eastern, Mongour

Dialects: 0

Professing Buddhists: 70%

Practising Buddhists: 55%

Christians: 0%

Scripture: none

***Jesus* film:** none

Gospel Recordings: Tu: Minhe

Christian Broadcasting: none

ROPAL code: MJG

Status of Evangelization

91%

9%

0%

A   B   C

A = Have never heard the gospel
B = Have heard the gospel but have not become Christians
C = Are adherents to some form of Christianity

A 1987 Chinese study reported 30,000 speakers of the Mongour language.[1] This figure has grown to about 40,000 today. The Mongour live primarily in Minhe County in the eastern part of Qinghai Province in western China. Minhe, formerly known as Shangchuankou, lies on the Huang Shui River. Minhe is situated east of the provincial capital Xining, a considerable distance from Huzhu County where the majority of the Tu people live.

Although the Mongour have been officially included as part of the Tu nationality, they speak a very different language and have a separate identity from the Tu. As one researcher explains, 'The Tu call themselves Mongol, except those living in Minhe, who form a minority, where the word is pronounced *Mongour*. This term has mistakenly been used by some Western scholars as the general name for all Tu.'[2]

The speakers of Mongour cannot communicate with other Tu in their own language and must revert to Chinese to be understood. 'Differences [between Tu and Mongour] are mainly phonological, but there are also lexical and grammatical differences.'[3] While Tu has many loanwords from Tibetan, Mongour contains numerous loanwords from Chinese. Mongour is considered 'the most divergent Mongolian language of all'.[4]

When the ancestors of today's Tu and Mongour people first came to Qinghai, the area was occupied by Tibetans, Uygurs and a group called the Shato. By the late 1300s, the Tu had divided into 16 clans. Eight clans were called *Tu* (White Mongol), five *Shato*, one *Black Mongol*, one *Turkish* (Uygur) and one Chinese.[5]

Revival Christian Church

The Mongour have several unique sexual customs. One is called 'marriage to the pole', whereby a girl stays with her family and takes in lovers. Any children born to her take her family's name. Another is the 'marriage to the girdle'—a Mongour girl sleeps with a guest, who upon departure leaves his girdle behind. In case the girl becomes pregnant, she would be 'married to the girdle'.[6] After child delivery, the mother and baby stay confined to a room for one month. Men are barred from entry and only the closest female relatives are allowed to enter.

Although the Mongour are nominally Buddhists, shamanism seems to hold most sway in their religious practices. Two types of shamans are active among the Mongour. 'White shamans' are used to heal sickness, while 'black shamans' bring vengeance on enemies. Another highly regarded religious figure is the *kurtain*. This is a person who allows himself to be possessed by an evil Daoist spirit.

By the 1920s Catholic missionaries were active in the Mongour region, but no church remains today. Missionary Frank Laubach issued a warning to the church in the 1930s: 'Millions in China will soon be reading. Are we going to give them reading matter? Will they be flooded with the message of Christ or with atheism? Will they read love or hate? This is the most stupendous, most arresting, most ominous fact, perhaps on this planet.'[7]

Monpa, But

The 1991 census in India recorded 675 members of the But Monpa tribe, up from 348 people in the 1981 census.[1] Almost all But Monpa inhabit the villages of Jeriagaon, Sellary, Khoitum, Ralung and Khoina in the Nafra Circle of West Kameng District of Arunachal Pradesh, north-east India. The But Monpa inhabit a hilly area 'surrounded by dense coniferous forests where the climate is cool and salubrious'.[2] The But Monpas call themselves Matchopa, Bootpa or Butpa.

This small tribe is one of six Monpa groups, each of which has been granted status as a Scheduled Tribe by the Indian government. The combined population of all Monpa in India is nearly 50,000.[3] Two distinct Monpa groups also live in Tibet.

Almost all Christian researchers have refused to list these six groups separately. It is generally assumed that because all six tribes call themselves 'Monpa' they must be one group and therefore do not need to be split down into these small components. This presumption is an error from an ethnolinguistic point of view. Others do not consider such numerically small groups worth mentioning. Our aim is to present all distinct people groups, regardless of size, as each is precious to the Saviour and the Bible states that *every* tribe, language and nation will have representatives worshipping around the throne of Jesus in heaven.

The term 'Monpa' is a generic one, used by the Tibetans to denote *mon* ('the low country') and *pa* ('belonging to'). The Monpa are, therefore, people 'belonging to the low country'. In reality, the various Monpa tribes of Arunachal Pradesh, including the

But, migrated into the region from diverse places at various times, 'differing with respect to their languages and many other cultural traits. . . . The languages of the Lish Monpas, Chug Monpas and But Monpas differ a lot from the rest of the Monpas, and closely resemble the languages of the Akas, Mijis and Sherdukpens.'[4]

The But Monpa are quite different from the other Monpa groups[5] and could probably be considered the least Buddhist of the various groups. K S Singh notes, 'Though they are listed under the greater Monpa group, except their dress they differ in all aspects (language, socio-cultural life and religion) from the other Monpa.'[6] In another book, Singh states, 'Except for the But Monpa, the rest of [the Monpa groups] belong to the Lamaistic school of Tibetan Buddhism. . . . It is interesting to note that the practice of pre-Buddhist shamanism still persists among them. However, the But Monpa have their own traditional faith, beliefs and festivals. Gradually they are being drawn into the greater fold of Buddhism.'[7] Despite the above indication that the But Monpa are not strong Buddhists, the 1981 census recorded 97.7 per cent of them as Buddhists and 0.86 per cent as Hindus, while 1.44 per cent did not state their religion.[8]

There are no known Christians among the But Monpa tribe, and less than 20 among all the Monpa groups in India. They are one of the most unreached and needy Buddhist groups in the Himalayas.[9]

Population:
745 (2000)
870 (2010)
1,010 (2020)
Countries: India
Buddhism: Tibetan
Christians: none known

Overview of the But Monpa

Other Names: Monba, Moinba, Monpa, Menba, Matchopa, Bootpa, Butpa, Shingjee, Rahungjee, Khoitumjee, Khonujee, Nagnoo

Population Sources:
675 in India (1991 census)

Language: Sino-Tibetan, Tibeto-Burman, Himalayish, Mahakiranti, Kiranti, Eastern

Dialects: 0

Professing Buddhists: 97%

Practising Buddhists: 50%

Christians: 0%

Scripture: none

Jesus **film:** none

Gospel Recordings: none

Christian Broadcasting: none

ROPAL code: MOB01

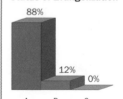

Status of Evangelization

88%

12%

0%

A   B   C

A = Have never heard the gospel
B = Have heard the gospel but have not become Christians
C = Are adherents to some form of Christianity

The Chugpa Monpa tribe live in just one location, Chug village, in north-east India. Chug village is within the Dirang District in the fascinating state of Arunachal Pradesh, home to dozens of relatively untouched tribes and colourful people groups. The Chugpa Monpa's homeland 'experiences severe cold weather during the winter months. During the monsoon the area receives heavy rainfall. Their houses can be marked from a long distance by prayer flags.'[1] The Chugpa Monpa were not counted separately in the 1981 Indian census, but in the 1971 census they numbered 483 people. Based on the 1991 census, they are now believed to number more than 800.

The oral traditions of the Chugpa say they migrated to their present location from the west and settled in the Sangti area of the Dirang Subdivision for a considerable period before moving on to their present location in a beautiful valley. Because of their different origins, the Chugpa Monpa language is quite distinct from other Monpa varieties spoken in the area, although they have learned to speak a Monpa lingua franca and Hindi in order to communicate with their neighbours. Despite their linguistic and cultural differences, the various Monpa groups share a certain uniformity in their appearance. Men and women wear maroon or black gowns and jackets, while Monpa men are fond of wearing their distinctive caps made of yak hair, which is both warm and waterproof.

Arunachal Pradesh is renowned for its incredibly wet weather—some meteorologists have labelled it the wettest place on earth. During the monsoon, it is common for an inch of rain to fall in Arunachal in an hour. Many different varieties of fruit and vegetables grow in this moist environment.

The diet of the Chugpa Monpa includes 'beef, pork, mutton, chicken and venison. The flesh of monkey is considered a taboo. . . . They drink *bangchen* (local beer) prepared out of rice or maize. . . . They also drink *ara* (distilled liquor). The Chug Monpas are fond of apples, oranges and plums.'[2]

Remarkably for a tiny people group who only inhabit one village, the Chugpa Monpa community has five social divisions, or clans: the Gumpa, Khumupa, Khumuthong-kor, Ngarmupa and Changmuchipa. In times past there were strict restrictions against individuals from the same clan marrying each other, but in recent times the village has relaxed these taboos due to their small numbers and their desire for survival. There have been some cases of intermarriage with people from the Sherdukpen, Dirang Monpa and Lish Monpa groups.

One hundred per cent of Chugpa Monpa profess Buddhism as their religion. They send their sons to Tibetan Buddhist monasteries in north India and maintain links with numerous other Buddhist tribes and people groups, including contacts inside Tibet. Lamas preside over birth, marriage and funeral rites. After a person dies, the lama decides whether the deceased should be buried, cremated, 'or if the body should be cut into 108 pieces and thrown into the river'.[3]

Although the people groups living on the southern plains of Arunachal Pradesh have witnessed tremendous Christian growth over the past 20 years, the gospel has yet to make an impact on the Chugpa Monpa.

Population:
817 (2000)
950 (2010)
1,110 (2020)
Countries: India
Buddhism: Tibetan
Christians: none known

Overview of the Chugpa Monpa

Other Names: Monba, Moinba, Monpa, Menba, Chug, Chung Monpa

Population Sources:
817 in India (2001, FMC South Asia)

Language: Sino-Tibetan, Tibeto-Burman, Himalayish, Mahakiranti, Kiranti, Eastern

Dialects: 0

Professing Buddhists: 100%

Practising Buddhists: 80%

Christians: 0%

Scripture: none

***Jesus* film:** none

Gospel Recordings: none

Christian Broadcasting: none

ROPAL code: MOB02

Photo credit: Dwayne Graybill

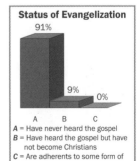

Status of Evangelization

91%

9%

0%

A   B   C

A = Have never heard the gospel
B = Have heard the gospel but have not become Christians
C = Are adherents to some form of Christianity

Monpa, Dirang

CHINA
Xizang (Tibet)

INDIA
Arunachal Pradesh

BHUTAN

Monpa Dirang

Population:
5,580 (2000)
6,500 (2010)
7,580 (2020)
Countries: India
Buddhism: Tibetan
Christians: 5

Overview of the Dirang Monpa

Other Names: Monba, Moinba, Monpa, Menba, Sangla

Population Sources:

5,050 in India (1991 census)

Language: Sino-Tibetan, Tibeto-Burman, Himalayish, Mahakiranti, Kiranti, Eastern

Dialects: 0

Professing Buddhists: 99%

Practising Buddhists: 85%

Christians: 0.1%

Scripture: none

Jesus **film:** none

Gospel Recordings: none

Christian Broadcasting: none

ROPAL code: MOB03

Status of Evangelization

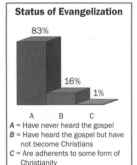

83%

16%

1%

A   B   C

A = Have never heard the gospel
B = Have heard the gospel but have not become Christians
C = Are adherents to some form of Christianity

The Dirang Monpa have been granted status in India as a Scheduled Tribe. Their population in the 1981 census was 3,599 (1,742 males and 1,857 females). This increased to 5,050 in the 1991 census. One of the alternate names for the Dirang Monpa is Sangla, which suggests that they may be related to the large Tsangla ethnic group of Bhutan, China and India, which numbers more than 250,000 people. More research needs to be done to determine the relationship between the Dirang Monpa and Tsangla languages.

The Dirang Monpa live in the Dirang Circle in the West Kameng District of Arunachal Pradesh in north-east India. The Dirang Monpa claim that they were the first inhabitants of the Dirang area. Some of their elders say their forefathers originated in eastern Bhutan, before migrating to their present location in India.

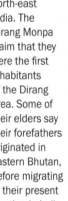

Dwayne Graybill

The diet of the Dirang Monpa consists of 'cereals, fish, meat, vegetables and *chhung* (local drink brewed from maize, rice, millet, wheat and buckwheat). Maize is the staple food item. . . . They eat beef, pork, mutton, fowls, yaks, *mithuns* and deer. The fruits consumed are apples, peaches, bananas, pomegranates and oranges.'[1]

Marriage in Dirang Monpa society is a simple procedure. A lama is hired to consult the horoscopes to determine the most auspicious time and day for a wedding to take place. Family members and friends gather at the bride's home. The lama simply places a white scarf, called a *katha*, around the necks of the bride and groom, blesses the couple, and they are married. A huge feast is held at which all the people, including children, often become intoxicated by consuming copious amounts of strong rice whisky.

The lamas perform many other roles in the community as well, in keeping with the important role that Tibetan Buddhism plays in the daily lives of Dirang Monpa society. After a baby is delivered, the mother is not allowed to leave the room for seven days. She is considered in a state of spiritual and physical pollution and nobody can visit her. When the baby is three days old, a lama is invited to name the child. 'After saying a prayer, he prepares a horoscope for the baby. The horoscope is consulted to choose a name for the child.'[2]

Not only is the Buddhist lama present at birth, but he also officiates at funerals. When there is a death, 'the body is carried to a nearby river and thrown into the water after being cut into 108 pieces [Tibetan Buddhists consider 108 to be an auspicious number]. If a person dies in an accident his or her body is buried. When a lama or an influential person dies, the body is cremated. . . . On the seventh day after the death a prayer is performed by the lama and a festoon is erected in front of the house of the deceased to satisfy the soul. On the ninth day, the last day of the mourning period, a feast is given.'[3]

Tibetan Buddhism has a strong grip on the lives of the Dirang Monpa. At the time of the 1981 census, 99.69 per cent of the Dirang Monpa stated that they believed in Buddhism, 0.25 per cent were Hindus, and just one individual claimed to be a Christian.[4] The previous Indian census, in 1971, had returned 100 per cent of the Dirang Monpa as Buddhists.

According to the eminent Indian anthropologist K S Singh, approximately 8,000 Kalaktang Monpa people live in the Kalaktang Circle of the West Kameng area of Tawang District in the north-east Indian state of Arunachal Pradesh.

The Kalaktang Monpa have been granted status in India as a Scheduled Tribe, but more research needs to be done to determine their ethnolinguistic relationship to other tribal groups, including the large Tsangla group. Although the Kalaktang Monpa language and culture appear to be quite different from those of most of the other Monpa groups, there are very few differences between the Kalaktang Monpa and the Dirang Monpa (despite the fact that the Indian authorities' investigations led them to grant separate tribal status to each group).

The Kalaktang Monpa are believed to be the original inhabitants of the Kalaktang circle, from which they take their name. In the past the Kalaktang Monpa did not possess a script, so their history was handed down in oral stories. Elderly Kalaktang Monpa men recall that their ancestors migrated to their present location from the Bumthang and Thalong areas in eastern Bhutan.

The Kalaktang Monpa have a rich culture. They are 'skilled in dyeing, weaving, paper-making, carpentry, cane and bamboo work. They perform some very popular forms of

a mask dance.'[1] Another source says, 'they have many pantomime dances which are generally performed during the annual festivals, both in the monasteries and in the villages. The *Ajilamu* and yak dances are very popular.'[2]

All Kalaktang Monpa were traditionally employed in farming or trading, but in recent years the Indian government has implemented various schemes and projects in the Kalaktang Monpa area. Consequently, many people have new occupations like office jobs, teaching and contract work. Medical centres, schools, banks and a postal system are now operating in the Kalaktang area.

All Kalaktang Monpa are thought to believe in Tibetan Buddhism. 'Their sacred place is called *goompha* which is adorned with the images of Lord Buddha and the Bodhisattvas (incarnations of Lord Buddha). The lama is their priest and his services are required to perform the birth, marriage and death rituals. Simultaneously they practise pre-Buddhistic animism or shamanism. The animistic priest, called *phrame*, cures diseases and removes evil spirits. . . . They share a common *goompha* (religious shrine) with the other Buddhist communities. Some of the Kalaktang Monpa send their children to the *goomphas* in the different parts of the country to acquire training in Lamaism. They have also established matrimonial and religious links with the other Monpas, Sherdukpens, Tibetans, Khambas and Membas.'[3]

There are no known Christians among the Kalaktang Monpa tribe. Their communities are extremely tightly sealed, and people generally are not open to outside influence. Much prayer is needed before the gospel will be able to penetrate this precious unreached people group.

Population:
8,450 (2000)
9,850 (2010)
11,500 (2020)
Countries: India
Buddhism: Tibetan
Christians: none known

Overview of the Kalaktang Monpa

Other Names: Monba, Moinba, Monpa, Menba, Tsangla

Population Sources:
8,000 in India (1995, K S Singh)

Language: Sino-Tibetan, Tibeto-Burman, Himalayish, Mahakiranti, Kiranti, Eastern

Dialects: 0

Professing Buddhists: 100%

Practising Buddhists: 90%

Christians: 0%

Scripture: none

Jesus **film:** none

Gospel Recordings: none

Christian Broadcasting: none

ROPAL code: MOB04

Status of Evangelization

83%
17%
0%

A   B   C

A = Have never heard the gospel
B = Have heard the gospel but have not become Christians
C = Are adherents to some form of Christianity

Monpa, Lishpa

More than 2,000 Lishpa Monpa people inhabit hilly terrain near the Dirang administrative centre in the West Kameng District of Arunachal Pradesh in north-east India. 'They are distributed in three villages—Lish, Lish Gompache and Lish Gompalok. Their habitat is surrounded by dense pine forests. It has a cool and salubrious climate with moderate to heavy rainfall.'[1] Their main village of Lish is located just three kilometres (two mi.) away from Dirang town.

The Lishpa Monpa, who actually call themselves 'Kishpi' in their own language, are considered the most different of all the Monpa groups in India. One source states, 'The Lishpas differ from the rest of the Monpas with regard to language, origin and culture.'[2] Their distinctiveness is no doubt due to the fact that they claim to have come from Tibet, before migrating down into today's India. Other Monpa groups say they migrated from Bhutan and areas to the west.

Dwayne Graybill

The renowned contemporary linguist George van Driem has said, 'Lishpa is a small group whose language, on the basis of available reports, belongs to the Kho-Bwa cluster. However, the Lishpa pass themselves off as "Monpa", a title to which the Lishpa are arguably entitled in view of the vague meaning of the term "Mon" and the large number of groups in Arunachal Pradesh, Bhutan and adjacent portions of Tibet who are designated by it. However, the Lishpa are linguistically quite distinct from the large East Bodish population group in Kameng District which goes primarily by the name of "Monpa" and amongst whom the Lishpa settlements are dispersed.'[3]

The 1971 census in India recorded 100 per cent of Lishpa Monpa people as Buddhists. The 1981 census returned 99.94 per cent of them as followers of Buddhism, in addition to one individual who declared he or she was a Hindu. It's possible that individual may have ticked the wrong box on the census questionnaire![4]

Despite this almost complete profession of Buddhism, the Lishpa Monpas practise a curious mixture of traditional Tibetan Buddhism combined with shamanism and witchcraft. One source notes, 'The Lishpa profess a form of Lamaistic Buddhism, which has been mixed up with some local beliefs and practices. The lama imparts religious teaching among them. The Lishpa practice witchcraft and sorcery and are engaged in curing diseases.'[5] Another publication states, 'Their shamanistic priests are called *frimpa*. . . . A witch-doctor or shaman is called *bonpu*. Besides Lord Buddha and his different incarnations, the Lishpas have a traditional community deity known as Phu or Lishpu (the hill deity). . . . The Lishpas also send their sons to different monasteries in India to acquire a training in Lamaism.'[6]

There has never been a single known Christian among the Lishpa Monpa. Outreach to them has proven difficult. The Monpa are bound in extreme spiritual darkness. Prospective missionaries to them should be trained in spiritual warfare. A group of Naga evangelists who moved to Arunachal Pradesh to reach the Monpa in 2001 faced tremendous demonic opposition and intimidation.

CHINA
Xizang (Tibet)

INDIA
Arunachal Pradesh

BHUTAN

Monpa Lishpa

Population:
2,060 (2000)
2,400 (2010)
2,800 (2020)
Countries: India
Buddhism: Tibetan
Christians: none known

Overview of the Lishpa Monpa

Other Names: Monba, Moinba, Monpa, Menba, Lish, Lishpa, Lish Monpa, Kishpi

Population Sources:
1,567 in India (1981 census)

Language: Sino-Tibetan, Tibeto-Burman, Himalayish, Mahakiranti, Kiranti, Eastern

Dialects: 0

Professing Buddhists: 100%

Practising Buddhists: 85%

Christians: 0%

Scripture: none

Jesus film: none

Gospel Recordings: none

Christian Broadcasting: none

ROPAL code: MOB05

Status of Evangelization
91%

9%

0%

A   B   C

A = Have never heard the gospel
B = Have heard the gospel but have not become Christians
C = Are adherents to some form of Christianity

A 1987 study reported 5,000 speakers of Medog Monpa living in China.[1] The majority are located in Medog County in southern Tibet. A few are also found in the Dongjiu area of Linzhi County. All Monpa in Tibet are located within the vast Menyu Prefecture. One linguist states, 'The Medog Monpa live mainly in Medog County in Tibet as well as Siang District of Arunachal Pradesh. This is a very small group . . . with the majority in India, quite distinct linguistically from the [Tsangla].'[2] Cut off for most of the year due to snow and landslides, Medog was the last county in China to become accessible to land vehicles. In 1994 a road was built there for the first time. Medog contains many Bengali tigers and 40 species of other rare, protected animals.[3]

An unspecified number of Monpa people living in the state of Arunachal Pradesh, India, are believed to speak the same language as the Medog Monpa of Tibet. More research needs to be conducted to determine which of the several distinct Monpa groups in India correspond to this group. The Medog Monpa language has been influenced more by Tibetan than by the Tsangla language. Medog Monpa is not a tonal language, while Tsangla contains four tones. Many Medog Monpa are bilingual in Tibetan, and many can read the Tibetan script.[4]

Unlike some of the Tsangla, whom the Chinese authorities counted as part of the Tibetan nationality, it appears that all of the Medog Monpa have been counted as part of the Monpa nationality. The Medog Monpa became poverty stricken following the

implementation of a feudal system imposed on them by the Zhuba Geju faction in the 14th century. For generations they were effectively slaves of the Tibetans.

The Monpa are known for their hospitality. They have a great love for music, singing and dancing. 'Most of them are able to play the traditional bamboo flute, a short thick instrument with four finger holes. . . . Their silversmiths are skillful in designing bracelets, earrings, necklaces and other ornaments.'[5] At Monpa weddings, the bride's uncle is the most honoured guest. According to tradition, he 'finds fault in everything, complaining the meat slices are too thick and the drinks too cheap. He bangs on the table with his fists, glowering angrily at everyone who passes. He behaves in this way to test the groom's family and observe their reactions.'[6]

The majority of Monpa follow Tibetan Buddhism. Some, however, still maintain their traditional beliefs in unseen gods, demons and ancestral spirits. Shamans and some Buddhist monks frequently use magic to cure the sick.

Most Medog Monpa are completely unaware that Christ came two millennia ago and died for their sin. No missionaries were allowed to work in this area of Tibet in the past. There is not a single known Christian fellowship or church within the entire Menyu Prefecture of Tibet.

Population:
6,590 (2000)
8,200 (2010)
10,100 (2020)
Countries: China, India
Buddhism: Tibetan
Christians: none known

Overview of the Medog Monpa

Other Names: Cangluo Monba, Medog Monba, Canglo Monba, Northern Monba, Motuo Monba, Eastern Monba

Population Sources:
5,000 in China (1987, *Language Atlas of China*)
also in India

Language: Sino-Tibetan, Tibeto-Burman, Himalayish, Mahakiranti, Kiranti, Eastern

Dialects: 0

Professing Buddhists: 85%

Practising Buddhists: 35%

Christians: 0%

Scripture: none

Jesus **film:** none

Gospel Recordings: none

Christian Broadcasting: none

ROPAL code: MOB

Status of Evangelization

92%

8%

0%

A **B** **C**

A = Have never heard the gospel
B = Have heard the gospel but have not become Christians
C = Are adherents to some form of Christianity

Photo credit: Dawyne Graybill

Monpa, Tawang

Approximately 8,000 members of the Tawang Monpa tribe live in the secluded and mysterious state of Arunachal Pradesh in north-east India. They are one of the largest Monpa groups in India and, due to their proximity to the large town of Tawang, one of the most influential. Tawang is strategically located a short distance from the meeting of the borders of the three nations of India, China and Bhutan. Many major festivals and Buddhist ceremonies are held in Tawang, and visitors come from all parts of the state to participate.

In recent years Arunachal Pradesh has opened to foreign tourism, and visitors from all around the world come to Tawang, though only in small numbers at the present time. One local tourist brochure proclaims, 'Moored high up in the mountain ranges of the Himalayas, at 3,500 metres [11,500 feet] above sea level is Tawang—the beautiful land of the Monpas. With sobriquets like "The Hidden Paradise" or "Land of the Dawn-lit Mountains", this land evokes images of awesome mountain views, remote hamlets, quaint and sleepy villages, magical gompas, tranquil lakes and a lot more.'[1]

The Tawang Monpa are named after their town, which in turn is named after the Tawang Monastery located there. This group, which has been granted status as a Scheduled Tribe in India, call themselves Brahmi Monpa,[2] while their language is called Monkit. The Tawang Monpa are different from other Monpa groups in terms of both language and culture. Despite these differences, most researchers lazily presume that the various groups who call themselves 'Monpa' must all be the same. This is far from true, as the generic term 'Monpa' is used to designate people living in the lower areas of the Himalayas, rather than to indicate a cohesive ethnolinguistic or historic group.

The diet of the Tawang Monpa is varied. They eat and drink 'pulses, fish, meat, vegetables and *bung chung* (local beer brewed from maize, rice, millet, wheat or buckwheat). . . . They consume milk products like *churpi*, ghee and butter. They eat beef, pork, mutton and the meat of fowl and yak. They also eat venison and the flesh of wild boar. The fruits consumed are oranges, peaches, pomegranates, apples and sugarcane.'[3]

The 1981 census returned 99.94 per cent of Tawang Monpa as Buddhists, as well as four individuals who claimed to be Hindu. Tawang is the spiritual centre of the area and home to several important monasteries, including the Tawang Monastery, where many festivities and traditional dances are held every year. Other important Buddhist landmarks include the 460-year-old Urgelling Monastery, which was the birthplace of the sixth Dalai Lama; the Rigyalling Monastery; and the more distant Taktsang Monastery. Together these institutions house more than 1,000 monks, 700 of which reside at Tawang Monastery alone.

In the past few years a few Tawang Monpa individuals, mostly young people, have believed in Jesus Christ. They immediately faced strong pressure from their families and communities to renounce their new faith. Some did, but others counted the cost and continue to follow Christ as Lord. The Christians who brought the gospel to Tawang have been persecuted.[4]

CHINA
Xizang (Tibet)
INDIA
Arunachal Pradesh
BHUTAN
Monpa Tawang

Population:
7,350 (2000)
8,550 (2010)
10,000 (2020)
Countries: India
Buddhism: Tibetan
Christians: 10

Overview of the Tawang Monpa

Other Names: Monba, Moinba, Monpa, Menba, Monkit
Population Sources:
6,503 in India (1981 census)
Language: Sino-Tibetan, Tibeto-Burman, Himalayish, Mahakiranti, Kiranti, Eastern
Dialects: 0
Professing Buddhists: 99%
Practising Buddhists: 90%
Christians: 0.1%
Scripture: none
***Jesus* film:** none
Gospel Recordings: none
Christian Broadcasting: none
ROPAL code: MOB06

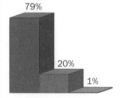

Status of Evangelization

79%

20%

1%

A   B   C
A = Have never heard the gospel
B = Have heard the gospel but have not become Christians
C = Are adherents to some form of Christianity

Dwayne Graybill

Population:
46,000 (2000)
53,700 (2010)
66,100 (2020)

Countries: China
Buddhism: Tibetan
Christians: 100

Overview of the Mosuo

Other Names: Mosso, Moso, Lushi, Hli-khin, Musu, Moxie, Mo-hseih, Jang

Population Sources:

40,000 in China (1991, Shi Yuoyi)

Language: Sino-Tibetan, Tibeto-Burman, Lolo-Burmese, Naxi, Eastern Naxi

Dialects: 0

Professing Buddhists: 95%

Practising Buddhists: 70%

Christians: 0.2%

Scripture: none

Jesus **film:** none

Gospel Recordings: Mosuo

Christian Broadcasting: none

ROPAL code: none

Status of Evangelization

83%

16%

1%

A   B   C

A = Have never heard the gospel
B = Have heard the gospel but have not become Christians
C = Are adherents to some form of Christianity

A 1991 study counted 40,000 Mosuo people,[1] living on both sides of the Sichuan-Yunnan border in south-west China. The Mosuo are primarily concentrated around the shores of beautiful Lugu Lake. Lugu is one of the highest inhabited lake areas in China, at an altitude of 2,685 metres (8,800 ft.) above sea level. Lion Mountain, home to the goddess Gammo, the chief Mosuo deity, rises majestically over the northern shore. No roads led to the lake until 1982. Before that time the Mosuo area was only accessible by foot or on horseback.

The Mosuo have been officially included as part of the Naxi nationality in China. The Mosuo deeply resent this and despise being called Naxi. The two groups have different languages, religions and cultures. Although distantly related to the Naxi, Mosuo speakers are not able to communicate with them in their own language and generally revert to Chinese in order to do so. According to Mosuo legends, the ancestors of today's Naxi and Mosuo migrated down from the Tibetan Plateau about 1,000 years ago.[2] Part of the group stopped at Lugu Lake and became today's Mosuo people, while the remainder continued south until they reached Lijiang, where today they are the Naxi. After many centuries of separation, the two groups have developed major ethnolinguistic differences.

For centuries the Mosuo have been a matri-archal and matrilineal society. The *azhu* system means that all property and assets are transferred to the female side of the

Julian Hawken

family, from mother to youngest daughter. Even the family name is passed down from the mother. Instead of taking a husband, Mosuo women are traditionally able to have 'walk-in' relationships. Men are only allowed to visit their lovers at night. They must leave the woman's house early the next morning and return to their mother's home. If a child is born, the responsibility to raise the child falls to the mother and her brothers. Often the identity of the father is not known at all. Despite pressure from the government to discontinue the *azhu* system, a 1994 study revealed that 60 per cent of the Mosuo still follow this way of life.[3]

Tibetan Buddhism has a strong grip on the Mosuo. Because the Mosuo have no written language, 'shamans had to memorize the equivalent of 71 volumes of text and recited them word for word during funerals, births and other events. From the first utterance to the last, a master's recitation took up to 60 hours.'[4] One source states, 'The pantheon of Mosuo deities includes thousands of invisible beings who reside in heaven and in purgatory and throughout the natural world. Every plant, animal and major geographical landmark has its own deity, and often the Mosuos believe such gods have demonic counterparts. Life, and the world itself, is one long struggle for power between good and evil.'[5]

There had never been a known Mosuo believer until recently, when a Mosuo family came to Christ under quite extraordinary, supernatural circumstances.[6] Today there are about 100 Mosuo believers.

LAOS

THAILAND Nan

Phrae

Population:
1,570 (2000)
1,710 (2010)
1,870 (2020)
Countries: Thailand
Buddhism: Theravada
Christians: none known

Overview of the Mpi

Other Names: Mpi-mi, Ma'pri, Kaw

Population Sources: 1,500 in Thailand (2000, J Schliesinger [1995 figure])

Language: Sino-Tibetan, Tibeto-Burman, Lolo-Burmese, Loloish, Southern, Phunoi

Dialects: 0

Professing Buddhists: 65%

Practising Buddhists: 30%

Christians: 0%

Scripture: none

Jesus **film:** none

Gospel Recordings: none

Christian Broadcasting: none

ROPAL code: MPZ

Status of Evangelization

69%

31%

0%

A   B   C

A = Have never heard the gospel
B = Have heard the gospel but have not become Christians
C = Are adherents to some form of Christianity

More than 1,500 people belonging to the Mpi ethnic group inhabit two villages in northern Thailand: Ban Dong Village in Muang District of Phrae Province and Ban Sagern in Tha Wang Pha District of Nan Province. The Mpi's Northern Thai neighbours call them *Kaw*, but the Mpi consider this name derogatory.

The Mpi are not found in any other countries, although their language reveals a close link between the Mpi and other Tibeto-Burman speaking tribes such as the 40,000 *Phunoi* of Laos, Thailand and Vietnam; the 8,000 *Bisu* of China and Thailand; and the 1,000 *Pyen* of Myanmar. Linguists report that there is some mutual intelligibility between Mpi and these three languages, which are related to the numerous Yi languages of southern China. The 'Yi' are a minority group invented by the Chinese authorities to define more than a hundred distinct tribes and Tibeto-Burman languages across several provinces of southern China. Each of these groups calls itself by a different ethnic name. The combined population of the 'Yi' nationality is more than eight million. The Mpi are unique in that the majority are Buddhists, whereas all Yi groups in China believe in polytheism, except for a few who are Christians.

The Mpi in Thailand were only 'discovered' by an American Peace Corps volunteer in 1967, who took an interest in them and later published the first Mpi dictionary. Despite the small population of those who speak it, the Mpi language has been

Xayographix

extensively studied and documented.[1]

The two Mpi villages are some distance apart. The Mpi of Ban Sagern in Nan Province claim that they were brought to Thailand as war captives in the late 1700s from Xishuangbanna in south-west China. Today their village is in a rural area and they depend heavily on their farming skills to make a living.

The Mpi of Ban Dong in Phrae Province, on the other hand, say that their ancestors were taken from southern China to become elephant handlers, or *mahouts*, in the armies of northern Thailand. After arriving in Thailand they settled in Chiang Rai Province, where they intermarried with local Chinese. Later they migrated into Phrae Province where they live to this day. The Mpi of Ban Dong live near Phrae City, with its many factories and industries, so many of them are employed as wage earners for Thai companies. The village also generates considerable income by making and selling brooms.

Despite their widespread geographic, economic and social differences, the Mpi from each area retain regular contact and intermarry with each other.

The Mpi are outwardly Buddhists who retain many traditional animistic beliefs. 'They strongly believe in the guardian spirit *chao fa*, which is the protector of the village and the house. The Mpi have altars in their houses for honouring this spirit. Every morning, offerings of food and drinks are placed at the altar. . . . The Mpi also believe in the spirit of the land and in malevolent spirits. The latter cause unnatural deaths. Ancestor worship is practiced within Buddhist concepts.'[2] There are no known Christian believers among the Mpi.

Approximately 70,000 Mru people live near the point where the three nations of Myanmar, Bangladesh and India meet. The majority of Mru (more than 40,000) live within the Yoma District and the Arakan hills of Rakhine State in western Myanmar.[1] Population figures for tribes in Myanmar are notoriously difficult to gauge. There has been no official census taken in Myanmar since the British conducted one in 1931![2] At that time there were 13,766 Mru.[3] A further 200 Mru villages—containing between 20,000 and 25,000 people—are located in the picturesque Chittagong Hills in south-east Bangladesh. There they live a semi-nomadic existence in a strategic border area that is off-limits to visitors.[4] Less than 2,000 Mru also reportedly live across the border in Tripura and in the Puruliya and Hugli (Hoogly) districts of West Bengal, India.[5]

Julian Hawken

The Mru practise a mixture of Buddhism and animism. In Myanmar the Buddhist influence is strong, with over 80 per cent adhering to Theravada Buddhism. Among the Mru in Bangladesh there is less Buddhist influence. They believe in *Torai* ('the Great Spirit'). The Mru explain that when Torai gave different tribes their written scripts he wrote the Mru script on a banana leaf, but an animal ate it before they could learn it.[6] Most Mru in India are Hindus.

A few years ago a tremendous power encounter took place, which resulted in several thousand Mru in Myanmar becoming Christians. In 1997 there were several Christian Mru villages. The main Buddhist temple in the area could not make the Christians recant, so they decided to persecute them into submission. The monks hired a gang of rough men to visit the Christian villages, burn down the churches and pastors' homes and beat the Christians. A group of these brutal men was dispatched from the main town. As they crossed a mountain pass on their way to the first Mru village, a freak thunderstorm struck. A bolt of lightning hit the persecutors, killing them all instantly. Another lightning bolt hit the 300-year-old Buddhist temple, burning it to the ground.

A second team of thugs—armed with chains and clubs—was dispatched by raft to another Christian village located on the banks of the local river. As their raft floated downstream to their destination, a heavy, unseasonable fog settled on the river. The men couldn't see a thing in front of them, including a fast-moving barge that slammed into their raft, sinking it and causing many of the would-be persecutors to drown. When news of these events circulated, the Mru acknowledged that God had judged the monks and the hired men because of their plans to attack the Christians. Many Mru put their faith in Christ as a result.[7]

There are few Christian believers among the Mru in Bangladesh. One mission that recently built a school for the Mru reported, 'This semi-nomadic tribe could be considered the most primitive tribe of Bangladesh. Mru men wear G-strings. The women are topless and wear only 10-inch long hand woven black skirts wrapped around their hips.'[8] After hearing about plans for the new school, 'The Mru villagers were ecstatic and enthusiastic. They donated bamboo and lumber from their fields. One of the village leaders signed a document donating four acres of land for the use of the school.'[9]

Population:
66,700 (2000)
75,100 (2010)
85,700 (2020)
Countries: Myanmar, Bangladesh, India
Buddhism: Theravada
Christians: 5,000

Overview of the Mru

Other Names: Mro, Murung, Niopreng, Mrung, Mru Chin, Khammi, Khami

Population Sources: 43,139 in Myanmar (2002, Myanmar Faces and Places)
17,811 in Bangladesh (1981 census)[10]
1,547 in India (1991 census)

Language: Sino-Tibetan, Tibeto-Burman, Mru

Dialects: 0

Professing Buddhists: 55%

Practising Buddhists: 40%

Christians: 7.4%

Scripture: New Testament 1994; Portions 1934

Jesus film: none

Gospel Recordings: Mru

Christian Broadcasting: none

ROPAL code: MRO

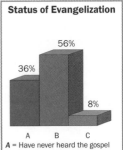

Status of Evangelization

A = 36%
B = 56%
C = 8%

A = Have never heard the gospel
B = Have heard the gospel but have not become Christians
C = Are adherents to some form of Christianity

Mugali

A 1998 study listed a population of 3,557 Mugali people in north-west Nepal.[1] Their homeland, which can only be reached by foot, is one of the most remote of any Buddhist group in the world. The Mugali inhabit 13 villages in the Mugu Kara area of the Mugu District of Karnali Zone.[2] The main village of Mugu is located 3,400 metres (11,150 ft.) above sea level. The Mugali comprise only about one-tenth of the total population in their district, which is just 30 kilometres (19 mi.) from the Chinese border. To get to Mugu, visitors must 'climb out of the Karan valley and move along the base of a narrow gorge to the north-west of Mount Syanan. At an altitude of approximately 11,500 feet this gorge widens into a V-shaped, rock-strewn valley. It is a quarter mile wide at this point . . . with the east and west being hemmed in by rockslides which are joined to the steep sides of the mountains, which reach a height of almost 19,000 feet. Mugu village lies at the bottom of this valley on the left hand side of the Mugu River.'[3] Small, scattered groups of Mugali people also live in the districts of Jumla, Dolpa, Surket, Baihang and Bajura.

Mugali homes are quite unique. They construct three-storey houses out of stone and wood. 'The flat roofs are made of wood, then covered with a mud mixture. Each storey consists of a single room with no windows. There is a door on each floor and there are small holes in the walls for ventilation. The ground floor, called the *goth*, is where livestock is kept. The next level, or *chhipra*, contains their store of grain and salt. The upper floor, or *koga*, is used as a living room and kitchen. A notched ladder provides access between floors.'[4]

There is a wide economic disparity between the Mugali people living in Mugu town and those in the small surrounding hamlets. Many Mugu residents are traders who sell and barter goods in the bazaars of north-west Nepal and across the border into Tibet. They live in relative comfort compared to the Mugali farmers, whose land is undeveloped and poor. The neighbours of the Mugali have a saying, '"Mugali people prosper on trade; otherwise, they are paupers". . . . They used to maintain large herds of yak, sheep and goats but their numbers have declined after the access to Tibetan pastures was blocked.'[5]

All Mugali people follow Tibetan Buddhism. They are closely tied culturally and ethnically to Tibet. 'Most village priests are married agriculturists, not the typical monks you would expect to see. They mainly worship the god named "Chomdendae" which is a four-legged creature holding a flower and a prayer rosary.'[6]

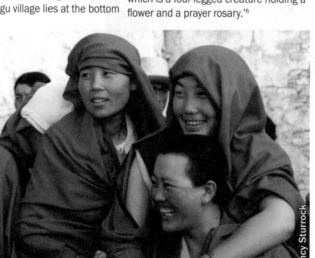

Gospel recordings are available in the Kham dialect of Mugali, but this resource has not been used much. There are no known Mugali Christians. One source laments, 'Only a very small percentage of Mugalis have ever heard the name of Jesus and the vast majority have had no exposure at all to the gospel message. They are very open and friendly to outsiders, but are also highly protective of their cultural and religious identity. . . . It is difficult to determine their receptivity because so little Christian work has been done amongst them.'[7]

Population:
3,700 (2000)
4,610 (2010)
5,700 (2020)
Countries: Nepal
Buddhism: Tibetan
Christians: none known

Overview of the Mugali

Other Names: Mugu, Mug'um, Khan, Mugali Tamang

Population Sources:
3,557 in Nepal (2000, B Grimes [1998 figure])

Language: Sino-Tibetan, Tibeto-Burman, Himalayish, Tibeto-Kanauri, Tibetic, Tibetan, Central

Dialects: 1 (Mugali Kham)

Professing Buddhists: 100%

Practising Buddhists: 75%

Christians: 0%

Scripture: none

Jesus **film:** none

Gospel Recordings: Kham: Mugali

Christian Broadcasting: none

ROPAL code: MUK

Status of Evangelization
92%

8%

0%

A   B   C
A = Have never heard the gospel
B = Have heard the gospel but have not become Christians
C = Are adherents to some form of Christianity

Approximately 1,000 members of the Na ethnic group live in the Gumsing, Taying, Esnaya, Lingbing, Tongla, Yeja, Reding, Redi and Dadu villages of the Taksing Circle in the Upper Subansiri District of Arunachal Pradesh, India. The Na area—which is lined with beautiful pine trees—is situated at an altitude of 2,300 metres (7,500 ft.) above sea level. The Subansiri River, known locally as the Nyrsi, flows through the western part of their habitation. Because of the high altitude, the Na area is cold all year round.

The 1981 Indian census did not list a separate population for the Na, but in 1995 a Na village headman stated that there were 978 people in the community.[1] The earlier 1971 census did have a category for the Na, but they returned a figure of only 238 people.

The Na say that their progenitor was a god named Shiju. 'As stated by the people themselves, there was a placed called Lung in the north, which is at a distance of three to four days by foot from Taksing. The Chadar clan of the community first migrated to Taksing and settled there. They were followed by other people via the Sarli route.'[2]

After arriving in their present location in India the Na were oppressed by the Tibetans, who objected to them leaving Tibet. This may suggest that the Na were formerly serfs of the Tibetans, before they fled to safety. 'It was the Nishings who took the initiative to bring about amity between the Tibetans and the Nas. . . . Consequently the Nas even started barter trade with the Tibetans.'[3]

The Na language falls within the Tani branch of the Tibeto-Burman family. It is related to Tagin, a language spoken by more than 30,000 people in Arunachal Pradesh. The Na speak their language in their own villages, but they use Hindi to communicate with outsiders. Some of the educated Na are able to speak English.

Although all Na people claim that they follow Tibetan Buddhism, their religious practices seem more akin to shamanism and spirit appeasement than to orthodox Buddhism. One source notes, 'They worship various spirits at home. The *nyibu* (shaman) is called for the rituals. One of their prominent deities is called *Yulo*. Earlier lamas were also called to drive away evil spirits by reading the *chhu* (sacred prayers) from the Buddhist scriptures. The Nas visit the monastery at least once a week for prayers. The lamas are now called for religious functions and festivals.'[4]

Almost every part of Na society is strongly influenced by these Buddhist-shamanist beliefs and practices. Even when selecting a partner for marriage, the Na summon a shaman to perform divination to determine whether the match will be blessed by the spirits. 'The final selection of the groom and bride depends on confirmation through the divination of eggs and chicken liver.'[5] The shaman kills a chicken and inspects the lines and patterns on the liver. He is supposed to be able to predict the future by these signs.

There are no known Christians among the Na people. Their remote area has experienced very little gospel witness throughout history. A recent source states that there are 975 Christians out of a total population of 50,086 in the the Upper Subansiri District,[6] but most of these Christians are from the Adi and Tagin people groups.

CHINA
Xizang (Tibet)

Arunachal
Pradesh

INDIA

Na

Population:
1,060 (2000)
1,230 (2010)
1,440 (2020)
Countries: India
Buddhism: Tibetan
Christians: none known

Photo credit: Dwayne Graybill

Overview of the Na

Other Names: Na-Tagin, Nga, Nah

Population Sources:
978 in India (1995, K S Singh)

Language: Sino-Tibetan, Tibeto-Burman, North Assam, Tani

Dialects: 0

Professing Buddhists: 100%

Practising Buddhists: 55%

Christians: 0%

Scripture: none

Jesus **film:** none

Gospel Recordings: none

Christian Broadcasting: none

ROPAL code: none

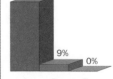

Status of Evangelization

91%

9%

0%

A   B   C

A = Have never heard the gospel
B = Have heard the gospel but have not become Christians
C = Are adherents to some form of Christianity

Newar

Approximately 1.3 million Newar people live in Nepal, India and Bhutan. The 1991 Nepal census listed 1,041,090 Newar people living throughout Nepal, concentrated in the densely populated Kathmandu Valley. The Newari language was spoken by 690,000 people in Nepal in 1991, or 66.3 per cent of their population. An additional 117,000 Newar inhabit 17 states in India,[1] with smaller communities in Bhutan and Bangladesh.[2]

The Newar are believed to be the original inhabitants of Nepal. In fact, the name Nepal is derived from 'Newar'.[3] They founded the city of Kathmandu and have a written history going back 2,500 years, recording their rich and diverse culture.[4] Although numerous warring tribes and rulers have come and gone over the centuries, the Newar continued to establish their kingdom and civilization. Today the term 'Newar' is a broad term covering people with different physical appearances and who speak both the Tibeto-Burman Newar language and Indo-European Nepali.[5] Rather than being a tribe or cohesive ethnic group, the Newar are people belonging to a common civilization and identity.

Xayographix

Although the majority of Newar people are Hindus and only one-third of their population professes Buddhism, the Newar are included in this book because there are more than half a million Buddhist Newaris. Many scholars believe that the Newar were once predominantly Buddhists, but centuries of influence from the south has reversed this situation so that today Hinduism holds sway with the majority. Certain Newar castes are born Buddhist. These include the highest ranking Bajracharya, who are Buddhist priests by profession, Shakya (goldsmiths), Udas (weavers), Tamrakar (copper workers), Jyapu (farmers), Kumal (potters), Chitrakar (artisans), Salmi (oil pressers), Pode (eaters of dead animals) and Chyame (garbage collectors).[6]

The Newar are somewhat unique in that their religious observances are a mixture of Hinduism and Buddhism, so intricately interwoven that it is impossible to separate them. If anything, their faith could almost be called Hinduistic Buddhism. One source states, 'Ask a Newar whether he's Hindu or Buddhist, the saying goes, and he'll answer "yes". After fifteen centuries of continuous exposure to both faiths, the Newars of the Kathmandu Valley have concocted a unique synthesis of the two.'[7] Another says, 'Both parties [Hindus and Buddhists] visit and worship the same deities in Hindu and Buddhist temples. In fact, many of the temples and shrines in Kathmandu Valley have both Hindu and Buddhist deities often adjacent to each other.'[8] Such a blending of faiths 'is best illustrated by the attribution of Buddhist Avalokiteswara and Hindu Matsyendranath to a purely local deity, Bunga-dya'.[9]

There were very few Christians in Nepal until the 1980s. Between then and the present time there has been a tremendous explosion of Christian growth. Thousands of Newar have also believed in Christ for the first time. Still, less than two per cent of Newar today are Christians.

Overview of the Newar

Other Names: Newari, Nepal Bhasa, Newah

Population Sources:
1,041,090 in Nepal (1991 census)
117,000 in India (2004, FMC South Asia)
1,700 in Bangladesh (2004, FMC South Asia)
also in Bhutan

Language: Sino-Tibetan, Tibeto-Burman, Himalayish, Mahakiranti, Newari

Dialects: 7 (Dolkhali, Sindhupalchok Pahri, Totali, Citlang, Kathmandu-Pathan-Kirtipur, Baktapur, Baglung)

Professing Buddhists: 30%

Practising Buddhists: 15%

Christians: 1.5%

Scripture: New Testament 1986

Jesus **film:** available

Gospel Recordings: Newari: Vaglung; Newari: Bhaktapur; Newari: Kathmandu; Newari: Patan; Newari: Pokhara; Newari: Porde

Christian Broadcasting: none

ROPAL code: NEW

Population:
1,382,800 (2000)
1,736,200 (2010)
2,139,500 (2020)

Countries: Nepal, India, Bangladesh, Bhutan

Buddhism: Mahayana

Christians: 20,000

Status of Evangelization

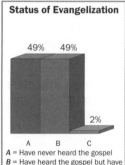

49%   49%

2%

A   B   C
A = Have never heard the gospel
B = Have heard the gospel but have not become Christians
C = Are adherents to some form of Christianity

Nubri

A 1992 source listed 3,200 Nubri people living in the Gandaki Zone of central Nepal.[1] They inhabit villages in the North Gorkha District, near the Nepal border with China, 'along the upper reaches of the Buri Gandaki River, west of and including Prok village, between Himal Chuli and Manaslu Himal on the west, and Ganesh Himal on the east. The local people view Sama as the regional center.'[2] The Nubri villages are situated on mountain slopes up to 4,000 metres (13,120 ft.) above sea level. Some of the more isolated villages take days to reach by foot. The area inhabited by the Nubri is part of the 'roof of the world'. The spectacular Himal Chuli stands at 7,892 metres (25,886 ft.), the Ganesh Himal at 7,406 metres (24,292 ft.), but the mighty Manaslu tops them both at 8,162 metres (26,771 ft.).

Another source says that the Nubri are 'concentrated in and around Larkye, in the valley through which the headwaters of the Bhalu Khola or "bear river" flow. The Bhalu Khola, a tributary of the Budhi Gandaki, is said to be known in the local Tibetan dialect as the Nupri, whence the name of the people.'[3]

Despite the searing peaks of the world's highest mountain range, the Nubri area still receives the monsoon rains from the Indian plains. 'As a consequence the landscape is lush and green, and the fields support

Julian Hawken

good harvests of corn in addition to the staple grains.'[4] Many Nubri men and women are traders who walk vast distances into other areas of Gorkha District as well as across the

border into Tibet. They take grain and merchandise from Nepal and trade it with Tibetans for wool and salt. The Gandaki and Siar valleys serve as two important trade routes into Tibet. The town of Larke (or Larkye) is situated on the Tibetan border.

The Nubri language is part of the Central Tibetan branch of Tibeto-Burman. Despite the small population

of this group, the Nubri speak four dialects. The dialect spoken in Prok is the most different from the others, and Nubri people from outlying areas sometimes have difficulty communicating with the Nubri who live in Prok. Linguistic surveys show that Nubri shares 67 per cent lexical similarity with Dolpo, 65 per cent with Loba, 59 per cent to 64 per cent with the Central Tibetan spoken in Lhasa, 55 per cent with Sherpa, and only 14 per cent to 31 per cent with Kutang Ghale, who share the north Gorkha District with the Nubri.[5]

Tibetan Buddhism is the religion of all Nubri. It shapes the identity of the people, who say, 'To be Nubri is to be Buddhist.' There is an interesting story relating to the Pung-gyen monastery on the east slopes of the Manaslu Himal. In the winter of 1953 the monastery was destroyed and all its inhabitants killed by an avalanche, soon after an unsuccessful attempt to scale the peak by a team of Japanese mountaineers. 'Immediately the local people concluded that the mountain god had become angry at them for allowing foreigners to trespass upon the holy sanctuary and had hurled the avalanche down in his fury. The following year the Japanese returned but were not given passage to the slopes, and it was not until 1956 that they finally succeeded in conquering Manaslu, at the same time contributing a large sum of money toward the building of a new Pung-gyen *gomba*.'[6]

Overview of the Nubri

Other Names: Nubripa, Nubriba, Larke, Kutang Bhotia, Larkye, Nupri, Larkye Bhote, Larkye Tibetans, Nupra, Nupraba

Population Sources:
3,200 in Nepal (2000, B Grimes [1992 figure])

Language: Sino-Tibetan, Tibeto-Burman, Himalayish, Tibeto-Kanauri, Tibetic, Tibetan, Central

Dialects: 4 (Sama, Lho, Namrung, Prok)

Professing Buddhists: 100%

Practising Buddhists: 65%

Christians: 0%

Scripture: none

***Jesus* film:** none

Gospel Recordings: Nubri

Christian Broadcasting: none

ROPAL code: KTE

Status of Evangelization

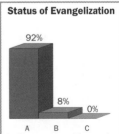

A = Have never heard the gospel
B = Have heard the gospel but have not become Christians
C = Are adherents to some form of Christianity

Population:
3,800 (2000)
4,700 (2010)
5,800 (2020)
Countries: Nepal
Buddhism: Tibetan
Christians: none known

CHINA
Xizang (Tibet)
NEPAL
Gandaki
INDIA
Nubri

Nupbi

Population:
2,000 (2000)
2,550 (2010)
3,250 (2020)
Countries: Bhutan
Buddhism: Tibetan
Christians: none known

Overview of the Nupbi

Other Names: Nupbikha

Population Sources:

2,000 in Bhutan (2000, P Hattaway)

Language: Sino-Tibetan, Tibeto-Burman, Himalayish, Tibeto-Kanauri, Tibetic, Tibetan, Eastern

Dialects: 0

Professing Buddhists: 100%

Practising Buddhists: 65%

Christians: 0%

Scripture: none

***Jesus* film:** none

Gospel Recordings: none

Christian Broadcasting: none

ROPAL code: NUB

Status of Evangelization

85%

15%

0%

A   B   C

A = Have never heard the gospel
B = Have heard the gospel but have not become Christians
C = Are adherents to some form of Christianity

More than 2,000 people belonging to the Nupbi ethnic group live in and around the town of Trongsa in central Bhutan. Trongsa is the capital of the district of the same name. One source describes Trongsa as 'smack in the middle of the country, separated from both the east and the west by high mountain passes. The town has had a large influx of immigrants from Tibet, and Bhutanese of Tibetan descent run most shops here. The Tibetans are so well assimilated into Bhutanese society that there is almost no indication of Tibetan flavor in the town.'[1]

The Nupbi people speak a language that is closely related to Bumthang. The Bumthang live further east than the Nupbi, with the western extent of their territory extending to Trongsa. A linguistic report states, 'The dialect spoken in Trongsa, called Nupbikha, a descriptive term which essentially denotes no more than "language of the west", is linguistically a dialect of Bumthang, although the speakers do not feel themselves to be Bumthangpas.'[2] Nupbi is part of the Eastern Tibetan branch of the Tibeto-Burman family. Their language 'appears to be archaic in that they preserve initial clusters which do not even occur in Classical Tibetan'.[3]

Being Tibetan Buddhists, the Nupbi practise sky burial, in which the dead person's corpse is taken to the top of a hill, brutally cut into pieces with an axe and left for the vultures and other birds of prey to devour. In

2003, two young American travellers stumbled across a Tibetan sky burial ceremony. They reported, 'We have witnessed a lot of wild stuff in the last week. We went to a sky burial, and it was the worst thing we have ever seen. As we came closer to a rock formation we started seeing the worst sight ever. Clothes were scattered all over the hillside then I spotted a human skull, then as we got near the rocks, dozens of skulls, spinal columns, rib cages, skull caps, legs, arms and every other body part. We were in the middle of hundreds of bones, with no one around. We looked at the hillside 100 feet away and saw at least 80 vultures sitting and waiting. They were at least four feet high each one of them. We came back at daybreak. Two monks walked up the hill to the site and later a truck came with four men in it. They dumped a bag and out of it fell a dead naked old woman, shaved head, and frozen stiff. They tied her neck to a one-foot stake and cut into her back. The monks chanted mantras, and the other men screamed a horrible scream that I will never forget. The hillside of vultures began to stir as the men cut a piece from the woman's back, threw it in the air and screamed like a vulture's scream. Then in a fury like demons, 50 vultures swooped down from the hills screaming and yelling like Satan himself. They tore into the body and within seconds bowels, body parts, and blood were everywhere. It was horrible. The men smashed the spinal column with a hatchet and the brains were offered to the vultures like an offering. . . . '[4]

There has never been a Christian community among the Nupbi people. For centuries their ancestors have lived and died without the slightest knowledge of the gospel, their bodies devoured by birds of prey.

Insights for Missions to Theravada Buddhists

Alex G Smith

Reaching Theravada Buddhists is a tough task. They do not have common points of contact from biblical revelation like Muslims or Jews, nor do redemptive analogies, such as those found in the traditions of many animistic tribal peoples, abound. Theravada Buddhism proposes a highly integrated philosophical system that is primarily atheistic and totally dependent on self-effort.

The Buddhist world

Although the vast Buddhist world is concentrated in East Asia, it encircles the globe, primarily through the diaspora of Chinese and Southeast Asian peoples, as well as the overseas Japanese. At the beginning of the 21st century, the number of Buddhists worldwide exceeded 700 million. Many more Chinese could be added to this total, since over 50 years of iron-fisted Chinese Communist control has not wiped out two millennia of Buddhist philosophy and thinking.

Buddhism has many faces among the various groups who have adopted it. It has often spread among peoples whose prevailing religion was animism.[1] Although the religious structure of Buddhism was able to achieve dominance over traditional belief systems among these peoples, it did not dislodge these beliefs entirely. Today, hundreds of unreached people groups are identified with Buddhism. There are two broad schools of Buddhism. Mahayana, the 'large vehicle', accounts for about 90 per cent of Buddhists, primarily Chinese, Japanese and Korean. About 16 million of this school adhere to a Tibetan (or Tantric) form of Buddhism in Tibet, Nepal, Mongolia, Bhutan and the nations that formerly comprised the Soviet Union. Theravada, the 'small vehicle', is the second school, with about 140 million adherents, primarily in Myanmar (formerly Burma), Thailand, Sri Lanka (formerly Ceylon), Cambodia and Laos. Buddhism also gained some popularity in the West in the 1960s and 1970s, mostly through American soldiers taking home Asian war brides as well as through the influx of Southeast Asian refugees.

The historical spread of Buddhism

The seeds of Theravada Buddhism were sown five

Burmese monks outside their temple in Myanmar. The 35-million Burmese are the largest Theravada Buddhist people group in the world.

Create International

hundred years before Christ through the teachings of Gautama Siddharta, who claimed to be enlightened as the Buddha. For the first three centuries, little Buddhist expansion occurred. It was confined largely to northern India and Nepal. Then, under King Asoka of Magadha in India, Buddhism began to expand rapidly. Through his patronage, Asoka built 84,000 stupas (monuments commemorating Buddha), pronounced edicts exhorting the people to follow Buddhist precepts and sent missionaries far and wide across his vast kingdom. These missionaries helped consolidate his conquests through teaching a peaceable religious doctrine.

Missionary monks also travelled the Silk Road into China and followed the trade routes to other lands as they spread the teaching of the Buddha. Then, under the Muslim conquests of the 12th century, Buddhism began to decline. Expansion seemed to have run its course.

Judeo-Christian encounter

During the intertestamental period four hundred years before Christ, a missionary movement of the Diaspora Pharisees reached as far as China.[2]

During this time, Pharisees must have had contact with Buddhists travelling the same roads.

Certainly the Nestorian Christians from the late 5th century AD had considerable interaction with Buddhists in China, primarily of the Mahayana school, but the Nestorian church did not survive because of syncretism and severe persecution. In spite of centuries of significant Christian missions, both Catholic and Protestant, to the Buddhist world, little church planting and growth has resulted, with the possible exception of South Korea, where about one-third of the population are now part of the church. Koreans had the advantage of having an indigenous concept of God, 'Hananim', which provided a vital point of contact for the gospel.

Today, Christians who live among Buddhist peoples generally make up less than one per cent of the population. Any significant growth that has occurred has usually been among tribal animist peoples.

Shortcomings

The failure of missions to make a significant impact, especially on Theravada Buddhists, is due to both Buddhist barriers and missiological weaknesses. We need to consider three major Buddhist barriers in particular:

A young girl from the Palaung Shwe tribe relaxes after helping in the field in Shan State, Myanmar.

Myanmar Faces and Places

Two mischievous Shan boys at play in Shan State, Myanmar.

1. *Its eclectic nature:* Buddhism has adeptly adjusted to the religio-cultural milieu of the peoples adopting it. In order to survive, Buddhism selected and incorporated essential cultural elements into its system, just as Hinduism did when it reclaimed Buddhist India back into the Hindu fold. Like Hinduism, Buddhism comes in many shapes and forms: in China, it is mixed with Taoism and Confucianism; in Japan, with Shintoism, Confucianism and ancestral worship; in Korea, with shamanism and Confucianism.

   Theravada Buddhism incorporated animistic spirits of the folk religion of the people into its worship, such as the 'Bon' in Sri Lanka, the 'Nats' in Myanmar, and the 'Phii' in Thailand and Laos. Lacking rituals and life cycles of their own, Buddhists also integrated Brahman (Hindu) rituals into their syncretistic mix. Buddhists would go even further to accept elements of Christianity as well, but there would be no room for a unique Christ. They even adapt Christian institutions. In 1880, the Young Men's Buddhist Society was formed in Sri Lanka.

   In Thailand and Laos, school children parade weekly in the uniforms of Boy Scouts and Girl Guides under Buddhist guise.

2. *Buddhist solidarity:* Buddhist philosophy is all pervasive, permeating the concepts and world-views of a people and saturating their culture, language, education and attitudes with Buddhistic viewpoints. In fact, the social solidarity of Buddhism is so strong that the national identity of the people comes from Buddhism. To be Thai or Burmese means to be Buddhist

3. *Theological barriers:* Paul A Eakin summarized many historical and doctrinal similarities between Buddhism and Christianity.[3] But there are significant differences in theological content, meaning and concepts, especially with regard to the doctrines of God, humankind, sin, salvation and the future. As D T Niles points out, the final category in Buddhism is death; in Christianity, it is life.[4]

   A leading Buddhist scholar, Bhikkhu Buddhadasa Indapanno, in comparing Christianity and Buddhism equated God with karma, rejecting God's personality in favour of impersonal 'nature' as the cause in life. He also identifies God the Creator with Buddhism's *avijja*, meaning 'lack of knowledge' or 'ignorance', a term which Buddhists identify as the cause of all evil and suffering.[5]

These theological barriers are so diametrically opposed to biblical truth that great discernment is necessary, even though superficial similarities appear to exist.

The first of these three major Buddhist barriers, its eclecticism, puts pressure on the church to remain faithful in a syncretistic society. The second, Buddhist solidarity, threatens the identity and survival of the church in Buddhist-dominated nations and means that those who dare to stand out as Christians will suffer isolation. The Japanese have a saying: 'The nail that sticks up will be pounded down.' The theological barriers put Christians in a constant defensive mode under subtle, persistent pressure to compromise their beliefs and reintegrate with society.

Missiological weakness

1. *Mission strategy:* The 'mission station approach' was common throughout the colonial period. In its time, it may have been the only viable way to help Christians survive and to get the church started. But the 'gathered, conglomerate' often separates converts from their people and society and seldom has had a major impact on the core of

Buddhist people groups. Christian missions and their churches were seen as outside intrusions and foreign imports to be avoided like the plague. Frequently, converts were considered traitors.

Another weakness common to mission strategy in the late 19th and early 20th century was in the area of the philosophy of

Buddhist monks take a trishaw in Phnom Penh, Cambodia.

ministry. To 'civilize' and to 'Christianize' were thought to be synonymous, so mission was deeply involved in both. In the process, a major tension arose between evangelism and education. Which should come first? Which should have priority? My book *Siamese Gold* contains a case study examining what happened in Northern Thailand between 1914 and 1940.[6]

A change of priority in policy and strategy emphasized schools, education and other institutions to the detriment of a growing movement of the churches among the

Buddhist population. This movement was arrested, or rather, a ripe harvest of christian converts was largely neglected and withered due to lack of pastoral care. The new policy, to educate Buddhists first so that they could be better evangelized later, curtailed reaping the already receptive harvest in progress. As funds, personnel and even national evangelists and pastors were transferred into the educational and institutional work, the churches struggled on, but the harvest of over 16,000 newly baptized people was lost. While the church could have tripled its 1914 membership in the North by 1940, its growth rate dropped and plateaued.

2. *Ineffective communication:* Too often evangelism revolves around the problem of definitions, especially in cultures saturated with Buddhism. One who proclaims the gospel cannot transfer meaning across cultures, and Buddhists who hear the message will only decipher bits of information. Often the Buddhist's assessment of Christianity and Buddhism is, 'They are just the same.' This response indicates that inadequate communication has taken place. One should not destroy faith as a quality. But in the process of transferring faith from non-gods to the true and living God, we need to give priority to communicating biblical concepts accurately. Premature decisions based on an incomplete understanding of Christian truth may inoculate Buddhists against the gospel.

3. *Lack of indigeneity:* Buddhist societies often view the church as an alien form and a foreign institution of the West. Frequently, the church looks more like an imported monstrosity. Its buildings, forms, music and methods are often so different from those of the Buddhist society around it. While of necessity there will be differences, too often the church sticks out like a sore thumb or 'a nail that must be pounded down.'

Strengths of Buddhist missions

Overall, the evangelization of Buddhists has been like squeezing a rubber ball—once the hand's pressure on the ball is released, the ball immediately springs back into its original form unchanged!

But four significant positive results arose from

A monk mows the temple lawn at Mae Hong Son, Thailand.

the valiant efforts and years of sacrifice of godly missionaries and national believers who have tried to penetrate Buddhist society, albeit with little success.

1. Gospel *seeds planted:* Much pioneering, sweat and tears in witness and seed sowing among Buddhists over the years laid the foundations for an expected harvest. 'We will reap . . . if we do not give up.[7]

2. *The church survived:* During the last century and a half, small churches have been planted and, against all odds, they have survived. Signs today indicate that they are beginning to stir and grow afresh. Some small people movements to Christ have occurred. For instance, Dr Daniel McGilvary a Presbyterian missionary to the Lao in Northern Thailand, saw an increase from 150 to 7,000 baptized in the 30 years between 1884 and 1914. Today, churches in Northern Thailand still form the strength and backbone of Christianity in that Buddhist land.

3. *Christian leaders trained:* With pressure on the church to survive, missions took seriously their role to develop leaders locally, through theological training and lay programmes. Today's church leadership in Thailand and Sri Lanka is no longer the uneducated farmers of yesterday. Many respected national leaders with degrees, training and experience are leading the churches forward in Buddhist countries. This provides hope for the future.

4. *Goodwill established:* One benefit of Christian hospitals and educational institutions, with their high standards, has been the generation of a large amount of goodwill. The nationalization of many of these institutions under Buddhist governments, however, has reduced their evangelistic potential. While these Christian institutions have not produced a major breakthrough in church growth, they have helped to break down some prejudice against Christianity. Some holistic, integrated farming experiments, such as those conducted by Jim Gustafson among Northeast Thai Buddhists, appear to encourage church growth. Where missionaries have helped Buddhists economically, the result has been greater receptivity to the gospel. In fact, where in

Statues of Buddha preside over a beautiful park in Vientiane, Laos.

Xayographix

the past a patron role has been utilized, small and lasting church movements have been established.

One of the difficulties is extracting oneself from that patron role without being seen as insincere in terms of the people's expectations. When missionaries step back from running everything and hand the church over to local control, some people perceive this as a rejection. It is also important to avoid creating a sense of dependence on the patron in the process of development.

These four strengths can be built upon and they can be integrated into a wider strategy for reaching Theravada Buddhists.

A young novice monk with a bowl full of cash donated to the temple.

Create International

Keys for strategy

The following twelve suggestions come from years of observation and experience in working with Buddhists. Each suggestion is like a pearl which has grown around some irritation and pain. Strung together, these pearls may prove to be helpful for strategizing ministries among Buddhist peoples. Each key is important.

1. *The indispensable—spiritual warfare:* Jesus said, 'I will build my church.[8] Essentially, mission is the activity of God, the Holy Spirit. Since Christ has chosen to use human vessels to accomplish evangelization, we must take part in spiritual warfare while depending totally on him.[9] Prayer is therefore a crucial ingredient as we pull down spiritual strongholds.[10]

    There is no point attacking Buddhism or using apologetic arguments. Buddhists are more likely to come to Christ as a result of seeing demonstrations of God's power (the miraculous). The folk Buddhists' capacity for the gospel should be studied, especially their fear of demons and ancestral spirits. Spiritual warfare and confrontation need to be made at these animistic cracks in the Buddhist walls.

2. *Efficient concentration—focus on one people group at a time:* Too often, people working among Buddhist groups have treated different groups as if all different groups were the same. When Christians identify a particular people group and try to understand that group, they are better able to establishes a basis for acceptance, communication and repeated contact. Time spent doing this also allows opportunity for diffusion of the message throughout the group.

3. *Connecting point—felt needs:* More study needs to be devoted to identifying points of contact related to the felt needs of the particular people. Some of the felt needs among Theravada Buddhists in Asia are sickness (often related to the demonic world), bondage and fear of demons, concerns about black magic and witchcraft, uncertainty

with regard to the future and karmic fatalism. Therefore, it is possible to approach Buddhists by applying the gospel in the areas of spiritual and physical healing, freedom from demonic oppression, protection from sorcery, and hope and certainty for the future.

4. *The specific goal—church planting movements:* Planting an individual church among the people is insufficient. The great missions statesman Dr Donald McGavran often talked about developing 'clusters of churches'. A church movement that proliferates churches must be the aim. Each will be a functioning church in true worship of God, in welcoming others into the fellowship and in reaching out in witness and service to the surrounding community. Evangelism is necessary, but its goal must be responsible participation in local churches.

5. *Effectual communication—receptor feedback:* While the communicator must clearly understand the biblical message, it is essential that he or she also listen to the receptor for feedback in order to know what is actually being understood. This cyclical feedback process will help clarify the conceptualization of the gospel and enable evangelists to see what the actual response over time is. Reaching people at their level of understanding and listening to how God is working in their lives, step by step, always makes for good evangelism—no matter how long it takes.

Effective communication also needs to be couched in indigenous forms, symbol, analogy, stories and word pictures relevant to the target audience.

Forms of communication with a local flavour[11] such as ethnic song and music, indigenous dance-drama and other arts should be investigated and adapted for witness and teaching.

6. *The crucial process—parallel witness and nurture:* Too often, delaying evangelism in order to consolidate through Christian education interrupts the flow of continuing

outreach, making it difficult to stimulate strong outreach again. Like the two rails of a train track, both evangelism and discipling should be kept running simultaneously. Also, it is very important to keep converts among their own people and culture so that they model their new faith among their relatives and friends and thus maintain contact with them—these relationships are important for spreading the gospel message.

7. *The logistical dynamic—family-oriented approach:* Focusing on the whole family or group is a wise and biblical approach. Using the natural bridges of relationships, we should permeate the whole extended family or group with the gospel. The primary relationships among Asian Buddhist peoples are those of nuclear or extended families or even village web relationships.

8. *The holistic strategy—comprehensive planning:* Practical steps and processes should be laid out from start to finish, with a view to reaching the set goal. Detailed strategies and plans with a clear means of evaluation through each phase of the church planting movement should be drawn up. These plans should cover everything from initial reconnaissance to extension of the church and mission.

9. *The essential division of labour—two groups of leaders:* Leaders working in the church in discipleship are the pastors and shepherds. Another set of leaders, reaching out to the unchurched community, may be classified as 'fishermen'. The church needs both types of leaders. The shepherds help the church grow where it is. The fishermen help the church go where it isn't.

We earnestly need to pray for and develop shepherds with the passion of fishermen, and fishermen with the hearts of shepherds.

10. *The continuing momentum—lay movements:* Each Christian is a most valuable agent of the gospel for church planting and extension. Christians are in daily contact with the society in which they work and live. Church leaders must stimulate lay movements

Xayographix

Thousands of Theravada Buddhists worship at Tad Luang in Vientiane, Laos.

and encourage lay teams to serve—both in evangelizing the community and in nurturing new believers.

Lay people provide a rich pool of gifts, abilities, resources, personnel and energy necessary for keeping the momentum of the Christ-ward movement going. Home discipleship groups, evangelistic Bible studies, community friendship groups and voluntary association projects are essential for ongoing evangelization and church planting.

11. *The vital flexibility—missionary roles:* During the process of evangelization, the missionary as well as the national church planter need to adjust their roles according to the stage of church development. Their functions at the pioneer stage would be quite different from those at the partnership stage. Those working with several churches at various stages of development may need to fulfil a different role in each situation.

Workers also need to fill basic roles such as learner, model and servant leader. Those filling pioneer and paternal roles should move on to the next stage as soon as it is practical to do so. Although it is difficult to change roles from time to time, this flexibility is vital for the growth and advancement of the churches.

12. *The final product—indigenous churches and missions:* Evaluating the whole process helps to determine how truly indigenous the church is. It is especially important to assess its identity with the people group and its level of the full expression of Christ and the gospel to its own society. Are adequate 'functional substitutes' being employed for those crucial areas of culture that would leave voids apart from relevant application from the Bible?

Does the church movement have indigenous missions reaching out to other people groups?

The following three R's are the bottom line for evaluation: Does it have the *respect* of the Buddhist community? Is it taking *responsibility* under the Lord for ministry to the society of which it is a part? Is it exhibiting *resourcefulness* in evangelizing its Buddhist neighbours and in coping with opposition from without?

Stimulating strong church movements among all the unreached Buddhist peoples demands much wisdom, training, sensitivity and perseverance. Reaching classical Buddhists may be a tough task, but it is by no means an impossible one.

Notes

This article, which was originally published in the *International Journal of Frontier Missions* 10.3 (July 1993), has been revised and updated for this edition.

1. Kenneth Scott Latourette, *Introducing Buddhism* (New York: Friendship Press, 1958) 43.

2. Richard R DeRidder, *The Dispersion of the People of God* (Kampen: Kok, 1971).

3. Paul A Eakin, *Buddhism and the Christian: An Approach to Buddhists in Thailand* (Bangkok: R Hongladaromp, 1956) 27f.

4. D T Niles, *Buddhism and the Claims of Christ* (Richmond, Virginia: John Knox Press, 1967) 34–35.

5. Bhikkhu Buddhadasa Indapanno, *Christianity and Buddhism* (Bangkok: Sinclaire Thompson Memorial Lectures, Fifth Series, 1967) 66–67.

6. Alex G Smith, *Siamese Gold: The Church in Thailand* (Bangkok: Kanok Bannasan, 1982) 145f.

7. Gal 6:9.

8. Matt 16:18.

9. John 15:5.

10. 2 Cor 10:3–5.

11. Alex G Smith, *The Gospel Facing Buddhist Cultures* (Taichung, Taiwan: Asia Theological Association, 1980) 10–11

Myanmar Faces and Places

A lady from the Pa-O tribe takes a shower.
Will she ever know the inward cleansing that Christ offers?

The 3,200 Nyahkur people comprise one of Thailand's least known tribes. They inhabit valleys surrounded by lush hills in the three central Thailand provinces of Chaiyaphum, Nakhon Ratchasima and Phetchabun. The majority of Nyahkur are in Chaiyaphum. Most live in mixed villages with Isan and Thai people.

The self-name of this tribe is *Nyahkur*, which means 'people of the forest'. The Thais call them *Chaobon*, meaning 'people of the hills'. The Nyahkur consider this latter term derogatory.

Despite their small numbers, the Nyahkur are considered a historically important group. Many linguists believe that their language is a link between Mon and Khmer. One scholar says, 'Their language contains so many Khmer and Mon words that some linguists consider the language as a bridge . . . even more closely related to ancient Mon than to the modern Mon dialect.'[1]

The Nyahkur people have been described as 'addicted to borrowing'.[2] This has caused them to be trapped in poverty and a never-ending cycle of financial woe. As early as 1919, an anthropologist called the Nyahkur a 'disappearing society' due to rampant disease, alcohol addiction and other destructive vices.[3]

When the Nyahkur get married, a bride price must be paid. These days the average price is 30,000 *baht* (about US$700). The value of a bride is measured 'by her ability as a worker, upon her beauty, especially her fair skin, and finally on the wealth of her parents'.[4] The record price paid for a pretty Nyahkur girl is 60,000 *baht*.

In the past the Nyahkur were animists enslaved to powerful demons. In recent decades, due to the influence of their Thai and Isan neighbours, they have embraced Buddhism. Practically all Nyahkur now claim to be Buddhists. In reality, however, they have retained most of their former animistic practices and placed a veneer of Buddhism over them. The Nyahkur 'still believe in many superstitions that affect every area of their lives. [They believe in] various spirits that inhabit the surroundings: village guardian spirits, mountain spirits, and soil spirits. . . . The spirits are called *nthock*. Evil spirits are blamed for almost everything that goes wrong. The Nyahkur wear charms and amulets, such as Buddhist images, necklaces of beads and old silver coins which are believed to protect against injuries, illness, and other sorts of evils. It is said that only the wearing of a necklace made of flat pieces of copper . . . has the power to protect against *nthock lakthep*, the most powerful of all the evil spirits.'[5]

Despite more than 20 years of missionary effort, there are no known Nyahkur Christians today. A team of missionaries first moved into the village of Ban Wang Ai Pho in 1982, and they have worked there since. One source says, 'They were not successful in baptizing the Chaobon [Nyahkur] people, because of the superstitious and animistic nature of their beliefs. But they were very successful in studying and preserving Chaobon culture and they gave a helping hand in social, health, administrative and human matters.'[6]

Population:
3,140 (2000)
3,430 (2010)
3,750 (2020)
Countries: Thailand
Buddhism: Theravada
Christians: none known

Overview of the Nyahkur

Other Names: Nyakur, Niakuol, Niakuoll, Nhyakhur, Chaubun, Chaobun, Chaobon

Population Sources: 3,000 in Thailand (2000, J Schliesinger [1995 figure])

Language: Austro-Asiatic, Mon-Khmer, Monic

Dialects: 0

Professing Buddhists: 95%

Practising Buddhists: 75%

Christians: 0%

Scripture: none

Jesus film: none

Gospel Recordings: none

Christian Broadcasting: none

ROPAL code: CBN

Status of Evangelization

91%
9%
0%

A   B   C

A = Have never heard the gospel
B = Have heard the gospel but have not become Christians
C = Are adherents to some form of Christianity

Nyaw

Approximately 120,000 people belonging to the Nyaw ethnic group live in north-east Thailand and central Laos. More than 80,000 Nyaw are found in the Thai provinces of Sakhon Nakhon,[1] Nakhon Phanom,[2] Mukdahan[3] and Nong Khai.[4] All of these locations are near the Thai-Lao border, which is marked by the great Mekong River. In Thailand the Nyaw share their communities with Isan, So and Thavung people. They all seem to get along well, even though the So and Thavung speak completely unrelated Mon-Khmer languages.

One source states that about 30,000 Nyaw also live in Laos.[5] They inhabit the Pakkading, Pakxan and Borikhan districts of Borikhamxai Province, and the Hinboun District of Khammouan Province.[6]

The common belief among the Nyaw people in Thailand is that their ancestors migrated from a place along the Laos-Vietnam border area. Others claim that the Nyaw came from the Xishuangbanna (Sipsong-panna) area of south-west China, although no people groups in China today identify themselves by this name.

Although the historical origins of the Nyaw are shrouded in mystery, linguistic studies reveal that the Nyaw language is closely related to Isan and the variety of Lao spoken in Luang Prabang, the largest city in Laos.[7] One researcher has given a more detailed analysis: 'Although the Nyaw have specific characteristics of Northern Tai in their language, they speak quite varying dialects in their different locations.'[8] Nyaw people living in 26 different villages in northern Thailand were studied. 'From the

phonetic point of view, the Nyaw tones in these villages differ so distinctively from each other that they produce 26 accents. These accents could be divided into three major dialects based on tonal systems, namely four-tone, five-tone and six-tone systems.'[9]

A Nyaw marriage is customarily arranged by a go-between who negotiates with the families of the bride and groom over the size of the bride price. These days the price may be as high as 60,000 *baht* (about $1,500). One source states that a large number of young Nyaw women have become prostitutes in Bangkok and Pattaya.[10] After the death of parents, the family house is left to the child (usually the youngest daughter) who had taken care of the parents in their old age.

Almost all Nyaw in Thailand consider themselves Thera-vada Buddhists, while in Communist Laos the strength of their adherence to Buddhism is not so strong. They believe in a variety of spirits and supernatural beings. The most feared is *pu jao*, the spirit of the village. Once a year, the Nyaw sacrifice pigs and chickens to this protector spirit.

There are a few scattered Nyaw Christians in both Thailand and Laos, although in both countries they live in areas with few known churches. Most Nyaw people have no access to the gospel, even though those in Thailand live in a country with freedom of religion.

No Bible or audio recordings exist in the Nyaw language, but work is underway in Thailand to produce the first Nyaw Scriptures.[11]

Paul Hattaway

Population:
118,560 (2000)
136,000 (2010)
156,700 (2020)
Countries: Thailand, Laos
Buddhism: Theravada
Christians: 100

Overview of the Nyaw

Other Names: Tai Yor, Yor, Nyo, Tai Nyo, Ngeou, Jo, Yo, Au, Ou, Ngo, Tai No

Population Sources: 80,000 in Thailand (2001, J Schliesinger [1999 figure])[12]
30,000 in Laos (2001, J Schliesinger [1990 figure])[13]

Language: Tai-Kadai, Kam-Tai, Be-Tai, Tai-Sek, Tai, Southwestern, East Central, Lao-Phutai

Dialects: 3

Professing Buddhists: 95%

Practising Buddhists: 40%

Christians: 0.1%

Scripture: none; work in progress

Jesus **film:** none

Gospel Recordings: none

Christian Broadcasting: none

ROPAL code: NYW

Status of Evangelization

77%
22%
1%

A   B   C
A = Have never heard the gospel
B = Have heard the gospel but have not become Christians
C = Are adherents to some form of Christianity

According to one researcher, 10,000 Nyenpa people live in central Bhutan. They inhabit the western half of the Trongsa District, as well as areas of south-east Wangdue Phodrang District. Linguist George van Driem has given a detailed description of where the Nyenpa language, called Nyenkha, is spoken: 'Nyenkha is spoken primarily on the eastern slopes of the Black Mountains overlooking the Mangdechu River. . . . On the west bank of the Mangdechu, the language is spoken as far north as the village of Simphu and as far south as the village of Kala across the river from Zhamgang. Nyenkha is also spoken in several villages to the east of the Mangdechu between Trongsa and Zhamgang, including Taktse, Usa and Trashidingkha. Nyenkha is also spoken on the western slopes of the Black Mountains in the villages of Phobjikha, Rid'ang and D'angchu and in surrounding hamlets of Wangdue Phodrang District.'[1]

The ethnic name of this group, Nyenpa, or 'people of Nyen', is probably derived from the term *Ngenlung*, or 'ancient region'. This is the name the Tibetan sage Kunkhen Longchen Ramjam used to refer to west-central Bhutan in the 14th century. The name of their language, *Nyenkha*, literally means 'ancient language'.

Tibetan Buddhism has had a spiritual stronghold on the area for more than 1,000 years. Bhutan is officially a Buddhist monarchy. The state supports about 5,000 monks in various institutions known as the *sangha*. The current chief abbot of Bhutan and the head of the monastic establishment is known as the Je Khenpo.

He is the 70th elected chief abbot since the office was created in 1637. The Je Khenpo is considered the spiritual leader of Bhutan and is the only person other than the king who is allowed to wear the saffron scarf which symbolizes supreme religious authority.

In the West, Buddhism has been portrayed as a religion of peace and tolerance, but Christians in Bhutan have had very different experiences. Many have been imprisoned, beaten, fined and persecuted for their faith in Christ. In October and November 2002, reports came out of Bhutan of mass persecution of Christians. On 24 September 2002, 40 Christians in Bhutan were arrested and tortured for their faith. When church leaders challenged the government about this action, they were told, 'We will persecute the Christians and put an end to them in Bhutan.'[2]

Another report stated, 'The Bhutanese government has begun a religious-cleansing operation and in the process, they identified 500 Christian families and deported them. The methodology of identification of the Christians was novel. The government authorities went to the 300 public schools and offered chocolates to the unsuspecting and innocent school children. They asked the Christian students to raise their hands. The innocent juveniles raised their hands. Then the authorities obtained the names and addresses of the children. With the addresses collected, the authorities raided the Christian homes and forced them to flee the country. The terrified Bhutanese Christians ran for their lives and took refuge in India and Nepal.'[3]

Population:
12,550 (2000)
16,100 (2010)
20,600 (2020)
Countries: Bhutan
Buddhism: Tibetan
Christians: none known

Overview of the Nyenpa

Other Names: Nyenkha, Ngenkha, Henkha, Lap, Mangsdekha, Mangdekha, Chutobikha, Mangdebikha

Population Sources:

10,000 in Bhutan (2001, G van Driem [1991 figure])

Language: Sino-Tibetan, Tibeto-Burman, Himalayish, Tibeto-Kanauri, Tibetic, Tibetan, Eastern

Dialects: 2 (Phobjikha, Chutobikha)

Professing Buddhists: 100%

Practising Buddhists: 70%

Christians: 0%

Scripture: none

Jesus **film:** none

Gospel Recordings: none

Christian Broadcasting: none

ROPAL code: NEH

Dwayne Graybill

Status of Evangelization

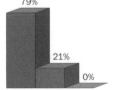

79%

21%

0%

A   B   C

A = Have never heard the gospel
B = Have heard the gospel but have not become Christians
C = Are adherents to some form of Christianity

Ole

CHINA
Xizang (Tibet)

BHUTAN
Wangdue
Phodrang

INDIA

Ole

Population:
630 (2000)
800 (2010)
1,000 (2020)
Countries: Bhutan
Buddhism: Tibetan
Christians: none known

Overview of the Ole

Other Names: Olekha, Ole Monpa, Monkha, Black Mountain

Population Sources:

500 in Bhutan (2001, G van Driem [1991 figure])

Language: Sino-Tibetan, Tibeto-Burman, Himalayish, Tibeto-Kanauri, Tibetic, Tibetan, Eastern

Dialects: 3 (Ole, Southern, Northern)

Professing Buddhists: 100%

Practising Buddhists: 55%

Christians: 0%

Scripture: none

***Jesus* film:** none

Gospel Recordings: none

Christian Broadcasting: none

ROPAL code: OLE

Status of Evangelization

98%

2%   0%

A   B   C

A = Have never heard the gospel
B = Have heard the gospel but have not become Christians
C = Are adherents to some form of Christianity

A remote area of central Bhutan is home to a small ethnic group called Ole. They inhabit the south-eastern part of Bhutan's Wangdue Phodrang District, within the aptly named Black Mountains. The Ole inhabit seven villages in all, comprising 86 households with an estimated population of about 500 individuals.[1] The Black Mountains are a 'southern spur of the Himalayas, which runs from north to south over a distance of some 200 km [123 miles], separating western from central Bhutan. The range was so called by the British because of its dense forest cover and its formidable and precipitous, dark escarpments.'[2] The highest peak in the area, Mount Jod'ushingphu, is a sacred mountain to the Ole. The Black Mountains are home to many rare animal and bird species, including the serow, the great-pied hornbill and the rare golden langur.

The ethnic name of this group differs depending on the location and name of their local clan. Linguist George van Driem was the first scholar to study this small group. He decided to simply call their language 'Black Mountain' after the region they inhabit. Van Driem explains, 'Their language is known as *Monkha* . . . although those living in Rukha village are wont to call their language *Olekha* "the Ole language" after the local clan name. Strictly speaking, it is correct only to refer to the Black Mountain dialect spoken in Rukha and Riti as *Olekha*. . . . I use the term Black Mountain Monpa or just Black Mountain to distinguish this group from

Dwayne Graybill

the other ethnolinguistic groups in the eastern Himalayan region which designate themselves as "Monpa".'[3]

It seems that the Ole's homeland once lay further south than its present position. They may have been pushed northward by the sudden influx of Nepali people into southern Bhutan. The Ole language has baffled and thrilled linguists, who see it as an extremely rare archaic language that has managed to survive to the present day. One scholar notes, 'The Ole represented the old vanguard of the ancient East Bodish population, separated from the remaining East Bodish groups at an early period, and lived beyond the range of Tibetan cultural influence. In contrast to other East Bodish language communities, the original Ole style of housing is not Bhutanese, nor were their native religious practices Buddhist.'[4]

Since the time they migrated into the Buddhist regions of central Bhutan, the Ole have gradually adopted a veneer of Buddhism. Today they all profess to be Buddhists, but in reality they have merely added this religion to their centuries-old shamanistic rituals and beliefs. It is not Buddhist monks who preside over Ole religious ceremonies, but rather Bon male and female shamans. They have 'also retained and incorporated native animist religious practices. The Ole of Rukha still avoid eating goat's meat or mutton, thus observing the very same dietetic taboo as many Rai peoples of eastern Nepal.'[5]

Christianity has yet to make any impact upon this small and fascinating people group.

MYANMAR
Shan State

Mae
Hong Son

Kayah
State

THAILAND

Padaung

Population:
50,000 (2000)
56,200 (2010)
63,100 (2020)
Countries: Myanmar,
Thailand
Buddhism: Theravada
Christians: 8,000

Overview of the Padaung

Other Names: Karen: Padaung,
Kayang, Long-Neck Karen,
Padong, Kayan, Ka-kaung,
Lae Kur

Population Sources: 40,900
in Myanmar (2000, B Grimes
[1983 figure])

500 in Thailand (2000, J
Schliesinger [1995 figure])

Language: Sino-Tibetan, Tibeto-
Burman, Karen, Sgaw-Bghai,
Bghai, Eastern

Dialects: 0

Professing Buddhists: 50%

Practising Buddhists: 25%

Christians: 15%

Scripture: none

***Jesus* film:** none

Gospel Recordings: Padaung,
Karen: Padaung

Christian Broadcasting: none

ROPAL code: PDU

Status of Evangelization

70%

15%   15%

A   B   C

A = Have never heard the gospel
B = Have heard the gospel but have
not become Christians
C = Are adherents to some form of
Christianity

Around 50,000 Padaung people live in the thick forests west of the Salween River and around the Pekon Hills, in Kayah State and southern Shan State of eastern Myanmar. Their traditional homeland is north-west of Loikaw town. Today they are concentrated in seven villages centred around their biggest village, Bangpe. Five hundred Padaung also live in Thailand, inhabiting three villages within Muang District of Mae Hong Son Province, very near the border with Myanmar.[1] The Padaung first arrived in Thailand in 1988 when they fled fighting between Burmese troops and ethnic minorities in Kayah State.

In their own language the Padaung call themselves *Ka-kaung*, which means 'people who live on the hilltops'. The Padaung language is closely related to that of the Lahta tribe in Myanmar. It is part of the Karen branch of the Tibeto-Burman family.

For centuries the Padaung women have been a source of curiosity because of their custom of wearing up to 32 gold-coloured brass neck coils. Once they were even brought to the court in Mandalay for official inspection. In the past girls adopted their neck rings on their fifth birthday and added one more coil each year until they were married. These days the custom is fading in Myanmar. Women in only three villages reportedly still practise it.

In Thailand, however, many Padaung women have continued the practice out of economic necessity. After their tribe moved into the country from Myanmar they settled along the border, but they were prohibited from cultivating the land because they were not Thai citizens. Tourist agencies saw an opportunity to make money from the

strange-looking Padaung women. Hordes of camera-clicking tourists have flocked on pre-arranged visits to photograph the 'long neck' women, as they have come to be known.[2]

There are several theories surrounding the origins of the custom. Some say it was to protect the women from tiger attacks in the jungle, as tigers usually attack humans by biting their throats. Others claim that the Padaung are descended from swans, so they elongate their necks in a bid to look

like their ancestors. 'Another tale records that the Padaung tribe was originally called Lae Khoe, and ruled over the Burmese people. Later, the Burmese and ethnic groups . . . joined forces to fight against the Lae Khoe and drove them off their land. During the war a young Lae Khoe princess escaped. She wrapped the tribe's sacred gold-coloured Padaung plant around her neck and declared that if the Lae Khoe failed to regain their land, she would never take it off. Since then, the Lha Khoe have been known as the Padaung.'[3]

The Padaung's religious beliefs are a curious mix. One source says, 'The majority of the Padaung are Buddhists, but their religion is tempered with animist beliefs and practices. Due to the existence of a Roman Catholic mission for about 100 years in their homeland in Myanmar, some of the Padaung are Christians.'[4]

215

Palaung, Pale

Approximately 300,000 Pale Palaung people live across a widespread area of three countries. The vast majority (more than 95%) live in a 16,000 square-kilometre (10,000 sq. mi.) area of northern and central Myanmar. Their main population centre is in southern Shan State around the towns of Kalaw and Namtu.[1] Population estimates for the Pale Palaung in Myanmar range from 190,000 to 290,000. Nobody is certain of figures in Myanmar due to the fact that no government has held a census for more than 70 years. In the 1931 census the Pale Palaung numbered 138,746.[2]

In China, the Pale Palaung number approximately 8,500. They live in Luxi County of western Yunnan Province, just a few miles from the border with Myanmar. The 1995 Thailand census counted a total of just 1,937 Pale Palaung people. Some sources say that the real number of this group in Thailand may be closer to 5,000. They moved into the Fang District of Thailand's Chiang Mai Province in 1983 to flee fighting in Myanmar. Their main village is on a mountain ridge literally atop the Thailand-Myanmar border. Just yards away, Thai and Burmese border guard posts face each other.

In China, the Pale Palaung have been combined with the Shwe Palaung, Rumai Palaung and the Riang to form the official De'ang minority group.[3] Although the four groups share much in common, their languages are different and they usually live in separate communities. The self-name of these Palaung groups is Ta-ang, which means 'rock people'. Palaung is a Burmese word.

The Pale Palaung have been Buddhists for many centuries. They were possibly converted by the Shan, who still exert a strong influence over the Palaung to this day. Every Palaung village has a temple, and it is considered a great honour for families when their sons become monks.[4] The Palaung also

Paul Hattaway

'strongly believe in spirits, called ganam. These supernatural powers exist in all natural surroundings, for instance in the water, forest, sky, trees, village and houses. Offerings to the spirits are most often made by ordinary people, although identification of the spirit causing illness or misfortune is made by a sorcerer, called pho moo muang. The meat of the sacrifices is boiled before offering it to the spirits. Each Palaung village has a spirit house, located some distance outside the village, and spirit gates to protect malevolent spirits from entering the village.'[5]

Very few Pale Palaung have come to Christ. Kachin Christians in Myanmar have attempted to reach them in recent years, with limited success, while a few families have converted to Christ among the Pale Palaung in China. For years, gospel radio broadcasts in the Pale Palaung language have sown seed throughout their widespread villages.

Those few Pale Palaung who come to faith in Christ invariably face strong opposition from their families and local communities, who believe that such decisions offend the evil spirits that control the Pale Palaung people and can bring disaster. In the mid-1990s, about a dozen Christian Palaung families in Myanmar were expelled from their villages and their homes were dismantled.[6]

Population:
300,260 (2000)
337,100 (2010)
378,600 (2020)
Countries: Myanmar, China, Thailand
Buddhism: Theravada
Christians: 300

Overview of the Pale Palaung

Other Names: De'ang Pale, Ngwe Palaung, Silver Palaung, Pale, Palay, Benglong, Bonglung, Bonglong, Penglung, Darang, Manton, Nam Hsan, Ta-ang, Bulei, Palong, Polaung, Da-ang, Da-eng, Di-ang, Bulai, Pulei, Southern Ta'ang

Population Sources:
190,000 to 290,000 in Myanmar (2000, B Grimes)
8,260 in China (2000, P Hattaway)
1,937 in Thailand (1995 census)

Language: Austro-Asiatic, Mon-Khmer, Northern Mon-Khmer,

Palaungic-Khmuic, Palaungic, Eastern Palaungic, Palaung

Dialects: 2 (Bulei, Raojin)

Professing Buddhists: 99%

Practising Buddhists: 70%

Christians: 0.1%

Scripture: work in progress

Jesus film: available

Gospel Recordings: Pale; Palaung Pale

Christian Broadcasting: available

ROPAL code: PCE

Status of Evangelization

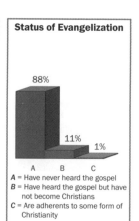

A = Have never heard the gospel
B = Have heard the gospel but have not become Christians
C = Are adherents to some form of Christianity

More than 140,000 Rumai Palaung inhabit a widespread area of northern Shan State in northern Myanmar (formerly called Burma).[1] They live in mountains that are, on average, about 5,000 to 8,500 feet above sea level. Many Rumai Palaung earn a living in simple agriculture and low-skilled manual jobs, such as collecting tea leaves. Others are rumoured to be involved with the illicit drug trade that predominates in this part of Asia, close to the Golden Triangle. Between 4,000 and 5,000 Pale Palaung inhabit China's Yunnan Province, in Longchuan and Ruili counties a short distance from the China-Myanmar border.[2]

In China the Rumai Palaung have been combined with the Pale Palaung, Shwe Palaung and Riang groups to form the official *De'ang* minority. The Rumai Palaung language is related to Shwe Palaung and Pale Palaung, yet it is distinct. Speakers from each language group share some words and expressions but must revert to a common language such as Shan in order to effectively communicate with one another. Rumai Palaung has been influenced by Tai languages such as Shan and Tai Mao much more than the three other Palaung varieties.

The Palaung people claim to be the original inhabitants of Myanmar. Chinese records show that they were living along the Nujiang River in north-west Yunnan Province as early as the 2nd century BC.[3] The Chinese also claim that the Palaung have been living in Myanmar for 2,000 years. Those who remain in China today are probably the descendants of small groups of people who migrated across the border into Yunnan to escape fighting between the British and tribal peoples in the early 1900s.

The Rumai Palaung have a traditional drum they call the *gelengdang*, which is made from a hollowed tree trunk. Its ends are covered with ox hides. Before using it, they fill it with water 'through a hole in its body to make the ox-hide and inside of the drum damp so that the desired resonance can be produced'.[4]

The Palaung believe that their first ancestor, Phu Sawti, was hatched from a serpent's egg. Their belief in this legend has contributed to the style of traditional dress worn by many Palaung women today. From their early teens, 'women wear 40 or 50 cane hoops apiece, one resting upon another to a depth of a foot around their hips. The undulating movement when they walk resembles a snake's motion.'[5]

There are probably more Christians among the Rumai Palaung than among any of the other Palaung groups, due to influences from the Kachin and other tribal Christians in northern Myanmar, yet the total number of believers among them amounts to only about one half of one per cent.

The Rumai Palaung still view Christianity as a strange religion. They believe that they have the truth in Buddhism, and they are fearful of the spiritual consequences if they should change their religion and stop appeasing the demons that they and their ancestors have been enslaved to for hundreds of years.

CHINA
Yunnan

Shan State

MYANMAR

Palaung Rumai

Population:
141,640 (2000)
159,000 (2010)
178,600 (2020)
Countries: Myanmar, China
Buddhism: Theravada
Christians: 600

Overview of the Rumai Palaung

Other Names: De'ang Rumai, Humai, Rumai, Ruomai, Black Palaung, Rummai, Rummai Palaung

Population Sources: 137,000 in Myanmar (2000, B Grimes)[6]
4,640 in China (2000, P Hattaway)

Language: Austro-Asiatic, Mon-Khmer, Northern Mon-Khmer, Palaungic-Khmuic, Palaungic, Eastern Palaungic, Palaung

Dialects: 0

Professing Buddhists: 98%

Practising Buddhists: 70%

Christians: 0.4%

Scripture: none

***Jesus* film:** none

Gospel Recordings: none

Christian Broadcasting: none

ROPAL code: RBB

Cooperative Baptist Fellowship

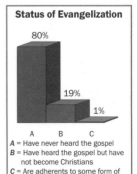

Status of Evangelization

80%

19%

1%

A   B   C

A = Have never heard the gospel
B = Have heard the gospel but have not become Christians
C = Are adherents to some form of Christianity

Palaung, Shwe

Population:
187,000 (2000)
209,900 (2010)
235,800 (2020)
Countries: Myanmar, China
Buddhism: Theravada
Christians: 500

Overview of the Shwe Palaung

Other Names: De'ang Shwe, Golden Palaung, Shwe, Ta-ang, Samlon Ta-ang

Population Sources: 148,000 in Myanmar (2000, B Grimes [1982 figure])

5,970 in China (2000, P Hattaway)

Language: Austro-Asiatic, Mon-Khmer, Northern Mon-Khmer, Palaungic-Khmuic, Palaungic, Eastern Palaungic, Palaung

Dialects: 15

Professing Buddhists: 96%

Practising Buddhists: 65%

Christians: 0.2%

Scripture: none

Jesus **film:** none

Gospel Recordings: Palaung

Christian Broadcasting: none

ROPAL code: SWE

Status of Evangelization

83%

16%

1%

A   B   C

A = Have never heard the gospel
B = Have heard the gospel but have not become Christians
C = Are adherents to some form of Christianity

Approximately 200,000 Shwe Palaung people inhabit areas of northern Shan State in northern Myanmar (formerly Burma). The main geographical centre of the Shwe Palaung in Myanmar is the town of Namshan, home to about 15,000 people.[1] An additional 6,000 Shwe Palaung live in Zhenkang and Baoshan counties in the western part of China's Yunnan Province, where they are part of the officially recognized De'ang minority. The Shwe Palaung are also known as the 'Golden Palaung' due to the style of the women's dress.

Many Palaung people believe that they were once brothers with the Karen, even though today the Palaung speak a Mon-Khmer language and the Karen speak a completely unrelated Tibeto-Burman language. The Palaung tell a story about how the two brothers were separated: 'The two tribes went out hunting with the intent of sharing their food with each other. The Karen caught an elephant, and a huge feast was held for all to enjoy as much meat as they could eat. The Palaung, however, could only manage to catch a porcupine. They skinned it and cooked the small amount of meat for the Karen to eat. The Karen didn't mind, as they thought the Palaung had only been able to catch a small animal. But when they finished their meal, they saw the large pile of needles and claimed the Palaung had only given them a small portion of their meat. The two groups have been separated ever since that time, but even

today many Palaung long to be reconciled with their Karen brothers. Some Palaung homes in Myanmar have an opening on one side, signifying that the Karen are welcome to return to live with them.'[2]

Although almost all Palaung in Myanmar are Buddhists, they are influenced by two schools of Buddhism—the Shan form and the Burmese form. Although each belongs to the Theravada sect, there are subtle differences in practice and style. Before Buddhism entered the region hundreds of years ago, the Palaung were spirit-worshippers and every village had its own shaman, or spirit-priest. Little has changed today, except that now the leading Buddhist monk usually adopts that role in the life of the community. 'Illness is attributed to the actions of evil spirits and the services of a diviner / medical practitioner serve to identify and counteract the proper spirit. . . . Ordinary people make a variety of offerings to placate them.'[3]

Although only a very small number of Palaung are Christians, one missionary report of a trip to Myanmar in 2003 gave encouraging signs that God is quietly working among Palaung people. The report said, 'We found individuals and pockets of Palaung who were believers in several areas. Some live in conditions as described in Hebrews 11:38. Some of their children have died from malaria, which is rampant near rivers and brooks. They hardly have enough to survive. . . . Their faces lit up when we came and they were very glad to have people come to help share the Good News with their friends, who are still in fear of hell and demonic forces, which they believe live inside trees and rocks.'[4]

Myanmar Faces and Places

Population:
678,900 (2000)
763,000 (2010)
857,000 (2020)
Countries: Myanmar, Thailand
Buddhism: Theravada
Christians: 12,000

Overview of the Pa-O

Other Names: Taungthu, Karen: Pa-O, Black Karen, Pa-U, Pa'o, Pa Oh, Taungtu, Pao Karen, Pao, Tau-soo

Population Sources:
560,000 in Myanmar (2000, B Grimes [1983 figure])
900 in Thailand (2000, J Schliesinger [1995 figure])

Language: Sino-Tibetan, Tibeto-Burman, Karen, Pa'o

Dialects: 2 (Southern Pa-O [Myanmar], Northern Pa-O [Thailand])

Professing Buddhists: 80%

Practising Buddhists: 60%

Christians: 1.7%

Scripture: Portions 1912

Jesus film: available

Gospel Recordings: Taungthu; Pa-O; Karen: Black

Christian Broadcasting: available

ROPAL code: BLK

Status of Evangelization

58%
40%
2%

A   B   C
A = Have never heard the gospel
B = Have heard the gospel but have not become Christians
C = Are adherents to some form of Christianity

Approximately 700,000 Pa-O people live in Southeast Asia. The large majority inhabits the south-western part of Shan State in Myanmar. The geographical centre of the Pa-O could be considered the mountains around the towns of Taunggyi and Kalaw.[1] A smaller number of Pa-O live in Mon State, Karen State and as far south as the Tanintharyi (formerly Tenasserim) Division on the Gulf of Martahan in the southern tip of Myanmar.

An additional 900 Pa-O live inside Thailand, inhabiting four villages within the Muang District of Mae Hong Son Province.[2] The Pa-O in Thailand fled Myanmar in 1975 because of the terrible social upheavals and human rights abuses committed by the military junta.

The Pa-O are called *Taungthu* by the Burmese, which means 'hill people'. The British colonialists called them *Black Karen* because most Pa-O women wear black or dark blue dresses. The Pa-O language shows them to be part of the great collection of Karen groups in Myanmar and Thailand, which together number as many as five million people in 20 language groups. Many Pa-O do not even know of this connection to the Karen, however, and consider themselves a unique people group.[3]

The Pa-O believe that their ancestors 'fled north to Shan State from the Mon City of Thaton, in Lower Burma, after the overthrow of the Mon King Manuha in the eleventh century by King Anawrahta of Pagan'.[4] This defeat took place in 1057. Today the Pa-O are the second most numerous ethnic

Myanmar Faces and Places

group in Shan State after the Shan.

One key area in which the Pa-O differ from other Karen groups is in their religious beliefs. While most of the Karen are either animists or Christians, the Pa-O have been a strong Buddhist group for many centuries. Buddhism has influenced all Karen groups to some degree, but Buddhism dominates every area of the lives and communities of the Pa-O. In Myanmar, most Pa-O villages can be identified by the magnificent wooden temples that are constructed on the outskirts of their villages.

Although one estimate puts the number of Pa-O Christians at around 12,000 (1.7%),[5] most Pa-O Buddhists have steadfastly rejected all efforts to evangelize them. One source states, 'The Pa-O people are Buddhists. They consider ordination as a novice even greater merit than ordination as a monk. During the first day of the novice ordination ceremony, called *poi sang long*, the sounds of drums, gongs and cymbals echo between the mountain ridges, when boys with shaved heads are taken from their homes to the temple. . . . However, they still retain animist beliefs to some extent, but much less than the Pwo and Sgaw Karen. They worship spirits, such as the house and tree spirits and spirit shrines are located outside villages or near pagodas, where offerings can be made.'[6]

Missionaries first translated Scripture portions into Pa-O in 1912, and the *Jesus* film is now available in their language.

Phuan

Population:
310,300 (2000)
357,600 (2010)
414,000 (2020)
Countries: Thailand, Laos
Buddhism: Theravada
Christians: 800

Overview of the Phuan

Other Names: Lao Phuan, Phu Un, Phouan, Puan, Phoan, Poan, Phuon, Phu-uen

Population Sources:
200,000 in Thailand (2001, J Schliesinger [1999 figure])
96,000 in Laos (1995, L Chazee)

Language: Tai-Kadai, Kam-Tai, Be-Tai, Tai-Sek, Tai, Southwestern, East Central, Chiang Saeng

Dialects: 0

Professing Buddhists: 95%

Practising Buddhists: 90%

Christians: 0.2%

Scripture: none

Jesus film: none

Gospel Recordings: none

Christian Broadcasting: none

ROPAL code: PHU

Status of Evangelization

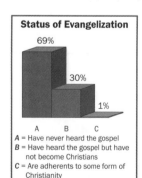

69%
30%
1%

A   B   C

A = Have never heard the gospel
B = Have heard the gospel but have not become Christians
C = Are adherents to some form of Christianity

More than 300,000 members of the Phuan ethnic group live in Thailand and Laos in Southeast Asia. The majority—more than 200,000—live in at least ten provinces of central and north-east Thailand, especially in Udon Thani, Lopburi and Sukkothai provinces.[1] French researcher Laurent Chazee estimated a further 96,000 Phuan people living in Laos in 1995.[2] In Laos they inhabit six different provinces and regions in the central and northern parts of the country.[3] The main location of the Phuan is near the Plain of Jars in Xiangkhoang Province. The Plain of Jars is an ancient collection of huge stone jars, believed to be around 2,000 years old. No one is sure why they were made or what they were used for. Most of the huge jars weigh between 600 kilograms and one ton (1,300 to 2,200 lb.). The largest weighs six tons (13,200 lb.).

The Phuan in Thailand were taken as captives of war and forcibly removed to Thailand at various times between 1792 and 1890 after the collapse of the Lan Xang ('Million Elephants') kingdom in Laos. They were ordered to render manual labour for noble Siamese families.

Today the Phuan are one of the proudest and most socially prominent of the 'tribal Tai' groups. Their language, which is closely related to Northern Tai, Tai Dam and Song, is spoken in almost all Phuan homes. In the past the Phuan used their own script, but it has become obsolete. The Phuan are proud of their ethnicity and not intimidated

by larger groups such as the Thai or Lao.[4] One researcher has found that the Phuan are 'proud of their physical appearance. Both sexes have fairer skin, are taller, have longer noses and more oval faces than the members of other Tai kin groups.'[5]

Buddhism is not only the religion of almost all Phuan people; it is the centre of their social existence. Every Phuan village in Thailand and most villages in Laos have their own temples. 'Many of the older Phuan women visit the temple on a daily basis during lunch and dinner times. They carry food in their baskets to the temple hall where they meet with other elderly Phuan women to enjoy themselves, eating and chatting.'[6]

The Phuan also live in bondage and fear of a complex hierarchy of evil spirits. The most important is *tha phu ban*, the protective spirit of the village. The Phuan make offerings of fruit, rice whiskey and other delicacies to the spirit which, if placated, is believed to grant favours to the people. If a favour is given, the Phuan sacrifice a chicken or a pig in honour of the spirit.

There is a small yet significant number of Christians among the Phuan both in Thailand and Laos. One tourist book on Laos suggests that there are a considerable number of Phuan Christians near Oakxan in Borikhamxai Province: 'The local population is predominantly Phuan, a tribal Thai group; many are Christian, which makes them doubly suspicious in the eyes of the Lao authorities.'[7]

Paul Hattaway

Approximately 400,000 Phutai people live across three countries in Southeast Asia: Laos[1] (154,000), Vietnam (150,000) and Thailand[2] (70,000). Phutai may also live in south-west Yunnan Province, China. A number of Phutai refugees were granted asylum in the USA. A small community has lived in the Los Angeles area since the late 1970s.

In all of the countries where they live, it is difficult for researchers to identify the Phutai because they have merged with other communities. In Vietnam they have not been granted status as a distinct ethnic group, but they are one of many sub-groups lumped together under the official 'Thai' minority. In Laos, the 1995 census listed a population of 472,458 Phutai people, but this inflated figure included groups such as the Tai Dam (Black Tai), Tai Kao (White Tai) and Tai Deng (Red Tai). Although ethnically they are distinct, there are only slight differences between the languages of these groups.[3] The name *Phutai* has a generic meaning, 'Tai people', which further complicates attempts to classify them. Despite this murky situation, some other ethnic groups envy the Phutai because of their rich cultural heritage. They are a proud people who still preserve their traditions.

Many Phutai in Vietnam, and to a lesser degree in Laos, remain animists, with minimal Buddhist influence.[4] Buddhism is stronger among the Phutai in Thailand, but worldwide only about 50 per cent of Phutai people identify themselves as Buddhists.

Each Phutai village in Thailand has one or more female shamans, called *moi yau*. They are responsible for mediating between the Phutai people and the spirit world. During certain times they go into trances and give messages from the spirit world or from the Phutai ancestors. The *moi yau* are both feared and highly respected by the Phutai.

Even those Phutai who say they are Buddhists mix their faith with the worship of 25 different spirits. 'Every year during the third lunar month the Phutai gather for the *Pi Tian* ("Spirit of Heaven") festival. People relax and unwind by riding horses, elephants and shooting arrows, etc. The focal point of the festival is a ritual at which the whole community gathers and offers sacrifices and prayers to the spirit that they believe resides in paradise above. After waiting for some time, the Phutai believe there is a moment when the spirit actually comes down from heaven. The normally-reserved Phutai dance and jump for joy, and often . . . healing takes place. Despite this remarkable ceremony, there are few Phutai who have ever accepted Jesus Christ, who is the Holy Spirit who gives lasting joy.'[5]

Today there are several hundred Phutai Christians in Laos, both Catholic and Protestant, and a similar number in Thailand. The vast majority of Phutai people, however, have never heard the gospel. Their strong sense of community often results in the Phutai being resistant to change and outside influence. Consequently, few have ever broken away to follow Christ.

Population:
388,500 (2000)
460,900 (2010)
548,400 (2020)
Countries: Laos, Vietnam, Thailand, USA, possibly China
Buddhism: Theravada
Christians: 900

Overview of the Phutai

Other Names: Phu Tai, Putai, Puthay, Poutai

Population Sources: 154,400 in Laos (2001, P Johnstone and J Mandryk)

150,000 in Vietnam (1993, P Johnstone)

70,000 in Thailand (2001, J Schliesinger [1999 figure])

also in USA; possibly China

Language: Tai-Kadai, Kam-Tai, Be-Tai, Tai-Sek, Tai, Southwestern, East Central, Lao-Phutai

Dialects: 0

Professing Buddhists: 50%

Practising Buddhists: 25%

Christians: 0.2%

Scripture: none

Jesus film: none

Gospel Recordings: Phu Tai

Christian Broadcasting: none

ROPAL code: PHT

Christian Far East Ministry

Status of Evangelization

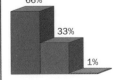

66%
33%
1%

A   B   C

A = Have never heard the gospel
B = Have heard the gospel but have not become Christians
C = Are adherents to some form of Christianity

Puman

Approximately 18,000 Puman people inhabit areas of south-west China. One source says that 'they number in the tens of thousands and can be found today living in Yunnan Province, especially in an area located between Baoshan, the Wuliang Hills and down to Simao, Lancang, Gengma and Zhenkang'.[1]

The Puman have been officially included as part of the Bulang nationality in China, although one linguist notes that the two groups are 'not very closely related'.[2]

Create International

The Puman are part of the great Mon-Khmer race of Asia. Over the centuries, the Mon-Khmer splintered into numerous groups that today are spread as far as India's Nicobar Islands and Indonesia. One linguist notes, 'Not all Pumans speak Puman as their native tongue. The Pumans living in the region between Zhenkang and Yunxian no longer speak Puman but have adopted Chinese as their native language.'[3]

The Puman traditionally cast lots every year before a statue of Buddha to determine where they should farm. Puman women adorn themselves with colourful head scarfs, often decorated with pieces of silver in the shape of shells or fish. This has baffled experts, since their region is located far from the coast.[4]

Most Puman are devoted believers in Theravada Buddhism. 'Larger Puman villages have a monastery and a special house for Buddhist images, since their religion is a syncretic mix of traditional animism and Theravada Buddhism.'[5]

In south-west China various Buddhist groups retain many stories regarding the coming of a Saviour, a blessed one who fits the description of Jesus Christ in many respects. Missionary William Clifton Dodd, who travelled extensively throughout the region in the 1930s, was intrigued to learn of some of the characteristics of this Thera-vada Buddhist messiah: 'His coming is to be preceded by a falling away from the practice of religion, morality and righteousness. His forerunner shall level every mountain, exalt every valley, make crooked places straight, and rough places smooth. . . . Only the pure in heart and life shall be able to see him. But those who see are to be delivered from the thralldom of rebirth. He is to be recognized by his pierced hand. And his religion shall be introduced from the south [Christianity came into southern Yunnan from Thailand], by a man with a white face and a long beard [a description that fits both Donald McGilvary and Dr Wilson—the first missionaries to bring the gospel to this part of China].'[6]

Despite their belief in a Saviour, most Puman have yet to hear about Jesus Christ. Few Christians have ever endeavoured to take the gospel to these people locked away in remote mountains and deep forests. Consequently, there has never been a known Christian fellowship among the Puman people, nor has there even been a single known Puman believer.

CHINA

Yunnan

MYANMAR

Puman

Population:
16,520 (2000)
21,300 (2010)
26,200 (2020)
Countries: China
Buddhism: Theravada
Christians: none known

Overview of the Puman

Other Names: U, P'uman, Wa-la, Phuman

Population Sources:

12,000 in China (1987, D Bradley)

Language: Austro-Asiatic, Mon-Khmer, Northern Mon-Khmer, Palaungic-Khmuic, Palaungic, Western Palaungic, Angkuic

Dialects: 0

Professing Buddhists: 100%

Practising Buddhists: 75%

Christians: 0%

Scripture: none

Jesus film: none

Gospel Recordings: Blang: Puman

Christian Broadcasting: none

ROPAL code: UUU

Status of Evangelization

87%

13%

0%

A   B   C

A = Have never heard the gospel
B = Have heard the gospel but have not become Christians
C = Are adherents to some form of Christianity

Pumi, Northern

A widespread, isolated section of south-west Sichuan Province in China is home to approximately 40,000 Northern Pumi people. Most are located in and around Muli County, described as 'a rich possession. The rivers, especially the Litang, carry gold and produce a considerable revenue.'[1] Northern Pumi is also spoken in Zuosuo and Yousuo districts of Yanyuan County and in the Sanyanlong and Dabao districts of Jiulong County.[2] Seven thousand Northern Pumi live in the Yongning District of Ninglang County in northern Yunnan Province.

In the past, the Northern Pumi were commonly known as *Xifan*, a derogatory Chinese name meaning 'barbarians of the west'—a name applied not only to this group but sometimes also used for all Tibetans. Older sources listed them as the Chrame people, a name also used in *Operation China*.[3] Linguistic sources, however, consistently label this group as the Northern Pumi. The Chinese government does not recognize the Northern Pumi as a distinct ethnic minority, but they have simply included those living in Sichuan as part of the Tibetan nationality based on their culture and religion. Consequently, the Northern Pumi in Sichuan almost always identify themselves as Tibetans when speaking with visitors, even though they have a separate language and history from their Tibetan neighbours.[4] The 7,000 Northern Pumi in northern Yunnan Province have been counted as part of the Pumi nationality.

The Northern Pumi language—which has three tones and five dialects—shares 60 per cent lexical similarity with Southern Pumi, which is spoken in Yunnan Province. The Southern Pumi have not been included in this book because they are primarily animists and polytheists. Few are adherents of Buddhism.

A Northern Pumi king presided over the former Buddhist monastery town of Muli until the 1950s. The king once 'held sway over a territory of 9,000 square miles—an area slightly larger than Massachusetts'.[5] The rulers of Muli 'are said to be of Manchu origin. They were given the sovereignty of the kingdom in perpetuity in recognition of valorous services rendered to Yungcheng, the famous Manchu emperor, who ascended the throne in 1723.'[6] The king ruled with 'absolute spiritual and temporal sway'[7] over his subjects. 'The villagers occupy wooden shanties scattered over the hillsides below the town. They are very poor, and live in constant fear of the lama king and his parasitic satellites.'[8] The king of Muli was fond of feeding visitors 'dried legs of mutton and yak cheese . . . propelled by squirming maggots the size of a man's thumb'. Rock's group gave theirs to beggars, who 'fought for it like tigers'.[9]

All Northern Pumi adhere to Tibetan Buddhism. Their religion is a major part of their ethnic and cultural identity. They are one of the most unreached people groups in China, with no known Northern Pumi church or Christian believer. In recent years a small number of faith-filled Christians have ventured into Muli and become advocates for the Northern Pumi people, although there are still no known believers among this precious and unique group today.

Population:
39,000 (2000)
48,100 (2010)
59,200 (2020)
Countries: China
Buddhism: Tibetan
Christians: none known

Overview of the Northern Pumi

Other Names: Xifan, Hsifan, Northern Pumi, Chrame, Ch'rame, Tshomi, Sichuan Pumi

Population Sources:
30,000 in China (1987, *Language Atlas of China*)

Language: Sino-Tibetan, Tibeto-Burman, Tangut-Qiang, Qiangic

Dialects: 4 (Tuoqi, Sanyanlong, Taoba, Zuosuo)

Professing Buddhists: 100%

Practising Buddhists: 95%

Christians: 0%

Scripture: none

***Jesus* film:** none

Gospel Recordings: none

Christian Broadcasting: none

ROPAL code: PMI

Status of Evangelization

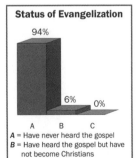

94%

6%   0%

A   B   C

A = Have never heard the gospel
B = Have heard the gospel but have not become Christians
C = Are adherents to some form of Christianity

China Advocate

Qiang, Cimulin

A Chinese source lists a 1990 figure of 9,800 speakers of Cimulin Qiang living in five districts within Heishui (Black Water) County in north-west Sichuan Province, China.[1] The total Qiang population in the 1990 census was 198,252. This figure is the total of the populations of 11 smaller linguistic groups, of which just four could accurately be described as Buddhist. Qiang is actually the Chinese term for these people. Their self-name is *Rma*. 'The Chinese character for *Qiang* is a combination of *yang* (sheep) and *ren* (people), with the composite meaning of "people tending sheep".'[2]

The Cimulin Qiang language is very different from other varieties of Qiang. Cimulin Qiang, which is a Northern Qiang language, is not tonal, whereas Southern Qiang varieties all have between two and six tones.[3] Many of the Cimulin Qiang are bilingual in Tibetan, while others living near the towns are able to speak Chinese. In addition, more than 50,000 speakers of Northern Qiang dialects have been categorized under the Tibetan nationality—and so these days they

have lost their Qiang identity and think of themselves as Tibetans.[4]

Qiang history dates back as far as the Western Zhou Dynasty (1100–771 BC), when considerable numbers of Han Chinese migrated west and formed mixed communities with the Di and Qiang.[5] They found themselves living in a buffer zone between the Chinese and Tibetans, and they have absorbed aspects of both cultures.[6]

One of the most important Qiang festivals is called *Jishanhui*, which women are not allowed to attend. A cow or sheep is sacrificed on an altar to the god of the mountains. They pray for a good harvest and for peace for the village.

The Northern Qiang language groups, including the Cimulin Qiang, have embraced Tibetan Buddhism more zealously than the Southern Qiang

Nancy Sturrock

because of centuries of influence from neighbouring Tibetans. The Northern Qiang also worship a multitude of Chinese and Tibetan deities, of which the sky god is considered the greatest. In addition, shamans, witches and mediums are located throughout the countryside. In 1994 one Christian interviewed a Qiang sorceress at a temple reputed to be 1,000 years old. The woman told the visitor, '"I have the power to put people into a trance and make their spirits leave their bodies and travel to hell. Usually, we can then call their spirits back, but sometimes it doesn't work, and the person dies and is trapped in hell forever." When we told her about a God who has the power to take her spirit to heaven, she was delighted and wanted to know more.'[7]

Most Qiang people, like this sorceress, have absolutely no awareness of the gospel. There are a few Northern Qiang Christians, including some families living in Songpan. 'There are no church buildings any more, but still Christian believers.'[8] It is not known, however, if there are any Christians specifically among the Cimulin Qiang group.

Overview of the Cimulin Qiang

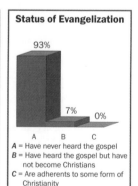

Other Names: Chiang: Cimulin, Chi'ang, Cimulin, Tz'u-mu-lin Ch'iang

Population Sources:

9,800 in China (1998, Liu Guangkun [1990 figure])

Language: Sino-Tibetan, Tibeto-Burman, Tangut-Qiang, Qiangic, Northern Qiang

Dialects: 0

Professing Buddhists: 70%

Practising Buddhists: 25%

Christians: 0%

Scripture: none

***Jesus* film:** none

Gospel Recordings: none

Christian Broadcasting: none

ROPAL code: CNG03

Population:
12,600 (2000)
16,300 (2010)
20,100 (2020)
Countries: China
Buddhism: Tibetan
Christians: none known

Status of Evangelization

93%

7%

0%

A   B   C

A = Have never heard the gospel
B = Have heard the gospel but have not become Christians
C = Are adherents to some form of Christianity

Population:
18,060 (2000)
23,300 (2010)
28,700 (2020)
Countries: China
Buddhism: Tibetan
Christians: none known

Overview of the Luhua Qiang

Other Names: Chiang: Luhua, Chi'ang, Luhua

Population Sources:

14,000 in China (1998, Liu Guangkun [1990 figure])

Language: Sino-Tibetan, Tibeto-Burman, Tangut-Qiang, Qiangic, Northern Qiang

Dialects: 0

Professing Buddhists: 90%

Practising Buddhists: 30%

Christians: 0%

Scripture: none

Jesus **film:** none

Gospel Recordings: none

Christian Broadcasting: none

ROPAL code: CNG04

Status of Evangelization

88%

12%

0%

A   B   C

A = Have never heard the gospel
B = Have heard the gospel but have not become Christians
C = Are adherents to some form of Christianity

The Chinese linguist Liu Guangkun estimated a 1990 figure of 14,000 speakers of the Luhua Qiang language living in north-west Sichuan Province in western China.[1] The Luhua Qiang language is spoken in the Luhua, Shashiduo, Yangrong, Zegai, Ergulu and Zhuogedu districts of Heishui (Black Water) County in the Aba Prefecture. Heishui County had a total population of 58,000 in the 1990 census, of which 49,600 (85.5%) speak Qiang languages.

Although they belong to the officially-recognized Qiang nationality and speak Qiang, many of the Qiang in Heishui County call themselves Tibetans when speaking in Chinese but *Rma* in their own language.

Luhua Qiang is one of four distinct varieties of Northern Qiang in China. One researcher has noted, 'Although Qiang does not have a large population, their language is divided into many dialects, and they are not intelligible from one to another. Even worse, each village uses a different dialect. It is therefore very difficult to research.'[2]

For a long period of time before 1949, the Qiang lived in primitive conditions. A feudal landlord economy dominated production. Many of these poor peasants eventually lost their land due to excessive and unfair taxation. They became hired labourers and wandered from place to place to make a living. Today's Luhua Qiang people grow corn, red peppers, potatoes, cabbages, beans and wheat. They also grow a fruit called *whadjou*. In their mud-brick homes they keep pigs, sheep, goats, chickens and some cattle.

Most Luhua Qiang have converted to Tibetan Buddhism under the influence of their Khampa Tibetan neighbours.

While outwardly they identify themselves as Buddhists, only a minority actively participate in Buddhist rituals. The ancient Qiang animistic religion is also present. White stones are not only representative of Qiang gods but are also a symbol of good fortune. Some Qiang believe that 'bringing a white stone into a house on New Year's Day will bring more property. So, when they visit a neighbour or relative . . . they present a white rock and shout "Property comes!" The host receives it carefully and then welcomes their blessing wholeheartedly by carefully placing it next to the ancestral tablets or the image of a deity.'[3]

China Advocate

Foreign missionaries who worked in the Qiang region in the late 1800s recounted this fascinating story of a brief encounter with an unknown tribe: 'Years ago a deputation from Ngapa came . . . with a request for pith helmets, guns and Bibles. Their interest in the Gospel, like the order, seemed mixed, but . . . eleven years later, the writer met a Prince from Ngapa who greedily bought up 500 [Scripture] portionettes. "No," [the Prince] said, "they are not for sale. My people are interested in this Gospel."'[4]

This interesting story reflects the interest in the gospel that the Qiang people still have today. They are unreached not because they are resistant to the claims of Christ, but rather because few have ever been presented with the gospel in such a way that they could comprehend it and make an intelligent decision to accept or reject the Saviour.

Qiang, Mawo

Population:
15,480 (2000)
19,950 (2010)
24,500 (2020)
Countries: China
Buddhism: Tibetan
Christians: none known

Overview of the Mawo Qiang

Other Names: Chiang: Mawo, Mawo

Population Sources:

12,000 in China (1998, Liu Guangkun [1990 figure])

Language: Sino-Tibetan, Tibeto-Burman, Tangut-Qiang, Qiangic, Northern Qiang

Dialects: 0

Professing Buddhists: 95%

Practising Buddhists: 30%

Christians: 0%

Scripture: none

Jesus film: none

Gospel Recordings: none

Christian Broadcasting: none

ROPAL code: none

Status of Evangelization

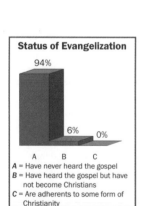

94%

6%

0%

A   B   C

A = Have never heard the gospel
B = Have heard the gospel but have not become Christians
C = Are adherents to some form of Christianity

In 1990 there were 12,000 speakers of the Mawo Qiang language reported in China. They live wholly within the borders of Heishui County (in the districts of Mawo, Zhawo, Shuangliusuo, Xi'er, Hongyan and E'en) in north-western Sichuan Province.[1]

The Mawo Qiang are one sub-group of the official Qiang national-ity in China, which numbers approximately 240,000 people. Out of this total, however, only about 85,000 are Buddhists and the rest practise traditional animism mixed with Chinese religions. The Mawo Qiang are one of the northern Qiang language groups who are Tibetan Buddhists due to their close proximity to the Tibetan people for many centuries. Some Qiang claim to be descended from sheep, hence the character for their name. (The upper radical of the Chinese character for Qiang defines 'sheep', the lower one 'son'.)

Mawo Qiang is one of four varieties of Northern Qiang spoken in Sichuan Province. It takes its name from Mawo District, which was the location chosen by scholars to study this language. Many Mawo Qiang are bilingual in Tibetan or multilingual in both Tibetan and the Sichuan dialect of Mandarin Chinese.

In the past, entire Qiang communities were wiped out because of plagues and disease. In recent years the government has given mass treatment for black fever and hookworm to the Qiang, which has greatly reduced the danger of these epidemics breaking out.

Qiang men and women typically wear homespun linen gowns with sheepskin vests called *guagua*. They wear their vests with the fur turned inward during cool weather and turned outward during rainy weather. Qiang women wear embroidered

shoes called Yun Yun shoes. An old legend says that, long ago, a Han girl named Yun Yun enjoyed close friend-ship with her Qiang sisters and taught them spinning, weaving and embroidery. One day Yun Yun and her Qiang sisters went up a mountain to cut firewood and got caught in a storm; Yun Yun slipped and fell into a deep valley, leaving behind only her embroidered shoes. In memory of Yun Yun the Qiang girls wear shoes patterned after hers and call them Yun Yun shoes. Unmarried girls often send their painstakingly embroidered shoes as gifts to the man they love. When they marry, they place several pairs in their dowry.[2]

One of the festivals celebrated by the Qiang is called *Zhuanshan* ('Mountain Circling'). In the past, villagers led an ox and carried food and wine up a mountain to sacrifice to the mountain gods. Monkeys, wild boars and rats, all made of paper, were set on fire to symbolize the destruction of the pests that devoured the Qiang's grain.

The Mawo Qiang are possibly the most unevangelized of the Qiang groups in China. Their language is very different from that of the Southern Qiang language groups, which contain most of the known Qiang believers.

Yadu Qiang is spoken by more people than any other Qiang language in China. The majority of the approximately 30,000 Yadu Qiang live in the Chibusu, Yadu, Qugu and Weicheng districts of Maoxian County in Sichuan Province and in the Waboliangzi and Se'ergu districts of Heishui County farther to the north.[1]

Yadu Qiang is one of 11 groups that make up the official Qiang nationality in China. The Yadu Qiang language is part of the Northern Qiang group. Although languages of the Northern Qiang appear to be more homogeneous than the Southern Qiang languages, which are clearly distinct from one another, Yadu Qiang speakers must still use Chinese or Tibetan to communicate with other Northern Qiang speakers.

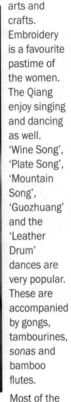
China Advocate

Although the Qiang are no longer considered a matriarchal society, women still play a leading role in agriculture and usually have the final say in the family. Young couples often live with the wife's family after the wedding. Until recently, early marriages were common among the Qiang. It was not unusual for a boy to marry between the ages of seven and ten, and women between 12 and 18. Qiang women sing a sarcastic song to their guests. 'It is the sixth moon, and the wheat flowers are blooming in the field. My husband is still an infant drinking milk. How long will it be before he grows up?' One of the games the Qiang play at festivals is called egg snatching. They place a number of rocks on the ground and, while one person guards them, others try to snatch them. Whoever gets the most wins the contest. Another Qiang favourite is the log-pushing contest. Two people grab the log and try to push each other out of a circle. Whoever succeeds wins.

The Qiang have their own unique cultural arts and crafts. Embroidery is a favourite pastime of the women. The Qiang enjoy singing and dancing as well. 'Wine Song', 'Plate Song', 'Mountain Song', 'Guozhuang' and the 'Leather Drum' dances are very popular. These are accompanied by gongs, tambourines, *sonas* and bamboo flutes.

Most of the Yadu Qiang living in Heishui County have been thoroughly assimilated to Tibetan culture and religion. They follow Tibetan Buddhism, mixed with polytheism and animism. Prayer flags and prayer beads are two of the common Buddhist symbols they have borrowed from the Tibetans.

Despite the fact that the Yadu Qiang have the largest population of the Qiang groups in Sichuan, there are no known Christians among them. Those in Maoxian County live nearer the Qiang believers, but there are major linguistic differences that make it difficult for the Yadu Qiang to understand the gospel from Southern Qiang speakers. The Yadu Qiang living in Heishui County have even less chance of hearing the gospel. They live alongside Tibetan nomads who are also completely untouched by Christianity.

Population:
29,650 (2000)
38,200 (2010)
47,000 (2020)
Countries: China
Buddhism: Tibetan
Christians: none known

Overview of the Yadu Qiang

Other Names: Chiang: Yadu, Yadu, Ya-tu Ch'iang

Population Sources:
23,000 in China (1998, Liu Guangkun [1990 figure])

Language: Sino-Tibetan, Tibeto-Burman, Tangut-Qiang, Qiangic, Northern Qiang

Dialects: 0

Professing Buddhists: 70%

Practising Buddhists: 25%

Christians: 0%

Scripture: none

***Jesus* film:** none

Gospel Recordings: none

Christian Broadcasting: none

ROPAL code: CNG01

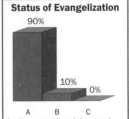

Status of Evangelization
90%
10%
0%
A   B   C
A = Have never heard the gospel
B = Have heard the gospel but have not become Christians
C = Are adherents to some form of Christianity

Qixingmin

According to a 1982 Chinese ethnographic survey, 3,000 Qixingmin (pronounced 'chee-shing-min') people live in Shuicheng and Weining counties in western Guizhou Province and in Qiubei County in Yunnan Province (where they may be better known as *Boren*).[1] This ethnically diverse area contains many Yi and Miao sub-groups in addition to the majority Han Chinese population.

In the 1982 China census the Chinese authorities did not list the Qixingmin under any of the recognized nationalities but instead placed them in a list of *Undetermined Minorities*. In 1985 they were reclassified under the Bai nationality—people who live more than 300 miles away in the Dali Prefecture of west-central Yunnan.[2] One source says that the identification of the Qixingmin ethnicity is a problematic one, primarily because they are known by three different ethnic names: *Qixingmin*, *Jing Ren* and *Bai Erzi*.[3]

Although the Qixingmin language, which may be called *Bo*, has never been studied in depth, it was mentioned in passing as a newly discovered language in a Chinese linguistic journal.[4] Today most Qixingmin are adequately bilingual in Mandarin Chinese, and their mother tongue is in an endangered state.

The Qixingmin have lived in their present location for at least 400 years. During the Ming (1368–1644) and Qing (1644–1911) dynasties the Qixingmin were better known as *Bai Erzi*. During the Qing Dynasty they lived in mixed communities with the Yizi, Bouyei, Miao and a group called the Baolu.

Despite their small numbers, the Qixingmin have a fierce reputation among their neighbours, who claim that the Qixingmin have hot tempers, that they are stubborn, and that they fight all the time. Visitors to a Qixingmin home are required to leave the house through a different door than the one by which they entered. The door is of great importance to the Qixingmin. Both the doors and the entrances to their villages are protected by regular cleansing ceremonies.

The Qixingmin's strong adherence to Mahayana Buddhism is one of the things that makes them a unique people in their area. They are a Buddhist enclave surrounded by numerous animistic and Christian communities. Most Qixingmin use prayer beads to help them meditate, while some men become monks and join monasteries for extended periods of time, which is considered a great honour to their families.

The Qixingmin are an unreached people group with no known believers, despite the fact that many have been exposed to the gospel from Han, Miao and Yi believers living in the Weining and Shuicheng areas. The ethnic identity of the Qixingmin is integrally linked with Buddhism: to be a Qixingmin is to be Buddhist. The cost of going against their culture and the threat of probable expulsion from their communities for those who become Christians have proven to be obstacles too great for the Qixingmin to overcome. Most churches in the area no longer attempt to evangelize them.

Population:
4,560 (2000)
5,890 (2010)
7,250 (2020)
Countries: China
Buddhism: Mahayana
Christians: none known

Overview of the Qixingmin

Other Names: Jing Ren, Bao Erzi, Bo, Boren

Population Sources:
3,000 in China (1982, *Minzu Shibie Wenxian Ziliao Huibian*)

Language: Sino-Tibetan, Tibeto-Burman, Unclassified

Dialects: 0

Professing Buddhists: 100%

Practising Buddhists: 85%

Christians: 0%

Scripture: none

Jesus film: none

Gospel Recordings: none

Christian Broadcasting: none

ROPAL code: none

Photo credit: International Mission Board

Status of Evangelization

58%

42%

0%

A   B   C

A = Have never heard the gospel
B = Have heard the gospel but have not become Christians
C = Are adherents to some form of Christianity

Population:
8,460 (2000)
10,420 (2010)
12,800 (2020)
Countries: China
Buddhism: Tibetan
Christians: none known

Overview of the Queyu

Other Names: Zhaba, Hokow

Population Sources:

7,000 in China (1991, *Encyclopedic Dictionary of Chinese Linguistics*)

Language: Sino-Tibetan, Tibeto-Burman, Tangut-Qiang, Qiangic

Dialects: 0

Professing Buddhists: 100%

Practising Buddhists: 45%

Christians: 0%

Scripture: none

***Jesus* film:** none

Gospel Recordings: none

Christian Broadcasting: none

ROPAL code: QEY

Status of Evangelization

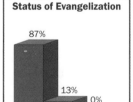

A = Have never heard the gospel
B = Have heard the gospel but have not become Christians
C = Are adherents to some form of Christianity

Seven thousand speakers of the Queyu (pronounced 'chue-yoo') language were reported in a 1991 Chinese study.[1] It is expected that this figure grew to 8,460 by the year 2000 and that it will have increased to 10,420 by 2010.

The Queyu inhabit the three counties of Xinlong, Yajiang and Litang in the large Garze Prefecture, which covers a vast area of western Sichuan Province in western China. Their two main villages are called You Laxi and Xhi Tuoxi. About 2,486 people lived in these villages in 1990.[2] Litang Township lies at an altitude of 4,700 metres (15,400 ft.) above sea level. The Queyu area was formerly part of the Kham Province of Tibet, until it was invaded and incorporated into China in the 1950s. The area has seen many horrific human rights abuses during Chinese rule, with many Tibetans being killed or imprisoned. One source states, 'The Queyu are one of the most unknown of the Qiangic speaking Tibetans. Most Tibetans and Chinese in surrounding counties have never heard of them. It is not known if any foreigners have ever travelled to this extremely remote mountainous area.'[3]

The Queyu have been officially counted as part of the Tibetan nationality, primarily because they follow the Tibetan Buddhist religion. Linguistically, however, the Queyu are closer to the Qiang minority. The Queyu language has four tones.

In the Tuanjie Township of Yajiang County

the people call themselves *Zhaba*, although they speak the same language as the Queyu there. They should not be confused with another Qiangic language group called *Zhaba* who live in the Zhamai District, also within the Garze Prefecture. The Zhaba are profiled separately in this book.

In late 1955, Chinese authorities ordered the monks of the large Litang Monastery to make an inventory of the monastery's possessions for tax assessment. The monks refused to oblige. In February 1956, the People's Liberation Army responded by laying siege to the Litang Monastery. Several thousand monks and farmers, many armed with farm imple-ments, defended the monastery. Chinese aircraft bombed Litang, destroying the monastery and killing hundreds of people. The Tibetans, outraged by the attack, spread the conflict to the surrounding towns of Dege, Batang and Chamdo.[4]

All Queyu profess to be Tibetan Buddhists, although there are also many aspects of shamanism and black magic in their religious practices.

Protestant and Catholic missionaries worked in the Litang area until the early 1950s. Today there is a small Protestant church among the Khampa Tibetans in Litang County,[5] and there are some Catholics in Yajiang.[6] Most people in the area, however, have never heard the name of Christ, and there are no known Queyu believers. The situation has changed little since this report in 1922: 'This region is not only without a resident missionary, but even the scouts of Christianity have barely touched it except at one or two points. . . . What is more serious is the fact that many border mission centres are undermanned or not manned at all.'[7]

Rakhine

Population:
2,123,500 (2000)
2,397,200 (2010)
2,706,600 (2020)

Countries: Myanmar,
Bangladesh, India

Buddhism: Theravada

Christians: 19,100

Overview of the Rakhine

Other Names: Arakanese,
Maghi, Morma, Yakan,
Yakhang, Rakhain, Mogh,
Magh, Marma, Mash, Mag,
Maga, Mugg

Population Sources:
1,900,000 in Myanmar (2002,
Myanmar Faces and Places)

200,000 in Bangladesh (2001,
P Johnstone and J Mandryk)

18,230 in India (1981 census)

Language: Sino-Tibetan,
Tibeto-Burman, Lolo-Burmese,
Burmish, Southern

Dialects: 2 (Marma, Rakhine)

Professing Buddhists: 75%

Practising Buddhists: 50%

Christians: 0.9%

Scripture: Portions 1914

Jesus film: available

Gospel Recordings: Arakanese;
Marma

Christian Broadcasting: none

ROPAL code: MHV

Status of Evangelization

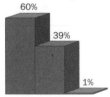

60%

39%

1%

A   B   C

A = Have never heard the gospel
B = Have heard the gospel but have
not become Christians
C = Are adherents to some form of
Christianity

The majority of Rakhine (1.9 million) live in the state of Myanmar that bears their name—Rakhine State—which until recently was also known as Arakan State.[1] They are concentrated in 'hilly, coastal areas, crisscrossed by multiple rivers, including the Lemro and Kaladan. It receives a great amount of rainfall and is largely covered by jungle. . . . The area is fairly sparsely populated, with very few large towns or cities. Sitwe [125,000] is by far the largest city in the area, and also the centre of trade. Other notable towns include Maungdaw, Buthidaung, Mrauk-U, Thandwe and Toung-gok. Otherwise, the population is primarily rural, living in the hills, forests, or along the sea.'[2] Visiting Rakhine State is like stepping back in time. Little has changed in the past 50 years. Motor vehicles are extremely rare, with ox carts and bicycles being the preferred way to get around. In the major city, Sittwe, electricity is only available for five hours (6 to 11 p.m.) every day.

In Bangladesh, more than 200,000 Rakhine live in the Chittagong Hills area in the south-east part of the country. The two dialect groups of Rakhine live separately in Bangladesh. The speakers of the Marma dialect live in the hills, while the Rakhine speakers live along the coast.[3] Approximately 20,000 Rakhine live in Tripura State of north-east India, where they are listed as the *Mag* Scheduled Tribe.[4]

The Rakhine live at the gateway between Southeast Asia and the Indian subcontinent. They have 'long been influenced by their proximity to India and have formed strong trading links with the sub-continent. They claim a long history of independence and ruled their own kingdom at Mrauk-U

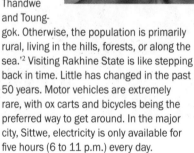

Myanmar Faces and Places

until 1784 AD.'[5] Identifying the Rakhine is a topic of debate. One source asks, 'Are the Rakhine actually Burmese with Indian blood, Indians with Burmese characteristics, or a separate race?'[6]

The Rakhine language is part of the Tibeto-Burman family. It has been described as 'one of the better known varieties of non-standard Burmese with profound pronunciation and vocabulary differences from the Burmese'.[7] In Myanmar about 80 per cent of Rakhine are Buddhists, while the 1981 census of India recorded 98.7 per cent of Rakhine in that country as Buddhists.[8] Theravada Buddhism was reputedly established during the reign of King Chandra Surya in AD 146,[9] as evidenced by their recorded historical books.[10]

Most of the remaining 20 per cent of Rakhine in Myanmar are Muslims, except for a small number of Christians and Hindus. The Muslim Rakhine have a long history of cultural clashes with their Buddhist brothers, often resulting in bloodshed. The most recent fighting took place in April 2001. There are also about 300,000 Rohinga Muslims in the north of Rakhine State, but they are related ethnolinguistically to the Bengalis of Bangladesh and India.

Missionaries translated portions of the Bible into Rakhine in 1914, but these are no longer in use. Less than one per cent of the Rakhine believe in Christ. Almost all of the believers are members of Catholic or Baptist churches. The Rakhine remain a sizeable people group largely forgotten by the Christian world.

More than 30,000 members of the Saek tribe live in central Laos and adjacent areas of north-east Thailand. Approximately 19,000 inhabit the Hinbouan and Grommarol districts of Khammouan Province in Laos, while an additional 11,000 make their home in Thailand's Sakon Nakhon Province.[1] The Saek are not the same as the tribe with a similar-sounding name, the Sach of Laos. The 1,100 Sach people speak a Viet-Muong language. Until about ten years ago linguists believed that the Saek language was part of the Mon-Khmer family, but today they agree that it is part of the Tai-Kadai family. Today most Saek people are bilingual in the national languages of Lao and Thai.[2]

Because they have no written history, finding out where the Saek originated is difficult. According to the Saek's own oral stories, they believe they came from areas of Thua Thien-Hue Province in Vietnam, some distance south of where they live today. This would explain why the Saek language contains some Vietnamese words, even though there are no Saek people left in Vietnam today.[3]

The migrations of the Saek may be explained by the fact they are a peace-loving people. Whenever they had conflict with other tribes they preferred to pack up their meagre possessions and move away rather than to stay and fight. Between 150 and 200 years ago, the Saek first migrated across the Mekong River into Thailand. 'The Saek have a legend about the angel *Ong mu,* which led them from Laos to their new destination in Thailand. *Ong mu* is the most respected supernatural being

Christian Far East Ministry

in Saek beliefs, and the guardian of the village and its inhabitants.'[4]

Although the majority of Saek people are nominally Buddhist, there is a stark difference between those living in Laos, who have less Buddhist influence, and those in Thailand who have Buddhist temples in every sizeable village. One source in Laos states, 'Although they are surrounded by Buddhism, most of the Saek in Laos adhere to their traditional ethnic beliefs [animism]. For example, ancestor worship (praying to deceased ancestors for help and guidance) is a common practice. Because these spirits are thought to cause illness, they have to be appeased through offerings.'[5]

Descriptions of the Saek in Thailand, however, show them to be more orientated towards Buddhism, while retaining their animistic beliefs. 'The Saek are Buddhists and they have pagodas in their villages. In spite of their Buddhist religion, the Saek still believe in spirits. Traditionally they worship their ancestors and make offerings to the guardian spirit of the village, to the house spirit and to several other spirits of the rivers, mountains and trees. Before harvest, the land spirit is appreciated with sacrifices of chicken and wine whisky. The Saek still have shamans, called *moi yau,* who cure sick villages and placate the spirits who cause the sickness.'[6]

The extent of Christianity among the Saek is difficult to gauge, due to their high level of assimilation to neighbouring people groups. There may be a small number of Saek Christians in both Laos and Thailand. Missionaries produced gospel recordings in the Saek language in 1966, but the majority of this tribe has yet to hear the gospel.

Overview of the Saek

Other Names: Sek, Seak, Tai Sek, Tai Set, Set, Xaek, Xek, Xec

Population Sources: 15,000 in Laos (1990, Asian Minorities Outreach)

11,000 in Thailand (2000, J Schliesinger [1995 figure])

Language: Tai-Kadai, Kam-Tai, Be-Tai, Tai-Sek, Sek

Dialects: 2 (Na Kadok, Khammouan)

Professing Buddhists: 55%

Practising Buddhists: 30%

Christians: 0.2%

Scripture: none

Jesus film: none

Gospel Recordings: Saek; Sek; Thai Saek

Christian Broadcasting: none

ROPAL code: SKB

Population:
30,400 (2000)
36,400 (2010)
43,800 (2020)

Countries: Laos, Thailand

Buddhism: Theravada

Christians: 50

Status of Evangelization

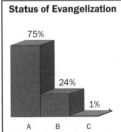

A = 75%
B = 24%
C = 1%

A = Have never heard the gospel
B = Have heard the gospel but have not become Christians
C = Are adherents to some form of Christianity

Samtao

Although more than 12,500 Samtao people are spread over four countries in Southeast Asia, they live primarily within the Mekong River Basin. The region is hot and humid most of the year, with monsoon rains between April and October.

Various sources report widely differing figures for Samtao populations, but most agree that the majority of Samtao live in the eastern part of Shan State in Myanmar, especially in mountain villages north-east of Kengtung City. Several thousand Samtao live in the Xishuangbanna Prefecture in Yunnan Province, China. Estimates of Samtao people in China range from 100[1] to 24,000![2]

The only countries where the number of Samtao people is more certain are Laos (2,213 Samtao according to the 1995 census, living in six villages within Luang Namtha and Bokeo provinces) and Thailand, where just 100 Samtao people inhabit the village of Ban Hin Taek Noc in the Mae Salong District of Chiang Rai Province. They have been in Thailand for at least three generations and have lost contact with Samtao communities in other countries.

The confusion surrounding the classification of the Samtao is due to their many ethnic names and language that has borrowed many words from other varieties. In Myanmar the Samtao were formerly part of an alliance of three tribes: Samtao, Samtuan and Sen Chun.

Regardless of their present status, the Samtao are known to have enjoyed a long and rich history. 'More than two thousand years ago, Han expansion reached Samtao country. By the Tang Dynasty of the seventh and eighth centuries, Samtaos had begun to distinguish themselves ethnically from surrounding peoples, acquiring a sense of group identity based on language and religion.'[3]

Wherever the Samtao have lived, they have absorbed aspects of neighbouring groups. In Laos, practically every aspect of Samtao culture mirrors that of the Lu and Lao. In China the Samtao have assimilated to the predominant Lu and are bilingual in that language.[4] The Lu converted the Samtao to Theravada Buddhism many centuries ago. When missionary William Clifton Dodd visited them in the early 1900s he remarked, 'These Sam Tao are the branch of the aboriginal stock found all over Indo-China. . . . The Sam Tao have been Buddhists for 900 years, and are the best Buddhists we have met.'[5]

Today there are a few Samtao Christians. One source states, 'The primary religion of the Samtao people . . . is nominally Buddhism. Less than one per cent have become Christians. . . . They also believe in spirits inhabiting the surroundings, such as the spirits of the house, the village, the trees, the sky, the forest and others. They also worship their ancestors. Once a year after harvest the Samtao hold an agricultural ceremony. They sacrifice chickens—and when they can afford also pigs—to the mother of rice.'[6]

CHINA
Yunnan

MYANMAR
Shan State

Luang Namtha
Bokeo
LAOS
Chiang Rai

THAILAND

Samtao

Population:
12,600 (2000)
14,400 (2010)
16,500 (2020)

Countries: Myanmar, China, Laos, Thailand

Buddhism: Theravada

Christians: 120

Overview of the Samtao

Other Names: Samtau, Samtuan, Saamtaav, Col, Sam Tao, Sen Chun, Xamtao, Lua

Population Sources: 6,000 in Myanmar (2000, P Hattaway)[7]

4,000 in China (2000, P Hattaway)

2,213 in Laos (1995 census)

100 in Thailand (2000, J Schliesinger [1995 figure])

Language: Austro-Asiatic, Mon-Khmer, Northern Mon-Khmer, Palaungic-Khmuic, Palaungic, Western Palaungic, Angkuic

Dialects: 0

Professing Buddhists: 90%

Practising Buddhists: 50%

Christians: 0.9%

Scripture: none

Jesus film: none

Gospel Recordings: none

Christian Broadcasting: none

ROPAL code: STU (Samtao) and XKO (Kiorr)

Dwayne Graybill

Status of Evangelization

75%

24%

1%

A   B   C

A = Have never heard the gospel
B = Have heard the gospel but have not become Christians
C = Are adherents to some form of Christianity

Behind the White-Washed Walls

Bryan Lurry

Bryan Lurry hails from Irving, Texas. After graduating from the University of North Texas with an accounting degree, he used his skills in Christian service in Asia, where he lived for five years. During this time Bryan came into contact with Shan Theravada Buddhist monks and was afforded the opportunity—over several months—to share the gospel and his life with the monks inside their temple.

Bryan had never received training in how to reach Buddhists, and he knew little of their ways and beliefs. Almost all of his learning was by trial and error. Yet his testimony shows us that there is no substitute for a heart of passion—passion first for the Lord Jesus Christ and passion for people. Many of us view Buddhist monks as mystical, unreachable figures with their long robes, shaven heads and monastic lifestyles. Some Christians may subconsciously view them as figures to be avoided, even demonically inspired religious rivals.

By sharing his life with the monks on their own level, Bryan came to see the monks as they really are—normal young men with desires, hopes, dreams and fears; men who live in desperate need of a personal relationship with the Lord Jesus Christ and who inwardly cry out for spiritual truth. It is hoped that those with a burden to reach Buddhists will learn from Bryan's unique experiences and will never consider Buddhist monks

'off limits' to gospel witness as large parts of the Body of Christ appear to have done through history.

Their idols are silver and gold, made by the hands of men. They have mouths, but cannot speak; eyes, but they cannot see; they have ears, but cannot hear, noses, but they cannot smell; they have hands, but cannot feel, feet, but they cannot walk; nor can they utter a sound with their throats. Those who make them will be like them, and so will all who trust in them. (Psalm 115: 4–8, NIV)

God's new and exciting call

Not long after my arrival in Asia in 1998 I felt the Lord Jesus Christ give me quite an intense burden for the Theravada Buddhist monks and novices that live in numerous temples throughout the city in which I was living. And so I began to visit the temples when time would allow, primarily on the weekends when I had time off work. I rode my bicycle, stopping at each temple along my path. In and around the temples I read Scripture passages, praised God in song and prayed that God would be glorified and known in all places where people do not acknowledge him as Lord.

Though I wanted to share the truth of Jesus Christ directly with these monks and novices, I never could quite make a connection with these

Novice monks leave the temple early in the morning to gather alms from the community.

International Mission Board

men. Why? There were many reasons, I told myself: my language ability was inadequate; these men did not really want to hear about Jesus; and many other such excuses. It was not until January 2000 that circumstances brought me to the point where I needed to make a connection with these mystical monks and novices.

I went through some rough spiritual battles in the beginning, and I soon realized that I had to seek much prayer support from my family and friends back home if I was to continue ministering to Buddhist leaders. Once the prayer support increased, I began to see the Lord work in amazing ways.

During a trip to a temple I met with two young men, a Shan Buddhist monk named Viboon, and a Shan Buddhist layman named Laan. We talked about lots of things, and specifically about a plan that I believed the Lord had given to me. I offered to teach them English each day using Bible stories, and I asked Laan to teach me about Shan Theravada Buddhism. We decided to meet at 10:00 a.m. at the temple the following morning.

This was the true beginning of the research assignment. Little did I realize that later on I would be teaching a regular Bible study, discussing the meaning of life with an abbot who had been shot through the face during his time as a Shan State soldier and going to study Buddhism in a class of 30 monks and novices. Had my eyes been open to what the Lord was going to do, I would never have believed it.

Overcoming external obstacles

Two of the primary obstacles I had to overcome as I commenced this ministry to the monks were the mystical nature of the temples and opposition from pharisees.

I must admit that the temples intimidated me. I saw many items that discouraged me from entering. At some temples, fierce-looking statues of creatures with long fangs and sharp claws guard the entrances. Guarding the main hall of many temples are two large statues of dragons with their multiple heads on either side of the staircase. In addition, images of lions, snakes and creatures that are half-bird and half-man adorn most temples.

If such images were on the outside of the temple, what would I find on the inside? I half imagined that these creatures would somehow come to life and attempt to harm me.

Only through immersing myself in the truth of God's word and through prayerful dependence on the Lord for his strength and protection was I able to overcome my fears and learn to disregard the apparent mystical nature of the temples.

Another obstacle I needed to overcome was that of the pharisees. Having read of Jesus' dealings with the Pharisees, I imagined that they were just a peculiar group of men with long beards and majestic robes. I came to see clearly, however, that the pharisaic spirit is still alive within the Body of Christ and still fighting against the Son of God—just as the Pharisees did two thousand years ago.

The words of Jesus in Matthew 28:18–20 command me, and all Christians, to go into all the world and make disciples of all people. This was my full intention. I wanted to engage with the monks and learn about their religion so that I could effectively share the truth of Jesus Christ with them. It seemed reasonable to me, but evidently it did not seem that way to all Christians.

I was shocked by the negative criticisms I received regarding the work I was doing among these lost people called monks and novices. Perhaps I shouldn't have been surprised, considering how many American Christians still refuse to witness to other races within their own communities.

A pharisee sees no purpose in taking time to study another religion. These people feared that by doing so my mind might be 'polluted' and I might lose my faith in Jesus Christ as the only 'Way, truth and life'. Such an insecure believer in Christ will never be able to effectively reach out to people of other faiths. If a person has such a shallow assurance and knowledge of the truth of Christianity that they fear it will be eroded by the error of another faith, then they would be better to stay at home and seek a personal, intimate relationship with the risen Lord before attempting missionary work. William Booth, the founder of the Salvation Army, once said he wanted to start a Holy Spirit rescue shop a yard from the gates of hell. Such a bold statement only stems from the heart of a believer completely secure in Christ and in his salvation.

I believe that one reason missionaries are making so little impact on the Buddhist world is that we have been too busy preaching and not spending enough time listening to the people to whom we are ministering. I wanted to hear their hearts. Their religion surely identifies their heart. Thus, I needed to help some Christians understand that a believer in Christ need not fear another religion, and that by understanding the other religion a Christian will be better equipped for effective ministry.

It's all about relationship

Another manifestation of the spirit of the Pharisees that I faced was the 'leave those people alone; they're happy just as they are' attitude. It seemed particularly abhorrent to some people—professing Christians included—that someone would try to convert the clergy of one religion over to another religion.

My response was that I didn't want to convert anyone to another 'religion'. To merely influence Buddhists to follow a new set of rules and regulations would be a waste of time. My desire was not that these monks, my friends, would change their religion, but that they would enter into a living, intimate, vibrant personal love affair with the Lord of lords and King of kings, Jesus Christ. I wanted them to find in him all the answers to their deepest questions and longings.

This is the one major difference between true Christianity and Buddhism (or any other religion for that matter): Christianity is a *relationship* with a living, personal God, not a set of dos and don'ts.

Most missionaries and Asian Christians seem to avoid ministry to Buddhist monks, novices and nuns based on their perception that they are somehow more 'evil' than 'normal' people because of their zeal and commitment to Buddhism. The focus of outreach in Buddhist countries, therefore, is on laymen and women. The general thinking is that if a person is so committed to Buddhism that he joined a temple, then he must be much more resistant to the gospel than an individual working in a secular job.

In fact, I found the exact opposite to be true.

Those who do service in Buddhist temples (or mosques, etc.) may actually be the people in their

International Mission Board

Befriending a monk at the temple.

communities who are most open and receptive to the gospel. Perhaps the very act of joining a temple shows that their hearts are searching for truth, whereas many secular people may be more indifferent or closed to hearing the claims of Christ.

By ignoring outreach to the leaders of other religions, we may be missing out on a crucial opportunity to bring Christ to a country or a people group. Jesus always spent time with those religious leaders who were seeking for truth. To Nicodemus, a Pharisee and member of the Jewish ruling council, Jesus personally explained the mystery of salvation (John 3:1–21).

Later, Jesus revealed himself to Saul on the road to Damascus and saved him (Acts 9:1–19). Saul had violently persecuted the church, but this did not deter God from taking Saul's misplaced religious zeal and using it for his glory.

Despite my disappointment that not everyone was as excited as I was about what God was doing among my new Buddhist friends, I continued in the knowledge that he wants all people to know Jesus the Christ, including Theravada Buddhist monks and novices.

Building bridges

Initially I had little information from which to formulate a strategy to share the gospel with Buddhist monks. But, as I learned more about what 'makes them tick', three main bridge-building possibilities presented themselves: English teaching, a Buddhism study and a Bible study.

I was afraid that one or more of these activities might prematurely end, so I reminded myself that these were three distinct bridges, each of which could help me build relationships with the monks.

The first bridge was established when I offered to teach English at the temple. Initially I thought I would have just one student, Laan, who was very excited by my offer. I told him that I would teach from my only curriculum book, a collection of stories taken from the Christian Bible. He did not mind at all and, in fact, was actually pleased. One of his friends had recently become a Christian and he wanted to know more about Christianity. Gradually, more students joined my class.

Each day, from Monday to Friday, I taught for one hour. The stories were short, usually with between five and ten new vocabulary words. The students had to use the new words in a sentence as part of their homework assignment, which took them just a few minutes. I had never taught English before, and this method enabled me to teach without having to spend a lot of time preparing the lessons.

We generally held the classes inside the main hall of the temple, but occasionally we moved to a smaller building if there were too many distractions, such as the arrival of groups of pilgrims, visiting monks from other temples, telephone calls or other interruptions.

No one seemed at all concerned that we were studying the Bible right inside the main hall of a Buddhist temple!

The second bridge I endeavoured to build was my study of Theravada Buddhism. I genuinely wanted to learn all I could so that I would be better able to minister to individuals who follow this religion. This study also gave me a chance to interact with my friends at the temple. I was much more accepted by the monks and novices because I had a purpose for being at the temple. I was a foreigner who was attempting to understand their religion.

As the days and weeks went by I asked them many questions—sometimes perhaps too many. They appreciated and trusted the fact that I was genuinely interested.

The third bridge was Bible study. Initially I thought that I would only be able to share God's word during my English classes, but God had other plans. One day during our English lesson—which had grown to a class of four monks—we read the story of Noah's flood. Laan wrote in his journal, 'I am Buddhist but I want to learn another religion.'

After class, Laan drove me to a local store where we sat down and ordered a couple of Cokes. I told him that I had noticed his interest in Christianity and wondered if he was interested in studying more. I told him I was willing to spend a few hours each

Teaching English to monks in the temple.

I never expected God would give me an opportunity to teach his word right inside a Buddhist temple!

International Mission Board

met a Christian before. Other monks and novices who joined our Bible study over the ensuing weeks knew little or nothing about even the basics of Christianity.

We held our Bible study in the main hall of the temple from 5:30 p.m. to about 7:00 p.m. each evening. We had scheduled the class to finish at this time because monks and novices were required to attend a chanting session back at the temple each day starting at 7:00 p.m. Interestingly, those who attended the Bible study never seemed concerned about returning to the temple in time for the chanting session. Often they missed it altogether.

We began at the very beginning of the Bible with the account of creation. Buddhists have very different beliefs about how the world came into existence, so we had many good discussions about the differences. I was glad that we started there. Only later did I come to realize how difficult it was for the monks to imagine a Creator God who wants to have a relationship with people. I initially thought that I should waste little time getting to the stories about Jesus, so they could understand the gospel. But without laying a foundation for understanding from the Old Testament, the New Testament would have actually meant very little to them. Over the weeks, more and more monks and novices from the temple joined our Bible study until we had quite a sizeable group meeting in a circle on the floor.

We had lots of fun, and I made the class creative so they would enjoy coming. I learned as much from my new friends as they learned from me. Sometimes I asked questions so I could specifically see what their responses would be. For example:

week teaching him the Bible, in addition to our English and Buddhism classes. He said he was indeed interested and wanted to know if a novice monk named Viboon could also study the Bible with us. Holding back my overwhelming joy, I calmly said that I didn't think that would be a problem!

The daily Bible studies

During our very first Bible study it became apparent to me that both Laan and Viboon really wanted to learn about Christianity. They immediately asked the two main questions that most Buddhist monks seem to have: 1. What is the list of rules that Christians must follow? and 2. Why did Jesus die on the cross?

Laan explained that he had several friends who had converted to Christianity, but he knew nothing about their beliefs or faith. Viboon had never even

1. *Was God right to destroy Sodom?* Interestingly, each student stated that God was right to destroy Sodom.

2. *Where was Jesus born?* No one knew, but the guesses included 'heaven' and 'India'.

3. *What is something you like about Christianity?* They all liked the fact that it teaches people to do good deeds.

4. *What is something you don't like about Christianity?* Jao Bu answered that he didn't like the fact that once someone was in hell he had to stay there for ever and had no hope of getting out. Laan disliked the fact that a person only gets one life on earth.

5. *Is there such a thing as Truth?* They all agreed that there are many truths, not just one.

Our Bible studies were not without problems. The fact that they were held right inside the temple caused a stir. Often visitors came and went through the main hall. Occasionally someone would stop, become involved in our study, and argue. Once a monk from the neighbouring temple saw our Bible study in progress and decided to join in. He proceeded to light his cigarette and tell me that a Buddhist does not need the help of Jesus Christ or the Holy Spirit because a Buddhist can control himself to the point that he will not sin. I found his claims to be quite ironic, spoken through the smoky haze as he puffed on his cigarette.

Revealing answers

Meanwhile, the English classes continued every day in the temple. One day I sensed that the students were getting a little bored, so I asked them some fun questions to stimulate conversation. Such a light-hearted approach is often the best way to remove tension and to get a glimpse into a person's heart. Some of the questions I asked were:

1. *If you had a million dollars, what would you do?* Jao Bu said he would give some of the money to the temple and use the rest to travel the world and build a house. Laan replied that he would give some of the money to his mother, some to impoverished schools in Shan State (Myanmar) and would use some to travel to America and experience democracy.

2. *If you knew you had only 24 hours left to live, what would you do and what would you choose for your last meal?* Jao Bu said he would pray for two hours about his next life and would then travel to visit his daughter. He would eat bread and drink milk for his last meal.

Laan said he would visit all his friends for one last time and then would get himself a large pizza.

3. *If you could change* one *thing about yourself, what would it be?* Jao Bu said he would like to be stronger and taller. He would also change his nose so it would be like my big nose and would have white skin.

Laan also said that he would rather have white skin.

Viboon cheekily said that he would have five additional wives like Jao Bu (before joining the temple, Jao Bu had indeed been married to six women at one time).

4. *Why did you become a Buddhist monk or novice?* Viboon said that because his mother breastfed him when he was a baby, it was best to enter the temple to 'repay' her for her kindness. She was gaining merit for his obedience in becoming a novice, and he was gaining merit because Gautama Buddhist said it was good to obey your parents. Viboon now felt that he could not leave the temple, because his parents had decided he should stay. He will not have the opportunity to make his own decision while they are alive.

The strong influence of parents in the Shan culture was evident in so many ways. I once asked whose parents followed Buddha's teaching correctly. They said that all of them do, and that none of their parents sinned.

5. *What is the most difficult Buddhist teaching to follow?* Viboon said that it was the rules that prohibit monks from eating dinner. Jao Bu said the path to achieving *nirvana* was too difficult, while Laan said the prohibition against drinking alcohol was the most difficult Buddhist teaching to obey.

6. *Are there any reasons why you would consider leaving the temple?* I was quite surprised and shocked when my students expressed their desire to leave the temple in order to be soldiers in the Shan Independence Army, which has been fighting the Burmese military for decades. They didn't see a contradiction in the fact that, as monks, they are literally not supposed to kill a mosquito, much less another human being.

These men, despite being clothed in robes of the priestly class, still have a strong patriotic desire to be part of the force that wins military and political freedom for their people from the 'oppressive' Burmese. Laan bluntly told me, 'I hate the Burmese because they rape and kill my people.'

Laan later left the temple, moved away and became a soldier in the Shan Independence Army. His desire came to fruition.

One day Viboon announced that he didn't want to be a novice any longer but the abbot, who raised Viboon, didn't want him to leave the temple. Viboon was also concerned because he knew his leaving would hurt his mother, so he decided to stay on for the time being. Viboon procured a monk / novice identity card from Thailand that allowed him to travel anywhere. What he really wanted to do was to move to Bangkok, get a job and earn lots of money.

Later, Viboon also told me that if he gave up being a novice and became a Christian, he could never go back and become a monk. It was interesting that he was thinking such things, contemplating becoming a Christian, when I had never mentioned such a scenario before.

must make a pilgrimage. I explained how a Tibetan Buddhist person would make a pilgrimage by prostrating himself from his home all the way to Lhasa, sometimes a distance of hundreds of miles. This surprised them, and they commented that Tibetan Buddhism was obviously a strict religion. The Theravada Buddhist monks do not need to make pilgrimages, except perhaps to visit all of the temples in the area from time to time. Neither do they prostrate themselves before images of Buddha.

When asked if they ever took a vow of silence, they said that a vow of silence is common in the Buddhist religion, but that the monks and novices at their temple don't practise it. When I asked why

As time went by, I developed close friendships with some of the monks.

Daily practices of the monks

Observing normal temple life was one of my main sources of information about Theravada Buddhism. I found many of their daily practices deeply interesting, and some were very surprising.

The local people provide food for the meals of the monks and novices. However, I also saw monks use personal money to purchase snacks. Once I saw the abbot eating ice cream after the noon hour and asked Viboon why he was allowed to eat after noon (which monks are prohibited to do). Viboon responded that ice cream does not qualify as food and therefore can be eaten at any time. This also applies to fruit, nuts and seeds.

One day I asked if Theravada Buddhist monks

they didn't participate in this practice they simply said that it was impossible to do and that all of the novices would 'faint' if they tried.

I was somewhat surprised to find that the monks did not believe that Gautama Buddha taught people not to eat meat. They claimed that he did not prohibit meat, although it was good to be a vegetarian if possible. Though a monk or novice cannot kill an animal, if someone else kills one and offers it to the temple, the monks can eat the meat without any sense of guilt. They also said that if a monk makes a vow not to eat certain meat, and then does so, he does wrong. A 'being' in hell will record his offence, which can only be wiped off the record when the monk performs enough good deeds to offset the sin.

Novices are always required to wear their robes, even while taking a shower and when sleeping. Monks are allowed to remove their robes for up to three days. There are 227 rules that monks must follow concerning their robes—how to wash them, iron them and so on.

All of the monks and novices are required to shave their heads once a month, in obedience to Gautama Buddha's teaching. In Thailand I noticed that monks also shaved their eyebrows, while in other Southeast Asian countries they didn't. My friends explained that Thai monks had an interesting historical reason for shaving their eyebrows. When Myanmar was at war with Thailand, Myanmar would send spies, posing as Buddhist monks, to gain information. The Thai monks began to shave their eyebrows so that the false Burmese monks would be easy to catch. The rule has remained to this day.

I found that the monks and novices had a very shallow knowledge of Buddhist teachings. Once when I asked questions about Buddhism and the reasons for certain practices, my friends showed me their book with a reference number attached to a certain subject. When I asked what the number meant, they said it referred back to a place in the *Tripitaka*—the summary teaching book of Buddhist rules and practices. When I asked if we could trace the reference back and look at the original text we tried, but to no avail. They just didn't understand how the reference system worked, as they had never even looked at the *Tripitaka*. I couldn't understand how they could simply not care about their own god's words, and I shared my frustration with them. It seemed to me that they accepted almost every Buddhist teaching based on tradition rather than conviction.

Inner freedom or a religious prison?

During our discussions it became apparent that my friends would all seriously consider leaving the temple if an opportunity for love and marriage should arise. The more I got to know these men, the more I realized how 'normal' they truly are. They struggle with desires and temptations like young men anywhere, and they have deep-seated ambitions to experience all that life has to offer. Years of suppressing their desires didn't help to remove them. If anything, the continual effort they expended in pushing desire down into their hearts only fanned the flames of temptation, making them even more curious about those things they were forbidden to experience. It's no wonder that many high-ranking Buddhist monks have fallen into sexual scandal and other sins in recent years. It is clear that the only way for a person to overcome sin and temptation is through the blood of Jesus Christ, and not by human effort and obeying laws and regulations. The same principle applies to all people, regardless of their religion or creed—recent scandals in the Roman Catholic priesthood around the world testify to this truth.

Only Jesus can set people free from the power of sin and death.

As I met with my friends at the temple every day and got to know them well, it dawned on me that these monks and novices are basically living in a prison. Following are some of the similarities I observed between this Buddhist temple and a prison:

I showed the 'Jesus' film to the monks right inside the temple. Here is the scene where Christ is crucified, showing his love for all people, including these precious young Buddhists.

International Mission Board

- Separation from society
- Limited visits from friends and family
- Possible transfers to another facility (temple)
- Care and funding by society
- Frequent difficulty reintegrating into society
- Prevalence of homosexuality
- Boredom
- Excessive television watching
- Bad food
- No privacy
- Silent periods
- Opportunity to reform
- Daily chores
- Communal meals
- Facing a trial
- Coming judgement day

The monks and novices are generally dissatisfied. Why is this? They have the perfect opportunity to follow Buddha's teaching. They have few distractions to prevent them living out what Buddha desired for himself and for all people. The cares of their world are few, yet they are not satisfied.

I believe they are dissatisfied because they have yet to discover truth. If ever there was a segment of society that wanted and needed to be free, it is these Buddhist monks and novices. *So if the Son sets you free, you will be free indeed'* (John 8:36, NIV).

A motley crew

Viboon and I took a stroll one day around the idols in the temple. He told me that every idol there represented a spirit that had been unable to achieve *nirvana* but had at one time been a person living in the world. I asked how idols are produced, as many of them have grotesque expressions of violence and fury. It was difficult for him to clearly explain, but he said that when a man has a dream or vision inspired by a spirit, the man will have the inspiration to make an idol of that being. He writes a magic spell on a piece of aluminium, rolls it up and places it inside the idol. A ceremony with chanting will then take place, to 'ordain' the idol. At that point the idol is believed to possess power and can affect a person.

One Tuesday, our discussion got somewhat touchy as the Bible story for the day was about worshipping idols and false gods. How was I to explain that the Bible was including Buddhists in this group? I explained it as sensitively as I could, but I got the point across. Laan did a lot of laughing

at my attempts to explain it sensitively because he understood exactly what the passage meant!

I shared my testimony and told my students that I had been attempting to follow God's commandments for 31 years and had not been successful. I further explained that God had thankfully provided a substitute for me, the sacrifice of Jesus Christ, to satisfy God's high standard. As carefully as I knew how, I explained that I could now enter heaven because Christ died for my sins. They still questioned why I wouldn't like to come back for a second spin in the world (reincarnation). I told them that when I die I will be in heaven worshipping God for all eternity and will have no desire to come back to this world.

They seemed to understand, but I felt so frustrated by my inability to really explain fully with my lips what was exploding inside my heart. May God forgive my inability! As I lay down on my bed that night I prayed that the Holy Spirit would take his word and convict their hearts of their need for Jesus.

Once I taught them what it means for a Christian to 'pray'. I explained that a believer in Christ can pray anywhere, at any time, and is actually talking with the Creator God. They balked at the thought. I said, 'Fine. I'm not asking you to believe that God is listening. I'm just simply telling you what a Christian believes is happening when he prays.' This whole concept is so strange to Buddhist monks that they usually just dismiss it as foolish talk.

Before I went to the temple for the first time, a Christian friend encouraged me to consider the religious passion of the Buddhist people while ministering to them.

After about four months, I had come to see that the monks and novices are a motley crew, brought together for various reasons, from various places, all with different expectations and hopes for the future. I discovered that these monks, at least in this particular temple, had little or no passion at all for Buddhism. None of them had any interest in living a devout life pursuing religious truths. The single most passionate thing about these specific monks and novices was their mutual hatred of the Burmese.

I am not implying that all monks are like the ones in this temple that I had befriended, but it did make me wonder.

During one Bible lesson we read about the miracle of Jesus turning water into wine. They

The happiest I ever saw my friends: eating pizza at my house!

understood the story but seemed quite unimpressed. They told me about a monk living in Shan State who could perform the same miracle whenever he wanted to. Laan had met a man who could levitate off the ground, and a woman who went into trances and told the future. Oh, how Satan has confused things!

I realized that telling about miracles in the Bible was not the most effective method of reaching the Shan people. Unlike the sceptical Western world, which says, 'Show us a miracle and we'll believe,' the Shan already knew about the reality of the supernatural world. How, then, could I find a way to share Christ's reality with them?

As I continued to work with the monks I grew to love them very much. It hurt me to see them lost, drifting in a sea of lies and sin. I just wanted to show them that I cared and wanted them to know the truth. They have not received much out of this life besides hurt, pain and anger.

When I attended a friend's wedding in another city, I left the temple for several days. During these days I missed my friends at the temple and realized we had grown quite close during our time together.

Surprisingly, my friends expressed the same feeling when I returned to the temple. They had missed me.

I wanted to know what they had missed. Was it the English classes? The Bible studies? They helped me to understand that it was the love and acceptance I showed them that they had missed. They receive little genuine love and friendship from their parents, friends or other monks and novices.

I came to understand that if a Christian, regardless of nationality or ethnicity, is able to love people such as these Buddhist monks because of the love of God in his or her heart, they will respond favourably. The language of love is an internationally recognized language.

Social outings

One day Laan had a question for me. While I was away he had been reading the Bible and had a question. Since I was unavailable he decided to visit a lady named Jane. She is a seamstress who attends church. When Laan asked her a question about the Bible she scolded him for reading his Bible. She said that it was not his religion, and he shouldn't be asking questions.

The 'Pharisees' were still around! I couldn't believe it—a person who claimed to be a Christian was scolding a 'seeker' for reading the Bible and trying to find some answers.

Over the following weeks I grew even closer to the monks, especially the three who had faithfully attended the classes from the very beginning. It was also one of the most personally trying times in my Christian life. Why? Because I had told three young Buddhist monks that if they sought the Lord with all their hearts they would find him. I was trying desperately to hold on to God's promises and to have faith that God would fulfil the promise in these three young men's lives. I have a desire to see them set free, but I cannot imagine the desire that God must have to see them set free.

About a month before I ended my ministry at the temple I was given a copy of the *Jesus* film in the Shan language. I began to consider what an effective tool the video could be in helping the monks and novices come to a saving faith in Christ.

The abbot of the temple gave permission to show the film in the temple, saying it would be good for educational purposes. About twenty monks and novices sat through the entire production from start to finish. During the film as Jesus taught I heard many exclamations of 'oh' as the Buddhist watchers apparently agreed with his teachings.

Towards the end of the movie, during the crucifixion scene, I noticed Viboon draw his knees up to his chest and let out some sounds of pain and anguish as the nails were hammered into Jesus' hands and feet.

After the movie finished most of the monks and novices stood up, turned around and walked away. This was to be expected, as they are not supposed

Serving hungry bodies and hungry souls.

International Mission Board

to show any emotion. Three of my closest friends, however, gave me feedback. Nong simply gave me the thumbs up, showing that he appreciated the film. Jao Bu said that it was an excellent film, while Sombat said that he now understood more clearly the life of Jesus.

Although I can't report any great rush of conversions because of the movie, I knew that the seed of God's word was sown deeply into the hearts of these men, and that in due time a harvest would be reaped.

I wonder what heaven thought that night, as twenty monks who many in the Christian world consider to be 'un–reachable' watched and heard a portrayal of the life of Jesus Christ right on the wall of their Buddhist temple.

Easter arrived, and I wanted to do something special to celebrate with my friends. I decided to have a pizza party at my home for those monks and novices who wanted to come. On Good Friday I invited them to come over for lunch. Nine monks and novices, including the abbot, arrived and we enjoyed pizza—the first time for many of them. It was exciting to see them take a ball of sticky rice and then eat the rice and pizza together. We had a wonderful time of laughter and fun, as the monks unwound and relaxed away from the strict atmosphere of the temple.

After the meeting I presented each one with a copy of the Gospel of John in Shan. They all took the gifts reverently and promised to read from chapter 17 to the end, to learn the meaning of Good Friday and Easter.

After four months of spending time with my friends I had grown quite attached. As the days flew quickly by, I realized I would soon have to leave and would miss them terribly. On my last day, I invited my four closest friends on an excursion. We drove a four-wheel drive pick-up into the remote countryside. After driving for about an hour we had to cross a swollen river that had risen due to heavy rain the previous day. After several futile attempts to drive across we realized it was impossible, so we all

got out of the vehicle and considered our options. We waded out into the water to see how deep it was. My two best friends at the temple pulled up their robes, making shorts, and followed.

When the water rose to near waist-high I playfully splashed my friends. The next thing I knew, the monks started a full-on water fight and we were all drenched! How we laughed and laughed!

Reflections on a special time

This experience in the river will remain as one of my abiding memories of my special time with my Buddhist friends. This was the time when I fully understood that despite their orange robes, shaven heads and very different vocations, these young men were just like me. They just wanted to live life to the full, to love and to laugh.

At the beginning of my adventure I considered Buddhist monks to be mystical, and even somewhat intimidating, figures. For some special reason, God has allowed us this unique opportunity to bond.

I left that part of the world and returned to America to continue my studies for a time, until the Lord moves me on to my next assignment. I arranged for a local pastor to follow up the seed that had been sown in the lives of those young men, which he eagerly did.

* * *

Thank you for letting me share some of my experiences with you. I hope that Christians will never again consider Buddhist monks to be unapproachable. I pray that they will no longer be overlooked, and that efforts will be specifically focused on winning this people group to Jesus Christ.

I have shared some of my friendships with men such as Laan, Viboon, Jao Bu and others, but they are just a few precious souls in one temple nestled in the hills of Southeast Asia. In the next valley are more temples, with more spiritually hungry young men, men with whom Jesus longs to enter into a relationship.

Hundreds of thousands of Buddhist monks and novices live scattered throughout Asia, trapped inside temples of silver and gold. Each one is a precious soul to the Lord Jesus Christ.

Who will go and reach them?

The 3.4 million Shan people are one of the most prestigious of the Tai groups in Southeast Asia. They are concentrated throughout the state that bears their name—Shan State—in north-east Myanmar.[1] For a generation, the Shan Independence Army has fought against the Burmese military in a bid to gain independence. Thousands have died, but the Shan appear no closer to their goal than they were at the beginning of their struggle.

The Shan in Myanmar are the descendants of a large group who migrated southward from China in the 12th century. There are still many people in China today who are ethnically related to the Shan—such as the Tai Mao and Tai Nua—but research has shown that there is just one village remaining in China today whose inhabitants speak the same language as the Shan of Myanmar.[2] The Shan call themselves *Tai Yay*—meaning 'Great Tai'.[3]

Over the years many Shan have migrated across the border into northern Thailand, where today they number more than 60,000 people in the provinces of Chiang Rai, Chiang Mai and Mae Hong Son. A small group of Shan lives on the other side of Thailand in Mukdahan Province near the Thai-Lao border.

The Shan language is part of the large Tai linguistic family.[4] Southern Shan was traditionally written using a script similar to Burmese, 'which does not distinguish tone or some vowels'.[5]

The Shan have been firm believers in Theravada Buddhism almost since its introduction in Myanmar in the 5th century AD. Today more than 99 per

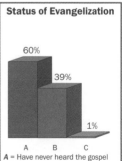

Myanmar Faces and Places

cent of Shan people are Buddhists. 'Gold-coloured temples are scattered throughout the jungles and mountains of Shan State. All Shan community life is centred around their religion. Unlike most Buddhists who believe in *karma*, the Shan believe they are protected from evil by the spiritual power of Buddha idols and spirits.'[6]

Traditionally each Shan family has sent at least one son to a temple at the age of seven or eight, where they receive both a secular and religious education from the Buddhist monks.

Missionaries first started reaching out to the Shan in 1860. They worked hard at translating the Scriptures into Shan. They first published portions of the Bible in 1871, followed by the New Testament in 1882 and the whole Bible in 1892.[7] The script that the missionaries used was the Burmese-like orthography, which most Shan believers today do not like. Several years ago a new Shan Bible, using a modern-day script, was published.

Historically, few Shan have responded to the gospel even though there are many vibrant churches in Shan State among other ethnic groups. The Shan tend to look down on their tribal neighbours, which creates a barrier of acceptance when the gospel is preached to them. In recent years, however, some encouraging breakthroughs have appeared among the Shan in Myanmar and among Shan refugees in Thailand. God has used tools such as gospel radio broadcasts in Shan and the Shan *Jesus* film to expose many thousands of Shan people to the message of eternal life for the first time.

Overview of the Shan

Population:
3,260,500 (2000)
3,663,000 (2010)
4,115,000 (2020)
Countries: Myanmar, Thailand, China, USA
Buddhism: Theravada
Christians: 30,000

Other Names: Tai Yai, Tai Yay, Sha, Tai Shan, Sam, Thai Yai, Thai Yay, Great Thai, Tai Luang, Ngio, Ngiow, Ngiaw, Ngiao, Ngeo, Niou, Ngiou, Ngieo, Nyaw, Sham, Sen, Tai Jai, Burmese Shan

Population Sources: 3,200,000 in Myanmar (2001, P Johnstone and J Mandryk)
60,000 in Thailand (2001, P Johnstone and J Mandryk)
500 in China (2000, P Hattaway)
also in USA and probably other Western nations

Language: Tai-Kadai, Kam-Tai, Be-Tai, Tai-Sek, Tai,

Southwestern, East Central, Northwest
Dialects: 0
Professing Buddhists: 95%
Practising Buddhists: 65%
Christians: 0.9%
Scripture: Bible 1892; New Testament 1882; Portions 1871
Jesus film: available
Gospel Recordings: Shan
Christian Broadcasting: available
ROPAL code: SJN

Status of Evangelization

60%
39%
1%

A   B   C
A = Have never heard the gospel
B = Have heard the gospel but have not become Christians
C = Are adherents to some form of Christianity

Sherdukpen

CHINA
Xizang (Tibet)

Arunachal Pradesh

INDIA

MYANMAR

Sherdukpen

Population:
3,040 (2000)
3,540 (2010)
4,130 (2020)
Countries: India
Buddhism: Tibetan
Christians: 20

Overview of the Sherdukpen

Other Names: Ngnok

Population Sources:

2,952 in India (1991 census)

Language: Sino-Tibetan, Tibeto-Burman, Himalayish, Tibeto-Kanauri, Tibetic, Tibetan, Unclassified

Dialects: 2 (Thungjee Ngnok, Sanjee Ngook)

Professing Buddhists: 98%

Practising Buddhists: 90%

Christians: 0.7%

Scripture: none

Jesus film: none

Gospel Recordings: none

Christian Broadcasting: none

ROPAL code: SDP

Status of Evangelization

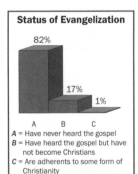

82%

17%

1%

A   B   C

A = Have never heard the gospel
B = Have heard the gospel but have not become Christians
C = Are adherents to some form of Christianity

Approximately 3,000 Sherdukpen people inhabit the Bomdila Subdivision of the West Kameng District of Arunachal Pradesh in north-east India. The three main villages are Rupa,[1] Shergaon and Jigaon. The 1971 census figure returned 1,635 Sherdukpen. This increased to 2,096 by the 1981 census and to 2,952 in 1991. A small number of Sherdukpen have moved down to the Assam plains.

The Sherdukpen language is part of the Kanauri branch of the Tibeto-Burman family. There are dialect differences between the Sherdukpen spoken in different villages. The dialect spoken by the inhabitants of Rupa village is called Thungjee Ngnok, while the other main dialect is called Sanjee Ngook.[2] The Sherdukpen culture and language are strange in that they are quite distinct from the other Tibeto-Burman varieties in Arunachal Pradesh. This suggests that this group migrated into the area from far away.

The Sherdukpen's oral history says that 'they originated from the marriage of a Tibetan prince with a princess of Assam, possibly of Kachari origin'.[3] Some scholars have thought that the Sherdukpen and some of the Monpa living in the Kameng District originated in eastern Bhutan because of the many cultural similarities that these groups share. Today, visitors to the region can easily identify the Sherdukpen because their dress is totally different from that of other peoples. The men's dress consists of a shawl, waist belt, jacket and a cap made of yak's hair. The Sherdukpen women wear a white cotton or silk gown called a *sinka*.

Dwayne Graybill

Buddhism first came to the Sherdukpen in the mid-1700s. The strength of Buddhist belief among this group can be seen from figures returned in the 1981 census, when 2,087 out of the 2,096 Sherdukpen people declared themselves Buddhists. The remaining nine individuals included a few who said they were Hindus, and some who filled their form out incorrectly!

The Buddhist lamas, known as *chize*, double as shaman priests among the Sherdukpen. They perform weddings and funerals and act as mediators between the spirit world and the community. Before a wedding can take place, a suitable bride price must be negotiated between the families of the bride and groom. The groom's family must come up with an acceptable form of payment to compensate the bride's family for all the years of expense and effort they spent in raising the girl. Traditionally, the bride price is 'two sheep, two yaks and a piece of *endi* cloth [a shawl]. . . . The most common form of marriage is a negotiated arranged one. The parents of both the boy and the girl arrange the marriage. The girl is ritually eloped by the boy's parents and their relatives. These days love marriages are increasing in number.'[4] After the bride price has been settled, a Buddhist lama is called in to consult the horoscopes to determine the best time and day for the wedding to take place.[5]

For countless centuries the Sherdukpen people, few in number yet unique, lived and died without any knowledge of the gospel. The 1991 census returned just 13 Sherdukpen people who declared themselves as Christians.

The Sherpa, despite being a relatively small group, are one of the most well-known peoples of Asia. Approximately 80,000 Sherpa inhabit both sides of the Himalayan Range. The majority live in India, where more than 45,000 live primarily in the Darjeeling District of West Bengal and in the states of Sikkim and Arunachal Pradesh.[1]

More than 30,000 Sherpa live in Nepal, especially in the Solu Khumbu District and around the famous town of Namche Bazaar.[2] An additional 3,000 live in Bhutan. In Tibet, the exact Sherpa population is uncertain. Various publications have listed 'a mere 400',[3] '800 speakers in China'[4] and 'no more than 1,000'.[5] The Sherpa in Tibet inhabit parts of Dinggye, Tingri and Zhangmu counties. Tingri County is directly on the road from Kathmandu to Lhasa, a route frequented by many tour groups during the summer months. Small numbers of Sherpa have dispersed to South Korea and the USA in recent years. These numbers do not include the Helambu Sherpa, who speak a different language. The Helambu Sherpa have been profiled separately in this book.

The name *Sherpa* means 'eastern people'. It is believed that all Sherpa once lived in Tibet before their descendants migrated west in the 15th century. 'At that time, a Mongol King attempted to force them to convert to his sect of Buddhism. The people fled to the Khumbu region.'[6] A Chinese account states, 'They believe themselves to be descendants of Tibetans from the Kham region in

Nancy Sturrock

Sichuan Province. Many, many years ago, their ancestors, returning from a pilgrimage to Buddhist temples in India and Nepal, settled down here.'[7] The Sherpa are distinguishable from Tibetans 'in part because their faces are smaller and they wear a colourful apron on their backside rather than the front'.[8]

Because the Sherpa language is related to Tibetan, most can communicate in a simple form of Tibetan.[9] Few of the 20,000 Sherpa in the Darjeeling area of India are still able to speak Sherpa.[10]

For many, the name Sherpa is inextricably linked to the mystique of Mount Everest, the highest mountain on earth. The first men to climb Mount Everest were New Zealander Sir Edmund Hillary and Sherpa Tenzing Norgay in 1953. Numerous Sherpa guides have since led foreign climbing teams up the world's highest peak.[11]

The Sherpa are Tibetan Buddhists, although 'with far less piety than the Tibetans. To have . . . a Buddhist statue and to recite or chant scriptures is all they do by way of religious practice.'[12] The *Gyawa* festival takes place 49 days after the death of a loved one. The Sherpa eat as much food as they can during the festival, believing that the food will nourish the loved one who has died.

In 1985, a Sherpa boy in Nepal had a vision in which Jesus visited him. The boy's conversion was followed by the gradual conversion of his extended family and several families in his village. The boy later went to Bible school and returned to pastor the local church in his village.[13] There are reported to be at least a few dozen Christian Sherpas around the Mt Everest region in Nepal.[14]

Overview of the Sherpa

Other Names: Sharpa, Sharpa Bhotia, Xiaerba, Serwa, Xiarba

Population Sources:
45,400 in India (2001, FMC South Asia)
30,000 in Nepal (2000, B Grimes [1998 figure])[15]
3,000 in Bhutan (1995, *Languages of Bhutan*)
800 in China (1996, B Grimes [1994 figure])
also in South Korea and USA

Language: Sino-Tibetan, Tibeto-Burman, Himalayish, Tibeto-Kanauri, Tibetic, Tibetan, Southern

Dialects: 3 (Solu, Khumbu, Ramechaap)

Professing Buddhists: 98%

Practising Buddhists: 90%

Christians: 0.1%

Scripture: Portions 1977; work in progress

Jesus **film:** available

Gospel Recordings: Sherpa: Solu

Christian Broadcasting: none

ROPAL code: SCR

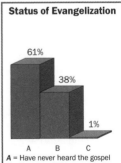

Status of Evangelization

61%

38%

1%

A B C

A = Have never heard the gospel
B = Have heard the gospel but have not become Christians
C = Are adherents to some form of Christianity

Population:
79,650 (2000)
95,400 (2010)
114,300 (2020)
Countries: India, Nepal, Bhutan, China, South Korea, USA
Buddhism: Tibetan
Christians: 40

Shixing

A 1983 report listed 2,000 speakers of the Shixing (pronounced 'sher-shing') language in China, 'living along the fast-flowing Shui Luo River and its downstream tributary, the Chongtian River',[1] in the First District of Muli County in southern Sichuan Province.

This group is one of the most remote and isolated people groups in the world. One prayer guide states, 'They live a good six days' travel from Chengdu and the only foreigners that have travelled here are linguists and a few professional mountain climbers. . . . The few people who have travelled there for research travel from Muli City. It takes one day of riding a bus on a terrible road, and two days of travelling by horse and foot.'[2] Mountain trails leading to the Shixing villages rise to an altitude of 4,680 metres (15,000 ft.). One early visitor to the area described the remarkable variation in terrain: 'We found the stifling heat in the gorges of the Shou Chu next to unbearable, especially as we passed from cool forest regions to a temperature of over 100° Fahrenheit within a couple of hours. . . . We found wild flowers, anemones, blue poppies and many primroses of all colours, forming a veritable carpet of exquisite designs.'[3]

The name *Shixing* means 'iron people'. The Northern Pumi call their Shixing neighbours *Xumi,* or *Sumu*. Recently the Shixing language has been found to belong to the Qiangic linguistic branch. When explorer Joseph Rock visited the Shixing in 1930, he remarked that their language 'seems to be a mixture of Nashi [Naxi], Tibetan and Hsifan [Northern Pumi]; yet it is not understood by any of the three'.[4]

The area inhabited by the Shixing has a long and rich history. Their villages are 'guarded by watchtowers erected by powerful Naxi kings several hundred years ago'.[5] The Naxi's interest in the region may have been due to the abundance of gold once found in the Shui Luo River. The great Naxi king, Mutien Wang, extensively mined the river.[6]

The Shixing live isolated lives farming rice and maize on thin strips of land leading down to the river. Their villages are 'peculiar conglomerations of huts built one against the other, with flat roofs, permitting one to step from house to house over the entire village'.[7]

All Shixing are Tibetan Buddhists; they were converted centuries ago. Outside many of their homes one will find *mani* piles (pyramids of white stones) that are engraved with the sacred Tibetan prayer, *Om mani padme hum*—'Hail the Jewel of the Lotus'. In the past the Shixing lived under the rule of the Northern Pumi king in Muli and his powerful religious rulers.

The Muli region in south-west Sichuan Province is one of the most gospel-neglected places on earth. No missionaries are known to have worked there in the past. There has never been a known believer or Christian fellowship among this group. The nearest believers to the Shixing are some minority Christians in northern Yunnan, but they are still a considerable distance away over some of the most remote terrain in the world.[8]

Population:
2,780 (2000)
3,430 (2010)
4,200 (2020)
Countries: China
Buddhism: Tibetan
Christians: none known

Overview of the Shixing

Other Names: Shihing, Shuhin, Xumi, Shishing, Sumu

Population Sources:
2,000 in China (1983, Sun Hongkai)

Language: Sino-Tibetan, Tibeto-Burman, Tangut-Qiang, Qiangic

Dialects: 0

Professing Buddhists: 100%

Practising Buddhists: 45%

Christians: 0%

Scripture: none

***Jesus* film:** none

Gospel Recordings: none

Christian Broadcasting: none

ROPAL code: SXG

China Advocate

Status of Evangelization

98%

2% 0%

A B C

A = Have never heard the gospel
B = Have heard the gospel but have not become Christians
C = Are adherents to some form of Christianity

Approximately 30,000 Sikkimese people inhabit all four districts of Sikkim, but they are concentrated in North Sikkim District near the Chinese border. 'They live in hilly terrain, of high altitude and cold climate, where there is high rainfall with medium snowfall and high humidity with dense forests.'[1] A migrant community of Sikkimese has moved down into the Darjeeling District of West Bengal. The 1981 census in India returned 22 Sikkimese Bhotia people living in Tripura State.

The Sikkimese are among the most complicated Buddhist groups profiled in this book. The Indian government has granted 'Scheduled Tribe' status to the 'Bhotia' tribe, but this is 'a generic term for several groups of people inhabiting the ranges along the snowy peaks of the Himalayas'.[2] The term Bhotia comes from *Bhot*, or *Bod*, the traditional name for people of Tibetan origin. The groups combined by the Indian authorities include many different ethnicities and languages, ranging from Jammu and Kashmir in north-west India all the way across to Arunachal Pradesh in north-east India.[3] In what follows here we are referring to people in the state of Sikkim who now have a sense of common identity and who speak the Sikkimese language.[4] These groups include 'the Chumipa (people from the Chumbi valley), Dhopthapa (inhabitants of Dhopta), Trompa or Do-mu-pa (inhabitants of Do-mu), Lachengpa (people of Lacheng valley) and Lachungpa (people of Lachung valley)'.[5] The Drukpa (people who originated in Bhutan) living in Sikkim are often considered part of this group, but

we have profiled the Drukpa separately in this book. The various ethnic segments of the Sikkimese migrated into the state at various times throughout history, including a recent influx of refugees from Tibet since the Chinese occupation in the 1950s. People from all different communities come together to celebrate Buddhist festivals and holidays, which creates good unity and relationships between them.

The Sikkimese language is part of the Tibeto-Burman family. It shares 65 per cent lexical similarity with Dzongkha of Bhutan and just 42 per cent with Tibetan.[6]

Being of Tibetan origin, it is not surprising that the Sikkimese people strongly believe in Tibetan Buddhism. The 1981 census returned 98.21 per cent of Sikkimese Bhotia as followers of Buddhism, 1.42 per cent as Hindus, 0.34 per cent as Christians and the rest as Muslims.

Today approximately 200 Sikkimese have believed in Jesus Christ—just 0.7 per cent of their population. About 100 Sikkimese Christians live inside Sikkim, while others live in the heavily-evangelized Darjeeling area in West Bengal. Some of those who have decided to follow Christ have been excommunicated from their villages. One source states, 'The Sikkimese Bhotia have portions of the Bible available in their own language, and there are eight missions agencies currently targeting them. Intercession and increased missions efforts are still needed. The small number of believers (about 1 per cent) need discipleship materials to encourage and strengthen them in their Christian walk.'[7]

(photo credit, vertical) Dwayne Graybill

CHINA
Xizang (Tibet)

Sikkim

BHUTAN

NEPAL

INDIA

Sikkimese

Population:
28,600 (2000)
33,300 (2010)
38,900 (2020)
Countries: India
Buddhism: Tibetan
Christians: 200

Overview of the Sikkimese

Other Names: Sikkim Bhotia, Sikkimese Bhotia, Sikkim Bhutia, Dandzongka, Danjongka, Danyouka, Denjonbg, Denjongkha, Denjongpa, Denjonke, Denjonka, Lachengpa, Lachungpa, Sikami, Bhotia, Bhutia, Lhori

Population Sources:
28,600 in India (2000, B Grimes [1996 figure])

Language: Sino-Tibetan, Tibeto-Burman, Himalayish, Tibeto-Kanauri, Tibetic, Tibetan, Southern

Dialects: 0

Professing Buddhists: 98%

Practising Buddhists: 85%

Christians: 0.7%

Scripture: none

***Jesus* film:** none

Gospel Recordings: Sikkimese

Christian Broadcasting: none

ROPAL code: SIP

Status of Evangelization

65%

34%

1%

A   B   C

A = Have never heard the gospel
B = Have heard the gospel but have not become Christians
C = Are adherents to some form of Christianity

Singhpo

Population:
3,940 (2000)
4,600 (2010)
5,360 (2020)
Countries: India
Buddhism: Theravada
Christians: 70

Overview of the Singhpo

Other Names: Sing-fo, Kachin, Jingpo, Jingpho, Kaku, Ka Khyen

Population Sources:
3,569 in India (1991 census)

Language: Sino-Tibetan, Tibeto-Burman, Jingpho-Konyak-Bodo, Jingpho-Luish, Jingpho

Dialects: 0

Professing Buddhists: 98%

Practising Buddhists: 90%

Christians: 1.8%

Scripture: Portions 1907

Jesus **film:** none

Gospel Recordings: none

Christian Broadcasting: none

ROPAL code: SGP

Status of Evangelization

71%

27%

2%

A   B   C

A = Have never heard the gospel
B = Have heard the gospel but have not become Christians
C = Are adherents to some form of Christianity

The 4,000 members of the Singhpo tribe primarily live in the Changlang and Lohit districts of the north-east Indian state of Arunachal Pradesh. They 'inhabit the plain regions of these districts, and the area is drained by the Tengapani and Nao-Dihing rivers. Their habitat is surrounded by dense forests of the tropical moist deciduous type.'[1] In addition a small, unspecified number of Singhpo people live across the border in the Margherita Subdivision of Tinsuria District in Assam State, as well as in the Lakhimpur and Sibsagar districts.

The Singhpo have experienced strong population growth. The 1961 Indian census listed 982 Singhpo people. The population increased to 1,567 in 1971; to 2,353 in 1981; and to 3,569 in 1991. This group has an extremely high birth rate. The average number of children born to a Singhpo woman is 5.6, although only 3.95 survive past infancy.[2]

The Singhpo are one of the most intriguing tribes in India today.[3] The name 'Singhpo' is a variation of 'Jingpo'. The Jingpo are a large ethnic group of more than 500,000 living in northern Myanmar and areas of western Yunnan Province in south-west China.[4] The Jingpo in these two countries are predominantly Christians or animists, with very little Buddhist influence. Among the Singhpo of India, however, Buddhism is a stronghold and almost all people follow it. The Singhpo migrated into India about a century before the gospel was first introduced to their cousins in Myanmar and China, and they consequently have missed out on believing in Christianity to this present time.

The forefathers of the Singhpo migrated from northern Myanmar in 1793, settling in the plains of Tirap District in Arunachal Pradesh.[5] The reason for their migration is unclear, although one source says that 'They arrived at their present habitat when a reign of terror was let loose by the Ahom king, Gaurinath Singha.'[6] Arriving in their present location, the Singhpo 'drove out the Khamtis from the lowlands under the Patkoi hills'.[7]

In more-than two centuries since their arrival, the Singhpo have lost connection

Dwayne Graybill

with their counterparts in other nations, and they have gradually developed distinct linguistic, cultural and religious traits. Due to their close interaction with the Khamti tribe, who speak a language from the Tai family, the Singhpo language has changed markedly from its original Tibeto-Burman form.[8] One source states that now Singhpo only shares a 50 per cent lexical similarity with Jingpo in Myanmar.[9] This figure makes more sense when we compare English and German, which share a 60 per cent lexical similarity.[10]

The 1981 census of India records 98.51 per cent of Singhpo as followers of Theravada Buddhism, 0.72 per cent as Hindus and just three people as Christians. The 1991 census, however, returned 70 Christians. One source notes, 'The Singhpo religion is a peculiar blend of Buddhism and their traditional religion. Besides Lord Buddha, they worship some benevolent and malevolent spirits. Their traditional and Buddhist priests are known as *disamba* and *chowsra*, respectively.'[11] There are a very few Singhpo Christians today. One survey of Arunachal Pradesh concluded, 'They are more open to the gospel now than ever before.'[12]

An Overview of Buddhism in Sri Lanka

Tilak Rupasinghe and Vijay Karunaratne

Sri Lanka, formally known as Ceylon, is a beautiful tropical island off the south-eastern tip of India. Famed for its gems and its tea, Sri Lanka is also well known as one of the world's most enduring centres of Theravada Buddhism. Buddhism has shaped the history and the culture of Sri Lanka for over two thousand years. Today, approximately 70 per cent of its 18 million people would call themselves Buddhists. Sri Lankans generally perceive their island to be the home of the form of Buddhism they consider most orthodox and the closest to the teachings of the Lord Buddha himself. They gladly welcome many foreigners—often from the West—who seek to study and follow the path of the Enlightened One.

Sri Lankan Buddhism, however (like Buddhism wherever it has gone), has displayed throughout its history a remarkable ability to adapt to changing times and the influx of many cultures. It is this ability that gives Sri Lankan Buddhism its unique shape.

A Sinhalese Buddhist monk in Sri Lanka.

Julian Hawken

From its inception to the present, three streams have merged to produce what is known and practised as Buddhism in Sri Lanka today. The first stream, referred to here as *traditional orthodoxy*, is high religion and constitutes the traditional and historical expressions of Buddhism in Sri Lanka. It traces its roots to the arrival of the first Buddhist missionaries from India and to the establishment of accepted and well-recognized Buddhist institutions, beliefs and practices. These include such things as monastic orders, the Buddhist scriptures, Buddhist doctrines (such as the Four Noble Truths and The Eightfold Path) and Buddhist rituals (such as the chanting of religious texts known as *pirith*). This is Buddhism proper and is probably best expressed in capsule form as the 'Three Refuges': the Buddha, the *Dharma* (the teaching of the Buddha) and the *Sangha* (Sri Lankan Buddhism's monastic structure). When Sri Lankan Buddhists speak of their religion—especially to non-Buddhists—it is this kind of Buddhism they normally have in mind.

The second stream that has shaped Sri Lankan Buddhism is *folk Buddhism*. Sometimes termed 'low religion', it is here that the supernatural intersects the lives of the island's Buddhists. Folk Buddhism traces its roots to both the spirit religions of Sri Lanka's original peoples and to the influence of Hinduism brought to Sri Lanka by South Indian invaders.

The third stream shaping Sri Lankan Buddhism is called by some anthropologists *protestant Buddhism*. Birthed in the late 19th century, protestant Buddhism is the product of a period of reformation popularly known as the 'controversies'—a period that significantly shaped many of the expressions and attitudes of Buddhism in Sri Lanka today. It is the blend of these three streams—orthodox, folk and protestant Buddhism—that has produced the kind of Buddhism commonly practised in Sri Lanka today.

Traditional Buddhist orthodoxy

Buddhism gained its first foothold on the island of Lanka around 250 BC with the arrival of the Indian missionary Mahinda Thero. Mahinda was very likely the son of King Asoka, the great missionizing Buddhist emperor of India. According to Sri Lanka's ancient chronicle *The Mahavamsa*, Mahinda's first converts in Sri Lanka were none other than the Lankan king, Devanampiya Tissa, and some of his key subjects. Tissa's conversion is commemorated annually on *Poson Poya,* the full moon day occurring in the month of June.

Following in Mahinda's footsteps, his sister Sanghamitta also came to Sri Lanka. She brought with her some bodily relics of the Buddha, and a branch of the sacred Bo-tree in north India under which the Buddha had attained enlightenment. The branch was planted at Lanka's then seat of government, the north-central city of Anuradhapura, and its descendant to this day survives as a much revered object of veneration. This, and other relics of the Buddha, continue to be potent symbols of the establishment of Buddhism on the island. Perhaps the most important of the relics is the left eye-tooth of the Buddha, brought to Sri Lanka in AD 311 and enshrined in the *Dalada Maligawa,* the Temple of the Tooth, in the central hill capital of Kandy. It is a 'national treasure of great value and a tangible token of the attachment of the Sinhalese to the doctrine of the [Buddha]'.[1]

Buddhism's roots in Sri Lankan soil were further strengthened by the introduction of the Buddhist scriptures to the island. Known as the *Tripitaka,* or 'Three Baskets', these writings became Theravada Buddhism's Bible—a canon that provides the source of much of our knowledge of Buddhism to this day. Initially handed down orally in the Pali language (a vernacular dialect of Sanskrit), the *Tripitaka* was brought to Sri Lanka by Mahinda. It was here, some time in the second half of the first century BC, that the full canon of the *Tripitaka* was written down for the first time. Transcribed in the Pali language, the preservation of these scriptures (which had been lost in India at a comparatively early date) is seen as 'one of the landmark contributions of the Sinhalese to world literature'.[2] Indeed, the complete canon of the

Tripitaka survives only in Pali and has undoubtedly contributed to Sri Lanka's claim to be the home of true Buddhist orthodoxy.

In a very real sense, Sri Lanka's monks may be credited with saving the Theravada tradition. Although Theravada had once spread from India all over south-east Asia, it had nearly died out there due to aggressive competition from Hinduism and Islam. It was from Sri Lanka that Theravada monks spread their tradition to Burma, Thailand, Malaysia, Cambodia and Laos, and from these lands to Europe and the West generally. In this sense, Sri Lanka has been a 'missionary nation' from its earliest days. This missionary dynamic continues to find expression and support in modern Buddhist institutions in Sri Lanka. Buddhist missionary ventures in the West are actively supported and applauded.

While Sri Lankan Buddhism has often had a

Colombo, the capital of Sri Lanka, is one of Asia's most beautiful cities.

missionary face, it has also always been closely identified with the ethnic identity of the Sinhala race. Ethnically, the Sinhala people make up over 70 per cent of Sri Lanka's population, and the vast majority of the Sinhala population would without hesitation identify themselves as Buddhists. Indeed, it would not be too far-fetched to say that, for most Sinhala people, to be a true Sinhala is to be a Buddhist. Sinhala myth, according to Sri Lanka's ancient chronicle the *Mahavamsa,* fosters this by telling us that Prince Vijaya, the immigrant north Indian prince who is believed to have founded the Sinhala race, was given protection by *Sakka,* the king of gods, at the Buddha's own direction. This protection was to enable Vijaya to establish Buddhism in the island. Thus the marriage of Sinhala identity and Buddhism goes back a long way. This means that Sinhala culture and language are often seen to be vehicles for Sri Lankan Buddhism, and vice versa. Conversion to Christianity (or any other religion) is often seen as a betrayal of one's own culture, language and history.

Undoubtedly the most significant Buddhist institution in Sri Lanka is the *Sangha*, the Buddhist monastic priesthood. While the monastery is meant to serve primarily as a place where monks can study, meditate and pursue the higher goal of *nirvana*, it has also been regarded from the start as the repository, guardian and promoter of Sri Lankan Buddhism, and by extension of the Sinhala identity. From the humblest village priest to the heads of the most powerful monastic orders, the *Sangha* speaks with a voice that no politician can afford to ignore. It is for this reason that Sri Lanka's Buddhist clergy are among the most politically active in the world. In the long and protracted civil war that has been fought against the Tamil separatists in the north of the island, one of the most vociferous and consistent voices speaking for the unity of the state and the predominance of Sinhala political control has been that of the Buddhist clergy. Without at least the tacit backing of the *Sangha* it is doubtful that any permanent political solution will be forged.

The reason for this is not difficult to discern. Beginning with Mahinda's conversion of the Lankan king Devanampiya Tissa, Buddhism has always known the patronage and support of indigenous Sri Lankan governments, whether ancient monarchy or modern democracy. In ancient Sri Lanka, ruling kings were the secular heads of Buddhism, and one of their major duties was to protect and promote Buddhism. The first duty of a king on ascending the throne was to express his loyalty to Buddhism by giving alms, building monasteries, and so on, for the welfare of the religion. This patronage by local monarchs encouraged the spread of Buddhism into every part of the country. While the political patronage of Buddhism suffered a major setback during the 400-odd years of colonial rule, the practice has been energetically revived in post-independence Sri Lanka. Buddhism today is given pride of place in the constitution and the government spends vast sums of money for Buddhist activities. Buddhist ceremonies attend virtually every government event, from the opening of parliament to the departure of the national cricket team for sporting events overseas.

Thus Sri Lankan Buddhism, in its formal structures and traditional institutions, sees itself as the guardian and the promoter of a pure and orthodox—albeit *Theravada*—Buddhism. It is rightly proud of its links to the Pali canon and actively seeks to promote its message through missionary activity. Sri Lankan Buddhism also functions as a guardian of the Sinhala identity and seeks to maintain this by fostering the links between government and *Sangha*, and between politics and religion.

Folk Buddhism

Traditional orthodoxy does not, however, account for the full religious expression of Sri Lankan Buddhists. Another major stream of Buddhism, concerned with the world of spirits, gods and planetary deities, is referred to here as *folk Buddhism*.

In the orthodox Theravada Buddhism of Sri Lanka, ultimate salvation is attained by final escape from the unending cycle of life and death, sorrow and happiness, health and sickness. This escape can only be achieved by the elimination of personal desire and the ultimate elimination of any personal identity. Known as *nirvana*, this ultimate salvation is the ideal goal of all Sinhala Buddhists. It is, however, a long road to walk. The actual attainment of *nirvana* is generally considered to be a goal beyond the immediate grasp of most ordinary Buddhists today. Involving highly sophisticated meditation, it may take thousands of life cycles to perfect. As one anthropologist has put it, 'the crucial problem facing Sinhalese religion is that the central ideal, salvation, … is itself practically unattainable.'[3] Faced with such distant salvation, the ordinary Buddhist turns his attention to the more attainable goal of happier rebirth. If one cannot reach an immediate full salvation, progress is still possible by performing good deeds and making merit (*pinkama*) resulting in happier rebirths. In this way a progressive series of rebirths bridges the gap between this life and the distant *nirvana*.

The problem remains, however, that this still tends to be a prescription for life to come, offering answers for the 'there and then' but little in the way of practical help for the 'here and now'. The everyday life of a Sri Lankan Buddhist, like the lives of most people everywhere, is full of worries, concerns and very real needs. The neighbour's encroachment on one's land, the son's looming university entrance exams or the mother-in-law's persistent ill health all call for a very present help in times of trouble. An appeal to the animistic world of gods, devils, planets and stars fills this gap left by Buddhist orthodoxy.

Prior to the arrival of Buddhism in the island, Sri Lankans were animists and polytheists with a well-developed regional demon-deity system. This indigenous religion catered primarily to the daily needs of people who lived in constant fear of capricious gods and evil spirits. As such, it provided a way of dealing with the 'here and now'. Buddhism's entrance onto the scene did not replace this system. Rather, Buddhism incorporated these traditional beliefs as a complementary religious system that addressed a part of the human experience (the problems and fears of *this* life) that orthodox Buddhism did not overtly address. While Buddhism was accepted as the state religion, traditional cultic practices continued to offer hope and relief for the cares and concerns of daily life.

This residual animism was modified and expanded with the arrival in Sri Lanka of Tamil invaders from south India, who brought with them the influence of Hinduism. Over time, the identities of many of the primary gods of the Hindu pantheon merged with those of local Sri Lankan deities. Sri Lankan Buddhism, with its scheme of progressive rebirths on the road to *nirvana,* was able to incorporate these gods into its theology as supernatural fellow travellers working their way, along with all living things, towards the common goal of *nirvana.* The four primary deities in the Sri Lankan pantheon have also in a sense been 'nationalized', as they are considered the guardian deities of the island as well as the protectors and preservers of Buddhism on the island.

These gods (or *devas*) continue to play a significant role in the daily religious lives of Sri Lankan Buddhists. They are considered to have great powers, and millions seek out their priests and temples (which are quite distinct from orthodox Buddhist priests and temples) for help with the daily problems of life. The primary shrine of one of these gods, located in the southern Sri Lankan town of Kataragama, is said to attract almost as many pilgrims as the Temple of the Tooth in Kandy.

While the worship and the institutions of these deities are often considered quite distinct from orthodox Buddhism, the fact is that both systems go hand in hand and together form basic components of Buddhist practice in Sri Lanka. They are parallel systems that practically serve each other, catering as they do to different levels of need. A visual illustration of the extent to which these two streams intermingle is the fact that deity shrines are often incorporated within the very confines of many Buddhist temples.

This intermingling is also clearly reinforced in the celebration of Sri Lankan Buddhism's premier festival, the Kandy *Dalada Perahera* (the procession of the tooth of the Buddha). This festival, which takes place in the city of Kandy every July or August, takes the form of a nightly procession around central Kandy. In this procession the tooth of the Buddha is paraded atop a massive tusker elephant appropriately costumed for the occasion. The tooth is accompanied by a large retinue of dancers, drummers, temple

At the fish markets in Kandy, Sri Lanka.

Paul Hattaway

functionaries, political patrons and elephants. All of this, however, represents only the first fifth of the procession. Following the retinue associated with the *dalada* (the tooth of the Buddha), each of the four major guardian deities of Lanka are honoured in a similar fashion. Elephants, dancers, drummers, temple functionaries and patrons associated with each of the major deity shrines in Kandy follow in succession, resulting in a parade that often involves close to a hundred elephants and a thousand participants. Thus annually, and in the most public way, the close connection between Sri Lankan Buddhism and deity worship is reinforced.

The idyllic island of Sri Lanka has been deeply affected by a 20-year civil war between the Buddhist Sinhalese and the Hindu Tamils.

The propitiation of deities is not the only area in which the supernatural world intersects with the everyday world of Sri Lankan Buddhists. Evil spirits and astrology play significant roles in their lives as well, and they are also served by their own distinctive functionaries and rituals. Charms and counter-charms, evil eye and evil mouth, horoscopes and palmistry, propitious times and 'bad times' are all part and parcel of the way most Sri Lankan Buddhists view and deal with the events of their lives. Fear of evil influences shapes the lives of most Sri Lankan Buddhists in some way, and the propitiation and manipulation of deities and evil spirits are very common ways of dealing with this fear. Astrology, too, is a major influence in the life of a Sri Lankan Buddhist. Horoscopes are cast at birth and are used to make major decisions throughout life. Major events, whether personal rites of passage or public commemorations, are always scheduled according to the positioning of certain stars or planets. Weddings, business ventures and travel schedules will be ordered according to auspicious or inauspicious times.

While Buddhist purists will sometimes look askance at these practices as accretions that have nothing to do with real Buddhism, the fact is that they combine with orthodox Buddhism to form the total religious expression of the Sri Lankan Buddhist.

Certainly the practices of folk Buddhism are not confined to the simple and the uneducated. Clever politicians, well-heeled businessmen, university professors and students preparing for major exams are all among an urban elite who actively make use of these avenues of power.[4]

There are, in fact, elements of the metaphysical that persist within the precincts of Buddhism proper. Doctrinally, the Buddha has no role to play as a supernatural being. He has transcended humanity by attaining release, or *nirvana,* and thus (unlike the Buddha of Tibetan Buddhism) is technically beyond being of any 'on site' help for this-worldly problems. However, while he is not worshipped as an interceding god in the conventional sense, the Buddha is venerated at virtually every ritual. The major events of his life are honoured and celebrated with much enthusiasm.[5] One cannot escape the Buddha's presence in the form of countless Buddhist symbols and Buddha statues wherever one goes in Sri Lanka. The relics of the Buddha in particular tend to import this sense of his presence. Relics may be bodily remains (such as his tooth in Kandy), things he used or places he went.[6] Such relics are believed by most to emanate special powers and blessings.[7]

The tooth of the Buddha in Kandy has also traditionally served to legitimize political power. From approximately the 12th century, it has been thought to be a symbol of sovereignty. The tooth has been captured in wars of political domination, moved to new sites of government and elaborately protected in special buildings. It is interesting that even today, when a new government is sworn in, or when foreign dignitaries visit the island, one of the first acts is to visit the Temple of the Tooth in Kandy and pay special homage to the tooth of the Buddha.[8]

The most pervasive Buddhist ritual in Sri Lanka is the *pirith* ceremony. *Pirith* is a collection of certain Buddhist texts that are chanted at important private or public events. It is quite common now to have *pirith* chanted on government radio to commence daily programming. Though the primary purpose of the *pirith* is ostensibly for the purpose of meditation and gaining merit, practically it functions as safety-rune, warding off evil and ensuring blessing. A well-known and oft-repeated text speaks clearly of the healing powers of the *pirith* and its capacity to bring blessing:

> *To ward off all calamities, to bring to fulfillment all rich blessings, for the destruction of all suffering, for the destruction of all fear and for the destruction of all disease and sickness, recite ye the Piritta.*

While Buddhist monks chant the text of the chosen *pirith,* a white thread or string is held by all those present (the *pirith nula*). On completion of the ceremony, the string is cut into smaller pieces and tied around the necks or wrists of those present and is thought to bring protection and blessing to them.

Thus it is that both within traditional orthodox Buddhism and alongside it in the practices and structures of folk Buddhism, the Sinhala people of Sri Lanka appeal to the powers of the supernatural to help them cope with the uncertainties and needs of their increasingly complicated lives.

Protestant Buddhism

With the arrival of the Portuguese in the early 16th century, Sri Lanka entered the era of Western colonialism. For the next 450 years the island was dominated by three successive colonial regimes—the Portuguese, the Dutch and the British—each of whom ruled for approximately 150 years. Western power entered the scene at a time when the institutions of Sri Lankan Buddhism were in a period of decline. The first Portuguese arrivals found local feuding and growing indiscipline in the monasteries and so had little difficulty in rapidly establishing themselves in the maritime provinces. With the

Portuguese in power, Buddhism in Sri Lanka lost its age-old traditional state patronage. Ardent Catholics, the Portuguese persecuted the Buddhists, destroying their temples and sacred objects in an effort to eradicate Buddhism and force the population to embrace Christianity. The subsequent Dutch rule did little better. Throughout the Portuguese and Dutch periods, conversion through coercion, often at the point of the sword, produced many public 'Christians'—and many bitter memories. Today, one of the greatest impediments to the Christian faith among Sri Lankan Buddhists remains these collective memories as a bitter legacy of the time.

Two significant factors undoubtedly contributed to Buddhism's preservation during this period. The first is that the central kingdom of Kandy remained independent and undefeated, providing a haven for battered Buddhism and a platform for the beginnings of much-needed monastic reforms. The second is simply that harsh European attempts to impose the Christian faith virtually ensured the eventual revival of Buddhism.

The arrival of the British at the end of the 18th century brought some respite to the scene. Many religious restrictions were lifted, and Buddhism once again began to grow. After a long period of suppression, freedom now gave Buddhism the 'oxygen' it needed to revive. And indeed, during the latter part of the 19th century, Sri Lankan Buddhism underwent a remarkable revival and reform. It is this reform that added the third stream that shapes modern Sri Lankan Buddhism.

Interestingly enough, the resurgence of Buddhism was directly linked to the activities of zealous Protestant missionaries from the West. While missionary methods thankfully no longer used overt coercion, evangelistic strategy now focused on education, polemics and the use of the press. A veritable tide of tracts and treatises was produced— attacking Buddhism in vitriolic and insensitive language and offending Buddhist sensibilities. Sri Lankan Buddhists, eventually discovering the value of the press for themselves, responded in kind. A cycle of written and oral controversies between Buddhist and Christian leaders followed, culminating in what has come to be known as 'The Panadura Debates'.

Held in August 1873, these were a series of public debates between leading members of the Buddhist and Christian clergies, climaxing in a final and decisive debate in the coastal town of Panadura. Whatever the actual outcome of the debates was, the perceived outcome is clear. The Buddhists won the day. Covered intensively by the press and followed closely by an aware and increasingly literate public, the debates were seen as a clear demonstration of the superiority of Buddhist teaching over Christian dogma. Sri Lankan Buddhists, past and present, regard the debates as a highly significant event in their religious history. According to one Buddhist writer, the debates were 'the fortunate event that saved Buddhism from being destroyed by the foreign missionaries backed by the then government'.[9] Another says that the debates 'closed down a dark period in Lankan Buddhism and ushered in a new bright era'.[10]

What is clear is that the period of the controversies, culminating in the Panadura debates, sparked the emergence of a rather new kind of Buddhism in Sri Lanka which continues to influence Buddhists to this day. The debates significantly restored Buddhist self-confidence and provided the major impetus for what some anthropologists call *protestant Buddhism*.

Leading the charge were two great revivalists who had been greatly influenced by the course of the debates, a Sinhala nationalist by the name of Anagarika Dharmapala, and an American theosophist, Colonel Henry Olcott, who had converted to Buddhism. The activities of Dharmapala and Olcott brought about a remarkable transformation in traditional Sri Lankan Buddhism which can still be seen today. With their encouragement and leadership, resurgent Buddhism began to borrow and exploit many

A young Sinhalese girl in Sri Lanka.

of the methods the missionaries themselves had brought to the island. Olcott in particular advised his followers to emulate the tactics of what he called 'our great enemy, Christianity'. He encouraged the formation of Buddhist missionary societies modelled on Christian missionary societies,[11] and he advised his followers to emulate Christian Sunday schools. He introduced fund-raising campaigns, encouraged the development of Buddhist colleges and Sunday schools, organized Buddhist preaching tours, wrote Buddhist catechisms and even encouraged prayers for healing in the name of Buddha. It was through his agitation in 1885 that the British colonial government recognized *Wesak* as a public holiday. Thus the revival of Buddhism in Sri Lanka was conditioned and shaped by the very Christianity with which the Buddhists were contending. It is ironic that the Christian missionaries who wished to spread their faith throughout the island provided the models and methods that propelled the creation of this new and vital form of protestant Buddhism. Today, many of the institutions of protestant Buddhism are at the forefront of attempts to protect the Sinhala Buddhist identity and to limit the growth of the church and the Christian faith in the island.

Over 50 years have gone by since Sri Lanka achieved her independence from Great Britain. This has meant 50 years of unfettered opportunity for Sri Lankan Buddhism to prosper under the patronage of a Sinhala-dominated government and with the impetus and energy of a revived Buddhism. This 50-year window of opportunity, however, has not been the success story one might have expected. Sri Lanka, 50 years on, is a society devastated by major

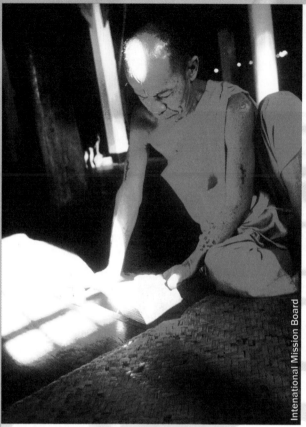

this vision and begin to believe in God's great agenda for their nation. It should be the Christian voice that expresses the greatest confidence in God's eternal purposes for their country. As the church has done so and God's people have begun to grow, the price to pay has escalated. Persecution and intimidation have moved from a theoretical possibility to an actual reality. In the last ten years many churches have been burned, believers threatened and pastors beaten. Through it all, the church needs to continue to be a sign—albeit a *Sri Lankan* sign clearly understood by her Buddhist compatriots—of God's kingdom. For as surely as God's word is true, the day will come when the island of Sri Lanka will be 'filled with the knowledge of the glory of God as the waters cover the sea'.

Notes

1. H R Perera, *Buddhism in Sri Lanka: A Short History* (Kandy: Buddhist Publication Society, 1988), 34–35.

2. Chandra Richard de Silva, *Sri Lanka: A History* (New Delhi: Vikas Publishing, 1994) 57.

3. Michael M Ames, 'Magical Animism and Buddhism: A Structural Analysis of Sinhalese Religious System', *Journal of Asian Studies* (1964) 21.

4. Some years ago, a particular alignment of the planets during one week in April was deemed so inauspicious that a healthy percentage of the government chose to organize their vacations abroad for the duration.

5. *Wesak*, celebrated in May, honours the birth, enlightenment and death of the Buddha and is the most important celebration of the Buddha as a person.

6. Mt Siri Pada, or Adam's Peak as it is popularly known, is Sri Lanka's fourth highest mountain. It is believed to have the imprint of the Buddha's foot imbedded at its peak, and it is the focus of pilgrimage for thousands every year.

7. The arrival of rain in April 2002, breaking a long spell of drought over large areas of the island, was attributed by many to a public exposition of the tooth of the Buddha in Kandy as the rains first broke.

8. In 1997 the Temple of the Tooth was attacked by Tamil 'Tiger' terrorists, whose aim has been to achieve independence for the Tamil-dominated north of the island. Their attack was undoubtedly calculated with the political symbolism of the tooth (and the temple) in mind.

9. Gunaratne and de Silva, 'The Debate of the Century', 17.

10. Perera, *Buddhism in Sri Lanka*, 81.

11. Through Olcott's encouragement, the Young Men's Buddhist Association was founded in 1896.

Intenational Mission Board

An elderly monk studying.

social problems. The nation's suicide rate is one of the highest in the world. Alcoholism and paedophilia are major problems. A Marxist insurrection in the late 1980s saw some 30,000 young people disappear forever. An 18-year civil war in the north has taken the lives of over 65,000 of the cream of the nation's youth. Resignation or emigration have often seemed the only real answers open to the people of Sri Lanka.

It is in this kind of context that God's church has finally begun to grow in Buddhist Sri Lanka. In Christ, the shape of eternity can begin to look a lot more promising than the *nirvana* that orthodox Buddhism offers. In Christ there can be a deliverance from the fear of evil spirits, unpredictable deities and distant planets that no folk Buddhism can offer. In Christ there can be healing from the wounds of injustice, oppression and ethnic hatred, both from the colonial past and the war-torn present. In Christ there can be hope for the redemption of the nation, its land, its language, its culture and its people. Sri Lankan Christians are the first who need to catch

Approximately 16 million members of the Sinhalese ethnic group live throughout the world. They are the dominant people of Sri Lanka, the beautiful island situated off the south-east coast of India. In Sri Lanka, where they comprise about 75 per cent of the nation's population, they primarily inhabit the verdant central and south-western areas. There are an additional 1.5 million Sinhalese people scattered around the world.[1]

The Sinhalese are one of the few Buddhist peoples in the world that speak a language from the Indo-European linguistic family. Sinhalese is closely related to the language spoken in the Maldives, but the Maldivians are almost completely Muslims, while most Sinhalese are Buddhists. The Sinhalese have absorbed much Hindu influence because of their close proximity to India. This influence can be seen today, for example, in the many castes (which are unusual for a Buddhist group) among the Sinhalese people.

Paul Hattaway

The Sinhalese first arrived in Sri Lanka at least 300 years before the Christian era. Various colonial powers have controlled Sri Lanka (formerly called Ceylon) for much of its history. The Portuguese, Dutch and British all had turns running the island for almost 450 years. The British finally relinquished control in 1948, and Sri Lanka was granted independence. Since that time the Sinhalese have been in almost constant conflict with the Hindu Tamils in the north of the country, who demand an independent state. The three million Tamils in Sri Lanka have been funded by their Tamil cousins in India, where they number more than 60 million. Full-scale war was declared in 1983, which has resulted in tens of thousands of deaths.

Buddhism was introduced to Sri Lanka in the 3rd century AD. Over the centuries, the strong Theravada sect of Buddhism blossomed among the Sinhalese. They are responsible for the spread of Theravada Buddhism to much of Southeast Asia. The Pali script was also exported from Sri Lanka and became the basis for orthographies such as Thai, Burmese and Khmer.[2] Today, Buddhism among the Sinhalese has become extremely syncretistic. It is not unusual to see statues of Mary, Jesus, Hindu deities and Buddha worshipped together.

According to tradition, Sri Lanka first received the gospel from the Apostle Thomas in the early days of the Christian era. In AD 537, a Nestorian reported numerous churches on the island. The Portuguese assumed control of Sri Lanka in 1505 and introduced Catholicism, followed by the Dutch who forced many Sinhalese to convert to the Reformed Church.[3] The Sinhalese Bible was translated in 1823. Today there are some huge Pentecostal churches in Colombo City, and approximately 4 per cent of the Sinhalese people follow Christ.

Buddhist leaders have reacted furiously in recent years to the strong evangelistic efforts of Christians. Mobs of Buddhists, often led by monks, have burned down dozens of churches, stabbed pastors and even a six-year-old pastor's son, poisoned Christians' wells and beaten numerous church-goers.[4] They have forced a change in the Sri Lankan constitution, making it illegal for people of one faith to proselytize people of other faiths.

Overview of the Sinhalese

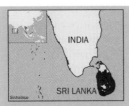

INDIA

SRI LANKA

Sinhalese

Population:
15,558,200 (2000)
17,098,500 (2010)
18,791,200 (2020)
Countries: Sri Lanka, Singapore, India, Maldives, USA, Canada, United Kingdom, Australia, New Zealand, Thailand, United Arab Emirates, Malaysia, Midway Islands, Saudi Arabia
Buddhism: Theravada
Christians: 620,000

Other Names: Sinhala, Singhalese, Singhala, Cingalese, Chingalese

Population Sources:
14,045,000 in Sri Lanka (2001, P Johnstone and J Mandryk [2000 figure])
12,000 in Singapore (2000, B Grimes [1993 figure])
2,800 in India (2001, FMC South Asia)
1,500 in Maldives (2001, FMC South Asia)
also in the USA, Canada, United Kingdom, Australia, New Zealand, Thailand, United Arab Emirates, Malaysia, Midway Islands, Saudi Arabia

Language: Indo-European, Indo-Iranian, Indo-Aryan, Sinhalese-Maldivian
Dialects: 1 (Rodiya)
Professing Buddhists: 90%
Practising Buddhists: 60%
Christians: 4%
Scripture: Bible 1823
Jesus film: available
Gospel Recordings: Sinhalese
Christian Broadcasting: available
ROPAL code: SNH

Status of Evangelization

61%

35%

4%

A   B   C

A = Have never heard the gospel
B = Have heard the gospel but have not become Christians
C = Are adherents to some form of Christianity

So

Approximately 150,000 So people live on both sides of the Laos-Thailand border in Southeast Asia. More than 110,000 live in western Laos, especially in northern Savannakhet Province and the southern half of Khammouan Province. An additional 30,000 So people inhabit 53 villages in north-east Thailand.[1] They are the descendents of prisoners of war who were brought to Thailand after the Siamese sacked Vientiane in 1827.[2] Since their arrival in Thailand, the So 'have struggled to avoid the Thai government's policy of gentle assimilation. The So feel the education policies of Thailand are especially designed to assimilate them to Thai society and culture.'[3]

There may also be So communities in Vietnam, but this is difficult to determine due to the confusing ethnolinguistic makeup of the So people. It seems that there are several sub-groups among this group, with their dialects overlapping with those of other related peoples. In Laos the So are usually called 'Mangkong', while some linguists call the So language 'Western Bru'. The Mangkong are also located in Vietnam, where they are part of the official Bru-Van Kieu minority group.[4]

The So in Thailand are more Buddhist than their counterparts in Laos, where the majority are spirit-worshippers with less Buddhist influence. Overall only about half of the So people in Asia claim to be Buddhists, and the number who actively practise Buddhism is significantly less. Relatively few attend temples or enroll their sons as monks. One source says, 'The So people are nominally Buddhists and they are very spirit

conscious, fearing most the deadly *phi pop*. In former days, individuals believed to be possessed by this evil spirit were ruthlessly killed by the village community.'[5]

There are approximately 2,000 Christians among the So in Laos, primarily in Khammouan Province. Overseas Missionary Fellowship and the Swiss Brethren had missionaries working among them in the 1950s and 1960s. 'They saw whole villages accept Christ, mostly the result of people being delivered from demonic oppression and the supernatural healing of sickness. By the time all foreign missionaries were expelled from Laos in 1975, they had left behind a strong and evangelizing So church. They have endured great persecution and hardship from the Communist authorities in recent years, but most have stood firm in their Christian faith.'[6]

In Thailand several missionaries have attempted to reach the So, including Bob and Eileen West of New Tribes Mission, who translated Scripture portions into the So language in 1980. 'They have spent fifteen years in Thai So villages, translating Bible portions and evangelistic books into their dialects. . . . Although they often show an intense interest in Scripture, the So have not yet overcome the spiritual barriers that prevent them from knowing the King of Kings. Their families and relatives all fear that if any one of them abandons worship of the spirits, the entire family will be punished. Consequently, only a few have accepted Christ to date, barely enough in any one place to form a church.'[7]

Population:
135,400 (2000)
165,800 (2010)
203,400 (2020)
Countries: Laos, Thailand, Vietnam
Buddhism: Theravada
Christians: 3,000

Overview of the So

Other Names: Kha So, Kah So, Thro, Mangkong, Mang-koong, Makong, So Makon, Mankoong, Mang Cong, Sou, Tro, Leun, Leung, Leu, Muong Leung, Luun, Ruul

Population Sources:
92,321 in Laos (1995 census)[8]
30,000 in Thailand (2000, J Schliesinger [1995 figure])[9]
also in Vietnam

Language: Austro-Asiatic, Mon-Khmer, Eastern Mon-Khmer, Katuic, West Katuic, Brou-So

Dialects: 6 (So Trong, So Slouy, So Phong, So Makon, Chali, Kaleu)

Professing Buddhists: 50%

Practising Buddhists: 20%

Christians: 2%

Scripture: Portions 1980; work in progress

***Jesus* film:** none

Gospel Recordings: Makong; So: Ban Lao; So: Muang Luang; So: Nhommarath; So: Phalane

Christian Broadcasting: none

ROPAL code: SSS

Status of Evangelization

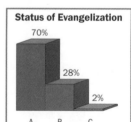

70%

28%

2%

A   B   C

A = Have never heard the gospel
B = Have heard the gospel but have not become Christians
C = Are adherents to some form of Christianity

Approximately 40,000 members of the Sogwo Arig tribe live in a remote part of western China. They inhabit Tsanggar Gonpa, a district within Tongde County in the Hainan Golog Prefecture, and parts of neighbouring He'nan County.[1] Tongde lies to the east of the Yellow River in Qinghai Province. The Qinghai Plateau—at a minimum elevation of 3,500 metres (11,500 ft.) above sea level—is snowbound nine months of the year and turns into a muddy bog the other three months. The area is home to the *Darakar Tredzong* (White Monkey Fortress), considered one of the three most sacred sites in all of the Amdo Tibetan areas.

The Sogwo Arig is a Mongolian tribe living in the midst of countless small Tibetan clans in one of the most remote locations in the world. Over the course of many centuries, the Sogwo Arig language and culture have gradually been assimilated by the Tibetans. Still today, however, Tibetans in the area know that the Sogwo Arig are of Mongol ancestry and view them as a separate people.[2]

The Sogwo Arig language became practically extinct during the course of the 20th century. Today they speak the Amdo Hbrogpa Tibetan language, but they retain various words in their vocabulary that reveal their Mongolian ancestry.

The Sogwo Arig claim to have been the Mongol rulers of Henan Province. A surprised French explorer discovered this fact in 1906, when the Sogwo Arig prince signed a letter with the title 'King of Henan'. Vicomte d'Ollone explains, 'When the Mongols were expelled from China, the dynasty of the kings of Ho-Nan [Henan]—kings without a kingdom—retired to their steppes; and when in their turn the Manchus seized the empire [1644] they utilized the Mongols for the purpose of holding the Tibetans in check, for which reason a horde was sent to establish itself in this region.'[3] The Sogwo Arig continued to be led by a succession of kings until the 1950s, when the Communist authorities stripped the Sogwo Arig royal family of its authority.

Today one of the few remaining Sogwo Arig cultural features is their Mongolian style of *yurt*. Sogwo Arig men will not leave their homes without being armed with their rifle. When they go on hunting expeditions, they take wooden tripods for resting their weapons on when firing.[4]

All Sogwo Arig are followers of either Tibetan Buddhism or Bon. They worship at crude sacrificial altars, constructed of yak dung piled about three feet high, upon which they regularly offer animal sacrifices to various gods and demons.

Hidden away in communities almost inaccessible to the outside world, the Sogwo Arig are virtually untouched by Christianity. Intrepid evangelists will need to overcome severe weather, rugged terrain, linguistic and cultural barriers and fierce packs of dogs which the Sogwo Arig have trained to attack strangers.

Photo credit: Nancy Sturrock

Population:
37,000 (2000)
47,700 (2010)
58,700 (2020)
Countries: China
Buddhism: Tibetan
Christians: none known

Overview of the Sogwo Arig

Other Names: Sokwo Arik, Arig Tibetan, Alike, A-li-k'oa, Tatze, Sohkwo

Population Sources:
35,000 in China (1998, Asian Minorities Outreach)

Language: Sino-Tibetan, Tibeto-Burman, Bodic, Bodish, Tibetan, Northern Tibetan

Dialects: 0

Professing Buddhists: 97%

Practising Buddhists: 65%

Christians: 0%

Scripture: none

Jesus **film:** none

Gospel Recordings: none

Christian Broadcasting: none

ROPAL code: none

Status of Evangelization

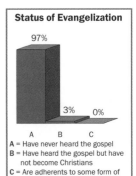

A = Have never heard the gospel
B = Have heard the gospel but have not become Christians
C = Are adherents to some form of Christianity

Song

THAILAND

Population:
45,400 (2000)
49,600 (2010)
54,200 (2020)
Countries: Thailand
Buddhism: Theravada
Christians: 400

Overview of the Song

Other Names: Lao Song, Tai Song, Thai Song, Lao Song Dam, Chao Song, Thai Soang

Population Sources: 45,000 in Thailand (2001, J Schliesinger [1999 figure])[1]

Language: Tai-Kadai, Kam-Tai, Be-Tai, Tai-Sek, Tai, Southwestern, East Central, Chiang Saeng

Dialects: 0

Professing Buddhists: 90%

Practising Buddhists: 55%

Christians: 0.9%

Scripture: Portions

Jesus **film:** none

Gospel Recordings: none

Christian Broadcasting: none

ROPAL code: SOA

Status of Evangelization

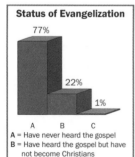

77%

22%

1%

A   B   C

A = Have never heard the gospel
B = Have heard the gospel but have not become Christians
C = Are adherents to some form of Christianity

More than 45,000 people belonging to the Song ethnic group inhabit a widespread area in central Thailand. They are distributed in the eight provinces of Phetchabun, Phitsanulok, Nakhon Sawan (Tha Tako District), Ratchaburi (Chom Bung District), Suphan Buri (Song Phinong District), Kanchanaburi, Chumphon and Nakhon Pathom (Muang District).[2]

The renowned researcher Erik Seidenfaden first noted the existence of the Song people in the 1950s.[3] He discovered that they were originally Tai Dam (Black Tai) people who were forcibly moved to Thailand from their homeland east of the town of Luang Prabang in Laos.[4]

Joachim Schliesinger adds: 'in the late eighteenth and nineteenth centuries, the Siamese armies raided the region several times and took tens of

Paul Hattaway

thousands of Tai Dam people to Thailand as war captives. The first Siamese military involvement in that area occurred . . . in the early 1780s, extending to the late nineteenth century. Most of the Song arrived in Thailand in two major waves. The first wave was taken as war captives by the Siamese army during the time of King Phra Nangklao (1824–1851). The second arrived in the 1870s.'[5] The captives were made to work on construction projects and also had to defend the court against frequent Chinese raids at the time. Consequently they spread out over a wide area of Thailand, from Phitsanulok Province in the north to Chumphon in southern Thailand, a distance of almost one thousand kilometres (620 mi.).

Although ethnically and linguistically[6] the Song have been shown to be a branch of the large Tai Dam ethnicity, they now have their own identity and sense of cohesiveness that qualify them as a separate people group.[7] Today 'the descendants of the Tai Dam captives do not consider themselves as Tai Dam but as Lao Song. . . . Song identity is now defined in part by a common recognition of a distinct historic experience and common opposition to the dominant culture and political society following relocation.'[8]

Song women wear a distinctive traditional costume consisting of a dark blue dress with white, bright blue or yellow vertical stripes. Until the 1980s the Song refused to intermarry with people from outside their group, but in recent years this has relaxed and they now intermarry freely with Thai, Isan and Chinese people.

One of the major characteristics that sets the Song apart from the Tai Dam is religion. While most Tai Dam in Laos, Vietnam and China are animists,[9] the Song in Thailand have overwhelmingly converted to Theravada Buddhism, although they still retain many of their traditional beliefs as well. Every Song village has its own shaman, called *mo sen*, who acts as a mediator between the people and the spirits.

Throughout the course of many generations since their ancestors first arrived in Thailand, the Song people have lived and died with very few of their number ever having heard of Jesus Christ. Today, less than one per cent of Song people are Christians.

Stod Bhoti

According to a 1996 source, 2,500 people belonging to the Stod Bhoti language group live along the Stod, Khoksar and upper Mayar valleys in the Lahul region of Himachal Pradesh in northern India.[1] The region has been described as having 'an inhospitable terrain with little vegetation as the area falls in the arid zone. . . . It has very scanty rainfall. Stone boulders and loose rocks keep falling all over and on small patches of terraced fields, which are usually near the river beds.'[2]

The classification of this small group is extremely problematic. In India the government has granted 'Scheduled Tribe' status to the 'Bhotia' and also the 'Bodh' of Himachal Pradesh. These two terms are generic names given to people of Tibetan origin across northern India and Nepal, and they are sometimes even used as a religious designation for all Buddhist people. It is said that the people who came from Tibet prior to 1962 are referred to as Bodhs, while those who have migrated across the border in the past forty years are called Tibetans. The total number of 'Bodh' people within the state at the time of the 1981 census was 22,635. These broad classifications, however, are of little value when trying to determine ethnic and linguistic divisions among the cold and remote mountains in the northern part of the state. Even the 2,500 people living in the three valleys given as the location of the Stod Bhoti (the Stod, Khoksar and Mayar valleys) may constitute three separate language groups and five sub-groups. Stod and Khoksar reportedly have 85 per cent mutual intelligibility, but Stod and Mayar only share 75 per cent intelligibility and there is a mere 62 per cent intelligibility

between Khoksar and Mayar.[3] Linguists say that there usually needs to be an 80 per cent mutual intelligibility between the speakers of two languages or dialects in order for them to be able to communicate in a meaningful manner.

Tibetan Buddhism is the preferred religion of all Stod Bhoti people in India, although Hindu influence is being seen more and more. The Stod Bhoti have their own monasteries, temples and lamas. The people are considered extremely superstitious and live in constant fear of evil spirits. They believe that they must vigilantly perform rituals and offerings to placate the deities—otherwise the spirit could take offence and bring disaster on their community.

One source summarized the religious practices of the Stod Bhoti as follows: 'The most learned of the lamas usually belong to the yellow sect and are called Bara Lama or *giani* (learned). . . . [The Stod

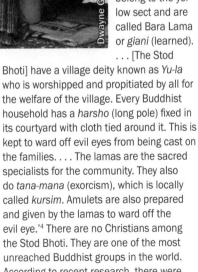
Dwayne Graybill

Bhoti] have a village deity known as *Yu-la* who is worshipped and propitiated by all for the welfare of the village. Every Buddhist household has a *harsho* (long pole) fixed in its courtyard with cloth tied around it. This is kept to ward off evil eyes from being cast on the families. . . . The lamas are the sacred specialists for the community. They also do *tana-mana* (exorcism), which is locally called *kursim*. Amulets are also prepared and given by the lamas to ward off the evil eye.'[4] There are no Christians among the Stod Bhoti. They are one of the most unreached Buddhist groups in the world. According to recent research, there were just three Christians in the whole of Lahul District with a population of 13,030.[5]

Population:
2,660 (2000)
3,100 (2010)
3,600 (2020)
Countries: India
Buddhism: Tibetan
Christians: none known

Overview of the Stod Bhoti

Other Names: Stod, Tod, Tod-kad, Stod-Kad, Lahul Bhoti, Bodh, Bhoti, Bhot

Population Sources:
2,500 in India (2000, B Grimes [1996 figure])

Language: Sino-Tibetan, Tibeto-Burman, Himalayish, Tibeto-Kanauri, Tibetic, Tibetan, Central

Dialects: 3 (Stod, Khoksar, Mayar)

Professing Buddhists: 100%

Practising Buddhists: 85%

Christians: 0%

Scripture: none

***Jesus* film:** none

Gospel Recordings: none

Christian Broadcasting: none

ROPAL code: SBU

Status of Evangelization
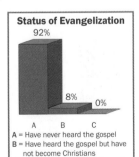

A = Have never heard the gospel
B = Have heard the gospel but have not become Christians
C = Are adherents to some form of Christianity

263

Tai Bueng

Population:
5,700 (2000)
6,200 (2010)
6,800 (2020)
Countries: Thailand
Buddhism: Theravada
Christians: none known

Overview of the Tai Bueng

Other Names: Tai Berng, Lao Bueng, Lao Berng

Population Sources: 5,600 in Thailand (2001, J Schliesinger [1998 figure])

Language: Tai-Kadai, Kam-Tai, Unclassified

Dialects: 0

Professing Buddhists: 100%

Practising Buddhists: 95%

Christians: 0%

Scripture: none

Jesus film: none

Gospel Recordings: none

Christian Broadcasting: none

ROPAL code: none

Status of Evangelization

93%

7%

0%

A   B   C

A = Have never heard the gospel
B = Have heard the gospel but have not become Christians
C = Are adherents to some form of Christianity

Few people have ever heard of the existence of the 5,700 Tai Bueng people of central Thailand. They live in two villages within the Phatthana Nikhom District of Lopburi Province, north of Bangkok. Ban Klok Salung is the larger of the two villages and is considered 'pure Tai Bueng'. Its approximately 5,000 residents still maintain many traditional customs. The smaller village is called Ban Manao Hwan and is home to about 600 Tai Bueng and families from other ethnic groups.

Quite simply, no one knows much about the origins of the Tai Bueng people. The name *bueng* means 'big', or 'great'— therefore they consider themselves the Great Tai, but they are not to be confused with the Tai Yay (Shan) people of northern Thailand and Myanmar, whose name carries the same meaning. Researcher Joachim Schliesinger points out that 'There are no known Tai Bueng communities in Laos or Vietnam, nor can any of them explain from where and how the designation derived. They insist strongly that they are Tai Bueng people distinct from other Tai groups.'[1] Not until linguists visit the Tai Bueng and conduct extensive comparative research can an accurate picture be drawn of how the Tai Bueng language relates to other Tai varieties in Southeast Asia.[2]

Some of the older Tai Beung people claim that their ancestors migrated to their present location in Thailand more than 200 years ago, from a place in north-eastern Laos called Muang Ou Then. They don't know why they made such a long journey,

but several other groups first entered Thailand from Laos as war captives during this same period.

Unlike many small tribal groups who have largely been assimilated to Thai culture, the Tai Beung women still wear their distinctive clothes—a traditional *chong kaben* dress with a heavy silver belt around the waist.

Tai Beung men are keen fishermen. They live near the Pa Sak River, which has an abundant supply of fish. The Tai Beung use homemade wooden boats to go fishing and also construct traps of thinly sliced bamboo. The Thai government has constructed a dam on the river, with the result that half of the people in Ban Manao Hwan had to relocate to avoid the raised water line. Besides rice, 'sugar cane and corn are cultivated as cash crops. The Tai Beung also grow cotton, vegetables and fruits such as banana, jackfruit, melons and mangoes.'[3]

It would be safe to assume that all Tai Beung people are Buddhists. Each of their villages has its own temple, and the people zealously observe all of the Buddhist festivals and rituals. 'The temple at Ban Manao Hwan, including its *vihar, sala,* bell tower and quarters for the monks, will be flooded when the Pa Sak River dam is completed; all religious relics and removable items will be relocated to a new site.'[4]

Christianity has not made any impact among the Tai Bueng. They remain an unreached and unevangelized group without any known Christians in their midst.

Christian Far East Ministry

CHINA

MYANMAR
Shan State
Luang
Namtha

LAOS

THAILAND
Tai Doi

Population:
360 (2000)
450 (2010)
570 (2020)
Countries: Laos, Myanmar
Buddhism: Theravada
Christians: none known

Overview of the Tai Doi

Other Names: Doi

Population Sources: 320 in Laos (1995, L Chazee)
also in Myanmar

Language: Austro-Asiatic, Mon-Khmer, Northern Mon-Khmer, Palaungic-Khmuic, Palaungic, Western Palaungic, Angkuic

Dialects: 0

Professing Buddhists: 70%

Practising Buddhists: 25%

Christians: 0%

Scripture: none

***Jesus* film:** none

Gospel Recordings: none

Christian Broadcasting: none

ROPAL code: none

Status of Evangelization

87%

13%

0%

A   B   C

A = Have never heard the gospel
B = Have heard the gospel but have not become Christians
C = Are adherents to some form of Christianity

The *Tai Doi*—whose name simply means 'mountain people'—are a tiny little-known group living on both banks of the Mekong River in Southeast Asia. In 1995, a total of 320 Tai Doi people (in 54 families) inhabited three villages in the Long District of Luang Namtha Province in north-west Laos. The names of the three villages are Muang Kham, Dondchay and Muong.[1] The Tai Doi have lived in Long District of Luang Namtha in Laos for at least five generations. In April 1994, some 19 Tai Doi families reportedly left the village of Muang Kham with all of their possessions and walked two days to join Lu and Tai Dam villages.[2] A small number of Tai Loi are also located on the other side of the Mekong River in the eastern part of Myanmar's Shan State.

There is some confusion regarding the differences between Tai Doi and Tai Loi. The authoritative *Ethnologue* lists Tai Doi as a dialect of Tai Loi and places it under the Palaungic branch of the Mon-Khmer language family,[3] while the *Atlas des Ethnies et des Sous-Ethnies du Laos* places Tai Loi under the Tai section and even states that the Tai Doi language is close to Tai Dam, while their culture is similar to that of the Lu.[4] It is likely that the Tai Doi are a Mon-Khmer speaking group, but the confusion is caused by the fact that they have lived for centuries surrounded by Tai-speaking peoples and have absorbed many linguistic and cultural influences. The Tai Loi live further to the north, near the borders of Laos, China and Myanmar.

Neither group is even mentioned in official literature on ethnic groups in Laos.

The Tai Doi share their villages with Lu and Akha people. Each Tai Doi house contains two families. Shamans are consulted to locate the most auspicious place to build before construction begins, which usually ends up being near a river or stream.

The Lu have been influential in converting their Tai Doi neighbours to Buddhism. The Tai Doi also worship their ancestors once a year. Both the animistic and ancestor worship practices of the Tai Doi do not stop them from claiming to be Theravada Buddhists. Many Tai Doi people in Laos and Myanmar are animists, appeasing a variety of spirit beings of which they live in fear. If anything goes wrong during the course of the year, such as a poor crop or an accident, the blame is always placed on the family involved for having done something wrong to offend the spirits. Buddhist monks and shamans are summoned, and for a price they chant and pray over the family, seeking to correct the spiritual imbalance that has caused the spirits to display their displeasure.

Missionary organizations have generally refused to place any importance on small tribes like the Tai Doi, and researchers have been hesitant to profile them, preferring to focus on the larger groups instead. Consequently, few prayers have ever been spoken on behalf of the Tai Doi. They remain an unevangelized and unreached people group with little access to the gospel.

Myanmar Faces and Places

Tai Gapong

More than 3,200 Tai Gapong people live in Southeast Asia. At least 2,000 inhabit a single village in Thailand—Ban Varit in Waritchaphum District of Sakhon·Nakhon Province. There are about 500 homes in Ban Varit, most of which are inhabited by Tai Gapong families, along with some ethnic Phutai and Yoy people.

The Tai Gapong say that they originated in Borikhamxai Province, Laos, in a district known as Gapong, from which they took their name. No district or town called Gapong exists in Laos today, but the 1,200 Tai Gapong in Laos today inhabit Ban Nahuong, about 25 kilometres (15 mi.) south of the town of Ban Nape in eastern Borikhamxai Province, near the Lao border with Vietnam.

According to Joachim Schliesinger, 'the ancestors of the Tai Gapong in Thailand migrated westwards from . . . central Laos, crossed the Mekong and settled in their present location in 1844 or 1845. The reason for their migration is unclear; they may have been taken as war captives and resettled across the Mekong River by the Siamese army, or migrated voluntarily.'[1]

In their language, *Gapong* means 'brain'—therefore the autonym of this interesting group means 'Brainy Tai'. Other Tai groups call them Phutai, but although the Tai Gapong say they are distantly related to the Phutai, they are now a distinct tribe with their own customs, history and dialect. In fact, even the Phutai who live in the Tai Gapong village in Thailand consider

them different.

For generations, Tai Gapong women have worn an elaborate traditional dress that sets them apart from other tribes. It consists of a short skirt that falls just below the knees, 'with white, red, brown and yellow horizontal stripes at its lower part, a long-sleeved dark coloured vest buttoned in the middle with silver coins and decorated with red bands along the hem, collar and sleeve-ends. In the past, Tai Gapong women wore a silver belt, silver ear-rings, silver necklaces and silver anklets.'[2]

All Tai Gapong people in Thailand are Buddhists, while among those in Laos the situation is not so clear. Although many Tai Gapong families in Laos claim to be Buddhists, their ceremonies and rituals are dominated by animistic practices.

Even in Thailand the Tai Gapong reportedly 'believe in an array of spirits, such as the spirit of the village, the spirit of the house, the spirit of the water, the spirit of the tree, but their most important spiritual being is *chao pu mahaesak*, an angel-like being, humanized in the form of a man-like statue in his shrine. The Tai Gapong honour *chao pu mahaesak* annually on a specific day with flowers, whisky, rice and other small sacrifices.'[3]

Because few people are even aware of the existence of the Tai Gapong people, little or no Christian outreach has ever been conducted among them. Only a very few Tai Gapong have heard the gospel. They continue—as they have for centuries—to live their lives without the slightest knowledge of Jesus Christ or his salvation.

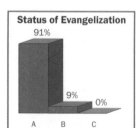

Population:
3,200 (2000)
3,690 (2010)
4,300 (2020)
Countries: Thailand, Laos
Buddhism: Theravada
Christians: none known

Overview of the Tai Gapong

Other Names: Tai Kapon, Tai Kapong, Tai Capong, Phu Tai Gapong

Population Sources: 2,000 in Thailand (2001, J Schliesinger [1999 figure])

1,200 in Laos (2001, J Schliesinger)

Language: Tai-Kadai, Kam-Tai, Be-Tai, Tai-Sek, Tai, Southwestern, East Central, Lao-Phutai

Dialects: 0
Professing Buddhists: 75%
Practising Buddhists: 45%
Christians: 0%
Scripture: none
Jesus **film:** none
Gospel Recordings: none
Christian Broadcasting: none
ROPAL code: none

Status of Evangelization

91%

9%

0%

A   B   C

A = Have never heard the gospel
B = Have heard the gospel but have not become Christians
C = Are adherents to some form of Christianity

Approximately 10,000 Tai He live in Borikhamxai Province in central Laos. They are concentrated in the Viangthong and Khamkeut districts, while smaller numbers of Tai He inhabit the Pakkading and Pakxan districts.[1] The area inhabited by the Tai He is well-watered and hilly. Numerous small and distinct ethnic groups live in central Laos. Despite the fact that the Tai He view themselves as a distinct people group, the Tai He remained unknown until Laurent Chazee, the French ethnographer, first listed them in 1995 as one of his 119 ethnic groups in Laos.[2]

days . . . by ordinary travel it will take from five to seven weeks to cover it, according to the stage of the water.'[3]

The Tai He practise a mixture of Buddhism and animism. In some villages, the Buddhist monks double as spirit priests, or shamans. Their role is to mediate between the spiritual world and the Tai He community. Because of this, the people greatly fear the shaman-monks. Sometimes the more respected monks take on even more roles in the community, such as those of counsellor and village advisor.

Population:
9,000 (2000)
11,350 (2010)
14,300 (2020)
Countries: Laos
Buddhism: Theravada
Christians: none known

Xayographix

An early missionary summarized the effects that shamanism had on the common people: 'This belief in witchcraft is often caused by the ruling class to forward selfish interests or to wreak their vengeance upon an offending family, thus taking an unfair advantage through the aid of a superstition that they themselves believe in. The awful shadow cast over Laos life by these superstitions is simply indescribable. The people are religiously like frightened children in the dark. They call and cry to one another, but are only the more frightened by the sounds and echoes of one another's voices, and in their gropings they start and scream as they touch one another, deeming it a devil instead of a friend. They stumble, they reel to and fro, they fall and cry out in a death agony that they would rather abide in the present unknown evil than to be launched into the future unknown.'[4]

There are no known churches or Christians among the unreached Tai He people group. They are still waiting to hear the good news of Jesus Christ.

Today visitors can easily reach Borikhamxai Province by mini-bus from the capital city Vientiane, which in turn is a short flight from Bangkok. Missionaries in the past experienced much more difficult ordeals travelling to areas of Laos. Lillian Johnson Curtis, a missionary in the late 1800s and early 1900s, described her travel from Bangkok to Laos: 'There is but one way of reaching the land of the Laos, unless, indeed, you may wish to go to Burma and take the tedious and expensive overland trip either by pony or elephant. If you follow in the footsteps of those who have gone before, you will go to Bangkok and there take passage in one of the unique Laos boats that come down to trade each year on the high water. The upper reaches of the river are exceedingly dangerous, as many rapids and narrow rocky gorges are found in the mountain-passes. . . . The journey can be cut in time to some eighteen or twenty

Overview of the Tai He

Other Names: He

Population Sources: 8,000 in Laos (1995, Asian Minorities Outreach)

Language: Tai-Kadai, Kam-Tai, Unclassified

Dialects: 0

Professing Buddhists: 60%

Practising Buddhists: 35%

Christians: 0%

Scripture: none

Jesus film: none

Gospel Recordings: none

Christian Broadcasting: none

ROPAL code: none

Status of Evangelization

88%

12%

0%

A   B   C

A = Have never heard the gospel
B = Have heard the gospel but have not become Christians
C = Are adherents to some form of Christianity

Tai Khang

More than 5,600 Tai Khang people live in northern and central Laos. 'They are concentrated in the Xam-Tai District of Houaphan Province, near the Vietnam border. A few spill across into the Nongkhet District of Xiangkhoang Province, while a Diaspora group live further south in the Viangthong District of Borikhamxai Province.'[1]

The Tai Khang population is expected to grow quickly in the coming years, numbering more than 7,000 in 2010 and estimated to grow to almost 9,000 by 2020. Laos has one of the highest birth rates in the world. 'In some communities, women have ten or more children. Children are seen as a great blessing, especially in rice-farming areas where as many hands as possible are needed to work in the fields.'[2] It is possible that Tai Khang people also live inside Vietnam, where they may be part of the official Thai minority group.

There is some debate about whether the main religion of the Tai Khang should be listed as animism or Buddhism, although a recent booklet by the Overseas Missionary Fellowship has listed them as a Buddhist group.[3] Another report states, 'The Tai Khang are traditionally animists, but in recent decades they have come under the influence of Buddhism more as ethnic Lao expand to some of the more far-flung parts of the nation.'[4]

According to one Christian missionary, the history of Buddhism in Laos dates back to around the 5th century AD,

Christian Far East Ministry

when 'there came missionaries from Ceylon [Sri Lanka] into the Laos provinces bearing with them the sacred scriptures of the Buddhists. We might say that these missionaries were very successful, for they were not persecuted or stoned, nor killed and they had the reward of seeing the people by villages and towns embracing their teachings. How different was the reception and spread of this religion from the true religion which the white-faced missionaries brought fourteen centuries afterwards! The secret lay in the fact that Buddhism was not exclusive while Christianity was; Buddhism allowed its adherents to retain their old system of spirit-worship, while Christianity said, Ye cannot serve two masters. Buddhism simply supplemented the existent faith, adding hereto a moral code and a clerical literature, while Christianity insisted, first, put off the old man with his deeds. . . . And so Buddhism flourished and became the nominal religion of the land, save of a few hill tribes here and there. But the old religion [animism] brought down with the Tais from the valley of the Yangtsi still lived and ruled men's hearts.'[5]

The twin strongholds of animistic spirit-worship and Theravada Buddhism continue to grip the hearts of the Tai Khang to this day. There are no known Christians among them. One book laments, 'Without hope in this world or the next, the Tai Khang of Laos have little awareness of the gospel. A few may have listened to gospel radio broadcasts in the Tai Dam or Lao languages, but most remain completely ignorant of the claims of Christ or their need for the Savior.'[6]

Population:
5,620 (2000)
7,090 (2010)
8,950 (2020)

Countries: Laos, possibly in Vietnam

Buddhism: Theravada

Christians: none known

Overview of the Tai Khang

Other Names: Kang, Tai Khaang, Tay Khang, Khang

Population Sources: 5,000 in Laos (1995, Asian Minorities Outreach)
possibly also in Vietnam

Language: Tai-Kadai, Kam-Tai, Unclassified

Dialects: 0

Professing Buddhists: 55%

Practising Buddhists: 25%

Christians: 0%

Scripture: none

Jesus film: none

Gospel Recordings: none

Christian Broadcasting: none

ROPAL code: TNU (Tay Khang) and possibly KYP (Kang)

Status of Evangelization

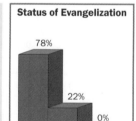

A = Have never heard the gospel
B = Have heard the gospel but have not become Christians
C = Are adherents to some form of Christianity

78% — A
22% — B
0% — C

Population:
450 (2000)
570 (2010)
710 (2020)
Countries: Laos
Buddhism: Theravada
Christians: none known

Overview of the Tai Laan

Other Names: Tai Lan, Laan
Population Sources: 400 in Laos (1995, Asian Minorities Outreach)
Language: Tai-Kadai, Kam-Tai, Unclassified
Dialects: 0
Professing Buddhists: 55%
Practising Buddhists: 30%
Christians: 0%
Scripture: none
***Jesus* film:** none
Gospel Recordings: none
Christian Broadcasting: none
ROPAL code: none

Status of Evangelization

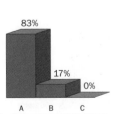

83%

17%

0%

A   B   C

A = Have never heard the gospel
B = Have heard the gospel but have not become Christians
C = Are adherents to some form of Christianity

One of the smallest and least-known Buddhist people groups in the world is the 450-strong Tai Laan of north-central Laos.

They inhabit a few villages in the Kham District of Xiangkhoang Province in Laos, less than 100 kilometres (62 mi.) from the Vietnam border. 'Formerly, their home was in an isolated part of Laos and they had little contact with other people. Now, since the construction of Highway No. 6 the Tai Laan have gained exposure to outside people, thoughts and merchandise.'[1]

Very little is known about the Tai Laan people. Until recently their existence was not known outside of their area, and little research has been conducted since. While one source lists their religion as animism, with 'a degree of Buddhist influence',[2] another booklet lists the Tai Laan as one of the Buddhist people groups of northern Laos.[3]

Many people in Laos say they are Buddhists, but even a casual look at their daily religious practices shows them to be animists, worshipping and appeasing a wide variety of demonic spirits, as well as other spirits the people consider benevolent. It is often during important celebrations and events that groups like the Tai Laan resort to Buddhist rituals. For the Tai Laan, one such event is the burial of their dead.

A Christian missionary once related her experiences of a Buddhist funeral in Laos: 'The thoughtful and devout always secure the presence of a monk at the deathbed. He recites passages from the sacred books, which few understand, because of their being expressed in Pali instead of the vernacular, and he sprinkles the dying with holy water. . . . If the family of the dead is very poor and cannot afford a cremation, the body is tightly wrapped in a cloth and either laid in a box or tied in a mat. It is then lashed to a pole and is borne to the forest on the shoulders of two men. There a shallow grave is dug, the body buried, and the spot soon forgotten.'[4]

In recent years, Christianity has finally started to gain a small foothold in the nation of Laos. Early missionary endeavours sowed the seed for later harvest, often with the blood of the saints. 'In 1868 the first converts, eight in all, were arrested. Two were taken before the authorities and confessed that they had forsaken Buddhism. The death yoke was then put around their necks and a small rope was passed through holes in their ears and carried tightly over the beam of the house. After a night of torture they still refused to deny Christ and were told to prepare for execution. Taken off into the jungle, they were pounded to death with clubs and one of them who lived too long under this punishment was also thrust through the heart with a spear.'[5]

As yet, there are no reports of any Christians among the Tai Laan people. One book laments this and states, 'Hopefully, with the opening up of the area to the outside world, the gospel will also be one of the commodities imported to the Tai Laan. At this time, the Tai Laan have no awareness of the gospel. No Scriptures, recordings or other material exists in the Tai Laan language.'[6]

Christian Far East Ministry

Tai Loi

The Tai Loi is one of the smallest Buddhist people groups in the world, even though they inhabit areas in two—and possibly three—different countries.

The majority of Tai Loi (approximately 1,400) live in Namkham, in the extreme eastern part of Myanmar's Shan State. A further 500 live on the eastern bank of the Mekong River in the Long District of Luang Namtha Province in north-west Laos. More research needs to be done to determine whether the Tai Loi are also found to the north in Xishuangbanna Prefecture of Yunnan Province, China. The Tai Loi in Myanmar say that they have relatives in China.

There is some confusion about the identity of the Tai Loi and the identity of another small group, the Tai Doi. Both inhabit the same general areas in Myanmar and Laos. Some linguistic sources, including the *Ethnologue*, list Tai Doi as a dialect of Tai Loi.[1] More recent research, however, states that 'although it is clear the two groups are related, today they have different names and ethnic identities. They also speak different dialects. . . . The Tai Loi language is part of the Palaungic branch of Mon-Khmer, although many people presume they are a Tai-speaking group because of their appearance and the fact they live with the Lu. In fact, the Tai Loi reportedly now use the Lu script for reading and writing, even though their spoken language is from a completely different language family.'[2] Another source clarifies that the Tai Loi language is 'closest to Palaung Pale, it has

a lot of sound changes, separating it from Palaung in China also'.[3]

The famous Mekong River has divided the two Tai Loi communities in Myanmar and Laos. For centuries it has been the lifeblood and food source for the Tai Loi. Dr Vrooman, who accompanied Presbyterian missionary Daniel McGilvary on a trip down the Mekong in the early 1900s, wrote, 'The current . . . is very swift, in places so much so that it was dangerous to navigate. The river is nearly a mile wide in places; and where the channel is narrow it rushes along with frightful rapidity. No scenery is finer throughout the entire distance we travelled on it. Mountains rise from either bank to the height of three or four thousand feet. The river fills the bottom of a long winding valley; as we glided swiftly down it, there seemed to move in a panorama two half-erect hanging landscapes of woodland verdure and blossom.'[4]

The Mekong Delta is also one of the strongest Theravada Buddhist areas in Asia. Gold-coloured temple roofs can be seen through the palm branches on each side of the river, testimony to a centuries-old belief in Buddhism by the peoples of the region.

There are no known Christian believers among the Tai Loi in either Myanmar or Laos. A gospel recording does exist in the Tai Loi language, but it is rarely utilized because of the remoteness of this group.

Population:
1,930 (2000)
2,250 (2010)
2,630 (2020)
Countries: Myanmar, Laos, possibly China
Buddhism: Theravada
Christians: none known

Overview of the Tai Loi

Other Names: Loi, Doi, Wakut, Monglwe, Tailoi
Population Sources: 1,368 in Myanmar (2002, Myanmar Faces and Places)
500 in Laos (1995, Asian Minorities Outreach)
possibly also in China
1,500 in all countries (1981, S Wurm and S Hattori)
Language: Austro-Asiatic, Mon-Khmer, Northern Mon-Khmer, Palaungic-Khmuic, Palaungic, Western Palaungic, Angkuic
Dialects: 0
Professing Buddhists: 55%
Practising Buddhists: 25%
Christians: 0%
Scripture: none
***Jesus* film:** none
Gospel Recordings: Tai Loi
Christian Broadcasting: none
ROPAL code: TLQ

Status of Evangelization

80%

20%

0%

A   B   C

A = Have never heard the gospel
B = Have heard the gospel but have not become Christians
C = Are adherents to some form of Christianity

Julian Hawken

More than half a million Tai Mao people live in China and several neighbouring Southeast Asian nations. The majority, more than 350,000, live in the Dehong Dai Autonomous Prefecture in China's Yunnan Province.[1] They are part of the official Dai nationality in China, which includes more than ten Tai language groups.

Approximately 80,000 Tai Mao—sometimes called Mao Shan, or in Burmese *Shan Tayok*, meaning 'Chinese Shan'—are located in northern Myanmar near the Chinese border, centred around the towns of Namkham and Muse. A further 40,000 Tai Mao make their home in Laos and a mere 100 inhabit one village in northern Thailand.[2]

Many researchers lump the Tai Mao together with the Tai Nua and / or the Shan. Indeed, the Tai Mao spoken language is closely related to varieties of Shan spoken in northern Myanmar, but the two groups use different scripts. The Tai Mao use a 'square' orthography. 'This has been revised and improved, and is still in use in China.'[3]

The Tai Mao have long possessed an advanced culture. By the 13th century they had created a calendar, as well as written books explaining the eclipses of the sun and moon, and they had composed a number of poems, legends and fairy tales. One tale tells of a cataclysmic flood that long ago destroyed most of the people and animals of the world. Through intermarriage among the survivors, the people began to multiply so much that soon the land could not support the needs of so many people.

Myanmar Faces and Places

The Tai Mao are Theravada Buddhists, although aspects of animism and shamanism influence their belief system. The Tai Mao also revere family ancestral spirits, called *diulahagun*. Between mid-July and October every year the Tai Mao do not celebrate any social or religious activities, nor do they visit their relatives or arrange marriages. 'When the busy season is over, they hold the Door Opening Festival, during which time people beat gongs and drums, and dance . . . to announce the end of the farming season.'[4]

The Tai Mao are unevangelized, despite the fact that they live in a region with many Christian churches among the neighbouring peoples. Scripture portions were translated into Tai Mao in 1931. Missionary John Kuhn of the China Inland Mission conducted meetings among the Tai Mao in China in the 1940s. He reported there were 'some fifty thousand people right on that spot and without a single witness to the Gospel. . . . We preached to a group in a home . . . a young lad in his late teens raised his hand to say "I will let the Saviour in". He belonged to the Kang clan of the [Tai Mao] race. I sat and gazed at the young Kang as the first convert in all that area!'[5]

For several years Far East Broadcasting has broadcast gospel radio programmes in the Tai Mao language, which they label 'Chinese Shan'. This, along with some coordinated outreach by local Christians, has resulted in a small but growing Tai Mao church in both China and Myanmar.

Overview of the Tai Mao

Other Names: Kang, Kong, Chinese Shan, Maw, Mao, Dai Mao, Tai Long, Tai Nuea, Dehong Dai, Dehong, Tai Dehong, Tai Le, Dai Le, Tai Loe, Dai Loe, Tai Mo, Dai Mo, Mao Shan, Mau, Northern Shan, Shan Tayok, Tai Che, Tai Khe, Tai Lhong, Tai Yai

Population:
509,700 (2000)
566,500 (2010)
630,800 (2020)
Countries: China, Myanmar, Laos, Thailand, possibly Vietnam
Buddhism: Theravada
Christians: 600

Population Sources:
350,000 in China (1990, A Diller)
72,400 in Myanmar (2000, B Grimes [1983 figure])
35,000 in Laos (1995, L Chazee)
100 in Thailand (2001, J Schliesinger [2000 figure])
possibly also in Vietnam

Language: Tai-Kadai, Kam-Tai, Be-Tai, Tai-Sek, Tai, Southwestern, East Central, Northwest

Dialects: 3 (Southwestern, East Central, Northwest)

Professing Buddhists: 85%

Practising Buddhists: 65%

Christians: 0.1%

Scripture: Portions 1931

Jesus film: none

Gospel Recordings: Tai Mao

Christian Broadcasting: available in 'Chinese Shan'

ROPAL code: TDD01

Status of Evangelization

66%
33%
1%

A   B   C

A = Have never heard the gospel
B = Have heard the gospel but have not become Christians
C = Are adherents to some form of Christianity

Tai Nua

Population:
135,600 (2000)
172,800 (2010)
212,900 (2020)
Countries: China
Buddhism: Theravada
Christians: 20

Overview of the Tai Nua

Other Names: Dai Nuea, Tai Nuea, Paiyi, Tai Nue, Tai Nu, Dai Na

Population Sources:

100,000 in China (1987, D Bradley)

Language: Tai-Kadai, Kam-Tai, Be-Tai, Tai-Sek, Tai, Southwestern, East Central, Northwest

Dialects: 0

Professing Buddhists: 50%

Practising Buddhists: 20%

Christians: 0.1%

Scripture: none

Jesus **film:** none

Gospel Recordings: none

Christian Broadcasting: none

ROPAL code: TDD

Status of Evangelization

80%

19%

1%

A   B   C

A = Have never heard the gospel
B = Have heard the gospel but have not become Christians
C = Are adherents to some form of Christianity

There is a great deal of confusion regarding the names used to classify the various Tai groups in China. Many publications call the Tai in the Dehong Prefecture *Tai Nua*, a name meaning 'northern Tai'. The Tai in Dehong are profiled in this book under the name *Tai Mao*, according to the classification of linguist David Bradley, who says that 'The Tai Nua or "Northern Tai" live in south-western Yunnan along river valleys; they number about 100,000.'[1] Those groups in Laos and Thailand who call themselves *Tai Nua* have also been included as *Tai Mao*. The Tai Nua discussed here are a group found only in Yunnan Province in China.[2]

The confusion of names is caused partly by 'the Chinese tendency to group languages together into nationalities, exemplified by the Dai nationality, which includes all the Southwestern Tai languages of China'.[3] Linguists have pointed out that Tai Nua is 'a name given to at least two quite different south-western branch groups'.[4] Indeed, Tai Nua, Tai Mao and Shan are on one hand distinct, and yet they are also related! It is difficult to determine where one language stops and the other starts. The situation is not black and white, but one vernacular gradually evolves into another.

After a Tai Nua wedding ceremony, the bridegroom goes to live with his bride's family. Traditionally he must take with him gifts of tea, rice, meat, bananas, four eggs and two salted fish for his new in-laws. Upon arrival, the village elder takes the packets

of tea and rice out to the road and calls on the spirits of heaven and earth to witness the marriage. He then ties a white thread around the wrist of the bride seven times, and once around the wrist of the groom, to indicate their unbreakable commitment to each other.[5]

Although they are nominally Theravada Buddhists, the Tai Nua have mixed many aspects of animism and polytheism into their beliefs. The very first Tai god was Shalou, the god of hunting. 'Before a hunt, sacrifices were . . . offered to Shalou to avert danger and to ensure success in the hunt.'[6] Buddhism has less of a grip on the Tai Nua than it does on the Tai Mao north-west of them in the Dehong Prefecture, or on the Lu who live south of them. The Tai Nua region has fewer temples and monasteries, and the main connection many Tai Nua have to Buddhism is through the observance of Buddhist rites at births, weddings and funerals.

There are just a few known Christians among the Tai Nua. Very little outreach is presently focused on bringing the gospel to them. Part of the problem is that visitors often struggle to see the difference between the Tai Nua and local Han Chinese, as many of those living near towns have become assimilated. Little improvement in the spiritual condition of the Tai Nua has taken place since the 1920s when one missionary lamented, 'There is not a missionary working south of Kunming to Mohei. . . . I am here alone and my little candle is the only light. Yet in these mountains are thousands of tribes-men who have never heard of the Gospel.'[7]

Photo credit: Create International

Approximately 4,000 members of the Tai Pao ethnic group inhabit areas of central Laos in Southeast Asia. Laos—despite its relatively small population of about six million people—is home to more than 140 tribes and ethnolinguistic groups.[1] Many of them are small in number, like the Tai Pao.

The Tai Pao villages are located in the Viangthong, Khamkeut and Pakkading districts of Borikhamxai Province, Laos.[2] Their communities are found at the border where these three districts intersect. The Tai Pao live near another small Buddhist group, the Tai He, and in fact may be related to them. Neither language has been researched by linguists to determine mutual intelligibility. The *Ethnologue* reports 'Classification problems, probably due to migration. Survey needed.'[3]

The religious world-view of the Tai Pao people is 'a mixture of animism and Theravada Buddhism. Such a religious intertwining has existed in Laos since Buddhism was introduced.'[4]

In Laos today, even professing Buddhists continue to seek the guidance of the spirits in matters that may benefit them. For example, thousands of people visit mediums in an effort to divine 'lucky numbers' which could help them win the lottery.

Contemporary author Grant Evans comments, 'The destabilizing of Lao culture and society . . . [has] seen people flock to all varieties of religious consultants in an attempt to find some orientation and

meaning in all of these changes. . . . This is especially evident in what I call "lottery mania" and the attempt to get rich quickly. . . . Every time I sat down with a Lao the conversation would drift toward lottery numbers and how to divine them: through dream interpretation, consultations with monks or nuns who would be asked for numbers, or other spirit mediums. With the collapse of socialist ideology no other explanations are offered for the confusions thrown up by economic, social and cultural change, and religious belief in all its variety has rapidly filled the gap.'[5]

One of the new and growing influences in Laos in recent years is Christianity. Although there have been small numbers of Christians—both Protestant and Catholic—in Laos for more than a century, since 1990 the Christian community in Laos has more than tripled in size. This has come about despite the fact that the Communist authorities in Laos have spared no effort to stop the spread of Christianity. Periodic crackdowns occur throughout the country, and there always seem to be a number of church leaders in prison in Laos at any given time.

Despite these encouraging developments, the small Tai Pao tribe has yet to experience God's grace. They remain an unreached people group with no known Christians. For the Tai Pao, 'maintaining their culture is equally as important as their religious beliefs. Accordingly, the few Tai Pao who have been exposed to the Gospel have not seriously considered it, believing that to become a Christian would be a disgrace against their culture and heritage as a Tai Pao.'[6]

Population:
3,710 (2000)
4,680 (2010)
5,900 (2020)
Countries: Laos
Buddhism: Theravada
Christians: none known

Overview of the Tai Pao

Other Names: Pao, Tay Pao

Population Sources: 3,300 in Laos (1995, Asian Minorities Outreach)

Language: Tai-Kadai, Kam-Tai, Unclassified

Dialects: 0

Professing Buddhists: 55%

Practising Buddhists: 25%

Christians: 0%

Scripture: none

Jesus **film:** none

Gospel Recordings: none

Christian Broadcasting: none

ROPAL code: TPO

Photo credit: Paul Hattaway

Status of Evangelization

79%

21%

0%

A   B   C

A = Have never heard the gospel
B = Have heard the gospel but have not become Christians
C = Are adherents to some form of Christianity

Tai Phake

According to scholar Anthony Diller of the Australian National University, several thousand Tai Phake people live in the north-east Indian state of Assam.[1] They are concentrated in five villages on the banks of the Burddihing (also called Dihing) River in Dibrugarh District in the extreme north-east of the state. The Tai Phake people originally lived further to the east in Mogoung.[2]

Various researchers agree that the Tai Phake language is a Southwestern Tai language, similar to Shan, which is spoken by more than three million people in north-east Myanmar, south-west China and northern Thailand. The name Tai Phake 'is derived from the term *pha*, meaning king or chief and *ke*, meaning an official, as they claim they are descendants of the Tai Royal officials. They are also referred to as Phakial and use Gohain or Phake as surnames.'[3]

Few people have ever heard of the Tai Phake because the Indian government has ignored their requests for official recognition. They have not been granted status either as a Scheduled Tribe or Scheduled Caste in India, leaving them somewhat anonymous and politically powerless.

Undoubtedly the Tai Phake are a remnant from the days when the Tai-speaking Ahom ruled the area. The Ahom kings reigned from Sibsagar in Assam for more than 600 years before the arrival of the British.[4] Most of the Ahom people were assimilated into Assamese culture and gradually lost the use of their mother tongue and now speak Assamese. Some small pockets of people, including the Tai Phake, appear to have survived the assimilation process and retain their language and culture to this day.[5] Other surviving Tai languages in north-east India include Khamti, Khamiyang, Aiton and Turung.

All Tai Phake people profess Theravada Buddhism as their religion. They brought Buddhism with them when they first migrated from Myanmar (Burma) and have retained their religion over the centuries, although they are now influenced by Hinduism as well as animistic practices. Every Tai Phake village has its own Buddhist temple. Their communities are divided into two categories: the secular and the clergy. The villagers are hard workers who produce Sali paddy, mustard, arum and potatoes. The Buddhist monks, however, are exempt from farm work. 'The Tai Phake observe six festivals which are intimately related with the worship of Lord Buddha. They are *Poi Chang Ken, Luicheti, Poi Nen Hok, Meiko Chumfai, Poi Nen Chi* and *Poi Kathin*. . . . The [Tai Phake monks] accept cooked food and water from the neighboring non-Phake communities and visit their households. Intercommunity marriages especially with the Buddhist groups are not looked at with contempt.'[6]

Christianity has failed to make much of an impact in this remote part of Assam. There are no known churches or Christians among the Tai Phake people. Their identity is bound up in their belief in Buddhism, so for an individual or family to break away from the status quo and believe in Christ is difficult.

Population:
4,600 (2000)
5,400 (2010)
6,350 (2020)
Countries: India
Buddhism: Theravada
Christians: none known

Overview of the Tai Phake

Other Names: Phake, Phakial, Phakey, Faake, Palke
Population Sources:
'several thousand' in India (1990, A Diller)
Language: Tai-Kadai, Kam-Tai, Be-Tai, Tai-Sek, Tai, Southwestern, East Central, Northwest
Dialects: 0
Professing Buddhists: 100%
Practising Buddhists: 95%
Christians: 0%
Scripture: none
Jesus film: none
Gospel Recordings: none
Christian Broadcasting: none
ROPAL code: PHK

Status of Evangelization

85%

15%

0%

A   B   C
A = Have never heard the gospel
B = Have heard the gospel but have not become Christians
C = Are adherents to some form of Christianity

Myanmar Faces and Places

Population:
18,050 (2000)
20,600 (2010)
24,500 (2020)
Countries: Laos, Thailand
Buddhism: Theravada
Christians: 40

Overview of the Tai Wang

Other Names: Tai Wang Angkham, Tai Wang Na Yom, Phu Tai Wang

Population Sources: 10,000 in Laos (2003, P Hattaway)

8,000 in Thailand (2001, J Schliesinger [1999 figure])

Language: Tai-Kadai, Kam-Tai, Be-Tai, Tai-Sek, Tai, Southwestern, East Central, Lao-Phutai

Dialects: 0

Professing Buddhists: 98%

Practising Buddhists: 70%

Christians: 0.2%

Scripture: none

Jesus film: none

Gospel Recordings: none

Christian Broadcasting: none

ROPAL code: none

Status of Evangelization

83%

17%

0%

A   B   C

A = Have never heard the gospel
B = Have heard the gospel but have not become Christians
C = Are adherents to some form of Christianity

One of the least-known people groups in Southeast Asia is the Tai Wang. More than 10,000 live in several villages in the Viraburi District of Savannakhet Province in central Laos, while an additional 8,000 Tai Wang live in and around the city of Phanna Nikhom in Sakhon Nakhon Province, north-east Thailand. In fact, Tai Wang is the main ethnic group living in the town of Phanna Nikhom, which lies on national highway number 22, about an hour's drive from the Thailand-Laos border.

Like many tribes and ethnic groups in this part of the world, the Tai Wang in Laos and Thailand were separated by a tumultuous history. In 1843, the ancestors of the Tai Wang who live in Thailand were captured as prisoners of war by the Siamese army and taken across the Mekong River from their homeland in central Laos to their present location in Thailand.[1] For two generations they were forced to render manual labour for the Thai authorities.

In Laos the government does not recognize the Tai Wang as a distinct people group but has combined them—along with several other loosely related tribes—with the Phutai minority. Indeed, the Tai Wang do share some cultural and linguistic similarities with the Phutai, but as one scholar has stated, the 'languages are comparable but dissimilar. The Tai Wang speak a more distinctive Lao language variety.'[2] Historically and socially, the Tai Wang do consider themselves a separate people group, while at the same time they acknowledge their connection to the Phutai on a wider scale.

In the past the Tai Wang women wore a

traditional black dress decorated with 'several rows of colored horizontal stripes at the lower part, a long-sleeved vest buttoned with small silver coins in front and decorated with red bands along the hem. . . . Every woman wore a heavy bracelet and a heavy silver belt.'[3] These days the women do not wear their traditional dress on a daily basis, but they do wear a modified form of it during important festivals when young Tai Wang maidens dress up in their best clothes in the hope of attracting the eye of a young suitor from a neighbouring village.

Until the 1970s the Tai Wang were very skilled at weaving cotton clothing on their large traditional looms. These days this skill has all but disappeared, as the practical Tai Wang have found it much easier to buy the modern clothing sold in markets and shops.

Xayographix

The economic backbone of the Tai Wang community in Thailand is agriculture. 'They are well known for producing watermelon seeds, which are exported as far away as Europe and the USA. They also grow peanuts, cucumber, chilies, paprika and cotton.'[4]

Almost all Tai Wang people in Laos and Thailand believe in Theravada Buddhism. They also worship a spirit known as *san chao pu sae na narong* which, they believe, protects their villages.

There are thought to be a small number of Christians among the Tai Wang. Most of this precious people group live and die without the slightest knowledge of the name of Jesus Christ.

275

Tak Bai Thai

More than 24,000 people living at the border of southern Thailand and northern Malaysia belong to the unique yet little-known Tak Bai Thai people group. In Thailand, approximately 20,000 Tak Bai Thai inhabit the three provinces nearest the Thai-Malay border: Narathiwat,[1] Pattani[2] and Yala. The geographical centre of the Tak Bai Thai people is the district that bears their name, Tak Bai, in Narathiwat Province. Tak Bai is just a mile or two from the Malaysian border.

Additional communities of Tak Bai Thai people are in Peninsula Malaysia.[3] 'When Kelantan came under British colonial rule in 1909, and the borders of Malaysia were fixed, the Tak Bai Thai were thus suddenly divided. Several thousand Tak Bai Thai live still across the border in Kelantan state of Malaysia who have family members in and around Tak Bai District in Thailand.'[4]

The Buddhist Tak Bai Thai live alongside Southern Thai and Pattani Muslims. The groups are tolerant of each other, though they keep their distance and have little close contact. Conflicts sometimes arise over land use. The Tak Bai Thai own almost all the land in the areas where they live, while the Muslims have almost none. This has led to tensions as the Muslims sometimes encroach illegally onto the Tak Bai Thai land, building houses and huts without permission.

Most ethnographic research on Thailand lists the Tak Bai Thai as part of the Southern Thai language group, but their vernacular is very different.[5] It has been described as 'a rather distinct and ancient Tai dialect, which developed differently from most of the modern Tai dialects spoken in Thailand today. Tak Bai Thai is very different from the Southern Thai language; it is more a mixture of northern and central Thai dialects, but articulated in the fast manner as the Southern Thai usually speak. Some words are exactly the same as the Thai speak in the Sukkothai area [in north-central Thailand].'[6]

Christian Far East Ministry

In fact, linguist Marvin Brown has found that the Tak Bai Thai language is similar to that spoken by people in Sukkothai in AD 1250.[7] It is not beyond the realm of possibility, therefore, that the Tak Bai Thai people along today's Thailand-Malaysia border are the descendants resulting from an interesting historical incident. Joachim Schliesinger says that 'when King Ramkhamhaeng of Sukkothai extended the power of his kingdom deep into the Malay peninsula in the late thirteenth century, he resettled thousands of Thai people from the Sukkothai region to the south, most probably to strengthen his foothold in this far corner of the kingdom. . . . They brought with them Buddhism and built many Buddhist temples in and around Pron, establishing Buddhism in the southern areas of the Malay peninsulas before Islam was introduced.'[8]

More than 700 years after they arrived in the area, the Tak Bai Thai people are still zealous Buddhists. Having to fight off the advances of Islam has made them even stronger in their faith and even more resistant to change. Few have ever heard of Jesus Christ, and a mere handful have put their trust in him.

Overview of the Tak Bai Thai

Population:
24,000 (2000)
26,600 (2010)
29,700 (2020)
Countries: Thailand, Malaysia
Buddhism: Theravada
Christians: 20

Other Names: Pak Tai, Pak Thai, Paktay, Takbai Thai, Thai Tak Bai

Population Sources: 20,000 in Thailand (2001, J Schliesinger [2000 figure])
'several thousand' in Malaysia (2001, J Schliesinger)

Language: Tai-Kadai, Kam-Tai, Be-Tai, Tai-Sek, Tai, Southwestern, Southern

Dialects: 0

Professing Buddhists: 99%
Practising Buddhists: 80%
Christians: 0.1%
Scripture: none
Jesus **film:** none
Gospel Recordings: none
Christian Broadcasting: none
ROPAL code: SOU01

Status of Evangelization

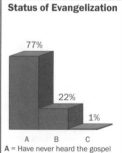

A = Have never heard the gospel
B = Have heard the gospel but have not become Christians
C = Are adherents to some form of Christianity

The Thai Way of Meekness

Ubolwan Mejudhon

Christians have long lamented the lack of progress of the gospel in Thailand. After more than 200 years of missionary enterprise, less than one per cent of Thai people have faith in Christ. Thai Christian Ubolwan Mejudhon examines some of the reasons behind the Thais' apparent resistance to Christianity—which may have more to do with the methods employed by the messengers than with the message itself.

Thailand is my beloved country. Outsiders call Thailand 'the land of smiles', but I call her 'my mother land'. I think Thailand smiles at outsiders, but Thailand sobs, cries and laughs with me because we belong to each other. That sense of belonging between Thailand and me gives me a good cultural identity.

Buddhism embraced me from birth. I learned Buddhism through persons whose lives pointed to Buddha's teaching. I remember how my mother cared for the poor and faced suffering with quiet courage. Suffering never harmed her but created in her more empathy and understanding for others.

Buddhism taught me through sight, sound and stories. My upbringing was a time of peace, of joy. There were no drunkards on the street or gun-firing in my hometown, Cholburi. Young men entered the monkhood, and many lay people vowed to keep the five Buddhist precepts. Relatives and friends shouted and danced with joy, leading novices to Buddhist temples. In the city, high school bands marched through the town, celebrating with gigantic candles. Most people watched and celebrated. Monks beat drums and bells in special rhythms—ta-loom-toom-meng—repeatedly. My heart leaped with joy, absorbing Buddhism in the Thai way, the way of meekness. I learned about Buddhism through the communities that participated in Buddhist rituals—it was a relational and inductive education.

Buddhism bonded me to spiritual truth in a meek way, a Thai way. For Buddhists, story is life and life is story. Where there is no story, there is no life. Thailand allowed me to seek and find truth by my own initiative.

I became a teacher, teaching Buddhist philosophy to engineering students in a university, beginning in 1968.

In 1971, I was sent to study 'Teaching English as a Second Language' at Victoria University, Wellington, New Zealand. I got lost in the streets, feeling confused, frightened and sad. I realized that I did not belong in this land. I was a sojourner, losing my mental map. I held fast to my Buddhism and Thai culture. I gently discipled people around me with acts of kindness, knowing that they were sad, too. When an Indonesian lady lost her costly train ticket, I loaned her some money. When my Thai roommate was sad and confused, I brought her a bunch of daffodils and asked permission to read a portion of Buddhist scripture to her. I found that Thai meekness effectively eased the pain of living abroad.

Then one day I met a Christian from Korea. I was surprised. 'He should be a Buddhist, not a Christian,' I thought. I observed that he spoke loudly when he talked about Christianity and Jesus, in season and out of season. I felt offended and planned to convert him to Buddhism. Therefore I invited him to dialogue with me about religions. It turned out I did

Buddhism is deeply ingrained into Thai life and culture. An elderly lady places an offering into a monk's bowl, 6 a.m. Mae Hong Son in Thailand.

International Mission Board

277

not have any chance to speak. He talked long and loudly. I listened to him, learning good things about Christianity which I would apply to my life. I was truly surprised that Hong Sung Chul expected me to believe in Jesus so soon. I wanted to discuss his religion; I did not want to be converted. I showed him pictures of my country so we would change the topic. I was offended when his face showed disgust as he looked at a picture of a gorgeous gold statue of Buddha. He said it was an idol.

A monk flicks holy water on a man, Wat Phrasing, Chiang Mai, Thailand.

That evening I learned that Christians were not meek, but assertive. Through Hong Sung Chul, I met many Christians. Most of them were eager to share with me how to be saved. Most of them had negative ideas about Buddha and Buddhism. I felt like a lone lamb among wolves. The things that helped me keep fellowship with them were their sincerity and honesty, which Buddhism and Thai culture taught me to detect. Moreover, God did reveal to me personally that he existed. I wanted to learn who Jesus was. I read the Bible, some Christian books, some atheistic books, and I observed Christian lives.

Nine days before I returned to Thailand I met another Christian, Mr Gordon Junck. He didn't witness to me, but I became a Christian. The elderly missionary spoke positively about Buddha and Buddhism. He simply said, 'Buddha was a very good man, but Jesus is God, daughter.' Then he gently hugged me and said goodbye. He said the word 'daughter' gently, and his grandfatherly hug linked me to the heavenly Father.

The way of meekness led me to Christ. That night, 28 October 1971, I became a Christian myself. My heart was filled with joy because of my renewed relationship with God. I believed I was Thai, and I loved my country even more. I wanted to share with my people that Jesus was the true, living God, and that he could help us fulfil all Buddhist precepts. He could transform lives, because he was God of all nations. However, when I returned to Thailand at the end of 1971, I found that I could not be Christian and Thai.

If my heart was a cup containing water which was Thai, Jesus had expanded that cup to love humankind beyond nationalities and races. However, Western Christianity filled my cup with oil and fire above the water. These three elements struggled within me. I learned that witnessing was very important for Christians in Thailand. I learned how to witness from other Christians in Thailand, using Western forms of witnessing which they saw as the one and only way. I argued with the Thai on the basis of rational, propositional truth about Christianity, but most Thais refused to argue with me. They are meek.

Distributing tracts was an alternative. Day in and day out, I roamed the streets, giving tracts to the Thai. Policemen used to stop me, suspecting I was a leftist. Leftists stopped me, thinking I was one of them. I gave tracts to both policemen and leftists. Many times I went to Buddhist monasteries to persuade monks to become Christians. The sympathetic look on their faces told me they considered me eccentric. I kept on witnessing in various ways. I wanted monks to read the Bible. When monks asked for food in the morning, I put small Bibles in their sacred bowls.

My friends and relatives complained that my ways of witnessing were weird. At that time I praised the Lord, thinking Christians should be accused and persecuted. I thought these people did not understand. I simply did the good things all Christians in the world were doing in order that this perishing world would be saved.

From time to time, however, a small, still voice seemed to ask me, 'Where has the gracious Ubolwan gone? Why have you become like a crusader?' I pushed these questions out of my mind because they disturbed me. I thought Thais could not be Thai and Christian. That thought disrupted my cultural identity because I forsook the Thai way of meekness.

At present, Thai Christians lose their cultural identity because they cannot be Christian and Thai in the Thai way of meekness. Thai Christianity follows Western methods of discipling which alienate Thai Christians from the Thai way of meekness, a dominant value of Thai culture. As a result, the spreading of the gospel suffers when Christians, Christianity and churches are perceived by the Thai as violating the Thai way of meekness in their presentation of the gospel, discipling and disciplining. Such evangelizing violates self-identity, grateful relationships, smooth interpersonal relationships and flexibility and adaptation in Thai culture. Thai Christian converts cannot fit in with their social networks and kinsmen because of their aggressive ways of witnessing, which are influenced by Western methods rooted in a different cultural context.

The discipling and disciplining of Christian churches in Thailand follow the same route. Discipleship training is direct, cognitively oriented, instantaneous, passing on information without significant relational bonding. Thai Christians find it hard to move progressively to Jesus Christ, who is the centre of their faith in the fullness of the Holy Spirit, as they lack living models of Christ in their Christian lives. They lose their cultural identity, their ties with social networks and kinsmen, and they cannot quite understand how to live victorious lives as Christians. When they fall due to secularism and temptations, the churches discipline them in such a way that they 'lose face' and the ties with their Christian brethren. As a result, they lose almost all of their identity. It is difficult for Thai Christians to keep their faith in Jesus Christ, whom they love, when they cut themselves off from their cultural, natural and social roots. Spreading the gospel in Thailand has been difficult for more than 150 years because Christians in Thailand do not practise the Thai way

of meekness.

Thai individuals prefer group harmony, especially close family ties and smooth interpersonal relations, while American children are taught at any early age to be assertive, self-expressive and individualistic so that they will fit well with their egalitarian system. Thai children are taught to be obedient, polite and subdued, so that they will live in harmony with their own hierarchical social order.

It is difficult for Westerners to understand the Thai, because Westerners emphasize the cognitive domain. Westerners use their heads to classify people into categories and move people up or down the civilization or moral development scale. The Thai

Monks in a procession at Tad Luang, Vientiane, Laos.

use their hearts to classify people as friends or foes, insiders or outsiders. Everything is an end in itself for Westerners; everything is a means to an end to preserve self-identity and relationship for the Thai. As a result, Westerners are outward explorers. They visit the moon and stars. Easterners are inward explorers; all world religions originated in the East.

Christians in Thailand do not study Thai culture to find out what Thai identity is, what creates Thai identity or what successful ways Thai people use to introduce change in ideology and behaviour. Christians in Thailand do not question the intelligibility, validity and credibility of the methods they use in discipling. They simply suffer the consequences; Christians make up less than one per cent of the population in Thailand after more than 150 years of witnessing.

After 23 years of faithfully following Western methods of discipleship, I struggle with many questions. Are these the methods Thai Christians have used for more than 150 years since Protestantism entered Thailand? What has been the result? How do non-Christian Thais perceive and explain Christians, Christianity and the churches? Has not the time come for us Christians to evaluate our past and present? Would Jesus use Western methods in the Thai cultural context? Can one be Thai and Christian at the same time? Why or why

were people of influence among the Thais in the four regions of Thailand where the local cultural context was different. My sample is an effort to be representative. The interview questions follow.

First, the research interviews suggest that the Thais interviewed (100 per cent) believe in self-worth, that we are all equal. Everybody is worthy of being respected, because all are human beings. One former university instructor mused, 'Do not think that Westerners are better than Thais. We are equal, because we are human beings alike. I feel that Thai Christians worship Westerners.' A respondent confirmed, 'Thai respect all religions. Our king honours all faiths.'

The respondents also had strong self-confidence. An engineer declared, 'Christian are boring. They have no self-identity or self-confidence. They throw all kinds of problems to God and use no brain or abilities.' A high school girl agreed,

On the way to worship Buddha: a night-time procession at Tad Luang in Vientiane, Laos.

Xayographix

not? What makes one a Thai? Is it the Thai way of meekness? How can one be both Christian and Thai? How can Thai Christians construct their own ways of discipling, which are key factors in spreading the gospel in Thailand? Lastly, what is the role of the Thai way of meekness for Christian missions in Thailand?

Research interviews with Thai Buddhists on the Thai Way of meekness

As I struggled to find answers to these and other questions, I interviewed 57 non-Christian Thais. My criteria for choosing the non-Christian interviewees were: 1) they had considerable knowledge of the gospel and the Christian church and had known Christians for more than three years; 2) they had a good understanding of Thai culture; 3) they

'I think God is very important to Christians. In all things, Christians refer to God, God, God. I feel that Christians do not depend on themselves.'

Thai Buddhists interviewed admire self-confidence. They like those who try their best to solve their immediate problems before turning to unseen powers. They believe human lives should have purpose, and those who do not first stand on their own feet lack confidence, are lazy and psychologically sick. A Buddhist engineer manager voiced the caring concern: 'It is obvious that Christians can never get many strong leaders as long as the leaders of Christians in Thailand do not clarify the expressions, 'trust completely in God', 'in everything turn to God' and 'everything will be fine if you trust in God.' The Thai interpret these expressions as doing nothing, hanging your destiny on fate.'

The self-identity and self-confidence of the Thai interviewees suggested the following taboos: 1) do not trample Buddhism; 2) do not force or persuade Thais to make an instant decision; 3) do not challenge Thais; and 4) do not contrast religions.

A Buddhist who has worked with Christians for more than 15 years calmly observed:

> Christians attack Buddha images which Buddhists respect. My mother taught me to respect Christianity, their churches and crosses. I listen to my young staff members blaspheme the sacred protector of Thailand whom I love. I feel despised. Christians did not give me a chance to speak up when we had religious disagreements . . . Why can't these aggressive, new Christians learn from the gentleness and politeness of old, ecumenical Christians whom I admire?

Another young man from a slum community related:

> Ten of my friends and I received Protestant scholarships for ten years. We were forced to attend a church every Sunday. In the church, the pastor forced us to be Christian. As long as the scholarships continued to flow, we could stand being forced.
>
> When the scholarships were terminated, we attended a Catholic school where the priest did not force or give any scholarships. Many of my friends became Catholic priests.

An interviewee lamented, 'I do not like missionaries who distribute many things to Thai youngsters and persuade them to be Christian.' A university graduate confided, 'Usually, I respect Christians, but I always feel a bondage whenever I invade a Christian boundary. Buddhism creates no bondage. Christianity requires me to attend church every Sunday. I am tired. I want to be free!'

While Americans enjoy challenge, these Thai interviewees detest the word. A man complained about a Christian lady who said to him, 'I want to challenge you to support this organization.' He mumbled, 'Challenge! That is a sensuous, sexual, stimulating word.' A school teacher taught me, 'If Christians challenge me, I will challenge them back. Don't ever dare to challenge Thais.'

The interviewees detested the contrast between religions, although they liked to compare good teaching in various faiths. Most of them echoed the response of one who said, 'Don't contrast religions. Don't be boastful of your own religion.'

Non-Christian interviewees concluded that Christians should be Christian and Thai. Thai-ness gave self-identity to the Thai. As one respondent pointed out, 'People of all faiths in Thailand must be good Thai citizens. We do not segregate people because of their faith.' A high school girl proposed, 'People in Thailand must cherish Thai culture regardless of their faith. They must respect hierarchy. Elderly people, parents and teachers must be respected.'

Second, respondents (65 per cent) valued the grateful relationship orientation. An administrator voiced his confusion about a Christian, 'I don't understand why she always thanks God but never thanks me.' Another teacher commented about his Christian brother, 'I prepared a meal for him. He did not take time to thank me, but he thanked God.'

An interviewee suggested, 'Good persons must help others with honesty and sincerity and without hidden agendas.' A respondent added, 'Thais cherish generosity. Generosity in time of crisis brings about grateful relationships.'

Third, next to self-identity and grateful relationships, interviewees (70 per cent) emphasized smooth relationships. A non-Christian commented, 'I observe that Christians are egocentric. Leaders lack reasons. Christians do not hold my heart in good consideration. Christians lack trust in non-Christians.' Another interviewee vented his anger, 'Christians are aggressive and threatening. If you do not believe in Jesus, you'll go to hell. Why do Christians attack other religions?' A lady shared her feelings, 'I cannot help but ask myself why Christians are extremely aggressive, and act unbecomingly.' A manager voiced his perception, 'The voice and the tone of Christian preachers are aggressive. I feel oppressed, unhappy and manipulated. They do not respect time, place and persons.' One respondent gives the following advice:

> We are Thais, we can communicate smoothly. We don't have to confront each other. A good person must have a smooth relationship with other fellowmen. Thais who have religion in their hearts will be humble, gentle and are not rough or rude.

Fourth, the interviewees (47 per cent) confirmed the important role of flexibility and adjustment orientation. A Buddhist teacher in a Christian school expressed her concept of Thai's flexibility and adjustment, 'I believe in both religions,

Young Thai men pray and burn incense before an altar in Chiang Mai, Thailand.

participating in religious festival and worship. A high school kid related, 'I like Christmas Eve. The school provides a lot of cookies and communal activities to enjoy.' A lady shared, 'I like Christian worship. It is fun to sing. We also like humorous preachers who tell us funny stories.' I observed that these non-Christians responded to the interview questions seriously, and the lack of small talk was obvious during interviewing.

Most non-Christians (70 per cent) suggested that Christian churches should participate in the communal activities as far as they can. A businessman related:

I attend a Christian church with my friend. I stand up, sit down and sing with Christians. Christians never participate in communal activities. I observe that Christians are good musicians. Why don't they play music for people in the community so they would be a part of the community?

All of those interviewed feel an overwhelming distaste for forceful communication; chatterboxes who ignore time, place and situation; over-persuasive communicators; challenging, controlling, aggressive messages; and messages which violate their personal lives by being boastful, proud, unintelligible, disuniting and which pin others against the wall. All Thai non-Christians interviewed spoke negatively about the witnessing approaches designed by James Kennedy in Evangelism Explosion III and Bill Bright of Campus Crusade for Christ International.

A high school girl spoke about the Evangelism Explosion III approach. 'I would be upset. It is ridiculous and strange. I do not know who will die first, the interrogator or me. I would simply walk away. I do not want anyone to talk about death. It is a depressive issue.'

Another Buddhist who had attended a Christian church for ten years answered one of the questions with these words: 'Are you crazy? Out of the blue, you come to talk with me about religion. That is attacking, really attacking. I do not trust strangers who ask these kinds of questions, especially Westerners. I would walk away.'

In preaching the gospel, Christians should explain the teaching of the Bible without contrasting

Buddhism and Christianity. I bring some needs to Buddha; I bring some needs to Jesus.' A Buddhist bluntly said, 'Christians are narrow-minded. Their world is narrow and suitable for legalists.' Another respondent suggested, 'Christians should dialogue with Buddhists and listen to their ideas and needs, because each religion is unique. Christians should listen to Buddhists' agreements and disagreements. Then we should learn to adapt ourselves.' A scholar related, 'When my friend is critically ill, I ask a spirit to help her. Will you please pray for her too? Perhaps God will listen to his servant?'

A housewife said to me: 'Christians do not get along with others, or live simple lives as ordinary folks who cooperate with others. Christians call themselves brethren, but all others non-believers, secular people, and the lost. They separate themselves from us. They segregate people. How can they call us to come to their faith?'

A respondent in the south expressed her disappointment: 'Christians provide no activities in which Buddhists can participate.' An interviewee in the north-east said, 'Christians detest Buddhist ceremonies, and they do not hide their disgust.' A student in Bangkok suggested, 'Christian churches should not isolate themselves from outside society. Christians should not perceive outsiders as strangers or people outside their fellowship.'

Seventh, the answers of respondents (24 per cent) mentioned the value of fun and pleasure. The fun and pleasure they spoke about came from it with that of Buddhism. Buddhists will do the contrasting on their own. Christians should proclaim the goodness of Christianity, showing a harmony between their lives and faith which should be above the often amoral and destructive Buddhist behaviour patterns. Then non-Christians will ask themselves, 'Why?' Christians should leave non-Christians free to think on their own and avoid arguing, which will only shadow the Christian image from the Thai perspective.

The other powerful natural bridge is 'Thai-ness'. Non-Christians who were interviewed said repeatedly, 'Thailand does not have Thai Buddhists, Thai Moslems or Thai Christians. We have just Thais. Christianity differentiates people as Thai Buddhists and Thai Christians. Thailand does not segregate people. All are Thais.' Whenever I started the interview by talking about the goodness of Thai-ness, Thai culture and Thailand, the dialogue flowed. Interviewees and I seemed to be in one mind and one spirit. The main concern of non-Christian Thais was, 'Christianity destroys our culture. The children disobey the parents when they convert and they act fanatic, and aggressive.'

A university student of religious study suggested:

Christians cannot explain the existence of God with doctrines to the Thai. Understanding about the concept of God comes from seeing first the harmony between Christians' views and their way of life. Dialoguing is helpful. I do not want to know about the attributes and miracles of God or his redemption but I want to know about what he taught concerning morality. Then naturally the issue will turn to God's existence. The Thai accept the ten commandments, but Christians start with redemption which blows our minds, because we do not understand that concept. If Christians continue to approach the Thai like that, they waste their time, and good things in Christianity will be rejected.

Xayographix

A woman places an offering in a spirit house outside an apartment complex in Chiang Mai, Thailand.

A respondent suggested, 'Christians can bring up religious issues only when they have deep relational bonding with non-believers. They should be sensitive to time, place and occasion. Most of all, they should learn to be vulnerable.'

A teacher gave advice about improper manners in communication concerning religion, 'When Christians disagree with non-Christians, Christians should not show disruptive emotion with their facial expressions, body movement, tone of voice or eye movements. They should stop showing disgust when people with whom Christians dialogue do things differently.'

Interviewees (79 per cent) thought Christian messengers were aggressive and 89 per cent of interviewees perceived that the Christian message was unintelligible. A lady complained, 'Christians did not take my heart into consideration. Some are good people but when they open their lips unkind and aggressive words pour out. Some gentle Christians never witness to me about Christ. The ones who did offended me.'

The Buddhist Thais interviewed obviously perceive Christians first of all as salesmen and saleswomen. Preachers are perceived as salesmen, lecturers, politicians, debaters and even magicians. All Christians can talk about is religion—at all times, in all places, to all people, and they are perceived as weird and foreign.

One young man interviewed pointed out:

Christian preachers confuse me. I do not really know who they are. What are their roles and statuses in Thai society? At the pulpit, they shout like politicians or public salesmen. When they come down, they joke and act like ordinary people, very ordinary, too ordinary. They are not monks because they wear no special robes. Who are they? I do not know what kind of pronouns I should use when talking with them.

All non-Christian Thais interviewed believed that Thais can be Christian and Thai in the Thai way if they learn to do the following: 1. demonstrate the congruence between words and deeds (93 per cent); 2. create deep relational bonding with non-Christians and their communities without a hidden agenda before sharing the gospel (65 per cent); 3. communicate the gospel with Thai manners and methods, following the suggestions they gave concerning messengers and messages as well as the Thai perception of religion (96 per cent), and 4. dialogue about the gospel without being forceful (65 per cent).

The conversion story of a group of gangster leaders

Now that we had learned how many Buddhists viewed Christianity, we were ready to put our knowledge into practice. Our church settled near a slum in Bangkok, Thailand in 1986. Children and

A young Thai monk.

International Mission Board

teenagers from the slum enjoyed playing soccer and basketball games in the church grounds. I observed a group of hooligans who came to play soccer regularly. People were scared to bother with them. However, I was curious to know who they were and why they ended up with drugs and alcohol at such a young age. The town where I was born was famous for hooligans and gangsters. When I was young, our family moved into a new area and my father invited a gangster from the area to our home and introduced all of the family members to him. I observed him closely; he was much like other people. Since then, I have been curious as to how a person turns into a hooligan. Therefore, one evening I approached the scariest looking one. I clumsily asked him for a suggestion about how to tell the children to collect all the garbage they had thrown on the ground before they went home. The man shouted, and immediately all the children cleaned the church garden.

After that I made it a point to talk with them every evening. I asked about their work, families and education. They told me they cleaned the windows of a high-rise building but were cheated out of their pay. They were always looking for jobs and were available to work most of the time. All of them were high school graduates and wanted to learn English so it would be easier for them to find jobs. I offered to teach them English at no cost. We were a funny mix of students and teacher. I lost most of my voice and found it painful to teach English pronunciation; my students took drugs and got drunk, swaying into the classroom, but they attended the class regularly. I never talked about Jesus or religious things. I wanted them to improve God's image within them. They were clever and polite. I taught them for two hours after work, using the best air-conditioned classroom. I asked their team to guard our church when we invited the Thai traditional drama team from Payap University to perform on Christmas Eve, because thousands of people would flood in. They received good pay, but one church member voiced his concern, 'Sister you are making friends with hooligans.'

Almost a year passed, and I still never talked about Jesus but kept teaching them English. One day I lost my voice almost completely, and it was very painful to talk. One of them said, 'Teacher, why do you try so hard to teach us? We are stupid. We can't learn a thing. Why don't you just stop teaching?' I did not know what to say. I just looked at them, because I loved them. Then I offered to test their personality types, so they would know their skills and find the right kinds of jobs. We sat and worked on the test. The leader of the team broke down and wept openly, pouring his heart out. He came from a good family, but his father had left the family when he was young. The leader was shocked and ran away to live by himself in the jungle for a year before he returned to live with his friends. I didn't know what to do or say, so I just listened. That night I asked permission to pray for them and I told them briefly about how Jesus had helped me in my difficulty. They asked me for Bibles. I gave them the books of Matthew and John. After that they often came to discuss the Bible after playing soccer.

Somjit was the first one to join our prayer meeting. That was a special night, because we tried to contextualize our Wednesday worship in the Thai style. We tried to imitate the Thai folk music rhythm. The opening song should start with the booming of a gong, which we did not have. Therefore, we all beat the table to make it boom like a gong. The Thai song traditionally starts with a prolonged chanting—ho-he-ho-he-ho-he-ho-hew three times, but none of us know how to do it. Somjit helped with the howling. Then we sang a lively song, invited all to pray and beat the table drum. A lady spontaneously stood up and danced to the music. She bowed to me inviting me to dance with her, so we danced to the rhythm in a worshipping spirit. Everybody prayed their hearts out. Somjit told me later that it was an awesome night; the Christian prayer meeting was festive. At the end of the prayer meeting we celebrated with a special song and another dance. Then we meditated silently. Somjit did the opposite. He prayed out loud, 'God, if you exist, you know I need a job. Please give me a job within a week. Then I will believe in you.'

The following week, Somjit returned. He said, 'God gave me a job at the City Bank as a manager's driver. They chose me because my English was better than that of the other applicants.' Then another student came to believe and told his mother. His mother came to watch the Thai traditional drama from Payap University. A member of our church happened to sit next to her and prayed for her painful legs. She was healed and later on became a believer and witnessed to another widow who was all by herself. The widow had no place to live, so the church built her a small home even though she was not a Christian. Recently a fire broke out in the slum area and she shared her small place in Christ-like ways with individuals who had lost everything. Within two years, four of them accepted Christ and have remained faithful believers. The testimony of Somjit's life demonstrates that Jesus' meekness fulfils the Thai ideal of meekness in Thai converts. Moreover, the Holy Spirit also helps Thai Christians progressively bond with Jesus, their living God, in their world-view and ethos.

Julian Hawken

A Thai novice monk reads a gospel booklet. Literature distribution may not be the most effective way to present the gospel to Thai people.

The conversion of a Thai Chinese family

The *Kama* and *Ahosikarma* ritual can be used to heal the broken relational bonding between new converts and their families. Our church informally performed this ritual of reconciliation with a Thai Chinese family whose father punished his children severely, to the point of shooting them, when they became Christians. During a Chinese sacred time, the two leaders of our church carried Chinese sacred objects, four yellow pears, on a plate to his door. The action signified the willingness to pay respect to a respectable authority. The symbolic action softened the father's heart and he allowed the leaders of the church to salute him, which signified forgiveness granted to some degree. Not many words were said, but the meaning was understood.

Later on, his shop was robbed, and he was wounded in the fighting. The pastor was the first one to visit him, and eventually he and the whole family became Christian through the cooperative work of many Christians.

Conclusion

Why should Christians in Thailand reconcile with the Thai? The research interview confirmed the unspoken, broken relationship between Christians in Thailand and the Thai. Colonization, modernization, the Vietnam War and aggressive forms of Christian mission wounded the smooth relationships between the Thai and Christians. Colonization took away many parts of the kingdom of Thailand and drained Thailand financially. Modernization destroyed rural communities and Thai culture. The Vietnam War brought about the problems of prostitution and the change in the value system wherever American military bases were located. The problem lingers to this day. At present Americans, both non-Christians and Christians, denigrate Thailand without mentioning the problems that American armies created. A Korean missionary smashed Buddha images and ran away, leaving the wounded relationships for Thai Christians to bear. Another group of Japanese missionaries shouted the gospel into a Buddhist temple and posted gospel messages on trees all over Thailand, believing that they were doing God's will. The research interview reveals the anger and negative attitudes towards the gospel and Christians in Thailand because of these aggressive missions.

Many parents harbour deep resentment and bitterness towards Christianity, Christians and churches because a church in Bangkok manipulates and brainwashes their children in the name of Jesus. As Thai Christians we should find fault with our own actions because, from the beginning, we have related the name of Jesus with Westerners. Missionaries come and go, Thai Christians grieve. While the church which uses the motivation of fear grows, many Thai parents and Thai Christians grieve.

The research findings demonstrate that it is important for Christians in Thailand to reconcile with the Thai because reconciliation is an important element in Thai relational culture. Indifference shown towards broken fellowship or wounded relationships will block the smoothness of the gospel communication. Christians in Thailand should stop offensive kinds of mission and try the way of meekness, which fits both the biblical standard and Thai culture. Christians need to think and pray about these problems.

Notes

This article is based on Ubolwan Mejudhon's doctoral dissertation 'The Way of Meekness: Being Christian and Thai in the Thai Way' (Asbury Theological Seminary, E Stanley Jones School of World Mission and Evangelism, 1997).

International Mission Board

Two lines of monks pass each other on the street in Mae Hong Son, Thailand.

Approximately 700,000 to 900,000 Eastern Tamang people live in the eastern and central parts of Nepal, concentrated in and around the nation's capital Kathmandu and in numerous villages in the north-east, south and east of the city.[1] There are also several thousand Tamang people living in India, in the lower Teesta valley and Rangit valley of Sikkim, as well as in parts of West Bengal and Uttar Pradesh.[2] Three thousand Tamang reportedly live in south-west Bhutan.[3] A small diaspora community of Tamang people reportedly lives in western Myanmar. The majority of the Tamang prefer to live on hills between 1,500 and 2,200 metres (4,920 to 7,200 ft.) above sea level. Some prefer to live at even higher altitudes, while others have migrated down to the hot plains.

At the time of the 1991 Nepal census, the Tamang returned a total figure of 1,018,252 people—5.5 per cent of Nepal's population. This makes them the second largest tribal group in Nepal after the Magar. Linguists, however, have identified five distinct Tamang languages among them. Each group has been profiled separately in this book, starting with the Eastern Tamang.

The name *Tamang* means 'horse trader'. They are generally very poor people. Many are employed in menial jobs (some are porters in Kathmandu, for example, or stone carriers at the rock quarries). One source notes that 'The Tamangs live in the high hills east, north, south and west of Kathmandu valley. They are commonly seen on the streets of the capital city carrying large basket loads of goods by headstraps, the men and boys dressed in loincloths and long, usually black, tunics . . . always with a *khuhuri* knife stuck at the waistband.'[4]

Some scholars have identified as many as 40 different clans among the Tamang in Nepal. Each clan is distinguished by slight cultural and dialect differences.

The majority of Tamang follow Tibetan Buddhism, 'but mix this heavily with animism and somewhat with Hinduism. Their priests, or lamas, have a dominant role in the community and perform ceremonies for funerals, to ensure a certain deity's protection on crops, etc. Perhaps the most powerful person in society is the shaman, however, who exorcises demons, and interacts with the spirit world.'[5]

Since the 1980s, a tremendous revival has broken out among many of Nepal's ethnic groups, and the Tamang are one of the most blessed in this regard. One Tamang pastor in 1991 reportedly oversaw '43 fellowships with a total congregation of 32,000 people'.[6] When asked why the Tamang people were so open to the gospel, the pastor responded, 'It is God's time for us. My people were once filled with fear, but when Jesus Christ came, we were turned from fear to faith. My people worshipped many, many spirits and had to offer continual sacrifices. Even if we were on the verge of starvation we still had to offer our food as sacrifices to the gods. . . . We have to cast out demons all the time. I used to be a lama priest and had a knowledge of the spirits. I can recognize the demonic forces of the different villages. I pray against them and command them to be gone in the name of Jesus.'[7]

(caption, sideways:) Gospel Recordings Nepal

Population:
877,800 (2000)
1,086,600 (2010)
1,345,200 (2020)
Countries: Nepal, India, Bhutan, Myanmar
Buddhism: Tibetan
Christians: 70,000

Overview of the Eastern Tamang

Other Names: Murmi, Nishung, Lama, Tamanglama

Population Sources:
584,097 to 718,048 in Nepal (2000, B Grimes [based on 1991 census])
3,000 in India (2000, P Hattaway)
3,000 in Bhutan (1995, *Languages of Bhutan*)
also in Myanmar

Language: Sino-Tibetan, Tibeto-Burman, Himalayish, Tibeto-Kanauri, Tibetic, Tamangic

Dialects: 3 (Outer-Eastern Tamang, Central-Eastern Tamang, Southwestern Tamang)

Professing Buddhists: 70%

Practising Buddhists: 35%

Christians: 8%

Scripture: Portions

Jesus **film:** available

Gospel Recordings: Tamang: Eastern

Christian Broadcasting: none

ROPAL code: TAJ

Status of Evangelization

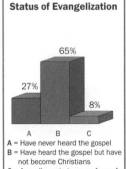

A = Have never heard the gospel
B = Have heard the gospel but have not become Christians
C = Are adherents to some form of Christianity

Tamang, Eastern Gorkha

CHINA
Gandaki
NEPAL
INDIA
Tamang Eastern Gorkha

Population:
4,750 (2000)
5,900 (2010)
7,300 (2020)
Countries: Nepal
Buddhism: Tibetan
Christians: 300

Overview of the Eastern Gorkha Tamang

Other Names: Murmi, Nishung, Lama, Tamanglama

Population Sources:

3,000 to 4,000 in Nepal (2000, B Grimes [1992 figure])

Language: Sino-Tibetan, Tibeto-Burman, Himalayish, Tibeto-Kanauri, Tibetic, Tamangic

Dialects: 2 (Kasigaon, Kerounja)

Professing Buddhists: 80%

Practising Buddhists: 55%

Christians: 6%

Scripture: none

Jesus film: none

Gospel Recordings: none

Christian Broadcasting: none

ROPAL code: TGE

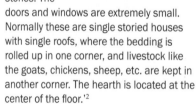

Status of Evangelization

59%
35%
6%

A   B   C

A = Have never heard the gospel
B = Have heard the gospel but have not become Christians
C = Are adherents to some form of Christianity

A linguist in 1992 estimated that there were between 3,000 and 4,000 Eastern Gorkha Tamang people living in north-central Nepal.[1] This group, which is different from the four other Tamang groups on the basis that they speak a separate language, inhabits villages south and east of the small township of Jagat, in the north Gorkha District of Gandaki Zone. The Eastern Gorkha Tamang's location is beautiful, with pristine forests clinging to the mountain slopes. Their villages are located at altitudes ranging from 600 to 1,800 metres (approximately 2,000 to 5,900 ft.) above sea level. Tamang houses are 'clustered at one place to make up a dense village within which there are constructed many cobble-stone paths for movement. Most of these houses consist of stone walls, thatched or wooden planked roofs held down by stones. The doors and windows are extremely small. Normally these are single storied houses with single roofs, where the bedding is rolled up in one corner, and livestock like the goats, chickens, sheep, etc. are kept in another corner. The hearth is located at the center of the floor.'[2]

The language of the Eastern Gorkha Tamang is part of the Tamangic branch of the Tibeto-Burman family. It reportedly contains 76 per cent to 77 per cent lexical similarity with Northwestern Tamang; 77 per cent to 79 per cent with Western Tamang; 70 per cent to 73 per cent with Southwestern Tamang; and 63 per cent to 73 per cent with Eastern Tamang.[3] This Tamang group is interesting in that the people actually refer to themselves as Gurung, and not as Tamang, even though their language is very different from any Gurung varieties and has been proven to be Tamangic.

The most popular musical instrument of the Tamang is the *damphu*, 'a circular structure about 1½ feet in diameter and covered on one side with a goat skin, stretched by means of a bamboo spike shooting inwards at the center. . . . The *dhampu* is considered an important and compulsory item in the lives and activities of the Tamangs, from birth, through life, till death. . . . According to the Tamang belief, a man named Wang Dorjee went into the jungle to hunt. He is supposed to have killed a *ghoral* (wild mountain goat) and skinned it. . . . He cut a branch of a *koiralo* tree and made a ring with the wood. Then he stretched the goat's skin over this wooden frame and fastened

Gospel Recordings Nepal

it to the edges with bamboo nails. Then he beat on the skin and heard the emergence of a soft sound. Wang spread the word of his invention and popularized the instrument.'[4]

Most Eastern Gorkha Tamang people are followers of Tibetan Buddhism, although some of those living at lower altitudes have come under the influence of Hinduism. One source notes, 'Tamangs follow the Nyingmapa sect of Buddhism whereby the practicing lamas are permitted to lead a family life; marriage among such families has created a class of upper stratum distinct from the ordinary peasants.'[5]

In recent years a significant number of Eastern Gorkha Tamang have put their trust in Christ. Pastor Prem Tamang of Gorkha said, 'Ours is a New Testament church. We read what the Bible says and we implement it. The church is built on the scriptures and our daily walk with God.'[6]

Estimates based on the 1991 census have found that there were at least 55,000 Northwestern Tamang people living in Nepal's Bagmati Zone. They are concentrated in Nuwakot District, along a mountainous strip. Some Northwestern Tamang have migrated out of the mountains and onto the sun-drenched plains in southern Nepal. The Nepal census gave an overall figure of more than one million Tamang people and did not differentiate between different language groups.

There are several conflicting reports about the origins of the Tamang people. According to a legend prevalent among the Hindu Tamang, it is said they were created from Lord Siva or, in other words, that their ancestor is Lord Siva.

Gospel Recordings Nepal

Others say that their ancestors were members of the Tibetan King Songtsen Gampo's cavalry, who came across the Himalayas and settled in the hills of Nepal long ago. 'The Tamangs of Nuwakot believe that almost a thousand years ago, there lived an anti-Buddhist king in Tibet called Galang Marma or Gyalbo Lunder. He was victorious over the Buddhists and set fire to many gompas. He then forced the lamas to marry and become civilians. Many icons and statues of the Buddha were destroyed too, but not all the lamas were subdued. Some managed to escape with their lives ... In this way, those lamas settled down in what are now Rasuwa and Nuwakot districts located north of the Kathmandu valley.'[1] These conflicting stories indicate that the Tamang people are not from one ethnic root, but from a collection of different tribes scattered across Nepal.

Northwestern Tamang women can easily be identified by their striking appearance.

They 'wear ornaments such as gold or silver earrings called *bhuntil* or *biru*, gold or silver bangles called *singikarmu mugs* (semi-precious stone) and gold ornaments called *gahu*. . . . Gold or silver *jantar* (square amulets hung on the chest on a string or a necklace) are also worn by both sexes.'[2]

The religious beliefs of the Northwestern Tamang are a combination of shamanism, Tibetan Buddhism and Hinduism. Those living in higher altitudes are generally more inclined towards Buddhism, while those at lower altitudes have come under more Hindu influence. For both groups, however, traditional spirit-worship dominates. One source notes that 'The Tamangs of the northern regions, while making or constructing houses make a statue of *ratilila* and keep it at a place where the people can see it while walking to and fro on the village paths. This is done because the Tamangs believe that this ensures warding off of evil spirits, no chance for lightning or *vajra* to strike their houses, and the wife of the house will not have to remain barren.'[3] Tamang lamas usually marry the daughters of other lamas and teach their sons to succeed them as lamas. Füerer-Haimendorf notes, 'In this way a class of lamas has grown up and though neither strictly endogamous nor formally privileged, this class now forms an upper stratum distinct from the ordinary cultivators.'[4] In recent years, 'quite a number of Tamang have become Christians, and they are actively reaching out to their own people'.[5]

CHINA

Bagmati

NEPAL

INDIA

Tamang Northwestern

Population:
66,700 (2000)
82,600 (2010)
102,300 (2020)
Countries: Nepal
Buddhism: Tibetan
Christians: 2,000

Overview of the Northwestern Tamang

Other Names: Murmi, Nishung, Lama, Tamanglama

Population Sources:
55,000 or more in Nepal (2000, B Grimes [based on 1991 census])

Language: Sino-Tibetan, Tibeto-Burman, Himalayish, Tibeto-Kanauri, Tibetic, Tamangic

Dialects: 1 (Dhading)

Professing Buddhists: 65%

Practising Buddhists: 30%

Christians: 3%

Scripture: none

Jesus film: none

Gospel Recordings: Tamang: Dhadhing; Tamang: Rasua

Christian Broadcasting: none

ROPAL code: TMK

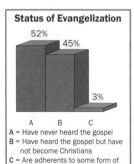

Status of Evangelization

52%

45%

3%

A   B   C

A = Have never heard the gospel
B = Have heard the gospel but have not become Christians
C = Are adherents to some form of Christianity

Tamang, Southwestern

Approximately 140,000 Southwestern Tamang people live in the *terai* (plains of southern Nepal), especially in the Chitwan area of Nayayani Zone, western Makwanpur District, as well as areas south and southeast of these districts. The Southwestern Tamang language also extends into the western part of Kathmandu District in Bagmati Zone. There is also a group of Tamang living across the border in the Dehra Dun area of the Indian state of Uttar Pradesh. They say they came from Tamgaluijn in Nepal in the late 1700s. Today only the elderly Tamang in Uttar Pradesh can still speak their mother tongue—the rest use Nepali and Hindi.

The Southwestern Tamang in Nepal have been more exposed to outside influence than any other Tamang group. Consequently, they are in the process of assimilation to Hindu culture and religion and are losing many of their ancient and colourful traditions. One source notes: 'The Tamang language, culture and traditions are rich. They were already described as a powerful nation in historic inscriptions going as far back as the third century, attesting to their ancient civilization. They are Buddhists, and their script originates from Tibetan. . . . The archives of Tamang religious scriptures are rich, varied and vast, [with their] categorizations of royal priests, raconteurs of history and other scholastic divisions of labor.'[1]

One of the primary locations of this group is the Chitwan District. The area is famous for the Royal Chitwan National Park, which is home to more than 400 rhinos and 80 tigers, as well as leopards, crocodiles, deer, monkeys, 50 other species of mammals and over 400 different types of birds. Chitwan is a precious refuge for these wild animals amidst an area of dense popula-

tion, searing heat and sickening pollution. In 1973 the rhino population had fallen to 100 and there were only 20 tigers left, but Nepali government intervention has since ensured that their numbers have increased, much to the delight of the thousands of tourists who visit Chitwan every year.

Although many Southwestern Tamang still profess Buddhism as their religion, Hinduism is making rapid inroads at its expense. Christianity has also experienced explosive growth in recent years. This growth is not without problems and lack of understanding, however. One evangelist was summoned to pray for a woman suffering from acute stomach pain. 'As he approached the house he heard what

Gospel Recordings Nepal

sounded like someone beating on a drum. The village was essentially animist and he assumed the witch doctor, renowned for his drum-beating antics, had arrived ahead of him. Upon entering the house, however, he saw that it was not the witch doctor but the woman's husband, who was fervently beating her on the head with his Bible. "In the name of Jesus be healed," he chanted between the blows. After explaining correct Biblical doctrine for praying over the sick, he asked the woman how she felt. Though she had been in agony before her husband's unorthodox beating, she could now stand and said the pain was gone. "Are you alright?" the evangelist asked. "No," she replied. "I have a headache."'[2]

Population:
132,400 (2000)
163,900 (2010)
202,900 (2020)
Countries: Nepal, India
Buddhism: Tibetan
Christians: 7,000

Overview of the Southwestern Tamang

Other Names: Murmi, Nishung, Lama, Tamanglama

Population Sources:

109,051 in Nepal (2000, B Grimes [based on 1991 census])

also in India

Language: Sino-Tibetan, Tibeto-Burman, Himalayish, Tibeto-Kanauri, Tibetic, Tamangic

Dialects: 0

Professing Buddhists: 50%

Practising Buddhists: 20%

Christians: 5.3%

Scripture: none

***Jesus* film:** none

Gospel Recordings: none

Christian Broadcasting: none

ROPAL code: TSF

Status of Evangelization

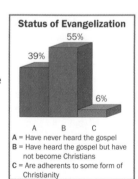

A = Have never heard the gospel
B = Have heard the gospel but have not become Christians
C = Are adherents to some form of Christianity

CHINA
Gandaki
Bagmati
NEPAL
Narayani
Tamang Western INDIA

Population:
388,900 (2000)
481,500 (2010)
596,100 (2020)
Countries: Nepal
Buddhism: Tibetan
Christians: 30,000

Overview of the Western Tamang

Other Names: Murmi, Nishung, Lama, Tamanglama

Population Sources:

186,408 to 320,350 in Nepal (2000, B Grimes [based on 1991 census])

Language: Sino-Tibetan, Tibeto-Burman, Himalayish, Tibeto-Kanauri, Tibetic, Tamangic

Dialects: 2 (Trisuli, Rasuwa)

Professing Buddhists: 65%

Practising Buddhists: 35%

Christians: 7.7%

Scripture: New Testament 1990

***Jesus* film:** none

Gospel Recordings: Tamang: Western

Christian Broadcasting: none

ROPAL code: TDG

Status of Evangelization

63%
29%
8%

A   B   C
A = Have never heard the gospel
B = Have heard the gospel but have not become Christians
C = Are adherents to some form of Christianity

After the 1991 Nepal census results were examined, researchers gave a very broad population range of between 186,408 and 320,350 Western Tamang people living in central Nepal.[1] They are concentrated in the Bagmati Zone, as well as into the eastern part of the Gandaki Zone (Gorkha District) and on the plains in Nayayani Zone. Nuwakot, Rasuwa and Dhading are three districts with significant numbers of Western Tamang.

Gospel Recordings Nepal

For approximately 1,000 years, the Tamang have professed Buddhism. 'There are Buddhist temples in every sizeable village. The gods and the religious paintings in the temples are all in the Sherpa style; the religious texts are all in the Tibetan script.'[2]

When a Tamang person dies, an unusual custom is observed. 'If the deceased is a rich person, then it is customary to light 108 oil lamps (clarified butter lamps) surrounding the corpse. The moment death claims the person, the body is raised so that the waist and knees can be bent and the whole person kept in the lotus posture, by placing the corpse in a large copper or earthenware pot or any other such large vessel. . . . Rich persons use *ghyu* and oil poured into the vessel to immerse half the body, while the poorer folks use water. Until the lama communicates the auspicious time for the removal of the corpse, various

edibles like rice, curry and pulses are placed all around the corpse. . . . The last rites for the corpse are preferentially done on a hilltop rather than on the river banks and burials are fewer than cremations. While the corpse is being consumed by flames, the lama sits nearby continually reading the sacred scriptures. While this is going on, the lamas are offered food brought along with the funeral procession. This they consume while reading the sacred books and the corpse is burning. This is customary and not considered dishonorable.'[3]

Since the 1980s, thousands of Western Tamang people have become Christians. In 1990, the Western Tamang became the only Tamang group to have the New Testament translated into their language.

God is working in many miraculous ways to reach this group. One evangelist named D B Tamang recalls how his mother become ill, and his father, the animistic priest, prayed to his gods for her healing. 'He sacrificed several goats and chickens, but her health continued to deteriorate. Soon they ran out of chickens and goats and while the priest went to a nearby village to buy more animals for sacrifice, the mother died. In his grief Tamang went to the Buddhist lama and pleaded with him to restore his mother's life. The lama visited the house and chanted prayers for several hours, but to no avail. Having no other recourse at a time like this, Tamang decided to call a group of Christians from a nearby village. . . . God raised Tamang's dead mother back to life. Seeing the miracle, Tamang went into the house and brought out all the family idols and burned them saying he had no use for them now. That day he and his family, along with 20 households totaling more than 160 people, accepted the Lord.'[4]

CHINA
Arunachal Pradesh
Assam
INDIA

Tangsa Tikhak

Population:
530 (2000)
620 (2010)
730 (2020)
Countries: India
Buddhism: Tibetan
Christians: 50

Overview of the Tikhak Tangsa

Other Names: Tikhak

Population Sources:

409 in India (1981 census)

Language: Sino-Tibetan, Tibeto-Burman, Jingpho-Konyak-Bodo, Konyak-Bodo-Garo, Konyak

Dialects: 0

Professing Buddhists: 60%

Practising Buddhists: 25%

Christians: 9.4%

Scripture: Tangsa New Testament 1992

Jesus **film:** none

Gospel Recordings: none

Christian Broadcasting: none

ROPAL code: NST12

Status of Evangelization

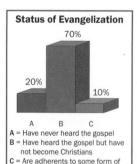

70%
20%
10%
A   B   C
A = Have never heard the gospel
B = Have heard the gospel but have not become Christians
C = Are adherents to some form of Christianity

The 1981 census of India listed a population of just 409 Tikhak Tangsa people (186 males and 223 females). They live in the Manmao, Nampong, Miao and Bordumsa circles of the Changlang District in south-eastern Arunachal Pradesh, India. A few of them also live in the Dibrugarh District of Assam.

The Tikhak are one of 15 different Tangsa tribes in India,[1] totalling 16,475 people according to the 1981 Indian census. Several Tangsa groups are also located across the border in western Myanmar. Among the 15 Tangsa groups in India, only two could be considered majority Buddhist: the Tikhak and the Yongkuk. The rest are Hindus, animists and Christians, and so have not been included in this book. In alphabetical order, the other Tangsa groups in India are the Havi (98% Hindu); Jugli (66% Hindu); Kimsing (62% Christian); Lungchang (95% animist); Lungphi (60% Hindu); Lungri (88% Hindu); Morang (46% Hindu, 38% Christian); Mosang (65% Hindu); Muklom (52% animist); Ronrang (98% Christian); Sangwal; Sankey (75% Christian); and the Tonglim (animist).[2]

The name *Tikhak* reportedly can mean either 'proficient basket makers or those who produce a peculiar coughing sound'.[3] They originated further to the east in a place called Mukcha in the Patkoi Range. About 150 years ago, for reasons unknown, they migrated away from their homeland to their present location.

One way to distinguish the Tikhak from other Tangsa tribes is by their dress. 'The men's lower dress called *impayan* (a

Dwayne Graybill

handwoven *lungi*) has red, green, brown and white squares. The women's lower dress *naitak* (also a handwoven *lungi*) has different vertical stripes intersected by broad horizontal black stripes. The men also use the *takot-khuka* (kind of head dress).'[4]

There is some confusion regarding the religious beliefs of the Tikhak Tangsa. The 1981 census returned 60 per cent of them as Buddhists, 32 per cent as Hindus, 6.3 per cent as Christians and 1.7 per cent as followers of 'other religions' (i.e., animism). At the time of the census, six out of every ten Tikhak Tangsa people stated that they were Buddhists. Other reports seem to imply that most Tikhak people are animists. 'The Tikhak religion consists of beliefs in different benevolent and malevolent spirits. The community believes in the concept of a god named *fra* or *pra.* No worship or sacrifice is offered to the *fra.* They worship the house deity called *Matai* once a year for the well-being of the family. *Lumrong* is worshipped for the protection of their entire area from natural calamities. . . . The *tumsa* (priest) is an expert in detecting evil spirits, in diagnosing and curing diseases, in predicting the future, and in presiding over the worship ceremonies. Thus he is respected by all. . . . A large number of Tikhaks have embraced Christianity, while some of them profess Buddhism.'[5]

Although for now the Tikhak Tangsa are classified as a majority Buddhist group, they are surrounded by Christians. Close to 50 per cent of the Tangsa people overall are now Christians. The Tangsa New Testament was published in 1992, although it is not known if the Tikhak Tangsa are able to read it.

The Yongkuk Tangsa tribe is the smallest Buddhist people group profiled in this book. In the 1981 India census their total population was given as just 59. They inhabit the Old Dokpe and Kamlao villages in the Manmao Circle in Changlang District. Changlang is located in the extreme north-eastern part of Arunachal Pradesh in north-east India, just north of the state of Nagaland and west of the international border with Myanmar. The Yongkuk region is 'covered with thick tropical vegetation with a variety of animal life, including elephants, tigers, bears, deer, monkeys, reptiles and birds'.[1]

The name Yongkuk is a compound of two words: *yong* means 'water', and *kuk* means 'upper', or 'higher'. 'The name thus implies "the people of the head waters of a river". The Yongkuks believe they originated at a place in the south known as Masoi Sinrapum. During their migration they crossed the Tennai Wakrup River and the Patkoi range, and established their first village in their present habitat in the Namchik River valley now known as Chhotam Pinjam. Among the Tangsas they are considered the first settlers in the Manchik valley.'[2]

The Yongkuk language is one of 15 Tangsa varieties in India.[3] *Tangsa*

Dwayne Graybill

means 'hill people'. Yongkuk is part of the Tibeto-Burman language family, reportedly close to the Nocte Naga language.[4] They also speak Assamese, Hindi and Nepali with outsiders.

In the past the Yongkuk Tangsa were a much larger group, but due to intermarriage with people from other ethnic groups their numbers have gradually decreased until today they are threatened with extinction. Despite their tiny numbers, the Yongkuk Tangsas still retain many of their

traditional customs. They are 'experts in spinning, weaving and basket-making. Folk-songs, folk-tales, folklore and folk-dances form part of their cultural heritage. Their musical instruments are the harp, flute, drum and bronze cymbal.'[5]

Out of the 59 Yongkuk Tangsa individuals recorded in the 1981 census, 55 people stated they were Buddhists, two were Christians, one Hindu, and one person was returned under 'other religions' (i.e., animism). Despite this confession of Buddhism, however, researchers tend to suggest that shamanism and animistic rituals are the dominant spiritual strongholds among this group. One source notes, 'The Yongkuks believe in a supernatural power, spirits and deities. They have three types of sacred specialists. They are the *fithang* (spiritual leader and diviner), *walangta* (astrologer and medicine man) and *tangsan* (who conducts the worshipping sessions and sacrifices). The festival of *Lamrong* is celebrated in the month of March in which pigs and chickens are sacrificed in each house to propitiate the deities for better health and a good crop.'[6]

Since the 1981 census, when just two individuals declared themselves as Christians, it is not thought that there have been any new breakthroughs for the gospel among this small group. K S Singh notes, 'Only a few persons of the community have adopted Christianity, and they have given up the traditional faith.'[7]

Population:
77 (2000)
90 (2010)
105 (2020)
Countries: India
Buddhism: Tibetan
Christians: 2

Overview of the Yongkuk Tangsa

Other Names: Yongkuk

Population Sources:
59 in India (1981 census)

Language: Sino-Tibetan, Tibeto-Burman, Jingpho-Konyak-Bodo, Konyak-Bodo-Garo, Konyak

Dialects: 0

Professing Buddhists: 93%

Practising Buddhists: 30%

Christians: 2.6%

Scripture: Tangsa New Testament 1992

Jesus film: none

Gospel Recordings: none

Christian Broadcasting: none

ROPAL code: none

Status of Evangelization

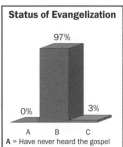

A = Have never heard the gospel
B = Have heard the gospel but have not become Christians
C = Are adherents to some form of Christianity

Taungyo

More than 560,000 Taungyo people live in central Myanmar. At the time of the most recent census held in Myanmar (then called Burma) in 1931, the Taungyo numbered just 22,296.[1] They are 'primarily located in mountainous valleys of southwest Shan State and southeast Mandalay Division. They border the vast dry zone to the west and the mountains and forests of the Shan State to the east. The Taungyo share their homeland with several other groups indigenous to the area, including the Pa-O, Palaung, Shan and Danau. Most of the area they inhabit has been deforested for agricultural use.'[2]

The centre of the Taungyo homeland could be said to be the town of Pindaya in Shan State. Pindaya contains a population of 25,000 people, the majority of whom are Taungyo, while most of the villages surrounding the town are also full of Taungyo people. It is common for two to three generations of the same family to live together under one roof. In many respects the Taungyo do not have a strong sense of self-identity as many other peoples in Myanmar do. They see themselves as linked to the Burmese people, with their main differences being cultural.

Linguistically, the Taungyo language is a variety of Burmese, but the people differ ethnically and culturally. When the Taungyo speak Burmese, they do so with a very strong accent. One source says that they have been 'influenced by the culture and speech of the Shans and Pa-Os among whom they live. . . . They may have

been refugees from Tavoy in Mon State, south-east Burma, or have been brought as slaves to Shan State, where they soon intermarried with locals. . . . Taungyo men wear a costume similar to the Shans, but the women are easily distinguishable by their heavy silver earrings and bracelets. They also wear heavy brass coils on their legs. If they are married, the rings are worn just under the knee; if they are single, they wear silver rings around the ankles.'[3]

Almost all Taungyo people believe in Theravada Buddhism. In rural areas they also practise *nat* (spirit) worship. Often the practitioners of this form of animism walk deep into the forests, where they conduct rituals to call on certain protective spirits. Some spirits are considered benevolent, while others are malevolent.

Most of the festivals that the Taungyo celebrate coincide with the Buddhist calendar in Myanmar. The Taungyo do have one festival in March each year that is unique to their group. During this time the people are expected to make donations to the local monks and monastery.

Less than one per cent of Taungyo people believe in Jesus Christ. Because of their linguistic relationship with Burmese, missionary organizations have not found it worthwhile to produce Taungyo-specific Scripture translations or media. One researcher has stated, 'Of the unreached groups of Myanmar, the Taungyo are one of the most readily accessible. Foreigners are legally permitted to travel to Pindaya, the city of highest Taungyo concentration, and home to a budding trekking industry.'[4]

Population:
560,000 (2000)
629,400 (2010)
707,500 (2020)
Countries: Myanmar
Buddhism: Theravada
Christians: 3,000

Overview of the Taungyo

Other Names: Taru, Dawe, Dawai, Tawe-Tavoy, Toru

Population Sources: 560,935 in Myanmar (2003, Myanmar Faces and Places)

Language: Sino-Tibetan, Tibeto-Burman, Lolo-Burmese, Burmish, Southern

Dialects: 0

Professing Buddhists: 98%

Practising Buddhists: 75%

Christians: 0.6%

Scripture: none

Jesus **film:** none

Gospel Recordings: none

Christian Broadcasting: none

ROPAL code: TCO

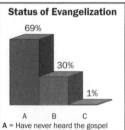

Status of Evangelization

69%
30%
1%

A B C

A = Have never heard the gospel
B = Have heard the gospel but have not become Christians
C = Are adherents to some form of Christianity

More than 100,000 Tavoyan people inhabit a long coastal stretch of the Tanintharyi Division (known as Tenasserim prior to 1989) in southern Myanmar.[1] There are five major ethnic groups present in the Tanintharyi Division, which runs parallel with Thailand in the thin tract of land that separates the Andaman Sea from the Gulf of Thailand. The Tavoyan inhabit the northern part of the state, centred around their ancient homeland of Dawei City.

A small number of Tavoyan people have made their way across the border and now live in refugee camps inside Thailand. They fled to Thailand to escape oppression at the hands of the Burmese authorities. In the mid-1990s, more than 15,000 local civilians were forced to work on the construction of the Ye to Dawei railway. The inhumane conditions resulted in hundreds of deaths. The railway was not constructed for tourism or trade, but to help the Burmese military rapidly deploy troops to the troubled border areas.

Many young Tavoyan men in Dawei have been forced to attend Burmese military training to counter insurgency groups. Today there are at least 22 rebel armies operating against the Burmese in Myanmar. One of the least known of these is the small Tavoyan army in the Tanintharyi Division. For centuries the Tavoyan people have been peace loving and gentle people, but their patience has been pushed to the limit by the evil activities and abuses of the Burmese junta. Even after arriving in Thailand, one group of refugees was reportedly attacked by a battalion of Myanmar's 62nd Infantry.[2]

The 1931 Burmese census returned a figure of 156,507 Tavoyan people[3]—higher than today's estimate. It is difficult to identify the Tavoyans today because of their close ethnic and linguistic affinity to the Burmese majority. It is not easy to judge where one group stops and the other begins. One book says, 'Most of the people living in the [Tanintharyi] Division are of Burmese ethnicity, although splitting hairs one can easily identify Tavoyan and Myeik sub-groups of the Burmese who enjoy their own dialect, cuisine and so on.'[4]

The Tavoyan people qualify for inclusion in this book because, in addition to cultural differences, their dialect is different enough from standard Burmese to make communication difficult. The *Ethnologue* states that Tavoyan is 'one of the better known varieties of nonstandard Burmese with profound pronunciation and vocabulary differences from Burmese'.[5]

The main Tavoyan town of Dawei (formerly known as Tavoy) has been inhabited for at least 500 years. As early as 1586, the town was one of the main producers of tin in Asia, supplying all of India. In the mid-1700s the town became the possession of the Ayutthaya rulers in today's Thailand, who used it as a trade port.

The American Baptists worked in the Tavoyan area for many decades, but most of their converts were from among the Karen people. They found the Buddhist Tavoyans slow to respond to the gospel—a pattern that continues to this day. Only about one in every thousand Tavoyan people today are Christians.

Population:
100,500 (2000)
112,900 (2010)
126,900 (2020)
Countries: Myanmar, refugees in Thailand
Buddhism: Theravada
Christians: 100

Overview of the Tavoyan

Other Names: Tavoy, Dawei, Tavoya
Population Sources: 100,000 in Myanmar (2002, Myanmar Faces and Places)
500 in Thailand (2003, P Hattaway)
Language: Sino-Tibetan, Tibeto-Burman, Lolo-Burmese, Burmish, Southern
Dialects: 0
Professing Buddhists: 98%
Practising Buddhists: 85%
Christians: 0.1%
Scripture: none
Jesus **film:** none
Gospel Recordings: none
Christian Broadcasting: none
ROPAL code: TVN

Status of Evangelization
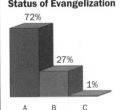

A = Have never heard the gospel
B = Have heard the gospel but have not become Christians
C = Are adherents to some form of Christianity

Tebbu

Gansu
Qinghai
Sichuan
Tebbu

Population:
20,000 (2000)
24,600 (2010)
30,300 (2020)
Countries: China
Buddhism: Tibetan
Christians: none known

Overview of the Tebbu

Other Names: Tebbus, Tewu, Tewo, Tewo Tibetans

Population Sources:

20,000 in China (2000, P Hattaway)

Language: Sino-Tibetan. Tibeto-Burman, Unclassified (possibly Qiangic)

Dialects: 2 (Upper Tebbu, Lower Tebbu)

Professing Buddhists: 95%

Practising Buddhists: 40%

Christians: 0%

Scripture: none

Jesus film: none

Gospel Recordings: none

Christian Broadcasting: none

ROPAL code: none

Status of Evangelization

96%

4%   0%

A   B   C

A = Have never heard the gospel
B = Have heard the gospel but have not become Christians
C = Are adherents to some form of Christianity

More than 20,000 Tebbu people live in one of the most dramatically remote regions of China. They inhabit villages in the midst of the imposing Min Shan Mountains along the Bailong River and its tributaries in southern Gansu Province, cut off from the rest of the world by their surroundings. The Tebbu are dispersed throughout rugged Tewo County and possibly into the eastern part of Zhugqu County.

When Joseph Rock visited the Tebbu in the 1920s he said, 'The Min Shan, extending from east to west, is composed of fantastic limestone crags cut into huge turrets and pinnacles. . . . Its northern slopes are cut into numerous deep valleys, densely forested with spruces, firs and rhododendrons, which debouch into the Tao River. The ridges and spurs separating these valleys . . . resemble huge sleeping dragons who guard the Tebbu Land.'[1] Rock also noted, 'There are ten thousand of these warlike people belonging to the Tebbu tribe. . . . These wild Tebbus that inhabit the most romantic spot of all China will perhaps remain an ethnological riddle; they call themselves Tewu, and are divided into two or perhaps three clans known as the Upper or Shan Tebbu, the Lower or Ha Tebbu, and the most refractory of all, the Tara Tebbu. . . . Today the Tebbu Land is practically closed to foreigners and Chinese alike, and he risks his life indeed who enters that forbidding natural fortress which the Tebbus claim for their own.'[2]

Little has changed in the years since Rock's visit. The Tebbu homeland is still dangerous for visitors, and the people still wild and unpredictable. The Tebbu in China have largely become invisible to the outside world, due to the fact that the government has lumped them together under the general Tibetan nationality, even though the Tebbu are very different—historically, culturally and linguistically. Although almost all Tebbu people profess Tibetan Buddhism as their religion, shamanist and animist rituals undergird all of their religious practices.

Christian and Missionary Alliance workers Edwin and Carol Carlson worked in this part of Gansu from 1922 to 1948. Their son, Bob Carlson, recalls the history of the outreach among the Tebbu people: 'It can be said that we were not received there with open arms, for my father was able to rent a house only because the landlord was having a dispute with the rest of the village, and figured the most spiteful thing he could do was to rent to foreigners. When we came on furlough in 1934, the men of a nearby village got together and burned the house to the ground.'[3]

The famous missionary Robert Ekvall lived for a number of years in Lhamo, better known on today's maps as Langmusi. Carlson notes, 'He had many friends among the Tebbus. In 1940, as the direct result of the death of his wife Betty, a majority of the people in one Tebbu village became Christians. Bob left Lhamo in 1941 and, because of the war, was not able to return. Subsequently my dad had some contact with the believers up until 1948. What became of those believers is something I would dearly love to know!'[4] It is now more than half a century since anything was heard about the Tebbu Christians. There is no evidence to suggest that their faith was passed on to the next generation.

Nancy Sturrock

Love Letters from Afar

Ubolwan Mejudhon

Christians have long lamented the lack of progress of the gospel in Thailand. After more than 200 years of missionary enterprise, less than one per cent of Thai people express faith in Christ. When Thai Christian Ubolwan Mejudhon went to study in New Zealand in the early 1970s, she found her life dramatically changed through a relationship with Jesus Christ. This article shares a few of the touching, personal letters between Ubolwan and her Buddhist fiancé. These precious letters give us a valuable insight into the difficulties Christians face as they try to share their faith with Buddhists. These letters also warn us not to have a confrontational spirit, which creates barriers between the Christian and non-Christian, and they encourage us to gently and respectfully share Christ without attacking the beliefs of those who don't yet know him as their Lord.

In 1970, Nantachai Mejudhon and I decided to marry, but at about the same time both of us secured scholarships to study abroad. Nantachai pursued graduate studies in the United States. In 1971, I went to the University of Victoria in Wellington, New Zealand. Both of us intended to be Buddhist missionaries during our years abroad. At the end of that same year, however, I dedicated my life to Jesus Christ. My conversion initiated an airmail letter debate in which Nantachai and I exchanged about 600 letters, trying to convince each other of our beliefs.

We would like to share a few of our experiences with you, in the hope that they will help you to understand more of the way Thai people—and many Buddhist people in general—think of the gospel. It is not accurate to say that Thais are resistant to the gospel. The great majority have simply never heard it in a way that is culturally acceptable and understandable to them.

Nantachai is completely Thai in the fabric of his life. One of the glorious moments of his childhood was his encounter with the queen of King Rama VII.

He always tells his children:

My parents brought me to the king's palace when I was four years old. They wanted me to officially submit myself as the king's subject. I sat still waiting for the queen so long that finally I ran and climbed up to sit on the king's throne. At that moment, the queen walked down the staircase and saw me. My parents were shocked because I had committed one of the greatest crimes and I was doomed to death. The Queen Rampaipannee smiled graciously and said, 'What a cute boy! You are courageous.' She gave me gold jewellery with her name on it.

The gentle way that the queen dealt with him caused Nantachai to be totally loyal to the Thai monarchy.

Nantachai met me when he was a member of the faculty of engineering at Prince of Songkla University. Nantachai taught mechanical engineering, and I taught English and Buddhist philosophy. When he first saw me, he thought, 'A lovely lady! Good for a girlfriend! How can I get to know her?' He soon pushed the thought out of his mind, however, because I was always busy with my job. Later, though, he asked me to help

him with his English, and I consulted him about Buddhism. Nantachai observed that I loved to pick wild flowers to fill my tiny vase, so he left flowers on my desk every morning. As our fellowship grew, Nantachai found we shared much in common—love for the king, the nation, Buddhism, classical music, nature, flowers and the poor. At long last Nantachai proposed and planned to marry me when he returned from the United States in 1972. He urged me to be a missionary of Buddhism while I studied in New Zealand in 1971.

My background and upbringing

King Rama VI gave 'Hachawanich' as the surname of my family because my uncle was a governor of a province. This background gives me pride and identity. As a result, from a young age I read many biographies about Thai royalty. I listened to stories from my mother and aunts concerning the goodness of our kings. My eyes glowed with excitement; my heart swelled with gratitude as I absorbed the gracious sacrifices of our good kings.

When I went to a pre-university school, my excellent teacher of history made me proud of our nation. She told us how our country disarmed colonialism with gentleness, gracious generosity and graceful strategies. Some Western scholars call the Thai mechanism of escape cowardly or full of double talk, but the Thai call it a Thai way of meekness. It takes great courage for a Thai leader to appear weak and intimidated for the sake of the country. The Thai mechanism of escape kept our country free for more than 800 years, and I am proud to be part of its heritage.

Buddhism is the other heritage that Thailand tenderly passed on to me. Buddhism was one of my mother's lifelines, and going to temples brought me joy. My father died when I was 13 years old. His

death left me with questions: 'Where is he now? Is he happy or sad? How can I escape from hell?' In 1967 my oldest brother, who was just 21 years old, was killed in an accident. His death caused great pain and raised more questions about life. What is the purpose of living? I took a course in Buddhist philosophy to find the answers. However, my Buddhist professor left a challenge with me. 'We cannot explain away the existence of God philosophically,' he said. I kept asking myself, 'Why not?'

Then I taught Buddhist philosophy at Prince of Songkla University, where I met Nantachai. Then, in 1971, I attended the University of Victoria in Wellington, New Zealand.

At that time, sheep and the gospel of Jesus filled New Zealand. In one of our final exams, we were asked to paraphrase the biblical story of the Good Samaritan. Various external readings in literature were filled with 'Jesus died for your sins.' When we went shopping, we saw Salvation Army officers singing songs on the street. My friends always wondered what kind of soldiers they were. While we stopped to talk on the street, a Salvation Army member approached us with 'Do you know Jesus . . .' I quickly and proudly finished his line, '. . . died for your sins?' He walked away. Back in the classroom, at least two students made their Christian faith known. One came from Indonesia, the other from Korea.

I heard about Jesus on 21 July 1971 from my Korean friend, Hong Sung Chul. I considered his witness assertive, aggressive and boastful because I realized he wanted to convert me, as did other evangelical Christians I came to know. During that time God revealed himself to me. While I looked at nature, I heard a still, small voice say to me 'God is the Creator. He is wonderful.' Then my search began for this God who spoke to me.

However, aggressive witness turned me off even though I loved the Christians' honesty and high ethical conduct. I became a Christian through a meek

Joyous Buddhism. Three ladies make offerings during a Buddhist ceremony at Tad Luang in Vientiane, Laos.

Xayographix

Christian who let God win my soul. He cooperated with God by saying the right thing, at the right time, in the right tone, with a proper manner that fit my Thai world-view. I became a Christian on 28 October 1971.

Love letters

The leaves of the trees in San Luis Obispo, California, slowly transformed their dresses from green to yellow, red and brown. An old leaf danced in the wind and gently fell on the pavement where a young engineer from Thailand was heading home. For Nantachai Mejudhon, two things mattered in all seasons: a postman and a mail box. That day he received four letters from his girlfriend, Ubolwan Hachawanich, who was studying in Wellington, New Zealand. He eagerly sat down at his study desk to read those precious letters. However, the exuberant joy on his face slowly changed into glaring shock as his eyes moved across those lines. He sat down and reread them. Then he walked around the bedroom rereading these pages. He locked himself in the bathroom and reread those letters many times more. Each time, the haunting message ate up more of his heart and mind. He felt he was dying inside. The letter said:

Julian Hawken

A group of novice monks in Thailand.

31 October 1971

My Dearest Brother,

It took such a long time to write this letter. I'm afraid with all of my heart that my letter will cause you great pain. However, I can no longer hold it to myself because I have never lied to you. I have to share the truth that I experienced. I have to share it with you because you are my love and we should hold no secret between us.

All your life, you always ask three questions:

1) Where do we come from? 2) What is the purpose of life? and 3) What is life after death? These are your questions and my questions, our questions. Now I have found all the answers in Jesus Christ . . .

You may wonder how these things took place. I have met many New Zealanders who are true Christians. We have exchanged our religious points of view. I came to realize that even though Buddhism and Christianity are different religions there were many things in common but the terms were different. However, the way of reaching the truth in Christianity is different from ours. The realization and understanding of Dharma (God) takes place in the heart, and not in the head. As a result, our spirits are tamed automatically and Dharma (God) remains always in us. . . .

On Sunday night, 25 October, I attended the evening service with Mrs Smyth. I knew later on that people at the church prayed that I could understand God. That night I could not sleep, my heart and mind were aggressively disturbed by some spiritual waves. On Tuesday night after I returned from Mr And Mrs Junck's place (Mr Junck was the preacher of the Sunday evening service), I felt like sincerely praying as the Christians suggested. Early on 28 October around five o'clock in the morning, I felt deep happiness such as I had never experienced before. I felt clean inside. I had the feeling of mercy and kindness towards others. I no longer feel the sinful nature in me. I simply know that I have the power to live out God's word. . . . Please do not feel sorrowful or angry. . . . May God protect you and bless you with happiness, peace, calm and a warm heart.

Lots of love,

Ubolwan

Nantachai's heart was like a falling leaf. He was desperately confused. Many questions rushed through his mind. He questioned, 'Is she converted to be a Christian? Why did she keep on studying Christianity when I asked her to stop? What is her hidden agenda? Is there any man behind this? Who deceived her? What will happen to our love and marriage? Who is this Jesus who steals Ubolwan from me? How did he dare to share Ubolwan's heart with me? How dare Jesus, Christians and Ubolwan put me in an unresolved dilemma? If I am against her, I probably will lose her. If I agree with her, I lose my identity. I will be a disgrace to my family and a laughing stock to my friends.'

All of his dreams seemed to disappear into thin air. He became a living dead person, carrying the burden of study and unsolved questions. However, Nantachai answered my letter with tenderness and gentleness, with firm Buddhist advice, yet with persuasive suggestions.

3 November 1971

My Dearest Sister,

I am surely glad that you have a peaceful mind. . . . I think I understand the feeling you experienced that night and that morning. I know how you feel. I understand the state of your mind—how deep and how peaceful. I know and understand because I received it when I was seventeen years old. . . .

It was not Jesus or Christians, prayers or the image of the cross . . . but you, yourself caused it to happen. Your heart and feeling did it. Whoever tries to understand Jesus' mercy to humankind and uses one's heart and mind to depend on him, taking refuge in him, meditating and concentrating as much as possible on his grace, that one will absorb more of his goodness. . . . Those who are enlightened in Buddha's knowledge, seeing the light of life, must be intellectual, patient exceedingly in various qualities and they must take his truth seriously. . . . If you walked that way and it helped you to *understand life more easily, you should be proud and take courage to accept that way. It doesn't matter whether you believe in Buddha, Jesus or other religious founders or even in nothing. The improvement of yourself is what counts. . . . I want you to understand this one thing—you did it yourself. No one causes this experience. Jesus Christ did not do it. You suggested to me to try this experience. . . . Even though I believe firmly in Buddhism, I do not close the door of my heart. Truth is truth and it challenges searching and reasonable dialogue. . . . I shall try to contact Protestant churches and try it myself. It will be quite difficult for me because Buddhism is my barrier. . . . However, I will try to accept Jesus Christ as my Saviour. I think I can try and see what will take place. . . . Meditating on Jesus' grace, endurance, perseverance and sacrifice to realize his graciousness is good. . . .*

I want to share with you about my personality. I am a man of strong determination. If I want to do something, I will accomplish it no matter how much I will suffer. . . . If I believe I should accomplish a certain thing by certain methods, none can stop me, my mother, you, or anybody. . . .

I cannot let anything be more important than our love. Love is more important than anything. Whenever I reach the truth of life, Dharma

Monks receive a drenching from the monsoon rains.

(God), I will immediately leave laymanhood.
. . .

Those who are in love must share a lot in common. . . . Therefore we should follow changes in each of us. We share one good quality, speaking truthfully to each other. When you or I change for better or for worse, we must not hide it from each other. We should try to follow up and keep similarity between us. Do not let misunderstanding or distant places cause gaps between us. Gaps in marriage occur when one fails to compromise, to be flexible and to assimilate with another. . . . What is your idea about this?

Miss you most,

    Nantachai

Buddhist nuns, dressed in white, at a procession to Tad Luang in Vientiane, Laos.

Xayographix

I had already returned to Thailand and was staying in my home in Cholburi, looking forward to my next move to Prince of Songkla University in the south of Thailand, when Nantachai's letter reached me. The dialogue continued as I wrote back as follows:

13 November 1971

Dearest Brother,

I have just received your letter dated 3 November with a thankful heart. I both agree and am against some of your ideas and would love to express my opinions. . . .

You explained that the experience I had was normal. It occurred because I had faith in Jesus' goodness; therefore his goodness entered my heart. Your argument is probably true, but when I studied Buddha's Dharma for a long time, having firm faith in him, I did not have such a quality in my heart. Why? I affirm that something took place in my heart. It is not gradual improvement of my heart as I usually tried to practice . . . but I had no purity of mind. When sufferings attacked me I could not help myself. However, now I have confidence that I can face all things with happiness. . . .

I plead with you not to forsake your proving. If we don't know whether God or the Holy Spirit exists we should prove it. Without proving, all we can do is assume some probabilities. If we would love to know the truth we should prove it.

You also mentioned the truth of life. I asked myself why we were born. We are born with a purpose. For Buddha, the search for nirvana (the extinction of all desires) was the noble truth. The highest purpose in Christianity is to know God. The Bible gives three meanings of God: God is love, God is spirit and God is personal. . . .

Seeking for the truth in Buddhism starts with forsaking sins, doing good, creating the peaceful mind. How can we forsake sins completely when we know that we are full of avidya (ignorance)? We, therefore, cannot forsake sins and do good with purity of heart. . . . You and I know how much we long for purity of hearts . . . Christians seek first the peaceful mind. Then they proceed to practice the precepts and Dharmas with the help of Jesus. Perhaps my saying needs proving because it seems unreasonable. However, I think the longing to act righteously does not ignite within us but the righteousness we see in others ignites it. Therefore it should be all right when Christians bond their hearts and minds to God, who probably is Buddhism's nirvana, or the Holy Spirit, which is the living Dharmas (truths). All my sayings need proving . . .

On 27 November 1971, Hong visited me to follow up my newfound faith. He read Proverbs 29:13 to me: 'Where there is no vision, the people are unrestrained' (NASB). Hong encouraged me to win the souls of the Thai to Christ. He suggested that I seriously try to win Nantachai to Christ. He said, 'It is better for Nantachai to be saved but lose his mind than perish in hell.' My heart went out for Nantachai's suffering. However, I did not want him to perish. I had none to turn to except Hong, whom I respected as a spiritual teacher. He explained to me that marriages between Christians and non-Christians do not work. He asked me to promise not to marry a non-Christian. After Hong's visit, my words to Nantachai reflected a new set of mind well expressed in the following excerpts:

Yawning worship: Lao women wait to present offerings to Buddhist monks at Tad Luang in Vientiane, Laos.

19 November 1971

You asked me whether I have changed my religion. I apologize for my lack of clarity in this matter. I have to share with you honestly that I did change my religion to Christianity. I have firm beliefs in three things: 1) I am a sinner; 2) Jesus Christ died on the cross as my Saviour; 3) my understanding about Buddhism is that

all Dharmas (truth) Buddha taught he wanted us to put into practice. Now, I am a Protestant Christian. I affirm that I feel no regret about my conversion. I am glad and proud that I received the good thing so that I can serve others spiritually. . . . If our heart is not clean, no matter how clever we are we cannot help others well. . . .

I appreciate your mention of gaps in marriage. I am afraid of these gaps. I am truly afraid. If we marry and we have to divorce because of these gaps, I think I'd better be single. I will wait for you all of my life if you truly seek the truth without putting off the search. Each day predicts our future. If we have the gaps today, tomorrow we cannot marry and be happy.

May God bless you.

Love you most,

Ubolwan

My letter postponing the engagement deeply hurt Nantachai. The loss of honour and spiritual trust from me was beyond his ability to cope. His life became very stressful. From then on, my letters were forceful and oppressive; I tried to convert Nantachai through indoctrination. I simply followed the way I was trained by other Christians. Nantachai's friend had to keep my letters away while Nantachai took his examination. Many nights he drank himself to sleep. His love for me mattered most. Any slight chance of losing me was unbearable. He responded with frustration.

29 November 1971

Don't let the differences of our religions destroy our wisdom. Use wisdom and the power of love to solve every problem. You told me that you chose Christianity and walked that way for me and our love. You used to write to me asking for my love and understanding, and I granted that honestly. I still love you and I am not angry at you. I understand you. Later on, you asked me to study so that I would get the experience. Even though I was a devoted Buddhist, I did my searching. On my two feet I searched Christianity. . . . You should understand how hard it was. . . . What's next? . . . Please tell me directly. What is in your heart?

Young Lao ladies in traditional dress in Vientiane, Laos.

Paul Hattaway

30 November 1971

This morning I (Nantachai) walked downtown and sat alone in the church. I felt peaceful and I walked towards the altar. With more sincerity than ever, I talked to Jesus Christ, 'Lord Jesus, I open the door of my life and accept you as my Saviour. Please make me the kind of person that you want me to be.'

I was afraid that others would overhear my prayer and consider me eccentric. . . . I know that you want me to be happy at all times with a peaceful mind. Therefore, you try hard . . . you try to be my leader in religion.

31 November 1971

I need encouragement, which you may not know. I would give you an example. I do not lie to you. When I received the letter telling me to postpone the engagement and marriage until I had a peaceful mind, knowing Christ, I could not do the examination the following day.

Then, I asked my friend to collect letters from the mail box. He kept your letters, being afraid I could not sleep and talked in my sleep.

Nantachai's Thai friends were angry with me, as were his relatives. The Thai community in San Luis Obispo discussed my conversion and witness. They concluded that I used my conversion to break my relationship with Nantachai, who was struggling at the university, or that I had a new boyfriend who was a Christian. Most of Nantachai's friends suggested that he find a new girlfriend. Nantachai's mother wrote a negative letter about me for the first time, considering me a woman without gratitude to our country.

On 20 December 1971, I received confirmation from the Holy Spirit that Nantachai would be my life partner, and I wrote to Nantachai:

20 December 1971

My new year gift for you is given from God. I do hope that you will be happy and satisfied. God confirmed to me that he created you to be my life partner. . . . I therefore believe that you will find him soon. . . .

God is with us everywhere in the creation. He is in the high mountains, the beautiful sky, cool wind and blooming flowers. He loves us and gives us freedom to believe. He does not force us to believe or plead with us to believe. . . . Please do not think I force you, because I have a reason. Life is uncertain. Who can tell when death comes? Who can be certain that our hopes and dreams will come true? Therefore, our priority is to hold on to the truth and the time is now. I will talk about this for the last time. I will cause no more trouble.

God's confirmation created a sensible spirit in me. Now my letters were not as pushy as those in the past. My correspondence during this period demonstrated gentle ways of sharing the goodness of

God in the creation and in answering prayers. While I gently witnessed, Nantachai made good progress, as an excerpt below demonstrates:

31 December 1971

Today I went downtown and bought three Christian books. I believe more in the existence of God. I should have more faith if I clearly find him. I believe because of the following reasons: 1) I receive peace when I read the Bible. It seems to me that not the lettering but God is teaching me. 2) I understand more about his love towards us sinful people for whom he died on the cross. It makes me feel that I should love him and love others as he loves us. 3) Now he is one of my refuges. When I am weak, it seems that he knows and encourages me to walk in the way of righteousness . . . I know he loves me and I have another wonderful refuge, and 4. I understand more about love.

However, the time between January and April 1972 was a difficult period for Nantachai. He was torn between his deep love for Buddha and Christianity. In one letter he explained how Buddhism helped him to see the goodness in Christianity.

18 January 1972

My process of learning in the past and at present is different from yours; this is why I find it's hard to believe in many things. I have to study step by step. I have to study thoroughly. My mind asks many questions until I am satisfied with answers I can believe. The thing which I firmly believe cannot be pulled out. Buddhism cannot be taken from me. As days go by, Buddhism gets deeper because the more I study the more I realize now precious it is to my life. Buddhism has no master. Buddhists who study Christianity do not serve two masters. Other religions have their masters. . . . I know what Buddhism is. I am happy to accept Buddhism and Christianity 100 per cent.

20 January 1972

I sit and reflect about the action of the monks and the teaching in the Bible. I am proud of the monks' behaviour. . . . They confess sins to

each other every evening. They live their lives according to 'If you have two shirts, give one to your neighbours;' 'Sell your properties and distribute them and follow me.' (Acts 2: 44–45). . . . There are many teaching in the Bible which the monks lived up to. . . . Therefore the monks live up to Dharmas (truths in religion) in the Bible more than many professing Christians.

Xayographix

A Thai woman prays fervently to Buddha.

28 January 1972

I am not a non-believer. I simply am not a 100 per cent believer.

14 February 1972

I agree with you that the way of Christianity is more practical. It is not ignorant, but it is beyond reason. The Bible says that men and nature are finite. We cannot understand everything about God who is infinite. . . . I sent you books about Buddhism in order for you to understand me. My wording is the reflection of my personal belief of Buddhism. If you perceive me with your world-view, which is based on Christianity, our thought patterns are not in one accord. However, if we try to understand the feeling of the one we love and continue to help one another, we will feel much better.

During this time Nantachai prayed to accept Christ every time Campus Crusade for Christ's staff approached him. Nothing happened. Every night he meditated about Jesus Christ, lived by Christian ethics and studied the Bible in a cell group and nothing happened. At the cell group, Nantachai experienced a powerful way of witnessing, a vulnerable kind of non-verbal witnessing. One evening, while Nantachai was waiting for the leader of the cell group, he found the leader crawling into the room. He was out of his mind because he got drunk. Nantachai felt sorry for the man and for himself. He questioned seriously, 'Is the spiritual search worth all my energy and effort?' The next morning he found the leader at the university library. The man walked to him and apologized for his misbehaviour. His deep sorrow and sincerity challenged Nantachai to feel the other dimension of Christianity, the repentance and confession of sin. After that he made up his mind to attend a church on Sunday.

In that small Presbyterian church, Nantachai sat in the back pew. He wanted to observe everything. At the beginning of the service, two African students sang 'Amazing Grace'. Nantachai was stunned by the radiant, shining faces of his African friends. 'I thought all Africans believe in primal religion . . . what a radiant, beaming spirit!' he reflected. Then people turned to hug each other saying, 'I love you.' Nantachai froze when a man beside him said, 'I love you, Nantachai,' and hugged him. Nantachai felt a clean, moving spirit in that church. 'Perhaps this is the Holy Spirit Ubolwan mentioned,' he thought on his way back home.

On 24 April I freely committed Nantachai to my Saviour, Jesus Christ. The following is an excerpt from the record of my experience:

During the past six months, I was full of worries and anxiety concerning you. . . . When I walked in quiet places, tears found their way on my face. It seemed to me that salvation was far away from you. Tonight I received four of your letters claiming your firm belief in Buddhism. I was deeply discouraged. At last I found a verse in the Bible, 'I do not want anyone else because God is enough.' I asked myself about my faith in him and my understanding of his grace. I asked myself whether I could accept this Scripture with all my heart. I found that I did not have much faith in God. I used my own ability to persuade you, but I have never committed you to him, who is our guidance. I demanded things to serve my own will. Therefore I knelt down and prayed honestly, 'I commit Nantachai

Young monks at play in Luang Prabang, Laos.

into your hands. I am willing to receive all the consequences according to your will. I will not make any decision unless your will is clear.' Since then I made the decision not to write to you or get your letters. I felt such peace in my heart. There is no more anxiety.

This incident occurred on 24 April 1972, and my letter reached Nantachai after his conversion. Nantachai described his conversion in the following way, as these excerpts from his correspondence reveal.

An elderly Thai monk resting.

International Mission Board

2 May 1972

This letter will bring you much happiness. It is the letter you have waited for such a long time. My dear sister, I met God. I committed everything in my life to Christ. I experience joy which I had never received before. It is such a different kind of joy. It occurs by itself in my heart. I only accept that I am a sinner and I cannot help myself from suffering; therefore I accept him as my only Saviour. That joy overflows my heart. While writing the letter I still feel that joy. It is so different from the happiness which comes from peace in Buddhism. It is joy and hope in my heart which will lead me to do all things with confidence in him. Dear sister, I had never dreamed that I would receive these things. I had tried like this for so many nights, many months. I was stubborn and arguing using my personal reasons. . . . Now I understand how much you love me. I write this letter with tears in my

eyes, remembering your love and understanding towards me, when I could not understand and argued seriously. Please forgive me.

Now he gives me life. I feel my life is purer. I feel that God is within me. . . . I used to think that we can live righteously and that happiness resulting from living righteously is the same in all religions. Buddhism could teach us as well as Christianity. However, joy comes from purity of heart when one receives Christ and commits one's life to him. Then we can live holy lives. I know that when I share this with others they will not understand. But I will keep on telling them and trying to explain this to everyone as you did to me. . . .

That night I read a book written by Billy Graham. While reading, I felt great joy and understood Christianity better. My heart was softened and I felt great joy, and I prayed to him, 'I am a sinner and I cannot get rid of all sins with my ability. I accept you as my Saviour who saved me from these sins. Please open my heart for me to feel more flooding joy.' I know he has accepted me and has opened my heart.

When I think back over the lessons we learned during this difficult yet wonderful time, they can be divided into three categories: 1) the Western way of discipling non-Christian Thais; 2) confirmation of the Thai way of meekness; and 3) the Holy Spirit and the discipleship of non-Christian Thais. By the Western way I mean the way of Westernized Christians who tried to influence Nantachai.

The Western way of discipling non-Christian Thais

The witness of Hong, the Salvation Army officer and the ten staff members of Campus Crusade for Christ reflects the either / or world-view of Christians who are influenced by the West, where power is held in high regard. Even though Hong is a Korean Christian, Korean Christianity was greatly influenced by Westerners, and so he was more like them in his methods. Hong singled out Nantachai's spirituality and ignored Nantachai's physical, mental and social needs. Hong believed that it was better for Nantachai to have a mental breakdown but be saved rather than to perish in hell.

The superior and negative attitudes of Christians towards non-Christians exhibited themselves in my letter of 19 November 1971, which I wrote after being discipled by Hong. I no longer thought that I could learn anything from Nantachai, but had decided that he had to learn from me. I considered myself a crusader who was endeavouring to save his soul. Therefore my correspondence became forceful and threatening. I confronted Nantachai and tried to indoctrinate him with information, using our future marriage to pressurize him. I disregarded his pleading to leave him alone for a while so he could study for the examination. My behaviour pattern of witness derived from the fear that Nantachai would go to hell if he did not believe in Jesus. I did what Christian taught me to do.

As a result, Nantachai stopped reading my letters and asked his friends to take away the letters for a while. Nantachai's friends and relatives are angry with me to this day. His roommate, who is Nantachai's best friend, refused to attend our wedding. Friends and folks considered Christians and Christianity unkind, selfish and fanatic. This either / or world-view of Christians drove Nantachai to the brink of breakdown.

Confirmation of the Thai way of meekness

The evidences elucidate the world-view of the Thai as power through weakness. This world-view shaped Nantachai's life and conversion. Submission to the Thai world-view is important to the Thai. The confession of a Christian who had become drunk helped Nantachai understand Christian honesty, repentance and confession of sin. The power of weakness ignited its dynamic power when I stopped pushing him to make a decision for Christ and committed him to God. Nantachai was free to choose his faith, and he chose Christ. Nantachai's conversion flowed with the Thai cultural grain of the Thai way of meekness.

Ego-orientation had a great impact upon Nantachai and me. The atmosphere of our country during Nantachai's youth influenced Nantachai to have strong self-identity based on pride in the freedom of our country and Thai heroes. He also absorbed this value from the words and deeds of his parents. His father rejected bribery and corruption, preferring to be poor and faithful to his king and country. His sophisticated knowledge of high Buddhism gave him peace of mind, contentment and a strong self-identity.

Extracts from correspondence revealed that Nantachai reacted aggressively when I violated his self-identity by manipulating him to be Christian.

Thais have strong self-identity. Nantachai and I did not feel inferior to Western Christians before our conversion. It is interesting to observe that I lost self-confidence and self-identity, humanly speaking, after my conversion. I relied heavily on the instruction of other Christians and did not question their suggestions. Nantachai demonstrated the firmness of his identity under spiritual oppression. Nantachai's personality and behaviour patterns revealed the ego-orientation of the Thai way of meekness. As our model suggests, the Thai are first and foremost ego-oriented, having strong self-esteem and a love for freedom.

Grateful relationship orientation exhibited itself in both Nantachai and me. The gentle way that the queen dealt with him caused Nantachai to be totally loyal to the Thai royal monarchy. Nantachai's parents brought him up with grateful relationships towards his country, Thailand. Grateful relationships towards Buddhism permeated Nantachai's being, and he expressed this in his correspondence. His letter written after his conversion stated his gratefulness for my love and understanding. I was grateful to the Thai royal monarchy because King Rama VI bestowed on me the family's surname. I was grateful to Buddhism, which comforted me in time of loss, and so I dedicated myself to teach Buddhist philosophy. However, this grateful relationship orientation influenced me to blindly follow the suggestions of Westernized Christians without critical thinking. Apart from this negative effect, grateful relationship orientation mingles in the fabric of Thai, elucidating the Thai way of meekness.

Nantachai's conversion and mine demonstrate that discipling non-believers requires seeking, finding and bonding. I sought the truth of Christ and initiated the religious discussion with Hong. I agreed to go and discuss with Mr Gordon Junck. When Nantachai determined to seek Christ by himself, he found the truth in Jesus Christ.

The fact that Nantachai's friends and relatives bore the burden of Nantachai's sorrow illustrated the Thai way of meekness. Their community-oriented value system influenced them to help Nantachai in times of life crisis by providing him with comfort, advice and companionship. For the Thai, life is not like an isolated island but a bunch of bananas in which interdependence plays an important role. Nantachai and his friends' cooperative effort in solving a life crisis flowed along the cultural grain of the Thai way of meekness.

Nantachai's conversion suggested that achievement in Thai culture demanded respect for authority and interpersonal relationships. Non-believers are authority. They have their own right to accept or reject the gospel. My friendship with Nantachai helped him realize that I discovered something extraordinary that he did not understand yet. My respect for his individualism at long last encouraged him to press on the spiritual search. This evidence confirms hierarchy, relationship and individualism as important elements of Thai social structure.

The Holy Spirit and the discipling of non-Christian Thais

Our experiences showed that the Holy Spirit worked through the Thai way of meekness. The Spirit used a gentle servant of God like Gordon Junck to lead me to Christ. The Holy Spirit led me to forsake the aggressive way of witness and to trust fully in him by telling me ahead of time about Nantachai's conversion. The Holy Spirit used the community of faith in worship, two African singers, the confession of a Christian who had become drunk and Billy Graham's books to lead Nantachai to know the living Saviour.

The Holy Spirit is above culture, but he chooses to work through the culture. The Holy Spirit worked through the Thai world-view of power though weakness. He certified the unplanned witness and made use of vulnerable but honest Christians to reveal himself to Nantachai. The Holy Spirit worked through those whose attitudes were humble and who practised gentle behaviour patterns. In short, those Christians who follow the incarnational model of Christ are powerful instruments of God for the Thai. The Holy Spirit did contextualize the theology of discipling for the Thai. He acknowledged that discipling is a progressive process for Thais. He also used Thai tools in discipling such as symbols, ceremonies, living models, formal and informal teaching.

Often I wonder, 'What will happen if missionaries and Thai Christians follow the way of the Holy Spirit and allow the gospel to flow along the Thai cultural grain?'

Notes

This article is based on Ubolwan Mejudhon's doctoral dissertation 'The Way of Meekness: Being Christian and Thai in the Thai Way' (Asbury Theological Seminary, E Stanley Jones School of World Mission and Evangelism, 1997).

Create International

Waiting for God's love letter from heaven: a Burmese man in contemplative mood.

Approximately 28 million Central Thai people are the main ethnolinguistic group in the country of Thailand. More than 200,000 Central Thais also live scattered in many nations around the world. Wherever a Thai restaurant can be found serving its delicacies, a Central Thai can usually be found nearby. Unlike other Asian peoples such as the Chinese, Indians or Vietnamese, the Thais have not spread out around the globe in such great numbers. Most Thais are happy to remain in their homeland.

The number of Central Thai in Thailand is difficult to estimate because of the high level of overlapping between languages that occurs. Because Central Thai is the national language used in education and media, the majority of the 60 million people in Thailand can speak it. About five million ethnic Chinese people living in Thailand now speak Central Thai as their first language.

The Thai people love their country, their king and their culture.[1] They have a very strong sense of national identity, reinforced by the fact that theirs is the only country in Asia never to be controlled by a colonial power. The Thais are proud of their independence. They changed their name from Siam to *Thailand* (meaning 'Land of the Free') in 1939. The Thais have many sayings that reflect their stubborn resistance to change, such as 'We have been neighbours of the Chinese for four thousand years but we don't use chopsticks!'[2]

Thai people are known around the world for their gentleness and friendliness, which has given birth to Thailand's nickname as 'The Land of Smiles'. They place great value on meekness, tolerance and humility.[3] Underneath this happy veneer, however, lie major social ills that the Thais do not readily acknowledge, such as the more than one

million people working in the sex industry, rampant AIDS, drug abuse and corruption.

The identity of the Thai people is wrapped up in their culture, of which Buddhism is a major component.[4] It is a common saying that '"To be Thai is to be Buddhist". This cultural-religious tie has given Thailand a reputation for being a "graveyard for missions".'[5] Christianity has had a presence in Thailand for almost 500 years. Catholic

Paul Hattaway

priests accompanied a Portuguese embassy to the nation in 1511. Protestant work commenced more than three centuries later, in 1816. To this day, work among the Thais has been slow. As late as 1957, '140 years after the beginning of resident Protestant Missions, Henry McCorkle correctly observed that Thailand had "more Buddhist temples than Protestant church members".'[6] Over the past century, many godly Christian men and women have faithfully sowed the seed of the word of God, and a small yet significant Christian minority is beginning to emerge in Thai society.[7]

Today there are an estimated 100,000 Central Thai Christians worldwide (four out of every 1,000 people). The Central Thai remain one of the largest, yet most accessible, unreached groups in the world.

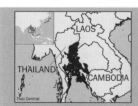

Overview of the Central Thai

Other Names: Thai, Central Thai, Siamese, Thai Khom, Thai Klang, Tai Noi, Standard Thai, Bangkok Thai

Population Sources:
20,000,000 to 25,000,000 in Thailand (1990, A Diller)
100,000 in Taiwan (2001, P Johnstone and J Mandryk)
37,000 in Myanmar (2003, Joshua Project II)
35,000 in Singapore (2001, P Johnstone and J Mandryk)
28,000 in Cambodia (2001, P Johnstone and J Mandryk)
20,000 in Malaysia (2003, Joshua Project II)
14,416 in USA (1996 B Grimes—1970 figure)
10,000 in Japan (2003, Joshua Project II)[8]

Language: Tai-Kadai, Kam-Tai, Be-Tai, Tai-Sek, Tai, Southwestern, East Central, Chiang Saeng

Dialects: 0

Professing Buddhists: 98%

Practising Buddhists: 55%

Christians: 0.4%

Scripture: Bible 1883; New Testament 1843; Portions 1834

Jesus film: available

Gospel Recordings Thai, Thai: Central

Christian Broadcasting: available

ROPAL code: THJ

Population:
27,498,200 (2000)
30,060,200 (2010)
32,861,700 (2020)

Countries: Thailand, Taiwan, Myanmar, Singapore, Camodia, Malaysia, USA, Japan, Australia, Brunei, Canada, United Arab Emirates, Finland, China, Laos, United Kingdom, France, Germany, New Zealand and many other nations

Buddhism: Theravada

Christians: 100,000

Status of Evangelization

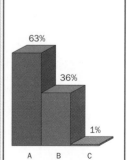

A = Have never heard the gospel
B = Have heard the gospel but have not become Christians
C = Are adherents to some form of Christianity

A 63%
B 36%
C 1%

Thai, Northern

Approximately six-and-a-half million Northern Thai people live in north and north-west Thailand. For the past 800 years, the Northern Thai have been centred in and around Chiang Mai—Thailand's second largest city after Bangkok. In addition to Chiang Mai, the Northern Thai can be found in the provinces of Chiang Rai, Nan, Phrae, Phayao, Lampang, Lamphun, Tak, Nan, Mae Hong Son and Uttaradit.

A small community of less than 10,000 Northern Thai lives in Laos.[1] Others live scattered around the world in countries like Singapore, the USA, Australia and the United Kingdom.

The first kingdom founded by the Northern Thai is believed to have been the state of Yonok in the Chiang Saen area in AD 773.[2] Later, as thousands of people migrated southward from southern China, King Mengrai united several Tai tribes and founded the great Lanna ('million rice fields') Kingdom at Chiang Rai in the late 13th century.[3] In 1296, Mengrai founded the city of *Chiang Mai* (which means 'New Town') and moved his capital there. Over the next 250 years Lanna flourished until its eventual downfall to the Burmese in 1556.

Right up until 1939, when Chiang Mai was formally incorporated into the modern Thai nation, the Northern Thais viewed themselves differently from the Isan and Central Thai (Siamese), with whom they often waged cruel wars.[4] In the 1770s, Chau Prasat Tawng, the King of Siam, 'laid the country waste, plundered their villages, and brought away many

Paul Hattaway

thousand captives to be slaves forever more. The [Northern Thai] king . . . underwent cruelties of which it is a shame even to speak. . . . He was confined to a large iron cage, exposed to the burning sun, and obliged to proclaim to everyone that the King of Siam was great and merciful.'[5]

The Northern Thai language is distinct from other Thai varieties.[6] They have their own script, called Yuan, which is similar to the orthography used by the Lu. Today, while most rural Northern Thai people continue to speak their own language in the home,[7] the ability to read Yuan has diminished.

The Northern Thai have believed in Buddhism for 1,000 years. In 1330 they sponsored their own monks to travel to Ceylon (Sri Lanka) and India to study 'the purest form of Buddhism at its root'.[8] Like other Theravada Buddhists, the Northern Thai today mix their beliefs with numerous animistic rituals.[9]

Protestant missionaries have faithfully worked in northern Thailand for about 150 years.[10] While many of the tribal peoples in the region have responded to the gospel in large numbers, progress among the Northern Thai has been painstakingly slow. In recent years the city of Chiang Mai has emerged as a regional missions hub and is home to about 2,000 foreign missionaries and their children. Strangely, however, most of them are engaged in work in places like China, Vietnam and Myanmar, while many of those focusing on Thailand work with the hill tribes.[11] Few are reaching out to Thai Buddhists. This strange situation may mean that there are more foreign missionaries than there are ethnic Thai Christians in Chiang Mai.

Overview of the Northern Thai

Other Names: Yuan, Lanna, Lan Na, Lanatai, Phyap, Phayap, Payap, Kammuang, Kammyang, Myang, Kam Mu'ang, Mu'ang, Khon Mung, Khon Myang, Tai Nya, La Nya, Western Laotian, Tai Yuan, Youon, Youanne, Youe, Yonok, Yonaka, Yon, Yun, Yoan, Khon Muang, Muang Lan Na, Lan Na Thai, Khon, Khon Mang, Lao Yuan, Nhuane, Lao Phung Dam

Population Sources:
6,500,000 in Thailand (2001, P Johnstone and J Mandryk)
9,750 in Laos (1999, Asian Minorities Outreach)
also in Singapore, USA, Australia, United Kingdom and many other nations

Language: Tai-Kadai, Kam-Tai, Be-Tai, Tai-Sek, Tai, Southwestern, East Central, Chiang Saeng

Dialects: 3 (Nan, Bandu, Tai Wang)

Professing Buddhists: 95%

Practising Buddhists: 65%

Christians: 0.6%

Scripture: Bible 1927; New Testament 1914; Portions 1867; work in progress

Jesus film: available

Gospel Recordings: Northern Thai

Christian Broadcasting: available

ROPAL code: NOD

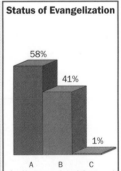

Status of Evangelization

- 58%
- 41%
- 1%

A = Have never heard the gospel
B = Have heard the gospel but have not become Christians
C = Are adherents to some form of Christianity

Population:
6,509,700 (2000)
7,116,800 (2010)
7,780,700 (2020)

Countries: Thailand, Laos, Singapore, USA, Australia, United Kingdom and other nations

Buddhism: Theravada

Christians: 40,000

LAOS

THAILAND

Thai Northern

More than five million speakers of the Southern Thai language live in a total of 14 provinces in the arm of south Thailand that reaches down to Malaysia. There are many thousands of people of Southern Thai origin living in the USA, England and other Western nations around the world, but because they identify themselves simply as 'Thai' in those places, it is difficult to estimate the number of Southern Thai living overseas.

The main areas of Southern Thai inhabitation are the provinces of Chumphon, Nakhon Sri Thammarat, Phatthalung, Ranong, Phang Nga, Phuket, Krabi, Trang, Surat Thani, Pattani and the four provinces bordering Malaysia: Narathiwat, Satun, Songkhla and Narathiwat. The region—squeezed between the idyllic Andaman Sea and the Gulf of Thailand—includes famous tourist spots like Phuket and Krabi, which are visited by millions of tourists every year.

The differences between the Southern Thai and other Thai are principally linguistic.[1] The Southern Thai language is called Dambro, which has been described as 'a group of dialects more distantly related to other Thai languages. The border dialects are quite distinct from others. Eighty-one per cent use Southern Thai in the home, 8.5 per cent use Central Thai, 10.5 per cent use both.'[2]

Many historians believe that the region now inhabited by the Southern Thai was once filled with Malay people. The Thais came down from southern China about 1,000 years ago, driving most of the Malays southward. 'They intermixed with . . . the Mon and Khmer . . . and with the Malay and Negritoes who also inhabited the area.

International Mission Board

Because of their mixed origin, many Southern Thai still differ somewhat in appearance from their Central Thai neighbors to the north, being of a darker hue.'[3]

Interestingly, about 1.5 million of the Southern Thai are Sunni Muslims. The strong Islamic influences come from Malaysia, and also from the 1.5 million Pattani Malays, who live alongside the Southern Thais yet are ethnolinguistically distinct from them.[4]

Both Buddhism and Islam appear to have arrived in Southern Thailand at about the same time during the 13th century. Nakhon Sri Thammarat became a 'center for the diffusion of a new school of Theravada Buddhism based on teachings from Ceylon [Sri Lanka]. From Nakhon Sri Thammarat monks carried the new form of Buddhism to the Angkorian Empire [Cambodia], Sukkothai [Central Thailand], and Lanna [Northern Thailand].'[5]

With such a religious battle for the hearts of the Southern Thai between Islam and Buddhism, it is not surprising that Christianity has failed to make much of an impact among this large unreached people group. 'Although several mission agencies are laboring among the Southern Thai, response has been low. Less than 1 per cent of the Southern Thai are Christians and the majority have never heard a clear presentation of the gospel. The Bible and the *Jesus* film have not been translated into the Dambro language and no Christian broadcasts are available to the Southern Thai.'[6]

THAILAND
Narathiwat
Pattani
Songkhla
Yala
MALAYSIA
Thai Southern

Population:
5,465,000 (2000)
5,973,200 (2010)
6,528,700 (2020)
Countries: Thailand, Malaysia, USA, United Kingdom, Australia
Buddhism: Theravada
Christians: 27,000

Overview of the Southern Thai

Other Names: Dambro, Southern Thai, Thai Malay

Population Sources: 5,000,000 in Thailand (1990, A Diller)

also in Malaysia, USA, United Kingdom, Australia

Language: Tai-Kadai, Kam-Tai, Be-Tai, Tai-Sek, Tai, Southwestern, Southern

Dialects: 1 (Thai Malay)

Professing Buddhists: 70%

Practising Buddhists: 45%

Christians: 0.5%

Scripture: none

***Jesus* film:** none

Gospel Recordings: Thai: Southern

Christian Broadcasting: none

ROPAL code: SOU

Status of Evangelization

75%

24%

1%

A   B   C

A = Have never heard the gospel
B = Have heard the gospel but have not become Christians
C = Are adherents to some form of Christianity

Thakali

The 1991 census in Nepal returned 13,731 members of the Thakali ethnic group, of which 7,113 (51.8%) were still able to speak the Thakali language. They primarily inhabit the Thak Sat Soe area in Thak Khola in the southern part of the Mustang District. Mustang is located within the Dhawalagiri Zone of north-central Nepal. Others have spread out into the 'Myagdi, Baglung, Parbat, Kaski, Gulmi, Syangja, Palpa and Rupendehi districts. The thirteen major Thakali villages are spread on the western bank of the Kali Gandaki Gorge through which flows the Kali River.'[1] The Thakali region is spectacular, flanked by the massive Annapurna Himal and the Dhawalagiri Himal, with peaks rising to 8,090 metres (26,535 ft.).

The Nepal government acknowledges the Thakali as one of the 61 ethnic groups of their nation. They also officially acknowledge the Marphali, Thintan and Syangtan as separate groups, even though they 'resemble the Thakalis in every conceivable way'.[2] There are four major clan divisions among the Thakali: namely Chhyoki, Salki, Dhimchen and Bhurki.[3]

Thakali men traditionally obtain their brides by abducting a girl when she is gathering wood in the forest or fetching water from a stream. She is taken back to the boy's home for several days, after which notification is sent to the girl's parents, bidding them to agree to the marriage.

For centuries the Thakali dominated the salt trade of western and central Nepal, trading southward into India and northward into Tibet. This has made them one of the wealthiest groups in Nepal today. Although the Thakali language is part of the Tibeto-Burman family, they are making a 'conscious effort to dilute their Bhotia [Tibetan] connection. The trend is towards identification with Hindu castes or better-known ethnic groups.'[4]

The present transition of the Thakali culture is also seen in their religion. 'Thak Khola is located in the zone where Tibetan cultural influences from the north come into contact with Hindu cultural influences from the south. Thus a mixture of native cultural elements and elements brought in and assimilated from the outside can be witnessed. This syncretism is above all reflected in religion, which is here a combination of animistic, pre-Buddhistic elements joined with Buddhist and Hindu ones. Adherents of Catholicism are now found among the migrated Thakalis and some Thakalis in Kathmandu call themselves atheists.'[5] One source notes, unflatteringly: 'Even the once proud tradition of becoming Buddhist monks is more or less extinct today, and only those old monks and nuns are upholding the traditional religion and beliefs, while the others consider these as the skeleton in their cupboards and wait for the death of these old monks and nuns so that once and for all they can bury the past.'[6]

Although the Thakali have been coming under many influences in recent years, Christianity has not been one of them. 'This group is still almost completely unreached with the gospel. A few have heard of and even accepted Christ, but there is still no Thakali speaking church and no Bible in their language.'[7]

Population:
16,600 (2000)
20,600 (2010)
25,500 (2020)
Countries: Nepal
Buddhism: Tibetan
Christians: 70

Overview of the Thakali

Other Names: Tapaang, Thaksya

Population Sources:
13,731 in Nepal (1991 census)

Language: Sino-Tibetan, Tibeto-Burman, Himalayish, Tibeto-Kanauri, Tibetic, Tamangic

Dialects: 3 (Tukche, Marpha, Syang)

Professing Buddhists: 50%

Practising Buddhists: 30%

Christians: 0.4%

Scripture: none

Jesus film: none

Gospel Recordings: Thakali; Thakali: Tingaun

Christian Broadcasting: none

ROPAL code: THS

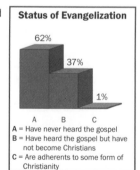

Status of Evangelization

62%

37%

1%

A   B   C

A = Have never heard the gospel
B = Have heard the gospel but have not become Christians
C = Are adherents to some form of Christianity

Photo credit: International Mission Board

CHINA
Xizang (Tibet)
Janakpur
Bagmati
NEPAL
Sikkim
INDIA
Thami

Population:
23,900 (2000)
29,600 (2010)
36,700 (2020)
Countries: Nepal, China, India
Buddhism: Tibetan
Christians: 300

Overview of the Thami

Other Names: Thangmi

Population Sources:

19,103 in Nepal (1991 census)

460 in China (2000, P Hattaway)

280 in India (2001, FMC South Asia)

Language: Sino-Tibetan, Tibeto-Burman, Himalayish, Tibeto-Kanauri, Western Himalayish, Eastern

Dialects: 2 (Eastern Thami, Western Thami)

Professing Buddhists: 55%

Practising Buddhists: 20%

Christians: 1.3%

Scripture: none

Jesus film: none

Gospel Recordings: Thami

Christian Broadcasting: none

ROPAL code: THF

Status of Evangelization

70%

28%

2%

A   B   C

A = Have never heard the gospel
B = Have heard the gospel but have not become Christians
C = Are adherents to some form of Christianity

The 1991 Nepal census listed 19,103 Thami people,[1] living in the Dolakha District of Janakpur Zone and the Sindhu Palchok District of Bagmati Zone in Nepal.[2] More than 100 Thami villages are dispersed over a distance of three days' walk, or approximately 40 miles, in the hills of east-central Nepal.[3] Several hundred Thami also live across the border in Zhangmu County, Tibet. The Thami were originally a nomadic tribe who settled east of Kathmandu. Their legends state that the first Thami couple gave birth to seven sons and seven daughters. In order to find suitable marriage partners, they were allowed to marry each other.[4] In recent years some Thami have migrated to the state of Sikkim in India in search of jobs.[5]

The Thami language is one of the few from the so-called Eastern Himalayish branch of Tibeto-Burman. Linguist Mark Turin has recently written many excellent linguistic and ethnographic studies on the Thami.[6] Thami is related to the Baraamu language of Nepal, a group of approximately 7,000 people—mostly animists and Hindus—who live in Nepal's Gandaki Zone. Thami, which does not have its own script, is still spoken in all Thami homes in Nepal, while Nepali is used for communication with outsiders.

Many Thami men in Nepal are employed as stonecutters. Their work is backbreaking and poorly paid. Neighbouring groups have taken advantage of the Thami for centuries, oppressing them and forcing them to live a hand-to-mouth existence. The Thami

were not allowed to possess any land before 1995. In recent years many Thami families have stopped work as stonecutters and carriers, after they came to see that families engaged in this occupation slowly became extinct, as the family members died prematurely from the work.[7] Many Thami women wear large gold earrings and nose rings. Some still wear traditional *labaedas*—clothing made from plants that are beaten and woven together.[8] The main diet of the Thami is fish and a porridge made with maize flour.

The religious adherence of the Thami is 'not purely Hindu or Buddhist. They worship deities which are not at all in any of the major religions. They tend towards Buddhism though they use the rituals of the Hindu religion in their marriage ceremonies.'[9] Three days after the birth of a child, 'the house is cleaned with cow dung and water. The people are sprinkled with cow urine to purify them. The baby is then named in accordance with the day of birth.'[10]

International Mission Board

Between 20 and 30 Thami people in Nepal received Christ in 1993 after listening to gospel recordings in their language.[11] Christian workers reported an 'open heaven' as the Thami in Nepal eagerly received the message of salvation. The believers meet in a small church building. In 1997, when a missionary visited an elderly Thami Buddhist monk, the former found that his arrival was expected. The monk explained to the surprised visitor: 'I had a vision two years ago that a foreigner would come and give me a little golden book about the truth. I have been praying and watching each day. I know you are that man.'[12]

Thavung

Population:
1,110 (2000)
1,250 (2010)
1,450 (2020)
Countries: Thailand, Laos
Buddhism: Theravada
Christians: none known

Overview of the Thavung

Other Names: Thavong, Thaveung, Thavueng, Aheu, So, Phon Soung

Population Sources: 750 in Thailand (1996, M Ferlus)[1]

200 to 300 in Laos (1996, M Ferlus)[2]

Language: Austro-Asiatic, Mon-Khmer, Viet-Muong, Thavung

Dialects: 0

Professing Buddhists: 75%

Practising Buddhists: 40%

Christians: 0%

Scripture: none

***Jesus* film:** none

Gospel Recordings: none

Christian Broadcasting: none

ROPAL code: THM

Status of Evangelization

88%

12%

0%

A   B   C

A = Have never heard the gospel
B = Have heard the gospel but have not become Christians
C = Are adherents to some form of Christianity

The tiny Thavung tribe numbers approximately 1,100 people. According to the French linguist Michael Ferlus,[3] in 1996 a total of 750 Thavung people inhabited three villages within the Song Daw District of Sakon Nakhon Province in north-east Thailand. Across the border in Laos, Ferlus estimated that between 200 and 300 Thavung live on the banks of the Theun River, east and south of Lak Sao in the Khamkeut District of Khammouan Province and in Borikhamxai Province.

Despite their small size, the Thavung are a fascinating group. Many scholars have tried to trace their history. It seems that they were once part of a larger group in Laos or eastern Vietnam that splintered as clans or families migrated to different areas. After generations of living separately, they developed linguistic and cultural differences. There seems to be strong evidence that the Thavung are closely related to the Phonsung and Kha Tong Luang tribes in Laos. Together, all three tribes are sometimes called *Aheu*. Most people in Thailand, including even their near neighbours, call them 'So'.[4]

The Thavung of Thailand share their villages with people from the Isan and Tai Yor groups. Although they inhabit the same village, the homes of people from each tribe are separated. During religious festivals and other social gatherings all the inhabitants come together to celebrate.

The Thavung are hard-working agriculturists. Their main cash crop is glutinous rice. They also grow maize, cassava, cotton and

Xayographix

tobacco. To supplement their diets the Thavung hunt 'rats, birds and all kind of game in the forest with arrows, stone slings and flintlocks. . . . They gather mushrooms, wild bananas, coconuts, snails, crabs, frogs, crickets, larvae and cicadas. Wild herbs are used for medical treatment of sickness.'[5]

While the Thavung say they are Buddhists, like numerous other groups in this part of the world their main underlying belief is in spirit-worship. Buddhism is a veneer over a complex array of animistic rituals. Their most important guardian spirit is called *pu yao*, who the Thavung believe protects the village. They appear to have borrowed their belief in this spirit from their Tai Yor neighbours. The Tai Yor construct spirit houses in each village to honour the *pu yao*. On special occasions, such as the Chinese New Year, the Thavung join the Tai Yor in sacrificing pigs and rice wine as they pray to their protector at the spirit house.

There are no known Christians among the Thavung people in either Thailand or Laos. Because of their small numbers and close-knit communities, the Thavung village leaders seek to keep out outside influences in a bid to protect their threatened way of life. As a result, the few Thavung who have been exposed to the gospel have had little interest in it. Because the Thavung are not officially recognized in either Thailand or Laos, few people have heard of their existence.

Population:
23,000 (2000)
25,800 (2010)
29,000 (2020)
Countries: Myanmar
Buddhism: Theravada
Christians: none known

Overview of the Thet

Other Names: That, Sakkya, Shakama

Population Sources: 23,000 in Myanmar (2002, Myanmar Faces and Places)

Language: Sino-Tibetan, Tibeto-Burman, Jingpho-Konyak-Bodo, Jingpho-Luish, Luish

Dialects: 0

Professing Buddhists: 100%

Practising Buddhists: 75%

Christians: 0%

Scripture: none

Jesus film: none

Gospel Recordings: none

Christian Broadcasting: none

ROPAL code: none

Status of Evangelization

67%

33%

0%

A   B   C

A = Have never heard the gospel
B = Have heard the gospel but have not become Christians
C = Are adherents to some form of Christianity

According to Myanmar Faces and Places, an organization that produces excellent calendars on the country of Myanmar, there are 23,000 Thet people living in the northern part of Rakhine State and southern Chin State in western Myanmar. The Thet are related to, and live near, the Dainet tribe.

Although a number of books and articles mention the Thet people in passing, there is no exhaustive research available on them. The *Ethnologue* merely refers to Thet as an alternate name for the Kado language, which is part of the Tibeto-Burman family. Six dialect groups, including the Thet, are listed for the Kado in Myanmar.[1] One other source suggests that the Thet are the same as the Chakma Buddhist people of Bangladesh, but the Chakma speak a language from the Indo-European linguistic family—so the two groups are completely unrelated, except for their mutual adherence to Theravada Buddhism.

More exhaustive research needs to be conducted in this remote and politically-sensitive part of Asia to determine the relationship between the Thet, Sak and Kado. It remains uncertain whether these names all represent distinct ethnic identities, or if they are all varieties of the one larger ethnic component. In the 1931 Burmese census all of these groups were classified under the category 'Sak', which returned a population of 51,820.[2] The *Ethnologue* gives a 1983 population of 128,500 for these groups.[3]

Create International

Most sources only give small, isolated nuggets of information about the Thet people. One says, 'Living in Rakhine State, the Thet are one of the oldest and smallest tribal groups from the age of Pyu. They are known by foreign scholars as the Sakkya tribe and famous for their large earrings made of silver and bamboo.'[4] Some tourism websites include a visit to a Thet village on the itinerary for a trip to the ruins of the Buddhist kingdom of Mrauk-U. One Burmese commercial enthusiastically states, 'A full day of sightseeing. Trekking tours as well as drives with horse carriages in and around Mrauk-U. You will remain reverential in the ruins of ancient temples. . . . You will be amazed by the almost gothic-like atmosphere in an intact Buddha temple . . . and you will meet people from the Thet tribe with huge holes in their ears. And in the evening the Buddhist monks will preach in ancient monasteries old prayers from time immemorial.'[5]

Richard Diran, in his book *The Vanishing Tribes of Burma*, has a full-page photograph of an elderly Thet woman. The description of the image says, 'This Thet (or Shakama) woman from the Kaladan River region in [Rakhine] State broke down and cried after I photographed her, amazed that anyone would be interested in her people today. In 1919, C C Lowis said the Thet were practically disappearing from [Rakhine] State, remarking that only 230 villagers had returned themselves as Thet in the census of 1901.'[6]

One thing that is certain, however, is that the Thet people have been strong believers in Theravada Buddhism for many centuries. There are no known Christians among them.

315

Tibetan, Central

More than one million speakers of the Central Tibetan language live scattered throughout Central Asia—and now in many nations around the world where they have been dispersed as refugees during the past 50 years. Approximately 740,000 speakers of Central Tibetan live in the city of Lhasa and surrounding counties in the Tibet Autonomous Region, now part of China.[1] Approximately 150,000 live in India,[2] 100,000 in Nepal and 70,000 in Bhutan.

Tourists in Lhasa often find that the city falls short of the mystique they desire, although it has certainly improved since Thomas Manning described it in the early 1800s: 'There is nothing striking, nothing pleasing in its appearance. The habitations are begrimed with smut and dirt. The avenues are full of dogs, some growling and gnawing bits of hide which lie about in profusion, and emit a charnel-house smell; others limping and looking livid; others ulcerated; others starving and dying and pecked at by the ravens; some dead and preyed upon. In short, everything seems mean and gloomy.'[3]

Although the Tibetans strongly maintain that they are one people and are opposed to any attempts to classify them separately, the Tibetan nationality clearly divides into numerous linguistic components.[4] Central Tibetan—which has five dialects—is considered the most prestigious Tibetan language, as is the language of Lhasa, the hub from which the Tibetan world emanates.

Written records of Tibetan history have survived from the 7th century AD, but it

International Mission Board

is known that nomadic tribes roamed Tibet as early as the 2nd century BC. The cradle of Tibetan civilization is the Yarlung Valley area, about 80 kilometres (49 mi.) south-east of Lhasa. There, according to tradition, the union of a monkey and a she-devil created the Tibetan race. Around AD 600 the warrior-king of Yarlung, Namri Gampo, unified the clans of Tibet.

He acquired a princess from Nepal and another one from China to be his wives. Under the persuasion of these two women, he combined the ancient polytheistic faith—which was a mixture of magic, divination, demon worship and sacrifices—with Buddhist teachings. The Buddhist religion is the lifeblood of the Tibetan people

In the 1950s, the Chinese took full control of Tibet. Hundreds of thousands of Tibetans have been killed,[5] and hundreds of temples and monasteries demolished. In many ways, all that this opposition seems to have done is strengthen Buddhism among the Tibetans.

Tibet has long posed one of the greatest challenges for Christianity. Timothy, the Nestorian patriarch in Baghdad (778–820), referred to Christians in Tibet and indicated that he was willing to assign a missionary to them.[6] In 1892 Hudson Taylor said, 'To make converts in Tibet is similar to going into a cave and trying to rob a lioness of her cubs.'[7] Today there are just one or two small Tibetan fellowships in Lhasa[8] and small pockets of believers among refugees in India and Nepal.[9] Chinese Christians trying to reach Tibetans often encounter strong opposition from the monks. At least five evangelists have been stoned to death since 1988.[10]

Overview of the Central Tibetans

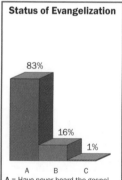

Population:
1,044,500 (2000)
1,282,000 (2010)
1,574,100 (2020)

Countries: China, India, Nepal, Bhutan, Switzerland, Taiwan, USA, Norway, France, Australia, United Kingdom, New Zealand

Buddhism: Tibetan

Christians: 200

Other Names: Zang, Wei, Weizang, Bhotia, Phoke, Dbus, Dbustsang, Lhasa, Lhasa Tibetan, U, Bhokha, Pohbetian, Tebilian, Tibate

Population Sources:
569,300 in China (1987, Language Atlas of China)
124,280 in India (1994, India Missions Association)
60,000 in Nepal (1973, Summer Institute of Linguistics)
50,000 in Bhutan (1987, D Bradley)
1,500 in Switzerland
also in Taiwan, USA, Norway, France, Australia, United Kingdom, New Zealand

Language: Sino-Tibetan, Tibeto-Burman, Himalayish, Tibeto-Kanauri, Tibetic, Tibetan, Central

Dialects: 5 (Lhasa, Chushur, Phanpo, Testhang, Lunrtse)

Professing Buddhists: 98%

Practising Buddhists: 90%

Christians: 0.1%

Scripture: Bible 1948; New Testament 1885; Portions 1862

Jesus film: available

Gospel Recordings: Lhasa; Tibetan: Colloquial

Christian Broadcasting: available

ROPAL code: TIC

Status of Evangelization

- A = Have never heard the gospel — 83%
- B = Have heard the gospel but have not become Christians — 16%
- C = Are adherents to some form of Christianity — 1%

A Tibetan Monk's Story

Nyima Chothar

I am a Tibetan and this is my story.

West of Lhasa is the province of Tsang, with its largest city, Shigatse, and greatest monastery, Tashilhunpo. Tashilhunpo dates from the time of the first Dalai Lama, Gedyn Druba (1391–1472). It is the seat of the succession of the Panchen Lamas, and the bodies of all the Panchen Lamas are buried there. Near Shigatse, the Panchen Lamas have two palaces: Kun Khyab Ling and the Dechen Potrang.

In the fire-serpent year (1917) in the little village of Chum in Namling County, I was born to a family of farmers. Until I was six years old, I lived with my parents and sisters at home. When I was small, I used to play at being a monk: beating the drums, blowing the white conch shell, setting up the special offerings called *tormas* and imitating the sacred dances. My parents encouraged me by giving me red and yellow clothing, just like the monks wear.

Before I was seven, my parents went to their master to ask permission for me to enter the monastery. One could not just decide to become a monk on one's own—one had to ask permission. Hence my parents had to seek their lord's permission for me to become a monk.

Father's older brother, my uncle, was a monk in Ganden Choklor. When I was six years old, he enrolled me as a novice monk, even though, according to the monastery rules, I should have been seven. Since I wasn't yet seven, my uncle told me: 'You must say that you are seven years old. If you don't, you can't stay in the monastery.' The two of us then went before the abbot. He said to me:

'I have a few questions for you—first, are you the son of a blacksmith?'

'No, sir.'

'Second: Are you the son of a butcher?'

'No, sir.'

'Third: Aren't you younger than seven years old?'

'I myself am just six, but my uncle said I had to say that I was seven.'

The abbot looked at my red-faced uncle and laughed.

'Since you have spoken truthfully to me, you are worthy to be a monk. In the future you will be an honest man.' Then the abbot gave me my new name—Nyima Chothar.

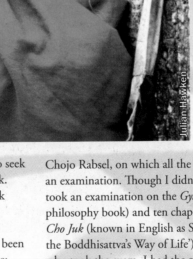

Julian Hawken

At the time I became a monk I had no idea what the monks did. I just knew they wore nice clothes and ate good food. Because I was still so young, for a year I did no study, but only played. My uncle loved me and took care of me. Our monastery was on a hill, and the monks had to carry me on their shoulders as they went up and down the stairs.

From the time I was eight until I was eleven, I studied the Tibetan language and the whole course of study known as Chojo Rabsel, on which all the monks had to pass an examination. Though I didn't have to, I also took an examination on the *Gyan Juk* (a Buddhist philosophy book) and ten chapters of another book, *Cho Juk* (known in English as Santdeva's 'Guide to the Boddhisattva's Way of Life'). Out of the 60 boys who took the exam, I had the good fortune to receive the first place prize—a *khatag*, or Tibetan ceremonial scarf.

Though I was a good student, I was still disobedient, and my uncle and my teacher punished me many times. Some of us would run away from the monastery, but our parents would catch us and return us there. Two of my friends and I fled to the top of a high mountain and stayed there for some time. After our food ran out, we ate the mountain birds' eggs. When we came down from the mountain our parents found out about this and caught us and returned us to the monastery, where we were whipped many times. After that I didn't want to stay with my uncle any more and so I lived apart from him, studying Buddhist philosophy and logic.

I asked my parents for permission to go to Lhasa, and I prepared clothes and food for the nine-day journey by horse and mule. When I reached Lhasa I stayed in Sera Monastery's Je College, where about 30 monks were studying Buddhist philosophy. I stayed there for two years, diligently studying the scriptural commentaries called Namdel, and the Buddhist scriptures known as the Prajnaparamita.

One day I went to Drepung Monastery to continue my studies. Some monks saw me as I was on my way, and they greeted me respectfully when they saw the special clothes I was wearing. Since I was quite proud, this made me glad.

At the Tibetan New Year holiday, when the rules of the monastery became more liberal, the monks gambled with dice and were allowed to play various kinds of games. In gambling with my friends I lost all my money and possessions.

Once I went out into Lhasa and the nearby villages to recite Buddhist texts. Sometimes, when someone had died, I went to recite the text known as the *Bardo Thodol*. Tibetans believe that when someone dies, their spirit wanders in an intermediate state called the *Bardo* before taking rebirth. During this time, the person's spirit is terrified by visions of wrathful gods. It is believed that the person can be delivered from fear by hearing this scripture, hence the name *Bardo Thodol* (which means 'deliverance through hearing the Bardo'). When a monk conducts such ceremonies, he receives so much good food and money for his services that he doesn't need to do any other kind of work. Often young monks don't think about the needs of the sick and the dying, but only about the money they receive for doing the ceremony.

From the Potala Palace to Bhutan

One day my teacher came to me and said: 'The Dalai Lama's bodyguard at the Potala needs a servant. Will you go?' I was glad to hear this and told him that I would, for I was happy to have the chance to live there. I stayed about a year with the bodyguard. For others it was difficult to see or meet the Dalai Lama,

Julian Hawken

The Potala Palace viewed from Jokhang Temple in Lhasa, Tibet.

Crowds of pilgrims wait in the courtyard of the Potala Palace in Lhasa.

Julian Hawken

When we got there, the Bhutanese people received us warmly. Wherever we went they offered us food and free places to stay. Even families living far away would call us to come and stay in their houses. A few families asked us to come and serve as their house-lamas. The Bhutanese people have great faith and respect for their religion, and we stayed there for more than a year.

but we saw him every day. At that time I was 13 or 14 years old.

I received a letter from my mother requesting that I return home immediately. It took me eight days by horse and mule to return to Shang. I was glad that I could stay with my family for a few months. I was also glad that I had kept my vows and could return as a monk. I had to go back into the service of the bodyguard, and I asked my parents' permission to leave. But my mother would not give me permission. She said, 'You don't need to go so far away from me. Why not stay in a monastery that is nearby?' I thought, 'There's no better monastery around here than Tashilhunpo. It would be good to stay there.' I told this to my parents, who were very pleased, and gave their permission.

The monks at Tashilhunpo liked to go to the park and gamble, and my friends and I used to go with them. If the *Pon Po* (monk in charge of discipline) came along, we would all run away. If we couldn't get away and he caught us, he would whip us many times. Part of the problem was that my section of monks was from the region of Tibet called Nghari, and his was from Gu-Ge. The Gu-Ge section was constructing a new building, and all the young monks had to go to work at the site. My friends and I didn't go and, knowing that the Pon Po would punish us, three of us fled from the monastery to the country of Bhutan.

In February 1950 one of my fellow monks lived with a Bhutanese woman. I thought to myself, 'I would never do that.' But, as the Tibetan proverb says, 'Whatever you think you will do, your fate will be determined by your deeds in your previous life.' On the fourth day of the sixth Tibetan month is the festival commemorating the preaching of the Buddha's first sermon. Early in the morning the monks and nuns and former monks of that area come together to worship the goddess Dolma. In the evening all of us drank Tibetan beer and hard liquor until we were out of our minds. That night four of us broke our monastic vows with Bhutanese women. Feeling very sad, and knowing that I'd shamed my parents, I didn't want to stay there any more. I felt deep regret, but there was no way to repent and take it back.

A strange new teaching

In January 1951 I went back to Phari, near the border between Tibet and Bhutan. I got a well-paid job carrying loads of wool across the Himalayas from Phari to Kalimpong, and carrying kerosene back again from Kalimpong to Phari. After a year, the man I was working for went out of business, and I went to Calcutta to work as a cook. But it was so hot there that I could hardly eat, and I lost my strength.

I found I had come down with malaria, and I was unable to work. I intended to return to Tibet by way of Bhutan and, taking leave of my employer, went to Baxaduars on the border between Bhutan and India. There were many Bhutanese families in that place. As I wasn't able to work, I put on monk's clothes and went out to recite the Buddhist scriptures in return for alms. But my illness got worse, and I became very sick.

There was a Christian hospital in that town, run the hospital, washing and bandaging the patients' wounds. Morning and evening I went with them to the mission worship service.

In the Bible they'd given me I read about the God who made the sky, the earth, the ocean, the trees, and all that is in the world. There it was written that God created the earth's birds and animals and all the ocean's creatures. The Bible said that God made the first man and woman, and by disobeying God's command these two became sinners. Their sin spread

International Mission Board

A man runs through burning bales of straw as part of a Buddhist festival in Bhutan.

by a Finnish mission. A Finnish lady named Miss Hellin Hukka gave me good treatment, and my illness became better in the course of a month. With good food and medicine, I regained my strength. I thought that the hospital people were very kind.

Miss Hukka exchanged the Buddhist books from which I'd been reading for a big book called a Bible. I was still going out to recite scriptures in the homes of the Bhutanese, but Miss Hukka encouraged me not to go, but to enter her employment. But without her knowledge I went out anyway. I was teaching her Tibetan for an hour each afternoon, and she was teaching me English.

While I stayed there I watered the garden and helped her with the many patients who came to to all humankind, making us all sinners.

But according to our Buddhist religion, the world arose by itself. A monkey, the emanation of the god Chenrezig, was the father of all men, and a rock-demoness, the emanation of the goddess Dolma, was the mother of all. That was the way humankind began.

I had to think about which story was true.

The Christians' Bible said that, after this, people still did not obey God, and God willed to destroy them all. In the book of Isaiah I read, 'There is no God but God. Gods and idols are not God, and making sacrifices to them is pointless. For though they have eyes, they cannot see; and though they have ears, they cannot hear.'

I thought, 'How is that? If this is true, all the religion I've practised so far is worthless. This Christian religion is unsuitable for Tibetans,' and I quit reading. But morning and evening I went to worship with the Christians and acted as though I believed, for they were taking care of me.

One day a Bhutanese girl named Sangey came to the hospital with a sore on her foot. This had been treated in her own country, but still had not gotten better, so she had come to Baxaduars for treatment. Her sore smelled awful, but nevertheless I washed it, put medicine on it, and bandaged it every day; and after a month it was healed. I got to like her, and she liked me. We decided to live together, but Miss Hukka found out about it and spoiled our plans by sending Sangey to Darjeeling. I was unhappy about this and left Baxaduars for Darjeeling, thinking that these Christians were nasty people who intruded on other people's business, for we had decided to live together, and Miss Hukka had come between us.

The new teaching follows me

On the two-day trip to Darjeeling, I was glad to be rid of those Christians and their Bible. Miss Hukka found out I'd left and phoned Darjeeling to call Sangey back to Baxaduars. When I found out I was without a wife, I was broken-hearted. I put my things in a local boarding house and went to the market, where I met a tall Englishman named Mr Ernest Shingler. I was very glad to meet him and he shook my hand like an old friend.

He asked, 'What is your name?'

Young novice monks study in Kalimpong temple near Darjeeling, India.

Dwayne Graybill

I told him and he replied, 'I've heard that name before. I have some work you could do. Are you interested?'

I was happy to tell him yes, and went with him. He arranged a small room for me to stay in, and every afternoon I taught him and his wife Tibetan. He asked me if I'd heard about the Jesus religion. I told him I had, and he gave me another Bible, just like the one I'd left in Baxaduars.

I had said I would never believe in this Jesus religion, but it seemed that I wasn't hearing of any other! I thought, 'Perhaps it is my fate to learn it!' and I began to read the Bible and pray.

Though I thought I was a Christian, and others said I'd become one, I was really only going through the motions.

Because I'd studied Buddhism for so many years, I couldn't leave it. Occasionally I still said mantras and recited texts, and I still believed in the Buddhist gods and idols. The Christians were very devout, but I wondered why they made no offerings to their God. 'After all, it isn't a sin to make offerings,' I thought.

One day, when I was reading the Bible's book of Isaiah, I found these words: 'From one tree a man cuts a piece of wood, throws it in the fire and cooks his food. From another he makes an idol and bows down to it, praying to it: "Save me!" but the idol doesn't answer and it cannot save' (Isa 44:15).

After reading this, my faith in the Buddhist gods diminished.

Mr Shingler kept coming for his Tibetan lessons three times a week, and praying with him made me feel much better and did me much good. There was a Bible school at a place called Mirig, and I did a course in the Gospel of John.

When I finished the whole course, I got a certificate. Through this, God deepened my understanding of my new faith and brought about many changes in my thinking. I stopped wandering about at night and quit many of my former bad habits.

I was ill with a fever and cough when a Pentecostal preacher from South India came to our hospital. Through his prayers a number of the patients were healed. After praying for some of the patients, he came to me.

'Do you believe in Jesus?' he asked.

'I believe in Jesus,' I replied, and the evangelist was glad.

He asked, 'Do you believe that if you pray to Jesus your illness will get better?'

A granddad and grandson at a Buddhist ceremony in Bhutan.

'I do,' I replied. And he put his hands on me and prayed in a loud voice, much to the amazement of the other patients who were looking on. Some of the other patients were also healed by the power of his prayer. He told me he would return the next day, then left.

The following day he came back and encouraged me, saying, 'In the book of Second Corinthians, chapter six, verse two, it says "In the time of my favour I heard you; in the day of salvation I helped you. Now is the time to believe; today is the day of salvation".'

And he also read from 1 Peter 2:24: 'He himself bore our sins in his body on the cross, so that we might die to sins and live to righteousness; by his wounds you have been healed.'

The evangelist said, 'Now your disease is healed. If you believe this, you have no more sickness, and you can go home.'

I felt the disease had left my body and I felt at peace in my mind. I believed I had been healed.

God gives me a new heart

In January, when I returned home and Mr Shingler and his wife saw me, they asked how it was that I'd gotten out of the hospital. I told them the whole story, and they were very happy and praised God. A week later Mr Shingler and I went to Karshang Hospital, a large Catholic centre, where I had an X-ray, which the doctors said was fine.

We both went home rejoicing. I believed that my Saviour Jesus had healed me, and I gave him thanks.

I read in the book of Ephesians, chapter four, verses 22 and 23: 'With regard to your former way of life, put off your old self, which is being corrupted by deceitful desires, to be made new in the attitude of your minds; and to put on the new self, created to be like God in righteousness and holiness.'

In the book of Hebrews, chapter ten, verse 17, it says: 'I will remember their sins and lawless acts no more. And where these have been forgiven, there is no longer any sacrifice for sin.' And in verse 22: 'Let us draw near to God with a sincere heart in full assurance of faith, having our hearts sprinkled to cleanse us from a guilty conscience, and having our bodies washed with pure water.'

After reading these words, I received a new heart.

Traditional Bhutanese dancers at a Buddhist festival in Thimphu, Bhutan.

I turned away from my adultery, drinking and other sins and, confessing them, left them all behind. All my sins were washed away by the blood of the Lord Jesus. Now I was a real Christian!

Because I had studied Buddhism for so long, it took me three years to come to faith in Christ.

I was baptized by Pastor Nathaniel in November 1955 at the Finnish Mission in Ghoom, near Darjeeling. Because the weather was cold, the church people had poured a great deal of hot water into the place where I was to be baptized, but the air was so cold that this had little effect. My friends wanted to give me special help, because I was the first Tibetan they'd baptized.

After my baptism many people asked me what kind of work I was going to do. 'I don't know,' I replied; 'I'll do whatever God tells me.'

While without work, I met an old friend. His wife and a relative of mine had a restaurant. I joined them as a cook's helper and, while the owner was away, as manager. I worked there for about six months. Before I came, a young Tibetan woman from Lhasa named Rigdzin Wangmo also started to work with them. We liked one another and, after arranging matters with our friends, we were married in the restaurant. A few months later, Rigdzin

Wangmo got sick and had to have a small operation. When she recovered we took leave of our friends and left for Calcutta, for I'd promised my earlier employer that I'd come back.

We stayed in Calcutta from September to March. While we were there, in February 1957, the Dalai Lama and the Panchen Lama came to India. They stayed at the Grand Hotel and we met them both. The Dalai Lama asked us about our country and our work, what plans we had for the future, and many other detailed questions.

'We plan to return to Tibet,' we told him. But he replied, 'If you go back to Tibet it won't do any good. Keep on doing the very thing you're doing now. Don't steal or fight; live peaceably with others; be diligent; and you'll be happy.'

My wife believes in Jesus

After Mr Shingler and Miss Withey and many other people talked to Rigdzin about Christ, she repented and believed in the Lord Jesus Christ. She was baptized in 1957 at El Shaddai Church. We had our second wedding, this time a Christian one. We both began to work for the Lord, preaching and helping refugees.

In 1959 the Chinese invaded Tibet and many Tibetans arrived in India. Many individual churches began to help the Tibetan people. Because we were Tibetan Christians, they asked us to help them. We gave out Christian books where the Tibetans were staying, but after a few minutes some monks came and took them all away.

With all the books gone, we were on our way back when a policeman came up behind us and said, 'The chief wants to see you.' So back we went with the police chief.

There in his hands were the books we'd given to the monks! He threw them in front of us and demanded, 'Who sent you here?'

. 'The Lord,' we replied.

'Who's he? You two aren't allowed here; go back the way you came. If you come around here again I'll put you in prison!'

While we were on our way back we saw many monks carrying our books under their robes. 'If you still have any like these, bring them back tomorrow!' they said.

We stayed there and gave out the rest of our literature. When we saw monks we would talk to them about Christ.

God gave us a child in Petong, whom we named Yacob Tshering. His birthday was 5 February 1960.

This is the story of how God saved a Tibetan monk and made him his child.

The Lord has been good to us all these years. My family has continued to serve him among Tibetans all along the Himalayan range. We have taught in schools, treated the sick, preached the gospel often and started a home for ill and poor Tibetans.

God graciously intervened on my life journey and set me on a new path to heaven. Please pray for my fellow Tibetans, that they too would have their eyes opened to see that Jesus Christ is the one true Saviour that they inwardly long for.

Notes

This article has been adapted with permission from a 1995 booklet by the same title, which may be ordered from Samdan Publishers, PO Box 2119, Kathmandu, Nepal.

International Mission Board

A little girl prays to Buddha in Bhutan.
Will the light of the gospel shine upon her generation?

CHINA
Xizang (Tibet)

NEPAL

INDIA

Tibetan Gtsang

Population:
661,200 (2000)
814,900 (2010)
1,004,400 (2020)
Countries: China, Nepal, India
Buddhism: Tibetan
Christians: 50

Overview of the Gtsang Tibetans

Other Names: Xigatse Tibetans, Xigatze Tibetans, Xigatze, Gyantse, Sagya, Tsang, Xigaze Tibetans

Population Sources:

457,700 in China (1987, *Language Atlas of China*)

50,000 in Nepal (1987, D Bradley)

also in India

Language: Sino-Tibetan, Tibeto-Burman, Himalayish, Tibeto-Kanauri, Tibetic, Tibetan, Central

Dialects: 10 (Reng, Pungmo, Kag, Lo, Gyasumdo, Kyidgrong, Dingri, Zhiskartse, Gyalrtse, Nadkarrtse)

Professing Buddhists: 99%

Practising Buddhists: 96%

Christians: 0.1%

Scripture: Tibetan Bible 1948; New Testament 1885; Portions 1862

Jesus **film:** none

Gospel Recordings: none

Christian Broadcasting: none

ROPAL code: TIC01

Status of Evangelization

84%

15%

1%

A   B   C

A = Have never heard the gospel
B = Have heard the gospel but have not become Christians
C = Are adherents to some form of Christianity

Almost 700,000 Tibetans belong to the Gtsang Tibetan language group. They are located in a wide geographical area, stretching east to west over roughly the entire length of the Tibet-Nepal border. Gtsang is spoken in the cities of Xigaze and Gyantse, the second and fourth largest cities in Tibet respectively. The main attraction of Gyantse is the immense pagoda, or *Kumbun*, built by Rapten Kunsang Phapa (1389–1442). Approximately 60,000 Gtsang Tibetans also live in Nepal, throughout northern parts of the country as well as in Kathmandu, the nation's capital.

The Gtsang Tibetan language—which has 10 dialects[1]—is a variety of Central Tibetan. It is largely intelligible with Lhasa and Ngahri Tibetan, although speakers can struggle to communicate with each other depending on their accents and how much exposure they have had to other varieties of Central Tibetan.[2] Despite their differences in speech, all Tibetans use the same Sanskrit-based orthography. In the 7th century, King Songtsen Gampo sent his minister, Thonmi Sambhota, to India, where he produced the script.

Xigaze, the capital of Tibet from 1618 to 1642, is the traditional seat of the Panchen Lama, Tibet's second most powerful ruler after the Dalai Lama. In 1954 the city was nearly destroyed by floods. After putting down a revolt in 1959, the Chinese imprisoned 400 monks in the Tashilhunpo Monastery.

The *Xigaze* New Year festival is held in the first week of the 12th lunar month. Thousands of visitors have flocked to Gyantse since 1408 for the annual horse racing and archery show. Captain O'Conner, the British trade agent at Gyantse in the

early 1900s, described the Gtsang Tibetans as 'superstitious indeed to the last degree, but devoid of any deep-rooted religious convictions or heart-searchings, oppressed by the most monstrous growth of monasticism and priest-craft which the world has ever seen.'[3]

The Gtsang region is home to several Buddhist sects, including the *Nyingmapa* (Ancient), *Kagyupa* (Oral Transmission) and *Sakya* (Gray Earth) schools. After the death of the Panchen Lama in 1989, the Chinese filled his position with their own choice of successor. In May 1995, the exiled Dalai Lama announced a new Panchen Lama who was immediately rejected by the Chinese. Monks at the Tashilhunpo Monastery and a number of lay Tibetans rioted in protest. Eighty monks were interrogated by the police, and the city of Xigatse was sealed off for several days.

Jesuit missionary Antonio de Andrade arrived in Tibet from India in 1624 by disguising himself as a Hindu pilgrim. 'Andrade outwitted hostile local officials, made his way north to the Himalayas, endured

China Advocate

altitude sickness and snow blindness, fought his way over a 17,900-foot pass into Tibet, and finally reached Tsaparang. . . . There he impressed the king and queen with his piety, and they gave him permission to return, establish a mission, and preach the Gospel.'[4] A revolution in Tsaparang in 1635 abruptly ended the Jesuit mission. Today there are a few Gtsang Tibetan Christians.

Tibetan, Jone

Approximately 100,000 Jone (pronounced 'Joe-nee') Tibetans inhabit Jone (Zhuoni) and Lintan counties in the south-western part of Gansu Province in western China, 'and east from there in the Bawa area of the Gannan Tibetan Autonomous Prefecture'.[1] A small number live in adjacent parts of northern Sichuan Province. Some publications have incorrectly given their location as the 'Yunnan-Tibet border'.[2] This group's name was previously spelled *Choni*, and they still appear in many publications by that name. The Tao River flows through Jone County.

In 1928 the explorer Joseph Rock discovered the Jone Tibetans. He wrote, 'I—in common with some 300 million Chinese and perhaps as many foreigners—was totally unaware of the existence of the Choni [Jone Tibetans].'[3] A more recent source explains that although the Chinese government officially considers them part of the Tibetan nationality, 'the people of this tribe have their own way of life. Due to their complex tribal structure, their lifestyle, customs, housing and costumes are visibly different from those of most Tibetans, making them a unique branch. As the tribe's women sport a hair-do with three thick plaits, locals call them *Sangemao* in the local Chinese dialect, literally meaning "three bundles of hair".'[4]

Jone was the site of an independent Tibetan kingdom until 1928, when Chinese General Fengyu Shang stripped the prince of his title and confiscated his land.[5]

A detailed history of the Jone appeared in a 1928 *National Geographic* article: 'The prince represents the twenty-second generation, but is not of direct descent. His ancestors, a Tibetan official family, left their own country and made their way across Sichuan and the Min Shan Range . . . to the Tao River in 1404, conquering and pacifying the tribes and villages on the way. Upon informing the Imperial Court in [Beijing] of their conquest of the territory for the Chinese Empire, they were made hereditary chiefs of Choni and the subjugated tribal lands. At the same time the Emperor, Yung Lo, gave them a seal and the Chinese name Yang.'[6] Today many Jone Tibetans still have the surname Yang.[7]

Jone formerly contained a huge Buddhist monastery, 'containing 172 buildings and 3,800 monks at its zenith'.[8] The Jone Tibetans' homes show that they are very religious people. 'On the right side of the sitting room an enclave enshrines the statue of a god accompanied by bamboo arrows wrapped with *hada* (a long piece of silk used as a greeting gift among Tibetans and Mongolians), scripture scrolls and similar items.'[9]

A 1922 mission report stated, 'The prince of Choni alone governs 48 clans and we can easily travel among these clans, as the prince is friendly and would protect us. . . . If we had the workers to employ we would press toward the west from the line we are now occupying.'[10] Today there are about 200 Jone Tibetan believers in Lintan County, to the north-west of Jone County. A church was constructed in 1997—the first ethnic Tibetan fellowship in Gansu Province. 'One woman sold her hair, and another family sold their TV to help build the new church.'[11]

Population:
100,200 (2000)
123,400 (2010)
152,000 (2020)
Countries: China
Buddhism: Tibetan
Christians: 200

Overview of the Jone Tibetans

Other Names: Choni, Chona, Chone, Jone, Cone, Choni Tibetan, Zhuoni Tibetan, Sangemao, Sangemao Tibetans

Population Sources:
77,000 in China (1987, *Language Atlas of China*)

Language: Sino-Tibetan, Tibeto-Burman, Himalayish, Tibeto-Kanauri, Tibetic, Tibetan, Northern

Dialects: 2 (Nongqu, Hebian)

Professing Buddhists: 95%

Practising Buddhists: 70%

Christians: 0.2%

Scripture: none

***Jesus* film:** none

Gospel Recordings: none

Christian Broadcasting: none

ROPAL code: CDA (Choni) and KHG06 (Jone)

Status of Evangelization

73%

26%

1%

A   B   C

A = Have never heard the gospel
B = Have heard the gospel but have not become Christians
C = Are adherents to some form of Christianity

Despite having an approximate population of only 50,000, the Nghari Tibetan language is spoken over a vast area of western Tibet. Nghari Prefecture, which has an area of 306,000 square kilometres (119,340 sq. mi.), lies north of the Himalayas at an average altitude of 4,500 metres (14,760 ft.) above sea level.[1] An unspecified number of Nghari Tibetans are also located in northern Nepal.

Almost all Nghari Tibetans are nomads, struggling to survive in the bleak conditions.[2] Their lifestyles have changed little over the last 1,000 years and they still have little technology or machinery. The inhabitants of the Nghari region of Tibet are also known as the *Chang Tang* (Northern Plain) Tibetans. Although they are ethnically Tibetan, they speak a language different from other Tibetan varieties. The Nghari Tibetan language group has seven dialects, named after their principal towns of habitation.[3]

The Tibetan alphabet consists of 30 consonants and four vowels, in addition to six symbols used for Sanskrit words.

Western Tibet is a holy site for the followers of the four religions of Buddhism, Hinduism, Jainism and Bon. Every year, thousands of pilgrims flock to the sacred Mount Kailas, a 6,714-metre (22,021 ft.) peak near Tibet's border with India and Nepal. Immersion in one of two holy lakes south of Mount Kailas is believed to release people from their sins for a lifetime. Pilgrims who trek to the top of the 5,640-metre-high (18,500 ft.) Dolma Pass are believed to be born again in the process. Folk Tibetans believe in a hell divided into eight hot and eight cold levels. Sinners are made to suffer until they have worked off their demerits. During the Cultural Revolution (1966–76), ten of the 13 monasteries in the region were demolished.

The favoured kind of burial for most Tibetans is 'wind burial'. The corpse is cut into small pieces and laid out on an exposed rock for vultures and ravens to eat. In the 1980s tourists in Lhasa secretly tried to take photographs of the ritual, an act considered a major offence by Tibetans. 'An Australian tried to hide up the mountain and take telephoto pics. Whilst hopping around on the skyline, he scared the birds away—an exceptionally evil omen. The irate burial squad gave chase brandishing knives and showered him with rocks.' Another group of tourists was 'bombarded with rocks, chased with knives or threatened with meaty leg-bones ripped straight off the corpse'.[4]

The first recorded Tibetan church was built by Jesuit missionaries in Lhasa in 1726. Twenty-seven baptized converts and 60 inquirers attended the church. 'At the end of April, 1742, a new convert named Pu Tsering publicly refused to bow before the Dalai Lama. . . . This threw the town into an uproar. . . . Twelve of the Christians were flogged with 20 lashes each. The missionaries fled to Nepal, but their church was attacked by a mob who destroyed everything except the church bell.'[5]

Today there are no known Christians among the Nghari Tibetans.

Tibetan Nghari

Population:
49,900 (2000)
61,500 (2010)
75,700 (2020)
Countries: China, Nepal
Buddhism: Tibetan
Christians: none known

Overview of the Nghari Tibetans

Other Names: Nghari, Ngharis, Mngharis, Drokpa, Drokwa, Drokba, Chang Tang Tibetans, Chang Tang Nomads

Population Sources:
38,400 in China (1987, *Language Atlas of China*)
also in Nepal

Language: Sino-Tibetan, Tibeto-Burman, Himalayish, Tibeto-Kanauri, Tibetic, Tibetan, Central

Dialects: 7 (Rutog, Gartok, Zamda, Burang, Coqen, Gerze, Xigaze)

Professing Buddhists: 100%

Practising Buddhists: 60%

Christians: 0%

Scripture: Tibetan Bible 1948; New Testament 1885; Portions 1862

Jesus **film:** none

Gospel Recordings: none

Christian Broadcasting: none

ROPAL code: TIC03

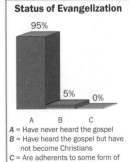

Status of Evangelization

95%

5%

0%

A   B   C

A = Have never heard the gospel
B = Have heard the gospel but have not become Christians
C = Are adherents to some form of Christianity

Photo credit: Julian Hawken

CHINA
Xizang (Tibet)
Sichuan
INDIA
MYANMAR
Yunnan
Tibetan Shangri-la

Population:
74,800 (2000)
92,100 (2010)
113,500 (2020)
Countries: China, Switzerland
Buddhism: Tibetan
Christians: 2,000

Overview of the Shangri-La Tibetans

Other Names: Tibetan: Zhongdian, Zhongdian Tibetans, Chung-tien Tibetans, Chongtien, Rgyalathang

Population Sources:

60,740 in China (1990, Asian Minorities Outreach)

also in Switzerland

Language: Sino-Tibetan, Tibeto-Burman, Himalayish, Tibeto-Kanauri, Tibetic, Tibetan, Northern

Dialects: 0

Professing Buddhists: 95%

Practising Buddhists: 70%

Christians: 2.6%

Scripture: Tibetan Bible 1948; New Testament 1885; Portions 1862

Jesus film: none

Gospel Recordings: Zang: Xiaozhongdian; Zang: Weixi; Zang: Deqing

Christian Broadcasting: none

ROPAL code: none

Status of Evangelization

64%
33%
3%

A   B   C

A = Have never heard the gospel
B = Have heard the gospel but have not become Christians
C = Are adherents to some form of Christianity

Approximately 75,000 linguistically-distinct Tibetans inhabit villages in Shangri-La (formerly Zhongdian), Weixi and Lijiang counties in the north-western part of Yunnan Province, China. According to the 1990 Chinese census, 50,302 live in Shangri-La County, 8,581 in Weixi and 1,849 in Lijiang. The extent of their territory seems to extend to the Hengduan Pass between the towns of Shangri-La and Deqen, located farther to the north.[1] Beyond the pass, the dialect changes markedly. *Hengduan* literally means 'cut off vertically'.[2] A few Shangri-La Tibetan families have reportedly migrated to Switzerland.[3]

Operation China profiles this group under the name *Tibetan, Zhongdian*. Recently the Chinese authorities officially changed the name of the town and county where this group lives from Zhongdian to Shangri-La, hoping to cash in on the mysterious place name first written about in the 1933 James Hilton novel *Lost Horizons*.[4] The Shangri-La Tibetans wear a different traditional dress from all other Tibetans. The women prefer to wear a cone-shaped headdress which is wrapped up inside a scarf.

Researchers who have travelled into Tibetan areas of northern Yunnan Province report that the dialect variation between Shangri-La and Deqen is enough to seriously affect mutual intelligibility between Tibetans from the two areas.[5] Local legends say that the ancestors of the Shangri-La Tibetans were Qiang people who came to the area, fought and overcame the locals in battle, and eventually became assimilated to Tibetan ways. This would explain the linguistic, clothing and cultural differences between

Julian Hawken

them and other Tibetan groups today.[6]

The majority of Shangri-La Tibetans adhere to Tibetan Buddhism. The large Jietang Songlin Monastery, which houses several hundred monks, is located just to the north of Shangri-La Township.

Although many Christians today think of the Tibetans as completely untouched by Christianity, there is a significant Catholic presence among the Shangri-La Tibetans. 'The story actually began in 1852 when an intrepid young missionary named Pére Renou arrived in Yunnan and headed for its northwest corner, reaching Dongzhulin, a Khampa monastery two-thirds of the way from Zhongdian to Deqen. There the young priest, disguised as a Chinese merchant, befriended the head lama. . . . Pére Renou and his little brand of hardy priests managed to erect churches in several Tibetan villages.'[7] Today, a large French-style cathedral still stands at Tchronteu, near Weixi.[8] 'The purpose of the monks of Saint Bernard was to minister to all in need who travelled over the high mountain trails in trade and commerce. Their most valuable helpers were huge Saint Bernard dogs—half Swiss and half Tibetan. In the city of Weixi, the monks, helped by the Cluny Sisters of Saint Joseph and two Tibetan nuns, ran a mission school attended by children from Sikkim, Nepal, Bhutan and Tibet.'[9] Presently, a Catholic priest is responsible for 9,500 Tibetan believers in his area. Of these, about 7,500 belong to the Southern Khampa group and 2,000 to the Shangri-La Tibetans.

An Overview of Tibetan Buddhism

Dorje

Of the major branches of Buddhism, probably the most widely recognized around the world today, is Tibetan Buddhism. Tibetan Buddhism is luring thousands of American and European youths into becoming devotees of its philosophy. The god-king Dalai Lama is Tibetan Buddhism's charismatic spokesman and figurehead. Although Buddhism in Tibet was originally part of the Mahayana school, there is no doubt that Tibetan Buddhism today has an identity, philosophy and creed of its own, separate from the Mahayana Buddhism practised by the Chinese, Koreans, Japanese and other peoples in eastern Asia. It is certainly distinct from the Theravada school of Buddhism adhered to by people in many Southeast Asian nations such as Thailand, Laos, Cambodia, Sri Lanka and Myanmar (Burma).

Tibetan Buddhism has a far-reaching influence, and despite its name it is far from being confined to Tibet, or Tibetan people. Scholars also refer to this form of Buddhism as Tantric Buddhism, while the Chinese refer to it as Lamaism (a term that many Tibetans consider offensive). The seed of Tibetan Buddhism was first planted among Tibetan peoples and Tibetan culture, but it has now spread far and wide into China, India, Nepal, the mysterious hermit-kingdom of Bhutan, Mongolia, the Siberian plains in Russia, and even into the universities and board rooms of North America and every Western nation on the face of the earth.

Although details are sketchy, it is generally believed that Buddhism first reached Tibet around 600 AD. The cradle of Tibetan civilization was the Yarlung valley, southwest of Lhasa. The warrior-king of Yarlung, Namri Gampo, unified the clans of Tibet. His son, Song Tsen Gampo, acquired two princesses to be his wives—one from Nepal and the other from China. Under their persuasion, Gampo is believed to have allowed the introduction of Buddhist teachings into Tibet for the first time.

In the Middle Ages the Tibetans spread their faith across most of Central Asia. By shrewd alliances and occasional military conquests, they converted the Mongols and other Asian peoples to their religion. When they had finished, dozens of peoples from the Himalayas to Siberia, and from China to the banks of Russia's Volga River, had professed Tibetan Buddhism. All of these diverse peoples looked to Tibet as their holy land, and to Lhasa as their holy city, the centre of the Tibetan Buddhist world.

By the late 18th century Tibetan Buddhism had stopped expanding and turned inward. With the rise of British power in neighbouring India in the late 1700s, the Tibetans grew suspicious of foreign motives and closed their country to outsiders. Tibet remained securely aloof from the rest of the world throughout the 19th century but, with the dawn of the 20th century, its shell of isolation began to crack. A British military expedition into Tibet in 1904 was

Approximately 20 million Tibetan Buddhists live across a vast area of Central Asia in some of the most remote places in the world.

International Mission Board

followed by a Chinese expedition in 1910, forcing the Dalai Lama to seek temporary refuge in India. Both the Chinese and British expeditions brought home to the Tibetans that just because they were not interested in the outside world, the reverse was not necessarily true.[1]

By 1949, the situation on Tibet's frontiers had changed ominously. To the east, Tibet's giant neighbour China was in the throes of a civil war. Complete Communist victory seemed imminent. Tibet's small, ill-equipped army was completely unprepared to meet the battle-hardened Chinese. By 1951 the Chinese had effectively annexed Tibet, provoking its people to armed resistance. Sporadic guerrilla warfare exploded into a full-scale

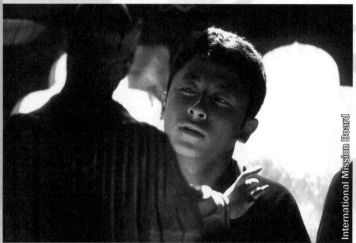

A young Drukpa man in Bhutan closely inspects an idol.

revolt against Chinese rule in the spring of 1959. In the fighting that followed, the Dalai Lama and thousands of his followers were forced to flee across the world's highest mountains to India, where they began the task of rebuilding their shattered lives and creating a focus of Tibetan culture and religion outside their homeland.

The short-lived revolt in Tibet was crushed. The militantly antireligious Communists began a campaign of terror against Tibetan Buddhism. Hundreds of monasteries were destroyed and their inhabitants shot or sent to labour camps. The Tibetan people had entered a long night of suffering from which they would not emerge for many years.

In 1962 the Dalai Lama summed up some of the ways the Tibetan people have been persecuted: 'Tens of thousands of our people have been killed, not only in military actions, but individually and deliberately. They have been killed without trial . . . Fundamentally they have been killed because they would not renounce their religion. They have not only been shot, but beaten to death, crucified, burned alive, drowned, vivisected, starved, strangled, hanged, scalded, buried alive, disemboweled and beheaded. These killings have been done in public. Men and women have been killed while their own families were forced to watch, and small children have even been forced to shoot their parents.'[2]

Though Buddhism had suffered a nearly mortal blow in Tibet, it began to flourish anew in the Tibetan refugee camps of India. Monks taught in newly established monasteries, set up schools and translated Tibetan religious texts into English and other European languages. Other monks went abroad to study and spread their faith among a generation of increasingly alienated Western youth. Within ten years, this restless generation had successfully transplanted Tibetan Buddhism from the Indian subcontinent to the West. Thousands of young people came face-to-face with what until then had been an obscure Central Asian religion. In the United States alone it has been estimated that over 100,000 Americans have become Tibetan Buddhists, and that number continues to grow thanks to a network of Tibetan Buddhist study centres.

The emergence of a Tibetan style of Buddhism

When Buddhism first reached Tibet it encountered a powerful resident shamanistic religion called Bon. At the time, Tibet was a land of primitive tribes who scraped out an existence from the wilds of the Central Asian plateau. Life for most Tibetans was a short, violent battle with numbing cold, sudden storms and other Tibetans. It is little wonder that Tibet's original religion tried to control this hostile environment with magical rites and sacrifices.

Some of the rites seem to have concerned a single supreme deity associated with the sky. This deity was very powerful, but remote and disinterested in the affairs of humankind. Other rites of more immediate importance concerned a host of spirit beings, ghosts, demons, locality spirits and house deities that had to be satisfied by animal, or occasionally human, sacrifices.[3]

The central figure in these bloody rites was the shaman, whose job it was to present the sacrifices, appease the spirits with magic, heal the sick and even control the weather. The shaman specialized in a kind of ecstatic trance that let him travel to the spirit world and serve as a medium for the ghosts of the dead. In addition to the shaman, there were also magicians and healers who had the power to control gods, demons and locality spirits.[4]

Except for human sacrifice, all of these beliefs and practices would find their way into Tibetan Buddhism. The Bon religion was never replaced by Buddhism, but rather found its full expression under the cover of its Buddhist cloak. Today Tibetan lamas and monks have assumed the role of the Bon shaman, mediating between the spirit world and the community. The past decade has even seen the emergence of monasteries that have turned away from Buddhism and are now exclusively Bon, especially in the eastern Tibet border areas, which today lie within the Chinese provinces of Gansu, Sichuan and Qinghai.[5]

A cult called *tantra* also took its place among the central teachings of Tibetan Buddhism. As Tibetan scholars explained it, Buddha reserved his supposed Tantric teachings for only a handful of his most promising followers.[6]

In fact, *tantra* (or *vajrayana*) is a mystery religion that appeared in north India between the seventh and tenth centuries AD. *Tantra* tried to break through illusion by exploring the union of opposites. Ritual sexual intercourse was the central liturgy in *tantra*. The gods were often depicted as locked in sexual embrace, often under the sponsorship of Shiva, the Hindu god of death and destruction.

Tantra's occult practices were kept secret by handing them down only from guru to disciple. Its most striking feature is its technique of occult visualization. The Tantric master gives each student a deity, which the student is to visualize. These deities, most of which appear in wrathful or monstrous forms, are supposed to be able to help the student achieve liberation. As students visualize, they try to become what they see, and in fact some Tibetan Buddhists claim to be able to actually materialize demons in front of them. In Tantric thinking, by

A group of monks at the Muli Monastery in Sichuan Province, China.

visualizing a liberated being, you can become one yourself.

Every Tibetan Buddhist culture has men and women who specialize in sorcery: compelling spirits to do human bidding. These sorcerers, more properly known as shamans, specialize in trances, exorcisms, curses and weather control. There are also witches who are believed to harm others with magical powers.

In a typical encounter, a medium will enter a trancelike state during which he moans, sweats, writhes and cries out in an abnormal voice. Some mediums demonstrate superhuman strength during their trances by twisting metal objects with their bare hands, or by jumping up and down with heavy weights on their backs.[7] After demonstrating possession by the spirits, a medium's words are taken as the utterance of whatever spirit possesses him.

These factors, and many others, have resulted

China Advocate

in Tibetan Buddhism looking very different from other forms of Buddhism today. Although almost all Tibetan people would unhesitatingly identify themselves as Buddhists if asked, their faith is a complex layered concoction. The line between Buddhism, shamanism and animism is blurred. Folk Tibetan Buddhists live in a world that teems with malignant, aggressive and violent spirits who can cause great mischief if not properly handled. Evil spirits lurk in all of life's shadows, waiting for the chance to strike. The ordinary Tibetan, or Ladakhi, or Bhutanese, lives in constant fear of these spirits and the evil they bring. No trouble is too great, no journey too long and no cost too high to avoid evil spirits, or to placate them once they have been offended.

Most Tibetan Buddhists, like most people everywhere, are less concerned about discovering the ultimate truths of the universe than about solving the problems of everyday life. A sick child, a potential business deal or simply getting enough to eat are problems that demand immediate attention. To solve problems like these, the peoples of the Tibetan Buddhist world rely on the shamanistic and animistic beliefs of their remote ancestors. These beliefs, mixed with some of the simpler teachings of Buddhism, make up the everyday religion of most people in the Tibetan Buddhist world.

The various Tibetan Buddhist sects

Beginning in the 9th century, a succession of scholar-monks laid the foundations of the major schools of Tibetan Buddhism. Known as the Great Translators, these men played a key role in giving Tibetan Buddhism its Tantric character.

The followers of these translator-teachers formed themselves into several quite distinct schools. The Gelugpa sect became the dominant school of Tibetan Buddhism.

The poet Milarepa (c.1052–1135) founded the Kargyupa sect of Tibetan Buddhism. The Kargyupas

A pile of 'mani' stones on the roadside in Sichuan Province, China. On each stone is inscribed the sacred prayer: 'Om mani padme hum' ('Hail the Jewel of the Lotus').

A man meticulously carves a prayer onto a 'mani' stone in Dharamsala, India. Millions of rocks have been carved throughout the Tibetan Buddhist world.

were hermits and never became very successful on the Tibetan religious scene. They soon split into a bewildering variety of sub-sects of which one, the Drukpa, became dominant. The Drukpa established themselves in the Himalayan kingdoms of Ladakh and Bhutan, where they remain predominant today. Drukpa-ruled Bhutan was the world's first officially Tibetan Buddhist state.[8]

The burst of religious creativity that gave rise to the Kargyupas and other orders of Tibetan Buddhism continued for over four hundred years. When it was over, Tibetan Buddhism had arranged itself in a spectrum of orders with varying degrees of emphasis on shamanist and Tantric beliefs. Most conservative were the Nyingma, whose doctrines followed the occult paths of their founder, the Tantric wizard Padma Sambhava. Next came the Sakyas, a slightly reformed sect which arose about the time of Milarepa. Somewhat less occult-orientated was Milarepa's Kargyupa order and its descendants the Drukpas. Least occultic were the Kadampas, who were about to undergo a major reformation at the hands of one of Tibetan Buddhism's greatest figures.

A monk from north-east Tibet named Tsong Khapa (c. 1357–1419) was troubled by the loose discipline of his fellow monks. He launched a series of reforms in monastic organization and discipline which earned him wide respect. He was so successful that his Kadampa order became known as the Gelugpa ('virtuous way') sect. To consolidate their founder's reforms, the Gelugpa order built several monasteries that would one day be the most powerful in all Tibet. The group also came to be known as the Yellow Hat sect.

With the rise of the great Gelugpa monasteries, the foundations of Tibetan Buddhism were complete. In the eight hundred years since the reign of Song Tsen Gampo, the Tibetans had sifted through nineteen centuries of Indian religious thought and selected Tantric Buddhism as the prize they sought above all else. Enshrined at the heart of the doctrine and backed by increasingly powerful monasteries, Tantric Buddhism was ready to begin an age of expansion that would take it to the farthest

Once a year this huge 'thangka' (mural) is brought out during a festival at the Muli monastery in Sichuan Province, China.

corners of Central Asia.

The Dalai Lamas

After the Mongolian world empire disintegrated in the 14th century, the Mongol tribes themselves continued to be led by the descendants of the great khans. Tibetan involvement with these later khans gave Tibetan Buddhism its most famous institution and spread Lamaism across much of Central Asia.

In the mid 1500s the head of the Tumed branch of the Mongols, Altan Khan, became the ruler of a new Mongol confederacy. In 1578 he met with Sonam Gyatso, the head lama of the Gelugpa sect. Together the Tibetan monk and the Mongol Khan formed a relationship of priest and king, complete with honorific titles. Sonam Gyatso received the Mongol name Ta-le (rendered in English as Dalai) Lama, meaning 'Ocean of Wisdom'.

There was more to their meeting than words. Altan Khan, who had made Tantric Buddhism the state religion of Mongolia the year before, received the blessing of Tibetan Buddhism's most respected leader. In return, he supported Sonam Gyatso's Gelugpa order over its rivals for power in Tibet. For his part, Sonam Gyatso gained the right to travel and preach in Mongolia, where he enjoyed remarkable success in extending the power and influence of Tibetan Buddhism. Together, Altan Khan and Sonam Gyatso began a revival of Tibetan Buddhism that has been called the greatest single influence on Mongol life and culture.[9]

Sonam Gyatso died in Mongolia in 1588, and his death forced the Gelugpas to find a new Dalai Lama. They borrowed from the Karmapa sect the idea of a line of reincarnating monks: as one such

of Chenrezi, the Buddha of compassion, and built the great Potala Palace in Lhasa.

The present Dalai Lama, Tenzin Gyatso, is the fourteenth. While some Tibetan activists have publicly expressed their displeasure at his methods—claiming he has compromised the Tibetan people because of his unwillingness to talk about an independent Tibetan nation—there is no doubt he remains hugely popular with the vast majority of Tibetan Buddhist people.

An ideal of non-violence

A welcome from the women of Dongla village in Sichuan Province, China. The large breastplates worn by the women contain Buddhist symbols and talismans to ward off evil spirits.

Paul Hattaway

In the spring of 1948 the Austrian traveller Heinrich Harrer, then a refugee in Tibet, was placed in charge of 1,500 men who were constructing a dike in front of the Dalai Lama's Summer Palace in Lhasa. The work frequently came to a halt as workmen discovered an earthworm or other small creature at the tip of a shovel. The dirt was carefully moved and the creature set aside in a safe place before digging resumed. No one wanted to be guilty of killing an animal.[10]

monk died, his successor would be 'discovered' in a child born about the same time of the previous lama's death. If a child passed various mystical tests, he was taken to a monastery and raised as a monk. Sonam Gyatso's two predecessors were given the title posthumously, and they are now known as the first and second Dalai Lamas.

The fifth Dalai Lama, Ngawang Gyatso, was one of Tibetan Buddhism's greatest figures. An able administrator and politician, he was the first Dalai Lama to assume complete control of Tibet. He united the country after a bitter civil war, proclaimed himself and his four predecessors to be incarnations

After the Chinese had annexed Tibetan areas in the 1950s they were astounded to find the rivers and lakes of Tibet teeming with an over-abundance of fish, due to the Tibetans' refusal to kill any living creature. The Chinese, having a somewhat opposite view of the food chain, used explosives in many lakes to kill thousands of fish at a time, sending them by the truckload back to the marketplaces of China for immediate consumption. Whole varieties of fish are believed to have become extinct in a short period of time.

The doctrine of non-violence has a long history in Buddhism, and Tibetan Buddhists have interpreted it chiefly for the benefit of animals. Because of possible harm to animals, food and sin share a strange association in the Tibetan Buddhist world. Farming is thought to be sinful because breaking up the soil inevitably kills some of the worms and insects that live in it. Although they eat meat, deliberately killing animals for food is considered very sinful, and if possible Tibetans will have it done by someone of another religion (usually a Muslim). Thus the simple act of eating imposes a burden of guilt on Tibetan Buddhists that can scarcely be imagined by those of other faiths.[11]

Even unconsciously taking life is sinful. Killing small insects by stepping on them is a frequent cause of unknowingly committed sin. So serious is it that the monks say a magic formula to guarantee that

Buddhist monks blow long horns at the Muli Monastery in Sichuan Province, China.

every little creature that dies under their feet will be reborn in paradise.[12]

It is little wonder, then, that many Tibetans who gain some exposure to Christianity are soon horrified at what they find. One Buddhist lama was urged to read a copy of the Bible. When he read it, he was shocked to find detailed instructions about the killing of animals, instructions for God's chosen people to go to war, and a God who was described as 'angry' and 'jealous'. When the lama read about the life of Jesus, he found that it was the head lamas who condemned Jesus to death. (The Tibetan Bible translates Matthew 20:18–19 and other passages using the term 'head lama' for 'chief priest'.)

As the lama read the Gospels, he realized that the Christians based their religion on a blood sacrifice, which he found deeply offensive. The shedding of blood for religious purposes had ended long ago in the Tibetan Buddhist world. The lama decided he could never follow such a strange religion, and he closed his Bible for the last time. His two Christian visitors later heard of his comments and urged their friends to pray for the lama's 'hardness of heart'.

In summary, what is needed in the Tibetan

An elderly woman turns a Tibetan Buddhist prayer wheel, or 'manichorkor'. Every time it spins, the scroll inside the cylinder is believed to release prayers to the heavens. Muli County in Sichuan Province, China.

Buddhist world are Christians who have solid spiritual foundations, who can live holy lives in the context of a Tibetan Buddhist culture, who can speak the right language well, and who can think like Tibetan Buddhists. If they can live out the Christian life in a locally understandable way, their living example will provide a powerful testimony to the peoples of the Tibetan Buddhist world.

Notes

1. For a fascinating account of the British expedition, see Sir Francis Younghusband, *India and Tibet* (London: John Murray, 1910; repr. Hong Kong: Oxford University Press, 1985).

2. Gyatso Tenzin (Dalai Lama XIV), *My Land and My People* (New York: McGraw-Hill, 1962).

3. Some authorities think that cannibalism was also a part of these rituals (see L Austine Waddell, *The Buddhism and Lamaism of Tibet* (New Delhi: Heritage Publishers) 518. Marco Polo also attributes cannibalism to the Tibetans (*The Travels of Marco Polo* [New York: Penguin, 1958] 110).

4. For an excellent discussion of Tibet's pre-Buddhist religion, see Robert Ekvall, *Religious Observances in Tibet* (Chicago: University of Chicago, 1964) 38.

5. The largest Bon monastery (housing several hundred Bon monks) is located in Tongren County, Qinghai Province. Others are scattered across various townships. Bon monks are distinguished from their Tibetan Buddhist counterparts by the colour of their robes, by the fact that they are allowed to marry, and by the absence of Buddha idols in their temples. Bon monks circle monasteries and stupas in an anti-clockwise direction, instead of the clockwise direction practised by Buddhists.

6. Klesang Gyatso, *Buddhism in the Tibetan Tradition: A Guide* (London: Routledge & Kegan Paul, 1984) 104–5.

7. The sociologist Robert Ekvall has described these behaviours in mediums in north-eastern Tibet (*Religious Observances in Tibet*, 27). Heinrich Harrer has given a similar description (*Seven Years in Tibet* [Los Angeles: J P Tarcher, 1981] 204–6).

8. Until recently Bhutan was the world's *only* official Buddhist nation, but in the past several years Mongolia and Tuva in Russia have also declared themselves Buddhist states.

9. American University, *Area Handbook for Mongolia* (Washington: U S Government Printing Office, 1970) 58.

10. Harrer, *Seven Years in Tibet*, 234.

11. Ekvall, *Religious Observances in Tibet*, 76.

12. Waddell, *Buddhism and Lamaism of Tibet*, 213.

A Khampa nomad herds her family's yaks near the spectacular Lake Jadeite in Sichuan Province, China.

Population:
20,000 (2000)
24,600 (2010)
30,300 (2020)
Countries: China
Buddhism: Tibetan
Christians: none known

Overview of the Shanyan Tibetans

Other Names: Shanyan

Population Sources:

20,000 in China (2000, P Hattaway)

Language: Sino-Tibetan, Tibeto-Burman, Himalayish, Tibeto-Kanauri, Tibetic, Tibetan, Unclassified

Dialects: 0

Professing Buddhists: 100%

Practising Buddhists: 60%

Christians: 0%

Scripture: none

Jesus film: none

Gospel Recordings: none

Christian Broadcasting: none

ROPAL code: none

Status of Evangelization

99%

1%   0%

A   B   C

A = Have never heard the gospel
B = Have heard the gospel but have not become Christians
C = Are adherents to some form of Christianity

More than 20,000 people living in the extraordinarily remote Shanyan District of Baiyu County in China's north-western Sichuan Province belong to the little-known Shanyan Tibetan ethnic group. Although the Chinese government does not differentiate between the Shanyan Tibetans and the main Tibetan nationality, Baiyu County contained 39,543 people at the time of the 1990 census, of which 36,591 (92.5%) were Tibetans. The majority of these are Shanyan Tibetan people.

The Tibetan name for Shanyan means 'rough terrain'. To reach the Shanyan Tibetans, visitors must first travel to Litang and Batang in the far west of Sichuan, a journey that can take up to several days from the provincial capital Chengdu. From there local buses go to Baiyu, although the route is often closed by landslides and road collapses. Travelling the 56 kilometres (35 mi.) from Baiyu to Shanyan is an even more treacherous affair, requiring travel by horseback over the 5,000-metre-high (16,400 ft.) Dalong ('Big Dragon') Mountain, 'through primitive forests, bushland and grassland and rocky hills. Moreover, it spans several temperature zones and makes 51 sudden turns.'[1] One visitor said, 'Shaking with fear, I rode the best russet horse in the township along a trail carved in sheer cliffs at an altitude of 2,000 metres (6,500 ft.) high above the roaring Jinsha River.'[2] The Jinsha River forms the border between Sichuan and Tibet.

The Shanyan Tibetans are culturally, ethnically and linguistically different from the Khampa Tibetans who also live in this remote region. When talking about his ancestors, a Shanyan Tibetan named Dorji

Wengxiong said, 'We came from areas on the upper reaches of the Yarlung Zangbo River in present-day Nghari Prefecture in Tibet. We are Tibetans and not local Khampa people. . . . Our ancestors kept moving east until they came to the Jinsha River. So far, we have lived here for 40 to 50 generations. Up to the 1950s, there were 18 *gebas* [clans], with about 20,000 people in Shanyan.'[3] Although historically the Shanyan Tibetans came from far western Tibet, their present home is a vast distance of more than 1,000 kilometres (620 mi.) from their original homeland. The hundreds of years of separation have resulted in the Shanyan Tibetans evolving into a distinct people group with a language no longer intelligible with Nghari Tibetan varieties.

Nancy Sturrock

Documents from the Qing Dynasty report 'this tiny area had defied imperial rule for over 200 years by relying on the dangerous terrain and the bravery of its people. To bring them under control, the court has sent expeditions on several occasions.'[4] It was not until October 1910 that the Shanyan Tibetans finally came under Chinese rule.

Most Shanyan Tibetans are Buddhists of the Nyima sect. They 'seldom invite lamas to chant sutras for them, as is required for religious events in other areas. Instead, they do it themselves while drinking. In old times, before setting off for a battle, all adult males would gather to slaughter an ox, drink and chant sutras. After drinking, they took an oath. Then, with a string of prayer beads or a pebble, they practiced divination to predicate their luck in the battle.'[5]

The Shanyan Tibetans are completely unreached by the gospel. They pose one of the greatest challenges of any Buddhist group in the world today.

337

Approximately 30,000 speakers of the Tinan language inhabit the central Himalayas on both sides of the India-China border. They live on the slopes of mountains that pierce the sky up to 7,000 metres (22,960 ft.) above sea level. The majority of Tinan are located in India where more than 24,000 live in the Spiti and Lahul District, which is situated in the lower Chandra-Bhaga Valley in the northern part of the state of Himachal Pradesh.[1] The main Tinan village in India is Gondla.

Smaller numbers of Tinan live in China. Linguists C F and F M Voegelin listed a 1977 population of between 450 and 1,600 Tinan living in western Tibet.[2] Geographic and political barriers keep this small group separated from contact with the outside world.

The Tinan—who are counted under the Tibetan nationality in China—are also known as *Lahuli* and *Bhotia*. In India they are one of the ethnic components in the officially-recognized *Lahaula* tribe.[3] The term *Bhotia* refers to people of Tibetan stock in general. The name *Lahuli* is also a generic term used to describe the inhabitants of the Lahul District, which was formerly controlled by the British.[4]

Although culturally there is little difference between the Tinan and other Tibetan peoples, their language is what qualifies them as a separate group. Tinan is a distinct language that is part of a group of several West Himalayish / Kanauri languages.[5] Other Tibetans cannot understand Tinan, which has 56 per cent to 63 per cent lexical similarity with Chamba Lahuli, 32 per cent to 37 per cent with Bunan, 21 per cent with Spiti and only 13 per cent with Central Tibetan.[6]

The region inhabited by the Tinan people was part of the Ladakhi Kingdom in the 10th century. Border clashes in the area in the 1950s and 1960s resulted in the Chinese seizing a large tract of land from India. The region, which is home to the Tinan people who live inside Tibet, is called Aksai Chin.

Tinan men are skillful merchants and traders. The women are known for their independence. 'Since their husbands are usually off on trading expeditions, the women feel free to take more than one husband. The men trade salt, grain and wool to other people in the Himalayan region and in the process sometimes become quite wealthy.'[7]

The majority of Tinan people are Tibetan Buddhists, although a number of families have converted to Hinduism. The strength of Tibetan Buddhism in northern India depends to a great extent on the prosperity and generosity of the Tinan. 'They, in turn, feel spiritually secure because of the religious merit they gain by dispensing charity and generously supporting the temples.'[8]

There are a handful of Tinan Christians in India, but none exist on the Tibetan side of the border. Few of the Tinan have ever heard of Jesus Christ. Mission work in Lahul began after Karl Gutzlaff challenged the Moravians to begin a mission in Tibet. 'The first missionaries, A W Heyde and E Pagell, settled down in Kyelang, a Tibetan village in the province of Lahul.'[9] Scripture portions were translated into Tinan in 1908 but have been out of print since 1915. Gospel recordings are currently available in the Tinan language.

Population:
29,350 (2000)
34,400 (2010)
40,300 (2020)
Countries: India, China
Buddhism: Tibetan
Christians: 20

Overview of the Tinan

Other Names: Lahuli Tinan, Lahuli, Bhotia of Lahul, Lahauli, Lahouli, Rangloi, Gondla, Tinani, Teenan, Gondhla, Lahaula

Population Sources:
24,534 in India (1994, India Missions Association)
450 to 1,600 in China (1977, C Voegelin and F Voegelin)

Language: Sino-Tibetan, Tibeto-Burman, Himalayish, Tibeto-Kanauri, Western Himalayish, Kanauri

Dialects: 0

Professing Buddhists: 80%

Practising Buddhists: 60%

Christians: 0.1%

Scripture: Portions 1908

Jesus **film:** none

Gospel Recordings: Lahouli Tinan

Christian Broadcasting: none

ROPAL code: LBF

Photo credit: Dwayne Graybill

Status of Evangelization

A = Have never heard the gospel — 91%
B = Have heard the gospel but have not become Christians — 8%
C = Are adherents to some form of Christianity — 1%

More than 150,000 Torgut Mongolians live alongside Kazak and Uygur communities in north-west China's Xinjiang Region.[1] Many live in the verdant Junggar Basin. The Junggar landscape consists primarily of grasslands, which are amply watered by the region's abundant rainfall. An unspecified number of Torgut also live in Russia 'between the Volga and the Don [rivers], east of the Caspian and north of the Caucasus'.[2] The Torgut language as spoken in China may now differ so markedly from the Torgut spoken in Russia that the two should be considered separate ethnolinguistic peoples.

Although the Torgut are a sub-group of the Kalmyk-Oirat, in China they view themselves as ethnically separate even though their languages are basically the same. They have been described as 'a law unto themselves, with their Tibetan religion, Mongolian language and unspeakable customs'.[3]

Torgut history closely mirrors that of the Kalmyk-Oirat. They migrated from Xinjiang to Russia in 1628, where they lived until 1771 when Russian pressure forced most Torgut to flee back to China. Thousands died of starvation or were killed and plundered by bandits on the return journey to Xinjiang.[4]

Folk dancing is a favourite pastime of the Torgut. The *bielgee*, or 'dance of the body', originated during the Qing (Manchu) Dynasty. Large public gatherings were outlawed because the Manchus feared a Mongol uprising. Traditional dances had to be performed privately inside the yurt, where there was little legroom. The dancers expressed themselves by using their arms, legs and other parts of their bodies in rhythmic movements.[5]

Although all Torgut claim to be Tibetan Buddhists, many practise shamanism. The black magic and secret arts of the Mongol shamans were vividly described 700 years ago, when Marco Polo challenged the Great Khan to become a Christian. He replied, 'On what grounds do you desire me to become a Christian? . . . You see that these sorcerers do what they will. When I sit at the table the cups in the middle of the hall come to me full of wine or other beverages without anyone touching them, and I drink from them. They banish bad weather in any direction they choose and perform many marvels. And, as you know, their idols speak and give them predictions as they ask. . . . If I am converted to the faith of Christ and become a Christian . . . these sorcerers, who with their arts and sciences achieve such great results, could easily compass my death.'[6]

There is no church today among the Torgut of China, despite the past efforts of self-sacrificing missionaries. During the Boxer Rebellion of 1900, 'seven Alliance missionaries and seven children tried to flee on camels. . . . Robbers intercepted them and took everything, even their clothes. In the trauma two of the missionaries gave birth. French missionary priests found the fourteen and the two infants naked in the desert and subsisting on roots. The priests gave them covering and took them back to the Catholic mission station. . . . The Boxers killed them with guns and swords, then set fire to the church.'[7]

Population:
146,000 (2000)
188,300 (2010)
232,000 (2020)
Countries: China, Russia
Buddhism: Tibetan
Christians: none known

Overview of the Torgut

Other Names: Torgot, Torgut Mongolians, Xinjiang Mongols

Population Sources:
106,000 in China (1987, *Language Atlas of China*)
also in Russia

Language: Altaic, Mongolian, Eastern, Oirat-Khalkha, Oirat-Kalmyk-Darkhat

Dialects: 0

Professing Buddhists: 100%

Practising Buddhists: 60%

Christians: 0%

Scripture: none

Jesus film: none[8]

Gospel Recordings: none

Christian Broadcasting: none

ROPAL code: KGZ03

Status of Evangelization

A = Have never heard the gospel
B = Have heard the gospel but have not become Christians
C = Are adherents to some form of Christianity

Tsangla

More than quarter of a million Tsangla people live in the eastern Himalayan Range. The largest numbers (approximately 170,000) are located in eastern and south-eastern areas of the small Buddhist kingdom of Bhutan, especially in Trashigang and Dungsam. More than 50,000 live in neighbouring parts of Arunachal Pradesh, India, especially in the Tawang and Kameng districts,[1] while a further 35,000 inhabit the southern part of Chinese Tibet, particularly in Cona County.[2] Others are scattered far to the north-east in Medog (Motuo) County.

In Bhutan, Tsangla houses 'are made of stone and wood, and are usually built on stilts in dispersed settlements along the mountain slopes. Larger settlements have monasteries called *dzongs*, where prayer flags and prayer wheels are a common sight. A local variety of cattle known as *mithun* is a valued form of wealth and is sacrificed at religious ceremonies. Pigs and goats are also raised to sell and to use as sacrifices.'[3]

There is some confusion about the classification of the Tsangla people. Although they are officially recognized as a 'Scheduled Tribe' in India, in China they have been counted as part of the Monba nationality—yet the Monba in China speak two very different languages, designated as

Cona Monba and Medog Monba according to their locations. Cona Monba (Tsangla) is 'quite distinct linguistically'[4] from Medog Monba, in areas of 'phonology, vocabulary, and

Dwayne Graybill

grammar'.[5] The speakers of the two languages struggle to communicate with each other.[6] Tsangla has four tones, while Medog Monba does not contain any tones at all.[7]

Nearly three centuries ago, the Tsangla people migrated across the Himalayas from the Moinyu area in south-east Tibet. The Tsangla in India also claim to have migrated from Bhutan.[8]

Many rural Tsangla practise 'river burial', by which a corpse is cut into

108 pieces and hurled into a rushing river to be washed away. Their Tibetan neighbours consider this to be the lowest form of burial and only use it for children and lepers. Tsangla silversmiths are renowned for their skill in making intricate jewelry and ornaments.

Although most Tsangla are outwardly Tibetan Buddhists, the majority continue to practise shamanistic and polytheistic rituals. The Tsangla believe that all disease is caused by demons. They feel that they are forced to sacrifice their valuable cattle and horses in order to pacify these angry demons so that they will cease to cause the affliction. They also believe that humans can be demons who cause sickness. A boy or girl who marries into a 'demon family' also becomes a demon. Therefore 'demon families' are only allowed to intermarry.[9] In addition to their Buddhist beliefs, each Tsangla villages 'has its *sibdag*, or "god of the soil", which must constantly be appeased, and each house has its god, *tab-lha*, who must not be offended.'[10]

Most Tsangla are unreached and geographically inaccessible to the gospel. A number of Tsangla have heard the gospel, however, due to the existence of short-wave gospel radio broadcasts in the Tsangla language and the recent translation of the *Jesus* film into Tsangla.

Overview of the Tsangla

Other Names: Sangla, Tshangla, Cona Monba, Monba: Cona, Cuona Monba, Central Monba, Moinba, Menba, Monpa, Mompa, Momba, Menpa, Memba, Southern Monba, Sharchagpakha, Sarchapkkha, Shachopkha, Shachobiikha

Population Sources:
138,000 in Bhutan (2001, G van Driem [1991 figure])[11]
46,000 in India (1997, India Missions Association)
30,000 in China (1987, *Language Atlas of China*)

Language: Sino-Tibetan, Tibeto-Burman, Himalayish, Tibeto-Kanauri, Tibetic, Bodish,

Tshangla

Dialects: 8 (Northern Tsangla, Southern Tsangla, Matchopa Nagnoo, Chug, Sangla, Kalaktang, Kishpignag, Monkit)

Professing Buddhists: 80%

Practising Buddhists: 35%

Christians: 0.1%

Scripture: Portions

Jesus film: Tsangla

Gospel Recordings: Bhutanese Tsangla

Christian Broadcasting: available (FEBC)

ROPAL code: TSJ

Population:
255,000 (2000)
315,100 (2010)
390,800 (2020)
Countries: Bhutan, China, India
Buddhism: Tibetan
Christians: 100

CHINA
Xizang (Tibet)
BHUTAN
INDIA
Arunachal Pradesh
Tsangla

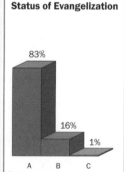

Status of Evangelization

83%

16%

1%

A   B   C

A = Have never heard the gospel
B = Have heard the gospel but have not become Christians
C = Are adherents to some form of Christianity

Population:
5,160 (2000)
6,400 (2010)
7,900 (2020)
Countries: Nepal
Buddhism: Tibetan
Christians: none known

Overview of the Tsum

Other Names: Tsumge, Siar, Siyar, Chumba, Shar, Tsumba

Population Sources:

2,200 to 3,500 in Nepal (2000, B Grimes [1980 figure])

Language: Sino-Tibetan, Tibeto-Burman, Himalayish, Tibeto-Kanauri, Tibetic, Tibetan, Central

Dialects: 0

Professing Buddhists: 100%

Practising Buddhists: 70%

Christians: 0%

Scripture: none

Jesus film: none

Gospel Recordings: none

Christian Broadcasting: none

ROPAL code: TTZ

Status of Evangelization

A = Have never heard the gospel
B = Have heard the gospel but have not become Christians
C = Are adherents to some form of Christianity

According to a 1980 source, between 2,200 and 3,500 Tsum people live along the southern slopes of the Himalayan Range in central Nepal.[1] In the 25 years since this estimate was made, it is thought that the population of the Tsum may have grown to exceed 5,000. The Tsum inhabit a number of villages in the northern Gorkha District of the Gandaki Zone, a short distance away from the China-Nepal border. The main Tsum village is called Chongong (also known as Chekampar).

Chongong is one of the overnight stops for trekkers doing the Langtang Trek. One guide book states, 'The trail descends through forest to the Langtang Khola at 1,890 metres [6,200 feet] then follows the river upstream, crossing from the southern to northern bank to reach Chongong at 2,380 metres [7,800 feet] . . . the villages around are in Tibetan style with stone walls around the fields and herds of yaks.'[2] Unlike the barren Tibetan Plateau to the north, the Tsum area receives the monsoon rains. 'As a consequence the landscape is lush and green, and the fields support good harvests of corn in addition to the staple grains.'[3]

The Tsum are also known as the Chumba, or Shar, because they live along the banks of the Shar (Eastern) River. Official books issued by the Nepali government tend to call them by these alternate names.

The closest neighbours to the Tsum are the Nubri people, who live along the upper reaches of the Buri Gandaki River just

Gospel Recordings Nepal

to the west.[4] The Tsum area is just north of Ganesh Himal, which stands at 7,406 metres (24,292 ft.) above sea level.

The Tsum speak a Central Tibetan language, but linguistic studies have shown that it only shares 71 per cent to 78 per cent lexical similarity with Nubri, 60 per cent to 66 per cent with Lhasa Tibetan and 66 per cent with Kyerung.[5] Few Tsum can speak more than a few words and phrases of Nepali. Their isolated mountain hideout has separated them from the main body of Nepali culture and language, and in most ways they are more aligned with Tibet than with Nepal. Many Tsum are traders, carrying grain and modern appliances from Nepal to Tibet, where they trade their goods for salt and wool.

Tibetan Buddhism dominates the lives of the Tsum people. Every family follows Buddha. They depend on lamas to keep peace between their communities and the spirits, and they spare no effort to placate the demons that can bring disaster to the Tsum's communities if they are offended. One visitor commented, 'The people of Nubri and Tsum are Buddhists . . . actively so, quite possibly because of their close proximity to and greater commerce across the northern frontier with Tibet.'[6]

Very few Tsum people have ever been exposed to the gospel of Jesus Christ. Most are too busy with their daily lives to care enough to seek the truth. Most are content to follow Buddha, as countless generations of their ancestors have done before them.

Approximately 200,000 Tu people live in north-west China, especially in the Huzhu Tu Autonomous County in Qinghai Province. Others are scattered throughout other parts of Qinghai, as well as in neighbouring areas of Gansu Province.[1]

The Tu—who are one of China's 55 official minorities—believe they are descended from white feathers that were left behind by a flock of cranes.[2] The Tibetans consider the Tu to be a part of the Tibetan nationality and accuse the Chinese of trying to weaken the unity of the Tibetan world by granting the Tu a separate identity. There is no doubt, however, that the Tu are distinct from the Tibetans historically, culturally and linguistically. There are two different languages spoken among the Tu: Huzhu, which is profiled here, and Mongour, which is covered separately in a profile under that name.

The existence of the Tu was first recorded in 1227, when a Mongol garrison was dispatched to control the area that the Tu still inhabit today. The troops remained there and later married women from local tribes. A bronze statue of the first Mongol general still stands in the Youning Monastery. A historian says, 'Their ancestors are believed to be the Tuguhuns who moved in the third and fourth centuries to Gansu and Qinghai provinces and mingled with local people of different nationalities. Places where the Tu people live in compact communities are still called Tuhun in the Tu language.'[3]

Even after 800 years of isolation, 60 per cent of Tu vocabulary is still Mongolian in nature. In 1979, a Tu script based on the Roman alphabet was created. It soon became popular among the Tu. The script is taught in local Tu schools today. A massive 70,000-entry Tu-Chinese dictionary was published in 1988. There are 11 different dialects within the Tu language. The Tu living in Datong County can now only speak Chinese. In addition, more than 4,000 ethnic Tu people speak Bonan as their mother tongue.[4]

Until recently, Tu girls were expected to be married by the age of 15. After that age, the girl was considered 'married to heaven'. Even today, if a Tu woman is still single by the time she reaches her mid-20s, she is allowed to sleep around, thus saving herself from disgrace in the eyes of the community. The entire Tu village raises any resulting children. Unmarried Tu women wear a single ponytail to advertise their status to prospective partners.

Dwayne Graybill

The Tu are ardent followers of Tibetan Buddhism. Their main religious centre is the Youning Monastery, founded in 1604. Shamans and mediums are also active among the Tu. The annual *Nadun* festival focuses around the *fala*, a Tu medium who 'impales himself with as many as 12 iron nails and is possessed by the spirit of the Erlang god'.[5]

Prior to the forced deportation of missionaries from China in the early 1950s, a handful of Tu Christians attended Han Chinese churches in the area.[6] Although there are just a few known Christians among the Tu today, there are about 400 Han Chinese believers living in the mountains 25 kilometres from Huzhu. They interact with the Tu and even speak the Tu language.

Population:
199,800 (2000)
250,200 (2010)
308,200 (2020)
Countries: China
Buddhism: Tibetan
Christians: 10

Overview of the Tu

Other Names: Huzhu, White Mongols

Population Sources:
191,624 in China (1990 census)[7]

Language: Altaic, Mongolian, Eastern Mongolian, Mongour

Dialects: 11 (Aragwa, Fulannara, Khalchiguor, Linxia, Mingho, Naringuor, Sanchuan, Datong, Tienyu, Wuyangpu, Yongjing)

Professing Buddhists: 98%

Practising Buddhists: 80%

Christians: 0.1%

Scripture: none

Jesus film: none

Gospel Recordings: none

Christian Broadcasting: none

ROPAL code: MJG

Status of Evangelization

86%

13%

1%

A   B   C

A = Have never heard the gospel
B = Have heard the gospel but have not become Christians
C = Are adherents to some form of Christianity

CHINA

INDIA

Assam

MYANMAR

Turung

Population:
1,000 (2000)
1,160 (2010)
1,350 (2020)
Countries: India
Buddhism: Theravada
Christians: none known

Overview of the Turung

Other Names: Shyam, Tairong, Tairung

Population Sources:

1,000 in India (2000, P Hattaway)

Language: Tai-Kadai, Kam-Tai, Be-Tai, Tai-Sek, Tai, East Central, Northwest

Dialects: 0

Professing Buddhists: 100%

Practising Buddhists: 85%

Christians: 0%

Scripture: none

Jesus **film:** none

Gospel Recordings: none

Christian Broadcasting: none

ROPAL code: TRY

Status of Evangelization

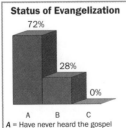

72%

28%

0%

A   B   C

A = Have never heard the gospel
B = Have heard the gospel but have not become Christians
C = Are adherents to some form of Christianity

Members of the little-known Turung ethnic group live in the Golaghat Subdivision of Jorhat District in Assam, north-east India. Small numbers also live in Karbi Aleng District.

Little or no research has ever been conducted on this small group. What is known about them is that they are a Tai-speaking people who migrated into north-east India from northern Burma (now Myanmar) in 1825. Despite the similar name, the Turung are not the same as the Derung tribe of northern Myanmar and south-west China. The Derung area is not far away from the Turung's habitation, but the Derung speak a completely different language belonging to the Tibeto-Burman family.

The *Ethnologue* notes that Turung is a 'nearly extinct' Northwest Tai language.[1] Out of the 70 Tai languages listed in the book, Turung is unique in that it is not closely related to any other variety and has been given its own category as the only group in the Northwest Tai branch. The Turung are also conversant in Assamese and Hindi.

The Turung have not been officially acknowledged as either a Scheduled Tribe or a Scheduled Caste in India. K S Singh notes, 'However, they enjoy the facilities extended to the Scheduled Tribes by introducing themselves as a Tai-speaking group. . . . The community has two subgroups, namely Taioi / Durung and Drarai. These sub-groups are further segmented into several clans like Lungking, Namchog, Chaopu and Chewan. Shyam and Turung are used as surnames.'[2]

The Turung are allowed to intermarry with the members of just two other ethnic groups—the Aiton and the Khamiyang. These two groups share many similarities with the Turung as small Tai-speaking tribes living in the Brahmaputra Valley. They are not allowed to intermarry with other neighbouring groups such as the Nepali, Karbi and Kachari, even though the Turung maintain harmonious relationships with all three of these groups. Before a Turung wedding is allowed to proceed, a suitable bride price must be agreed upon and paid. The price is dependent on a number of factors including the beauty of the bride and the economic and social status of the groom's family.

Rice cultivation is the main occupation of the Turung. They are not vegetarians and consume various kinds of meat. In recent years some Turung have obtained office and clerical jobs for the local government and private companies.

Dwayne Graybill

All Turung people profess Theravada Buddhism as their religion. They have their own monks and places of worship. Their faith is important to them, as it is the main link they still possess that ties them to their ancestors and culture. It is for this reason that they zealously retain relationships with other Tai Buddhist groups in the region.

Although Christianity has exerted a growing influence in Assam, and a massive number of Christians live nearby in Nagaland, no Turung people are known to have put their faith in Christ so far. For a person to do so would be considered disgraceful to the Turung. This pressure has hindered the introduction of the gospel to this precious group.

More than 250,000 Tuva people inhabit the region where the three nations of Russia, Mongolia and China intersect. The majority (215,000) live in the Tuva Republic of Russia, radiating out from the capital Kyzl. More than 34,000 Tuva live in north-west Mongolia, especially in the Hövsgöl and Hovd Aimags. An additional 3,000 Tuva people live across the border in the Xinjiang Region of north-west China, primarily in the Burjin, Habahe, Fuyun and Altay counties of Altay Prefecture.

Tuva was declared an independent state by the Tsarist government in Russia in 1912. At the same time, Mongolia gained independence from China. Freedom was short-lived, however. Tuva became a Russian protectorate in 1914. In 1944 it was integrated into the Soviet Union. The Tuva live in a 'harsh mountainous region that has an intense climate. The summers are hot and dry with temperatures reaching 43 degrees Celsius (110°F). The winters are bitterly cold with temperatures dropping to –61 degrees Celsius (–78°F).'[1]

The Tuva in Mongolia and China are diaspora groups who migrated to their present locations in the early 1800s. In the late 1800s the Tuva in China started to call themselves Mongolians 'to avoid oppression by the then ruling Qing Dynasty, and to enjoy the favored status of the Mongolians, who were allies of the Manchurian court'.[2]

Asian Report

Tuva is a Turkic language. Because of contact with other peoples, 90 per cent of the Tuva in China can speak Kazak and 30 per cent can speak Kalmyk-Oirat.[3] Most can also speak Mandarin. In Mongolia, the Tuva are bilingual in Mongolian. 'The use of the [Tuva] language is rapidly declining on both sides of the China-Mongolia border',[4] although it is reportedly still spoken by most Tuva children.

The majority of Tuva in all three of the countries they inhabit believe in Tibetan Buddhism. Tibetan missionaries converted them in the 1700s.[5] In the 1930s the Soviets destroyed nearly all Buddhist monasteries, and a number of monks were put to death. The persecution caused a decline in Buddhism among the Tuva. Since the collapse of the Soviet Union, Buddhism has experienced a renaissance among the Tuva in Russia, aided by visits by the Dalai Lama and other high-ranking Buddhist leaders.

The Buddhist faith of the Tuva is coupled with the strong influence of shamanism. 'Ceremonies are held on the 7th and 49th days after someone's death. The soul is believed to remain in the body of the deceased for seven days, then depart for the "kingdom of the dead," reaching its ultimate destination on the 49th day. The Tuva believe that all natural elements contain spirits that must be appeased with offerings. The people are dependent on shamans to cure the sick by magic and communicate with the spirits.'[6]

In Russia there are a reported '17 registered evangelical Tuva churches'.[7] One Tuva believer in Russia was recently martyred. His death was reported on television, causing a growth of interest in the gospel among many people.[8]

Overview of the Tuva

Other Names: Tuvin, Uryangkhai, Altai Uryangkhai, Altai Uriangkhai, Altai Tuva, Tuwa, Monchak, Monjak, Soyon, Shor, Urinkhai, Uryankhai-Monchak, Tuvinian, Tuba, Tannu-Tuva, Soyod, Soyot, Tuvan, Tuvia, Diba, Kök, Mungak, Tuva-Uriankhai, Tuwa-Uriankhai, Tyva, Tofa, Tokha

Population:
252,300 (2000)
258,800 (2010)
266,400 (2020)

Countries: Russia, Mongolia, China

Buddhism: Tibetan

Christians: 2,000

Population Sources:

215,000 in Russia (2001, P Johnstone and J Mandryk [2000 figure])
34,000 in Mongolia (2001, P Johnstone and J Mandryk [2000 figure])
3,000 in China (1993, J Janhunen)

Language: Altaic, Turkic, Northern

Dialects: 7 (Kokchulutan, Khowsogol Uigur, Central Tuvin, Western Tuvin, Northeastern Tuvin [Todzhin], Southeastern Tuvin, Tuba-Kizhi)

Professing Buddhists: 90%

Practising Buddhists: 55%

Christians: 0.8%

Scripture: Portions 1996; work in progress

Jesus film: available

Gospel Recordings: none

Christian Broadcasting: none

ROPAL code: TUN

Status of Evangelization

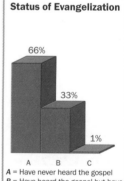

66%

33%

1%

A   B   C

A = Have never heard the gospel
B = Have heard the gospel but have not become Christians
C = Are adherents to some form of Christianity

Approximately 75 million Vietnamese people live throughout the world. More than 70 million inhabit all parts of Vietnam. In the aftermath of the Vietnam War (which ended in 1975), refugees made their way to dozens of countries around the globe. Today there are large communities of Vietnamese in different parts of the world including 1.2 million in the USA; 300,000 in France; and 150,000 in Australia.

The Vietnamese, who call themselves Kinh or Jing, have a long history. Their ancestors were already occupying northern Vietnam 2,000 years ago. In 1471 they destroyed the Chamba kingdom and migrated to the southern extremities of Vietnam. The Chinese ruled Vietnam as a vassal state from about 200 BC to AD 938. Their influence has been felt by all generations of Vietnamese since. Ethnic, cultural and dialect differences continue to exist between Vietnamese from the north of the country and those from the south.

Theravada Buddhism was brought to Vietnam from India by pilgrims at the end of the 2nd century AD. At about the same time, Chinese monks introduced Mahayana Buddhism. Neither sect of Buddhism enjoyed widespread popularity until centuries later. Between the 10th and 13th centuries,

Julian Hawken

Buddhism received royal patronage. Today, Mahayana Buddhism is by far the largest Buddhist sect in Vietnam—with approximately 40 million adherents[1]—although there is Theravada influence in the south of the country among both Khmer and Vietnamese people. If asked their religion, 'the Vietnamese are likely to say that they are Buddhist, but when it comes to family or civic duties they are likely to follow Confucianism while turning to Taoist conception in understanding the nature of the cosmos. . . . The function of the Vietnamese Buddhist monk is to minister to the spiritual and superstitious needs of the peasantry, but it is largely up to him whether he invokes the lore of Taoism or the philosophy of Buddhism. A monk may live reclusively on a remote hilltop or he may manage

a pagoda on a busy city street. And he may choose to fulfil any number of functions: telling fortunes, making and selling talismans, advising whether a house should be constructed, reciting incantations at funerals or even performing acupuncture.'[2]

Catholic missionaries from Portugal, Spain and France began work in Vietnam in the 16th century. By 1685 there were already an estimated 800,000 Catholics in Vietnam.[3] Many believers were martyred for their faith.[4]

Protestant work did not get underway until the early 1900s. The Christian and Missionary Alliance spearheaded the Protestant enterprise. Today there are an estimated 6.2 million Vietnamese Christians in Vietnam. This figure includes about 5.8 million Catholics and only 400,000 Protestants, who meet in both government-sanctioned churches and illegal house church gatherings.[5] Persecution of Christians continues throughout the country, with dozens of pastors in prison at any given time.

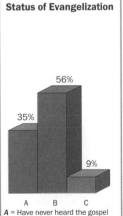

Overview of the Vietnamese

Other Names: Viet, Kinh, King, Gin, Jing, Ching, Annamese

Population Sources:
69,373,700 in Vietnam (2001, P Johnstone and J Mandryk)
1,200,000 in USA (2001, P Johnstone and J Mandryk)
620,000 in Cambodia (2001, P Johnstone and J Mandryk)
300,000 in France (2001, P Johnstone and J Mandryk)
150,000 in Australia (2001, P Johnstone and J Mandryk)
104,000 in Thailand (2001, P Johnstone and J Mandryk)
89,000 in Laos (2001, P Johnstone and J Mandryk)[6]
60,000 in Germany (1999, Asian Minorities Outreach)
60,000 in Canada (1999, Asian Minorities Outreach)[7]

Language: Austro-Asiatic, Mon-Khmer, Viet-Muong, Vietnamese

Dialects: 3 (Northern, Central, Southern)

Professing Buddhists: 65%

Practising Buddhists: 35%

Christians: 9%

Scripture: Bible 1916; New Testament 1914; Portions 1890

Jesus film: available

Gospel Recordings: Vietnamese; Vietnamese: Hue; Vietnamese: North; Vietnamese: South

Christian Broadcasting: available

ROPAL code: VIE

Population:
72,031,700 (2000)
83,340,700 (2010)
96,425,100 (2020)

Countries: Vietnam, USA, Cambodia, France, Australia, Thailand, Laos, Germany, Canada, China, United Kingdom, Norway, Netherlands, New Caledonia and many other nations

Buddhism: Mahayana, some Theravada

Christians: 6,500,000

Status of Evangelization

A — 35%
B — 56%
C — 9%

A = Have never heard the gospel
B = Have heard the gospel but have not become Christians
C = Are adherents to some form of Christianity

CHINA
Xizang (Tibet)

NEPAL
Mechi
Sikkim
W Bengal

INDIA
Walung

Population:
16,000 (2000)
19,700 (2010)
24,300 (2020)
Countries: Nepal, India
Buddhism: Tibetan
Christians: 10

Overview of the Walung

Other Names: Ulang, Walungge, Olangchung, Olangchung Gola, Walunggi Keccya, Walungpa, Walungba, Holung

Population Sources:

10,000 to 15,000 in Nepal (2000, B Grimes)

1,000 in India (2000, P Hattaway)

Language: Sino-Tibetan, Tibeto-Burman, Himalayish, Tibeto-Kanauri, Tibetic, Tibetan, Central

Dialects: 0

Professing Buddhists: 95%

Practising Buddhists: 75%

Christians: 0.1%

Scripture: none

Jesus **film:** none

Gospel Recordings: none

Christian Broadcasting: none

ROPAL code: OLA

Status of Evangelization

77%

22%

1%

A   B   C

A = Have never heard the gospel
B = Have heard the gospel but have not become Christians
C = Are adherents to some form of Christianity

More than 15,000 Walung people (who are also known as Olangchung, Walungchung, Holung and Walungge) live in the northern part of the Taplejung District of Mechi Zone in far eastern Nepal. They inhabit about a dozen villages, the five largest of which are named Walungchung, Yangma, Gunsa, Lilip and Lungtung.[1] One source notesm: 'The upper Tamur in Taplejung District has a number of Bhotia [Tibetan] settlements. The largest is Walungchung, once a flourishing *gola* (mart) for transaction of goods between Tibet and Darjeeling. The houses are built of stone walls with wooden shingle roofs. Crops include barley, wheat and potato. The people adhere to Buddhism and their chief deity at the Walungchung

livelihoods as middlemen on the route between Tibet and India. In 1972 one book reported, 'Many successful and rich traders are in residence here. . . . Exports to Tibet include grain, cotton thread and material, sugar, cigarettes, matches and other such goods generally of Indian origin, in exchange for wool, woolen carpets and Tibetan salt. . . . Yak, mules and *dzums* are used by traders as pack animals. Sar is the nearest town in Tibet, about a four or five day's journey from the border.'[4] When modern roads and transportation killed trade through the Walung area, many of the people were left in turmoil as they had completely relied on trade as their source of income. There were few crops planted in

International Mission Board

gompa is Chenrezi. . . . The Walung people have been hit hard by the decline in Tibetan trade and many have migrated to Darjeeling, Kathmandu and Hile.'[2] Approximately 1,000 Walung people now live in the Darjeeling District of West Bengal in India.

The Walung are believed to have migrated south from Tibet several hundred years ago, before settling in their present location. Their language has evolved over the years, so that today it reportedly shares 71 per cent lexical similarity with Lhasa Tibetan; 68 per cent with Dolpo, Loba and Kyerung; and 66 per cent with Lhomi, Helambu Sherpa and Baragaunle.[3] These linguistic relationships show the Walung's historical link to Tibet.

For generations the Walung dominated trade in this part of Nepal, earning their

the Walung villages, and few kept animals. Tibetan Buddhism is the religion of almost all Walung people. The main village of Walungchung has a large monastery that was built more than 200 years ago. Monks from Lhasa were often invited to come down to the Walung area to reside at the monastery.

The Walung are a desperately needy unreached people group. They have no Scripture, *Jesus* film or gospel recordings in their language. Few have ever been exposed to the gospel in a meaningful way that would allow them to intelligently accept or reject Christ. In 1958 the first four Walung boys attended a missionary school in Darjeeling, but the Walung's homeland in Nepal remains a spiritually barren land.

The 1991 *Encyclopedic Dictionary of Chinese Linguistics* lists a population of 2,000 Wutun people in China.[1] They live in three main villages: Wutun Xiazhuang, Wutun Shangzhuang and Jiangchama, located in the Longwu District of Tongren County in the eastern part of Qinghai Province.

The Chinese government does not recognize the Wutun as a separate people group but includes them under the Tu nationality. The Wutun resist this classification and insist on their own identity. There are also ethnic Tu people in the same area, but the two groups cannot understand each other's languages. Neighbouring Tibetans refer to the Wutun as *Sanggaixiong*, meaning 'the centre of the lion'.

The Wutun language is a mixture of Chinese, Mongolian and Tibetan. Their vocabulary contains just under 60 per cent Chinese and 20 per cent Tibetan words. Most linguists believe that Wutun is either 'a variety of Chinese heavily influenced by Tibetan or perhaps a Tibetan language undergoing relexification with Chinese forms'.[2] Most Wutun men are able to read Chinese, while the Tibetan script is used for religious purposes.

According to Wutun oral history, a long time ago a Tibetan king sent soldiers from Lhasa to where the Wutun now live to drive off other groups in the area. The soldiers stayed and married local women. Together they eventually became the Wutun people. The Wutun children began to speak their mother's language and could not speak Tibetan—the language of their fathers—so they lost their original language.[3] Today all Wutun family names are Tibetan-language names and not Tu names.

The Wutun are skilled artists. Buddhist scenes and the Buddha himself are the most common subjects of their paintings. They claim their artistic skills came about because the original soldiers studied art in Nepal.[4]

Tibetan Buddhism is the only religion among the Wutun. They are fanatical believers. Their whole ethnic identity is bound up in their faith. Although they do not have their own temples, the Wutun frequent Tibetan temples in the Tongren area. Like all Buddhists, the Wutun believe that they will end up in a state of bliss after death. But, being better and more privileged, they believe they will go there directly, while other Buddhists achieve enlightenment only after going through many trials and testings.[5]

The Wutun have an almost complete lack of knowledge about the existence of Christianity. In the 1920s and 1930s there were Christian and Missionary Alliance workers nearby. In 1996, a 74-year-old Wutun man told a visitor, 'When I was a small boy I heard something about this Jesus religion, but I did not understand. There are no believers in any other religions among us Wutun except for Buddhism. We are not interested in any new religions because we know that we have the best and only true religion in the world.'[6]

Population:
2,450 (2000)
3,070 (2010)
3,782 (2020)
Countries: China
Buddhism: Tibetan
Christians: none known

Overview of the Wutun

Other Names: Wutunhua, Wutu, Sanggaixiong

Population Sources:
2,000 in China (1987, *Encyclopedic Dictionary of Chinese Linguistics*)

Language: Mixed Language: Chinese-Tibetan-Mongolian

Dialects: 0

Professing Buddhists: 100%

Practising Buddhists: 100%

Christians: 0%

Scripture: none

***Jesus* film:** none

Gospel Recordings: none

Christian Broadcasting: none

ROPAL code: WUH

Photo credit: Dwayne Graybill

Status of Evangelization

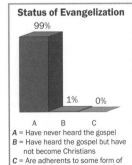

99%

1%

0%

A   B   C

A = Have never heard the gospel
B = Have heard the gospel but have not become Christians
C = Are adherents to some form of Christianity

Xiangcheng

More than 11,000 people who inhabit a valley in and around the township of Xiangcheng in China's south-west Sichuan Province speak a distinct language and possess their own unique historical heritage.[1] The region is extremely remote. One visitor described Xiangcheng: 'The town looked magnificent. The solid residential houses were all built with big blocks of stone, but their windows tended to be very small, probably for the purpose of defense, in addition to keeping warm. We were told that in the old days, horse drivers were afraid of bandits here.'[2] The Xiangcheng build beautiful houses, which have white rocks on the roofs like those of the Qiang people. Xiangcheng homes are square-shaped, two stories high, with colourful decorations around the window frames.

They are very different from the houses of their neighbours, the Khampa.

The Chinese government has not recognized the Xiangcheng as an independent minority but has included them as part of the Tibetan nationality. As a result, few people are aware of their existence. One source states, 'The Xiangcheng people identify themselves as the descendants of Tibetan, Naxi, and Subi people. . . . In his southern expedition, Kublai Khan of the Yuan Dynasty (1271–1368) brought a great number of Subi people of Mongolian origin here to settle down in Xiangcheng. Ruins of ancient castles can still be found here.'[3]

It appears that the Xiangcheng language is a mixture of several elements. They speak their own language within their families, but most use Khampa Tibetan when speaking to outsiders. Xiangcheng may be a Qiangic language.

For centuries the Xiangcheng area has remained virtually untouched—a remote outpost along the ancient caravan route that linked Yunnan with Tibet and Sichuan. One writer has noted, 'Xiangcheng's geographic location provides a unique strategic location, which perhaps has also nurtured the firm character of the Xiangcheng people. Xiangcheng controls Zhongdian to the south, defends the ancient Yunnan-Tibet route in the west, and blocks the Sichuan-Tibet route from Batang to Dajianlu [now Kangding]. Since ancient times Xiangcheng has been contested by all strategists.'[4]

When Joseph Rock visited in 1930, he found that the Xiangcheng territory was ruled by Sashatimba, a bandit chief based at the Sangpiliang Monastery. 'Other bandit chiefs assist Sashatimba to rule the land. Together they loot and rob and murder. They even go on journeys of many weeks to hold up caravans or loot peaceful settlements. No Chinese dares to enter the [Xiangcheng] territories.'[5]

The Xiangcheng are zealous believers in Tibetan Buddhism, as evidenced by the numerous Buddhist temples and pagodas throughout the region.[6] Their remoteness and strong faith in Buddhism has resulted in the Xiangcheng being one of the most untouched people groups in China, although a few years ago one young man believed in Christ and travelled to Kunming City to learn more of the Bible. He has proven a zealous disciple with a strong desire to reach his own people.

China Advocate

Population:
11,160 (2000)
13,750 (2010)
16,900 (2020)
Countries: China
Buddhism: Tibetan
Christians: 5

Overview of the Xiangcheng

Other Names: Hsiangcheng, Qagcheng Tibetan, Phyagphreng

Population Sources:
10,000 in China (1995, Asian Minorities Outreach)

Language: Sino-Tibetan, Tibeto-Burman, Unclassified (possibly Qiangic)

Dialects: 0

Professing Buddhists: 95%

Practising Buddhists: 85%

Christians: 0.1%

Scripture: none

Jesus film: none

Gospel Recordings: none

Christian Broadcasting: none

ROPAL code: none

Status of Evangelization

91%

8%

1%

A   B   C

A = Have never heard the gospel
B = Have heard the gospel but have not become Christians
C = Are adherents to some form of Christianity

According to one study, 'The Yakha are a tribal group of almost 26,000 people living in nearly 600 villages throughout the mountains of eastern Nepal. They are found throughout the Koshi Zone but are primarily just south of the city of Chainpur.'[1] Yakha communities are spread across the Tehrathum, Sankuwasawa and Dhankuta districts within Koshi Zone. From one end of their territory in Nepal to the other is a distance of approximately 80 kilometres (49 mi.). Other sources list between 8,000 and 10,000 speakers of the Yakha language in Nepal.[2]

because of their exposure to Nepalese and Indian culture.'[7] Buddhist influence is strongest among the Yakha in the Sankhwasawa District, but it is more diluted the further south they are found.

Not only are the different accounts of the Yakha's religion confusing, but also a great variety of opinion exists on the status of Christianity among them. One source claims, 'Many Yakhas have heard the name of Jesus, and received Christian literature, but have not yet understood the message of the cross and Christianity. There are about

Population:
35,260 (2000)
43,200 (2010)
53,000 (2020)
Countries: Nepal, India
Buddhism: Tibetan
Christians: 900

Nancy Sturrock

Overview of the Yakha

Other Names: Yakkha, Yakkhaba, Yakkhaba Cea, Yakkhaba Sala, Dewansala, Roi, Yakthomba

Population Sources:

29,400 in Nepal (1997, Bethany World Prayer Center [2000 figure])

5,860 in India (2001, FMC South Asia)

Language: Sino-Tibetan, Tibeto-Burman, Himalayish, Mahakiranti, Kiranti, Eastern

Dialects: 3 (Northern Yakha, Southern Yakha, Eastern Yakha)

Professing Buddhists: 55%
Practising Buddhists: 20%
Christians: 3%
Scripture: none
Jesus film: none
Gospel Recordings: Yakha
Christian Broadcasting: none
ROPAL code: YBH

A migrant community of Yakha has moved to north-east India. Approximately 4,900 live in the Darjeeling District of West Bengal and 960 in Sikkim.[3] The majority of Yakha people in West Bengal believe in Hinduism, whereas almost all Yakha in Sikkim are Buddhists. One source says, 'There are a few of them scattered in all the districts of Sikkim. . . . Their natural environment is hilly terrain, moderately cold, humid, and without snowfall.'[4]

The Yakha language is one that fascinates scholars. It appears to be related to Rai and Limbu, yet it has features that are distinctive from both. Yakha is part of the Eastern Kiranti branch of the Tibeto-Burman family.[5]

There are conflicting reports regarding the religious beliefs of the Yakha. One source says, 'They are traditionally animists, but have adopted many of the Hindu customs and beliefs.'[6] Another states, 'Most identify themselves as Buddhists. A few have embraced Hindu customs and beliefs

750 believers scattered throughout Yakha villages, which is about 3 per cent of the total Yakha population.'[8]

A second report gives a less enthusiastic appraisal of the gospel among this group. 'Christianity is considered a low-caste or foreign religion. As a result, many Yakha are very anti-Christian and would excommunicate from their communities any who become Christian. This kind of threatened separation from the tribe is a formidable barrier to most in the Yakha culture. . . . One key to reaching the Yakha with the gospel, however, may be their desire and deep respect for traits such as honesty and kindness. Believers who have opportunities to live Christ-filled lives before the Yakha may be able to gain their respect and point them to the Author of Life.'[9] Among the Yakha in India, 'some have recently become Christianized. They are those who know the least about their language, culture and ethnic feelings.'[10]

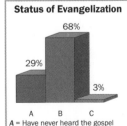

Status of Evangelization

68%
29%
3%

A   B   C

A = Have never heard the gospel
B = Have heard the gospel but have not become Christians
C = Are adherents to some form of Christianity

Yong

MYANMAR
Chiang Rai
THAILAND
Chiang Mai
Lamphun
Yong

Population:
12,000 (2000)
13,100 (2010)
14,300 (2020)
Countries: Thailand, possibly Myanmar
Buddhism: Theravada
Christians: none known

Overview of the Yong

Other Names: Tai Yong, Nyong

Population Sources: 12,000 in Thailand (2003, Joshua Project II)

possibly also in Myanmar

Language: Tai-Kadai, Kam-Tai, Be-Tai, Tai-Sek, Tai, Southwestern, Unclassified

Dialects: 2 (Eastern, Western)

Professing Buddhists: 100%

Practising Buddhists: 75%

Christians: 0%

Scripture: none

Jesus **film:** none

Gospel Recordings: none

Christian Broadcasting: none

ROPAL code: YNO

Status of Evangelization

68%

32%

0%

A   B   C

A = Have never heard the gospel
B = Have heard the gospel but have not become Christians
C = Are adherents to some form of Christianity

More than 12,000 members of the Yong ethnic group live in scattered parts of northern Thailand. They inhabit villages within three provinces: Lamphun (Muang, Pasang, Ban Hong and Mae Tha districts); Chiang Mai and Chiang Rai.

Joachim Schliesinger, in his excellent book *Tai Groups of Thailand*, quotes a population source of between 240,000 and 320,000 Yong people in Thailand. This high figure is unlikely, since if it were correct the Yong would be one of the largest ethnic groups in northern Thailand. As it is, few people outside of their immediate areas have ever heard of them.

Schliesinger states that the Yong 'are in fact ethnic Lu people who once lived in Muang Yong of today's Shan State of Burma. As is common practice among Tai peoples, the Tai Yong derived their new group name from their location at Muang Yong. . . . The King of Siam ordered the Chiang Mai rulers to launch several military raids north and west into the [Shan, Khun and Yong] villages and towns to capture the inhabitants and resettle them as war captives to Chiang Mai, Lamphun and Lampang. The largest influx of Yong occurred in 1805, when 10,000 people were taken from Muang Yong to be resettled in northern Thailand.'[1]

The first Yong arrivals in Thailand settled in the Pasang District of Lamphun Province. They named their village Ban Vieng Vong. This remains an active Yong habitation to this day. At Ban Vieng Vong, 'the Yong reinforced ritual power and social stratifica-

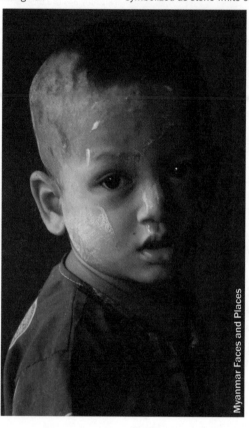

Myanmar Faces and Places

tion. The oldest monastery in Ban Vieng Vong shelters the four guardian spirits of their former Muang Yong in Burma, which they took with them when they were resettled.'[2] The names of these four idols, symbolized as stone white elephants, are *suranna, pittiya, lakkhana* and *thewada*. They are considered sacred to the Yong people, who not only worship and appease these spirit beings, but who also see their identity and history as a people intricately bound up with the safe transport of these idols from their original homeland.

The Yong language is a member of the Southwestern Tai linguistic branch. There are numerous languages in this group, with speakers dispersed over a wide geographical area from India to Laos. Most of the Southwestern Tai groups are strong believers in Theravada Buddhism.[3]

Although Buddhism is the chosen religion of the Yong people, their beliefs are heavily mixed with animistic ritual and spirit-worship. The Yong 'honor the spirit of the land and the ancestral spirits and believe in many other spirits of the surroundings. On full moon in June, the villagers flock to the local spirit shrine to make sacrifices . . . of pig heads, chicken, and nine different kinds of fruit.'[4]

There are no known Christian believers among the Yong. They are blinded by their deep religious devotion to idols and traditions and in need of much prayer.

MONGOLIA
CHINA
Qinghai
Yonzhi

Population:
3,270 (2000)
4,030 (2010)
4,950 (2020)
Countries: China
Buddhism: Tibetan
Christians: none known

Overview of the Yonzhi

Other Names:

Population Sources:

3,000 in China (1996, Asian Minorities Outreach)

Language: Sino-Tibetan, Tibeto-Burman, Himalayish, Tibeto-Kanauri, Tibetic, Tibetan, Northern

Dialects: 0

Professing Buddhists: 60%

Practising Buddhists: 25%

Christians: 0%

Scripture: none

***Jesus* film:** none

Gospel Recordings: none

Christian Broadcasting: none

ROPAL code: none

Status of Evangelization

100%

0%   0%

A   B   C

A = Have never heard the gospel
B = Have heard the gospel but have not become Christians
C = Are adherents to some form of Christianity

More than 3,000 members of the Yonzhi tribe, a nomadic Tibetan people group, live in a virtually inaccessible area of eastern Qinghai Province in north-west China. They primarily inhabit the Heha Chen Valley, near the town Tibetans call Cheb Chu. The Yonzhi area lies within Gonghe County, east of the Yellow River. The imposing Anye Machen Mountain range, considered sacred by all Tibetans, lies to the east of the Yonzhi tribe. The highest peak is the 6,282-metre (20,604 ft.) Machen Gangri. In the short summer months the area comes alive with flowers. 'Red and blue poppies, bright, fresh, and unharmed, looked happily out of their bed of snow. . . . The scenery became more and more beautiful as we descended. The little meadows, clearings in the juniper forest, were full of flowers . . . out in all their glory.'[1] The Yonzhi share their homelands with many blue sheep, gazelles and wolves.

The Yonzhi are a distinct ethnic group who live in a remote area that has changed little for hundreds of years. The Chinese government does not recognize them as a distinct ethnicity. Instead, they are considered to be a part of the Golog, who in turn are officially counted as part of the Tibetan nationality in China. The Yonzhi speak a variety of Golog Tibetan, the regional language. Few have any knowledge of Chinese.

For countless generations the Yonzhi have lived simple lives, unaffected by events in the rest of the world. Joseph Rock, the

Julian Hawken

famous botanist and explorer, stumbled across the Yonzhi in 1929. He recalls, 'The people were astonished at sight of our party. One asked, "Why this array of arms and force when visiting our territory?" We continued up the valley to the very foot of [Anye Machen], the mountain god of the Yonzhi tribe. The last few tents we passed were cursed by some plague, the nomads said. The inmates lay dying outside, covered with yak-hair rugs.'[2]

The Yonzhi are nomadic, living in yak-hair tents and moving every few weeks to find new pastures for their yaks, sheep and goats. In addition to Tibetan Buddhism, the Yonzhi worship Anye Machen, the Yonzhi's mountain deity. The Yonzhi believe that the nearby Anye Machen Mountain contains a powerful god of the same name. He is often represented in pictures riding a white horse, with the sun and a rainbow to his right and the moon to his left. 'All Tibetans worship Anye Machen; every monastery has either a picture or image of him. *Anye* means "old man" and corresponds to our "saint". *Ma* means "peacock" and *chen* "great".'[3]

The Yonzhi are one of the most unreachable people groups in China—if not the entire world. Their region is snowbound for most of the year with temperatures plummeting to minus 40 degrees Celsius (–40°F). The Yonzhi move around frequently, relocating their homes and herds to new pastures. Their communities are only accessible by foot or horseback. To the Yonzhi, the gospel remains untold. It is possible that no Yonzhi has ever heard the name of Jesus Christ.

Yoy

More than 8,000 Yoy people live on both sides of the Mekong River in Southeast Asia. The majority—about 7,000—inhabit villages in the north-east Thailand province of Sakhon Nakhon. They are dispersed over three districts: Akat Amnuai,[1] Phang Khon[2] and Sawang Daen Din.

An additional 1,000 Yoy make their homes in the central Laos province of Kham-mouan. They live in a few villages at the intersection of three districts: Nakay, Grom-marol and Bourapha. These districts are in the eastern part of the province, not far from the Laos-Vietnam border. The Yoy claim that they also have relatives living in Vietnam, but specific details or numbers have yet to be obtained.

The origins of the Yoy people are obscure. Although few research-ers have ever studied this group, each seems to put forward a different theory on where the Yoy came from. One theory is that they originated in southern China where their ancestors, the Zhuang and Bouyei, are among the largest of China's minority nationali-ties today—each numbering in the millions. A branch of this group migrated firstly into Vietnam, and later into Laos and Thailand. Only extensive linguistic research can determine whether the Yoy language can be linked to these Northern Tai varieties in China, to see if this first theory holds any weight.

The second theory is that the Yoy are ethnic Giay people, a quarter of a million of whom live on both sides of the China-Vietnam border today. The Giay language is also a Northern Tai variety.

The third theory is that the Yoy are in fact Saek people. Indeed today the Saek live in the same areas of both Laos and Thailand as the Yoy do.[3] While this may originally have been true, there is no doubt that today the Saek and Yoy have distinct ethnic identities.[4]

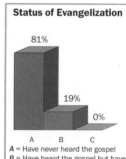

Christian Far East Ministry

While the origins of the Yoy may be obscure, there is no doubt that the Yoy in Thailand entered from Laos in the 19th century. Their existence was recorded in the Siamese records of 1857. In Thailand the Yoy call themselves Lao Yuai. They are hard-working farmers who harvest glutinous rice and maize as their staple crops. 'Other crops include cassava, basil, beans, onions, tomatoes, papaya, jackfruit, bananas and melons. Some families cultivate cotton.'[5]

The Yoy are professing Bud-dhists, although a close inspec-tion of their religious practices reveals a regular dependence on spirit-appeasement and animism. Elements of ancestor worship are also present.

Outside each Yoy village, the people construct a spirit shrine where at certain times of the year the villagers come and make offerings of pigs and chickens to the protective spirit they believe can bring them good luck, wealth and happiness in the coming year. If they do not keep peaceful relations with this spirit, the Yoy believe disaster will befall their community.

The Yoy live in a part of Southeast Asia with few known churches. They have lived for centuries with little knowl-edge of Christianity. Not surprisingly, there are no known believers among the Yoy today.'[6]

Overview of the Yoy

Other Names: Tai Yoy, Tai Yoi, Yoi, Yooi, Yooy, Yoe, Yay, Du'o'i, Duoi, Dioi, Giy, Yuai, Yueai, Lao Yuai

Population Sources: 7,000 in Thailand (2001, J Schliesinger [1998 figure])

1,000 in Laos (1995, Asian Minorities Outreach)

also in Vietnam

Language: Tai-Kadai, Kam-Tai, Be-Tai, Tai-Sek, Tai, Unclassified

Dialects: 0

Professing Buddhists: 80%

Practising Buddhists: 55%

Christians: 0%

Scripture: none

Jesus film: none

Gospel Recordings: none

Christian Broadcasting: none

ROPAL code: YOY

Population:
8,250 (2000)
9,250 (2010)
10,300 (2020)
Countries: Thailand, Laos, Vietnam
Buddhism: Theravada
Christians: none known

Status of Evangelization

81%

19%

0%

A   B   C

A = Have never heard the gospel
B = Have heard the gospel but have not become Christians
C = Are adherents to some form of Christianity

Population:
4,810 (2000)
5,800 (2010)
7,150 (2020)
Countries: China
Buddhism: Tibetan
Christians: 50

Overview of the Enger Yugur

Other Names: East Yugur, Enger, Mongolian Yugur, Shira Yugur, Shera Yugur, Eastern Yogor, Yugar, Yugu, Yogor, Huihe, Huihu, Huangtou Huihe, Sali Weiwu, Sali Weiwuer, Sali Uygur, Xila Weiguer, Xila Yugur

Population Sources:

4,000 in China (1987, *Language Atlas of China*)

Language: Altaic, Mongolian, Eastern Mongolian, Mongour

Dialects: 0

Professing Buddhists: 65%

Practising Buddhists: 40%

Christians: 0.9%

Scripture: none

***Jesus* film:** none

Gospel Recordings: East Yugur

Christian Broadcasting: none

ROPAL code: YUY

Status of Evangelization

72%
27%
1%
A   B   C

A = Have never heard the gospel
B = Have heard the gospel but have not become Christians
C = Are adherents to some form of Christianity

The small Yugur (not to be mistaken for the Muslim *Uygur*) people group lives in the Gansu corridor in north-west China. They are one of the more unique people groups in China, speaking two completely unrelated languages. The Enger (Eastern) Yugur live in the eastern part of the Sunan Yugur Autonomous County in northern Gansu Province.[1] Their main locations are in Kangle, Hongshiwo and Qinglong townships of Kangle District in Sunan Yugur County, and Dongtan and Beitan townships of Huangcheng District. A 1987 study listed 4,000 speakers of Enger Yugur, representing about a third of all Yugur. The Yugur region was largely unknown and cut off from the world for centuries until the completion of the Lanzhou-Urumqi railway line in 1963, which passes through the Yugur area.

The Enger Yugur, who speak a Mongolian language, have been combined with the

International Mission Board

Turkic-speaking Saragh Yugur to form the official Yugur minority in China. Only a handful of people living in the Dahe District of Sunan County can speak both Yugur languages. Enger Yugur is closely related to Bonan, Tu, Dongxiang and Mongolian. 'Its phonology is closer to the first three languages, whereas in vocabulary and grammar it is somewhat more akin to Mongolian.'[2] A significant number of Yugur, living in Jiuquan, Huangnibao and parts of Sunan County, can now speak only Chinese. In addition, some Yugur are bilingual in the Tibetan language.

Most scholars believe that the Yugur are descended from a nomadic tribe known as the Huiqu.[3] The Huiqu were first recorded during the Tang Dynasty (AD 618–907). In the mid-800s, 'heavy snowfall, combined with an attack from the forest-dwelling Kirgiz from the north, forced the Yugurs to flee their Mongolian homeland.'[4] They moved to Gansu, where they came under the control of the Tibetans.

The Yugur practise wind burials, similar to the tradition of the Tibetans. Dead corpses are cut up into pieces and taken to a mountaintop where ravens and other birds of prey come and devour the flesh. Historically the Yugur were divided into nine separate clans. Each clan controlled its own herding area.

When the Yugur first arrived in the area in the 9th century they believed in Manichaeanism. The Tibetans soon converted them to Buddhism. Today most Yugur remain followers of Tibetan Buddhism. In recent years there has been a revival of ancient shamanism and the cult of the 'Emperor of Heaven', Han Tengri.

Although few Enger Yugur today have ever heard the name of Jesus Christ, the region had many Christians in the past. The Ongkuts developed a widespread Christian culture, as we know from the many Christian crosses found by archaeologists.[5] The Yugur are thought to be the descendants of this tribe. When Marco Polo visited Dunhuang, near the Yugur's homeland, he reported, 'It is true there are some Turks who hold to the religion of the Nestorian Christians.'[6] In 1992 the first contemporary Enger Yugur people believed in Christ. Today there are approximately 50 Christians.

Yugur, Saragh

Approximately 10,000 Saragh (Western) Yugur live in the western part of the Sunan Yugur Autonomous County, in the narrow northern corridor of Gansu Province, China. The nearest town to the Saragh Yugur is Zhangye. Other Saragh Yugur communities are located in the Dahe and Minghua districts and in the Huangnibao area near Jiuquan City in western Gansu.

The Saragh Yugur, also known as *Yaofuer*, are the Turkic half of the official Yugur nationality. They live in a separate area from the Enger Yugur. Whereas Enger Yugur is a Mongolian language, Saragh

the Uygurs in Xinjiang, who also speak a Turkic language. A small number of people migrated back inside the wall to avoid the conflict between the Turfan and Hami rulers. They are believed to be the Yugur's ancestors.

Many Saragh Yugur live in yak-hair yurts. A visitor who comes by horseback should leave his whip, rifle, ammunition and all meat outside the yurt. The Yugur believe that the god of hair dresses in red and rides a reddish horse, so visitors dressed in red are not allowed inside a Yugur home.[4] The Yugurs are heavy drinkers. Each evening

Population:
9,870 (2000)
11,880 (2010)
14,600 (2020)
Countries: China
Buddhism: Tibetan
Christians: 50

International Mission Board

Overview of the Saragh Yugur

Other Names: West Yugur, Saragh, Saraygh, Sarig, Ya Lu, Yellow Uighur, Sari Yogur, Yuku, Yugu, Yohur, Yaofuer

Population Sources:

8,197 in China (1990, Asian Minorities Outreach)

Language: Altaic, Turkic, Eastern

Dialects: 0

Professing Buddhists: 60%

Practising Buddhists: 30%

Christians: 0.5%

Scripture: none

Jesus **film:** none

Gospel Recordings: none

Christian Broadcasting: West Yugur

ROPAL code: YBE

Yugur is a completely different language—a member of the Turkic family. The two Yugur groups have little contact with each other, but when they do meet they must use Chinese to communicate. One expert notes that Saragh Yugur 'still preserves many features of the language of medieval Turkic literature'.[1] Because they do not have their own script, written Chinese is in common use among the Yugur.

The Tibetans controlled the Yugur region until the Tangut state of Xixia conquered them in 1028.[2] The Tanguts, in turn, were annihilated by the Mongols in the early 1200s. The Chinese finally assumed control of the area during the Ming Dynasty (1368–1644). There were 300,000 Yugurs at that time, most of whom were living outside the Great Wall at Jiayuguan,[3] farther to the west of their present location. Today, their descendants are no longer called Yugur and probably have become part of

meal is followed by strong alcohol. Revelry often goes on far into the next morning. They do not consider themselves to be good hosts unless their guests get drunk.

The Saragh Yugur adhere to a mixture of Tibetan Buddhism and shamanism. Each family clan has a shaman who consults the spirit world for them.

This group had no knowledge whatsoever of Christianity until 1997, when about 15 Saragh Yugur believed in Christ after watching the *Jesus* film in Mandarin.[5] This number grew to around 50 believers by May 2000. The authorities in Sunan are strongly opposed to the introduction of Christianity. During the 1980s and early 1990s one mission agency sent workers several times to distribute gospel literature among the Yugur, but on every occasion the workers were arrested before they could complete their task.[6]

Status of Evangelization

82%

17%

1%

A   B   C

A = Have never heard the gospel
B = Have heard the gospel but have not become Christians
C = Are adherents to some form of Christianity

Architecture of the Buddhist World

Each of the Buddhist countries in Asia has its own distinctive style of architecture, which reflects local culture and Buddhist beliefs. In this section we present a pictorial display of some of them.

1

2

3

1. Temples at the Grand Palace in Bangkok, Thailand. [Paul Hattaway]
2. The Potala Palace, the centre of the Tibetan Buddhist world, in Lhasa, Tibet. [Julian Hawken]
3. A sea of thousands of colourful lanterns to celebrate Buddha's birthday. Beomeosa Temple, Pusan, South Korea. [Paul Hattaway]

5

4

6

7

8

4. A 500-year-old Buddhist pagoda in Guangzhou, southern China. [Paul Hattaway]
5. Doi Suthep Temple brilliantly lit up at night. Chiang Mai, Thailand. [Xayographix]
6. Monks at the Gongga Langjiling Monastery in Sichuan, China. [China Advocate]
7. The Swyambu Temple in Kathmandu, Nepal. [Nancy Sturrock]
8. Worshippers at the famous Shwedagon Pagoda in Yangon (Rangoon), Myanmar. [Myanmar Faces and Places]

9

10

11

12

13

14

9.   A Tuvan church in Kyzyll, Tuva, Russia. [Nancy Sturrock]

10. One temple in a land of ten thousand temples, Myanmar. [Nancy Sturrock]

11. The world's largest idol: the 520 metre (1,705 feet) high bronze Buddha at Po Lin Monastery on Lantau Island, Hong Kong.

12. The amazing Shwedagon Pagoda complex in Yangon (Rangoon), Myanmar. [Create International]   [International Mission Board]

13. Tad Luang temple complex in Vientiane, Laos. [Xayographix]

14. Typical Burmese-style temples in Myanmar. [Xayographix]

15. One of the many temples in Durbar Square in Kathmandu, Nepal. [Paul Hattaway]
16. Typical Newari architecture around the window of a house in Bhaktapur, Nepal. [David Treat]
17. Resident monks of a monastery in Muli County in Sichuan, China. [China Advocate]

CHINA
Xizang (Tibet)

INDIA

Za

Population:
500 (2000)
610 (2010)
750 (2020)
Countries: China
Buddhism: Tibetan
Christians: none known

Overview of the Za

Other Names: Deng Za, Zayu

Population Sources:

500 in China (2000, P Hattaway)

Language: Sino-Tibetan, Tibeto-Burman, Unclassified

Dialects: 0

Professing Buddhists: 100%

Practising Buddhists: 55%

Christians: 0%

Scripture: none

Jesus film: none

Gospel Recordings: none

Christian Broadcasting: none

ROPAL code: none

Status of Evangelization

98%

2%   0%

A   B   C

A = Have never heard the gospel
B = Have heard the gospel but have not become Christians
C = Are adherents to some form of Christianity

Approximately 500 people belonging to an ethnic group called the Za live in a remote area of south-eastern Tibet. The Za, who were originally a collection of tribal peoples including relatives of today's Geman Deng people, live between Xiachayu and the Wanong Valley in Zayu County. Very few foreigners have ever ventured into this extremely remote part of China.

The Za ethnic group is one of the most fascinating examples of ethnic fusion in China today. The ancestors of the Za are believed to have been the same as today's Geman Deng people, but Tibetan political and religious leaders entered the area about 200 years ago and exerted their influence over the people there. The result is a new ethnic group that the Tibetans call Za, who speak a distinct language from the Deng and who practise different customs. The Za were not counted under any official nationality in the 1990 China census but instead were included in a list of 'Undetermined Minorities'.

Chinese linguist Sun Hongkai, who visited the Za in 1976, wrote, 'Today the Za people only use their own language at home; outside the home they use Tibetan. The language that they use at home is about 60 per cent Tibetan loanwords, and the grammar is also basically Tibetan. Recent Geman Deng immigrants into this area can only understand about 30 per cent of the speech of the Za people. . . . Two hundred years of language contact, because of political, economic, cultural and religious dominance, caused one language to be heavily influenced by another and gradually lose its unique characteristics. In the recognition and comparison of this type of language we see how social factors play a crucial role in the process of language change in contact situations. Za is an

unclassified part of the Tibeto-Burman language family.'[1]

Two hundred years ago, the Tibetans entered this area and set up a combined rule of government and religion, and subsequently the original inhabitants of the area slowly became Tibetanized. The Tibetans ruled the Za with an iron fist. The Za were not even allowed to travel outside the area without prior permission of the monk or administrator. Today, the Za have changed from the Geman Deng so much that they deserve to be viewed as a distinct ethnolinguistic group.[2]

China Advocate

The Za have lost the use of all of their original customs and festivals; these are still practised by Geman Deng people who lived outside the influence of Tibetan rule. Culturally, the Za have become identical to the Tibetans. The forefathers of the Za people were polytheists, worshiping nature and a host of spirits. When the Tibetans took over the area long ago, however, they converted the Za to the Tibetan Buddhist religion.

Christianity has yet to make its presence felt in the isolated part of Tibet inhabited by the Za. Few roads led into the area until recently. Contact between the Za and the outside world is now possible. Today, the Za remain unaware of the existence of Christianity and are a completely unreached people group.

Zakhring

CHINA Xizang (Tibet)

INDIA
Arunachal Pradesh

MYANMAR

Zakhring

Population:
320 (2000)
380 (2010)
440 (2020)
Countries: India
Buddhism: Tibetan
Christians: none known

Overview of the Zakhring

Other Names: Meyor, Charumba

Population Sources:

249 in India (1981 census)

Language: Sino-Tibetan, Tibeto-Burman, Unclassified

Dialects: 2 (Lower Zyphe, Upper Zyphe)

Professing Buddhists: 100%

Practising Buddhists: 100%

Christians: 0%

Scripture: none

Jesus film: none

Gospel Recordings: none

Christian Broadcasting: none

ROPAL code: ZKR

Status of Evangelization

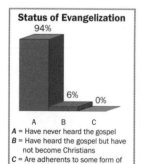

94%

6%

0%

A   B   C

A = Have never heard the gospel
B = Have heard the gospel but have not become Christians
C = Are adherents to some form of Christianity

Much confusion surrounds the tiny, little-known Zakhring tribe of north-east India. They inhabit the hilly terrain and the banks of the Lohit River in the Walong and Kibithoo area (Hayuliang Subdivision) of the Lohit District in Arunachal Pradesh.

The 1981 census returned a figure of just 14 Zakhring people. However, 235 additional people identified themselves under the ethnic name 'Meyor', which is a synonym for the Zakhring. Together, then, the total population for this group was 249. In the years since the 1981 census the population for the Zakhring is thought to have surpassed 300. To further complicate their identification, various sources note that neither Zakhring nor Meyor is the name these people use for themselves. In their own language they call themselves Charumba.

Regardless of their small size and the multiplicity of names, the Indian government has granted official status to this group as a Scheduled Tribe, under the name Zakhring.

Scholar Dutta Choudhury says the Zakhring arrived from the north (Tibet) in two waves of migration—the first in the late 1800s and the second wave a few years later in the early 1900s.[1] These two separate migrations may explain why such a small group of a few hundred people speak two distinct dialects, which the *Ethnologue* labels Lower Zyphe and Upper Zyphe.[2] When they first arrived in the Lohit District they 'had to face bitter opposition from the Mishmis. However, the Zakhring migrants overcame the opposition and settled in and around Walong.'[3]

The Zakhring enjoy close relationships with the Tibetans and Monpa, and intermarriage with these groups is encouraged. Many Tibetan refugees live nearby. In both the 1971 and 1981 censuses, 100 per cent of Zakhring people declared themselves to be followers of Buddhism. Zakhring art reflects their origins in Tibet and their faith in Tibetan Buddhism. The Zakhring 'paint scrolls and murals, make wooden images of Buddha and produce some hand painted wooden objects and masks'.[4]

Elements of the pre-Buddhist Bon religion seem to have been retained by the Zakhring. 'The Zakhring's Buddhism is tinged with beliefs in animism and shamanism. Their shamanistic priest is known as *kahu* who practises witchcraft. He is often called in to cure a person suffering from a disease. Besides Lord Buddha and the Bodhistatvas, the Zakhrings also have a community deity or village deity known as *Yong* or the deity of the hills. Thus each village has a separate *Yong*.'[5]

The tiny Zakhring tribe must rank as one of the most unreached Buddhist people groups in the world. They are isolated in a small area that has little or no access to gospel witness. There has never been a known Christian among the Zakhring. One Christian source states, 'They are a small and insignificant tribe mostly dependent on others. They do not have a Bible nor literature of their own. They are in need of development.'[6]

Dwayne Graybill

According to the India Missions Association, 28,099 Zangskari people live in one of the most remote and harshest areas of the world, in the north Indian state of Jammu and Kashmir.[1] The Zangskaris dwell between the Himalayas and the Indus River Valley. The Zangskari homeland is located between the Ladakhi people and the Purik people. Another source gives a much lower figure of just 8,000 to 10,000 speakers of the Zangskari language.[2] A small number of Zangskaris may also live across the border into Tibet. This is almost impossible to verify, due to the simple fact there is no set border between the two countries. Each claims significant tracts of territory as their own, and the inhabitants of the region wander about as they please without any restrictions.

The Zangskar area is a ruggedly attractive desert landscape with minimal rainfall throughout the year. Farmers must water their crops from melted snow and river water. The winters are long and difficult, with temperatures plummeting to minus 30 degrees Celcius (–22°F) for weeks on end, bringing a halt to all travel and communications.

Zangskar is virtually untouched by the modern world, isolated by a ring of high peaks. The lowest pass in the area is the Pensi La at 4,418 metres (14,500 ft.).

Many ethnolinguistic sources combine the Zangskari people together with the Ladakhi and do not acknowledge their distinctiveness. The Indian government has done this, not granting official status to the Zangskaris. Although culturally and religiously the two groups are basically the same, in the areas of language and history the two are different. One source states, 'The Zangskari people are independent and proud and by their geographical situation quite separate from the rest of Ladakh, with their own royal family—the local King of Pandum and Zangla.'[3]

Linguistically the Zangskari language is closer to the Champa language than to Ladakhi.[4] The Zangskaris use the Tibetan script for religious and secular purposes. The original inhabitants of Zangskar were the Mon people, an Indo-European group who today only number in the hundreds. In the past they dominated Zangskar. When A H Francke visited Zangskar in the late 1800s he reported, 'Zangskar was once entirely in the hands of the Mons. The ruins of their old castles are still called "Mon-castles". Then the country was conquered by the Tibetans, and remained a Tibetan country until the Mons came back about seventy years ago and reconquered it. . . . Among the ruins of the settlements of the ancient Mons of Zangskar I discovered imposing remains of ancient Buddhist art, and more and more the conviction grew upon me that the settlement must have had some connection with the pre-Lamaist Buddhism.'[5]

Today the Zangskari people remain overwhelmingly Buddhist.[6] There are no known Christians among them. Portions of the Bible were translated into the Zangskari language in 1945, but these have been out of print since 1951. Little has changed over the centuries. Most Zangskari people are still waiting to hear the gospel for the first time.

Population:
28,099 (2000)
32,750 (2010)
38,200 (2020)
Countries: India, possibly China
Buddhism: Tibetan
Christians: none known

Overview of the Zangskari

Other Names: Zanskari, Zaskari

Population Sources:
28,099 in India (2001, India Missions Association)
possibly also in China

Language: Sino-Tibetan, Tibeto-Burman, Himalayish, Tibeto-Kanauri, Tibetic, Tibetan, Western

Dialects: 0

Professing Buddhists: 90%

Practising Buddhists: 70%

Christians: 0%

Scripture: Portions 1945

Jesus film: none

Gospel Recordings: none

Christian Broadcasting: none

ROPAL code: ZAU

Photo credit: Julian Hawken

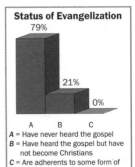

Status of Evangelization
79%
21%
0%

A   B   C

A = Have never heard the gospel
B = Have heard the gospel but have not become Christians
C = Are adherents to some form of Christianity

Zhaba

A 1983 source listed 15,000 people belonging to the Zhaba ethnolinguistic group in China.[1] They live in parts of Yajiang and Daofu counties within the vast Garze Tibetan Autonomous Prefecture in western Sichuan Province. The area was originally part of Kham Province in Tibet until the Chinese annexed it. One source states, 'The Zhaba live a hard life in a land of fast winding rivers and high mountains. Most of the Zhaba live along the Xianshui River that flows from Daofu to Yajiang.'[2]

The main centre is Zhaba township in southern Daofu County. The town, which boasts a population of 5,200, has had no electricity or telephone lines since 1997, when the government banned logging because of environmental concerns. The logging industry had been extremely profitable, so when the companies pulled out, the electricity and phone lines were unplugged too.

Although the Zhaba are culturally Tibetans, their language is part of the Qiangic branch of Tibeto-Burman, totally unintelligible to surrounding Tibetans. When Marco Polo passed through rural Tibetan areas in the 13th century he found unique local customs. Polo wrote, 'No man of that country would on any consideration take to wife a girl who was a maid; for they say a wife is worth nothing unless she has been used to consort with men. . . . When travellers come that way, the old women of the place get ready, and take their unmarried daughters . . . to whomsoever will accept them. . . . In this manner people travelling in that way

. . . shall find perhaps 20 or 30 girls at their disposal.'[3] Promiscuity continues to be rife among the Zhaba. A 1950s survey of the Garze area found the rate of venereal diseases was 40 per cent among people in peasant areas and 50.7 per cent among people living in the pasture areas.[4]

Most people in the area acknowledge that the Zhaba were the original inhabitants. 'They say they came to this area after being defeated in the Mongol wars in northern China.'[5] Throughout history their society has been matriarchal. Today, 'in some of the distant villages the women still have control over the family, with the father taking care of his sister's children, not his own. When a couple wants to get married, it is not the fathers who discuss the potential marriage, but the brothers of the mothers of the prospective bride and groom.'[6]

The Zhaba worship a wide variety of demons and ghosts. These influences date back to the pre-Buddhist Tibetan religion of Bon. Today the Zhaba's religion continues to be a mixture of Buddhism and Bon. 'There is a Bon temple just north of Zhaba town, which has three groups using the monastery, 30 monks being there at any given time. Every Zhaba village has a temple and its own Holy Mountain where the villagers go to worship on special holidays.'[7]

There are no known Christians among the Zhaba, although there are a few Tibetan Catholics further west near Litang.

Population:
20,900 (2000)
25,750 (2010)
31,700 (2020)
Countries: China
Buddhism: Tibetan
Christians: none known

Overview of the Zhaba

Other Names: Zaba, Zhaboa, Buozi

Population Sources:
15,000 in China (1983, Sun Hongkai)

Language: Sino-Tibetan, Tibeto-Burman, Tangut-Qiang, Qiangic

Dialects: 2 (Western Zhaba, Eastern Zhaba)

Professing Buddhists: 100%

Practising Buddhists: 85%

Christians: 0%

Scripture: none

Jesus **film:** none

Gospel Recordings: none

Christian Broadcasting: none

ROPAL code: ZHA

Photo credit: China Advocate

Status of Evangelization

98%

2%

0%

A   B   C

A = Have never heard the gospel
B = Have heard the gospel but have not become Christians
C = Are adherents to some form of Christianity

Notes to the Profiles

Aiton

1. Cited in Barbara F Grimes, *Ethnologue: Languages of the World* (14th edn, CD-ROM version, 2000).
2. K S Singh ed., *India's Communities: A–G* (People of India IV; Delhi: Oxford University Press and Anthropological Survey of India, 1998) 72.
3. See G C Sharma Tahkur, *The Plain Tribes of Lakhimpur, Dibrugarh, Sibsagar and Nowgong* (Gauhati: Tribal Research Department, Government of Assam, 1972).
4. Singh, *India's Communities: A–G*, 73.

Amdo, Hbrogpa

1. Australian Academy of the Humanities and the Chinese Academy of Social Sciences, *Language Atlas of China: C–11* (Hong Kong: Longman Group, 1987) describes each of the four main Amdo language groups profiled in this volume as 'vernaculars'. Grimes describes them as dialects, but notes 'those listed as dialects may not be intelligible with each other'. See Grimes, *Ethnologue* (13th edn, 1996) 540. In the author's opinion, after field surveys in 1995 and 1996, the four main identified Amdo languages are definitely mutually unintelligible, with dozens of additional dialects spoken across the vast Amdo region. The four main languages listed here can at best be described as the common trade languages spoken in four main geographical regions. There is a lack of reliable linguistic research conducted in the Amdo area. Detailed research could reveal many more mutually unintelligible languages spoken among the Amdo. Jackson Tianshin Sun, 'Review of Zangmian Yu Yuyin Han Cohui [Tibeto-Burman Phonology and Vocabularies]', *Linguistics of the Tibeto-Burman Area* 15.2 (1992) 73–113, has studied and classified 23 Amdo dialects, including Golog varieties. Most of the names are based on locations.
2. David Bradley, 'East and South-East Asia', in *A World of Language: Papers Presented to Professor S. A. Wurm on His 65th Birthday* (ed. Donald Laycock and Werner Winter; Canberra: The Australian National University, 1987) 170.
3. The Amdo groups live in Huangnan, Hainan, Haibei and Haixi prefectures in Qinghai Province; in Gannan Prefecture and Tianzhu County of south-western Gansu Province; and in parts of the Aba and Ganzhi prefectures in northern Sichuan Province.
4. Vanya Kewley, *Tibet: Behind the Ice Curtain* (London: Grafton Books, 1990) 392.
5. There are several large Bon monasteries in the Gansu-Qinghai border area, including the towns of Tongren and Xiahe. Bon monks are allowed to marry, and they circle temples in a counter-clockwise direction, unlike Tibetan Buddhists.
6. Milton T Stauffer ed., *The Christian Occupation of China* (Shanghai: China Consultation Committee, 1922) 281.
7. Ibid.
8. Douglas Allen, 'Tibet: The Continuing Story', *China and the Church Today* (February 1986) 14–15. Even though this article states that the believers were Amdo Tibetans, it is possible this event occurred among the Jone Tibetans in southern Gansu Province (see the *Tibetan, Jone* profile below).
9. Ralph Covell, *The Liberating Gospel in China: The Christian Faith Among China's Minority Peoples* (Grand Rapids: Baker Books, 1995) 80.
10. *Pray for China* (Hong Kong: Christian Communications Ltd., April 1996).

Amdo, Rongba

1. Australian Academy and CASS, *Language Atlas of China*, C-11.
2. It is important to note that even though the name 'Rongba' has socio-economic connotations, this group, and the other Amdo groups profiled, have been included because of linguistic differences. This book attempts to deal only with those Buddhist groups who are ethnically and/or linguistically distinct.
3. *Beijing Review*, 27 June 1983.
4. Marku Tsering, *Sharing Christ in the Tibetan Buddhist World* (Pennsylvania: Tibet Press, 1988) 49.

Amdo, Rongmahbrogpa

1. Australian Academy and CASS, *Language Atlas of China*, C-11.
2. A good linguistic survey of the Rongmahbrogpa Amdo language is: Charlene Makley, Keith Dede, Hua Kan and Wang Qingshan, 'The Amdo Dialect of Labrang', *Linguistics of the Tibeto-Burman Area* 22.1 (1999) 97–127.
3. Li Wuzi, 'Monks and Nuns at the Labrang Monastery', *China Tourism* 229 (August 1999) 22.
4. Joseph F Rock, 'Seeking the Mountains of Mystery', *National Geographic* (February 1930) 143–44. On a trip to Xiahe in 1995, the author observed that there was still a simmering tension between the Amdo and Hui. The Amdo were incensed at the plans of the Hui to build a large mosque, which would have been higher than the monastery roof. The Amdo threatened to smash the mosque to the ground if the Muslims proceeded with the construction.
5. Tsering, *Sharing Christ in the Tibetan Buddhist World*, 52.
6. Stauffer, *The Christian Occupation of China*, 281.

Amdo, Rtahu

1. Grimes, *Ethnologue* (13th edn, 1996) 540.
2. Bradley, 'East and South-East Asia', 170.
3. Buckley and Strauss, *Tibet*, 9.
4. Ibid., 25.
5. Stauffer, *The Christian Occupation of China*, 281.

Angku

1. Global Evangelization Movement (GEM), 'World's Peoples Listed by Country, Part 1', unpublished report (1995).
2. S A Wurm and Shiro Hattori eds., *Language Atlas of the Pacific Area* (Canberra: The Australian Institute of the Humanities and the Japan Academy, 1981) list a 1981 figure of 1,000 Kiorr in Laos. The Kiorr are also known as the Con.
3. James S Olson, *An Ethnohistorical Dictionary of China* (Westport, CT: Greenwood Press, 1998) 168.
4. Grimes, *Ethnologue* (11th edn, 1988) 446.
5. Inez de Beauclair, *An Introduction to the Southwestern Peoples of China* (Chengdu: West China Union University, 1945) 9.
6. Olson, *An Ethnohistorical Dictionary of China*, 168.

Bai

1. According to the 1990 Chinese census, there were 88 counties or municipalities in China that recorded more than 500 Bai people. In descending order, the largest are: Dali (Yunnan) 281,730; Eryuan (Yunnan) 198,196; Heqing (Yunnan) 138,397;

Jianchuan (Yunnan) 137,689; Yunlong (Yunnan) 136,917; Sangzhi (Hunan) 92,755; Lanping (Yunnan) 81,243; Binchuan (Yunnan) 40,940; Dafang (Guizhou) 37,536.

2. According to Li Shao-ni, as cited in Stuart Milliken, 'SIL China Nationalities and Languages Files' (unpublished research paper, Guangzhou, 1993).

3. David Y H Wu, 'Culture Change and Ethnic Identity Among Minorities in China', 16, in Chiao Chien and Nicholas Tapp, eds., *Ethnicity and Ethnic Groups in China* (Hong Kong: The Chinese University of Hong Kong, 1989).

4. John Kuhn, *We Found a Hundred Tribes* (London: CIM, 1945) 12.

5. Wu, 'Culture Change and Ethnic Identity', 15.

6. Martin M C Yang, 'Peoples and Societies in Yunnan (Part I)', *Journal of Ethnology and Sociology* 16 (Taipei, 1978) 21–112.

7. Robert Ramsey explains the enigma of the Bai language: 'The language that they speak has not been shown to be related to any other. It has elements that look like Tibeto-Burman; others that look like Tai or Mon-Khmer; and some tantalizing ones that look like Chinese on several levels. But none of these prove a genetic affinity. Who then are the Bai? . . . In the PRC the Bai are classed as a Tibeto-Burman people, and their language is put into the Yi branch of that language family. This classification is premature. It is still not known what, if any, language family Bai belongs to, much less what branch.' Robert S Ramsey, *The Languages of China* (Princeton: Princeton University Press, 1987) 290.

8. David Wu, 'Culture Change and Ethnic Identity', 17.

9. Grimes, *Ethnologue* (13th edn, 1996) 541.

10. Himsey Hui, 'The Bai', *China and the Church Today* (October 1985) 15.

11. 'Ethnic Groups in Yunnan', *Bridge* (September–October 1990).

12. *Chinese Prayer Letter and Ministry Report (CPLMR)* 119 (December 1991–February 1992).

13. See *World Pulse*, 19 April 1996.

14. Kuhn, *We Found a Hundred Tribes*, 12–13.

Baragaunle

1. Grimes, *Ethnologue* (14th edn, 2000).

2. Tamla Ukyab and Shyam Adhikari, *The Nationalities of Nepal* (Kathmandu: Ministry of Local Development National Committee for Development of Nationalities, 2000) 10.

3. Grimes, *Ethnologue* (14th edn, 2000).

4. Two excellent articles on the Mustang region are: Michel Peissel, 'Mustang: Remote Realm in Nepal', *National Geographic* (October 1965) 579–604; and Galen Rowell, 'Annapurna: Sanctuary for the Himalaya', *National Geographic* (September 1989) 391–405.

5. Hugh Finlay, Richard Everist and Tony Wheeler, *Nepal: A Lonely Planet Travel Survival Kit* (Hawthorn, Australia: Lonely Planet Publications, 1997) 378.

6. Ukyab and Adhikari, *The Nationalities of Nepal,* 10.

7. Dor Bahadue Bista, *The People of Nepal* (Kathmandu: Ratna Pustak Bhandar, 1972) 192.

Barua

1. K S Singh ed., *Tripura* (People of India XLI; Calcutta: Seagull Books and Anthropological Survey of India, 1996) 50.

2. Singh, *India's Communities: A–G*, 314.

3. Dharmadhar Mahasthabir, *Saddharmer Panarutthan* (Calcutta: Das Brothers, 1371, repr. n.d.) 17.

4. Singh, *India's Communities: A–G*, 315.

5. Ibid.

Beda

1. Sachchidananda R R Prasad ed., *Encyclopaedic Profile of Indian Tribes*, I (New Delhi: Discovery Publishing House, 1998) 82.

2. Singh, *India's Communities: A–G*, 344.

3. Prasad, *Encyclopaedic Profile of Indian Tribes,* 82.

4. See H A Rose ed., *Glossary of the Tribes and Castes of the Punjab and North-West Frontier Province* (Lahore: Civil and Military Gazette Press, 1919) 345.

5. Prasad, *Encyclopaedic Profile of Indian Tribes,* 83.

6. Stauffer, *The Christian Occupation of China*, 278.

Bonan, Tongren

1. *Mission Frontiers* (April 1995).

2. Buliash Todaeva, 'Einige Besonderheiten

der Paoan-Sprache', *Acta Orientalia Hungaricae* 16 (1963) 175–97.

3. Henry G Schwartz, *The Minorities of Northern China: A Survey* (Bellingham: Western Washington University Press, 1984) 139.

4. See Christoph Baumer, 'Archaic Shaman Dance of Tongren', *China Tourism* 243 (October 2000) 54–59.

5. Olson, *An Ethnohistorical Dictionary of China*, 31.

6. Stauffer, *The Christian Occupation of China*, 266.

7. See Covell, *The Liberating Gospel*, 75.

Brokpa

1. George van Driem, *Languages of the Himalayas*, II (Leiden: Brill, 2001) 871.

2. Ibid., 867.

3. Personal report from SP Prayer Network, Australia.

4. Van Driem, *Languages of the Himalayas*, II, 867.

Brokpa, Brokkat

1. Van Driem, *Languages of the Himalayas*, II, 867.

2. Stan Armington, Bhutan (Hawthorn, Australia: Lonely Planet Publications, 1998) 206.

3. Van Driem, *Languages of the Himalayas*, II, 867.

4. Ibid.

Bulang

1. An interesting Chinese government publication on the Bulang people is put out by the Editing Group of Yunnan Province, *Investigation of the Society and History of the Bulang Minority* (3 vols; Kunming: Yunnan People's Publishing House, 1986). Also see Wang Guoxiang, *The Bulangs, Flowers, Love Songs and Girls* (Kunming: Yunnan Education Publishing House, 1995).

2. The main Bulang village in Thailand is called Ban Huewy Khun in Mae Sai District of Chiang Rai Province. The second main location is in Ban Lua Pattana in Mae Chan District.

3. The Bulang language has been comprehensively studied. Some of the linguistic papers available include Karen L Block, 'Discourse Grammar of First Person Narrative in Plang', University of Texas (Arlington, 1994); Block, 'What Makes a Story in Plang?', *Mon-Khmer Studies* 26 (1996); and Debbie Paulsen, 'A

Phonological Reconstruction of Proto-Plang', *Mon-Khmer Studies* 18–19 (1992).

4. Grimes, *Ethnologue* (14th edn, 2000).
5. Hattaway, *Operation China*, 90.
6. Joachim Schliesinger, *Ethnic Groups of Thailand: Non-Tai-Speaking Peoples* (Bangkok: White Lotus Press, 2000) 114.
7. *CPLMR* 119 (December 1991–February 1992).
8. The Bulang are recognized as an official minority group in China, and their population in the 1990 census was given as 82,280. This figure includes several smaller groups (Angku, Puman, Kong Ge and Samtao) that have distinct ethnic identities and speak languages that are similar to, yet different from, Pulang. The population of these groups was subtracted when I made my estimate for the Bulang in China (see Paul Hattaway, *Operation China: Introducing All the Peoples of China* [Carlisle: Piquant Publishing, 2000] 90).

Bumthang

1. Van Driem, *Languages of the Himalayas*, II, 908.
2. Ibid., 910. See pp 908–10 for a more comprehensive analysis of the Bumthang language.
3. Grimes, *Ethnologue* (14th edn, 2000).
4. Armington, *Bhutan*, 216.

Buriat, China

1. Juha Janhunen and Tapani Salminen, *UNESCO Red Book on Endangered Languages: Northeast Asia* (Helsinki, Finland: University of Helsinki, 1996).
2. Slaviska Missionen, *Pray for Us* prayer booklet (Stockholm, 1995).
3. Issachar Frontier Missions Research, *Mongolia Challenge Report: A Summary of Current Spiritual Needs and a Strategy for Response* (Seattle, WA: Issachar, 1984) II, 2, i.
4. Ibid.
5. Kang Jie, 'The Buryats from Siberia', *China Tourism* 83 (n.d.) 30.
6. Slaviska Missionen, *Pray for Us*.

Buriat, Mongolia

1. Bethany World Prayer Center, 'The Northern Mongolian of Mongolia'.
2. Olson, *An Ethnohistorical Dictionary of China*, 37.
3. Bethany World Prayer Center, 'The

Northern Mongolian of Mongolia'.
4. Tsering, *Sharing Christ in the Tibetan Buddhist World*, 7.

Buriat, Russia

1. See K V Vyatkina, 'The Buryats', in M G Levin and L P Potapov eds., *The Peoples of Siberia* (Chicago: University of Chicago Press, 1964) 203–42.
2. See Don Belt, 'The World's Great Lake', *National Geographic* (June 1992) 2–40; and Pyotr Zubkhov, 'Buryatia: A Republic on Lake Baikal', *Soviet Life* 378 (1988) 41–46.
3. 'The Buryats', prayer brochure published anonymously (c.2000).
4. See Ross Marlay, 'Buryats', in James S Olson, Lee Brigance Pappas and Nicholas C J Pappas eds., *Ethnohistorical Dictionary of the Soviet and Russian Empires* (Westport, CT: Greenwood Press, 1994).
5. Anonymous, 'The Buryats'.
6. 'Buriat-Mongolian Mission, Siberia', *The Evangelical Magazine and Missionary Chronicle* 11 (July 1883) 328–31.
7. William Swan, *Missionary Magazine* (October 1937) 499–500.
8. Marshall Broomhall, *The Bible in China* (London: CIM, 1934) 128–29. The script used in this original Buriat translation is now obsolete, and a new translation work is in progress.
9. William Swan, *Letters on Missions* (Boston: Perkins and Marvin, 1831) 179, as cited in Covell, *The Liberating Gospel*, 119. It is worth paraphrasing here an excellent 1876 summary of the mission among the Buriat. This comes from an article entitled 'Traces of the Old Buriat Mission', *Chinese Recorder* 7.2 (March–April 1876) 81–90: 'A mission among the Buriats, a Mongolian tribe living under the authority of Russia, was commenced by the Rev. E. Stallybrass and the Rev. W. Swan, who left England in the year 1817–18. The mission was established first at the town of Selinginsk, and afterwards also on the Ona; but in 1841 the emperor Nicholas broke up the mission, and the missionaries retired from the field. . . . The missionaries were not Russians, and lived not in the ameliorated Siberia of today, but in the old dismal Siberia of half a century ago. To be in Siberia then, was to be pretty well out of the world; and for Englishmen and Scotchmen to be there, meant a degree of isolation and solitariness that must have been hard to bear.

No telegraphs then, and postal facilities were very meager. They were foreigners in a strange land, looked on with suspicion by the government, the ecclesiastics, and the people; and above all were utterly beyond the range of Christian sympathy. And there they were year after year, learning the language, translating the Scriptures, preaching the gospel, and instructing the ignorant adults and children. They had gone to Siberia—not to seek to bring them over from the faith of the Greek Church—but to seek the conversion of the Buddhistic Buriats; so remembering their aim, they removed themselves as much as possible from the Russian inhabitants; and surrounded themselves with, and sought friendships among the Buriats. This was severing the last link that bound them to the civilized world, and rendering their isolation pretty nearly complete. . . . A strange spectacle were those missionaries in Siberia, to the Russians who dwelt in the various towns. The Russians could not understand them, and seem never to have been weary of talking about them, and wondering and laughing at them. . . . When a few people could be assembled, something like a service would be held; when only individuals could be got at, conversation was used. Schools too were established, with the hope of raising up an instructed, and if possible Christian generation. But the great work which they ever returned to, as their other missionary duties permitted them, was the translation of the Bible into the language of the Buriats. But this was no light task for two men to accomplish; but they did complete it, and printed and published the Old Testament in Siberia. Russia, it seems, had let the missionaries go on unmolested till they were beginning to be successful, and then she stopped them. The ecclesiastics in Siberia are generally supposed to be the real cause of the suspension of the mission. . . . What argument was advanced against the continuance of the mission perhaps cannot now be known, but one thing can be mentioned, which may have something to do with it. Even a quarter of a century after the missionaries left Siberia, all converts were spoken of as belonging to the English, or rather as being Englishmen. The converts

themselves knew better; but the mass of the people, Russians and Buriats, seem to have regarded conversion to Christianity as a desertion of Russia and a going over to England. . . .
It may be asked then, what did all the zeal, labour, and ability of the old missionaries accomplish? The answer is—a score also of converts, the translation of the Bible, and an indefinite moral influence. As to the converts, some remain to this present day members of the Greek Church, and apparently good, warm-hearted, intelligent Christians. As to the original number, perhaps they were not so many as 20; perhaps there were more. But even though there were a few more than the larger number, that were a small harvest to reap after 20 years' labor of two or three men. The translation of the Bible into the Mongolian language, opened up the sealed Book of the Scriptures to the Buriats of Siberia and to the Mongols of Mongolia. No small result this. The translation is not by any means perfect, partaking of the imperfections of all first versions of the Bible in any language; but the work has been well understood in Siberia, and, for the most part, quite serviceable in the various regions of Mongolia and the Chinese Empire.'

10. Patrick Johnstone and Jason Mandryk, *Operation World: When We Pray God Works* (Carlisle: Paternoster Lifestyle, 2001) 549.

Burmese

1. The most recent census in Burma/Myanmar was conducted in 1931 by the British colonial rulers. At that time, the Burmese numbered 8,596,031. See Colin Metcalf Dallas Enriquez, *Races of Burma* (Delhi: Indian Government Manager of Publications, 1933) 126.
2. The Burmese in Bangladesh speak *Bomang*, a different dialect from the standard Burmese spoken in Myanmar.
3. Buddhism among the Burmese is mixed with *nat*, or spirit-worship. See Y Rodrigue, *Nat-Pwe: Burma's Supernatural Sub-Culture* (Edinburgh: Kiscadale, 1992); M Spiro, *Burmese Supernaturalism* (Englewood Cliffs, NJ: Prentice-Hall, 1967); and Sir R C Temple, *The Thirty-seven Nats: A Phase of Spirit-Worship Prevailing in Burma* (London: W Griggs, 1906).

4. A superb coffee-table type pictorial book on the peoples of Myanmar is Richard K Diran, *The Vanishing Tribes of Burma* (London: Weidenfeld and Nicolson, 1997).
5. Remarkably, Judson's 1835 translation of the Bible is still the most used and loved translation in Myanmar today.
6. Edward Judson, *The Life of Adoniram Judson* (New York: Anson D Randolph, 1883) 150.
7. Maung Shwe Wa, *Burma Baptist Chronicle* (Rangoon: Burma Baptist Convention, 1963) 135.
8. Also: 7,105 in India (2003, Joshua Project II); 3,014 in Cambodia (2003, Joshua Project II); 557 in Sri Lanka (2003, Joshua Project II); 500 in Germany (2003, Joshua Project II); 416 in Laos (1995 census); also in many other nations around the world.

Chak

1. Taken from the www.icbl.org website.
2. See Khine Tun Shwe, *A Guide to Mrauk-U: An Ancient City of Rakhine* (Myanmar, 1993).
3. Michael Clark and Joe Cummings, *Myanmar (Burma)* (Hawthorn, Australia: Lonely Planet Publications, 2000) 432.
4. Ibid., 433.

Chakma

1. 'The Chittagong Hill Tracts (CHT) had a chequered history. In 1895 at the time of the redemarcation of areas among the different authorities (Assam, Bengal and Burma) a part of the CHT was sliced out and added to Lushai Hills of Assam from Bengal and as a result the size and area of the CHT was reduced from 5419 sq. miles to 5093 sq. miles. As a consequence, the Chakma inhabitants in the transferred land became the inhabitants of Lushai Hills in Assam' (Prasad, *Encyclopaedic Profile of Indian Tribes*, I, 161).
2. See Singh, *Tripura*, 112–17.
3. Grimes, *Ethnologue* (14th edn, 2000) cites a 1987 population from ABWE (Association of Baptists for World Evangelism) of 300,000 Chakma in India, and 560,000 total in both countries, but other sources do not agree with such a high figure for Chakma in India.
4. 1981 census figure.
5. Two early books on the Chittagong Hill Tracts were written by Thomas

Lewin when the area was under British colonial rule and considered part of British India. See Thomas Herbert Lewin, *The Hill Tracts of Chittagong and the Dwellers Therein: With Comparative Vocabularies of the Hill Dialects* (Calcutta: Bengal Press, 1869); and *Hill Proverbs of the Inhabitants of the Chittagong Hill Tracts* (Calcutta: Bengal Secretariat Press, 1873). Another interesting early book is Emil Riebeck, *The Chittagong Hill-Tribes: Results of a Journey Made in the Year 1882* (trans. A H Keane; London: Asher and Co., 1885).
6. Van Driem, *Languages of the Himalayas*, II, 570.
7. Richard S Ehrlich, 'Far from World's Eyes, Religious War Rages in Bangladesh', *Washington Times* (26 May 1987).
8. See S P Talukdar, *The Chakmas: Life and Struggle* (Delhi: Gian Publishing House, 1988). The Bengalis have tried to forcibly convert the Chakma to Islam. One monk recalls what happened in 1986 when Chakma in Panchari were attacked simply because they were not Muslims: 'One day 13 of us went to market. . . . The Bangladesh Rifles (paramilitary force) and settlers caught us and out of 13, nine were killed and four of us escaped. The reason was that we were not Muslims; they wanted us to be Muslims to take Islam. It was in the market itself and some of the people were also caught up from around. Among the people whom they caught was my wife. They cut her with *daos* (machete)—some of the marks on her neck are still there. . . . They also tried to cut me with *daos* on the neck. Luckily my shirt collar was thick and I escaped from being killed. As they killed the others they shouted: 'Oh Chakmas, will you not become Muslims? If you refuse we will kill you now.' A Buddhist monk from the temple at Kalanal described to Amnesty International the persistent harassment of the Jumma villagers by the military personnel and the settlers: 'For many months now soldiers have been regularly visiting us and slaughtering cows in our shrine. . . . They always said that if we did not agree to this (conversion to Islam) they would come one day and kill us. On the morning of 1 May they carried out their threat by escorting a group of

two to three hundred settlers, some of whom were dressed in the uniform of home guards, to our village and began their depredations by attacking Buddha Vihar (the temple). Most of us were, however, able to flee but soldiers pounced on Purnananda Bhikku (one of the monks) and after beating him with rifle butts handed him over to the Muslims who threw him into the shrine which was by now on fire. He died. Later when I met more people from my village they said that two young girls of the village had been raped mercilessly by troops and Muslims and then killed with bayonets.' For more information, see www.angelfire.com/ab/jumma/religion.html.

9. K S Singh, *The Scheduled Tribes* (People of India III; Calcutta: Oxford University Press, Anthropological Survey of India, 1997) 204. See also P C Basu, 'The Social and Religious Ceremonies of the Chakma', *Journal and Proceedings of the Asiatic Society of Bengal* 27.2 (1931) 213–23.

10. Indian Research Teams, *Peoples of India: Christian Presence and Works Among Them* (India Missions Association, May 1997) 88.

Chali

1. Van Driem, *Languages of the Himalayas*, II, 913–14.
2. Ibid., 914.
3. Armington, *Bhutan*, 13.

Champa

1. The Champa were mentioned in the 1926 article by E von Eickstedt, 'The Races and Types of Western and Central Himalayas', *Man in India* (June 1926) 237–76.
2. Singh, *The Scheduled Tribes*, 206–7.
3. Ibid., 207–8.
4. Prasad, *Encyclopaedic Profile of Indian Tribes*, I, 171.

Chaungtha

1. Grimes, *Ethnologue* (14th edn, 2000).
2. Myanmar Faces and Places, Chaungtha profile, unpublished, 2003.
3. Enriquez, *Races of Burma*, 127.
4. Taken from the Chaungtha profile on the www.seamist.org website.
5. Ibid.

Chhairottan

1. For more on Mustang, see Clara Marullo, *The Last Forbidden Kingdom: Mustang, Land of Tibetan Buddhism* (London: Thames and Hudson, 1995).
2. Ukyab and Adhikari, *The Nationalities of Nepal*, 17.
3. Two excellent articles on the Mustang region are Peissel, 'Mustang: Remote Realm in Nepal' and Rowell, 'Annapurna: Sanctuary for the Himalaya'.
4. Taken from the www.earthboundexp.com website.
5. Ibid.
6. An interesting book on the Khampa resistance is Michael Peissel, *Cavaliers of Kham: The Secret War in Tibet* (London: Heinemann, 1972).
7. Some say Mao threatened to take over Nepal if the king of Nepal failed to quell the uprising in its territory.
8. Finlay et al., *Nepal*, 382.

Chimtan

1. Ukyab and Adhikari, *The Nationalities of Nepal*, 19.
2. Bista, *The People of Nepal*, 193.
3. Ibid.

Chong

1. The names of the four villages are Ban Nam Khun, Ban Ban Klong Po, Ban Ta Kien Tong, and Ban Kichagud.
2. Schliesinger, *Ethnic Groups of Thailand*, 71.
3. Ibid., 74.

Chuanlan

1. Samuel Clarke, *Among the Tribes in South-West China* (London: Morgan and Scott, 1911) 10.
2. Zhang Xiaosong, 'Tunbao People: Descended from Frontier Soldiers', *China Tourism* 274 (May 2003) 42.
3. Ibid., 45.

Chuanqing

1. *Minzu Shibie Wenxian Ziliao Huibian, Minzu Yanjiu Cankao Ziliao* [Compilation of the Classified Nationality Literature in Nationality Research Reference Material] (Guiyang: Guizhousheng Minzu Yanjiusuo, 1982, Chinese language) 68. In 1952, their population was given as 'more than 200,000'. Fei Xiaotong, 'Xin Zhongguo

de Minzuxue Yanjiu yu Fazhan', [Studies in and Development of Ethnography in New China], in Lin Yuehua, *Minzuxue Yanjiu* [Studies in Ethnography] (Beijing: Zhongguo Shehui Kexue Chubanshe, 1985, Chinese language).
2. Some sources state that the Chuanqing have been officially included in the Han nationality, however, this is not true. This misconception is based on the English translation of Fei Xiaotong's 'On the Question of Identification of Nationalities in China', *Chinese Social Sciences* 1 (1980) 66–69, but the Chinese version of the same article simply says 'we consider them Chinese', 167. Both the *Minzu Shibie Wenxian Ziliao Huibian*, 68–72, and the *Guizhou Nianjian* 1985 [*Guizhou Annual* 1985] (Guiyang: Guizhou Renmin Chubanshe, 1985) 341, say the Chuanqing remain the largest unclassified group in China.
3. Fei Xiaotong, 'On the Question of Identification of Nationalities in China', 98–100.
4. Clarke, *Among the Tribes in South-West China*, 9. One sub-group of the Chuanqing was known as the Fang Teo Ren ('Phoenix-Headed People') in reference to the headdress of the women. Ibid., 10.
5. *Minzu Shibie Wenxian Ziliao Huibian*, 68.
6. Leo J Moser, *The Chinese Mosaic: The Peoples and Provinces of China* (Boulder, CO: Westview Press, 1985).
7. Wu Dong, 'The Tunbao Honouring Mothers Festival', *China Tourism* 262 (May 2002) 69.
8. A recent figure for Catholics in Guizhou has not been published, but there were 100,000 before 1949. See *Bridge* (July–August 1987).

Dainet

1. Enriquez, *Races of Burma*, 77.
2. Ibid.
3. Diran, *The Vanishing Tribes of Burma*, 164.
4. Ibid., 225.
5. See Khine Tun Shwe, *A Guide to Mrauk-U*.
6. Clark and Cummings, *Myanmar (Burma)*, 432.

Dakpa

1. Armington, *Bhutan*, 246.
2. Ibid.

3. Bethany World Prayer Center's profile, 'The Dakpa of Bhutan', actually profiles the Brokpa.
4. Van Driem, *Languages of the Himalayas*, II, 915.
5. See Brian Houghton Hodgson, 'Sifán and Hórsók Vocabularies', *Journal of the Asiatic Society of Bengal* 22 (1853).
6. Van Driem, *Languages of the Himalayas*, II, 916.

Danau

1. Diran, *The Vanishing Tribes of Burma*, 202.
2. Grimes, *Ethnologue* (14th edn, 2000).
3. Confidence in the *Ethnologue* figure is further eroded as the same Danau entry goes on to doubt the existence of the Danau in Myanmar at all! 'It may be in Thailand or China rather than, or in addition to, Myanmar. Investigation needed.' The Danau are certainly present in Myanmar in large numbers, but there is no record of them in either China or Thailand.
4. Enriquez, *Races of Burma*, 127.
5. 'Danau (Danu) Group of Myanmar (Burma)', profile on www.seamist.org.
6. Clark and Cummings, *Myanmar (Burma)*, 354.
7. Mission Outreach, *Asia Prayer Focus*, June 2000.
8. Ibid.
9. Ibid.
10. Ibid.

Dariganga

1. See Grimes, *Ethnologue* (14th edn, 2000).
2. J Bolortuya, 'Eastern Aimag Offers Visual Paradise for Travelers', on the *Virtual Mongolia Online Magazine*.
3. Ibid.
4. Bethany World Prayer Center, 'The Dariganga of Mongolia'.

Dokhpa

1. This is based on an evaluation of the 1931 Indian census, which listed them in areas now controlled by Pakistan. In 1931 Pakistan had not yet been formed and was part of India. The Dokhpa may have all moved back into Indian-controlled Kashmir. FMC South Asia estimates a possible 960 Dokhpa in Pakistani Kashmir.
2. Singh, *The Scheduled Tribes*, 253. It is uncertain where Grimes' 1981 census figure for the Dokhpa of 3,000 people came from (Grimes, *Ethnologue* [13th edn, 1996] 573).

3. Singh, *The Scheduled Tribes*, 253.
4. Ibid.
5. Ibid., 254.

Dolpo

1. The Christian ministry Gospel Recordings has listed their Dolpo recording under both Nepal and China, indicating that they believe the same language is spoken across the border in Tibet.
2. Grimes, *Ethnologue* (14th edn, 2000).
3. An excellent article on the Karnali area of Nepal is Barry C Bishop, 'Karnali, Roadless World of Western Nepal', *National Geographic* (November 1971) 656–89.
4. Bista, *The People of Nepal*, 195.
5. An excellent article featuring the Dolpo people is Eric Valli and Diane Summers, 'Himalayan Caravans', *National Geographic* (December 1993) 5–35.
6. Dr Rajesh Gautam and Asoke K Thapa-Magar, *Tribal Ethnography of Nepal*, I (Delhi: Book Faith India, 1994) 182.
7. Frontier Missions Center for Himalayan Peoples, *Pray for the Peoples of Nepal: A 30 Day Prayer Guide for the Unreached Peoples of Nepal* (Cimmaron, CO: YWAM, n.d.).

Dowaniya

1. See Singh, *India's Communities*, 3 vols.
2. Singh, *India's Communities: A–G*, 882.
3. Grimes, *Ethnologue* (14th edn, 2000).
4. Singh, *India's Communities: A–G*, 883.

Drukpa

1. See 'Unmasking the Dragon: The Drukpa of Bhutan', a prayer profile on the International Mission Board's website: www.tconline.org.
2. Singh, *The Scheduled Tribes*, 153. See also pp 254–56 for a profile of the Drukpa.
3. Van Driem, *Languages of the Himalayas*, II, 891.
4. P W Asia, 'Drukpa of Bhutan: a UPG in Need of Adoption!' (Prayer profile, Singapore, *c.*1998).
5. Indian Research Teams, *Peoples of India*, 88–89.
6. Paraphrased from Ethnos Asia, 'Prayer Focus: A Prayer Guide to Access-Restricted Nations in Asia' 69 (December 2002). The testimony concludes: 'During the period that we were translating the New Testament, I was led to start a fellowship for the backslidden believers. Together with

two evangelists, the small fellowship grew in number. Our first miracle was the healing of an old crippled man. Because of the miracle healing, 18 came to the Lord. A series of miracles followed with the healing of a madman and many sick people in the village. More were added to the fellowship. Over 27 families had committed their lives to the Lord. In that same year, we planted two fellowships, one in Trongsa, Central Bhutan and the other one in Phuentsholing, south Bhutan. By 2001, we had planted another fellowship in the north of Bhutan and another in Gelephu, in the south. Today, with six evangelists, the Lord's work is being carried out, no matter what the situation is. We are now witnessing to 13 of the 20 districts of Bhutan.'

Dura

1. Gautam and Thapa-Magar, *Tribal Ethnography of Nepal*, I, 192, note: 'The Durras of Lamjung are a minority population in comparison with the local Gurungs and during a study carried out in 1983–84, their total population count in said area was estimated at 3,000 heads, while in sum total it was a mere 4,500 heads which comprised the whole Durra tribe on a national census basis.'
2. Van Driem, *Languages of the Himalayas*, II, 811. Van Driem notes: 'Dura settlements include Hadi Khola, Bangre, Besi Bengre, Sindure, Dhuseni, Neta, Tandrankot, Candigau, Bhorletar, Bhangu, Malin, Arikose and Kuncha. The Dura hamlets of Sisaghat and Ramthumki on the Madi river are relatively new settlements which were established by Dura who came relatively recently.'
3. Ukyab and Adhikari, *The Nationalities of Nepal*, 25.
4. Van Driem, *Languages of the Himalayas*, II, 812.
5. Gautam and Thapa-Magar, *Tribal Ethnography of Nepal*, I, 206

Dzala

1. Van Driem, *Languages of the Himalayas*, II, 871.
2. Armington, *Bhutan*, 248.
3. Van Driem, *Languages of the Himalayas*, II, 914.
4. Ibid.

Ergong

1. *Qiangic Speaking Tibetans* (an unpublished prayer guide produced by an anonymous missionary, 2000).
2. See Sun Hongkai, 'Chuanxi Minzu Zoulang Diqu de Yuyan' in *Xinan Minzu Yanjiu* (Chengdu: Sichuan Minzu Chubanshe, 1983, Chinese language). According to Jonathon Evans (personal communication, August 1999), Ergong (Horpa) speakers inhabit central and eastern Daofu County (Chengguan District, Wari, Xiajia and Muru townships of Wari District, Shazhong Township of Bamei District); and central and north-western Danba County (Geshiza, Bianer, and Dandong townships of Dasang District, Donggu Township in Chuangu District, Bawang and Jinchuan townships of Jinchuan District) of Garze Prefecture, an area traditionally known as the five parts of Horpa territory. Scattered communities are also reported in adjacent Luhuo County (Renda Township of Xialatuo District) and Xinlong County (in Manqing, Zhuwo and Duozhan townships of Hexi District).
3. *Qiangic Speaking Tibetans.*
4. See Sun Hongkai, 'Review of Zangmian Yu Yuyin Han Cohui' [Tibeto-Burman Phonology and Vocabularies] *Linguistics of the Tibeto-Burman Area* 15.2 (1992) 73–113; and James A Matisoff, 'Languages and Dialects of Tibeto-Burman', *STEDT Monograph II Series* (Berkeley: University of California, 1988).
5. See Brian Houghton Hodgson, 'Sifán and Hórsók Vocabularies'; also Hodgson, 'On the Tribes of Northern Tibet (Horyeul and Sokyeul) and of Sifan', in *Essays on the Languages, Literatures, and Religions of Nepal and Tibet* (London: Trubner and Co., 1874). The Ergong were also discussed by J H Edgar, 'The Horpa of the Upper Nya or Yalung', *Journal of West China Border Research Society* (1932).
6. *Qiangic Speaking Tibetans.*
7. Ibid.

Ersu

1. According to *Qiangic Speaking Tibetans*, the Ergong live in Shijin, Yanyuan, Ganluo, Yuexi, western Mianning, northern Muli and southern Jiulong counties. Three Ersu villages are within Jiulong County: between 1,000 and 2,000 live in Xia Ka District of Jiulong, and an additional 1,000 Ersu live in other parts of the county.
2. Olson, *An Ethnohistorical Dictionary of China*, 73.
3. See Sun Hongkai trans., 'Languages of the Ethnic Corridor in Western Sichuan', *Linguistics of the Tibeto-Burman Area* 13.1 (Spring 1990) 2.
4. Grimes, *Ethnologue* (13th edn, 1996) 547.
5. Matisoff, 'Languages and Dialects of Tibeto-Burman'.
6. *Qiangic Speaking Tibetans.*
7. Audrey Muse, 'A Profile of the Jiarong People of China', (unpublished report, May 1996).

Gahri

1. Grimes, *Ethnologue* (14th edn, 2000). One Indian researcher believes this figure is too high, but estimates for Gahri are difficult to make because it is primarily a linguistic term.
2. Michael Buckley and Robert Strauss eds., *Tibet: A Travel Survival Kit* (Hawthorn, Australia: Lonely Planet Publications, 1986) 249.
3. In *Operation China* I listed this group as Bunan, but the consensus among researchers now seems to be that they should be called the Gahri.
4. Singh, *The Scheduled Tribes*, 680.
5. Grimes, *Ethnologue* (14th edn, 2000).
6. Singh, *The Scheduled Tribes*, 680.

Gara

1. See K S Singh ed., *Himachal Pradesh* (People of India XXIV; Delhi: Anthropological Survey of India, 1996) 642–45.
2. Prasad, *Encyclopaedic Profile of Indian Tribes*, 284.
3. Singh, *The Scheduled Tribes*, 281.
4. Ibid.
5. Ibid.

Ghale, Kutang

1. Grimes, *Ethnologue* (14th edn, 2000).
2. Ibid.
3. Jan Salter and Harka Gurung, *Faces of Nepal* (Lalitpur, Nepal: Himal Association, 1996) 45–47.

Ghale, Northern

1. Van Driem, *Languages of the Himalayas*, II, 987.
2. Ibid., 984.
3. Grimes, *Ethnologue* (14th edn, 2000).

4. For linguistic studies that examine Ghale, see Warren William Glover, *Sememic and Grammatical Structures in Gurung* (Nepal) (Kathmandu: Summer Institute of Linguistics, 1974); Yoshio Nishi, 'Five Swadesh 100-word Lists for the Ghale Language – A Report on the Trek in the Ghale Speaking Area in Nepal', 158–94 in Hajime Kitamura ed., *Anthropological and Linguistic Studies of the Gandaki Area in Nepal* (Monumenta Serindica 10; Tokyo: Institute for the Study of Languages and Cultures, 1982); Nishi, 'A Brief Survey of the Linguistic Position of Ghale', *Bulletin of the Faculty of Law and Literature*, XVI (Matsuyama: Ehine University, 1983) 27–49; and Holly Smith, 'Ambiguous Segments in Ghale', paper presented at the 19th annual Conference of the Linguistic Society of Nepal, Tribhuvan University, Kirtipur (26 November 1998).
5. Bista, *The People of Nepal*, 88.
6. Ibid., 90.

Ghale, Southern

1. Grimes, *Ethnologue* (14th edn, 2000).
2. Gautam and Thapa-Magar, *Tribal Ethnography of Nepal*, I, 242.
3. Van Driem, *Languages of the Himalayas*, II, 987.
4. Salter and Gurung, *Faces of Nepal*, 47.
5. Bista, *The People of Nepal*, 87–88.
6. *Global Prayer Digest* 13.5 (May 1994).

Golog

1. Galen Rowell, 'Nomads of China's West', *National Geographic* (February 1982) 244.
2. Colin Mackerras, *China's Minorities: Integration and Modernization in the Twentieth Century* (Hong Kong: Oxford University Press, 1994) 243.
3. Rock, 'Seeking the Mountains of Mystery', 131.
4. Rowell, 'Nomads of China's West', 244.
5. Rock, 'Seeking the Mountains of Mystery', 131.
6. Grimes, *Ethnologue* (12th edn, 1992) 517.
7. Unfortunately, because many Golog areas are still virtually inaccessible to outsiders, no recent anthropological or linguistic research has been conducted there. The Golog still consist of numerous small ethnolinguistic or ethno-social groups. Joseph Rock, on his 1929 trip through the region (see

'Seeking the Mountains of Mystery',
140–72) briefly mentions more than
a dozen tribes, clans and groups of
Golog. These include the Lhardi
tribe, the fearless Ngura nomads, the
Amchok robber tribe, the Rimong
tribe (described as the most powerful
Golog group), the Kangsar tribe who
lived west of the Yellow River, the
Kanggan, the Tsokhar tribe, a Golog
tribe called the Ngawa who had
their own king, the Gartse tribe, the
Butsang, the Shahrang robber tribe
living in the Ba valley, and a clan
called the Jazza who are not a Golog
tribe. Missionary Robert Ekvall, in
his book *The Lama Knows: A Tibetan
Legend is Born* (New Delhi: Oxford
and IBH Publishing, 1979) mentions
numerous Golog tribes from his
experience living in the area prior to
1949. On just one page of his book
(p 75) Ekvall mentions the 'Archong,
Gon-mong, Bu-wha-thsang, Lu-di-
thsang, Kangghan, Kang-gsar, Gsar-
ta'. Despite the political and social
upheavals in the decades since this
information was published, most or
all of these groups still exist in their
separate forms. Whether they still
retain ethnolinguistic distinctions or
whether they are now merely social
distinctions is unknown. It is hoped
that research will permit the inclusion
of some or all of these groups in
future editions of this work.
8. Rowell, 'Nomads of China's West', 244.
9. Stauffer, *The Christian Occupation of
China*, 282.

Gong

1. Zhang Weiwen and Zeng Qingnan, *In
Search of China's Minorities* (Beijing:
New World Press, 1993) 240.
2. Schliesinger, *Ethnic Groups of Thailand*,
195.

Gongduk

1. Van Driem, *Languages of the Himalayas*,
II, 463–64.
2. A report on the Gongduk language
appears in van Driem, *Languages of the
Himalayas*, II, 463–68.
3. Grimes, *Ethnologue* (14th edn, 2000).
4. Van Driem, *Languages of the Himalayas*,
II, 464.
5. The 2,500 Lhokpu people have not been
profiled in this book because they are
not Buddhists. The Lhokpu practice
an indigenous religion in which native
deities such as *Tenglha* 'God of the

Heavens figure prominently. The
Lhokpu are the only native Bhutanese
who have not adopted Buddhism and
who bury their dead' (Ibid., 804).
6. Three articles on Bhutan's history and
culture are: Burt Kerr Todd, 'Bhutan,
Land of the Thunder Dragon',
National Geographic (December 1952)
713–54; Desmond Doig, 'Bhutan:
Mountain Kingdom Between Tibet
and India', *National Geographic*
(September 1961) 384–415; and
John Scofield, 'Bhutan Crowns a New
Dragon King', *National Geographic*
(October 1974) 546–71.
7. Cited in Armington, *Bhutan*, 9.

Groma

1. Grimes, *Ethnologue* (13th edn, 1996)
548.
2. Covell, *The Liberating Gospel*, 33.
3. The 1995 Joshua Project listed a
population of 14,000 Groma in India,
but later databases produced by the
Joshua Project removed this figure and
simply noted that the Groma also live
in India.
4. See Ernest Herbert Cooper Walsh, *A
Vocabulary of the Trowoma Dialect of
Tibetan Spoken in the Chumbi Valley
(So far as it Differs from Standard
Tibetan) together with a Corresponding
Vocabulary of Sikkimese and of Central
(Standard) Tibetan (Given for the
Purpose of Comparison)* (Calcutta:
The Bengal Secretariat Book Depot,
1905).
5. Grimes, *Ethnologue* (13th edn, 1996)
548.
6. Missions Advanced Research Center
[MARC], 'Bhots in the State of
Sikkim', *World Christianity: South
Asia* (California: MARC Publications,
n.d.).
7. Leslie Lyall, *A Passion for the Impossible*
(Chicago: Moody Press, 1965) 158.
8. *DAWN Report* 32 (November 1997) 6.

Guiqiong

1. See Sun Hongkai, 'Chuanxi Minzu
Zoulang Diqu de Yuyan'.
2. Dong Zhaofu, 'Jiaowai Luhen'
[Recollections of a Trip to the
Frontiers], *Bianzheng Gonglun* (1930).
3. Sun Hongkai, 'Chuanxi Minzu Zoulang
Diqu de Yuyan', 11.
4. Wu Wenhui and Zhu Jianhua, 'Xikang
Renkou Wenti, Shang' [Xikang
Population Problems, 1]. *Bianzheng
Gonglun* III, n.d.
5. Eileen Crossman, *Mountain Rain: A

New Biography of James O Fraser
(Singapore: OMF, 1982) 144.

Gurung, Eastern

1. Van Driem, *Languages of the Himalayas*,
II, 958–59.
2. This is based on an evaluation of the
1931 Indian census, which lists
them in areas now controlled by
Bangladesh. In 1931 Bangladesh had
not yet been formed and was part
of India. The Gurung may have all
moved back into India and Nepal.
2. Salter and Gurung, *Faces of Nepal*, 45.
4. The Glover family have written
more about the Gurung languages
than anyone else. Some of their
works include: Jessie R Glover,
Conversational Gurung (Canberra:
Pacific Linguistics, 1979); Warren
William Glover, *Sememic and
Grammatical Structures in Gurung
(Nepal)* (Kathmandu: Summer
Institute of Linguistics, 1974); Warren
William Glover and J K Landon,
'Gurung Dialects', in Ronald L
Trail ed., *Papers in South-East Asian
Linguistics*, No. 7 (Canberra: Pacific
Linguistics, 1980); Warren William
Glover, 'Gurung Phonetic Summary',
in *Bodic Languages*, I (Kathmandu:
Summer Institute of Linguistics,
1969); Warren William Glover and
Jessie R Glover, *A Guide to Gurung
Tone* (Kathmandu: Summer Institute
of Linguistics, 1972); Warren William
Glover, Jessie R Glover and Deu
Bahadur Gurung, *Gurung-Nepali-
English Dictionary with English-
Gurung and Nepali-Gurung Indicies*
(Canberra: Pacific Linguistics, 1977).
5. Grimes, *Ethnologue* (14th edn, 2000).
6. An amazing article featuring the
Gurung people has been written
by Eric Valli and Diane Summers,
'Honey Hunters of Nepal', *National
Geographic* (November 1988) 660–71.
7. Bethany World Prayer Center, 'The
Eastern Gurung of Nepal'.
8. Frontier Missions Center for Himalayan
Peoples, *Pray for the Peoples of Nepal*.

Gurung, Western

1. Singh, *India's Communities: A–G*,
1152–54.
2. Gautam and Thapa-Magar, *Tribal
Ethnography of Nepal*, I, 258.
3. Bethany World Prayer Center, 'The
Western Gurung of Nepal'.
4. Ibid.

Hakka

1. Hakka population estimates for various provinces in China for the year 2000 are: Guangdong (8.1 million); Jiangxi (5.9 million); Guangxi (4.2 million); Fujian (2.6 million); Hong Kong (210,000) and Hunan (170,000).
2. Chinese Academy of Social Sciences (CASS), *Information China,* III (London: Pergamon Press, 1989) 1249.
3. Stauffer, *The Christian Occupation of China,* 351.
4. Australian Academy and CASS, *Language Atlas of China, B–13.*
5. Stauffer, *The Christian Occupation of China,* 352.
6. Bethany World Prayer Center, 'The Hakka of China'.
7. Stauffer, *The Christian Occupation of China,* 353.
8. William Robson, *Griffith John: Founder of the Hankow Mission* (New York: Fleming H Revell, *c.*1890) 47.
9. See Ming, 'A Young Woman Evangelist in a Booming Town', *Bridge* 52 (March–April 1992) 12. For testimonies of Hakka Christians and other excellent Hakka information, see Jessie Gregory Lutz and Rolland Ray Lutz, *Hakka Chinese Confront Protestant Christianity 1850–1900: With the Autobiographies of Eight Hakka Christians, and Commentary* (Armonk, NY: M E Sharpe, 1998).
10. 19,200 in French Polynesia (2000, B Grimes [1997 figure]); 6,000 in Panama (1981, MARC); 6,000 in Suriname (2000, B Grimes); 5,000 in French Guiana (2000, B Grimes); 3,000 in Brunei (2000, B Grimes [1979 figure]). Also in Mauritius, New Zealand, South Africa, the United Kingdom, the USA, Canada, Jamaica, Sri Lanka, Philippines, Australia, Kenya, Netherlands, France, Germany, Brazil, Trinidad.

Han Chinese, Cantonese

1. Moser, *The Chinese Mosaic,* 17, 36.
2. Australian Academy and CASS, *Language Atlas of China, A–5.*
3. Aby Zeid, *Achbar ul Sin wal Hind* [Observations Upon China and India], cited in John Foster, *Church of the T'ang Dynasty* (London: SPCK, 1939) 130.
4. Robson, *Griffith John,* 22.
5. Stauffer, *The Christian Occupation of China,* 161.
6. 29,400 in Thailand; 20,000 in New

Zealand; 6,000 in Philippines; 4,500 in Costa Rica; 3,500 in Brunei; 680 in Nauru. Also in Laos, Panama, Australia, Netherlands, the United Kingdom, Honduras, Mauritius, South Africa and many other nations of the world. These figures are derived from various sources, including Grimes, *Ethnologue* (14th edn, 2000) and Johnstone and Mandryk, *Operation World* (2001).

Han Chinese, Gan

1. Stauffer, *The Christian Occupation of China,* 122.
2. Moser, *The Chinese Mosaic,* 120.
3. James and Marti Hefley, *China! Christian Martyrs of the 20th Century: An Excerpt from 'By Their Blood'* (Milford, MI: Mott Media, 1978) 32.
4. Ibid.

Han Chinese, Hainanese

1. Moser, *The Chinese Mosaic,* 197.
2. Storey, *China,* 743.
3. 'The Church on Hainan Island: Past and Present', *Bridge* 27 (January–February 1988) 4.
4. Ibid.
5. *Bridge* (June 1992).
6. *Bridge* (December 1989).

Han Chinese, Huizhou

1. Australian Academy and CASS, *Language Atlas of China, B–11.*
2. See Ping-Ti Ho, *Studies on the Population of China 1368–1953* (Cambridge, MA: Harvard University Press, 1959) 240–44.
3. Moser, *The Chinese Mosaic,* 113.
4. Grimes, *Ethnologue* (13th edn, 1996) 544.
5. Moser, *The Chinese Mosaic,* 115.
6. Ibid., 117.
7. Ibid., 112.
8. Ibid., 117.

Han Chinese, Jin

1. Australian Academy and CASS, *Language Atlas of China, B–7.*
2. Moser, *The Chinese Mosaic,* 76.
3. Huang Xianlin ed., *Zhongguo Renkou: Guangxi Fence* [China's Population: Guangxi Volume], (Beijing: Zhongguo Caizheng Jingji Chubanshe, 1988, Chinese language).

Han Chinese, Mandarin

1. Johnstone and Mandryk, in their *Operation World* (2001 edn), list

Chinese populations for numerous countries. There are dozens of other countries with Chinese communities, but no population figures are available. Following, in descending order, are where the Chinese live around the world, and the size of their communities. Note that these figures refer simply to 'Chinese' communities, and do not distinguish between different Chinese languages. However, in most cases the majority are Mandarin-speaking Chinese. There are 21,796,000 in Taiwan; 8,520,000 in Indonesia; 6,447,000 in Thailand; 5,650,000 in Malaysia; 2,746,000 in Singapore; 1,900,000 in the USA; 1,596,000 in Myanmar; 1,595,000 in the Philippines; 1,120,000 in Vietnam; 930,000 in Canada; 450,000 in Australia; 350,000 in Cambodia; 252,000 in Japan; 250,000 in the United Kingdom; 180,000 in Brazil; 180,000 in France; 168,000 in North Korea; 150,000 in Panama; 115,000 in Peru; 100,000 in South Korea; 70,000 in Netherlands; 66,000 in Costa Rica; 60,000 in Madagascar; 51,200 in Brunei; 50,000 in Italy; 40,000 in South Africa; 38,000 in Mexico; 35,000 in Mauritius; 33,000 in Jamaica; 30,000 in Argentina; 30,000 in Spain; 20,000 in Belgium; 20,000 in Cuba; 20,000 in Guatemala; 15,000 in Tanzania; 14,000 in Ecuador; 10,000 in Nicaragua; 10,000 in Paraguay; 9,000 in Colombia; 9,000 in the Dominican Republic; 8,000 in Fiji; 8,000 in Sweden; 7,000 in French Polynesia; 6,000 in Belize; 6,000 in Bolivia; 6,000 in Norway; 6,000 in Trinidad and Tobago; 5,000 in French Guiana; 5,000 in Guyana; 5,000 in Honduras; 4,000 in East Timor; 3,000 in the Czech Republic; 3,000 in the Solomon Islands; 2,500 in Guam; 2,000 in Austria; 2,000 in Chile; 2,000 in El Salvador; 2,000 in Micronesia; 2,000 in Puerto Rico; 1,000 in the Seychelles; 900 in Nauru; 250 in Tonga; 150 in Dominica. There are also approximately 30,000 Chinese working (mostly illegally) in Israel, and another 30,000 Chinese in Laos.

2. Taken from Ralph Covell's article in this volume, 'Buddhism and the Gospel in China'. See also Ralph Covell, *Confucius, the Buddha, and Christ* (Maryknoll, NY: Orbis Books, 1986) 133–50.

3. P Yoshiro Saeki, *The Nestorian Documents and Relics in China* (Tokyo: Maruzen, 1951) 57f, 456.
4. Samuel Hugh Moffett, *A History of Christianity in Asia,* I: *Beginnings to 1500* (San Francisco: HarperSanFrancisco, 1992) 293.
5. See note 1 for a full listing.
6. See note 1 for a full listing. These figures are derived from various sources, including Grimes, *Ethnologue* (14th edn, 2000) and Johnstone and Mandryk, *Operations World* (2001).
7. The dialects in their clusters are as follows: *Northeastern Mandarin* (82 million speakers in 1987): Jiaoning, Tongxi, Yanji, Zhaofu, Changjin, Nenke, Jiafu, Zhanhua; *Beijing* (18 million): Jingshi, Huaicheng, Chaofeng, Shike; *Jilu* (Beifang) (83.6 million): Laifu, Dingba, Tianjin, Jizun, Luanchang, Fulong, Zhaoshen, Xingheng, Liaotai, Canghui, Huangle, Yangshou, Juzhao, Zhanghuan; *Jiaoliao* (28.8 million): Qingzhou, Denglian, Gaihuan; *Zhongyuan* (169.4 million): Zhengcao, Cailu, Luoxu, Xinbeng, Pingyang, Jiangzhou, Xiezhou, Guanzhong, Qinlong, Longzhong, Nanjiang; *Lanyin* (11.7 million): Jincheng, Yinwu, Hexi, Tami; *Southwestern Mandarin* (200 million): Chengyu, Yaoli, Baolu, Qianbei, Kungui, Minjiang, Renfu, Yamian, Lichuan, Ebei, Wutian, Cenjiang, Qiannan, Guiliu, Changhe; *Jianghuai* (67.2 million): Hongchao, Tairu, Huangxiao.

Han Chinese, Min Bei

1. Australian Academy and CASS, *Language Atlas of China*, B–12.
2. Grimes, *Ethnologue* (13th edn, 1996) 545.
3. Ibid.
4. Arthur de C Sowerby, 'By the Waters of the Min', *China Journal* 10 (1929) 22.
5. Ibid., 25.
6. Moser, *The Chinese Mosaic*, 166.
7. Arthur Christopher Moule and Paul Pelliot, *Marco Polo: The Description of the World* (2 vols; London: Routledge, 1938) 350.
8. The Min Bei Christians today prefer to use the standard Chinese Scriptures, rather than the translation in their own language.

Han Chinese, Min Dong

1. Information in the *Ethnologue* has confused research into the Min Dong

Chinese. The 1996 *Ethnologue* (p 545) gives no population for the Min Dong in China, but the 2000 edition gives their total population for all countries as 247,000 'or more'. The 'more' happens to be about nine million more! The 247,000 figure is the total of the populations given for all the Southeast Asian countries where the Min Dong language is spoken. In other words, the 2000 edition still does not list a population for Min Dong in China. The confusion probably stems from the fact that the Min Dong figures are incorrectly included under the Min Bei population. The authoritative 1987 *Language Atlas of China* lists 7,526,000 Min Dong in China and divides the various Min groups in a way that is supported by numerous other sources.
2. Moser, *The Chinese Mosaic*, 31.
3. Ibid., 163.
4. J E Walker, 'Shao-wu in Fuh-kien: A Country Station', *Chinese Recorder* (September–October 1878) 349.
5. Moule and Pelliot, *Marco Polo*, 347.
6. 'Along the Fujian Coast', *Bridge* (January–February 1986) 4.

Han Chinese, Min Nan

1. Grimes, *Ethnologue* (13th edn, 1996) 545.
2. Moffett, *A History of Christianity in Asia*, 458.
3. Henry Yule and Henri Cordier, *Cathay and the Way Thither: Being a Collection of Medieval Notices of China* (4 vols; Delhi: Munshiram Manoharlal, 1998) 191–94.
4. James M Hubbard, 'Problems in China', *National Geographic* (August 1900) 297.
5. 'Along the Fujian Coast', *Bridge* (January–February 1986) 4.

Han Chinese, Pinghua

1. Australian Academy and CASS, *Language Atlas of China*, B–14.
2. Ibid.
3. William Clifton Dodd, *The Tai Race: Elder Brother of the Chinese* (Cedar Rapids: The Torch Press, 1923) 148. Several excellent Chinese linguistic studies of the Pinghua language include Li Wei, 'Guangxi Lingchuan Pinghua de Tedian', *Fangyuan* 4, 251–54; and Zhang Junru, 'Ji Guangxi Nanning Xinxu Pinghua', *Fangyuan*, 241–50.

4. Clarke, *Among the Tribes in South-West China*, 58–59.
5. Stauffer, *The Christian Occupation of China*, 148.

Han Chinese, Puxian

1. Moser, *The Chinese Mosaic*, 173.
2. Leo Moser says that this is the result of a strong emphasis on sports in the local school system which dates back at least to 1878 (*The Chinese Mosaic*, 173). At that time, according to Rao Fengqi, 'champions of races were treated like scholars who had come in first in the imperial examinations. They were draped with red silk over their shoulders, flowers were pinned on their chests and they were given a parade through the streets' (Rao Fengqi, 'Why Does Putian County Produce So Many Athletes?' *China Reconstructs* [May 1983] 55–56).
3. Moser, *The Chinese Mosaic*, 174.
4. William Marsden trans., *The Travels of Marco Polo* (New York: Dell, 1961) 300–1.
5. 'Along the Fujian Coast', *Bridge* (January–February 1986) 4.
6. 'Putian Church: Different Traditions, New Developments', *Amity News Service* (June 1997).

Han Chinese, Wu

1. Australian Academy and CASS, *Language Atlas of China*, B–9. Grimes, in *Ethnologue* (13th edn, 1996) 545, cites a 1984 figure of 77,175,000 Wu speakers.
2. Moser, *The Chinese Mosaic*, 144.
3. Ibid., 145.
4. Moule and Pelliot, *Marco Polo*, 263. Polo calls Zhenjiang by the name 'Quengianfu'.

Han Chinese, Xiang

1. Grimes, in *Ethnologue* (13th edn, 1996) 545, cites a 1984 figure of 36,015,000 Xiang speakers.
2. William Barclay Parsons, 'Hunan: The Closed Province of China', *National Geographic* (October 1900) 393.
3. Lin Shao-Yang, *A Chinese Appeal to Christendom* (1911).
4. Olson, *An Ethnohistorical Dictionary of China*, 365.
5. Ibid., 364.
6. *Eastern Express*, Hong Kong (5 October 1995).
7. Robson, *Griffith John*, 60–61.
8. 'Difficulties in Hunan Province', *Bridge* 10 (March–April 1985) 3.

Han Tai

1. Zheng Lan, *Travels through Xishuangbanna: China's Subtropical Home of Many Nationalities* (Beijing: Foreign Languages Press, 1981) 4.
2. Asian Studies Institute, 'The Dai People of Southeast Asia' (unpublished report, 1996) 14.
3. Bethany World Prayer Center, 'The Shan of Southeast Asia.'
4. Asian Minorities Outreach, 'The Black Tai', *Newsletter* 36 (December 1995).
5. Asian Minorities Outreach, *The 50 Most Unreached People Groups of China and Tibet* (Chiang Mai, Thailand: AMO Publishing, 1996) 8.
6. Asian Studies Institute, 'The Dai People of Southeast Asia', 4.

Hdzanggur

1. Rock, 'Seeking the Mountains of Mystery', 162–63.
2. Ibid., 163.
3. Ibid., 162.
4. Various sources have documented human rights abuses against Tibetans of Radja Monastery. One of them, taken from the www.bosold.net website, has the 1997 testimony of a Buddhist monk called Lobsang Dhargay: 'The worst torture I endured was when I was handcuffed with my arms around a hot chimney and left there for a whole day without food or water. The scorching heat of the chimney resulted in blisters all over my body. There was water running from the blisters and my wounds were stinging painfully from heavy perspiration.' The report goes on to say, 'He was detained in Golok Prison for a year without trial. With every interrogation he was beaten with sticks, kicked, punched and shocked all over his body with an electric cattle prod. He escaped Tibet on April 2, 1997 and reached Dharamsala, India on April 28, 1997.'
5. Taken from the Tibetan Center for Human Rights and Democracy (TCHRD) website, 14 October 2003.

Helambu Sherpa

1. Frontier Missions Center for Himalayan Peoples, *Pray for the Peoples of Nepal.*
2. Bethany World Prayer Center, 'The Helambu Sherpa of Nepal'.
3. Frontier Missions Center for Himalayan Peoples, *Pray for the Peoples of Nepal.*
4. Ibid.

Hu

1. Grimes, *Ethnologue* (11th edn, 1988) 449.
2. *Encyclopedic Dictionary of Chinese Linguistics (EDCL)* [Zhongguo Yuyanxue Dacidian] (Nanjing: Jiangxi Educational Publishing House, 1991) 594.
3. Olson, *An Ethnohistorical Dictionary of China*, 168–69.

Huay

1. See Schliesinger, *Ethnic Groups of Thailand*, 85–89.
2. Ibid., 85.
3. Ibid., 88.

Huayao Tai

1. Asian Studies Institute, 'The Dai People of Southeast Asia', 17. According to the 1990 census, a total of 39,094 Dai people were living in Xinping County and 21,444 in Yuanjiang County. Most of these are Huayao Tai.
2. Stauffer, *The Christian Occupation of China*, 349. Also see Dodd, *The Tai Race.*
3. Personal communication with a Lu (November 1997).
4. Xie Shixun, 'The Floral-Belted Dais of the Red River', *China Tourism* 78 (n.d.) 67.
5. See Li Ping, 'The Flower Street Festival of the Dai', *China Tourism* 165 (April 1994) 79–81; and Shen Zhi, 'The Resplendent Flower-Waist Dais', *China Tourism* 263 (June 2002) 58–62. Shen Zhi says, 'January 13th of the lunar calendar is the "Lesser Huajie" for the flower-waist Dais. Dai girls bedeck themselves in their festive best, donning silver bracelets, earrings, chains and bells. They collect meticulously-crafted clothes, skirts, flowery sashes, fragrant pouches and embroidered kerchiefs in a woven bamboo basket and put on their woven bamboo hats. Then, they gather on the street. There they take out all the things and spread them out in an orderly fashion, waiting for their sweethearts to come. While playing flutes, the young men wander around, looking for their ideal spouse. If a young man finds someone he likes, he approaches her, takes her pouch of kerchief and then leaves. The girl then gathers up her belongings and follows him to a place where they can profess their feelings. . . . The silver ornament and the pouch of kerchief

then become items of betrothal. May 6th of the lunar calendar is called the "Greater Huajie".' (p 60).
6. See Shen Zhi, 'The Resplendent Flower-Waist Dais', 60–61.

Intha

1. Enriquez, *Races of Burma*, 127.
2. Clark and Cummings, *Myanmar (Burma)*, 432.
3. Grimes, *Ethnologue* (14th edn, 2000).
4. Diran, *The Vanishing Tribes of Burma*, 112.
5. Clark and Cummings. *Myanmar (Burma)*, 432.
6. Diran, *The Vanishing Tribes of Burma*, 112.

Isan

1. For further reading on Isan history and development, see Nrong Ketudat, 'Ethnic Groups in Northeastern Thailand', *The Bangkok World* (1 February 1970); Pira Sudham, *People of Esarn* (Bangkok: Siam Media International Books, 1987); Peter Rogers, *Northeast Thailand: From Prehistoric to Modern Times* (Bangkok: DK Book House, 1996); Erik Seidenfaden, *The Thai Peoples: Book 1, The Origins and Habitation of the Thai Peoples with a Sketch of their Material and Spiritual Culture* (Bangkok: The Siam Society, 1958); and J L Taylor, *Forest Monks and the Nation State: An Anthropological and Historical Study in Northeastern Thailand* (Singapore: Institute of Southeast Asian Studies, 1993).
2. *The Isaan People: Destined for Destruction or Redeemed for Rebirth?* (people group profile, Mark and Helen Caldwell, November 1997).
3. Grimes, *Ethnologue* (14th edn, 2000).
4. Peter Rogers, *A Window on Isan: Thailand's Northeast* (Bangkok: Edns Duang Kamol, 1989).
5. The Summer Institute of Linguistics (SIL) estimated between 15 million and 23 million Isan-speaking people in Thailand in 1995 (Grimes, *Ethnologue* [14th edn, 2000]). The lower figure of 15 million came from an earlier 1983 study.

Japanese

1. Also 20,000 in Singapore; 19,000 in Bolivia; 18,000 in Hong Kong (China); 15,000 in Paraguay; 10,000 in Taiwan; 3,500 in Micronesia; 3,000 in Guam; 1,700 in Dominican

Republic; and 1,200 in Panama. All of these figures are taken from Johnstone and Mandryk, *Operation World* (2001). There are dozens of other countries with Japanese communities, but no population figures are available. Grimes, *Ethnologue* (14th edn, 2000) lists the following additional countries where Japanese is spoken: American Samoa, Belize, Canada, Germany, Mongolia, New Zealand, Northern Mariana Islands, Palau, Philippines. More than 5,000 Japanese have remained in China since they were left behind after the Second World War (see Hattaway, *Operation China*, 225).

2. The Okinawan Islands—home to several distinct language groups known collectively as Ryukyuan—are not included in this study because Buddhism has not made an impact among them as it has on other Japanese on the major islands. One book notes, 'The result of a survey shows that 1.7% of the population [in Okinawa] are Buddhist believers and 0.3% Shintoists. Unlike other prefectures, traditional Buddhism and Shintoism are not rooted here. Instead, popular folklore beliefs based on ancestor worship are integral parts of the Okinawan's life' (Operation Japan Publishing Committee and Japan Evangelical Missionary Association, *Operation Japan: Japan in Focus, a Handbook for Prayer* [2000 edn] 195).

3. There are numerous stirring accounts of this gruesome event. One of them was given by an early Jesuit missionary in Michael Cooper, *Rodrigues the Interpreter: An Early Jesuit in Japan and China* (New York: Weatherhill, 1994) 138–39: 'There on the morning of Wednesday 5 February 1597 the twenty-six Christians were clamped and tied to a semicircle of crosses. Lines of soldiers armed with lances and muskets surrounded the site to keep back the crowds. Only Rodrigues and Pasio were allowed to stand within the circle by the side of the crosses and comfort the martyrs in their agony. As the sympathetic spectators pressed forward, the guards used their staves and clubs to beat them back, and both priests were sometimes caught in the melee and struck with blows. Of the twenty-six victims, four were Spaniards, one was Mexican,

another was Indo-Portuguese, while the rest were Japanese. Two of the Japanese who died on that day had not been included in the original list of condemned Christians, but had insisted on joining the group. Among the twenty-six were Thomas, aged fifteen years; Antonio, thirteen; and Luis, twelve; the boys showed incredible courage and resolution, and from their crosses they sang the psalm 'O Children, Praise the Lord'. All of them could have obtained instant reprieve by renouncing their religion, and in fact the compassionate Hansaburo had done his utmost to save Luis. The martyrs were not left to die lingering deaths on the crosses, and two pairs of executioners swiftly dispatched them with lance thrusts.'

4. David B Barrett, George T Kurian and Todd M Johnson eds., *World Christian Encyclopedia, Second Edition: A Comparative Survey of Churches and Religions in the Modern World, Volume 1, The World by Countries: Religionists, Churches, Ministries* (New York: Oxford University Press, 2001) 415.

5. Ibid., 412.

6. Ibid.

Jiarong, Chabao

1. Muse, 'A Profile of the Jiarong People of China'.

2. Lin Xiangron, *Jiarongyu Yufa* (Chengdu: Sichuan Minzu Chubanshe, 1993, Chinese language) 412.

3. Wu Wenhui and Zhu Jianhua, 'Xikang Renkou Wenti, Shang', as cited in Mackerras, *China's Minorities*, 130.

4. Ibid.

5. Ibid.

6. *Qiangic Speaking Tibetans*.

7. Ibid.

Jiarong, Guanyingqiao

1. Jonathon Evans, personal communication (August 1999).

2. Ibid.

3. *Qiangic Speaking Tibetans*.

Jiarong, Shangzhai

1. Evans, personal communication (August 1999).

2. See Qu Aitang, 'Jiarongyude Fangyan: Fangyan Huafen he Yuyan Shibie' [Jiarong Dialects: Issues in Dialect Subclassification and Language Recognition], *Minzu Yuwen* 4 and 5 (1990, Chinese language).

3. Evans, personal communication (August

1999).

4. See Lin Xiangron, *Jiarongyu Yufa*, 526.

5. Fei Xiaotong, as cited in Sun Hongkai, 'Languages of the Ethnic Corridor in Western Sichuan', 1–2.

6. *Qiangic Speaking Tibetans*.

Jiarong, Sidabao

1. Evans, personal communication (August 1999).

2. Bradley, 'East and South-East Asia', 168.

3. Evans, personal communication (August 1999).

4. Muse, 'A Profile of the Jiarong People of China'.

5. Ge Jialin, 'The Jiarong Tibetans Celebrate Their Harvest', *China Tourism* 166 (May 1994) 58.

6. Muse, 'A Profile of the Jiarong People of China'.

7. Ibid.

Jiarong, Situ

1. Lin Xiangron, *Jiarongyu Yufa*, 411. The Hong Kong Association of Christian Missions lists a specific figure of 138,394 Jiarong (including the Situ Jiarong). J-O Svantesson, in a personal communication (1990), lists a figure of 100,000 speakers of Jiarong, as cited in Grimes, *Ethnologue* (13th edn, 1996) 551.

2. Evans, personal communication (August 1999).

3. Vladimir Li, *Some Approaches to the Classification of Small Ethnic Groups in South China* (Prague: Institute of Oriental Studies, n.d.).

4. Fei Xiatong, 'On the Question of Identification of Nationalities in China', *Chinese Social Sciences* 1 (1980) 147–62.

5. In recent years there have been numerous linguistic studies of the Jiarong languages. Some of these include Lin Xiangron, 'Sound System of the Zhuo Keji (Ma'erkang) Dialect of Jiarong', *Yuyin Yanjiu* 2 (1988); also Lin Xiangron, *Jiarongyu Yufa*; Ma Changshou, 'Jiarong Minzu Shehui Shi', *Minzuxue Yanjiu Jikan* 4 (1944); Qu Aitang, 'Jiarongyu Gaikuang', *Minzu Yuwen* 2 (1984) and 'Jiarongyude Fangyan: Fangyan Huafen He Yuyan Shibie'; Yasuhiko Yashuda, *A Historical Study of the Jiarong Verb System* (Tokyo: Seishido, 1984); and Jackson Tianshin Sun, 'Caodeng rGyalrong Phonology: A First Look', *Linguistics of the Tibeto-Burman Area* 17.2 (1994).

6. *Qiangic Speaking Tibetans.*
7. Muse, 'A Profile of the Jiarong People of China'.

Jirel

1. Cited in Grimes, *Ethnologue* (14th edn, 2000).
2. Eleven of the Jirel villages are named: Jiri, Sikri, Kavre, Dung, Okma, Yarsa, Jhakhu, Chatpu, Darkha, Manganga and Chetrangu. Gautam and Thapa-Magar, *Tribal Ethnography of Nepal*, I, 300.
3. Van Driem, *Languages of the Himalayas*, II, 863.
4. Gautam and Thapa-Magar, *Tribal Ethnography of Nepal*, I, 300.
5. Two ladies, Esther Strahm and Anita Maibaum, have published several articles on the Jirel language, including: 'Jirel Phonetic Summary', in Maria Hari ed., *Tibeto-Burman Phonemic Summaries* (Kathmandu: Tribhuvan University and the Summer Institute of Linguistics, 1971); 'Jirel Texts', in Austin Hale ed., *Clause, Sentence, and Discourse Patterns in Selected Languages of Nepal* (Norman, OK: Summer Institute of Linguistics, 1973); 'Clause Patterns in Jirel', in Austin Hale, 'Collected Papers on Sherpa, Jirel', *Nepal Studies in Linguistics 2* (Kirtipur: SIL and Institute of Nepal and Asian Studies, 1975); and 'Verb Pairs in Jirel', in Yogendra Prasad Yadava and Warren William Glover eds., *Topics in Nepalese Linguistics* (Kathmandu: Royal Nepal Academy, 1999).
6. Grimes, *Ethnologue* (14th edn, 2000).
7. Gautam and Thapa-Magar, *Tribal Ethnography of Nepal*, I, 306.
8. Ibid., 305.

Kagate

1. See Monika Hoehlig and Maria Hari, *Kagate Phonemic Summary* (Kathmandu: Summer Institute of Linguistics and Institute of Nepal and Asian Studies of Tribhuvan University, 1976).
2. Van Driem, *Languages of the Himalayas*, II, 864.
3. Grimes, *Ethnologue* (14th edn, 2000).
4. K S Singh ed., *Sikkim* (People of India XXXIX; Calcutta: Seagull Books and Anthropological Survey of India, 1993) 78.
5. Grimes, *Ethnologue* (14th edn, 2000).
6. Singh, *Sikkim*, 80.
7. Ibid., 81.

Kaike

1. Cited in Grimes, *Ethnologue* (14th edn, 2000).
2. Van Driem, *Languages of the Himalayas*, II, 978.
3. See James F Fisher, 'A Vocabulary of the Kaike Language', unpublished report presented to the Institute of Nepalese Studies of Tribhuvan University, Kirtipur (March 1971).
4. Van Driem, *Languages of the Himalayas*, II, 977.
5. Ibid., 978–79.
6. James F Fisher, *Trans-Himalayan Traders, Economy, Society and Culture in Northwest Nepal* (Berkeley: University of California Press, 1986) 130.

Kaleung

1. Schliesinger, *Ethnic Groups of Thailand*, 61.
2. See Surat Warangrat, 'Kaloeng', *Muang Boran Journal* 7.3 (1987); and James R Chamberlain, 'The Tai Dialects of Khammouan Province: Their Diversity and Origins', Sixteenth International Conference on Sino-Tibetan Language and Linguistics, 16–18 September (Seattle, WA, 1983).
3. Schliesinger, *Ethnic Groups of Thailand*, 61–62.

Kalmyk-Oirat

1. Issachar Frontier Missions Research, *Mongolia Challenge Report*, II, 2, i.
2. See Paula G Rubel, *The Kalmyk Mongols: A Study in Continuity and Change* (Bloomington: Indiana University Publications, 1967).
3. Bethany World Prayer Center, 'The Kalmyk-Oirat'.
4. Edward Murray, 'With the Nomads of Central Asia: A Summer's Sojourn in the Tekes Valley, Plateau Paradise of Mongol and Turkic Tribes', *National Geographic* (January 1936) 48.
5. CASS, *Information China*, III, 1274.
6. Murray, 'With the Nomads of Central Asia', 48.
7. Because of major historical influences, a translation produced for the Kalmyk-Oirat in Russia will not be useable among the Kalmyk-Oirat in either Mongolia or China. The Kalmyk-Oirat language in Russia has been heavily influenced by Russian, while in China the Kalmyk-Oirat use the *tod* script, which is different from the traditional Mongolian downward

script.
8. The *Jesus* film is available in Kalmyk, but it was translated for the Kalmyk living in Russia and contains many loanwords that are not used in China.

The Oirat in China are not able to understand it.

Kayah, Western

1. Myanmar Faces and Places, 'Profile of the Kayah'.
2. Ibid. Also see F K Lehman, 'Burma: Kayah Society as a Function of the Shan-Burma-Karen Context', in J Steward ed., *Contemporary Change in Traditional Societies* (Chicago: University of Illinois, 1967).
3. For superb photographs of the Kayah people in traditional dress, see the outstanding book by Diran, *The Vanishing Tribes of Burma*, 126–131.
4. Grimes, *Ethnologue* (14th edn, 2000).
5. Myanmar Faces and Places, 'Profile of the Kayah'.
6. Grimes, *Ethnologue* (14th edn, 2000) cites a 1987 figure of 210,000 Western Kayah in Myanmar.

Khamiyang

1. K S Singh ed., *Arunachal Pradesh* (People of India XIV; Calcutta: Anthropological Survey of India, 1995) 173.
2. According to FMC South Asia (personal communication, May 2004) there were 1,500 Khamiyang in India (2001 estimate) of which 1,060 lived in the Lohit District of Arunachal Pradesh.
3. Singh, *The Scheduled Tribes*, 503.
4. Ibid.
5. The 1981 census found that 44% of Khamiyang speak Assamese, 30% speak Tai in some form or another, and 23% speak languages not specified to census takers.
6. Singh, *Arunachal Pradesh*, 173.

Khampa, Eastern

1. The 1981 census of India listed 1,221 'Khamba' people in Himachal Pradesh, and 342 'Khampa' in Arunachal Pradesh, at opposite ends of the Himalayan Range. Those in Himachal Pradesh would have come from the Western Khampa group in China, while those in Arunachal Pradesh say they originated in Zayu, Tibet, which would place them in the Southern Khampa group. There are undoubtedly many hundreds of

Eastern Khampa among the tens of thousands of Tibetan refugees who have fled since the Chinese occupation began in the 1960s, but their numbers are impossible to determine.

2. Bradley, 'East and South-East Asia', 170.
3. Grimes, *Ethnologue* (13th edn, 1996) 553.
4. Sertar, in north-west Sichuan Province, is home to the famous Larong Pancavidya Buddhist Institute. Not only do thousands of Tibetans study there, but also 500 Han Chinese students who desire to know more about Buddhist teachings. See Huang Yanhong, 'A Buddhist Land of 3,000 Women: The Larong Pancavidya Institute in Sertar', *China Tourism* 228 (July 1999) 46–57.
5. Joseph F C Rock, 'Konka Risumgongba: Holy Mountain of the Outlaws', *National Geographic* (July 1931) 43.
6. Mackerras, *China's Minorities*, 71.
7. Buckley and Strauss, *Tibet*, 16. Throughout the 1960s Khampa rebels, from their base in Mustang, Nepal, continued to mount spasmodic attacks on the Chinese from across the border. This was ended only after Mao Zedong apparently personally threatened the king of Nepal. See the Chhairottan profile in this book for more information.
8. Tsering, *Sharing Christ in the Tibetan Buddhist World*, 86.
9. Covell, *The Liberating Gospel*, 50.
10. Tony Lambert, 'Christianity and Tibet', *Pray for China Fellowship* (OMF International, April 1996).
11. Stauffer, *The Christian Occupation of China*, 278.

Khampa, Northern

1. Australian Academy and CASS, *Language Atlas of China*, C–11.
2. In the late 1990s, severe winter storms decimated the Northern Khampa. Tens of thousands of yaks and other animals froze to death, and hundreds of people were killed by the cold or by the ensuing starvation. Various aid agencies have worked to alleviate the Northern Khampa's suffering.
3. *The Edge* 2.3 (Fall 1997).
4. Cited by Pamela Logan, *Lifestyle* (October–November 1994).
5. Heinrich Harrer, *Seven Years in Tibet* (London: Pan Books, 1953) 94.

Khampa, Southern

1. Grimes, *Ethnologue* (13th edn, 1996)

540, numbers 520,000 Atuence, a figure that has been used by the Joshua Project and other people group lists. However, the location given ('Yunnan-Tibet border') in no way supports such a large population. All Tibetans numbered only 101,500 in Yunnan Province in 1985 *(Yunnan Nianjian 1986*, 454). The regions across the borders in southern Tibet and south-west Sichuan, where the same language is spoken, are relatively sparsely populated. The 1987 Australian Academy and CASS, *Language Atlas of China, C–11*, lists the Tibetan language in this area as Southern Kham and gives a population of 134,300. This figure includes speakers from both the Southern Khampa (73,560) and the Shangri-La Tibetan (60,740) language groups, which have been profiled separately in this book. There were a total of 20,484 Tibetans living in Zayu County, Tibet, according to the 1990 census.

2. John Morse, personal communication (January 1998). In the early 1990s a dispute with the Myanmar authorities resulted in the rejection of Tibetans' citizenship that forced most Tibetans to go back across the border into China. Some have returned since then.
3. An outstanding article on the Deqen region is Liu Dongping and Cheng Weidong, 'Deqen: A Highland in the Hengduan Mountains', *China Tourism* 245 (December 2000) 19–41.
4. For a detailed account of a Westerner's visit to the Deqen region, see Wade Brackenbury, *Yak Butter and Black Tea: A Journey into Forbidden China* (Chapel Hill: Algonquin Books, 1997) 25–33.
5. One interesting article on languages in the area is Hanny Feurer and Yang Fuquan, 'Greetings Among Naxi and Kham Tibetans on Yunnan's High Plateau', *Linguistics of the Tibeto-Burman Area* 22.1 (1999) 11–58.
6. Tian Qui, 'The Tibetans of Deqen', *China Tourism* 108 (n.d.) 30.
7. See Tony Lambert, 'The Challenge of China's Minority Peoples', *Chinese Around the World* (April 1991) 9, and 'Christianity and Tibet', *Pray for China Fellowship* (April 1996).
8. 'A handful of the 700 church members are Naxi, the remainder are Tibetans. The church's Tibetan priest, who is only 27 years old, completed four

year's study at the Catholic seminary in Beijing' (personal communication, 3 November 1997). Dianna Lau, 'From Yunnan to Tibet', *China Tourism* 261 (April 2002), has a section entitled 'Yanjing's Catholic Church' (pp 22–23) which documents her visit to the church in Yanjing and also includes a picture of the inside of the sanctuary. 'From its outer appearance, I never would have believed it was a true Catholic church. I was only convinced by the Christian murals and the image of Jesus Christ on the altar. Interestingly, however, above each of the murals a *hada* was hung, adding a uniquely Tibetan flavour. . . . We were told that Mass is held twice a day, in the morning and evening. Most of the attendants are elderly villagers, as the younger ones are busy with work or have gone elsewhere to do business. Having taken some pictures, we saw many local Tibetans gathered in front of the one-storey houses on either side of the church. At their feet were baskets of fresh grapes. It turned out that it was the church's grape-collection day. The French missionaries had not only brought the Bible to the village but also the knowledge of growing grapes and making wine.'

9. See Covell, *The Liberating Gospel*, 44–51.
10. Joseph F C Rock, 'Through the Great River Trenches of Asia', *National Geographic* (August 1926) 155.
11. Stauffer, *The Christian Occupation of China*, 282.
12. Alex Buchan, 'Catholic Church Hangs on in Tibet', *Compass Direct* (September 1998). According to the priest, 'the Catholic community is very poor, nomadic, and has only had a church since 1986. Their knowledge of the faith is not strong.' Of this total of 9,500 Catholics, about 7,500 are Southern Khampa and 2,000 are Shangri-La Tibetans.

Khampa, Western

1. Bradley, 'East and South-East Asia', 170.
2. Cynthia Beall and Melvyn Goldstein, 'The Remote World of Tibet's Nomads', *National Geographic* (June 1989) 771.
3. 'In Uttar Pradesh they are distributed in Dearma and Byans villages of Pithoragarh District, where they are called as Shah Khampa; in Spiti Division of Himachal Pradesh as

Piti Khampa; in Kinaur as Khunnu Khampa; in Kullu as Neondi Khampa; in Chamba as Thava Khampa; in Lahul as Gharja Khampa' (Singh, *Himachal Pradesh*, 314).

4. See David Plymire, *High Adventure in Tibet* (Springfield, MO: Gospel Publishing House, 1959).

5. Stauffer, *The Christian Occupation of China*, 276.

Khamti

1. Lila Gogoi, *The Tai Khamtis of the North-East* (New Delhi: Omsons Publications, 1990).

2. Bethany World Prayer Center, 'The Khamti Shan of Myanmar'.

3. FMC South Asia (personal communication, May 2004) estimate 9,580 Khamti in Lohit District; 810 in Changlang; 137 in Lower Subsansiri; 100 in Tirup; and 111 in Dibang Valley.

4. Singh, *Arunachal Pradesh*, 179. FMC South Asia (personal communication, May 2004) estimate that 3,090 Khamti in Assam inhabit Tinsuria District; 2,300 inhabit Lakhimpur District; 1,220 inhabit Dhemaji District; 500 inhabit Dibrugarh District; 43 inhabit Cachar; and 17 inhabit North Cachar Hills. All of these estimates are 2001 figures.

5. See Philip Richard Thornhagh Gurdon, 'On the Khamtis', *Journal of the Royal Asiatic Society* (1895).

6. See S Dutta Choudhury, *Arunachal Pradesh District Gazetteers: Lohit District* (Shillong: Director of Information and Public Relations, Government of Arunachal Pradesh, 1978).

7. Singh, *Arunachal Pradesh*, 179.

8. Ibid.

9. Ibid., 181. Also see J Sarkar, 'A Note on Avoidance of Direct Exchange of Bride Among the Khamptis of Arunachal Pradesh', *Man in India* 57 (1977).

10. See B Kaundinya, *Monastic Buddhism Among the Khamtis of Arunachal* (New Delhi: National Publishing House, 1986).

11. Singh, *The Scheduled Tribes*, 502.

12. The Khamti in Kachin State of Myanmar live in one of the areas in Asia most densely populated with Christians. There are 60,000 Rawang Christians living nearby, as well as Christian Lisu and members of other ethnic groups. All but a few Khamti, however, have steadfastly stuck to their Buddhist beliefs.

13. 'There is no confirmation of their presence in China, although some publications mention the possibility of Khamtis living in China. If so, it is probable they have been assimilated to the related Dai groups in Yunnan Province' (Hattaway, *Operation China*, 577).

Kheng

1. See van Driem, *Languages of the Himalayas*, II, 871.

2. Ibid., 910.

3. Grimes, *Ethnologue* (14th edn, 2000).

4. Van Driem, *Languages of the Himalayas*, II, 910.

5. Ibid., 910–11.

6. Tsering, *Sharing Christ in the Tibetan Buddhist World*, 55–56.

Khmer

1. The Khmer live primarily in Surin, Sisaket, Buriram, Ubon Ratchathani, Nakhon Ratchasima and Korat provinces. All of these Thai provinces border northern Cambodia. Many of the Khmer in Thailand were refugees who escaped the Khmer Rouge slaughter between 1975 and 1979, while other Khmer communities have been established in Thailand for centuries. Some sources have separated the Khmer in Thailand from those elsewhere and labelled them the Northern Khmer, based on linguistic differences. However, these differences are minor and speakers of Khmer in Thailand and Khmer in Cambodia and elsewhere have no problem understanding each other. For this reason we have combined the Central Khmer and Northern Khmer into this one profile.

2. The Khmer in Vietnam are found in the provinces of Soc Triang, Tra Vinh, Kien Giang, An Giang, Can Tho, Dong Nai, Song Be, Tay Ninh and in Ho Chi Minh (formerly Saigon) City (Asian Minorities Outreach, *The Peoples of Vietnam* [Chiang Mai, Thailand: AMO Publishing] 46).

3. They live in the Attapu and Champasak provinces (Asian Minorities Outreach, *Faces of the Unreached in Laos: Southeast Asia's Forgotten Nation* [Chiang Mai, Thailand: AMO Publishing, 1999] 45).

4. There are numerous books available that deal with the reign of the Khmer Rouge in Cambodia. One of the better overviews is David P Chandler, *A History of Cambodia* (Westview Press, 1996).

5. An encouraging book tracing the spiritual transformation taking place in Cambodia is Don Cormack and Peter Lewis, *Killing Fields, Living Fields* (Grand Rapids: Kregel Publications, 2001). A remarkable autobiography of one young Khmer boy who survived the killing fields and later became a Christian is Sokreaksa S Himm, *The Tears of my Soul* (London: Monarch Books, 2003).

6. Based on a figure of 83.3% of Cambodia's population of 11,167,719 (Johnstone and Mandryk, *Operation World*) 137.

7. SIL (Summer Institute of Linguistics) estimated 1,000,000 Khmer in Thailand in 1991.

8. Johnstone and Mandryk (*Operation World*, 675) have listed a 2000 population of 1.1 million Khmer in Vietnam.

9. Northern Khmer in Thailand further divides into three sub-dialects: Buriram, Surin and Sisaket.

Khorat Thai

1. Seidenfaden, *The Thai Peoples: Book 1.*

2. Wilheim Credner, *Siam: Das Land der Tai* (Stuttgart: J Engelhorns Nachfolger, 1935).

3. Joachim Schliesinger, *Tai Groups of Thailand: Volume 2, Profile of the Existing Groups* (Bangkok: White Lotus Press, 2001) 7.

4. A good linguistic study of Khorat Thai is Narumol Chantrasupawong, *Classifiers in Khorat Thai Spoken in Ban Thap Prang, Tambol Krathok, Amphoe Chok Chai, Nakhon Ratchasima Province* (MA thesis, Chulalongkorn University, 1985).

5. Schliesinger, *Tai Groups of Thailand*, 9.

6. Ibid., 12.

Khowa

1. Although this group has been labelled Khowa by the Indian government, they apparently are unhappy with this designation and want to be identified as Bugun.

2. There are also Bugun speakers in the nearby hamlets of Kaspi, Mangopam, Lichini (Bamphu) Ramo, Namphri, Chithu, Sachida, Pani-Phu, Dichin and Bicham (van Driem, *Languages of the Himalayas*, II, 476). Only two Khowa villages are accessible by road.

3. Singh, *Arunachal Pradesh*, 185.
4. Due to classification difficulties, the 1991 census returned just 29 Khowa people in India. It seems that most were returned under a different ethnic group for reasons that are unclear.
5. Van Driem, *Languages of the Himalayas*, II, 476.
6. Ivan M Simon, 'The Khoa Language', *Resarun* (1976) 100–03.
7. Rinchin Dondrup, *Bugun Language Guide* (Itanagar: Directorate of Research of the Government of Arunachal Pradesh, 1990).
8. J N Chowdhury, *Arunachal Pradesh: From Frontier Tracts to Union Territory* (New Delhi: Cosmo Publications, 1983) 25.
9. Prasad, *Encyclopaedic Profile of Indian Tribes*, II, 438.
10. Ibid.
11. Singh, *Arunachal Pradesh*, 186–87.

Khuen

1. The Khuen in Laos 'live in the Nale, Sing and Viangphoukha districts of Luang Namtha Province in north-west Laos. A few Khuen spill across the border into the western part of Oudomxai Province. The Khuen share the region with communities of Nguan, Samtao and Kim Mun people' (Asian Minorities Outreach, *Faces of the Unreached in Laos*, 53).
2. *Encyclopedic Dictionary of Chinese Linguistics*, 594.
3. Dodd, *The Tai Race*, 237.
4. Ibid., 239.
5. Ibid., 240.

Khun

1. See Schliesinger, *Tai Groups of Thailand*, 125.
2. 'Possibly not in Thailand' (Grimes, *Ethnologue* [14th edn, 2000]).
3. Schliesinger, *Tai Groups of Thailand*, 125.
4. See Anatole-Roger Peltier, *Tai Khoeun Literature* (Bangkok: Duang Kamol, 1987).
5. Schliesinger, *Tai Groups of Thailand*, 126.
6. Ibid., 125.
7. Ibid., 128–129.
8. Personal communication (May 1997). Both the Lu and the Khun use the same script, based on the Mon alphabet. Although the two dialects are different, the Khun Christians told us that the differences were minor. Incidentally, there were also Scripture

portions translated specifically into Khun in 1938.

Kinnaura

1. See Shiva Chandra Bajpai, *Kinnaur: A Restricted Land in the Himalaya* (New Delhi: Indus Publishing Company, 1991).
2. Singh, *Himachal Pradesh*, 336.
3. Grimes, *Ethnologue* (14th edn, 2000).
4. Three good linguistic sources on Kinnauri were written by Thomas Grahame Bailey, 'Kanauri Vocabulary in Two Parts: English-Kanauri and Kanauri-English', *Journal of the Royal Asiatic Society* (1910); 'Kanauri Vocabulary in Two Parts: English-Kanauri and Kanauri-English', *Journal of the Royal Asiatic Society* (1911); and 'Kanauri Vocabulary in Two Parts', *Journal of the Royal Asiatic Society* 13 (1910).
5. See ibid. The 1981 Indian census found that the Kinnaura community speaks a total of 21 different languages, including 91% Kinnauri, 6% Hindi, nearly 1% Urdu and 0.7% Arabic. Interestingly, 130 Kinnaura returned Khandeshi as their first language. Khandeshi is spoken over 1,000 km (620 mi.) to the south.
6. Singh, *Himachal Pradesh*, 336.
7. Ibid., 341.
8. Singh, *The Scheduled Tribes*, 534.
9. Tony Hilton and Kumaradass, *Adopt – A District of Himachal Pradesh* (Chennai: People India Research and Training Institute, 1998) 88.

Korean

1. Robert Storey and Alex English, *Korea* (Hawthorn, Australia: Lonely Planet Publications, 2001) 15.
2. Schwartz, *The Minorities of Northern China*, 210.
3. Johnstone and Mandryk, *Operation World* (2001) 387.
4. Ibid., 385, states that there are 1,082,000 Buddhists in North Korea (4.5% of the population).
5. Moffett, *A History of Christianity in Asia*, 461.
6. Barrett et al., *World Christian Encyclopedia*, 683.
7. The numbers of Christians in South Korea appear to have plateaued in recent years. Church division, legalism and lack of vision have caused diminished growth. The dominant Presbyterian church, especially, has experienced numerous splits along

theological lines.
8. There are also 70,000 in Brazil; 35,000 in Argentina; 20,000 in Kyrgyzstan; 10,000 in Paraguay; 5,000 in Guam; and 3,000 in Singapore. All of these figures, unless noted, are taken from Johnstone and Mandryk, *Operation World* (2001 edn). There are dozens of other countries with Korean communities, but no population figures are available. Grimes, *Ethnologue* (14th edn, 2000) lists the following additional countries where Korean is spoken: American Samoa, Australia, Bahrain, Belize, Brunei, Canada, Germany, Mauritania, Mongolia, New Zealand, Northern Mariana Islands.

Kucong

1. Hattaway, *Operation China*, 258.
2. Asian Minorities Outreach, *The Peoples of Vietnam*, 53–54.
3. These include Long, Viangphouka and Luang Namtha districts in Luang Namtha Province, and Tonpheung and Meung districts in Bokeo Province (Asian Minorities Outreach, *Faces of the Unreached in Laos*, 58).
4. Hattaway, *Operation China*, 258.
5. Zheng Lan, *Travels Through Xishuangbanna: China's Subtropical Home of Many Nationalities* (Beijing: Foreign Languages Press, 1981) 17.
6. One of the greatest revival stories in history took place among the Lahu of Burma and China in the early 1900s. A small number of Kucong were converted, but generally the revival impacted the Lahu more. One of the main trigger points for the revival was the Lahu belief in a supreme god named *G'ui Sha*. 'When American Baptist missionary William Young first preached the gospel to the Lahu in northern Burma in 1901, they exclaimed, "We as a people have been waiting for you for centuries. . . . We even have meeting houses built in some of our villages in readiness of your coming." Many of the Lahu men wore strings on their wrists. They explained, "We Lahu have worn [strings] like these since time immemorial. They symbolize our bondage to evil spirits. You alone, as the messenger of G'ui Sha, may cut these manacles from our wrists—but only after you have brought the lost book of G'ui Sha to our very hearths!" Lahu tribesmen came all the way from China to hear Young preach. Six

thousand Lahu were baptized in 1905 and 1906. Today there are between 35,000 and 50,000 Lahu Christians in China' (Hattaway, *Operation China,* 265).

7. Covell, *The Liberating Gospel,* 226.

8. T'ien Ju-K'ang, *Peaks of Faith: Protestant Mission in Revolutionary China* (Leiden: E J Brill, 1993) 136.

9. Derived from a 1988 source of 30,000 Kucong in China (1988, *Yunnan Nianjian*).

10. Laurent Chazée, *Atlas des Ethnies et des Sous-Ethnies du Laos* (Vientiane: Laurent Chazée, 1995) estimates 1,600 Kucong in Laos in 16 villages. Grimes, *Ethnologue* (14th edn, 2000) lists a population of 20,000 Kucong in Laos but does not give a source. It is likely that this figure refers to all Lahu in Laos, of which the Kucong are only one part.

11. Cited in Grimes, *Ethnologue* (13th edn, 1996) 554.

Kui

1. Other population estimates for the Kuy in Thailand are much higher, including 300,000 (1992 by Diffloth, cited in Grimes, *Ethnologue* [14th edn, 2000]) and 217,000 in Johnstone and Mandryk, *Operation World* (2001) 618.

2. Johnstone and Mandryk, *Operation World,* 395, estimate 51,200 in Laos.

3. Smaller numbers also live in Buriram and Roi Et provinces, in addition to thousands who have migrated to Bangkok in search of work.

4. The majority live in Savannakhet Province, in addition to Saravan, Xekong and Champasak.

5. 'All districts of Preah Vihear, eastern Siem Reap, northern Kampong Thom, western Stung Traeng and several areas of Kratie Province' (Grimes, *Ethnologue* [14th edn, 2000]).

6. Schliesinger, *Ethnic Groups of Thailand,* 41.

7. Asian Minorities Outreach, *Faces of the Unreached in Laos,* 108.

8. Schliesinger, *Ethnic Groups of Thailand,* 45.

9. Chazée, *Atlas des Ethnies et des Sous-Ethnies du Laos,* 93.

Kurtop

1. Van Driem, *Languages of the Himalayas,* II, 911.

2. Armington, *Bhutan,* 237.

3. Ibid., 239.

4. Ibid., 18.

Kyerung

1. GEM, 'World's Peoples Listed by Country'.

2. Grimes, *Ethnologue* (13th edn, 1996) 729.

3. Grimes, *Ethnologue* (14th edn, 2000).

Ladakhi

1. The Joshua Project originally listed a figure of 12,000 Ladakhi in China, which was also used in the 1996 book by Asian Minorities Outreach, *The 50 Most Unreached People Groups in China and Tibet.* Grimes' *Ethnologue* (14th edn, 2000) continues to use this figure. Subsequent research, however, has shown this figure to be far too high. All researchers that I consulted who are familiar with the area deny the possibility of so many Ladakhi within Tibet. The Joshua Project also lowered their figure to 2,400 in China before the publication of the Bethany World Prayer Center prayer profiles.

2. For an account of the Chinese invasion see W E Garrett, 'Mountain Top War in Remote Ladakh', *National Geographic* (May 1960).

3. See R S Man, *The Ladakhi: A Study in Ethnography and Change* (Calcutta: Anthropological Survey of India, 1986).

4. Grimes, *Ethnologue* (13th edn, 1996) 586.

5. See David Llewellyn Snellgrove, Hugh Richardson and Tadeusz Skorupski, *The Cultural Heritage of Ladakh,* I: *Central Ladakh* (Warminster: Aris and Phillips, 1977).

6. See Thomas J Abercrombie, 'Ladakh: The Last Shangri-La', *National Geographic* (March 1978) 332–59.

7. Hellmut de Terra, 'On the World's Highest Plateaus', *National Geographic* (March 1931) 331–32.

8. Stauffer, *The Christian Occupation of China,* 278.

9. Ibid., 281.

10. One such group is the Delhi-based Cooperative Outreach of India, who conduct medical clinics and evangelism in Ladakh. They have reported more than a dozen Ladakhi people coming to Christ and being discipled in the past few years. In 1999, a short-term mission team from Phoenix in the United States travelled to Ladakh to work with COI. One

of the team members reported, 'God took my life and challenged me in every way. I will never be the same again. We did all we could to show His love to the Ladakhi people, until our hearts broke. We hiked into the mountains that were so high our lungs felt like they would burst through lack of oxygen. We slept in tents on the ground and moved from village to village each day. We shared the gospel, distributed Scripture books and gospel cassettes, helped with medical clinics run by our Indian translators, sang songs, played with the Ladakhi children. . . . One team member even brought his scissors and spent hours cutting people's ragged hair until his fingers were swollen and aching. But most of all we prayed for the souls of these people who have absolutely no concept about a Creator God or why He would send His Son into the world to die for them. We loved the Ladakhis, and they loved us back. All of this was done with the knowledge that these precious people would probably never again have the chance to hear about Jesus. We knew that we were among the most unreached of the unreached in the world, and felt God's overwhelming compassion for them. I can't wait to go back' (Asian Minorities Outreach, 'The Ladakhis' *Newsletter* 55 (December 1999).

Lao

1. This official figure probably includes the populations of smaller ethnic groups in Laos, such as the Phutai. Laurent Chazée estimates that just 1.7 million Lao people are in Laos (*The Peoples of Laos: Rural and Ethnic Diversities* [Bangkok: White Lotus Press, 1999] 39), while linguistic sources list as many as three million Lao-speakers in the country. Adult literacy of Lao in Laos is estimated at 75% (86% for men and 65% for women).

2. Schliesinger estimated between 10,000 to 20,000 Lao in Thailand (Schliesinger, *Tai Groups of Thailand,* 13). The Lao in Thailand inhabit parts of Phitsanulok, Uttaradit, Nan, Phrae and Phayao provinces.

3. Also 11,940 in Vietnam (2003, Joshua Project II); 1,700 in Argentina (2003, Joshua Project II); also in Australia, United Kingdom and many other Western nations of the world.

4. Two good accounts of Lao history by Martin Stuart-Fox are: *A History of*

Laos (Cambridge: Harvard University Press, 1977); and *The Lao Kingdom in Lan Xang: Rise and Decline* (Bangkok: White Lotus Press, 1998).

5. Schliesinger, *Tai Groups of Thailand*, 17.
6. Daniel McGilvary, *A Half Century among the Siamese and the Lao* (New York: Fleming H Revell, 1912) 405.
7. Lillian Johnson Curtis, *The Laos of North Siam, as Seen Through the Eyes of a Missionary* (Bangkok: White Lotus Press, 1903, repr. 1998) 133.

Lao Ga

1. See Schliesinger, *Tai Groups of Thailand*.
2. Probably the only two linguistic studies that mention the Lao Ga are Sirikul Kitiharakul, *Relations between Community Closeness and Lexical Choice of the Lao Khrang Community at Ban Nong Kraphu, Tambon Ban Luang, Amphoe Son Tum, Nakhon Pathom* (MA thesis, Chualongkorn University, 1996) and Wilailuck Daecha, *A Comparative Study of the Phonology of Six Tai Dialects Spoken in Amphoe Tha Tako, Changwat Nakhon Sawan* (MA thesis, Chulalongkorn University, 1987).
3. Schliesinger, *Tai Groups of Thailand*, 21.
4. Ibid., 25.

Lao Krang

1. Including the Kogmor subdistrict of Thap Than District.
2. Manoram District.
3. Including the village of Ban Nong Kraphi in Don Tum District.
4. Tha Tako District.
5. One linguistic study of the Lao Krang language is Kitiharakul, *Relations between Community Closeness and Lexical Choice of the Lao Khrang Community at Ban Nong Kraphu*. Mention of Lao Krang is also made in Daecha, *A Comparative Study of the Phonology of Six Tai Dialects;* and Kanchana Panka, *The Phonological Characteristics of Lao Dialects in Amphoe Muang, Nakhon Pathom* (MA thesis, Chulalongkorn University, 1980).
6. The Lao Khang are an animistic group profiled in Asian Minorities Outreach, *Faces of the Unreached in Laos*, 116.
7. Schliesinger, *Tai Groups of Thailand*, 38.
8. Ibid., 39.

Lao Lom

1. See Schliesinger, *Tai Groups of Thailand*, 41.

2. Ibid., 41–42.
3. Ibid., 44.

Lao Ngaew

1. Schliesinger, *Tai Groups of Thailand*, 46.
2. Ibid., 47.
3. These include Pornsri Chinchest, *Lao Ngaew Tones in Citation Forms and in Connected Speech* (MA thesis, Chulalongkorn University, 1989); Tanakorn Sungkep, *A Phonological Study of Lao Ngaeo with Comparisons to Five Tai Dialects* (MA thesis, Mahidol University, 1983); and Wilailuck Daecha, *A Comparative Study of the Phonology of Six Tai Dialects*.
4. Schliesinger, *Tai Groups of Thailand*, 49–50.
5. Ibid., 50.

Lao Ti

1. Erik Seidenfaden, 'Siam's Tribal Dresses', *Journal of the Siam Society* 21.2 (1929).
2. Schliesinger, *Tai Groups of Thailand*, 60.
3. Ibid., 63.
4. Ibid., 64–65.

Lao Wieng

1. Ban Rai District.
2. Tha Tako District.
3. Schliesinger, *Tai Groups of Thailand*, 66–67.
4. Ibid., 70.

Lap

1. Van Driem, *Languages of the Himalayas*, II, 866.
2. John Scofield, 'Life Slowly Changes in a Remote Himalayan Kingdom', *National Geographic* (November 1976) 669, 675.
3. Tsering, *Sharing Christ in the Tibetan Buddhist World*, 79–80.
4. 'The Church in Bhutan', *Go Magazine* (Interserve, 2002) 10–11.

Lawa, Eastern

1. Grimes, *Ethnologue* (14th edn, 2000).
2. Schliesinger, *Ethnic Groups of Thailand*, 101. See also Georges Condominas, *From Lawa to Mon, from Saa' to Thai: Historical and Anthropological Aspects of Southeast Asian Social Spaces* (trans. S Anderson; Canberra, 1990).
3. See Kraisri Nimmanahaeminda, 'The Lawa Guardian Spirits of Chiang Mai', *Journal of the Siam Society* 55.2 (1967).

4. Schliesinger, *Ethnic Groups of Thailand*, 104–5.
5. An excellent article on the Lawa is Peter Kunstadter, 'Living With the Gentle Lua', *National Geographic* (July 1966).

Lawa, Western

1. Ma Yin, *China's Minority Nationalities* (Beijing: Foreign Languages Press, 1989) 276–77.
2. T'ien Ju-K'ang, *Peaks of Faith*, 31.

Lemo

1. Francis Kingdon Ward, *The Land of the Blue Poppy* (Cambridge: Cambridge University Press, 1913) 230.
2. Dwayne Graybill, personal communication (September 1997).
3. 'Tremendous Success in Small Minority Area', *New China News Agency* (25 November 1958).

Lepcha

1. Van Driem, *Languages of the Himalayas*, II, 819, states that there are 'over a thousand speakers of Lepcha in south-western Bhutan, where there are a number of Lepcha villages in Samtsi District, in Denchukha north of the Amochu, or Tursa Khola.' The Lepcha in Bhutan migrated there from Sikkim.
2. Van Driem states that there were only 'roughly a hundred Lepcha households reported in Ilam district in eastern Nepal in 1986, settled mainly in the villages of Namsalin, Phikkal, Kolbun, Panckanya, Kanyam, Sri Antu and Cisopani' (ibid.).
3. There is a large amount of English-language literature available on the Lepcha. Some of the best include Indira Awasty, *Between Sikkim and Bhutan: The Lepchas and Bhutias of Pedong* (New Delhi: D K Publishers, 1979); Tapan Chattopadhyaya, *Lepchas and their Heritage* (Delhi: B R Publishing, 1990); A K Das and S K Banerjee, *The Lepchas of Darjeeling District* (Calcutta: Cultural Research Institute, 1962); A R Foning, *Lepcha: My Vanishing Tribe* (New Delhi: Sterling Publishers, 1987); Geoffrey Gorer, *Himalayan Village: An Account of the Lepchas of Sikkim* (London: Michael Joseph, 1938) and *The Lepchas of Sikkim* (New Delhi: Cultural Publishing House, 1983); C J Morris, *Living with the Lepchas: A Book about Sikkim Himalayas* (London: Toronto Heinemann,

1938); H Siiger and J Rischel, *The Lepchas: Culture and Religions of a Himalayan People* (Copenhagen: Natural Museum, 1967); and R N Thakur, *Himalayan Lepchas* (New Delhi: Archives Publishers, 1988).
4. Colonel George Byers Mainwaring, *A Grammar of the Rong (Lepcha) Language, as it Exists in the Dorjiling and Sikkim Hills* (Calcutta: Baptist Mission Press, 1876) xviii–xx. Two other good early articles are Archibald Campbell, 'Note on the Lepchas of Sikkim, with a Vocabulary of their Language', *Journal of the Asiatic Society of Bengal* 4 (1840); and John Avery, 'On the Language of the Lepchas', *Journal of the American Society: Proceedings at New York, October 28th and 29th, 1885* 13 (1889). A more recent linguistic survey of Lepcha is Nicholas C Bodman, 'On the Place of Lepcha in Sino-Tibetan: A Lexical Comparison', *Linguistics of the Tibeto-Burman Area* 11.1 (1988) 1–26. The 1981 Indian census found that 63% of this group speak Lepcha as their first language, 33% speak Nepali and 1% speak some form of Tibetan/Bhotia.
5. Dr Joseph Dalton Hooker, *Himalayan Journals; or, Notes of a Naturalist in Bengal, the Sikkim and Nepal Himalayas, the Khasia Mountains, and c.*, I (London: John Murray, 1854) 117–118.
6. See C de Beauvoir Stocks, 'Folk-lore and Customs of the Lap-chas of Sikhim', *Journal of the Asiatic Society of Bengal* 21 (1927).
7. Indian Research Teams, *Peoples of India*, 99.

Lhomi

1. Van Driem, *Languages of the Himalayas*, II, 866.
2. Hattaway, *Operation China*, 290.
3. Olavi Vesalainen and Mraja Vesalainen, *Lhomi Phonetic Summary* (Kirtipur: Summer Institute of Linguistics and Institute for Nepal and Asian Studies, 1976). Also see the Vesalainens', 'Clause Patterns in Lhomi', *Pacific Linguistics B* 53 (1980).
4. Van Driem, *Languages of the Himalayas*, II, 865.
5. Grimes, *Ethnologue* (14th edn, 2000).
6. *Global Prayer Digest* 5 (May 1994).
7. Hattaway, *Operation China*, 290.

Loba

1. Two excellent articles on the Mustang region are: Peissel, 'Mustang: Remote Realm in Nepal' and Rowell, 'Annapurna: Sanctuary for the Himalaya'.
2. See the Baragaunle profile in this book for more information.
3. Grimes, *Ethnologue* (14th edn, 2000).
4. Gautam and Thapa-Magar, *Tribal Ethnography of Nepal*, II, 20.
5. Asian Minorities Outreach, 'The Loba', *Newsletter* 49 (June 1998).

Lu

1. In China the Lu are considered the major component in the officially-recognized Dai minority nationality, which includes several other people groups and languages.
2. Especially in the north-eastern areas of Shan State, from the western bank of the Mekong River across to Kengtung City and beyond. In Myanmar the Lu are somewhat difficult to separate from the other related Tai-speaking groups in the area, including the Shan.
3. The Lu inhabit a widespread area of northern Laos, the majority being in Phongsali, Luang Namtha and Bokeo provinces east of the Mekong River.
4. The Thailand Lu live in the northern provinces of Chiang Rai (especially Chiang Khong District), Phayao (Chiang Kham and Chiang Muan districts), Nan (Pua, Thung Chang and Tha Wang Pha districts), Lamphun and Lampang.
5. In Vietnam, despite their small size, the Lu are recognized as one of the official minority groups of that nation. They live in Lai Chau Province in the extreme north-west of Vietnam, not far from the Lu homeland in southern China.
6. Hattaway, *Operation China*, 494.
7. For a comprehensive record of Lu legends, see Zhu Liangwen, *The Dai (Or the Tai and their Architecture and Customs in South China)* (Kunming: The Science and Technology Press of Yunnan, 1992); and John Hoskin and Geoffrey Walton eds., *Folk Tales and Legends of the Dai People: The Thai Lue in Yunnan* (Bangkok: DD Books, 1992).
8. Zhu Liangwen, *The Dai*, 15. For a comprehensive study on religious practices among the Lu, see T'ien Ju-K'ang, *Religious Cults of the Pai-I*

Along the Burma-Yunnan Border (New York: Cornell University Monograph, 1986); Baba Yuji, 'The Ritual of the Guardian Spirit of the Tai-Lue and its Social Background: A Case Study of Nan Province in Northern Thailand', *Fifth International Conference on Thai Studies* (London, 1993); and Baba Yuji, 'Migration and Spirit Cult: The Case Study on Tai-Lue Villages in Nan Province, Northern Thailand', *First International Conference on Thai Studies* (Chiang Mai, 1996).

Malimasa

1. As most people doubt the existence of this group, two separate population sources are cited here.
2. Matisoff, 'Languages and Dialects of Tibeto-Burman'.
3. Rock, 'Through the Great River Trenches of Asia', 161.
4. Ibid., 163.
5. Personal communication (September 1997).
6. Grimes, *Ethnologue* (13th edn, 1996) 558.
7. For an account of their work see Christian Simonnet, *Thibet, Voyage au Bout de la Chrétienté* (Paris: Editions du Monde Nouveau, 1949).
8. *Great Missionaries to China* (Grand Rapids: Zondervan, 1947) 111.
9. George Sweeting, *More than 2000 Great Quotes and Illustrations* (Texas: Word Publishing, 1985) 184.

Man

1. FMC South Asia, personal communication (May 2004).
2. 1,814 Man people in 1991.
3. 768 people.
4. 550 of the 585 Man people in Meghalaya live in the West Garo Hills, in addition to 27 in the East Khasi Hills and only 8 in the East Garo Hills.
5. Singh, *The Scheduled Tribes*, 749.
6. Ibid.
7. Ibid., 750.

Manangba

1. Perdita Phole, *Useful Plants of Manang District: A Contribution in the Ethnobotany of the Nepal-Himalaya* (Stuttgart: Franz Steiner Verlag, 1990).
2. Finlay et al., *Nepal*, 379.
3. Bista, *The People of Nepal*, 201.
4. Ibid., 202.

Manchu

1. Fifty-four per cent of all Manchu in China live in Liaoning Province (1990 census).
2. Kevin Sinclair, *The Forgotten Tribes of China* (Canada: Cupress, 1987) 43.
3. Grimes, *Ethnologue* (13th edn, 1996) 556.
4. CASS, *Information China*, III, 1248. According to the 1990 census there were 419 counties or municipalities in China that recorded more than 500 Manchu people. In descending order, the largest are: Xiuyan (Liaoning) 436,235; Fengcheng (Liaoning) 428,617; Qinglong (Hubei) 336,080; Kaiyuan City (Liaoning) 326,145; Beizhen (Liaoning) 320,524; Xingcheng City (Liaoning) 265,255.
5. Schwartz, *The Minorities of Northern China,* 149. See also Ch'en Chieh-hsien, 'The Decline of the Manchu Language in China During the Ch'ing Period (1644–1911)', in *Altaica Collects: Berichte und Vorträge der XII. Permanent International Altaistic Conference (3.–8. Juni 1974 in Bonn/Bad Honney)* (Wiesbaden: Otto Harrassowitz 1976).
6. Janhunen and Salminen, *UNESCO Red Book*.
7. Australian Academy and CASS, *Language Atlas of China*, C–5.
8. Grimes, *Ethnologue* (13th edn, 1996) 556.
9. In recent years there has been somewhat of a revival in the Manchu language, and it is even being taught to children in some schools in Heilongjiang.
10. Ramsey, *The Languages of China*, 216–17.
11. See Jerry Norman, *A Concise Manchu-English Lexicon* (Seattle: University of Washington Press, 1978); Norman and Paul Georg Von Mollendorf, *A Manchu Grammar with Analyzed Texts* (Shanghai: American Presbyterian Mission Press, 1892).
12. 'Chinese records report that the Suzhen sent tribute to the kings of the Western Zhou in the eleventh century BC' (Schwartz, *The Minorities of Northern China*, 145).
13. Bethany World Prayer Center, 'The Manchu of China'.
14. Stauffer, *The Christian Occupation of China,* 252.
15. Hefley, *China! Christian Martyrs of the 20th Century*, 35–37: 'Chang Sen had been converted after being struck blind in mid-life. Before his conversion he had been known

as *Wu so pu wei te*, meaning "one without a particle of good in him". A gambler, woman-chaser and thief, he had driven his wife and only daughter from home. When he was stricken blind, neighbors said it was the judgment of the gods for his evil doing. On hearing rumours that the Boxer soldiers were coming to kill Chang, the local believers hid him in a cave. The soldiers arrived and soon they had rounded up about fifty Christians for execution. "You're fools to kill all these," a resident told them. "For every one you kill, ten will spring up while that man Chang Sen lives. Kill him and you will crush the foreign religion." The Boxers promised to spare the fifty if someone would take them to Chang. No one volunteered. Finally when it appeared the Boxers would kill the fifty, one man slipped away and found Chang to tell him what was happening. "I'll gladly die for them," Chang offered. . . . He was bound by local authorities and taken to the temple of the god of war, and commanded to worship. "I can only worship the One Living and True God," he declared. . . . The blind evangelist was put in an open cart and driven to the cemetery outside the city wall. . . . When they reached the cemetery, he was shoved into a kneeling position. Three times he cried, "Heavenly Father, receive my spirit." Then the sword flashed, and his head tumbled to the ground. The Boxers refused to let the Christians bury his body. Instead, fearful of a report that Blind Chang would rise from the dead, they forced the believers to buy oil and burn the mangled remains. . . . The local Christians were thus spared persecution'.
16. See Asia Harvest, 'Revival in Heilongjiang', *Newsletter* 70 (April 2003); and *Newsletter* 71 (June 2003). These newsletters list many remarkable testimonies from the house churches about how the gospel has grown in Heilongjiang Province since the early 1990s. These are also available on the Asia Harvest website: www.asiaharvest.org.
17. Also 2,695,675 (1964 census); 2,418,931 (1953 census).

Manmet

1. Cited in Grimes, *Ethnologue* (14th edn, 2000).
2. Asian Studies Institute, 'The Dai People of Southeast Asia', 19.

Matpa

1. Armington, *Bhutan*, 61.
2. Ibid., 54. The *World Christian Encyclopedia* (2001) 117, gives a 2000 population of 2.124 million, the same figure as Johnstone and Mandryk's *Operation World*. These publications probably base their population estimates on official United Nations figures. Critics of the lower figure, however, believe the government has artificially created it to suit its own political interests, not wanting to acknowledge the large number of Nepali and Indian migrants who have flooded into the country in the past few decades.
3. See Scofield, 'Life Slowly Changes in a Remote Himalayan Kingdom', 658–83; and Bruce W Bunting, 'Bhutan: Kingdom in the Clouds', *National Geographic* (May 1991) 79–101.

Minyak

1. See Sun Hongkai, 'Chuanxi Minzu Zoulang Diqu De Yuyan'.
2. Rock, 'Konka Risumgongba', 399.
3. Joseph F Rock, 'The Glories of the Minya Konka', *National Geographic* (October 1930) 411.
4. Although most people in China have never heard of the Minyak, surprisingly their language has been studied extensively, starting in the 1850s when B H Hodgson compiled a small lexicon of the language. See Hodgson, 'Sifán and Hórsók Vocabularies'. Other more recent Minya studies include Huang Bufan, 'Muyayu', in Dai Qingxia et al., *Zangmianyu Shiwu Zhong* (Beijing: Yanshan Press, 1991); Sun Hongkai, 'Qiangyu Zhishu Wenti Chutan', in *A Collection of Articles on the Nationality Languages* (Xining: Qinghai University Press, 1982).
5. *Encyclopedic Dictionary of Chinese Linguistics*, 544.
6. *Qiangic Speaking Tibetans*.
7. Ibid.
8. Rock, 'Konka Risumgongba', 399.
9. Ibid., 411.

Mon

1. Mon leaders in Myanmar claim a figure of over four million. The fact that there has been no official census in Myanmar since 1931 makes their claims impossible to verify. In 1931 there were 337,000 Mon people. Many Mon in Myanmar have been absorbed into the Burmese ethno-cultural sphere, and it is mostly the Mon living in southern Mon State who still retain their language and strong sense of identity.
2. Many good books and articles have been written on the Mon of Thailand. Some include Christian Bauer, *Mon Language and Literature in Thailand* (London: University of London, 1981) and 'Language and Ethnicity: The Mon in Burma and Thailand', in Gehan Wijeyewardene ed., *Ethnic Groups across National Boundaries in Mainland Southeast Asia* (Singapore: Australian National University, Institute of Southeast Asian Studies, 1990); and Emmanuel Guillon, *The Mons: A Civilization of Southeast Asia* (trans. and ed. James V Di Crocco; Bangkok: The Siam Society, 1999).
3. Enriquez, *Races of Burma*, 126.
4. For information about the ancient Mon language see Gerald Diffloth, *The Dvaravati Old Mon Language and Nyah Kur* (Bangkok: Chulalongkorn University, 1984). R Halliday has produced three helpful books and articles on the Mon: 'Immigration of the Mons into Siam', *Journal of the Siam Society* 10.3 (Bangkok, 1913); 'The Mons in Siam', *Journal of the Burma Research Society* 12 (Rangoon, 1922); and *A Mon-English Dictionary* (Bangkok: Siam Society, 1922).
5. Schliesinger, *Ethnic Groups of Thailand*, 31.
6. An interesting article on the ancient Mon kingdom is H L Shorto, 'The 32 Myos in the Medieval Mon Kingdom', *Bulletin of the School of Oriental and African Studies* 26 (1963).
7. The world-famous Shwedagon Pagoda in Yangon (Rangoon) was built in a part of the city formerly controlled by the Mon, and many scholars believe that the Mon built it. Today, the Kyaiktiyo Pagoda in Mon State is one of the most wondrous sights in Myanmar. It is a gigantic gold-coloured rock that is perched right on the end of a cliff at the top of Mt Kyaikto. The Mon believe that the rock is held steadfastly in place by a single strand of Buddha's hair.
8. 'The Mons of Myanmar', prayer profile on the International Mission Board website: www.tconline.org.
9. Schliesinger, *Ethnic Groups of Thailand*, 33.

Mon, Ladakh

1. Prasad, *Encyclopaedic Profile of Indian Tribes*, III, 706.
2. Singh, *The Scheduled Tribes*, 818.
3. Ibid., 817–18.
4. See A H Francke, *A History of Western Tibet: One of the Unknown Empires* (Delhi: Motilal Banarsidass Publishers, 1998) 15–19.
5. Prasad, *Encyclopaedic Profile of Indian Tribes*, III, 706.
6. Wahid Saddiq, *Ladakh between Earth and Sky* (Bombay: B I Publications, 1981) 14; cited in Prasad, *Encyclopaedic Profile of Indian Tribes*, III, 706.

Mongol

1. CASS, *Information China*, III, 1249. According to the 1990 census there were 313 counties or municipalities in China that recorded more than 500 Mongol people. In descending order, the largest Mongol populations are in: Ke'erqin Zuoyizhongqi (333,436); Ke'erqin Zuoyihouqi (261,678); Tongliao City (188,192); Ke'erqin Youyizhongqi (184,347); Ke'erqin Youyiqianqi (161,183); Zalaite (151,927); Fuxin (Liaoning) (138,763); Naiman (130,019); and Kalaqin (120,466). All of these are in the *Inner Mongolian Autonomous Region* unless otherwise stated.
2. Grimes, *Ethnologue* (13th edn, 1996) 557. In my book *Operation China* I profiled the Mongols and the Khalkha Mongols separately. Input from linguists and researchers since has convinced me that linguistic differences between the two are not great enough to classify them as two different ethnolinguistic groups. Mongols from Inner Mongolian areas of China and Mongols from the far reaches of the nation of Mongolia have no problem communicating with each other. The major linguistic differences between the two lie in the different usage of written scripts.
3. Johannes Reimer, *Operation Soviet Union* (Fresno, CA: Logos, 1990).
4. Rev G H Bondfield, 'Mongolia, a Neglected Mission Field', as cited in Stauffer, *The Christian Occupation of China*, 268.
5. Plano Carpini, as cited in Moffett, *A History of Christianity in Asia*, 68.
6. John Stewart, *The Nestorian Missionary Enterprise: A Church on Fire* (Edinburgh: T & T Clarke, 1923) 159.
7. Ibid., 143–44.
8. Covell, *The Liberating Gospel*, 129.
9. Moule and Pelliot, *Marco Polo*, 79.
10. *CPLMR* 119 (December 1991– February 1992).
11. Due to the efforts of Chinese house church Christians in China, a tremendous revival has broken out in parts of eastern and north-east Inner Mongolia. One major house church movement claims that 500,000 people in Inner Mongolia came to Christ between 2000 and 2003, of which approximately 10 per cent are ethnic Mongols and the rest Han Chinese. In the early 1900s, claims were often made of large numbers of Mongol believers in China, but these often stemmed from a misunderstanding of the figures reported for Catholics in Inner Mongolia. In the early 1920s the Roman Catholic Church listed 105,695 baptized converts in Inner and Outer Mongolia, especially in the regions of Suwei Bashan, Alashan and Olanbor (see Stauffer, *The Christian Occupation of China*, 274) and 200,000 Catholics by 1940 (J Leyseen, *The Cross Over China's Wall* [Beijing: The Lazarist Church, 1941], 138). However, 'the large majority of these were Han Chinese, and few were Mongolians', (Covell, *The Liberating Gospel*, 131). The 1922 report is brought into focus with the note, 'As far as is known, most of the work is on behalf of Chinese and little direct evangelistic activity is carried on among the Mongols' (Stauffer, *The Christian Occupation of China*, 274). One critic of the Catholic work in Inner Mongolia noted that 'very often the incentive held out to the heathen is an economic one. The converts are invited to live on the land, each family is given an ox, a plow, a small field and sufficient seed' (Mrs A B Magnuson, as cited in Hefley, *China! Christian Martyrs of the 20th Century*, 43).
12. Johnstone and Mandryk, *Operation World*, 451.

Mongol, Sichuan

1. One source says that the Sichuan Mongols historically were Mosuo people. If that is true, their language today probably retains linguistic influence from Naxi. See Charles F McKhann, 'The Naxi and the Nationalities Question', in Stevan Harrell ed., *Cultural Encounters on China's Ethnic Frontiers* (Seattle, WA: University of Washington Press, 1995) 61.
2. Target Ministries, personal communication (March 1997).
3. Ibid. 'They have some vocabulary which has been passed down. I remember them saying their word for table was one such word.'
4. Rock, 'The Land of the Yellow Lama', *National Geographic* (April 1925) 463.
5. Rock, 'Konka Risumgongba', 26.
6. Target Ministries, personal communication (March 1997).
7. Ibid.
8. Ibid.

Mongour

1. Australian Academy and CASS, *Language Atlas of China*, C–2. There were a total of 38,005 members of the Tu nationality living in Minhe County according to the 1990 census. Most of these are ethnic Mongour, but some may be ethnic Tu.
2. Schwartz, *The Minorities of Northern China*, 109.
3. Zhaonasitu, as cited in Milliken, 'SIL China Nationalities and Languages Files'.
4. Ramsey, *The Languages of China*, 201.
5. Schwartz, *The Minorities of Northern China*, 109.
6. Ibid., 113–14.
7. Marjorie Medary, *Each One Take One: Frank Laubach, Friend to Millions* (New York: David McKay, 1954) 80–81.

Monpa, But

1. Their numbers had decreased alarmingly from 555 in the 1971 census.
2. Singh, *Arunachal Pradesh*, 218.
3. See D K Duarah, *The Monpas of Arunachal Pradesh* (Itanagar: Directorate of Research of the Government of Arunachal Pradesh, 1990).
4. Ibid., 216.
5. See Bibhas Dhar, 'The Monpas of Khategthang Area, alias, the Tsanglas: A Brief Ethnographic Account', in S

Karotemprel ed., *The Tribes of North-East India* (Calcutta: Firma K L M Ltd., 1984) 295–306.
6. Singh, *Arunachal Pradesh*, 218.
7. Singh, *The Scheduled Tribes*, 819.
8. Ibid., 821.
9. Interestingly, the India Missions Association, which is the largest Christian research organization in India, lists a total number of 3,750 Monpa Christians in India, out of a total population of 29,730 (Indian Research Teams, *Peoples of India*, 124). If true, this would mean that 12.61 per cent of Monpa people are Christians. This figure must be presumed to be an error, as all other sources working in Arunachal Pradesh state that there is a very small number of Monpa believers, a veritable handful and no more than a few dozen. The Rev P C Muanthanga, *The Harvest Field of Arunachal Pradesh* (Shillong: NEIBMCC: Carey Research and Communication Centre, 1998) 11, states: 'Only one or two Monpas have become Christians and the vast majority have not received the Gospel till now'.

Monpa, Chugpa

1. Singh, *Arunachal Pradesh*, 223.
2. Ibid.
3. Singh, *The Scheduled Castes*, 822. On this custom see also the profile below on the Dirang Monpa.

Monpa, Dirang

1. Singh, *Arunachal Pradesh*, 228.
2. Ibid., 229.
3. Ibid., 229–30.
4. Singh, *The Scheduled Tribes*, 824.

Monpa, Kalaktang

1. Singh, *The Scheduled Tribes*, 825.
2. Singh, *Arunachal Pradesh*, 235.
3. Ibid.

Monpa, Lishpa

1. Singh, *Arunachal Pradesh*, 237.
2. Ibid.
3. Van Driem, *Languages of the Himalayas*, II, 477–78.
4. Due to classification problems, the 1991 census in India returned just 12 Lishpa Monpa people. The rest appear to have been counted under the all-encompassing 'Monpa' category.
5. Singh, *The Scheduled Tribes*, 827.
6. Singh, *Arunachal Pradesh*, 241.

Monpa, Medog

1. Australian Academy and CASS, *Language Atlas of China*, C–6.
2. Bradley, 'East and South-East Asia', 170.
3. He Guanghua, 'The Lost Horizons of Medog', *China Reconstructs* (March 1995) 47–50. An excellent article on the rugged geography of the Medog area is Hong Yang, 'Adventures in the Namjagbarwa Canyon of Tibet', *China Tourism* 214 (May 1998).
4. See Sun Hongkai, Lu Shaozun, Zhang Jichuan and Ouyang Jueya, *The Languages of the Menba, Luoba and Deng Peoples* (Beijing: Chinese Social Science Publishing House, 1980).
5. Bethany World Prayer Center, 'The Men-Pa'.
6. Zhang and Zeng, *In Search of China's Minorities*, 139.

Monpa, Tawang

1. 'Tawang: A Hidden Paradise beyond Imagination' (Tawang, Arunachal Pradesh: District Tourism Promotion Committee, n.d.).
2. Singh, *Arunachal Pradesh*, 243.
3. Ibid.
4. In May 2004, local Buddhist lamas forced the first ever Monpa church in Tawang to close.

Mosuo

1. Shi Youyi ed., *Folkways of China's Minority Nationalities* (Southwest) (Chengdu: Huayi Publishing House, 1991), 44.
2. A good account of Mosuo history can be found in McKhann, 'The Naxi and the Nationalities Question', 54.
3. Matt Forney, 'Total Recall', *Far Eastern Economic Review* (29 May 1997) 70. The government opposes everything that doesn't line up with the majority Han culture, which they consider supreme.
4. Ibid. In 1997, only two shamans were still able to recite the entire text, but seven children were being trained to know the chants in order to retain the Mosuo culture.
5. Olson, *An Ethnohistorical Dictionary of China*, 247.
6. See Tribes and Nations Outreach, *Kindreds* 7.2 (Bangkok, 1996).

Mpi

1. Several linguistic studies include J G Harris et al., *A Mpi Dictionary: Working Papers in Phonetics and*

Phonology (Bangkok: Thai and Minority Language Research Project I.1, 1976); James A Matisoff, *Mpi and Lolo-Burmese Microlinguistics* (Tokyo: Institute for the Study of Languages and Cultures of Asia and Africa, 1978); and Sittichai Sah-Iam, *Phrases and Clauses in the MPI Language at Ban Dong, Phrae Province* (Bangkok: Mahidol University, MA thesis, 1984).
2. Schliesinger, *Ethnic Groups of Thailand*, 191.

Mru

1. The Mru should not be confused with the similarly-named Maru tribe of Kachin State in northern Myanmar. Although both groups speak a language from the Tibeto-Burman linguistic family, they are not closely related.
2. In the current political climate in Myanmar, with several armed insurgencies taking place at any given time, it is unlikely that the government has either the resources or the will-power to conduct a census. Overall, there are 22 different armed opposition groups in Myanmar! A census that returns higher-than-expected populations for a certain group like the Shan or Kachin could give impetus to the independence movements in those areas; while a census that returns smaller figures than expected for such groups would likely be seen as rigged. A good source for information about the insurgency problem in Myanmar is Martin Smith, *Ethnic Groups in Burma: Development, Democracy and Human Rights* (London: Anti-Slavery International, 1994).
3. Enriquez, *Races of Burma*, 126.
4. The national policy in Bangladesh is meant to prohibit outsiders from moving to the Mru area so that the Mru can retain their traditional culture. In recent years, however, armed Bengali farmers have reportedly entered the Mru area and seized their land. The Mru have taken up arms against them in retaliation. See Bethany World Prayer Center, 'The Mru of South Asia'.
5. The Mru in India are not recognized as an official ('scheduled') tribe by the Indian government, although their population was noted separately in the 1991 census (1,547) and in the 1981 census (1,231). There were 70 Mru

Christians in India, according to the 1991 census.
6. Bethany World Prayer Center, 'The Mru of South Asia'.
7. A Western missionary familiar with these events related this testimony to me in 1999. A Mru later confirmed it.
8. *Prayer Focus*, Ethnos Asia *Newsletter* 40 (Bangkok, July 2000).
9. Ibid. The report goes on to say, 'Two leaders from the nearby Khumi [Chin] tribe heard the news and came to join in this discussion. They have also longed for a primary school for their children for a very long time. They reported, "Thirty families in our village are ready to abandon their old faith." They have no one to teach them about Christianity. Maybe, when the school is established, they will learn more about this new faith.'
10. The Association of Baptists for World Evangelism (ABWE) estimated 20,000 Mru in Bangladesh in 1999.

Mugali

1. Cited in Grimes, *Ethnologue* (14th edn, 2000). The Bethany World Prayer Center profile 'The Mugali of Nepal' incorrectly lists a 1990 population of 39,800.
2. The names of some of their 13 villages are Mugu, Dolphu, Maha, Chyute, Krimi, Mangri, Wongri, Katik and Daura. See Ukyab and Adhikari, *The Nationalities of Nepal*.
3. Gautam and Thapa-Magar, *Tribal Ethnography of Nepal*, II, 72.
4. Bethany World Prayer Center, 'The Mugali of Nepal'.
5. Salter and Gurung, *Faces of Nepal*, 13.
6. Frontier Missions Center for Himalayan Peoples, *Pray for the Peoples of Nepal*.
7. Ibid.

Na

7. Singh, *Arunachal Pradesh*, 266.
2. Ibid.
3. Ibid., 269.
4. Ibid., 268.
5. Ibid., 267.
6. Maunthanga, *The Harvest Field of Arunachal Pradesh*, 6.

Newar

1. According to FMC South Asia, there are 89,000 Newar in West Bengal (57,000 in Darjeeling District; 22,000 in Jalpailguri; and 7,000 in Medinapur District); and 25,600 in Sikkim (of which 11,000 are in the East Sikkim

District). For further information on the Newar in India, see K S Singh ed., *India's Communities: N–Z* (People of India VI; Delhi: Oxford University Press and Anthropological Survey of India, 1998) 2634–35; and Gopal Singh Nepali, *The Newars* (Bombay: United Asia Publications, 1965).
2. FMC South Asia reports 1,700 Newar in Bangladesh, 750 in Dhaka. In Bangladesh they are Hindus.
3. See John Burton-Page, 'The Name "Nepal"', *Bulletin of the School of Oriental and African Studies* 16.3 (1954). The name of this group should actually be spelled 'Newah', but it has been labelled 'Newar' for so long that it has become the commonly accepted way to spell it in English. There is a Newah Association in Nepal that strongly insists the spelling be changed.
4. See K P Chattopadhyaya, 'An Essay on the History of Newar Culture', *Journal of the Asiatic Society of Bengal* 19.10 (1923).
5. In India, 107,000 Newar speak Nepali as their first language; 4,730 speak Bengali; just 4,200 speak Newari; and 900 speak Hindi (FMC South Asia, personal communication [May 2004]).
6. Gautam and Thapa-Magar, *Tribal Ethnography of Nepal*, 119.
7. Taken from the http://dg.ian.com website.
8. Bista, *The People of Nepal*, 25.
9. Salter and Gurung, *Faces of Nepal*, 55.

Nubri

1. Citied in Grimes, *Ethnologue* (14th edn, 2000).
2. Ibid.
3. Van Driem, *Languages of the Himalayas*, II, 862.
4. Bista, *The People of Nepal*, 203.
5. Grimes, *Ethnologue* (14th edn, 2000).
6. Bista, *The People of Nepal*, 204–5.

Nupbi

1. Armington, *Bhutan*, 210.
2. Van Driem, *Languages of the Himalayas*, II, 908.
3. Ibid.
4. Email newsletter from *Travel the Road* (20 December 2003). Travel the Road is a production team of two young men who travel to various remote parts of the world, filming unreached people groups. Their programmes have been shown on Christian

television in the USA, although it is highly unlikely that the gruesome scenes described in this report will ever be shown in public.

Nyahkur

1. Schliesinger, *Ethnic Groups of Thailand*, 35.
2. Ibid., 38.
3. See Erik Seidenfaden, 'Some Notes about the Chaubun: A Disappearing Society', *Journal of the Siam Society* 12.3 (1919); and Seidenfaden, 'Further Notes About the Chaubun, etc.', *Journal of the Siam Society* 13.3 (1920).
4. Schliesinger, *Ethnic Groups of Thailand*, 39.
5. Ibid., 30–40.
6. Ibid., 35.

Nyaw

1. Muang, Kut Bak, Song Dao and Warit Chaphum districts.
2. Tha Uthen, Na Wa and Phon Sawan districts.
3. Wan Yai and Don Tan districts.
4. Tha Bo District.
5. Schliesinger, *Tai Groups of Thailand*, 159.
6. Asian Minorities Outreach, *Faces of the Unreached in Laos*, 122. The Nyaw are profiled as the 'Tai Nyo' in this book.
7. Grimes, *Ethnologue* (13th edn, 1996) 789.
8. Schliesinger, *Tai Groups of Thailand*, 159.
9. Ibid., 160. His information appears to have come from Kanjana Koowatthanasiri, *The Tones of Nyo* (MA thesis, Chulalongkorn University, 1980).
10. Schliesinger, *Tai Groups of Thailand*, 163.
11. Asian Minorities Outreach, *Faces of the Unreached in Laos*, 122.
12. In 1990, Anthony Diller of the Australian National University estimated 50,000 speakers of the Nyaw language in Thailand. Citied in Grimes, *Ethnologue* (13th edn, 1996) 789.
13. This figure in Laos may be too high.

Nyenpa

1. Van Driem, *Languages of the Himalayas*, II, 913.
2. The Voice of the Martyrs, 'The Persecution and Prayer Alert' (Wednesday, 30 October 2002).
3. *Friday Church News Notes*, 'Bhutanese

Christians Flee to India for Life' (1 November 2002).

Ole

1. Van Driem, *Languages of the Himalayas*, II, 919. Grimes, *Ethnologue* (14th edn, 2000) lists a population of 1,000 Ole people, but this is based on an earlier estimate by van Driem, which he later adjusted to be lower. There may be closer to 1,000 people who identify themselves with this ethnic group, but there are only 500 remaining who can still speak the Ole language.
2. Van Driem, *Languages of the Himalayas*, II, 917.
3. Ibid., 918.
4. Ibid., 881–82.
5. Ibid., 919.

Padaung

1. The names of their villages in Thailand are Ban Nai Soi, Ban Nam Pieng Din and Ban Huai Suea Thao. See Schliesinger, *Ethnic Groups of Thailand*, 222.
2. Some people have complained that the Padaung women have become little more than exploited zoo animals, with tour operators getting rich from their appearance while paying the Padaung as little money as possible. Several years ago an unscrupulous Thai businessman was imprisoned after he was caught illegally smuggling some Padaung women into Thailand so he could make money with them. The women were returned to Myanmar.
3. Schliesinger, *Ethnic Groups of Thailand*, 223–24.
4. Ibid., 227.

Palaung, Pale

1. 'The mountainous north of Myanmar's Shan State is the traditional homeland of the Silver Palaung. This region varies in elevation from 5,000 to 8,500 feet and is significantly cultivated. Uncultivated areas are covered in forest. Their villages are usually located near a stream or river. This area is prone to violent storms in the rainy season and, because of deforestation and erosion, landslides are a major problem. Many Silver Palaung also live in the south-western part of Shan State, near the Inle Lake area, though not on the lake itself' (Myanmar Faces and Places, 'Silver Palaung Profile' [unpublished, 2003]).
2. Enriquez, *Races of Burma*, 127. This

figure probably included all of the different Palaung groups, not only the Pale.

3. See Hattaway, *Operation China*, 110.
4. See Min Naing, *Palaungs of Burma* (Rangoon: Ministry of Culture, 1960).
5. Schliesinger, *Ethnic Groups of Thailand*, 100.
6. See Asian Minorities Outreach, 'The Palaung', *Newsletter* 38 (March 1996).

Palaung, Rumai

1. The main centre of the Rumai Palaung is the town of Namshan in northern Shan State, yet 'very few Rumai Palaung actually live in Namshan, but this is their market town' (Myanmar Faces and Places, 'Rummai Palaung Profile' [unpublished, 2003]).
2. See Hattaway, *Operation China*, 111.
3. Zhang and Zeng, *In Search of China's Minorities*, 228.
4. Ibid., 232
5. *Global Prayer Digest* 8.9 (September 1989).
6. Carl F and Florence M Voegelin, *Classification and Index of the World's Languages* (New York: Elsevier North Holland, 1977) listed 139,000 total Rumai in Myanmar and China in 1977.

Palaung, Shwe

1. Myanmar Faces and Places, 'Golden Palaung Profile' (unpublished, 2003).
2. Hattaway, *Operation China*, 112.
3. C Peter Wagner and Edward Dayton, *Unreached Peoples '79* (Elgin, IL: David Cook, 1979).
4. Personal communication with a missionary among the Palaung (20 April 2003).

Pa-O

1. 'The Pa-O extend west to the Shan State / Mandalay Division border, east beyond Ho-Pong, south to near the Kayah / Shan State border, and north beyond Pindaya, with small pockets located in Karen and Kayah States' (Myanmar Faces and Places, 'Pa'o Karen Profile' [unpublished, 2003]).
2. The names of their villages in Thailand are Ban Hwe Sarop, Ban Hwe Khan, Ban Pong Yam and Ban Hti Ta Maung. See Schliesinger, *Ethnic Groups of Thailand*, 214.
3. See William D Hackett, *The Pa-O People of the Shan State, Union of Burma: A Sociological and Ethnographic Study of*

the *Pa-O (Taungthu) People* (Cornell University, PhD thesis, 1953).
4. Diran, *The Vanishing Tribes of Burma*, 76.
5. Myanmar Faces and Places, 2003.
6. Schliesinger, *Ethnic Groups of Thailand*, 216–17.

Phuan

1. In Thailand the Phuan live in the provinces of Lopburi (Ban Mi and Khok Samrong districts), Udon Thani, Roi Et, Sukkothai, Uttaradit, Nakhon Nayok, Prachin Buri, Nakhon Sawan (Tha Tako District), Phetchaburi, Ratchaburi (Photharam District) and Bangkok City.
2. Chazée, *Atlas des Ethnies et des Sous-Ethnies du Laos.*
3. In Laos, the Phuan live in the provinces of Xiangkhoang, Borikhamxai, Oudomxai and Houaphan as well as in Vientiane Municipality and the Xaisomboun Special Region.
4. Three excellent resources on the Phuan are Wichian Wongwiset, *The Phuan of Thailand (Thai Phuan)* (Bangkok: Wattana Phanit, 1982); Snit Smuckarn, *Peasantry and Modernization: A Study of the Phuan in Central Thailand* (PhD thesis, University of Hawaii, 1972) and 'A Culture in Search of Survival: The Phuan of Thailand and Laos' (New Haven: Yale University Press Center for International and Area Studies, Monograph Series 31, 1988).
5. Schliesinger, *Tai Groups of Thailand,* 82.
6. Ibid., 83.
7. Joe Cummings ed., *Laos* (Singapore: Lonely Planet, 3rd edn, 1998) 271.

Phutai

1. In Laos the Phutai are concentrated in the southern arm of the country—in Khammouan, Savannakhet, Champasak and Saravan provinces—while some communities are also located in the northern provinces of Oudomxai and Luang Prabang.
2. The Phutai of Thailand inhabit the north-eastern provinces of Nakhon Phanom (Na Kae, Ru Nu Nakhon and That Phanom districts); Sakhon Nakhon (the Phu Phan hills); Mukdahan (Muang, Don Tan and Nikhom Kham Soi districts); and Kalasin (Khao Wong District). The Phutai in Thailand all migrated from Khammouan Province in Laos (Schliesinger, *Tai Groups of Thailand*, 89).

3. See Chamberlain, 'The Tai Dialects of Khammouan Province'.
4. See Thomas A Kirsch, 'Development and Mobility among the Phu Tai of North-east Thailand', *Asian Survey* 6.7 370–378 and *Phu Thai Religious Syncretism: A Case Study of Thai Religion and Society* (PhD thesis, Harvard University, 1967).
5. Asian Minorities Outreach, *Faces of the Unreached in Laos*, 89.

Puman

1. Olson, *An Ethnohistorical Dictionary of China*, 280.
2. Grimes, *Ethnologue* (13th edn, 1996) 563.
3. Olson, *An Ethnohistorical Dictionary of China*, 280.
4. Jun Feng, 'Xishuangbanna: Homeland of Minorities', *China Tourism* 72 (n.d.) 35.
5. Olson, *An Ethnohistorical Dictionary of China*, 281.
6. Dodd, *The Tai Race,* 334.

Pumi, Northern

1. Rock, 'The Land of the Yellow Lama', 467. A total of 34,616 'Tibetans' were living in Muli County according to the 1990 census. The majority of these are Northern Pumi people.
2. Lu Shaozun, *Pumi Yu Fangyan Yanjiu* (Beijing: Minorities Publishing House, 2001) 6.
3. Ethno-historian Leo Moser writes, 'As far back as the Shang times, the known world was conceived as a system of concentric circles or squares. At the centre was the Shang capital. Surrounding it were the lands under the direct sovereignty of the Shang; surrounding these were a zone of feudal states . . . under a loose Shang hegemony; surrounding that were the outer states, in which semibarbarian or barbarian peoples resided. The barbarians were often called *sifang*, or "[people of the] four directions"' (Moser, *The Chinese Mosaic*, 23).
4. When writing *Operation China* I struggled to find a name for this group. I didn't want to call them by the derogatory name *Xifan*, even though they are most commonly know by this name. After carefully reading through Joseph Rock's articles from the 1920s and 1930s, I found that Rock mentioned their self-name was *Chrame* (See Rock, 'Konka Risumgongba', 1). I therefore called this group Chrame, as I felt there was

no better alternative available. Since the publication of *Operation China*, however, people who have visited this group have told me that nobody was familiar with the name Chrame, which Rock had used more than 70 years ago. The people today simply call themselves Tibetans, and some don't mind identifying themselves as Xifan, despite the connotations of that Chinese name. Linguistic research, however, labels the language as Northern Pumi, so I have used this name here.
5. Rock, 'The Land of the Yellow Lama', 467.
6. Ibid.
7. Rock, 'Konka Risumgongba', 19.
8. Ibid.
9. Rock, 'The Land of the Yellow Lama', 477.

Qiang, Cimulin

1. Liu Guangkun, *Maqo Qiangyu Yanjiu* (Chengdu: Sichuan Minzu Chubanshe, 1998). According to James Matisoff, the Cimulin Qiang have a 'speaker population of about 9,000, primarily distributed in the vicinity of Cimulin in Xiaoheishui District; specifically, the villages of Ermulin, Rewo, Wumushu, Ciba and Qinglanggou' (Matisoff, 'Languages and Dialects of Tibeto-Burman').
2. 'The Stone, A Guardian of Life: The Qiang: Keeping a Unique Stone Culture' (unpublished report [1998] 3).
3. Huang Bu-Fan (1987) 33, as cited in Milliken, 'SIL China Nationalities and Languages Files'.
4. J-O Svantesson, personal communication (1990), as cited in Grimes, *Ethnologue* (12th edn, 1992) 526.
5. CASS, *Information China*, III, 1249.
6. An excellent overview of the Qiang is Huang Yanhong, 'The Qiang People', *China Tourism* 202 (May 1997) 62–67.
7. Asian Minorities Outreach, 'The Qiang', *Newsletter* 27 (June 1994).
8. Thomas F Torrance Jr, 'Journal of My First Visit to Hong Kong, Chengdu and Wenchuan, April 22 to June 3, 1994' (unpublished report, Edinburgh, 1994) 41.

Qiang, Luhua

1. Liu Guangkun, *Maqo Qiangyu Yanjiu*. According to James Matisoff, the Luhua Qiang 'take their name from

a village in Sichuan province, China. Speaker population of about 12,000, primarily distributed in the vicinity of Luhua in Heishui County; specifically, the villages of Sandagu, Shashiduo, Yang'er, Zegai, Ergulu, Shangyinshan and Shangyangshan' (Matisoff, 'Languages and Dialects of Tibeto-Burman').

2. 'The Stone, A Guardian of Life', 4.
3. Ibid., 14.
4. Stauffer, *The Christian Occupation of China*, 277. Although missionaries presumed his motive for buying so many was to make money by reselling them, the prince assured them that he wanted them to help his people.

Qiang, Mawo

1. Liu Guangkun, *Maqo Qiangyu Yanjiu*. According to James Matisoff, the Mawo Qiang 'take their name from a village in Sichuan province, China. Speaker population of about 15,000, primarily distributed in the vicinity of Mawo in Heishui County; specifically, the villages of Zhawo, Esi, Hongyan, Xi'er, Shuangliushu, Xiayinshan and Xiayangshan' (Matisoff, 'Languages and Dialects of Tibeto-Burman').

2. Another source, 'The Stone, A Guardian of Life', 7–8, records a completely different legend about the origins of the Yun Yun shoes. . . . 'When a Qiang man was travelling from the north to the south, he met a violent person . . . who fought with him. Although the Qiang man was unable to win in the beginning, on the second night of the battle he had a dream. In his dream, a god told him that the Qiang people needed to jump up so the clouds were under their feet and with the help of the white rock, they would be able to win the battle. After actually winning, they wore the cloud shoes to remember this important time in their history. The shoes also became a symbol of protection for the Qiang people and a good gift to express affection between a man and a woman.'

Qiang, Yadu

1. Liu Guangkun, *Maqo Qiangyu Yanjiu*. According to James Matisoff, the Yadu Qiang 'take their name from a village in Sichuan province, China. Speaker population of more than 10,000, primarily distributed in the vicinity of Wabuliangzi in southern Heishui

County, and Chibusu in northern Maoxian County; specifically, the villages of Qugu, Heping, and Weicheng' (Matisoff, 'Languages and Dialects of Tibeto-Burman').

Qixingmin

1. *Minzu Shibie Wenxian Ziliao Huibian*, 56.
2. *Guizhou Nianjian* 1985.
3. *Minzu Shibie Wenxian Ziliao Huibian*, 56.
4. See the Introduction to Zhang Jimin, 'Lajiyu yu Gelaoyu de Guanxi', *Minzu Yuwen* 3 (1992, Chinese language) 19–27.

Queyu

1. *Encyclopedic Dictionary of Chinese Linguistics*, 543.
2. *Qiangic Speaking Tibetans*.
3. Ibid.
4. See Peissel, *Cavaliers of Kham*.
5. Lambert, 'Christianity and Tibet'.
6. Ibid.
7. Stauffer, *The Christian Occupation of China*, 276.

Rakhine

1. The most recent census in Burma / Myanmar was conducted in 1931 by the British colonial rulers. At that time, the Rakhine numbered 208,251 (Enriquez, *Races of Burma*, 126).
2. Myanmar Faces and Places, 'Profile of the Rakhine'.
3. Grimes, *Ethnologue* (14th edn, 2000). FMC South Asia (personal communication, May 2004) listed a much higher figure of 358,000 Rakhine (*Mag*) in Bangladesh, primary in Chittagong District (168,000), Rangamati District (49,000), Cox Bazar (43,000), Khagrachhari (41,000) and Bandarban (28,000). Approximately 75 per cent of the Rakhine in Bangladesh speak Rakhine and 25 per cent speak Bengali.
4. FMC South Asia (personal communication, May 2004) listed a much higher figure of 47,800 *Mag* (Rakhine) in India, of which 42,000 are Buddhists, 5,500 Hindus and 200 Christians. In India, FMC South Asia say 42,000 are dispersed in Tripura State (36,300 in South Tripura District and 5,000 in North Tripura District). A further 5,500 live in West Bengal (2,600 in Jalapaiguri District and 850 in Parganas North District).

5. Diran, *The Vanishing Tribes of Burma*, 160.
6. Clark and Cummings, *Myanmar (Burma)*, 425.
7. Grimes, *Ethnologue* (14th edn, 2000).
8. Singh, *The Scheduled Tribes*, 701.
9. Diran, *The Vanishing Tribes of Burma*, 160.
10. The historical Buddhist centre of the Rakhine was at Mrauk-U. The temple complex was founded in 1433 and today contains more than 70 ruins that can be visited by tourists. For a good account of the Mrauk-U history and temples, see Clark and Cummings, *Myanmar (Burma)*, 432–41.

Saek

1. Some of the main Saek areas in Thailand include Ban Adsamart in Muang District; Ban Pailom and Ban Dongsamo in Na Wa District; and Ban Bawa in Si Songkhram District (Schliesinger, *Ethnic Groups of Thailand*, 56).
2. See L N Morev, *The Sek Language* (Moscow, 1988).
3. See James R Chamberlain, 'The Origin of the Sek: Implications for Tai and Vietnamese History', *The Journal of the Siam Society* 86.1 and 2 (1998).
4. Schliesinger, *Ethnic Groups of Thailand*, 56.
5. Bethany World Prayer Center, 'The Saek of Laos'.
6. Schliesinger, *Ethnic Groups of Thailand*, 59–60.

Samtao

1. Grimes, *Ethnologue* (14th edn, 2000). It's possible that this low figure only refers to those who are still able to speak the Samtao language.
2. Schliesinger, *Ethnic Groups of Thailand*, 116.
3. Olsen, *An Ethnohistorical Dictionary of China*, 298.
4. See Hattaway, *Operation China*, 469.
5. Dodd, *The Tai Race*, 213.
6. Schliesinger, *Ethnic Groups of Thailand*, 120.
7. Although some sources state that there are just 100 or less Samtao in Myanmar, Olsen (*An Ethnohistorical Dictionary of China*, 298) confirms 'Most Samtaos live today in the north-eastern region of . . . Myanmar (Burma) but several thousand can also be found across the border in the Yunnan Province of China.'

Shan

1. The most recent census held in Myanmar was in 1931. At the time there were 1,037,406 Shan returned, but this figure probably included other smaller Tai-speaking groups in Shan State (Enriquez, *Races of Burma*, 126).

2. The village is 'located in a remote area that juts into Myanmar, in a densely forested and mountainous region . . . in the Dehong Prefecture of western Yunnan Province' (Hattaway, *Operation China*, 479).

3. There are numerous books and articles about the Shan. Some of the more interesting ones include Wilbur Willis Cochrane, *The Shans* (Rangoon: Government Printing Press, 1915); Archibald R Colquhoun, *Amongst the Shans* (London: Field and Tuer, 1885); Leslie Milne and Wilbur Cochrane, *Shans at Home* (New York: Paragon Book Reprint Co., 1970); and Chao Tzang Yawnghwe, *The Shan of Burma: Memoirs of a Shan Exile* (Singapore: Australian National University Institute of Southeast Asian Studies, 1987).

4. Missionary Josiah N Cushing produced three interesting early linguistic studies on the Shan language: *Grammar of the Shan Language* (Rangoon: American Baptist Mission Press, 1871); *Elementary Handbook of the Shan Language* (Rangoon: American Baptist Mission Press, 1888); and *A Shan and English Dictionary* (Rangoon: American Baptist Mission Press, 1914).

5. Grimes, *Ethnologue* (13th edn, 1996) 722–23.

6. Hattaway, *Operation China*, 479.

7. The American Baptist Mission Press wrote a linguistic manual for the study of Shan. See F Bigg-Wither, *A Guide to the Study of Shan* (Rangoon: American Baptist Mission Press, 1911).

Sherdukpen

1. A study on the Sherdukpen of Rupa village was done as part of the 1971 Indian census. See Roy Burman, B K ed., 'Socio-Economic Survey of Rupa: A Sherdukpen Village in Arunachal Pradesh', in *Census of India, 1971. Series 1, India, Part C VI* (New Delhi: Controller of Publications, 1975).

2. Probably the only thorough study of the Sherdukpen language is

Rinchin Dondrup, *A Hand Book on Sherdukpen Language* (Itanagar: Directorate of Research on the Government of Arunachal Pradesh, 1990).

3. Singh, *Arunachal Pradesh*, 288.

4. Ibid., 289.

5. For more interesting information on Sherdukpen culture and society, see R R P Sharma, *The Sherdukpen* (Shillong: Research Department, NEFA Administration, 1961). See also Prasad, *Encyclopaedic Profile of Indian Tribes*, IV, 916–18.

Sherpa

1. According to FMC South Asia (personal communication, May 2004), 23,900 live in the Darjeeling District of West Bengal; 7,300 in Sikkim (5,200 in South Sikkim District and 2,200 in West Sikkim District); and an additional 4,000 inhabit the Jalpaiguri District of Arunachal Pradesh.

2. The Khumbu dialect of Sherpa is spoken 'north from Namche Bazaar. [The Solu dialect] is the southern region including the villages of Gumdi, Sete, Junbesi, Phaplu and Sallery; around Rolwaling, the northern border of Janakpur District and Taplejung, Mechi District. There may also be some around Lukla' (Grimes, *Ethnologue* [14th edn, 2000]).

3. Xu Yixi, *Headdresses of Chinese Minority Nationality Women* (Hong Kong: China Film Press, 1989) 49.

4. Grimes, *Ethnologue* (13th edn, 1996) 561.

5. Gu Shoukang, 'The Sherpas: Hardy Folk of the Himalayas', *China Tourism* 54 (n.d.) 10.

6. Bethany World Prayer Center, 'The Helambu Sherpa of Nepal'.

7. Gu Shoukang, 'The Sherpas', 12.

8. Bradley, 'East and South-East Asia', 170.

9. There have been several comprehensive linguistic studies on the Sherpa language. See Austin Hale ed., 'Collected Papers on Sherpa, Jirel', *Nepal Studies in Linguistics* 2 (Kirtipur: SIL and the Institute of Nepal and Asian Studies, 1975) xii, 176; and Burkhard Schttelndreyer, 'Narrative Discourse in Sherpa', *SIL Publications in Linguistics and Related Fields: Papers on Discourse* 51 (Dallas: SIL, 1978) 248–66.

10. Bethany World Prayer Center, 'The Helambu Sherpa of Nepal'.

11. Two excellent *National Geographic* articles on the Sherpa are by Desmond

Doig, 'Sherpaland: My Shangri-La', *National Geographic* (October 1966) 545–77; and Jim Carrier, 'Gatekeepers of the Himalaya: Nepali's Sherpa People Prosper amid Dizzying Change as Climbers and Trekkers Descend Upon their Mountain Home', *National Geographic* (December 1992) 70–89.

12. Gu Shoukang, 'The Sherpas', 12. The best account of Sherpa religious practices is Sherry B Ortner, *Sherpas through their Rituals* (Cambridge: Cambridge University Press, 1978). See also James F Fisher and Sir Edmund Hillary, *Sherpas: Reflections on Change in Himalayan Nepal* (Berkeley: University of California Press, 1990).

13. Scott Anderson, personal communication (1996).

14. Johnstone, *Operation World* (1993) 406.

15. Johnstone and Mandryk, *Operation World* (2001) 469, list a population of 158,000 Sherpa in Nepal, but no other sources list such a high figure.

Shixing

1. See Sun Hongkai, 'Chuanxi Minzu Zoulang Diqu de Yuyan'. For a recent account of the Shuilo River see Jon Bowermaster, 'Rapid Descent: First Run Down the Shuilo River', *National Geographic* (November 1996) 116–29.

2. *Qiangic Speaking Tibetans*.

3. Rock, 'Konka Risumgongba', 30.

4. Ibid.

5. Ibid., 34.

6. Ibid.

7. Ibid.

8. In 2003 one Christian researcher made the arduous visit to the Shixing people. In part, he reported, 'Needless to say, it was very difficult to get to them. Hence, it is now becoming more and more understandable why there have not been any "workers" that have gone to them in the past. . . . When I got there, I immediately looked for transportation to Shuiluo, the area that the Shixing live. The Shixing call themselves in their own language *Xumu* (Shoo-moo). *Xu* means "rice", *Mu* means "people" in their own language. Shuiluo is actually a large area of several villages. There are several villages in that area where the Shixing are a majority. Some of the villages are only other Tibetans. The Shixing that I met would tell me that the only thing

that made them different than the Tibetans is that they have a different language. I also observed that they are not quite as religious . . . . One of the surprising things is that although there are no telephones (cell phones don't even work up there), very little electricity, no paved roads, no clean water and poor health care, there are several satellite TVs. I later found out that one of China's main goals in development is to have everyone in the empire within "TV range". The Shixing are a very warm-hearted people. I couldn't go past one house practically without being invited in for a drink of yak butter tea, a taste of walnuts, pomegranates, pears, very small peaches and other local fruits. The Shixing are farmers, growing corn and rice as staples and they also raise livestock. The people groups of Shuiluo tend to be taller than the Han Chinese. There is a saying in Shuiluo that goes "the mountains, people and horses are big, but the chickens, goats and cows are small!" And it is true, I have never seen a skinner cow' (personal communication [10 February 2004]).

Sikkimese

1. Singh, *Sikkim*, 23.
2. Singh, *The Scheduled Tribes*, 149. See also B B Chatterjee, *Bhotia of Indo-Tibetan Border of Uttarakhans* (Varansai: Institute of Gandhian Studies, 1975) and S C Bose, *Land and the People of the Himalayas* (Calcutta: Indian Publications, 1968).
3. See R R Prasad, *Bhotia Tribals of India* (New Delhi: Gian Publishing House, 1989).
4. See C Y Salisbury, *Mountaintop Kingdom: Sikkim* (Delhi: Vikas Publishing House, 1972).
5. Singh, *The Scheduled Tribes*, 153.
6. Grimes, *Ethnologue* (14th edn, 2000).
7. Bethany World Prayer Center, 'The Sikkimese Bhotia of India'.

Singhpo

1. Singh, *The Scheduled Tribes*, 1080.
2. P B S V Padmanabham, *A Demogenetic Profile of Singphos* (unpublished report submitted to the director, Anthropological Survey of India, 1981).
3. See Paul C Dutta, *The Singhpos* (Itanagar: Directorate of Research on the Government of Arunachal

Pradesh, 1990).
4. See Hattaway, *Operation China*, 233.
5. S Dutta Choudhury, 'The Singhpos', *North-Eastern Affairs, India* 2.1 (1973) 94–96.
6. Singh, *Arunachal Pradesh*, 293.
7. Prasad, *Encyclopaedic Profile of Indian Tribes*, IV, 929.
8. See Kamalesh Das Gupta, *A Phrase Book in Singhpo* (Shillong: Director of Information and Public Relations of Arunachal Pradesh, 1979).
9. Grimes, *Ethnologue* (14th edn, 2000).
10. Ibid.
11. Singh, *The Scheduled Tribes*, 1081. See also Tapan Kumar M Baruah, *The Singhpos and their Religion* (Shillong: Director of Information and Public Relations of Arunachal Pradesh, 1977).
12. Muanthanga, *The Harvest Field of Arunachal Pradesh*, 18.

Sinhalese

1. Johnstone and Mandryk, *Operation World*, 586. The neighbouring countries of India and Maldives have just 2,800 and 1,500 Sinhalese respectively (FMC South Asia, personal communication [May 2004]).
2. See R C Childers, 'Notes on the Sinhalese Language: Proofs of the Sanskritic Origin of Sinhalese', *Journal of the Royal Asiatic Society* 8 (1876).
3. See Barrett et al., *World Christian Encyclopedia*, 695.
4. Just a few accounts of persecution of Christians in Sri Lanka by the Buddhists include Alex Buchan, 'Sri Lanka and Christian Persecution', *Compass Direct* (1 July 2000) and the Voice of the Martyrs, 'The Persecution and Prayer Alert' (31 July 2002).

So

1. Primarily in the provinces of Mukdahan (Dong Luang District), Sakhon Nakhon (Muang and Kusuman districts) and Nakhon Phanom (Na Wa and Tha Uthen districts). 'Most of the So communities in Thailand are located between the large inland lake Nong Han of Sakhon Nakhon Province and the Mekong River, as well as on the slopes of the Phu Pan Range and along the Songkram River' (Schliesinger, *Ethnic Groups of Thailand*, 51).
2. For an interesting look at the So of Laos

more than 50 years ago, see André Fraisse, 'Les tribus So de la province de Cammon', *Bulletin de la Société des Etudes Indochinoises* 25 (Saigon, 1950).
3. Asian Minorities Outreach, *Faces of the Unreached in Laos*, 105.
4. In *Faces of the Unreached in Laos* (1999) I profiled the Mangkong and So as two separate groups, but later research has led me to believe that the two groups were doubly counted. The 1995 Laos census called the So group *Mangkong* and did not differentiate between them and the So.
5. Schliesinger, *Ethnic Groups of Thailand*, 54.
6. Asian Minorities Outreach, *Faces of the Unreached in Laos*, 72.
7. *Global Prayer Digest* 9.11 (November 1990).
8. Johnstone and Mandryk, *Operation World* (2001) 395, listed a figure of 120,000 So in Laos.
9. Ibid., 618, listed a figure of 58,000 So in Thailand.

Sogwo Arig

1. According to the 1990 census there were 22,506 Mongols in He'nan County and only 320 in Tongde County. It is possible that other ethnic Sogwo Arig in Tondge were counted as part of the Tibetan nationality.
2. Good pictures of the Sogwo Arig can be seen in Rock, 'Seeking the Mountains of Mystery', 142.
3. Henri Marie Gustave Vicomte d'Ollone, *In Forbidden China: The d'Ollone Mission 1906–09, China-Tibet-Mongolia* (London: T Fisher Unwin, 1912) 283.
4. Ekvall, *The Lama Knows*, mentions the 'Sohkwo' tribe several times. Ekvall lived and worked in this part of China prior to 1949.

Song

1. SIL estimated there to be 20,000 to 30,000 speakers of the Song language in 1982.
2. Schliesinger, *Tai Groups of Thailand*, 51.
3. See Seidenfaden, *The Thai Peoples: Book 1*.
4. See also two sources in Thai: Buruphat Somsong, '[An Account of the Lao Song and Their Immigration]' *Phu Thai Journal* 5.14 (1983); and Niphon Senaphitak, [*The Story of the Thai Song*] (Bangkok: Sam Nao, 1978).
5. Schliesinger, *Tai Groups of Thailand*,

51–52.
6. See Daecha, *A Comparative Study of the Phonology of Six Tai Dialects*.
7. See also two reports by Bert F Sams, 'Black Tai and Lao Song Dam: The Divergence of Ethnocultural Identities', *Journal of the Siam Society* 76 (1988) and *Tradition and Modernity in a Lao Song Village of Central Thailand* (PhD thesis, University of California, Los Angeles, 1987).
8. Schliesinger, *Tai Groups of Thailand*, 53.
9. The Tai Dam did not qualify for inclusion in this book because only a small minority of their population believes in Buddhism.

Stod Bhoti

1. Grimes, *Ethnologue* (14th edn, 2000).
2. Singh, *Himachal Pradesh*, 113.
3. Grimes, *Ethnologue* (14th edn, 2000).
4. Singh, *Himachal Pradesh*, 117–18.
5. Hilton and Kumaradass, *Adopt – A District of Himachal Pradesh*, 88.

Tai Bueng

1. Schliesinger, *Tai Groups of Thailand*, 109.
2. The Tai Bueng were mentioned in one linguistic source, see Jerry W Gainey and Theraphan L Thongkum, *Language Map of Thailand* (Bangkok: Central Institute of English, 1977).
3. Schliesinger, *Tai Groups of Thailand*, 111.
4. Ibid., 112.

Tai Doi

1. Chazée, *Atlas des Ethnies et des Sous-Ethnies du Laos*, 51.
2. Ibid.
3. Grimes, *Ethnologue* (13th edn, 1996) 699.
4. Chazée, *Atlas des Ethnies et des Sous-Ethnies du Laos*, 51.

Tai Gapong

1. Schliesinger, *Tai Groups of Thailand*, 120.
2. Ibid., 121.
3. Ibid., 123.

Tai He

1. Asian Minorities Outreach, *Faces of the Unreached in Laos*, 113.
2. Chazée, *Atlas des Ethnies et des Sous-Ethnies du Laos*.
3. Curtis, *The Laos of North Siam*, 25–26.
4. Ibid., 243.

Tai Khang

1. Asian Minorities Outreach, *Faces of the Unreached in Laos*, 116.
2. Ibid.
3. OMF Mekong Center, *30 Days of Prayer for Northern Laos* (Thailand: Mekong Center, 2002).
4. Asian Minorities Outreach, *Faces of the Unreached in Laos*, 116.
5. Curtis, *The Laos of North Siam*, 224.
6. Asian Minorities Outreach, *Faces of the Unreached in Laos*, 116.

Tai Laan

1. Asian Minorities Outreach, *Faces of the Unreached in Laos*, 117.
2. Ibid.
3. OMF Mekong Center, *30 Days of Prayer for Northern Laos*.
4. Curtis, *The Laos of North Siam*, 154.
5. Robert E Speer, *Missionary Principles and Practice: A Discussion of Christian Missions and of Some Criticisms upon Them* (London: Fleming H Revell, n.d.) 404.
6. Asian Minorities Outreach, *Faces of the Unreached in Laos*, 117.

Tai Loi

1. Grimes, *Ethnologue* (14th edn, 2000).
2. Asian Minorities Outreach, *Faces of the Unreached in Laos*, 118.
3. Grimes, *Ethnologue* (14th edn, 2000).
4. Dodd, *The Tai Race*, 232.

Tai Mao

1. According to the 1990 China census, there were 107,907 Dai people in Luxi County; 37,796 in Ruili; 30,506 in Lianghe; and 23,755 in Longchuan. The majority of these are Tai Mao. Of these, however, only those in Ruili, and some in Zhenfang County (between Ruili and Luxi), call themselves 'Tai Mao'. The rest call themselves 'Tai Nua', only it is pronounced 'Tai Le'. There are very slight dialect differences between those who identify themselves as Tai Mao and the Tai Le / Nua. The people profiled in our Tai Nua profile, however, are different from the Tai Mao. The situation is very confusing and even experienced researchers who travel frequently in the region do not agree on the terminology that should be used to differentiate Tai Mao from the Tai Nua. See note 2 to the Tai Nua profile for more discussion on this subject.

2. Ban Mao Mok Cham in Mae District near Fang in Chiang Mai Province (Schliesinger, *Tai Groups of Thailand*, 130). The Tai Mao in Thailand migrated there from Myanmar in the early 1970s.
3. Bradley, 'East and South-East Asia', 164.
4. Zhu Liangwen, *The Dai*.
5. Kuhn, *We Found a Hundred Tribes*, 5.

Tai Nua

1. Bradley, 'East and South-East Asia', 164.
2. Differentiating between the Tai Nua and Tai Mao is very complicated because of the overlapping of ethnic names. Geographical and linguistic divisions between the two are not clear. It is not possible to say, 'The Tai Nua stop here and the Tai Mao start there.' Most other ethnic groups in Asia can be divided this way, but the Tai groups tend to blur into each other and there are many shades of grey. The fact that there are numerous people in the China-Myanmar border area who refer to themselves by different names adds to the confusion. Hence we profile the Tai Nua and Tai Mao as in *Operation China*, going with David Bradley's linguistic definition of the two. This is not in keeping with the data of other missions research, most of which stems from the *Ethnologue* (which simply lists the Tai Mao as a dialect of Tai Nua). This classification does not, however, take into account important linguistic and ethnic differences. For the Tai Nua in China to receive the gospel in their heart language, media will need to be produced that differs from the Tai Mao media used in Dehong.
3. Bradley, 'East and South-East Asia', 164.
4. Anthony Diller, 'Tai Languages: Varieties and Subgroup Terms', *The Yunnan Project Newsletter* 25 (Canberra: Faculty of Asian Studies, Australian National University, June 1994).
5. *Global Prayer Digest* 14.4 (April 1995).
6. Zhu Liangwen, *The Dai*.
7. Stauffer, *The Christian Occupation of China*, 241.

Tai Pao

1. See Asian Minorities Outreach, *Faces of the Unreached in Laos*. This book profiles 138 distinct people groups in Laos, in a format similar to *Peoples of the Buddhist World*.
2. Asian Minorities Outreach, *Faces of the*

Unreached in Laos, 123.
3. Grimes, *Ethnologue* (13th edn, 1996) 699.
4. Asian Minorities Outreach, *Faces of the Unreached in Laos*, 123.
5. Grant Evans, *The Politics of Ritual and Remembrance: Laos since 1975* (Chiang Mai: Silkworm Books, 1998) 75.
6. Asian Minorities Outreach, *Faces of the Unreached in Laos*, 123.

Tai Phake

1. Citied in Grimes, *Ethnologue* (14th edn, 2000).
2. B C Allen, *Assam District Gazetteer 3* (1905).
3. Singh, *India's Communities: N–Z*, 3417.
4. See Ney Elias, *Introductory Sketch of the History of the Shans of Upper Burma and West Yunnan* (Calcutta, 1876).
5. B K Barua, *A Cultural History of Assam* (Guwahati: Bina Library, 2003).
6. Singh, *India's Communities: N–Z*, 3418.

Tai Wang

1. Schliesinger, *Tai Groups of Thailand*, 135.
2. Ibid.
3. Ibid., 136.
4. Ibid., 137.

Tak Bai Thai

1. Pron Subdistrict; Tak Bai, Sukhirin and Sungai Padi districts.
2. Sai Buri and Panare districts.
3. Few sources list the Tak Bai Thai as living in Malaysia, but one that does is Chantas Thongchuay, *Current Thai Dialects in Kelantan, Kedah and Perlis* (MA thesis, Chulalongkorn University, 1982).
4. Schliesinger, *Tai Groups of Thailand*, 166.
5. See Chailert Kitprasert, *A Tonal Comparison of Tai Dialects: Tai Bai Group* (MA thesis, Mahidol University, Nakhon Pathom, 1985).
6. Schliesinger, *Tai Groups of Thailand*, 165.
7. See Marvin J Brown, *From Ancient Thai to Modern Dialects and Other Writings on Historical Thai Linguistics* (Bangkok: White Lotus Press, 1960, repr. 1985).
8. Schliesinger, *Tai Groups of Thailand*, 166.

Tamang, Eastern

1. 'Outer-Eastern Tamang is spoken in eastern Sindhu Palchowk,

Ramechhap, Dolakha districts, and in most districts in eastern Nepal and parts of north-eastern India. Central-Eastern Tamang is spoken in most of Kabhre District, western Sindhu Palchowk, Lalitpur, Bhaktapur, Kathmandu, and eastern Nuwakot districts, and districts south of those. Southwestern Tamang is spoken in western Makwanpur and Chitwan districts and districts south and southwest of those' (Grimes, *Ethnologue* [14th edn, 2000]).
2. For information on the Tamang of India, see Singh, *Sikkim*, 172–77; Singh, *India's Communities: N–Z*, 3420–23; and S Munshi and U Lama, 'The Tamangs of Darjeeling: A Study of Group Identity', *Journal of the Indian Anthropological Society* 13.2–3 (1978).
3. 'Languages of Bhutan' map, unpublished (*c.*1995).
4. Bista, *The People of Nepal*, 55.
5. Frontier Missions Center for Himalayan Peoples, *Pray for the Peoples of Nepal*.
6. 'Black Bravery', *Asian Report* 24.3, Report 190 (May–June 1991).
7. Ibid.

Tamang, Eastern Gorkha

1. Grimes, *Ethnologue* (14th edn, 2000).
2. Gautam and Thapa-Magar, *Tribal Ethnography of Nepal*, II, 258.
3. Grimes, *Ethnologue* (14th edn, 2000).
4. Gautam and Thapa-Magar, *Tribal Ethnography of Nepal*, II, 279.
5. Salter and Gurung, *Faces of Nepal*, 49.
6. *Asian Report* 25.3, Report 195 (May–June 1992) 10–11.

Tamang, Northwestern

1. Gautam and Thapa-Magar, *Tribal Ethnography of Nepal*, II, 264.
2. Ibid., 259.
3. Ibid., 258.
4. Christoph von Füerer-Haimendorf, 'Ethnographic Notes on the Tamangs of Nepal', *Eastern Anthropologist* 4.3–4 (March–August 1956) 166–67.
5. Frontier Missions Center for Himalayan Peoples, *Pray for the Peoples of Nepal*.

Tamang, Southwestern

1. Ukyab and Adhikari, *The Nationalities of Nepal*, 61.
2. Andrew Wark, 'It's Time to Climb Higher', *Asian Report* 25.3, Report 195 (May–June 1992) 11.

Tamang, Western

1. See Grimes, *Ethnologue* (14th edn, 2000). See also Kesar Lall, 'The Tamangs', *Nepal Review* 1.3 (1969).
2. Bista, *The People of Nepal*, 61–62.
3. Gautam and Thapa-Magar, *Tribal Ethnography of Nepal*, II, 274–74.
4. Moa Pangnem, 'A Miracle for Tamang', *Asian Report* 29.3, Report 217 (May–June 1996) 8.

Tangsa, Tikhak

1. See Paul C Dutta, *The Tangsas of the Namchik and Tirap Valleys* (Shillong North-East Frontier Agency, 1959).
2. See Singh, *The Scheduled Tribes*, 1099–1128. FMC South Asia (personal communication [May 2004]) lists 33 different Tangsa tribes in India! Some of these are extremely small groups, with less than 50 people. For now there is not enough information available on these smaller groups, some of which are reportedly Buddhist, to profile them.
3. Ibid., 1122.
4. Singh, *Arunachal Pradesh*, 379.
5. Ibid., 383.

Tangsa, Yongkuk

1. Singh, *Arunachal Pradesh*, 391.
2. Ibid.
3. See Kamalesh Das Gupta, *The Tangsa Language: A Synopsis* (Shillong: Directorate of Research of the Government of Arunachal Pradesh, 1980). Another good linguistic study on Tangsa is Swapon Kumar Bandyopadhyay, 'A Tangsa Wordlist', *Linguistics of the Tibeto-Burman Area* 12.2 (1989) 79–91.
4. Grimes, *Ethnologue* (14th edn, 2000).
5. Singh, *The Scheduled Tribes*, 1127.
6. Singh, *Arunachal Pradesh*, 393–94.
7. Ibid., 394.

Taungyo

1. Enriquez, *Races of Burma*, 127.
2. Myanmar Faces and Places, 'Profile of the Taungyo'.
3. Diran, *The Vanishing Tribes of Burma*, 80.
4. Myanmar Faces and Places, 'Profile of the Taungyo'.

Tavoyan

1. Myanmar Faces and Places, 'Tavoyan Profile'.
2. Report from Amnesty International,

cited in Clark and Cummings, *Myanmar (Burma)*, 413.

3. Enriquez, *Races of Burma*, 127.
4. Clark and Cummings, *Myanmar (Burma)*, 413.
5. Grimes, *Ethnologue* (14th edn, 2000).

Tebbu

1. Joseph F Rock, 'The Land of the Tebbus', *Geographical Journal* 81. 2 (February 1933) 108.
2. Ibid., 108–10.
3. He continues: 'We were never able to live in Denga again, though visits to Dragsgumna presented no problem. In Dragsgumna our landlord came to the Lord. Four or five years later his wife, a certified battle-axe of a woman, came to the Lord and was baptized in Jone, where we were living at the time. Because of her changed life her two adult sons also believed' (Bob Carlson, personal communication [28 February 2001]). *Operation China* (2000) only listed the Tebbu people in an appendix recording 'Other Possible Groups'. As a result of reading *Operation China*, Carlson contacted me with information about this fascinating people group. His letter began, 'In Appendix I you refer to the Tebbus. This is a group with which my parents worked at various times . . .'
4. Bob Carlson, personal communication (28 February 2001).

Thai, Central

1. A helpful book that introduces Thai culture is William J Klausner, *Reflections on Thai Culture* (Bangkok: Suksit Siam, 1981).
2. The Thais are believed to have come southward from southern China about 1,000 years ago. See Sri Dvaravati Dhida Saraya, *The Initial Phase of Siam's History* (Bangkok: Muang Boran, 1999).
3. See the article in this book by Ubolwan Mejudhon, 'The Thai Way of Meekness' (p 277).
4. Kenneth E Wells has written some good books and articles on Thai Buddhism and missions history, including *Thai Buddhism* (Bangkok: Bangkok Times Press, 1939); 'Buddhism in Thailand: Its Sources of Strength', *International Review of Missions* XXXI (April 1942); and *History of Protestant Work in Thailand 1828–1958* (Bangkok: Church of Christ in Thailand, 1958).

5. Asian Minorities Outreach, *Faces of the Unreached in Laos*, 134.
6. Alex G Smith, *Siamese Gold: The Church in Thailand* (Bangkok: OMF Publishers, 1982) xxiii. Smith's excellent book is probably the most comprehensive overview of Christianity in Thailand ever written.
7. Another excellent account of missionary work in the early 20th century is Dodd, *The Tai Race*.
8. Also 9,000 in Australia (2003, Joshua Project II); 8,600 in Brunei (2001, P Johnstone and J Mandryk); 8,400 in Canada (2003, Joshua Project II); 3,000 in United Arab Emirates (1996, B Grimes [1986 figure]); 1,500 in China (2001, P Johnstone and J Mandryk); 1,000 in Finland (2003, Joshua Project II); 600 in Laos (1999, Asian Minorities Outreach) as well as in the United Kingdom, France, Germany, New Zealand and many other nations.

Thai, Northern

1. The Northern Thai (Tai Yuan) in Laos live in Bokeo Province (Houayxay and Pha-Oudom districts); Luang Namtha Province (Luang Namtha District); Oudomxai Province (Xai District); and Xaignabouri Province (Xaignabouri District). See Asian Minorities Outreach, *Faces of the Unreached in Laos*, 126.
2. Schliesinger, *Tai Groups of Thailand*, 184.
3. See Aroonrut Wichienkeeo and Wijeyewardene Gehan eds., *The Laws of King Mangrai* (Canberra: Australian National University, 1986).
4. Only recently the Northern Thai were referred to as *Lao Phung Dam*, or 'Black Bellied Lao', because of their custom of tattooing their stomachs, while the Isan were called *Lao Phung Kha* ('White Bellied Lao') because they did not tattoo their stomachs.
5. 'In this cage were placed with the prisoner a large mortar to pound him with, a larger boiler to boil him in, a hook to hang by, and a sword to decapitate him; also a sharp-pointed spike for him to sit on. His children were sometimes put in along with him' (Sir John Bowring, *The Kingdom and People of Siam* [Kuala Lumpur: Oxford University Press, 1857, repr. 1977] 62).
6. See Preeya Nokaeo, *Central Thai and Northern Thai: Linguistic and Attitudinal Study* (PhD thesis,

University of Texas, 1989).
7. According to Grimes, '87.5 per cent use Northern Thai in the home, 3 per cent use Central Thai, while 9.5 per cent use both' (*Ethnologue* [13th edn, 1996] 791).
8. Schliesinger, *Tai Groups of Thailand*, 185.
9. See Paul Cohen and Gehan Wijeyewardene eds., 'Spirit Cults and the Position of Women in Northern Thailand', *Mankind* 3 (1984); and Richard Davies, *Muang Metaphysics: A Study of Northern Thai Myth and Ritual* (Bangkok: Pandora, 1984). It could be said that the Northern Thai's religious view is one of 'whatever works'. During the time I lived in Chiang Mai, it was reported that a barren Thai peasant couple travelled to Chiang Mai seeking spiritual help to cure their condition. They visited the monks at Wat Phrasing, the main Buddhist temple, but their prayers and incantations did not help. They then heard about the former British monarch, Queen Victoria, whose statue stood outside the British consulate in Chiang Mai City. After praying before the statue, the couple returned home and soon after found that the wife was pregnant. When this news spread, the local Chiang Mai newspaper estimated that up to half of the entire population of Chiang Mai had come to the British consulate in a six-month period, prayerfully seeking divine blessings. In the end, the consulate removed Queen Victoria's statue because of the disturbance the crowds were causing to their daily operations.
10. The early Protestant missionary enterprise was headed by the Presbyterians; see McGilvary, *A Half Century among the Siamese and the Lao*. For a good overview of missions history in Thailand as a whole, see Smith, *Siamese Gold*.
11. Part of the reason for this is the fact that overt missionary activity is outlawed in almost every neighbouring country, such as Communist China, Laos and Vietnam. There are about 6,000 to 8,000 other foreigners living in Chiang Mai.

Thai, Southern

1. There are as many as seven tones in Southern Thai. See Anthony Diller, 'How Many Tones in Southern Thai?'

in Nguyen Dang Lien ed., *South-East Asian Linguistic Studies* 4 (Canberra: Pacific Linguistics, 1979).

2. Grimes, *Ethnologue* (13th edn, 1996) 791.
3. Schliesinger, *Tai Groups of Thailand*, 103.
4. There are many books written on the Southern Thai Muslims, but few on the Southern Thai Buddhists. Some of the more interesting on the Muslims include: Andrew Forbes ed., *The Muslims of Thailand* (2 vols; Ranchi: The Catholic Press, 1998); and Ministry of Foreign Affairs, *Islam in Thailand* (Bangkok, 1976). In March 2004, approximately 100 Muslims in Thailand were killed by police after they attacked various police stations throughout the area. The Thai prime minister quickly moved to downplay fears that these militants were linked to the al-Qaeda terrorists, saying that the attacks were part of a cultural grievance. Evidence suggests otherwise, although the Southern Thai Muslims and the Pattani people are upset at the overwhelming influence of Thai culture, language and Buddhism upon them.
5. Schliesinger, *Tai Groups of Thailand*, 106.
6. Asia Center for World Missions, *AC News and Views*, 17 (15–31 July 2002).

Thakali

1. Gautam and Thapa-Magar, *Tribal Ethnography of Nepal*, II, 281. The names of the 13 major Thakali villages are Tukuche, Khanti, Nabrikot, Bhurjungkot, Nagung, Dhampu, Tuti, Toglung, Kobang, Larjung, Lete, Sokung and Sirkung.
2. Ukyab and Adhikari, *The Nationalities of Nepal*, 45.
3. An excellent article on the Thakali is Mark Turin, 'Too Many Stars and Not Enough Sky: Language and Ethnicity among the Thakali of Nepal', *Contributions to Nepalese Studies* 24.2 (1997) 187–99.
4. Salter and Gurung, *Faces of Nepal*, 17.
5. Susanna von der Heide, *The Thakalis of North Western Nepal* (Kathmandu: Ratna Pustak Bhandar, 1988) 71. Von der Heide's book is one of the few books ever published specifically about one ethnic group in Nepal.
6. Gautam and Thapa-Magar, *Tribal Ethnography of Nepal*, II, 292–93.
7. Frontier Missions Center for Himalayan Peoples, *Pray for the Peoples of Nepal*.

Thami

1. There are conflicting reports on the population of the Thami in Nepal. While the official 1991 census figure is listed as 19,103, some sources list the census figure as 14,400 (see Grimes, *Ethnologue* [14th edn, 2000]). This lower figure probably refers to the number of speakers of the Thami language in Nepal, rather than to the members of the ethnic group as a whole. Other sources list 29,400 Thami in Nepal in 2000 (Bethany World Prayer Center, 'The Thami of Nepal'); 'spoken by upwards of 35,000 people' (van Driem, unpublished research page on the Thami, n.d.); and '30,000 in all' (Ukyab and Adhikari, *The Nationalities of Nepal*, 64). For an overview of the problem, see Mark Turin, 'Time for a True Population Census: The Case of the Miscounted Thangmi', *Nagarik* 2.4 (2000) 14–19.
2. Ukyab and Adhikari, *The Nationalities of Nepal*, 64, state that the Thami inhabit the villages of Susma, Chhamawati, Khepachagu, Alamyu, Bigu, Kalinchok, Lapilang and Lakuri Danda.
3. An unpublished fact sheet on the Thami says that they live in the following villages within Dolakha District: Suspa, Khopa, Baabre, Kalinchok, Lapilang, Boch and Dolakha. In Suspa Panchayat District their main village is called Suspachemoti. They also inhabit Piskar, Chokati and Thali.
4. See Mark Turin, 'By Way of Incest and the Golden Deer: How the Thangmi Came to be and the Pitfalls of Oral History', *Journal of Nepalese Studies* 3.1 (1999) 13–19.
5. See Singh, *India's Communities N–Z*, 3486.
6. See four excellent articles by linguist Mark Turin: 'The Thangmi Verbal Agreement System and the Kiranti Connection', *Bulletin of the School of Oriental and African Studies* 61.3 (1998) 476–91; 'Whence Thangmi? Historical Ethnography and Comparative Morphology', 451–77 in Yogendra Prasad Yadava and Warren William Glover eds., *Topics in Nepalese Linguistics* (Kathmandu: Royal Nepal Academy, 1999); 'Shared Words, Shared History? The Case of Thangmi and Late Classical Newar', *Journal of Newar Studies* 3 (1999) 9–17; and 'The Changing Face of Language and Linguistics in Nepal:

Some Thoughts on Thangmi', *Janjati* 1.3 (2000) 49–62.
7. Gautam and Thapa-Magar, *Tribal Ethnography of Nepal*, II, 324.
8. Frontier Missions Center for Himalayan Peoples, *Pray for the Peoples of Nepal*.
9. Gautam and Thapa-Magar, *Tribal Ethnography of Nepal*, II, 322.
10. Frontier Missions Center for Himalayan Peoples, *Pray for the Peoples of Nepal*.
11. *Sounds* (California: Gospel Recordings, Spring 1994).
12. *Advance* newsletter (August 1997).

Thavung

1. Schliesinger, *Ethnic Groups of Thailand*, 166, lists just 500 Thavung people in Thailand, living in two villages. Ferlus states that they are found in three villages.
2. Stephen A Wurm and Shiro Hattori, *Language Atlas of the Pacific Area* (The Australian Institute of the Humanities and the Japan Academy, 1981) lists 500 Thavung people in Laos.
3. Michael Ferlus, 'Langues et Peuples Viet-Muong', *Mon-Khmer Studies* 16 (1996).
4. See Benjamas Khamsakul, *The Attitude of So (Thavung) Ethnic Group toward their Own Language and Its Use: Case Study of Nong Waeng Village, Pathumwapi Subdistrict, Song Dao District, Sakon Nakhorn Province* (Bangkok: Mahidol University, MA thesis, 1988).
5. Schliesinger, *Ethnic Groups of Thailand*, 68–69.

Thet

1. Grimes, *Ethnologue* (14th edn, 2000).
2. Enriquez, *Races of Burma*, 126.
3. Grimes, *Ethnologue* (14th edn, 2000).
4. Taken from the www.mission.itu.ch website.
5. Taken from the www.asiatours.net website. See also Khine Tun Shwe, *A Guide to Mrauk-U: An Ancient City of Rakhine* (Myanmar, 1993).
6. Diran, *The Vanishing Tribes of Burma*, 161. The book Diran refers to is C C Lowis, *The Tribes of Burma* (Rangoon: Ethnographic Survey of India, 1919).

Tibetan, Central

1. According to the 1990 China census—which did not distinguish between different Tibetan ethnic groups or languages as this book has—there were 186 counties or municipalities

in China that recorded more than 500 Tibetan people. In descending order, the largest Tibetan populations are in: Lhasa City *(Tibet)* 96,431; Xiahe *(Gansu)* 86,671; Xigaze *(Tibet)* 76,246; Changdu *(Tibet)* 72,381; Mangkang *(Tibet)* 64,411; Nanmulin *(Tibet)* 61,014; Yushu *(Qinghai)* 59,630; Jiangda *(Tibet)* 59,585.

2. Tibetans in India can be found throughout the Himalayan states of Himachal Pradesh, Arunachal Pradesh, Assam and Sikkim, as well as in camps in Delhi, West Bengal and central India. According to the *CAF Prayer Bulletin* (April 2003), Tibetan exiles are found in New Delhi, Himachal Pradesh, Uttar Pradesh, Bihar, West Bengal, Sikkim, Nagaland, Meghalaya, Orissa, Maharashtra, Karnataka and Tamil Nadu. Of the 150,000 Tibetans in India, some 60,000 now live in South India. FMC South Asia (personal communication [May 2004]) gives more detailed analysis of the Tibetans in India. They list 124 different districts in India with Tibetan communities, including Arunachal Pradesh (12,700); Assam (1,000); Chhattisgarh (1,900); Uttaranchal (20,000); Uttar Pradesh (1,000); Himachal Pradesh (47,000); West Bengal (22,000); Jammu and Kashmir (8,000); Maharashtra (2,000); and Karnataka (31,000). Almost all of the Tibetans in Karnataka State live in the Mysore District.

3. Buckley and Strauss, *Tibet*, 23.

4. My aim is to classify groups according to 'mission significant' classifications—that is, how far the gospel can penetrate from one people group to another without encountering cultural, linguistic or other barriers. Using these criteria, the Tibetans are certainly a collection of more than a dozen different ethnolinguistic varieties. The Tibetans oppose such classifications, claiming that it weakens their unity as a race. They even argued for the inclusion of the Tu minority in the Tibetan nationality, despite the fact that the Tu speak a Mongolian language and have a separate historical identity.

5. The Dalai Lama presents a happy-go-lucky image to the world, but a recent book written in German by Victor Trimondi, *Der Schatten des Dalai Lama: Sexuality, Magie und Politik im tibetischen Buddhismus* [The Shadow

of the Dalai Lama: Sexuality, Magic, and Politics in Tibetan Buddhism] (Dusseldorf: Patmos, 1999) shows a very different side to the spiritual leader of Tibet. Trimondi was a personal friend and assistant to the Dalai Lama, converting to Tibetan Buddhism and travelling with the Dalai Lama for a number of years.

6. J Dauvillier, 'Temoignages Nouveaux sur le Christianisme Nestorien chez les Tibetans', in *Histoire et Institutions des Èglises Orientales au Moyen Age* (London: Varioum Reprints 2, 1983) 165.

7. William Carlsen, *Tibet: In Search of a Miracle* (New York: Nyack College, 1985) 37.

8. Lambert, 'The Challenge of China's Minority Peoples'.

9. The Tibetan gospel radio broadcasts, called 'Gawelylon', have had a tremendous impact upon many Tibetans, especially on those living in India and Nepal. In 2002 the producers received 22,000 response letters.

10. Alex Buchan, 'Buddhist Leaders Fail to Reckon with Persecution', *Compass Direct* (24 April 1998). In part, Buchan's article stated: 'In mainland China many house churches confirm that the most difficult harvest field is Tibet—"because the monks will chase, beat, even kill our evangelists" . . . One house church leader from Henan said, "Since 1988 we have had five evangelists stoned to death by Tibetan Buddhist monks in the provinces of Tibet, Qinghai and Gansu. . . . We think many Buddhists spread the gospel because their monks are so frightened and try to kill us, which makes the people ask what we have that makes their monks so afraid. In their overreaction is our opportunity."'

Tibetan, Gtsang

1. Bradley, 'East and South-East Asia', 170, lists 19 dialects of Gtsang Tibetan, but some of them are people groups we have profiled separately in this book.

2. Two good linguistic surveys of Gtsang Tibetan have been written by Felix Haller: 'A Brief Comparison of Register Tone in Central Tibetan and Kham Tibetan', *Linguistics of the Tibeto-Burman Area* 22.2 (1999) 77–97 and 'The Verbal Categories of Shigatse Tibetan and Themchen Tibetan', *Linguistics of the Tibeto-*

Burman Area 23.2 (2000) 175–91.

3. Cited in Buckley and Strauss, *Tibet*, 13.

4. Tsering, *Sharing Christ in the Tibetan Buddhist World*, 75.

Tibetan, Jone

1. Wu Pingguan, 'The Sangemao—Special Tibetans', *China Tourism* 268 (November 2002) 74.

2. Grimes, *Ethnologue* (13th edn, 1996) 546.

3. Joseph F Rock, 'Life among the Lamas of Choni', *National Geographic* (November 1928) 569.

4. Wu, 'The Sangemao—Special Tibetans', 74.

5. Rock, 'Life among the Lamas of Choni', 569.

6. Ibid.

7. Ibid., 576. When Rock visited there in 1928, he noticed that the gate to the Jone monastery bore an inscription by Emperor Kangxi (1710) in favor of Chih Lien, a Jone priest who had paid him a visit. In the past the Jone prince was selected by rules of succession. If a prince had two sons, the elder succeeded him and the second became the lama of the monastery. If there was only one son, he took both positions concurrently.

8. Ibid.

9. Wu, 'The Sangemao', 75.

10. Stauffer, *The Christian Occupation of China*, 281.

11. *Global Chinese Ministries* (Colorado: OMF, March 1998).

Tibetan, Nghari

1. An outstanding article on the Nghari Prefecture is Zheng Ligang, 'Into Remote Ngari: A Tour by Land-Rover', *China Tourism* 244 (November 2000) 18–45.

2. See Beall and Goldstein, 'The Remote World of Tibet's Nomads', 752–81.

3. Bradley, 'East and South-East Asia', 169.

4. Buckley and Strauss, *Tibet*, 141.

5. Tsering, *Sharing Christ in the Tibetan Buddhist World*, 78. Until recently, the church bell was held in a room in the basement of the Jokhang Temple in Lhasa, a sad reminder of the demise of Christianity from Tibet more than 250 years ago. In 1996 the bell was removed, possibly because so many foreigners were asking to see it.

Tibetan, Shangri-La

1. An excellent article on the region is Xie Guanghui, 'Into the World Called

Shangri-La', *China Tourism* 215 (June 1998) 35–51.

2. Tai Chi Yin, 'Timeless Plateau: Zhongdian', *China Tourism* 108 (n.d.) 24.

3. See Krisadawan Hongladarom, 'Rgylathang Tibetan of Yunnan: A Preliminary Report', *Linguistics of the Tibeto-Burman Area* 19.2 (1996) 69–92.

4. 'When British writer James Hilton published his book "Lost Horizon" in 1933, he might never have thought that so many people from different nations would have crazily followed his fictitious, mysterious story in search an ideal place. In the novel, four people . . . took the same plane to flee from British India where a revolution was in the making. Unexpectedly, the plane was hijacked and finally landed in a place full of snow mountains, lamaseries, and people from different ethnic groups living together in a harmonic and peaceful manner. Ever since the novel went off the press, many places in India, Pakistan, Nepal and China have claimed they are the very home to "Shangri-La". In the 1990s, most of the "Lost Horizon" fans or researchers turned their eyes to Deqing County in the Deqing Tibetan Autonomous Prefecture, Yunnan Province, where people could find almost everything the author described in his novel. People's interest in "Shangri-La" has brought a great opportunity to the Tibetan prefecture, which had for decades been plagued by poverty and a lack of ways to eradicate the poverty for local people. It has taken every chance to promote the Shangri-La-based local tourism industry, by trying hard to prove that it is the very place where the four fictitious foreigners had stayed and enjoyed the local culture, a mixture of the ethnic traditions of the Han People and Tibetans.' (*People's Daily* [August 13 2001]).

5. Linguistic studies on the Shangri-La (Zhongdian) Tibetan language include Hongladarom, 'Rgylathang Tibetan of Yunnan', 69–92; and Hpung Sarep, 'Rgylathang Tibetan of Yunnan: A Preliminary Report', *Linguistics of the Tibeto-Burman Area* 19.2 (1996) 93–184.

6. The Xiangcheng people who live across the Yunnan-Sichuan border to the north still retain many customs that are similar to those of the Qiang. The existence of the Xiangcheng supports the oral legend from Shangri-La.

7. Jim Goodman, 'Tibetan Christians in a Yunnan Village', *China Tourism* 215 (June 1998) 84.

8. Covell, *The Liberating Gospel*, 155.

9. Ibid., 51.

Tibetan, Shanyan

1. Shui Xiaojie, 'Visiting the Shanyan Tibetans', *China Tourism* 240 (July 2000) 67.

2. Ibid.

3. Ibid., 70.

4. Ibid., 67.

5. Ibid., 68–69.

Tinan

1. According to FMC South Asia (personal communication [May 2004]) there are great difficulties classifying the population of this group because Tinan is a linguistic classification. FMC South Asia suspects that the number of Tinan may be much lower, possibly around 8,000 in India.

2. Voegelin and Voegelin, *Classification and Index of the World's Languages*.

3. 'According to census reports, Lahauli is spoken by 18,728 persons in the region' (Singh, *The Scheduled Tribes*, 680).

4. *Operation China* lists this group as Lahuli Tinan. It has since become popular among researchers simply to call them Tinan and their language Tinani.

5. Bradley, 'East and South-East Asia', 169.

6. Grimes, *Ethnologue* (1996, 13th edn) 587. One good linguistic study of the Lahauli languages is Jag Deva Singh, 'Lahauli Verb Inflection', *Linguistics of the Tibeto-Burman Area* 12.2 (1989) 41–49.

7. *Global Prayer Digest* 8.7 (July 1989).

8. Ibid.

9. Covell, *The Liberating Gospel*, 57.

Torgut

1. The Torgut inhabit a widespread area of north and north-west Xinjiang, including the Ili Kazak Prefecture and the area north-west of Korla in central Xinjiang.

2. Grimes, *Ethnologue* (14th edn, 2000).

3. Murray, 'With the Nomads of Central Asia', 11.

4. Bethany World Prayer Center, 'The Kalmyk-Oirat'.

5. Issachar Frontier Missions Research, *Mongolia Challenge Report*, II, 2, i.

6. Moule and Pelliot, *Marco Polo*, 201.

7. Hefley, *China! Christian Martyrs of the 20th Century*, 18–19.

8. The *Jesus* film is available in Kalmyk, but it was translated for the Kalmyk living in Russia and contains many loanwords that are not used in China. The Torgut in China are not able to understand it.

Tsangla

1. The main Tsangla village in Arunachal Pradesh appears to be Bishing. Strangely, according to the 1981 Indian census, 2,679 'Memba' people living in the West Siang District of northern Arunachal Pradesh have been granted status as a Scheduled Tribe, separate from the Monpa groups. Other sources indicate that these Memba are in fact Tsangla people who speak the Tsangla language.

2. Australian Academy and CASS, *Language Atlas of China*, C–6. The 1990 census of China listed only 6,069 Monba people in Motuo County; 549 in Cona (Cuona) County; and 542 in Linzhi County. It is believed that many ethnic Monba people were officially counted as part of the Tibetan nationality, which explains the discrepancy between government figures and linguistic figures for the Monba.

3. Bethany World Prayer Center, 'The Sangla of Bhutan'.

4. Bradley, 'East and South-East Asia', 170.

5. Grimes, *Ethnologue* (14th edn, 2000).

6. One good linguistic study of the Tsangla language is Erik Andvick, 'Tshangla Verb Inflections', *Linguistics of the Tibeto-Burman Area* 16.1 (1993) 75–136.

7. *Encyclopedic Dictionary of Chinese Linguistics*, 538–39.

8. In Bhutan, the Tsangla language shares only 48 per cent lexical similarity with the national language Dzongkha.

9. Zhang Jianghua and Wu Congzhong, 'Tibet's Menba Nationality', *China Reconstructs* (July 1979) 55.

10. Asia Center for World Missions, 'The Sangla of Bhutan', *AC News and Views* 20 (October 2002).

11. Cited in Grimes, *Ethnologue* (14th edn, 2000). Johnstone and Mandryk, *Operation World* (2001), 110, list 131,000 Tsangla in Bhutan.

Tsum

1. Cited in Grimes, *Ethnologue* (14th edn, 2000).
2. Finlay et al., *Nepal*, 373.
3. Bista, *The People of Nepal*, 203.
4. See the profile on the Nubri in this book.
5. Grimes, *Ethnologue* (14th edn, 2000).
6. Bista, *The People of Nepal*, 203.

Tu

1. According to the 1990 census there were 21 counties or municipalities in China that recorded more than 500 Tu people. In descending order, the largest Tu populations are in: Huzhu (Qinghai) 57,147; Minhe (Qinghai) 38,005 [most of these are Mongour]; Datong (Qinghai) 34,753; Tianzhu (Gansu) 11,837; Tongren (Qinghai) 7,470 [some of these are Wutun]; Ledu (Qinghai) 6,587; Menyuan (Qinghai) 6,118.
2. *Global Prayer Digest* 10.6 (June 1991).
3. Chun Shizeng ed., *Chinese Nationalities* (Beijing: China Nationality Photography and Art Press, 1989) 54.
4. Australian Academy and CASS, *Language Atlas of China*, C–5.
5. *Global Prayer Digest* 12.9 (September 1993).
6. *CPLMR* 119 (December 1991–February 1992).
7. Previous censuses in China listed 159,426 Tu (1982); 77,349 (1964); and 53,277 (1954).

Turung

1. Grimes, *Ethnologue* (14th edn, 2000).
2. Singh, *India's Communities: N–Z*, 3536.

Tuva

1. Bethany World Prayer Center, 'The Tuvinian of Russia'.
2. *Frontiers Focus* 5.2.
3. Australian Academy and CASS, *Language Atlas of China*, C–5.
4. Janhunen and Salminen, *UNESCO Red Book*.
5. *Global Prayer Digest* 15.9 (September 1996).
6. Bethany World Prayer Center, 'The Tuvinian of Russia'.
7. *Call to Prayer* (November–December 1998). The Tuva Scriptures and *Jesus* film used by the Tuva in Russia are not understood by the Tuva in China, and possibly not by the Tuva in Mongolia.
8. *Global Prayer Digest* 15.9 (September 1996).

Vietnamese

1. Barrett et al., *World Christian Encyclopedia*, p 803, lists 39,533,909 Buddhists in Vietnam in mid-2000, although the Buddhism is highly mixed with other religious beliefs.
2. Daniel Robinson and Robert Storey, *Vietnam: A Travel Survival Kit* (Hawthorn, Australia: Lonely Planet, 1993) 57–58.
3. See Asian Minorities Outreach, *The Peoples of Vietnam*, 106.
4. See *The New Glories of the Catholic Church: Translated from the Italian by the Fathers of the London Oratory, at the Request of the Cardinal Archbishop of Westminster, with a Preface by His Eminence* (London: Richardson, 1859) 209–43; and Hefley, *China!*
5. The growth of the house churches among the Vietnamese has been slower than among the tribal peoples in the central and southern parts of Vietnam. Several significant house church movements have emerged in the past 15 years among the Vietnamese, each with a zeal for evangelism and a nationwide plan. North Vietnam remains a spiritually difficult place for the penetration of the gospel. It has been Communist for a generation longer than the south of Vietnam, and restrictions in the north seem to be generally stronger than in the south. One of the hindrances southern Vietnamese evangelists face is their accent, which immediately gives their identity away when they speak to a north Vietnamese. It makes it easier for the authorities to find and punish the Christian workers.
6. In Laos the Vietnamese inhabit small pockets of land throughout the nation, including the provinces of Xekong, Phongsali, Houaphan, Vientiane City, Khammouan, Saravan, Savannakhet and Champasak. See Asian Minorities Outreach, *Faces of the Unreached in Laos*, 137.
7. Also 27,000 in China (2001, P Johnstone and J Mandryk); 22,000 in the United Kingdom (1999, Asian Minorities Outreach); 15,000 in Norway (2001, P Johnstone and J Mandryk); 8,000 in Netherlands (1999, Asian Minorities Outreach); 3,000 in New Caledonia (2001, P Johnstone and J Mandryk); also in many other nations around the world.

Walung

1. Grimes, *Ethnologue* (14th edn, 2000).
2. Salter and Gurung, *Faces of Nepal*, 13–15.
3. Grimes, *Ethnologue* (14th edn, 2000).
4. Bista, *The People of Nepal*, 183.

Wutun

1. *Encyclopedic Dictionary of Chinese Linguistics*, 556.
2. Grimes, *Ethnologue* (13th edn, 1996) 564.
3. Dwayne Graybill, personal communication (October 1996).
4. Ibid.
5. Ibid.
6. Ibid.

Xiangcheng

1. There were a total of 22,325 people belonging to the Tibetan nationality in Xiangcheng, according to the 1990 census, about half of whom were Xiangcheng people and half Khampa Tibetans.
2. Xian Yanyun, 'In Search of the Ancient Tea Caravan Route', *China Tourism* 181 (August 1995), 75.
3. Ibid.
4. Ibid.
5. Rock, 'Konka Risumgongba', 17.
6. The main temple in Xiangcheng is the Sangpi Monastery, built in 1654 by Lobsang Gyatso, the fifth Dalai Lama. See Zheng Chengdong, 'Xiangcheng: At the Foot of Bamu Sacred Mountain', *China Tourism* 255 (October 2001) 34–42.

Yakha

1. Bethany World Prayer Center, 'The Yakha of Nepal'.
2. Werner Winter, 'Diversity in Rai Languages: An Inspection of Verb Stems in Selected Idioms', *Lingua Posnaniensis* 34 (1991) 141–56.
3. FMC South Asia, personal communication (May 2004).
4. Singh, *Sikkim*, 198.
5. For more information on Yakha linguistics, see van Driem, *Languages of the Himalayas*, II, 680–83.
6. Frontier Missions Center for Himalayan Peoples, *Pray for the Peoples of Nepal*.
7. Bethany World Prayer Center, 'The Yakha of Nepal'.
8. Frontier Missions Center for Himalayan Peoples, *Pray for the Peoples of Nepal*.
9. Bethany World Prayer Center, 'The Yakha of Nepal'.
10. Singh, *Sikkim*, 202.

Yong

1. Schliesinger, *Tai Groups of Thailand*, 152.
2. Ibid., 153.
3. One linguistic study of the Yong language is Wisuttira Neamnark, *Lamphun Yong Phonology: A Synchronis Comparative Study* (MA thesis, Chulalongkorn University, Bangkok, 1984). Linguists have found the Yong language to be closely related to Lu. The Yong in Thailand are also bilingual in Northern Thai.
4. Schliesinger, *Tai Groups of Thailand*, 156.

Yonzhi

1. Rock, 'Seeking the Mountains of Mystery', 173, 185.
2. Ibid., 173.
3. Ibid., 184.

Yoy

1. The villages of Ban Akat, Ban Wa Yai and Ban Chuam.
2. The village of Ban Ummau.
3. See the Saek profile in this book.
4. These three theories are summarized in Schliesinger, *Tai Groups of Thailand*, 178–79.
5. Ibid., 180–81.
6. Asian Minorities Outreach, *Faces of the Unreached in Laos*, 138.

Yugur, Enger

1. According to the 1990 census there were just two counties or municipalities in China that recorded more than 500 Yugur people: 8,813 were listed in Sunan County and 2,275 in Jiuquan City. The census did not distinguish between the two Yugur groups.
2., Schwartz, *The Minorities of Northern China*, 61.
3. 'Down the ages, the name of the ethnic group has changed on many occasions. In the Tang Dynasty (618–907) it was called "Huihe" and "Huihu"; in the Song Dynasty (960–1279) it was known as "Huangtou Huihe"; in the Yuan Dynasty (1271–1368) it was called "Sali Weiwu"; in the Ming Dynasty (1368–1644) it became "Sali Weiwuer [Uygur]"; and in the Qing Dynasty (1644–1911) it was renamed "Xila Weiguer [Yugur]". . . . In 1953, they chose the name "Yugur" which sounds like "prosperity and solidarity" in Chinese' (Tian Zicheng, 'The Fascinating Yugurs',

China Tourism 256 [November 2001] 68–69).
4. Schwartz, *The Minorities of Northern China*, 57.
5. P M Scott, 'Some Mongol Nestorian Crosses', *The Chinese Recorder* (February 1930) 104–8, and (November 1930) 704–6.
6. Moule and Pelliot, *Marco Polo*, 150.

Yugur, Saragh

1. Schwartz, *The Minorities of Northern China*, 60.
2. Ibid., 59.
3. Ma Yin, *China's Minority Nationalities*, 130.
4. Zhang and Zeng, *In Search of China's Minorities*, 74.
5. Personal communication (August 1997).
6. See Asian Minorities Outreach, *The 50 Most Unreached People Groups of China and Tibet*, 48.

Za

1. Sun Hongkai, 'On Nationality and the Recognition of Tibeto-Burman Languages', *Linguistics of the Tibeto-Burman Area* 15.2 (Fall 1992) 7–8.
2. See Wang Jian, 'Zayu People: Little Known to the Outside World', *China Tourism* 261 (April 2002) 26–27.

Zakhring

1. S Dutta Choudhury, 'The Singhpos', *North-Eastern Affairs, India* 2.1 (1973).
2. Grimes, *Ethnologue* (14th edn, 2000).
3. Singh, *Arunachal Pradesh*, 406.
4. Singh, *The Scheduled Tribes*, 1204. See A K Das, 'Style and Symbolic Motifs in the Art of Arunachal', in K K Ganguly and S S Biwas eds., *Rupanjali* (Calcutta: O C Ganguly Memorial Society, 1986) 207–9.
5. Singh, *Arunachal Pradesh*, 406.
6. Muanthanga, *The Harvest Field of Arunachal Pradesh*, 19.

Zangskari

1. Indian Research Teams, *Peoples of India*, 126.
2. 1984, Dayton and Wilson, cited in Grimes, *Ethnologue* (14th edn, 2000).
3. Taken from the www.leh-ladakh.com website.
4. Perhaps the only liguistic study that deals specifically with Zangskari is Hoshi Michiyo and Tondup Tsering, *Zangskar Vocabulary: A Tibetan Dialect Spoken in Kashmir* (Tokyo: Institute

for the Study of Languages and Cultures of Asia and Africa, 1978).
5. Francke, *A History of Western Tibet*, 16.
6. A fascinating book is by David Llewellyn Snellgrove, Hugh Richardson and Tadeusz Skorupski, *The Cultural Heritage of Ladakh*, II: *Zangskar and the Cave Temples of Ladakh* (Warminster: Aris and Phillips, 1980).

Zhaba

1. Sun Hongkai, 'Chuanxi Minzu Zoulang Diqu de Yuyan'. A later source listed only 7,700 Zhaba. See *Encyclopedic Dictionary of Chinese Linguistics* (1991) 542. The Zhaba are not the same as the Queyu, some of whom also call themselves Zhaba. The Queyu are profiled separately, above.
2. *Qiangic Speaking Tibetans*.
3. Marco Polo, *The Travels of Marco Polo: The Complete Yule-Cordier Edition* (New York: Dover Publications, 1903) 44.
4. Wang Duanyu, 'Lama Jiao Yu Zangzu Renkou' [Lamaism and the Population of the Tibetans], *Minzu Yanji* (1984) 46.
5. *Qiangic Speaking Tibetans*.
6. Ibid.
7. Ibid.

Appendix 1: Index of Alternative Names

Often the names of people groups are spelled a host of different ways. In addition to different spellings, many tribes and people groups are known by different names according to their location, language or clan names. The Rakhine people of Myanmar, for example, are also known as the Arakanese. Across the border in Bangladesh they are better known as the Marma, while in India the government has officially listed them under the name Mag. This index of 1,674 alternate names will hopefully assist the reader in avoiding confusion. This index lists all known names for each Buddhist group. The names in bold are the names used in the profiles.

Name	See
A	
Aheu	Thavung
Aiton	
Aitonia	Aiton
Aleng	Mon
Alike	Sogwo Arig
A-li-k'oa	Sogwo Arig
Altai Tuva	Tuva
Altai Uriangkhai	Tuva
Altai Uryangkhai	Tuva
Amchok	Golog
Amdo, Hbrogpa	
Amdo, Rongba	
Amdo, Rtahu	
Amoy	Han Chinese, Min Nan
Anduo	Amdo, Hbrogpa
Angku	
Annamese	Vietnamese
Anshuenkun	Khampa, Southern
Aouei	Kui
Arakanese	Rakhine
Arig Tibetan	Sogwo Arig
Atuence	Khampa, Southern
Atuentse	Khampa, Southern
Au	Nyaw
B	
Bahra Gaunle	Baragaunle
Bai	
Baihua	Han Chinese, Cantonese
Baihuo	Bai
Baini	Bai
Baizi	Bai
Bama	Burmese
Bamachaka	Burmese
Bamas	Burmese
Bangkok Thai	Thai, Central
Bao'an	Bonan, Tongren
Bao Erzi	Qixingmin
Baragaon	Baragaunle
Baragaun	Baragaunle
Baragaunle	
Baragaunle: Mustang	Baragaunle

Baraua	Barua
Bargu	Buriat, China
Bargu Buriat	Buriat, China
Barua	
Bawang Rong-ke	Ergong
Beda	
Bedar	Beda
Beijinghua	Han Chinese, Mandarin
Benglong	Palaung, Pale
Beta	Beda
Bhama	Burmese
Bhingi (#1)	Ghale, Northern
Bhingi (#2)	Ghale, Southern
Bhoka	Tibetan, Central
Bhot (#1)	Beda
Bhot (#2)	Stod Bhoti
Bhotte (#1)	Ghale, Northern
Bhotte (#2)	Ghale, Southern
Bhotte Ghale (#1)	Ghale, Northern
Bhotte Ghale (#2)	Ghale, Southern
Bhoti	Stod Bhoti
Bhotia (#1)	Beda
Bhotia (#2)	Sikkimese
Bhotia (#3)	Tibetan, Central
Bhotia of Bhutan	Drukpa
Bhotia of Dukpa	Drukpa
Bhotia of Lahul	Tinan
Bhoti Gurung	Baragaunle
Bhumtan	Bumthang
Bhutanese	Drukpa
Bhutia	Sikkimese
Black Karen	Pa-O
Black Mountain	Ole
Black Palaung	Palaung, Rumai
Blang	Bulang
Bo	Qixingmin
Bodh (#1)	Beda
Bodh (#2)	Stod Bhoti
Bonan, Tongren	
Bonglong	Palaung, Pale
Bonglung	Palaung, Pale
Boonan	Gahri
Bootpa	Monpa, But
Bopa	Ergong
Boren	Qixingmin

Bor-Khampti	Khamti
Bote (#1)	Ghale, Northern
Bote (#2)	Ghale, Southern
Bote Ghale (#1)	Ghale, Northern
Bote Ghale (#2)	Ghale, Southern
Bprang	Bulang
Braang	Bulang
Brang	Bulang
Brogpa (#1)	Amdo, Hbrogpa
Brogpa (#2)	Brokpa, Brokkat
Brokhpa	Dokhpa
Brokpa	
Brokpa (#2)	Dokhpa
Brokpa of Dah-hanu	Dokhpa
Brokpa of Dur	Brokpa, Brokkat
Brokpa, Brokkat	
Brokpake	Brokpa
Brokskad	Brokpa, Brokkat
Brokskat	Dokhpa
Broqpa	Dokhpa
Brukpa	Dokhpa
Buddhist Bonan	Bonan, Tongren
Buerzi	Ersu
Bulai	Palaung, Pale
Bulang	
Bulei	Palaung, Pale
Bumtang	Bumthang
Bumtangkha	Bumthang
Bumtanp	Bumthang
Bumthang	
Bumthangkha	Bumthang
Bumthapkha	Bumthang
Bunan	Gahri
Bunun	Khowa
Buoba	Minyak
Buozi	Zhaba
Bur'aad	Buriat, Mongolia
Buriat, China	
Buriat, Mongolia	
Buriat, Russia	
Buriat-Mongolian (#1)	Buriat, China
Buriat-Mongolian (#2)	Buriat, Mongolia
Buriat-Mongolian (#3)	Buriat, Russia
Burman	Burmese
Burmese	
Burmese Shan	Shan
Buryat (#1)	Buriat, China
Buryat (#2)	Buriat, Mongolia
Buryat (#3)	Buriat, Russia
Butpa	Monpa, But
Butsang	Golog
Byangskat	Champa
Byanskat	Champa

C

Cambodians	Khmer
Canglo Monba	Monpa, Medog
Cangluo Monba	Monpa, Medog
Cantonese	Han Chinese, Cantonese
Central Khmer	Khmer
Central Monba	Tsangla
Central Thai	Thai, Central
Chabao	Jiarong, Chabao
Chak	
Chakama	Chakma
Chakma	
Chali	
Chalikha	Chali
Chalipkha	Chali
Champa	
Champa Ladakhi	Champa
Changpa	Champa
Changs-skat	Champa
Changtang	Champa
Changtang Ladakhi	Champa
Chang Tang Nomads	Tibetan, Nghari
Chang Tang Tibetans	Tibetan, Nghari
Changthang	Champa
Chaobon	Nyahkur
Chaobun	Nyahkur
Chao Song	Song
Charumba	Zakhring
Chaubun	Nyahkur
Chaoxian	Korean
Chaungtha	
Chawng	Chong
Chawngma	Chakma
Chhairo	Chhairottan
Chhairo Tibetans	Chhairottan
Chhairottan	
Chiajung (#1)	Jiarong, Guanyingqiao
Chiajung (#2)	Jiarong, Shangzhai
Chiajung (#3)	Jiarong, Situ
Chi'ang (#1)	Qiang, Cimulin
Chi'ang (#2)	Qiang, Luhua
Chiang: Cimulin	Qiang, Cimulin
Chiang: Luhua	Qiang, Luhua
Chiang: Mawo	Qiang, Mawo
Chiang: Yadu	Qiang, Yadu
Chiarong (#1)	Jiarong, Chabao
Chiarong (#2)	Jiarong, Guanyingqiao
Chiarong (#3)	Jiarong, Shangzhai
Chiarong (#4)	Jiarong, Sidabao
Chiarong (#5)	Jiarong, Situ
Chimada	Chimtan
Chimang	Chimtan

Chimtan	
Chimtan Tibetans	Chimtan
Chinese: Hui	Han Chinese, Huizhou
Chinese: Qiongwen	Han Chinese, Hainanese
Chinese Shan	Tai Mao
Ching	Vietnamese
Chingalese	Sinhalese
Chocangacakha	Matpa
Chomo	Groma
Chomo Tibetan	Groma
Chona	Tibetan, Jone
Chone	Tibetan, Jone
Chongtien	Tibetan, Shangri-La
Choni	Tibetan, Jone
Choni Tibetan	Tibetan, Jone
Chong	
Chrame	Pumi, Northern
Ch'rame	Pumi, Northern
Chuanchun	Chuanlan
Ch'uan-chun-tsi	Chuanlan
Chuanlan	
Chuangqing	Chuanqing
Chuanqing	
Chug	Monpa, Chugpa
Chumba	Tsum
Chumbi Tibetan	Groma
Chung Monpa	Monpa, Chugpa
Chung-tien Tibetans	Tibetan, Shangri-La
Chuo-mu Tibetan	Groma
Chutobikha	Nyenpa
Cimulin	Qiang, Cimulin
Cingalese	Sinhalese
Col	Samtao
Color Belt Dai	Huayao Tai
Con	Angku
Cona Monba	Tsangla
Cone	Tibetan, Jone
Cuoi	Kui
Cuona Monba	Tsangla
Cur	Khmer
Cu Tho	Khmer

D

Da-ang	Palaung, Pale
Da-eng	Palaung, Pale
Daduwa	Gurung, Eastern
Dagpa	Dakpa
Daignet	Dainet
Dai: Han	Han Dai
Dai Le (#1)	Lu
Dai Le (#2)	Tai Mao
Dai Loe	Tai Mao
Dai Lu	Lu

Dai Mao	Tai Mao
Dai Mo	Tai Mao
Dai Na	Tai Nua
Dainet	
Daingnet	Dainet
Da Jiao Ban	Chuanqing
Dakpa	
Dakpa (#2)	Brokpa
Dakpakha	Dakpa
Dali	Bai
Dambro	Thai, Southern
Danau	
Danaw	Danau
Dandzongka	Sikkimese
Danjongka	Sikkimese
Danu	Danau
Danyouka	Sikkimese
Daofuhua	Ergong
Dap (#1)	Brokpa
Dap (#2)	Dakpa
Darang	Palaung, Pale
Dariganga	
Dariganga Mongols	Dariganga
Dawei	Tavoyan
Dawai	Taungyo
Dawe	Taungyo
Da Xiuzi	Chuanqing
Dbus	Tibetan, Central
Dbustsang	Tibetan, Central
De'ang Pale	Palaung, Pale
De'ang Rumai	Palaung, Rumai
De'ang Shwe	Palaung, Shwe
Dehong	Tai Mao
Dehong Dai	Tai Mao
Deng Za	Za
Denjonbg	Sikkimese
Denjongka	Sikkimese
Denjongke	Sikkimese
Denjongkha	Sikkimese
Denjongpa	Sikkimese
Deqen Tibetans	Khampa, Southern
Deqin Tibetan	Khampa, Southern
Dewansala	Yakha
Dhopa	Dolpo
Di-ang	Palaung, Pale
Diba	Tuva
Dinenet	Dainet
Dioi	Yoy
Doi (#1)	Tai Doi
Doi (#2)	Tai Loi
Dokhpa	
Dokskat	Dokhpa
Dolpa	Dolpo

Dolpali	Dolpo
Dolpali Bhote	Dolpo
Dolpa Tibetan	Dolpo
Dolpo	
Dowaniya	
Drokba	Tibetan, Nghari
Drokpa (#1)	Dokhpa
Drokpa (#2)	Tibetan, Nghari
Drokwa	Tibetan, Nghari
Drukha	Drukpa
Drukke	Drukpa
Drukpa	
Drukpa (#2)	Dokhpa
Drukpha	Drukpa
Druku	Drukpa
Dry Land Dai	Han Tai
Dukpa	Drukpa
Dui	Kui
Duoi	Yoy
Du'o'l	Yoy
Duoxu	Ersu
Durbet	Kalmyk-Oirat
Duon	Lu
Dura	
Durra	Dura
Dzala	
Dzalakha	Dzala
Dzalamat	Dzala
Dzongkha	Drukpa

E

East Yugur	Yugur, Enger
Eastern Jiarong	Jiarong, Situ
Eastern Jyarung	Jiarong, Situ
Eastern Min	Han Chinese, Min Dong
Eastern Monba	Monpa, Medog
Eastern Tai	Lao
Eastern Yogor	Yugur, Enger
Enger	Yugur, Enger
Erankad	Gahri
Ergong	
Ersu	
Ersubuerzi	Ersu
Ersu Yi	Ersu
European Oirat	Kalmyk-Oirat

F

Faake	Tai Phake
Fangpa	Champa
Fang Teo Ren	Chuanqing
Flowery Belt Dai	Huayao Tai
Flowery Waist Dai	Huayao Tai

G

Gahra	Gahri
Gahri	
Galle (#1)	Ghale, Northern
Galle (#2)	Ghale, Southern
Galle Gurung (#1)	Ghale, Northern
Galle Gurung (#2)	Ghale, Southern
Gan	Han Chinese, Gan
Gara	
Garba	Gara
Garra	Gara
Gatse	Golog
Gesista	Ergong
Ggolo	Golog
Ghale (#1)	Ghale, Northern
Ghale (#2)	Ghale, Southern
Ghale Gurung (#1)	Ghale, Northern
Ghale Gurung (#2)	Ghale, Southern
Ghale, Northern	
Ghale, Southern	
Gin	Vietnamese
Giong	Gong
Giy	Yoy
Golden Palaung	Palaung, Shwe
Golog	
Golok	Golog
Gondhla	Tinan
Gondla	Tinan
Gong	
Gongduk	
Gongdubikha	Gongduk
Gongdukpa	Gongduk
Gongdupkha	Gongduk
Gon Shan	Khun
Great Thai	Shan
Groma	
Gromo	Groma
Guichong	Guiqiong
Guiqiong	
Gurkhal	Gurung, Western
Gurun	Gurung, Eastern
Gurung (#1)	Gurung, Eastern
Gurung (#2)	Gurung, Western
Gurung, Eastern	
Gurung, Western	
Guangdong	Han Chinese, Cantonese
Guangdong Hua	Han Chinese, Cantonese
Guanhua	Han Chinese, Mandarin
Guanyingqiao	Jiarong, Guanyingqiao
Guoyu	Han Chinese, Mandarin
Gurtu	Kurtop
Gwong Dung Waa	Han Chinese, Cantonese

Gyantse	Tibetan, Gtsang
Gyarong (#1)	Jiarong, Chabao
Gyarong (#2)	Jiarong, Guanyingqiao
Gyarong (#3)	Jiarong, Shangzhai
Gyarong (#4)	Jiarong, Sidabao
Gyarong (#5)	Jiarong, Situ
Gyarung (#1)	Jiarong, Chabao
Gyarung (#2)	Jiarong, Guanyingqiao
Gyarung (#3)	Jiarong, Shangzhai
Gyarung (#4)	Jiarong, Sidabao
Gyarung (#5)	Jiarong, Situ
Gyirong	Kyerung

H

Hahl	Mongol
Hahl Mongol	Mongol
Hainan Chinese	Han Chinese, Hainanese
Hainanese	Han Chinese, Hainanese
Hakka	
Hakka Chinese	Hakka
Halh	Mongol
Han Chinese, Cantonese	
Han Chinese, Gan	
Han Chinese, Hainanese	
Han Chinese: Hakka	Hakka
Han Chinese, Huizhou	
Han Chinese, Jin	
Han Chinese, Mandarin	
Han Chinese, Min Bei	
Han Chinese, Min Dong	
Han Chinese, Min Nan	
Han Chinese, Pinghua	
Han Chinese, Puxian	
Han Chinese, Wu	
Han Chinese, Xiang	
Han Dai	Han Tai
Hanghohua	Korean
Hanguk Mal	Korean
Han Tai	
Hdzanggur	
He	Tai He
Henghua	Han Chinese, Puxian
Henkha	Nyenpa
Hihin	Mongol, Sichuan
Hii-khin	Mongol, Sichuan
Hinghua	Han Chinese, Puxian
Hkamti	Khamti
Hkawa	Bulang
Hkun	Khun
Hkun Loi	Bulang
Hli-khin	Mosuo
Hockchew	Han Chinese, Min Bei
Hokchia	Han Chinese, Min Bei

Hokchiu	Han Chinese, Min Bei
Hokka	Hakka
Hokkien	Han Chinese, Min Nan
Hoklo	Han Chinese, Min Nan
Hokow	Queyu
Holung	Walung
Hor	Ergong
Hor-ke	Ergong
Horpa	Ergong
Horsok	Ergong
Horu	Ergong
Hoton	Han Chinese, Mandarin
Hsiang	Han Chinese, Xiang
Hsiangcheng	Xiangcheng
Hsifan	Pumi, Northern
Hsinghua	Han Chinese, Puxian
Hu	
Huangtou Huihe	Yugur, Enger
Huayao Tai	
Huichou	Han Chinese, Huizhou
Huihe	Yugur, Enger
Huihu	Yugur, Enger
Huizhou	Han Chinese, Huizhou
Humai	Palaung, Rumai
Hunan Chinese	Han Chinese, Xiang
Hunanese	Han Chinese, Xiang
Huzhu	Tu
Hwayao Dai	Huayao Tai
Hweichow	Han Chinese, Huizhou

I

Inntha	Intha
Intha	
Isan	
Issan	Isan

J

Jang	Mosuo
Jarong (#1)	Jiarong, Chabao
Jarong (#2)	Jiarong, Guanyingqiao
Jarong (#3)	Jiarong, Shangzhai
Jarong (#4)	Jiarong, Sidabao
Jarong (#5)	Jiarong, Situ
Jazyk	Kalmyk-Oirat
Jazza	Golog
Jiarong, Chabao	
Jiarong, Guanyingqiao	
Jiarong, Shangzhai	
Jiarong, Sidabao	
Jiarong, Situ	
Jin	Han Chinese, Jin
Jing	Vietnamese
Jingpho	Singhpo

Jingpo	Singhpo
Jing Ren	Qixingmin
Jinyu	Han Chinese, Jin
Jirel	
Jiri	Jirel
Jirial	Jirel
Jiripa	Jirel
Jo	Nyaw
Jone	Tibetan, Jone
Jonkha	Drukpa
Jyali	Beda
Jyayi	Beda

K

Kachin	Singhpo
Kagate	
Kagate Bhote	Kagate
Kagatey	Kagate
Kagati	Kagate
Kah So	So
Ka Khyen	Singhpo
Kaike	
Kaike (#2)	Dolpo
Kaikhe	Dolpo
Ka-kaung	Padaung
Kaku	Singhpo
K'ala	Angku
Kaleum	Kaleung
Kaleun	Kaleung
Kaleung	
Kalerng	Kaleung
Kalmuck	Kalmyk-Oirat
Kalmuk	Kalmyk-Oirat
Kalmyk-Oirat	
Kalmytskii	Kalmyk-Oirat
Kam	Khampa, Eastern
Kammuang	Thai, Northern
Kam Mu'ang	Thai, Northern
Kampuchean	Khmer
Kam Ti	Khamti
Kan	Han Chinese, Gan
Kanaura	Kinnaura
Kanauri	Kinnaura
Kanaury Anuskad	Kinnaura
Kanawara	Kinnaura
Kanawari	Kinnaura
Kanawi	Kinnaura
Ka-ne	Kaike
Kang (#1)	Khampa, Eastern
Kang (#2)	Tai Khang
Kang (#3)	Tai Mao
Kangba	Khampa, Southern
Kanggan	Golog

Kangsar	Golog
Kanorin Skad	Kinnaura
Kanorug Skadd	Kinnaura
Kar Bhote	Lhomi
Karen Padaung	Padaung
Karen: Pa-O	Pa-O
Karenni	Kayah, Western
Karieng Daeng	Kayah, Western
Karrenyi	Kayah, Western
Kathe Bhote	Lhomi
Kaw	Mpi
Kawa	Bulang
Kayah, Western	
Kayah Li	Kayah, Western
Kayan	Padaung
Kayang	Padaung
Ke	Hakka
Kebumtamp	Bumthang
Kebumtarp	Drukpa
Kechia	Hakka
Kehia	Hakka
Kejia	Hakka
Kek	Hakka
Ken	Kheng
Keng	Kheng
Keylong Boli	Gahri
Khalka	Mongol
Khalkha	Mongol
Khalmag	Kalmyk-Oirat
Khalong	Kaleung
Kham (#1)	Khampa, Eastern
Kham (#2)	Khampa, Northern
Kham (#3)	Khampa, Western
Khamba (#1)	Khampa, Eastern
Khamba (#2)	Khampa, Northern
Khamba (#3)	Khampa, Southern
Khamba (#4)	Khampa, Western
Khamen-Boran	Kui
Khami	Mru
Khamiyang	
Khamjang	Khamiyang
Khammi	Mru
Khampa, Eastern	
Khampa, Northern	
Khampa, Southern	
Khampa, Western	
Khampti	Khamti
Khampti Shan	Khamti
Khams	Khampa, Eastern
Khams-Bhotia	Khampa, Eastern
Khams-Yal	Khampa, Eastern
Kham Tai	Khamti
Khamti	

Khamti Shan	Khamti
Khamyang	Khamiyang
Khan	Mugali
Khandi Shan	Khamti
Khang	Tai Khang
Khanigaon	Kaike
Khantis	Khamti
Kha So	So
Khek	Hakka
Khen	Kheng
Kheng	
Khengkha	Kheng
Khenkha	Kheng
Khmer	
Khmer Krom	Khmer
Khoa	Khowa
Khoen	Khun
Khoitumjee	Monpa, But
Kho Me	Khmer
Khon	Thai, Northern
Khon Doi	Bulang
Khon Mang	Thai, Northern
Khon Muang	Thai, Northern
Khon Mung	Thai, Northern
Khon Myang	Thai, Northern
Khonujee	Monpa, But
Khorat	Khorat Thai
Khorat Thai	
Khouen	Khuen
Khowa	
Khuen	
Khuen (#2)	Khun
Khun	
Khun Shan	Khun
Khutsho	Kucong
Khween	Khuen
Kinara	Kinnaura
King	Vietnamese
Kinh	Vietnamese
Kinnara	Kinnaura
Kinnaura	
Kinnaura Yanuskad	Kinnaura
Kinnaurese	Kinnaura
Kinnauri	Kinnaura
Kinner	Kinnaura
Kinori	Kinnaura
Kiorr	Angku
Kishpi	Monpa, Lishpa
Kmajang	Khamti
Kok	Tuva
Kon	Lu
Kong	Tai Mao
Konka	Khampa, Eastern

Konkaling	Khampa, Eastern
Korean	
Kontoi	Bulang
Koonawure	Kinnaura
Kmer	Khmer
Krang	Lao Krang
Ku	Khmer
Kuan	Khuen
Kuanhua	Khuen
Kucong	
Kui	
Kui (#2)	Kucong
Kui Souei	Kui
Kui Sung	Kucong
Kunawar	Kinnaura
Kunawari	Kinnaura
Kuoy	Kui
Kur	Kucong
Kurteopkha	Kurtop
Kurtobikha	Kurtop
Kurtobi Zhake	Kurtop
Kurthopka	Kurtop
Kurthopkha	Kurtop
Kurtokha	Kurtop
Kurtop	
Kurtopa	Kurtop
Kurtopakha	
Kutang Bhotia	Nubri
Kutsung	Kucong
Kuy	Kui
Kuy Soung	Kucong
K'wa	Bulang
Kween	Khuen
Kwi	Kucong
Kwong	Gong
Kyango	Dokhpa
Kyerung	
Kyirong	Kyerung

L

Laan	Tai Laan
Labbu	Bai
Lachengpa	Sikkimese
Lachungpa	Sikkimese
Ladak	Ladakhi
Ladakh	Ladakhi
Ladakhi	
Ladaphi	Ladakhi
Ladhakhi	Ladakhi
Ladwags	Ladakhi
Lae Kur	Padaung
Lahaula (#1)	Gahri
Lahuala (#2)	Tinan

Lahauli	Tinan	Lao Phung Dam	Thai, Northern
Lahouli (#1)	Gahri	Lao Song	Song
Lahouli (#2)	Tinan	Lao Song Dam	Song
Lahu Adaw-aga	Kucong	Lao-Tai	Lao
Lahu Aga	Kucong	*Lao Ti*	
Lahul	Gahri	Laotian	Lao
Lahul Bhoti	Stod Bhoti	Laotian Tai	Lao
Lahuli (#1)	Gahri	Lao Wiang	Lao
Lahuli (#2)	Tinan	*Lao Wieng*	
Lahuli of Bunan	Gahri	Lao Wiengchan	Lao Wieng
Lahuli Tinan	Tinan	Lao Yuai	Yoy
La Hu Si	Kucong	Lao Yuan	Thai, Northern
Lahu Shi	Kucong	*Lap*	
Lahu Shi Kakeo	Kucong	Lap (#2)	Nyenpa
Lahu Xi	Kucong	Lap-cha	Lepcha
Laimo	Lemo	Larke	Nubri
Lakha	Lap	Larkye Bhote	Nubri
Lakhapa	Lap	Larkye Tibetans	Nubri
Lama (#1)	Tamang, Eastern	Lava	Lawa, Eastern
Lama (#2)	Tamang, Eastern Gorkha	Lavu'a	Lawa, Eastern
Lama (#3)	Tamang, Northwestern	Lawa (#1)	Gong
Lama (#4)	Tamang, Southwestern	Lawa (#2)	Lawa, Eastern
Lama (#5)	Tamang, Western	Lawa (#3)	Lawa, Western
Lanatai	Thai, Northern	*Lawa, Eastern*	
Lanna	Thai, Northern	*Lawa, Western*	
Lan Na	Thai, Northern	Leme	Bai
Lan Na Thai	Thai, Northern	*Lemo*	
Lao		*Lepcha*	
Lao Berng	Tai Bueng	Leu (#1)	Lu
Lao Bueng	Tai Bueng	Leu (#2)	So
Lao Di	Lao Ti	Leun	So
Laoeng	Kaleung	Leung	So
Lao Ga		Lhardi	Golog
Lao Gao	Lao Ga	Lhasa	Tibetan, Central
Lao Glang	Lao Krang	Lhasa Tibetan	Tibetan, Central
Lao Go	Lao Ga	Lhoket	Lhomi
Lao Grang	Lao Krang	*Lhomi*	
Lao Han (#1)	Chuanlan	Lhopas	Loba
Lao Han (#2)	Chuanqing	Lhori	Sikkimese
Lao Isan	Isan	Lila (#1)	Ghale, Northern
Lao Kaleung	Kaleung	Lila (#2)	Ghale, Southern
Lao Kang	Lao Krang	Lish	Monpa, Lishpa
Lao Kao	Lao	Lish Monpa	Monpa, Lishpa
Lao Khrang	Lao Krang	Lishpa	Monpa, Lishpa
Lao Klang	Lao Krang	Lisu	Ersu
Lao Krang		Lo	Bulang
Lao Lom		*Loba*	
Lao Lu	Lu	Lodak	Ladakhi
Lao-Lum	Lao	Lodokhi	Ladakhi
Lao Ngaew		Loi (#1)	Bulang
Lao Ngiaw	Lao Ngaew	Loi (#2)	Tai Loi
Lao-Noi	Lao	Lo Manthang	Loba
Lao Phuan	Phuan	Lo Montang	Loba

Long-Neck Karen	Padaung
Lopa	Loba
Lowa (#1)	Lawa, Eastern
Lowa (#2)	Loba
Lower Kinnauri	Kinnaura
Loyu	Loba
Lu	
Lua (#1)	Bulang
Lua (#2)	Samtao
Lue	Lu
Lugu Lake Mongols	Mongol, Sichuan
Luhua	Qiang, Luhua
Lu-k'ou	Lemo
Lum Lao	Lao
Lushi	Mosuo
Lusu	Ersu
Luun	So
L'wa	Lawa, Eastern
Ly	Lu

M

Made	Amdo, Hbrogpa
Mag	Rakhine
Magh	Rakhine
Maghi	Rakhine
Majia	Hakka
Makong	So
Malimasa	
Man	
Man (#2)	Burmese
Man (#3)	Manchu
Manang	Manangba
Manangay	Manangba
Manangba	
Manangbhot	Manangba
Manangbolt	Manangba
Manangi	Manangba
Manangpa	Manangba
Manchou	Manchu
Manchu	
Mandarin	Han Chinese, Mandarin
Mang Cong	So
Mangdebikha	Nyenpa
Mangdekha	Nyenpa
Mangkong	So
Mangkoong	So
Mangsdekha	Nyenpa
Manju	Manchu
Mankoong	So
Manmet	
Man Met	Manmet
Manmi	Manmet
Manmit	Manmet

Manton	Palaung, Pale
Mao	Tai Mao
Mao Shan	Tai Mao
Maphekha	Matpa
Ma'pri	Mpi
Marma	Rakhine
Mash	Rakhine
Matchopa	Monpa, But
Matpa	
Mau	Tai Mao
Maw	Tai Mao
Mawo	Qiang, Mawo
Medog Monba	Monpa, Medog
Mekong Tibetan	Khampa, Southern
Melhesti	Kinnaura
Memba	Tsangla
Menba (#1)	Monpa, But
Menba (#2)	Monpa, Chugpa
Menba (#3)	Monpa, Dirang
Menba (#4)	Monpa, Kalaktang
Menba (#5)	Monpa, Lishpa
Menba (#6)	Monpa, Tawang
Menba (#7)	Tsangla
Menggu	Mongol
Meng Zu	Mongol
Menpa	Tsangla
Meragsagstengkha	Brokpa
Mera Sagtengpa	Brokpa
Meyor	Zakhring
Mgolog	Golog
Mien	Khmer
Milakkha	Lawa, Eastern
Milchan	Kinnaura
Milchanang	Kinnaura
Milchang	Kinnaura
Minaro	Dokhpa
Minchia	Bai
Min Dong	Han Chinese, Min Dong
Minhe Tu	Mongour
Minkia	Bai
Min Nan	Han Chinese, Min Nan
Min Pei	Han Chinese, Min Bei
Minya	Minyak
Minya Tibetans	Minyak
Minyak	
Mira Sagtengpa	Brokpa
Miyao	Minyak
Mngharis	Tibetan, Nghari
Mogh	Rakhine
Mo-hseih	Mosuo
Moinba (#1)	Monpa, But
Moinba (#2)	Monpa, Chugpa
Moinba (#3)	Monpa, Dirang

Moinba (#4)	Monpa, Kalaktang
Moinba (#5)	Monpa, Lishpa
Moinba (#6)	Monpa, Tawang
Moinba (#7)	Tsangla
Mompa	Tsangla
Mon	
Mon (#2)	Mon, Ladakh
Monba (#1)	Monpa, But
Monba (#2)	Monpa, Chugpa
Monba (#3)	Monpa, Dirang
Monba (#4)	Monpa, Kalaktang
Monba (#5)	Monpa, Lishpa
Monba (#6)	Monpa, Tawang
Monba: Cona	Tsangla
Monchak	Tuva
Mon, Ladakh	
Monglwe	Tai Loi
Mongol	
Mongolian	Mongol
Mongolian Buriat	Buriat, Mongolia
Mongolian Yugur	Yugur, Enger
Mongol, Sichuan	
Mongor	Mongour
Mongou	Mongour
Mongour	
Monguor	Mongour
Monjak	Tuva
Monkha	Ole
Monkit	Monpa, Tawang
Monpa (#1)	Monpa, But
Monpa (#2)	Monpa, Chugpa
Monpa (#3)	Monpa, Dirang
Monpa (#4)	Monpa, Kalaktang
Monpa (#5)	Monpa, Lishpa
Monpa (#6)	Mompa, Tawang
Monpa (#7)	Tsangla
Monpa, But	
Monpa, Chugpa	
Monpa, Dirang	
Monpa, Kalaktang	
Monpa, Lishpa	
Monpa, Medog	
Monpa, Tawang	
Moonglair Khampti	Khamti
Morma	Rakhine
Moso	Mosuo
Mosso	Mosuo
Mosuo	
Motuo Monba	Monpa, Medog
Mou	Mon
Mountain Dai	Han Tai
Mousseur Luang	Kucong
Moxie	Mosuo

Mpi	
Mpi-mi	Mpi
Mro	Mru
Mru	
Mru Chin	Mru
Mrung	Mru
Mu'ang	Thai, Northern
Muang Lan Na	Thai, Northern
Mugali	
Mugali Tamang	Mugali
Mugg	Rakhine
Mugu	Mugali
Mug'um	Mugali
Mun	Mon
Mungak	Tuva
Munya	Minyak
Muong Leung	So
Murmi (#1)	Tamang, Eastern
Murmi (#2)	Tamang, Eastern Gorkha
Murmi (#3)	Tamang, Northwestern
Murmi (#4)	Tamang, Southwestern
Murmi (#5)	Tamang, Western
Murung	Mru
Musseh Kwi	Kucong
Mustang	Loba
Mustang Bhote	Loba
Mustang Tibetans	Loba
Musu	Mosuo
Mutanchi Rongkup	Lepcha
Muya	Minyak
Muyak	Minyak
Myan	Burmese
Myang	Thai, Northern
Myanmas	Burmese
Myen	Burmese

N

Na	
Nagnoo	Monpa, But
Nah	Na
Nama	Bai
Nam Hsan	Palaung, Pale
Na-Tagin	Na
Nepal Bhasa	Newar
Neshyangba	Manangba
Neshyangpa	Manangba
Nesyangba	Manangba
Ne Thu	Kucong
Newah	Newar
Newar	
Newari	Newar
Nga	Na
Ngaew	Lao Ngaew

Ngalong	Drukpa
Ngalop	Drukpa
Ngambo	Amdo, Hbrogpa
Nganshuenkuan	Khampa, Southern
Ngarung	Drukpa
Ngawa	Golog
Ngenkha	Nyenpa
Ngeo	Shan
Ngeou	Nyaw
Nghari	Tibetan, Nghari
Ngharis	Tibetan, Nghari
Ngiao	Shan
Ngiaw (#1)	Lao Ngaew
Ngiaw (#2)	Shan
Ngieo	Shan
Ngio	Shan
Ngiou	Shan
Ngiow	Shan
Ngnok	Sherdukpen
Ngo	Nyaw
Ngolok	Golog
Ngura	Golog
Nhuane	Thai, Northern
Nhuon	Lu
Ngwe Palaung	Palaung, Pale
Nhyakhur	Nyahkur
Niakuol	Nyahkur
Niakuoll	Nyahkur
Niopreng	Mru
Niou	Shan
Nishung (#1)	Tamang, Eastern
Nishung (#2)	Tamang, Eastern Gorkha
Nishung (#3)	Tamang, Northwestern
Nishung (#4)	Tamang, Southwestern
Nishung (#5)	Tamang, Western
Northeastern Jiarong	Jiarong, Chabao
Northeastern Mongolian	Buriat, China
Northeastern Thai	Isan
Northern Chinese	Han Chinese, Mandarin
Northern Gurung	Manangba
Northern Jiarong	Jiarong, Chabao
Northern Lawa	Lawa, Eastern
Northern Min	Han Chinese, Min Bei
Northern Monba	Monpa, Medog
Northern Pumi	Pumi, Northern
Northern Mongolian (#1)	Buriat, China
Northern Mongolian (#2)	Buriat, Mongolia
Northern Mongolian (#3)	Buriat, Russia
Northern Shan	Tai Mao
Nubri	
Nubriba	Nubri
Nubripa	Nubri
Nunpa	Lepcha

Nupbi	
Nupbikha	Nupbi
Nupra	Nubri
Nupraba	Nubri
Nyahkur	
Nyakur	Nyahkur
Nyarong	Khampa, Southern
Nyaw	
Nyaw (#2)	Shan
Nyenkha	Nyenpa
Nyenpa	
Nyeshang	Manangba
Nyishang	Manangba
Nyo	Nyaw
Nyong	Yong

O

Oirat	Kalmyk-Oirat
Olangchung	Walung
Olangchung Gola	Walung
Old Han (#1)	Chuanlan
Old Han (#2)	Chuanqing
Ole	
Olekha	Ole
Ole Monpa	Ole
Ou	Nyaw

P

Padaung	
Padong	Padaung
Pai	Bai
Pai-l	Lu
Pai-yi	Lu
Paiyi	Tai Nua
Pak Tai	Tak Bai Thai
Paktay	Tak Bai Thai
Pak Thai	Tak Bai Thai
Palaung, Pale	
Palaung, Rumai	
Palaung, Shwe	
Palay	Palaung, Pale
Pale	Palaung, Pale
Palke	Tai Phake
Palong	Palaung, Pale
Panchgaun	Baragaunle
Panchgaunle	Baragaunle
Pao	Pa-O
Pa-O	
Pa'o	Pa-O
Pa Oh	Pa-O
Pao	Tai Pao
Pao Karen	Pa-O
Pa-U	Pa-O

Pawang	Ergong
Payap	Thai, Northern
Peguan	Mon
Pei	Han Chinese, Mandarin
Penghua	Han Chinese, Pinghua
Penglung	Palaung, Pale
Pengwa	Han Chinese, Pinghua
Penhwa	Han Chinese, Pinghua
Phalpa	Champa
Phakial	Khamti
Phake	Tai Phake
Phakey	Tai Phake
Phakial	Tai Phake
Phoan	Phuan
Phoke	Tibetan, Central
Phoke Dolpa	Dolpo
Phon Soung	Thavung
Phouan	Phuan
Phou Lao	Lao
Phuan	
Phuman	Puman
Phuon	Phuan
Phutai	
Phu Tai	Phutai
Phu Tai Gapong	Tai Gapong
Phu Tai Wang	Tai Wang
Phu-uen	Phuan
Phu Un	Phuan
Phyap	Thai, Northern
Phyagphreng	Xiangcheng
Ping	Han Chinese, Pinghua
Pinghua	Han Chinese, Pinghua
Pinghwa	Han Chinese, Pinghua
Plaang	Bulang
Plang	Bulang
Poan	Phuan
Pohbetian	Tibetan, Central
Polaung	Palaung, Pale
Poonan	Gahri
Potinhua	Han Chinese, Mandarin
Poutai	Phutai
Prong	Bulang
Pu	Chuanqing
Puan	Phuan
Pula	Bulang
Pulang	Bulang
Pulei	Palaung, Pale
Puman	
P'uman	Puman
Pumi, Northern	
Punan	Gahri
Punti	Han Chinese, Cantonese
Pu Ren	Chuanqing

Putai	Phutai
Puthay	Phutai
Putian	Han Chinese, Puxian
Putonghua	Han Chinese, Mandarin
Pu-Xian	Han Chinese, Puxian

Q

Qagcheng Tibetan	Xiangcheng
Qalmaq	Kalmyk-Oirat
Qiang, Cimulin	
Qiang, Luhua	
Qiang, Mawo	
Qiang, Yadu	
Qinghai Bonan	Bonan, Tongren
Qiongwen	Han Chinese, Hainanese
Qixingmin	
Qotong	Han Chinese, Mandarin
Queyu	

R

Rahungjee	Monpa, But
Rakhain	Rakhine
Rakhine	
Rangloi	Tinan
Red Karen	Kayah, Western
Rgyalathang	Tibetan, Shangri-La
Rgyarong (#1)	Jiarong, Chabao
Rgyarong (#2)	Jiarong, Guanyingqiao
Rgyarong (#3)	Jiarong, Shangzhai
Rgyarong (#4)	Jiarong, Sidabao
Rgyarong (#5)	Jiarong, Situ
Rimong	Golog
Rman	Mon
Rmen	Mon
Roi	Yakha
Rong (#1)	Champa
Rong (#2)	Lepcha
Rongba	Amdo, Rongba
Rongke	Lepcha
Rong Kong	Lao
Rongkup	Lepcha
Rongpa (#1)	Amdo, Rongba
Rongpa (#2)	Lepcha
Rumai	Palaung, Rumai
Rummai	Palaung, Rumai
Rummai Palaung	Palaung, Rumai
Ruomai	Palaung, Rumai
Rupshu	Champa
Ruul	So

S

Saamtaav	Samtao
Saek	
Sanggaixiong	Wutun

Sagtengpa	Brokpa
Sagya	Tibetan, Gtsang
Sakkya	Thet
Sali Uygur	Yugur, Enger
Sali Weiwu	Yugur, Enger
Sali Weiwuer	Yugur, Enger
Sam	Shan
Samlon Ta-ang	Palaung, Shwe
Samtao	
Sam Tao	Samtao
Samtau	Samtao
Samtuan	Samtao
Sangemao	Tibetan, Jone
Sangemao Tibetans	Tibetan, Jone
Sangla (#1)	Monpa, Dirang
Sangla (#2)	Tsangla
Saragh	Yugur, Saragh
Saraygh	Yugur, Saragh
Sarig	Yugur, Saragh
Sari Yogur	Yugur, Saragh
Seak	Saek
Sek	Saek
Sen	Shan
Sen Chun (#1)	Bulang
Sen Chun (#2)	Samtao
Serwa	Sherpa
Set	Saek
Sha	Shan
Shachobiikha	Tsangla
Shachopkha	Tsangla
Shahrang	Golog
Shakama	Thet
Sham	Shan
Shan	
Shanghai Chinese	Han Chinese, Wu
Shanghainese	Han Chinese, Wu
Shangzhai	Jiarong, Shangzhai
Shan Tayok	Tai Mao
Shanyan	Tibetan, Shanyan
Shar	Tsum
Sharchapkkha	Tsangla
Sharchop	Drukpa
Sharpa	Sherpa
Sharpa Bhotia	Sherpa
Shera Yugur	Yugur, Enger
Sherdukpen	
Sher-feizu	Chuanqing
Sherpa	
Shertu	Chuanqing
Shi	Kucong
Shihing	Shixing
Shingjee	Monpa, But
Shing Saapa	Lhomi
Shingsaba	Lhomi
Shira Yugur	Yugur, Enger
Shishing	Shixing
Shixing	
Shong	Chong
Shor	Tuva
Shuba	Kagate
Shuhin	Shixing
Shui Dai	Lu
Shui-Pai-I	Lu
Shwe	Palaung, Shwe
Shyam (#1)	Khamiyang
Shyam (#2)	Turung
Shyuba	Kagate
Siamese	Thai, Central
Siar	Tsum
Sichuan Mongolians	Mongol, Sichuan
Sichuan Pumi	Pumi, Northern
Sidabao	Jiarong, Sidabao
Sikami	Sikkimese
Sikkim Bhotia	Sikkimese
Sikkim Bhutia	Sikkimese
Sikkimese	
Silver Palaung	Palaung, Pale
Sing-fo	Singhpo
Singhala	Sinhalese
Singhalese	Sinhalese
Singhpo	
Singsawa	Lhomi
Sinhala	Sinhalese
Sinhalese	
Sipsongpanna Dai	Lu
Situ	Jiarong, Situ
Siyar	Tsum
So	
So (#2)	Thavung
Soai	Kui
Sogwo Arig	
Sogwo Arik	Sogwo Arig
Sohkwo	Sogwo Arig
So Makon	So
Song	
Sou	So
Souei	Kui
Southern Min	Han Chinese, Min Nan
Southern Monba	Tsangla
Southern Ta'ang	Palaung, Pale
Southern Thai	Thai, Southern
Soyod	Tuva
Soyon	Tuva
Soyot	Tuva
Standard Thai	Thai, Central
Stod	Stod Bhoti

Stod Bhoti	
Stod-Kad	Stod Bhoti
Stotpa	Champa
Suai	Kui
Suay	Kui
Suei	Kui
Sui	Kui
Sumu	Shixing
Suoi	Kui
Syuba	Kagate
Syuuba	Kagate

T

Ta-ang (#1)	Palaung, Pale
Ta-ang (#2)	Palaung, Shwe
Tahu	Amdo, Rtahu
Tai Berng	Tai Bueng
Tai Bueng	
Tai Capong	Tai Gapong
Tai Che	Tai Mao
Tai Dehong	Tai Mao
Tai Doi	
Tai Gapong	
Tai He	
Tai Isan	Isan
Tai Jai	Shan
Tai Kaleun	Kaleung
Tai Kam Ti	Khamti
Tai Kang	Lao Krang
Tai Kapon	Tai Gapong
Tai Kapong	Tai Gapong
Tai Khaang	Tai Khang
Tai Khamti	Khamti
Tai Kham Ti	Khamti
Tai Khang	
Tai Khe	Tai Mao
Tai Khoen	Khun
Tai Khrang	Lao Krang
Tai-Khuen	Khun
Tai Khun	Khun
Tai Klang	Lao Krang
Tai Krang	Lao Krang
Tai L	Lu
Tai Laan	
Tai Lan	Tai Laan
Tai Lao	Lao
Tai Le	Tai Mao
Tai Lei	Lao Lom
Tai Lhong	Tai Mao
Tai Loe	Tai Mao
Tai Loei	Lao Lom
Tai Loi	
Tai Loi (#2)	Bulang

Tailoi	Tai Loi
Tai Lom	Lao Lom
Tai Long	Tai Mao
Tai Lu	Lu
Tai Luang	Shan
Tai Mao	
Tai Mo	Tai Mao
Tai No	Nyaw
Tai Noi	Thai, Central
Tai Nu	Tai Nua
Tai Nua	
Tai Nue	Tai Nua
Tai Nuea (#1)	Tai Mao
Tai Nuea (#2)	Tai Nua
Tai Nya	Thai, Northern
Tai Nyo	Nyaw
Tai Pao	
Tai Phake	
Tairong	Turung
Tairung	Turung
Tai Sek	Saek
Tai Set	Saek
Tai Shan	Shan
Tai Song	Song
Tai Wang	
Tai Wang Angkham	Tai Wang
Tai Wang Na Yom	Tai Wang
Tai Wieng	Lao Wieng
Tai Yai (#1)	Shan
Tai Yai (#2)	Tai Mao
Tai Yay	Shan
Tai Yoi	Yoy
Tai Yong	Yong
Tai Yor	Nyaw
Tai Yoy	Yoy
Tai Yuan	Thai, Northern
Takam	Chakma
Takanoon	Mon
Tak Bai Thai	
Takbai Thai	Tak Bai Thai
Takpa	Dakpa
Talaing	Mon
Taleng	Mon
Tamang, Eastern	
Tamang, Eastern Gorkha	
Tamanglama (#1)	Tamang, Eastern
Tamanglama (#2)	Tamang, Eastern Gorkha
Tamanglama (#3)	Tamang, Southwestern
Tamanglama (#4)	Tamang, Western
Tamang, Northwestern	
Tamang, Southwestern	
Tamang, Western	
Tamu (#1)	Gurung, Eastern

Tamu (#2)	Gurung, Western	*Thavung*	
Tamu Kyi	Gurung, Western	*Thet*	
Tangsa, Tikhak		Thet (#2)	Chakma
Tangsa, Yongkuk		Thro	So
Tannu-Tuva	Tuva	Tibas Skad	Kinnaura
Taofu	Ergong	Tibati	Tibetan, Central
Tapaang	Thakali	*Tibetan, Central*	
Tarali Kham	Kaike	Tibetan: Deqen	Khampa, Southern
Tarali Magar	Kaike	*Tibetan, Gtsang*	
Taru	Taungyo	*Tibetan, Jone*	
Tatze	Sogwo Arig	*Tibetan, Nghari*	
Taungthu	Pa-O	*Tibetan, Shangri-La*	
Taungtu	Pa-O	*Tibetan, Shanyan*	
Taungyo		Tibetan: Zhongdian	Tibetan, Shangri-La
Tau-soo	Pa-O	Ticherong	Kaike
Tavoy	Tavoyan	Tichurong	Kaike
Tavoya	Tavoyan	Tikhak	Tangsa, Tikhak
Tavoyan		*Tinan*	
Tawe-Tavoy	Taungyo	Tinani	Tinan
Tay Khang	Tai Khang	Tod	Stod Bhoti
Tay Po	Tai Po	Tod-kad	Stod Bhoti
Tebbu		Tofa	Tuva
Tebbus	Tebbu	Tokha	Tuva
Tebilian	Tibetan, Central	Tomo	Groma
Te'ch'in Tibetan	Khampa, Southern	Tongren	Bonan, Tongren
Teenan	Tinan	Torgot	Torgut
Teguan	Mon	*Torgut*	
Teochew	Han Chinese, Min Nan	Torgut Mongolians	Torgut
Tewo	Tebbu	Toru	Taungyo
Tewo Tibetans	Tebbu	Tosu	Ersu
Tewu	Tebbu	Tro	So
Thai	Thai, Central	Trowoma	Groma
Thai, Central		Tsak	Chakma
Thai, Northern		Tsakalingpaikha	Matpa
Thai, Southern		Tsamangpakha	Matpa
Thai Tak Bai	Tak Bai Thai	Tsang	Tibetan, Gtsang
Thai Isan	Isan	*Tsangla*	
Thai Khom	Thai, Central	Tsangla (#2)	Monpa, Kalaktang
Thai Khorat	Khorat Thai	Tshali	Chali
Thai Klang	Thai, Central	Tshalingpa	Chali
Thai Malay	Thai, Southern	Tshangkha	Lap
Thai Soang	Song	Tshangla	Tsangla
Thai Song	Song	Tshomi	Pumi, Northern
Thai Wiengchan	Lao Wieng	Tsokhar	Golog
Thai Yay	Shan	*Tsum*	
Thakali		Tsumba	Tsum
Thaksya	Thakali	Tsumge	Tsum
Thami		*Tu*	
Thangmi	Thami	Tuba	Tuva
That	Thet	Tun	Chuanqing
Thaveung	Thavung	Tunbao (#1)	Chuanlan
Thavong	Thavung	Tunbao (#2)	Chuanqing
Thavueng	Thavung	*Turung*	

Tuva

Tuvan	Tuva
Tuva-Uriankhai	Tuva
Tuvia	Tuva
Tuvin	Tuva
Tuvinian	Tuva
Tuwa	Tuva
Tuwa-Uriankhai	Tuva
Tyva	Tuva
Tz'u-mu-lin Ch'iang	Qiang, Cimulin

U

U (#1)	Puman
U (#2)	Tibetan, Central
Ugawng	Gong
U Gong	Gong
Ugong	Gong
U Kwang	Gong
Ulang	Walung
Upper Ladakhi	Champa
Urinkhai	Tuva
Uryangkhai	Tuva
Uryankhai-Monchak	Tuva

V

Vieng	Lao Wieng
Viet	Vietnamese
Vietnamese	
Volga Oirat	Kalmyk-Oirat

W

Wakut	Tai Loi
Wa-la	Puman
Walung	
Walungba	Walung
Walungge	Walung
Walunggi Keccya	Walung
Walungpa	Walung
Wannan	Han Chinese, Huizhou
Wei	Tibetan, Central
Weilate	Kalmyk-Oirat
Weizang	Tibetan, Central
Western Jiarong (#1)	Jiarong, Sidabao
Western Jiarong (#2)	Ergong
Western Jyarong	Jiarong, Sidabao
Western Laotian	Thai, Northern
Western Mongolian	Kalmyk-Oirat
West Yugur	Yugur, Saragh
White Mongols	Tu
Wiang	Lao Wieng
Wiang Papao Lua	Lawa, Eastern
Wu	Han Chinese, Wu
Wutu	Wutun
Wutun	

Wutunhua	Wutun

X

Xaek	Saek
Xamtao	Samtao
Xec	Saek
Xek	Saek
Xiaerba	Sherpa
Xiangcheng	
Xiarba	Sherpa
Xifan	Pumi, Northern
Xigatse Tibetans	Tibetan, Gtsang
Xigatze	Tibetan, Gtsang
Xigatze Tibetans	Tibetan, Gtsang
Xigaze Tibetans	Tibetan, Gtsang
Xila Weiguer	Yugur, Enger
Xila Yugur	Yugur, Enger
Xinjiang Mongol	Kalmyk-Oirat
Xinjiang Mongols	Torgut
Xinghua	Han Chinese, Puxian
Xinmin	Hakka
Xishuangbanna Dai	Lu
Xong	Chong
Xouay	Kui
Xuay	Kui
Xumi	Shixing

Y

Yadu	Qiang, Yadu
Yakan	Rakhine
Yakha	
Yakhang	Rakhine
Yakkha	Yakha
Yakkhaba	Yakha
Yakkhaba Cea	Yakha
Yakkhaba Sala	Yakha
Yakthomba	Yakha
Ya Lu	Yugur, Saragh
Yang Deang	Kayah, Western
Yangtsebikha	Dzala
Yaofuer	Yugur, Saragh
Ya-tu Ch'iang	Qiang, Yadu
Yay	Yoy
Yellow Lahu	Kucong
Yellow Uighur	Yugur, Saragh
Yo	Nyaw
Yoan	Thai, Northern
Yoe	Yoy
Yogur	Yugur, Enger
Yohur	Yugur, Saragh
Yoi	Yoy
Yolmo	Kagate
Yon	Thai, Northern

Yonaka	Thai, Northern
Yong	
Yongkuk	Tangsa, Yongkuk
Yonok	Thai, Northern
Yonzhi	
Yooi	Yoy
Yor	Nyaw
Youanne	Thai, Northern
Youe	Thai, Northern
Youon	Thai, Northern
Yoy	
Yuai	Yoy
Yuan	Thai, Northern
Yue	Han Chinese, Cantonese
Yueai	Yoy
Yue Chinese	Han Chinese, Cantonese
Yueh	Han Chinese, Cantonese
Yuet	Han Chinese, Cantonese
Yuet Yue	Han Chinese, Cantonese
Yueyu	Han Chinese, Cantonese
Yugar	Yugur, Enger
Yugu (#1)	Yugur, Enger
Yugu (#2)	Yugur, Saragh

Yugur, Enger	
Yugur, Western	
Yuku	Yugur, Saragh
Yul-Mi	Drukpa
Yun	Thai, Northern

Z

Za	
Zaba	Zhaba
Zakhring	
Zang	Tibetan, Central
Zangskari	
Zanskari	Zangskari
Zaskari	Zangskari
Zayu	Za
Zhaba	
Zhaba (#2)	Queyu
Zhaboa	Zhaba
Zhongdian Tibetans	Tibetan, Shangri-La
Zhuomu Tibetan	Groma
Zhuoni Tibetan	Tibetan, Jone
Ziral	Jirel
Zongkhar	Drukpa

Appendix 2: Language Affiliation Index

The following table shows the linguistic relationship that various Buddhist peoples share with one another. It is helpful for those developing evangelistic resources for a group to discover linguistic and probable historical roots and similarities between groups. The names of each of the groups profiled in this book appear italicized, in capital letters, along with their primary country in parenthesis. A group's linguistic affiliation can be traced through its various branches upward, to the language family in large letters at the top of each section. Buddhist groups speak languages from five different linguistic familes (Altaic, Austro-Asiatic, Indo-European, Sino-Tibetan, and Tai-Kadai), as well as two 'language isolates' (Korean and Japanese). Most of the information regarding each group's linguistic affiliation comes from Barbara Grimes (ed.), *Ethnologue: Languages of the World* (14th edition, 2000).

Altaic (14)
Mongolian
Eastern
Oirat-Khalkha
Khalkha-Buriat
####### Buriat (3)
BURIAT, CHINA (China)
BURIAT, MONGOLIA (Mongolia)
BURIAT, RUSSIA (Russia)
####### Mongolian Proper (2)
DARIGANGA (Mongolia)
MONGOL (China)
####### Oirat-Kalmyk-Darkhat (2)
KALMYK-OIRAT (Mongolia)
TORGUT (China)
Eastern Mongolian
Mongour (4)
BONAN, TONGREN (China)
MONGOUR (China)
TU (China)
YUGUR, ENGER (China)

Tungus
Southern
Southwest (1)
MANCHU (China)
Turkic
Eastern (1)
YUGUR, SARAGH (China)
Northern (1)
TUVA (Russia)

Austro-Asiatic (24)

Mon-Khmer
    Eastern Mon-Khmer
        Katuic
            West Katuic
                Brou-So *(1)*
                    SO (Laos)
                Kuay-Yoe *(1)*
                    KUI (Thailand)
        Khmer
            Central Khmer
                Southern Khmer
                    Northern Khmer *(1)*
                        KHMER (Cambodia)
        Monic *(2)*
            MON (Myanmar)
            NYAHKUR (Thailand)
        Pearic
            Western
                Chong *(1)*
                    CHONG (Cambodia)

    Northern Mon-Khmer
        Khmuic
            Mal-Khmu
                Khmu *(1)*
                    KHUEN (Laos)
        Palaungic-Khmuic
            Palaungic
                Eastern Palaungic
                    Danau *(1)*
                        DANAU (Myanmar)
                    Palaung *(3)*
                      PALAUNG, PALE (Myanmar)
                      PALAUNG, RUMAI (Myanmar)
                      PALAUNG, SHWE (Myanmar)
                Western Palaungic
                    Angkuic *(7)*
                      ANGKU (Myanmar)
                      HU (China)
                      MANMET (China)
                      PUMAN (China)
                      SAMTAO (Myanmar)
                      TAI DOI (Laos)
                      TAI LOI (Myanmar)

            Waic

                Bulang *(1)*
                    BULANG (China)

                Lawa *(2)*
                    LAWA, EASTERN (Thailand)
                    LAWA, WESTERN (China)

Viet-Muong

      Thavung *(1)*
         THAVUNG (Thailand)

      Vietnamese *(1)*
         VIETNAMESE (Vietnam)

   Unclassified *(1)*
      HUAY (Thailand)

Indo-European (8)

Indo-Iranian

   Indo-Aryan

      Eastern Zone

         Bengali-Assamese *(3)*
            BARUA (India)
            CHAKMA (Bangladesh)
            MAN (India)

      Northern Zone

         Eastern Pahari *(1)*
            DURA (Nepal)

      Northwestern Zone

         Dardic

            Shina *(3)*
               DOKHPA (India)
               GARA (India)
               MON, LADAKH (India)

         Sinhalese-Maldivian *(1)*
            SINHALESE (Sri Lanka)

Sino-Tibetan (148)
Chinese (17)
CHUANLAN (China)
CHUANQING (China)
HAKKA (China)
HAN CHINESE, CANTONESE (China)
HAN CHINESE, GAN (China)
HAN CHINESE, HAINANESE (China)
HAN CHINESE, HUIZHOU (China)
HAN CHINESE, JIN (China)
HAN CHINESE, MANDARIN (China)
HAN CHINESE, MIN BEI (China)
HAN CHINESE, MIN DONG (China)
HAN CHINESE, MIN NAN (China)
HAN CHINESE, PINGHUA (China)
HAN CHINESE, PUXIAN (China)
HAN CHINESE, WU (China)
HAN CHINESE, XIANG (China)
LEMO (China)

Tibeto-Burman
Bai (1)
BAI (China)
Bodic
Bodish
Tibetan
Northern Tibetan (7)
AMDO, HBROGPA (China)
AMDO, RONGBA (China)
AMDO, RONGMAHBROGPA (China)
AMDO, RTAHU (China)
GOLOG (China)
HDZANGGUR (China)
SOGWO ARIG (China)

Karen
Pa'o (1)
PA-O (Myanmar)
Sgaw-Bghai
Bghai
Eastern (1)
PADAUNG (Myanmar)
Kayah (1)
KAYAH, WESTERN (Myanmar)

Jingpho-Konyak-Bodo
  Jingpho-Luish
    Jinghpo (2)
      DOWANIYA (India)
      SINGHPO (India)
    Luish (2)
      DAINET (Myanmar)
      THET (Myanmar)
  Konyak-Bodo-Garo
    Konyak (2)
      TANGSA, TIKHAK (India)
      TANGSA, YONGKUK (India)

Lolo-Burmese
  Burmish
    Southern (6)
      BURMESE (Myanmar)
      CHAUNGTHA (Myanmar)
      INTHA (Myanmar)
      RAKHINE (Myanmar)
      TAUNGYO (Myanmar)
      TAVOYAN (Myanmar)
  Loloish
    Southern (2)
      GONG (Thailand)
      KUCONG (China)
    Phunoi (1)
      MPI (Thailand)
  Naxi (2)
    MALIMASA (China)
    MOSUO (China)

Mru (1)
  MRU (Myanmar)

North Assam
  Tani (1)
    NA (India)

Tangut-Qiang
  Gyarong (6)
    ERGONG (China)
    JIARONG, CHABAO (China)
    JIARONG, GUANYINGQIAO (China)
    JIARONG, SHANGZHAI (China)
    JIARONG, SIDABAO (China)
    JIARONG, SITU (China)

Qiangic (7)

   ERSU (China)
   GUIQIONG (China)
   MINYAK (China)
   PUMI, NORTHERN (China)
   QUEYU (China)
   SHIXING (China)
   ZHABA (China)

Northern Qiang (4)

   QIANG, CIMULIN (China)
   QIANG, LUHUA (China)
   QIANG, MAWO (China)
   QIANG, YADU (China)

Himalayish

Mahakiranti

Kiranti

Eastern (8)

   MONPA, BUT (India)
   MONPA, CHUGPA (India)
   MONPA, DIRANG (India)
   MONPA, KALAKTANG (India)
   MONPA, LISHPA (India)
   MONPA, MEDOG (China)
   MONPA, TAWANG (India)
   YAKHA (Nepal)

Newari (1)

   NEWAR (Nepal)

Tibeto-Kanauri

Tibetic

Bodish (1)

   TSANGLA (Bhutan)

Tamangic (14)

   CHHAIROTTAN (Nepal)
   CHIMTAN (Nepal)
   GHALE, KUTANG (Nepal)
   GHALE, NORTHERN (Nepal)
   GHALE, SOUTHERN (Nepal)
   GURUNG, EASTERN (Nepal)
   GURUNG, WESTERN (Nepal)
   MANANGBA (Nepal)
   TAMANG, EASTERN (Nepal)
   TAMANG, EASTERN GORKHA (Nepal)
   TAMANG, NORTHWESTERN (Nepal)
   TAMANG, SOUTHWESTERN (Nepal)
   TAMANG, WESTERN (Nepal)
   THAKALI (Nepal)

Lepcha (1)
LEPCHA (India)

Kanauri (1)
KAIKE (Nepal)

Tibetic

Tibetan (1)
GONGDUK (Bhutan)

Central (15)
BARAGAUNLE (Nepal)
DOLPO (Nepal)
HELAMBU SHERPA (Nepal)
KAGATE (Nepal)
KYERUNG (China)
LHOMI (Nepal)
LOBA (Nepal)
MUGALI (Nepal)
NUBRI (Nepal)
STOD BHOTI (India)
TIBETAN, CENTRAL (China)
TIBETAN, GTSANG (China)
TIBETAN, NGHARI (China)
TSUM (Nepal)
WALUNG (Nepal)

Eastern (8)
BUMTHANG (Bhutan)
CHALI (Bhutan)
DAKPA (Bhutan)
KHENG (Bhutan)
KURTOP (Bhutan)
NUPBI (Bhutan)
NYENPA (Bhutan)
OLE (Bhutan)

Northern (7)
KHAMPA, EASTERN (China)
KHAMPA, NORTHERN (China)
KHAMPA, SOUTHERN (China)
KHAMPA, WESTERN (China)
TIBETAN, JONE (China)
TIBETAN, SHANGRI-LA (China)
YONZHI (China)

Southern (9)
BROKPA (Bhutan)
BROKPA, BROKKAT (Bhutan)
DRUKPA (Bhutan)
GROMA (China)
JIREL (Nepal)
LAP (Bhutan)
MATPA (Bhutan)
SHERPA (Nepal)
SIKKIMESE (India)

Western (1)
ZANGSKARI (India)

Unclassified (3)
KHOWA (India)
SHERDUKPEN (India)
TIBETAN, SHANYAN (China)

Unclassified (1)
DZALA (Bhutan)

Western

Ladakhi (2)
CHAMPA (India)
LADAKHI (India)

Western Himalayish

Eastern (1)
THAMI (Nepal)

Kanauri (4)
BEDA (India)
GAHRI (India)
KINNAURA (India)
TINAN (India)

Unclassified (6)
MONGOL, SICHUAN (China)
QIXINGMIN (China)
TEBBU (China)
XIANGCHENG (China)
ZA (China)
ZAKHRING (India)

Tai-Kadai (40)
Kam-Tai
   Be-Tai
      Tai-Sek
         Sek (1)
            SAEK (Laos)
         Tai
            East Central
               Northwest (1)
                  TURUNG (India)
          Southwestern
            East Central
               Chiang Saeng (4)
                  PHUAN (Thailand)
                  SONG (Thailand)
                  THAI, CENTRAL (Thailand)
                  THAI, NORTHERN (Thailand)
               Northwest (12)
                  AITON (India)
                  HAN TAI (China)
                  HUAYAO TAI (China)
                  KHAMIYANG (India)
                  KHAMTI (Myanmar)
                  KHUN (Myanmar)
                  LAO LOM (Myanmar)
                  LU (China)
                  SHAN (Myanmar)
                  TAI MAO (China)
                  TAI NUA (China)
                  TAI PHAKE (India)
               Lao-Phutai (13)
                  ISAN (Thailand)
                  KALEUNG (Thailand)
                  KHORAT TAI (Thailand)
                  LAO (Laos)
                  LAO GA (Thailand)
                  LAO KRANG (Thailand)
                  LAO NGAEW (Thailand)
                  LAO TI (Thailand)
                  LAO WIENG (Thailand)
                  NYAW (Thailand)
                  PHUTAI (Laos)
                  TAI GAPONG (Thailand)
                  TAI WANG (Laos)

                                      Southern (2)
                                           TAK BAI THAI (Thailand)

                                           THAI, SOUTHERN (Thailand)

Unclassified (2)

                 YONG (Thailand)

                 YOY (Thailand)

Unclassified (5)

    TAI BUENG (Thailand)

    TAI HE (Laos)

    TAI KHANG (Laos)

    TAI LAAN (Laos)

    TAI PAO (Laos)

Mixed Language (1)

Chinese-Tibetan-Mongolian

    WUTUN (China)

Japanese (1)

    JAPANESE (Japan)

Korean (1)

    KOREAN (South Korea)

Unclassified (1)

    CHAK (Myanmar)

Appendix 3: Distribution of Buddhist Peoples by Country

Of the 238 Buddhist people groups profiled in this book, exactly 100 (42%) have communities located in more than one country. Buddhist groups are found in at least 94 countries around the world, and apart from possibly a few small countries in Africa and the South Pacific, there are probably Buddhist individuals in every nation on earth.

(Note: The names listed below are the names used in the Profiles in this book. In some cases, the name used by a group in one country is different from that used in another. See the Index of Alternative Names for clarification.)

CHINA (111): Amdo, Hbrogpa; Amdo, Rongba; Amdo, Rongmahbrogpa; Amdo, Rtahu; Angku; Bai; Bonan, Tongren; Bulang; Buriat, China; Burmese; Champa; Chuanlan; Chuanqing; Dolpo; Ergong; Ersu; Gahri; Golog; Groma; Guiqiong; Hakka; Han Chinese, Cantonese; Han Chinese, Gan; Han Chinese, Hainanese; Han Chinese, Huizhou; Han Chinese, Jin; Han Chinese, Mandarin; Han Chinese, Min Bei; Han Chinese, Min Dong; Han Chinese, Min Nan; Han Chinese, Pinghua; Han Chinese, Puxian; Han Chinese, Wu; Han Chinese, Xiang; Han Tai; Hdzanggur; Hu; Huayao Tai; Japanese; Jiarong, Chabao; Jiarong, Guanyingqiao; Jiarong, Shangzhai; Jiarong, Sidabao; Jiarong, Situ; Kalmyk-Oirat; Khampa, Eastern; Khampa, Northern; Khampa, Southern; Khampa, Western; Khamti; Khuen; Korean; Kucong; Kyerung; Ladakhi; Lawa, Western; Lemo; Lhomi; Lu; Malimasa; Manchu; Manmet; Minyak; Mongol; Mongol, Sichuan; Mongour; Monpa, Medog; Mosuo; Palaung, Pale; Palaung, Rumai; Palaung, Shwe; Phutai; Puman; Pumi, Northern; Qiang, Cimulin; Qiang, Luhua; Qiang, Mawo; Qiang, Yadu; Qixingmin; Queyu; Samtao; Shan; Sherpa; Shixing; Sogwo Arig; Tai Loi; Tai Mao; Tai Nua; Tebbu; Thai, Central; Thami; Tibetan, Central; Tibetan, Gtsang; Tibetan, Jone; Tibetan, Nghari; Tibetan, Shangri-La; Tibetan, Shanyan; Tinan; Torgut; Tsangla; Tu; Tuva; Vietnamese; Wutun; Xiangcheng; Yonzhi; Yugur, Enger; Yugur, Saragh; Za; Zangskari; Zhaba

INDIA (59): Aiton; Barua; Beda; Burmese; Chakma; Champa; Dakpa; Dokhpa; Dowaniya; Drukpa; Gahri; Gara; Groma; Gurung, Eastern; Gurung, Western; Kagate; Khamiyang; Khampa, Eastern; Khampa, Western; Khamti; Khowa; Kinnaura; Ladakhi; Lepcha; Lhomi; Man; Mon, Ladakh; Monpa, But; Monpa, Chugpa; Monpa Dirang; Monpa, Kalaktang; Monpa, Lishpa; Monpa, Medog; Monpa, Tawang; Mru; Na; Newar; Rakhine; Sherdukpen; Sherpa; Sikkimese; Singhpo; Sinhalese; Stod Bhoti; Tai Phake; Tamang, Eastern; Tamang, Southwestern; Tangsa, Tikhak; Tangsa, Yongkuk; Thami; Tibetan, Central; Tibetan,

Gtsang; Tinan; Tsangla; Turung; Walung; Yakha; Zakhring; Zangskari

THAILAND (58): Angku; Bulang; Burmese; Chong; Gong; Hakka; Han Chinese, Cantonese; Han Chinese, Hainanese; Han Chinese, Mandarin; Han Chinese, Min Dong; Han Chinese, Min Nan; Huay; Isan; Kaleung; Kayah, Western; Khmer; Khorat Thai; Khun; Kucong; Kui; Lao; Lao Ga; Lao Krang; Lao Lom; Lao Ngaew; Lao Ti; Lao Wieng; Lawa, Eastern; Lawa, Western; Lu; Mon; Mpi; Nyahkur; Nyaw; Padaung; Palaung, Pale; Pa-O; Phuan; Phutai; Saek; Samtao; Shan; Sinhalese; So; Song; Tai Bueng; Tai Gapong; Tai Mao; Tai Wang; Tak Bai Thai; Tavoyan; Thai, Central; Thai, Northern; Thai, Southern; Thavung; Vietnamese; Yong; Yoy

NEPAL (39): Baragaunle; Chhairottan; Chimtan; Dolpo; Drukpa; Dura; Ghale, Kutang; Ghale, Northern; Ghale, Southern; Gurung, Eastern; Gurung, Western; Helambu Sherpa; Jirel; Kagate; Kaike; Khampa, Eastern; Khampa, Western; Kyerung; Lepcha; Lhomi; Loba; Manangba; Mugali; Newar; Nubri; Sherpa; Tamang, Eastern; Tamang, Eastern Gorkha; Tamang, Northwestern; Tamang, Southwestern; Tamang, Western; Thakali; Thami; Tibetan, Central; Tibetan, Gtsang; Tibetan, Nghari; Tsum; Walung; Yakha

MYANMAR (37): Angku; Bulang; Burmese; Chak; Chaungtha; Dainet; Danau; Gurung, Western; Han Chinese, Mandarin; Intha; Kayah, Western; Khampa, Southern; Khamti; Khun; Kucong; Lao; Lawa, Western; Lu; Mon; Mru; Padaung; Palaung, Pale; Palaung, Rumai; Palaung, Shwe; Pa-O; Rakhine; Samtao; Shan; Tai Doi; Tai Loi; Tai Mao; Tamang, Eastern; Taungyo; Tavoyan; Thai, Central; Thet; Yong

LAOS (32): Angku; Burmese; Han Chinese, Cantonese; Han Chinese, Mandarin; Isan; Kaleung; Khmer; Khuen; Kucong; Kui; Lao; Lu; Nyaw; Phuan; Phutai; Saek; Samtao; So; Tai Doi; Tai Gapong; Tai He; Tai Khang; Tai Laan; Tai Loi; Tai Mao; Tai Pao; Tai Wang; Thai, Central; Thai, Northern; Thavung; Vietnamese; Yoy

UNITED STATES (26): Burmese; Hakka; Han Chinese, Cantonese; Han Chinese, Mandarin; Han Chinese, Min Nan; Han Chinese, Wu; Han Chinese, Xiang; Isan; Japanese; Kalmyk-Oirat; Khmer; Khuen; Korean; Kucong; Lao; Lu; Mongol; Phutai; Shan; Sherpa; Sinhalese; Thai, Central; Thai, Northern; Thai, Southern; Tibetan, Central; Vietnamese

BHUTAN (24): Brokpa; Brokpa, Brokkat; Bumthang; Chali; Dakpa; Drukpa; Dzala; Gongduk; Gurung, Eastern; Gurung, Western; Khampa, Eastern; Kheng;

Kurtop; Lap; Lepcha; Matpa; Newar; Nupbi; Nyenpa; Ole; Sherpa; Tamang, Eastern; Tibetan, Central; Tsangla

UNITED KINGDOM (18): Burmese; Hakka; Han Chinese, Cantonese; Han Chinese, Mandarin; Han Chinese, Min Nan; Han Chinese, Wu; Han Chinese, Xiang; Isan; Japanese; Khmer; Korean; Lao; Sinhalese; Thai, Central; Thai, Northern; Thai, Southern; Tibetan, Central; Vietnamese

AUSTRALIA (16): Hakka; Han Chinese, Cantonese; Han Chinese, Mandarin; Han Chinese, Wu; Han Chinese, Xiang; Isan; Japanese; Khmer; Korean; Lao; Sinhalese; Thai, Central; Thai, Northern; Thai, Southern; Tibetan, Central; Vietnamese

MALAYSIA (14): Burmese; Hakka; Han Chinese, Cantonese; Han Chinese, Hainanese; Han Chinese, Mandarin; Han Chinese, Min Bei; Han Chinese, Min Dong; Han Chinese, Min Nan; Han Chinese, Puxian; Isan; Sinhalese; Tak Bai Thai; Thai, Central; Thai, Southern

SINGAPORE (14): Hakka; Han Chinese, Cantonese; Han Chinese, Hainanese; Han Chinese, Mandarin; Han Chinese, Min Bei; Han Chinese, Min Dong; Han Chinese, Min Nan; Han Chinese, Puxian; Isan; Japanese; Korean; Sinhalese; Thai, Central; Thai, Northern

CANADA (13): Hakka; Han Chinese, Cantonese; Han Chinese, Mandarin; Han Chinese, Wu; Han Chinese, Xiang; Isan; Japanese; Khmer; Korean; Lao; Sinhalese; Thai, Central; Vietnamese

VIETNAM (12): Han Chinese, Cantonese; Han Chinese, Mandarin; Khmer; Kucong; Lao; Lu; Phutai; So; Tai Khang; Tai Mao; Vietnamese; Yoy

CAMBODIA (8): Burmese; Chong; Han Chinese, Mandarin; Khmer; Kui; Lao; Thai, Central; Vietnamese

GERMANY (8): Burmese; Hakka; Han Chinese, Wu; Japanese; Kalmyk-Oirat; Korean; Thai, Central; Vietnamese

BRUNEI (8): Hakka; Han Chinese, Cantonese; Han Chinese, Mandarin; Han Chinese, Min Bei; Han Chinese, Min Dong; Han Chinese, Min Nan; Korean; Thai, Central

NEW ZEALAND (8): Hakka; Han Chinese, Cantonese; Han Chinese, Wu; Japanese; Korean; Sinhalese; Thai, Central; Tibetan, Central

FRANCE (8): Hakka; Han Chinese, Mandarin; Han Chinese, Wu; Khmer; Lao; Thai, Central; Tibetan, Central; Vietnamese

MONGOLIA (7): Buriat, Mongolia; Dariganga; Japanese; Kalmyk-Oirat; Korean; Mongol; Tuva

RUSSIA (7): Buriat, Russia; Kalmyk-Oirat; Korean; Manchu; Mongol; Torgut; Tuva

TAIWAN (7): Hakka; Han Chinese, Mandarin; Han Chinese, Min Nan; Japanese; Kalmyk-Oirat; Mongol; Thai, Central

BANGLADESH (7): Burmese; Chak; Chakma; Gurung, Eastern; Mru; Newar; Rakhine

INDONESIA (6): Hakka; Han Chinese, Cantonese; Han Chinese, Mandarin; Han Chinese, Min Bei; Han Chinese, Min Dong; Han Chinese, Min Nan

PHILIPPINES (5): Hakka; Han Chinese, Cantonese; Han Chinese, Mandarin; Han Chinese, Min Nan; Japanese

PANAMA (4): Hakka; Han Chinese, Cantonese; Han Chinese, Mandarin; Japanese

NETHERLANDS (4): Hakka; Han Chinese, Cantonese; Han Chinese, Mandarin; Vietnamese

BRAZIL (4): Hakka; Han Chinese, Mandarin; Japanese; Korean

JAPAN (4): Han Chinese, Mandarin; Japanese; Korean; Thai, Central

ARGENTINA (4): Han Chinese, Mandarin; Japanese; Korean; Lao

NORTH KOREA (3): Han Chinese, Mandarin; Korean; Manchu

SRI LANKA (3): Burmese; Hakka; Sinhalese

MAURITIUS (3): Hakka; Han Chinese, Cantonese; Han Chinese, Mandarin

SOUTH AFRICA (3): Hakka; Han Chinese, Cantonese; Han Chinese, Mandarin

SOUTH KOREA (3): Han Chinese, Mandarin; Korean; Sherpa

PARAGUAY (3): Han Chinese, Mandarin; Japanese; Korean

APP 3: DISTRIBUTION BY COUNTRY

BELIZE (3): Han Chinese, Mandarin; Japanese; Korean

NORWAY (3): Han Chinese, Mandarin; Tibetan, Central; Vietnamese

GUAM (3): Han Chinese, Mandarin; Japanese; Korean

KYRGYZSTAN (3): Kalmyk-Oirat; Korean; Mongol

FRENCH POLYNESIA (2): Hakka; Han Chinese, Mandarin

FRENCH GUIANA (2): Hakka; Han Chinese, Mandarin

JAMAICA (2): Hakka; Han Chinese, Mandarin

TRINIDAD & TOBAGO (2): Hakka; Han Chinese, Mandarin

COSTA RICA (2): Han Chinese, Cantonese; Han Chinese, Mandarin

NAURU (2): Han Chinese, Cantonese; Han Chinese, Mandarin

HONDURAS (2): Han Chinese, Cantonese; Han Chinese, Mandarin

PERU (2): Han Chinese, Mandarin; Japanese

ITALY (2): Han Chinese, Mandarin; Han Chinese, Wu

MEXICO (2): Han Chinese, Mandarin; Japanese

BOLIVIA (2): Han Chinese, Mandarin; Japanese

DOMINICAN REPUBLIC (2): Han Chinese, Mandarin; Japanese

MICRONESIA (2): Han Chinese, Mandarin; Japanese

AMERICAN SAMOA (2): Japanese; Korean

NORTHERN MARIANA ISLANDS (2): Japanese; Korean

UZBEKISTAN (2): Kalmyk-Oirat; Korean

UNITED ARAB EMIRATES (2): Sinhalese; Thai, Central

SWITZERLAND (2): Tibetan, Central; Tibetan, Shangri-La

SURINAME (1): Hakka

KENYA (1): Hakka

MADAGASCAR (1): Han Chinese, Mandarin

SPAIN (1): Han Chinese, Mandarin

BELGIUM (1): Han Chinese, Mandarin

CUBA (1): Han Chinese, Mandarin

GUATEMALA (1): Han Chinese, Mandarin

TANZANIA (1): Han Chinese, Mandarin

ECUADOR (1): Han Chinese, Mandarin

NICARAGUA (1): Han Chinese, Mandarin

COLOMBIA (1): Han Chinese, Mandarin

FIJI (1): Han Chinese, Mandarin

SWEDEN (1): Han Chinese, Mandarin

GUYANA (1): Han Chinese, Mandarin

EAST TIMOR (1): Han Chinese, Mandarin

CZECH REPUBLIC (1): Han Chinese, Mandarin

SOLOMON ISLANDS (1): Han Chinese, Mandarin

AUSTRIA (1): Han Chinese, Mandarin

CHILE (1): Han Chinese, Mandarin

EL SALVADOR (1): Han Chinese, Mandarin

PUERTO RICO (1): Han Chinese, Mandarin

SEYCHELLES (1): Han Chinese, Mandarin

TONGA (1): Han Chinese, Mandarin

DOMINICA (1): Han Chinese, Mandarin

PALAU (1): Japanese

UKRAINE (1): Kalmyk-Oirat

KAZAKHSTAN (1): Korean

BAHRAIN (1): Korean

MAURITANIA (1): Korean

MALDIVES (1): Sinhalese

MIDWAY ISLANDS (1): Sinhalese

SAUDI ARABIA (1): Sinhalese

ISRAEL (1): Han Chinese, Mandarin

FINLAND (1): Thai, Central

NEW CALEDONIA (1): Vietnamese

PAKISTAN (1): Dokhpa

Bibliography

Abercrombie, Thomas J, 'Ladakh: The Last Shangri-La'. *National Geographic* (March 1978) 332–59.

Albrecht, Gerd, 'Recent Mani Settlements in Satun Province, Southern Thailand'. *Journal of the Siam Society* 86, Part 1 and 2 (1998).

Alhuwaila, H P S, *Hermit Kingdom: Ladakh*. New Delhi: Vikas Publishing House, 1980.

Allen, B C, *Assam District Gazetteer* 3 (1905).

Allen, Charles, *A Mountain in Tibet*. London: Futura, 1982.

Allen, Douglas, 'Tibet: The Continuing Story'. *China and the Church Today* (February 1986).

Alley, Rewi, *Folk Poems from China's Minorities*. Beijing: New World Press, 1982.

Amir Hassan, *Meet the Tribes of Uttar Pradesh*. Guragaon: Academic Press, 1982.

Amity News Service, 'Putian Church: Different Traditions, New Developments' (June 1997).

Amundsen, Edward, *In the Land of the Lamas: The Story of Trashilhamo, a Tibetan Lassie*. London: Marshall Brothers, 1910.

An Chunyang and Liu Bohua eds., *Where the Dai People Live*. Beijing: Foreign Languages Press, 1985.

Anderson, Edward F, *Plants and People of the Golden Triangle: Ethnobotany of the Hill Tribes of Northern Thailand*. Portland: Timber Press, 1993.

Anderson, John P, 'A Journey along a Part of the Siam-Burma Frontier'. *Journal of the Siam Society* 28.2 (1924).

—, 'Some Notes about the Karens in Siam'. *Journal of the Siam Society* 17.2 (1923).

Anderson, K E, 'Elements of Pwo Karen Buddhism'. In S Egerod and P Sorenson eds., *Lampang Report* (Copenhagen: Scandinavian Institute of Asia Studies, 1976).

Andvick, Erik, 'Tshangla Verb Inflections'. *Linguistics of the Tibeto-Burman Area* 16.1 (1993) 75–136.

Appleton, George, *The Christian Approach to the Buddhist*. London: Edinburgh House Press, 1958.

Aris, Michael, *Bhutan: The Early History of a Himalayan Kingdom*. Warminster: Aris and Phillips, 1979.

Armington, Stan, *Bhutan*. Hawthorn,

Australia: Lonely Planet Publications, 1998.

Asia Center for World Missions, *AC News and Views* 17 (15–31 July 2002).

—, 'The Sangla of Bhutan'. *AC News and Views* 20 (October 2002).

Asia Harvest, 'Revival in Heilongjiang, Part 1'. *Newsletter* 70 (April 2003).

—, 'Revival in Heilongjiang, Part 2'. *Newsletter* 71 (July 2003).

Asian Minorities Outreach [now Asia Harvest]. *Faces of the Unreached in Laos: Southeast Asia's Forgotten Nation*. Chiang Mai, Thailand: AMO Publishing, 1999.

—, *The 50 Most Unreached People Groups of China and Tibet*. Chiang Mai, Thailand: AMO Publishing, 1996.

—, *The Peoples of Vietnam*. Chiang Mai, Thailand: AMO Publishing, 1998.

—, 'The Amdo Tibetans'. *Newsletter* 40 (July 1996).

—, 'The Black Thai'. *Newsletter* 36 (December 1995).

—, 'The Chrame'. *Newsletter* 51 (December 1998).

—, 'The Khmu'. *Newsletter* 47 (November 1997).

—, 'The Ladakhis'. *Newsletter* 55 (December 1999).

—, 'The Loba'. *Newsletter* 49 (June 1998).

—, 'The Palaung'. *Newsletter* 38 (March 1996).

—, 'The Pumi'. *Newsletter* 31 (February 1995).

—, 'The Qiang'. *Newsletter* 27 (June 1994).

—, 'The Tibetans'. *Newsletter* 30 (December 1994).

Asia Prayer Focus. Newsletter of Mission Outreach (New Zealand, June 2000).

Asian Report. Magazine of Asian Outreach International. 24.3, Report 195 (May–June 1991).

—, 25.3, Report 195 (May–June 1992) 10–11.

Asian Studies Institute, 'The Dai People of Southeast Asia'. (unpublished report, 1996).

Asia Watch, *A Modern Form of Slavery: Trafficking of Burmese Women and Girls into Brothels in Thailand*. New York, 1993.

Assam Government, *Tribes of Assam Plains: A Profile*. Gauhati: Directorate of Welfare, 1980.

Aston, William George, 'A Comparative

Study of the Japanese and Korean Languages'. *Journal of the Royal Asiatic Society* 6.3 (1879).

Atkinson, Edwin Felix Thomas, *The Himalayan Districts of the North-Western Provinces of India*. 3 vols. Allahabad: The North-Western Provinces and Oudh Government Press, 1882, 1884, 1886.

Aung, M H, *Folk Elements in Burmese Buddhism*. Oxford, 1962.

—, *A History of Burma*. New York: Columbia University Press, 1967.

Aung Thwin, M, *Pagan: The Origins of Modern Burma*. Honolulu: University of Hawaii Press, 1985.

Australian Academy of the Humanities and the Chinese Academy of Social Sciences, *Language Atlas of China*. Hong Kong: Longman Group, 1987.

Avedon, John, *In Exile from the Land of Snows*. New York: Alfred A Knopf, 1984.

Avery, John, 'On the Language of the Lepchas'. *Journal of the American Society: Proceedings at New York, October 28th and 29th, 1885* 13 (1889).

Awasty, Indira, *Between Sikkim and Bhutan*. Delhi: B R Publishing, 1978.

Aymonier, Étienne, *Khmer Heritage in Thailand, with Special Emphasis on Temples, Inscriptions and Etymology*. Bangkok: White Lotus Press, 1901, repr. 1999.

—, *Khmer Heritage in the Old Siamese Provinces of Cambodia*. Bangkok: White Lotus Press, 1901, repr. 1999.

Backus, Mary ed., *Siam and Laos as Seen by Our American Missionaries*. Philadelphia: Presbyterian Board, Wescott and Thomson, 1884.

Baddeley, John F, *Russia, Mongolia, China*. New York: 1919.

Bahadpur, K P ed., *Castes, Tribes and Cultures of India: Assam*. Delhi: Ess Ess Publications, 1977.

Bailey, Thomas Grahame, *The Languages of the Northern Himalayas, being Studies of Twenty-Six Himalayan Dialects*. Asiatic Society Monographs 12, London: The Royal Asiatic Society, 1908.

—, 'Kanauri Vocabulary in Two Parts: English-Kanauri and Kanauri-English'. *Journal of the Royal Asiatic Society* (1910).

—, 'Kanauri Vocabulary in Two Parts: English-Kanauri and Kanauri-

English'. *Journal of the Royal Asiatic Society* (1911).

—, 'Kanauri Vocabulary in Two Parts'. *Journal of the Royal Asiatic Society* 13 (1910).

—, *Linguistic Studies from the Himalayas, Being Studies in the Grammar of Fifteen Himalayan Dialects.* London: Royal Asiatic Society, 1915.

Bai Yu, 'Life in Baima: Near the Yellow River Source'. *China Tourism* 138 (December 1991).

Bajpai, Shiva Chandra, *Kinnaur: A Restricted Land in the Himalaya.* New Delhi: Indus Publishing Company, 1991.

Bajracharya, Purna Harsha, 'Newar Marriage Customs and Festivals'. *Southwestern Journal of Anthropology* 14.4 (1959).

Bandyopadhyay, Swapon Kumar, 'A Tangsa Wordlist'. *Linguistics of the Tibeto-Burman Area* 12.2 (1989) 79–91.

Baradoloi, Muktinath, *Land of the Hornbill and Myna.* Shillong: North-East Frontier Agency Research Department, 1964.

Bardoloi, B N et al., *Tribes of Assam.* Guwahati: Tribal Research Institute, 1987.

Bare, Garland, 'The T'in and Kha Phai'. *A Background Study for a Conference of American Bible Society Personnel and American Church of Christ Missionaries.* Pua, Nan Province, Thailand, 1961.

Barkataki, S, *Tribes of Assam.* New Delhi: National Book Trust, 1969.

Barnouw, Victor, 'Eastern Nepalese Marriage Customs and Kinship Organisation'. *Southwest Journal of Anthropology* 11 (1955).

Barth, Fredrik, *Ethnic Groups and Boundaries.* Boston: Little, Brown and Co., 1969.

Barrett, David B ed., *World Christian Encyclopedia.* New York: Oxford University Press, 1982.

—, and George T Kurian and Todd M Johnson eds., *World Christian Encyclopedia, Second Edition: A Comparative Survey of Churches and Religions in the Modern World, Volume 1: The World by Countries: Religionists, Churches, Ministries.* New York: Oxford University Press, 2001.

—, *World Christian Encyclopedia, Second Edition: A Comparative Survey of Churches and Religions in the Modern*

World, Volume 2: The World by Segments: Peoples, Languages, Cities, Topics. New York: Oxford University Press, 2001.

Barrett, David B and Todd M Johnson, *World Christian Trends AD 30—AD 2200: Interpreting the Annual Christian Megacensus.* Pasadena, CA: William Carey Library, 2001.

—, 'Annual Statistical Table on Global Mission: 1999'. *International Bulletin of Missionary Research* 23.1 (1999).

Barua, B K, *A Cultural History of Assam.* Guwahati: Bina Library, 2003.

Barua, S N and Surenda Nath, *Tribes of the Indo-Burman Border, a Sociological History of the Inhabitants of the Paktai Range.* 1991.

Baruah, Tapan Kumar M, *The Singhpos and their Religion.* Shillong: Director of Information and Public Relations of Arunachal Pradesh, 1977.

Bassenne, Marthe, *In Laos and Siam.* Bangkok: White Lotus Press, 1912, repr. 1994.

Basu, P C, 'The Social and Religious Ceremonies of the Chakma'. *Journal and Proceedings of the Asiatic Society of Bengal* 27.2 (1931) 213–23.

Baudesson, Henry, *Indochina and Its Primitive People.* London: Hutchinson and Co., *c.*1930.

Bauer, Christian, *Mon Language and Literature in Thailand.* London: University of London, 1981.

—, 'Language and Ethnicity: The Mon in Burma and Thailand'. In Gehan Wijeyewardene ed., *Ethnic Groups across National Boundaries in Mainland Southeast Asia* (Singapore: Australian National University, Institute of Southeast Asian Studies, 1990).

Baumer, Christoph. 'Archaic Shaman Dance of Tongren'. *China Tourism* 24.3 (October 2000) 54–59.

Bawden, Charles R, *The Modern History of Mongolia.* London: Weidenfeld and Nicholson, 1968.

—, *Shamans, Lamas and Evangelicals.* London: Routledge and Kegan Paul, 1985.

Beall, Cynthia and Melvyn Goldstein, 'The Remote World of Tibet's Nomads'. *National Geographic* (June 1989) 752–81.

Beauvoir Stocks, C de, 'Folk-lore and Customs of the Lap-chas of Sikhim'. *Journal of the Asiatic Society of Bengal*

21 (1927).

Beaver, R Pierce et al., *Eerdmans' Handbook to the World's Religions.* Grand Rapids: Eerdmans, 1982.

Bechert, Heinz and Richard Gombrich, *The World of Buddhism.* London: Thames and Hudson, 1984.

Bedi, Rajesh and Ramesh Bedi, *The Trans Himalayan Kingdom.* New Delhi: Roli Books International, 1981.

Bekaert, Jacques, *Cambodian Diary 1: Tales of a Divided Nation, 1983–1986.* Bangkok: White Lotus Press, 1997.

—, *Cambodian Diary 2: A Long Road to Peace, 1987–1993.* Bangkok: White Lotus Press, 1998.

Bell, Sir Charles Alfred, *The People of Tibet.* Oxford: Clarendon Press, 1928.

—, *Tibet, Past and Present.* Oxford: Clarendon Press, 1924.

—, *The Religion of Tibet.* Oxford: Clarendon Press, 1931; Delhi: Motilal Banarsidass, 1992.

Belt, Don, 'The World's Great Lake'. *National Geographic* (June 1992) 2–40.

Benedict, Paul K, *Kinship in Southeastern Asia.* Harvard University, Cambridge, PhD thesis, 1941.

—, *Austro-Thai Language and Culture, with a Glossary of Roots.* New Haven: Human Relations Area Files Press, 1975.

—, 'Languages and Literatures of Indochina'. *Far Eastern Quarterly* 6.4 (1947).

Bethany World Prayer Center, 'Central Bhotia of Bhutan'. Prayer Profiles 1997.

—, 'Eastern Bhotia'.

—, 'The Black Tai'.

—, 'The Arakanese of India'.

—, 'The Athpare Rai of Nepal'.

—, 'The Bantawa Rai of Nepal'.

—, 'The Bhutanese of Bhutan'.

—, 'The Burmese'.

—, 'The Burmese of Bangladesh'.

—, 'The Burmese of India'.

—, 'The Burmese of Malaysia'.

—, 'The Burmese of Thailand'.

—, 'The Burmese Shan'.

—, 'The Cambodian of Laos'.

—, 'The Central Khmer of Thailand'.

—, 'The Central Khmer of Vietnam'.

—, 'The Central Tai of Thailand'.

—, 'The Chamlinge Rai of Nepal'.

—, 'The Chiang of China'.

—, 'The Dakpa of Bhutan'.

—, 'The Danuwar Rai of Nepal'.

—, 'The Dariganga of Mongolia'.

—, 'The Diaspora Han Chinese'.

—, 'The Durbet of Mongolia'.

—, 'The Eastern Gurung of Nepal'.

—, 'The Eastern Magar of Nepal'.

—, 'The Galle Gurung of Nepal'.

—, 'The Gurung of Bhutan'.

—, 'The Hakka of China'.

—, 'The Helambu Sherpa of Nepal'.

—, 'The Hill Tribes of Myanmar'.

—, 'The Japanese of Japan'.

—, 'The Japanese of Thailand'.

—, 'The Kalinge Rai of Nepal'.

—, 'The Kalmyk of Russia'.

—, 'The Kalmyk-Oirat'.

—, 'The Khalka Mongol of Mongolia'.

—, 'The Kham Magar of Nepal'.

—, 'The Khamti Shan of Myanmar'.

—, 'The Kui of Thailand'.

—, 'The Kulunge Rai of Nepal'.

—, 'The Lalung of India'.

—, 'The Lao of Laos'.

—, 'The Lao of Vietnam'.

—, 'The Lepcha of Bhutan'.

—, 'The Lhoba of India'.

—, 'The Limbu of India'.

—, 'The Limbu of Nepal'.

—, 'The Loba of Nepal'.

—, 'The Lu of Laos'.

—, 'The Lu of Myanmar'.

—, 'The Lu of Thailand'.

—, 'The Maghi of Bangladesh'.

—, 'The Manchu of China'.

—, 'The Men-pa'.

—, 'The Mru of South Asia'.

—, 'The Mugali of Nepal'.

—, 'The Nepalese of Nepal'.

—, 'The Newar of Nepal'.

—, 'The Northeastern Tai of Thailand'.

—, 'The Northern Khmer of Thailand'.

—, 'The Northern Mongolian of Mongolia'.

—, 'The Palaung of Myanmar: A Cluster of 5 Palaung Groups'.

—, 'The Phu Tai of Laos'.

—, 'The Ryukyuan of Japan'.

—, 'The Saam Rai of Nepal'.

—, 'The Saek of Laos'.

—, 'The Sampange Rai of Nepal'.

—, 'The Sangla of Bhutan'.

—, 'The Shan of Southeast Asia'.

—, 'The Sherpa of India'.

—, 'The Sherpa of Nepal'.

—, 'The Shin of India'.

—, 'The Sikkimese Bhotia of India'.

—, 'The Sinhalese of Sri Lanka'.

—, 'The Southern Tai of Thailand'.

—, 'The Tai of Malaysia'.

—, 'The Talaing of Thailand'.

—, 'The Tamachhange Rai of Nepal'.

—, 'The Tangchangya of Bangladesh'.

—, 'The Thami of Nepal'.

—, 'The Thulunge Rai of Nepal'.

—, 'The Tibetans of Nepal'.

—, 'The Tribes of Northeast Thailand'.

—, 'The Tsun-Lao of Vietnam'.

—, 'The Tuvinian of Mongolia'

—, 'The Tuvinian of Russia'.

—, 'The Western Gurung of Nepal'.

—, 'The Western Lawa of China'.

—, 'The Western Magar of Nepal'.

—, 'The White Tai of Vietnam'.

—, 'The Yakha of Nepal'.

— 'Tibetans in India'.

Berval, Rene de, *Kingdom of Laos: The Land of the Million Elephants and the White Parasol*. Saigon: France-Asie, 1959.

Beyer, Stephan V, *The Classical Tibetan Language*. Albany: State University of New York Press, 1992.

Bharadwaji, L, *A History of Burma*. Rangoon, 1951.

Bhardwaj, A N, *The Problems of Scheduled Castes and Scheduled Tribes in India*. New Delhi: Light and Life Publications, 1979.

Bhargava, Bhawani Shanker, *The Criminal Tribes: A Socio-Economic Study of the Principal Criminal Tribes and Castes in Northern India*. Lucknow: Universal Publications, 1946.

Bhasin, Veena, *Ecology, Culture and Change: Tribals of Sikkim Himalayas*. New Delhi: Inter-India Publications, 1989.

Bhowmick, K L et al., *Tribal India: A Profile in Indian Ethnology*. Calcutta: World Press, 1971.

Bickel, Balthasar, 'Introduction: Person and Evidence in Himalayan

Languages'. *Linguistics of the Tibeto-Burman Area* 23.2 (2000).

Bigg-Wither, F, *A Guide to the Study of Shan*. Rangoon: American Baptist Mission Press, 1911.

Bigandet, Paul A, *An Outline of the History of the Catholic Burmese Mission from the Year 1720 to 1887*. Rangoon: Hanthawaddy Press, 1887.

Birender Singh, R K, 'Special Tables for Scheduled Castes and Scheduled Tribes'. In *Census of India, 1981* (New Delhi: Controller of Publications, 1988).

Bisch, J, *Why Buddha Smiles*. London: Collins, 1964.

Bishop, Barry C, 'Karnali, Roadless World of Western Nepal'. *National Geographic* (November 1971) 656–89.

Bisht, B S, *Tribes of India Nepal Tibet Borderland: A Study of Cultural Transformation*. New Delhi: Gyan Publishing House, 1994.

Bista, Dor Bahadur, *The People of Nepal*. Kathmandu: Ratna Pustak Bhandar, 1972.

Blanchard, Wendell et al., *Thailand: Its People, Its Society, Its Culture*. New Haven: Human Relations Area Files Press, 1957.

Blanford, Carl E, *Chinese Churches in Thailand*. Bangkok: Suriyaban, 1975.

Block, Karen L, 'Discourse Grammar of First Person Narrative in Plang'. Arlington: University of Texas, 1994.

—, 'What Makes a Story in Plang?' *Mon-Khmer Studies* 26 (1996).

Blofeld, J, *People of the Sun: Encounters in Siam*. London: Hutchison, 1960.

Board of Foreign Missions, *Siam Mission*. Centennial Series, New York: The Board of Foreign Missions of the Presbyterian Church in the USA, 1937.

Bodman, Nicholas C, 'On the Place of Lepcha in Sino-Tibetan: A Lexical Comparison'. *Linguistics of the Tibeto-Burman Area* 11.1 (1988) 1–26.

Bolortuya, J, 'Eastern Aimag Offers Visual Paradise for Travelers'. *Virtual Mongolia Online Magazine*.

Bondfield, G H, 'Mongolia, a Neglected Mission Field'. In Milton T Stauffer ed., *The Christian Occupation of China* (Shanghai: China Consultation Committee, 1922).

Boon Chuey Srisavasdi, *The Hill Tribes of Siam*. Bangkok: Khun Aroon, 1963.

Booz, Patrick R, *Yunnan: Southwest China's Little-Known Land of Eternal Spring*. Lincolnwood, IL: Passport Books, 1987.

Bose, J K, *Glimpses of Tribal Life in North East India*. Calcutta: Institute of Social Research and Applied Anthropology, 1980.

Bose, N K, *Tribal Life in India*. New Delhi: National Book Trust, 1971.

—, *Some Indian Tribes*. New Delhi: National Book Trust, 1973.

Bose, S C, *Land and the People of the Himalayas*. Calcutta: Indian Publications, 1968.

Boutsavat, V and G Chapelier, 'Lao Popular Buddhism and Community Development'. *Journal of the Siam Society* 69.2 (1973).

Bowermaster, Jon, 'Rapid Descent: First Run Down the Shuilo River'. *National Geographic* (November 1996) 116–29.

Bowles, Gordin T, *The People of Asia*. New York: Charles Scribner, 1977.

Bowring, Sir John, *The Kingdom and People of Siam*. Kuala Lumpur: Oxford University Press, 1857, repr. 1977.

Brackenbury, Wade, *Yak Butter and Black Tea: A Journey into Forbidden China*. Chapel Hill: Algonquin Books, 1997.

Bradley, David, 'East and South-East Asia'. In Donald C Laycock and Werner Winter eds., *A World of Language: Papers Presented to Professor S A Wurm on his 65th Birthday* (Canberra: The Australian National University, 1987).

Bridge. 'Along the Fujian Coast'. (January–February 1986).

—, 'Difficulties in Hunan Province'. 10 (March–April 1985).

—, 'Ethnic Groups in Yunnan'. (September–October 1990).

—, 'The Church on Hainan Island: Past and Present'. 27 (January–February 1988).

Broomhall, Marshall. *The Bible in China*. London: CIM, 1934.

Brother Yun with Paul Hattaway, *The Heavenly Man: The Remarkable True Story of Chinese Christian Brother Yun*. London: Monarch Books, 2001.

Brown, Arthur Judson, 'A Modern Apostle of Siam: A Sketch of the Life and Work of the Rev Eugene P Dunlap, DD'. *Missionary Review of the World* (June 1918).

Brown, Marvin J, *From Ancient Thai to Modern Dialects and Other Writings on Historical Thai Linguistics*. Bangkok: White Lotus Press, 1960, repr. 1985.

Bruk, Solomon Il'ich, *Peoples of China, Mongolian People's Republic, and Korea*. Washington, DC: US Joint Publications Research Service 1710, 1959.

—, 'Distribution of National Minorities in the People's Republic of China'. In Stephen P Dunn and Ethel Dunn eds., *Introduction to Soviet Ethnography* 2 (Berkeley, CA: Highgate Road Social Science Research Station, 1958).

Bruksasri, Wanat and John McKinnon, eds., *The Highlanders of Thailand*. Kuala Lumpur: Oxford University Press, 1983.

Buchan, Alex, 'Buddhist Leaders Fail to Reckon with Persecution'. *Compass Direct* (24 April 1998).

—, 'Catholic Church Hangs on in Tibet'. *Compass Direct* (September 1998).

—, 'Sri Lanka and Christian Persecution'. *Compass Direct* (1 July 2000).

Buchanan, Claudius. *Christian Researches in Asia: With Notices of the Translation of the Scriptures into the Oriental Languages*. Boston: Armstrong and Cornhill, 1811.

Buckley, Michael and Robert Strauss, eds., *Tibet: A Travel Survival Kit*. Hawthorn, Australia: Lonely Planet Publications, 1986.

Budge, Ernest A W, *The Monks of Kublai Khan Emperor of China*. London: Religious Tract Society, 1928.

Bull, Geoffrey T, *When Iron Gates Yield*. London: Hodder and Stoughton, 1955.

Bunting, Bruce W, 'Bhutan: Kingdom in the Clouds'. *National Geographic* (May 1991) 79–101.

'Buriat-Mongolian Mission, Siberia'. *The Evangelical Magazine and Missionary Chronicle* 11 (July 1883) 328–31.

Burling, Robbins, *Hill Farms and Padi Fields: Life in Mainland Southeast Asia*. Englewood Cliffs, NJ: Prentice Hill, 1965.

Burton-Page, John. 'The Name "Nepal"'. *Bulletin of the School of Oriental and African Studies* 16.3 (1954).

Butler, John, *A Sketch of Assam with some Account of Hill Tribes, by an Officer*. London: Smith, Elder and Co., 1847.

Byles, M, *Journey into Burmese Silence*. London: Allen and Unwin, 1962.

Caldwell, Mark and Helen, *The Isaan People: Destined for Destruction or Redeemed for Rebirth?* (people group profile, November 1997).

Campbell, Archibald, 'Note on the Lepchas of Sikkim, with a Vocabulary of their Language'. *Journal of the Asiatic Society of Bengal* 4 (1840).

Caplan, L, *Land and Social Change in East Nepal*. London: Routledge and Kegan Paul, 1970.

Carey, Fred, 'A Trip to the Chinese Shan States'. *Geographical Journal* 14.4 (1899).

Carey, William, *Adventures in Tibet*. Chicago: Student Missionary Campaign Library, 1901.

Carlsen, William, *Tibet: In Search of a Miracle*. New York: Nyack College, 1985.

Carné, Louis, *Travels on the Mekong*. Bangkok: White Lotus Press, 1872, repr. 1995.

Carrier, Jim, 'Gatekeepers of the Himalaya: Nepali's Sherpa People Prosper amid Dizzying Change as Climbers and Trekkers Descend upon their Mountain Home'. *National Geographic* (December 1992) 70–89.

Census of India, 1961. Delhi: Manager of Publications, 1966.

Central Institute of Indian Languages, *Distribution of Languages in India in States and Union Territories*. Mysore, 1973.

Chaiwan, Saad, *The Christian Approach to Buddhists in Thailand*. Bangkok: Suriyaban Publishers, 1975.

Chakrabarti, Mukul and D Mukhopadhyay, *Indian Tribes*. Calcutta: Saraswat Library, 1971.

Chamberlain, James R, 'The Tai Dialects of Khammouan Province: Their Diversity and Origins'. *Sixteenth International Conference on Sino-Tibetan Language and Linguistics, 16–18 September*. Seattle, WA, 1983.

—, 'The Origin of the Sek: Implications for Tai and Vietnamese History'. *The Journal of the Siam Society* 86, Part 1 and 2 (1998).

Chandler, David P, *A History of Cambodia*. Boulder, CO: Westview Press, 1996.

Chang Jen-Kai [Zhang Ren-Gai], 'The Minority Races of South Szechuen'. *China Monthly Review* 122.4 (1952).

Chang Kun, 'A Comparative Study of the Southern Ch'iang Dialects'. *Monumenta Serica* 26 (1967).

Chantrasupawong, Narumol, *Classifiers in Khorat Thai Spoken in Ban Thap Prang, Tambol Krathok, Amphoe Chok Chai, Nakhon Ratchasima Province.* Chulalongkorn University, MA thesis, 1985.

Chao, Jonathon ed., *The China Mission Handbook: A Portrait of China and its Church.* Hong Kong: Chinese Church Research Centre, 1989.

Chao Tzang Yawnghwe, *The Shan of Burma: Memoirs of a Shan Exile.* Singapore: Australian National University Institute of Southeast Asian Studies, 1987.

Charbonnier, Jean, *Guide to the Catholic Church in China 1989.* Singapore: China Catholic Communication, 1990.

Chatterjee, B B, *Bhotia of Indo-Tibetan Border of Uttarakhans.* Varansai: Institute of Gandhian Studies, 1975.

Chattopadhyay, Sudhakar, *Racial Affinities of North East Indian Tribes.* New Delhi: Munshiram Manoharlal, 1973.

Chattopadhyaya, Alaka, *Atisa and Tibet.* Delhi: Motilal Banarsidass, 1967.

Chattopadhyaya, Kamaladevi, *Tribalism in India.* New Delhi: Vikas Publishing House, 1978.

Chattopadhyaya, K P, 'An Essay on the History of Newar Culture'. *Journal of the Asiatic Society of Bengal* 19.10 (1923).

Chattopadhyaya, Tapan, *Lepchas and their Heritage.* Delhi: B R Publishing, 1990.

Chaudhuri, Mamata, *Tribes of Ancient India.* Calcutta: Indian Museum, 1977.

Chazée, Laurent, *Atlas des Ethnies et des Sous-Ethnies du Laos.* Vientiane: Laurent Chazée, 1995.

—, *The Peoples of Laos: Rural and Ethnic Diversities.* Bangkok: White Lotus Press, 1999.

Ch'en Chieh-hsien, 'The Decline of the Manchu Language in China During the Ch'ing Period (1644–1911)'. In *Altaica Collects: Berichte und Vorträge der XII. Permanent International Altaistic Conference (3.–8. Juni 1974 in Bonn/Bad Honneg)* (Wiesbaden: Otto Harrassowitz, 1976).

Ch'en, Kenneth K S, *Buddhism in China: A Historical Survey.* Princeton: Princeton University Press, 1964.

Chen Shuren, 'Muni Gully: Wonderland of Nature'. *China Tourism* 110 (n.d.).

Chen Yunguang and Zhang Heping, 'Flower Gathering Festival at Boyu'. *China Tourism* 115 (n.d.).

Cheng Te-k'un and Liang Ch'ao-t'ao [Zheng Dekun and Liang Zhaotao], 'An Introduction to the Southwestern Peoples of China'. *West China Union University Museum Guidebook* 7 (Chengdu, 1945).

Chiao Chien and Nicholas Tapp eds., *Ethnicity and Ethnic Groups in China.* Hong Kong: The Chinese University of Hong Kong, 1989.

Childers, R C, 'Notes on the Sinhalese Language: Proofs of the Sanskritic Origin of Sinhalese'. *Journal of the Royal Asiatic Society* 8 (1876).

China Pictorial Publications, *Minority Peoples in China.* Beijing: China Pictorial Publications, 1987.

Chinchest, Pornsri, *Lao Ngaew Tones in Citation Forms and in Connected Speech.* Chulalongkorn University, MA thesis, 1989.

Chinese Academy of Social Sciences (CASS), *Information China.* London: Pergamon Press, 1989.

Chinese Prayer Letter and Ministry Report (CPLMR) 119 (December 1991–February 1992).

Chit, K M, *Burmese Legends.* Bangkok: Tamarind Press, 1984.

Choedon, Yeshi and Norbu Dawa, *Tibet.* London: Tiger Books, 1997.

Chopra, P N, *Sikkim.* New Delhi: S Chand, 1979.

Chowdhury, J N, *Arunachal Pradesh: From Frontier Tracts to Union Territory.* New Delhi: Cosmo Publications, 1983.

Chun Shizeng ed., *Chinese Nationalities.* Beijing: China Nationality Photography and Art Press, 1989.

Chu Thai Son ed., *Vietnam: A Multicultural Mosaic.* Hanoi: Foreign Languages Publishing House, 1991.

Clark, Michael and Joe Cummings, *Myanmar (Burma).* Hawthorn, Australia: Lonely Planet Publications, 2000.

Clarke, Samuel, *Among the Tribes in South-West China.* London: Morgan and Scott, 1911.

Cochrane, Wilbur Willis, *The Shans.* Rangoon: Government Printing Press, 1915.

Coedès, George, *Les Langues de l'Indochine.* Paris: University of Paris, 1949.

Coehlo, V H, *Sikkim and Bhutan.* New Delhi: Indraprastha Press, 1967.

Cohen, Paul and Gehan Wijeyewardene eds., 'Spirit Cults and the Position of Women in Northern Thailand'. *Mankind* 3 (1984).

Colquhoun, Archibald Ross, *Across Chryse, Being the Narrative of a Journey of Exploration through the South China BorderLands from Canton to Mandalay.* 2 vols. London: Sampson Low, Marston, Searle and Rivington, 1883.

—, *Amongst the Shans.* London: Field and Tuer, 1885.

— 'On the Aboriginal and Other Tribes of Yunnan and the Shan Country'. *Anthropological Institute of Great Britain and Ireland* 13.1 (1884).

Collister, Peter, *Bhutan and the British.* London: Serindia Publications, 1987.

Cooper, Michael, *Rodrigues the Interpreter: An Early Jesuit in Japan and China.* New York: Weatherhill, 1994.

Cooper, Robert G, 'The Tribal Minorities of Northern Thailand: Problems and Prospects'. *Southeast Asian Affairs* IV (1979).

Condominas, Georges, *From Lawa to Mon, from Saa' to Thai: Historical and Anthropological Aspects of Southeast Asian Social Spaces.* Translated by S Anderson. Canberra, 1990.

Cormack, Don and Peter Lewis, *Killing Fields, Living Fields.* Grand Rapids: Kregel Publications, 2001.

Covell, Ralph, *Confucius, the Buddha, and Christ.* Maryknoll, NY: Orbis Books, 1986.

—, *The Liberating Gospel in China: The Christian Faith among China's Minority Peoples.* Grand Rapids: Baker Books, 1995.

Credner, Wilheim, *Siam: Das Land der Tai.* Stuttgart: J Engelhorns Nachfolger, 1935.

Crooke, W, *The Tribes and Castes of the North-Western India.* 4 vols. Calcutta: Superintendent Government Printing Press, 1896.

Crossman, Eileen, *Mountain Rain: A New Biography of James O Fraser.* Singapore: OMF, 1982.

Cummings, Joe ed., *Laos.* Singapore: Lonely Planet, 3rd edn, 1998.

Cunningham, Alexander, *Ladakh: Physical, Statistical and Historical, with Notice of the Surrounding Countries.* New Delhi: Sagar Publications, 1964.

Cupet, P, *Among the Tribes of Southern Vietnam and Laos*. Bangkok: White Lotus Press, 1891, repr. 1998.

Curtis, Lillian Johnson, *The Laos of North Siam, as Seen through the Eyes of a Missionary*. Bangkok: White Lotus Press, 1903, repr. 1998.

Cushing, Josiah N, *Grammar of the Shan Language*. Rangoon: American Baptist Mission Press, 1871.

—, *Elementary Handbook of the Shan Language*. Rangoon: American Baptist Mission Press, 1888.

—, *A Shan and English Dictionary*. Rangoon: American Baptist Mission Press, 1914.

d'Ollone, Henri Marie Gustave Vicomte, *In Forbidden China: The d'Ollone Mission 1906–09, China-Tibet-Mongolia*. London: T Fisher Unwin, 1912.

—, *Langues des Peuples non Chinois de la Chine* 6.27–28. Paris: E Leroux, 1912.

d'Orleans, Henri Philippe Marie Prince, 'From Yun-nan to British India'. *Geographical Journal* 7 (1896).

Daecha, Wilailuck, *A Comparative Study of the Phonology of Six Tai Dialects Spoken in Amphoe Tha Tako, Changwat Nakhon Sawan*. Chulalongkorn University, MA thesis, 1987.

Dai Qingxia et al., *Zangmianyu Shiwu Zhong*. Beijing: Yanshan Press, 1991, Chinese language.

Dalton, Edward Tuite, *Descriptive Ethnology of Bengal*. Calcutta: Government Printing Press, 1872.

Dang Nghiem Van, Chu Thai Son and Luu Hang, *The Ethnic Minorities in Vietnam*. Hanoi: The Gioi Publishers, 1993.

Das, A K and S K Banerjee, *The Lepchas of Darjeeling District*. Calcutta: Cultural Research Institute, 1962.

—, et al., *Handbook on Scheduled Castes and Scheduled Tribes of West Bengal*. Calcutta: Tribal Welfare Department, West Bengal, 1966.

—, 'Style and Symbolic Motifs in the Art of Arunachal'. In K K Ganguly and S S Biwas eds., *Rupanjali* (Calcutta: O C Ganguly Memorial Society, 1986).

—, *West Bengal Tribes through Photographs*. Calcutta: Cultural Research Institute, West Bengal, 1964.

Das, Bhuban Mohan, *Anthropometry of the Tribal Groups of Assam*. Miami: Field Research Project, 1970.

Das, Nava Kishor, *Ethnic Identity, Ethnicity and Social Stratification in North-East India*. New Delhi: Inter-India Publications, 1989.

Das, Sarat Chandra, *Journey to Lhasa and Central Tibet*. London: Murray, 1902.

Das, Shivatosh, *Life Style of Indian Tribes: Locational Practice*. 3 vols. Delhi: Gian Publishing House, 1986–89.

—, *The People of the Eastern Himalayas*. New Delhi: Sagar Publications, 1978.

Das Gupta, Kamalesh, *An Introduction to Central Monpa*. Shillong: Phililogical Section of the Research Department of the North-East Frontier Agency, 1968.

—, *A Phrase Book in Singhpo*. Shillong: Director of Information and Public Relations of Arunachal Pradesh, 1979.

—, *The Tangsa Language: A Synopsis*. Shillong: Directorate of Research of the Government of Arunachal Pradesh, 1980.

Datta, Ray B, *Tribal Identity and Tension in North-East India*. New Delhi: Omsons Publications, 1989.

Dauvillier, J, 'Témoignages Nouveaux sur le Christianisme Nestorien chez les Tibetans'. In *Histoire et Institutions des Eglises Orientales au Moyen Age* (London: Varioum Reprints 2, 1983).

Davies, Henry Rodolph, *Yun-nan: The Link between India and the Yangtze*. Cambridge: Cambridge University Press, 1909.

Davies, Richard, *Muang Metaphysics: A Study of Northern Thai Myth and Ritual*. Bangkok: Pandora, 1984.

DAWN Report 32 (November 1997).

Deb, Arabinda, *Bhutan and India: A Study in Frontier Relations (1772–1865)*. Calcutta: Firma KLM Ltd., 1976.

de Beauclair, Inez, *An Introduction to the Southwestern Peoples of China*. Chengdu: West China Union University, 1945.

—, *Tribal Cultures of Southwest China*. Taiwan: The Chinese Association for Folklore, 1974.

— 'Ethnic Groups'. In Hellmut Wilheim ed., *A General Handbook of China* (New Haven: HRAF Press Monograph 55, 1956).

De Fillipi, Fillipo, *An Account of Tibet: The Travels of Ippolito Desideri of Pistola, 1712 to 1727*. London: George Routledge and Sons, 1932.

Delaporte, Louis and Francis Garnier,

A Pictorial Journey along the Old Mekong: Cambodia, Laos, and Yunnan. Bangkok: White Lotus Press, 1866, repr. 1998.

Desideri, Ippolito, *An Account of Tibet: The Travels of Ippolito Desideri of Pistola, SJ 1712–1727*. London: George Routledge and Sons, 1932.

De Terra, Hellmut, 'On the World's Highest Plateaus'. *National Geographic* (March 1931) 331–32.

Deuri, R K, *The Sulungs*. Shillong: Research Department of the Government of Arunachal Pradesh, 1983.

Dhammananda, K Sri, 'Do You Know?' Key-note speech given at the opening ceremony of the 14th YBAM Bienniel Convention. (This article was viewed on a website that is no longer active.)

Dhar, Bibhas, 'The Monpas of Khategthang Area, alias, the Tsanglas: A Brief Ethnographic Account'. In S Karotemprel ed., *The Tribes of North-East India* (Calcutta: Firma KLM Ltd., 1984).

Dhida Saraya, Sri Dvaravati, *The Initial Phase of Siam's History*. Bangkok: Muang Boran, 1999.

Diemberger, Hildegard, 'Gangla Tshechu, Beyul Khenbalung'. In C Ramble and M Brauen eds., *International Seminar on the Anthropology of Tibet and the Himalaya* (Zurich: Ethnographic Museum of the University of Zurich, 1993).

Diffloth, Gerard, 'The Wa Languages'. *Linguistics of the Tibeto-Burman Area* 5.2 (1980).

—, *The Dvaravati Old Mon Language and Nyah Kur*. Bangkok: Chulalongkorn University, 1984.

Diller, Anthony, 'Tai Languages: Varieties and Subgroup Terms'. *The Yunnan Project Newsletter* 25 (Canberra: Faculty of Asian Studies, Australian National University, June 1994).

—, 'How Many Tones in Southern Thai?' in Nguyen Dang Lien ed., *South-East Asian Linguistic Studies*. Canberra: Pacific Linguistics 4, 1979.

Diran, Richard K, *The Vanishing Tribes of Burma*. London: Weidenfeld and Nicolson, 1997.

Djang, W B, 'The Decline and Possible Future of a Great Race: The Ch'iang People'. Manuscript, New Haven: Yale Divinity School, 1948.

Dodd, William Clifton, *The Tai Race: Elder*

Brother of the Chinese. Cedar Rapids: The Torch Press, 1923.

Doig, Desmond, 'Bhutan: Mountain Kingdom between Tibet and India'. *National Geographic* (September 1961) 384–415.

—, 'Sherpaland: My Shangri-La'. *National Geographic* (October 1966) 545–77.

Dommen, Arthur, *Laos: Keystone of Indochina*. Boulder, CO: Westview Press, 1985.

Dondrup, Rinchin, *A Handbook on Sherdukpen Language*. Itanagar: Directorate of Research on the Government of Arunachal Pradesh, 1990.

—, *Bugun Language Guide*. Itanagar: Directorate of Research of the Government of Arunachal Pradesh, 1990.

Dong Zhaofu, 'Jiaowai Luhen' [Recollections of a Trip to the Frontiers]. *Bianzheng Gonglun* (1930), Chinese language.

Doyle, Edward and Samuel Lipsman, *The Vietnam Experience: Setting the Stage*. Boston: Boston Publishing Co., 1981.

Dreyer, June Elizabeth Tuefel, *China's Forty Millions: Minority Nationalities and National Integration in the People's Republic of China*. Cambridge, MA: Harvard University Press, 1976.

Dube, S C ed., *Tribal Heritage of India (Ethnicity, Identity and Interaction)*. New Delhi: Vikas Publishing House, 1977.

Dube, S M, *Modernisation and Elites in Arunachal Pradesh*. New Delhi: Controller of Publications, 1977.

Dupuis, J, *A Journey to Yunnan and the Opening of the Red River to Trade*. Bangkok: White Lotus Press, repr. c.1998.

Duarah, D K, *The Monpas of Arunachal Pradesh*. Itanagar: Directorate of Research of the Government of Arunachal Pradesh, 1990.

Dutta Choudhury, S, *Arunachal Pradesh District Gazetteers: Lohit District*. Shillong: Director of Information and Public Relations, Government of Arunachal Pradesh, 1978.

—, 'The Singhpos'. *North-Eastern Affairs, India* 2.1 (1973) 94–96.

Dutta, Paul C, *The Tangsas of the Namchik and Tirap Valleys*. Shillong North-East Frontier Agency, 1959.

—, *The Singhpos*. Itanagar: Directorate of Research on the Government of Arunachal Pradesh, 1990.

Dutta, Shoshee Chunder, *Wild Tribes of India*. London: Gilbert and Revington, 1884.

Eakin, Paul A, *Buddhism and the Christian Approach to Buddhists in Thailand*. Bangkok: R Hongladaromp, 1956.

Eastern Express. Hong Kong (5 October 1995).

Eberhard, Wolfgram, *China's Minorities: Yesterday and Today*. Belmont: Wadsworth Publishers, 1982.

—, *The Local Cultures of South and East Asia*. Leiden: Brill, 1968.

Editing Group of Yunnan Province, *Investigation of the Society and History of the Bulang Minority*. 3 vols. Kunming: Yunnan People's Publishing House, 1986.

Edgar, J H, *High Altitudes: Missionary Problems in Kham or Eastern Tibet*. Chengdu: Canadian Mission Press, n.d.

—, 'The Ancient Yong and Possible Survivals in Szechwan'. *Journal of West China Research Society* 6 (1933).

—, 'The Horpa of the Upper Nya or Yalung'. *Journal of West China Border Research Society* (1932).

Edmonson, Jerold A ed., *Kadai: Discussions in Kadai and SE Asian Linguistics*. Arlington: University of Texas, 1990.

—, *Languages of the Vietnam-China Borderlands*. Arlington: University of Texas, 1996.

—, and David B Solnit, *Comparative Kadai: The Tai Branch*. Arlington: University of Texas, 1997.

Ehrlich, Richard S, 'Far from World's Eyes, Religious War Rages in Bangladesh'. *Washington Times* (26 May 1987).

Ekvall, Robert B, *The Lama Knows: A Tibetan Legend is Born*. New Delhi: Oxford and IBH Publishing, 1979.

Ekvall, Robert L, *Gateway to Tibet*. Harrisburg: Christian Publications, 1938.

—, *Religious Observances in Tibet*. Chicago: University of Chicago Press, 1964.

Elias, Ney, *Introductory Sketch of the History of the Shans of Upper Burma and West Yunnan*. Calcutta, 1876.

Elias, Norbert, *A History of the Moghuls of Central Asia*. Translated by E Dennison Ross. London: Curzon Press, 1895.

Elwin, Verrier, *India's North-East Frontier in the Nineteenth Century*. London:

Oxford University Press, 1959.

—, *A Philosophy for NEFA*. Itanagar: Directorate of Research, 1957.

—, *Myths of the North East Frontier of India*. Shillong: North-East Frontier Agency, 1958.

—, *A New Deal for Tribal India*. Delhi: Manager of Publications, 1963.

—, *The Tribal World of Verrier Elwin: An Autobiography*. Bombay: Oxford University Press, 1964.

—, and V Price Coverley, *The Hill People of North East India*. London: Oxford University Press, 1960.

Embree, John Fee and Lilia Ota Dotson, *Bibliography of the Peoples and Cultures of Mainland Southeast Asia*. New York: Russel and Russel, 1972.

—, and William Leroy Thomas, *Ethnic Groups of Northern Southeast Asia*. New Haven: Yale University, 1950.

Encyclopedic Dictionary of Chinese Linguistics (EDCL) [Zhongguo Yuyanxue Dacidian]. Nanjing: Jiangxi Educational Publishing House, 1991.

Enriquez, Colin Metcalf Dallas, *Races of Burma*. Delhi: Indian Government Manager of Publications, 1933.

—, *A Burmese Arcady*. London, 1923.

Enwall, Joakim ed., *Hmong Writing Systems in Vietnam: A Case Study of Vietnam's Minority Language Policy*. Stockholm: Center for Pacific Asia Studies at Stockholm University, 1995.

Ethnic Cultures Publishing House, *Vietnam: Image of the Community of 54 Ethnic Groups*. Vietnam News Agency, 1996.

Ethnos Asia, 'Prayer Focus: A Prayer Guide to Access-Restricted Nations in Asia'. 40 (July 2000).

—, 69 (December 2002).

Evans, Grant, *Lao Peasants under Socialism*. New Haven: Yale University Press, 1990.

—, *The Politics of Ritual and Remembrance: Laos since 1975*. Chiang Mai: Silkworm Books, 1998.

Evans-Pritchard, Sir Edward E, *Peoples of the Earth* 13. London: Tom Stacey, 1973.

Far Eastern and Russian Institute, *A Regional Handbook on the Inner Mongolia Autonomous Region*. New Haven: HRAF Press, 1956.

Fay-Cooper, Cole, *The Peoples of Malaysia*. New York: D Van Nostrand Company, 1945.

Fei Xiatong [Fei Hsiao Tung], 'China Minorities Nationalities'. *Far Eastern Economic Review* 13.3 (1952).

—, 'On the Question of Identification of Nationalities in China'. *Chinese Social Sciences* 1 (1980) 147–62.

—, 'Xin Zhongguo de Minzuxue Yanjiu yu Fazhan'. [Studies in and Development of Ethnography in New China]. In Lin Yuehua, *Minzuxue Yanjiu* [Studies in Ethnography] (Beijing: Zhongguo Shehui Kexue Chubanshe, 1985), Chinese language.

Fergusson, W N, *Adventure, Sport and Travel on the Tibetan Steppes*. London: Constable and Company, 1911.

—, 'The Tribes of North-Western Se-chuan'. *Geographical Journal* 32.6 (1910).

Ferlus, Michel, 'Langues et Peuples Viet-Muong'. *Mon-Khmer Studies* 16 (1996).

Ferrars, Max and Bertha, *Burma*. London: William Clowes and Sons, 1901.

Feurer, Hanny and Yang Fuquan, 'Greetings among Naxi and Kham Tibetans on Yunnan's High Plateau'. *Linguistics of the Tibeto-Burman Area* 22.1 (1999) 11–58.

Finlay, Hugh, Richard Everist and Tony Wheeler, *Nepal: A Lonely Planet Travel Survival Kit*. Hawthorn, Australia: Lonely Planet Publications, 1997.

Fisher, James F, 'A Vocabulary of the Kaike Language'. An unpublished report presented to the Institute of Nepalese Studies of Tribhuvan University, Kirtipur (March 1971).

—, *Trans-Himalayan Traders, Economy, Society and Culture in Northwest Nepal*. Berkeley, CA: University of California Press, 1986.

—, and Sir Edmund Hillary, *Sherpas: Reflections on Change in Himalayan Nepal*. Berkeley: University of California Press, 1990.

Foning, A R, *Lepcha: My Vanishing Tribe*. New Delhi: Sterling Publishers, 1987.

Forbes, Andrew ed., *The Muslims of Thailand*. 2 vols. Ranchi: The Catholic Press, 1998.

—, *Khon Muang: People and Principalities of North Thailand*. Bangkok: Teak House Books, 1997.

—, and David Henley, *The Haw: Traders of the Golden Triangle*. Bangkok: Teak House Books, 1997.

Forney, Matt, 'Total Recall'. *Far Eastern Economic Review* (29 May 1997).

Forrest, George, 'Journey on Upper Salwin: October–December 1905'. *Geographical Journal* 32 (1908).

—, 'The Land of the Crossbow'. *National Geographic* (February 1910).

Foster, B L, *Ethnicity and Economy: The Case of the Mons in Thailand*. University of Michigan, PhD thesis, 1972.

—, *The Social Organization of Four Thai and Mon Villages*. New Haven: Human Relations Area Files, 1977.

Foster, John, *Church of the T'ang Dynasty*. London: Society for the Propagation of Christian Knowledge, 1939.

Fouser, Beth, *The Lord of the Golden Tower—King Prasat Thong and the Building of Wat Chaiwatthanaram*. Bangkok: White Lotus Press, 1996.

Fraisse, André, 'Les tribus So de la province de Cammon'. *Bulletin de la Société des Etudes Indochinoises* 25 (Saigon 1950).

— 'Les tribus Sek et Kha de la province de Cammon'. *Bulletin de la Société des Etudes Indochinoises* 25 (Saigon 1950).

Francke, A H, *A History of Western Tibet: One of the Unknown Empires*. Delhi: Motilal Banarsidass Publishers, repr. 1998.

Freeman, Michael, *Hilltribes of Thailand*. Bangkok: Asia Books, 1989.

Friday Church News Notes, 'Bhutanese Christians Flee to India for Life'. (1 November 2002).

Frontier Missions Center for Himalayan Peoples, *Pray for the Peoples of Nepal: A 30 Day Prayer Guide for the Unreached Peoples of Nepal*. Cimmaron, CO: YWAM, n.d.

Fryer, F W R, *Tribes on the Frontier of Burma*. 1907.

Fuchs, Stephen, *The Aboriginal Tribes of India*. Madras: Macmillan Press, 1973.

Gaide, L, 'Notice Ethnographique sur les Principales Races Indigènes de la Chine Meridionale (Yun-nam en Particulier) et du Nord de l'Indo-Chine'. *Annales d'Hygiene et de Medicine Coloniales* 5 (1903).

Gainey, Jerry W and L Thongkum Theraphan, *Language Map of Thailand*. Bangkok: Central Institute of English, 1977.

Gan-Chadhari, Jagadis, *Tripura: The Land and its People*. Delhi: Leeladevi Publishers, 1980.

Ganguly, K K and S S Biwas eds., *Rupanjali*. Calcutta: O C Ganguly Memorial Society, 1986.

Garnier, Francis, *Travels in Cambodia and Part of Laos*. Bangkok: White Lotus Press, 1885, repr. 1996.

—, *Further Travels in Laos and Yunnan*. Bangkok: White Lotus Press, 1886, repr. 1996.

Garrett, W E, 'Mountain Top War in Remote Ladakh'. *National Geographic* (May 1960).

Gautam, M K, *Socio-Cultural Change in Tribal India*. Leiden: Natural Museum of Ethnology, 1963.

Gautam, Dr Rajesh and Asoke K Thapa-Magar, *Tribal Ethnography of Nepal*. 2 vols. Delhi: Book Faith India, 1994.

Geddes, William R, *The Hill Tribes of Thailand*. SEATO Record IV, 1965.

Ge Jialin, 'The Jiarong Tibetans Celebrate Their Harvest'. *China Tourism* 166 (May 1994).

Ge Lin, 'The Qiang People and Their Ancient Castles'. *China Tourism* 59 (n.d.).

Gervaise, Nicolas, *The Natural and Political History of the Kingdom of Siam*. Bangkok: White Lotus Press, 1688, repr. 1998.

Ghurye, G S, *The Scheduled Tribes*. Bombay: Popular Book Depot, 1959.

Gilmour, James, *Among the Mongols*. London: The Religious Tract Society, 1882.

Ginsburgs, George and Michael Mathos, *Communist China and Tibet: The First Dozen Years*. The Hague: Martinus Nijhoff, 1964.

Global Evangelization Movement, 'World's Peoples Listed by Country, Part 1'. Unpublished report, 1995.

Global Prayer Digest 8.7 (July 1989).

— 8.9 (September 1989).

— 9.11 (November 1990).

— 10.6 (June 1991).

— 12.9 (September 1993).

— 13.5 (May 1994).

— 14.4 (April 1995).

— 15.9 (September 1996).

Glover, Jessie R, *Conversational Gurung*. Canberra: Pacific Linguistics, 1979.

Glover, Warren William, *Sememic and Grammatical Structures in Gurung (Nepal)*. Kathmandu: Summer Institute of Linguistics, 1974.

—, and J K Landon, 'Gurung Dialects'. In

Ronald L Trail ed., *Papers in South-East Asian Linguistics 7* (Canberra: Pacific Linguistics, 1980).

—, 'Gurung Phonetic Summary'. In *Bodic Languages* (Kathmandu: Summer Institute of Linguistics 1, 1969).

—, and Jessie R Glover, *A Guide to Gurung Tone*. Kathmandu: Summer Institute of Linguistics, 1972.

—, Jessie R Glover and Deu Bahadur Gurung, *Gurung-Nepali-English Dictionary with English-Gurung and Nepali-Gurung Indicies*. Canberra: Pacific Linguistics, 1977.

Go Magazine, 'The Church in Bhutan'. Interserve, 2002.

Gogoi, Lila, *The Tai Khamtis of the North-East*. New Delhi: Omsons Publications, 1990.

Gogoi, Padmeswar, *The Tai and the Tai Kingdoms with a Fuller Treatment of the Tai-Ahom Kingdoms*. Gauhati: Department of Publication of Gauhati University, 1968.

—, *Tai-Ahom Religion and Customs*. Gauhati: Publication Board of Assam, 1976.

Goodden, Christian, *Three Pagodas: A Journey Down the Thai-Burmese Border*. Halesworth: Jungle Books, 1996.

—, *Around Lan-Na: A Guide to Thailand's Northern Border*. Halesworth: Jungle Books, 1999.

Goodman, Jim, 'Tibetan Christians in a Yunnan Village'. *China Tourism* 215 (June 1998).

Gorer, Geoffrey, *Himalayan Village: An Account of the Lepchas of Sikkim*. London: Michael Joseph, 1938.

—, *The Lepchas of Sikkim*. New Delhi: Cultural Publishing House, 1983.

Goulart, Peter, *The Forgotten Kingdom*. London: John Murray, 1957.

—, *The Princes of the Black Bone: Life in the Tibetan Borderland*. London, 1958.

Graham, David Crockett, *The Customs and Religions of the Ch'iang*. Washington, DC: Smithsonian Institute, 1958.

—, *Folk Religion in Southwest China*. Washington, DC: Smithsonian Institute, 1961.

—, *Songs and Stories of the Ch'uan Miao*. Washington, DC: Smithsonian Institute, 1954.

Graham, W A, *Siam*. 2 vols. London: Alexander Moring, 1924.

Graw, T C, *Hand Book of Castes and Tribes Employed in the Tea Estates in North-East India*. Calcutta: Indian Tea Association, 1924.

Great Missionaries to China. Grand Rapids: Zondervan, 1947.

Greene, Stephen Lyon Wakeman, *Absolute Dreams: Thai Government under Rama VI, 1919–1925*. Bangkok: White Lotus Press, 1999.

Gregory, John W and C J Gregory, *To the Alps of Chinese Tibet*. Philadelphia: J B Lippincott, 1924.

Grimes, Barbara F ed., *Ethnologue: Languages of the World*. Dallas: SIL, 11th edn, 1988.

—, *Ethnologue: Languages of the World*. Dallas: SIL, 12th edn, 1992.

—, *Ethnologue: Languages of the World*. Dallas: SIL, 13th edn, 1996.

—, *Ethnologue: Languages of the World*. CD-Rom version, 14th edn, 2000.

Grose, F S, *Tribes of the Shan States*. Mandalay, 1922.

Grousett, Rene, *The Empire of the Steppes: A History of Central Asia*. Translated by N Walford. New Brunswick: Rutgers University Press, 1970.

Grunfeld, A Tom, *The Making of Modern Tibet*. London: M E Sharpe, 1987.

Gurdon, Philip Richard Thornhagh, 'On the Khamtis'. *Journal of the Royal Asiatic Society* (1895).

Gryaznov, Mikhail, *The Ancient Civilizations of Southern Siberia*. New York: Cowles Publishing, 1969.

Guillon, Emmanuel, *Notes sur le Bouddhisme Mon*. Göttingen: Vandenhoeck and Ruprecht, 1983.

—, *The Mons: A Civilization of Southeast Asia*. Translated and edited by James V Di Crocco. Bangkok: The Siam Society, 1999.

Guizhou Nianjian [Guizhou Annual], Guiyang: Guizhou Renmin Chubanshe, 1985, Chinese language.

Gunn, Geoffrey C, *Theravadins, Colonists and Commissars in Laos*. Bangkok: White Lotus Press, 1998.

Gu Shoukang, 'The Sherpas: Hardy Folk of the Himalayas'. *China Tourism* 54 (n.d.).

Gustafson, James, 'Syncretistic Rural Thai Buddhism'. Fuller Theological Seminary, Pasadena, CA, MA thesis.

Gyatso, Kelsang, *Buddhism in the Tibetan Tradition: A Guide*. London: Routledge and Kegan Paul, 1984.

Hackett, William D, *The Pa-O People of the Shan State, Union of Burma: A Sociological and Ethnographic Study of the Pa-O (Taungthu) People*. Cornell University, PhD thesis, 1953.

Haldipur, Krishna, *Around the Hills and Dales of Arunachal Pradesh*. Shillong: North-Eastern Hill University, 1985.

Hale, Austin ed., *Clause, Sentence, and Discourse Patterns in Selected Languages of Nepal*. Norman, OK: Summer Institute of Linguistics, 1973.

—, 'Collected Papers on Sherpa, Jirel'. *Nepal Studies in Linguistics 2*. Kirtipur: SIL and Institute of Nepal and Asian Studies, 1975.

Hall, D G E, *A History of South-East Asia*. London: Macmillan, 1955.

Hall, G L, *Golden Boats from Burma*. Macrae Smith, 1961.

Haller, Felix, 'A Brief Comparison of Register Tone in Central Tibetan and Kham Tibetan'. *Linguistics of the Tibeto-Burman Area* 22.2 (1999) 77–97.

—, 'The Verbal Categories of Shigatse Tibetan and Themchen Tibetan'. *Linguistics of the Tibeto-Burman Area* 23.2 (2000) 175–91.

Hallett, Holt S, *A Thousand Miles on an Elephant in the Shan States*. Bangkok: White Lotus, repr. 1988.

Halliday, R, 'Immigration of the Mons into Siam'. *Journal of the Siam Society* 10.3 (Bangkok, 1913).

—, 'The Mons in Siam'. *Journal of the Burma Research Society* 12 (Rangoon, 1922).

—, *A Mon-English Dictionary*. Bangkok: Siam Society, 1922.

Halpern, Joel M, *Government, Politics, and Social Structure in Laos: A Study of Tradition and Innovation*. Monograph Series 4. New Haven: Yale University Press, 1964.

Hammerton, J A ed., *Tribes, Races and Cultures of India and Neighbouring Countries*. Delhi: Mittal Publications, 1984.

Hanks, Lucien M et al. eds., *Ethnographic Notes on Northern Thailand*. Ithaca, NY: Cornell University, Southeast Asia Program, 1965.

—, *Gazeteer for 1964, 1969, 1974: Maps of Ethnic Settlements of Chiang Rai Province North of the Mae Kok River, Thailand*. Ithaca, NY: Cornell University, Southeast Asia Program, 1975.

Hari, Maria ed., *Tibeto-Burman Phonemic*

Summaries. Kathmandu: Tribhuvan University and the Summer Institute of Linguistics, 1971.

Harmand, F J, *Laos and the Hilltribes of Indochina*. Bangkok: White Lotus Press, 1997.

Harrell, Stevan ed., *Cultural Encounters on China's Ethnic Frontiers*. Seattle: University of Washington Press, 1995.

Harrer, Heinrich, *Ladakh*. Innsbruck: Penguin Verlag, 1978.

—, *Return to Tibet*. Harmondsworth: Penguin, 1985.

—, *Seven Years in Tibet*. Los Angeles: J P Tarcher, 1981.

Harris Hilton, D and H Tony E Samuel, *Uttar Pradesh: Before the Throne of God*. Chennai: People India Research, 1999.

Harris, J G et al., *A Mpi Dictionary: Working Papers in Phonetics and Phonology*. Bangkok: Thai and Minority Language Research Project 1.1, 1976.

Hasnain, Nadeem, *Tribal India Today*. New Delhi: Harman Publications, 1986.

Hattaway, Paul, *China's Unreached Cities 1: A Prayer Guide for 52 of China's Least Evangelized Cities*. Chiang Mai, Thailand: AMO Publishing, 1999.

—, *China's Unreached Cities 2: A Prayer Guide for 52 of China's Least Evangelized Cities*. Chiang Mai, Thailand: Asia Harvest, 2003.

—, *Operation China: Introducing All the Peoples of China*. Carlisle: Piquant Publishing, 2000.

—, *Back to Jerusalem: Three Chinese House Church Leaders Share their Vision to Complete the Great Commission*. Carlisle: Piquant Publishing, 2003.

Heber, A Reeve and Kathleen M Reeve, *In Himalayan Tibet*. London: Secretary Service, 1926.

Heberer, Thomas, *China and its National Minorities: Autonomy or Assimilation?* New York: M E Sharpe, 1989.

Heckendorf, George, *Church Growth Survey of North East Thailand*. Bangkok, December 1971.

Hefley, James and Marti, *China! Christian Martyrs of the 20th Century: An Excerpt from 'By Their Blood'*. Milford, MI: Mott Media, 1978.

He Guanghua, 'The Lost Horizons of Medog'. *China Reconstructs* (March 1995) 47–50.

Heissig, Walther, *The Religions of Mongolia*. Berkeley, CA: University of California Press, 1980.

Heritage Research, 'People of Nepal'. *Journal of Nepal Sociology* (October 1991).

Hickey, Gerald C and Jesse Wright, *The Hill People of Northern Thailand: Social and Economic Development*. Chiang Mai: Chiang Mai University, 1978.

Hilton, Tony and Kumaradass, *Adopt—A District of Himachal Pradesh*. Chennai: People India Research and Training Institute, 1998.

Himm, Sokreaksa S, *The Tears of my Soul*. London: Monarch Books, 2003.

Hinkhouse, Paul M, 'William Clifton Dodd: Apostle to the Tai'. *Missionary Review of the World* (February 1920).

Hinton, Peter ed., *Tribesmen and Peasants in North Thailand*. Chiang Mai: Tribal Research Center, 1969.

Hodgson, Brian Houghton, 'On the Aboriginies of the Sub-Himalayas'. *Journal of the Asiatic Society of Bengal* 16 (1847).

— 'On the Tribes of Northern Tibet (Horyeul and Sokyeul) and of Sifán'. In *Essays on the Languages, Literatures, and Religions of Nepal and Tibet* (London: Trubner, 1874).

—, 'Sifán and Hórsók Vocabularies'. *Journal of the Asiatic Society of Bengal* 22 (1853).

Hoefer, H J, *Burma*. Hong Kong: APA Productions, 1981.

Hoehlig, Monika and Maria Hari, *Kagate Phoenmic Summary*. Kathmandu: Summer Institute of Linguistics and Institute of Nepal and Asian Studies of Trubhuvan University, 1976.

Holladay, J S and T W Bevan, 'The Lawa of Umphai and Middle Me Ping'. *Journal of the Siam Society* 32.1 (1940).

Hongladarom, Krisadawan, 'Rgylathang Tibetan of Yunnan: A Preliminary Report'. *Linguistics of the Tibeto-Burman Area* 19.2 (1996) 69–92.

Hong Yang, 'Adventures in the Namjagbarwa Canyon of Tibet'. *China Tourism* 214 (May 1998).

Hopfe, Lewis M, *Religions of the World*. New York: Macmillan Publishing Company, 4th edn, 1987.

Hooker, Joseph Dalton, *Himalayan Journals; or, Notes of a Naturalist in Bengal, the Sikkim and Nepal Himalayas, the Khasia Mountains, and c*. 2 vols. London: John Murray, 1854.

Hoshi Michiyo and Tondup Tsering, *Zangskar Vocabulary: A Tibetan Dialect Spoken in Kashmir*. Tokyo: Institute for the Study of Languages and Cultures of Asia and Africa, 1978.

Hoskin, John and Geoffrey Walton eds., *Folk Tales and Legends of the Dai People: The Thai Lue in Yunnan*. Bangkok: DD Books, 1992.

Hu, S Y, 'Ethnobotany of the Gia-rung Tribe'. Manuscript, New Haven: Yale Divinity School, n.d.

Huang Baoshan, *Snowy Mountains and Grasslands: Travels in Northwestern Sichuan*. Beijing: Foreign Languages Press, 1990.

Huang Bufan, 'Muyayu'. In Dai Qingxia et al., *Zangmianyu Shiwu Zhong* (Beijing: Yanshan Press, 1991), Chinese language.

Huang Xianlin ed., *Zhongguo Renkou: Guangxi Fence* [China's Population: Guangxi Volume]. Beijing: Zhongguo Caizheng Jingji Chubanshe, 1988, Chinese language.

Huang Yanhong, 'A Buddhist Land of 3,000 Women: The Larong Pancavidya Institute in Sertar'. *China Tourism* 228 (July 1999) 46–57.

—, 'The Qiang People'. *China Tourism* 202 (May 1997) 62–67.

Hubbard, James M, 'Problems in China'. *National Geographic* (August 1900).

Huc, Abbe, *Christianity in China, Tartary and Thibet*. London: Brown, Green, Longmans and Roberts, 1857.

Hudden, Alfred C, *Head-Hunters*. London, 1932.

Huffman, Franklin E, *Bibliography and Index of Mainland Southeast Asian Languages and Linguistics*. New Haven: Yale University Press, 1986.

Hugoniot, Richard D ed., *A Biographical Index of the Lesser Known Languages and Dialects of India and Nepal*. Waxhaw: SIL, 1970.

Hui, Himsey, 'The Bai'. *China and the Church Today* (October 1985).

Hutchison, E W and E Seidenfaden, 'The Lawa in Northern Siam'. *Journal of the Siam Society* 27.2 (1935).

Hutton, J H, *Census of India, 1931: With Complete Survey of Tribal Life and Systems*. 3 vols. Delhi: Gian Publishing House, 1986.

Iijima, Shigeru, 'The Thakali, a Central

Himalayan Tribe'. *The Japanese Journal of Ethnology* 24.3 (1960).

Iila, Nai Pan, *The Dvaravati Old Mons and the New Mon Immigrants in Thailand*. Bangkok: Chulalongkorn University, 1996.

Indian Government, *Report on Scheduled Tribes*. Delhi: Ministry of Home Affairs, 1960.

—, *The Report of the Advisory Committee on the Revision of Lists of Scheduled Tribes*. Delhi: Manager of Publications, 1965.

—, *The Tribal People of India*. Delhi: Manager of Publications, 1973.

India Missions Association, *Go into All: Andaman and Nicobar, Chandigarh, Dadra and Nagar Haveli, Daman and Diu, Delhi, Goa, Lakshadweep, Pondicherry and Sikkim*. Chennai: India Missions Association, 1997.

—, *Go into All: Haryana, Himachal Pradesh, Jammy and Kashmir and Punjab*. Madras: India Missions Association, 1995.

—, *Go into All: Uttar Pradesh*. Chennai: India Missions Association, 1997.

—, *Let My People Go, Volume V: Haryana State, Himachal Pradesh State, Jammu and Kashmir State, Punjab State*. Madras: India Missions Association, 1995.

—, *Let My People Go, Volume VII: Uttar Pradesh State*. Madras: India Missions Association, 1996.

—, *Let My People Go, Volume X: West Bengal State*. Chennai: India Missions Association, 1996.

— and the FMC Research Teams, *Unreached Mega Peoples of India*. Chennai: India Missions Association, 1999.

Indian Research Teams, *Peoples of India: Christian Presence and Works among Them*. India Missions Association, May 1997.

International Mission Board, 'Unmasking the Dragon: The Drukpa of Bhutan'. A prayer profile on the IMB website: www.tconline.org.

—, 'The Mons of Myanmar'. Prayer profile on IMB website.

Iorns, Magallanes, C J and M Holick eds., *Land Conflicts in Southeast Asia: Indigenous Peoples, Environment and International Law*. Bangkok: White Lotus Press, *c.*1998.

Issachar Frontier Missions Research, *Mongolia Challenge Report: A Summary of Current Spiritual Needs and a Strategy for Response*. Seattle, WA: Issachar, 1984.

Izikowitz, Karl Gustav, *Lamet, Hill Peasants in French Indochina*. Göteborg, 1951.

Jagchid, Sechin and Paul Hyer, *Mongolia's Culture and Society*. Boulder, CO: Westview Press, 1979.

Janhunen, Juha and Tapani Salminen, *UNESCO Red Book on Endangered Languages: Northeast Asia*. Finland: University of Helsinki, 1996.

Jia Lin, 'Over the Dadu River'. *China Tourism* 60 (n.d.).

Jeffrey, J H, *Khams*. Devon: Arthur H Stockwell, 1974.

Jennar, Raoul M, *Cambodian Chronicles, 1989–1996: Volume 1: Bungling a Peace Plan, 1989–1991*. Bangkok: White Lotus Press, 1998.

Jest, Corneille, 'Les Thakali'. *Ethnographic* 9.58–59 (1964–65).

Jesuit Fathers, *The Catholic Directory of Thailand*. Bangkok: Jesuit Fathers, 1967.

Jigmei, Ngapo Ngawang, et al., *Tibet*. London: Frederick Muller, 1981.

Johnstone, Patrick, *Operation World*. Grand Rapids: Zondervan, 1993.

— and Jason Mandryk, *Operation World: When We Pray God Works*. Carlisle: Paternoster Lifestyle, 2001.

Johnston, Sir Reginald Fleming, *From Peking to Mandalay: A Journey from North China to Burma through Tibetan Ssuch'uan and Yunnan*. London: John Murray, 1908.

Jottrand, Mr and Mrs Émile, *In Siam: The Diary of a Legal Advisor of King Chulalongkorn's Government*. Bangkok: White Lotus Press, 1905, repr. 1996.

Judson, Edward, *The Life of Adoniram Judson*. New York: Anson D F Randolph and Co., 1883.

Jun Feng, 'Xishuangbanna: Homeland of Minorities'. *China Tourism* 72 (n.d.).

Jun Su, 'A Trip to the Three Islands Inhabited by the Jing People'. *China Tourism* 77 (n.d.).

Kambunratana, Prachuap et al., *Survey of the Hill Tribes and Minority Groups in Northern Thailand*. Bangkok: Ministry of Education, 1987.

Kang Jie, 'The Buryats from Siberia'. *China Tourism* 83 (n.d.).

Kansakar, Tej R, 'Multilingualism and the Language Situation in Nepal'. *Linguistics of the Tibeto-Burman Area* 19.2 (1996).

Kar Chaudhari, Amalendubikasa, *Tribal Songs of North-East India with Special Reference to Arunachal Pradesh*. Calcutta: Firma K L Mukhopadhyay, 1984.

Karnow, Stanley, *Vietnam: A History*. New York: The Viking Press, 1983.

Karotemprell, S ed., *Tribes of North-East India*. Calcutta: Firma K L Mukhopadhyay, 1984.

Katzner, Kenneth, *The Languages of the World*. New York: Funk and Wagnalls, 1977.

Kauffman, H E, 'Some Social and Religious Institutions of the Lawa (N.W. Thailand)'. *Journal of the Siam Society* 60.2 (1972).

Kaundinya, B, *Monastic Buddhism among the Khamtis of Arunachal*. New Delhi: National Publishing House, 1986.

Kesar Lall, 'The Tamangs'. *Nepal Review* 1.3 (1969).

Ketudat, Nrong, 'Ethnic Groups in Northeastern Thailand'. *The Bangkok World* (1 February 1970).

Kemp, Hugh P, *Steppe by Step*. London: Monarch / OMF / Interserve, 2000.

Kewley, Vanya, *Tibet: Behind the Ice Curtain*. London: Grafton Books, 1990.

Khaing, Mi Mi, *Burmese Family*. London: Longmans and Green, 1946.

Khamsakul, Benjamas, *The Attitude of So (Thavung) Ethnic Group toward their own Language and its Use: Case Study of Nong Waeng Village, Pathumwapi Subdistrict, Song Dao District, Sakon Nakhorn Province*. Bangkok: Mahidol University, MA thesis, 1988.

Kirkpatrick, W, *An Account of the Kingdom of Nepal*. London: W Miller, 1811.

Kirsch, Thomas A, 'Development and Mobility among the Phu Tai of Northeast Thailand'. *Asian Survey* 6.7.

—, *Phu Thai Religious Syncretism: A Case Study of Thai Religion and Society*. Harvard University, PhD thesis, 1967.

Kitamura, Hajime ed., *Anthropological and Linguistic Studies of the Gandaki Area in Nepal*. Monumenta Serindica 10. Tokyo: Institute for the Study of Languages and Cultures, 1982.

Kitiharakul, Sirikul, *Relations between Community Closeness and Lexical Choice of the Lao Khrang Community at Ban Nong Kraphu, Tambon Ban Luang, Amphoe Son Tum, Nakhon*

Pathom. Chualongkorn University, MA thesis, 1996.

Kitprasert, Chailert, *A Tonal Comparison of Tai Dialects: Tai Bai Group*. Mahidol University, Nakhon Pathom, MA thesis, 1985.

Klausner, William J, *Reflections on Thai Culture*. Bangkok: Suksit Siam, 1981.

Komonkitiskun, Jiranan, 'Lawa Pronouns'. *Mon-Khmer Studies* 21 (1992).

Koowatthanasiri, Kanjana, *The Tones of Nyo*. Chulalongkorn University, MA thesis, 1980.

Kotturan, George, *The Himalayan Gateway: History and Culture of Sikkim*. New Delhi: Sterling, 1983.

Krader, Lawrence, *Peoples of Central Asia*. Indiana University Press, 1971.

—, *Social Organization of the Mongol Turkic Pastoral Nomads*. The Hague: Mouton, 1963.

Kremmer, Christopher, *Stalking the Elephant Kings: In Search of Lao*. Chiang Mai: Silkworm Books, 1997.

Kuhn, John, *We Found a Hundred Tribes*. London: China Inland Mission, 1945.

Kunstadter, Peter ed., *South East Asia Tribes, Minorities and Nations*. 2 vols. Princeton: Princeton University Press, 1967.

—, *Research on the Lua and Skaw Karen Hill People of Northern Thailand, with Some Practical Implications*. Bangkok, 1964.

—, *The Future of Upland Tribal People in the Nations of Southeast Asia: Lua' and Karen Hill Peoples of Northwest Thailand*. Princeton: Princeton University, 1965.

—, *The Lua (Lawa) of Northern Thailand: Aspects of Social Structure, Agriculture, and Religion*. Princeton: Princeton University, Research Monograph 21, 1965.

—, 'Living With the Gentle Lua'. *National Geographic* (July 1966).

—, 'Residential and Social Organization of the Lawa of Northern Thailand'. *Southwestern Journal of Anthropology* 22.1 (1966).

—, ed., *Southeast Asian Tribes, Minorities and Nations*. 2 vols. Princeton: Princeton University Press, 1967.

— 'Hill and Valley Populations in Northwest Thailand'. In Peter Hinton ed., *Tribesmen and Peasants in North Thailand* (Chiang Mai: Tribal Research Center, 1969).

—, 'Animism, Buddhism, and Christianity: Religion in the Life of Lua People of Pa Pae, Northwestern Thailand'. In John McKinnon and Wanat Bhruksasri eds., *Highlanders of Thailand* (Kuala Lumpur: Oxford University Press, 1983).

—, *Highland Populations in Northern Thailand*. Honolulu: East-West Population Institute, 1978.

Labbé, Armand J, *Ban Chiang: Art and Prehistory of Northeast Thailand*. Santa Ana: Bowers Museum, 1985.

Lacouperie, Terrien de, *Languages of China before the Chinese*. London, 1887.

Lafitte, Gabriel, and Alison Ribush, *Happiness in a Material World: The Dalai Lama in Australia and New Zealand*. Melbourne: Lothian, 2002.

Lal, Parmanand and B K Dasgupta, *Lower Siang People: A Study in Ecology and Society*. Calcutta: Anthropological Survey of India, 1978.

Lambert, Tony, *The Resurrection of the Chinese Church*. Illinois: OMF, 1994.

—, 'The Challenge of China's Minority Peoples'. *Chinese around the World* (April 1991).

—, 'Christianity and Tibet'. *Pray for China Fellowship* (April 1996).

Languages of Bhutan. An unpublished study by an anonymous researcher, *c*.1995.

Larson, Frans August, *Larson, Duke of Mongolia*. Boston: Little, Brown and Co., 1930.

—, *On Tramp among the Mongols*. Boston: Little, Brown and Co., n.d.

Latourette, Kenneth Scott, *A History of Christian Missions in China*. New York: Macmillan, 1929.

—, *A History of the Expansion of Christianity*. 7 vols. New York: Harper, 1937.

—, *Introducing Buddhism*. New York: Friendship Press, 1958.

Lattimore, Owen, *Mongolian Folktales and Stories*. Ulan Bator.

Lau, Dianna, 'From Yunnan to Tibet'. *China Tourism* 26.1 (April 2002).

Lausanne Committee for World Evangelization. *The Thailand Report— Christian Witness to Buddhists* 15. Wheaton: Lausanne Committee for World Evangelization, 1980.

Laycock, Donald C and Werner Winter eds., *A World of Language: Papers Presented to Professor S A Wurm on his 65th Birthday*. Canberra: The Australian National University, 1987.

Lazzarotto, Angelo S, *The Catholic Church in Post-Mao China*. Hong Kong: The Holy Spirit Study Center, 1983.

Leach, Edmund, *Political Systems of Highland Burma: A Study of Kachin Social Structure*. London: Bell, 1954.

Learner, Frank Doggett, *Rusty Hinges: A Story of Closed Doors Beginning to Open in North-East Tibet*. London: CIM, 1933.

Le Bar, Frank M, Gerald C Hickey and John K Musgrave, *Ethnic Groups of Insular Southeast Asia*. New Haven: HRAF Press, 1972.

—, *Ethnic Groups of Mainland Southeast Asia*. New Haven: HRAF Press, 1964.

Le Bar, Frank and Adrienne Suddard eds., *Laos: Its People, Its Society, Its Culture*. New Haven: HRAF Press, 1960.

Lee, Chae-Jin, *China's Korean Minority: The Politics of Ethnic Education*. Boulder, CO: Westview Press, 1986.

Lee, Jacob D H ed., *China's 55 Ethnic Minorities*. Watson, Australia: YWAM Institute of Asian Studies, 1995.

Lefèvre, E, *Travels in Laos: The Fate of Sip Song Pana and Muong Sing (1894– 1896)*. Bangkok: White Lotus Press, 1897, repr. 1995.

Lehman, F K, 'Burma: Kayah Society as a Function of the Shan-Burma-Karen Context'. In J Steward ed., *Contemporary Change in Traditional Societies* (Chicago: University of Illinois, 1967).

Lei Hongan, *Traditional Religious Beliefs of the Minority Nationalities*. Kunming: Yunnan Ethnic Research Institute, 1984.

Le May, Reginald, *An Asian Arcady: The Land and Peoples of Northern Siam*. Cambridge: Heffer and Sons, 1926.

Levin, M G and L P Potapov eds., *The Peoples of Siberia*. Chicago: University of Chicago Press, 1964.

Levine, Nancy E, *The Dynamics of Polyandry, Kinship, Domesticity, and Population on the Tibetan Border*. Chicago: University of Chicago Press, 1988.

Lewin, Thomas Herbert, *The Hill Tracts of Chittagong and the Dwellers Therein: With Comparative Vocabularies of the Hill Dialects*. Calcutta: Bengal Press, 1869.

—, *Hill Proverbs of the Inhabitants of the Chittagong Hill Tracts*. Calcutta:

Bengal Secretariat Press, 1873.

Lewis, Paul W and Elaine Lewis, *Peoples of the Golden Triangle*. New York: Thames and Hudson, 1984.

Leyseen, J, *The Cross over China's Wall*. Beijing: The Lazarist Church, 1941.

Lim, David and Steve Spaulding eds., *Sharing Jesus in the Buddhist World*. Pasadena, CA: William Carey Library, 2003.

Lin Shao-Yang, *A Chinese Appeal to Christendom*. 1911; publisher's name not available.

Lintner, B, *Land of Jade: A Journey through Insurgent Burma*. Edinburgh: Kiscadale, 1990.

Lin Xiangron, *Jiarongyu Yufa*. Chengdu: Sichuan Minzu Chubanshe, 1993, Chinese language.

—, 'Sound System of the Zhuo Keji (Ma'erkang) Dialect of Jiarong'. *Yuyin Yanjiu* 2 (1988), Chinese language.

Lin Yuehua, *Minzuxue Yanjiu* [Studies in Ethnography]. Beijing: Zhongguo Shehui Kexue Chubanshe, 1985, Chinese language.

Liu Dongping and Cheng Weidong. 'Deqen: A Highland in the Hengduan Mountains'. *China Tourism* 245 (December 2000).

Liu Guangkun, *Maqo Qiangyu Yanjiu*. Chengdu: Sichuan Minzu Chubanshe, 1998, Chinese language.

Li Ping, 'The Flower Street Festival of the Dai'. *China Tourism* 165 (April 1994) 79–81.

Li, Vladimir, *Some Approaches to the Classification of Small Ethnic Groups in South China*. Prague: Institute of Oriental Studies, n.d.

Li Wei, 'Guangxi Lingchuan Pinghua de Tedian'. *Fangyuan* 4, Chinese language.

Li Wuzi, 'Monks and Nuns at the Labrang Monastery'. *China Tourism* 229 (August 1999).

Logan, Pamela, *Lifestyle* (October–November 1994).

Lord, Donald C, *Mo Bradley and Thailand*. Grand Rapids, Eerdmans, 1969.

Loti, Pierre, *Siam*. London: T Werner Laurie, 1929.

Loup, Robert, *Martyr in Tibet: The Heroic Life and Death of Father Maurice Tourney, St Bernard Missionary to Tibet*. New York: David McKay Co., 1956.

Lovett, Richard, *James Gilmour and His Boys*. London: Religious Tract Society, 1894.

—, *James Gilmour of Mongolia*. London: Religious Tract Society, 1893.

Lowis, C C, *Tribes of Burma*. Rangoon: Ethnographic Survey of India, 1909.

Lu Shaozun, *Pumi Yu Fangyan Yanjiu*. Beijing: Minorities Publishing House, 2001, Chinese language.

Lutz, Jessie Gregory and Rolland Ray Lutz, *Hakka Chinese Confront Protestant Christianity 1850–1900: With the Autobiographies of Eight Hakka Christians, and Commentary*. Armonk, NY: M E Sharpe, 1998.

Lyall, Leslie, *A Passion for the Impossible*. Chicago: Moody Press, 1965.

McCarthy, James, *Surveying and Exploring in Siam*. London: John Murray, 1902.

McCaskill, Don and Ken Kampe eds., *Development or Domestication? Indigenous Peoples of Southeast Asia*. Chiang Mai: Silkworm Books, 1997.

McDonald, Rev N A, *A Missionary in Siam (1860–1870)*. Bangkok: White Lotus Press, 1871, repr. 1999.

McFarland, Bertha Blount, *Our Garden Was so Fair: The Story of Mission in Thailand*. New York: Fleming H Revell, 1943.

—, *McFarland of Siam*. New York: Vantage Press, 1958.

McFarland, George Bradley, *Historical Sketch of Protestant Missions in Siam 1828–1928*. Bangkok: The Bangkok Times Press, 1928.

McGilvary, Daniel, *A Half Century among the Siamese and the Lao*. New York: Fleming H Revell, 1912.

McKhann, Charles F, 'The Naxi and the Nationalities Question'. In Stevan Harrell ed., *Cultural Encounters on China's Ethnic Frontiers* (Seattle: University of Washington Press, 1995).

McKinnon, John and W Bhrukrasri eds., *Highlanders of Thailand*. Kuala Lumpur: Oxford University Press, 1983.

McLeish, Alexander, *Christian Progress in Burma*. London: World Dominion Press, 1929.

MacDonald, A W, 'Les Tamang vus par un d'eux'. *Homme* 6.1 (1966).

MacGregor, John, *Through the Buffer State: Travels in Borneo, Siam, Cambodia, Malaya and Burma*. Bangkok: White Lotus Press, 1896, repr. 1994.

Ma Changshou, 'Jiarong Minzu Shehui Shi'. *Minzuxue Yanjiu Jikan* 4 (1944), Chinese language.

Mackerras, Colin, *China's Minorities: Integration and Modernization in the Twentieth Century*. Hong Kong: Oxford University Press, 1994.

Mahasthabir, Dharmadhar, *Saddharmer Panarutthan*. Calcutta: Das Brothers, 1371, repr. n.d.

Mainwaring, Colonel George Byers, *A Grammar of the Rong (Lepcha) Language, as it Exists in the Dorjiling and Sikkim Hills*. Calcutta: Baptist Mission Press, 1876.

Majupuria, Indra, *Marriage Customs in Nepal: Traditions and Wedding Ceremonies among Various Nepalese Ethnic Groups*. Kathmandu: Tribhuvan University, 1989.

Makley, Charlene, Keith Dede, Hua Kan and Wang Qingshan, 'The Amdo Dialect of Labrang'. *Linguistics of the Tibeto-Burman Area* 22.1 (1999).

Ma Nai Hui and Su Jun Hui eds., *China's Minority Nationalities*. Beijing: China Nationalities Photographic Art Publishing, 1988.

Man, R S, *The Ladakhi: A Study in Ethnography and Change*. Calcutta: Anthropological Survey of India, 1986.

Missions Advanced Research Center [MARC]. 'Bhots in the State of Sikkim'. *World Christianity: South Asia*. California: MARC Publications, n.d.

Marini, G F de A, *A New and Interesting Description of the Lao Kingdom (1642–1648)*. Bangkok: White Lotus Press, 1663, repr. 1998.

Marlay, Ross, 'Buryats'. In James S Olson, Lee Brigance Pappas and Nicholas C J Pappas eds., *Ethnohistorical Dictionary of the Soviet and Russian Empires* (Westport, CT: Greenwood Press, 1994).

Marsden, William trans., *The Travels of Marco Polo*. New York: Dell, 1961.

Marullo, Clara, *The Last Forbidden Kingdom: Mustang, Land of Tibetan Buddhism*. London: Thames and Hudson, 1995.

Matisoff, James A, *Mpi and Lolo-Burmese Microlinguistics*. Tokyo: Institute for the Study of Languages and Cultures of Asia and Africa, 1978.

—, 'Languages and Dialects of Tibeto-Burman'. *STEDT Monograph II*

Series. Berkeley, CA: University of California, 1988.

—, *Languages of Mainland Southeast Asia.* Cambridge: Cambridge University Press, 1982.

Maung Shwe Wa, *Burma Baptist Chronicle.* Rangoon: Burma Baptist Convention, 1963.

Ma Xueliang, 'Minority Languages of China'. *China Reconstructs* 3.3 (1954).

Ma Yin, *China's Minority Nationalities.* Beijing: Foreign Languages Press, 1989.

Mayoury, Ngaosyvathn, *Lao Women: Yesterday and Today.* Vientiane: Lao State Publishing, 1982.

Medary, Marjorie, *Each One Take One: Frank Laubach, Friend to Millions.* New York: David McKay, 1954.

Meeker, Oden, *The Little World of Laos.* New York: Charles Scribner's Sons, 1959.

Mehra, G N, *Bhutan.* New Delhi: Vikas, 1974.

Metford, Beatrix, *Where China Meets Burma.* London: Blackie and Son, 1935.

Michael, John F, *The North-East Frontier of India.* Delhi: Vivek Publishing House, 1973.

Milliken, Stuart, 'SIL China Nationalities and Languages Files'. Unpublished report, Guangzhou, 1993.

Milne, Leslie and Wilbur Cochrane, *Shans at Home.* New York: Paragon Book Reprint Co., 1970.

Minford, John, trans., *Favourite Folktales of China.* Beijing: New World Press, 1983.

Ming, 'A Young Woman Evangelist in a Booming Town'. *Bridge* 52 (March–April 1992).

Ministry of Foreign Affairs, *Islam in Thailand.* Bangkok, 1976.

Minzu Shibie Wenxian Ziliao Huibian, Minzu Yanjiu Cankao Ziliao [Compilation of the Classified Nationality Literature in Nationality Research Reference Material]. Guiyang: Guizhousheng Minzu Yanjiusuo, 1982, Chinese language.

Miri, Sujata ed., *Religion and Society of North-East India.* New Delhi: Vikas Publishing House, 1980.

Missions Frontiers. Pasadena, CA: US Center for World Mission, April 1995.

Moffett, Samuel Hugh, *A History of*

Christianity in Asia, I: *Beginnings to 1500.* San Francisco: HarperSanFrancisco, 1992.

Moore, George, *The Lost Tribes and the Saxons of the East and of the West, with New Views of Buddhism and Trs. of Rock Records in India.* London: Longman Green, 1861.

Morev, L N, *The Sek Language.* Moscow, 1988.

Morganthaler, Hans, *Impressions of the Siamese-Malayan Jungle.* Bangkok: White Lotus Press, 1923, repr. 1994.

Morice, A, *People and Wildlife in and around Saigon.* Bangkok: White Lotus Press, 1875, repr. 1997.

Morris, C J, *Living With the Lepchas: A Book about Sikkim Himalayas.* London: Toronto Heinemann, 1938.

Morse, Eugene, *Exodus to a Hidden Valley.* New York: Reader's Digest Press, 1974.

Moser, Leo J, *The Chinese Mosaic: The Peoples and Provinces of China.* Boulder, CO: Westview Press, 1985.

Moses, L and S A Halkovic, *Introduction to Mongolian History and Culture.* Bloomington: University of Indiana Press, n.d.

Moule, Arthur Christopher, *Christians in China before the Year 1550.* London: SPCK, 1930.

—, and Paul Pelliot. *Marco Polo: The Description of the World.* 2 vols. London: Routledge, 1938.

Muanthanga, Rev P C, *Directory of Churches and Missions in N E India.* Shillong: Carey Research and Communication Center, 1997.

—, *The Harvest Field of Arunachal Pradesh.* Shillong: Carey Research and Communication Center, 1998.

—, *The Harvest Field of Tripura.* Shillong: Carey Research and Communication Center, 1998.

Munier, Christophe, *Sacred Rocks and Buddhist Caves in Thailand.* Bangkok: White Lotus Press, 1998.

Munshi, S and U Lama, 'The Tamangs of Darjeeling: A Study of Group Identity'. *Journal of the Indian Anthropological Society* 13.2–3 (1978).

Murray, Edward, 'With the Nomads of Central Asia: A Summer's Sojourn in the Tekes Valley, Plateau Paradise of Mongol and Turkic Tribes'. *National Geographic* (January 1936).

Muse, Audrey, 'A Profile on the Jiarong

People of China'. Unpublished report (May 1996).

Myanmar Faces and Places, Unpublished prayer profiles of a variety of people groups in Myanmar, 2003.

Myrdal, Jan, *The Silk Road: A Journey from the High Pamirs and Ili through Sinkiang and Kansu.* New York: Pantheon Books, 1979.

Nagano, Yasuhiko, *A Historical Study of the Jiarong Verb System.* Tokyo: Seishido, 1984.

Nagi, Thakur Sen, *Scheduled Tribes of Himachal Pradesh: A Profile.* Simla, self-published, 1976.

Naing, Min, *Palaungs of Burma.* Rangoon: Ministry of Culture, 1960.

—, *Races of Burma.* Rangoon: Ministry of Culture, 1960.

Nair, P T, *Tribes of Arunachal Pradesh.* Guwahati: Spectrum Publications, 1985.

Nairne, W P, *Gilmour of the Mongols.* London: Hodder and Stoughton, 1924.

Nandy, Raj, *North and North Eastern Frontier Tribes of India.* Delhi: Cultural Publishing House, 1983.

Nationalities Affairs Commission of Guangxi Zhuang Autonomous Region, *The Yao Nationality.* Nanning: People's Publishing House, 1990.

National Statistics Center, *Laos Census 1995: Preliminary Report 2: Results on the Province and District Level.* Vientiane, 1995.

Nawigamune, Wanna, *Chiang Mai and the Hill Tribes.* Bangkok: Sangdad Publishing, 1992.

Neale, Frederick A, *Narrative of a Residence in Siam.* London: National Illustrated Library, 1852.

Neamnark, Wisuttira, *Lamphun Yong Phonology: A Synchronis Comparative Study.* Chulalongkorn University, MA thesis, 1984.

Neiss, P, *Travels in Upper Laos and Siam.* Bangkok: White Lotus Press, *c.*1890, repr. 1997.

Nepali, Gopal Singh, *The Newars.* Bombay: United Asia Publications, 1965.

Neterowicz, Eva M, *The Tragedy of Tibet.* Washington, DC: The Council for Social and Economic Studies, 1989.

Netland, Harold, 'Vajrayana (Tibetan Buddhism)'. In *Evangelical Dictionary of World Missions* (ed. A Scott Moreau;

Grand Rapids: Baker Books, 2000).

New China News Agency, 'Tremendous Success in Small Minority Area' (25 November 1958).

New Glories of the Catholic Church, The. Translated from the Italian by the Fathers of the London Oratory, at the Request of the Cardinal Archbishop of Westminster, with a Preface by His Eminence. London: Richardson, 1859.

Niles, D T, *Buddhism and the Claims of Christ.* Richmond: John Knox Press, 1967.

Nimmanahaeminda, Kraisri, 'The Lawa Guardian Spirits of Chiang Mai'. *Journal of the Siam Society* 55.2 (1967).

Nishi, Yoshio, 'Five Swadesh 100-word Lists for the Ghale Language—A Report on the Trek in the Ghale Speaking Area in Nepal'. Pp. 158–94 in Hajime Kitamura ed., *Anthropological and Linguistic Studies of the Gandaki Area in Nepal.* Monumenta Serindica 10. Tokyo: Institute for the Study of Languages and Cultures, 1982.

—, 'A Brief Survey of the Linguistic Position of Ghale'. *Bulletin of the Faculty of Law and Literature.* Matsuyama: Ehine University, 1983.

Nokaeo, Preeya, *Central Thai and Northern Thai: Linguistic and Attitudinal Study.* University of Texas, PhD thesis, 1989.

Norbu, Dawa, *Red Star over Tibet.* New Delhi: Sterling, 1987.

Norbu, Thubten Jigme and Colin M Turnbull, *Tibet: Its History, Religion and People.* New York: Penguin Books, 1987.

Norman, Jerry, *A Concise Manchu-English Lexicon.* Seattle: University of Washington Press, 1978.

—, and Paul Georg Von Mollendorf, *A Manchu Grammar with Analyzed Texts.* Shanghai: American Presbyterian Mission Press, 1892.

Nuechteriein, Donald E, *Thailand and the Struggle for Southeast Asia.* Ithaca, NY: Cornell University Press, 1965.

O'Connor, V C S, *The Silken East.* 2 vols. London: Hutchinson and Co., 1904.

—, *Mandalay and Other Cities in Burma.* London: Hutchinson and Co., 1907.

Okanda, F E, 'The Newars of Nepal'. *Natural History* 66.4 (1957).

Oldfield, H A, *Sketches from Nepal.* London: Allen, 1880.

Olson, James S, *An Ethnohistorical Dictionary of China.* Westport, CT: Greenwood Press, 1998.

—, Lee Brigance Pappas and Nicholas C J Pappas eds., *Ethnohistorical Dictionary of the Soviet and Russian Empires.* Westport, CT: Greenwood Press, 1994.

OMF Mekong Center, *30 Days of Prayer for Northern Laos.* Thailand: Mekong Center, 2002.

Operation Japan Publishing Committee and Japan Evangelical Missionary Association, *Operation Japan: Japan in Focus, a Handbook for Prayer*, 2000 edn.

Orléans, Henri d', *Around Tonkin and Siam: A French Colonialist View of Tonkin, Laos and Siam.* Bangkok: White Lotus Press, 1892, repr. 1999.

Ortner, Sherry B, *Sherpas through their Rituals.* Cambridge: Cambridge University Press, 1978.

Osborne, Milton E, *The French Presence in Cochinchina and Cambodia: Rule and Response (1859–1905).* Ithaca, NY: Cornell University Press, 1969.

Pachen, Ani and Adelaide Donnelley, *Sorrow Mountain: The Remarkable Story of a Tibetan Warrior Nun.* London: Transworld, 2000.

Padhy, Krishn Singh and P C Satapathy, *Tribal India.* New Delhi: Ashish Publishing House, 1989.

Padmanabham, P B S V, *A Demogenetic Profile of Singphos.* Unpublished report submitted to the director, Anthropological Survey of India, 1981.

Page, Homer, *The Little World of Laos.* New York: Charles Scribner's Sons, 1959.

Panchani, Chander Sheikhar, *Arunachal Pradesh: Religion, Culture and Society.* Delhi: Konark Publishers, 1989.

Pangnem, Moa, 'A Miracle for Tamang'. *Asian Report* 29.3, Report 217 (May–June 1996).

Pan, Hla, 'Mon Literature and Culture over Thailand and Burma'. *Journal of the Burma Research Society* 41 (Rangoon, 1958).

Panka, Kanchana, *The Phonological Characteristics of Lao Dialects in Amphoe Muang, Nakhon Pathom.* Chulalongkorn University, MA thesis, 1980.

Parkin, Robert, *A Guide to Austroasiatic Speakers and their Languages: Oceanic Linguistics Special Publication* 23.

Honolulu: University of Hawaii Press, 1991.

Parsons, Hy, 'Aborigines in West China'. *Missionary Review of the World* 54.2 (1931).

Parsons, William Barclay, 'Hunan: The Closed Province of China'. *National Geographic* (October 1900).

Patterson, George, *Requiem for Tibet.* London: Aurem, 1990.

Paulsen, Debbie, 'A Phonological Reconstruction of Proto-Plang'. *Mon-Khmer Studies* 18–19 (1992).

Peace Books Company, *Life Styles of China's Ethnic Minorities.* Hong Kong, 1991.

Peachey, Titus and Linda, 'Religion in Socialist Laos'. *Southeast Asian Chronicle* 91 (1983).

Peissel, Michael, *Cavaliers of Kham: The Secret War in Tibet.* London: Heinemann, 1972.

—, 'Mustang: Remote Realm in Nepal'. *National Geographic* (October 1965) 579–604.

Peltier, Anatole-Roger, *Tai Khoeun Literature.* Bangkok: Duang Kamol, 1987.

People's Daily (13 August 2001).

Perera, H R, *Buddhism in Sri Lanka: A Short History.* Kandy: Buddhist Publication Society, 1988.

Perazic, Elizabeth, 'Little Laos: Next Door to Red China'. *National Geographic* (January 1960).

Pfanmuller, Klein, *Burma the Golden.* Hong Kong: APA Productions, 1982.

Phillips, David J, *Peoples on the Move: Introducing the Nomads of the World.* Carlisle: Piquant, 2001.

Phole, Perdita, *Useful Plants of Manang District: A Contribution in the Ethnobotany of the Nepal-Himalaya.* Stuttgart: Franz Steiner Verlag, 1990.

Ping-Ti Ho, *Studies on the Population of China 1368–1953.* Cambridge, MA: Harvard University Press, 1959.

Plymire, David, *High Adventure in Tibet.* Springfield: Gospel Publishing House, 1959.

Polo, Marco, *The Book of Ser Marco Polo, the Venetian, Concerning the Kingdoms and Marvels of the East.* 2 vols. Translated by Henry Yule. London: John Murray, 1903.

—, *The Travels of Marco Polo.* New York: Penguin, 1958.

—, *The Travels of Marco Polo: The Complete*

Yule-Cordier Edition. New York: Dover Publications, 1903.

Poppe, Nicholas, *Mongolian Language Handbook.* Washington, DC: Center for Applied Linguistics, 1970.

Population Reference Bureau, *1998 World Population Data Sheet.* Washington, DC: Population Reference Bureau, 1998.

Pradhan, Prachanda, 'Mechanism of Social Control in the Sherpa Community'. *Vasudha* 13.5 (1969–70).

Prapas, Charusathira, *Thailand's Hill Tribes.* Bangkok: Ministry of Interior, 1967.

Prasad, R R, *Bhotia Tribals of India.* New Delhi: Gian Publishing House, 1989.

Prasad, Sachchidananda R R ed., *Encyclopaedic Profile of Indian Tribes.* 4 vols. New Delhi: Discovery Publishing House, 1998.

Prawdin, Michael, *The Mongol Empire: Its Rise and Legacy.* London: Allen and Unwin, 1940.

Pray for China. Hong Kong: Christian Communications Ltd., April 1996.

Preecha, Chaturabhand, *People of the Hills.* Bangkok: Duang Kamol, 1980.

Pro Mundi Vita, *Thailand in Transition: The Church in a Buddhist Country.* Brussels: Pro Mundi Vita Centrum Informationis, 1973.

Purcell, Victor, *The Chinese in S E Asia.* London: Oxford University Press, 1965.

PW Asia, 'Drukpa of Bhutan: A UPG in Need of Adoption!' Prayer profile, Singapore (*c.*1998).

Qiangic Speaking Tibetans. An unpublished prayer guide produced by an anonymous missionary, 2000.

Qu Aitang, 'Jiarongyude Fangyan: Fangyan Huafen he Yuyan Shibie' [Jiarong Dialects: Issues in Dialect Subclassification and Language Recogniton]. *Minzu Yuwen* 4 and 5 (1990, Chinese language).

Raghaviah, V, *Tribal Revolts.* Nellore: Andhra Rashtra Adimjati Sevak Sangh, 1971.

—, *Tribes of India.* 2 vols. New Delhi: Bharatiya Adimjati Sevak Sangh, 1972.

Rakow, Regina Meg. *Laos and Laotians.* Honolulu: University of Hawaii Center for Southeast Asian Studies, 1992.

Ramsey, S Robert, *The Languages of China.*

Princeton: Princeton University Press, 1987.

Rangsrisht, Vejvant ed., *Thailand: Past and Present.* Bangkok: Publicity Committee Ninth Pacific Science Congress, 1957.

Rao Fengqi, 'Why Does Putian County Produce So Many Athletes?' *China Reconstructs* (May 1983) 55–56.

Raza, Moonis and Aijazuddin Ahmad, *An Atlas of Tribal India.* New Delhi: Concept Publishing Company, 1990.

Regmi, D R, *Ancient and Medieval Nepal.* Lucknow: Prem Printing Press, 1952.

Reimer, Johannes, *Operation Soviet Union.* Fresno, CA: Logos, 1990.

Richardson, Don, *Eternity in their Hearts.* California: Regal Books, 1981.

Richardson, Hugh E, *Tibet and Its History.* London: Oxford University Press, 1962.

Riebeck, Emil, *The Chittagong Hill-Tribes: Results of a Journey Made in the Year 1882.* Translated from the German by Prof A H Keane, London: Asher and Co., 1885.

Rijnhart, Susie Carson, *With the Tibetans in Tent and Temple.* Chicago: Fleming H Revell, 1901.

Risley, H H, *The Tribes and Castes of Bengal.* 2 vols. Calcutta: Bengal Secretariat Press, 1891.

—, *Study of Ethnology in India.* London: Anthropological Institute, 1891.

Rizvi, Janet, *Ladakh: Crossroads of High Asia.* Delhi: Oxford, 1983.

Robinson, Daniel and Robert Storey, *Vietnam: A Travel Survival Kit.* Hawthorn, Australia: Lonely Planet, 1993.

Robinson, Joan, 'National Minorities in Yunnan'. *Eastern Horizon* 14.4 (1975).

Robinson, W, *A Descriptive Account of Assam to which is Added a Short Account of the Neighbouring Tribes.* London: Ostell and Lepage, 1841.

Robson, William, *Griffith John: Founder of the Hankow Mission.* New York: Fleming H Revell, *c.*1890.

Rock, Joseph F C, *The Ancient Nakhi Kingdom of Southwest China.* 2 vols. Cambridge: Harvard University Press, 1947.

— 'The Glories of the Minya Konka'. *National Geographic* (October 1930).

— 'Konka Risumgongba: Holy Mountain of the Outlaws'. *National Geographic* (July 1931).

—, 'The Land of the Tebbus'. *Geographical Journal* 81.2 (February 1933).

—, 'The Land of the Yellow Lama'. *National Geographic* (April 1925).

—, 'Life among the Lamas of Choni'. *National Geographic* (November 1928).

—, 'Seeking the Mountains of Mystery'. *National Geographic* (February 1930) 140–72.

—, 'Through the Great River Trenches of Asia'. *National Geographic* (August 1926).

Rockhill, William Woodville, *The Land of the Lamas.* New York: Century Company, 1891.

Rodrigue, Y, *Nat-Pwe: Burma's Supernatural Sub-Culture.* Edinburgh: Kiscadale, 1992.

Rogers, Peter, *A Window on Isan: Thailand's Northeast.* Bangkok: Editions Duang Kamol, 1989.

—, *Northeast Thailand: From Prehistoric to Modern Times.* Bangkok: DK Book House, 1996.

Rong Mei, 'On the Sichuan-Tibet Highway'. *China Tourism* 74 (n.d.).

Rose, Archibald, 'The Reaches of the Upper Salween'. *Geographical Journal* 34.6 (1909).

—, and J Coggin Brown, 'Lisu (Yawyin) Tribes of the China-Burma Frontier'. *Royal Asiatic Society of Bengal* 3 (1911).

Rose, H A ed., *Glossary of the Tribes and Castes of the Punjab and North-West Frontier Province.* Lahore: Civil and Military Gazette Press, 1919.

Roux, Emile, *Searching for the Sources of the Irrawaddy.* Bangkok: White Lotus Press, 1999.

Rowell, Galen, 'Annapurna: Sanctuary for the Himalaya'. *National Geographic* (September 1989) 391–405.

—, 'Nomads of China's West'. *National Geographic (*February 1982).

Rowney, Horatio Bickerstaffe, *The Wild Tribes of India.* London: Thomas De La Rue and Company, 1824.

Roy Burman, B K ed., 'Socio-Economic Survey of Rupa: A Sherdukpen Village in Arunachal Pradesh'. In *Census of India, 1971* (Series 1, India, Part C VI; New Delhi: Controller of Publications, 1975).

Rubel, Paula G, *The Kalmyk Mongols: A Study in Continuity and Change.* Bloomington: Indiana University

Publications, 1967.

Ruohamäki, Olli-Pekka, *Fishermen No More? Livelihood and Environment in Southern Thai Maritime Villages*. Bangkok: White Lotus Press, 1999.

Saeki, P Yoshiro, *The Nestorian Documents and Relics in China*. Tokyo: Maruzen, 1951.

Saha, Sudhanshu Bikash ed., *Tribes of Tripura: A Historical Survey*. Agartala: Rupall Book House, 1986.

Sah-Iam, Sittichai, *Phrases and Clauses in the MPI Language at Ban Dong, Phrae Province*. Mahidol University, Bangkok, MA thesis, 1984.

Saihoo, Patya, *The Hill Tribes of Northern Thailand*. Bangkok, 1970.

Saklani, Girija, *The Uprooted Tibetans in India*. New Delhi: Cosmo, 1984.

Salisbury, C Y, *Mountaintop Kingdom: Sikkim*. Delhi: Vikas Publishing House, 1972.

Salter, Jan and Harka Gurung, *Faces of Nepal*. Lalitpur, Nepal: Himal Association, 1996.

Sams, Bert F, 'Black Tai and Lao Song Dam: The Divergence of Ethnocultural Identities'. *Journal of the Siam Society* 76 (1988).

—, *Tradition and Modernity in a Lao Song Village of Central Thailand*. University of California, Los Angeles, PhD thesis, 1987.

Samuel, H Tony and Subhro Sekher Sircar, *West Bengal: Before the Throne of God*. Chennai: People India Research, 1999.

San Antonio, Gabriel Quiroga de, *A Brief and Truthful Relation of Events in the Kingdom of Cambodia*. Bangkok: White Lotus Press, repr. 1998.

Sarep, Hpung, 'Rgylathang Tibetan of Yunnan: A Preliminary Report'. *Linguistics of the Tibeto-Burman Area* 19.2 (1996) 93–184.

Sarkar, Jayanta, 'A Note on Avoidance of Direct Exchange of Bride among the Khamptis of Arunachal Pradesh'. *Man in India* 57 (1977).

—, *Society, Culture and Ecological Adaptation among Three Tribes of Arunachal Pradesh*. Calcutta: Anthropological Survey of India, 1987.

Schram, Louis M J, *The Monquors of the Kansu-Tibetan Frontier, Part I: Their Origin, History and Social Organization*. Philadelphia: American Philios. Society, 1954.

—, *The Monquors of the Kansu-Tibetan Frontier, Part III: Records of the Monquor Clans*. Philadelphia: American Philios. Society, 1961.

Schliesinger, Joachim, *Ethnic Groups of Thailand: Non-Tai-Speaking Peoples*. Bangkok: White Lotus Press, 2000.

—, *Tai Groups of Thailand, Volume 2: Profile of the Existing Groups*. Bangkok: White Lotus Press, 2001.

—, *Hill Tribes of Vietnam*. 2 vols. Bangkok: White Lotus Press, 1997, 1998.

Schtetelndreyer, Burkhard, 'Narrative Discourse in Sherpa'. In *SIL Publications in Linguistics and Related Fields: Papers on Discourse* 51 (Dallas: SIL, 1978) 248–66.

Schwartz, Henry G, *The Minorities of Northern China: A Survey*. Bellingham: Western Washington University Press, 1984.

Scofield, John, 'Bhutan Crowns a New Dragon King'. *National Geographic* (October 1974) 546–71.

—, 'Life Slowly Changes in a Remote Himalayan Kingdom'. *National Geographic* (November 1976) 658–83.

Scott, P M, 'Some Mongol Nestorian Crosses'. *The Chinese Recorder* (February 1930) 104–8; (November 1930) 704–6.

Scott, Sir George, 'Among the Hill Tribes of Burma: An Ethnological Thicket'. *National Geographic* (March 1922).

Sebok, Thomas A ed., *Linguistics in East Asia and Southeast Asia* 2: *Current Trends in Linguistics*. The Hague: Mouton, 1967.

Seidenfaden, Erik, 'Some Notes about the Chaubun: A Disappearing Society'. *Journal of the Siam Society* 12.3 (1919).

—, 'Further Notes about the Chaubun'. *Journal of the Siam Society* 13.3 (1920).

—, 'Siam's Tribal Dresses'. *Journal of the Siam Society* 21.2 (1929).

— 'The Lawa: Additional Note'. *Journal of the Siam Society* 17.1 (1923).

— 'The Kui People of Cambodia and Siam'. *Journal of the Siam Society* 39.2 (1952).

—, *The Thai Peoples: Book 1, The Origins and Habitation of the Thai Peoples with a Sketch of their Material and Spiritual Culture*. Bangkok: The Siam Society, 1958.

Sen, Sipra, *The Tribes of Meghalaya (Bibliography)*. Delhi: Mittal Publications, 1985.

—, *Arunachal Pradesh and the Tribes: Select Bibliography*. Delhi: Gian Publishing House, 1986.

Senaphitak, Niphon, *[The Story of the Thai Song]*. Bangkok: Sam Nao, 1978, Thai language.

Sharma, Devidatta, *Tribal Languages of Himachal Pradesh*. Delhi: Mittal Publications, 1989.

Sharma, R R P, *The Sherdukpen*. Shillong: Research Department, NEFA Administration, 1961.

Sharma Thakur, G C, *The Plain Tribes of Lakhimpur, Dibrugarh, Sibsagar and Nowgong*. Gauhati: Tribal Research Department, Government of Assam, 1972.

Sharma, T C and D N Majumadar eds., *Eastern Himalayas: A Study on the Anthropology Tribalism*. New Delhi: Cosmo Publications, 1979.

Shen Zhi, 'The Resplendent Flower-Waist Dais'. *China Tourism* 263 (June 2002) 58–62.

Shi Youyi ed., *Folkways of China's Minority Nationalities (Southwest)*. Chengdu: Huayi Publishing House, 1991.

Shiratori, Yoshiro, *Visual Ethnography: The Hill Tribes of South East Asia*. Japan: Kodansha, 1978.

Shorto, H L, *A Dictionary of Modern Spoken Mon*. London: Oxford University Press, 1962.

—, 'The 32 Myos in the Medieval Mon Kingdom'. *Bulletin of the School of Oriental and African Studies* 26 (1963).

—, et al. *Bibliographies of Mon-Khmer and Tai Linguistics*. London: Oxford University Press, Oriental Bibliographies 2, 1963.

Shresstha, Lila Raj, 'The Thami'. *The Rising Nepal*. Kathmandu: The Gorkhapatra Corporation, 18 March 1966.

Shui Xiaojie, 'Visiting the Shanyan Tibetans'. *China Tourism* 240 (July 2000).

Shwe Lu Maung, *Burma: Nationalism and Ideology*. Dhaka: University Press, 1989.

Siiger, H and J Rischel, *The Lepchas: Culture and Religions of a Himalayan People*. Copenhagen: Natural Museum, 1967.

Silva, Chandra Richard de, *Sri Lanka: A History*. New Delhi: Vikas Publishing, 1994.

Simon, Ivan M, 'The Khoa Language'. *Resarun* (1976).

Simonnet, Christian, *Thibet, Voyage au Bout de la Chrétienté*. Paris: Editions du Monde Nouveau, 1949.

Sinclair, Kevin. *The Forgotten Tribes of China*. Canada: Cupress, 1987.

Singer, Noel F, *Burmah: A Photographic Journey 1855–1925*. Stirling, UK: Paul Strachan—Kiscadale Ltd., 1993.

Singh, B K ed., *An Introduction to the Tribal Language and Culture of Manipur*. Imphal: Manipur State Kala Akad, 1976.

Singh, Jag Deva, 'Lahauli Verb Inflection'. *Linguistics of the Tibeto-Burman Area* 12.2 (1989) 41–49.

Singh, K S ed., *Arunachal Pradesh*. People of India XIV. Calcutta: Anthropological Survey of India, 1995.

—, *Himachal Pradesh*. People of India XXIV. Delhi: Anthropological Survey of India, 1996.

—, *India's Communities: A–G*. People of India IV. Delhi: Oxford University Press and Anthropological Survey of India, 1998.

—, *India's Communities: H–M*. People of India V. Delhi: Oxford University Press and Anthropological Survey of India, 1998.

—, *India's Communities: N–Z*. People of India VI. Delhi: Oxford University Press and Anthropological Survey of India, 1998.

—, *Manipur*. People of India XXXI. Calcutta: Seagull Books and Anthropological Survey of India, 1998.

—, *Meghalaya*. People of India XXXII. Calcutta: Seagull Books and Anthropological Survey of India, 1994.

—, *Mizoram*. People of India XXXIII. Calcutta: Seagull Books and Anthropological Survey of India, 1995.

—, *Nagaland: People of India* XXXIV. Calcutta: Seagull Books and Anthropological Survey of India, 1994.

—, *Our Tribal Heritage*. Ranchi: Regional Development Commissioner, 1989.

—, *People of India*. An Introduction I. Calcutta: Anthropological Survey of India; New Delhi: Oxford University Press, 1992.

—, *Sikkim*. People of India XXXIX. Calcutta: Seagull Books and Anthropological Survey of India, 1993.

—, *The Scheduled Castes*. People of India II. Calcutta: Oxford University Press and Anthropological Survey of India, 1999.

—, *The Scheduled Tribes*. People of India III. Calcutta: Oxford University Press and Anthropological Survey of India, 1997.

—, *Tribal Situation in India*. Simla: Indian Institute of Advanced Studies, 1972.

—, *Tribal Society in India: An Anthropo-historical Perspective*. Delhi: Manohar Publications, 1985.

—, *Tripura*. People of India XLI. Calcutta: Seagull Books and Anthropological Survey of India, 1996.

Singh, Nagendra, *Bhutan: A Kingdom in the Himalayas*. New Delhi: Thomson, 1972.

Singh, Raghubir, 'A Rare Visit to a World unto Itself'. *National Geographic* (November 1988).

Singhanetra-Renard, Anchalee, 'Overview of Highland Minorities in Mainland South-East Asia'. *Indochina-Sub-Regional Highland Peoples Programme, United Nations Volunteers*. Chiang Mai: Chiang Mai University, 1998.

Sinha, B B, *Society of Tribal India*. Delhi: B R Publishing, 1982.

Sinha, Kamaleshwar, *Meghalaya: Triumph of the Tribal Genius*. Delhi: Indian School of Social Department, 1970.

Sino-Tibetan Etymological Dictionary and Thesaurus (STEDT), *Description of the Sino-Tibetan Language Family*. Berkeley, CA: University of California, Department of Linguistics, 1996.

Skinner, G William, *Chinese Society in Thailand: An Analytical History*. Ithaca, NY: Cornell University Press, 1957.

—, *Leadership and Power in the Chinese Community of Thailand*. Ithaca, NY: Cornell University Press, 1958.

Slaviska Missionen, *Folkboken: Folkgrupperna I OSS, Baltikum och Kina*. Sweden, 1998.

—, *Pray for Us*. Prayer booklet, Stockholm, 1995.

Smith, Alex G, *Buddhism through Christian Eyes . . . Etc., including The Gospel Facing Buddhist Cultures*. Littleton, CO: OMF, 2001.

— 'Status of Christianity—Country Profile: Thailand'. Monrovia: MARC Publications, 1974.

—, *Siamese Gold: The Church in Thailand*. Bangkok: OMF Publishers, 1982.

—, *Strategy to Multiply Rural Churches: A Central Thailand Case Study*. Bangkok: OMF Publishers, 1977.

Smith, Holly, 'Ambiguous Segments in Ghale'. Paper presented at the 19th annual Conference of the Linguistic Society of Nepal, Tribhuvan University, Kirtipur (26 November 1998).

Smith, Martin, *Ethnic Groups in Burma: Development, Democracy and Human Rights*. London: Anti-Slavery International, 1994.

—, *Burma: Insurgency and the Politics of Ethnicity*. London: Zed Books, 1991.

Smithies, M ed., *The Mons*. Bangkok: The Siam Society, 1986.

Smuckarn, Snit, *Peasantry and Modernization: A Study of the Phuan in Central Thailand*. University of Hawaii, PhD thesis, 1972.

—, 'A Culture in Search of Survival: The Phuan of Thailand and Laos'. New Haven: Yale University Press Center for International and Area Studies. Monograph Series 31 (1988).

Snellgrove, David, *Buddhist Himalaya: Travels and Studies in Quest of the Origins and Nature of Tibetan Religion*. Oxford: Cassirer, 1957.

—, *Himalayan Pilgrimage*. Oxford: Cassirer, 1961.

—, *Four Lamas of Dolpo: Tibetan Biographies*. 2 vols. Oxford: Bruno Cassirer, 1967.

Snellgrove, David and Hugh Richardson, *A Cultural History of Tibet*. Colorado: Prajna Press, 1980.

Snellgrove, David Llewellyn, Hugh Richardson and Tadeusz Skorupski, *The Cultural Heritage of Ladakh. Volume I: Central Ladakh*. Warminster: Aris and Phillips, 1977.

—, *The Cultural Heritage of Ladakh. Volume II: Zangskar and the Cave Temples of Ladakh*. Warminster: Aris and Phillips, 1980.

Somsong, Buruphat, '[An Account of the Lao Song and Their Immigration]' *Phu Thai Journal* 5.14 (1983), Thai language.

Sounds. Newsletter of Gospel Recordings. California (Spring 1994).

Sowerby, Arthur de C, 'By the Waters of the Min'. *China Journal* 10 (1929).

Speer, Robert E, *Missionary Principles and Practice: A Discussion of Christian Missions and of Some Criticisms upon Them*. London: Fleming H Revell, n.d.

Spiro, M, *Burmese Supernaturalism*. Englewood Cliffs, NJ: Prentice-Hall, 1967.

Srisavasdi, Boon Chuey, *The Hill Tribes of Thailand*. Bangkok: Bamrung Nukhoulkit Press, 1963.

Starling, Lucy, 'A Century of Missions in Siam'. *Missionary Review of the World* (January 1929).

—, *Dawn over the Temple Roofs*. New York: World Horizons, 1960.

Stauffer, Milton T ed., *The Christian Occupation of China*. Shanghai: China Consultation Committee, 1922.

Stein, R A, *Tibetan Civilization*. London: Faber and Faber, 1972.

Storey, Robert et al. eds., *China: A Travel Survival Kit*. Hawthorn, Australia: Lonely Planet Publications, 1994.

—, and Alex English, *Korea*. Hawthorn, Australia: Lonely Planet Publications, 2001.

Steward, J ed., *Contemporary Change in Traditional Societies*. Chicago: University of Illinois, 1967.

Stewart, John, *The Nestorian Missionary Enterprise: A Church on Fire*. Edinburgh: T & T Clarke, 1923.

Stevenson, Henry Noel Cochrane, 'The Hill Peoples of Burma'. *Burma Pamphlets* 6 (London: Longmans, 1944).

Stevenson, Paul Huston, 'The Chinese-Tibetan Borderland and Its Peoples'. *China Journal* 6 (1927).

—, 'Notes on the Human Geography of the Chinese-Tibetan Borderland'. *Geographical Review* 22 (1932).

Strachan, P, *Pagan*. Singapore: Kiscadale Publishing, 1989.

Strahm, Esther and Anita Maibaum, 'Jirel Phonetic Summary'. In Maria Hari ed., *Tibeto-Burman Phonemic Summaries* (Kathmandu: Tribhuvan University and the Summer Institute of Linguistics, 1971).

—, 'Jirel Texts'. In Austin Hale ed., *Clause, Sentence, and Discourse Patterns in Selected Languages of Nepal* (Norman,

OK: Summer Institute of Linguistics, 1973).

—, 'Clause Patterns in Jirel'. In Austin Hale. 'Collected Papers on Sherpa, Jirel'. *Nepal Studies in Linguistics 2*. (Kirtipur: SIL and Institute of Nepal and Asian Studies, 1975).

—, 'Verb Pairs in Jirel'. In Yogendra Prasad Yadava and Warren William Glover eds., *Topics in Nepalese Linguistics* (Kathmandu: Royal Nepal Academy, 1999).

Stuart, Arabella, *The Lives of Mrs Ann H Judson and Mrs Sarah B Judson*. Buffalo: Miller Orton and Mulligan, 1854.

Stuart-Fox, Martin, *A History of Laos*. Cambridge: Harvard University Press, 1977.

—, *Laos: Politics and Society*. London: Frances Publishers, 1986.

—, *The Lao Kingdom in Lan Xang: Rise and Decline*. Bangkok: White Lotus Press, 1998.

Sudham, Pira, *People of Esarn*. Bangkok: Siam Media International Books, 1987.

Sungkep, Tanakorn, *A Phonological Study of Lao Ngaeo with Comparisons to Five Tai Dialects*. Mahidol University, MA thesis, 1983.

Sun Hongkai, 'A Brief Account of my Research Work, with an Appended Bibliography'. *Linguistics of the Tibeto-Burman Area* 10.1 (1987).

—, 'Chuanxi Minzu Zoulang Diqu de Yuyan'. In *Xinan Minzu Yanjiu*. (Chengdu: Sichuan Minzu Chubanshe, 1983), Chinese language.

—, 'Languages of the Ethnic Corridor in Western Sichuan'. *Linguistics of the Tibeto-Burman Area* 13.1 (1990).

—, 'On Nationality and Recognition of Tibeto-Burman Languages'. *Linguistics of the Tibeto-Burman Area* 15.2 (1992).

—, 'A Preliminary Investigation into the Relationship between Qiong Long and the Languages of the Qiang Branch of Tibeto-Burman'. *Linguistics of the Tibeto-Burman Area* 12.1 (1989).

—, Lu Shaozun, Zhang Jichuan and Ouyang Jueya, *The Languages of the Menba, Luoba and Deng Peoples*. Beijing: Chinese Social Science Publishing House, 1980.

—, 'Qiangyu Zhishu Wenti Chutan'. In *A Collection of Articles on the Nationality*

Languages (Xining: Qinghai University Press, 1982).

—, 'Caodeng rGyalrong Phonology: A First Look'. *Linguistics of the Tibeto-Burman Area* 17.2 (1994).

—, 'Review of Zangmian Yu Yuyin Han Cohui' [Tibeto-Burman Phonology and Vocabularies]. *Linguistics of the Tibeto-Burman Area* 15.2 (1992) 73–113.

Swan, William, *Letters on Missions*. Boston: Perkins and Marvin, 1831.

—, *Missionary Magazine* (October 1937) 499–500.

Swaurp, R and Ranveer Singh, *Social Economy of a Tribal Village in Indo-Tibetan Border*. Delhi: Mittal Publications, 1988.

Syamananda, Rong, *A History of Thailand*. Bangkok: Thai Watana Panich, 1973.

Tai Chi Yin, 'Timeless Plateau: Zhongdian'. *China Tourism* 108 (n.d.).

Taik, A A, *Visions of Shwedagon*. Bangkok: White Lotus Press, 1989.

Talukdar, S P, *The Chakmas: Life and Struggle*. Delhi: Gian Publishing House, 1988.

Tambiah, S J, *Buddhism and the Spirit Cults in Northwest Thailand*. Cambridge: Cambridge University Press, 1970.

Tanbuali, Maga Canla, *The State of Buddhist Religion in the Lao People's Democratic Republic*. Bangkok: Khana Sasanikachon, 1977.

'Tawang: A Hidden Paradise beyond Imagination'. Tawang, Arunachal Pradesh: District Tourism Promotion Committee, n.d.

Taylor, J L, *Forest Monks and the Nation State: An Anthropological and Historical Study in Northeastern Thailand*. Singapore: Institute of Southeast Asian Studies, 1993.

Taylor, R H, *The State in Burma*. London: C Hurst, 1987.

Teichman, Eric, *Travels of a Consular Officer in Eastern Tibet*. London: Cambridge University Press, 1922.

Temple, Sir R C, *The Thirty-seven Nats: A Phase of Spirit-Worship Prevailing in Burma*. London: W Griggs, 1906.

Tenzin, Gyatso (Dalai Lama XIV), *My Land and My People*. New York: McGraw-Hill, 1962.

—, *Freedom in Exile: The Autobiography of the Dalai Lama of Tibet*. London:

Abacus, 1990.

—, *The Good Heart: His Holiness the Dalai Lama Explores the Heart of Christianity and of Humanity*. Boston: Wisdom Publications, 1996.

Terwiel, B J, *Monks and Magic: An Analysis of Religious Ceremonies in Central Thailand*. London: Curzon Press, 1979.

Thakur, R N, *Himalayan Lepchas*. New Delhi: Archives Publishers, 1988.

The Edge 2.3 (Fall 1997).

'The Stone, A Guardian of Life: The Qiang: Keeping a Unique Stone Culture'. Unpublished report, 1998.

Thomas, David D, *Mon-Khmer Subgroupings in Vietnam*. The Hague: Mouton, 1966.

Thompson, H Gordon, 'From Yunnanfu to Peking along the Tibetan and Mongolian Borders'. *Geographical Journal* 67 (1926).

Thongchuay, Chantas, *Current Thai Dialects in Kelantan, Kedah and Perlis*. Chulalongkorn University, MA thesis, 1982.

Time Magazine, South Pacific Edition (29 April 2002).

Tian Qui, 'The Tibetans of Deqen'. *China Tourism* 108 (n.d.).

Tian Zicheng, 'The Fascinating Yugurs'. *China Tourism* 256 (November 2001).

T'ien Ju-K'ang, *Peaks of Faith: Protestant Mission in Revolutionary China*. Leiden: E J Brill, 1993.

—, *Religious Cults of the Pai-i along the Burma-Yunnan Border*. New York: Cornell University Monograph, 1986.

Tiley, Chodag, *Tibet, the Land and the People*. Beijing: New World Press, 1988.

Todaeva, Buliash, 'Einige Besonderheiten der Paoan-Sprache'. *Acta Orientalia Hungaricae* 16 (1963) 175–97.

Todd, Burt Kerr, 'Bhutan, Land of the Thunder Dragon'. *National Geographic* (December 1952) 713–54.

Torrance, Thomas, *China's First Missionaries: Ancient Israelites*. Chicago: Daniel Shaw, repr. 1988.

—, *The History, Customs and Religion of the Chi'ang, an Aboriginal people of West China*. Shanghai: 1920.

—, 'Notes on the West China Aboriginal Tribes'. *West China Border Research Society* 5 (1932).

Torrance, Thomas F, Jr, 'Journal of my First Visit to Hong Kong, Chengdu and Wenchuan, April 22 to June 3, 1994'. Unpublished report, Edinburgh, 1994.

— 'A Visit by Thomas F Torrance to Chengdu, the Capital of Sichuan, and to Weichou and Chi'ang villages in Wenchuan County, the upper Min Valley, Sichuan, October 4–18, 1986'. Unpublished report, Edinburgh, 1986.

'Traces of the Old Buriat Mission'. *Chinese Recorder* 7.2 (March–April 1876) 81–90.

Trail, Ronald L ed., *Papers in South-East Asian Linguistics 7*. Canberra: Pacific Linguistics, 1980.

Tribes and Nations Outreach, *Kindreds* 7.2 (Bangkok, 1996).

Tribal Research Society, *The Hill Tribes of Thailand*. Chiang Mai: The Technical Service Club, 1995.

Trimondi, Victor, *Der Schatten des Dalai Lama: Sexualität, Magie und Politik im tibetischen Buddhismus* [The Shadow of the Dalai Lama: Sexuality, Magic, and Politics in Tibetan Buddhism]. Dusseldorf: Patmos, 1999.

Tsering, Marku, *Sharing Christ in the Tibetan Buddhist World*. Upper Darby, PA: Tibet Press, 2nd edn, 1993.

Tucci, Giuseppe, *The Religions of Tibet*. Berkeley: University of California Press, 1980.

Tucker, Ruth A, *From Jerusalem to Irian Jaya: A Biographical History of Christian Missions*. Grand Rapids: Zondervan, 1983.

Tun Shwe, Khine, *A Guide to Mrauk-U: An Ancient City of Rakhine*. Myanmar, 1993.

Turin, Mark, 'Too Many Stars and Not Enough Sky: Language and Ethnicity among the Thakali of Nepal'. *Contributions to Nepalese Studies* 24.2 (1997) 187–99.

—, 'The Thangmi Verbal Agreement System and the Kiranti Connection'. *Bulletin of the School of Oriental and African Studies* 61.3 (1998) 476–91.

—, 'Whence Thangmi? Historical Ethnography and Comparative Morphology'. In Yogendra Prasad Yadava and Warren William Glover eds., *Topics in Nepalese Linguistics* (Kathmandu: Royal Nepal Academy, 1999) 451–77.

—, 'By Way of Incest and the Golden Deer: How the Thangmi Came to Be and the Pitfalls of Oral History'.

Journal of Nepalese Studies 3.1 (1999) 13–19.

—, 'Shared Words, Shared History? The Case of Thangmi and Late Classical Newar'. *Journal of Newar Studies* 3 (1999) 9–17.

—, 'The Changing Face of Language and Linguistics in Nepal: Some Thoughts on Thangmi'. *Janjati* 1.3 (2000) 49–62.

—, 'Time for a True Population Census: The Case of the Miscounted Thangmi'. *Nagarik* 2.4 (2000) 14–19.

Turpin, F H, *History of the Kingdom of Siam and the Revolutions that Have Caused the Overthrow of the Empire up to 1770*. Bangkok: White Lotus Press, repr. 1997.

Tweed, Thomas A, 'Nightstand Buddhists and other Creatures: Sympathizers, Adherents, and the Study of Religion'. In Duncan Ryuken Williams and Christopher S Queen eds., *American Buddhism: Methods and Findings in Recent Scholarship* (Surrey: Curzon Press, 1998).

Ukyab, Tamla and Shyam Adhikari, *The Nationalities of Nepal*. Kathmandu: Ministry of Local Development National Committee for Development of Nationalities, 2000.

Upcraft, W M, 'The Wild Men of Szechuan'. *Chinese Recorder* (October 1892).

US Department of the Army, *Minority Groups in Thailand*. Ethnographic Study Series, Pamphlet 550–107. Washington, DC: US Government Printing Press, 1970.

Valli, Eric and Diane Summers, 'Himalayan Caravans'. *National Geographic* (December 1993) 5–35.

—, 'Honey Hunters of Nepal'. *National Geographic* (November 1988) 660–71.

Van Driem, George, *Languages of the Himalayas*, II. Leiden: E J Brill, 2001.

Van Dyck, Howard, *William Christie: Apostle to Tibet*. Harrisburg: Christian Publications, 1956.

Vansittart, E, 'The Tribes, Clans and Castes of Nepal'. *Journal of the Asiatic Society of Bengal* 63.4, Part 1, 1894; Guragon, India: Vintage Books, repr. 1992.

Vesalainen, Olavi and Marja, 'Clause Patterns in Lhomi'. *Pacific Linguistics* B 53 (1980).

—, 'Lhomi Phonetic Summary'. (Kathmandu: SIL and the Institute of Nepal and Asian Studies, 1976).

Vietnam News Agency, *Vietnam: Image of the Community of 54 Ethnic Groups*. The Ethnic Publishing House, 1996.

Voegelin, Carl F and Florence M Voegelin, *Classification and Index of the World's Languages*. New York: Elsevier North Holland, 1977.

Voice of the Martyrs, 'The Persecution and Prayer Alert'. (30 October 2002).

—, 'The Persecution and Prayer Alert'. (31 July 2002).

von der Heide, Susanna, *The Thakalis of North Western Nepal*. Kathmandu: Ratna Pustak Bhandar, 1988.

von Eickstedt, E, 'The Races and Types of Western and Central Himalayas'. *Man in India* (June 1926) 237–76.

Von Füerer-Haimendorf, Christoph, *Caste and Kin in Nepal, India and Ceylon*. London: Asia Publishing House, 1966.

—, 'Ethnographic Notes on the Tamangs of Nepal'. *Eastern Anthropologist* 4.3–4 (March–August 1956) 166–67.

—, 'Elements of Newar Social Structure'. *Journal of the Royal Anthropological Institute* 86.2 (1956).

—, *Highlanders of Arunachal Pradesh: Anthropological Research in North-East India*. New Delhi: Vikas Publishing House, 1982.

—, *Himalayan Barbary*. London: John Murray, 1956.

—, 'Moral Concepts in Three Himalayan Societies'. *Indian Anthropology*. London: Asia Publishing House, 1962.

—, 'Pre-Buddhist Elements in Sherpa Belief and Ritual'. *Man* 55.61 (1955).

—, *The Sherpas of Nepal*. London: John Murray, 1964.

—, *Tribes of India: A Struggle for Survival*. Delhi: Oxford University Press, 1985.

Von Füerer-Haimendorf, Christoph, E Schueider, Toni Hagen and G O Dhyrenfurth, *The Sherpas of the Khumbu Region*. London: Oxford University Press, 1963.

Vyatkina, K V, 'The Buryats'. In M G Levin and L P Potapov eds., *The Peoples of Siberia* (Chicago: University of Chicago Press, 1964).

Waddell, L Austine, *The Buddhism and Lamaism of Tibet*. New Delhi: Heritage, 1979.

—, *The Tribes of the Brahmaputra Valley*. Delhi: Sanskaran Prakashan, 1970.

Wagner, C Peter and Edward Dayton, *Unreached Peoples '79*. Colorado: David Cook, 1979.

Wagner, Elizabeth, *Tearing Down Strongholds: Prayer for Buddhists*. Hong Kong: Living Books for All, 1988.

Wahid Saddiq, *Ladakh between Earth and Sky*. Bombay: B I Publications, 1981.

Walker, Anthony R, *Farmers in the Hills: Ethnographic Notes on the Upland People of North Thailand*. Singapore: Suvarnabhumi Books, 1986.

Walker, J E, 'Shao-wu in Fuh-kien: A Country Station'. *Chinese Recorder* (September–October 1878).

Walsh, Ernest Herbert Cooper, *A Vocabulary of the Trowoma Dialect of Tibetan Spoken in the Chumbi Valley (So far as it Differs from Standard Tibetan), together with a Corresponding Vocabulary of Sikkimese and of Central (Standard) Tibetan (Given for the Purpose of Comparison)*. Calcutta: The Bengal Secretariat Book Depot, 1905.

Wan, F C, 'Unforgettable Times with Our Lhoba Friends'. *China Tourism* 70 (n.d.).

Wang Guoxiang, *The Bulangs, Flowers, Love Songs and Girls*. Kunming: Yunnan Education Publishing House, 1995.

Wang Jia, 'The Siyueba Festival at Jiwei'. *China Tourism* 107 (n.d.).

Wang Jian, 'Zayu People: Little Known to the Outside World'. *China Tourism* 261 (April 2002).

Wang, Mary T, 'A Remote Tribe in West China'. *China Magazine* 16.5 (1946).

Wang Duanyu, 'Lama Jiao Yu Zangzu Renkou' [Lamaism and the Population of the Tibetans]. *Minzu Yanji* (1984), Chinese language.

Warangrat, Surat, 'Kaloeng'. *Muang Boran Journal* 7.3 (1987).

Ward, Francis Kingdon, *From China to Hkamti Long*. London: Edward Arnold, 1924.

—, *The Land of the Blue Poppy*. Cambridge: Cambridge University Press, 1913.

—, *The Mystery Rivers of Tibet*. London: Seeley, Service and Co., 1923.

Wark, Andrew, 'It's Time to Climb Higher'. *Asian Report* 25.3, Report 195 (May–June 1992).

Wells, Kenneth E, *Thai Buddhism*. Bangkok: Bangkok Times Press, 1939.

—, 'Buddhism in Thailand: Its Sources of Strength'. *International Review of Missions* XXXI (April 1942).

—, *History of Protestant Work in Thailand 1828–1958*. Bangkok: Church of Christ in Thailand, 1958.

Wenk, Klaus, *Thai Literature: An Introduction*. Bangkok: White Lotus Press, 1995.

Wen Yu, 'The Personal Endings of the Verb in the Jyarung Language as Spoken at Paslok'. *Studia Serica* 1.4 (1940).

White, John Claude, *Sikkim and Bhutan: Twenty-One Years on the Northeast Frontier (1887–1908)*. Delhi: Vivek, 1971.

White Lotus Press, *Guide to the Tipitaka—An Introduction to the Buddhist Canon*. Bangkok: White Lotus Press, 1993.

Wichienkeeo, Aroonrut and Gehan Wijeyewardene eds., *The Laws of King Mangrai*. Canberra: Australian National University, 1986.

Wijeyewardene, Gehan ed., *Ethnic Groups across National Boundaries in Mainland Southeast Asia*. Singapore: Australian National University, Institute of Southeast Asian Studies, 1990.

—, ed., 'The Theravada Compact and the Karen'. *Sojourn: Social Issue in Southeast Asia* 2.1 (1987).

Williams, Duncan Ryuken and Christopher S Queen eds., *American Buddhism: Methods and Findings in Recent Scholarship*. Surrey: Curzon Press, 1998.

Winter, Werner, 'Diversity in Rai Languages: An Inspection of Verb Stems in Selected Idioms'. *Lingua Posnaniensis* 34 (1991) 141–56.

Winter, Ralph D and David A Fraser, 'World Mission Survey'. In *Perspectives on the World Christian Movement: A Reader* (Pasadena, CA: William Carey Library, 3rd edn, 1999).

Wong Chung Fai, 'The Felt-Hatted Baima'. *China Tourism* 115 (n.d.).

—, 'A Mountain Hamlet in Zhugqu'. *China Tourism* 115 (n.d.).

Wong How-Man, 'Peoples of China's Far Provinces'. *National Geographic* (March 1984).

Wongwiset, Wichian, *The Phuan of Thailand (Thai Phuan)*. Bangkok: Wattana Phanit, 1982.

World Pulse. (19 April 1996).

Wright, A, *Buddhism in Chinese History*. Stanford: Stanford University Press, 1959.

Wright, Arnold and Oliver T Breakspear, *Twentieth-Century Impressions of Siam*. Bangkok: White Lotus Press, 1903, repr. 1994.

Wu, David Y H, 'Culture Change and Ethnic Identity among Minorities in China'. In Chiao Chien and Nicholas Tapp eds., *Ethnicity and Ethnic Groups in China* (Hong Kong: The Chinese University of Hong Kong, 1989).

Wu Dong, 'The Tunbao Honouring Mothers Festival'. *China Tourism* 262 (May 2002).

Wu Pingguan, 'The Sangemao—Special Tibetans'. *China Tourism* 268 (November 2002).

Wurm, Stephen A ed., *Atlas of the World's Languages in Danger of Disappearing*. Paris: UNESCO, 1996.

Wurm, Stephen A and Shiro Hattori, *Language Atlas of the Pacific Area*. The Australian Institute of the Humanities and the Japan Academy, 1981.

Wu Wenhui and Zhu Jianhua, 'Xikang Renkou Wenti, Shang' [Xikang Population Problems, 1]. *Bianzheng Gonglun* III (n.d.), Chinese language.

Wu Zhouming, 'The Ancient Trail in Sichuan'. *China Tourism* 59 (n.d.).

Xian Yanyun, 'In Search of the Ancient Tea Caravan Route'. *China Tourism* 181 (August 1995).

Xiao Yang, 'Vietnamese Refugees in China'. *Bridge* 9 (January–February 1985).

Xie Guanghui, 'Into the World Called Shangri-La'. *China Tourism* 215 (June 1998) 35–51.

Xie Shixun, 'The Floral-Belted Dais of the Red River'. *China Tourism* 78 (n.d.).

Xinan Minzu Yanjiu. Chengdu: Sichuan Minzu Chubanshe, 1983, Chinese language.

Xu Yixi ed., *Headdresses of Chinese Minority Nationality Women*. Hong Kong: China Film Press, 1989.

Yadava, Yogendra Prasad and Warren William Glover eds., *Topics in Nepalese Linguistics*. Kathmandu: Royal Nepal Academy, 1999.

Yang, Martin M C, 'Peoples and Societies in Yunnan (Part I)'. *Journal of Ethnology and Sociology* 16 (Taipei, 1978) 21–112.

Yan Wenbian, Zhang Pen and Gu Qing eds., *Dai Folk Legends*. Beijing: Foreign Languages Press, 1988.

Yashuda, Yasuhiko, *A Historical Study of the Jiarong Verb System*. Tokyo: Seishido, 1984.

Young, Oliver Gordon, *The Hill Tribes of Northern Thailand*. Bangkok: The Siam Society, Monograph 1, 1974.

Younghusband, Sir Francis, *India and Tibet*. London: John Murray, 1910.

Yuji, Baba, 'The Ritual of the Guardian Spirit of the Tai-Lue and its Social Background: A Case Study of Nan Province in Northern Thailand'. *Fifth International Conference on Thai Studies* (London, 1993).

—, 'Migration and Spirit Cult: The Case Study on Tai-Lue Villages in Nan Province, Northern Thailand'. *First International Conference on Thai Studies* (Chiang Mai, 1996).

Yule, Henry and Henri Cordier, *Cathay and the Way Thither: Being a Collection of Medieval Notices of China*. 4 vols., Delhi: Munshiram Manoharlal, repr. 1998.

Yunnan Nianjian [Yunnan Annual] (Kunming: Yunnan Nianjian Zazhishe, 1985, 1986, 1988), Chinese language.

Zago, Marcel, *Rites et Ceremonies en Milieu Bouddhiste Lao*. Rome: Universita Georgiana Documenta Missionala 6, 1972.

Zeid, Aby, *Achbar ul Sin wal Hind* [Observations upon China and India]. In John Foster, *Church of the T'ang Dynasty* (London: SPCK, 1939).

Zhang Jianghua and Wu Congzhong, 'Tibet's Menba Nationality'. *China Reconstructs* (July 1979).

Zhang Jimin, 'Lajiyu yu Gelaoyu de Guanxi'. *Minzu Yuwen* 3 (1992), Chinese language.

Zhang Junru, 'Ji Guangxi Nanning Xinxu Pinghua'. *Fangyuan*, Chinese language.

Zhang Weiwen and Zeng Qingnan, *In Search of China's Minorities*. Beijing: New World Press, 1993.

Zhang Xiaosong, 'Tunbao People: Descended from Frontier Soldiers'. *China Tourism* 274 (May 2003).

Zheng Chengdong, 'Xiangcheng: At the Foot of Bamu Sacred Mountain'. *China Tourism* 255 (October 2001) 34–42.

Zheng Lan, *Travels through Xishuangbanna: China's Subtropical Home of Many Nationalities*. Beijing: Foreign Languages Press, 1981.

Zheng Ligang, 'Into Remote Ngari: A Tour by Land-Rover'. *China Tourism* 244 (November 2000) 18–45.

Zheng Ming, 'Mountain Ceremony of the Tibetans of Southern Gansu'. *China Tourism* 125 (November 1990).

Zheng Peng, *Our Beautiful Xishuangbanna*. Shenzhen: Meiguang Colour Printing, n.d.

Zhu Liangwen, *The Dai (Or the Tai and their Architecture and Customs in South China)*. Kunming: The Science and Technology Press of Yunnan, 1992.

Zubkhov, Pyotr, 'Buryatia: A Republic on Lake Baikal'. *Soviet Life* 378 (1988) 41–46.

Zwalf, W, *Heritage of Tibet*. London: British Museum, 1981.

Contact Information

Now that you have read about the peoples of the Buddhist world, you may want to become involved in reaching them with the gospel. The following interdenominational ministries all focus on reaching out to Buddhists and will be glad to hear from you.

Asia Harvest

Web: www.asiaharvest.org
A Christian organisation that works with church leaders throughout Asia.

Asia Pacific Institute of Buddhist Studies (APIBS)

Email: alan.Johnson@agmd.org
Based in Baguio, Philippines, APIBS runs training programmes specifically aimed at reaching the wider Buddhist world.

Back to Jerusalem (BTJ)

Web: www.backtojerusalem.com
This website details the efforts of the church in China to reach the surrounding nations, many of which are Buddhist, with the gospel.

Billionhours/Billionwait

Web: www.billionhours.org and www.onebillionwait.org
These two websites are dedicated to raising one billion hours of prayer for the salvation of the Buddhist world. They display prayer updates, news of prayer summits, links to resources and a prayer guide to help you intercede effectively for Buddhists.

Central Asia Fellowship (CAF)

Email: tbwcentral@psmail.net
Contact CAF for information regarding partnerships, networking, training, resources and prayer mobilization for the Tibetan Buddhist world.

Gospel Recordings

Email: sg@gospelrecordings.com
Web: www.globalrecordings.net
Contact Gospel Recordings for information on any of the cassette tapes that are listed in the profiles in *Peoples of the Buddhist World.*

Overseas Missionary Fellowship (OMF)

Email: asmith@omf.org
Dr Alex Smith of OMF, an acknowledged authority on Buddhism, is available to conduct training sessions and seminars, give presentations and speak at conferences on how Christians can work effectively in the Buddhist world.

Sonrise Center for Buddhist Studies

Web: www.sonrisecenter.org
The Sonrise Center for Buddhist Studies was founded in 1988 as a virtual learning community. It offers resources, online courses and the latest information from a Christian perspective on global trends and issues pertaining to Asian religions and cultures. Its founding director, James C Stephens, was a Buddhist youth leader (1970–1984) prior to his Christian conversion.

South East Asia Network (SEANET)

Web: www.seanetwork.org
The website of SEANET aims to equip churches for effective outreach to the Buddhist nations of Asia.

Other titles by Paul Hattaway available from Piquant Editions:

Contact info@piquant.net
or visit www.piquanteditions.com
or www.asiaharvest.org

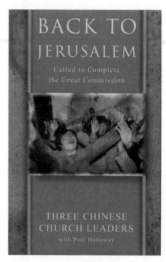

The Heavenly Man: The Remarkable True Story of Chinese Christian Brother Yun
Brother Yun with Paul Hattaway
ISBN 1-903689-23-6

Back to Jerusalem: Called to Complete the Great Commission
Brother Yun, Peter Xu Yongze and Enoch Wang with Paul Hattaway
ISBN 1-903689-03-1

Operation China: Introducing all the Peoples of China
Paul Hattaway (with 704 full-colour photographs)
ISBN 0-9535757-5-6 / CD-ROM version: ISBN 1-903689-19-8